The Story of
the People, the Places, and the Cultures

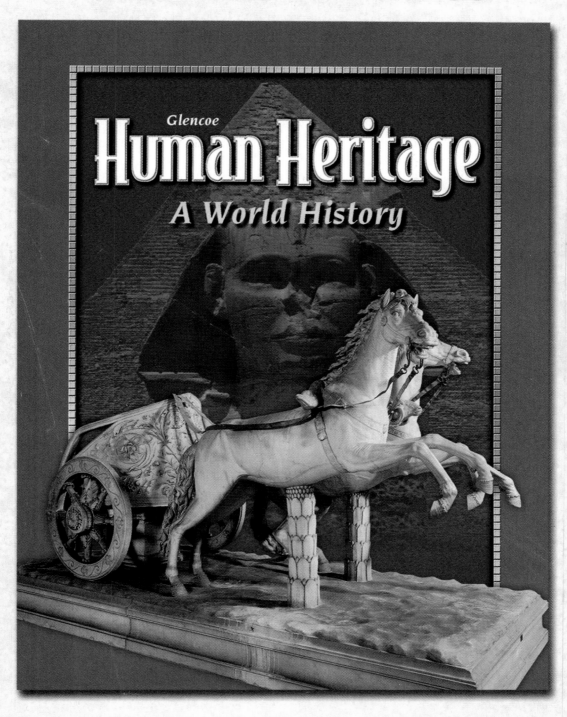

Glencoe

Human Heritage
A World History

Resources for You . . .
Resources for Every Student, Every Day!

For Chapter Overviews, Student Activities, Self-Check Quizzes, Puzzles, and other resources, go to humanheritage.glencoe.com

Vocabulary and Guided Reading

Hands-On History Lab Activities

Enrichment Activities

Cooperative Learning Activities

Reading Essentials and Study Guide

Reproducible Lesson Plans

Primary Source Readings

Videodisc Bar Code Correlation

Spanish Chapter Digests
Audiocassettes Activities and Tests

Block Scheduling

Spanish Summaries and Glossary

Teacher's Wraparound Edition

Glencoe
Human Heritage
A World History

Help Spanish-Speaking Students:
• Review Chapter Content
• Master New Material
• Prepare for Quizzes and Tests

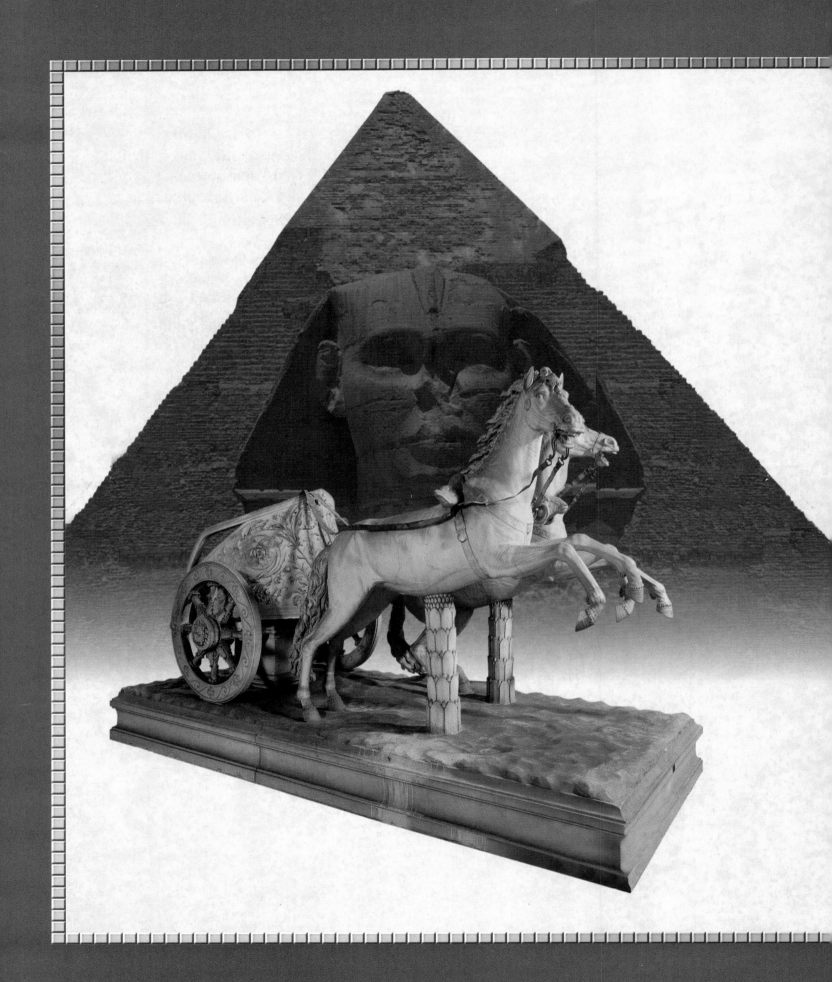

Teacher's Wraparound Edition

Glencoe
Human Heritage
A World History

Visit the Glencoe Web site at **socialstudies.glencoe.com** for chapter-based activities you and your students can explore for this and other Glencoe Social Studies books. There you will also find online versions of our *Time/Glencoe Current Events Update, Economics Update,* and many more exciting resources!

Miriam S. Greenblatt

Peter S. Lemmo

Glencoe McGraw-Hill

New York, New York   Columbus, Ohio   Woodland Hills, California   Peoria, Illinois

AUTHORS

Miriam Greenblatt is a writer, editor, and educational consultant who has traveled extensively in Asia, Africa, and Latin America. During the past 30 years, she has contributed to more than 45 elementary, junior high, and high school social studies texts and ancillaries, and has written almost a dozen history books for teenagers. A graduate of Hunter College of the City of New York and the University of Chicago, Greenblatt is a former teacher and a member of the National Association of Scholars and the Illinois Council for Social Studies. She is listed in *Who's Who in America 2000* and *Who's Who in the World 2000*.

Peter S. Lemmo is a high school teacher in the New York City school system, where he has taught since 1970. A graduate of the City College of New York and the City University of New York, he has trained student teachers and contributed to several books. Lemmo has been instrumental in developing pilot instructional programs and curricula and was rated an exemplary teacher by the State Education Department of New York. He is also a member of the National Council for the Social Studies, the Association for Supervision and Curriculum Development, and other professional organizations, and he has traveled extensively in more than 55 countries.

Glencoe/McGraw-Hill

Printed in the United States of America

Send all inquiries to:
Glencoe/McGraw-Hill
8787 Orion Place
Columbus, OH 43240-4027

ISBN 0-07-821619-2 (Student Edition)

ISBN 0-07-821620-6 (Teacher's Wraparound Edition)

1 2 3 4 5 6 7 071 06 05 04 03 02 01 00

ACADEMIC CONSULTANTS

Jerrold Green, Ph.D.
Director
Middle East Studies Center
University of Arizona
Tucson, Arizona

Al Naklowycz, Ph.D.
President
Ukranian-American Academic
  Association of California
Carmichael, California

Joseph R. Rosenbloom, Ph.D.
Professor of Classics
Washington University
St. Louis, Missouri

Sayyid M. Syeed, Ph.D.
Director
International Institute of Islamic
  Thought
Herndon, Virginia

TEACHER REVIEWERS

Richard Ammentorp
Schaumburg School District
Schaumburg, Illinois

Robin Harrison Black, Ph.D.
Winburn Middle School
Lexington, Kentucky

Rick Boeglin
Richardson North Junior High
  School
Richardson, Texas

Margaret Gray, Ph.D.
Vigo County School
  Corporation
Terre Haute, Indiana

Kathleen A. Grotto
West Orange Senior High
  School
West Orange, New Jersey

Dianne Hill
Muskogee Public Schools
Muskogee, Oklahoma

Joseph Scheideler
Canton Junior/Senior High
  School
Collinsville, Connecticut

Table of Contents

Table of Contents

Table of Contents

Features

Charts, Diagrams, and Illustrations

Map Study

MAP STUDY

NCSS Correlation

Theme	1	2	3	4	5
Culture and Traditions	4, 5	1, 2	1, 2, 3	2, 3, 4	1, 2
Continuity and Change	1, 2, 5	1, 2	1	2	1, 2
Geography and History	1, 2, 3, 4, 5	1, 2	1, 2	1, 2, 4	1, 2
Individual Action	5	1, 2	1, 2	1, 2, 4	1, 2
Groups and Institutions		1, 2	1, 2	2, 3, 4	1, 2
Government and Democracy		2	1, 2	2, 3	2
Economic Factors	3	2	1, 2	3, 4	
Science and Technology			3	5	
Global Connections	1		2, 3	3, 5	
Civic Rights and Responsibilities					
Skill Category/ Specific Skill	Map Skills/ Understanding a Mercator Projection Critical Thinking Skills/ Understanding Cause and Effect	Map Skills/ Determining Relative Location	Critical Thinking Skills/ Distinguishing Fact from Fiction Map Skills/ Identifying Physical Features	Map Skills/ Reading Map Legends	

Theme	11	12	13	14	15
Culture and Traditions	1, 2	1, 2	1, 2, 3	4	1, 2, 3
Continuity and Change	1	2	2	2, 5	2, 4
Geography and History			1	2, 3, 4, 5	1, 4
Individual Action	1, 2	1, 2	2	1, 3, 5	1, 2, 3, 4
Groups and Institutions	1	1	2	2, 5	3, 4
Government and Democracy	2	1, 2	3	1, 3, 5	1, 2, 4
Economic Factors		2	1, 2	3, 4	2, 4
Science and Technology	2				
Global Connections		2	3	3, 4	2
Civic Rights and Responsibilities	2			1	1
Skill Category/ Specific Skill			Map Skills/ Reading a Political Map		Critical Thinking Skills/ Recognizing the Main Idea

*The section numbers set in red indicate the central theme of the section.

NCSS Correlation

Theme	6	7	8	9	10
Culture and Traditions	1, 2	1, 2, 3	1, 2, 3, 5, 6	1, 2	1, 2, 3, 4
Continuity and Change	1, 2	3	5, 6	2	3, 4
Geography and History	1, 2	1, 3	4, 5, 6	1, 2	1, 3
Individual Action	1, 2	1, 2, 3	1, 2, 5, 6	1, 2	1, 2, 3
Groups and Institutions	1, 2	3	1, 5	1, 2	1, 3
Government and Democracy		1, 3			1, 3
Economic Factors	1	2, 3	1, 2, 3, 5, 6	1, 2	2, 3
Science and Technology		2	2, 5		
Global Connections	1, 2		1, 2, 3		
Civic Rights and Responsibilities					1, 2, 3
Skill Category/ Specific Skill	Map Skills/ Reading a Map Scale Critical Thinking Skills/Making Comparisons		Map Skills/ Reading Latitude	Map Skills/ Reading Longitude	Map Skills/Reading Physical Maps Crtitcal Thinking Skills/ Recognizing Bias

Theme	16	17	18	19	20
Culture and Traditions	1, 2, 3	1	1, 3	1, 2	1, 2
Continuity and Change	2, 3	1	3	1, 2	1, 2
Geography and History	2, 3	2	2	1, 2	1, 3
Individual Action	1, 2	1	1, 2, 3	2	1, 2
Groups and Institutions	1, 2, 3	1, 2	1, 2, 3	1, 2	2, 3
Government and Democracy		1, 2		2	
Economic Factors		2	3	2	1
Science and Technology					
Global Connections	1, 2	2	3	1, 2	3
Civic Rights and Responsibilities					
Skill Category/ Specific Skill			Technology Skills/ Developing Multimedia Presentations Map Skills/ Understanding Inset maps		Map Skills/ Tracing Historical Routes

NCSS Correlation

Theme	21	22	23	24	25	
Culture and Traditions	1, 2, 3	1, 2, 3	1, 2, 3, 4	1, 2, 3, 4	1, 2, 3, 4	
Continuity and Change	1, 2, 3, 4	1, 2	1, 2, 3, 4	2	2	
Geography and History	1, 2, 4	1, 2	1, 2, 4	1, 4	4	
Individual Action	2, 3	1, 2	2, 3, 4	1, 2, 4	2, 3, 4	
Groups and Institutions	1, 2, 3, 4	1, 2	1, 2, 3, 4	2, 3, 4	1, 2, 3, 4	
Government and Democracy	1, 2	1	2, 4	1, 2	1, 2	
Economic Factors	1, 4	2	1, 2	1, 4	4	
Science and Technology		3			4	
Global Connections	3, 4	1, 3			4	
Civic Rights and Responsibilities				1, 4		
Skill Category/ Specific Skill	Critical Thinking Skills/Making Generalizations		Map Skills/ Analyzing Historical Maps		Technology Skills/ Using the Internet Map Skills/ Determining Exact Location	

Theme	31	32	33	34	35	
Culture and Traditions	1, 2, 3	1, 2, 3	2, 4	1	1, 2, 3	
Continuity and Change	1, 2, 3	1, 2, 3	3, 4, 5	1, 2	1, 2, 3	
Geography and History	1, 2, 3, 4, 5	1, 2	2, 4	1, 2	1, 2	
Individual Action	1, 3	1, 2, 3	1, 3, 4, 5	1, 2	1, 2, 3	
Groups and Institutions	2, 3, 4	1, 2, 3	1, 3, 4	1, 2	2, 3	
Government and Democracy	1, 2, 3, 4, 5, 6	1, 2, 3	4	1, 2	1, 2, 3	
Economic Factors	1, 2, 3, 4, 5, 6	1, 2, 3	2, 3, 4, 5	1, 2	1, 2, 3	
Science and Technology		3	1, 2, 3, 4, 5	1		
Global Connections	1, 2, 3, 4, 5, 6	1, 3	1, 2, 3, 4, 5	2	1, 2	
Civic Rights and Responsibilities	3	1, 2, 3	4	1	1, 2	
Skill Category/ Specific Skill		Map Skills/ Reading a Military Map Technology Skills/ Building a Database			Map Skills/ Comparing Historical Maps Critical Thinking Skills/Predicting Consquences	

*The section numbers set in red indicate the central theme of the section.

NCSS Correlation

Theme	26	27	28	29	30
Culture and Traditions	1, 2, 3, 4, 5	1, 2, 3, 4, 5	1, 2, 3, 4, 5	1, 2, 3, 4, 5	
Continuity and Change	2, 3, 5	2, 4, 5	1	2, 3	1, 2
Geography and History	1, 2, 3	1, 2, 4, 5	1	5, 6	1, 2, 3
Individual Action	3, 4, 5	1, 2, 3, 4	1, 2, 3, 4, 5	1, 2, 3, 4, 5	1, 2, 3
Groups and Institutions	2, 3, 4	2, 5	1, 4	1, 2, 3, 4, 5, 6	2
Government and Democracy	3	1, 2, 3, 4, 5	1, 4, 5	4, 5, 6	1, 2, 3
Economic Factors	1, 2, 3, 4	1, 3	1, 3		1, 2, 3
Science and Technology		3, 4	1, 3		1
Global Connections	1		3	2, 3	1, 2, 3
Civic Rights and Responsibilities			1		
Skill Category/ Specific Skill				Critical Thinking Skills/Drawing Conclusions	Map Skills/ Reviewing Map Legends

Theme	36	37	38	39
Culture and Traditions	1, 2, 3, 5	1, 2, 3	2, 3	1, 2, 3
Continuity and Change	2, 3	1, 2, 3	1, 3	1, 2, 3
Geography and History	1, 2, 3, 4	1, 2, 3	1	1, 2
Individual Action	2, 3, 4	1, 2, 3	1, 2, 3	1, 2, 3
Groups and Institutions	3	2, 3	2, 3	1, 2, 3
Government and Democracy	1, 2, 3, 4, 5	1, 2	1, 2, 3	1, 2, 3
Economic Factors	1, 2, 3, 4, 5	1, 2, 3	1, 2, 3	1, 2, 3
Science and Technology	1, 3	1	1	3
Global Connections	2, 3, 4, 5	1, 2, 3	1, 3	1, 2, 3
Civic Rights and Responsibilities	5	2	1, 3	1, 2, 3
Skill Category/ Specific Skill			Technology Skills/ Using an Electronic Spreadsheet	Map Skills/ Reading a Demographic Map

Teacher Planning and Support

New!
Daily Questions in Social Studies focus on Geography, Economics, Cultures, Citizenship, and History!

Hands-On History Lab Activities

GLENCOE SOCIAL STUDIES
Guide to Using the Internet

GLENCOE SOCIAL STUDIES
School-to-Work Handbook

Heritage
World History

Ready-To-Use Activities:
• provide students Internet applications
• extend Social Studies concepts
• develop multimedia literacy

Activity Cards
WORLD GAMES

WORLD ACTIVITY CARDS ACTIVITY CRAFTS

COUNTRIES OF THE WORLD
COUNTRIES OF THE WORLD
FLASH CARDS
GLENCOE

Geography and
Map Activities

TEACHER'S ANNOTATED EDITION
BUILDING SKILLS IN
GEOGRAPHY

Glencoe
Human Heritage

GLENCOE SOCIAL STUDIES
OUTLINE MAP
RESOURCE BOOK

Glencoe Social Studies
Making a World of Difference

The World – Physical/Political

BUILDING SKILLS IN
GEOGRAPHY

Richard G. Boehm   James F. Petersen   Larry E. Bybee

A text-workbook based on the five
major geographical themes of:

• Location

• Place

• Region

• Movement

• Human/Environment Interaction

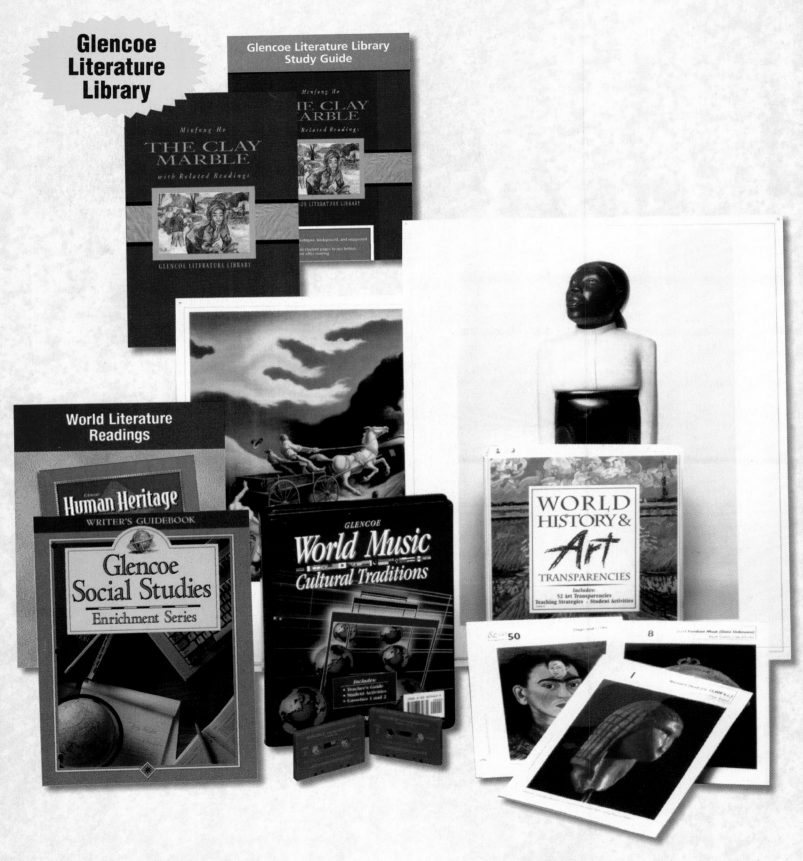

Glencoe Literature Library

Glencoe Literature Library Study Guide

Minfong Ho
THE CLAY MARBLE
with Related Readings

GLENCOE LITERATURE LIBRARY

Minfong Ho
THE CLAY MARBLE
with Related Readings

World Literature Readings

Human Heritage
WRITER'S GUIDEBOOK

Glencoe Social Studies
Enrichment Series

GLENCOE
World Music
Cultural Traditions

Includes:
• Teacher's Guide
• Student Activities
• Cassettes 1 and 2

WORLD HISTORY & Art TRANSPARENCIES

Includes:
52 Art Transparencies
Teaching Strategies · Student Activities

Primary Source
Readings

Enrichment
Activities

Cooperative Learning
Activities

Glencoe
Human Heritage
A World History

Ready-to-Use
Activities:
• Provide Collaborative Learning
• Include High-Interest Formats
• Enrich Learning Through
  Hands-On Experience

n Heritage
rld History

GLENCOE SOCIAL STUDIES
World History
Primary Source Document
Library

Includes:
• More than 200 primary source
  documents
• Audio document library
• Teacher strategies and
  activities
• Full text search and va
  browsing functions
• Guided tour...and ma
  convenient features

Glencoe Social S
T E C H N O L

GLENCOE SOCIAL STUDIES
World History
Primary Source Document
Library

Windows &
Macintosh
Version 1.0

P/N G17012 01
ISBN 0-02-821701-2

Glencoe
McGraw-Hill

© Copyright by The McGraw-Hill Companies, Inc.
All Rights Reserved. 10/00

GLENCOE
FOODS
AROUND THE
WORLD

Spanish Chapter Digests
Audiocassettes Activities and Tests

Glencoe
Human Heritage
A World History

This Resou...
• Includes Activitie...
Accompany Audi...
• Provides Assess...

Mc Graw Hill Glencoe
McGraw-Hill

Spanish
Summaries and Glossary

Glencoe
Human Heritage
A World History

Help
Spanish-Speaking
Students:
• Review Chapter Content
• Master New Material
• Prepare for Quizzes and Tests

Human Heritage

Human Heritage

ABCNEWS INTERACTIVE™

Turning Points in World History from ABCNews InterActive™ highlights the historical events that changed the world and its people.

Videotapes

From the lives of the famous to the lives of the infamous, from ancient times to today, from the battlefields of war to the monuments of peace, **A&E Home Video, Biography,** and **The History Channel** videotapes bring the full panorama of history into your classroom.

NATIONAL GEOGRAPHIC SOCIETY

The prestigious **National Geographic Society** has teamed with Glencoe to provide your students with a variety of interactive videodiscs, CD-ROMS, transparencies, and posters to extend and enrich the study of world history.

OVERVIEW

Unit 1 serves as an introduction to the study of world history and geography and sets the stage for the development of civilization.

➤ **Chapter 1** acquaints the students with the five fundamental geographic themes that geographers use to study the earth, and with geographical features. It also discusses how scientists uncover clues that help them piece together what happened in the distant past.

➤ **Chapter 2** deals with prehistory and the various stages of development people went through before civilization evolved.

UNIT OBJECTIVES

After reading Unit 1, students will be able to:

1. identify important geographic themes.

2. explain ways in which geography has influenced the course of history.

3. specify how scientists work together to learn about the past.

4. describe how hunters and food gatherers and food producers lived during prehistoric times.

UNIT PROJECT

Have students select five major achievements of prehistoric people that have been most important to humankind. Ask them to rank the achievements, listing the most important first. Then, working in groups, create a display of these achievements, bringing prehistoric life into the classroom. Finally, have them write a paragraph explaining the achievement and how important it was to the development of civilization.

UNIT 1 # Place and Time

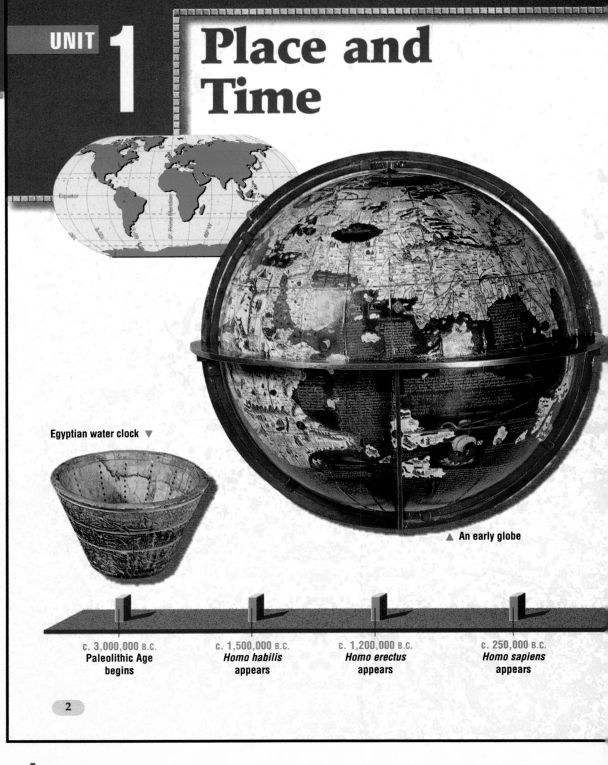

Egyptian water clock ▼

▲ An early globe

c. 3,000,000 B.C.
Paleolithic Age begins

c. 1,500,000 B.C.
Homo habilis **appears**

c. 1,200,000 B.C.
Homo erectus **appears**

c. 250,000 B.C.
Homo sapiens **appears**

2

ABOUT THE UNIT OPENING

Examining Artifacts

Ask students how these two artifacts illustrate the Unit title. *(The globe shows places on the earth; the water clock shows a way of keeping time.)* Tell students that historians use two question words—*where* and *when*—to study place and time. Encourage students to use these words to form questions about the following topics in Unit 1: early humans, the start of farming, the first cities.

Global Chronology

Refer students to the unit time line above. Explain that *c.* means "about" and that B.C. means "before Christ." Ask students to explain what the time line covers. *(major events in prehistory)* About how long did the Paleolithic Age last? *(about 2,992,000 years)* About how long after the Neolithic Age began did writing develop? *(about 3,500 years)*

Multimedia Activity

Surfing the Net
Archaeology

Archaeologists have uncovered many prehistoric *artifacts*, or objects made by people. These artifacts have helped historians piece together the stories of cultures before the invention of writing. To learn more about discoveries in the United States, visit the Internet.

Getting There

Follow these steps to gather information about archaeological sites in your state or in a state near your region.
1. Pick a search engine, such as Excite, Lycos, Yahoo, WebCrawler, etc.
2. Type in the main search word *archaeology*. Then add words to focus your research. Words might include *prehistoric, North America, Native Americans*.
3. Explore links the search engine brings up on the screen. (Links point the way to Web sites on the Internet.)
4. Click on links that provide information on the subject of your research.

Hands-On Activity

Pick a current archaeological dig in the state of your choice. Design a historical marker that might be placed at this site. The marker should include a description of the site's location, estimated dates that early people lived at the site, the name of these people (if available), and important discoveries made.

PRIMARY SOURCES
Library

See pages 674–675 for a primary source reading to accompany Unit 1.

c. 100,000 B.C. **Cro-Magnons appear**

c. 8000 B.C. **Neolithic Age begins**

c. 6500 B.C. **Catal Hüyük established**

Journal Notes

When did people appear on the earth? What factors have influenced where and how people have lived? Note details as you read.

Geographic Location

Unit 1 focuses mainly on the continents of Africa, Europe, and Asia, where archaeologists have found the remains and artifacts of prehistoric people. However, developments here impacted the whole world.

GLENCOE TECHNOLOGY

Videodisc
Use the MindJogger to preview the unit content.

MindJogger Videoquiz

Unit 1
Disc 1 Side A

 Also available in VHS.

INTRODUCING THE UNIT

Write the following quotation on the chalkboard from Cicero, a Roman statesman and orator: *"Not to know what happened before one was born is to remain a child."* Have students brainstorm the meaning of the quotation. Ask them how we can overcome ignorance about our past. (*by studying history*)

RECORDING JOURNAL NOTES

Help students begin writing in their journals by asking them to name the factors that have influenced where people have lived. Tell students to note details about these factors in their journals as they read this unit.

PRIMARY SOURCES
Library

Items in the Primary Sources Library for this unit focus on Mary Leakey's work at Olduvai Gorge. Elements include:
• Selection from *National Geographic* article by Mary Leakey
• Photograph of Leakey at work

For additional primary source documents, have students use the World History Primary Source Document CD-ROM.

Chapter 1 Planning Guide

Objectives	Reproducible Resources	Multimedia Resources
Section 1 **Five Themes of Geography** Describe how the five themes of geography help explain what a place is like and why it is like that.	Reproducible Lesson Plan Chapter 1 Vocabulary and Guided Reading Activity Reading Essentials and Study Guide 1-1 Chapter 1 Cooperative Learning Activity Chapter 1 Chart and Graph Skill Activity Section 1 Quiz Unit 1 Hands-On History Lab	Vocabulary PuzzleMaker Interactive Tutor Self-Assessment Software ExamView® Pro Testmaker Glencoe Skillbuilder Interactive Workbook, Level 1
Section 2 **Land, Water, and Climate** Explain how landforms, waterways, and climate have shaped history.	Reproducible Lesson Plan Reading Essentials and Study Guide 1-2 Chapter 1 Geography and Map Activity Section 2 Quiz	Teaching Transparency and Activity 1B Vocabulary PuzzleMaker Interactive Tutor Self-Assessment Software ExamView® Pro Testmaker Glencoe Skillbuilder Interactive Workbook, Level 1
Section 3 **Natural Resources** Describe how natural resources have shaped history.	Reproducible Lesson Plan Reading Essentials and Study Guide 1-3 Section 3 Quiz	Vocabulary PuzzleMaker Interactive Tutor Self-Assessment Software ExamView® Pro Testmaker Glencoe Skillbuilder Interactive Workbook, Level 1
Section 4 **Legends** Analyze the importance of legends in the study of history.	Reproducible Lesson Plan Reading Essentials and Study Guide 1-4 Unit 1 World Literature Readings 1 & 2 Section 4 Quiz	Vocabulary PuzzleMaker Interactive Tutor Self-Assessment Software ExamView® Pro Testmaker Glencoe Skillbuilder Interactive Workbook, Level 1
Section 5 **Archaeology** Summarize how archaeology helps scientists learn about ancient civilizations	Reproducible Lesson Plan Reading Essentials and Study Guide 1-5 Chapter 1 Activity Book Activity Chapter 1 Enrichment Activity Unit 1 Primary Source Readings 1 & 2 Section 5 Quiz	Teaching Transparency and Activity 1A Vocabulary PuzzleMaker Glencoe Skillbuilder Interactive Workbook, Level 1
Chapter 1 **Review and Evaluation**	Chapter 1 Reteaching Activity Chapter 1 Performance Assessment Activity Spanish Summary and Glossary Chapter 1 Test	Vocabulary PuzzleMaker Interactive Tutor Self-Assessment Software Glencoe Skillbuilder Interactive Workbook, Level 1 Audiocassettes* ExamView® Pro Testmaker

*Also available in Spanish.

Presentation Plus!

Use Glencoe's **Presentation Plus!** multimedia teacher tool to easily present dynamic lessons that visually excite your students. Using Microsoft® PowerPoint, you can customize the presentations to create your own personalized lessons.

Interactive Lesson Planner

Planning has never been easier! Using this CD-ROM, organize your week, month, semester, or year with all the help you need. The **Interactive Lesson Planner** gives you access to all of the blackline masters which accompany *Human Heritage*.

✓ PERFORMANCE ASSESSMENT ACTIVITIES

Climate Maps   Tell students to create a simple outline map of the world showing the continents. Ask them to add major climate zones to their maps and to create a key. As students read the chapter, have them locate and mark each place that they read about. Discuss differences between climate zones, and identify places with climates similar to where students live.

CHAPTER RESOURCES

LITERATURE ABOUT THE PERIOD

Courlander, Harold. *The King's Drum, and Other African Tales.* Harcourt, 1962. Folktales from Africa south of the Sahara

READINGS FOR THE STUDENT

Demko, George, Jerome Agel, and Eugene Boe. *Why in the World: Adventures in Geography.* Anchor, 1992. Multifaceted look at geography through the relationship of people and the earth.

READINGS FOR THE TEACHER

Natoli, Salvatore J., ed. *Strengthening Geography in the Social Studies: National Council for the Social Studies, Bulletin 81.* NCSS/SSSS. Ideas for teaching geographic concepts.

KEY TO ABILITY LEVELS

Teaching strategies have been coded for varying learning styles and abilities.

L1   Level 1 activities are **basic** activities and should be within the ability range of all students.

L2   Level 2 activities are **average** activities and should be within the ability range of the average to above-average student.

L3   Level 3 activities are **challenging** activities designed for the ability range of above-average students.

ELL   ELL activities should be within the ability range of English Language Learning students.

Teacher's Corner

INDEX TO NATIONAL GEOGRAPHIC MAGAZINE

The following articles relate to this chapter:

Note: Since many of the Magazine's articles emphasize the broad geographical themes mentioned in this chapter, students are encouraged to explore its back issues (see magazine CD-Rom listing under Additional National Geographic Society Products), For instance, see:
- "Revolutions in Mapping," by John Noble Wilford, February 1998.
- "The Most Ancient Americans," by Rick Gore, October 1997.
- "Iceland's Trial by Fire," photos by Steve Winter, May 1997.
- "The Iceman: Lone Voyager From the Copper Age," by David Roberts, June 1993.
- "Finding a Pharaoh's Funeral Bark," by Farouk El-Baz, April 1988.
- "A Buried Roman Town Gives Up Its Dead," by Joseph Judge, December 1982.

NATIONAL GEOGRAPHIC SOCIETY PRODUCTS AVAILABLE FROM GLENCOE

To order the following, call Glencoe at 1-800-334-7344:
- *PicturePack: Physical Geography of the World (Transparencies)*
- *STV: World Geography (Videodisc)*
- *Picture Atlas of the World (CD-ROM)*
- *GeoBee (CD-ROM; Software)*
- *PicturePack: World Geography Library (Transparencies)*

ADDITIONAL NATIONAL GEOGRAPHIC SOCIETY PRODUCTS

To order the following, call National Geographic at 1-800-368-2728:
- *The Complete National Geographic: 108 Years of National Geographic Magazine on CD-ROM (CD-ROMs)*
- *Exploring Your World: The Adventure of Geography (Book)*
- *World (Laminated Desk Maps)*
- *Geography: Five Themes for Planet Earth (Video)*
- *National Geographic World Atlas for Young Explorers (Book)*

Access *National Geographic's* new dynamic MapMachine Web site and other geography resources at:
http://www.nationalgeographic.com/
http://www.nationalgeographic.com/maps/

OVERVIEW

Chapter 1 links the five themes of geography to the study of the earth. It also shows how legends and archaeology help historians learn about the past.

➤ **Section 1** describes the five themes of geography.

➤ **Section 2** discusses the kinds of landforms, waterways, and climates found on the earth.

➤ **Section 3** describes the natural resources on the earth.

➤ **Section 4** explains how legends have been used to obtain clues to the past.

➤ **Section 5** examines the importance of archaeology.

CHAPTER OBJECTIVES

After reading Chapter 1, students will be able to:

1. describe how the five themes of geography help explain what a place is like and why.

2. explain how landforms, waterways, climate, and natural resources have shaped history.

3. discuss why legends are important to the study of history.

4. summarize how archaeology helps scientists learn about ancient civilizations.

EXAMINING ARTIFACTS

Point out that history is more than written words. Ask students what the bronze plaque and Stonehenge tell them about the early people who designed them. What other sources of information on the past can they name?

PERFORMANCE ASSESSMENT ✓

Use the Performance Assessment activities on page 4B to help you evaluate students as they complete the chapter.

4

CHAPTER 1

Geography and History

3,000,000 B.C.–present

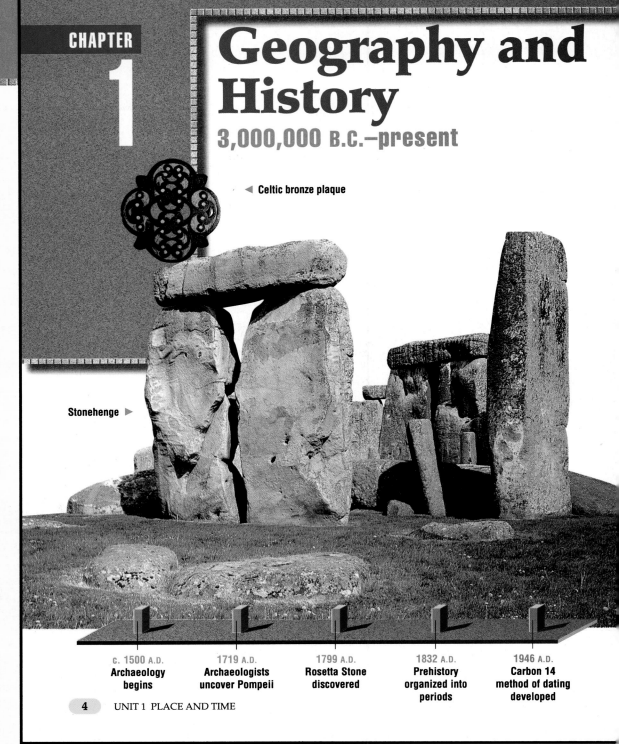

◀ **Celtic bronze plaque**

Stonehenge ▶

c. 1500 A.D.	1719 A.D.	1799 A.D.	1832 A.D.	1946 A.D.
Archaeology begins	**Archaeologists uncover Pompeii**	**Rosetta Stone discovered**	**Prehistory organized into periods**	**Carbon 14 method of dating developed**

4 UNIT 1 PLACE AND TIME

TEACHING RESOURCES

Chapter Focus

 Read to Discover

- How the five themes of geography help explain what a place is like and why.
- How landforms, waterways, climate, and natural resources have shaped history.
- How legends have been important to the study of history.
- How archaeology helps scientists learn about ancient civilizations.

 Terms to Learn
landforms
tectonic plates
glaciers
river system
archaeology
artifacts

 People to Know
Geradus
  Mercator
Mary Leakey
Frank Libby

 Places to Locate
Mount Everest
Nile River
Egypt
Pompeii

Why It's Important   Many scientists believe that people have been living on the earth for more than 2 million years. Where and how they lived was influenced greatly by the kind of land on which they lived. In many ways, the relationship between people and their environment has been the center of world history.

HISTORY Online
Chapter Overview
Visit the *Human Heritage* Web site at **humanheritage.glencoe.com** and click on **Chapter 1—Chapter Overviews** to preview this chapter.

SECTION 1 Five Themes of Geography

Geography is the study of the earth and of the ways people live and work on it. Geography helps explain why people live the way they do. Geography also helps explain the past by answering questions about why certain events occurred where they did. Geographers use five themes to help explain what a place is like and why it is like that.

Location   The location theme helps answer the question "Where is it?" For example, where is Kenya? That question can be answered by saying that Kenya is located on the huge continent of Africa.

There are two types of location: absolute and relative. **Absolute location** refers to the exact location of a place on the earth's surface. For example, the capital of Kenya—Nairobi—is located at one place and one place only. No other place on Earth has exactly the same location.

✓ **Reading Check**
How does **geography** help explain the past?

✓ **Reading Check**
What does **absolute location** tell you about a place?

GEOGRAPHY ACTIVITIES
📁 Chapter 1 Geography and Map Activity
📁 Social Studies Outline Map Resource Book

INTERDISCIPLINARY CONNECTIONS
📁 Unit 1 World Literature Readings 1 & 2
🎨 World History & Art Transparency 1, *Woman's Head*
🎧 World Music: Cultural Traditions

EXTENSION AND ENRICHMENT
📁 Unit 1 Primary Sources Reading 1
💿 World History Primary Source Document Library CD-ROM

📁 Chapter 1 Enrichment Activity
📁 Foods Around the World

ASSESSMENT AND EVALUATION
📁 Chapter 1 Performance Assessment Activity
📁 Chapter 1 Section Quizzes 1–1, 1–2, 1–3, 1–4, 1–5
📁 Chapter 1 Test
💿 Chapter 1 ExamView® Pro Testmaker Software
🎧 Chapter 1 Digests Audiocassettes Activities and Tests

SPANISH RESOURCES
📁 Chapter 1 Spanish Chapter Summary and Glossary
🎧 Chapter 1 Spanish Chapter Digests Audiocassettes Activities and Tests

---

HISTORY Online
Chapter Overview introduces students to chapter content and key terms. Have them access **Chapter 1 Overview** at **humanheritage. glencoe.com**

FOCUS

🔔 Bellringer
Write the following question on the chalkboard: *What factors have influenced the clothes you are wearing today?*

Motivational Activity
Ask students to share their reasons for wearing the clothes they have on today. Direct the responses by asking such questions as: Why are you wearing a shirt instead of a warm sweater?

GUIDE TO READING

Reading Strategy
Ask students to read "Why It's Important" and summarize the chapter's main theme. *(The relationship between people and their environment has helped shape human history.)* **L1**

Vocabulary Precheck
Ask students to define each of the "Terms to Learn." Have a volunteer consult the dictionary for any unfamiliar words. **L1** **ELL**

💾 Use the Vocabulary PuzzleMaker for Chapter 1 to create a crossword puzzle. **L1**

📁 Assign Chapter 1 Vocabulary and Guided Reading Activity.

📁 Assign Reading Essentials and Study Guide 1-1.

✓ **Reading Check Answers**
Geography helps to explain why events occurred where they did.
Absolute location refers to the exact location of a place on the earth's surface.

TEACH

Guided Practice

PLACE   A place such as the Moi Avenue in Mombasa, Kenya, shown here can be described easily. It is the avenue with the huge crossed elephant tusks. **What other details could be included in a description of this place?**

 Reading Check
How do you determine a place's **relative location?**

Relative location refers to the position of a place in relation to other places. Nairobi is located north of Mt. Kilimanjaro, west of the Indian Ocean, and southeast of Lake Turkana. Using this information, Nairobi can be found on a map of Africa if Mt. Kilimanjaro, the Indian Ocean, and Lake Turkana are located. A place may be described with many different locations.

Place   The theme of place answers the question "What is the place like?" Places can be described by their physical characteristics such as climate, mountains, deserts, bodies of water, plants, and animals.

Places can also be described by their human characteristics. These characteristics tell how many people live in a place, what language they speak, and what they do for a living. Knowing about a place's soil and about how its people make a living tells more about it than just its location. The physical and human characteristics of Nairobi, for example, make it a place that is different from Tokyo.

Human/Environmental Interaction

The theme of human/environmental interaction deals with how people use, adapt to, or change their environment. People respond to their environment in different ways. Sometimes they *adapt*, or adjust, to it. For example, people wear light clothing in a hot place and warm clothing in a cold place. At other times, people *modify*, or change, their environment. They may irrigate dry land to grow crops or build a dam to keep a river from flooding.

Ancient people adapted to their environment. They hunted animals and gathered fruit. Later, they changed the environment by farming the land and raising livestock.

Movement

The theme of movement looks at how people and places are linked together. Every day you have contact with people around the world. Your breakfast may include fruit from Latin America. You may ride to school in a bus, truck, or car made in Japan or Germany.

Movement has brought the world's people closer together. Transportation—the movement of goods and people—allows people to use products made in places thousands of miles away. Modern transportation lets people themselves travel thousands of miles in a matter of hours. The movement of people has been important in world history. The bringing of ideas to a new location has changed many cultures.

Albedo The amount of light a planetary surface reflects, or bounces back into space, is called "albedo." Albedo comes from the Latin word *albus*, meaning "whiteness." White has a much higher albedo, or ability to reflect light, than black. That's why people wear white clothes in summer or in hot climates.

INTERACTION Many acres of American forests have been cut to supply lumber products to a growing nation, as this photograph shows. Many new trees are planted to replace those removed. **What theme of geography is represented by this action?**

CAPTION ANSWER

human/environmental interaction

 VIDEODISC
STV: World Geography, Vol. 2: Africa and Europe

Side One, Frames 00001-49739
Title: *Africa*
Subject: Geographic contrasts and how people and animals have affected the natural environment of Africa
Ask: What continues to happen geologically in the Great Rift Valley?
(volcanic activity)

COOPERATIVE LEARNING

Organize the class into five groups. Have each group prepare five questions about a particular place. Each question should be about a different theme of geography. Allow time for the group to research the place they choose in order to ask appropriate questions and to know the answers to their questions. Have the groups present their questions and quiz each other, perhaps in a competition format.

Assign Chapter 1 *Cooperative Learning Activity* in the TCR.

L1 **Geography: Regions** Help students understand the concept of regions by making a list on the chalkboard of all the ways the students can think of to divide the United States into regions based on physical features and on human features. **ELL**

L2 **Critical Thinking** Ask students to chart an example of each kind of region: physical features, human features, economic, and a functional region other than those mentioned in their text. Have them add one region they think of themselves to their charts, also. Have students compare charts and note similarities and differences.

Linking Across Time

Answers will vary, but most students will probably focus on the computer's word processing speed, memory, and ability to access information and communicate with people via the Internet.

Communication—the movement of ideas and information—allows people to see or hear what is happening in their community or in another part of the world. People receive almost instant information by newspaper, radio, telephone, television, computer, and satellite.

The movement of people has been especially important in world history. People brought ideas and culture from one place to another. Sometimes those ideas changed the culture in the new location.

Regions To make it easier to study the world, geographers generally organize the world into regions. Geographers may define a region by its physical features, such as the kind of land found there. The Sahara is a desert region. Or they may define a region by its human features, such as the religion the people practice, the language they speak, or the way they earn a living. A region that shares a common language, such as Quebec where most people speak French, is such a region. Other regions might be economic, such as a "corn belt," or political, such as a region where the same type of political system is followed.

A type of region that has developed as human civilization has developed is a functional region. A functional region is an area where there is a central focus, such as a city. The characteristics of the region decrease as one moves away from the focus, or the city.

Linking Across Time

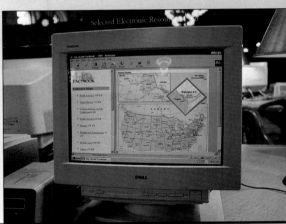

Written Communication Ever since people wrote their first clay tablets more than 5,000 year ago (left), they have been looking for easier and quicker ways to write. Perhaps no invention has affected written communication more than the computer (right). **How has the computer speeded up the movement of ideas and information?**

8   UNIT 1 PLACE AND TIME

MEETING SPECIAL NEEDS

The chapters in this textbook are organized in outline form to aid student understanding of the material. Point this out to students by creating on the chalkboard an outline of Chapter 1. Explain to students that the title of the chapter is the title of the outline; section titles can be used for Roman Numerals I, II, III; subsection titles can be used for A, B, C; and the topic sentence in the paragraphs can be used for 1, 2, 3.

Also to aid students' readability and understanding, social studies terms are first presented in boldface and then defined in context. Other unfamiliar terms are italicized and then defined. Have students find examples of these aids by scanning Chapter 1.

Refer to *Inclusion for the Middle School Social Studies Classroom: Strategies and Activities* for additional resources.

Section 1 Assessment

1. **Define:** geography, absolute location, relative location.
2. What five themes do geographers use to study the earth?
3. Why do geographers organize the world into regions?

Critical Thinking

4. **Making Comparisons** How does the theme of location differ from the theme of place?

Graphic Organizer Activity

5. Draw a diagram like this one, and use it to summarize information on each of the five themes used by geographers.

Five Themes				
1.	2.	3.	4.	5.

Use **Interactive Tutor Self-Assessment Software** to review Section 1.

L2 **Art** Have students work in small groups to create clay relief diagrams showing the four kinds of landforms. Have them label these landforms and add other geographic features if they choose. **ELL**

Reading Check Answer
The four kinds of **landforms** include mountains, hills, plateaus, and plains. **Elevation** describes height above sea level, and **relief** describes changes in height.

SECTION 2 Land, Water, and Climate

Photographs of the earth taken from space show a contrast of water and land beneath huge swirls of white clouds. These photographs reflect three of the things geographers study: land, water, and climate.

Landforms Land covers about 30 percent of the surface of the earth. Land is made up of four main kinds of **landforms,** or natural features of the earth's land surface. These landforms are mountains, hills, plateaus, and plains. Geographers describe each landform by its **elevation,** or height above sea level, and its **relief,** or changes in height.

Mountains are the highest of the world's landforms. They rise at least 2,000 feet, or 610 meters, above sea level. One of the peaks in the Himalaya (him uh lā' uh) Mountains in central Asia is Mount Everest, the world's highest mountain. It towers 29,028 feet, or 8,848 meters, above sea level. Other mountain ranges, like the Appalachians (ap uh lā' chunz) in the eastern United States, are not as high. Mountains generally have high relief.

Hills are lower than mountains. They rise from 500 to 2,000 feet, or 152 to 610 meters, above sea level. They generally have moderate relief. Plateaus are raised areas of flat or almost flat land. Plateaus can vary in elevation from 300 to 3,000 feet, or 91 to 914 meters, above sea level. Most of them have low relief.

Plains are large areas of flat or gently rolling land. They generally rise less than 1,000 feet, or 305 meters, above sea level and have low relief. The world's largest plain is the North European Plain, which stretches for more than 1,000 miles, or 1,609 kilometers, from the western coast of France to the Ural Mountains in Russia.

Reading Check
What are the four main kinds of **landforms?** How do geographers use **elevation** and **relief** to describe landforms?

Island Tips Some of the world's islands are really mountain summits—the tips of volcanoes that have risen from the sea. The highest summit in Hawaii, Mauna Kea, rises 13,796 feet, or 4,205 meters, above sea level. However, when measured from its base, Mauna Kea stands 32,000 feet, or 9,750 meters—taller than Mount Everest.

GEOGRAPHY AND HISTORY
Mountain ranges vary in age as well as height. The Himalayas are young mountains, having been formed about 25 million years ago. The Appalachians, which were formed about 225 million years ago, are among the oldest mountains in the world.

Use the **Vocabulary Puzzle-Maker** to create crossword and word search puzzles.

Section 1 Assessment Answers

1. geography, study of the earth and the ways people live and work on it (p. 5); absolute location, the exact location of a place on the earth's surface (p. 5); relative location, the position of a place in relation to other places (p. 6)
2. location, place, human/environmental interaction, movement, regions
3. to make it easier for them to study the world

4. Answers will vary but students might indicate that place gives more specific details about a place, and location describes a place's relation to other places.
5. Summaries should reflect the information on location, place, human/environmental interaction, movement, and regions on pp. 5–8.

Assign the Chapter 1 **Section 1 Quiz** in the TCR. Testmaker available.

Surface Changes From Inside the Earth The land surface of the earth is constantly changing. Most changes are caused by forces from deep within the earth, usually heat and pressure.

Heat and pressure are caused by the structure of the earth itself. The inside of the earth is made up of three separate layers. At the center of the earth is the **core.** The inner part of the core is solid rock, and the outer part of the core is made up of melted rock. Around the core is the **mantle,** which is made up mostly of hot, solid rock. Floating on the melted outer part of the mantle is a thin layer of rock, sand, and soil called the **crust.** The crust may be from 3 to 30 miles, or 5 to 49 kilometers, thick.

Heat from the core—the hottest part of the earth—causes the rock in the mantle to rise. This puts pressure on the crust and causes it to move. In recent years, scientists have come to believe that the crust does not move in one piece but in separate sections called **tectonic** (tek ton' ik) **plates.** These plates move very slowly, about 0.8 to 2 inches, or 2 to 5 centimeters, a year. Plates can move together, move apart, or slide past one another.

This movement of the plates explains what geographers call **continental drift.** Most geographers believe that about 220 million years ago, all the continents of the world formed one huge land mass named Pangaea (pan jē' uh). Over time, the plates

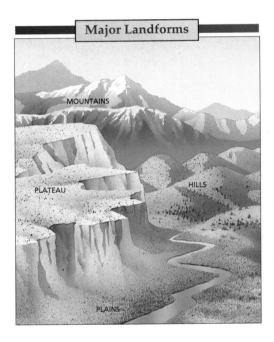

Major Landforms

MOUNTAINS

PLATEAU

HILLS

PLAINS

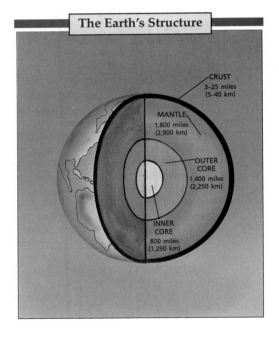

The Earth's Structure

CRUST
3–25 miles
(5–40 km)

MANTLE
1,800 miles
(2,900 km)

OUTER CORE
1,400 miles
(2,250 km)

INNER CORE
800 miles
(1,290 km)

Tectonic Plates

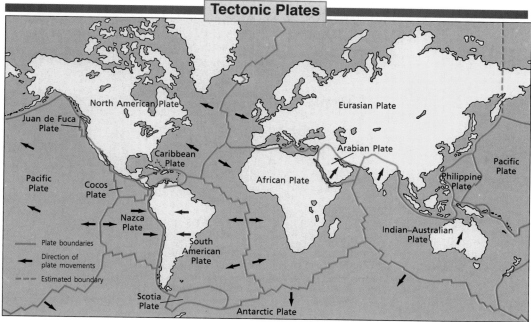

North American Plate

Juan de Fuca Plate

Eurasian Plate

Caribbean Plate

Arabian Plate

Pacific Plate

Pacific Plate

Cocos Plate

African Plate

Philippine Plate

Nazca Plate

South American Plate

Indian–Australian Plate

- Plate boundaries
- Direction of plate movements
- Estimated boundary

Scotia Plate

Antarctic Plate

moved and Pangaea split into seven continents. Some plates, such as the ones on which Africa and South America are located, moved apart. Other plates, such as the plates on which India and most of Asia are located, collided. The crust where these two plates met was squeezed upward to form the Himalayas.

Plate movement also creates **volcanoes.** These are cone-shaped mountains made when melted rock called lava flows up from the earth's mantle, cracks the crust, and then cools into solid rock. The Hawaiian Islands, for example, were formed by volcanoes that thrust up from the ocean floor millions of years ago.

Plate movements can also cause **earthquakes,** or sudden shifts in the earth's crust. These often happen when tectonic plates slide past one another. About 800,000 earthquakes occur each year with only about 50,000 of them strong enough for people to even feel them. A strong earthquake, however, can cause loss of life and serious property damage.

Both volcanoes and earthquakes are generally found along the edges of the earth's tectonic plates. They are so common around the Pacific Ocean that geographers call one area the "Ring of Fire."

The tectonic plates are still moving. Most geographers believe that thousands of years from now, California, which is on

MAP STUDY

LOCATION The idea that the continents were once joined and then slowly drifted apart is called the continental-drift theory. **According to the plate map, which plate is colliding with the South American plate along the west coast of South America?**

✓ Reading Check
How are **volcanoes** formed? What is a common cause of **earthquakes?**

MAP STUDY
Answer

Nazca Plate

✓ Reading Check Answer
Plate movements create **volcanoes** and are a common cause of **earthquakes.**

LINKING PAST TO PRESENT

There have been several serious earthquakes in the United States. In 1906, an earthquake that caused a great fire in San Francisco left more than 500 dead or missing. A 1989 earthquake in the same location killed dozens. Although this earthquake was quite strong, buildings have been constructed to withstand strong earthquakes and fireproof materials have been used in construction.

COOPERATIVE LEARNING

Organize the class into two groups. Assign volcanic eruptions to one group and earthquakes to the other group. Tell each group to make a list of natural disasters caused by these surface changes from inside the earth. Then have members work together to research information about the natural disasters on their list and to prepare an oral report and bulletin-board display of their subject.

L3 **Critical Thinking** Have students contrast the surface changes of forces from inside the earth with the surface changes of forces from outside the earth. *(Students should note that forces from inside the earth cause sudden, drastic changes in the earth's surface and are usually destructive. Forces from outside the earth are more gradual in nature and can either help or hurt people.)*

L2 **Geography: Human/Environmental Interaction** Have a volunteer read aloud a description of the Dust Bowl in the 1930s from an encyclopedia or history book. Discuss the human/environmental interaction that contributed to this disaster as a volunteer writes the causes on the chalkboard. Have students create a graphic organizer that shows the results of your discussion.

EARTHQUAKE DISASTERS   Mexico has experienced many earthquakes that have caused terrible loss of life and property. These earthquakes most often occur without warning. **What causes an earthquake?**

a different plate from most of the United States, will be located far off the west coast of Canada.

Surface Changes From Outside the Earth   Forces from outside the earth also cause changes on its surface. Three main forces are wind, water, and ice. All three reshape the land by a process called erosion (i rō′ zhuhn), in which rock and soil are moved from one place on the earth's surface to another. These forces can either help or hurt people.

An example of helpful wind erosion can be found in the plains of northern China, where large amounts of wheat and other food crops are grown. The plains are covered with a thick, rich, yellowish soil called *loess* (les) which was carried there by winds blowing from deserts to the west. On the other hand, during the 1930s winds blew away so much of the soil in the central part of the United States that the area became known as the Dust Bowl.

Water erosion that is helpful can be seen in the Mekong (may′ kawng) River of Southeast Asia. This river carries rich soil down from the mountains and spreads it over the lowlands, creating one of the most fertile areas in the world. Harmful water erosion occurs when the Huang Ho (hwong huh) in northern China overflows its banks and floods farms and homes.

Ice erosion has also caused changes on the earth's surface and in people's lives. Four times in the last 500,000 years, during

12   UNIT 1 PLACE AND TIME

EXTENDING THE CONTENT

The edges of the Pacific Ocean basin (which are generally the same as the borders of the Pacific plate plus some smaller plates) have come to be called the "Ring of Fire" because most of today's active volcanoes are located here. In North America, the Ring includes Alaska's Aleutians, the Cascade Range (where Mount St. Helens erupted), and Mexico's Popocatepetl. It continues southward through Central America and down the western edge of South America into Antarctica. On the other side of the Pacific are Japan's Fujiyama, the Southern Alps of New Zealand, and mountains in the Philippines and Indonesia.

what are called the Ice Ages, great ice sheets called **glaciers** spread out from the North and South poles. The ice drove people and animals away, smoothed hills into plains, created lakes, and dug new channels for rivers.

Landforms in History   All through history, landforms have played an important part in helping people decide where to live. People stayed away from mountainous areas where travel was difficult or where the air was so thin that it was hard to breathe. Instead, people settled mostly in plains and hilly areas where the soil was rich enough for crops to grow.

Landforms also have made a big difference in the political relationships of people. In ancient times the Greeks lived in many different city-states. One reason the Greeks did not join together to form a nation was that their communities were separated from one another by a landform—mountains.

Waterways   About 70 percent of the earth's surface is covered with water. The largest waterways in the world are the four oceans—the Atlantic, the Pacific, the Indian, and the Arctic.

✔ **Reading Check**
How did **glaciers** affect human and physical geography?

MAP STUDY

PLACE Scientists believe that in the last two million years glaciers have covered large areas of the earth's surface during the Ice Ages. **What continents were affected the most by the Ice Ages?**

✔ **Reading Check Answer**
Glaciers drove people and animals away, smoothed hills into plains, created lakes, and dug new channels for rivers.

L3 **Critical Thinking** Ask students to explain the duality of the Mississippi River in bringing both prosperity and devastation to the people who live along it. Have some students research the flood of 1993 and create a graph or chart showing loss of acres of farmland, lives, and destroyed property. Have other students research the economic prosperity enjoyed by those who earn their living from the river, creating a chart or graph of dollars earned and jobs generated. Have the two groups share their charts.

DID YOU KNOW

The Atlantic Ocean was named by the Romans after the Atlas Mountains that rose at the western end of the Mediterranean Sea. The Alantic got its name from two Latin words meaning "in the middle of the land." The Pacific Ocean was named by Spanish explorer Ferdinand Magellan, who found it calm and peaceful after his stormy voyage around Cape Horn.

Ice Ages

Map of the world showing continents and oceans during the Ice Ages, with latitude lines at 60°N, 30°N, 0°Eq, 30°S, 60°S and longitude lines at 120°W, 60°W, 0°, 60°E, 120°E.

Labels: ARCTIC OCEAN, NORTH AMERICA, EUROPE, ASIA, PACIFIC OCEAN, ATLANTIC OCEAN, AFRICA, PACIFIC OCEAN, SOUTH AMERICA, INDIAN OCEAN, AUSTRALIA, ANTARCTICA

Ice Sheets in the Paleolithic Age

miles 0 / 2000 / 4000
kilometers 0 / 2000 / 4000 / 6000

N

MEETING SPECIAL NEEDS

Help English Language Learning students learn the geographical terms that are discussed in this chapter. Have the class use their textbook and geographical reference materials to create a list of geographical features. Next, ask students to group related terms into the following categories: landforms, waterways. Organize the students into two groups and assign one category to each group. Have each student in the group define and illustrate one or more terms. When all the students have finished their assignments, compile the definitions and illustrations into an illustrated dictionary to use as a class reference.

📂 Refer to *Inclusion for the Middle School Social Studies Classroom: Strategies and Activities* for additional resources.

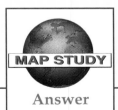
MAP STUDY

Answer

North America, Europe, Asia, and Antarctica

Reading Check
What is the longest **river system** in the world?

Reading Check
How is **climate** shaped by movements of the earth?

Reading Check
How can a place's **latitude** help you predict temperatures in the area?

Smaller bodies of salt water are known as seas. They are usually partly surrounded by land. Bodies of water that are completely surrounded by land are known as lakes. The world's largest fresh-water lake is Lake Superior in North America. It is about 350 miles, or 563 kilometers, long and 160 miles, or 257 kilometers, wide.

Waterways that empty into another body of water are known as rivers. Most rivers begin high in mountains or hills. A river and all the streams that flow into it make up a **river system.** The longest river system in the world is the Nile, which flows about 4,160 miles, or 6,693 kilometers, from its source in the highlands of central Africa to its mouth on the Mediterranean Sea.

Waterways in History Like landforms, waterways have played an important part in helping people decide where to live. People's earliest homes were along the banks of rivers and other waterways. These bodies of water provided them with a means for travel and trade, drinking water, irrigation for crops as farming developed. Thus, river valleys were often sites for villages and cities. Animals also used waterways for food and drinking water, so the riverbanks were good hunting grounds.

Climate and the Sun The pattern of weather of a place over many years is **climate.** The most important thing that shapes climate is the sun. The sun provides the earth with heat and light. All parts of the earth, however, do not receive the same amount of sunlight.

As the earth moves through space, it *rotates,* or spins like a top. Geographers say that it spins on its *axis,* an imaginary line that runs through the earth's center from the North Pole to the South Pole. It takes one day of 24 hours for the earth to spin around completely.

Besides rotating, the earth moves around the sun in an almost circular path called an *orbit.* This motion, known as a *revolution,* takes one year of 365¼ days to complete. It is the earth's revolution around the sun that causes the seasons.

Seasons vary from one part of the world to another. The earth's axis, instead of being straight up and down, is tilted at an angle. This means that places in the Northern Hemisphere are tilted toward the sun from March to September. As a result, these places have spring and summer at that time. During these same months, however, the Southern Hemisphere is tilted away from the sun. There it is fall and winter. Six months later, from September to March, conditions reverse, and the seasons are the opposite.

Climate Zones The amount of heat from the sun a place receives depends on its **latitude,** or distance north or south of the

EXTENDING THE CONTENT

Making a list of the world's longest rivers is not an easy task. Some references use only the length of the river itself, while others use the length of the entire river system. For example, the Mississippi River itself is 2,348 miles (or 3,779 km) long and ranks twelfth in length in the world. Some sources will rank the Mississippi the third longest river because they consider the combined Mississippi-Missouri rivers for length—3,880 miles (or 6,240 km).

The Earth's Revolution

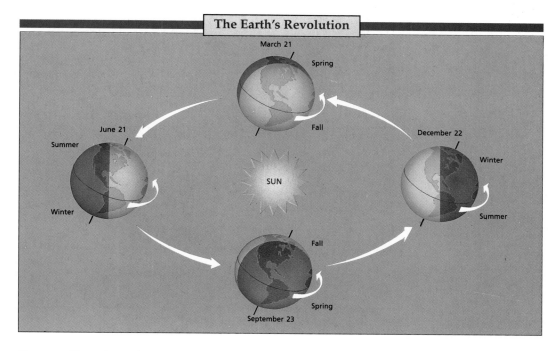

Equator. Rays from the sun are most direct at the Equator. Geographers often organize the earth into three climate zones based on latitude.

The **tropical zone,** also called the tropics, is the area between the Tropic of Cancer and the Tropic of Capricorn. The tropical zone always receives the most direct rays of the sun. Most places in the tropics are hot year-round.

The **temperate** (tem'puh ruht) **zone** is found in both the area between the Tropic of Cancer and the Arctic Circle in the Northern Hemisphere, and the area between the Tropic of Capricorn and the Antarctic Circle in the Southern Hemisphere. The sun's rays reach the temperate zone at a slant for part of the year and almost directly for the rest of the year. As a result, the weather in this zone is generally cold in winter and warm in summer.

The **polar zone** is the area north of the Arctic Circle and south of the Antarctic Circle. This area receives no sunlight at all during part of the year and only slanting rays during the rest of the year. As a result, the climate in the polar zone is very cold, and few people live there.

Climate, Water, and Wind   In addition to the sun, climate is shaped by large bodies of water, which keep the temperature of a place from getting too hot or too cold. Water gains or

Reading Check
Where is the **tropical zone** located?

Reading Check
What type of weather is found in each **temperate zone?**

Reading Check
Why is the **polar zone** very cold?

16

Reading Check Answer
Prevailing winds blow from a certain ("prevailing") direction most of the year. **Ocean currents** are steady streams of either hot or cold water.

Reading Check Answer
Mountains affect **precipitation** by causing air to rise, which in turn cools the air and forces it to drop its moisture.

MAKING CONNECTIONS

➤➤ **Science** In the days of sailing ships, experienced sea captains and navigators took advantage of their knowledge of the winds to make long voyages that seem almost unbelievable today.

NATIONAL GEOGRAPHIC SOCIETY

CD-ROM
Picture Atlas of the World
You and your students can see the challenges and solutions involved in making maps by viewing the Mapping Our World animation "Round Earth on Flat Paper."

Record Rain Cherrapunji, India, holds the world's record for annual rainfall. From August 1860 to August 1861, monsoons dumped 1,042 inches, or 2,647 centimeters, on the town. That's a downpour!

Reading Check
How did **prevailing winds** get their name? What are **ocean currents?**

Reading Check
How do mountains affect **precipitation?**

MONSOON Monsoons are very important to the agriculture of southern Asia. The wet, or summer, monsoons bring moisture necessary for farming to the area. Here, an Indian farmer struggles to plow his fields in the midst of monsoon winds and rain. **How do monsoons differ from prevailing winds?**

loses heat more slowly than land. Also, air over a lake is cooler than air over the land.

Climate is also shaped by the movement of air and ocean water. Air that moves is called wind. Some winds are known as **prevailing** (pri vā′ lēng) **winds** because they blow from a certain direction almost all the time. Other winds are called monsoons because they change direction according to the season of the year. Monsoons often bring heavy rainfall. Ocean water that flows in a steady stream is called an **ocean current.** Both winds and ocean currents carry heat or cold and moisture all over the world. Ocean currents that flow from the Equator toward the poles warm the lands they pass. Currents that flow from the poles to the Equator cool the land they pass.

Climate and Altitude   Climate is also shaped by altitude. The higher the altitude, the colder the climate. In the tropical zone, people often prefer living in highlands rather than lowlands because the highland temperatures are more comfortable. The ancient Incas settled in the Andes Mountains of Peru instead of along the Pacific coast for that reason. Mountains also affect **precipitation**—the falling of moisture such as rain or snow. As the air rises over mountains, it cools and drops its moisture.

16   UNIT 1 PLACE AND TIME

EXTENDING THE CONTENT

The pattern of prevailing winds worldwide is due to temperature differences and to the earth's rotation, which deflects winds from a straight-line path. At the Equator, for instance, rising warm air causes clouds and uncertain breezes where a ship might be motionless for days. Immediately to the north and south are two bands of trade winds, cool easterly winds that blow slight-

ly toward the Equator. In the middle latitudes, the earth's rotation makes the prevailing winds westerlies. These winds are stormier and more erratic than the trade winds. For early European explorers, though, they provided a dependable route homeward from the Americas across the Atlantic.

Understanding a Mercator Projection

Because Earth is a sphere, no flat map can show its whole surface. Mapmakers use different **projections** (pruh jek´ shuhns), or ways of representing Earth on a flat surface.

One projection used often is a Mercator (muhr kāt´ uhr) projection. Named after Gerardus Mercator, a Flemish mapmaker of the 1500s, it is made by wrapping paper around a globe. A light shining from the center of the globe projects Earth's features onto the paper. This allows the map to be traced.

The parts of the map that are most like the earth are where the paper touches the globe, such as at the Equator. The parts that are most *distorted* (dis tort´ ed), or twisted out of shape, are where the paper does not touch the globe such as near the poles.

Map Practice

1. **Which of the earth's climate zones is shown most accurately?**
2. **Which is most distorted?**
3. **Is the shape of North America more accurate on this map or on a globe? Why?**

World Climate Zones

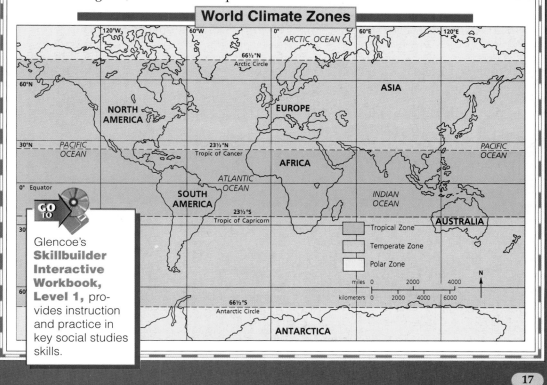

Glencoe's **Skillbuilder Interactive Workbook, Level 1,** provides instruction and practice in key social studies skills.

17

SPOTLIGHT ON: WORLD CLIMATE

Factors of climate can change as has been shown in recent years all over the world. Much of Africa north of the Equator receives very little rainfall. In this area is the world's largest tropical desert—the Sahara. However, at one time the Sahara was a fertile region that supported a thriving civilization. Because of a gradual lack of rainfall, most of this area is now uninhabitable. On the southern border of this desert is the Sahel, which in Arabic means *coastal land.* Between 1968 and 1974 a drought in the Sahel destroyed livestock and caused the starvation of many West Africans.

MAP SKILLS

TEACH

UNDERSTANDING A MERCATOR PROJECTION

Instruct the students to read the instructional part of the feature. Ask: Why can't a flat map show the whole surface of the earth? *(because the earth is a sphere)* How is a Mercator map projection made? *(by wrapping paper around a globe, shining a light from the center of the globe onto the paper, and tracing the map)* Which parts of the Mercator projection are most like the earth? *(parts where the paper touches the globe, such as at the Equator.)* Direct students to study the map. Ask: Which continent is more accurate on a Mercator projection, South America or Asia? Why? *(South America, because it is located closer to the Equator than Asia is)*

Next, have students work in small groups to study other projections. Assign each group one of the following projections: conic, sinusoidal, polar, Goode's interrupted equal-area projection, Robinson, or Gall-Peters. Have students find an example of their projection, explain how it is made, and describe its inaccuracies. Have each group present their findings.

Assign the Chapter 1 **Geography and Map Activity.**

Answers to Map Practice

1. Tropical Zone
2. Polar Zone
3. The globe representation is more accurate because no flat map can accurately represent a sphere.

17

Fun Facts...

Climate Early Greeks classified climates based on what they knew about Greece and areas to the south and north. They called their own climate *temperate* because it posed few problems of shelter and clothing. They believed the area south of the Mediterranean Sea became hotter, so they called these lands *torrid*. Cold winds from the north led them to call that area *frigid*.

Climate in History

Climate, like land and waterways, plays an important part in shaping history. It helps determine where people live, what kind of clothes they wear, what kind of houses they build, and what crops they grow. It also affects the speed with which they work and the kinds of things they do for entertainment. Since climate is something humans cannot control, it has affected civilizations since prehistoric times.

Sometimes climate affects the way a country behaves towards its neighbors. Climate has also helped decide the outcomes of wars. For example, many of Russia's harbors stay frozen during much of the year. In the past, Russia has often gone to war with other countries in order to capture land for warm water ports. Climate was also one reason the Russians were able to stop the invasions of French ruler Napoleon Bonaparte (nuh pō' lē uhn bō' nuh part) in the 1800s and German ruler Adolf Hitler in the 1940s. The Russians were used to the bitter cold and snow of their country's winter, whereas the invaders were not.

COLD CLIMATE This buoy has become frozen in the St. Petersburg Harbor during the cold Russian winter. Such waterways have been important many times in Russia's history. **What has the lack of warm water ports and harbors caused Russia to do in the past?**

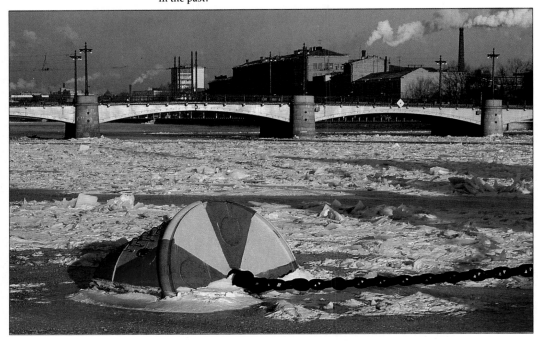

MEETING SPECIAL NEEDS

Have interested students research the affects of climate on the soldiers who fought in such wars as Vietnam and the Persian Gulf War. Encourage them to interview any participants in these wars that they happen to know. Have them explain their findings in an oral report to the class.

Refer to *Inclusion for the Middle School Social Studies Classroom: Strategies and Activities* for additional resources.

Section 2 Assessment

1. **Define:** landforms, elevation, relief, core, mantle, crust, tectonic plates, continental drift, volcanoes, earthquakes, erosion, glaciers, river system, climate, latitude, tropical zone, temperate zone, polar zone, prevailing winds, ocean current, precipitation.
2. What are some of the ways landforms and waterways have been important to history?
3. Into what climate zones do geographers often organize the earth?

Critical Thinking

4. **Making Generalizations** How does climate affect the way that you live?

Graphic Organizer Activity

5. Draw a diagram like this one, and use it to show the four kinds of landforms and to list examples of each landform in your community or state.

💾 Use **Interactive Tutor Self-Assessment Software** to review Section 2.

L2 **Geography: Region** Organize students into seven groups to make natural resource maps of the continents. Assign each group one of the continents. Have a member of each group present its map to the class. Discuss which continent appears to be most abundant in resources and what implications there might be as a result. **ELL**

L3 **Critical Thinking** Ask students to consider why some countries think of their people as their most important natural resource. What countries would be most likely to think this way? *(China, India)* Why?

SECTION 3 Natural Resources

Natural resources are materials found in nature. Some, such as air, are found everywhere. Others, such as oil, are found only in certain areas. Some places have many natural resources, while others have few.

Kinds of Natural Resources There are different kinds of natural resources. Some resources helpful to people include air, water, soil, sunlight, minerals, fossil fuels, forests, and animal life. Some of these—air, water, soil, and sunlight—are essential for any kind of life to exist. They are the most important natural resources.

Other natural resources, while not essential for life, are important because they enable people to live better. One such resource is **minerals,** or nonliving substances found beneath the earth's surface. Throughout history, people have used such minerals as iron, copper, tin, gold, and silver to make tools, weapons, jewelry, and money. Fossil fuels, such as coal, oil, and natural gas, provide the energy needed to heat homes and power machines.

Natural resources become valuable only when people learn how to use them. For example, during the 1200s Marco Polo left his native city of Venice, in present-day Italy, and traveled to

✔️ **Reading Check**
What are some examples of **natural resources?**

✔️ **Reading Check**
Why have **minerals** been important to people throughout history?

✔️ **Reading Check Answer**
Examples of **natural resources** include air, water, soil, sunlight, minerals, fossil fuels, forests, and animal life.

✔️ **Reading Check Answer**
People have used **minerals** to make tools, weapons, jewelry, and money.

Section 2 Assessment Answers

1. All terms are defined in the text Glossary.
2. Landforms and waterways played an important part in where people lived and their political relationships.
3. the tropical, temperate, and polar zones
4. Answers will vary but should give examples of the way climate affects the way they live.

5. The diagrams should include examples of the mountains, hills, plateaus, and plains in your community or state. (You might use the presence and/or absence of these landforms to discuss the unique features of your region, as would be the case in states on the Great Plains, along the Rockies, etc.)

Assign the Chapter 1 **Section 2 Quiz** in the TCR. Testmaker available.

L1 **Art** Have students find pictures in newspapers and magazines or draw illustrations of renewable resources and nonrenewable resources. Then divide a bulletin board in half. Title one side "Renewable Resources" and the other side "Nonrenewable Resources." Display pictures and illustrations on the bulletin board. Use the bulletin board to start a discussion of how the students can conserve their use of nonrenewable resources.

L3 **Geography: Human/Environmental Interaction** Have students research laws passed in their state to control the pollution of the air, soil, and water. Ask them to present their findings in an oral report to the class. Have the class decide if any additional laws are needed.

Reading Check Answer
Renewable resources can be replaced; **nonrenewable resources** cannot.

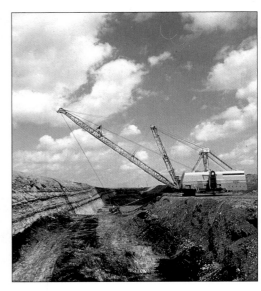

MINERALS Some natural resources are found beneath the ground and are called minerals. Oil and coal are two minerals for which people drill and mine underground. The oil well shown here (left) is in the jungles of Nigeria. Coal mining in North Dakota is also shown (right). **What are other examples of minerals?**

Reading Check
How do **renewable resources** and **nonrenewable resources** differ from each other?

China. A few years after returning home, he wrote a book about the wonderful things he had seen on his journey. One of these was a black rock, now known as coal, which the Chinese dug out of the ground and burned to keep themselves warm. The Venetians (vi nē' shuhnz) doubted Marco Polo. They had not used coal as the Chinese had. People later changed their minds about coal when they began using it as a fuel to power steam engines and to process steel.

Some resources can be replaced as they are used. These are **renewable resources.** For example, American farmers who lived in the Dust Bowl of the 1930s were able to get back their once-rich soil. To do this they used better ways of farming and planted trees to keep the soil from being blown away. Other natural resources cannot be replaced as they are used. These are **nonrenewable resources.** For example, once fossil fuels and most minerals are used up, they will be gone forever.

In recent years, people have become more and more concerned about making better use of the world's natural resources. Some countries have passed laws to slow down the pollution of the air, water, and soil. Scientists also are trying to develop new sources of energy.

20 UNIT 1 PLACE AND TIME

COOPERATIVE LEARNING

Ask the class to name important resources that need to be conserved, as you write responses on the chalkboard. Organize the students into as many groups as there are items on the list. Have each group investigate efforts being made to conserve its resource. Have each group also brainstorm other ways in which their resource might be conserved. After each group has completed its work, ask each to participate in a round-table discussion in which group members take turns suggesting ways to conserve their assigned resource.

Natural Resources in History   Natural resources affected the location and growth of settlements all through history. The sharing of these resources has also been important. Rich soil and plenty of water made farming possible and led to the rise of cities. Asians and Europeans came into contact with one another partly because Europeans wanted the silks and spices of Asia that had been cultivated. Modern industry started in countries that had large amounts of coal and iron ore for making steel. During the 1800s, the discovery of gold in California, South Africa, Australia, and Alaska caused hundreds of thousands of people to move to those areas.

Section 3 Assessment

1. **Define:** natural resources, minerals, renewable resources, nonrenewable resources.
2. What resources are needed for life?

Critical Thinking

3. **Demonstrating Reasoned Judgment** Why do you think people have become more interested in making better use of the world's natural resources?

Graphic Organizer Activity

4. Create a diagram such as this one, and use it to show examples of how natural resources have helped shape history.

RENEWABLE RESOURCES Soil is considered a renewable resource. Some human activities, like the strip mining of coal (left), use up the land. With careful management, however, such areas can be reclaimed, or made productive again (right). **What are some examples of nonrenewable resources?**

💾 Use **Interactive Tutor Self-Assessment Software** to review Section 3.

CAPTION ANSWER

fossil fuels and most minerals such as copper, tin, and gold

DID YOU KNOW

Oil takes millions of years to form, and the earth's supply is limited. Industrialized countries like the United States consume far more oil than they produce and must import large amounts. Many experts believe that the world's fossil fuels will be used up if steps are not taken to limit their consumption and to find alternative energy sources.

L2 **Science** Have students research to find out about alternative energy sources. Then have them make a diorama showing one of the alternative energy sources being used or applied.

Section 3 Assessment Answers

1. natural resources, materials found in nature (p. 19); minerals, nonliving substances found beneath the earth's surface (p. 19); renewable resources, resources that can be replaced (p. 20); nonrenewable resources, resources that cannot be replaced (p. 20)
2. air, water, soil, and sunlight
3. Answers will vary but might include that people are afraid resources will be used up,

and they want to stop pollution of these resources.
4. Examples should come from "Natural Resources in History" on this page. Encourage students to add more than four examples, either from Section 3 or from their own knowledge of history.

Assign the Chapter 1 **Section 3 Quiz** in the TCR. Testmaker available.

L2 **Critical Thinking** Ask students why they think people developed legends to explain their past.

L3 **Writing** Have students imagine that they were living long ago, when there were no scientific explanations for natural occurrences. Have students write a legend explaining thunder and lightning.

Use the **Vocabulary Puzzle-Maker** to create crossword and word search puzzles.

✔ **Reading Check Answer**
Legends help explain the past.

✔ **Reading Check**
What are the purposes of **legends?**

SECTION 4 Legends

People have always been interested in learning about the past. Every group of people on the earth has **legends**, or folktales, that help to explain the past. These legends began as stories that were spoken or sung. People passed them down from generation to generation.

A Chinese Legend The Chinese have a legend about the beginnings of China. It says that the universe was a huge egg. When the egg split open, the upper half became the sky, and the lower half became the earth. Out of the split egg came P'an Gu (pan gū), the first man. Each day for 18,000 years P'an Gu grew taller, the sky grew higher, and the earth grew thicker. Then P'an Gu died. His head split and became the sun and the moon. His blood filled the rivers and the seas. His hair became the forests and the meadows. His perspiration became the rain. His breath became the wind and his voice, the thunder.

22 UNIT 1 PLACE AND TIME

MULTICULTURAL PERSPECTIVES

Every culture has at least one creation myth or legend. The following is a Norse myth as told in Bulfinch's classic *Mythology: The Age of Fable.*

There was once no heaven above nor earth beneath, but only bottomless deep, and a world of mist in which flowed a fountain. Twelve rivers flowed from this fountain, and when they had flowed far from their source, they froze into ice . . .

Southward from the world of mist was the world of light. From this flowed a warm wind upon the ice and melted it. The vapours rose in the air and formed clouds, from which sprang Ymir, the Frost giant, and his progeny [children] and the cow Audhumbla, whose milk

An African Legend   The Africans have a legend about why the sun shines more brightly than the moon. It says that God created the Moon and then the Sun. Because the Moon was bigger and brighter, the Sun became jealous and attacked the Moon. They fought and wrestled until the Sun begged for mercy. Then they wrestled again. This time the Sun threw the Moon into the mud. Dirt splashed all over the Moon, and it was no longer as bright as before. To stop the fighting, God stepped in. He told the Sun that from then on it would be brighter than the Moon and would shine during the day for kings and workers. He told the Moon that from then on it would shine only at night for thieves and witches.

A Rumanian Legend   The Rumanians have a legend about the creation of mountains and valleys. It says that when God finished making the heavens, He measured them with a little ball of thread. Then He started to create the earth to fit under them. A mole came along and offered to help. So God let the mole hold the ball of thread while He created the earth.

STONEHENGE   Many legends have been told about the ancient ruins of Stonehenge in Great Britain, shown here. These stones are arranged in an unusual formation believed to date back to prehistoric times. **How do modern people learn about ancient legends such as the stories about Stonehenge?**

Independent Practice

L2 **Language Arts** Have students research legends about a group of people they are interested in. Every culture can be found represented in the library. Ask students to prepare a reading of one legend for the class. Have them write the name of the legend and its topic on a notecard and attach it to a wall map of the world showing where the culture it represents exists, or did exist.

DID YOU KNOW ??

It is believed that Stonehenge was built in three phases from 2800 to 1500 B.C. Besides being used for tribal gatherings and religious ceremonies, the stones were probably used to find out when major astronomical happenings would occur.

CAPTION ANSWER

People passed them down from generation to generation. After people developed writing, they wrote down their legends.

MULTICULTURAL PERSPECTIVES

afforded nourishment and food to the giant . . . While she [the cow] was one day licking the salt stones there appeard at first the hair of a man, on the second day the whole head, and on the entire form endowed with beauty, agility, and power. This new being was a god, from whom and his wife, a daughter of the giant race sprang the three brothers Odin, Vili, and Ve.

They slew the giant Ymir, and out of his body formed the earth, of his blood the seas, of his bones the mountains, of his hair the trees, of his skull the heavens, and of his brain clouds, charged with hail and snow. Of Ymir's eyebrows, the gods formed Midgard (middle earth), destined to become the abode of man.

While God was weaving and shaping the earth, the mole let out the thread little by little. God was too busy to notice that at times the mole let out more thread than it should have. When God was finished, He was amazed to find that the earth was too big to fit under the heavens.

The mole, seeing what it had done, was afraid. It ran off and buried itself. God sent the bee to find the mole and ask it what should be done. But when the bee found the mole, it would not answer the question.

The bee hid in a flower, hoping the mole would think it was alone and start talking to itself. Sure enough, the mole thought out loud. It said that it would squeeze the earth so that the mountains would stick up and the valleys would sink down. Then the earth would be small enough to fit under the heavens. Upon hearing this, the bee buzzed off. The mole heard the buzzing and became angry. It put a curse on the bee, saying, "Henceforth, feed on yourself."

The bee told God what the mole had said. God squeezed the flat earth so that the mountains rose up, the valleys sank down, and the earth fit under the heavens. God then turned the mole's curse into a blessing. Ever since, the bee makes its own honey, while the mole lives underground and is afraid to come out.

Other Legends

These Chinese, African, and Rumanian legends are about the creation of the world. This is not true of all legends. Many are about the deeds of godlike men and women or about strange and wonderful lands. Other legends explain natural elements such as the placement of stars or why a maple tree has red leaves. Some even explain geographic features such as mountains and rivers.

After people developed writing more than 5,000 years ago, they wrote down their legends. Many came to be thought of as fact. In recent years, **archaeologists,** or scientists who study the remains of past human life, and **anthropologists,** or scientists who study the origin and development of humans, became curious about how much of certain legends was fiction and how much was fact. This led them to search out the truth of some of the legends.

✓ **Reading Check** What type of work is done by **archaeologists?** What do **anthropologists** study?

Section 4 Assessment

1. **Define:** legends, archaeologists, anthropologists.

Critical Thinking

2. **Analyzing Information** What legends do you know? What do they try to explain?

Graphic Organizer Activity

3. Draw a diagram like this one, and use it to show the order of events in one of the legends in this section.

☐ → ☐ → ☐ → ☐ → ☐

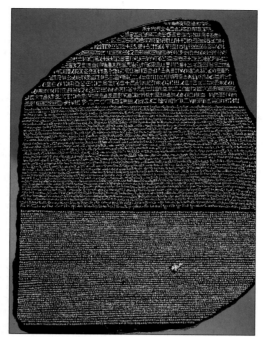

EGYPTIAN ARTIFACTS   Archaeologists have uncovered many artifacts in Egypt. This spearhead (left), from about 15,000 B.C., is one of the oldest objects found in the region. The Rosetta Stone (right), from around 200 B.C., is one of the most famous archaeological finds. On it is carved a decree issued by Egyptian priests to honor a leader. **What kinds of objects can be considered artifacts?**

SECTION 5 Archaeology

Archaeology, or the study of the remains of past human life and cultures, began about 500 years ago. At that time, some Europeans dug up old marble statues and ornaments made by the ancient Greeks and Romans and sold them for a great deal of money. Scientists began to study these **artifacts,** or things made by people. They found they could learn from the artifacts how people lived long ago. People who lived in ancient times did not leave many written records.

Artifacts do not have to be works of art. They can be anything made by people such as weapons, tools, or pottery. The earliest artifacts are pieces of hard rock that were chipped into cutting or digging tools or into weapons.

✓ **Reading Check**
How did **archaeology** get its start?

✓ **Reading Check**
What information did scientists discover from the study of **artifacts?**

DID YOU KNOW
In recognition of the earth's diverse religions, some people use the letters C.E. (Common Era) instead of A.D. (*anno Domini*, or "in the year of our Lord," referring to the birth of Christ) and B.C.E. (Before the Common Era) instead of B.C. (before Christ).

💾 Use the **Vocabulary Puzzle-Maker** to create crossword and word search puzzles.

✓ **Reading Check Answer**
Archaeology got its start when some Europeans dug up old marble statues and ornaments made by the ancient Greeks and Romans and sold them for a lot of money.

✓ **Reading Check Answer**
Artifacts show scientists how people lived in ancient times.

PRIMARY SOURCES
Library
You might assign "African Origins," from pages 674–675 of the Primary Sources Library.

MULTICULTURAL PERSPECTIVES

In today's world, dolls are considered toys, but archaeological evidence suggests that in ancient times dolls played an important part in adult life as well. Ritual dolls, probably used in fertility rites, have been found in Europe from France to Russia, from the Aurignacian culture that existed there some 40,000 years ago.

People in History

Mary Nicol Leakey
1913–1996

Paleoanthropologist

At age 11, Mary Nicol Leakey visited a cave filled with prehistoric paintings. The cave inspired her to become a paleoanthropologist—a person who studies prehistoric humans and prehumans. She later left England for East Africa. Here she discovered prehuman footprints more than 3.6 million years old! For more on this discovery, see pp. 674–675.

Archaeological Finds   About 1700, some Italian farmers discovered they were living on top of an ancient Roman city named Herculaneum (huhr kyul lā′ nē uhm) that had been buried for more than 1,000 years. In 1719 archaeologists began uncovering the city. After more than 50 years, they uncovered not only Herculaneum but also another Roman city called Pompeii (pom pā′). These cities contained, among other things, fine houses, theaters, streets, and temples. More importantly, from what they found, the archaeologists learned exactly how ancient Romans lived.

The discovery of Herculaneum and Pompeii was followed in 1799 by one of the greatest of all archaeological discoveries. This was the finding in Egypt of the Rosetta Stone, a slab of stone on which are carved ancient Egyptian picture-writing and its Greek translation. Although scholars knew the Greek language well, they had not been able to *decipher,* or explain the meaning of, the ancient Egyptian language. The Rosetta Stone was a two-

POMPEII   The Roman city of Pompeii was buried under the mud and lava from a volcanic eruption in 79 A.D. Discovered in the middle 1700s, the site has provided much information on Roman life and art, such as this wall painting from a home. **What other ancient Roman city was discovered in the 1700s?**

EXTENDING THE CONTENT

When archaeologists excavated Pompeii, they found restaurants with games and wine on the table, bakeries with bread in the oven, and family pets in the houses. They found comfortable townhouses with colorful tiled floors, paintings on the walls, and elegant furnishings. Many had central gardens with pools, fountains, benches, and statues. In Pompeii's warm climate, people spent much time outside in the family garden. Less wealthy people often lived in small rooms over shops or in apartments.

When people first began to investigate the past, many saw it as a "treasure house" of statues, paintings, and jewelry to be col-

Archaeological Sites

Archaeological Sites map showing: BLACK SEA, CASPIAN SEA, GREECE, Sesklo, TURKEY, Catal Hüyük, CYPRUS, Khirokitia, MEDITERRANEAN SEA, SYRIA, MESOPOTAMIA, Tigris River, Euphrates River, Jarmo, IRAN, ISRAEL, Jericho, IRAQ, EGYPT, Nile River, PERSIAN GULF, SAUDI ARABIA. Legend: ■ Major Digs. miles 0 200 400; kilometers 0 200 400 600.

MAP STUDY

LOCATION Archaeologists carefully piece together information gathered at archaeological sites. **What archaeological site is found near the Tigris and Euphrates rivers?**

language dictionary that gave them the key to the meaning of Egyptian picture-writing. Now they could learn much more about the history of Egypt and its people.

A great many archaeological finds have been made since the discovery of the Rosetta Stone. For example, between 1850 and 1950 archaeologists uncovered five lost civilizations. In 1988 they discovered the oldest known piece of cloth, woven 9,000 years ago. Archaeologists continue to make discoveries in many parts of the world. This can be especially difficult because often only small pieces of artifacts are found. Thus archaeologists have only hints or clues about people of past civilizations.

Dating Archaeological Remains   After archaeologists *excavate*, or dig into the earth, to uncover remains of the past, they have to *date*, or find the age of, the remains. In 1832 Christian J. Thomsen, a Danish archaeologist, divided early human history into three *ages*, or periods. These ages were based on the

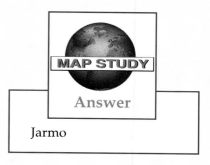

EXTENDING THE CONTENT

lected and sold. During this period of history, tombs were looted, temples were destroyed, and gold objects melted down. Wealthy private collectors took home objects they could find. Victorious generals systematically cleaned out the tombs and temples of conquered lands. With the development of archaeology as a science, came more responsibility and more public interest in historical findings.

material people used for tools and weapons during them. Thomsen named these ages the Stone Age, the Bronze Age, and the Iron Age. Later, scientists also divided the Stone Age into three shorter periods of time—old, middle, and new. Scientists relied on common sense when unearthing artifacts. They assumed that older artifacts would be found beneath more recent ones.

Still later, archaeologists realized that the material used for tools and weapons was not as important as how people got their food. So they divided early human history into two general periods. During the first period, people were food gatherers. During the second period, they were food producers.

To tell the date of an archaeological find, scientists first used trees. Each year, trees form a new growth ring. Scientists counted the number of rings in a wooden object, such as a house beam, and compared the pattern with the rings of a tree whose age they knew. In that way, they could identify dates as far back as 3,000 years earlier.

ARCHAEOLOGICAL SITES Archaeological research is a major method of learning about ancient civilizations. Specialized techniques and tools are required for successful research. This archaeological excavation (left) is at the Agora in Athens, Greece. The archaeologist shown (right) is searching for artifacts with a metal detector. **What do bones, animal remains, and tools tell archaeologists about a people?**

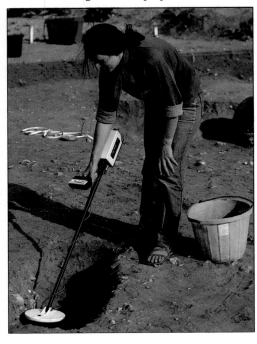

SPOTLIGHT ON: WILLARD FRANK LIBBY

Willard Frank Libby was born in 1908 in Grand Valley, Colorado. He taught chemistry at the University of California at Berkeley from 1933 until 1945. From 1945 until 1959, he was a member of the Institute for Nuclear Studies and the chemistry department at the University of Chicago. It was during this period that he made his famous discovery about carbon 14 dating. In 1960, in large part for this discovery, he won the Nobel Prize for chemistry.

Understanding Cause and Effect

You know that if you watch television instead of completing your homework, you will receive poor grades. This is an example of a cause-and-effect relationship. This cause—watching television instead of doing homework—leads to an effect—poor grades.

When you look for why or how an event or chain of events took place, you are developing the skill of understanding cause and effects.

CAUSES AND EFFECTS

CAUSES
- Europeans dig up artifacts for sale.
- Scientists study these artifacts.
- Artifacts provide information on the past.

↓

Start of Archaeology

↓

EFFECTS
- Lost civilizations are uncovered.
- Early human history is divided into periods.
- New methods of dating are devised.

Glencoe's **Skillbuilder Interactive Workbook, Level 1,** provides instruction and practice in key social studies skills.

Learning the Skill A *cause* is any person, event, or condition that makes something happen. What happens as a result is known as an *effect*. These guidelines will help you identify cause and effect:

- Look for "clue words" that alert you to cause and effect, such as *because, led to, brought about, produced,* and *therefore.*
- Look for logical relationships between events, such as "She did this and then that happened."

In a chain of historical events, one effect often becomes the cause of other effects. The chart on this page shows such a chain of events.

Skill Practice

Study the cause-and-effect chart on this page. Then answer the questions below.

1. **What were some of the causes of the start of archaeology?**
2. **What were some of the effects of archaeology upon history?**
3. **What effect do you think the discovery of lost civilizations has had upon our view of the past?**

CRITICAL THINKING SKILLS

TEACH

Understanding Cause and Effect

You might introduce this lesson by asking students to write down one good thing that happened to them in the past week. Call on a volunteer to share his or her experience. Ask the student these questions: "What caused this event to happen?" "What was the effect of the event on your life?"

Use the following diagram to display the student's responses.

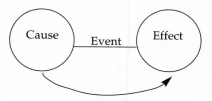

Ask the rest of the class to create similar diagrams showing the cause and effect of the experiences that they wrote down. Use this exercise to introduce the skill lesson and questions on this page.

Answers to Skill Practice

1. Europeans dug up artifacts for sale. The scientists who studied these artifacts discovered important information about the past.

2. Lost civilizations were uncovered. Early human history was divided into periods, and new methods of dating were developed.

3. Answers will vary, but encourage students to appreciate the effect of the past on our present-day lives. (For example, you might refer students to the "Linking Across Time" feature in each chapter of this book.)

TEAM TEACHING STRATEGIES

Science Working with a science teacher, distribute pictures of tree stumps with differing sizes of rings to small groups of students. Have them speculate on the cause of these differences. (*Abundant rainfall produces wide rings; dry years produce narrow rings.*) Explore the effects of differing rainfall patterns on the way people live.

Next, review with students how scientists have used trees to help date archeological objects. (*Answers should reflect information on page 28.*) Then, ask students what additional information a tree stump or wooden object might provide to archaeologists. (*information on the weather or climate at an ancient site, reasons people may or may not have farmed, reasons people abandoned a site, etc.*)

Ask students to summarize the main points of the chapter, orally or in writing. Discuss the answers to the Section and Chapter Review questions.

Evaluate

Assign the Chapter 1 **Performance Assessment Activity** in the TCR.

Administer the **Chapter 1 Test** found in the TCR. Testmaker available.

Reteach

Have students work in small groups to explain what they discovered about the four "Chapter Focus" objectives on page 5.

Assign the Chapter 1 **Reteaching Activity** in the TCR.

Enrich

Have students research and report on one of the archaeological sites on the map on page 27.

Assign Chapter 1 **Enrichment Activity** in the TCR.

CLOSE

Have the students prepare a time capsule that would include artifacts that best represent their lives and cultures today.

💾 Use **Interactive Tutor: Self-Assessment Software** to review Section 5.

Self-Check Quiz gives students an interactive chapter tutorial. Have them access *Chapter 1 Quiz* at **humanheritage.glencoe.com**

In 1946 an American scientist named Willard Frank Libby discovered that all living things contain a radioactive element called carbon 14. After plants, animals, and humans die, the carbon 14 gradually disappears. By measuring how much carbon 14 a skeleton or the remains of a wooden boat contain today, scientists can figure out about how old the object is as far back as about 30,000 years.

Section 5 Assessment

1. **Define:** archaeology, artifacts.
2. Why did scientists begin to study artifacts?
3. Why was the discovery of the Rosetta Stone important?

Critical Thinking

4. **Predicting Consequences** What would you like about being an archaeologist? What would you dislike?

Graphic Organizer Activity

5. Draw a diagram like the one below, and use it to show the three major periods in early human history.

Chapter Summary & Study Guide

1. Geographers use five themes to study the earth: location, place, human/environmental interaction, movement, and regions.
2. Four major kinds of landforms—mountains, hills, plateaus, and plains—make up 30 percent of the surface of the earth.
3. The surface of the earth is constantly undergoing change.
4. About 70 percent of the earth's surface is covered by water.
5. Climate is shaped by many factors, including the sun, large bodies of water, winds and ocean currents, and altitude.
6. Geographers divide the earth into climate zones based on latitude: the tropical zone, the temperate zone, and the polar zone.
7. Examples of natural resources include air, water, sunlight, minerals, fossil fuels, forests, and animal life.
8. Renewable resources can be replaced. Nonrenewable resources are gone forever when used up.
9. Legends have helped people explain the past.
10. Archaeologists study artifacts to learn how people lived long ago.
11. Since 1946, scientists have used the carbon 14 method of dating to identify the age of artifacts.

Self-Check Quiz

Visit the *Human Heritage* Web site at **humanheritage.glencoe.com** and click on *Chapter 1—Self-Check Quiz* to assess your understanding of this chapter.

Section 5 Assessment Answers

1. archaeology, the study of human remains (p. 25); artifacts, things made by people (p. 25)
2. to learn how people lived long ago
3. It gave scholars the key to the meaning of Egyptian picture-writing.
4. Answers will vary but students should give specific examples that relate to an archaeologist's job.
5. The periods include the Stone Age, Bronze Age, and Iron Age.

Assign the Chapter 1 **Section 5 Quiz** in the TCR. Testmaker available.

Assessment

Using Key Terms

Imagine you are writing an explanation for a younger student of how geography has shaped history. Use the following words to describe in a simple way how landforms, waterways, and climate have influenced history.

landforms	tectonic plates	glaciers
climate	elevation	river system
natural resources	archaeology	artifacts
	erosion	

Understanding Main Ideas

1. What are the four major kinds of landforms?

2. What do geographers believe caused Pangaea to split into seven continents?

3. How has erosion both helped and hurt people?

4. Why did early people settle along the banks of waterways?

5. Why are air, water, soil, and sunlight important natural resources?

6. How have people's views about natural resources changed in recent years?

7. How is the carbon 14 test used as a dating tool?

Critical Thinking

1. In what climate zone would you prefer to live? Why?

2. "It is important to plan the use of the world's natural resources." What is your opinion of this statement? Explain.

3. Why is it important to identify the date of artifacts as exactly as possible?

4. How do ideas about the past change as more knowledge becomes available?

Graphic Organizer Activity

History Create a diagram like this one, and use it to show some of the archaeological finds that have changed history.

Archaeological Discoveries — Example, Example, Example, Example

Geography in History

Movement Look at the map on page 13 that shows how far ice sheets moved during the Ice Ages. What descriptive statements could you make about the movement of ice north of the Equator compared to south of the Equator?

Using Your Journal

Review any details you may have noted about the geographical factors that have influenced history. Choose three of these factors and write a short essay explaining how these factors influence your life today.

31

Bonus Test Question

For Chapter 1 Test
You are living in an area where you receive no sunlight for part of the year and slanted rays the rest of the year. You see a bear. What color is it? *(white—polar bear)*

Using Your Journal

Essays will vary but should include concrete references to modern examples. You might call on volunteers to read their essays and discuss them with the class.

Geography in History

There was greater movement of ice north of the Equator than south of the Equator.

Assessment Answers

Using Key Terms

Explanations will vary but should include all the vocabulary words to describe how these have influenced history.

Understanding Main Ideas

1. mountains, hills, plateaus, and plains

2. continental drift

3. Sometimes wind erosion contributes to making land rich for farming, as in China. Or erosion can destroy people's way of life, such as the Dust Bowl.

4. because they provided drinking water, fish and other food, good hunting grounds, rich soil for farming, water for irrigation, and easier trade and travel

5. because they are needed for any kind of life to exist

6. They are passing laws to slow down pollution and trying to develop new sources of energy.

7. dates artifacts older than those that can be dated by using trees

Critical Thinking

1. Answers will vary, but students should provide reasons.

2. Answers will vary but should include that natural resources are necessary to maintain life.

3. Answers will vary but should include that exact dating helps reconstruct history.

4. Answers will vary.

Graphic Organizer Activity

Examples include: Herculaneum, Pompeii, Rosetta Stone, lost civilizations discovered since 1850, 9,000–year old piece of cloth discovered in 1988, any of the sites on the map on page 27

Chapter 2 Planning Guide

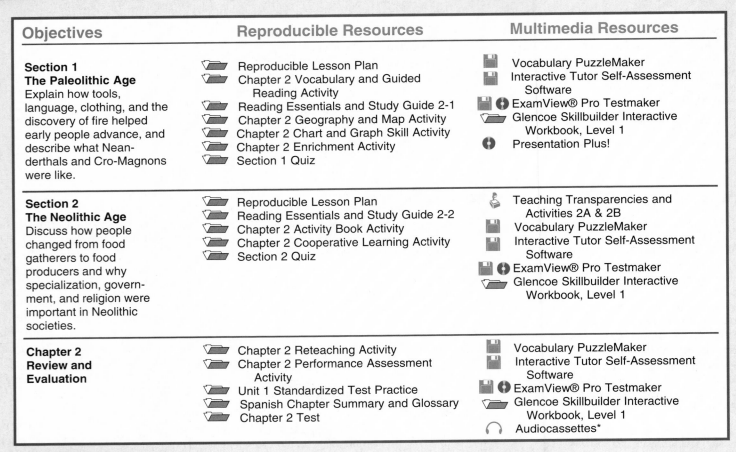

Objectives	Reproducible Resources	Multimedia Resources
Section 1 **The Paleolithic Age** Explain how tools, language, clothing, and the discovery of fire helped early people advance, and describe what Neanderthals and Cro-Magnons were like.	Reproducible Lesson Plan Chapter 2 Vocabulary and Guided Reading Activity Reading Essentials and Study Guide 2-1 Chapter 2 Geography and Map Activity Chapter 2 Chart and Graph Skill Activity Chapter 2 Enrichment Activity Section 1 Quiz	Vocabulary PuzzleMaker Interactive Tutor Self-Assessment Software ExamView® Pro Testmaker Glencoe Skillbuilder Interactive Workbook, Level 1 Presentation Plus!
Section 2 **The Neolithic Age** Discuss how people changed from food gatherers to food producers and why specialization, government, and religion were important in Neolithic societies.	Reproducible Lesson Plan Reading Essentials and Study Guide 2-2 Chapter 2 Activity Book Activity Chapter 2 Cooperative Learning Activity Section 2 Quiz	Teaching Transparencies and Activities 2A & 2B Vocabulary PuzzleMaker Interactive Tutor Self-Assessment Software ExamView® Pro Testmaker Glencoe Skillbuilder Interactive Workbook, Level 1
Chapter 2 **Review and Evaluation**	Chapter 2 Reteaching Activity Chapter 2 Performance Assessment Activity Unit 1 Standardized Test Practice Spanish Chapter Summary and Glossary Chapter 2 Test	Vocabulary PuzzleMaker Interactive Tutor Self-Assessment Software ExamView® Pro Testmaker Glencoe Skillbuilder Interactive Workbook, Level 1 Audiocassettes*

*Also available in Spanish.

Presentation Plus!

Use Glencoe's **Presentation Plus!** multimedia teacher tool to easily present dynamic lessons that visually excite your students. Using Microsoft® PowerPoint, you can customize the presentations to create your own personalized lessons.

Interactive Lesson Planner

Planning has never been easier! Using this CD-ROM, organize your week, month, semester, or year with all the help you need. The **Interactive Lesson Planner** gives you access to all of the blackline masters which accompany *Human Heritage*.

✓ PERFORMANCE ASSESSMENT ACTIVITIES

Time Line Have students create an illustrated time line tracing the progression of early people from prehistory to the establishment of the first cities. The time line should depict how early people may have looked, what they wore, where they lived, and the tools they used.

CHAPTER RESOURCES

LITERATURE ABOUT THE PERIOD

Auel, Jean M. *The Clan of the Cave Bear*. Bantam, 1984. A Cro-Magnon girl is adopted by a Neanderthal tribe.

READINGS FOR THE STUDENT

Johanson, Donald and James Shreece. *Lucy's Child: The Discovery of a Human Ancestor*. William Morrow and Company, Inc., 1989. An account of Johanson's return to Africa in 1986.

READINGS FOR THE TEACHER

Gowlett, John. *Ascent to Civilization: The Archaeology of Early Man*. Knopf, 1984. The rise and development of human culture revealed by archaeological finds.

Pfeiffer, John. *The Emergence of Humankind*. Harper & Row, 1985. The unfolding story of human evolution and the human condition.

KEY TO ABILITY LEVELS

Teaching strategies have been coded for varying learning styles and abilities.

L1 Level 1 activities are **basic** activities and should be within the ability range of all students.

L2 Level 2 activities are **average** activities and should be within the ability range of the average to above-average student.

L3 Level 3 activities are **challenging** activities designed for the ability range of above-average students.

ELL ELL activities should be within the ability range of English Language Learning students.

NATIONAL GEOGRAPHIC SOCIETY — Teacher's Corner

INDEX TO NATIONAL GEOGRAPHIC MAGAZINE

The following articles relate to this chapter:

- "Saharan Rock Art," by David Coulson, June 1999.
- "The Dawn of Humans," by Lee Berger, August 1998.
- "The Dawn of Humans," by Rick Gore, September 1997.
- "The Dawn of Humans," by Rick Gore, July 1997.
- "The Dawn of Humans," by Rick Gore, May 1997.
- "The First Steps," by Rick Gore, February 1997.
- "Neanderthals," by Rick Gore, January 1996.

NATIONAL GEOGRAPHIC SOCIETY PRODUCTS AVAILABLE FROM GLENCOE

To order the following, call Glencoe at 1-800-334-7344:

- *PicturePack: Physical Geography of the World (Transparencies)*
- *STV: World Geography (Videodisc)*
- *Picture Atlas of the World (CD-ROM)*
- *PicturePack:World Geography Library (Transparencies)*

ADDITIONAL NATIONAL GEOGRAPHIC SOCIETY PRODUCTS

To order the following, call National Geographic at 1-800-368-2728:

- *Wonders of the Ancient World: National Geographic Atlas of Archaeology (Book)*
- *Read & Explore: Painters of the Cave, by Patricia Lauber (Literature Kit)*

Access *National Geographic's* new dynamic MapMachine Web site and other geography resources at:

http://www.nationalgeographic.com/
http://www.nationalgeographic.com/maps/

THE HISTORY CHANNEL. HOME VIDEO. Biography

The following videotape program is available from Glencoe to enrich Chapter 2:

- **The Fate of the Neanderthals**
  0-7670-0233-4

To order, call Glencoe at 1-800-334-7344. To find classroom resources to accompany many of these check:

A&E Television: http://www.aetv.com
The History Channel: http://www.historychannel.com

OVERVIEW

Chapter 2 deals with the Paleolithic and Neolithic ages.

➤ **Section 1** focuses on the life-style of the earliest humans—the food gatherers of the Paleolithic, or Old Stone, Age.

➤ **Section 2** describes the developments of the Neolithic, or New Stone, Age—the beginning of farming, the domestication of animals, and the formation of villages.

CHAPTER OBJECTIVES

After reading Chapter 2, students will be able to:

1. explain how tools, language, clothing, and the discovery of fire helped early people advance.

2. summarize what Neanderthals and Cro-Magnons were like.

3. describe how people changed from food gatherers to food producers.

4. discuss why specialization, government, and religion were important in Neolithic societies.

EXAMINING ARTIFACTS

These artifacts show the skills and talents of early humans. The Paleolithic ivory carving—barely one and a half inches high—depicts the face of a *Homo sapien* crafted sometime between 30,000 and 20,000 B.C. By this time, early humans had spread out of Africa and into the more temperate zones of the world. Explore how these artifacts help dispel stereotypes about prehistoric "cave people."

PERFORMANCE ASSESSMENT ✓

Use the Performance Assessment Activities on page 32B to help you evaluate students as they complete the chapter.

Prehistoric People
8000 B.C.–3000 B.C.

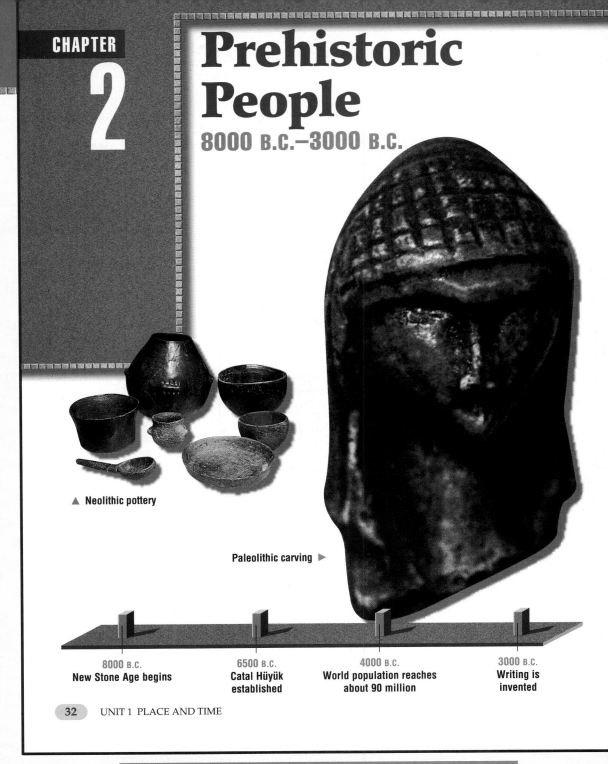

▲ **Neolithic pottery**

Paleolithic carving ▶

8000 B.C.	6500 B.C.	4000 B.C.	3000 B.C.
New Stone Age begins	**Catal Hüyük established**	**World population reaches about 90 million**	**Writing is invented**

TEACHING RESOURCES

TEACHER PLANNING AND SUPPORT

- Reproducible Lesson Plan
- Block Scheduling Implementation Guide
- Videodisc Bar Code Correlation
- Presentation Plus!

REVIEW AND REINFORCEMENT

- Reading Essentials and Study Guide 2-1, 2-2
- Chapter 2 Vocabulary and Guided Reading Activity
- Vocabulary PuzzleMaker Software
- Teaching Transparencies 2A & 2B
- Chapter 2 Reteaching Activity

- Chapter 2 Activity Book Activity
- Chapter 2 Chart and Graph Skill Activity
- Interactive Tutor Self-Assessment Software
- Chapter 2 Digests Audiocassettes Activities and Tests

APPLICATION AND HANDS-ON ACTIVITIES

- Unit 1 Hands-On History Lab Activity

Chapter Focus

📖 Read to Discover

- How tools, language, clothing, and the discovery of fire helped early people advance.
- What Neanderthals and Cro-Magnons were like.
- How people changed from food gatherers to food producers.
- Why specialization, government, and religion were important in Neolithic societies.

Terms to Learn	**People to Know**	🌐 **Places to Locate**
prehistory	Lucy	Olduvai Gorge
civilization	Neanderthals	Jericho
migrate	Cro-Magnons	Catal Hüyük
specialization		

Why It's Important   Most archaeologists believe people have lived on the earth for millions of years. The period of time before the invention of writing is called **prehistory**. It lasted until about five thousand years ago, when people learned how to write. Through the use of artifacts, archaeologists have traced the milestones that paved the way from prehistory to the rise of **civilization**—a time when people progressed culturally and began to live in cities.

Chapter Overview
Visit the *Human Heritage* Web site at **humanheritage.glencoe.com** and click on *Chapter 2—Chapter Overviews* to preview this chapter.

✓ **Reading Check**
When did **prehistory** end? What helped bring about the rise of **civilization?**

SECTION 1   The Paleolithic Age

Although there were no written records during prehistory, scientists have learned a great deal about prehistoric people. They have learned how early human beings lived and what important discoveries they made. Scientists also think they know why people moved out of Africa to other parts of the world.

Many scientists believe that until about 900,000 years ago people lived only on the grasslands of eastern and southern Africa. Then the earth's climate changed—it became colder. Ocean water froze into huge glaciers that spread out from the North and South poles. As the ice sheets grew, the sea level fell and uncovered land that had been under water. Land bridges then connected Africa to both southern Europe and southwestern Asia.

Chapter Overview introduces students to chapter content and key terms. Have them access **Chapter 2 Overview** at **humanheritage.glencoe.com**

FOCUS

📹 Bellringer

Write the following question on the chalkboard: *If you were marooned on a desert island, what tools would you need to survive?*

Motivational Activity

Ask students to list the tools they would need to survive on a desert island. Have a volunteer write them on the chalkboard. Discuss how studying the tools left by prehistoric people can help us to understand our past.

GUIDE TO READING

Reading Strategy

Ask students to read "Why It's Important" and summarize the chapter's main theme. *(that developments during prehistory paved the way for the rise of civilization)* **L1**

Vocabulary Precheck

Ask students to define each of the "Terms to Know." Have a volunteer consult the dictionary for any unfamiliar words. **L1 ELL**

💾 Use the Vocabulary PuzzleMaker for Chapter 2 to create a crossword puzzle. **L1**

🗂 Assign Chapter 2 Vocabulary and Guided Reading Activity.

🗂 Assign Reading Essentials and Study Guide 2-1.

✓ **Reading Check Answer**
Prehistory ended about five thousand years ago. The invention of writing and the rise of cities helped bring about the rise of **civilization.**

GEOGRAPHY ACTIVITIES

- 🗂 Chapter 2 Geography and Map Activity
- 🗂 Social Studies Outline Map Resource Book

INTERDISCIPLINARY CONNECTIONS

- 🗂 Unit 1 World Literature Reading 1
- 💻 Focus on World Art Print 6, *Cycladic Harpist*
- 🎧💿 World Music: Cultural Traditions

ENRICHMENT AND EXTENSION

- 🗂 Unit 1 Primary Sources Reading
- 💿 World History Primary Source Document Library CD-ROM
- 🗂 Foods Around the World

- 🗂 Chapter 2 Extension Activity

ASSESSMENT AND EVALUATION

- 🗂 Chapter 2 Performance Assessment Activity
- 🗂 Chapter 2 Section Quizzes 2-1, 2-2
- 🗂 Chapter 2 Test
- 🗂 Unit 1 Standardized Test Practice
- 💾💿 Chapter 2 ExamView® Pro Testmaker Software
- 🎧 Chapter 2 Digests Audiocassettes Activities and Tests

SPANISH RESOURCES

- 🗂 Chapter 2 Spanish Chapter Summary and Glossary
- 🎧 Chapter 2 Spanish Chapter Digests Audiocassettes Activities and Tests

Guided Practice

L1 **Daily Life** Ask the students to write a short essay explaining how tools, language, clothing, and the discovery of fire helped early people advance. Have students share their essays with the class. Ask the students to rank the innovations in the order of importance. Then have students draw conclusions about the importance of tools, language, clothing, and the discovery of fire in the advancement of early people. **ELL**

✓ **Reading Check Answer**
Early people were able to **migrate** out of Africa by making their way around the northern deserts and across land bridges.

CAPTION ANSWER

the oldest or strongest men in the band

✓ **Reading Check**
How did early people **migrate** out of Africa?

People were able to **migrate**, or make their way, around the desert of northern Africa and across the land bridges. Between about 900,000 and 700,000 years ago, people made their way into Europe and Asia. Much later, between about 40,000 and 15,000 years ago, they also migrated to the Americas.

Scientists call the first age in which people lived the Paleolithic (pā lē uh lith' ik) Age, or Old Stone Age. It lasted from about 2.3 million years, until 10,000 years ago. During this period, people obtained their food by hunting and gathering.

Obtaining Food Paleolithic people lived in small **bands**, or groups, of about 30 members. When the food supply was good, the bands grew to about 40 or 50 members. Most of the group members lived to be no more than 20 or 25 years old. More than half of the children died from illnesses or were killed by animals before their first birthdays.

The people within a group lived and worked together and shared their food. They fed and cared for people who became injured or sick.

GROUP LIFE Experts believe that most early people lived in groups made up of several families. Here, a group of hunters use stones to sharpen tools. Two men carry a large animal killed in a hunt, as a few women tend fires near their tents. **Who were the leaders in a group of prehistoric people?**

COOPERATIVE LEARNING

Divide the class into small groups to prepare a bulletin-board display showing the history of crops such as wheat, barley, corn, rice, potatoes, yams, and cotton. Each group's contribution should graphically portray the crop, when and where it originated, and where it is grown now. Below the graphics, students should include information about the cultivation of the crop then and now, and the economic importance of the crop then and now. Each group member should have a specific task. Have each group discuss its contribution before posting it on the bulletin board.

EARLY TOOLS For more than 2 million years, prehistoric people lived by hunting animals and gathering plants. They used tools made of wood and stone. The wooden tools have decayed. Archaeologists, however, have found many stone tools. **For what purposes did prehistoric people use stone tools?**

Each band searched for food within an area known as its **home territory.** This usually covered about two square miles, or five square kilometers, for every band member. There were campsites at various places throughout the home territory. The band stayed at a campsite until the available food supply was used up and then moved.

Women and children gathered berries, nuts, fruit, and eggs out of bird and turtle nests. They poked sticks into bee nests to get honey and into the ground to dig roots.

Men of the group obtained meat. They caught fish using their bare hands and hunted small animals with sticks and stones. Occasionally, they were able to kill a large animal that was too young, too old, or too badly hurt to run away. A good kill meant that the group would have enough meat to last for several days.

Making Tools Life for hunters and gatherers became easier when they learned to make tools. At first the only tools people had were sticks and stones they found on the ground. Soon they learned to shape stones to make them more useful.

✔ **Reading Check**
What were some of the features of a band's **home territory?**

Oldest Tools In 1995, archaeologists working in Ethiopia found stone spear points more than 2.6 million years old, making them the earliest tools found on earth.

GEOGRAPHY AND HISTORY
People in Europe, Africa, and western Asia usually made their tools of flint, a stone found on the surface of Earth. In eastern Asia, where there was not much flint, people made their tools of quartz.

✔ **Reading Check Answer**
A band's **home territory** usually covered about two square miles (five square kilometers) and included campsites at various places.

EXTENDING THE CONTENT

Some scientists are predicting global warming, an increase in global average temperatures. Unlike the natural forming and melting of glaciers in prehistory, human activities are responsible for much global warming. Trapping of heat by gases in the atmosphere, such as carbon dioxide, results in a greenhouse effect. Burning fossil fuels is one human activity that releases carbon dioxide in the air.

People in History

Lucy
c. 3,200,000 B.C.

Hominid Skeleton

Lucy made headlines in 1974 when two scientists—Donald C. Johanson and Tom Gray—discovered her skeleton in the deserts of Ethiopia. They named her after a popular Beatles song, "Lucy in the Sky with Diamonds." Although Lucy walked the earth 3.2 million years ago, her skeleton was nearly complete. She gave the world its first look at an early prehuman.

The earliest shaped stones are known as *Olduvan pebble tools*, named after the Olduvai Gorge in eastern Africa where they were first discovered. Pebble tools were made from pebbles or stones about the size of a fist. The toolmaker hit one pebble with another removing chips and creating a jagged cutting edge. This edge was sharp enough to cut the meat off of small animals' bones, split animal bones, and chop up plants.

Later people learned to knock long, sharp-edged chips called flakes from stones and use them as tools. Using flakes for knives they could butcher, or cut up, animals as big as elephants quickly and efficiently. People also used flakes to scrape one end of a wooden branch into a sharp point for a digging stick or a meat skewer.

Making Fire   People also learned to make fire during the Paleolithic Age. The first fires they knew about were made by nature, such as those started by lightning. Eventually, people discovered how to make fire themselves. They created a spark by rubbing two sticks or stones together, or rapidly turning a stick in a hole in a dry log.

People used fire to keep themselves warm and dry. They also used it as a weapon, throwing burning sticks of wood at animals to drive them away. Sometimes they used fire to drive big animals into mudholes. The heavy animals would sink in the mud and people could then kill them.

People also used fire to clear out brush and undergrowth. Finally, people used fire to cook food. Cooked food was much easier to chew and digest than raw food. As a result, people spent less time eating and more time doing other things.

Seeking Shelter   Early people usually camped out in the open. They protected themselves from the wind by digging pits in the ground or by crouching in dry river beds. They also took shelter under an overhanging rock or piled up brush.

At first, early people used caves only for such emergencies as escaping from a sudden storm or a large animal. By about 100,000 years ago, however, people in China, western Europe, and southwestern Asia were living in caves most of the time.

Making Clothing   After hunters began killing large animals, they found that the animal skins could be used for protection and warmth. They scraped the skins clean and then laid them out in the sun to dry. Later, people discovered that pounding fat into the skin while it was drying would make it softer.

At first people wrapped the skins around themselves. Later, they learned how to fasten the skins together. Clothing made a big difference in where people lived. Before they had clothing, most people stayed in areas that were warm and dry. Once they

36   UNIT 1 PLACE AND TIME

EXTENDING THE CONTENT

A ravine 295 feet (or 90 m) deep in northern Tanzania, known as Olduvai Gorge, is part of the Great Rift Valley, a series of valleys that extends all the way north to Syria. The sides of the ravine resemble a layer cake of different strata laid bare by the cutting action of ancient rivers. A prehistoric lake had swamped old bones with sediment and later disappeared. Through millennia, nearby volcanoes spewed ash over Olduvai, creating the distinct strata. In 1959 the Leakeys made major discoveries in the deepest and oldest layers at Olduvai.

PREHISTORIC PEOPLE   There were two types of early *Homo sapiens*, Neanderthals and Cro-Magnons. From the remains of these two peoples, scientists have tried to reconstruct how they might have looked. These models show the facial features of the Neanderthal (left) and a Cro-Magnon (right). **In what areas of the world did the first people most likely live?**

had clothing to protect them from the weather, they were able to move into areas that were cooler and wetter.

Developing Language   In addition to learning to make tools, fire, and clothing, early people developed language. Before they learned to talk, early people simply made sounds, or pointed to objects, to express meaning. Hand signals were probably used for common things such as water, food, animals, and weapons. Gradually because of new social needs, sounds and hand signals were no longer enough. The development of language was a great human achievement. It made it possible for people to work together, share ideas, and pass on their beliefs and stories. The younger generations could learn more easily from the older generation and greater progress was made in all areas of civilization.

The Neanderthals   The first people on Earth are known as *Homo habilis* (hō mō huh bil' uhs), or "skillful man." Next came *Homo erectus* (hō' mō ē rekt' uhs), or "man who walks upright." Then, between about 300,000 and 200,000 years ago, came *Homo sapiens* (hō' mō sāp' ē uhnz), or "man who thinks."

Then... & Now

Languages There may be 2,000 to 10,000 languages in the world today. Dialects, or variations within a language, range from about 20,000 to more than 50,000. The largest native language in the world is Chinese, but among the many dialects are Mandarin, Cantonese, Wu, Min, Xiang, Kan, and Hakka.

CHAPTER 2 PREHISTORIC PEOPLE   **37**

LINKING PAST TO PRESENT

In 1992, a skull fragment that had been sitting in a tray at the National Museum of Kenya for 25 years was given a closer look. New dating methods reveal the fragment to be 2.4 million years old, which makes it the earliest known remains of the genus *Homo* by 500,000 years.

The following videotape program is available from Glencoe to enrich Chapter 2:

- **The Fate of the Neanderthals**

To find classroom resources to accompany this video, check the following home page:

A&E Television:
http://www.aetv.com

MULTICULTURAL PERSPECTIVES

Hadar in Ethiopia is part of the Great Rift Valley. At Hadar, sediments along shores of ancient lakes are reappearing because of earth movements and erosion. In the 1970s, Dr. Donald Johanson and a French geologist, Maurice Taieb, mounted an expedition into the area. The now world-famous fossilized skeleton "Lucy" was found in 1974. Later, other spectacular hominid finds at Hadar were made at just one site. The remains of at least 13 individuals were found jumbled together. Johanson dubbed this collection of more than 200 bones the "First Family."

There are two kinds of *Homo sapiens*. The first is the Neanderthal (nē an' der tahl), named after the Neander River in Germany where their remains were first discovered in 1856. Since then, other Neanderthal remains have been found throughout Europe and in parts of Asia and Africa. Scientists estimate that about 1 million Neanderthals were living at any one time.

Neanderthal people were good hunters. They used traps to catch birds and small animals. They used *pitfalls* to catch large animals like the rhinoceros and the elephant. A pitfall was a large hole that was covered with branches, leaves, and earth. As an animal ran across this hole, it crashed through the covering and fell into the pit. The hunters would then kill the animal with spears.

Neanderthals were also builders. In northern areas, for example, they made houses by covering a framework of mammoth bones with animal skins. More bones piled on the bottoms of the skins prevented them from being blown away. As many as 30 people lived in such a house during the cold months of the year. They improved cave dwelling by digging drainage ditches in caves and designing rock protection for entrances.

According to experts, Neanderthals were also the first people to bury their dead. Archaeologists have found graves of people from this time in which they discovered the remains of flowers, tools, and food.

Linking Across Time

The Aborigines Archaeologists have found spearheads and cave paintings showing that hunters traveled to Australia more than 40,000 years ago. Their descendants call themselves the Aborigines (ab uh rij' uh nēz) and live much as their ancestors did (far right). **Why does the study of traditional cultures provide valuable information about the past?**

MULTICULTURAL PERSPECTIVES

Most people still imagine Neanderthal people as looking like the Hollywood stereotype—stooping and gorilla-like. Actually, according to anthropologist Richard Leakey, the people of Neanderthal times could probably (with the right clothes) pass unnoticed in a modern crowd. They were fairly short, stocky, muscular, with powerful shoulders and arms, but were taller than earlier *Homo erectus* and *Homo habilis*, and walked about as upright as we do. One reason for the common stereotype is that the first, classic Neanderthal skeleton, found in 1856, was of a man whose severe arthritis had bent his neck and spine and enlarged his joints.

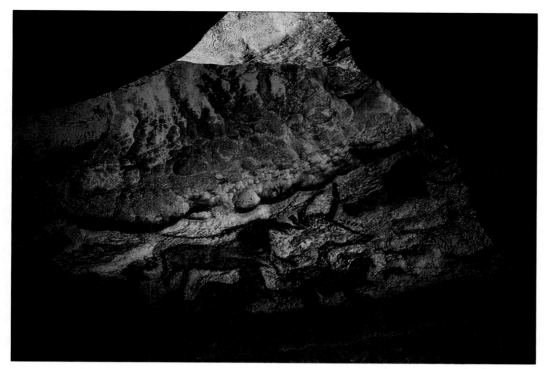

PREHISTORIC HORSE   This prehistoric painting of a horse was found on the wall of a cave in Lascaux, France. Early art such as this always showed the animal's profile. **What can scientists learn about Cro-Magnon people from looking at their art?**

LINKING PAST TO PRESENT

Ask students to name groups of people in recent history, or contemporary life, who have used bone, antler, and ivory to fashion needles, fishing hooks, combs, tools, and other items.

CAPTION ANSWER

about their ceremonies, traditions, and history

The Cro-Magnons

The second kind of *Homo sapiens* is the Cro-Magnon (krō mag' nahn), named after a rock shelter in France where their remains were first discovered in 1868. Cro-Magnons appeared in North Africa, Asia, and Europe about 100,000 years ago. Archaeologists consider them the first modern human beings.

Cro-Magnons were very skillful toolmakers. They invented the *burin*, which resembles a chisel. By using the burin, people could make other tools and objects from antler, bone, ivory, and shell, as well as stone and wood.

Using new tools made Cro-Magnons better hunters thus increasing their food supply. Points of antler or bone fastened to the end of wooden sticks could penetrate the hides of larger animals. People fashioned antler and bone into *spear throwers*, or devices that made spears fly through the air faster and farther. This allowed hunters to stay a greater distance from animals making hunting less dangerous.

First Razors Cro-Magnons may have invented the first razors. Some Cro-Magnon cave paintings portray beardless men, and Cro-Magnon graves contain sharpened shells—the first razors. Later peoples hammered razors out of bronze or iron.

CHAPTER 2 PREHISTORIC PEOPLE   **39**

SPOTLIGHT ON: CRO-MAGNONS

Archaeologists have unearthed evidence that prehistoric men were shaving as early as 18,000 B.C. Some Cro-Magnon cave paintings portray beardless men, and early Cro-Magnon gravesites contain sharpened shells that were the first razors. Later, people hammered razors out of bronze, and eventually, out of iron. Mirrors were first water ponds, and then highly polished metal.

Use **Interactive Tutor Self-Assessment Software** to review Section 1.

Fun Facts....

The Flute The first musical instrument invented by early humans was the flute. Carved bone flutes date back more than 30,000 years.

Another important tool that Cro-Magnons invented was the axe, which they used to cut down trees and hollow out the logs to make canoes. In southeastern Asia, they cut down stalks of bamboo and tied them together with vines to make rafts. Winds or ocean currents then carried the rafts to other lands. It is likely that this is how people reached Australia about 40,000 years ago.

Cro-Magnons also fashioned bone, ivory, and shell into body ornaments, such as necklaces and rings. They decorated their clothing with bone or ivory beads. They played music on flutes carved from long, hollow bones.

Cro-Magnons were artists as well as toolmakers. They carved statues out of ivory and bone or molded them out of clay. They covered the walls of some caves in western Europe, Africa, and South America with pictures painted brightly with paints made from minerals. The pictures show mostly animals, such as horses, bulls, and deer, but also show outlines and patterns of lines, dots, and curves.

Many anthropologists think cave paintings may have had religious significance. Cro-Magnons believed that animals had spirits. They thought that painting an animal's picture gave people power over its spirit and would help them find and kill the animal. Anthropologists think the cave paintings may have been a kind of textbook about Cro-Magnon ceremonies, traditions, or history.

Cro-Magnon bands cooperated, often hunting large animals together. This required them to jointly agree on rules and the first true leaders. Every year or so, they held social gatherings, where they exchanged information about the movement of animal herds and traded materials such as amber and shells.

Section 1 Assessment

1. **Define:** prehistory, civilization, migrate, bands, home territory.
2. Why did early people begin to move out of Africa and into other parts of the world about 900,000 years ago?
3. How did tools change in the Paleolithic Age?

Critical Thinking

4. **Analyzing Information** What do you think was the most important advancement made by early people? Explain.

Graphic Organizer Activity

5. Draw a diagram like this one, and use it to compare ways of life followed by the Neanderthals and Cro-Magnons. Be sure to include the accomplishments of each.

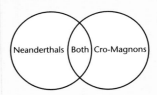

Neanderthals | Both | Cro-Magnons

DOMESTICATING ANIMALS Early people painted scenes of their hunting and food-producing activities. Here, a cave painting from North Africa shows cattle being herded. Some cattle are tied to a rope, while women and children do chores. **What was the importance of learning to herd animals?**

SECTION 2 The Neolithic Age

In the Neolithic (nē uh lith′ ik), or New Stone Age, about 8000 B.C., people changed from food gatherers to food producers. Over several thousand years they began to obtain most of their food from farming. This brought about such great changes in the way they lived that experts call the beginning of farming the Neolithic Revolution.

Farmers and Herders Two important discoveries brought on the Neolithic Revolution. One was learning to grow food. The other was learning to herd animals.

Experts believe that people discovered that seed from wild grains, such as wheat and barley, could be planted and harvested. This probably came about when they noticed that new shoots had grown from spilled grain. Scientists believe agriculture developed independently in different parts of the world. In southwestern Asia early people grew wheat and barley and in

Student Web Activity
Visit the *Human Heritage* Web site at **humanheritage.glencoe.com** and click on *Chapter 2— Student Web Activities* to find out more about the Neolithic Age.

CAPTION ANSWER
It helped people change from food gatherers to food producers.

DID YOU KNOW
The expanded food supply increased the average life expectancy of people to 30 years.

Use the **Vocabulary Puzzle-Maker** to create crossword and word search puzzles.

HISTORY Online
Student Web Activity objectives, goals, and answers can be found at the *Chapter 2 Web Activity Lesson Plan* at **humanheritage.glencoe.com**

---

eastern Asia they grew millet, rice, and soy beans. In Mexico they grew corn, squash, and potatoes, and they grew peanuts and a grain called sorghum in Africa.

People probably learned they could herd animals when a hunting band built fences to enclose a herd of wild animals they had chased into a ravine. The hunters killed one animal at a time, saving the rest for later. Soon captured animals began to lose their fear of people and became **domesticated,** or tamed, and the hunters became herders. In time, Neolithic people were breeding animals to improve the animals' qualities. People also began using certain animals such as donkeys, camels, and llamas as pack animals.

The Neolithic Revolution greatly increased people's food supply. With more food available, the **population**, or number of people, began to grow. Experts think there were about 5 million people in the world in 8000 B.C. Within 4,000 years the population grew to about 90 million. People were also living longer.

Early Villages Once people began to produce food, they were able to settle in one place. They built permanent shelters and formed villages of about 150 to 200 people in areas with a good soil and water supply.

POTTERY MAKING   Neolithic people learned the art of baking clay pottery. Baked clay, unlike sun-dried clay, will not disintegrate in water. In this picture, men are covering the oven so that the pots inside will bake. **How did Neolithic people use pottery?**

EXTENDING THE CONTENT

Farming in the Neolithic period began at different times in different parts of the world—and the influence of crops and animals that were raised in those first centuries still can be seen in the traditional diet and cuisine in various parts of the world. In the Fertile Crescent, Mesopotamians began farming about 8,000 B.C. As in every early farming culture, the basic crop was a cereal grain. In the Middle East the original crops were wheat, barley, and other cereal grains, along with garden crops such as peas, beans, squash, and yams.

EARLY VILLAGES Archaeologists today continue to dig up artifacts of early people. These scientists have uncovered the sites of several ancient villages. **How do archaeologists know they have found the site of a prehistoric village?**

The earliest known villages in the world have been found in southwestern Asia. Two of the oldest are Jericho (jer´ uh kō) in present-day Israel (iz´rē uhl), which dates back to about 8000 B.C. and Abu Hureyra (ah bu hu rā´ rah) in present-day Syria, which was established about 500 years later. Another early village is Catal Hüyük (kat' uhl hū´ yūk) located in present-day Turkey. People lived there from about 6500 to 5700 B.C.

Archaeologists know a great deal about Catal Hüyük because it was struck by a fire that blackened rather than destroyed wooden and cloth objects. The blackening helped preserve the objects. Evidence shows the houses in Catal Hüyük were made of sun-dried mud brick. They had flat roofs made of reeds plastered over with mud. The walls and roofs were supported by a *post-and-lintel,* or a horizontal length of wood or stone placed across two upright poles. The post-and-lintel was an important contribution to architecture because it enabled buildings to support weight above an open space.

As protection against attack, the houses in this village had two or three rooms and no doors. People went in and out of the houses through a hole in the roof by using a ladder. The houses were crowded together on the side of a hill. The floors were covered with rushes, or grasslike plants, and sleeping platforms were covered with mats.

First Farmers Many archaeologists believe that women invented the practice of agriculture. In societies of hunter-gatherers, women collected fruits, nuts, and seeds. As they did so, they probably noticed that plants sprouted where seeds fell. Only with the invention of the plow did men take over the job of farming.

CHAPTER 2 PREHISTORIC PEOPLE **43**

EXTENDING THE CONTENT

Based on the appearance of the first complete Neanderthal skeleton found in the mid-1800s, at La Chapelle-aux-Saints, France, the image of a clumsy Neanderthal made sense—slouching along, stooped, with bowed legs. Later physical anthropologists discovered, however, that the skeleton was of a man who had suffered from arthritis. The first researcher had not recognized the signs of the disease. Then, in 1957, archaeologists investigating a cave at Shanidar, in northern Iraq, found a skeleton of a 40-year-old Neanderthal man with a paralytic birth defect. That disabled Neanderthals survived suggests that members of the community must have taken care of one another.

TEACH

Determining Relative Location

Have the students read the introduction to the feature. Ask: When facing the North Pole, what is the direction to the left? *(west)* What are cardinal directions? *(the four main directions of north, south, east, and west)* Why are northeast, northwest, southeast, and southwest known as intermediate directions? *(They are located between the cardinal directions.)*

Explain to students that most maps have a directional compass or an arrow on them to point north. Once north is known, the other directions can be found. Draw an arrow with an *N* above it on the chalkboard. Ask students to create a complete directional compass using the arrow and including the cardinal and intermediate directions.

Direct students to the map of "Sites of Early People." Ask: What Cro-Magnon site is northeast of Teshik-Tash? *(Malta)* In which direction is Cro-Magnon from Neanderthal? *(southwest)*

Provide students with a map of their state. Have them locate their community and ask them to determine the location of their community relative to other places shown on the map.

Assign the Chapter 2 **Geography and Map Activity** in the TCR.

Answers to Map Practice

1. Cro-Magnon and Le Moustier
2. Boskop
3. southeast

Determining Relative Location

Most maps show direction, or the line or course along which something is pointing or facing. Understanding direction makes locating places, whether on a map on in a town, much easier.

All directions heading toward the North Pole are north (abbreviated N), and all directions heading toward the South Pole are south (S). When facing the North Pole, the direction to the right is east (E) and to the left is west (W). These four main directions are called **cardinal directions.**

There are also four other directions, which are known as intermediate directions. This is because they are located between the cardinal directions. The direction between north and east is northeast (NE) and between north and west is northwest (NW). The direction between south and east is southeast (SE) and between south and west is southwest (SW).

Map Practice

1. **What sites are located southwest of Neanderthal?**
2. **Which site is south of Broken Hill?**
3. **In which direction is Ngandong from Teshik-Tash?**

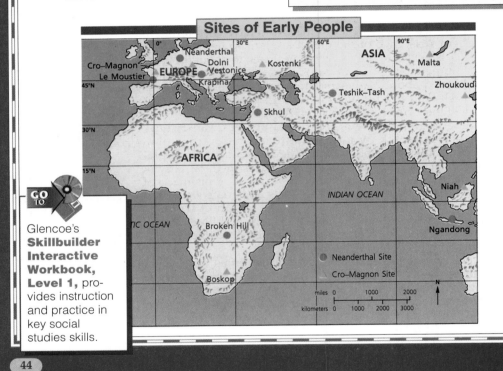

Sites of Early People

Glencoe's **Skillbuilder Interactive Workbook, Level 1,** provides instruction and practice in key social studies skills.

SPOTLIGHT ON: EARLY PEOPLE

The fascinating prehistoric art of the Lascaux Caves was in danger of disappearing because of people entering the caves and changing the atmospheric conditions. Once the visits to the cave had been cancelled and the original climatic conditions recreated, the cave art returned to the state it was in on the day of its discovery. French officials closed the caves and built an exact replica of them nearby for the public to visit.

Among the houses stood open courtyards with large ovens for baking bread. Beyond the houses were vegetable gardens, apple orchards, fields of grain, and pastures where sheep and cattle grazed.

Specialization

A result of increased food supplies was **specialization**, or the development of occupations. Fewer people were needed to produce food so they began to do jobs that had nothing to do with food. They became potters, weavers, and metal workers. They exchanged the things they made for grain, fruit, and meat.

Specialization was aided by a number of developments. One was that people learned to make pottery by baking clay. They used pottery for carrying and storing food, and for cooking. This enabled them to add such things as soups and stews to their diet.

In addition, people learned to weave cloth. People took wool from sheep, spun it into thread, and wove the thread into cloth on a loom, which was invented during the Neolithic Age. They dyed the cloth bright colors and used it for clothing.

Neolithic people also learned to work metals. They picked up lumps of copper, lead, gold, and silver that they found lying on the ground and hammered these metals into beads and jewelry. Soon they learned how to shape the metal into weapons. Because metals found on the ground were scarce, however, people continued to work mostly in stone, bone, and wood.

Government

Another development of Neolithic times was village government. It was more complex than government in earlier times due to land ownership. People's lives depended on the use of a given piece of land. As a result, people began to protect what they had. They set boundaries and passed their land on to their children.

Even so, disputes often arose over land ownership. To keep order in Neolithic villages, a single chief was chosen. Besides settling disputes, the chief, with the help of a small group of people, directed village activities.

Religion

Experts believe that the chiefs of most Neolithic villages were also priests. They handled religious duties for the village which included offering prayers for things people needed, such as rich soil, healthy animals, and water for crops.

At first, Neolithic people prayed to the forces of nature that they saw around them. After a time, they created gods and goddesses to represent these forces. The most important was the Earth Mother, the goddess of fertility. Many of the houses in Catal Hüyük, for example, had altars for this goddess.

✔ Reading Check
How did **specialization** develop in Neolithic times?

Religion Four out of five people in the world say they practice some form of religion. The five largest world religions are Christianity, Islam, Hinduism, Buddhism, and Judaism.

CHAPTER 2 PREHISTORIC PEOPLE **45**

Videodisc

Use the MindJogger to review students' knowledge of the unit

MindJogger Videoquiz

Unit 1
Disc 1 Side A

 Also available in VHS.

Reteach

Assign the Chapter 2 **Reteaching Activity** in the TCR.

Enrich

Have students write a simulated journal entry detailing an imaginary archaeological find. Have them describe the location, type of discovery, artifacts found, and method used to determine the age of their find.

Assign the Chapter 2 **Enrichment Activity** in the TCR.

CLOSE

Have students speculate as to why animals are the most common subject in prehistoric paintings that have been discovered.

Use **Interactive Tutor Self-Assessment Software** to review Section 2.

Self-Check Quiz gives students an interactive chapter tutorial. Have them access **Chapter 2 Quiz** at **humanheritage.glencoe.com**

Archaeologists believe that more elaborate religious customs and ceremonies appeared at this time. Neolithic people began to build separate altars and other places of worship for their many pagan gods and goddesses.

Section 2 Assessment

1. **Define:** domesticated, population, specialization.
2. What two important discoveries changed people from food gatherers to food producers?
3. What were two results of the increased food supply during the Neolithic Age?
4. What two roles did village chiefs play?

Critical Thinking

5. **Understanding Cause and Effect** How did learning to produce food lead early civilizations to develop villages?

Graphic Organizer Activity

6. Draw a diagram like this one, and use it to show the cause and effects of the development of farming.

Cause	Development of Farming	Effect
		Effect
		Effect

Chapter Summary & Study Guide

1. Prehistoric time can be divided into the Paleolithic and Neolithic Ages.
2. During the Paleolithic Age, people lived in small hunting-and-food-gathering bands.
3. Over time, Paleolithic people learned to make tools and clothes, developed language, and discovered how to make fire.
4. Early *Homo sapiens* included the Neanderthal and the Cro-Magnon.
5. The shift from food gathering to food producing brought so many changes that it has been called the Neolithic Revolution.
6. Food production made it possible for people to settle in one place and develop villages.
7. Increased food supplies in the Neolithic Age resulted in increased population and specialization.
8. Neolithic villagers learned to make pottery, invented the loom, and began to work metals.
9. Neolithic village government was led by a chief who settled disputes and directed village activities.

Self-Check Quiz

Visit the *Human Heritage* Web site at **humanheritage. glencoe.com** and click on **Chapter 2—Self-Check Quiz** to assess your understanding of this chapter.

Section 2 Assessment Answers

1. domesticated, tamed (p. 42); population, number of people (p. 42); specialization, development of occupations (p. 45)
2. farming and herding
3. population increased and specialization
4. They were rulers and priests.
5. People had to learn to produce food before they could settle in villages because farming provided a steady food supply and people no longer needed to hunt and gather food in nomadic bands.

6. Cause: discovered that seed from wild grains could be planted and harvested; Effects: increased food supply, growth of the world's population, rise of early villages, specialization, development of government (to settle land disputes), and so on.

Assign the Chapter 2 **Section 2 Quiz** in the TCR. Testmaker available.

Using Key Terms

Write a short description of a day in the life of a person who lived during the Paleolithic or Neolithic ages. Use the following words in your description.

prehistory   civilization   migrate
bands   home territory   domesticated
population   specialization

Understanding Main Ideas

1. What is the main difference between the Paleolithic and Neolithic ages?
2. Why did Paleolithic people move from place to place?
3. How did early men and women share the work of getting food?
4. How did the discovery of fire affect people's lives?
5. What difference did clothing make in the way people lived?
6. Why did the Cro-Magnons produce cave paintings?
7. How did increased food supplies cause increased population?
8. Why did people in the Neolithic Age begin to take up different occupations?
9. How did people in the Neolithic Age change their form of government?

Critical Thinking

1. Do you think the development of farming should be called a revolution? Explain.
2. What would you have liked about living in Catal Hüyük? What would you have disliked?
3. How would you have organized work activities if you had been a village chief?

Graphic Organizer Activity

Economics Draw a diagram like this one, and use it to show the steps leading up to the rise of villages in the Neolithic Age. (Add "steps" as necessary.)

Rise of Villages

Geography in History

Place When early people began to build shelters, they used some geographic features to decide where they would build their homes. What features affected their choice of building sites? How might geography affect their choice of building materials?

Using Your Journal

Review any details you may have noted about what early people went through as civilization developed. Pay special attention to new ideas and skills. Write an essay explaining how one of their discoveries or inventions set the stage for cultures to develop.

47

Using Key Terms

Descriptions will vary but should include all the vocabulary words..

Understanding Main Ideas

1. the way people got food
2. to search for food
3. Women gathered berries, nuts, eggs, roots; men hunted.
4. It enabled early people to cook food, keep warm, frighten animals, and refine weapons.
5. It protected early people from the weather, enabling them to move to cooler and wetter regions.
6. They thought that creating an animal in paint gave them a kind of magic power over its spirit.
7. More food was available to support larger numbers of people, and people lived longer.
8. When fewer people were needed to produce they began to take up jobs that had nothing to do with food production.
9. They chose a chief to settle disputes and direct village activities.

Critical Thinking

1. Answers will vary but should indicate that farming was a momentous development.
2. Answers will vary but should include specific examples.
3. Answers will vary but should reflect Neolithic work and tools.

Graphic Organizer Activity

Steps might include: rise of farming and domestication of animals, increased population, construction of permanent shelters, specialization, etc.

? Bonus Test Question

For Chapter 2 Test
Imagine you are a Neolithic person who has just survived an avalanche. How might this natural disaster make life harder? How might it make life easier? *(Answers will vary.)*

Using Your Journal

Essays will vary but should include specifics about one development. You might call on volunteers to read their essays to the class.

Geography in History

Answers may vary but should include consideration of mountains, rivers and streams, valleys, and swamps.

FOCUS

Objectives

After reading the Around the World for Unit 1, your students will be able to:

1. locate parts of Africa where prehistoric art is found.

2. identify types of animals herded by prehistoric peoples in Africa.

3. appreciate prehistoric art as a form of historic evidence.

Bellringer

Ask students to describe the Sahara. (*Most students will focus on its qualities as a desert, using adjectives such as hot, dry, sandy, and so on.*)

Motivational Activity

Refer students to the Around the World feature, pointing out that the Sahara was once a vast, wet grassland. Ask: Which of the animals in the pictures on pages 48–49 probably would not survive in the Sahara today? (*crocodile, giraffe, cattle*)

TEACH

Geography: Location Refer students to the map on page 48. Tell them that prehistoric art has been found on every continent except Antarctica. Africa, however, has some of the world's oldest art, including paintings that may reach back more than 40,000 years. Ask: In what parts of Africa are most prehistoric paintings found? (*southern and southeastern Africa*) Where are most engravings found? (*northern Africa, particularly the Sahara, Morocco, and Egypt's Nile Valley*)

PREHISTORIC PEOPLES OF THE SAHARA

During the prehistoric era, the Sahara—the world's largest desert—looked nothing like it does today. Vast grasslands stretched across a broad open plain. Rivers and shallow lakes shimmered in the sun. The land was wet and green enough to support bands of hunters and some of the earth's earliest communities of herders.

Between 10,000 and 4,000 years ago, the area's climate changed. The rains stopped falling and the temperatures rose. The grasslands, rivers, and lakes disappeared. So did the prehistoric peoples who once lived there. However, they left behind a rich legacy of rock art that has kept their stories alive.

Prehistoric Art in Africa

Engravings
Paintings

▲ Africa has more prehistoric rock art sites than any other continent.

▲ In the dry desert of modern Libya, a life-size crocodile stretches across a rock. The engraving, carved about 9,000 years ago, captures a time when these giant reptiles soaked up the sun on the banks of ancient rivers.

48   UNIT 1

SPOTLIGHT ON: THE SAHARA

During the Ice Age, temperatures had been too cold for evaporation, and rainfall declined around the world. At this time, the Sahara was a vast, uninhabitable desert, much like today. When the Ice Age ended, however, clouds heavy with rain blew in from the Atlantic Ocean. As the clouds dropped their water, the desert shrank to a narrow strip and new rivers and lakes appeared. Lake Chad, which did not exist in 12,000 B.C., swelled to nearly 400,000 acres—an area nearly ten times its present-day size.

Evidence of the well-watered Sahara was discovered by astronauts in the late 20th century. Staring down at the earth from space shuttles, they saw the remains of ancient river beds beneath the shifting sands of the desert—glimpsing what the land may have looked like more than 4,000 years ago.

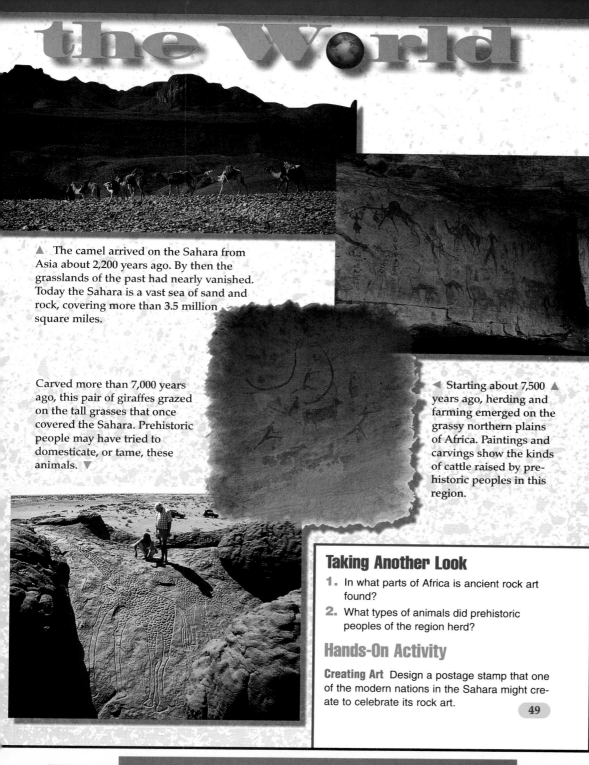

▲ The camel arrived on the Sahara from Asia about 2,200 years ago. By then the grasslands of the past had nearly vanished. Today the Sahara is a vast sea of sand and rock, covering more than 3.5 million square miles.

Carved more than 7,000 years ago, this pair of giraffes grazed on the tall grasses that once covered the Sahara. Prehistoric people may have tried to domesticate, or tame, these animals. ▼

◄ Starting about 7,500 ▲ years ago, herding and farming emerged on the grassy northern plains of Africa. Paintings and carvings show the kinds of cattle raised by prehistoric peoples in this region.

Taking Another Look

1. In what parts of Africa is ancient rock art found?
2. What types of animals did prehistoric peoples of the region herd?

Hands-On Activity

Creating Art Design a postage stamp that one of the modern nations in the Sahara might create to celebrate its rock art.

49

LINKING PAST TO PRESENT

The prehistoric rock art of the Sahara has stood the test of time. Working with stone chisels, artists chipped grooves so deep that even the scouring winds and sands of the Sahara have not worn them away. In some places, grooves still sink more than two inches into the stone faces where they were carved.

The biggest threat facing the prehistoric art is not the environment, but humans. Tourists wet the paintings to make colors more brilliant for photos. People retouch the art, thinking they will keep its magic alive. Worst of all, thieves chisel out engravings or paintings for sale.

Discuss with students why many historians and archaeologists fear the loss of this art. (*The art is a link with vanished cultures.*)

ASSESS

Check for Understanding

Have students answer the questions in **Taking Another Look** on page 49.

Enrich

Encourage students to create an illustrated version of the map on page 48. To find examples of rock art in each of the regions on the map, have students visit the Web site for the Trust for African Rock Art (TARA). Photographs by TARA's founder David Coulson can be found at: http://www.tara.org.uk

CLOSE

Ask students to speculate on why prehistoric peoples may have created rock art. (*for religious purposes, for decoration, to record important events, etc.*)

ANSWERS TO TAKING ANOTHER LOOK

1. Answers should reflect information on the map on page 48. You might point out that much of the art has been found in the cliffs and caves of Africa's most mountainous regions. Encourage students to suggest reasons for this. (*Sample Response: Prehistoric peoples found shelter and protection in these areas.*)
2. different kinds of cattle, camels

Hands-On Activity
Postage stamps should reflect information about prehistoric peoples in the feature and in Chapter 2.

Answers and Analyses

1C   Culture/Environment

On page 11, volcanoes and earthquakes are attributed to plate movement, and not to human habitation. Therefore, choices A and B can be eliminated. From the discussion of glaciers on pages 12–13, it is unreasonable to assume that humans could cause glaciers to advance. The way that people build their homes might affect wind and water, which are said on page 12 to cause erosion.

2J   Economics

The difference between renewable and non-renewable resources is discussed on pages 20–21. There it states that coal and minerals are nonrenewable, so choices F and G can be eliminated. Plastic is not a resource; instead, it is a product that is made from resources. Therefore, choice H can be eliminated.

A great number of standardized test questions are constructed to test essential vocabulary or concepts. Encourage students to learn specialized vocabulary by keeping a list of words with definitions on the side of the board.

3A   Culture/Environment

The first paragraph on page 22 states that legends are stories that help to *explain the past.* This information makes A the best choice.

Standardized Test Practice

Directions: Choose the *best* answer to each of the following multiple choice questions. If you have trouble answering a question, use the process of elimination to narrow your choices. Write your answers on a separate piece of paper.

1. The ways that people build their homes can cause which of the following surface changes to the earth?

   A   Earthquakes

   B   Volcanic eruptions

   C   Erosion

   D   Advancement of glaciers

> **Test-Taking Tip:**   Always read the question and *all* of the answer choices carefully. Avoid answers that seem extreme. For example, it is very unlikely that the way people build their homes could *cause* the *advancement of glaciers.* Therefore, you can eliminate answer D.

2   Some resources are nonrenewable, while others are renewable. Which of the following is an example of a renewable resource?

   F   Coal

   G   Minerals

   H   Plastic

   J   Timber

> **Test-Taking Tip:**   Think about the meaning of these terms. *Resources*, often referred to as "*natural resources*," are materials found in nature. Renewable resources can be replaced as they are used. *Nonrenewable resources* CANNOT be replaced. It is a good idea to keep a vocabulary list of new words as you read each new chapter. The **glossary** of your textbook can help you define these unfamiliar words.

3. Many early legends were created as ways to

   A   explain the creation of Earth

   B   explain where archaeological remains came from

   C   compare different societies

   D   introduce children to a tribe's language

> **Test-Taking Tip:**   Think of familiar examples to double-check your understanding of the question. Remember, sometimes more than one answer seems correct. For instance, though the telling of legends certainly helped children learn a tribe's language, that was not the primary reason they were created. Always choose the *best* answer.

4. The discovery of the Rosetta Stone allowed scientists to

   F   understand the fall of the Roman Empire

   G   understand the ancient Egyptian language

   H   understand how Pompeii was destroyed

   J   translate the ancient Greek language into English

> **Test-Taking Tip:**   This question asks you to remember a *fact* about the Rosetta Stone. The Rosetta Stone was one of the *most important* archaeological discoveries, since it was carved in *three languages*. Archaeologists already understood two of these languages, so this discovery allowed them to *decipher* the other. Only two answer choices discuss *languages*, so you can easily eliminate the others.

5. Which of the following CANNOT be shown on the map on the top?

A   True direction

B   Latitude and longitude

C   Accurate land shapes

D   The exact size of all continents

> *Test-Taking Tip:*   The map on the top is called a *Mercator projection*. Remember, a *map projection* is a way of representing a *round* earth on a *flat* piece of paper. What becomes distorted in a Mercator projection?

6. Which of the following is NOT considered an artifact?

F   A spearhead from ancient Egypt

G   A fossil of an extinct fish from the Paleolithic era

H   A clay water pitcher from the Shang dynasty

J   A silver bracelet from Pompeii

> *Test-Taking Tip:*   Another important term to remember is *artifact*. Artifacts are *things made by people*. Be careful when a question uses the words NOT or EXCEPT— overlooking these words is a common error. Look for the answer choice that does NOT fit.

7. During the Paleolithic Age, people lived in groups of 20 to 30 people. Increases in population within these bands were usually caused by

A   low average birth weight

B   discovery of safe migration routes

C   a stable food supply

D   frequent natural disasters

> *Test-Taking Tip:*   Eliminate answers that do not make sense. For example, answers A and D probably would probably cause a *drop* in population rather than an increase.

51

Answers and Analyses

4G   History

A description of the Rosetta Stone can be found on pages 26–27. There it states that the Rosetta stone gave scholars *the key to the meaning of Egyptian picture-writing.*

> Encourage students to use the process of elimination. They probably recall that the Rosetta Stone has to do with ancient languages, which will allow students to narrow the choices down to G and J, and then take a good guess.

5D   Geography

According to page 17, a Mercator projection *distorts* the shape and size of continents, especially in the areas farther away from the equator.

6G   Culture/Environment

On page 25, an artifact is defined as something *made by people*. Each of these is an example of something made by humans except for G.

7C   Culture/Environment

According to page 34, *When the food supply was good, the bands grew to about 40 or 50 members.*

> Remind students to read the question very carefully, because often one or more answer choices will be the exact opposite of the desired reponse. Choices A and D would *decrease*, not increase, the population.

Tested Objectives	
Questions	**Reading Objective**
1	Perceive relationships and recognize outcomes
2	Analyze information
3, 4	Identify central issues
5	Make comparisons
6, 7	Make inferences and generalizations

OVERVIEW

Unit 2 describes the emergence and development of civilization in the river valleys of the Middle East, South Asia, and China.

➤ **Chapter 3** discusses the rise of civilization in the Tigris-Euphrates Valley of Mesopotamia, focusing on Sumer as well as later Mesopotamian empires.

➤ **Chapter 4** summarizes how civilization developed in the Nile Valley of Egypt and highlights the Old, Middle, and New Kingdoms.

➤ **Chapter 5** deals with the Harappan civilization of the Indus River valley in India and Pakistan, and the Shang civilization of the Huang Ho River valley in China.

UNIT OBJECTIVES

After reading Unit 2, your students will be able to:

1. give examples of how the environment influenced the ways in which people of the river valleys lived.

2. discuss the early civilizations of Mesopotamia, Egypt, and the eastern river valleys in terms of their similarities and differences.

3. summarize the contributions made by the river valley civilizations to other civilizations.

UNIT PROJECT

Have students create a "You Are There" display to represent what they learn about these early civilizations. After dividing them into groups, have each group choose among the Sumerians, Babylonians, Egyptians, Harappans, and Shang to display. Students can decide what and how to present their material, in written, visual, or interactive formats.

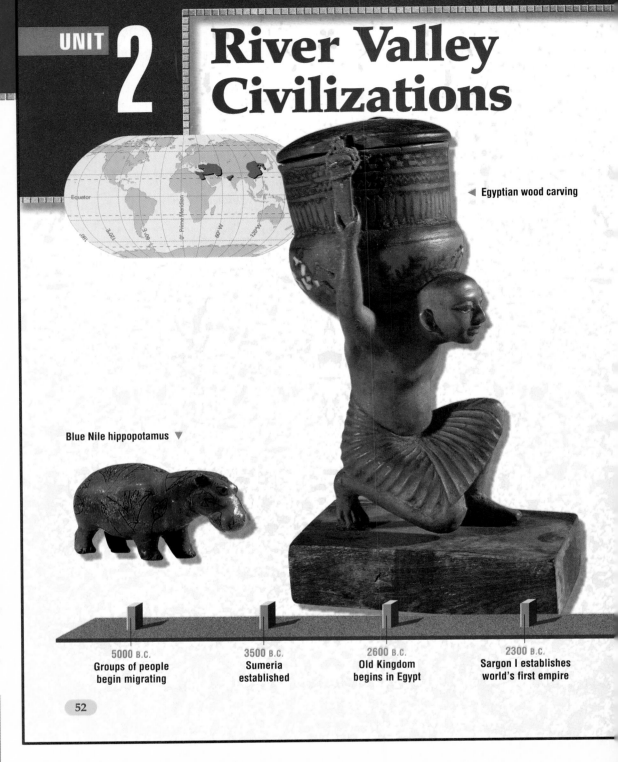

UNIT 2 # River Valley Civilizations

Equator

◀ Egyptian wood carving

Blue Nile hippopotamus ▼

| 5000 B.C. | 3500 B.C. | 2600 B.C. | 2300 B.C. |
| Groups of people begin migrating | Sumeria established | Old Kingdom begins in Egypt | Sargon I establishes world's first empire |

ABOUT THE UNIT OPENING

Examining Artifacts

Tell students that plants, animals, and scenes associated with the Nile River played an important role in Egyptian art. Use the carvings of the Egyptian water bearer and the river hippo as examples. Encourage students to speculate on reasons ancient peoples such as the Egyptians built the world's earliest civilizations along the banks of rivers.

Global Chronology

Refer students to the unit time line. Ask students to recall the meaning of B.C. and A.D. (*B.C. means "before Christ" and* A.D. *stands for* anno Domini *which means "in the year of the Lord."*) Ask students to explain what the time line covers. (*some major events in the early river valley civilizations in the Middle East, South Asia, and China*)

Multimedia Activity

Turning Points in World History
The Rise of Cities

Setting up the Video

Work with a group of your classmates to view "The Rise of Cities" on the videodisc *Turning Points in World History*.

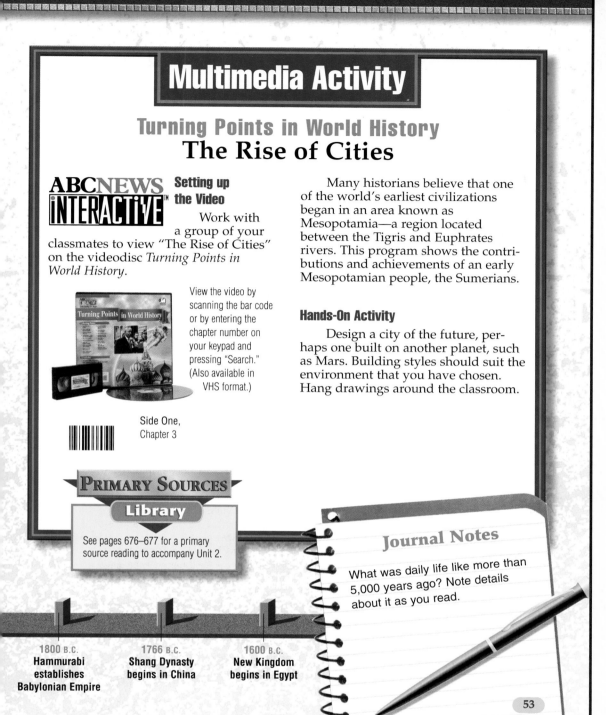

View the video by scanning the bar code or by entering the chapter number on your keypad and pressing "Search." (Also available in VHS format.)

Side One, Chapter 3

Many historians believe that one of the world's earliest civilizations began in an area known as Mesopotamia—a region located between the Tigris and Euphrates rivers. This program shows the contributions and achievements of an early Mesopotamian people, the Sumerians.

Hands-On Activity

Design a city of the future, perhaps one built on another planet, such as Mars. Building styles should suit the environment that you have chosen. Hang drawings around the classroom.

PRIMARY SOURCES
Library

See pages 676–677 for a primary source reading to accompany Unit 2.

Journal Notes

What was daily life like more than 5,000 years ago? Note details about it as you read.

1800 B.C.	1766 B.C.	1600 B.C.
Hammurabi establishes Babylonian Empire	Shang Dynasty begins in China	New Kingdom begins in Egypt

53

 Geographic Location

The civilizations discussed in this unit arose along the Tigris-Euphrates, Nile, Indus, and Huang Ho river valleys. Have students locate these rivers on the appropriate maps in their text Atlas. Then have volunteers locate them on a wall map of the world.

GLENCOE
TECHNOLOGY

Videodisc
Use the MindJogger to preview the unit content.

MindJogger Videoquiz

Unit 2
Disc 1 Side A

Also available in VHS.

INTRODUCING THE UNIT

Explain to the class that because the ancient civilizations studied in this unit developed in river valleys, they were alike in many ways. Ask students to brainstorm ways that river valley civilizations might be alike. (*They all developed ways of controlling floods and producing a surplus of food, allowing them time to focus on other cultural endeavors.*)

RECORDING JOURNAL NOTES

Have students write a description of a typical day in their lives. Then have volunteers read their descriptions, and write some details on the board. Explain to students that they could note these kinds of details as they read about early civilizations.

PRIMARY SOURCES
Library

Items in the Primary Sources Library for this unit focus on the development of justice in the ancient world. Elements include:
- Passages from Hammurabi's Code
- Carvings from the tablet on which the code was recorded

 For additional primary source documents, have students use the **World History Primary Source Document CD-ROM.**

Chapter 3 Planning Guide

Objectives	Reproducible Resources	Multimedia Resources
Section 1 **The Rise of Sumer** Describe how religion, family life, and government influenced Sumerian civilization.	Reproducible Lesson Plan Chapter 3 Vocabulary and Guided Reading Activity Reading Essentials and Study Guide 3-1 Chapter 3 Cooperative Learning Activity Chapter 3 Chart and Graph Skill Activity Chapter 3 Enrichment Activity Unit 2 Primary Sources Reading Unit 2 World Literature Reading 1 Section 1 Quiz Unit 2 Hands-On History Lab	Teaching Transparencies and Activities 3A & 3B ABCNEWS INTERACTIVE Turning Points in World History Vocabulary PuzzleMaker Interactive Tutor Self-Assessment Software ExamView® Pro Testmaker Glencoe Skillbuilder Interactive Workbook, Level 1 Presentation Plus!
Section 2 **Later Mesopotamian Empires** Explain why Hammurabi and his reforms were important.	Reproducible Lesson Plan Reading Essentials and Study Guide 3-2 Chapter 3 Geography and Map Activity Section 2 Quiz	Vocabulary PuzzleMaker Interactive Tutor Self-Assessment Software ExamView® Pro Testmaker Glencoe Skillbuilder Interactive Workbook, Level 1
Section 3 **Contributions** Describe how the Mesopotamian civilization contributed to other civilizations.	Reproducible Lesson Plan Reading Essentials and Study Guide 3-3 Section 3 Quiz	Vocabulary PuzzleMaker Interactive Tutor Self-Assessment Software ExamView® Pro Testmaker Glencoe Skillbuilder Interactive Workbook, Level 1
Chapter 3 **Review and Evaluation**	Chapter 3 Reteaching Activity Chapter 3 Performance Assessment Activity Spanish Chapter Summary and Glossary Chapter 3 Test	Vocabulary PuzzleMaker Interactive Tutor Self-Assessment Software ExamView® Pro Testmaker Glencoe Skillbuilder Interactive Workbook, Level 1 Audiocassettes*

*Also available in Spanish.

Presentation Plus!

Use Glencoe's **Presentation Plus!** multimedia teacher tool to easily present dynamic lessons that visually excite your students. Using Microsoft® PowerPoint, you can customize the presentations to create your own personalized lessons.

Interactive Lesson Planner

Planning has never been easier! Using this CD-ROM, organize your week, month, semester, or year with all the help you need. The **Interactive Lesson Planner** gives you access to all of the blackline masters which accompany *Human Heritage*.

✓ PERFORMANCE ASSESSMENT ACTIVITIES

Newspaper Articles Remind students that the elements of a newspaper article include *who, what, where, when, why,* and *how.* Have students choose an event from the chapter to write about in newspaper style. When the articles are completed, students can share them with the class.

CHAPTER RESOURCES

LITERATURE ABOUT THE PERIOD

Oppenheim, A. Leo. *Letters from Mesopotamia.* University of Chicago Press, 1967. A translation of business and personal letters found in cuneiform.

READINGS FOR THE STUDENT

Foster, Leila Merrell. *The Sumerians.* Watts, 1990. Discusses the rise and fall of the Sumerian civilization and includes several photographs of Sumerian artifacts.

Wetwood, Jennifer. *Gilgamesh, and Other Babylonian Tales.* Coward, McCann & Geoghegan, 1970. Retells ancient tales of Sumer and Babylon.

READINGS FOR THE TEACHER

Gailey, Harry A. *History of Africa Volume I: Earliest times to 1800.* Krieger, 1980. An overview of this period in African history.

Hawkes, Jacquetta, ed. *Atlas of Ancient Archaeology.* McGraw-Hill, 1974. Traces the patterns of ancient cultures and civilizations around the world.

KEY TO ABILITY LEVELS

Teaching strategies have been coded for varying learning styles and abilities.

L1 Level 1 activities are **basic** activities and should be within the ability range of all students.

L2 Level 2 activities are **average** activities and should be within the ability range of the average to above-average student.

L3 Level 3 activities are **challenging** activities designed for the ability range of above-average students.

ELL ELL activities should be within the ability range of English Language Learning students.

Teacher's Corner

INDEX TO NATIONAL GEOGRAPHIC MAGAZINE

The following articles relate to this chapter:

- "The Power of Writing," by Joel L. Swerdlow, August 1999.
- "Iraq: Crucible of Civilization," by Merle Severy, May 1991.

NATIONAL GEOGRAPHIC SOCIETY PRODUCTS AVAILABLE FROM GLENCOE

To order the following, call Glencoe at 1-800-334-7344:

- *PicturePack: Physical Geography of the World (Transparencies)*
- *PictureShow: Ancient Civilizations: Egypt and the Fertile Crescent (CD-ROM)*
- *PicturePack: Fertile Crescent (Transparencies)*
- *The Fertile Crescent (Poster Set)*
- *STV: World Geography (Videodisc)*
- *PictureShow: Ancient Civilizations Library (CD-ROMs)*
- *PicturePack: Ancient Civilizations Library, Part II (Transparencies)*

ADDITIONAL NATIONAL GEOGRAPHIC SOCIETY PRODUCTS

To order the following, call National Geographic at 1-800-368-2728:

- *National Geographic Atlas of World History (Book)*
- *Wonders of the Ancient World: National Geographic Atlas of Archaeology (Book)*

Access *National Geographic's* new dynamic MapMachine Web site and other geography resources at:
http://www.nationalgeographic.com/
http://www.nationalgeographic.com/maps/

OVERVIEW

Chapter 3 focuses on the development of civilization in Mesopotamia from around 3500 to 1800 B.C.

➤ **Section 1** describes the rise of Sumer and the development of city-states.

➤ **Section 2** discusses the effects of conquest on the development of Mesopotamia.

➤ **Section 3** presents the contributions of Mesopotamia.

CHAPTER OBJECTIVES

After reading Chapter 3, your students will be able to:

1. describe how religion, family life, and government influenced Sumerian civilizations.

2. explain why Hammurabi and his reforms were important.

3. name Mesopotamian contributions.

EXAMINING ARTIFACTS

Introduce Chapter 3 by asking students what the helmet suggests about how Sumer rose to power. *(through conquest)* What does it tell them about Sumer's wealth? *(that it possessed riches such as gold)* Explain that the carving is a portrait of a husband and wife found at a Sumerian temple. What can students infer about family relationships from this carving? *(that they were close)*

PERFORMANCE ASSESSMENT ✓

Use the Performance Assessment Activities on page 54B to help you evaluate students as they complete the chapter.

CHAPTER 3

Mesopotamia
3500 B.C.–1700 B.C.

Sumerian man and woman ▼

▲ Gold Sumerian warrior's helmet

3500 B.C.	2300 B.C.	1800 B.C.	1700 B.C.
Sumeria established	**Sargon I creates the world's first empire**	**Hammurabi conquers Akkad and Sumer**	**Tales of Gilgamesh started**

54 UNIT 2 RIVER VALLEY CIVILIZATIONS

TEACHING RESOURCES

TEACHER PLANNING AND SUPPORT

- 📂 Reproducible Lesson Plan
- 📂 Block Scheduling Implementation Guide
- 📂 Videodisc Bar Code Correlation
- 🔘 Presentation Plus!

REVIEW AND REINFORCEMENT

- 📂 Reading Essentials and Study Guide 3-1, 3-2, 3-3
- 📂 Chapter 3 Vocabulary and Guided Reading Activity
- 💾 Vocabulary PuzzleMaker Software
- 🖨 Teaching Transparencies 3A & 3B

- 📂 Chapter 3 Reteaching Activity
- 📂 Chapter 3 Cooperative Learning Activity
- 📂 Chapter 3 Activity Book Activity
- 📂 Chapter 3 Chart and Graph Skill Activity
- 💾 Interactive Tutor Self-Assessment Software
- 📼 Unit 2 MindJogger VideoQuiz

APPLICATION AND HANDS-ON ACTIVITIES

- 📂 Daily World History, Geography, and Culture Question
- 📂 Unit 2 Hands-On History Lab Activity

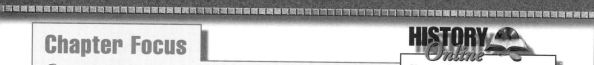

Chapter Focus

Read to Discover

- How religion, family life, and government influenced the civilization of Sumer.
- Why Hammurabi and his reforms were important.
- How the developments of Mesopotamia contributed to other civilizations.

 Terms to Learn

city-state
artisans
ziggurat
cuneiform
scribe
priest-kings
empire
culture
reform
reign

People to Know

Gilgamesh
Sargon I
Hammurabi

Places to Locate

Mesopotamia
Sumer
Ur
Babylon

HISTORY Online
Chapter Overview
Visit the *Human Heritage* Web site at **humanheritage.glencoe.com** and click on **Chapter 3—Chapter Overviews** to preview this chapter.

Why It's Important   The earliest known civilizations developed along the Tigris and Euphrates rivers, which begin in the mountains of eastern Turkey. The twin rivers each flow more than 1,000 miles, or 1,600 kilometers, southeast across a great plain in an area known as the Middle East. Then, the waters join and empty into the Persian Gulf. Today, the land between the two rivers is part of the country of Iraq. In ancient times, the area was called Mesopotamia (mes uh puh tay' mē uh), "the land between the rivers."

Around 4000 B.C., groups of people began migrating, or moving, into Mesopotamia. They developed so many new ideas that the area has been called the "cradle of civilization." The influence of Mesopotamia left a lasting impact on the ancient world.

SECTION 1   The Rise of Sumer

The people who settled in southern Mesopotamia about 3500 B.C. were a short, stocky, black-haired people called Sumerians (sū mer' ē uhnz). Their area of Mesopotamia was known as Sumer (sū' mŭhr).

HISTORY Online
Chapter Overview introduces students to chapter content and key terms. Have them access **Chapter 3 Overview** at **humanheritage.glencoe.com**

FOCUS

Bellringer

Write the following question on the chalkboard: *What is a cradle of civilization?* Have students write their responses.

Motivational Activity

Ask volunteers to share their explanations of a cradle of civilization. Ask: *What features would an area need in order to give birth to and encourage the growth of a civilization?* Suggest that students consider this question as they study the section.

GUIDE TO READING

Reading Strategy

Ask students to read "Why It's Important" and summarize the chapter's main theme. *(The people of Mesopotamia developed many new ideas and left a lasting impact on world civilization.)*

Vocabulary Precheck

Ask students to define each of the "Terms to Learn." Have a volunteer consult the dictionary for any unfamiliar words. **L1** **ELL**

Use the Vocabulary PuzzleMaker for Chapter 3 to create a crossword puzzle. **L1**

Assign Chapter 3 Vocabulary and Guided Reading Activity.

Assign Reading Essentials and Study Guide 3-1.

Guided Practice

L2 **Daily Life** Write the following question on the board: *"How did religion, family life, and government influence Sumerian civilization?"* Ask volunteers to write a script about daily life in Sumer that includes the following members of Sumerian society: a priest, a student, a scribe, and a woman. Explain that the script should answer the question on the board.

Direct the remaining members of the class to act as anthropologists whose job it is to answer the original question by observing the role-play.

Student Web Activity objectives, goals, and answers can be found at the **Chapter 3 Web Activity Lesson Plan** at humanheritage.glencoe.com

Sample responses: to prevent forgery, as proof of authority, and so on.

NATIONAL GEOGRAPHIC SOCIETY

Use these materials to enrich student understanding of Mesopotamian civilizations.

NGS PICTURESHOW CD-ROM
Egypt and the Fertile Crescent

NGS PICTUREPACK TRANSPARENCY SET
Fertile Crescent

Student Web Activity
Visit the *Human Heritage* Web site at **humanheritage.glencoe.com** and click on **Chapter 3—Student Web Activities** to find out more about the Sumerian civilization.

Sumerian civilization is the earliest known on Earth. For the first time, people began to control their physical environment. The Sumerians knew they had to control the twin rivers. The rivers flooded each spring. When the waters went down, natural *levees* (lev' ēz), or raised areas of soil, remained behind. The Sumerians built the levees even higher and used them to keep back the floodwaters. During summer when the land became dry, they poked holes in the levees. The river water that ran through the holes made channels in the soil. The Sumerians made the channels larger until they became canals. They used the water in the canals to irrigate their crops. The chief crop of the Sumerians was barley. The Sumerians also grew wheat, sesame, flax, fruit trees, date palms, and many different kinds of vegetables.

A system of irrigation canals took much planning. People had to learn to work together. In time, they became more organized. They set up governments to make laws so they would know what was expected of them. As the population grew, they began to build cities.

There was no building stone and little timber in Sumer. The Sumerians had to find other materials to use for their houses and public buildings. They mixed mud from the river with crushed reeds to make bricks. They left the bricks out in the sun to bake and then used them to build their cities. One of the great cities of

Official Seals   Around 3500 to 3400 B.C., officials in Mesopotamia started using cylinder seals (below) to mark goods and verify documents written in cuneiform on clay. Today governments around the world continue to use seals to mark documents such as the passports carried by United States citizens (right). **Why do you think governments stamp important documents with seals?**

56   UNIT 2 RIVER VALLEY CIVILIZATIONS

COOPERATIVE LEARNING

Organize the class into three groups. Have each group research information about one aspect of life in ancient Sumer, Akkad, or Babylon. Have groups prepare a class presentation, the subject and format of which they determine cooperatively. Subjects could include lifestyles, occupations, religious practices, or achievements. Formats could include role plays, lectures, and skits. Direct group members to decide what role each team member will play in gathering and presenting the material. Allow time after each presentation for discussion and questions.

 Assign Chapter 3 *Cooperative Learning Activity* in the TCR.

Sumer was Ur (uhr). The Sumerians were the first city-builders in this area of the world.

City-States

Each Sumerian city was considered a state in itself, with its own god and government. Each **city-state** was made up of the city and the farmland around it. Each city was surrounded by a wall of sun-dried brick. The wall had bronze gates that were opened during the day and closed at night to keep out lions and bandits.

Narrow, winding streets led from the gates to the center of the city. Near the center were the houses of the upper class—priests and merchants. These houses were two stories high with wooden balconies. The balconies looked out over courtyards around which the living quarters were built. The courtyards provided light and air for rooms. Outside walls were windowless to keep out heat from the sun and smells of the streets.

Behind the houses of the rich were the houses of the middle class—government officials, shopkeepers, and **artisans** (art' uh zuhnz), or skilled workers. These houses also were built around open courtyards but were only one story high. Farther out were the houses of the lower class—farmers, unskilled workers, and people who made their living by fishing.

The Sumerians were very proud of their cities. Often, one city-state would go to war with another city-state. They fought over boundary lines and to prove which city-state was stronger.

Religious and Family Life

At the center of each Sumerian city was a temple, called a **ziggurat** (zig' uh rat). The word "ziggurat" means "mountain of god" or "hill of heaven." Each ziggurat was made up of a series of square levels. Each level was smaller than the one below it. Great stairways led to the top of a ziggurat, which was believed to be the home of the city's chief god. Only priests could enter the home of the god.

Around the ziggurat were courts. The courts and the ziggurat were the center of Sumerian life. Artisans worked there. Children went to school there. Farmers, artisans, and traders stored their goods there. The poor were fed there. All great events were celebrated in this area.

The Sumerians believed that all the forces of nature, such as wind, rain, and flood, were alive. Because they could not control these forces, they viewed them as gods. In all, there were more than 3,000 Sumerian gods.

The Sumerians believed that at first there were only male gods. Then female gods appeared. The male gods found they had to work very hard to please the female gods. The male gods decided that they needed servants to do their work. So, from the mud of the rivers, they made humans who would be their servants. The Sumerians believed that they were on Earth only to

---

Reading Check
What areas made up each Sumerian **city-state?**

Reading Check
What are **artisans?**

Reading Check
What was the purpose of a **ziggurat?**

✓ **Reading Check Answer**
Each **city-state** was made up of a city and the farmland around it.

🔲 **Critical Thinking** Ask students to give possible reasons why the Sumerians had more than 3,000 gods who represented the forces of nature.

✓ **Reading Check Answer**
Artisans are skilled workers.

✓ **Reading Check Answer**
A **ziggurat** served as a temple and center of religious life.

VIDEODISC
Turning Points in World History

Side One
Chapter 3

Title: *The Rise of Cities*
Subject: The inventions of the Sumerians in Mesopotamia enabled people to live together in communities for the first time.
Ask: What led to the need for new forms of government in Mesopotamia? *(population growth)*

MEETING SPECIAL NEEDS

Encourage students who are tactile/kinesthetic learners to work in small groups to create models of a Sumerian city using materials of their choice. Direct students to use the information in the text and in historical reference books to help them construct the models. Display the models in the classroom.

📁 Refer to *Inclusion for the Middle School Social Studies Classroom: Strategies and Activities* for additional resources.

MAKING CONNECTIONS

➤➤ **Language Arts** Cuneiform was used by heterogeneous groups who spoke different languages. It served as the writing system for diverse cultures for some 3,000 years. Sumerians, Akkadians, Babylonians, Assyrians, Hittites, and Ancient Persians are among the peoples whose language was written in cuneiform. As a system of encoding, cuneiform was as widely used as the Latin alphabet is today.

DID YOU KNOW ??

Sumerian students had to memorize a list of about 600 word signs. They copied and recopied their lessons until they mastered them.

SUMERIAN PRAYING STATUES   To honor their gods, Sumerians left statues of themselves within their temple. These statues, standing with their hands clasped, were meant to offer prayers when the people were not present. **In how many gods did the Sumerians believe?**

serve the gods. If the gods were unhappy with them, their crops would not grow and they would not live a happy life. Therefore, the goal of each Sumerian was to please the gods.

Only priests, however, could know the will of the gods. This made Sumerian priests very powerful. For example, all land was owned by a city's god. But priests controlled and administered the land in the god's name. The priests also ran schools.

Schools were only for the sons of the rich. Poorer boys worked in the fields or learned a trade. Schools were made up of rooms off the temple courtyards. They were known as tablet houses because their main purpose was to teach students how to write. Students sat in rows on brick benches. They wrote with sharp-ended reeds on clay tablets about the size of a postcard. Sumerian writing was called **cuneiform** (kyū nē′ uh form). It was made up of hundreds of markings shaped like wedges.

✓ **Reading Check**
What was **cuneiform?**

Writing developed because people had to keep track of business deals. When people lived in villages, they knew everyone and could remember what goods they exchanged with whom. When cities arose, there were too many people and goods to remember. At first, the Sumerians used pictures to represent objects. Later, they used pictures to represent ideas. Still later, they used pictures to represent syllables.

✓ **Reading Check**
What were some of the places a **scribe** might work?

When a student graduated from school, he became a **scribe,** or writer. He worked for the temple, the palace, the government, or the army. Some scribes went to work for a merchant or set up their own businesses as public writers.

MULTICULTURAL PERSPECTIVES

Learning to write the hundreds of cuneiform symbols in ancient times was a long, difficult process. One clay tablet found in Sumer seems to be a composition that teachers gave their students for practice. Students wrote once, found their mistakes, scraped off the surface of the clay tablet, and wrote again. The following is an excerpt from a clay tablet. "First I had to recite my homework. Then I prepared my new tablet. I copied out the text that the supervisor gave me. Then I ate my lunch. After 'Break', the father of the tablet house asked me questions. Last of all, I was given a written task that I had to do in the tablet house. After my lessons I went straight home. My father heard me recite…"

Although only Sumerian males went to school, women did have rights. They could buy and sell property. They could run businesses and own and sell enslaved persons.

Although a woman handled her husband's affairs when he was away, the husband was the head of a household. He could divorce his wife by saying, "You're not my wife." If he needed money, he had the right to sell or rent his wife and children as enslaved persons for up to three years. He also arranged the marriages of his children.

Children were expected to support their parents when the parents became old and were also expected to obey older family members. All family members were to obey the gods and the priests.

Priests and Kings   At first, Sumerian priests were also kings of city-states. One of the most famous **priest-kings** was Gilgamesh (gil' ga mesh) of Uruk (ū' rūk). Tales told about Gilgamesh made him seem more like a god than a person. One tale written about 1700 B.C. is the oldest known story in the world.

In the story, Gilgamesh and his friend Enkidu (en' ki dū) travel the world performing great acts of courage. When Enkidu dies, Gilgamesh searches for a way to live forever. He learns that only the gods can live forever. Part of the Gilgamesh story tells of a great flood that covered the whole world. The account of the flood is very much like the biblical story of Noah and the ark.

The Sumerian priest-kings received advice from an assembly made up of free men. When war broke out with another city-state, the assembly would choose one of its members to serve as military leader until the war was over. As time went on, these leaders stayed in charge even after peace returned. By about 3000 B.C., they took the place of priests as permanent kings. At the same time, kingship became *hereditary* (huh red' uh ter ē), or passed down from parent to child.

Then...&Now

Cuneiform Today only about 250 people know how to read the more than 1 million cuneiform signs that make up the written Sumerian language. To change this, a team of language experts at the University of Pennsylvania is working on an 18-volume Sumerian dictionary. The team expects the work to be done sometime in the 2000s.

✓ **Reading Check**
Who was one of the most famous Sumerian **priest-kings?**

MAKING CONNECTIONS

➤➤ **Literature** Gilgamesh is the first known hero figure in literature. His story was the prototype for later epic poetry and may have influenced Homer's epics, the *Iliad* and the *Odyssey*.

✓ **Reading Check Answer**
One of the most famous Sumerian **priest-kings** was Gilgamesh.

GEOGRAPHY AND HISTORY
By 3000 B.C. the Sumerians had established 12 city-states in the Tigris-Euphrates Valley, including Ur, Uruk, and Eridu. The Fertile Crescent, as the area is often called because of its relatively rich topsoil and its curved shape, was able to support city-state populations ranging from 20,000 to 250,000.

💾 Use the **Interactive Tutor Self-Assessment Software** to review Section 1.

Section 1 Assessment

1. **Define:** city-state, artisans, ziggurat, cuneiform, scribe, priest-kings.
2. How did the Sumerians gain control of the twin rivers?
3. What was the center of Sumerian life?

Critical Thinking

4. **Making Comparisions**   How would you compare the lives of women in the time of Sumer to the lives of women in the modern world?

Graphic Organizer Activity

5. Draw a diagram like this one, and use it to show accomplishments of the Sumerians.

Accomplishments

Section 1 Assessment Answers

1. city-state, self-governing city (p. 57); artisans, skilled workers (p. 57); ziggurat, Sumerian temple (p. 57); cuneiform, Sumerian writing (p. 58); scribe, Sumerian writer (p. 58); priest-kings, Sumerian priests who were also kings (p. 59)
2. by building natural levees even higher
3. the courts and the ziggurat
4. Answers will vary. Students may point out that like Sumerian women, modern women can buy property and businesses.

Modern women, however, also can get an education, divorce, and cannot be enslaved.
5. Accomplishments might include: levees to control flooding, a system of irrigation canals, construction of brick cities, organization of city-states, development of a writing system, creation of literature such as the story of Gilgamesh.

Assign Chapter 3 **Section 1 Quiz** in the TCR. Testmaker available.

CRITICAL THINKING SKILLS

TEACH

Distinguishing Fact From Opinion

You might introduce this activity by asking students to complete these sentences on a sheet of paper:

The best song ever written is:

_____.

The best food ever created is:

_____.

Record student answers on the board under two heads: Best Song and Best Food. On top of these two columns, write the words "Differences in Opinion." Ask students to define the word "opinion." Use their answers to introduce the skills lesson and the accompanying questions.

Answers to Skill Practice

1. Fact. It can be proven by existing archaeological finds.
2. Opinion. Some people might think other accomplishments are more important. The sentence also includes the judgment word "greatest."
3. Fact. It can be proven by evidence found at the sites of ancient city-states such as Sumer.
4. Opinion. Women at the time might have seen their lives differently. The sentence also includes the judgment word "terrible."
5. Opinion. The statement cannot be proven. The sentence also includes the judgment word "better."

Distinguishing Fact From Opinion

Suppose a friend says, "Our school's basketball team is awesome. That's a fact." Actually, it is not a fact; it is an opinion. Are you able to tell the difference?

Learning the Skill A **fact** answers a specific question such as: What happened? Who did it? When and where did it happen? Why did it happen? Statements of fact can be checked for accuracy and proven. If your friend had said, "We have the highest-ranking team in the state," that could be a fact. We can look up the rankings of state teams and determine whether the statement is a fact.

An **opinion,** on the other hand, expresses beliefs, feelings, and judgments. Although it may reflect someone's thoughts, we cannot prove or disprove it.

An **opinion** often begins with phrases such as *I believe, I think, probably, it seems to me,* or *in my opinion.* It often contains words such as *might, could, should,* and *ought* and superlatives such as *best, worst,* and *greatest.* Judgment words that express approval or disapproval—such as *good, bad, poor,* and *satisfactory*—also usually indicate an opinion.

To distinguish between facts and opinions, ask yourself these questions:

- Does this statement give specific information about an event?
- Can I check the accuracy of this statement?
- Does this statement express someone's feelings, beliefs, or judgment?
- Does it include phrases such as *I believe,* superlatives, or judgment words?

Skill Practice

Read each numbered statement. Then tell whether each is a fact or an opinion, and explain how you arrived at your answer.

1. Sumerian civilization is the earliest known on Earth.
2. The greatest accomplishment of the Sumerians was their system of irrigation.
3. A temple called a ziggurat formed the center of Sumerian life.
4. Women in Sumeria had terrible lives.
5. The priest-kings were better rulers than the military leaders who took over power.

Glencoe's **Skillbuilder Interactive Workbook, Level 1,** provides instruction and practice in key social studies skills.

60

TEAM-TEACHING STRATEGY

Language Arts Work with a language arts teacher to develop a lesson on persuasive writing. Explain to students that people sometimes use facts to support an opinion. Illustrate this by distributing copies of letters to the editor from your local newspaper. Have students identify the main opinion expressed in each letter and the facts used to support that opinion.

Next, tell students to imagine that they are scribes working for Hammurabi. As they read Section 2, have students record his achievements. Assign groups of students to use these facts to write letters persuading conquered peoples to accept this opinion: "Hammurabi is the best ruler you could possibly have."

SECTION 2 Later Mesopotamian Empires

About 2400 B.C., the power of Sumer started to fade. New civilizations began to develop in Mesopotamia as conquerors moved in from nearby areas.

Sargon I   Sargon I (sar' gon) was a ruler from an area in northern Mesopotamia known as Akkad (ak' ad). About 2300 B.C., he moved his armies south and began to conquer the city-states of Sumer one by one. He united the conquered city-states with Akkad and became known as king of Sumer and Akkad. Thus, Sargon I created the world's first **empire** (em' pīr), or group of states under one ruler. He extended this empire to include all of Mesopotamia.

Under Sargon I, Akkadian became the language of the people. Sumerian was used only for religious purposes. The Akkadians, however, worshipped the Sumerian gods. They also wrote their language in Sumerian cuneiform. Sargon I ruled his empire for more than 50 years. Shortly after his death, the empire fell.

Hammurabi of Babylon   Following the death of Sargon I, the separate city-states again rose to power. Then, about 1800 B.C., a new group of people called Amorites (am' uh rīts) entered the Tigris-Euphrates Valley and built cities of their own. One of these cities was Babylon (bab' uh luhn). The king of Babylon, Hammurabi (ham uh rob' ē), conquered Akkad and Sumer and became ruler of a great new empire.

The people of Babylon took as their own many parts of the **culture,** or way of life, of the people they had conquered. For example, they took over the language of the city-states. They also worshiped the same Sumerian gods that the Akkadians had worshiped, but they gave those gods Babylonian names.

Hammurabi was a great conqueror. He extended his rule to the Mediterranean Sea. As ruler, he brought about many changes. He improved irrigation systems by building and repairing canals. He changed religion by raising the god of Babylon above all other gods. When the people began to worship this god as well as their own local god, they became more united. Hammurabi also reorganized the tax system and began a government housing program.

The **reform,** or improvement, for which Hammurabi became best known was a code of law. Each city-state had its own code. Hammurabi took what he believed were the best laws from each code. He put these together and then issued one code by which everyone in the empire was to live. Hammurabi wanted to make sure that his code was carried out fairly and justly. To do this, he

Reading Check
How did Sargon I build the world's first **empire?**
How did the people of Babylon borrow from the **culture** of other people?
For what **reform** is Hammurabi best known?

Hammurabi
c.1750 B.C.

Babylonian King

Hammurabi built an empire that stretched north from the Persian Gulf through the Tigris and Euphrates valleys and west to the Mediterranean Sea. He turned Babylon into one of the most powerful capitals of the ancient world.

Reading Check Answer
Sargon I built the world's first **empire** by conquering city-states and uniting them. Babylonians borrowed from the **culture** of other people by adopting the language of city-states and worshiping some of the same gods.
Hammurabi is best known for his **reform** of law.

PRIMARY SOURCES
Library

You might assign "The Pursuit of Justice," from pages 676–677 of the Primary Sources Library.

ABCNEWS
INTERACTIVE™

 VIDEODISC
Turning Points in World History

    Side One
Chapter 4

Title: *The Code of Hammurabi*
Subject: Hammurabi's written code of laws established justice and became the basis for rules and laws throughout the world.
Ask: How were punishments for crimes decided? *(Punishments were to fit the crimes, like the biblical saying, "an eye for an eye.")*

Use the **Vocabulary Puzzle-Maker** to create crossword and word search puzzles.

SPOTLIGHT ON: SARGON I

Sargon I tells his own story in an account found carved on a block of diorite. The story is similar to the biblical story of Moses.

"Of my father I know only his name . . . My mother was a priestess . . . She brought me into the world secretly . . . She took a basket of reeds, placed me inside it, covered it with pitch [tar], and placed me in the Euphrates. And the river, without which the land cannot live, carried me through part of my future kingdom . . . and bore me along to Akki, who fetched water to irrigate the fields. Akki made a gardener of me. In the garden that I cultivated Inanna [chief goddess] saw me. And she turned her favor toward me and promised to make me great."

MAP SKILLS

TEACH

Identifying Physical Features

Instruct the students to study the map on page 62 to answer the following questions:

What empire was located partly in the mountains? *(Hammurabi's empire)*

What seas border Asia Minor? *(Mediterranean Sea, Black Sea)*

Have the students look at the physical map of the Middle East on pages 678–679 in the textbook Atlas. Point out to students that this map uses many colors and grades of shading to show physical features. Ask the students to identify and locate physical features of the Middle East shown on this map.

Assign Chapter 3 **Geography and Map Activity** in the TCR.

Answers to Map Practice

1. Seas shown on the map in addition to the Mediterranean Sea are the Caspian Sea, the Black Sea, and the Red Sea.

2. Besides the Nile, the rivers shown on the map are the Tigris River and the Euphrates River.

3. The map and the map key indicate that there was an ancient coastline of the Persian Gulf.

Identifying Physical Features

Different physical features making up Earth's surface are often shown on maps. They include landforms, such as mountains, hills, plateaus, and plains. Physical features also include bodies of water, such as oceans, seas, lakes, and rivers.

Most maps use black boundary lines and color to point out water and land areas. Blue is generally used to show the size and shape of large bodies of water. For example, notice the Mediterranean Sea located west of Syria on the map below. Rivers, such as the Nile River in Egypt, are often shown by black lines. To distinguish rivers from boundaries, which are also shown by black lines, rivers are usually labeled.

Maps in this textbook use earth tone colors to point out land areas. Mountains are shown by shades of black. For example, there are mountains located where the Euphrates River begins but not where the river empties into the Persian Gulf.

Look at the map below, and answer the following questions:

Map Practice

1. **In addition to the Mediterranean, what seas are shown?**
2. **Besides the Nile, what rivers are shown?**
3. **How can you tell that the Persian Gulf coastline has changed over the years?**

Mesopotamia

Glencoe's **Skillbuilder Interactive Workbook, Level 1,** provides instruction and practice in key social studies skills.

SPOTLIGHT ON: MESOPOTAMIA

The area of Mesopotamia, in addition to being known as "the cradle of civilization," was also known as "the fertile crescent." It was given this name because the actual area was shaped like a crescent and the land was extremely fertile. Both the climate and the silt from the Tigris and Euphrates rivers added to its richness and productivity.

appointed royal judges. Judges who were not honest and witnesses who did not tell the truth were punished.

Hammurabi's code covered almost everything in daily life. A person was believed innocent until proven guilty. Once proven guilty, a person was punished. Punishments ranged from fines to death. There were no prison sentences. Members of the upper class generally were punished more severely than members of the middle or lower classes.

During Hammurabi's rule, Babylon became an important trade center. Babylonians exchanged their *surplus,* or extra, products for money or for the goods. People from other parts of the world came to trade, some from as far away as India and China. These traders paid gold and silver for the goods made by Babylonians.

Hammurabi ruled for more than 40 years. His **reign** (rān), or period of power, is known as the Golden Age of Babylon. After his death, however, the Babylonian Empire declined, and Mesopotamia was again divided into a number of small city-states.

Sculpture of a Sumerian Chariot

✓ **Reading Check**
What did people call the **reign** of Hammurabi?

Section 2 Assessment

1. **Define:** empire, culture, reform, reign.
2. What happened to Sumer under Sargon I's rule?
3. How did Hammurabi come to power?

Critical Thinking

4. **Using Reasoned Judgment** What do you think Hammurabi would say about the court system in the United States today?

Graphic Organizer Activity

5. Draw a diagram like this one, and use it show key events in the life of Hammurabi.

SECTION 3 Contributions

From the beginnings of Sumer until the death of Hammurabi, the influence of Mesopotamia on other civilizations was felt in many ways. Inventions, customs, and ideas of the Sumerian and Babylonian cultures were copied and, improved upon by other peoples.

The Sumerians developed the earliest known civilization in the world and has been called "the cradle of civilization." The oldest written records known are Sumerian. The Sumerians were the first people to write down their laws. Sumerian cuneiform became the model for other people's writing.

The Sumerians also invented many things such as the wheel, which helped transportation. Another was the plow, which made

Evaluate

Assign Chapter 3 **Performance Assessment Activity** in the TCR.

Administer **Chapter 3 Test** found in the TCR. Testmaker available.

Reteach

Organize students in small groups. Have pairs or individuals in each group outline a different section of the chapter. Have students regroup and compile the outlines into a chapter outline. Then have group members use the outline to quiz one another.

Assign Chapter 3 **Reteaching Activity** in the TCR.

Enrich

Assign Chapter 3 **Enrichment Activity** in the TCR.

CLOSE

Ask students to evaluate the following statement: *"The Golden Age of Babylon" is an appropriate name for Hammurabi's reign.*

💾 Use the **Interactive Tutor Self-Assessment Software** to review Section 3.

Self-Check Quiz gives students an interactive chapter tutorial. Have them access **Chapter 3 Quiz** at humanheritage.glencoe.com

---

it possible for farmers to grow more food with less effort. Still another was the sailboat, which replaced muscle power with wind power.

The people of Mesopotamia developed a 12-month calendar based on the cycles of the moon. The calendar marked the times for religious festivals and planting.

From Mesopotamia also came contributions in the field of mathematics. The people developed a number system based on 60. From that came the 60-minute hour, 60-second minute, and 360-degree circle. The people of Mesopotamia also used a clock that was operated by controlled drops of water.

Section 3 Assessment

1. Why was Mesopotamia called "the cradle of civilization"?
2. What did the people of Mesopotamia contribute to the field of mathematics?

Critical Thinking

3. **Determining Cause and Effect**
   How have inventions by the people of Mesopotamia helped shape present-day life?

Graphic Organizer Activity

4. Draw a diagram like this one, and use it to show facts that support this statement: Mesopotamia was "the cradle of civilization."

```
          Cradle of
         Civilization
 ┌────┐ ┌────┐ ┌────┐ ┌────┐
 │Fact│ │Fact│ │Fact│ │Fact│
 └────┘ └────┘ └────┘ └────┘
```

Chapter Summary & Study Guide

1. Civilization began in an area known as Mesopotamia, located between the Tigris and Euphrates rivers.
2. Sumer was the first known civilization in the world.
3. Sumerian civilization consisted of a series of city-states, the most important of which was Ur.
4. Each Sumerian city-state had its own chief god and government.
5. Sargon I of Akkad created the world's first empire in 2300 B.C.
6. About 1800 B.C., Hammurabi conquered Akkad and Sumer and established the Babylonian Empire.

7. Hammurabi unified the Babylonian Empire by setting up a single code of law and by raising the god of Babylon above all others.
8. Major contributions of the Mesopotamian civilizations include writing, the wheel, the plow, the sailboat, and a number system based on 60.

Self-Check Quiz

Visit the *Human Heritage* Web site at **humanheritage. glencoe.com** and click on **Chapter 3—Self-Check Quiz** to assess your understanding of this chapter.

Section 3 Assessment Answers

1. because the earliest known civilization developed there
2. a number system based on 60, which led to the 60-minute hour, 60-minute second, and 360-degree circle
3. Answers will vary, but might note that there would not be bicycles if the wheel had not been invented.

4. Facts might include any of the many accomplishments and inventions mentioned in this section, particularly those that influenced later civilizations such as our own.

Assign Chapter 3 **Section 3 Quiz** in the TCR. Testmaker available.

Assessment

Using Key Terms

Imagine that you are a visitor to ancient Mesopotamia. Use the following words in a letter home in which you describe what you have seen and experienced during your visit.

artisans	culture	empire
ziggurat	priest-kings	scribe
reform	cuneiform	city-state
reign		

Understanding Main Ideas

1. Why were the twin rivers important to Sumerian life?
2. Why was the ziggurat important to the Sumerians?
3. Who was Gilgamesh, and why was he important?
4. What did Sargon I accomplish?
5. What trading system did the people of Babylonia use?
6. What changes did Hammurabi bring to Mesopotamia?
7. What happened to people who broke Hammurabi's laws?
8. Why was the sailboat an important invention?

Critical Thinking

1. In what ways do you think your school is similar to or different from the schools in Sumeria?
2. What do you think would have happened to Sumer if it had suffered ten years of drought? How would the kingdom be affected?
3. Why do you think religion played such an important part in Sumerian life?

Graphic Organizer Activity

History Create a chart like this one, and use it to write newspaper headlines that tell the importance of each date to the history of Mesopotamia.

Date	Headline
3500 B.C.	
2300 B.C.	
1800 B.C.	
1700 B.C.	

Geography in History

Location Babylon became a major trading center. Refer to the map on page 62 and imagine that you are King Hammurabi. You must select the location for another settlement that you hope will also become a trading center. Where would you locate this settlement? Explain.

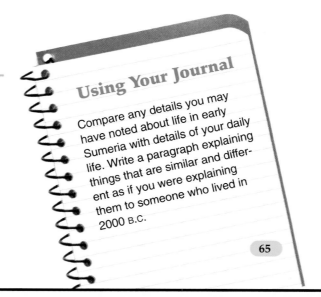

Using Your Journal

Compare any details you may have noted about life in early Sumeria with details of your daily life. Write a paragraph explaining things that are similar and different as if you were explaining them to someone who lived in 2000 B.C.

65

? Bonus Test Question

For Chapter 3 Test
The Sumerians developed ways of telling time and counting. What elements of that system remain today, and what parts have disappeared? *(the 60-minute hour, 360° circle; modern numbers are based on 10.)*

Using Your Journal

Journal entries will vary, but students should compare their way of life with that of Sumerians. You might call on volunteers to read their entries to the class.

Geography in History

Answers will vary, but could mention access to transportation, central location, and balance to Babylon's location.

Assessment Answers

Using Key Terms

Letters will vary. Students should include the terms in a letter home describing their visit to ancient Mesopotamia.

Understanding Main Ideas

1. They used water to irrigate crops, mud to make bricks, and fish and waterfowl for food.
2. because they were the center of Sumerian life—all great events were celebrated there
3. a famous priest-king; in a tale about him he learned that only the gods can live forever, and that people should take pride in what they do
4. He created the world's first empire.
5. They exchanged their surplus products for money or goods.
6. extended Babylonian rule, improved irrigation systems, raised god of Babylon above all other gods, reorganized tax system, began government housing program, codified laws
7. They were punished.
8. because it replaced muscle power with wind power

Critical Thinking

1. Answers will vary, but should show a knowledge of Sumerian education.
2. Answers will vary, but could note 10 years of drought could cause food and water shortages and cause Sumerians to migrate.
3. Answers will vary, but could note that Sumerians believed all forces of nature were alive, and that they were powerful gods.

Graphic Organizer Activity

Headlines will vary, but should reflect the importance of each of the events on the time line on page 54.

Chapter 4 Planning Guide

Objectives	Reproducible Resources	Multimedia Resources
Section 1 **The Nile** Analyze why the Nile River was so important to the growth of Egypt.	Reproducible Lesson Plan Chapter 4 Vocabulary and Guided Reading Activity Reading Essentials and Study Guide 4-1 Chapter 4 Geography and Map Activity Unit 2 World Literature Reading 2 Section 1 Quiz	Vocabulary PuzzleMaker Interactive Tutor Self-Assessment Software ExamView® Pro Testmaker Glencoe Skillbuilder Interactive Workbook, Level 1 Presentation Plus!
Section 2 **The Old Kingdom** Discuss how pharaohs, pyramids, and religious beliefs influenced the Old Kingdom of Egypt.	Reproducible Lesson Plan Reading Essentials and Study Guide 4-2 Chapter 4 Enrichment Activity Section 2 Quiz	Vocabulary PuzzleMaker Interactive Tutor Self-Assessment Software ExamView® Pro Testmaker Glencoe Skillbuilder Interactive Workbook, Level 1
Section 3 **The Middle Kingdom** Describe what happened during Egypt's Middle Kingdom.	Reproducible Lesson Plan Reading Essentials and Study Guide 4-3 Section 3 Quiz	Vocabulary PuzzleMaker Interactive Tutor Self-Assessment Software ExamView® Pro Testmaker Glencoe Skillbuilder Interactive Workbook, Level 1
Section 4 **The New Kingdom** Explain why Egyptian civilization grew and then declined during the New Kingdom.	Reproducible Lesson Plan Reading Essentials and Study Guide 4-4 Chapter 4 Cooperative Learning Activity Section 4 Quiz	Teaching Transparencies and Activities 4A & 4B Vocabulary PuzzleMaker Interactive Tutor Self-Assessment Software ExamView® Pro Testmaker Glencoe Skillbuilder Interactive Workbook, Level 1
Section 5 **Contributions** Summarize what the Egyptians contributed to other civilizations.	Reproducible Lesson Plan Reading Essentials and Study Guide 4-5 Chapter 4 Activity Book Activity Chapter 4 Chart and Graph Skill Activity Section 5 Quiz	Vocabulary PuzzleMaker ExamView® Pro Testmaker Glencoe Skillbuilder Interactive Workbook, Level 1
Chapter 5 **Review and Evaluation**	Chapter 4 Reteaching Activity Chapter 4 Performance Assessment Activity Spanish Chapter Summary and Glossary Chapter 4 Test	Vocabulary PuzzleMaker Interactive Tutor Self-Assessment Software Glencoe Skillbuilder Interactive Workbook, Level 1 Audiocassettes*

*Also available in Spanish.

Presentation Plus!
Use Glencoe's **Presentation Plus!** multimedia teacher tool to easily present dynamic lessons that visually excite your students. Using Microsoft® PowerPoint, you can customize the presentations to create your own personalized lessons.

 Interactive Lesson Planner

Planning has never been easier! Using this CD-ROM, organize your week, month, semester, or year with all the help you need. The **Interactive Lesson Planner** gives you access to all of the blackline masters which accompany *Human Heritage.*

✓ PERFORMANCE ASSESSMENT ACTIVITIES

Television Newscast Have students imagine they are television journalists carried back in time to ancient Egypt. Have them write and present a newscast-style report on an object or structure to be shown on the evening news.

CHAPTER RESOURCES

LITERATURE ABOUT THE PERIOD

Perl, Lila. *Mummies, Tombs, and Treasure: Secrets of Ancient Egypt.* Clarion Books, 1990. An account of ancient Egyptian beliefs about death and the afterlife.

READINGS FOR THE STUDENT

Morley, Jaquelin, Mark Bergin, and John James. *An Egyptian Pyramid.* Peter Bedrick, 1991. Explains how the pyramids were built and their purpose.

Rossini, Stephane. *Egyptian Hieroglyphics: How to Read and Write Them.* Dover, 1989. Describes the principles of Egyptian reading and writing.

READINGS FOR THE TEACHER

Bowman, Alan K. *Egypt after the Pharaohs.* Berkeley: University of California Press, 1986. History of Egypt 332 B.C.-642 A.D., portraying daily life, government, economy, architecture, and culture.

  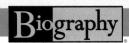

The following videotape programs are available from Glencoe:

- **Cleopatra: Destiny's Queen**
  1-56501-454-5

- **King Tut: The Face of Tutankhamen**
  1-56501-159-7

- **Mummies and the Wonders of Ancient Egypt**
  1-56501-773-0

To order, call Glencoe at 1-800-334-7344. To find resources to accompany these, check:

A&E Television: http://www.aetv.com
The History Channel: http://www.historychannel.com

NATIONAL GEOGRAPHIC SOCIETY — Teacher's Corner

INDEX TO NATIONAL GEOGRAPHIC MAGAZINE

The following articles relate to this chapter:

- "Valley of the Mummies," by Donovan Webster, October 1999.
- "Abusir Tomb," by Zahi Hawass, November 1998.
- "Valley of the Kings," Kent R. Weeks, September 1998.
- "The Magic of Paper," by Jon R. Luoma, March 1997.
- "The Imperiled Nile Delta," by Peter Theroux, January 1997.

NATIONAL GEOGRAPHIC SOCIETY PRODUCTS AVAILABLE FROM GLENCOE

To order the following, call Glencoe at 1-800-334-7344:

- *PicturePack: Ancient Egypt (Transparencies)*
- *PictureShow: Ancient Civilizations: Egypt and the Fertile Crescent (CD-ROM)*
- *PictureShow: Ancient Civilizations Library (CD-ROMs)*

ADDITIONAL NATIONAL GEOGRAPHIC SOCIETY PRODUCTS

To order the following, call National Geographic at 1-800-368-2728:

- *Egypt: Quest for Eternity (Video or Videodisc)*
- *GeoKit: Ancient Egypt (Multimedia Teaching Module)*
- *Mr. Mummy (Video)*
- *Pharaoh's Voyage for Eternity (Video)*
- *Who Built the Pyramids? (Video)*

Access *National Geographic's* new dynamic MapMachine Web site and other geography resources at:
http://www.nationalgeographic.com/
http://www.nationalgeographic.com/maps/

KEY TO ABILITY LEVELS

Teaching strategies have been coded for varying learning styles and abilities.

L1 Level 1 activities are **basic** activities and should be within the ability range of all students.

L2 Level 2 activities are **average** activities and should be within the ability range of the average to above-average student.

L3 Level 3 activities are **challenging** activities designed for the ability range of above-average students.

ELL ELL activities should be within the ability range of English Language Learning students.

OVERVIEW

Chapter 4 focuses on the changes in society during the Old, Middle, and New Kingdoms.

➤ **Section 1** explains the importance of the Nile River to the Egyptian civilization.

➤ **Section 2** discusses Egypt's Old Kingdom.

➤ **Section 3** describes Egypt's Middle Kingdom.

➤ **Section 4** traces the New Kingdom.

➤ **Section 5** presents Egyptian contributions.

CHAPTER OBJECTIVES

After reading Chapter 4, students will be able to:

1. analyze why the Nile River was so important to the growth of Egyptian civilization.

2. discuss how pharaohs, pyramids, and religious beliefs influenced the Old Kingdom.

3. describe what happened during Egypt's Middle Kingdom.

4. explain why Egyptian civilization grew then declined during the New Kingdom.

5. list Egyptian contributions.

EXAMINING ARTIFACTS

Tell students that the elaborate gold mask and intricately painted sandals were found in Egyptian tombs. Ask: What does the location of these artifacts tell you about the Egyptian people? *(that they held strong beliefs about death and the afterlife)*

PERFORMANCE ASSESSMENT ✔

Use the Performance Assessment activities on page 66B to help you evaluate students as they complete the chapter.

Egypt
3100 B.C.–671 B.C.

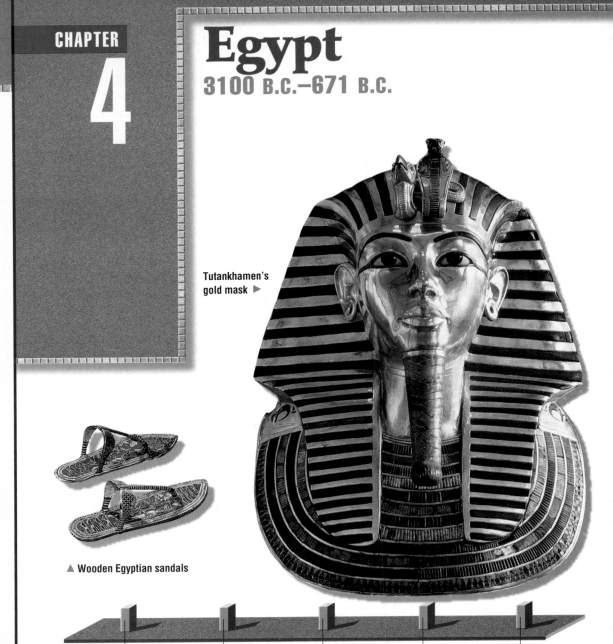

Tutankhamen's gold mask ▶

▲ Wooden Egyptian sandals

2600 B.C.	2300 B.C.	1786 B.C.	1550 B.C.	671 B.C.
Old Kingdom established	**Middle Kingdom begins**	**Hyksos invade Egypt**	**Ahmose founds the New Kingdom**	**Assyrians take over Egypt**

66   UNIT 2   RIVER VALLEY CIVILIZATIONS

TEACHING RESOURCES

TEACHER PLANNING AND SUPPORT

🗁 Reproducible Lesson Plan
🗁 Block Scheduling Implementation Guide
🗁 Videodisc Bar Code Correlation
💿 Presentation Plus!

REVIEW AND REINFORCEMENT

🗁 Reading Essentials and Study Guide 4-1, 4-2, 4-3, 4-4, 4-5
🗁 Chapter 4 Vocabulary and Guided Reading Activity
💾 Vocabulary PuzzleMaker Software
🖨 Teaching Transparencies 4A & 4B

🗁 Chapter 4 Reteaching Activity
🗁 Chapter 4 Cooperative Learning Activity
🗁 Chapter 4 Activity Book Activity
🗁 Chapter 4 Chart and Graph Skill Activity
💾 Interactive Tutor Self-Assessment Software

APPLICATION AND HANDS-ON ACTIVITIES

🗇 Daily World History, Geography, and Culture Question
🗇 World History Game Card 10
🗁 Unit 2 Hands-On History Lab Activity

Chapter Focus

 Read to Discover

- Why the Nile River was so important to the growth of Egyptian civilization.
- How Egyptian religious beliefs influenced the Old Kingdom.
- What happened during Egypt's Middle Kingdom.
- Why Egyptian civilization grew and then declined during the New Kingdom.
- What the Egyptians contributed to other civilizations.

 Terms to Learn

shadoof
pharaoh
pyramids
embalming
mummy
legend
hieroglyphic
papyrus

 People to Know

Narmer
Ahmose
Thutmose III
Hatshepsut
Amenhotep IV

 Places to Locate

Nile River
Punt
Thebes

Why It's Important The Egyptians settled in the Nile River Valley of northeast Africa. They most likely borrowed ideas such as writing from the Sumerians. However, the Egyptian civilization lasted far longer than the city-states and empires of Mesopotamia. While the people of Mesopotamia fought among themselves, Egypt grew into a rich, powerful, and unified kingdom. The Egyptians built a civilization that lasted for more than 2,000 years and left a lasting influence on the world.

Chapter Overview
Visit the *Human Heritage* Web site at **humanheritage.glencoe.com** and click on **Chapter 4—Chapter Overviews** to preview this chapter.

SECTION 1 The Nile

The Nile River flows north 4,145 miles, or 6,671 kilometers, from the mountains of central Africa to the Mediterranean Sea. The last 600 miles, or 960 kilometers, is in Egypt. There, the river cuts a narrow, green valley through the desert. Shortly before the Nile reaches the sea, it branches to form a fan-shaped area of fertile land called a *delta*. Most ancient Egyptians lived in this area. For a long time, they were protected from foreign invasions by the desert, the sea, and waterfalls called *cataracts* (kat' uh rakts).

Chapter Overview introduces students to chapter content and key terms. Have them access **Chapter 4 Overview** at **humanheritage.glencoe.com**

FOCUS

 Bellringer

Have students write the words *ancient Egypt* on their papers. Ask them to write words or phrases that come to mind when they think of ancient Egypt.

Motivational Activity

Call on volunteers to share their ideas about ancient Egypt. Write these on the chalkboard and have students notice the words and phrases that appear most often. (*Nile River, pharaohs, pyramids, fertile lands, mummies*) Have students copy any words or phrases that were not on their papers. Then tell them that they will learn the historical significance of these terms as they study the section.

GUIDE TO READING

Reading Strategy

Ask students to read "Why It's Important" and summarize the chapter's main theme. (*Egyptian civilization lasted a long time and left a lasting impression on world civilization.*)

Vocabulary Precheck

Ask students to define each of the "Terms to Learn." Have a volunteer consult the dictionary for any unfamiliar words. **L1** **ELL**

 Use the Vocabulary PuzzleMaker for Chapter 4 to create a crossword puzzle. **L1**

Assign Chapter 4 Vocabulary and Guided Reading Activity.

Assign Reading Essentials and Study Guide 4-1.

Guided Practice

L1 **Geography: Human/Environmental Interaction** Have students locate the Nile River on the map of Africa in the text Atlas. Point out the Delta of the Nile. Next, write the following phrase on the board: *Egypt: the gift of the Nile.* Inform students that this is a phrase coined by the historian Herodotus, and elicit from them the possible meanings of the phrase. Ask students how the Egyptians made use of the Nile River.

CAPTION ANSWER

the desert, the sea, and waterfalls called cataracts

✓ Reading Check Answer

A **shadoof** was used to lift water from the Nile to basins or bowl-shaped holes.

LINKING PAST TO PRESENT

The Aswan High Dam in southeastern Egypt was built in the 1960s partly to protect crops and people against seasonal flooding. The lack of this flooding, however, means that fertile soil is no longer deposited annually. Instead, farmers in the area rely on chemical fertilizers to make the soil fertile. Ask students to describe how the dam has changed the environment around the Nile.

💾 Use **Interactive Tutor Self-Assessment Software** to review Section 1.

NILE RIVER   Over thousands of years, the flooding of the Nile River has left rich soil all along its banks. The Nile River valley is only 3 percent of Egypt's land, yet most Egyptians live and work in this area. **What geographical features protected the Egyptians in the Nile River delta?**

The Egyptians had an advantage over the people of the other river valley civilizations. Every year, about the middle of July, the Nile overflowed its banks. The flood waters went down but left behind large amounts of rich soil good for growing crops.

Egyptian farmers planted their fields while the soil was still wet. To water their crops during the dry season, the Egyptians dug out *basins,* or bowl-shaped holes. They used a machine called a **shadoof** (shuh dūf′) to lift water from the Nile to the basins. The Egyptians raised flax, wheat, barley, and grapes.

✓ Reading Check
How was a **shadoof** used?

Section 1 Assessment

1. **Define:** shadoof.
2. Where did most Egyptians live?
3. How did the Egyptians control the Nile?

Critical Thinking

4. **Making Comparisons**   How did the Egyptians' use of the Nile River compare with the Sumerians' use of the Tigris and Euphrates rivers?

Graphic Organizer Activity

5. Draw a diagram like this one, and use it to show how the Nile River influenced Egyptian civilization. (Add more lines as needed.)

Section 1 Assessment Answers

1. shadoof, machine used to lift water (p. 68)
2. in the Nile delta
3. by building a system of basins and irrigation canals
4. Answers will vary, but could note both Egyptians and Sumerians depended on the rivers for living, and both civilizations controlled their environment. The Egyptians dug out basins and built irrigation canals to the fields. The Sumerians also built irrigation canals. The Egyptians raised flax, wheat, barley, and grapes. The Sumerians grew barley, wheat, sesame, flax, fruit trees, date palms, and vegetables.
5. Sample responses: cataracts served as protection, flooding left behind good soil, provided water to grow crops in dry season.

Assign the Chapter 4 **Section 1 Quiz** in the TCR. Testmaker available.

SECTION 2 The Old Kingdom

At first, Egypt was made up of two kingdoms. One was Upper Egypt, which lay in the southern part of the Nile River valley. The other was Lower Egypt, which lay in the north delta.

Narmer, also known as Menes (mē' nēz), was a king of Upper Egypt. About 3100 B.C., he led his armies from the valley north into the delta. He conquered Lower Egypt and married one of its princesses, uniting the two kingdoms. He wore a double crown, the high white one of the south and the shallow red one of the north. Narmer had many titles. He was called "Lord of Upper and Lower Egypt," "Wearer of Both Crowns," and "Lord of the Two Lands." He set up a new capital at Memphis, a city on the border between Upper and Lower Egypt.

About 2600 B.C., the Old Kingdom started in Egypt. It lasted for nearly 500 years. During the period of the Old Kingdom, Egyptian cities became centers of religion and government. Kings, priests, government officials, and artisans lived there.

Most Egyptians, however, did not live in cities. They lived on large estates along the banks of the Nile. The rich Egyptians who owned these estates lived in wood and brick houses with beautiful gardens and pools. Walls were decorated with brightly

GEOGRAPHY AND HISTORY

Direct students to the map of ancient Egypt on page 75. Explain that because the Nile River flows from central Africa into the Mediterranean Sea, or from south to north, the southern part of Egypt is actually Upper Egypt, and the northern half is actually Lower Egypt.

CAPTION ANSWER

The rich owned large estates and lived in elegant houses, while the poor farmed the land and lived in small mud-brick houses.

MAKING CONNECTIONS

➤➤ **Geography: Location** The Nile is the longest river in the world. Its two branches are the Blue Nile, which begins in the Ethiopian highlands, and the White Nile, which rises in Uganda and meets the Blue Nile at present-day Khartoum.

Use the **Vocabulary Puzzle-Maker** to create crossword and word search puzzles.

EGYPTIAN LIFE   Paintings from tombs offer much information about everyday life in ancient Egypt. Here, a wall painting shows a man and woman plowing and planting their fields. **How did the lives of the rich differ from those of the poor in Egypt?**

EXTENDING THE CONTENT

One reason we know a great deal about homes in ancient Egypt is that small models—called soul houses—often were included in the things buried with a person to assure him or her of a pleasant afterlife. The houses of both rich and poor were comfortable in the dry, hot climate. With almost no rain, it was practical to build mud-brick walls and flat roofs with vents to catch the breeze. Egyptians had less furniture in their homes than people today have—a few brightly colored chairs and stools, small tables, oil lamps, and chests for storing clothes. Beds were like cots, with tightly stretched cord springs.

Linking Across Time

Harvesting Wheat   Both men and women harvested the wheat crops that helped fuel the growth of ancient Egypt (left). Today some Egyptian farmers still harvest this crop by hand with a sickle (right), much as their ancestors did more than 3,000 years ago. **What is the connection between the flooding of the Nile and the production of wheat?**

colored paintings that showed scenes of daily life. A household was made up of an owner's family, servants, and artisans. The artisans were hired to build boats, weave linen, and make tools and pottery.

Most Egyptians, however, were farmers who lived in villages on the estates. At first, their houses were made of reeds and mud. Later, they were made of sun-baked mud-brick. These houses generally had only one room with a roof made of palm leaves. They were built on high ground so that they would be safe from the yearly flood. Egyptian farmers worked in the fields and took care of the cattle. When they were not farming, they built monuments, dug ditches, and repaired roads.

The Pharaoh   The Egyptians believed that the strength and unity of their country came from having a strong ruler. At first, Egyptian rulers were called kings. Later, they were called **pharaoh** (fār′ ō), meaning "great house." To Egyptians, the pharaoh was a ruler, a priest, and a god. He was the center of Egyptian life and ruled on Earth the way other gods ruled in heaven.

The pharaoh owned all the land in Egypt, but he gave gifts of land to rich Egyptians and priests. To make sure the land produced well, the pharaoh saw to it that dams and irrigation canals were built and repaired. The pharaoh also ordered the building of brick *granaries*, or buildings for storing grain. These were used to store grain from good harvests so people would not starve in times of bad harvests.

✓ **Reading Check**
How did the Egyptians view the **pharaoh?**

70   UNIT 2 RIVER VALLEY CIVILIZATIONS

MULTICULTURAL PERSPECTIVES

One thing that made the position of women strong in Egypt was the economic power of inheritance. Custom dictated that property descend from mother to daughter. Thus, to keep property in the family, pharaohs often married relatives.

The pharaoh also chose all government officials. They made certain that taxes were gathered and building permits were given out. Trade with other lands was in the pharaoh's hands. The word of a pharaoh was law.

The Egyptians believed that what happened to Egypt depended on the pharaoh's actions. As chief priest, the pharaoh carried out certain rituals. For example, he made the first break in the irrigation dikes each year to open the land to the water. When the water went down, he drove a sacred bull around the capital city. The Egyptians believed this ritual would make the soil rich so they could grow good crops. The pharaoh was the first to cut the ripe grain. Egyptians believed this would bring a good harvest.

Pharaohs were treated with great respect. Whenever they appeared in public, people played music on flutes and cymbals. They also bowed and "smelled the earth" or touched their heads to the ground.

The Pyramids   Another way the people of the Old Kingdom showed how they felt about the pharaohs was by building them great tombs called **pyramids** (pir' uh midz). Because the sun sank in the west, these "Houses of Eternity" were built on the west bank of the Nile. They were designed to protect the pharaohs' bodies from floods, wild animals, and robbers. The Egyptians believed the pharaohs would be happy after death if they had their personal belongings. Therefore, they placed a pharaoh's clothing, weapons, furniture, and jewelry in the pyramids.

A Big Pyramid
The Pyramid of Khufu (see photo) contains more than 2 million stone blocks that average 2 1/2 short tons, or 2.3 metric tons, each. The pyramid originally stood 481 feet, or 147 meters, high. Today its base covers about 13 acres, or 5 hectares.

Reading Check
What was the purpose of the **pyramids?**

L3 **Critical Thinking** Write the following criteria of a civilization on the board: *a writing system, a well-organized government, art and literature, and specialization of labor.* Ask students to write a brief explanation of how ancient Egypt met these criteria.

CAPTION ANSWER

Egyptians buried personal items, items of wealth, and any utilitarian and comfort items the King might need in the afterlife.

The following videotape program is available from Glencoe to enrich Chapter 4:

- **Pyramids of Giza**

To find classroom resources to accompany this video, check the following home page:
A&E Television:
http://www.aetv.com

PYRAMIDS AT GIZA   The pyramids were built at Giza on the Nile River. The largest pyramid once enshrined the body of King Khufu. **What items were probably buried with the King?**

COOPERATIVE LEARNING

Encourage students to study the illustrations in this chapter. Point out that ancient Egyptian paintings presented the human face and limbs in profile, while the upper torso, shoulders, and eyes were presented in front view. Suggest that they find more examples of ancient Egyptian art such as in *The Atlas of Ancient Egypt* by John Baines and Jaromír Málek. Once they are familiar with this art style, have students plan and create a mural using the Egyptian style of art to illustrate a scene from Egyptian daily life.

DID YOU KNOW ???

Enslaved persons were not employed in building the pyramids. Enslavement did not become common in Egypt until the New Kingdom, when conquests in Syria and Palestine brought in prisoners of war. Then enslaved persons built monuments and temples for the pharaohs in the New Kingdom.

MAKING CONNECTIONS

➤➤ **Language Arts** The term *underworld* had a different meaning for the ancient Egyptians than it has for most people today. To the Egyptians, it meant the cool, tree-shaded land of Osiris, where even the poor could rest.

CAPTION ANSWER

They tried to lead a good life and learn certain magic spells.

It took many people and much work to build the pyramids. Farmers worked on them during the three summer months that their fields were flooded. The workers used copper tools to cut huge granite and limestone blocks from quarries across the Nile Valley or in Upper Egypt. The blocks of rock were tied with ropes onto wooden sleds, pulled to the Nile, placed on barges filled with sand, and floated across the river. Other workers then unloaded the blocks and pulled them to the place where the pyramids were being built. Huge mud and brick ramps were built beside each of the pyramids. The workers dragged the blocks up the ramps to each new layer of the pyramid.

Religious Beliefs The Egyptians believed in many gods. Two of the most important gods were the river god Hapi (hop' ē) and the sun god Re (rā). The Egyptians depended on the river and the sun. The river brought them water and fertile soil, while the sun helped their crops to grow.

Another important god was Osiris (ō sī ris), god of the harvest and of eternal life. According to Egyptian legend, Osiris was an early pharaoh who gave his people laws and taught them farming. He and his wife Isis (ī'sis) ruled over the dead. The Egyptians believed that the souls of the dead went to the underworld. There, they were weighed on a scale. If a person had led a good life and knew certain magic spells, the scales balanced. Then, Osiris would grant the person life after death. To learn the correct magic spells, Egyptians studied a special book called the *Book of the Dead.*

Then... & Now

Mummies Today scientists are able to perform CAT scans on mummy cases, allowing the scientists to see inside, without opening the mummy case. Using computers, they turn the two-dimensional CAT-scan pictures into three-dimensional images of the mummies.

EGYPTIAN GODS The god Osiris ruled over the Egyptian underworld. Here, he sits in judgment as other animal-headed gods weigh a dead man's soul and record the results. The scales have balanced, so the dead man may enter the underworld. **How did Egyptians prepare for life after death?**

MEETING SPECIAL NEEDS

Encourage students who are tactile/kinesthetic learners to make dioramas, models, or diagrams of a pyramid under construction as described in the subsection titled "The Pyramids." Display the students' creations in the classroom.

📁 Refer to *Inclusion for the Middle School Social Studies Classroom: Strategies and Activities* for additional resources.

The Egyptians also used a process called **embalming** (em balm' ēng) to preserve the bodies of the dead. At first, they used the process to preserve the body of the pharaoh because they believed the soul could not live without the body. It was important for a pharaoh's soul to live after death. In that way, the pharaoh would continue to take care of Egypt.

Later, embalming was used to preserve other people as well as the pharaoh. To embalm a body, the Egyptians placed it in a wooden box and covered it with a chemical called natron. Natron dried up the water in the body, causing it to shrink. After the shrunken body had dried, it was wrapped with long strips of linen. The wrapped body was known as a **mummy.** The mummy of a poor person was often buried in a cave or in the sand. The mummy of a rich person was placed inside a special case or coffin. The coffin was then placed in a tomb.

✓ **Reading Check**
Why did the Egyptians develop the practice of **embalming?**

✓ **Reading Check**
What is a **mummy?**

Section 2 Assessment

1. **Define:** pharaoh, pyramids, embalming, mummy.
2. How did most Egyptians live during the Old Kingdom?
3. What did the Egyptians believe happened to a person after death?

Critical Thinking

4. **Making Comparisons** How were the pharaohs similar to and different from government leaders of the United States today?

Graphic Organizer Activity

5. Draw this diagram, and use it to compare the Egyptian burial practices for the rich and the poor.

Rich | Both | Poor

SECTION 3 The Middle Kingdom

About 2300 B.C., government officials, jealous of the pharaoh's power, took control of Egypt. Almost 200 years of confusion followed. Finally, new pharaohs brought peace and a new period called the Middle Kingdom.

Pharaohs had less power in the Middle Kingdom. After death, they were no longer buried in pyramids but in tombs cut into cliffs. Then the Egyptians began to trade with countries beyond the Nile Valley.

The Middle Kingdom came to an end in 1786 B.C., when Egypt was invaded by the Hyksos (hik' sōs), a people from western Asia. The Hyksos crossed the desert in horse-drawn chariots and used weapons made of bronze and iron. Egyptians had always fought on foot with weapons made of copper and stone and were defeated.

EGYPTIAN BRONZE ART

CHAPTER 4 EGYPT 73

Section 2 Assessment Answers

1. pharaoh, Egyptian king (p. 70); pyramids, tombs for pharaohs (p. 71); embalming, process to preserve bodies (p. 73); mummy, body wrapped with linen (p. 73)
2. Most Egyptians lived as farmers in villages on large estates along the Nile.
3. Their souls went to the underworld and were weighed on a scale. If the scales balanced, Osiris granted life after death.

4. Sample responses: Both provide for citizens and deal with foreign policy/trade. U.S. leaders are not considered gods.
5. Both were embalmed. The poor were buried in a cave or in the sand; the rich were placed in special coffins inside a tomb.

Assign the Chapter 4 **Section 2 Quiz** in the TCR. Testmaker available.

The Hyksos ruled Egypt for about 150 years. They copied some Egyptian customs but most Egyptians hated them. Around 1550 B.C., an Egyptian prince named Ahmose (ah mo' suh), using Hyksos weapons, led an uprising and drove the Hyksos out of Egypt.

Section 3 Assessment

1. How did the Middle Kingdom come about?
2. What ended Hyksos rule?

Critical Thinking

3. **Demonstrating Reasoned Judgment** Do you think the decrease in the pharaoh's power had a positive or negative effect on Egypt? Explain.

Graphic Organizer Activity

4. Draw a diagram like this one, and use it to compare the power of the pharaohs in the Old Kingdom and the Middle Kingdom.

Power of Pharaohs — Old Kingdom — Middle Kingdom

SECTION 4   The New Kingdom

Ahmose founded another line of pharaohs and began the period known as the New Kingdom. During this time, Egypt became richer and its cities grew larger.

During the New Kingdom, most pharaohs were no longer content to remain within the Nile Valley but marched their armies into lands to the east. It was during this period that the Egyptian empire was founded. One warrior-pharaoh, Thutmose III (thūt mō' suh), with an army of 20,000 archers, spear throwers, and charioteers, extended Egyptian control into Syria (sir' ē uh) and Palestine (pal' uh stīn).

One of the few pharaohs who was not interested in war and conquest was Hatshepsut (hat shep' sūt), Thutmose III's stepmother, who had ruled Egypt before her stepson. Her chief interests were trade and the building of temples. During her rule, Egyptian traders sailed along the coast of east Africa to the land of Punt. In the land of Punt, the Egyptians traded beads and metal tools and weapons for such things as ivory, a black wood called *ebony* (eb' uh nē), monkeys, hunting dogs, leopard skins, and *incense,* or material burned for its pleasant smell. The Egyptians had never seen most of these things. They welcomed the returning traders with a huge reception.

STATUE OF HATSHEPSUT

Religion   The Egyptians of the New Kingdom began to worship a new god. As the god of the city of Thebes, he had been called Amon. When Thebes became the capital of Egypt,

---

Reading Map Legends

In order to show information on maps, mapmakers use symbols. These are marks that stand for such things as places, directions, and features. Symbols include lines, dots, stars, and small pictures.

A list of symbols and what they stand for is called a **legend.** By reading legends, it is possible to identify empires, nations, religions, climates, and any other information that can be shown on a map.

For example, on the "Ancient Egypt" map below, notice that there are three symbols in the legend. Each symbol stands for the boundary of one of the Egyptian kingdoms. The broken line stands for the southern boundary of the Old Kingdom. The Middle Kingdom's boundary is shown by the dotted line. The area of the New Kingdom is shown in green.

Map Practice

1. **Which Egyptian kingdom included only the first cataract?**
2. **Which kingdom extended to the second cataract?**
3. **In which was Thebes located?**

Ancient Egypt

Southern Boundary, Old Kingdom
Southern Boundary, Middle Kingdom
New Kingdom, c. 1450 B.C.

miles 0   200   400
kilometers 0   200   400   600

N

75

Glencoe's **Skillbuilder Interactive Workbook, Level 1,** provides instruction and practice in key social studies skills.

MAP SKILLS

TEACH

READING MAP LEGENDS

Instruct the students to study the map on page 75 to answer the following questions:

What symbol should be added to the legend for cataracts? *(two short parallel lines)*

What symbol should be added to the legend for cities? *(a dot)*

Next, have the students refer to the map of Mesopotamia on page 62 to answer the following questions:

What symbol is used to show Hammurabi's Empire? *(the color brown)*

What symbol is used to show an ancient coastline? *(a dashed line)*

Assign Chapter 4 **Geography and Map Activity** in the TCR.

Answers to Map Practice

1. Old Kingdom
2. Middle Kingdom
3. all three kingdoms

SPOTLIGHT ON: ANCIENT EGYPT

Although Egypt's desert land is often thought of in connection with the camel, this animal was not actually brought to Egypt until 525 B.C. The most common beast of burden in ancient Egypt was the donkey. Lions also prowled the deserts of ancient Egypt, and cats, who were often mummified after they died, were a favorite house pet.

GUIDED PRACTICE

L3 **Critical Thinking** Have students write letters to the editor explaining their position on this question: Did religion play a greater role in Egyptian society than it does in our society today? Ask students to respond and support their response with reasons.

CAPTION ANSWER

The temples were built by enslaved persons.

MAKING CONNECTIONS

➤➤ **Language Arts** It was difficult to become a scribe. A student enrolled in school at age 5 and attended classes from sunup to sundown until age 17. Scribes, associated with the ruling class, did not have to work in the fields and were paid more than most Egyptians.

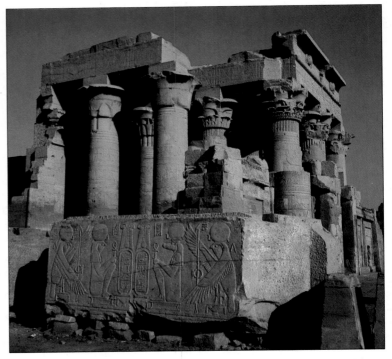

TEMPLE AT KOM OMBO Warring pharaohs of the New Kingdom built large temples to honor their gods. The stone block in front of this temple shows Egyptian hieroglyphs. This temple has many statues and monuments. **Who provided the labor to build temples?**

The Best Dentist
Egyptians could have benefited from regular trips to the dentist. Everyone, rich and poor, suffered from cavities, inflamed gums, and infections. A physician in the Old Kingdom named Hesire won the title of "Chief of the Tooth-doctors."

however, the Egyptians combined Amon with the sun god Re. They called the new god Amon-Re (ah' muhn ī a'). Amon-Re became the most powerful god of all. People built many temples in his honor. These were built, in part, by enslaved persons who had been captured by the warring pharaohs.

The temples were more than houses of worship. They were industrial centers. They gave work to sculptors and artisans who carved statues, built furniture, and made clothes for priests. They were treasuries, filled with copper, gold jewelry, glass bottles, bundles of grain, dried fish, and sweet-smelling oils. The temples were also schools—places where young boys were trained to be scribes. The right to become a scribe was passed on from father to son.

Scribes wrote religious works in which were spells, charms, and prayers. They kept records of the pharaohs' laws and lists of

---

MULTICULTURAL PERSPECTIVES

The wigs, cosmetics, and jewelry worn by the ancient Egyptians present a vivid image of these people. Generally, both men and women wore simply cut tunics and sheaths of draped, pleated, natural linen. Egyptian men and women's jewelry, wigs, and makeup, however, were elaborate and striking. They wore wigs or hairpieces with curls. Some Egyptians shaved their heads. Bold green (from powdered malachite) and black eye-liners were often worn. Red ocher was applied as lipstick and blusher. Henna colored their hair. Many Egyptians wore large necklaces that covered their chests. Earrings first became popular in the New Kingdom.

the grain and animals paid as taxes. They copied fairy tales and adventure stories and wrote down medical prescriptions.

There were several kinds of Egyptian writing. One was **hieroglyphic** (hī uhr uh glif' ik), or a kind of writing in which pictures stand for words or sounds. The Egyptians carved and painted hieroglyphs, or picture symbols, on their monuments. However, scribes needed an easier form of writing to keep records. So, they developed two other kinds of writing in which hieroglyphs were rounded off and connected.

Decline of Egypt   Over time, the priests of Amon-Re gained much power and wealth. They owned one third of Egypt's land and began to play a major role in the government. As time passed, the pharaoh's power declined.

Then, about 1370 B.C., a new pharaoh named Amenhotep IV (ah muhn hō' tep) came to the throne. He did not like the priests. He did not agree with them on what was good for Egypt. He wanted to return power to the pharaohs. Amenhotep IV closed the temples of Amon-Re and fired all temple workers. He set up a new religion that was different from the old religion because only one god was worshiped. This god was called Aton (ah' tuhn). Amenhotep IV changed his name to Akhenaton (ahk nah' tuhn), which means "Spirit of Aton." Only his family and close advisers, however, accepted the new religion.

HIEROGLYPHS   Ancient Egyptians viewed hieroglyphs as gifts from the gods. The pictures were first used as a way of keeping records. Later, they represented the sounds of spoken language. Here, hieroglyphs are painted on a coffin lid. **How did hieroglyphs differ from cuneiform?**

✔ Reading Check
What was **hieroglyphic** writing?

Tutankhamen
C. 1369 B.C.–1351 B.C.

Egyptian Pharaoh

Nicknamed the "boy king," Tutankhamen came to power at age 9. He pleased the priests by rejecting Akhenaton's religion. Although frail, he loved to race chariots and hunt animals. When he died at age 18, officials placed him in a treasure-filled tomb. The tomb's beautiful contents, discovered in 1922, made "King Tut" one of Egypt's most famous pharaohs.

✔ Reading Check Answer
Hieroglyphic writing uses pictures to stand for words or sounds.

Independent Practice

L1 **Writing** Instruct students to devise a rebus writing system and to write a sample sentence or phrase. Call on volunteers to write their samples and keys on the chalkboard. Discuss similarities and differences in the rebuses used. **ELL**

L2 **Language Arts** Write the following scenarios on the chalkboard:
1. You are a historian studying the New Kingdom of Egypt before the reign of Amenhotep IV. Describe the main events in the growth of Egyptian civilization.
2. You are a historian studying the New Kingdom of Egypt after the reign of Amenhotep IV. Describe the most important events in the decline of Egyptian civilization.

Tell students to choose one scenario and write the description of events. Have volunteers read their histories to the class.

CAPTION ANSWER

Hieroglyphs were picture symbols, while cuneiform was made up of hundreds of markings shaped like wedges.

COOPERATIVE LEARNING

Have the students write and perform a play about one of the people listed in the section. Divide the class into small groups. Have each group be responsible for researching the person chosen. Group members can volunteer for a specific task in the project, such as writing the script, acting, making costumes, finding props, writing and designing programs, and designing sets. At each stage of the project, all students should be given an opportunity to react to the group task. Then have the students present the play to other classes.

📁 Assign Chapter 4 *Cooperative Learning Activity* in the TCR.

Use **Interactive Tutor Self-Assessment Software** to review Section 4.

Reading Check Answer
Papyrus was made from a reed also called papyrus.

 Use the **Vocabulary Puzzle-Maker** to create crossword and word search puzzles.

After Amenhotep IV died, about 1360 B.C., his son-in-law Tutankhamen (tū tahng kah' muhn) became pharaoh. He was only nine years old. The priests made Tutankhamen return to the old religion. He died after ruling for only nine years.

Little by little, Egypt lost its power. One reason was the struggle between the priests and the pharaohs. Another was the pharaohs' attempts to keep neighboring countries under Egyptian control. Much energy and money was spent on war. Then, too, other peoples of the eastern Mediterranean were using iron weapons. Since Egypt had no iron ore, money was spent to bring in small amounts to make weapons.

By 1150 B.C., Egypt's empire was gone. Egyptian civilization kept growing weaker until Egypt was taken over by a people known as the Assyrians (uh sē' rē uhnz) in 671 B.C.

Section 4 Assessment

1. **Define:** hieroglyphic.
2. How did rulers of the New Kingdom expand trade?
3. Why did Egypt grow weak?

Critical Thinking

4. **Drawing Conclusions** In your opinion, which of the following pharaohs contributed the most to Egyptian civilization: Thutmose III, Hatshepsut, Amenhotep IV, or Tutankhamen? Explain.

Graphic Organizer Activity

5. Draw this diagram, and use it to show important events in the history of the New Kingdom. (Add boxes as needed.)

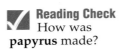

Reading Check
How was **papyrus** made?

SECTION 5 Contributions

The Egyptians made many contributions to other civilizations. One was a paper called **papyrus** (puh pī' ruhs). It was made from a reed also called papyrus. In order to write on papyrus, the Egyptians invented ink. The dry climate of Egypt preserved some writings so well that they can still be read today.

Papyrus had other uses. It was made into baskets and sandals. It was also tied in bundles to make columns for houses. Even rafts and riverboats were made of papyrus.

Other contributions of the Egyptians lay in the field of mathematics. They used a number system based on ten. They also

78 UNIT 2 RIVER VALLEY CIVILIZATIONS

---

used fractions and whole numbers. They used geometry to *survey*, or measure, land. When floods washed away the boundary markers that separated one field from the next, the Egyptians surveyed the fields to see where one began and the other ended.

The Egyptians knew the Nile flooded about the same time every year. They used this knowledge to make a calendar. The calendar had three seasons of 120 days each, and 5 special feast days for the gods.

The Egyptians also made contributions in the field of medicine. As dentists, eye doctors, animal doctors, and surgeons, Egyptian doctors were the first specialists in medicine. They were

Student Web Activity
Visit the *Human Heritage* Web site at **humanheritage.glencoe.com** and click on *Chapter 4—Student Web Activities* to find out more about Egyptian contributions.

MEDICAL PRACTICE IN ANCIENT EGYPT   Egyptian skill in medicine was highly valued in the Mediterranean area for 2,500 years. Here, an Egyptian doctor gives medicine to a patient. The doctor's assistant holds a scroll listing directions for treating the illness. **What kind of medical help did Egyptian doctors give their patients?**

Student Web Activity objectives, goals, and answers can be found at the *Chapter 4 Web Activity Lesson Plan* at **humanheritage.glencoe.com**

CAPTION ANSWER

Egyptians had dentists, eye doctors, animal doctors, and surgeons. Their physicians were the first to use splints, bandages, and compresses. They also treated such problems as indigestion and hair loss.

ASSESS

Check for Understanding

Ask students to summarize the main points of the chapter, orally or in writing. Discuss the answers to the Section and Chapter Assessments.

Evaluate

Assign the Chapter 4 **Performance Assessment Activity** in the TCR.

Administer the **Chapter 4 Test** in the TCR. Testmaker available.

MEETING SPECIAL NEEDS

If possible obtain a copy of the book *Ancient Lives: Daily Life in Egypt of the Pharaohs* by John Romer. Gather students who are auditory learners and read excerpts from the book to help the students understand the social customs and daily life of Egyptians. Involve students in a discussion about how their way of life compares to the lives of ancient Egyptians.

Refer to *Inclusion for the Middle School Social Studies Classroom: Strategies and Activities* for additional resources.

Reteach

For each section, have students write a sentence that summarizes the main concept. Call on volunteers to read their sentences. Have the class choose the best summary sentences for each section.

Assign Chapter 4 **Reteaching Activity** in the TCR.

Enrich

Have students research one of the people mentioned in the chapter and write a biographical sketch about them.

Assign Chapter 4 **Enrichment Activity** in the TCR.

CLOSE

Have students discuss the following question: Which contribution of the Egyptians to other civilizations was the most important? Why?

Use **Interactive Tutor Self-Assessment Software** to review Section 5.

the first to use splints, bandages, and compresses. They were masters at sewing up cuts and at setting broken bones. The Egyptians also treated such problems as indigestion and hair loss. For indigestion, they used castor oil. For hair loss, they used a mixture of dog toes, dates, and a donkey hoof.

Section 5 Assessment

1. **Define:** papyrus.
2. What mathematical contributions did the Egyptians make to civilization?
3. What medical contributions did the Egyptians make to other civilizations?

Critical Thinking

4. **Demonstrating Reasoned Judgment** Which Egyptian contribution do you think has had the greatest impact on life in the United States today?

Graphic Organizer Activity

5. Draw a diagram like this one, and use it to rate Egyptian contributions from most important to least important. (Add lines as needed.)

Most
_____
_____
_____
_____
Least

Chapter Summary & Study Guide

1. Egyptian civilization began in the Nile River valley over 5,000 years ago.
2. About 3100 B.C., Narmer united Upper and Lower Egypt.
3. The Old Kingdom began about 2600 B.C. and lasted for nearly 650 years.
4. Kings of Egypt became known as pharaohs and were viewed by Egyptians as rulers, priests, and gods.
5. During the Old Kingdom, pyramids were built as tombs for pharaohs.
6. The Egyptians worshiped many gods.
7. The Egyptians placed great importance on life after death and created a process to preserve bodies as mummies.
8. The Middle Kingdom began about 1950 B.C. and lasted until the Hyksos invasion of Egypt in 1786 B.C.
9. The New Kingdom began after Ahmose drove the Hyksos out of Egypt about 1550 B.C.
10. During the New Kingdom, most pharaohs were interested in conquest.
11. During the New Kingdom, priests became very powerful.
12. Amenhotep IV tried to establish a religion based on one god, but he failed.
13. Toward the end of the New Kingdom, Egypt began to decline.
14. Egyptian contributions to later civilizations included the use of geometry, surveying, and papyrus.

Section 5 Assessment Answers

1. papyrus, Egyptian paper (p. 78)
2. They used a number system based on 10, fractions and whole numbers, and geometry to survey the land.
3. They were the first to use splints, bandages, compresses, setting of broken bones, and treatment of indigestion and hair loss.
4. Answers will vary but could include the mention of any modern conveniences that were made possible by Egyptian ingenuity.
5. Answers will vary, but encourage students to name their choice for most important contribution and reasons for their selection.

Assign Chapter 4 **Section 5 Quiz** in the TCR. Testmaker available.

Assessment

Using Key Terms

Use the following list of words to write a newspaper article describing the contributions of the Egyptians.

sadoof   pharaoh   pyramids
embalming   mummy   legend
hieroglyphic   papyrus

Understanding Main Ideas

1. What did the Egyptians borrow from the Sumerians?
2. What did the Nile River give to the Egyptian people?
3. Why did the Egyptians show such great respect for the pharaoh?
4. What role did the Hyksos play in the development of Egyptian civilization?
5. What role did religion play in Egypt during the Old Kingdom? During the New Kingdom?
6. What kinds of writing did the Egyptians have, and why were they used?
7. What problems did flooding of the Nile River create, and how did the Egyptians try to solve them?
8. How did the Egyptians use the papyrus reed?

Critical Thinking

1. Do you agree with experts who call Egypt "the gift of the Nile"? Explain.
2. How was the government of Egypt similar to that of Babylonia? How was it different?
3. Do you think Amenhotep IV was wise in opposing the priests of Amon-Re? Explain.
4. Would you have like living in ancient Egypt? Why or why not?

Graphic Organizer Activity

History Create a chart like this one, and use it to compare characteristics of the Old Kingdom, Middle Kingdom, and New Kingdom of Egypt.

Old Kingdom	Middle Kingdom	New Kingdom

Geography in History

Human/Environmental Interaction
Note the area covered by ancient Egypt on the map on page 75. Why do you think the empire developed where it did, rather than expanding to the west or only to the south? Explain your answer.

Using Your Journal

Compare the effect of government on the lives of Egyptians with the effect of government on your daily life. Write a few short paragraphs explaining elements that are similar and those that are different.

81

Using Your Journal

Journal entries will vary, but students should compare the effects of Egyptian government on the lives of Egyptians with the effect of government on their own daily lives.

Geography in History

Answers will vary, but should include reliance on the Nile River and Mediterranean; proximity to people; and natural barriers.

Assessment Answers

Using Key Terms

Newspaper articles will vary but should use the vocabulary words listed.

Understanding Main Ideas

1. farming, seeds for wheat and barley, and writing
2. water and rich soil
3. because the pharaoh was considered a ruler, priest, and god
4. They introduced iron and bronze weapons and a new style of fighting.
5. During both the Old and New kingdoms religious rituals were carried out by the pharaoh and brought unity. Religion during Akhenaton's rule divided the people.
6. Hieroglyphic writing used on monuments; other writing to write religious works and records.
7. The floods washed away boundary markers, so the Egyptians surveyed fields. They also developed calendars to predict the floods.
8. for paper, baskets, sandals, columns for houses, rafts, and riverboats

Critical Thinking

1. Answers will vary, but note that Egypt needed the Nile .
2. Both held complete power. The ruler of Egypt was considered a god-king; the ruler of Babylon was not.
3. Answers will vary, but could say that this helped the decline of Egypt.
4. Answers will vary, but students should give explanations.

Graphic Organizer Activity

Entries will vary, but should show knowledge of the unique accomplishments of each kingdom.

Chapter 5 Planning Guide

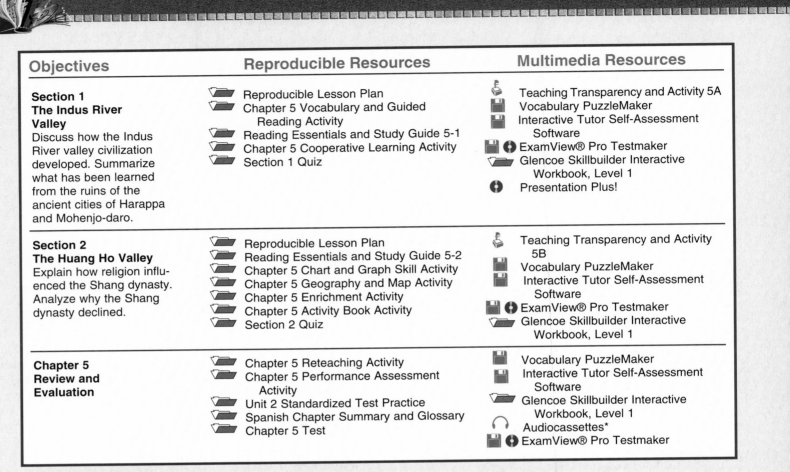

Objectives	Reproducible Resources	Multimedia Resources
Section 1 **The Indus River Valley** Discuss how the Indus River valley civilization developed. Summarize what has been learned from the ruins of the ancient cities of Harappa and Mohenjo-daro.	Reproducible Lesson Plan Chapter 5 Vocabulary and Guided Reading Activity Reading Essentials and Study Guide 5-1 Chapter 5 Cooperative Learning Activity Section 1 Quiz	Teaching Transparency and Activity 5A Vocabulary PuzzleMaker Interactive Tutor Self-Assessment Software ExamView® Pro Testmaker Glencoe Skillbuilder Interactive Workbook, Level 1 Presentation Plus!
Section 2 **The Huang Ho Valley** Explain how religion influenced the Shang dynasty. Analyze why the Shang dynasty declined.	Reproducible Lesson Plan Reading Essentials and Study Guide 5-2 Chapter 5 Chart and Graph Skill Activity Chapter 5 Geography and Map Activity Chapter 5 Enrichment Activity Chapter 5 Activity Book Activity Section 2 Quiz	Teaching Transparency and Activity 5B Vocabulary PuzzleMaker Interactive Tutor Self-Assessment Software ExamView® Pro Testmaker Glencoe Skillbuilder Interactive Workbook, Level 1
Chapter 5 **Review and Evaluation**	Chapter 5 Reteaching Activity Chapter 5 Performance Assessment Activity Unit 2 Standardized Test Practice Spanish Chapter Summary and Glossary Chapter 5 Test	Vocabulary PuzzleMaker Interactive Tutor Self-Assessment Software Glencoe Skillbuilder Interactive Workbook, Level 1 Audiocassettes* ExamView® Pro Testmaker

*Also available in Spanish.

Presentation Plus!

Use Glencoe's **Presentation Plus!** multimedia teacher tool to easily present dynamic lessons that visually excite your students. Using Microsoft® PowerPoint, you can customize the presentations to create your own personalized lessons.

 Interactive Lesson Planner

Planning has never been easier! Using this CD-ROM, organize your week, month, semester, or year with all the help you need. The **Interactive Lesson Planner** gives you access to all of the blackline masters which accompany *Human Heritage*.

✓ PERFORMANCE ASSESSMENT ACTIVITIES

Daily Life Organize students into groups of four. Suggest that students imagine that they are living during the time of the Shang dynasty. Have students in each group choose one of the following roles: a Shang ruler, a noble, a farmer, or a married woman. Tell the group members to describe their daily lives. Then ask students to make a chart comparing each person's way of life.

CHAPTER RESOURCES

LITERATURE ABOUT THE PERIOD

Chang, Richard F. *Chinese Mythical Stories*. Yale Far Eastern Publications, 1990. Legends and myths of China.

READINGS FOR THE STUDENT

National Geographic Society (Special Publications Division). *Mysteries of the Ancient World*. National Geographic Society, 1979. A collection of articles with photographs of ancient sites, including Harappa and Mohenjo-daro.

Oliphant, Margaret. *Atlas of the Ancient World*. Simon and Schuster, 1992. Survey of the ancient world cultures including those of India and China.

READINGS FOR THE TEACHER

Basham, A.L. *The Wonder That Was India*. Taplinger, 1967. A survey of the history of ancient India.

Teacher's Corner

NATIONAL GEOGRAPHIC SOCIETY PRODUCTS AVAILABLE FROM GLENCOE

To order the following, call Glencoe at 1-800-334-7344:

- *PicturePack: Physical Geography of the World (Transparencies)*
- *STV: World Geography (Videodisc)*
- *PicturePack: Ancient India*
- *PictureShow: Ancient Civilizations: India and China (CD-ROM)*
- *PictureShow: Ancient Civilizations Library (CD-ROMs)*
- *PicturePack: Ancient Civilizations Library, Part I (Transparencies)*

ADDITIONAL NATIONAL GEOGRAPHIC SOCIETY PRODUCTS

To order the following, call National Geographic at 1-800-368-2728:

- *National Geographic Atlas of World History (Book)*
- *Wonders of the Ancient World: National Geographic Atlas of Archaeology (Book)*

Access *National Geographic*'s new dynamic MapMachine Web site and other geography resources at:

http://www.nationalgeographic.com/
http://www.nationalgeographic.com/maps/

KEY TO ABILITY LEVELS

Teaching strategies have been coded for varying learning styles and abilities.

L1 Level 1 activities are **basic** activities and should be within the ability range of all students.

L2 Level 2 activities are **average** activities and should be within the ability range of the average to above-average student.

L3 Level 3 activities are **challenging** activities designed for the ability range of above-average students.

ELL ELL activities should be within the ability range of English Language Learning students.

OVERVIEW

Chapter 5 focuses on the development of the Harappan and Shang civilizations in South Asia and China.

➤ **Section 1** describes the Harappan civilization in the Indus River valley.

➤ **Section 2** explains the development of the Shang civilization in the Huang Ho Valley.

CHAPTER OBJECTIVES

After reading Chapter 5, students will be able to:

1. discuss how the Indus River valley civilization developed.

2. summarize what has been learned from the ruins at Harappa and Mohenjo-daro.

3. explain how religion influenced the Shang dynasty.

4. analyze why the Shang dynasty declined.

EXAMINING ARTIFACTS

Have students study the two objects on this page—a toy horse and a necklace. Based on what they have learned in earlier chapters, what would they assume about the level of the culture that produced these goods? (*Sample responses: people stayed in one place and could accumulate goods; probably had enough food to support a class of artisans; valued children and gave them toys*)

PERFORMANCE ASSESSMENT ✓

Use the Performance Assessment Activities on page 82B to help you evaluate students as they complete the chapter.

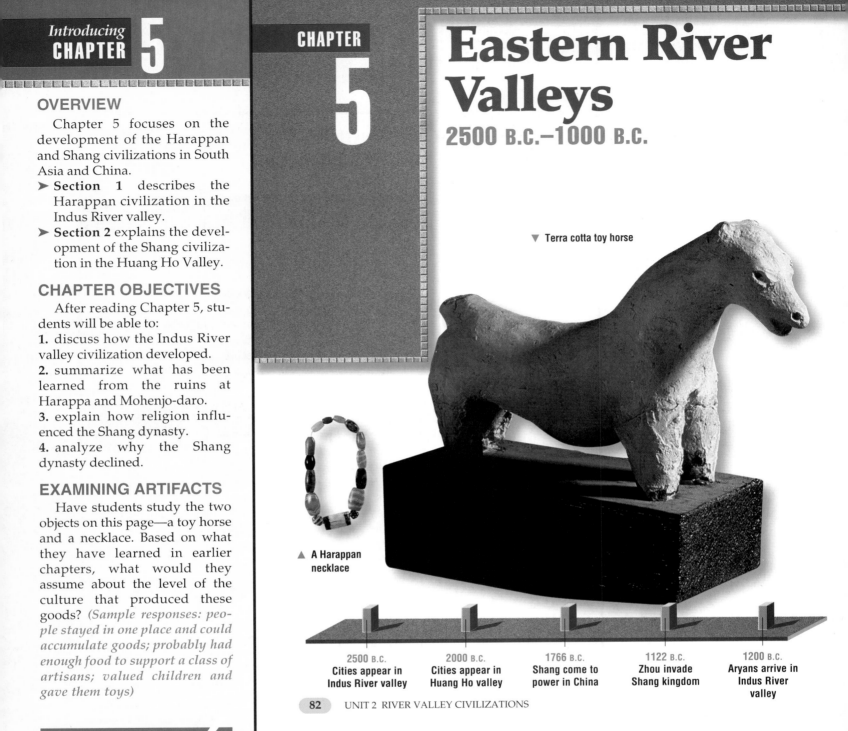

CHAPTER 5

Eastern River Valleys
2500 B.C.–1000 B.C.

▼ **Terra cotta toy horse**

▲ **A Harappan necklace**

2500 B.C.	2000 B.C.	1766 B.C.	1122 B.C.	1200 B.C.
Cities appear in Indus River valley	Cities appear in Huang Ho valley	Shang come to power in China	Zhou invade Shang kingdom	Aryans arrive in Indus River valley

82   UNIT 2 RIVER VALLEY CIVILIZATIONS

TEACHING RESOURCES

TEACHER PLANNING AND SUPPORT

🗁 Reproducible Lesson Plan
🗁 Block Scheduling Implementation Guide
🗁 Videodisc Bar Code Correlation
💿 Presentation Plus!

REVIEW AND REINFORCEMENT

🗁 Reading Essentials and Study Guide 5-1, 5-2
🗁 Chapter 5 Vocabulary and Guided Reading Activity
💾 Vocabulary PuzzleMaker Software
🖨 Teaching Transparencies 5A & 5B

🗁 Chapter 5 Reteaching Activity
🗁 Chapter 5 Cooperative Learning Activity
🗁 Chapter 5 Activity Book Activity
🗁 Chapter 5 Chart and Graph Skill Activity
💾 Interactive Tutor Self-Assessment Software
📼 Unit 2 MindJogger VideoQuiz

APPLICATION AND HANDS-ON ACTIVITIES

🗁 Daily World History, Geography, and Culture Question
🗁 Unit 2 Hands-On History Lab Activity

Chapter Focus

 Read to Discover

- How the Indus River valley civilization developed.
- What has been learned from the ruins of Harappa and Mohenjo-daro.
- How religion influenced the Shang dynasty.
- Why the Shang dynasty declined.

 Terms to Learn

planned
  communities
citadel
dynasty
ancestors
oracle bones
nobles

 People to Know

Harappans
Aryans
Yü the Great
Wu

🌐 **Places to Locate**

Indus River
Harappa
Mohenjo-daro
Huang Ho
  valley

Why It's Important By 2500 B.C., cities started to appear in the Indus Valley of South Asia. By 2000 B.C., they were being established in the Huang Ho (Yellow River) valley of China.

More isolated than the people of Mesopotamia or Egypt, the people of the eastern river valley civilizations were cut off from other parts of the world by high mountains, broad deserts, and large bodies of water. As a result, they became *self-sufficient*, or able to take care of nearly all their own needs. Compared to the Sumerians and the Egyptians, they did little trading with other parts of the world.

Because few artifacts have been found, much of what is known about the ancient eastern river valley civilizations comes from legends. Even so, available evidence points to unique and rich cultures that continue to interest archaeologists.

SECTION 1 The Indus River Valley

The Indus River flows through the countries known today as Pakistan and India. About 2500 B.C., a group of people called Harappans (huh rap' uhnz) settled in the valley of the Indus River. Although others had lived there before, the Harappans

GEOGRAPHY ACTIVITIES

- Chapter 5 Geography and Map Activity
- Social Studies Outline Map Resource Book

INTERDISCIPLINARY CONNECTIONS

- World Music: Cultural Traditions

ENRICHMENT AND EXTENSION

- World History Primary Source Document Library CD-ROM
- Chapter 5 Enrichment Activity
- Foods Around the World

ASSESSMENT AND EVALUATION

- Chapter 5 Performance Assessment Activity
- Chapter 5 Section Quizzes 5-1, 5-2
- Chapter 5 Test
- Chapter 5 Standardized Test Practice
- Chapter 5 ExamView® Pro Testmaker Software
- Chapter 5 Digests Audiocassettes Activities and Tests

SPANISH RESOURCES

- Chapter 5 Spanish Chapter Summary and Glossary
- Chapter 5 Spanish Chapter Digests Audiocassettes Activities and Tests

 HISTORY *Online*

Chapter Overview
Visit the *Human Heritage* Web site at **humanheritage.glencoe.com** and click on *Chapter 5—Chapter Overviews* to preview this chapter.

HISTORY *Online*

Chapter Overview introduces students to chapter content and key terms. Have them access **Chapter 5 Overview** at **humanheritage.glencoe.com**

FOCUS

📐 **Bellringer**

Write on the board: *How do you think mountains affected the lives of people in early civilizations?* Have students write a brief answer.

Motivational Activity

Have students read their thoughts about how mountains have affected civilizations. Then tell students that the early Indus River and Huang Ho valley civilizations were isolated from other civilizations by natural barriers such as high mountains. Ask students how isolation might affect a civilization. (*It forced them to take care of all their needs. They were unable to exchange ideas with other people.*)

GUIDE TO READING

Reading Strategy

Ask students to read "Why It's Important" and summarize the chapter's main theme. (*Because of geographic barriers, the eastern river valley civilizations developed self-sufficient and unique cultures known largely through artifacts and legends.*)

Vocabulary Precheck

Ask students to define each of the "Terms to Learn." Have a volunteer consult the dictionary for any unfamiliar words. **L1** **ELL**

💾 Use the Vocabulary PuzzleMaker for Chapter 5 to create a crossword puzzle. **L1**

☞ Assign Chapter 5 Vocabulary and Guided Reading Activity.

Guided Practice

L2 **Critical Thinking** Ask students to discuss how the Harappans controlled their environment in order to survive in the Indus Valley.

MAKING CONNECTIONS

►► **Geography: Region**
The Indus River rises in the Tibet region of China. When it reaches the plain, it receives water from five major tributaries. Its delta, unlike the Nile River delta and most other river deltas, is composed of clay and cannot be used for farming. The clay, however, was used to make bricks.

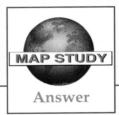

MAP STUDY

Answer

The Hindu Kush Mountains, the Himalaya Mountains, the Thar Desert, and the Arabian Sea would have helped protect the people of the Indus River valley from enemies.

---

were the first to create a civilization. Harappan civilization extended about 1,000 miles, or 1,600 kilometers, from the foothills of the Himalayas to the Indian Ocean. This area was more than twice the size of either Mesopotamia or Egypt.

The lives of the Harappan people were shaped by the Indus River. The river fertilized the land and made its soil rich. When the river flooded, however, it swept away everything in its path. People had to control the Indus in order to settle near it. To do this, they built dikes and dams. They cleared land for farming and built irrigation systems to bring water to dry areas. They grew barley, wheat, peas, melons, and dates and fished in the river.

The Harappans were the earliest known people to grow cotton. They spun the cotton, wove it into cloth, and dyed it bright colors. They produced cotton cloth hundreds of years before anyone else.

The Indus River influenced the way the Harappans built their cities. To protect cities from floods, the Harappans built them on raised mounds. They used river mud to make bricks, which they baked in the sun. Then they went one step further. They *fired*, or baked, some bricks in *kilns*, or ovens. They used these kiln-dried bricks as a covering over the mud bricks. The fired bricks were stronger and lasted much longer than sun-dried ones. The Harappans used fired bricks for houses and public buildings.

Early India

MAP STUDY

PLACE India is part of the triangle-shaped peninsula that forms the southern part of the continent of Asia. **What geographic features would have helped to protect the people of the Indus River valley from enemies?**

MEETING SPECIAL NEEDS

Have the students who are auditory learners view the film *India: Early Civilizations.* (See suggested Chapter Resources in the Chapter Planning Guide.)

Prior to viewing the film ask students to listen for the answer to the question: *How did the Indus River valley civilization develop?* After viewing the film hold a class discus-

sion. Ask: *What factors influenced the development of the Indus River valley civilization? What role did geographic isolation play? Was this role positive, negative, or both? Why?*

☞ Refer to *Inclusion for the Middle School Social Studies Classroom: Strategies and Activities* for additional resources.

Student Web Activity
Visit the *Human Heritage* Web site at **humanheritage.glencoe.com** and click on ***Chapter 5— Student Web Activities*** to find out more about Harappan civilization.

THE GREAT BATH AT MOHENJO-DARO   The people of Mohenjo-daro may have washed themselves at the Great Bath. It measured 40 feet, or 12 meters, long and 23 feet, or 7 meters, wide. To make the Bath watertight, they used cement, tar, and four layers of brick. **What was the purpose of the Great Bath?**

Harappa and Mohenjo-daro   Harappan civilization centered around two major cities, Harappa and Mohenjo-daro (mōhen′ jō dahr′ ō). These cities were about 400 miles, or 640 kilometers, apart. Many experts believe they were twin capitals.

Harappa and Mohenjo-daro are the oldest examples yet found of **planned communities,** or cities built to a definite plan. Both cities contained hundreds of small buildings. Some buildings served as homes, while others served as shops. The buildings were laid out on a planned street *grid*, or uniform network. The streets crossed each other at almost perfect right angles. The buildings that lined the streets were arranged in blocks of about the same size.

Most buildings were two stories high and were built around a courtyard, which opened into several rooms. Outer walls of buildings had no windows, and walls fronted on narrow lanes in such a way as to break the force of the wind. Almost every building had its own well, bathroom, and drains. The drains carried waste away from the houses and emptied it into drain holes lined with brick. These drains were cleaned often. This sanitation system helped protect the health of the Harappans.

The most important buildings of Harappa and Mohenjo-daro were built high above the houses and shops so as to be safe from neighboring peoples and floods. In each city, a **citadel** (sit′ uh duhl), or fortress, stood on a mound at least 40 feet, or 12 meters, high. It was surrounded by a thick brick wall. Inside the citadel at Mohenjo-daro was a huge watertight tank called the Great Bath. Some experts believe it was used for religious ceremonies. Next to

Reading Check
What are **planned communities?**

Reading Check
Where was a **citadel** located, and what did it look like?

Student Web Activity objectives, goals, and answers can be found at the ***Chapter 5 Web Activity Lesson Plan*** at **humanheritage.glencoe.com**

CAPTION ANSWER

It was used for religious ceremonies.

Reading Check Answer
Planned communities are cities built to a definite plan.

Reading Check Answer
A **citadel,** or fort, stood on a mound at least 40 feet (12 meters) high and was surrounded by a thick brick wall.

NATIONAL GEOGRAPHIC SOCIETY

Use these materials to enrich student understanding of Indus River valley civilizations.

NGS PICTURESHOW CD-ROM
India and China

NGS PICTUREPACK TRANSPARENCY SET
Ancient India

COOPERATIVE LEARNING

Divide the class into groups of five or six students. Have each group choose a topic from these suggestions: religion, architecture, city planning, farming, textiles, arts and crafts, commerce, and geography. Have groups research their topic as it pertains to Harappan civilization, and prepare a creative presentation about it. Students might create a song, skit, or collage of visuals. Suggest students assess their own project participation after their presentations.

📁 Assign Chapter 5 *Cooperative Learning Activity* in the TCR.

The sites of Harappa and Mohenjo-daro are located in present-day Pakistan. Some scholars believe that as civilizations collapsed in Harappa and Mohenjo-daro, many people fled southward from the Indus Valley to the tip of the Indian Peninsula. Known there as Dravidians, they re-established their culture, which has remained distinct from the rest of India. Connections between Tamil—a Dravidian language currently spoken in Sri Lanka—and the scattered samples of Harappan writing that are found on Harappan seals have been made.

L1 Critical Thinking Ask students to give reasons that might explain why most Harappan gods were female. **ELL**

No Showers?
Harappan bathrooms contained no bathtubs. People preferred to pour water over themselves from hand-held pitchers.

Sculpture of Harappan Priest-King

the Great Bath stood a huge granary. Traders from other areas who stopped at Mohenjo-daro most likely left their goods there.

Harappa also had a series of huge granaries. The floor of each granary was supported on low walls. In the walls were air holes that allowed air to move around in the granary. This kept the grain dry and prevented it from spoiling. Nearby were circular brick platforms. Each had a scooped-out area in the center where grain could be pounded.

Decline of the Harappans   No one knows for certain how Harappan civilization came to an end. One reason may have been that the Harappans used up their natural resources. For example, the Harappan farmers may have tried to raise more and more crops on the same plots. This would have robbed the soil of nutrients needed to make it fertile enough to produce well. Without good harvests, there would not have been enough food to feed everyone, especially if the Harappan population was increasing.

Another reason may have been that the Harappans cut down too many trees to fuel their ovens. Without tree cover, floods would have swept away the soil and forced people to leave their cities and farming villages. It is known that parts of Mohenjo-daro had to be rebuilt several times because of floods. At first, the city was rebuilt carefully. As time went on, however, new buildings were not made as well, and older ones were patched up. Then, too, the Harappans may have gotten tired of rebuilding and decided to move somewhere else.

A third reason may have been that the Indus River valley was invaded and all the Harappans were killed. Unburied skeletons of groups of men, women, and children have been found in the streets of Mohenjo-daro's ruins. Every skeleton showed some kind of injury.

All that is certain is that Harappan civilization began to change about 1700 B.C. Not only were homes no longer built as well, but pottery was no longer made as carefully. By 1200 B.C., a group of people called Aryans (ār' ē uhnz) had taken over the Indus River valley. Harappan civilization ceased to be.

Evidence of a Lost Civilization   Very little is known about the Harappan people and their civilization. As yet, no one has been able to read Harappan writing. There is no record of the civilization's political history. No royal tombs have been discovered. All that is known about Harappan religion is that there was more than one god, and most Harappan gods were female.

Much of what is known comes from the ruins of Harappa and Mohenjo-daro. There, archaeologists have found jewelry made of gold and a blue stone called lapis lazuli (lap' uhs laz' uh lē), as

EXTENDING THE CONTENT

The Aryans were an Indo-European group that seems to have migrated to the south and east from southern Russia. Nomadic herdsmen, they had horse-driven chariots, bronze axes, and bows and arrows. Their distinctive language persisted wherever they conquered. Indo-European is the language family name given to the Aryans' language—an ancestor to almost every European language. The Aryans had no artistic tradition and no written language, but they had a rich oral tradition of songs, proverbs, hymns, and rituals. These were later collected in the four religious books called the Vedas.

HARAPPAN SEAL This Harappan seal is 1 inch, or 2.5 centimeters, square. It shows a bull facing an incense burner. In eastern civilizations, the bull was a symbol of strength. The seal also shows Harappan writing. **What is unusual about Harappan writing?**

Then... **& Now**

Bangles Today, many people in India and Pakistan wear bangles—ring-shaped bracelets and anklets. So did the Harappans. To find out how the Harappans made their bangles, archaeologists in the 1980s and 1990s turned to present-day bangle makers. Using traditional methods, they gave archaeologists insights into how the Harappan bangle makers might have worked.

CAPTION ANSWER

No one has been able to decipher Harappan writing.

DID YOU KNOW

Soapstone is a soft stone composed mainly of talc and chlorite that has a soapy feel.

LINKING PAST TO PRESENT

Some Harappan seals had as their central figure the god Shiva, who later became a principal Hindu god.

Independent Practice

L1 History Have students research the excavation of Harappa or Mohenjo-daro and write a one-page journal entry from the viewpoint of an archaeologist at the site.

Use **Interactive Tutor Self Assessment Software** to review Section 1.

---

well as tools and weapons of stone, copper, and bronze. They have also found clay models of animals, rattles, dice, and toy carts with movable wheels.

One of the most important finds was a series of tiny seals made of soapstone. An animal and a line of writing were carved on each seal. The animals included tigers, elephants, rhinoceri, and crocodiles. This suggests that at one time much of the area was jungle. Most of the seals had a small hole in them and could be worn as necklaces or bracelets. The seals may have stated the names, titles, or trades of a person, family, or business. Experts believe the seals were used to stamp the wet clay that sealed packages of goods. Some Harappan seals have been found as far away as Sumer.

Section 1 Assessment

1. **Define:** planned communities, citadel.
2. How did the Indus River influence the Harappans?
3. What were some of the outstanding features of Harappa and Mohenjo-daro?

Critical Thinking

4. **Predicting Consequences** What do you think archaeologists would learn about the Harappans if they could read Harappan writing?

Graphic Organizer Acitvity

5. Draw a diagram like this one, and use it to summarize the accomplishments of the Harappans.

Harappans

Section 1 Assessment Answers

1. planned communities, cities built by design (p. 85); citadel, fortress (p. 85)

2. in the building of dikes and dams, cities, houses, and public buildings; and in farming and irrigation

3. planned street grids, a sanitation system, citadels, and huge granaries; Mohenjo-daro also had a Great Bath

4. Answers will vary, but students might suggest that archaeologists would learn about the daily life of the Harappans.

5. Sample accomplishments: planned communities, street grids, bathrooms, sanitation system, granaries, system of writing, use of seals, creation of jewelry and weapons, and so on

Assign Chapter 5 **Section 1 Quiz** in the TCR. Testmaker available.

88

➤➤ **Legends** Over the centuries the Chinese have developed many legends. One myth tells how the universe was created from the body of a giant named Pan Gu, who hatched from an egg. Another celebrates the deeds of a hero-king named Yao, a person in the form of a mountain.

Reading Check Answer
A **dynasty** is a ruling family.

CAPTION ANSWER

because there are no records of China's beginnings and no remains have been found

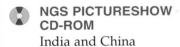

NATIONAL GEOGRAPHIC SOCIETY

Use these materials to enrich student understanding of China.

⦿ **NGS PICTURESHOW CD-ROM**
India and China

🖨 **NGS PICTUREPACK TRANSPARENCY SET**
Ancient China

💾 Use the **Vocabulary Puzzle-Maker** to create crossword and word search puzzles.

SECTION 2 The Huang Ho Valley

About 2000 B.C., or 500 years after the Harappans settled in the Indus River valley, a civilization developed in the Huang Ho valley of northern China. There are no records of its beginnings, and no remains have been found. For this reason, much of what happened comes from legend.

According to Chinese legend, a man-god named Yü the Great drove out the serpents and dragons that lived along the Huang Ho. He drained the land so that people could live there and grow crops. Yü founded a kingdom called Xia (shē′ ah) and united most of northern China under his rule.

Many experts believe that the early settlers of China chose the Huang Ho valley for their home because it was fertile. The river flooded every year, bringing rich soil with it.

The valley was cut off from other civilizations. The people there developed their culture without borrowing from other civilizations. By 1800 B.C., there were villages and farms all along the river. The people farmed the land and used the river for travel and trade. They made clay ovens, cupboards, benches, and pottery. They built small round clay houses with thatched roofs.

Reading Check
What is a
dynasty?

Cities of the Shang   The first records of Chinese civilization come from a **dynasty** (dī′ nuh stē), or ruling family, called Shang. The Shang came to power in 1766 B.C. They built the first Chinese

THE WISE MAN FU HSI   Chinese legends tell the stories of Yü and another man-god, Fu Hsi. Here, Fu Hsi points to eight geometric designs used to tell the future. **Why are legends important to historians studying early China?**

EXTENDING THE CONTENT

China's Huang Ho—formerly the Yellow River—took its name from the great amounts of yellow-brown silt, or loess, that it carries downstream. Through the years the river has been given other names. Its frequent disastrous floods have led people to call it "China's Sorrow," while the rich soil it deposits in the river valley has made it known as "China's Joy." The river flows about 3,000 miles eastward and empties into the Yellow Sea. It begins in the mountains of western China and makes a large loop northward in the middle of its course. The river's course has changed many times, creating the broad, fertile North China Plain.

Shang China

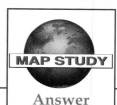

MAP STUDY

MOVEMENT The landforms of China contributed to the early isolation of the Chinese. **What geographical features would have discouraged the Shang people from movement to other lands or their contact with other people?**

MAP STUDY

Answer

The geographical features that would have stopped the Shang people from movement to other lands include the mountains to the west, the Gobi, the Yellow Sea, and the Pacific Ocean.

DID YOU KNOW ??

The buildings of the Shang people faced south to get as much sun as possible during the cold winter months.

cities. Most were designed in the same way. At the center stood a palace and a temple. Public buildings and the homes of high government officials were built around the palace. Within an outer district were workshops, burial grounds, and the homes of the workers.

Most of the Shang people, however, did not live in the city. The city was the home of the rich, the learned, and the skilled. Poorer people lived in the countryside. They were farmers who grew such grains as millet, wheat, and rice and raised cattle, sheep, and chickens. The farmers also produced silk, which was used to make clothes for the very rich. The Chinese produced silk hundreds of years before anyone else.

Spirits, Ancestors, and Kings   The Shang worshiped **spirits,** or supernatural beings, which they believed lived in mountains, rivers, and seas. The people believed they had to please the spirits. If the spirits became angry or unhappy, the people might suffer a poor harvest or lose a battle.

The Shang believed that **ancestors,** or those from whom one is descended, also influenced people's fortunes. So, they offered their ancestors food, wine, and special prayers. They hoped their ancestors would help them in time of need and bring them good fortune. Because of this respect for ancestors, family ties were very important to the Shang. They had rules about how family members should act toward one another. Children were taught to

✓ Reading Check
What role did **spirits** play in Shang religion?

✓ Reading Check
Why did the Shang respect their **ancestors?**

✓ Reading Check Answer
The Shang believed the **spirits** lived in the mountains, rivers, and seas, and that people needed to please the spirits to avoid misfortune.

✓ Reading Check Answer
The Shang believed that **ancestors** influenced people's fortunes.

MEETING SPECIAL NEEDS

Encourage students who are tactile/kinesthetic learners to prepare a bulletin board depicting the early history of China. Have the students discuss what should be included in the display. Some suggestions are maps showing what crops were grown, drawings of artifacts, and illustrations of the layout of an excavated city. Assign small groups to research and prepare each

topic with each student assuming responsibility for a specific task. Have the class design and assemble the bulletin-board display.

📁 Refer to *Inclusion for the Middle School Social Studies Classroom: Strategies and Activities* for additional resources.

People in History

Wu
c. 1000 B.C.

Zhou King

Wu, the ruler of a former Shang territory, led the attack against the last Shang emperor. The emperor was so cruel that many soldiers gave up without a fight. Wu, known as "the Military King," believed the gods wanted the Zhou dynasty to rule China, and he became the first Zhou ruler.

obey their parents and to honor older people. Wives were trained to obey their husbands.

The Shang believed that their kings received their power from the spirits of nature and their wisdom from their ancestors. For this reason, religion and government were tied closely together. An important duty of kings was to contact the spirits of nature to make sure they provided enough water for farming.

Kings also asked the advice of their ancestors before making important decisions. To do this, kings had questions scratched on a flat, polished piece of bone. The bone had a hole drilled in it, and a hot bar was put in the hole. Heat from the bar produced a pattern of cracks on the bone. The cracks were believed to be the ancestors' replies to a king's questions. A special interpreter gave the king the meaning of the ancestors' replies. These bones are known as **oracle** (ōr′ uh kuhl) **bones.** The writing on them is the oldest known form of Chinese writing.

Under the king was a large class of **nobles,** or people of high rank in a kingdom. They spent much of their time hunting, both for pleasure and as preparation for war. Nobles often fought with each other about land. They joined together only when they had to fight other people who refused to accept Shang rule.

Nobles rode into battle in horse-drawn bronze chariots. They wore bronze helmets and armor made of buffalo or rhinoceros hide. They were skilled in the use of the bow and arrow. Their

ORACLE BONES Shang rulers tried to learn the future by using oracle bones. Here, a turtle shell used for this purpose shows an early form of Chinese writing. **When did Shang rulers use oracle bones?**

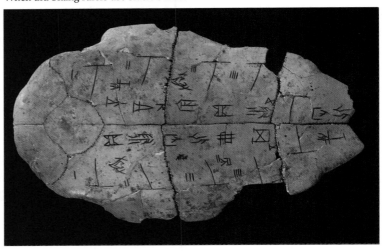

EXTENDING THE CONTENT

In addition to producing fine bronze objects, the people of the Shang dynasty carved beautiful ivory and jade statues. They wove silk into elegantly colored cloth for the upper class and fashioned pottery from kaolin, a fine white clay.

arrows had sharp points of bone or bronze. Soldiers marched on foot behind nobles' chariots. These soldiers generally were poor peasants whom the nobles had forced to leave their farms and join the army.

Decline of the Shang There was a great gap between rich and poor during the rule of the Shang. Rich Shang lived in the cities in wooden houses. They owned bronze weapons and ornaments and wore linen, wool, fur, and silk clothes. Poor Shang lived in the countryside and worked with wooden or stone tools. Their houses were thatched or mud huts or caves scooped out of the ground. Neither group felt any loyalty toward the other.

Many experts believe that this gap between rich and poor weakened the Shang civilization. In 1122 B.C., a people known as Zhou (jō) invaded the Shang kingdom. The Shang were not united enough to hold off the invaders, and their civilization came to an end.

Linking Across Time

Metal Casting Shang metalsmiths perfected a form of casting to create some of the finest bronze works the world has ever known (below). Metalsmiths still use molds to create everything from artworks to machine parts (right). **What conclusions can you draw about Shang technology?**

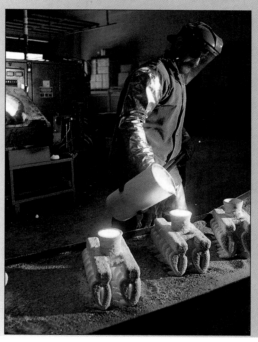

MULTICULTURAL PERSPECTIVES

The people of the Chinese dynasties believed that their rulers governed according to a principle known as a Mandate from Heaven. If rulers were just and effective, they received a mandate. If rulers did not govern properly—as indicated by poor crops or losses in battle—they lost the mandate to someone else who then started a new dynasty. This principle started with the Zhou dynasty.

L1 **Daily Life** Ask students to imagine themselves as a king, noble, soldier, or farmer during the Shang dynasty in ancient China. Have students write a diary entry describing a day in the life of the person they have chosen. Call on volunteers to read their diary entries to the class.

Linking Across Time

Conclusions will vary, but most students will conclude that the Shang excelled at bronze metalwork and turned metal casting into an art.

ASSESS

Check for Understanding

Ask students to summarize the main points of the chapter, orally or in writing. Discuss the answers to the Section and Chapter Assessment questions.

Evaluate

Assign Chapter 5 **Performance Assessment Activity** in the TCR.

Administer **Chapter 5 Test** in the TCR. Testmaker available.

Reteach

Have students survey the chapter and make a list of questions to test their knowledge of the chapter. Working in pairs, students can quiz each other.

Assign Chapter 5 **Reteaching Activity** in the TCR.

Ask students to bring to class illustrations of bronze objects made by the Shang and other dynasties. Allow students to discuss and list similarities and differences in the art.

Assign Chapter 5 **Enrichment Activity** in the TCR.

CLOSE

Have students write a paragraph describing the features of the Harappan civilization or the Shang dynasty that made them attractive to invaders.

 Use **Interactive Tutor Self-Assessment Software** to review Section 2.

Self-Check Quiz gives students an interactive chapter tutorial. Have them access **Chapter 5 Quiz** at humanheritage.glencoe.com

GLENCOE TECHNOLOGY

 Videodisc
Use the MindJogger to review students' knowledge of the unit.

MindJogger Videoquiz

Unit 2
Disc 1 Side A

Also available in VHS.

The Shang left behind a great gift to the rest of the world in their works of bronze. These include sculptures, cups, vases, fancy vessels, and a variety of other items used for religious purposes. Many art experts believe these are among the finest works of bronze ever made.

Section 2 Assessment

1. **Define:** dynasty, spirits, ancestors, oracle bones, nobles.
2. What were some of the Shang religious beliefs?
3. What may have been the reason for the decline of the Shang civilization?

Critical Thinking

4. **Formulating Questions** If world leaders today could use oracle bones, what questions might they want answered before making decisions?

Graphic Organizer Activity

5. Draw a diagram like this one, and use it to show the structure of a typical Shang city.

Chapter Summary & Study Guide

1. The eastern river valley civilizations began in the Indus River valley about 2500 B.C. and in the Huang Ho valley about 2000 B.C.
2. The first people to build a civilization in the Indus River valley were the Harappans.
3. The Harappans are believed to have been the first people to produce cotton cloth, bake bricks in ovens, and build sanitation systems.
4. The Harappan cities of Harappa and Mohenjo-daro are the oldest known planned communities.
5. No one knows for sure how the Harappan civilization ended, but the Aryans moved into and took over the valley about 1200 B.C.
6. The legendary kingdom of Xia probably was established in China about 2000 B.C.
7. The Shang started the first recorded Chinese dynasty around 1766 B.C.
8. The Shang believed spirits and ancestors influenced their lives.
9. The Shang developed the form of writing found on oracle bones and a method of making beautiful bronze artworks.
10. Shang civilization ended with the Zhou invasion of 1122 B.C.

Self-Check Quiz

Visit the *Human Heritage* Web site at **humanheritage. glencoe.com** and click on **Chapter 5—Self-Check Quiz** to assess your understanding of this chapter.

Section 2 Assessment Answers

1. dynasty, ruling family in China (p. 88); spirits, supernatural beings (p. 89); ancestors, those from whom one is descended (p. 89); oracle bones, bones to receive messages from ancestors (p. 90); nobles, people of high rank (p. 90)
2. Sample beliefs: worship of spirits, worship of departed ancestors, spiritual powers and duties of kings
3. the distance between the rich and poor

4. Answers will vary but should include questions about current affairs.
5. center—palace and temple; around the palace/temple—public buildings and homes of high government officials; outer district—workshops, burial grounds, homes of workers

Assign Chapter 5 **Section 2 Quiz** in the TCR. Testmaker available.

Using Key Terms

Imagine you are preparing a feature film about the civilizations in the Indus River and Huang Ho valleys. Use the following words in a brief summary describing the facts you plan to present in your film.

planned communities   citadel
dynasty   spirits
ancestors   oracle bones
nobles

Understanding Main Ideas

1. Why is so little known about the early life of people in the Indus River and Huang Ho valleys?
2. Why were Harappa and Mohenjo-daro unique places in which to live?
3. What were some of the possible reasons for the decline of the Harappans?
4. What evidence suggests that there was trade between Harappa and Sumer?
5. Why were family ties important to the Shang people?
6. How did Shang kings use oracle bones?
7. Why did the gap between the rich and poor help weaken the Shang?
8. What cultural contribution did the Shang leave to the world?

Critical Thinking

1. Why did people in the eastern river valleys borrow little from people in other regions?
2. What do you think may happen to a civilization if it uses up its natural resources? Why?
3. Do you think people today hold ancestors in the same high regard as the Shang? Explain.

Graphic Organizer Activity

Citizenship Create a diagram like this one, and use it to show the flow of power and authority in the Shang government. Groups that should appear on the chart include: artisans, farmers, king, spirits and ancestors, nobles. Which group appears at the top? At the bottom?

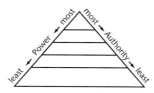

Geography in History

Place Refer to the map of early India on page 84. Note the location of the Indus civilizations and the geographic features that may have affected its development. Describe what other area of this region is a likely place for other civilizations to develop. Explain why.

Using Your Journal

Compare any details you may have noted about planned communities in Harappa and Mohenjo-daro with details about your own community. Create a chart illustrating the ways in which your community is similar and different.

93

Bonus Test Question

For Chapter 5 Test
The geographic locations of the Harrapan and Shang affected their quality of life. Which civilization would have been most affected by a monsoon that blew from the southwest? Explain. *(The Harrapans with coastal areas would be hit first and hardest. The Shang might get rains.)*

Using Your Journal

Charts will vary but should include information that explains ways in which students' communities are similar to and different from the planned communities in Harappa and Mohenjo-daro.

Geography in History

A likely place would be along the eastern coast and the Bay of Bengal, and along the Ganges River. Students should note access to water.

Using Key Terms

Summaries will vary. Students should use the words and terms to prepare a summary of a feature film about the civilizations in the Indus River and Huang Ho valleys.

Understanding Main Ideas

1. because very few remains have been found
2. because they were planned communities
3. They may have used up their natural resources or may have been invaded and killed.
4. Some Harappan seals have been found in Sumer.
5. because they respected their ancestors and believed they would bring the Shang people good fortune
6. Questions were scratched on a bone. Cracks on the bone were believed to be the ancestors' replies.
7. because it prevented them from uniting to hold off invaders
8. works of bronze

Critical Thinking

1. because they were cut off from other parts of the world by mountains, deserts, and water
2. Answers will vary, but should include that a civilization may die or its people may move.
3. Answers will vary but should explain students' reasons.

Graphic Organizer Activity

From top to bottom: spirits and ancestors, king, nobles, artisans, farmers

UNIT 2 Around

FOCUS

Objectives

After reading the Around the World for Unit 2, your students will be able to:

1. identify the location of the Hittite empire.

2. discuss the methods the Hittites used to control their empire.

3. explain the historical importance of the Hittite battle chariot.

Bellringer

Ask students who invented the chariot. *(Without prior historical knowledge, students will probably say the Egyptians, Greeks, or Romans—the chariot drivers most often seen in movies.)*

Motivational Activity

Explain to students that the world's earliest known chariot originated in Mesopotamia, around 3500 B.C. Then refer them to the feature on pages 94–95. Ask: What advantage did the Hittite battle chariot have over other chariots? *(Larger chariots held two soldiers, doubling Hittite fighting power.)*

TEACH

Geography: Location Divide students into pairs or small groups. Have them compare the map of the Hittite Empire on page 94 with the map of ancient Egypt on page 73. Ask: Which Egyptian territory do you think the Hittites most wanted to control? Why? *(Syria; because it bordered on the Hittite Empire)* If the Hittites wanted to invade Egypt, what route would they probably take? *(They would travel through Syria and Palestine and then into Lower Egypt.)*

THE HITTITES

Around 2000 B.C., the Hittites moved into Asia Minor from an area somewhere beyond the Black Sea. Within the next 700 years, they built an empire that rivaled Egypt in size and power. Although the Hittites adopted many of the customs of the people they conquered, they developed ideas and inventions of their own. One of the most important of these was the Hittite battle chariot—the weapon that allowed the Hittites to challenge the civilizations of Mesopotamia and Egypt.

Hittite Empire

BLACK SEA

ANATOLIA PLATEAU
ASIA MINOR

CASPIAN SEA

MEDITERRANEAN SEA

Tigris River

Euphrates River

EGYPT

Nile River

Hittite Empire at Peak

miles 0   200   400
kilometers 0   200   400

▲ In 1595 B.C., Hittite armies plunged deep into Mesopotamia to capture the city of Babylon. Although a rebellion forced the Hittite king to return home, Babylon never recovered from the attack. The Hittites went on to take control of lands stretching from the Aegean Sea in the west to the upper Euphrates River in the east.

◄ Deeply religious, the Hittites used the fury of the gods to threaten people who broke laws or treaties. A Hittite artist armed this god with a thunder hammer and a handful of jagged lightening bolts.

94   UNIT 2

SPOTLIGHT ON: THE HITTITES

Hittite women enjoyed a freedom unknown to women in Mesopotamia and Egypt. Laws allowed them to follow professions that elsewhere were held only by men. Clay tablets and seals found by archaeologists reveal that queens often ruled jointly with kings. Queens also had the right to act independently.

The best-known Hittite queen is Puduhepa, wife of Hattushili III. The couple ruled the Hittite Empire at its height of power. They hammered out a treaty of friendship with Ramses II, one of the greatest empire builders of the New Kingdom. The seal cut into the tablet bore the image of the king on one side and the queen on the other. To cement the friendship, the Hittite couple gave Ramses two of their daughters in marriage. The respect commanded by Puduhepa is evidenced by letters in which Ramses refers to her as "my sister."

the World

Some Hittite battle chariots carried two warriors—a driver and an archer. The larger and heavier battle chariots carried three—a driver and two armed soldiers. This allowed the Hittites to double their fighting power. ▼

◄ The Hittites preferred to rule by treaty rather than by force. They recorded the terms of these treaties on gold, silver, or iron tablets written in their own hieroglyphics or in cuneiform adopted from the Babylonians.

The royal seal of a Hittite king was imprinted on this clay tablet. ◄

The Hittites considered the sun goddess, called Arinna, the giver of all life. Known as "Queen of Heaven and Earth," she was honored with works of gold such as this statue. ►

Taking Another Look

1. Where did the Hittites build their empire?
2. What methods did they use to control their empire?

Hands-On Activity

Writing an Argument Write a list of arguments that an Egyptian soldier might have used to convince the pharaoh to adopt the all-new Hittite battle chariot.

95

ASSESS

Check for Understanding

Have students answer the questions in **Taking Another Look** on page 95.

Enrich

Ask students to create advertisements that a Hittite chariot maker might have used to sell one of the new three-person battle chariots.

CLOSE

Ask students to imagine they are the king of the Hittite Empire at the height of its power. How would they explain Hittite success? *(Most students will cite use of the battle chariot, but encourage them to understand the importance of treaties in extending Hittite power. Hittite kings, who also served as priests, would have undoubtedly also mentioned help from deities such as those mentioned on pages 94–95.)*

ANSWERS TO TAKING ANOTHER LOOK

1. Sample response: The Hittites built their empire on the Anatolian Plateau in Asia Minor. At its height, the empire extended from the Aegean Sea in the west to the upper Euphrates River in the east.

2. Although the Hittites used conquest to extend their holdings, they preferred to rule by treaty rather than by force.

Hands-On Activity
Arguments will vary, but might include the need to put more soldiers in the field, the proven success of the Hittite chariot in battle, and so on.

THE
PRINCETON
REVIEW

Standardized Test Practice

Answers and Analyses

1A   Civics

The rights of Sumerian women are discussed at the top of page 59. There it states that *they could run businesses.*

2J   History

According to page 57, a ziggurat had a religious and not an agricultural purpose. According to page 5, cuneiform was a system of writing. Therefore choices F and H can be eliminated. Even though they are in use today, feed troughs are not attributed to the Mesopotamians, so choice G can also be eliminated.

THE
PRINCETON
REVIEW   **TEST-TAKING TIP**

As with any specific question, students should begin by eliminating unreasonable choices. Since the question asks about agricultural inventions, choices F and H can be eliminated.

3B   Civics

According to page 61, before Hammurabi, each city-state had its own code. Hammurabi *took what he believed were the best laws from each code. He put these together and then issued one code by which everyone in the empire was to live.*

Directions: Choose the *best* answer to each of the following multiple choice questions. If you have trouble answering a question, use the process of elimination to narrow your choices. Write your answers on a separate piece of paper.

1. Sumerian society granted certain rights to women. Which of the following rights did Sumerian women have?

   A   They had the right to operate businesses.

   B   They had the right to vote in city-state elections.

   C   They had the right to attend the same schools as men.

   D   They had the right to join the Sumerian army.

   Test-Taking Tip: Eliminate answers that you know are incorrect. Since only the sons of the rich could attend school, you can eliminate answer C.

2. Which of the following Mesopotamian inventions is still used in agriculture today?

   F   Ziggurats

   G   Feed troughs

   H   Cuneiform

   J   Plows

   Test-Taking Tip: Make sure that you read the question carefully. The question asks for an invention used in *agriculture* (farming). Since *cuneiform* is *Sumerian writing,* it cannot be the correct answer.

3. The Code of Hammurabi was important because

   A   it punished unfair judges

   B   it established one set of laws for all city-states

   C   it protected confidential messages sent between judges

   D   it required prison sentences for people convicted of crimes

   Test-Taking Tip: Remember to read *all* the answer choices and pick the *best* answer. Although the Code of Hammurabi *did* punish unfair judges, this fact is not the *most important.* Which aspect of the Code was the most significant *change* from previous codes of law?

4. A major accomplishment of the societies of Mesopotamia and ancient Egypt, which allowed these civilizations to flourish, was

   F   the building of pyramids to honor rulers

   G   the teaching of English to children in school

   H   the use of waterways to irrigate crops

   J   the development of the 60-minute hour

   Test-Taking Tip: The key phrase in this question is: *which allowed these civilizations to flourish.* Some of these accomplishments are certainly important—we still use the 60-minute hour today—but they did not all contribute to the *basic survival* of these two civilizations.

96

5. The Mesopotamian, Egyptian, and Indus River Valley civilizations arose where they did because

A of advice from their religious leaders about where to settle

B there were so many hunting grounds in North Africa

C the rivers they settled near provided a means of transportation

D of the many renewable resources available nearby

Test-Taking Tip: Think about what these three civilizations had in common (they all settled in river valleys). Why was this geographical feature so important to the development of these societies?

6. The Egyptians made many contributions to other civilizations. Which of the following was NOT developed by the Egyptians?

A papyrus

B a number system based on ten

C medical splints and bandages

D city-states

Test-Taking Tip: Be careful—overlooking the words NOT or EXCEPT is a common error. Look for the answer that does NOT fit. Since the Egyptians *did* develop papyrus (a type of paper made from reeds), answer A is not the correct choice.

Ancient Egypt

7. According to the map above,

F ancient Egypt did not include Thebes

G the New Kingdom of Egypt included the Sahara

H the southern boundary of the Old Kingdom was near the 1st Cataract of the Nile

J Phoenicia was not part of the New Kingdom of Egypt

Test-Taking Tip: Use the map's *legend*, or *key*, to help you understand what the map's symbols represent. Make sure your answer is supported by information *on the map*. Do not rely on your memory.

 STOP

97

4H Culture/Environment

While the Egyptians built pyramids, the Mesopotamians did not; the Mesopotamians developed the 60-minute hour, but nothing is said about how the Egyptians kept time. Therefore, choices F and J can be eliminated. It is unreasonable to think that they taught English to students. Evidence for H can be found on pages 56 and 70.

THE PRINCETON REVIEW **TEST-TAKING TIP**

Remind students that when a question asks for something true of *both* civilizations, any choice that they know does not apply to one or the other can be eliminated.

5D Culture/Environment

Since the origin of villages and cities is tied to the possibility of agriculture, and farming requires irrigation, the best answer is the availability of natural resources such as water.

6D History

Since the Mesopotamians had city-states (according to page 61), they were not invented by the Egyptians.

7H Geography

According to the map, the southern boundary of the Old Kingdom is just south of the first cataract.

Tested Objectives	
Questions	**Reading Objective**
1	Identify supporting ideas
2, 7	Analyze information
3, 4	Identify central issues
5	Draw conclusions
6	Make inferences and generalizations

OVERVIEW

Unit 3 surveys the rise and fall of important kingdoms and empires in the ancient Middle East, Africa, and the Americas to 1500 A.D.

➤ **Chapter 6** describes the Phoenicians and the Hebrews and their interest in trade and religion, and their contributions to later civilizations.

➤ **Chapter 7** discusses the contributions of the Assyrians, Chaldeans, and Persians and examines how their empires were forged and maintained and how their ideas spread.

➤ **Chapter 8** explains the development of civilization in sub-Saharan Africa and the Americas, and how ideas spread through trade and through conquest of these civilizations.

UNIT OBJECTIVES

After reading Unit 3, your students will be able to:

1. give examples of the important cultural and religious contributions of the Phoenicians and the Hebrews.

2. explain how the rise of empires affected the early peoples of the Middle East.

3. characterize the kinds of empires that developed in Africa and the Americas.

UNIT PROJECT

Have students create a monument to one of the kingdoms and civilizations studied in Unit 3. Their goal is to research their civilization and devise and create a monument that represents the people and/or their achievements. Monuments can take any form students choose, such as an object, videotape, or story.

98

Ideas and Armies

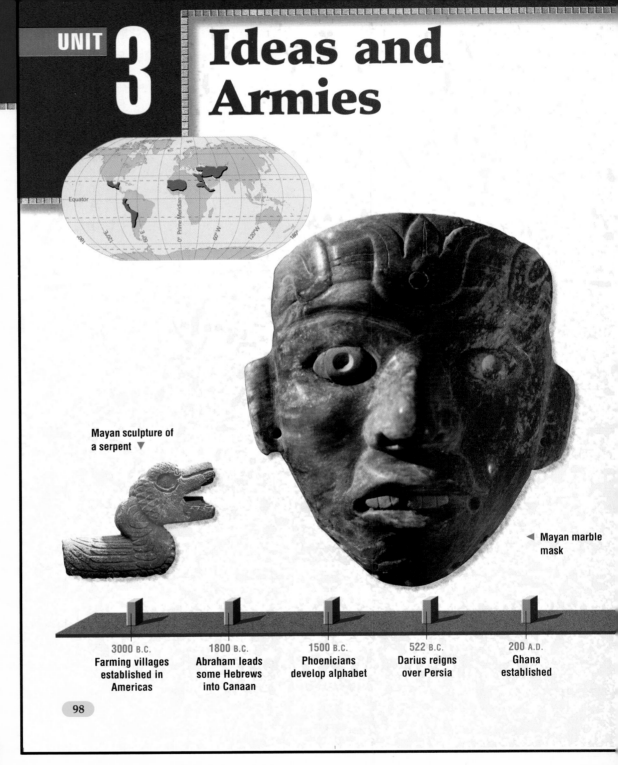

Mayan sculpture of a serpent ▼

◄ Mayan marble mask

3000 B.C.	1800 B.C.	1500 B.C.	522 B.C.	200 A.D.
Farming villages established in Americas	Abraham leads some Hebrews into Canaan	Phoenicians develop alphabet	Darius reigns over Persia	Ghana established

98

ABOUT THE UNIT OPENING

Examining Artifacts

Remind students that historians sometimes have to obtain information and draw conclusions about past civilizations based on artifacts alone. Refer students to the Mayan sculpture and mask on this page. Brainstorm with students what these artifacts tell them about the Maya, a people from Mesoamerica.

Global Chronology

Refer students to the unit time line above. Ask students about what year farming villages were established throughout the Americas. *(3000 B.C.)* Ask students what contribution the Phoenicians made to civilization in 1500 B.C. *(developed the alphabet)*

Multimedia Activity

Surfing the Net
The Maya

The Maya, a group of Native American people, rose to greatness in Central America between 300 and 800 A.D. These extraordinary architects and scientists built a civilization that still astounds the world with its accomplishments and beauty. Many of the ruins uncovered by archaeologists can be visited today. To find out more about these ruins, search the Internet.

Getting There

Follow these steps to gather information on Mayan architecture.
1. Pick a search engine, such as Excite, Lycos, WebCrawler, Yahoo, Infoseek, etc.
2. Type in the main search word *Maya*. Then add words to focus your search. Words might include *architecture, temples, ruins,* or *pyramids.*
3. Explore links that the search engine brings up on the screen. (Links point the way to Web sites on the Internet.)
4. Click on links that provide information on the subject of your research.

Hands-On Activity

Pick one of the ruins that interests you. Then design a postcard showing this site. On the back, write a note to a friend explaining where the ruins are located and why they are special.

PRIMARY SOURCES
Library

See pages 678–679 for a primary source reading to accompany Unit 3.

Journal Notes

What contributions to the modern world were made by civilizations more than 3,000 years ago? Note details about these contributions as you read.

600 A.D.
Mayan civilization reaches its peak

1240 A.D.
Kingdom of Mali established

1438 A.D.
Incan Empire founded

99

Geographic Location

The civilizations discussed in this unit were located in the Middle East; in northeastern, eastern, and western Africa; and in Central America and South America along the Andes Mountains. Have students locate these places in their text Atlas. Then have volunteers locate them on a wall map of the world.

GLENCOE
TECHNOLOGY

Videodisc
Use the MindJogger to preview the unit content.

MindJogger Videoquiz

Unit 3
Disc 1 Side A

Also available in VHS.

INTRODUCING THE UNIT

Refer students to the unit's title, "Ideas and Armies." Point out that many ideas have been transmitted peacefully through trade or forcefully through conquest. Ask students which ideas would probably be accepted more easily into a society. (*Ideas transmitted peacefully through trade.*)

RECORDING JOURNAL NOTES

Have students make a list of recent inventions that 3,000 years from now might be considered important. Call on volunteers to read their lists as you write responses on the chalkboard. Tell students to note in their journal details about the contributions to the modern world made by civilizations more than 3,000 years ago.

PRIMARY SOURCES
Library

Items in the Primary Sources Library for this unit focus on justice in the ancient world. Elements include:
• Oral history about Sundiata Keita, founder of Mali.
• Description of Mansa Musa's court

For additional primary source documents, have students use the **World History Primary Source Document CD-ROM.**

Chapter 6 Planning Guide

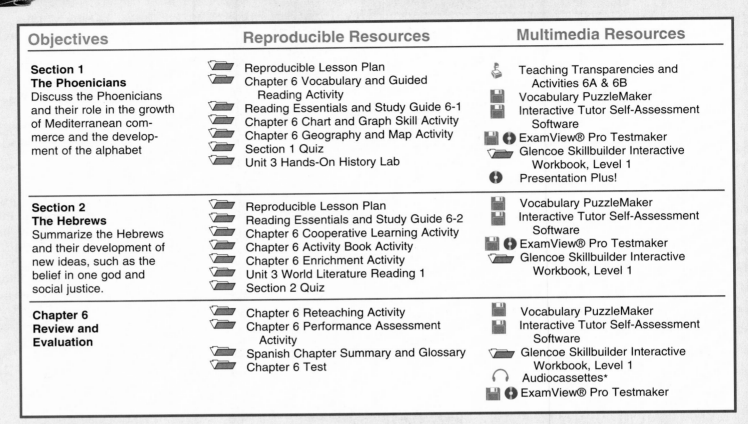

Objectives	Reproducible Resources	Multimedia Resources
Section 1 **The Phoenicians** Discuss the Phoenicians and their role in the growth of Mediterranean commerce and the development of the alphabet	Reproducible Lesson Plan Chapter 6 Vocabulary and Guided Reading Activity Reading Essentials and Study Guide 6-1 Chapter 6 Chart and Graph Skill Activity Chapter 6 Geography and Map Activity Section 1 Quiz Unit 3 Hands-On History Lab	Teaching Transparencies and Activities 6A & 6B Vocabulary PuzzleMaker Interactive Tutor Self-Assessment Software ExamView® Pro Testmaker Glencoe Skillbuilder Interactive Workbook, Level 1 Presentation Plus!
Section 2 **The Hebrews** Summarize the Hebrews and their development of new ideas, such as the belief in one god and social justice.	Reproducible Lesson Plan Reading Essentials and Study Guide 6-2 Chapter 6 Cooperative Learning Activity Chapter 6 Activity Book Activity Chapter 6 Enrichment Activity Unit 3 World Literature Reading 1 Section 2 Quiz	Vocabulary PuzzleMaker Interactive Tutor Self-Assessment Software ExamView® Pro Testmaker Glencoe Skillbuilder Interactive Workbook, Level 1
Chapter 6 **Review and Evaluation**	Chapter 6 Reteaching Activity Chapter 6 Performance Assessment Activity Spanish Chapter Summary and Glossary Chapter 6 Test	Vocabulary PuzzleMaker Interactive Tutor Self-Assessment Software Glencoe Skillbuilder Interactive Workbook, Level 1 Audiocassettes* ExamView® Pro Testmaker

*Also available in Spanish.

Presentation Plus!

Use Glencoe's **Presentation Plus!** multimedia teacher tool to easily present dynamic lessons that visually excite your students. Using Microsoft® PowerPoint, you can customize the presentations to create your own personalized lessons.

Interactive Lesson Planner

Planning has never been easier! Using this CD-ROM, organize your week, month, semester, or year with all the help you need. The **Interactive Lesson Planner** gives you access to all of the blackline masters which accompany *Human Heritage.*

Chapter 6 Planning Guide

✓ PERFORMANCE ASSESSMENT ACTIVITIES

Poster Have students make an illustrated map poster with key, for one civilization studied. Each poster should contain a map that shows the continent where the civilization existed, the cities that were the centers of the civilization, and major geographic features of the area. Map details can be shown visually in any way students choose. Display completed posters.

CHAPTER RESOURCES

LITERATURE ABOUT THE PERIOD

Herrmann, Siegfried. *A History of Israel in Old Testament Times*. Fortress Press, 1975. Focuses on the Old Testament as a history of early Israel, with evidence from sources other than the Bible.

READINGS FOR THE STUDENT

Asimov, Isaac. *The Land of Canaan*. Houghton Mifflin, 1971. Popularly written history of this small area and the different peoples who have occupied it since ancient times.

Chu, Daniel and Eliott Skinner. *A Glorious Age in Africa: The Story of Three Great African Empires*. Africa World, 1990. An illustrated review of the three earliest empires of West Africa.

READINGS FOR THE TEACHER

Davidson, Basil. *A History of West Africa, 1000–1800*. Longman, 1981. An early history of West Africa.

De Lange, N.R.M. *Atlas of the Jewish World*. Phaidon Press, 1984. A history of the Jewish people.

KEY TO ABILITY LEVELS

Teaching strategies have been coded for varying learning styles and abilities.

L1 Level 1 activities are **basic** activities and should be within the ability range of all students.

L2 Level 2 activities are **average** activities and should be within the ability range of the average to above-average student.

L3 Level 3 activities are **challenging** activities designed for the ability range of above-average students.

ELL ELL activities should be within the ability range of English Language Learning students.

NATIONAL GEOGRAPHIC SOCIETY

Teacher's Corner

INDEX TO NATIONAL GEOGRAPHIC MAGAZINE

The following articles relate to this chapter:

- "Beirut Rising," by Peter Theroux, September 1997.
- "The Three Faces of Jerusalem," by Alan Mairson, April 1996.

NATIONAL GEOGRAPHIC SOCIETY PRODUCTS AVAILABLE FROM GLENCOE

To order the following, call Glencoe at 1-800-334-7344:

- *PictureShow: Ancient Civilizations: Egypt and the Fertile Crescent* (CD-ROM)
- *PicturePack: Ancient Civilizations: The Fertile Crescent* (Transparencies)
- *PictureShow: Ancient Civilizations Library* (CD-ROMs)
- *PicturePack: Ancient Civilizations Library, Part II* (Transparencies)

ADDITIONAL NATIONAL GEOGRAPHIC SOCIETY PRODUCTS

To order the following, call National Geographic at 1-800-368-2728:

- *Jerusalem: Within These Walls* (Video or Videodisc)

Access *National Geographic's* new dynamic MapMachine Web site and other geography resources at:
http://www.nationalgeographic.com/
http://www.nationalgeographic.com/maps/

  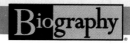

THE HISTORY CHANNEL®   A&E HOME VIDEO®   Biography®

The following videotape program is available from Glencoe:

- **King David**
  1-56501-833-8

To order, call Glencoe at 1-800-334-7344. To find classroom resources to accompany many of these check:

A&E Television: http://www.aetv.com
The History Channel:
http://www.historychannel.com

OVERVIEW

Chapter 6 focuses on the cultures of the Phoenicians and the Hebrews.

➤ **Section 1** discusses the Phoenicians and their role in the growth of Mediterranean commerce and the development of the alphabet.

➤ **Section 2** summarizes the Hebrews and their development of new ideas and the impact of religious beliefs on civilizations.

CHAPTER OBJECTIVES

After reading Chapter 6, students will be able to:

1. explain how trade helped the Phoenicians and the Hebrews build their civilizations.

2. identify the important cultural contributions made by the Phoenicians and the Hebrews.

3. describe the religious beliefs held by the Hebrews.

EXAMINING ARTIFACTS

Ask students what these artifacts tell them about the history of the Hebrews, or Israelites. *(that at some point they were held captive)* Based on the time line, where can students conclude the Hebrews lived? *(Canaan)* Explain that this chapter describes the importance of Canaan to the Hebrews and to the other peoples who lived there.

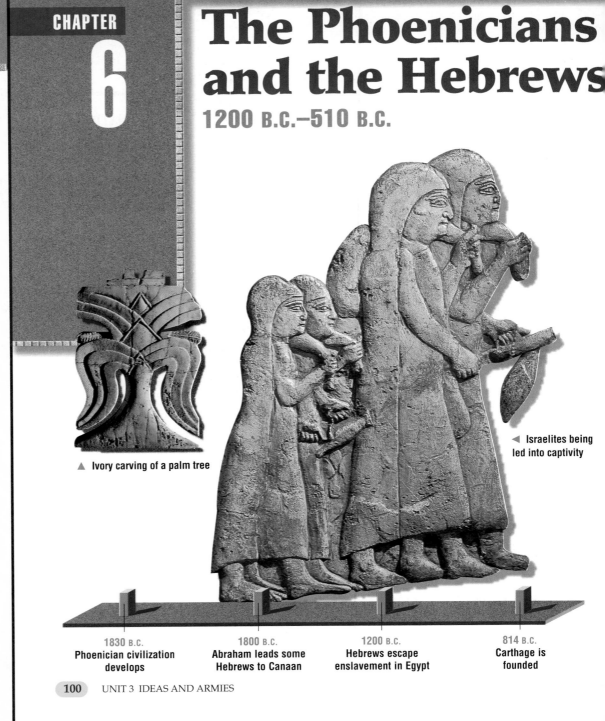

CHAPTER 6

The Phoenicians and the Hebrews

1200 B.C.–510 B.C.

▲ **Ivory carving of a palm tree**

◄ **Israelites being led into captivity**

1830 B.C.	1800 B.C.	1200 B.C.	814 B.C.
Phoenician civilization develops	**Abraham leads some Hebrews to Canaan**	**Hebrews escape enslavement in Egypt**	**Carthage is founded**

100   UNIT 3 IDEAS AND ARMIES

PERFORMANCE ASSESSMENT ✓

Use the Performance Assessment Activities on page 100B to help you evaluate students as they complete the chapter.

TEACHING RESOURCES

TEACHER PLANNING AND SUPPORT

- Reproducible Lesson Plan
- Block Scheduling Implementation Guide
- Videodisc Bar Code Correlation
- Presentation Plus!

REVIEW AND REINFORCEMENT

- Reading Essentials and Study Guide 6-1, 6-2
- Chapter 6 Vocabulary and Guided Reading Activity
- Vocabulary PuzzleMaker Software
- Teaching Transparencies 6A & 6B
- Chapter 6 Reteaching Activity
- Chapter 6 Cooperative Learning Activity

- Chapter 6 Activity Book Activity
- Chapter 6 Chart and Graph Skill Activity
- Interactive Tutor Self-Assessment Software
- Unit 3 MindJogger VideoQuiz

APPLICATION AND HANDS-ON ACTIVITIES

- Daily World History, Geography, and Culture Question
- Unit 3 Hands-On History Lab Activity

GEOGRAPHY ACTIVITIES

- Chapter 6 Geography and Map Activity
- Social Studies Outline Map Resource Book

Chapter Focus

 Read to Discover

- How trade helped the Phoenicians and the Hebrews build their civilizations.
- What important cultural contributions were made by the Phoenicians and the Hebrews.
- What religious beliefs were held by the Hebrews.

Chapter Overview

Visit the *Human Heritage* Web site at **humanheritage.glencoe.com** and click on **Chapter 6—Chapter Overviews** to preview this chapter.

Terms to Learn	People to Know	Places to Locate
treaties	Abraham	Canaan
holy of holies	Moses	Carthage
colonies	Saul	Jerusalem
descendants	David	Israel
social justice	Solomon	Judah
judge		
psalms		
prophets		
sabbath		

Why It's Important   At the eastern end of the Mediterranean Sea lies a piece of land shared today by Lebanon (leb' uh nuhn) and Israel. In ancient times, it was the bridge that connected Egypt and Mesopotamia, and it was known as Canaan (kā' nuhn). Soldiers, shepherds, and merchants who passed through Canaan carried new ideas and goods between Egypt and Mesopotamia.

Two groups—the Phoenicians and the Hebrews—settled in Canaan and formed small kingdoms. Each group was interested in trade and in learning. Through these peaceful activities, they made important contributions to later civilizations.

SECTION 1 The Phoenicians

The Phoenicians lived in the northern part of Canaan. Most of what is known about them comes from the Bible, the writings of other ancient peoples, and the ruins of their cities and ships.

Two different groups formed the Phoenician people. One was the Canaanites (kā' nuh nīts), who came from the desert south and east of Canaan. The Canaanites were herders who wandered from pasture to pasture. The second group was the Philistines (fil' uh stēnz), who came from the eastern Mediterranean near Greece. The Philistines were traders and shipbuilders.

INTERDISCIPLINARY CONNECTIONS

- Unit 3 World Literature Reading 1
- World Music: Cultural Traditions

EXTENSION AND ENRICHMENT

- Chapter 6 Enrichment Activity
- World History Primary Source Document Library CD-ROM
- Foods Around the World

ASSESSMENT AND EVALUATION

- Chapter 6 Performance Assessment Activity
- Chapter 6 Section Quizzes 6-1, 6-2
- Chapter 6 Test
- Chapter 6 ExamView® Pro Testmaker Software
- Chapter 6 Digests Audiocassettes Activities and Tests

SPANISH RESOURCES

- Chapter 6 Spanish Chapter Summary and Glossary
- Chapter 6 Spanish Chapter Digests Audiocassettes Activities and Tests

---

Chapter Overview introduces students to chapter content and key terms. Have them access **Chapter 6 Overview** at **humanheritage.glencoe.com**

FOCUS

 Bellringer

Ask students to solve the following money problem: What combination of 3 coins equals 20 cents if one of the coins is <u>not</u> a dime? *(see Motivational Activity)*

Motivational Activity

Ask students for the answer to the coin problem *(one of the coins is a dime so the correct combination is a dime and two nickels)* and poll how many students had the correct answer. Suggest that these students might have made good Phoenician traders. Explain to students that in this chapter they will learn about the Phoenician civilization who developed an elaborate and successful system of trade.

GUIDE TO READING

Reading Strategy

Ask students to read "Why It's Important" and summarize the chapter's main theme. *(The Phoenicians and Hebrews who settled in Canaan both made important contributions to history.)*

Vocabulary Precheck

Ask students to define each of the "Terms to Learn." Have a volunteer consult the dictionary for any unfamiliar words. **L1** **ELL**

Use the Vocabulary PuzzleMaker for Chapter 6 to create a crossword puzzle. **L1**

Assign Chapter 6 Vocabulary and Guided Reading Activity.

Assign Reading Essentials and Study Guide 6–1.

Guided Practice

L2 **Critical Thinking** Have students identify innovations of the Phoenicians, such as a working alphabet, sea routes plotted by the sun and stars, and signed peace agreements. Have students discuss how the Phoenicians benefited from being innovative.

Linking Across Time

Answers will vary, but students should understand that trade helped spread Middle Eastern culture and new ideas such as the Phoenician alphabet.

MAKING CONNECTIONS

➤➤ **History** Since there was no single power in Mesopotamia between 1200 and 900 B.C., small nations were able to prosper. For this reason, this period of time has been called the "era of small states."

L1 **Bartering** Explain to students that in early civilizations, people traded goods with one another since they did not have money systems. The name for this system is bartering. Divide the class into two "nations." Ask each group to decide on imaginary products to trade, the products' values, and a record keeping system. Then ask the nations to role-play a trade situation between the two groups. Discuss the results. **ELL**

The Growth of Trade   By 1200 B.C., the Phoenicians had built cities and towns along a narrow strip of land between the mountains and the sea. Although the land was rich, there was not enough to grow food for all of the people. For this reason, many Phoenicians turned to the sea to make a living.

The mountains near Phoenicia were covered with cedar forests. These forests provided wood that the Phoenicians used to build strong, fast ships. The Phoenicians started out as coastal traders. In time, they became widely traveled merchant shippers who controlled the trade of the Mediterranean. They exchanged cedar logs, cloth, glass trinkets, and perfume for gold and other metals. Many Phoenician ships were traveling workshops. Sailors who were also artisans carried their tools with them and worked on board the ships.

Phoenician sailors and explorers plotted their courses by the sun and stars. They traveled to places where no one else dared to go. They brought Middle Eastern culture to unexplored areas of the western Mediterranean. Some experts believe the Phoeni-

Linking Across Time

Glass Making   Artisans along the Phoenician coast discovered the art of glassblowing in the 1st century B.C. (below). This revolutionary technique remained in wide use until the late 1800s A.D. and is considered an art form today (right). **What role did Phoenician trade play in spreading new ideas?**

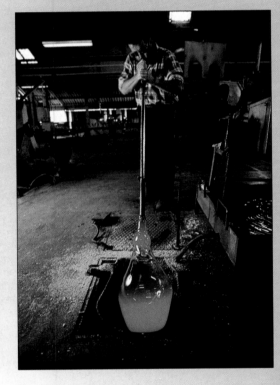

102

COOPERATIVE LEARNING

Have students work in groups to role play a business interaction between a Phoenician merchant and a new island trading partner. Explain that the role play should reveal differences in trading practices and the characters' reactions to these differences. Assign students in each group to one of these roles: Phoenician merchant, Phoenician ship captain, island merchant, island merchant's scribe. Students may add other appropriate characters. Have students research their roles and then work cooperatively with team members to plan the role play. After each team performs, ask the class to comment on its historical accuracy.

cians actually sailed around the west coast of Africa to India. They may even have sailed across the Atlantic Ocean to the Americas 2,000 years before Columbus.

From their business dealings, the Phoenicians learned the value of making agreements. They used the same idea to keep peace with their larger, more powerful neighbors. They signed peace **treaties,** or agreements between states or countries, in which they promised to supply free shipments of goods. In exchange for these shipments, the other countries agreed to guarantee Phoenician independence.

The Cities of Phoenicia   Phoenicia never became a united country. Mountains separated one group of Phoenicians from another. The only contact was through narrow mountain passes or by sea. As a result, Phoenicia remained a collection of independent city-states. The largest of these were Tyre (tīuhr), Byblos (bib' lus), Beirut (bā rūt'), and Sidon (sīd' uhn).

Though the people of all of these city-states spoke the same language and practiced the same religion, they did not always get along. The search for more profit from trade led to jealousy and quarrels among the city-states. The Phoenicians called themselves by the name of their city-states. Only people from other places called them Phoenicians.

At first, each city-state was ruled by a king who also served as high priest. In time, rich merchant families made the kings share their power with councils of merchants. Soon, the councils were telling the kings what to do.

Most Phoenician cities had stone walls around them for protection. Behind these walls stood the family-owned shops of merchants and artisans. Shopkeepers sold their goods outside their shops. Since wood was plentiful, many of the Phoenicians were carpenters and cabinetmakers. They also were very good at metalwork, which they learned from the Egyptians and the Mesopotamians.

Phoenician cities were very crowded. Streets were narrow and buildings were close together. Most buildings were made of stone or brick and had high narrow doors, windows, columns, and tiled roofs. Some houses had roof gardens.

Outside the walls of the city stood the port. It was the center of activity. Ships docked to load and unload goods. Phoenician merchants kept records of shipments of papyrus, gold, and linen from Egypt, pottery from Mesopotamia, and copper and hides from Cyprus (sī' pruhs). Goods were stored in great warehouses until they went to market in Phoenicia or were shipped overseas.

Phoenician cities were also important cloth-dyeing centers. The Phoenicians made an expensive purple dye that was in great demand. In fact, the name "Phoenician" means "of purple merchants." According to legend, a Phoenician god named

Book Names The name *Byblos* comes from a Greek word meaning "book." The Greeks gave the city its name because of the large amount of papyrus it exported. The English word *Bible* comes from the same term. The Bible, however, refers to Byblos by its original name—Gebal, a city inhabited since 7000 B.C.

Reading Check
How did the Phoenicians use **treaties** to keep the peace?

Reading Check Answer
Phoenician **treaties** promised free shipments of goods to countries that guaranteed Phoenician independence.

DID YOU KNOW
The importance of trade in the city-state of Tyre was recorded in the Bible:

Who was like Tyre . . .
In the midst of the sea?
When your waves were unloaded from the seas,
You satisfied many peoples;
With your great wealth and merchandise
You enriched the kings of the earth.
—Ezekiel 27:32-33

GEOGRAPHY AND HISTORY
Have students locate the present-day Lebanese cities of Tyre, Byblos, Beirut, and Sidon on a map of the Middle East.

NATIONAL GEOGRAPHIC SOCIETY

Use these materials to enrich student understanding of Phoenician culture.

NGS PICTURESHOW CD-ROM
Egypt and the Fertile Crescent

MEETING SPECIAL NEEDS

Instruct students who are visual learners to make drawings of a typical Phoenician market or ship. Have students use the descriptions in the textbook and other books for reference. Display the drawings in the classroom.

📖 Refer to *Inclusion for the Middle School Social Studies Classroom: Strategies and Activities* for additional resources.

L2 **Science** Ask students why they think the Phoenicians believed in many gods that were closely tied to nature. What characteristics of the different forces of nature makes this seem logical? **ELL**

Reading Check Answer
The **holy of holies** was the most sacred chamber in the temple. It was where Phoenicians kept the image or sacred stone of their god.

PHOENICIAN TOMB   The Phoenicians offered human sacrifices to please their gods. Inside this underground burial chamber at Carthage are clay urns that hold the ashes of victims who were sacrificed. **Why were human rather than animal sacrifices made to the Phoenician gods?**

Melqart (mel' kart) was walking along the seashore with his girlfriend Tyrus (tī' rus) and a dog. When the dog picked up a shellfish called *murex* (myuhr' eks) and bit into it, the dog's mouth turned purple. Tyrus liked the color so much that she said she would not marry Melqart unless he gave her a gown of that color. Melqart gave her the gown and started the dye-making trade in Phoenicia.

Gods and Goddesses   The Phoenicians believed in many gods who were closely tied to nature. Since they thought the gods met people only on hills and under trees, they worshiped only in these places at first. Later, they built temples. Each had an entrance hall, a main hall, and a **holy of holies,** or most sacred chamber, where the image or sacred stone of the god was kept. Sacrifices of wine, perfume, animals, and humans were made on a nearby stone altar. Only priests could offer these sacrifices. It was thought that this strengthened the power of the gods and kept them friendly toward people.

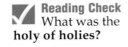

Reading Check
What was the **holy of holies?**

The Phoenicians believed in a life after death. At first, they buried their dead in clay *urns* (ernz), or ornamental vases. Later, influenced by Egyptian customs, they embalmed the bodies, wrapped them in linen, and placed them in stone coffins in hillside cemeteries.

104   UNIT 3 IDEAS AND ARMIES

EXTENDING THE CONTENT

The murex is a small edible sea snail common in the eastern Mediterranean. Its famous purple dye comes from a liquid produced by a small gland. Each snail produces only a few drops, which at one time were boiled down and concentrated to create a dye. One pound of dye required about 60,000 snails. Even today, huge mounds of shells can be seen piled near the ruins of ancient dye works.

Because of the smell from the snail shells, the dye "factories" were located some distances outside of town, downwind.

Carthage Some Phoenician sailors and traders set up trading posts along the coast of North Africa. Other Phoenicians built **colonies,** or permanent settlements, in these areas. These colonies soon turned into cities.

The most famous of these cities was Carthage (kar' thij), founded in 814 B.C. in present-day Tunisia (tū nē' zhē uh). Legend states the city was founded by a Phoenician princess named Dido (dī' dō). At first Dido ruled the city of Tyre. Her brother, however, thought that he should rule Tyre. So, he killed Dido's husband and overthrew Dido. She fled to North Africa where she and her followers built Carthage.

Carthage soon became a Mediterranean power. It was a great trading city. Ships from Carthage may have traveled to the British Isles in search of tin, a metal highly valued by merchants.

The Alphabet Through trade, the Phoenicians spread ideas as well as goods. Their most important gift was the idea of an alphabet. The Phoenicians did not invent the alphabet. They did, however, pass it on to other cultures.

At first, the Phoenicians used a system of picture writing. However, it was difficult to keep trade records this way. So, they looked for an easier writing system. They borrowed a simple version of Egyptian hieroglyphs from the people of the Canaanite towns that lay to the south. By the time the Canaanite system of writing reached Phoenicia, it had become an alphabet.

✔ **Reading Check**
Where did the Phoenicians build **colonies?**

HISTORY *Online*
Student Web Activity
Visit the *Human Heritage* Web site at **humanheritage.glencoe.com** and click on **Chapter 6— Student Web Activities** to find out more about Phoenician accomplishments.

ALPHABETS This chart shows how different alphabets developed from the Phoenician alphabet. The characters of the alphabets closely resemble each other. **On whose system of writing did the Phoenicians base their alphabet?**

Modern Characters	Ancient Phoenician	Ancient Hebrew	Ancient Greek	Early Roman	Greek Names
A	⨉ ⨶	✗	◁ A A	∏ ∧ A	Alpha
B	⅁ 9	५ ९	﹚ Ɛ	ß B	Beta
G	٦ ٦	٦٦	⟨ ⌐ ٦٦	C G	Gamma
D	△ ٩	٩△	△ ◁ △	△ D	Delta
E	ⱻ	ⱻ	ⱻ Ƒ Є	E	Epsilon
F	٦	⅄	₣₣⌐	F	Digamma
Z	Z	—	⎰	Z	Zeta
HE	ⴼ	E	⊟ H	H	Eta
TH	⊙	—	⊙	—	Theta
I	⌒ ⌒	⅂	⎰⎰	I	Iota

✔ **Reading Check Answer**
The Phoenicians built **colonies** along the coast of North Africa.

L3 **Mathematics** Have students locate the present-day Tunisian city of Carthage on a map of Africa. Point out that Carthage was once a colony of Phoenicia. Have students calculate the approximate distance between Carthage and Phoenicia and show the route that Phoenicians might have taken to travel from one to the other.

CAPTION ANSWER
the Canaanites to the south

HISTORY *Online*
Student Web Activity objectives, goals, and answers can be found at the **Chapter 6 Web Activity Lesson Plan** at humanheritage.glencoe.com

---

MEETING SPECIAL NEEDS

Have interested students use the alphabet chart on this page to write the following words using each alphabet shown: *bed, bad, fade, death.* Then have them choose their own word to write using one of the alphabets. Have students exchange and decipher each other's new words.

📁 Refer to *Inclusion for the Middle School Social Studies Classroom: Strategies and Activities* for additional resources.

➤➤ **Language** The Phoenician alphabet had 22 letters, all consonants, that were written from left to right. The Phoenicians gave each letter a name. The first letter was the picture of an ox, or *aleph*. The second letter was the picture of a house, or *beth*.

💾 Use **Interactive Tutor Self-Assessment Software** to review Section 1.

L2 **Culture** Remind students that the way of life of a group of people is referred to as its culture. Divide the class into two groups. Assign one group the Phoenicians and the other group the Hebrews. Direct each group to create a chart to show examples of the following information about their assigned culture group: beliefs, language, the arts, buildings, clothing, and law. Encourage students to use the textbook and other reference books. After the groups have completed their charts, create a master chart on the chalkboard. Discuss how the cultural contributions of the Phoenicians and the Hebrews may have influenced students' lives.

💾 Use the **Vocabulary Puzzle-Maker** to create crossword and word search puzzles.

The Canaanite system of writing had 22 symbols, or letters, from which any number of words could be formed. Since it was easy to use, the Canaanite system provided the writing system Phoenician traders needed for keeping records.

The Phoenicians made the Canaanite alphabet their own. They carried it to Europe, where the Greeks borrowed it and made a few changes. Later, the Romans borrowed it from the Greeks. Most western alphabets, including the English, are based on the Roman alphabet.

Section 1 Assessment

1. **Define:** treaties, holy of holies, colonies.
2. Why did the Phoenicians turn to trade to make a living?
3. How did the Phoenicians view their gods?

Critical Thinking
4. **Making Generalizations** Why is the alphabet a major contribution to civilization?

Graphic Organizer Activity
5. Draw a diagram like this one, and use it to show the causes and effects of the rise of Phoenician trade.

Causes → Rise of Phoenician Trade → Effects

SECTION 2 The Hebrews

Like the Phoenicians, the Hebrews, or Israelites, were a small group among the peoples of the ancient Middle East. Because of their religion, however, they have had a great influence on the world's civilizations. Their religion still exists today. It is called Judaism (jū' dē iz uhm).

Most early Hebrews were *nomadic* (nō mad' ik), or wandering, herders; some were traveling merchants. Leading long trains of donkeys loaded with goods, these merchants walked from one trading post to the next. The Hebrews followed a route that started from the city of Ur on the Euphrates River. There, Hebrew artisans made goods from gold, copper, and ivory. Hebrew merchants then stuffed the goods into bags, loaded them on donkeys, and started up the valley of the Tigris and Euphrates. At Harran (hah rahn'), a city near the Turkish mountains, they exchanged their goods for silver. Sometimes, merchants continued west and then south along the Mediterranean coast to trade with Egyptian, Phoenician, and Cretan (krēt' uhn) merchants.

Israelite Ivory Box

Section 1 Assessment Answers

1. treaties, agreements between states or countries (p. 103); holy of holies, most sacred chamber (p. 104); colonies, permanent settlements (p. 105)
2. because there was not enough land to grow food
3. as closely tied to nature
4. Answers will vary but should include that the spread of an alphabet provided an easy-to-use writing system. This increased trade because records could be kept, which increased contact with other civilizations.

5. Sample causes: location along the sea, scarcity of land to grow food, forests to build ships; Sample effects: control of Mediterranean trade, traveling workshops, exploration of uncharted areas, spread of Middle Eastern culture, use of treaties to keep peace

Assign Chapter 6 **Section 1 Quiz** in the TCR. Testmaker available.

ABRAHAM   Abraham taught the Hebrews to worship Yahweh. Here, Abraham is shown leading the Hebrews on their journey from Ur to Canaan. **Why did the Hebrews eventually leave Canaan?**

CAPTION ANSWER
A drought came, and they went to Egypt to get food.

DID YOU KNOW ???

In many cases, Hebrew words are written without vowels. The Israelites wrote YHVH as the name of God. Because later Israelites chose not to speak the name of God, the identity of the vowels and the correct pronunciation of the name is uncertain.

The God of Abraham   The story of the Hebrews and their god is written in the Bible. It states that Yahweh (yah′ wā), or God, made an agreement with Abraham. Abraham and his followers were to leave Ur and go to Canaan. There, they were to worship and obey Yahweh as the one true god. In exchange, Yahweh promised that they and their **descendants,** or offspring such as children, grandchildren, great-grandchildren, and so on, could always live in Canaan.

During ancient times, most people believed in many gods. These gods behaved like humans but were more powerful. The Hebrews, however, believed that Yahweh was different from humans. He did not get hungry or thirsty, marry, or have children. According to the Hebrews, Yahweh did only what was just and right, even though He was powerful and could do whatever He wanted.

Abraham and members of his household settled in Canaan around 1800 B.C. In Canaan, they raised flocks of sheep and grew wheat, figs, and olives. Abraham's grandson, Jacob, had 12 sons. Each son led a separate family group. These Hebrew groups later formed 12 Hebrew tribes. The Hebrews stayed in Canaan for about 100 years. Then, a drought came, and they went to Egypt where they could get food.

Reading Check
What did the agreement with Yahweh promise the **descendants** of Abraham's followers?

Reading Check Answer
The agreement with Yahweh promised that **descendants** of Abraham could always live in Canaan.

GEOGRAPHY AND HISTORY
By 3000 B.C. the Sumerians had established 12 city-states in the Tigris-Euphrates river valley, including Ur, Uruk, and Eridu. The Fertile Crescent, as the area is often called because of its relatively rich topsoil and its curved shape, was able to support city-state populations ranging from 20,000 to 250,000.

MULTICULTURAL PERSPECTIVES

According to the Book of Genesis 22:17-18 (RSV), God made the following promise to Abraham and his descendants if they would worship and obey him:
I will indeed bless you, and I will multiply your descendants as the stars of heaven and as the sand which is on the seashore. And your descendants shall possess the gate of their enemies, and by your descendants shall all the nations of the earth bless themselves, because you have obeyed my voice.

MAP SKILLS

TEACH

Reading a Map Scale

Instruct the students to read the map on page 108 to answer the following questions:

From north to south, how long is the Phoenician kingdom? *(approximately 175 miles, or 281 km)*

What is the distance from Tyre to Jerusalem? *(approximately 100 miles, or 161 km)*

Have students use the map of the Middle East and its map scale in the text Atlas to find the distances between five different places shown on the map. Ask volunteers to relate the distances.

Assign Chapter 6 **Geography and Map Activity** in the TCR.

Answers to Map Practice

1. approximately 60 miles, (96 km)

2. approximately 50 miles, (80 km)

3. approximately 150 miles, (241 km)

Reading A Map Scale

Maps provide many kinds of information. One thing maps can show is distance, or how far one point on a map is from another. To do this, most maps have scale.

A map scale shows the relationship between the distances on the map and the actual distances on Earth. The length of a scale represents a certain number of miles or kilometers on Earth. Using this scale, it is possible to figure actual distances between any two points on this map.

For example, to figure the distance between the cities of Beirut and Tyre, use a ruler to measure how far apart they are. Now, compare this length with the map scale. Since Beirut and Tyre are about one-half inch, or 1.3 centimeters, apart on the map, the actual distance between them on Earth is about 50 miles, or 80 kilometers.

Map Practice

1. **What is the distance between Sidon and Damascus?**
2. **From north to south, how long is the Dead Sea?**
3. **How far is it from Jerusalem to Beirut?**

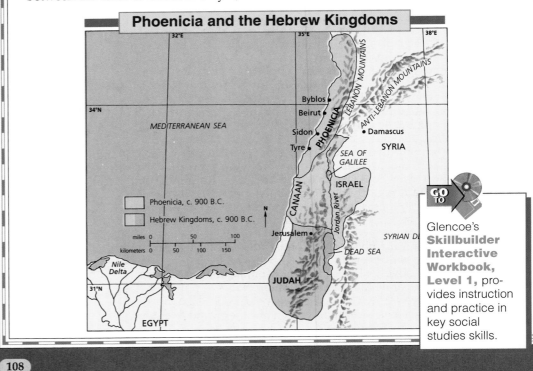

Phoenicia and the Hebrew Kingdoms

Glencoe's **Skillbuilder Interactive Workbook, Level 1,** provides instruction and practice in key social studies skills.

SPOTLIGHT ON: HEBREW KINGDOMS

According to the Old Testament, Moses led the Hebrew people to Palestine, the land of "milk and honey," but died before entering the area himself. Scripture states he was actually forbidden to enter Palestine as punishment because he had doubted God's word.

MOSES According to the Bible, Yahweh allowed Moses and the Hebrews to pass through the Red Sea. The waters then closed again, drowning the pharaoh and his army. **What important set of laws did God give Moses on Mount Sinai?**

GEOGRAPHY AND HISTORY

Explain to the students that present-day Jews commemorate the Exodus from Egypt and rededicate themselves to freedom each year during an eight-day celebration called Passover. Ask volunteers to research and trace the Hebrew's Exodus on a map of the Middle East for the rest of the class.

Independent Practice

L3 Critical Thinking Ask students to respond to the following: Many people accept the Bible as a collection of sacred writings. How might it also be a historical document?

Moses and the Ten Commandments After the Hebrews settled in Egypt, they were enslaved. About 600 years later, Moses, the Hebrew leader at the time, appeared before the pharaoh and told him to end Hebrew enslavement and let the Hebrews leave Egypt. The pharaoh at first refused but later agreed. Moses then led the Hebrews out of Egypt. The pharaoh again changed his mind and led his army in pursuit. According to the Bible, Yahweh parted the Red Sea to allow the Hebrews to cross and they escaped into the Sinai (sī' nī) Desert. They called their escape the *Exodus* (ek' suh duhs).

Life in the desert was hard, but Moses told the Hebrews not to give up. Moses led them to Mount Sinai. There, he climbed to the top of the mountain to receive a message from God. The Bible states that Yahweh told Moses that He would protect the Hebrews and lead them back to Canaan. In return, they were to renew the *covenant* (kuv' uh nuhnt), or agreement, with Him. They were to promise to obey certain laws, the most important of which became the Ten Commandments.

The Ten Commandments stated that the Hebrews were to give their loyalty only to Yahweh. They were not to worship other gods or idols (ī' dls). The Ten Commandments also taught that it was wrong to lie, steal, or murder, and that people should honor their parents and respect other people's property.

The Hebrews believed God was just, and they too should be just. They used laws to influence the way people behaved. Their

Ramses II No one knows for sure, but many scholars believe that Ramses II was the pharaoh who tried to stop the flight of Moses and the Hebrews out of Egypt. Ramses ruled Egypt for nearly 70 years and outlived a dozen of his sons.

CHAPTER 6 THE PHOENICIANS AND THE HEBREWS **109**

EXTENDING THE CONTENT

According to Exodus 20:2-14, in one version of the Bible, the Ten Commandments are:

You shall have no other gods beside me.

You shall not make for yourself a sculptured image. . . .

You shall not swear falsely by the name of the Lord your God. . . .

Remember the sabbath day and keep it holy. . . .

Honor your father and your mother. . . .

You shall not murder.

You shall not commit adultery.

You shall not steal.

You shall not bear false witness against your neighbor.

You shall not covet . . . anything that is your neighbor's.

▼ **Reading Check**
What does **social justice** mean?

People in History

Moses
c. 1400 B.C.–1300 B.C

Hebrew Prophet
During the Hebrew enslavement, the pharoah ordered the death of all Hebrew male infants. To save her son, Moses' mother put him in a papyrus basket and floated him down the Nile. Pharoah's daughter rescued the baby and raised him as her own. Moses later fled Egypt and worked as a shepherd until about age 80, when according to the Bible, Yahweh instructed him to free his people.

laws affected not only individuals but the whole community. The Hebrews believed in **social justice.** Everyone had a right to be treated fairly.

The Promised Land   Moses died shortly before the Hebrews reached Canaan. The Hebrews were afraid that without a strong leader they would not be able to enter Canaan. The people who already lived there had built many walled cities on hilltops. Soldiers in lookout towers guarded the cities against enemy attack. However, Joshua, a new leader and a good general, brought the Hebrews safely into the promised land.

Once they had settled in Canaan, the Hebrews became farmers and shepherds. They copied the Canaanites' tools and borrowed their alphabet. Canaan was rocky and dry. There was little water. So, during the two months of the rainy season, farmers collected and stored water in small caves or underground basins. During the dry season, they used what they had stored to irrigate their crops of olives, flax, barley, wheat, and grapes.

Most Hebrews lived in one-room houses. The room was divided in two, with one section slightly higher than the other. During the day, people cooked and did other household chores in the lower level. At night, donkeys and goats bedded down there, while the family slept on the upper level. The walls of the houses

HARVEST IN ANCIENT ISRAEL   Hebrew writers called Canaan "a land flowing with milk and honey." This area, however, had a dry climate and little water. The Hebrews had to work hard to farm the land. Hebrew farmers and their workers gathering the harvest are shown in this painting. **What crops did the Hebrews grow in Canaan?**

COOPERATIVE LEARNING

Organize the class into small groups. Suggest to each group that they are members of a school (or city) "commandment committee." It is their task to write a list of commandments to guide school behavior that they think will cover all necessary considerations and possibilities. Encourage groups to list commandments by priority.

Regroup the students and allow each group to share their commandments and poll their consensus.

🗂 Assign Chapter 6 *Cooperative Learning Activity* in the TCR.

Making Comparisons

Suppose you want to buy a portable compact disc (CD) player, and you must choose among three models. You would probably compare characteristics of the three models, such as price, sound quality, and size to figure out which model is best for you. In the study of world history, you often compare people from different cultures or regions. You might also compare people and events from one time period with those from a different time period.

Learning the Skill When making comparisons, you examine two or more groups, situations, events, or documents. Then you identify any similarities and differences. For example, the chart on this page compares the characteristics of two ancient civilizations.

When making comparisons, you first decide what items will be compared and determine which characteristics you will use to compare them. Then you identify similarities and differences in these characteristics.

PHOENICIAN AND HEBREW CIVILIZATIONS

CULTURAL CHARACTERISTIC	PHOENICIANS	HEBREWS
Homeland	Canaan	Canaan
Political organization	city-states	12 tribes
Method of rule	kings/merchant councils	kings/council of elders
Main occupations	artisans, merchants, shippers	herders, farmers, traders
Religion	belief in many gods closely tied to nature	belief in one all-powerful god
Main contribution	spread of an alphabet	idea of a single, just god

Skill Practice

Analyze the information on the chart on this page. Then answer these questions.

1. What items are being compared?
2. What characteristics are being used to compare them?
3. In what ways were the Phoenicians and the Hebrews similar?
4. In what ways were the two groups different?
5. Suppose you wanted to compare the Phoenician and Hebrew religions in more detail. What are some of the characteristics you might compare?

Glencoe's **Skillbuilder Interactive Workbook, Level 1,** provides instruction and practice in key social studies skills.

111

TEAM TEACHING STRATEGIES

Language Arts Invite the language arts teacher to explain the use of a Venn diagram in making comparisons. Then organize the class into groups, and have each group use a Venn diagram to compare the lives of David and Solomon. In an information-sharing session, compile a master diagram on the chalkboard. Ask students to note similarities and differences between the lives of these two leaders.

Next, instruct students to use the Venn diagram to create two "People in History" features like the one on page 110. Have them research missing information, such as estimated dates of birth and death, as well as other interesting details about David and Solomon. Also encourage students to illustrate their features, either with a photocopy of a painting or their own drawing.

TEACH

Making Comparisons

Introduce this lesson by writing the words "cat" and "dog" on the chalkboard. Ask students to name ways these two animals are alike. (*Both are mammals. They each have four legs, are covered with fur, are meat-eating predators, and so on.*) Then have students identify differences. (*Cats meow, dogs bark. Cats can climb trees, most dogs cannot. Cats belong to the feline family, dogs belong to the canine family.*)

Point out to students that they have just practiced the skill of making comparisons. Explain that comparing means looking for similarities and differences. Brainstorm some of the things that historians might compare. (*nations, regions, leaders, important events, cultures, etc.*) Then assign the skills lesson and accompanying questions.

Answers to Skill Practice

1. Phoenicians and Hebrews
2. items under "Cultural Characteristics"
3. Similarities might include: both lived in Canaan, both had kings, both traded.
4. Phoenicians were organized into city-states, the Hebrews into tribes. Phoenician occupations centered around trade, while many Hebrews worked as farmers and herders. The Phoenicians had many gods, the Hebrews had one. The Phoenicians contributed the alphabet, the Hebrews contributed the idea of one just god.
5. Sample response: number of gods, characteristics of the gods/god, worship practices, attitudes toward death, etc.

111

Reading Check Answer
A Hebrew **judge** settled disputes and led troops into battle.

Reading Check Answer
David wrote many of the **psalms** in the Bible.

Reading Check Answer
The **prophets** were persons claiming to have received messages from God. They criticized the way many Hebrews were living and reminded them of their duty to God and to one another.

Biography

The following videotape program is available from Glencoe to enrich chapter 6:

• **King David**

To find classroom resources to accompany these videos, check the following home page:

A&E Television:
http://www.aetv.com

were made of mud-brick or stone plastered with mud and white-washed. Floors were made of beaten clay. Wooden beams supported a flat, thatched roof, which was covered with clay.

Kings After Joshua died the 12 Hebrew tribes split apart. Each tribe was led by a council of elders. In times of crisis, a temporary leader called a **judge** settled disputes and led troops into battle.

In time, the Hebrews decided they needed a king to unite them. A warrior-farmer named Saul became their first king. He ruled well for several years. Toward the end of his reign, however, he lost the people's support. When Saul died in battle, David became the new king.

David reunited the Hebrews and defeated the Canaanites. He captured a Canaanite fortress and on that site established Jerusalem (juh rū′ suh luhm), the capital of the Hebrew kingdom. A fine musician, David wrote many of the **psalms** (sahms), or sacred songs, found in the Bible.

After David died, his son Solomon (sahl′ uh muhn) became king. Through trade and treaties with other lands, Solomon brought peace and made the Hebrew kingdom more powerful. He built a huge temple in Jerusalem out of limestone, cedar wood, and gold. It was designed and built by artisans from Phoenicia.

Solomon's wealth and wisdom became known all through the Middle East. Many Hebrews, however, were not happy with Solomon. They did not like working on his building projects or paying the high taxes he demanded. After Solomon died, the Hebrews in the northern part of the country set up their own separate kingdom called Israel. A southern kingdom, which was ruled from Jerusalem, became known as Judah. For nearly 200 years, the two kingdoms fought each other off and on. Gradually, both became weak enough for others to conquer.

The Prophets **Prophets,** or persons claiming to have messages from God, appeared in the Hebrew kingdoms. They came from cities and villages. They were teachers, farmers, and shepherds. They criticized the way the Hebrews were living. The rich were mistreating the poor, and government officials were accepting bribes. The prophets reminded the Hebrews of their duty to God and to one another. They warned the Hebrews that Yahweh would punish them if they did not return to His ways.

Some prophets added a new meaning to the laws of Moses. They taught that Yahweh was the god not only of Hebrews, but of everyone.

The people refused to listen to the prophets' warnings. Then, it was too late. Powerful neighbors took over the Hebrew kingdoms. After 722 B.C., the Israelites, the people of the northern kingdom, disappeared. Although the Judeans survived, most were forced to move to Babylonia in 586 B.C.

Reading Check
What was the role of a Hebrew **judge**?

Reading Check
Who wrote many of the **psalms** found in the Bible?

Reading Check
Who were the **prophets**, and what message did they deliver?

EXTENDING THE CONTENT

Solomon's Temple, though destroyed more than 2,500 years ago, is one of the best-known buildings of ancient times. From the description given in the First Book of Kings, we know even the names of artisans who worked on it. The temple had three rooms in a row, all 33 feet (11 m) wide; the outer porch, 16 feet (5 m) wide; the central hall or holy place, 66 feet (21 m) long; and steps leading up to the square inner chamber, or holy of holies, which was kept totally dark. The Ark of the Covenant was in the center of the holy of holies.

While in Babylonia, the Judeans, or Jews, made changes in their religion. Having lost the great temple at Jerusalem, they had to find some other way to worship God. They began meeting in small groups on the **sabbath,** or day of rest. The groups would pray and talk about their religion and history. The Jews wrote down their laws, sayings, and stories of the past on scrolls. The study of these writings led the Jews to value learning, and their teachers became important leaders.

Reading Check
What did Jews do on the **sabbath**?

The Jews spent 70 years in Babylonia before they were allowed to return to their homeland. They rebuilt Jerusalem and the temple. Under a scribe named Ezra, they wrote down the laws of Moses in five books called the *Torah* (tor' uh). Other writings were added later to make the Old Testament of the Bible.

HEBREW PROPHETS

Name	Teachings
Elijah c. 850 B.C.	Everyone should behave in a moral way.
Amos c. 755 B.C.	Prayers and sacrifices do not make up for bad deeds.
	Behaving justly is much more important than ritual.
Hosea 745-730 B.C.	God is a god of love and compassion who loves His people the way a father loves his children.
	God suffers when people turn from Him and do not follow His commandments.
Isaiah of Jerusalem 740-701 B.C.	People can have peace and prosperity only if they carry out God's will.
	The future depends on how justly one behaves in the present.
Micah 714-700 B.C.	Both rich and poor have to obey God's laws.
	It is important to "do justly, love mercy, and walk humbly with thy God."
Jeremiah 626-587 B.C.	Suffering is the result of wickedness.
	God will make a new covenant with the Jews in the future.
Ezekiel 593-571 B.C.	People are responsible for their own behavior.
Isaiah of Babylon c. 545 B.C.	God is the god of all people.
	God will free Israel and lead it back to the promised land

Reading Check Answer
The Jews met in small groups on the **sabbath** to pray and talk about religion.

L1 **Critical Thinking** Direct students to choose one of the teachings by a Hebrew prophet on the chart on page 113. Then have them explain the teaching in their own words.

ASSESS

Check for Understanding

Ask students to summarize the main points of the chapter, orally or in writing. Discuss the answers to the Section and Chapter Assessment questions.

Evaluate

Assign Chapter 6 **Performance Assessment Activity** in the TCR.

Administer **Chapter 6 Test** in the TCR. Testmaker available.

MEETING SPECIAL NEEDS

Discuss with students who are auditory learners what questions they would ask a rabbi about Judaism, if they had the opportunity. Ask a volunteer to record the questions.

If possible, arrange for a rabbi or religious resource person to speak to students, answering their questions in person. If a personal visit is not possible, ask the speaker to record the answers to the questions on tape. Play the recording for students.

Refer to *Inclusion for the Middle School Social Studies Classroom: Strategies and Activities* for additional resources.

Reteach

Have students work in groups to outline different subsections. Then have groups exchange their outlines and use them to quiz other members of their group.

Assign Chapter 6 **Reteaching Activity** in the TCR.

Enrich

Suggest students compare a psalm from the Book of Psalms to the lyrics of a modern song they know that also has a theme or message. Which is more understandable?

Assign Chapter 6 **Enrichment Activity** in the TCR.

CLOSE

Ask students to list places where people have historically practiced their religion, such as temples and churches. Then have them describe how Jews changed their rituals when they no longer had the Jerusalem Temple.

💾 Use **Interactive Tutor Self-Assessment Software** to review Section 2.

Self-Check Quiz gives students an interactive chapter tutorial. Have them access **Chapter 6 Quiz** at **humanheritage.glencoe.com**

Major Contributions The Hebrews were the first people to believe in one god. At first, they believed God was concerned only about them. They expected other people to worship many gods. Later, some prophets said God cared about all peoples and all nations.

The Hebrews were the first to believe in a just god. They believed individuals and society should likewise be just. Their laws were designed to teach people to treat one another fairly.

Section 2 Assessment

1. **Define:** descendants, social justice, judge, psalms, prophets, sabbath.
2. Where did the Hebrews trade? What goods did they trade?
3. What new ideas did the Hebrews develop and contribute to later civilizations?

Critical Thinking

4. **Demonstrating Reasoned Judgment** How was the Hebrew belief in one god important to civilization?

Graphic Organizer Activity

5. Draw a diagram like this one, and use it to show milestones in the history of the Hebrews. (Add boxes as needed.)

Chapter Summary & Study Guide

1. Phoenician civilization began to develop about 1830 B.C.
2. Phoenicians earned a living from the sea and from trade items such as cedar and purple dye.
3. One of the most important Phoenician contributions was the spread of an alphabet.
4. The Phoenicians set up colonies along the North African coast, including Carthage, founded in 814 B.C.
5. According to the Bible, God made an agreement with Abraham whereby the Hebrews could always live in Canaan if they would worship Him alone.
6. About 1200 B.C., the Hebrews escaped Egyptian bondage and, under Moses' leadership, made a new covenant with God, promising to obey the Ten Commandments.
7. An important Hebrew contribution was the belief in a single just god and a just society.

Self-Check Quiz

Visit the *Human Heritage* Web site at **humanheritage. glencoe.com** and click on *Chapter 6—Self-Check Quiz* to assess your understanding of this chapter.

Section 2 Assessment Answers

1. descendants, offspring (p. 107); social justice, equal treatment (p. 110); judge, settled disputes (p. 112); psalms, sacred songs (p. 112); prophets, had messages from God (p. 112); sabbath, day of rest (p. 113)
2. from Ur to Harran and along the Mediterranean coast; gold, copper, and ivory goods
3. the belief in a single god and a just society

4. Answers will vary.
5. Milestones will vary, but should reflect the chronological order of events in this section, starting with Yahweh's agreement with Abraham.

Assign Chapter 6 **Section 2 Quiz** in the TCR. Testmaker available.

Assessment

Using Key Terms

Imagine that you are a traveler to Canaan. Use the following words to write a letter home explaining the new ideas that you have learned about during your visit.

treaties   holy of holies   colonies
descendants   social justice   judge
psalms   prophets   sabbath

Understanding Main Ideas

1. Why were the Phoenicians successful long-distance sailors?
2. What were some of the features of a Phoenician city-state?
3. According to the Bible, what agreement did Yahweh make with Abraham?
4. Why did the Hebrews believe in social justice?
5. Why did the Hebrews make changes in their religion while living in Babylonia?

Critical Thinking

1. How can people who have very limited natural resources still manage to earn a living?
2. Why were language and religion by themselves not enough to unify the Phoenician people?
3. How does the idea that God is just affect the way people behave?
4. Explain the phrase, "Do justly, love mercy, and walk humbly with thy God."
5. Why do you think many people during this time believed that people should listen to prophets?

Graphic Organizer Activity

Culture Create a diagram like this one, and use it to compare Phoenician and Hebrew religious beliefs and practices.

Geography in History

Place The Hebrews moved from place to place within the same region along the Mediterranean Sea. Choose one of their migrations and describe the geography and features of the land through which they passed. Then make a map showing the route and the geographic features of their migration.

Using Your Journal

Review any details you may have noted about the contributions of the Phoenicians and the Hebrews. Write a paragraph explaining how these contributions have affected your life.

Assessment Answers

Using Key Terms

Letters will vary but should include that these are new ideas they have learned in Canaan.

Understanding Main Ideas

1. because of strong, fast ships, and plotted courses
2. Most were crowded, had stone walls around them for protection, with shops behind. The port lay outside the walls.
3. that if Abraham and his followers were to go to Canaan and obey Yahweh they could always live there
4. because they should be like God who was just
5. because they had lost the great temple at Jerusalem

Critical Thinking

1. Answers will vary but should include through trade.
2. because mountains separated groups of Phoenicians
3. Answers will vary but should include that if people believe God is just, they will behave justly.
4. Answers will vary but should include that justice should be tempered with love and mercy.
5. Answers will vary but could refer to the power the prophets had to incite the people.

Graphic Organizer Activity

Sample responses: both—worshiped in temples; Phoenicians—believed in many gods closely tied to nature, embalmed bodies, believed in life after death, practiced sacrifice; Hebrews—believed in one just god, worshiped on the sabbath, compiled sacred writings into the Torah and Old Testament

---

Bonus Test Question

For Chapter 6 Test

Who would be more likely to win achievement awards in the following—a Canaanite or Aegean: agriculture, mathematics, wool weaving, map making, desert survival, astronomy. (*probable answers: Canaanites, Aegeans, Canaanites, both, Canaanites, Aegeans*)

Using Your Journal

Paragraphs will vary but students might include the ways that the alphabet, the idea of treaties, the idea of one god, and the idea of social justice affect them.

Geography in History

Depending upon which migration students choose to describe, they should include arid, dry land; sand, mountains; little vegetation; rivers and/or Mediterranean Sea.

Chapter 7 Planning Guide

Objectives	Reproducible Resources	Multimedia Resources
Section 1 **The Assyrians** Discuss how the Assyrian civilization rose in Mesopotamia and expanded into neighboring lands.	Reproducible Lesson Plan Chapter 7 Vocabulary and Guided Reading Activity Reading Essentials and Study Guide 7-1 Chapter 7 Cooperative Learning Activity Chapter 7 Chart and Graph Skill Activity Section 1 Quiz	Vocabulary PuzzleMaker Interactive Tutor Self-Assessment Software ExamView® Pro Testmaker Glencoe Skillbuilder Interactive Workbook, Level 1 Presentation Plus!
Section 2 **The Chaldeans** Summarize the Chaldeans and their methods of ruling and increasing trade.	Reproducible Lesson Plan Reading Essentials and Study Guide 7-2 Section 2 Quiz	Vocabulary PuzzleMaker Interactive Tutor Self-Assessment Software ExamView® Pro Testmaker Glencoe Skillbuilder Interactive Workbook, Level 1
Section 3 **The Persians** Explain how Persian ideas spread through the forging of large empires, and how their social and religious life helped create a stable society.	Reproducible Lesson Plan Reading Essentials and Study Guide 7-3 Chapter 7 Geography and Map Activity Chapter 7 Enrichment Activity Chapter 7 Activity Book Activity Section 3 Quiz	Teaching Transparencies and Activities 7A & &B Vocabulary PuzzleMaker Interactive Tutor Self-Assessment Software ExamView® Pro Testmaker Glencoe Skillbuilder Interactive Workbook, Level 1
Chapter 7 **Review and Evaluation**	Chapter 7 Reteaching Activity Chapter 7 Performance Assessment Activity Spanish Chapter Summary and Glossary Chapter 7 Test	Vocabulary PuzzleMaker Interactive Tutor Self-Assessment Software Glencoe Skillbuilder Interactive Workbook, Level 1 Audiocassettes* ExamView® Pro Testmaker

*Also available in Spanish.

Presentation Plus!

Use Glencoe's **Presentation Plus!** multimedia teacher tool to easily present dynamic lessons that visually excite your students. Using Microsoft® PowerPoint, you can customize the presentations to create your own personalized lessons.

 ## Interactive Lesson Planner

Planning has never been easier! Using this CD-ROM, organize your week, month, semester, or year with all the help you need. The **Interactive Lesson Planner** gives you access to all of the blackline masters which accompany *Human Heritage.*

✓ PERFORMANCE ASSESSMENT ACTIVITIES

Friendly Letters   Instruct students to imagine that they are teenagers living in one of the civilizations described in the chapter. Tell them to write a letter to a friend in a neighboring city describing a day in their lives. Ask volunteers to share their letters with the class.

CHAPTER RESOURCES

READINGS FOR THE STUDENT

Jameson, Cynthia. *The Secret of the Royal Mounds: Henry Layard and the First Cities of Assyria.* Coward, McCann & Geoghegan, 1980. An illustrated account of the career of Layard, the discoverer of ancient Nineveh and one of the first scientific archaeologists.

Saggs, H.W. *Everyday Life in Babylonia and Assyria.* Dorset Press, 1987. Describes the life and customs of ancient Babylonians and Assyrians.

READINGS FOR THE TEACHER

Collins, Robert. *The Medes and the Persians: Conquerors and Diplomats.* McGraw-Hill, 1975. Recounts the daily lives, beliefs, and government of the ancient Persians.

Editors of Time-Life Books. *Lost Civilizations: Mesopotamia—The Mighty Kings.* Time-Life Books, 1995. A vividly illustrated look at civilizations in the Fertile Crescent.

KEY TO ABILITY LEVELS

Teaching strategies have been coded for varying learning styles and abilities.

L1 Level 1 activities are **basic** activities and should be within the ability range of all students.

L2 Level 2 activities are **average** activities and should be within the ability range of the average to above-average student.

L3 Level 3 activities are **challenging** activities designed for the ability range of above-average students.

ELL ELL activities should be within the ability range of English Language Learning students.

NATIONAL GEOGRAPHIC SOCIETY — Teacher's Corner

INDEX TO NATIONAL GEOGRAPHIC MAGAZINE

The following article relates to this chapter:

• "Iraq: Crucible of Civilization," by Merle Severy, May 1991.

NATIONAL GEOGRAPHIC SOCIETY PRODUCTS AVAILABLE FROM GLENCOE

To order the following, call Glencoe at 1-800-334-7344:

• *PicturePack: Physical Geography of the World* (Transparencies)
• *STV: World Geography* (Videodisc)
• *Picture Atlas of the World* (CD-ROM)
• *PicturePack: World Geography* (Transparencies)

ADDITIONAL NATIONAL GEOGRAPHIC SOCIETY PRODUCTS

To order the following, call National Geographic at 1-800-368-2728:

• *Arabia: Sand, Sea, and Sky* (Video)
• *Families of the World Series: Israel* (Video)
• *National Geographic Atlas of World History* (Book)
• *Wonders of the Ancient World: National Geographic Atlas of Archaeology* (Book)

Access *National Geographic*'s new dynamic MapMachine Web site and other geography resources at:
http://www.nationalgeographic.com/
http://www.nationalgeographic.com/maps/

OVERVIEW

Chapter 7 focuses on the Assyrian, Chaldean, and Persian empires and their contributions to the ancient Middle East.

➤ **Section 1** discusses the Assyrian civilization and its empire in Mesopotamia.

➤ **Section 2** explains the features of the Chaldean civilization and its city of Babylon.

➤ **Section 3** describes the contributions made by Persians to other civilizations.

CHAPTER OBJECTIVES

After reading Chapter 7, your students will be able to:

1. explain how the Assyrians established and maintained an empire in Mesopotamia.

2. describe what the Chaldean city of Babylon was like.

3. discuss how the Persians were able to rule an empire that stretched from Egypt to India.

EXAMINING ARTIFACTS

Ask students what these artifacts reveal about the Assyrians. *(Sample response: They possessed wealth and saw themselves—or their ruler—as strong as a lion.)* As students read through the chapter, direct them to decide whether a winged lion accurately represents the Assyrian people.

PERFORMANCE ASSESSMENT ✓

Use the Performance Assessment Activities on page 116B to help you evaluate students as they complete the chapter.

Military Empires
1400 B.C.–570 B.C.

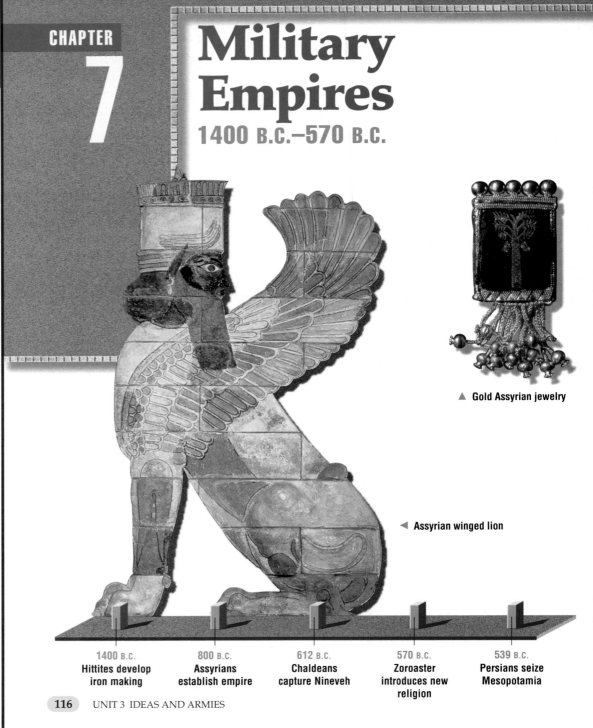

▲ **Gold Assyrian jewelry**

◀ **Assyrian winged lion**

1400 B.C.	800 B.C.	612 B.C.	570 B.C.	539 B.C.
Hittites develop iron making	**Assyrians establish empire**	**Chaldeans capture Nineveh**	**Zoroaster introduces new religion**	**Persians seize Mesopotamia**

116 UNIT 3 IDEAS AND ARMIES

TEACHING RESOURCES

TEACHER PLANNING AND SUPPORT

 Reproducible Lesson Plan
Block Scheduling Implementation Guide
Videodisc Bar Code Correlation
Presentation Plus!

REVIEW AND REINFORCEMENT

Reading Essentials and Study Guide 7-1, 7-2, 7-3
Chapter 7 Vocabulary and Guided Reading Activity
Vocabulary PuzzleMaker Software

 Teaching Transparencies 7A & 7B
Chapter 7 Reteaching Activity
Chapter 7 Cooperative Learning Activity
Chapter 7 Activity Book Activity
Chapter 7 Chart and Graph Skill Activity
Interactive Tutor Self-Assessment Software

APPLICATION AND HANDS-ON ACTIVITIES

Daily World History, Geography and Culture Question
Unit 3 Hands-On History Lab Activity

Chapter Focus

 Read to Discover

- How the Assyrians established and maintained an empire in Mesopotamia.
- What the Chaldean city of Babylon was like.
- How the Persians were able to rule an empire that stretched from Egypt to India.

 Terms to Learn

empires
smelting
provinces
caravans
astronomers

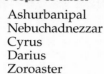 **People to Know**

Ashurbanipal
Nebuchadnezzar
Cyrus
Darius
Zoroaster

 Places to Locate

Nineveh
Babylon
Persepolis
Lydia

Why It's Important While the Phoenicians and the Hebrews were developing their civilizations, powerful kingdoms rose and fell in Mesopotamia. Built by the Assyrians, the Chaldeans (kal dē′ uhns), and the Persians, these kingdoms were not content to stay where their civilizations began. Rulers raised large armies and expanded into neighboring lands. They developed new ways of organizing their **empires**—territories governed by a single ruler or nation. They also increased trade. Through conquest and trade, these three empire-builders spread their ideas and customs over a wide area.

Chapter Overview
Visit the *Human Heritage* Web site at **humanheritage.glencoe.com** and click on *Chapter 7—Chapter Overviews* to preview this chapter.

☑ **Reading Check**
Which people used large armies to build powerful **empires** in Mesopotamia?

SECTION 1 The Assyrians

About 1,000 years after Hammurabi ruled, a people called Assyrians rose to power in Mesopotamia. Their country, Assyria, lay in the upper part of the Tigris River valley. The Assyrians spoke the same language and used the same writing system as the Babylonians.

The Assyrians were warriors. Experts believe their liking for war was influenced by geography. Assyria's rolling hills and rain-watered valleys did not provide protection against invaders. Assyrian shepherds and farmers had to learn to fight to survive. In time, fighting became a way of life.

The Assyrians built a powerful army. By 1100 B.C., they had defeated their neighboring enemies. By 800 B.C., they were strong enough to take over cities, trading routes, and fortresses throughout Mesopotamia.

CHAPTER 7 MILITARY EMPIRES **117**

Chapter Overview introduces students to chapter content and key terms. Have them access **Chapter 7 Overview** at **humanheritage.glencoe.com**

FOCUS

🔲 **Bellringer**

Write this saying on the chalkboard: *So passes away the glory of the world.* Ask students to write a sentence that explains the meaning of the word *glory* in this statement.

Motivational Activity

Discuss students' explanations of *glory*. Then ask the students to think about the world today and find examples of countries that are declining from a position of earlier glory.

☑ **Reading Check Answer**
The Assyrians, Chaldeans, and Persians used large armies to build **empires** in Mesopotamia.

GUIDE TO READING

Reading Strategy

Ask students to read "Why It's Important" and summarize the chapter's main theme. *(Through trade and conquest, the Assyrians, Chaldeans, and Persians spread ideas and customs throughout Mesopotamia.)*

Vocabulary Precheck

Ask students to define each of the "Terms to Learn." Have a volunteer consult the dictionary for any unfamiliar words. **L1** **ELL**

💾 Use the Vocabulary PuzzleMaker for Chapter 7 to create a crossword puzzle. **L1**

📂 Assign Chapter 7 Vocabulary and Guided Reading Activity.

📂 Assign Reading Essentials and Study Guide 7-1.

New Model The Hittites developed a chariot that could carry two soldiers *and* a driver. Other peoples, including the Egyptians, used a two-person chariot. With their three-person chariot, Hittites could field twice as many soldiers as their foes.

ASSYRIAN SOLDIERS   Assyrian kings often celebrated their victories by decorating palaces and temples with scenes of warfare. Here, a wall painting shows Assyrian soldiers killing enemy captives. **How was the Assyrian army organized?**

The Assyrian Army   The Assyrian army was well-organized. It was divided into groups of foot soldiers armed with shields, helmets, spears, and daggers. It also had units of charioteers, cavalry, and archers.

At first, the Assyrians fought only during summer when they did not have to be concerned about planting or harvesting crops. Later, as they took over more land, soldiering became a year-round job. When the Assyrians needed more soldiers, they hired them from other places or forced the people they had conquered to serve.

Assyrian power was due partly to their weapons, which were made of iron. Iron weapons are harder and stronger than weapons made of copper or tin. Iron had been used in the Middle East for many centuries. Until about 1400 B.C., however, it was too soft to be made into weapons. Then, a people called Hittites (hi′ tītz) developed a process of **smelting.** They heated iron ore, hammered out its impurities, and rapidly cooled it. The Assyrians borrowed the skill of smelting from the Hittites.

The Assyrians were cruel warriors. For several hundred years, their armies spread death and destruction throughout the Middle East. They were especially skilled in attacking cities. They tunneled under walls or climbed over them on ladders. They used beams mounted on movable platforms to ram holes through city gates. Once they captured a city, they set fire to its buildings and carried away its citizens and goods.

Anyone who resisted Assyrian rule was punished. Those who did not resist had to pay heavy taxes. The Assyrians also

 Reading Check How did the process of **smelting** work?

MULTICULTURAL PERSPECTIVES

Assyrians were the first hairstylists. They refined this styling so much that hairstyles became a major part of the culture. Assyrians even had laws specifying the hairstyles of people in certain jobs. They cut short hair into graduated tiers and arranged long hair in ringlets and curls. They oiled, perfumed, and tinted hair. They even curled hair with a fire-heated iron bar, the first known curling iron.

found a way to conquer people without fighting. They spread stories of their cruelty. Other people were so frightened by the stories that they would simply surrender.

Kings and Government   Assyria's kings were strong leaders. They had to be to rule an empire that extended from the Persian Gulf in the east to the Nile Valley in the west. Assyrian kings spent much of their time fighting battles and punishing enemies. However, they were also involved in peaceful activities. A great Assyrian king, Ashurbanipal (osh uhr bon' uh pol), started one of the world's first libraries. It held 25,000 tablets of hymns, stories, and biographies.

Assyrian kings had to control many peoples spread over a large area. To do this, they divided their empire into **provinces,** or political districts. They then chose officials to govern each province. The officials collected taxes and made certain the king's laws were obeyed.

All provinces were connected by a system of roads. Although only roads near major cities were paved, all were level enough for carts and chariots to travel on. Over the roads moved the trade of the empire. Government soldiers were posted at stations along the

 Reading Check
Why did the Assyrians divide their empire into **provinces**?

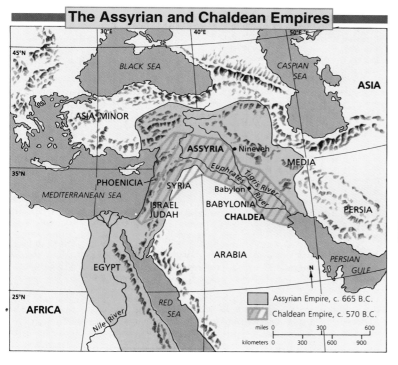

The Assyrian and Chaldean Empires

Assyrian Empire, c. 665 B.C.
Chaldean Empire, c. 570 B.C.

miles 0   300   600
kilometers 0   300   600   900

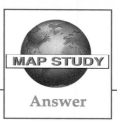

MAP STUDY

LOCATION The Assyrian and Chaldean empires were extensive. **What was the location of each of these empires in terms of latitude and longitude?**

119

SPOTLIGHT ON: ASHURBANIPAL

Ashurbanipal was both a brutal Assyrian king and a scholar. Since he was able to read and write Assyria's cuneiform writing, he collected every cuneiform tablet in the kingdom that he felt was worth saving. His collection was stored in his library at Nineveh. The collection included 22,000 tablets written in Sumerian, Babylonian, and Assyrian. These tablets represented 2,500 years of Mesopotamian written history and included letters, official documents, and dictionaries and studies of mathematics, astronomy, and botany.

Guided Practice

DID YOU KNOW ⁇

The ziggurat in Babylon is thought to be the Tower of Babel mentioned in the Book of Genesis, Chapter 11 of the Old Testament.

---

roads to protect traders from bandits. Messengers on government business used the stations to rest and to change horses.

In time, the empire became too large to govern. After Ashurbanipal died, various conquered peoples worked to end Assyrian rule. One group was the Chaldeans. In 612 B.C., they captured Nineveh (nin' uh vuh), the Assyrian capital. The Assyrian Empire crumbled shortly after.

Section 1 Assessment

1. **Define:** empire, smelting, provinces.
2. How was Assyria governed?
3. Why did the Assyrian Empire fall?

Critical Thinking

4. **Forming Conclusions** Do you think ruling by fear is an effective way to govern? Why or why not?

Graphic Organizer Activity

5. Draw a diagram like this one, and use it to show the cause and effects of the Assyrian warrior way of life.

SECTION 2 The Chaldeans

Like the Assyrians, the Chaldeans were warriors who conquered many different peoples. Under their king Nebuchadnezzar (neb uh kuhd nez' uhr), they extended their empire's boundaries as far west as Syria and Palestine. The Chaldeans called themselves Babylonians. This was because most Chaldeans were descendants of the people who made up Hammurabi's empire about 1,200 years earlier. They built a new capital at Babylon in which nearly 1 million people lived.

Babylon was the world's richest city up to that time. It had its own police force and postal system. Huge brick walls encircled the city. The walls were so wide that two chariots could pass on the road on top. Archers guarded the approaches to the city from towers built into the walls.

In the center of the city stood palaces and temples. A huge ziggurat reached more than 300 feet, or over 90 meters, into the sky. When the sun shone, its gold roof could be seen for miles.

The richness of the ziggurat was equaled by that of the king's palace. The palace had "hanging gardens." These were layered beds of earth planted with large trees and masses of flowering vines and shrubs. They seemed to hang in mid-air. Nebuchadnezzar built the gardens to please his wife, who missed the mountains and plants of her native land.

Seven Wonders Historians of the time counted the Hanging Gardens of Babylon among the Seven Wonders of the World. Other wonders included: the pyramids of Egypt, the statue of Zeus at Olympia, the temple of Artemis (Diana) at Ephesus, the mausoleum at Halicarnassus, the Colossus of Rhodes, and the lighthouse at Pharos.

120 UNIT 3 IDEAS AND ARMIES

To please the people, Nebuchadnezzar built a beautiful street near the palace. It was paved with limestone and marble and lined by walls of blue glazed tile. Each spring, thousands of pilgrims crowded into Babylon to watch a gold statue of the god Marduk (mar′ duhk) being wheeled along this street. The Chaldeans believed that the procession would make their crops grow. They also believed it would help keep peace in the empire.

Outside the center of Babylon stood houses and marketplaces. There, artisans made pottery, cloth, and baskets. These were sold to passing **caravans,** or groups of traveling merchants. Traders came to Babylon from as far away as India and Egypt. Trade helped make Babylon rich.

✓ Reading Check
How did **caravans** help Babylon grow rich?

CAPTION ANSWER

because Babylon was one of the world's richest cities and it needed protection

L1 Daily Life Provide students with an index card and suggest they imagine they are visitors in ancient Babylonia. They are to make a postcard to send to their families back in America. On one side of the postcard, students should draw an illustration of an area or a feature of the city of Babylon. On the other side of the postcard, students should write a note to their families giving their impressions of the city's appearance and the achievements and daily life of its people. Display the completed postcards on the bulletin board.

ENTRANCE TO BABYLON The Ishtar Gate was ancient Babylon's main entrance. It honored the goddess Ishtar and was covered with images of wild animals. **Why was Babylon surrounded by walls with gates?**

COOPERATIVE LEARNING

Have students use reference books in order to make a list of the Seven Wonders of the Ancient World. Then divide the class into seven groups. Assign each group a wonder of the ancient world to research and report on. Ask students to also list what they consider to be the Seven Wonders of the Modern World. Discuss their choices and compare them to the ancient wonders.

📁 Assign Chapter 7 *Cooperative Learning Activity* in the TCR.

Reading Check Answer
Astronomers study the heavens and the movement of heavenly bodies.

Independent Practice

L1 **Language Arts** Suggest students read more about the Assyrian cuneiform writing. Have them make a chart of some of its symbols and their meanings. Display the charts and have students explain whether or not they think cuneiform writing would be easier to learn and use than our writing. **ELL**

Use **Interactive Tutor Self-Assessment Software** to review Section 2.

Use the **Vocabulary Puzzle-Maker** to create crossword and word search puzzles.

Reading Check
What do **astronomers** study?

Babylon was also a center of science. Chaldean **astronomers,** or people who collect, study, and explain facts about the heavenly bodies, believed that changes in the sky revealed the plans of the gods. So, they studied the stars, planets, and moon. Once they knew the movement of heavenly bodies, they made maps that showed the positions of the planets and the phases of the moon. Babylonian astronomers made one of the first sundials. They also were the first to have a seven-day week.

Babylon was the center of a great civilization for many years. As time passed, though, the Chaldeans began to lose their power. They found it hard to control the peoples they had conquered. Then, in 539 B.C., Persians from the mountains to the northeast captured Babylon. Mesopotamia became just another part of the Persian Empire.

Section 2 Assessment

1. **Define:** caravans, astronomers.
2. What did the Chaldean astronomers contribute to science?
3. What led to the fall of the Chaldean Empire?

Critical Thinking

4. **Identifying Alternatives** Under whose rule—the Assyrian's or the Chaldean's—would you have preferred to live? Explain.

Graphic Organizer Activity
5. Draw a diagram like this one, and use it to describe Babylon.

SECTION 3 The Persians

Persian Pony Express
King Darius established a postal system that operated much like the American Pony Express. Postal stations were set up a day's ride apart. At each station, a fresh rider and horse would wait to take the mail from the incoming rider.

Originally, the Persians were part of the people known as Aryans. The Aryans were cattle herders from the grasslands of central Asia. About 2000 B.C., however, the Persians began to separate from other Aryans. They finally settled on a high plain between the Persian Gulf and the Caspian Sea, where they established Persia. Today, this region is called Iran (i ran'), or "the land of the Aryans." Modern Persians are Iranians (ir ā' nē uhnz).

The Persians lived peacefully in the highlands for over 1,000 years. They divided most of the country into large farms owned by nobles. The nobles spent most of their time riding horses and practicing archery. Their farms were worked by laborers.

There was little water on the hot plain. Farmers depended on streams that came down from the mountains. They dug underground tunnels from the springs to the fields. With water, farm-

Section 2 Assessment Answers

1. caravans, groups of traveling merchants (p. 121); astronomers, scholars who study the stars and planets (p. 122)
2. They made maps that showed the positions of the planets and the phases of the moon, made one of the first sundials, and were the first to use the seven-day week.
3. The Chaldeans found it hard to control the peoples they had conquered; some years, crops were poor and trade was slow; and in 539 B.C., the Persians captured Babylon.
4. Answers will vary but students must give reasons to support their opinions.
5. Sample descriptions: richest city, own police force and postal system, encircled by huge brick walls, guarded by archers atop towers, palaces and temples in center, huge ziggurat, hanging gardens, beautiful streets, Ishtar Gate, etc.

Assign Chapter 7 **Section 2 Quiz** in the TCR. Testmaker available.

Coins The practice of showing portraits (below) or symbols on coins stretches back to the Lydians, who invented the use of coins, and the Persians, who spread their use. In 2000, the United States government issued a new one-dollar coin with the portrait of Sacajawea (far right). **Why do archaeologists and historians consider coins a valuable source of evidence about the past?**

ers were able to grow wheat and barley and to pasture flocks of fat-tailed sheep.

Army and Empire   About 600 B.C., the Persians were conquered by the Medes (mēdz), a neighboring people. The Medes, however, were soon overthrown by the Persians under King Cyrus (sī' ruhs). Cyrus then organized an army to conquer new territory. The army grew until it numbered in the hundreds of thousands. Its officers were Persians, while its soldiers were either Persians or conquered peoples.

The best fighters in the Persian army were the Immortals. They earned this name because their number never fell below 10,000. When an Immortal became sick, was wounded, or died, another soldier took his place. The Immortals had the honor of leading the Persian army into battle.

Within a short time, the Persians ruled an empire that stretched from Egypt to India. The Persians were mild rulers who allowed their subjects to keep their own language, religion, and laws. The Persians believed loyalty could be won more easily with fairness than with fear or force. They wanted their subjects to pay taxes and to produce goods for trade. They felt these things would not be done if those under their rule were treated badly.

One of the strongest Persian kings was Darius (duh rī' uhs). He wanted a monument to honor his military victories. So, he brought artisans from many lands to build a grand palace-fortress-treasury in the capital city of Persepolis (puhr sep' uh luhs). Buildings with many columns were constructed on giant stone

Student Web Activity

Visit the *Human Heritage* Web site at **humanheritage.glencoe.com** and click on ***Chapter 7— Student Web Activities*** to find out more about Persian contributions.

Answers will vary but might include that coins show the beliefs of a people, important figures, system of money, extent of trade (based on distribution of the coins), and so on.

MAKING CONNECTIONS

➤➤ **Language Arts** Many English words come from Iran, or ancient Persia, by way of the Greek language. There are flower names such as *rose, jasmine, lilac,* and *narcissus*. There are food names, such as *asparagus, orange, peach, rice,* and *spinach*. Other words include *peacock, tapestry, tiara,* and *tiger*.

Student Web Activity objectives, goals, and answers can be found at the ***Chapter 7 Web Activity Lesson Plan*** at humanheritage.glencoe.com

MEETING SPECIAL NEEDS

Have students who are auditory learners debate the following topic: *Conquerors should maintain tight control over conquered peoples in order to keep their empires together.* Form two teams, one to defend the idea that conquerors should maintain tight control and the other to defend the idea that conquered peoples should be treated fairly.

After giving each team time to research and develop its arguments, have each team present their views.

📂 Refer to ***Inclusion for the Middle School Social Studies Classroom: Strategies and Activities*** for additional resources.

Most wealthy Persian men traveled on horseback or in a litter. They thought that only the lower class should be seen walking. Men wore their beards long and curled. They used makeup on their faces, colored their eyelids, and perfumed themselves.

LINKING PAST TO PRESENT

Zoroaster taught that one could love God only by loving humanity. In Zoroastrianism, the sun was considered the great cleansing power and fire, a symbol of purity. Today most followers of the religion live in India and are called Parsees, which means Persians.

People in History

Darius
c. 558 B.C.–486 B.C.

Persian King

Darius organized a vast empire. He wanted conquered people to pay taxes and to supply soldiers, but he respected their customs. He allowed the Jews to rebuild their temple in Jerusalem and consulted with Egyptian priests and Greek oracles in Asia Minor. However, he did not involve citizens in government. That innovation belonged to the Greek city-states that would challenge Darius near the end of his life.

platforms. In the gateways, workers carved figures that were half human and half beast. Persepolis became the most magnificent city in the empire.

Government Officials   The king did not govern alone. There were many officials to carry out his orders. They all spoke Aramaic (ar uh mā' ik). This was the language used by Middle Eastern merchants.

The king chose a governor, a secretary, and a general for each of the 20 provinces of the empire. These officials collected taxes of gold, silver, sheep, horses, wheat, and spices and sent them to the royal treasury in Persepolis. These officials also settled local quarrels and protected the people against bandits. Each reported separately to the king. This helped keep them honest. If one was stealing tax money, for example, the others were sure to report it. The king would then remove the dishonest official from office.

Another group of officials was the inspectors. Called "the Eyes and Ears of the King," they traveled throughout the empire. They decided whether people were able to pay their taxes. They also checked on rumors of possible rebellion. The inspectors never warned provincial officials they were coming. This made provincial officials careful about doing a good job.

The last group of officials was the judges. They made sure that the king's laws were carried out properly.

Family Life   The Persians lived in houses with pointed roofs and porches that faced the sun. Poor families had one-room houses. Noble families had houses with one set of rooms for men and another for women and children.

Persian families were large. Fathers ruled their families in much the same way the king ruled the empire. A father's word was law. Poor children worked with their parents. The children of nobles, however, were cared for by their mothers until they were five years old. Then, they were raised by enslaved people. Often, they did not see their fathers until they reached adulthood. Boys were trained to ride horses and draw a bow. Girls were trained to run households and raise children.

Rich women lived very sheltered lives. They spent most of their time at home apart from the men. If they had to leave the house, they stepped into a closed *litter,* or a carriage without wheels that was carried by servants. Poor women had more freedom, but they had to work hard.

Religion   At first, the Persians worshiped many gods. Then, about 570 B.C., a religious leader named Zoroaster (zōr' uh was tuhr) told the Persians about two gods. One god, Ahura Mazda (uh hūr' uh maz' duh), was wise and truthful. He created all good things in the world. The other god, Ahriman (ar' i muhn),

124   UNIT 3 IDEAS AND ARMIES

EXTENDING THE CONTENT

Kings Cyrus and Darius are given credit for setting up a postal system that served the main part of the Persian Empire. Along the Royal Road from Sardis in Asia Minor to Susa near the Persian Gulf, there were more than a hundred relay stations where mounted messengers could change horses. The Persian postal service was described by the Greek historian Herodotus in the following way: *Neither snow, nor rain, nor heat, nor gloom of night stays these couriers from the swift completion of their appointed rounds.*

made all evil things in the world. Ahura Mazda and Ahriman were at war with each other all of the time.

Zoroaster said human beings had to decide which god they would support. Zoroaster then listed the good and bad deeds a person performed. Good deeds were keeping one's word, giving to the poor, working the land, obeying the king, and treating others well. Bad deeds included being lazy, proud, or greedy. Zoroaster could tell from the list which god a person had chosen. He believed that in the end Ahura Mazda would defeat Ahriman. People who supported Ahura Mazda would enjoy happiness after death. Those who supported Ahriman would be punished.

Trade   The Persians thought they should be warriors, farmers, or shepherds. They refused to become traders. They believed that trade forced people to lie, cheat, and be greedy. They did, however, encourage trade among all peoples they conquered.

The Persians improved and expanded the system of roads begun by the Assyrians. One road, the Royal Road, ran more than 1,600 miles, or more than 2,560 kilometers. A journey that took three months before the Royal Road was built took only 15 days after it was completed. The Persians also opened a caravan route to China. Silk was first brought west along this route.

MAP STUDY

REGIONS The Persian Empire stretched from the Nile River to the Indus River, a distance of 3,000 miles, or 4,800 kilometers. Within this empire, the Persians ruled more than 50 million people. **Into what continents did the Persian Empire extend?**

The Persian Empire

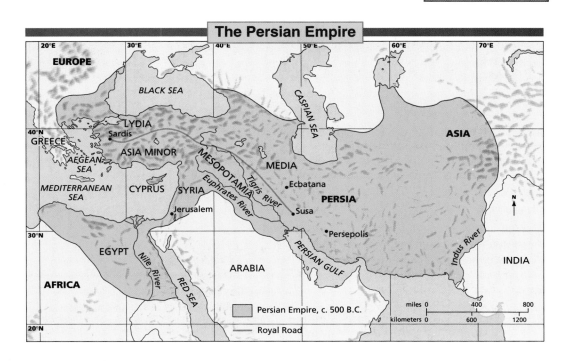

Persian Empire, c. 500 B.C.
— Royal Road

CHAPTER 7 MILITARY EMPIRES **125**

Reteach

Organize students into small groups to compose a song or rap that expresses the main ideas of one section in the chapter.

Assign Chapter 7 **Reteaching Activity** in the TCR.

Enrich

Have students investigate one of the people discussed in the chapter and write a biographical sketch of the person. Suggest authors present the biographical sketch to the class as if they are that person.

Assign Chapter 7 **Enrichment Activity** in the TCR.

CLOSE

Have students discuss this question: *Based on your reading of the chapter—which is more likely to bring about change in a culture—an idea brought to people through peaceful means or an idea forced on them?*

💾 Use **Interactive Tutor Self-Assessment Software** to review Section 3.

Self-Check Quiz gives students an interactive chapter tutorial. Have them access *Chapter 7 Quiz* at humanheritage.glencoe.com

---

The Persians spread the idea of using coins for money. The first known coins had been made in Lydia (lid' ē uh), a tiny kingdom in Asia Minor bordering on the Aegean Sea. After conquering Lydia, the Persian king decided to use gold coins in his empire. This helped to increase trade. It also changed the nature of trade. Merchants who had sold only costly goods began to sell everyday, cheaper things as well. They sold chickens, dried fish, furniture, clothing, and pots and pans. Since people could get more goods, they began to live better than they had before.

Section 3 Assessment

1. How did the Persians treat people they conquered?
2. What religious ideas did Zoroaster introduce to Persia?
3. In what ways did the Persians contribute to the growth of trade within their empire?

Critical Thinking

4. **Making Comparisons** How do the roles of government officials in the United States compare with the role of government officials in Persia?

Graphic Organizer Activity

5. Draw a diagram like this one, and use it to describe the government, economy, and religion of the Persian Empire.

Chapter Summary & Study Guide

1. About 800 B.C., the Assyrians built an empire in Mesopotamia.
2. The Assyrians used the Hittite process of smelting to make strong iron weapons.
3. The Assyrian Empire was divided into provinces linked by roads.
4. In 612 B.C., the Chaldeans captured the Assyrian capital of Nineveh.
5. Under Nebuchadnezzar, the Chaldeans built a new capital at Babylon, which quickly became a center of trade and science..
6. Around 539 B.C., the Persians added Mesopotamia to their empire.
7. The Persians divided their empire into provinces, each governed by various groups of officials.
8. About 570 B.C., Zoroaster taught a new religion in which good and evil took the form of two gods who were constantly fighting each other.
9. Though the Persians did not become traders themselves, they encouraged trade within their far-flung empire.

Self-Check Quiz
Visit the *Human Heritage* Web site at **humanheritage. glencoe.com** and click on *Chapter 7—Self-Check Quiz* to assess your understanding of this chapter.

Section 3 Assessment Answers

1. The Persians let them keep their own language, religion, and laws.
2. one good and one bad god, choosing a god, and punishment after death.
3. They improved the system of Assyrian roads, opened a caravan route to China, and spread coins.
4. Answers will vary but may include Persian officials were appointed, whereas U.S. officials are elected; both Persian and U.S. officials dealt with taxation, and in providing protection.
5. government—should reflect mild rule toward conquered peoples and descriptions on p. 124; economy—should emphasize importance of trade and descriptions on pp. 125–126; religion—should highlight Zoroaster and descriptions on pp. 124–125

Assign Chapter 7 **Section 3 Quiz** in the TCR. Testmaker available.

Assessment

Using Key Terms

Imagine you are writing a feature magazine article about the Assyrian and Chaldean empires. Use the following words in your article to describe some of the achievements made in these two empires.

empires smelting provinces
caravans astronomers

Understanding Main Ideas

1. What do experts believe influenced the Assyrians to become warriors?
2. What made the Assyrians such feared fighters?
3. Why did the Chaldeans call themselves Babylonians?
4. What was the importance of the god Marduk to the Babylonians?
5. What was the relationship between the Persians and the Aryans?
6. In Persian government, who were "the Eyes and Ears of the King," and what did they do?
7. How was family life in Persia alike for both the rich and poor?
8. Why did the Persians refuse to become traders?

Critical Thinking

1. How can the reputation of a group like the Assyrians affect how others act toward that group?
2. How did the introduction of coins affect trade?
3. How would you describe the Persian attitude toward trade, and how wise was this policy?

4. In which of the empires discussed in this chapter would you have chosen to live? Explain.

Graphic Organizer Activity

Citizenship Create a diagram like this one, and use it to compare the governments of the Assyrian and Persian Empires.

Geography in History

Human/Environmental Interaction
What changes in their environment did the Persians make that extended ideas started by the Assyrians and Chaldeans? Explain your answer.

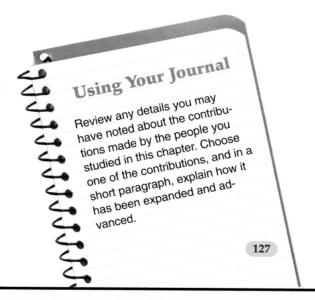

Using Your Journal

Review any details you may have noted about the contributions made by the people you studied in this chapter. Choose one of the contributions, and in a short paragraph, explain how it has been expanded and advanced.

127

Bonus Test Question
For Chapter 7 Test
What is smelting and why was this technology important to the development of a system of roads by the Assyrians? *(Smelting, the process of heating and cooling metal to form it, allowed the Assyrians to make weapons that made them successful conquerors.)*

Using Your Journal

Paragraphs will vary but should explain how the contribution has been expanded and advanced. You might call on volunteers to share their paragraphs with the class.

Geography in History

The Persians extended roads started by the Assyrians and maintained the division into provinces. Farming methods including irrigation canals were borrowed from the Chaldeans.

CHAPTER **7**

Assessment Answers

Using Key Terms

Articles will vary but students should use the words to describe these empires' achievements.

Understanding Main Ideas

1. Assyria's geography
2. They were cruel warriors who burned cities and carried away its citizens and goods.
3. Most were descendants of the people who had made up Hammurabi's empire.
4. They believed Marduk would make their crops grow and help keep peace.
5. The Persians were originally part of the Aryan people.
6. They were government officials who traveled throughout the empire to assess taxes and check on rumors of rebellion.
7. Both lived in houses with pointed roofs and porches that faced the sun, and both had large families ruled by the father.
8. because they believed that trade forced people to lie and cheat

Critical Thinking

1. Students should note that a reputation of strength or cruelty will cause fear.
2. It increased trade and the types of goods sold.
3. Answers will vary but should include Persians' aversion to trade that later changed.
4. Answers will vary.

Graphic Organizer Activity

Sample responses: both—ruled by kings, divided empire into provinces, used officials to collect taxes and enforce laws; Assyria—relied on fear, harsh punishment of resisters, levied heavy taxes; Persia—relied on fairness instead of force, used inspectors to keep king informed, appointed judges to control law

Chapter 8 Planning Guide

Objectives	Reproducible Resources	Multimedia Resources
Section 1 **Ancient African Kingdoms** Discuss how the ancient African civilizations of Kush and Asksum passed along elements of their culture to the world.	Reproducible Lesson Plan Chapter 8 Vocabulary and Guided Reading Activity Reading Essentials and Study Guide 8-1 Section 1 Quiz	Vocabulary PuzzleMaker Interactive Tutor Self-Assessment Software ExamView® Pro Testmaker Glencoe Skillbuilder Interactive Workbook, Level 1 Presentation Plus!
Section 2 **The Middle Kingdoms** Identify how West African kingdoms grew and developed.	Reproducible Lesson Plan Reading Essentials and Study Guide 8-2 Chapter 8 Cooperative Learning Activity Chapter 8 Chart and Graph Skill Activity Chapter 8 Geography and Map Activity Section 2 Quiz	Vocabulary PuzzleMaker Interactive Tutor Self-Assessment Software ExamView® Pro Testmaker Glencoe Skillbuilder Interactive Workbook, Level 1
Section 3 **East African Civilizations** Summarize how East African civilizations developed as trading regions.	Reproducible Lesson Plan Reading Essentials and Study Guide 8-3 Chapter 8 Enrichment Activity Unit 3 Primary Sources Reading Section 3 Quiz	Vocabulary PuzzleMaker ExamView® Pro Testmaker Glencoe Skillbuilder Interactive Workbook, Level 1
Section 4 **Path to the Americas** Explain why people crossed into the Americas.	Reproducible Lesson Plan Reading Essentials and Study Guide 8-4 Section 4 Quiz	Vocabulary PuzzleMaker Interactive Tutor Self-Assessment Software
Section 5 **Mesoamerica** Describe the kinds of civilizations that developed in Mesoamerica.	Reproducible Lesson Plan Reading Essentials and Study Guide 8-5 Chapter 8 Activity Book Activity Chapter 8 Enrichment Activity Section 5 Quiz	Vocabulary PuzzleMaker ExamView® Pro Testmaker Glencoe Skillbuilder Interactive Workbook, Level 1
Section 6 **The Incas** Characterize what life was like for the Inca of South America.	Reproducible Lesson Plan Reading Essentials and Study Guide 8-6 Chapter 8 Activity Book Activity Section 6 Quiz	Teaching Transparencies and Activities 8A & 8B Vocabulary PuzzleMaker ExamView® Pro Testmaker
Chapter 8 **Review and Evaluation**	Chapter 8 Reteaching Activity Chapter 8 Performance Assessment Activity Unit 3 Standardized Test Practice Spanish Chapter 8 Summary and Glossary Chapter 8 Test	Vocabulary PuzzleMaker Interactive Tutor Self-Assessment Software Glencoe Skillbuilder Interactive Workbook, Level 1 ExamView® Pro Testmaker Audiocassettes*

*Also available in Spanish.

Presentation Plus!

Use Glencoe's **Presentation Plus!** multimedia teacher tool to easily present dynamic lessons that visually excite your students. Using Microsoft® PowerPoint, you can customize the presentations to create your own personalized lessons.

 Interactive Lesson Planner

Planning has never been easier! Using this CD-ROM, organize your week, month, semester, or year with all the help you need. The **Interactive Lesson Planner** gives you access to all of the blackline masters which accompany *Human Heritage*.

✓ PERFORMANCE ASSESSMENT ACTIVITIES

A Geographical Journal Have students keep a geographical journal of the continents they will study in this chapter (Africa, North America, South America). Instruct them to sketch an outline map of each continent and to locate each empire or civilization as it is studied, along with any other information they choose.

CHAPTER RESOURCES

LITERATURE ABOUT THE PERIOD

Courlander, Harold. *A Treasury of African Folklore.* Crown Publishers, 1975. Collection of the oral literature, traditions, myths, and legends of Africa.

READINGS FOR THE STUDENT

Chu, Daniel, and Elliot Skinner. *A Glorious Age in Africa; the Story of Three Great African Empires.* Doubleday (Zenith Books), 1990. Illustrated account of Ghana, Mali, and Songhai.

Stuart, Gene S. *America's Ancient Cities.* National Geographic Society, 1988. Illustrated collection of essays on cultures of North America and Mesoamerica.

READINGS FOR THE TEACHER

Gallenkamp, Charles. *Maya: The Riddle and Rediscovery of a Lost Civilization.* Viking, 1985. Detailed account of the Mayas.

KEY TO ABILITY LEVELS

Teaching strategies have been coded for varying learning styles and abilities.

L1 Level 1 activities are **basic** activities and should be within the ability range of all students.

L2 Level 2 activities are **average** activities and should be within the ability range of the average to above-average student.

L3 Level 3 activities are **challenging** activities designed for the ability range of above-average students.

ELL ELL activities should be within the ability range of English Language Learning students.

Teacher's Corner

INDEX TO NATIONAL GEOGRAPHIC MAGAZINE

The following articles relate to this chapter:

- "Frozen in Time," by Johan Reinhard, November 1999.
- "Masai Passage to Manhood," by Carol Beckwith, September 1999.
- "Journey to the Heart of the Sahara," by Donovan Webster, March 1999.
- "New Inca Mummies," by Johan Reinhard, July 1998.

NATIONAL GEOGRAPHIC SOCIETY PRODUCTS AVAILABLE FROM GLENCOE

To order the following, call Glencoe at 1-800-334-7344:

- *PicturePack: Ancient Civilizations: Middle America (Transparencies)*
- *PicturePack: Ancient Civilizations: South America (Transparencies)*
- *PictureShow: Ancient Civilizations: Middle and South America (CD-ROM)*
- *PictureShow: Ancient Civilizations: Africa (CD-ROM)*
- *PicturePack: Ancient Africa (Transparencies)*

ADDITIONAL NATIONAL GEOGRAPHIC SOCIETY PRODUCTS

To order the following, call National Geographic at 1-800-368-2728:

- *Read & Explore: Discovering the Inca Ice Maiden,* by Johan Reinhard (Literature Kit)

Access *National Geographic*'s new dynamic MapMachine Web site and other geography resources at:
http://www.nationalgeographic.com/
http://www.nationalgeographic.com/maps/

  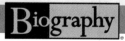

The following videotape programs are available from Glencoe:

- **Machu Picchu: City in the Sky**
  0-7670-0143-5
- **Peru: Warriors and Treasure**
  0-7670-1861-3
- **Secrets of the Aztec Empire**
  0-7670-0105-2

To order, call Glencoe at 1-800-334-7344. To find resources to accompany these, check:

A&E Television: http://www.aetv.com
The History Channel: http://www.historychannel.com

OVERVIEW

Chapter 8 focuses on the development of civilization in Africa and the Americas.

➤ **Section 1** discusses the Kush and Aksum civilizations.
➤ **Section 2** describes West African kingdoms.
➤ **Section 3** describes the contributions of the East African civilizations.
➤ **Section 4** explains why people migrated to the Americas.
➤ **Section 5** summarizes the civilizations of Mesoamerica.
➤ **Section 6** analyzes the Inca civilization of South America.

CHAPTER OBJECTIVES

After reading Chapter 8, students will be able to:
1. discuss how the ancient civilizations of Kush and Aksum passed along their culture.
2. summarize how West African and East African kingdoms developed because of trade.
3. explain how bands of people crossed into the Americas.
4. describe the civilizations that developed in Mesoamerica.
5. discuss Inca culture.

EXAMINING ARTIFACTS

Ask students what occupation they think the terra cotta figure holds. *(soldier)* Why? *(because both the figure and the horse are wearing armor)* Point to the gold disc, and have students speculate on the connection between the disc and rider. Have students review and revise their theories as they read the chapter.

PERFORMANCE ASSESSMENT ✓

Use the Performance Assessment Activities on page 128B to help you evaluate students as they complete the chapter.

128

CHAPTER 8

Africa & the Americas
6000 B.C.–1500 B.C.

◀ **Terra cotta horse and rider from Mali**

▲ **Gold Ashanti disc from Mali**

500 B.C.	750 B.C.	200 A.D.	700 A.D.	1240 A.D.	1400 A.D.
Mayan civilization begins	**Kushites conquer Egypt**	**Ghana founded**	**Shona settle in Zimbabwe**	**Kingdom of Mali established**	**Aztec Empire prospers**

TEACHING RESOURCES

TEACHER PLANNING AND SUPPORT

- Reproducible Lesson Plan
- Block Scheduling Implementation Guide
- Videodisc Bar Code Correlation
- Presentation Plus!

REVIEW AND REINFORCEMENT

- Reading Essentials and Study Guide 8-1, 8-2, 8-3, 8-4, 8-5, 8-6
- Chapter 8 Vocabulary and Guided Reading Activity
- Vocabulary PuzzleMaker Software
- Teaching Transparencies 8A & 8B
- Chapter 8 Reteaching Activities

- Chapter 8 Cooperative Learning Activity
- Chapter 8 Activity Book Activity
- Chapter 8 Chart and Graph Skill Activity
- Interactive Tutor Self-Assessment Software
- Chapter 8 MindJogger VideoQuiz

APPLICATION AND HANDS-ON ACTIVITIES

- Daily World History, Geography and Culture Question
- Unit 3 Hands-On History Lab Activity
- World History Game Card 3
- World History Craft Cards 9 and 10

Chapter Focus

Read to Discover

- How the ancient African civilizations of Kush and Aksum passed along elements of their culture.
- How West African kingdoms and East African civilizations grew because of trade.
- How Native Americans developed farming and other skills.
- What kinds of civilizations developed in Mesoamerica.
- What life was like for the Inca of South America.

HISTORY Online

Chapter Overview

Visit the *Human Heritage* Web site at **humanheritage.glencoe.com** and click on *Chapter 8—Chapter Overviews* to preview this chapter.

Terms to Learn	People to Know	Places to Locate
silent barter	Kashta	Meroë
pilgrimage	Piankhi	Timbuktu
population	Ezana	Zimbabwe
explosion	Sundiata Keita	Bering Strait
quipus	Mansa Musa	Tenochtitlán
	Sunni Ali	Kilwa
	Askia	
	Muhammad	
	Montezuma II	
	Pachacuti	

Why It's Important While armies carved out empires in the Middle East, civilizations developed in Africa south of the Sahara and in the Americas. Through conquest and trade, Africans and early Americans built great kingdoms and empires that rivaled civilizations elsewhere in the world.

SECTION 1 Ancient African Kingdoms

Other civilizations besides Egypt flourished in ancient Africa. Less is known about them than about Egypt. However, archaeologists have discovered enough remains to be able to tell what African civilizations were like.

Kush The first of these African civilizations was Kush. It lay south of Egypt on the Nile River in present-day Sudan (sū dan'). Its history began about 2000 B.C. At that time, the Kushites were nomadic cattle herders. They grazed long-horned cattle on a *savannah* (suh van' uh), or grassy plain.

During the New Kingdom, Egyptian armies conquered Kush. Kush remained part of Egypt for almost 500 years. Over

CHAPTER 8 AFRICA AND THE AMERICAS **129**

HISTORY Online

Chapter Overview introduces students to chapter content and key terms. Have them access *Chapter 8 Overview* at **humanheritage.glencoe.com**

FOCUS

Bellringer

Ask students to estimate what percentage of time they spend each day eating and sleeping—the basic functions of living.

Motivational Activity

Ask students to share their time estimates. Discuss how the ability to take care of basic needs influences the kind of life people can lead. Suggest that students recall this discussion as they study the empires and civilizations in this chapter.

GUIDE TO READING

Reading Strategy

Ask students to read "Why It's Important" and summarize the chapter's main theme. *(Through conquest and trade, peoples in Africa and the Americas built civilizations that rivaled those elsewhere in the world.)*

Vocabulary Precheck

Ask students to define each of the "Terms to Learn." Have a volunteer consult the dictionary for any unfamiliar words. **L1** **ELL**

💾 Use the Vocabulary PuzzleMaker for Chapter 8 to create a crossword puzzle. **L1**

🗀 Assign Chapter 8 Vocabulary and Guided Reading Activity.

🗀 Assign Reading Essentials and Study Guide 8-1.

GEOGRAPHY ACTIVITIES
🗀 Chapter 8 Geography and Map Activity
🗀 Social Studies Outline Map Resource Book

INTERDISCIPLINARY CONNECTIONS
🖼 World History & Art Transparency 8, *Gold Pendant Mask*
📖 Focus on World Art Print 11, *Presentation of Captives to a Maya Ruler*
🎧 World Music: Cultural Traditions

ENRICHMENT AND EXTENSION
🗀 Unit 3 Primary Sources Reading
🗀 Chapter 8 Enrichment Activity
💿 World History Primary Source Document Library CD-ROM

🗀 Foods Around the World

ASSESSMENT AND EVALUATION
🗀 Chapter 8 Performance Assessment Activity
🗀 Chapter 8 Section Quizzes 8-1, 8-2, 8-3, 8-4, 8-5, 8-6
🗀 Chapter 8 Test
🗀 Unit 3 Standardized Test Practice
💾🔊 Chapter 8 ExamView® Pro Testmaker Software
🎧 Chapter 8 Digests Audiocassettes Activities and Tests

SPANISH RESOURCES
🗀 Chapter 8 Spanish Chapter Summary and Glossary
🎧 Chapter 8 Spanish Chapter Digests Audiocassettes Activities and Tests

129

Guided Practice

L3 **Critical Thinking** Ask students to consider the significance of the Assyrian invasion of Kush. How did the inhabitants of Kush benefit from the invasion? How or what did they lose by the invasion? *(Benefits: learned iron-smelting, which helped them grow large amounts of grain and make iron goods for trade, which helped make Meroë a major trading center; Losses: forced to give up territory in Egypt)*

DID YOU KNOW ??

The most common Kushite symbols found on their pottery are the snake, the lion, and the lotus.

CAPTION ANSWER

Aksumite armies burned Meroë to the ground.

Fun Facts . . .

A Brave Queen One warrior-queen of Meroë, Amanirenas, challenged the Romans who seized Egypt after the death of Cleopatra. The Romans eventually drove Amanirenas back into Meroë, but she fought valiantly and her deeds are recorded in Greek and Roman histories of the time.

---

time, the Kushites learned many things from the Egyptians. They learned to worship the god Amon-Re. They learned how to work copper and bronze. They changed Egyptian hieroglyphs to fit their own language.

About 1160 B.C., Egypt's power declined. In time, the Kushites won back their independence. They set up a capital at Napata (nap' uht uh). From Napata, they sent caravans into Egypt. These caravans carried gold, ivory, ebony, and other goods to trade.

About 750 B.C., the Kushite king Kashta (kahsh' tuh) set out to conquer Egypt. He led his cavalry into Egypt and took some territory. His son Piankhi (pyahng' kē) completed the conquest and founded a dynasty that ruled Egypt for 70 years. However, during the 600s B.C., the Assyrians invaded Egypt. Armed with iron weapons, they drove the Kushites back to the south.

Despite their losses, the Kushites gained something from the Assyrians. They learned the secret of iron-smelting. Soon, Kushite farmers, using iron hoes, were growing large amounts of grain. Kushite blacksmiths were making iron knives and spears, which they exchanged for cotton textiles and other goods from India, Arabia, and China. Kush became a great trading nation.

Around 540 B.C., the Kushites moved their capital to Meroë (mār' ō ē). The city was on the Nile, which provided an avenue

KUSHITE PYRAMIDS   The Kushites copied many elements of Egyptian art, language, and religion. The pyramids near the cities of Meroë and Napata are imitations of Egyptian pyramids. The Kushite pyramids are smaller, however, and have more steeply sloped sides. **What happened to the city of Meroë?**

COOPERATIVE LEARNING

Organize the class into groups of three or four. Have each group select one culture studied in this chapter for further investigation. Each group should write a journal of an imagined archaeologist who has discovered artifacts from the selected culture. Every member of the group is responsible for researching the culture by using the text and library resources, taking notes during a group discussion about which artifacts to include, drawing pictures of artifacts, and drawing the location of the cultural group on a map.

for trade and transportation. Nearby were large deposits of iron ore and trees to fuel smelting furnaces. Meroë also lay in the center of good grazing land.

In Meroë, there was a huge temple dedicated to Amon-Re, with a long avenue of stone rams leading to its entrance. Sandstone palaces and houses of red brick filled the city. Walls of buildings were tiled in blue and yellow or covered with paintings. Small pyramids stood in the royal cemetery. Smelting furnaces poured forth huge columns of smoke, and around the furnaces lay heaps of shiny black *slag*, or waste from smelting.

Kush remained a great trading country for some 600 years, and then began to decline. As it declined, another kingdom rose to take its place. This was Aksum in present-day Ethiopia. About 350 A.D., Aksumite armies burned Meroë to the ground.

Aksum   Like Kush, Aksum was a trading country. Through ports on the Red Sea, Aksumite merchants served as middlemen for countries on the Mediterranean and in the Far East. They imported silks, spices, and elephants from India. They exported gold, ivory, and enslaved people from Africa. Jewish, Greek, and Arab merchants settled in Aksum.

It was most likely the Greeks who brought Christianity to Aksum. Emperor Ezana (ex zah' nuh), whose armies had destroyed Meroë, converted to Christianity in 324 A.D. This heritage was passed down to the present day.

Aksumites achieved many things. They developed a writing system. They learned to farm on *terraces* (ter' is uhz), or raised levels of land. They minted gold coins and built stone monuments 60 feet, or 18 meters, tall.

Over time, Aksum's power as a trading country began to decline. This was because other kingdoms began to interfere with Aksum's trade. After Arab armies swept across North Africa in the 600s A.D., the Aksumites retreated toward the *interior,* or inland areas, of their country. There, they lived in isolation for more than 1,000 years.

Aksumite Stone Monument

GEOGRAPHY AND HISTORY

Ethiopia is situated where Aksum once stood. As Aksum, it exerted a wide influence in the Horn of Africa, southern Arabia, the Red Sea, and as far west as Kush. With the spread of Islam, Aksum's foreign trade ended. Aksum was a small Christian area in the larger, Muslim East Africa. Its geographical isolation and being located on high plateaus helped the country keep its religious and cultural individuality.

Use **Interactive Tutor Self Assessment Software** to review Section 1.

Section 1 Assessment

1. How did the Kushites and Egyptians influence each other?
2. Why did the Kushites choose Meroë as their capital?

Critical Thinking

3. **Making Generalizations**   How were the kingdoms of Kush and Aksum influenced by other cultures?

Graphic Organizer Activity

4. Draw a diagram like this one, and use it to show the effects of iron-smelting on Kush. (Add boxes as needed.)

Section 1 Assessment Answers

1. Kushites learned to worship the god Amon-Re, how to work in copper and bronze, and to adopt hieroglyphs to fit their language. Egypt was ruled for a time by Kush and was also influenced through trade.
2. It was on the Nile, it lay near large deposits of iron ore and trees to fuel smelting furnaces, and it had good grazing land.
3. Answers will vary but Kushites learned iron-smelting from the Assyrians; they worshiped the same god and built pyramids like the Egyptians; Aksumites took Christianity from the Greeks.
4. Possible effects: made iron hoes, which increased grain production; made iron knives and spears for trade; moved capital to Meroë, where large deposits of iron ore and trees to fuel smelting could be found; grew into a great trading nation

Assign the Chapter 8 **Section 1 Quiz** in the TCR. Testmaker available.

L2 Communication Have two students act out a silent barter using modern objects and ask why this technique was used in Africa. *(to eliminate language problems, to show trust and good will)* Ask students how difficult or simple their simulated barter was. Would this be successful in modern times? Have the class discuss why effective trade was important to the growth of African kingdoms.

Reading Check Answer
In **silent barter,** Ghanian merchants and gold miners would exchange goods and gold without saying a word or even seeing each other.

LINKING PAST TO PRESENT

The present nation of Ghana is not located in the same area of West Africa as the empire of Ghana was located in the mid-1000s. The early empire of Ghana is now occupied by the countries of Mauritania and Mali.

DID YOU KNOW ???

Ancient Ghana's capital consisted of two cities connected by a road lined with houses. The king and soldiers lived in one city; Arab traders lived in the second city.

💾 Use the **Vocabulary Puzzle-Maker** to create crossword and word search puzzles.

SECTION 2 The Middle Kingdoms

Several large trading kingdoms arose in West Africa after 400 A.D. Their rise was aided by the knowledge of iron-smelting. This was most likely brought to West Africa by *refugees,* or people who flee for safety, from Kush.

Ghana The first of these trading kingdoms was Ghana (gah' nuh). Legend has it that Ghana was founded about 200 A.D. Around 350 A.D., the Ghanians learned how to smelt iron. With iron swords and lances, Ghanian warriors expanded the boundaries of their country. They also gained control over West Africa's major trade routes.

Along these trade routes, goods were carried by caravans of camels or donkeys. The most important goods were salt and gold. Caravans carried salt south from Taghaza (tuh gah' zuh) in present-day Algeria (al jir' ē uh). They returned north with gold from Wangara (wahn gar' uh), an area southwest of Ghana.

Ghanian merchants and Wangara gold miners used a trading technique called **silent barter.** Ghanian merchants would travel to a trading site along a river in Wangara. They would place salt and other goods on the ground and beat drums to signal the gold miners. Then, they would withdraw. Next, the gold miners would appear, look at the goods, and leave some gold. Then, they would withdraw. If the Ghanians thought they had received enough gold, they would take it and leave. If not, they would withdraw and wait for the miners to leave more gold. When the exchange was over, the Ghanians would trade the gold to merchants from North Africa. Often, the gold was shipped to Europe and Asia for sale.

Only gold dust could be used in trade. Nuggets became the property of the king, who controlled the economy. Legend has it that one nugget was so heavy that it served as a hitching post for the king's horses.

In 1042 A.D., Arabs from North Africa started a war against Ghana. They destroyed the capital and made the Ghanians give them tribute. Ghana managed to regain its independence but was not strong enough to survive.

Mali By 1240 A.D., Ghana was a part of Mali (mah' lē), the second large trading kingdom in West Africa. The king of Mali, whose army had conquered Ghana, was Sundiata Keita (sūn dē ah' tuh kī ' tuh), or "Hungering Lion."

Reading Check How did **silent barter** work?

Photograph of Camel Caravan

COOPERATIVE LEARNING

Divide students into three groups, and ask them to pretend they are members of Arab caravans visiting each of the three empires described in this section. Direct them to record their impressions of the journey, including the trip across the Sahara, in the form of journal entries. Call on members from each group to read the entries aloud. You might use this exercise to introduce the primary source reading by Arab scholar Ibn Fadl Allah al Omari on pages 678–679 of the **Primary Sources Library.**

📁 Assign Chapter 8 *Cooperative Learning Activity* in the TCR.

GOLD DESIGNS The gold mined in ancient Africa was often formed into intricate designs on jewelry and ceremonial ornaments. These pieces are elephant charms. **Who controlled most of the gold supply in ancient Ghana?**

Sundiata Keita did several things to make his kingdom strong. He reestablished the salt—gold trade, which the Arabs had disrupted. He organized a permanent army. He divided the kingdom into provinces, each headed by a general. The generals kept the peace and saw that there was enough food for the people. To strengthen ties with different groups in the kingdom, Sundiata Keita moved his capital from place to place.

Sundiata Keita wanted to impress the people with his power. When he appeared in public, trumpeters announced his arrival. He sat on an ebony throne under an arch made from large elephant tusks. He never spoke directly to people. Instead, requests were answered by servants standing at the foot of the stairs leading to the throne.

One of the most famous kings of Mali was Mansa Musa I (mahn' sah mū' sah), or King Moses I. One reason Mansa Musa was famous was because of a **pilgrimage** (pil' gruh mij), or religious journey, he made to Arabia in 1324–25. It took more than 14 months to cover the 3,000 miles, or 4,800 kilometers. Some 12,000 servants traveled with the king. Each carried a 4-pound, or 1.8-kilogram, gold bar. Mansa Musa gave many of these bars to poor

People in History

Mansa Musa I
c. 1337 A.D.

West African Emperor

A grandson or grand-nephew of the warrior king Sundiata Keita, Mansa Musa guided Mali to its height of power. Under his rule, Mali grew to the size of western Europe and, in terms of gold, it outdid the wealth of Egypt. Mansa Musa used his large army to secure safe passage of travelers and traders through his empire and to keep order for nearly 25 years.

Reading Check
What is a **pilgrimage?**

SPOTLIGHT ON: MANSA MUSA I

One of the most celebrated travelers of the Middle Ages was Mansa Musa I, ruler of Mali in the 1300s. Europeans who learned of his *hajj* included pictures of him holding a gold nugget on their maps of Africa. On his holy pilgrimage to Makkah, Musa stopped in Cairo where he visited the local sultan. Mansa Musa, who had brought a great deal of gold with him, gave it freely to needy people in Egypt and other places he traveled. When Mansa Musa and his entourage returned to Mali, he brought with him some of the brightest and most talented scholars and architects. His dream was to build great cities in Mali to be centers of learning. Mansa Musa's sharing of wealth created aftereffects on the Egyptian economy. So much gold was in circulation that it was devalued.

GEOGRAPHY AND HISTORY

The people of Songhai used the Niger River for military transportation and trade. They also built dikes and canals along the river.

L2 **Economics** Africa's early kingdoms became wealthy from the development of trade of natural resources. Ask students to read and report on current newspaper or magazine articles discussing how African nations today are working to increase trade or development of their natural resources.

💾 Use **Interactive Tutor Self-Assessment Software** to review Section 2.

people he met along the way. As a result of this trip, news of Mansa Musa and Mali reached as far as Europe.

In Arabia, Mansa Musa met a Spanish architect whom he brought back to Mali. There, the architect built a university in the trading city of Timbuktu (tim buhk tū′). It became a great center of learning and drew students from Europe, Asia, and Africa.

After 25 years, Mansa Musa's reign ended. The rulers who followed him were weak. Within 100 years after Mansa Musa's death, Mali lost its land to others.

Songhai   The kingdom that replaced Mali as the most powerful in West Africa was Songhai (song′ hī). By the late 1400s, it controlled almost all the land that had been part of Mali. Songhai also conquered other lands and became the largest of the three trading kingdoms.

The Sultan Sunni Ali, in 1464, ruled Songhai from the city of Gao. He maintained a huge army equipped with armor, camels and horses. He also had a large navy that patrolled the Niger River. Following Sunni Ali's death, Askia Muhammad came to power in Songhai. He extended the empire even more and culture flourished. Sultan Askia welcomed teachers, doctors, poets, students, and religious leaders from Asia and Europe.

Songhai was more organized than the other two kingdoms. It was divided into provinces and with a governor for each. Everyone used the same weights and measures and followed the same legal system. Only members of the ruling Songhai could become political leaders or join the cavalry. Other groups had special jobs, such as caring for the army's horses or serving at the royal court. Most enslaved people, often prisoners of war, worked as farmers.

Despite its power, Songhai lasted only 100 years. In 1591 A.D., the ruler of Morocco sent an army across the Sahara to seize Songhai's gold mines. Though only half of the Moroccan soldiers survived the trip, they had guns. They defeated Songhai's soldiers, who were armed only with swords and spears.

Section 2 Assessment

1. **Define:** silent barter, pilgrimage.
2. What were two important trade goods in West Africa?
3. How was the kingdom of Songhai organized?

Critical Thinking

4. **Making Inferences**   Why do you think Ghanian merchants set up a system called silent barter?

Graphic Organizer Activity

5. Draw a diagram like this one, and use it to summarize the accomplishments of the three great West African kingdoms.

West African Accomplishments		
Ghana	Mali	Songhai

(134)   UNIT 3 IDEAS AND ARMIES

Section 2 Assessment Answers

1. silent barter, system of trade in ancient Ghana (p. 132); pilgrimage, a religious journey (p. 134)
2. salt and gold
3. It was divided into provinces, each with a governor. Everyone used the same weights, measures, and legal system.
4. Answers will vary but might include that Ghanian merchants might have been dealing with people who did not speak their language.
5. Accomplishments should reflect the policies established by the rulers of each kingdom, particularly the growth of trade and the encouragement of learning.

Assign Chapter 8 **Section 2 Quiz** in the TCR. Testmaker available.

Reading Latitude

To measure distances north and south, mapmakers use imaginary lines on maps and globes. These are called lines of latitude and they run east and west around Earth. Lines of latitude are often called parallels because they never meet and remain the same distance from each other all the way around Earth.

Latitude is measured in degrees, as shown by the symbol °. The Equator, which is a line of latitude, is marked 0° because all other lines of latitude are measured from it. One degree of latitude equals about 69 miles, or 110 kilometers.

There are 90 lines of latitude from the Equator to each pole. Those lines north of the Equator are marked with an N. Those lines south of the Equator are marked with an S.

Map Practice

1. Which civilization was located closest to the Equator?
2. Which city, Timbuktu or Napata, was located closest to the 20°N line of latitude?
3. Which line of latitude runs through the center of the great trading civilization of Zimbabwe?

Early Africa

20°W · 20°E · 40°E
MEDITERRANEAN SEA
30°N · SAHARA DESERT · EGYPT
Taghaza ·
20°N · Timbuktu · Napata · Meroë · RED SEA
10°N
WANGARA
0°Eq
  Kush
  Aksum · ATLANTIC OCEAN
10°S
  Ghana · Kilwa
  Mali
20°S
  Zimbabwe
30°S · Trade Routes · INDIAN OCEAN
miles 0 · 500 · 1000
kilometers 0 · 500 · 1000 · 1500
N

GO TO

Glencoe's **Skillbuilder Interactive Workbook, Level 1,** provides instruction and practice in key social studies skills.

135

MAP SKILLS

TEACH

Reading Latitude

Instruct students to study the map on page 135 to answer the following questions:

Which city was located close to the 10° S line of latitude? *(Kilwa)*

Which city lies almost halfway between 20° N and 30° N lines of latitude? *(Taghaza)*

Between what two lines of latitude do most of the early empires and civilizations of Africa lie? *(10° N and 20° N)*

Ask students to make a generalization about early civilizations of Africa based on their latitude. *(Students' generalizations might include that the climate between 10° N and 20° N was conducive to farming and trade for early African civilizations.)*

Answers to Map Practice

1. Mali
2. Napata
3. 20°S

SPOTLIGHT ON: EARLY AFRICA

As trading grew in ancient Africa, so did the need for some form of currency or money. Paper currency and coins did not yet exist. Until the mid-fifteenth century, cowrie shells and trading beads were used as currency. Among some West African people, iron chains and spearheads were also used as money. Then, in the mid-1400s, while the Songhai Empire was rising, coins became popular. As always, gold nuggets were considered to be of great value by almost all peoples.

L1 Geography: Movement
Ask students to brainstorm the reasons why people today move from one geographic area to another. *(better climate, education, job opportunities, and religious or political freedom)* Ask students to compare these reasons for migration with those of early peoples.

Use the **Vocabulary Puzzle-Maker** to create crossword and word search puzzles.

SECTION 3 East African Civilizations

The growth of trading kingdoms in West Africa was matched by the rise of trading kingdoms and city-states in East Africa. Goods moved from the interior of East Africa to coastal markets, which, in time, became large city-states. Each of these had its own ruler and government.

Zimbabwe   One of the best-known trading kingdoms was Zimbabwe (zim bah' bwā). The people of Zimbabwe speak a language known as Bantu (ban' tū). Their ancestors, the Shona (shō' nuh), once lived in present-day Nigeria (nū jir' ē uh) in West Africa. About 100 A.D., a **population explosion,** or a large and sudden growth in population, took place. Since the land could not support the increased number of people, many Shona began to leave their homeland to look for new homes.

The Shona settled in Zimbabwe in East Africa about 700 A.D. There, they built towns using stones that were cut in such a way that they fitted together without mortar. The capital had houses, a fort, and a temple. The fort stood on top of a hill and was surrounded by a huge wall. Besides the temple, the enclosed area contained the houses of the chief and his officials.

The people of Zimbabwe viewed their chief as a god-king. They approached him by crawling on their stomachs. Officials imitated him. If he coughed, they coughed. When he ate, they ate. The chief kept his throne as long as he was in good health. When he grew old, however, he was expected to take poison. Then, a younger man would become chief, and Zimbabwe could remain strong.

Another reason Zimbabwe remained strong was trade. Its people traded gold, copper, and ivory from the interior to merchants from cities along Africa's east coast. From these cities, trade was carried on with Arabia, Persia, India, and China.

Kilwa   Another important trading city-state in East Africa was Kilwa (kil' wuh). From Kilwa, merchants sailed across the Red Sea and the Indian Ocean. The people of Kilwa collected heavy taxes from traders of other countries. They used their wealth to extend their power over neighboring city-states. They also used it to dress in fine cotton and silk and to fill their four-story houses with vases and hangings from India and China.

A culture known as Swahili (swah hē' lē) developed in Kilwa and other East African city-states. Many Arab traders had settled in the coastal cities. For this reason, Swahili culture is a mix of

Reading Check
How did a **population explosion** cause the Shona to leave their homeland?

Zimbabwe Ruins

EXTENDING THE CONTENT

Bantu is a language spoken over a very large area of Africa, from the fifth parallel of north latitude to the Republic of South Africa. A subgroup of the Benue-Congo group of Niger-Congo language family, Bantu includes the languages of Rwanda, Makua, Xhosa, and Zulu. Most Bantu languages are tonal, which means they use pitch to differentiate words that might be pronounced in the same way.

Arabic and African cultures. The Swahili language is a combination of Bantu and Arabic.

Section 3 Assessment

1. **Define:** population explosion.
2. How did the people of Zimbabwe view their leader?
3. How did the people at Kilwa use their wealth?

Critical Thinking

4. **Understanding Cause and Effect** A population explosion among the Shona caused many of these people to leave their homeland. What are some of the events or conditions that might cause people to leave their homelands today?

Graphic Orgainzer Activity

5. Draw a diagram like this one, and use it to show features of Swahili culture.

L2 **Culture** Organize tactile/kinesthetic learners into three groups. Assign each group one of the following Mesoamerican groups: the Olmecs, the Mayas, or the Aztecs. Each group should create a simple board game involving the history and people of their chosen civilization. Suggest they design a gameboard and basic rules for playing the game. Suggest each group invite other students to play their game.

Use **Interactive Tutor Self Assessment Software** to review Section 3.

NATIONAL GEOGRAPHIC SOCIETY

TRANSPARENCIES
Physical Geography of the World
Display the following to enrich student appreciation of the diverse environments settled by Native Americans.
2. Sonoran Desert, U.S.
3. Rocky Mountains, Canada
4. Grand Canyon, U.S.
6. Mississippi River, U.S.
8. Baffin Island, Canada
9. Appalachian Mountains, U.S.

 Use the **Vocabulary Puzzle-Maker** to create crossword and word search puzzles.

SECTION 4 Path to the Americas

Until about 25,000 years ago, there were no people in the Americas. Then, hunting-and-food-gathering bands began to cross into the Americas from Asia over a land bridge. This land bridge was formed during the last Ice Age. At that time, large amounts of ocean water were frozen into huge glaciers, and sea levels dropped. Today, this bridge is covered by the waters of the Bering Strait.

The bands came in search of food, following grass-grazing animals that had crossed earlier. The bands lived off their kill and also gathered wild plants. Over time, they spread all through the Americas. Experts believe people reached the southern tip of South America by about 9000 B.C.

About 7000 B.C., the last Ice Age ended. The climate became hotter and drier, and in many areas deserts took the place of grasslands. Large game almost disappeared. So, people had to find other ways of getting food.

By 6000 B.C., people in the Tehuacán (tā wah kahn') Valley south of present-day Mexico City had developed farming. By 3000 B.C., there were thousands of small farming villages all through the Americas. The most important crop was *maize* (māz), or corn.

Between 3000 B.C. and 1000 B.C., people developed such skills as weaving and pottery making. They grew peanuts, tomatoes, and potatoes. In a few areas, they built irrigation systems that helped support a growing population.

Section 3 Assessment Answers

1. population explosion, large and sudden growth in population (p. 136)
2. as a god-king
3. to extend their power over neighboring city-states, to dress in fine cotton and silk, and to fill their houses with riches from India and China
4. Answers will vary but might include that people leave their homes because of war, famine, disease, religious persecution, or simply hope of a better life.
5. Sample features: made up of city-states, traded with people across the Red Sea and Indian Ocean, mix of Arabic and African cultures, spoke a language made up Arabic and Bantu

Assign Chapter 8 **Section 3 Quiz** in the TCR. Testmaker available.

💾 Use **Interactive Tutor Self-Assessment Software** to review Section 4.

Independent Practice

L3 **Critical Thinking** Ask students to name the characteristics of a centralized government, as you write responses on the chalkboard. Have students form groups to describe what must happen in a civilization before a centralized government can form. *(division of labor—one group producing enough food, housing, and other necessities for the community; establishment of military or political force to maintain peace)*

HOME VIDEO.

The following videotape program is available from Glencoe to enrich Chapter 8:

• **The Maya**

To find classroom resources to accompany this video, check the following home page:

A&E Television:
http://www.aetv.com

💾 Use the **Vocabulary Puzzle-Maker** to create crossword and word search puzzles.

Section 4 Assessment

1. How did hunting-and-gathering bands travel to the Americas?
2. How long may it have taken for people to spread out over North and South America?
3. When and where did farming first appear?

Critical Thinking

4. **Understanding Cause and Effect** What do think caused hunting-and-gathering bands to push farther south into the Americas?

Graphic Orfanizer Activity

5. Draw a diagram like this one, and use it to show the cause and effects of the invention of farming in Mesoamerica.

```
┌────────┐     ┌──────────┐     ┌────────┐
│ Cause  │────▶│ Rise of  │────▶│ Effect │
└────────┘     │ Farming  │     └────────┘
               │          │────▶┌────────┐
               │          │     │ Effect │
               └──────────┘     └────────┘
                          └────▶┌────────┐
                                │ Effect │
                                └────────┘
```

SECTION 5 — Mesoamerica

As the number of people grew, societies became more complex. Several great civilizations rose in Mesoamerica, or Middle America, before 900 A.D. and others later.

The Olmecs One of the earliest civilizations in Mesoamerica was that of the Olmecs (ōl' meks). It came into being around 1000 B.C. About 900 years later, it disappeared mysteriously. The Olmecs had a great influence on other peoples of the area and was called the "mother culture." They developed planned cities, hieroglyphic writing, and a calendar.

The Olmecs lived along the southern coast of the Gulf of Mexico. Part of the year, the people farmed. The rest of the year they built stone cities, which were chiefly religious centers. The cities stood on top of huge hills. They had temples; sacred pools; and houses for priests, artists, and architects. The people lived in nearby villages. They visited the cities on festival and market days.

The Mayas Another great civilization, that of the Mayas (mī' uhz), began in Mesoamerica about 500 B.C. It reached its peak between 300 and 900 A.D. The Mayas lived in present-day southeast Mexico, Belize (buh lēz'), and Guatemala (gwah tuh mah' luh). Like the Olmecs, the Mayas lived in farming villages that surrounded religious cities. Mayan cities had temples and houses for priests and nobles.

The Mayas were great traders. Their cities, linked by roads paved with white cement, had busy marketplaces. Canoes handled local trade along the coasts.

Mayan Figure

Section 4 Assessment Answers

1. perhaps across a land bridge over the Bering Strait
2. from 23,000 B.C. to 9000 B.C., or about 14,000 years
3. By 6,000 B.C., people in the Tehuacán Valley south of present-day Mexico City had developed farming.
4. Answers will vary but could include the need for food, safety from attack, weather, or curiosity.
5. Sample responses: cause—end of last Ice Age and disappearance of most large game; effects—rise of farming villages, development of weaving and pottery making, construction of irrigation ditches, population growth

Assign Chapter 8 **Section 4 Quiz** in the TCR. Testmaker available.

Linking Across Time

Tortillas Mayan women rose at dawn to boil and grind corn for making the dough for tortillas—thin, round, flat breads. They then worked the dough by hand (left) before baking. Tortillas remain a basic part of the Mayan diet today (right), with women making tortillas in much the same way as their ancestors. **Why was maize (corn) important to the development of civilization in Mesoamerica?**

The Maya adapted their own hieroglyphs from the Olmecs. Mayan mathematicians came up with the idea of zero and a counting system based on 20. Mayan astronomers were able to predict when eclipses of the sun and the moon would take place. They developed a calendar, based on that of the Olmecs, with a year of 365 days. They also made cotton cloth and paper.

About 900 A.D., most Mayas abandoned their cities and disappeared. No one knows why. A plague may have broken out. Perhaps the soil could no longer produce enough food. War may have interfered with trade.

The Aztecs

Later, a third great civilization, that of the Aztecs, rose in Mesoamerica. About 1200 A.D., the Aztecs began moving south into the central valley of Mexico. Through military conquest, they expanded their empire to include all of central Mexico. By 1400 A.D., the Aztec Empire had 5 million people.

The Aztecs made the people they conquered pay tribute. This took the form of corn, clothing, rubber, and wood. It is believed that each year 2 million cotton cloaks alone were sent to the capital, Tenochtitlán (tā noch tē tláhn').

Tenochtitlán was built on an island in Lake Texcoco (teks kō' kō). *Causeways,* or paved roads, connected the island to the mainland. The city had pyramid-temples, palaces, gardens, zoos, schools, and markets. About 300,000 people lived there. Some dressed in feathered capes and cloaks of many colors. Women wore flowers and feathers in their hair.

Busy Markets Markets played an important part in the economic and social life of the Aztec. The market at Tlateloco was the largest in the ancient Americas. About 60,000 people may have visited the market each day.

CHAPTER 8 AFRICA AND THE AMERICAS **139**

Linking Across Time

Sample response: Maize was one of the first crops grown in the Mesoamerica and allowed for later cultural development.

LINKING PAST TO PRESENT

Tenochtitlán means "near the cactus." Legend has it that Huitzilopochli, the god of sun and war, told the Aztecs to build their city in the place where they found an eagle with a snake in its beak perched on a cactus. The eagle-snake cactus symbol appears on the modern Mexican flag.

The following videotape program is available from Glencoe to enrich Chapter 8:

- **Secrets of the Aztec Empire**

To find classroom resources to accompany this video, check the following home page:

A&E Television:
http://www.aetv.com

MULTICULTURAL PERSPECTIVES

Olmec priests wore jaguar skins, bright red robes, bird feathers, and flower-topped headdresses. They also filed their teeth and put semi-precious stones in them. Some nobles placed splint-like boards on their children's heads and wrapped them with cloth to create elongated skulls, which they thought were beautiful.

Painting of Aztec Farmer

To feed the people, the Aztecs had to create more farmland. They filled in parts of the lake and dug drainage canals. They planted crops in soil-filled reed baskets anchored in the lake. They also built *aqueducts* (ak' wuh dukts), or water channels, to bring fresh water to the city's reservoirs from mainland springs. Canoes delivered the water from the reservoirs to people's houses.

The Aztecs were a warlike people. War and religion were closely connected. The people worshiped two major gods. One was the rain god who stood for the peaceful life of farming. The other was the sun god who stood for war and expanding empire. The Aztecs believed that the sun god needed human sacrifices. They felt that if they did not make them, the sun would not rise in the morning. Victims were generally prisoners of war.

The Aztec Empire reached its height in the early 1500s under Montezuma II (mahn tuh zū' muh). During his reign, however, Spaniards, who had guns and horses, attacked the Aztecs. Easily defeated by the Spaniards, the Aztecs lost their empire.

Section 5 Assessment

1. What were some of the accomplishments of the Maya?
2. How did the Aztec Empire come to an end?

Critical Thinking

3. **Drawing Conclusions** Why do you think Mayan civilization ended?

Graphic Organizer Activity

4. Draw a diagram like this one, and use it to summarize the accomplishments of the three great Mesoamerican civilizations.

Mesoamerican Accomplishments		
Olmec	Maya	Aztec

SECTION 6   The Incas

About the same time the Aztecs moved south into central Mexico, the Incas moved out from Peru. They established an empire that stretched along the west coast of South America for about 2,500 miles, or 4,000 kilometers. By the 1500s, there were 12 million people in the Inca Empire.

Student Web Activity

Visit the *Human Heritage* Web site at **humanheritage.glencoe.com** and click on *Chapter 8— Student Web Activities* to find out more about the ancient civilizations of the Americas.

History   The Incas started out as farmers and shepherds. They built villages on the rocky slopes of the Andes Mountains. In the fertile valley below, they grew corn, potatoes, and other crops. On pastures above, they grazed alpacas (al pak' uhz) and llamas (lah' muhs).

In 1438, the Inca ruler Pachacuti (pah chuh kū' tē) conquered several neighboring peoples and founded the Inca Empire. He used several techniques to hold it together. He ordered

140   UNIT 3 IDEAS AND ARMIES

conquered peoples to worship the Inca sun god in addition to their own gods. He made the Inca language of Quechua (kech' wuh) the official language. He moved people who had been living under Inca rule into newly conquered lands. They helped spread Inca culture and watched for signs of rebellion.

Pachacuti also had a huge system of stone-paved roads built. Rope suspension bridges crossed canyons and rivers. Way stations with food, weapons, and other supplies needed by the Inca army were set up on the roads. Only soldiers and government officials were allowed to use the roads.

Inca Way of Life A ruler, known as the Inca, determined the way of life. Land belonged to the ruler and not to the people who worked it. Villagers paid taxes to the empire in two ways.

Growing Grains The Aztecs and Incas grew high-protein grains called amaranth and quinoa. Today these grains, native to the Americas, have become important in parts of India, Pakistan, Nepal, and China. Amaranth and quinoa, in the form of flour and cereals, have become common in U.S. health-food stores.

Early American Empires

MAP STUDY

HUMAN/ ENVIRONMENTAL INTERACTION
The Inca developed engineering skills that enabled them to build a large network of roads. **How did the environment of the Inca make road building more difficult?**

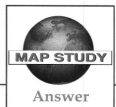

MAP STUDY

Answer

The Incas had to build roads through mountainous areas.

L1 **Geography: Location** Have students write five questions about the locations and relationships of places shown on the map of early American empires. Have students ask their questions to the class. **ELL**

ASSESS

Check for Understanding

Ask students to summarize the main points of the chapter, orally or in writing. Discuss the answers to the Section and Chapter Assessment questions.

Evaluate

Assign Chapter 8 **Performance Assessment Activity** in the TCR.

Administer **Chapter 8 Test** in the TCR. Testmaker available.

EXTENDING THE CONTENT

Sometimes called the "lost city of the Andes," the Incas' startling mountain fortress of Machu Picchu had never been seen except by local Native Americans until 1911. It was discovered by a Yale University expedition led by Hiram Bingham. The ruined city perches 8,000 feet (2,438 m), high in the mountains on a lush green ridge between two steep rocky peaks, about 50 miles (80 km) from Cuzco, Peru. It has a temple and citadel, as well as the ruins of many small stone houses. Thousands of worn stone steps connect the remains of farming terraces, squares, fountains, and aqueducts.

Reteach

Assign Chapter 8 **Reteaching Activity** in the TCR.

Enrich

Have students investigate the way in which the Mayas and Aztecs processed and prepared chocolate. If possible, encourage students to demonstrate the methods for the class.

Assign Chapter 8 **Enrichment Activity** in the TCR.

CLOSE

Hold a class discussion about why the kingdoms and civilizations described in this chapter declined.

Use **Interactive Tutor Self-Assessment Software** to review Section 6.

Self-Check Quiz gives students an interactive chapter tutorial. Have them access **Chapter 8 Quiz** at humanheritage.glencoe.com

---

They paid through their labor. This involved not only farming land, but also building roads and mining gold. In addition, they paid taxes in kind.

The Inca had to keep track of people and goods. Because there was no written language, special accountants used **quipus** (ke̅′ pū z), or counting devices, to do this. Quipus were made up of knotted strings of different colors. Each color represented a different item. The knots in each string stood for tens, hundreds, and so on. The spaces between the knots stood for zero.

The wealth of the Inca Empire was shown in the way the ruler lived. His palace was the size of a town. There were hundreds of rooms and thousands of servants. The Inca's bodyguards wore gold armor. The poles of the litter in which he was carried were covered with gold. A desire for this wealth was part of the reason the Spaniards destroyed the Inca Empire in the early 1500s.

✓ **Reading Check**
What were **quipus,** and how did the Inca use them?

Section 6 Assessment

1. **Define:** quipus.
2. How big was the Inca Empire at its peak?
3. How did Pachacuti hold the Inca Empire together?

Critical Thinking

4. **Demonstrating Reasoned Judgment** Suppose the Inca had the choice of keeping Pachacuti as their leader or electing a new one. Which choice do you think they would have taken? Explain.

Graphic Organizer Activity

5. Draw a diagram like this one, and use it to show the changes that Pachacuti brought to the Incan way of life.

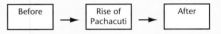

| Before | → | Rise of Pachacuti | → | After |

Chapter Summary & Study Guide

1. The Kushites and Egyptians influenced each other through conquest and trade.
2. The Aksumites destroyed Kush and later converted to Christianity.
3. The kingdoms of Ghana, Mali, and Songhai built West African empires based on a trade in salt and gold.
4. A population explosion led the Shona to build Zimbabwe in East Africa.
5. Kilwa and other coastal cities handled trade between Africa and Arabia, Persia, India, and China.
6. The Olmec and the Maya invented many new ideas, including forms of writing and a calendar.
7. The Aztec and the Inca built complex civilizations that lasted until the time of European arrival in the Americas.

Self-Check Quiz
Visit the *Human Heritage* Web site at **humanheritage. glencoe.com** and click on *Chapter 8—Self-Check Quiz* to assess your understanding of this chapter.

142   UNIT 3 IDEAS AND ARMIES

Section 6 Assessment Answers

1. quipus, Inca counting devices (p. 142)
2. 12 million people
3. He ordered conquered peoples to worship the Inca sun god, made Quechua the official language, and moved people who had been living under Inca rule into newly conquered lands.
4. Answers will vary but should include that some people would rather replace him with a less strict, less dictatorial leader. Others may want to keep him as a leader since he provided well for them.

5. Sample responses: *before*—made up of farmers and shepherds living in scattered villages; *after*—a large unified empire connected by roads and customs (also see answer to question 3)

Assign Chapter 8 **Section 6 Quiz** in the TCR. Testmaker available.

Using Key Terms

Imagine that you are putting together a photo display about ancient civilizations. You have found a photo that illustrates each of these terms:

silent barter   pilgrimage
population explosion   quipus

Use each term in a one-sentence caption describing what the photo shows.

Understanding Main Ideas

1. How did Ghana gain control of West African trade routes?
2. What was the effect of Mansa Musa's pilgrimage?
3. What was the main difference between the Mesoamerican civilizations that developed before and after 900 A.D.?
4. What did the Olmec contribute to other civilizations?
5. How did the Aztec treat the people they conquered?
6. Who directed and controlled the Incan way of life?

Critical Thinking

1. How do you think the development of African civilization might have been different if the Kushites did not develop iron-smelting?
2. Why was trade important to the growth of African civilization?
3. Which Mesoamerican civilization would you choose to live in? Why?
4. What contributions did early American civilizations make to present-day life in the United States?

Graphic Organizer Activity

History Draw two parallel time lines like the ones shown, and use them to compare important events in the early civilizations of Africa and the Americas. Sample events are provided to help you get started.

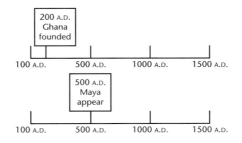

Geography in History

Location Compare the maps of early empires found on pages 135 and 141. What similarities in location of these civilizations can you find? What differences in location are there between the two areas?

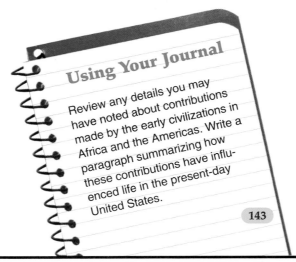

Using Your Journal

Review any details you may have noted about contributions made by the early civilizations in Africa and the Americas. Write a paragraph summarizing how these contributions have influenced life in the present-day United States.

143

Assessment Answers

Using Key Terms

Captions will vary but should include a descriptive sentence for the scene.

Understanding Main Ideas

1. by the use of iron swords and lances
2. News of Mansa Musa and Mali spread as far as Europe. Mansa Musa also met a Spanish architect while in Arabia and convinced him to help build a university in Timbuktu.
3. The earlier civilizations were peaceful, had rulers interested in learning, religion and trade; later civilizations were warlike, with religions marked by human sacrifice.
4. planned cities, hieroglyphic writing, a calendar
5. The Aztecs made them pay tribute and sacrificed some of them to the sun god.
6. the ruler

Critical Thinking

1. Answers will vary but should include lack of progress.
2. Answers will vary but should include that without trade, African civilizations would not have interacted.
3. Answers will vary but should include specific reasons.
4. Answers will vary.

Graphic Organizer Activity

Students should pick important dates highlighted in the chapter and arrange them at correct intervals on the time line.

Bonus Test Question
For Chapter 8 Test
You dig up pottery from a past civilization and know that it was made by the Olmec. What evidence helped you reach your conclusion? *(The pottery is adobe clay, was found near the ruins of a city, contains kernels of corn, etc.)*

Using Your Journal

Diary entries will vary. You might call on volunteers to read their entries to the class.

Geography in History

Similarities: both are contiguous, close to the Equator, and coastal; differences: Mesoamerican empires stretched north and bordered the Pacific Ocean; African kingdoms stretched east and bordered the Atlantic and Indian oceans.

FOCUS

Objectives

After reading the Around the World for Unit 3, your students will be able to:

1. state the length of time the Zhou held power.

2. discuss how the Zhou changed farming in the China.

3. recognize the artistic and musical accomplishments of the Zhou.

Bellringer

Starting with the drafting of the Constitution in 1787, ask students how long the United States government has been in existence. *(Students should subtract 1787 from the present date.)*

Motivational Activity

Refer students to the Around the World feature, pointing out that the Zhou dynasty ruled China for more than 800 years. Ask: What do the pictures on pages 144–145 reveal about what the Zhou achieved during this time span? *(Sample responses: built a great empire, used irrigation channels to grow rice, created artistic and musical works, developed a tradition of strong family ties)*

TEACH

Geography: Region Have students examine the map on page 144. Ask: What geographic features helped isolate China from the outside world? *(the mountains to the west and the ocean to the east)* Link this geographic isolation to the Zhou kings who considered the outside world as "uncivilized."

Next, divide the class into groups, and assign each group

144

THE ZHOU

The Zhou dynasty ruled for more than 800 years—the longest ruling dynasty in Chinese history. Zhou kings claimed they ruled according to a "mandate from heaven." However, this claim did not stop ambitious nobles from challenging their power. For the last 500 years of their rule, Zhou kings watched their empire crumble as warring states tried to seize control of China.

Despite the constant warfare, the Zhou dynasty oversaw many advancements. Achievements ranged from the development of new philosophies to the invention of new weapons.

▲ The Zhou ruled from 1028 B.C. to about 256 B.C. Boundaries changed constantly throughout this period. This map shows the Zhou Empire around the height of its power.

The Zhou introduced many advances in farming, including the irrigation channels used by Chinese farmers today. These channels allowed farmers to flood the fields used to grow rice. Production of rice became increasingly important as the Zhou extended their power into China's great river basins. ▼

SPOTLIGHT ON: THE ZHOU

The following are some details about daily life in China during the Zhou dynasty. You might want to share this information with students.

• Most people were poor farmers living in rural homes of mud and straw.

• Meals of peasants were mostly rice and vegetables, and rarely, meat.

• As many as 100 family members lived together under the rule of the oldest male relative.

• Males were more valued as family members than females.

• Peasant women made all of the clothing out of rough fabric. The wealthy wore silk.

• It was unusual for a peasant to travel outside of the village. Languages were not the same from region to region.

• Art objects and ornate furniture filled the homes of the wealthy.

the World

▲ The Zhou created ornate metal statues, such as this winged dragon.

The Zhou kings considered the outside world uncivilized. They prided themselves on their cultural accomplishments. These chimes come from a Zhou orchestra, which included flutes, drums, wooden clappers, and more. The chimes consist of 64 bronze bells ranging in size from 8 inches to 5 feet. ▼

The Zhou had strong family ties and traditions. These mourning figures honor a family member who has died. ▶

Bronze work, such as this three-legged bowl and ladle, were crafted by the Zhou. ▼

Taking Another Look

1. When did the Zhou dynasty begin and end?
2. What advancement in farming did Zhou rulers introduce?

Hands-On Activity

Writing an Announcement Write an announcement for a CD of music played on the bronze chimes created during the Zhou dynasty. Be sure to mention that the chimes still work perfectly after nearly 2,500 years. **145**

one of the cultures, kingdoms, or city-states studied in Unit 3. Tell students to imagine that they are representatives sent to visit the Zhou emperor. What will they take to prove the accomplishments of their homeland? **L1**

ASSESS

Check for Understanding

Have students answer the questions in **Taking Another Look** on page 145.

Enrich

Developments under the Zhou, such as the invention of iron plows and flood-control systems, increased food and helped make Zhou China the most densely populated country. Assign interested students to find out China's population rank today.

CLOSE

Assign students to review the accomplishments of the Shang on pages 88–92, and ask them to explore how the Zhou built on Shang achievements.

ANSWERS TO TAKING ANOTHER LOOK

1. The Zhou ruled from 1028 B.C. to about 256 B.C.
2. The Zhou introduced the irrigation channels used by Chinese farmers today. These channels helped control flooding and increased rice production.

Hands-On Activity
Advertisements will vary, but students should place the chimes in the context of world history, noting the great age of Chinese civilization and the region's early cultural development.

Standardized Test Practice

Answers and Analyses

1B   History

According to page 103, the Phoenicians were not unified under a single government, nor did they conquer distant lands (though they traded widely). Choices C and D can therefore be eliminated. Nothing is said about a system of numbers. On pages 105–106, however, it states that the Phoenicians took the alphabet and *carried it to Europe.*

2H   History

The top of page 103 states that the Phoenicians signed *treaties* according to which *they promised to supply free shipments of goods* in exchange for their independence.

3B   History

According to page 114, *The Hebrews were the first people to believe in one god.*

TEST-TAKING TIP

When several choices seem possible, students should re-read the question and look for a key word in the question that will help make one choice better than others. In this case, the key word is *first*. This information should help students eliminate several choices.

4F   Civics

The Ten Commandments mention neither an exchange system nor punishments for crimes; choices G and H can be eliminated. The Code of Hammurabi does not mention one god, so choice J can be eliminated. Therefore, F is the best choice.

Directions: Choose the *best* answer to each of the following multiple choice questions. If you have trouble answering a question, use the process of elimination to narrow your choices. Write your answers on a separate piece of paper.

1. **Which of the following statements about the Phoenicians is true?**

    A   The Phoenicians invented the system of numbers we use today.

    B   The Phoenicians introduced a written alphabet to Europe.

    C   The Phoenicians lived under a single, unified government.

    D   The Phoenicians used their navy to conquer and settle many distant lands.

    > *Test-Taking Tip:*   This question requires you to remember an important *fact* about the Phoenicians. Since the Phoenicians did not have a *single, unified government,* you can eliminate answer C.

2. **In what unique way did the Phoenicians protect themselves from being conquered by other nations?**

    F   They built a strong army that other nations feared.

    G   They conquered other countries and took over foreign governments.

    H   They signed peace treaties with neighboring countries.

    J   They created a strong, unified central government in their country.

    > *Test-Taking Tip:*   The important word in this question is *unique.* The Phoenicians certainly did not invent the idea of having a strong army (answer F). What *new idea* did they try?

3. **The Hebrews are thought to be the first people to**

    A   devise a moral code

    B   worship one god

    C   live in the desert area known as Canaan

    D   write down their religious legends

    > *Test-Taking Tip:*   Make sure that you read the question and *all* the answer choices carefully. Think back to the other cultures and civilizations you have studied. Do you remember if, for instance, the Egyptians wrote down their religious legends? They did so in hieroglyphics. Though the Hebrews *did* write down their religious legends, they were not the *first* people to do so. Therefore, you can eliminate answer D.

4. **The Ten Commandments and the Code of Hammurabi are similar because they both**

    F   say that people should respect each other and each other's property

    G   established a regulated exchange system

    H   lay out the proper punishments for different crimes

    J   instruct people to worship only one god

    > *Test-Taking Tip:*   This question asks you to make a *comparison.* Choose the answer that is true for *both* sets of laws. Eliminate any choice that is not true of either the Ten Commandments or the Code of Hammurabi. For instance, the Ten Commandments does not lay out punishments. Therefore, you can eliminate choice H.

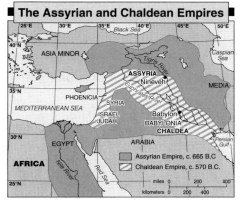

The Assyrian and Chaldean Empires

Use the map above to answer questions 5 and 6.

5. Approximately how far is it from Babylon to Nineveh?

A 100 miles

B 150 miles

C 300 miles

D 450 miles

Test-Taking Tip: Use the *map scale* to determine the distance from one point to another. If you do not have a ruler, you can use a small piece of paper to copy the length of the scale. Hold the paper next to the area you want to measure to help you estimate the distance.

6. Which of the following is east of Assyria?

F The Black Sea

G Media

H Phoenicia

J Israel

Test-Taking Tip: Study the map carefully before you choose an answer. Which way is *east* on a map?

7. What was something new and different about how the Persians traded?

A They kept track of trades using a written alphabet.

B They traded pots and pans in exchange for cloth.

C They only traded within their own country.

D They did business by using coins for money.

Test-Taking Tip: Notice that the question asks you to identify what was *new and different* about the Persians' method of trading. Was trading pots and pans for cloth a *new and different* idea?

STOP

147

Answers and Analyses

5C Geography

The scale on the bottom of the map indicates that the distance from Babylon to Nineveh is roughly 300 miles.

THE PRINCETON REVIEW TEST-TAKING TIP

All of the information needed to answer the question is on the map, but students need to read very carefully to avoid mistakes. In this case, students need to make sure that they do not confuse miles and kilometers on the scale.

6G Geography

According to the map, Phoenicia and Israel are west of Assyria, and the Black Sea is north of Assyria. The one choice that is east of Assyria is Media.

7D Economics

According to page 126, the Persians *spread the idea of using coins for money.*

THE PRINCETON REVIEW TEST-TAKING TIP

Students should scrutinize the language of the question to make sure they understand it thoroughly. The Phoenicians used an alphabet, so choice A cannot be right. Choice C is unlikely to be *new and different.*

Tested Objectives	
Questions	**Reading Objective**
1, 5, 6	Analyze information
2, 3	Identify supporting ideas
4	Make comparisons
7	Evaluate information

UNIT 4

The Greeks

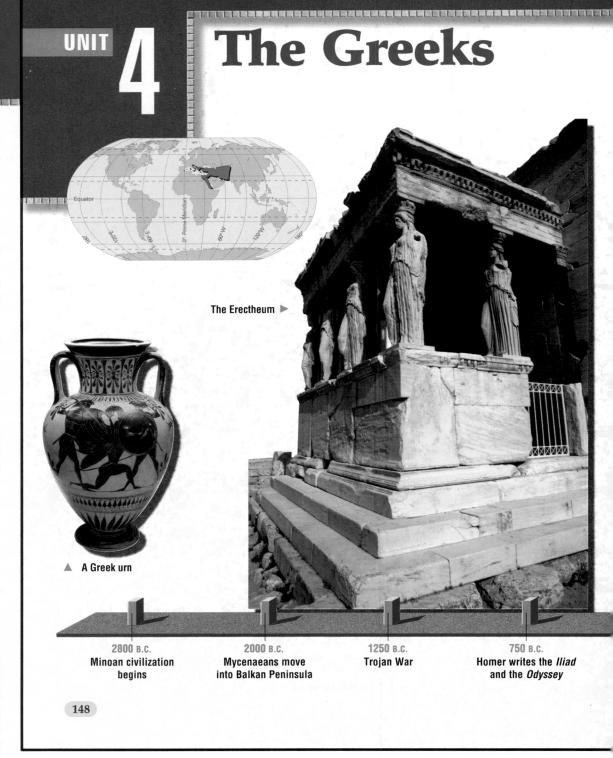

The Erectheum ▶

▲ A Greek urn

2800 B.C.	2000 B.C.	1250 B.C.	750 B.C.
Minoan civilization begins	Mycenaeans move into Balkan Peninsula	Trojan War	Homer writes the *Iliad* and the *Odyssey*

148

OVERVIEW

Unit 4 examines the history of the ancient Greeks from the rise of the Aegean civilizations to the conquest of Greece by the Romans.

➤ **Chapter 9** describes the Minoan and Mycenaean civilizations out of which Hellenic civilization grew.

➤ **Chapter 10** discusses the evolution of the polis as the political and geographic center of Greek life and examines in detail the city-states of Athens and Sparta.

➤ **Chapter 11** explains the major contributions made to western civilization by the Greeks of the Classical Age.

➤ **Chapter 12** summarizes the Hellenistic period from the Macedonian conquest to the coming of the Romans.

UNIT OBJECTIVES

After reading Unit 4, students will be able to:

1. discuss how the Greek culture developed.

2. describe how Greek culture spread.

3. summarize Greek contributions to western civilizations.

UNIT PROJECT

Have students imagine that they are one of the following: a Minoan priest-king, a Mycenaean seafarer, a Spartan warrior, an Athenian citizen, an Olympic athlete, Socrates, Plato, Aristotle, a Greek wife of Philip of Macedonia, Alexander the Great. Tell students that in these roles they maintained diaries. Have them write several diary entries describing special events in their lives. Ask students to make an oral presentation of their entries to the class.

ABOUT THE UNIT OPENING

Examining Artifacts

Ask students what two Greek accomplishments these artifacts show. *(architecture/sculpture and trial by jury)* Based on these artifacts, ask students to infer, or guess, some of the things the Greeks may have valued. *(Sample responses: art, beauty, justice, etc.)* Tell students that this unit will highlight Greek contributions to world civilization.

Global Chronology

Ask students to name time line entries that indicate this time period was turbulent. *(Trojan War, Persian Wars begin, Peloponnesian War)* Ask students to name time line entries that indicate culture flourished during this time. *(Homer writes* Iliad *and* Odyssey, *Golden Age of Athens begins)*

Multimedia Activity

Turning Points in World History
Democracy in Greece

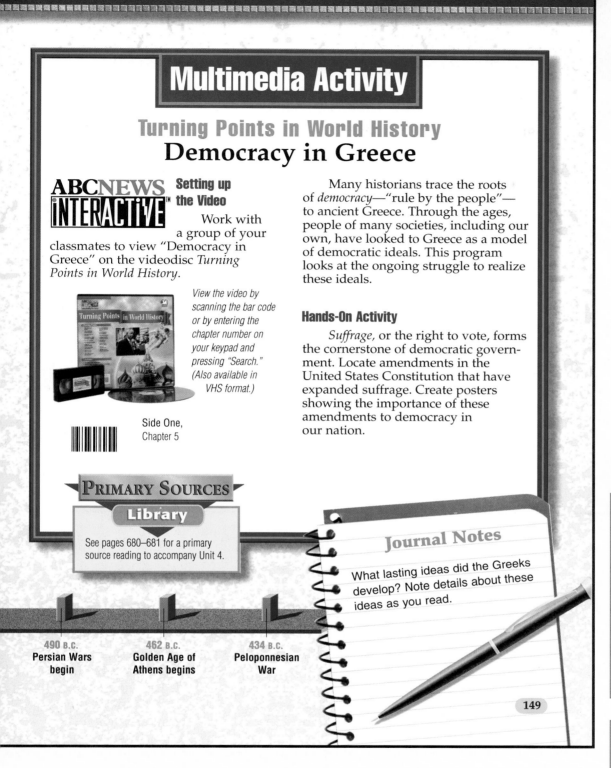

ABCNEWS INTERACTIVE™

Setting up the Video

Work with a group of your classmates to view "Democracy in Greece" on the videodisc *Turning Points in World History*.

View the video by scanning the bar code or by entering the chapter number on your keypad and pressing "Search." (Also available in VHS format.)

Side One, Chapter 5

Many historians trace the roots of *democracy*—"rule by the people"—to ancient Greece. Through the ages, people of many societies, including our own, have looked to Greece as a model of democratic ideals. This program looks at the ongoing struggle to realize these ideals.

Hands-On Activity

Suffrage, or the right to vote, forms the cornerstone of democratic government. Locate amendments in the United States Constitution that have expanded suffrage. Create posters showing the importance of these amendments to democracy in our nation.

PRIMARY SOURCES Library

See pages 680–681 for a primary source reading to accompany Unit 4.

490 B.C.
Persian Wars begin

462 B.C.
Golden Age of Athens begins

434 B.C.
Peloponnesian War

Journal Notes

What lasting ideas did the Greeks develop? Note details about these ideas as you read.

149

INTRODUCING THE UNIT

Construct a wheel graphic organizer on the board using Greece as the hub and the following headings on spokes coming out from the hub: *Geography, Culture, Important People, Lasting Contributions.* Have students call out ideas as you write responses on the wheel attached to the appropriate topic.

RECORDING JOURNAL NOTES

Help students begin writing in their journals by brainstorming ideas they think were developed by the Greeks. Write responses on the board. Have students note in their journal details about the contributions to the modern world that were developed by the Greeks.

PRIMARY SOURCES Library

Items in the Primary Sources Library for this unit focus on the role of women in Greek society. Elements include:
- Selection from Plato's *Republic.*
- Greek vase painting.

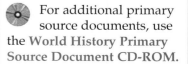 For additional primary source documents, use the **World History Primary Source Document CD-ROM.**

Geographic Location

The Greek civilizations discussed in this unit were located from the Mediterranean Sea eastward to the Indus Valley. Have students locate these places in their text Atlas and name the continents that this area includes. *(Europe, Africa, and Asia)*

Chapter 9 Planning Guide

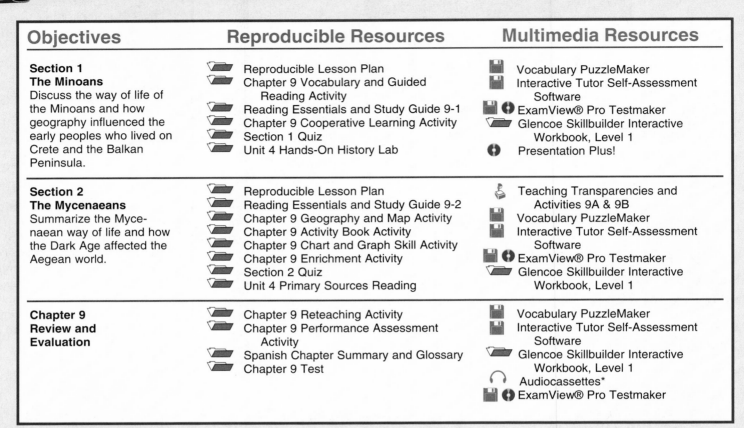

Objectives	Reproducible Resources	Multimedia Resources
Section 1 **The Minoans** Discuss the way of life of the Minoans and how geography influenced the early peoples who lived on Crete and the Balkan Peninsula.	Reproducible Lesson Plan Chapter 9 Vocabulary and Guided Reading Activity Reading Essentials and Study Guide 9-1 Chapter 9 Cooperative Learning Activity Section 1 Quiz Unit 4 Hands-On History Lab	Vocabulary PuzzleMaker Interactive Tutor Self-Assessment Software ExamView® Pro Testmaker Glencoe Skillbuilder Interactive Workbook, Level 1 Presentation Plus!
Section 2 **The Mycenaeans** Summarize the Mycenaean way of life and how the Dark Age affected the Aegean world.	Reproducible Lesson Plan Reading Essentials and Study Guide 9-2 Chapter 9 Geography and Map Activity Chapter 9 Activity Book Activity Chapter 9 Chart and Graph Skill Activity Chapter 9 Enrichment Activity Section 2 Quiz Unit 4 Primary Sources Reading	Teaching Transparencies and Activities 9A & 9B Vocabulary PuzzleMaker Interactive Tutor Self-Assessment Software ExamView® Pro Testmaker Glencoe Skillbuilder Interactive Workbook, Level 1
Chapter 9 **Review and** **Evaluation**	Chapter 9 Reteaching Activity Chapter 9 Performance Assessment Activity Spanish Chapter Summary and Glossary Chapter 9 Test	Vocabulary PuzzleMaker Interactive Tutor Self-Assessment Software Glencoe Skillbuilder Interactive Workbook, Level 1 Audiocassettes* ExamView® Pro Testmaker

*Also available in Spanish.

Presentation Plus!

Use Glencoe's **Presentation Plus!** multimedia teacher tool to easily present dynamic lessons that visually excite your students. Using Microsoft® PowerPoint, you can customize the presentations to create your own personalized lessons.

Interactive Lesson Planner

Planning has never been easier! Using this CD-ROM, organize your week, month, semester, or year with all the help you need. The **Interactive Lesson Planner** gives you access to all of the blackline masters which accompany *Human Heritage.*

✓ PERFORMANCE ASSESSMENT ACTIVITIES

Writing Have students write their own version of the *Iliad* using prose or poetry. Tell them to imagine they are one of the soldiers hidden inside the Trojan horse. They should describe their feelings as the horse is pulled into Troy by the Trojans, the ensuing battle, their escape from Troy, and their adventures on their way home.

CHAPTER RESOURCES

LITERATURE ABOUT THE PERIOD

Renault, *The King Must Die.* Random House, 1988. Retells the legend of Theseus's struggle with the Minotaur.

READINGS FOR THE STUDENT

Evslin, Bernard. *Heroes and Monsters of Greek Myth.* Scholastic, 1988. Retells many Greek myths.

READINGS FOR THE TEACHER

Cotterell, Arthur. *The Minoan World.* Charles Scribner's Sons, 1979. Surveys Minoan civilization.

Fine, John V. A. *The Ancient Greeks.* Belknap Press, 1983. Surveys the Greek world up to the accession of Alexander the Great.

KEY TO ABILITY LEVELS

Teaching strategies have been coded for varying learning styles and abilities.

L1 Level 1 activities are **basic** activities and should be within the ability range of all students.

L2 Level 2 activities are **average** activities and should be within the ability range of the average to above-average student.

L3 Level 3 activities are **challenging** activities designed for the ability range of above-average students.

ELL ELL activities should be within the ability range of English Language Learning students.

Teacher's Corner

INDEX TO NATIONAL GEOGRAPHIC MAGAZINE

The following articles relate to this chapter:

- "Ancient Greece, Part I: Echoes of the Heroic Age," by Caroline Alexander, December 1999.
- "Oldest Known Shipwreck Reveals Splendors of the Bronze Age," by George F. Bass, December 1987.
- "The Quest for Ulysses," by Tim Severin, August 1986.

NATIONAL GEOGRAPHIC SOCIETY PRODUCTS AVAILABLE FROM GLENCOE

To order the following, call Glencoe at 1-800-334-7344:

- *PicturePack: Physical Geography of the World (Transparencies)*
- *PictureShow: Ancient Civilizations: Greece and Rome (CD-ROMs)*
- *PicturePack: Ancient Greece (Transparencies)*
- *PicturePack: Ancient Civilizations Library, Part I (Transparencies)*

Access *National Geographic's* new dynamic MapMachine Web site and other geography resources at:

http://www.nationalgeographic.com/
http://www.nationalgeographic.com/maps/

  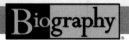

The following videotape program is available from Glencoe:

- **The Odyssey of Troy**
  0-7670-0132-X

To order, call Glencoe at 1-800-334-7344. To find classroom resources to accompany many of these videos, check the following home pages:

A&E Television: http://www.aetv.com
The History Channel:
http://www.historychannel.com

OVERVIEW

Chapter 9 introduces Minoan and Mycenaean cultures as forerunners of Greek civilization.

➤ **Section 1** discusses the way of life of the Minoans.

➤ **Section 2** explains the culture of the Mycenaeans.

CHAPTER OBJECTIVES

After reading Chapter 9, students will be able to:

1. describe what life was like for the Minoans.

2. discuss how geography influenced the people who lived on Crete and the Balkan Peninsula.

3. summarize what life was like for the Mycenaeans.

4. explain how the Dark Age affected the Aegean world.

EXAMINING ARTIFACTS

Have students identify the vehicle in the fresco. *(chariot)* Based on prior knowledge, call on a volunteer to name the chariot's most common use. *(as a weapon of war)* Direct students to find items in the time line that prove that the Mycenaeans engaged in warlike activities. Ask: What else can you infer about Mycenaean culture based on these artifacts? Tell students to evaluate their inferences as they read through the chapter.

PERFORMANCE ASSESSMENT ✔

Use the Performance Assessment activities on page 150B to help you evaluate students as they complete the chapter.

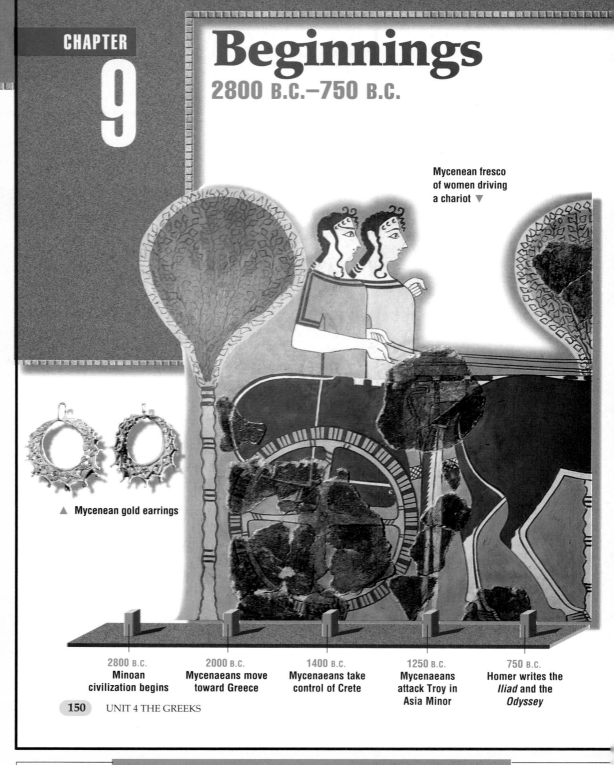

CHAPTER 9

Beginnings
2800 B.C.–750 B.C.

Mycenean fresco of women driving a chariot ▼

▲ **Mycenean gold earrings**

2800 B.C.	2000 B.C.	1400 B.C.	1250 B.C.	750 B.C.
Minoan civilization begins	Mycenaeans move toward Greece	Mycenaeans take control of Crete	Mycenaeans attack Troy in Asia Minor	Homer writes the *Iliad* and the *Odyssey*

150 UNIT 4 THE GREEKS

TEACHING RESOURCES

TEACHER PLANNING AND SUPPORT

🗁 Reproducible Lesson Plan
🗁 Block Scheduling Implementation Guide
🗁 Videodisc Bar Code Correlation
🔘 Presentation Plus!

REVIEW AND REINFORCEMENT

🗁 Reading Essentials and Study Guide 9-1, 9-2
🗁 Chapter 9 Vocabulary and Guided Reading Activity
💾 Vocabulary PuzzleMaker Software
 Teaching Transparencies 9A & 9B

🗁 Chapter 9 Reteaching Activity
🗁 Chapter 9 Cooperative Learning Activity
🗁 Chapter 9 Activity Book Activity
🗁 Chapter 9 Chart and Graph Skill Activity
💾 Interactive Tutor Self-Assessment Software
🔘📼 Unit 4 MindJogger VideoQuiz

APPLICATION AND HANDS-ON ACTIVITIES

🗁 Daily World History, Geography, and Culture Question
🗁 Unit 4 Hands-On History Lab Activity

Chapter Focus

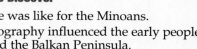

Read to Discover

- What life was like for the Minoans.
- How geography influenced the early peoples who lived on Crete and the Balkan Peninsula.
- What life was like for the Mycenaeans.
- How the "Dark Age" affected the Aegean world.

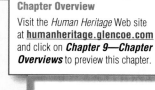

Chapter Overview
Visit the *Human Heritage* Web site at **humanheritage.glencoe.com** and click on *Chapter 9—Chapter Overviews* to preview this chapter.

Terms to Learn	People to Know	Places to Locate
bull leaping	Theseus	Crete
labyrinth	Homer	Balkan Peninsula
parchment	Odysseus	Troy
shrines	Helen	Asia Minor
megaron		Ionia
tenants		
civil wars		

Why It's Important   Greek civilization grew out of a combination of two earlier civilizations, Minoan (muh nō' uhn) and Mycenaean (mīsuh nē' uhn). Due to the geography of the land, both became great sea powers. Although their power was eventually destroyed, the Minoans and the Mycenaeans left an important *legacy* (leg' uh sē), or gift from the past, to the Greeks.

SECTION 1   The Minoans

Minoan civilization rose around 2800 B.C. on Crete (krēt), an island in the Mediterranean Sea. The Minoans, who were also known as Cretans, grew wheat, barley, grapes, and olives. When the olive groves and vineyards produced more than was needed, the Minoans traded the surplus for goods they could not grow or make on Crete.

Since there were many forests on Crete, the Minoans learned to work with wood and became good carpenters. They also learned to work with metal. They used their metalworking and carpentry skills to build ships and began to earn a living from trade instead of farming.

When pirates threatened them, the Minoans changed the way they built their ships so the ships could go faster. They made them slimmer, with two or three masts instead of one. The Minoans also put a deck over the heads of rowers to protect them.

GEOGRAPHY ACTIVITIES
- Chapter 9 Geography and Map Activity
- Social Studies Outline Map Resource Book

INTERDISCIPLINARY CONNECTIONS
- World Music Cultural Traditions

ENRICHMENT AND EXTENSION
- World History Primary Source Document Library CD-ROM
- Chapter 9 Enrichment Activity
- Foods Around the World

ASSESSMENT AND EVALUATION
- Chapter 9 Performance Assessment Activity
- Chapter 9 Section Quizzes 9-1, 9-2
- Chapter 9 Test
- Chapter 9 ExamView® Pro Testmaker Software
- Chapter 9 Digests Audiocassettes Activities and Tests

SPANISH RESOURCES
- Chapter 9 Spanish Chapter Summary and Glossary
- Chapter 9 Spanish Chapter Digests Audiocassettes Activities and Tests

---

Chapter Overview introduces students to chapter content and key terms. Have them access *Chapter 9 Overview* at **humanheritage.glencoe.com**

FOCUS

Bellringer
Ask students to write their favorite commercial jingle or slogan.

Motivational Activity
Discuss students' favorite jingles and ask volunteers to recite them. Ask students why some commercials are remembered. *(People usually remember things they hear, especially if it rhymes or is put to music.)* Tell students that in this chapter they will learn about a world-famous poet who wrote about the songs and legends that he had heard.

GUIDE TO READING

Reading Strategy
Ask students to read "Why It's Important" and summarize the chapter's main theme. *(The Minoan and Mycenaean cultures paved the way for the rise of Greek civilization.)*

Vocabulary Precheck
Ask students to define each of the "Terms to Learn." Have a volunteer consult the dictionary for any unfamiliar words. **L1** **ELL**

Use the Vocabulary PuzzleMaker for Chapter 9 to create a crossword puzzle. **L1**

Assign Chapter 9 Vocabulary and Guided Reading Activity.

Assign Reading Essentials and Study Guide 9-1.

TEACH

Guided Practice

L1 **Geography: Place** Ask students to locate Crete on the map of Western Europe in the text Atlas. Ask students to describe geographical features that offered protection to Minoan cities. *(seas and mountains)* **ELL**

✓ **Reading Check Answer**
Bull leaping was a form of bullfighting in which a young man grabbed a bull's horns, somersaulted onto its back, and did a back flip into a female partner's arms.

HISTORY Online

Student Web Activity objectives, goals, and answers can be found at the **Chapter 9 Web Activity Lesson Plan** at **humanheritage.glencoe.com**

MAKING CONNECTIONS

➤➤ **Legends** A legend of ancient Crete tells about the world's first robot. A huge bronze figure with the body of a man and the head of a bull guarded the island's coast. If enemies landed it would heat its body in fire, grab the invaders, and burn them to ashes.

Minoan Jar

✓ **Reading Check**
What was **bull leaping?**

HISTORY Online

Student Web Activity

Visit the *Human Heritage* Web site at **humanheritage.glencoe.com** and click on *Chapter 9—Student Web Activities* to find out more about the Minoans.

---

and placed a large wooden beam in the *prow,* or front part of the ship. This was used to smash a hole in enemy ships to sink them.

Over time, the Minoans drove off the pirates. By about 2000 B.C., Crete was the world's first important seafaring civilization. Minoan merchant ships traveled far to trade pottery, leather and bronze armor, and metal jewelry.

The People

The Minoans were a small people with bronzed skin and long dark hair. Men wore striped loincloths, long robes embroidered with flowers, or trousers that bagged at the knees. Women wore full skirts and short-sleeved jackets that laced in front. The Minoans had small waists and wore tight belts to show them off. They also wore jewelry, such as gold and silver earrings, necklaces, bracelets, and rings.

The Minoans spent their time in a variety of ways. Men farmed and fished. They raised cattle, long-horned sheep, and goats. They also served in the navy and the royal guard. Women performed household duties, attended sporting events, and went hunting in chariots.

The people of Crete loved sports. They built what was probably the world's first arena. It stood in the open air. Stone steps formed grandstands, where about 500 people could sit and watch the action. The king and the royal party had their own special box seats.

Boxing matches were held in the arena. **Bull leaping,** a form of bullfighting, was also held there. A young man and woman "fought" the bull together. The man would grab the bull's horns. As the bull raised its head to toss him, the man would do a somersault, landing on his feet on the bull's back. He would then do a back flip. Standing behind the bull, the woman would catch her partner as he landed. Many experts believe bull leaping was a religious ceremony as well as a sport.

Cities and Palaces

The Minoans built many cities, which were different from those of other ancient civilizations in two ways. At the heart of each Minoan city stood a palace rather than a temple. Also, Minoan cities did not have walls around them. Instead, people depended on the sea and navy for protection.

One of the largest cities of Crete was Knossos (kuh nahs' uhs). It covered about 28 acres, or 11.2 hectares. About one fifth of the area was taken up by a five-story palace that served as a government building, temple, factory, and warehouse. Its walls were built of stone and sun-dried brick framed with wooden beams. The Minoans decorated the inside walls with brightly colored *frescoes* (fres' kōs), or water color paintings made on damp plaster. The palace had bathrooms with bathtubs and flush toilets. It also had hot and cold running water and portable fireboxes to heat rooms.

MEETING SPECIAL NEEDS

Have visual learners study the Minoan frescoes found in this chapter and in other reference books. Point out to students the various shades and colors used in the frescoes. Have students work in small groups to create a fresco with small scraps of torn paper, colored with markers or crayons in the Minoan style. Topics from the Minoan culture could include: daily life, sports, city design, or religion. Provide each group with a large sheet of newsprint to use for the fresco. Display frescoes in the classroom.

📖 Refer to *Inclusion for the Middle School Social Studies Classroom: Strategies and Activities* for additional resources.

The palace had several entrances. Passageways and rooms formed a **labyrinth** (lab' uh rinth), or a network of paths through which it is difficult to find one's way. Because labyrinth means "double ax," the palace was called the "House of the Double Ax." The palace was also called by that name because it was filled with pictures, carvings, and bronze models of a double ax.

Sea captains, merchants, and shipbuilders lived in houses around the palace. Past their houses stood those of artisans who made beautiful cups and vases and designed delicate jewelry.

Houses were built side by side around courtyards. Most were two stories high. Lower walls were made of stone, upper walls of sun-dried brick. On the inside walls were painted scenes of daily life. Each house also had its own well and drains.

Many early Minoan houses had no entrance from the street. A person went in or out through the roof and lowered a ladder over the side of the house. Later, wooden doors and windows made of oiled and tinted **parchment** (parch' muhnt), or thin animal skin, were added.

☑ **Reading Check**
What is a **labyrinth?**

☑ **Reading Check**
How did Minoans use **parchment** in building their homes?

☑ **Reading Check Answer**
A **labyrinth** is a complicated network of paths.

☑ **Reading Check Answer**
Minoans used **parchment** for windows in their homes.

CAPTION ANSWER
boxing matches

L1 **Human/Environmental Interaction** Have students list occupations of Minoans. *(farmers, fishers, shepherds, sea captains, merchants, shipbuilders, artisans)* What did most of the occupations have in common? *(a connection with the sea)* Why would occupations related to the sea be plentiful in Minoan society? *(Crete is a small island surrounded by the sea.)*

DID YOU KNOW
The palace at Knossos was built around 2000 B.C. It was discovered in 1900 by Sir Arthur Evans, a British archaeologist.

BULL LEAPING   This painting from Knossos shows Minoans bull leaping. In the center, a man leaps over the bull's back. Another man grips the bull's horns so that it will lift its head and toss him. The woman behind the bull prepares to catch the leapers. **What other sporting event was held in a Minoan arena?**

COOPERATIVE LEARNING

Call on volunteers to research the story of Theseus and the Minotaur—a half bull, half human monster that lived inside a labyrinth at the Palace of Knossos. Meet with the volunteers to practice a retelling of the story to the class as a whole.

After students have presented the story, divide the rest of the class into groups, and have each group design murals depicting scenes from the myth. Assign the storytellers to coordinate the scenes prepared by each group. When students are done, display the murals, which might be drawn on posterboard, on a wall of the classroom.

📁 Assign Chapter 9 *Cooperative Learning Activity* in the TCR.

Rulers and Religion   The rulers of Crete were priest-kings.
They made the laws and represented the gods on Earth. The
priest-kings would climb to the top of Mount Juktas (yūk' tuhs) to
look for a sign from heaven that would tell them the will of the
gods. Then, they would tell their people what the gods wanted
them to do.

The Minoans had many gods. The main god was the Great
Goddess, Mother Earth. She made plants grow and brought
children into the world. To honor her, the Minoans built **shrines,**
or sacred places to worship, in palaces, on housetops, on hilltops,
and in caves. The people believed that hilltops led to heaven, and
caves led to the underworld.

Sacred horns made of clay and covered with stucco rested
against the back wall of each shrine. A hole between the horns
held a bronze double ax. Around the horns were clay models of
animals. People left offerings of human hair, fruit, flowers,
jewels, and gold at the shrines.

The Minoans believed that certain things were sacred. The
lily was their sacred flower. The king wore a plumed crown of
lilies and a lily necklace. The double ax was sacred. It stood for the
power of Mother Earth and the authority of the king. The dove
was sacred because it flew to the heavens.

MINOAN RELIGION   This Minoan fresco shows a religious ceremony. As a
musician plays the harp, two women and a man carry offerings to a shrine. The double
axes with birds sitting on them (left) are symbols of the Great Goddess. **What did
Minoans believe about the Great Goddess?**

154   UNIT 4 THE GREEKS

The Fall of the Minoans　No one is certain why Minoan civilization came to an end. What is certain is that about 1400 B.C., control of the sea and of Crete passed to the Mycenaeans.

Legend explains the fall of the Minoans with the story of Theseus (thee' sex uhs) and the Minotaur (min' uh tauhr). A young Greek prince named Theseus was brought to Knossos. He was to be sacrificed to the Minotaur, a huge monster the king kept in the palace labyrinth. The Minotaur had the body of a man and the head of a bull and lived on human flesh. Theseus was put into the labyrinth. He fought the monster with a magical sword and killed it. When the Minotaur died, the power of the Minoans died too.

Relief Sculpture of Minotaur.

Section 1 Assessment

1. **Define:** bull leaping, labyrinth, parchment, shrines.
2. What kind of government did the Minoans have?
3. How did cities in Crete differ from cities in other ancient civilizations?

Critical Thinking

4. **Making Generalizations**　How did geography influence the development of the Minoan civilization?

Graphic Organizer Activity

5. Draw a chart like this one, and use it to fill in details on Minoan civilization.

```
              Minoan Civilization
    ┌──────────┬─────────┬──────────┬─────────┐
  Economy     Cities   Religion    Sports
```

SECTION 2 　The Mycenaeans

The Mycenaeans came from the grasslands of southern Russia. Around 2000 B.C., small groups started making their way west into Europe and then south through the Balkan (bol' kuhn) Peninsula. Finally, they settled in the lowlands of Greece.

The Mycenaean kings built fortress-palaces on hilltops. In times of danger or attack, the people in the villages outside the palace walls took shelter within the palace. Its chief feature was the **megaron** (meg' uh ron), or a square room with a fireplace in its center. The king held council meetings and entertained in the megaron.

Land was divided into estates that were farmed either by enslaved people or by **tenants,** or people who live on and work another person's land. Landowners gave the king horses, chariots, weapons, wheat, farm animals, honey, and hides in exchange for protection. Tenants labored to supply many of these items.

Reading Check
How did Mycenaean kings use the **megaron?**
How did **tenants** earn a living?

CHAPTER 9 BEGINNINGS　**155**

Section 1 Assessment Answers

1. bull leaping, Minoan sport (p. 152); labyrinth, path network (p. 153); parchment, thin animal skin (p. 153); shrines, sacred places (p. 154)
2. They were ruled by priest-kings, who represented the gods.
3. At the heart of each city stood a palace, and cities did not have walls around them.
4. Answers will vary, but due to geography the Minoans became a sea power. Because of forests on Crete, the Minoans worked with wood. Because Minoan cities were near the sea, they did not have walls.
5. Items in each box should reflect innovations and achievements mentioned in the text. You might use these responses as examples: economy—world's first important seafaring nation; cities—palace at the center instead of a temple, no walls; religion—Great Goddess, Mother Earth, main deity; sports—bull jumping.

Assign Chapter 9 **Section 1 Quiz** in the TCR. Testmaker available.

Use the Interactive Tutor Self-Assessment Software to review Section 1.

L3 Critical Thinking Ask students to explain what purpose myths and legends about monsters might have served the Minoans. (*They might have provided supernatural explanations of actual events.*)

MAKING CONNECTIONS

➤➤ **Folklore** According to legend, Ariadne, the Minoan king's daughter, gave Theseus the clue of unwinding a ball of thread to help him find his way out of the labyrinth. After killing the Minotaur, Theseus escaped from Crete with Ariadne.

Reading Check Answer
Mycenaean kings used the **megaron** to hold council meetings and to entertain people. **Tenants** earned a living by working on another person's land.

DID YOU KNOW ??
The Mycenaeans got their name from their chief fortress-palace of Mycenae, which was excavated in 1876–1877 by a German amateur archaeologist named Heinrich Schliemann.

Use the Vocabulary Puzzle-Maker to create crossword and word search puzzles.

MAP SKILLS

TEACH

Reading Longitude

Ask students to study the map to answer the following questions:

Along which line of longitude is Mount Juktas located? *(25˚E)*

Between which two lines of longitude is Cyprus located? *(30˚E and 35˚E)*

Along what approximate line of longitude is Mycenae located? *(23˚E)*

Between which lines of longitude was the Minoan culture located? *(20˚E and 35˚E)*

Have students use the map of Western Europe in the text Atlas to create questions about the locations of places based on longitude. Have students ask a partner their questions.

Answers to Map Practice

1. 25˚E
2. Mycenae

Reading Longitude

To measure distances east and west on Earth, mapmakers use imaginary lines on maps and globes. These are called lines of **longitude,** or **meridians** (muh rid′ ē uhnz), and they run from the North Pole to the South Pole.

Like lines of latitude, meridians are measured in degrees. All meridians are measured from the Prime Meridian, a line of longitude that runs through Greenwich, England. The Prime Meridian is marked 0°. Those lines east of the Prime Meridian are marked with an E, from 1°E to 180°E. Those lines west of the Prime Meridian are marked with a W, from 1°W to 180°W. Unlike lines of latitude, meridians are not always the same distance from one another. They are farthest apart at the Equator, and closest together at the poles.

Lines of longitude are often used to help specify location. For example, it is much easier to find Troy on the map below if one knows that it is located at about 26°E.

Look at the map below, and answer the following questions:

Map Practice

1. **Along which line of longitude was Knossos located?**
2. **Which early Aegean city was located closest to 20°E?**

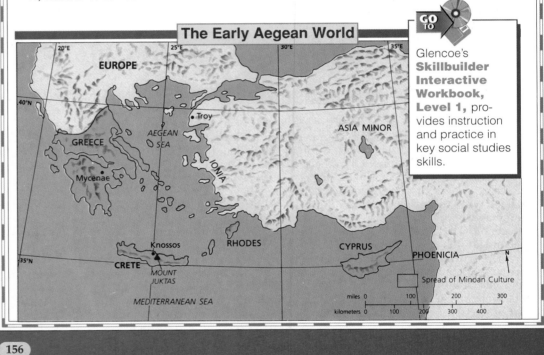

The Early Aegean World

Glencoe's **Skillbuilder Interactive Workbook, Level 1,** provides instruction and practice in key social studies skills.

SPOTLIGHT ON: THE AEGEAN WORLD

Archaeologists have unearthed relics of the Greek civilization by digging throughout the Aegean area. Artifacts have also been found in another treasury of sorts— the Mediterranean Sea. Many important and interesting relics have been found in the waters near Crete and Cyprus. Students may enjoy reading more about these discoveries in *Diving to the Past: Recovering Ancient Wrecks* by W. John Hackwell.

Linking Across Time

Greek Shipping   The seafaring tradition has continued from Mycenaean times (below) into the present. Today Greece is among the top ten shipping nations in the world (right). **What does the size of this modern Greek ship tell you about Greek trade today?**

Although they kept large herds of cattle, the Mycenaeans relied on hunting to get more meat. They hunted rabbit, deer, boar, wild bulls, and game birds. Women rode with the men in chariots during the hunt. When hunters were after big game, they used greyhounds. The game was captured with nets or killed with spears, slings, or bows and arrows.

Traders and Pirates   Shortly after the Mycenaeans settled in the lowlands of Greece, they were visited by Minoan traders from Crete. The Mycenaeans began to imitate Minoan gold and bronze work. They adapted Cretan script to their own language. They copied Minoan fashions. Most important of all, they learned how to build ships and how to navigate.

The Mycenaeans also began to grow olives. They made presses to squeeze oil from the olives. They used the oil for cooking, as fuel for lamps, and to rub on their bodies. They sold plain oil in large clay jars and perfumed oil in painted vases. Sale of the oil made the Mycenaeans rich. It also led to the founding of trading stations and settlements on nearby islands.

CHAPTER 9 BEGINNINGS   **157**

Linking Across Time

Sample answers: That Greeks still transport much of their goods by sea; that shipping still plays an important part in the Greek economy.

Independent Practice

L2 Daily Life Ask students to research and make a chart comparing the chief agricultural crops and occupations of the Mycenaeans to those of present-day Greeks.

DID YOU KNOW ??

Troy was discovered and excavated by Heinrich Schliemann in 1870. As he dug, Schliemann found nine cities at the site. The seventh city down is presumed to be Troy of the Trojan War period.

EXTENDING THE CONTENT

Gold was not a metal native to Mycenaean lands, but has been found in Mycenaean tombs and shaft graves. Historians believe that Mycenaean rulers either traded or fought to acquire gold and other riches. During this period, Egypt was the leading source of gold in the Mediterranean. It seems possible that mercenaries, or paid warriors, from Mycenae may have fought for the Egyptians and were paid in gold.

158

L1 **Writing** Have students imagine that they are traders who come to do business with the Mycenaeans. Tell them to write letters home describing Mycenaean fortress-palaces, land, occupations, and lifestyles. Have students share their letters.

LINKING PAST TO PRESENT

The events and heroes of the Trojan War, along with their later fates, became the subjects of the greatest Greek tragedies. For example, Euripedes' *Trojan Women* looks at the human aftermath of war in the fallen city. Aeschylus's *Oresteia*, a trilogy of poetic dramas about the ill-fated House of Atreus, begins with Agamemnon's homecoming from victory at Troy. Later writers throughout the world have also drawn on this famous story.

CAPTION ANSWER

from songs and legends that had been handed down by word of mouth

The following videotape program is available from Glencoe to enrich Chapter 9:

- **The Odyssey of Troy**

To find classroom resources to accompany this video, check the following home page:

A&E Television:
http://www.aetv.com

People in History

Homer
c. 700s B.C.

Greek Poet

Homer remains a mystery. Nobody knows what he looked like or exactly when he lived. Ancient Greek *bards*, or poets, called him the "Ionian bard," so maybe Homer came from Ionia. Tradition says Homer was blind, but he was not blind to history. Archaeologists have proven that many of the stories told by Homer actually took place. That means his poems are more than good literature—they are also good history.

Despite their success in trade, the Mycenaeans were warriors at heart. In battle, they used large hide shields with wooden frames, and fought with spears and swords. Their leaders wore fancy bronze armor. At first, the Mycenaeans fought one another. After they learned about shipbuilding and navigation, they outfitted pirate fleets and began to raid nearby lands. By about 1400 B.C., they had replaced the Minoans as the chief power of the Aegean world.

The Trojan War   The Mycenaeans are famous for their attack on Troy, a major trading city in Asia Minor. This attack probably took place during the middle 1200s B.C. At the time, the Trojans (trō' juhns) controlled the trade routes to the Black Sea. They made money by taxing the ships that carried grain and gold from southern Russia to Greece.

About 500 years after the Mycenaeans attacked Troy, a blind Greek poet named Homer (hō' muhr) composed a long poem about the event. He called his poem the *Iliad* (il' ē uhd). Homer also composed a poem called the *Odyssey* (ahd' uh sē), which tells about the wanderings of Odysseus (ō dis' ē uhs), a Mycenaean hero of the Trojan War. Homer drew his material for the two

THE TROJAN HORSE   The first Greek myths came from the Mycenaeans. Later, the poet Homer gathered these legends and used them to write his works. Here, a painting of the Trojan horse from Homer's poem the *Iliad* is shown. **Where did Homer get his material for the *Iliad* and the *Odyssey*?**

MULTICULTURAL PERSPECTIVES

Literature, sculpture, music, and even everyday speech still reflect the incidents and characters of the Trojan War. People who have never read a line of Homer's *Iliad* or Virgil's *Aeneid*, which finishes the story of Troy, are familiar with the story of the Trojan Horse. Some quotes from the story are familiar phrases, such as the reference to Helen: "Was this the face that launched a thousand ships?"

poems from songs and legends that had been handed down by word of mouth. He then added his own descriptions and details of everyday life.

According to Homer's account in the *Iliad*, the Trojan War was fought over a woman. The king of Troy had a son named Paris, who fell in love with Helen, the wife of a Mycenaean king. When Paris took Helen to Troy, her husband became angry. He formed an army and sailed after them. However, the walls of Troy were so tall, thick, and strong that the Mycenaeans could not get into the city. They had to camp on the plain outside the city walls.

After ten years of fighting, the Mycenaeans still had not taken Troy. Then, Odysseus suggested a way they could capture the city. He had the soldiers build a huge, hollow wooden horse. The best soldiers hid inside the horse, while the rest boarded their ships and sailed away.

The Trojans saw the ships leave and thought they had won the war. They did not know the Mycenaean ships would return after dark. The Trojans tied ropes to the wooden horse and pulled it into the city as a victory prize. When they fell asleep, the Mycenaean soldiers hidden inside the horse came out. They opened the city gates and let in the rest of the Mycenaean army. The Mycenaeans killed the king of Troy and burned the city. Then, with Helen, they returned to their homes.

A "Dark Age"   The Mycenaeans did not return to peaceful ways after crushing Troy. Instead, a series of **civil wars,** or wars between opposing groups of citizens, broke out. Within 100 years after the end of the Trojan War, almost no Mycenaean fortress-palaces were left. Soon after, a people called Dorians (dōr' ē uhns) entered Greece and conquered the Mycenaeans. Their iron swords were not as well made as Mycenaean bronze swords. Nevertheless, Dorian swords were stronger. Thousands of Mycenaeans fled the Greek mainland and settled in Aegean islands and on the western shore of Asia Minor. These settlements later became known as Ionia (ī ō' nē uh).

As a result of the civil wars and the Dorian invasion, the Aegean world entered a "Dark Age," which lasted until about 800 B.C. It was a time of wandering and killing. Overseas trade stopped. The people of the Aegean region forgot how to write and keep records. The skills of fresco painting and working with ivory and gold disappeared. The Aegean world was cut off from the Middle East, and the people had to create a new civilization on their own.

The people started over. Once again, herding and farming became the main ways of life. Local leaders ruled small areas. These leaders called themselves kings, but they were little more than chiefs. At first, the borders of the areas they ruled kept changing. In time, however, the borders became fixed, and each area became an independent community. The people of these

Mycenaean Goldwork

✓ Reading Check
How did **civil wars** weaken the Mycenaeans?

L1 **History** Have students imagine they were Mycenaeans who lived before and after the Dorian invasion. Tell them that they are responsible for writing two journal entries. In the first entry they should describe Mycenaean life before the Dorian invasion. In the second entry they should describe how their lives have changed.

✓ Reading Check Answer
After the **civil wars,** almost no Mycenaean fortress-palaces were left, making it easy for the Dorians to conquer Greece.

ASSESS

Check for Understanding

Ask students to summarize orally or in writing the main points of the chapter. Discuss the answers to the Section and Chapter Assessment questions.

Evaluate

Assign Chapter 9 **Performance Assessment Activity** in the TCR.

Administer **Chapter 9 Test** in the TCR. Testmaker available.

COOPERATIVE LEARNING

Organize the class into small groups and have each group find additional information about a Greek hero or heroine—either from the *Iliad* or *Odyssey* or from Greek myths. Each group should then write their own adventure involving their subject, and decide how it will be presented to the class. Some suggestions include acting out a myth, making a videotape, or presenting a choral reading.

Reteach

Have students use the key terms to describe the main concepts of the chapter.

Assign Chapter 9 **Reteaching Activity** in the TCR.

Enrich

Have students take turns reading aloud passages from the *Iliad* and the *Odyssey*. What do they like most and least about what they hear?

Assign Chapter 9 **Enrichment Activity** in the TCR.

CLOSE

Ask students to discuss which of the following statements is most true: *The early Greek people shaped their environment* OR *The early Greek people were shaped by their environment.*

💾 Use **Interactive Tutor Self-Assessment Software** to review Section 2.

Self-Check Quiz gives students an interactive chapter tutorial. Have them access **Chapter 9 Quiz** at humanheritage.glencoe.com

---

communities began calling themselves Hellenes (hel' ēns), or Greeks. They worked hard to redevelop their culture and to learn new crafts and skills. The civilization they created flourished from about the 700s B.C. until 336 B.C.

Section 2 Assessment

1. **Define:** megaron, tenants, civil wars.
2. In what ways were the Mycenaeans influenced by Minoan culture?
3. According to Homer, how did the Mycenaeans finally win the Trojan War?
4. What happened in the Aegean world during the "Dark Age"?

Critical Thinking

5. **Demonstrating Reasoned Judgment** Why was the growing of olives such an important development for the Aegean world?

Graphic Organizer Activity

6. Draw a diagram like this one, and use it to show the causes and effects of the Trojan War on the Mycenaeans.

Causes	→	Trojan War	→	Effects

Chapter Summary & Study Guide

1. Minoan civilization began to develop on the Mediterranean island of Crete around 2800 B.C.
2. The Minoans started as farmers but eventually turned to trade.
3. Since the Minoans depended on the sea and their ships for protection, their cities were not walled.
4. The Minoans worshiped many gods, the most important of which was the Great Goddess, Mother Earth.
5. Around 1400 B.C., the Mycenaeans took control of the Mediterranean.
6. Instead of cities, the Mycenaeans built fortress-palaces on hilltops.
7. The Mycenaeans learned many things from the Minoans, including a writing script and the skills of shipbuilding and navigation.

8. The Mycenaeans fought a lengthy war against Troy, described in two long poems, the *Iliad* and the *Odyssey*
9. After years of civil war, the Mycenaeans were conquered by the Dorians.
10. During the 300 years of the "Dark Age," the people of the Aegean area lost many of their skills and had to create a new civilization.

Self-Check Quiz

Visit the *Human Heritage* Web site at **humanheritage. glencoe.com** and click on **Chapter 9—Self-Check Quiz** to assess your understanding of this chapter.

Section 2 Assessment Answers

1. megaron, palace room with a center fireplace (p. 155); tenants, people who work another person's land (p. 155); civil wars, wars between opposing groups (p. 159)
2. They copied Minoan metalwork, adapted Cretan script, copied Minoan fashions, and learned how to build and navigate ships.
3. by hiding soldiers in a huge, hollow, horse and tricking the Trojans into dragging it inside their city
4. It was a time of wandering and killing, overseas trade stopped, people forgot how

to write, and artistic skills disappeared.
5. Answers will vary but could include the many uses of oil developed and the trade and the wealth it brought.
6. Sample responses: *causes*—Trojan control of trade routes to Black Sea; according to Homer, capture of Helen by Trojan king; *effects*—eruption of a series of civil wars, conquest by the Dorians, "Dark Age" for the Aegean world

Assign Chapter 9 **Section 2 Quiz** in the TCR. Testmaker available.

Assessment

Using Key Terms

Imagine that you are living among the early Greeks. Use the following words to write a paragraph describing the life of the Minoans and the Mycenaeans.

bull leaping   labyrinth   parchment
shrines   megaron   tenants
civil wars

Understanding Main Ideas

1. What civilizations combined to form Greek civilization?
2. In what ways were the Minoan people able to gain control of the Mediterranean Sea?
3. What do experts believe about the sport of bull leaping?
4. Why didn't Minoan cities have walls around them?
5. What were some of the features of the palace at Knossos?
6. What did the Mycenaeans build instead of cities?
7. How was the Trojan War described in the *Iliad*?
8. Why did the people of Greece have to create a new civilization?

Critical Thinking

1. How well did the Minoans use their natural resources? Explain your answer.
2. What effect did being an island civilization have on the Minoans?
3. What role did religion play in Minoan daily life?
4. In what ways would the Mycenaean civilization have been different if the people had not learned to build and sail ships?

Graphic Organizer Activity

Culture Create a before-and-after chart like the one shown, and use it to show what the Mycenaean civilization was like before and after contact with the Minoans.

Before → Contact with Minoans → After

Geography in History

Regions Refer to the map on page 156 as you think about the "Dark Age" of the Aegean region. What human actions and geographic factors made it possible for this period of history to last for 300 years?

Create a poster warning people about the events and geographic factors that led to the "Dark Ages."

Using Your Journal

Review any details you may have noted about the ideas developed by the Minoans. Write a magazine article describing what the Minoans did for sport and entertainment.

Bonus Test Question

For Chapter 9 Test

Imagine you are an archaeologist who has dug up artifacts you believe are Mycenaean. Describe two artifacts you have found and what each was used for. *(Answers will vary but should be supported by explanation.)*

Using Your Journal

Magazine articles will vary but should include the fact that Minoans changed the way ships were made so that they could go faster. The Minoans loved sports and built what was probably the world's first arena.

Geography in History

Answers will vary but should include references to the isolation caused by the sea, mountains, migrations, and civil wars.

Assessment Answers

Using Key Terms

Paragraphs will vary but should include comparisons.

Understanding Main Ideas

1. Minoan and Mycenaean
2. They built faster ships with a large wooden beam in the prow to smash and sink enemy ships.
3. that it was a religious ceremony as well as a sport
4. the people depended on the sea and navy for protection
5. It was five stories high, built of stone, framed with wood, and decorated with frescoes. It had bathrooms, several entrances, and labyrinths.
6. fortress-palaces
7. Paris took Helen to Troy. The Mycenaeans attacked Troy; they later built a huge wooden horse with soldiers hidden inside which was pulled into Troy. The Mycenaeans burned the city.
8. because their civilization was destroyed during the Dark Age

Critical Thinking

1. Answers will vary, but the Minoans used resources wisely.
2. It provided natural protection and also made travel and trade easier.
3. Answers will vary, but religion gave kings power.
4. Answers will vary but could include lack of development.

Graphic Organizer Activity

Answers should reflect information on pages 156–158. The most important change shown will be knowledge of shipbuilding and navigation, which allowed the Mycenaeans to expand their influence in the Aegean world.

Objectives	Reproducible Resources	Multimedia Resources
Section 1 **The Polis** Explain why the polis was the geographic and political center of Greek life.	Reproducible Lesson Plan Chapter 10 Vocabulary and Guided Reading Activity Reading Essentials and Study Guide 10-1 Section 1 Quiz Unit 4 Hands-On History Lab	Vocabulary PuzzleMaker Interactive Tutor Self-Assessment Software ABCNEWS INTERACTIVE Turning Points in World History ExamView® Pro Testmaker Glencoe Skillbuilder Interactive Workbook, Level 1 Presentation Plus!
Section 2 **Sparta** Describe life in Sparta, noting how Sparta was different from other Greek city-states, especially in regard to the role of women.	Reproducible Lesson Plan Reading Essentials and Study Guide 10-2 Section 2 Quiz	Vocabulary PuzzleMaker Interactive Tutor Self-Assessment Software ExamView® Pro Testmaker Glencoe Skillbuilder Interactive Workbook, Level 1
Section 3 **Athens** Discuss life in Athens, summarizing how the Persian War affected Greece, and describe how Athens controlled other city-states.	Reproducible Lesson Plan Reading Essentials and Study Guide 10-3 Chapter 10 Chart and Graph Skill Activity Chapter 10 Geography and Map Activity Unit 4 World Literature Reading 2 Chapter 10 Cooperative Learning Activity Section 3 Quiz	Teaching Transparencies and Activities 10A & 10B Vocabulary PuzzleMaker Interactive Tutor Self-Assessment Software ExamView® Pro Testmaker Glencoe Skillbuilder Interactive Workbook, Level 1
Section 4 **Decline of the City-States** Explain why Athens and the other Greek city-states declined.	Reproducible Lesson Plan Reading Essentials and Study Guide 10-4 Chapter 10 Activity Book Activity Chapter 10 Enrichment Activity Section 4 Quiz	Vocabulary PuzzleMaker Interactive Tutor Self-Assessment Software ExamView® Pro Testmaker Glencoe Skillbuilder Interactive Workbook, Level 1
Chapter 10 **Review and Evaluation**	Chapter 10 Reteaching Activity Chapter 10 Performance Assessment Activity Spanish Chapter Summary and Glossary Chapter 10 Test	Vocabulary PuzzleMaker Interactive Tutor Self-Assessment Software Glencoe Skillbuilder Interactive Workbook, Level 1 Audiocassettes* ExamView® Pro Testmaker

*Also available in Spanish.

Presentation Plus!

Use Glencoe's **Presentation Plus!** multimedia teacher tool to easily present dynamic lessons that visually excite your students. Using Microsoft® PowerPoint, you can customize the presentations to create your own personalized lessons.

 ## Interactive Lesson Planner

Planning has never been easier! Using this CD-ROM, organize your week, month, semester, or year with all the help you need. The **Interactive Lesson Planner** gives you access to all of the blackline masters which accompany *Human Heritage.*

✓ PERFORMANCE ASSESSMENT ACTIVITIES

Model   Have students work in small groups to create a model of a Greek city-state. Tell students to use the information from their textbook or from other reference books. The models should include: farming villages, fields, orchards, acropolis and its temple, and an agora. Display models in the classroom.

CHAPTER RESOURCES

LITERATURE ABOUT THE PERIOD

Renault, Mary. *The Last of the Wine.* Random House, 1975. A novel about Athens during the Peloponnesian War.

READINGS FOR THE STUDENT

Burrell, Roy. *The Greeks: Rebuilding the Past Series.* Oxford University Press, 1990.

Hamilton, Edith. *The Greek Way.* Norton, 1983. Story of the Greek spirit and mind told by great writers.

READINGS FOR THE TEACHER

Editors of Time-Life Books. *What Life Was Like at the Dawn of Democracy.* Time-Life Books, 1997. A look at classical Athens during the years 525 B.C.– 322 B.C.

Editors of Time-Life Books. *Greece—Temples, Tombs, and Treasures.* Time-Life Books, 1994. A colorful look at the history and art of Ancient Greece.

KEY TO ABILITY LEVELS

Teaching strategies have been coded for varying learning styles and abilities.

L1 Level 1 activities are **basic** activities and should be within the ability range of all students.

L2 Level 2 activities are **average** activities and should be within the ability range of the average to above-average student.

L3 Level 3 activities are **challenging** activities designed for the ability range of above-average students.

ELL ELL activities should be within the ability range of English Language Learning students.

NATIONAL GEOGRAPHIC SOCIETY — Teacher's Corner

INDEX TO NATIONAL GEOGRAPHIC MAGAZINE

The following articles relate to this chapter:

- Ancient Greece: Part II, "Ascent to Glory," by Caroline Alexander, February 2000.
- "When the Greeks Went West," by Rick Gore, November 1994.

NATIONAL GEOGRAPHIC SOCIETY PRODUCTS AVAILABLE FROM GLENCOE

To order the following, call Glencoe at 1-800-334-7344:

- *PictureShow: Ancient Civilizations: Greece and Rome (CD-ROM)*
- *PicturePack: Ancient Greece (Transparencies)*
- *PicturePack: Ancient Civilizations Library, Part I (Transparencies)*

ADDITIONAL NATIONAL GEOGRAPHIC SOCIETY PRODUCTS

To order the following, call National Geographic at 1-800-368-2728:

- *Wonders of the Ancient World: National Geographic Atlas of Archaeology (Book)*

Access *National Geographic's* new dynamic MapMachine Web site and other geography resources at:
http://www.nationalgeographic.com/
http://www.nationalgeographic.com/maps/

The following videotape program is available from Glencoe to enrich Chapter 10:

- **Mystical Monuments of Ancient Greece**
  0-7670-0012-9

To order, call Glencoe at 1-800-334-7344. To find classroom resources to accompany many of these videos, check the following home pages:

A&E Television: http://www.aetv.com
The History Channel:
http://www.historychannel.com

OVERVIEW

Chapter 10 discusses Greek city-states, particularly Sparta and Athens.

➤ **Section 1** discusses the development of the Greek polis.
➤ **Section 2** summarizes the way of life in Sparta.
➤ **Section 3** describes the growth of democracy in Athens and its dominance in the Delian League.
➤ **Section 4** analyzes the decline of the Greek city-states.

CHAPTER OBJECTIVES

After reading Chapter 10, students will be able to:

1. explain why the polis was the geographic and political center of Greek life.
2. describe what life was like in Sparta and Athens.
3. summarize how the Persian Wars affected Greece.
4. discuss how Athens controlled the other city-states.
5. explain why Athens and the other city-states declined.

EXAMINING ARTIFACTS

Tell students that Sparta and Athens were the two leading city-states in ancient Greece. Explain that the woman on the coin is the goddess Athena. Ask: What do these artifacts tell you about each city-state? *(Sample responses: Spartans had a strong army; the Athenians worshiped Athena and used coins for trade.)* Record answers for review at the end of the chapter.

PERFORMANCE ASSESSMENT ✓

Use the Performance Assessment activities on page 162B to help you evaluate students as they complete the chapter.

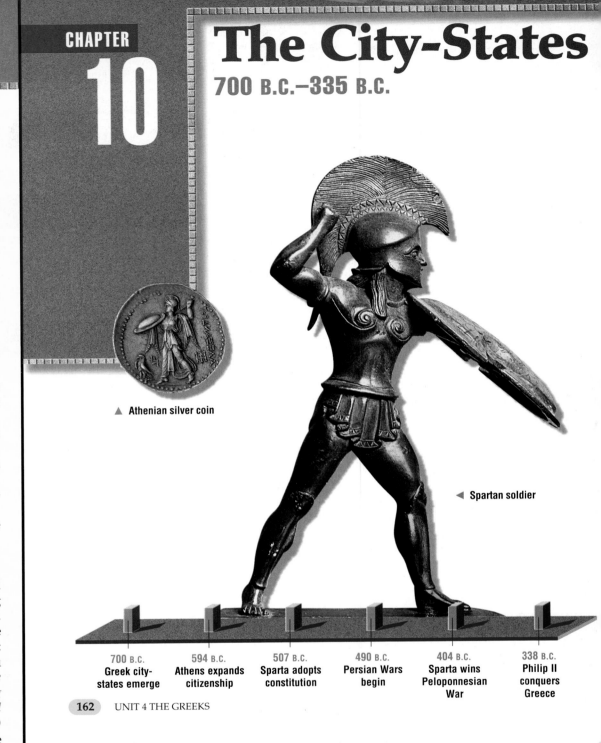

The City-States
700 B.C.–335 B.C.

▲ Athenian silver coin

◀ Spartan soldier

700 B.C.	594 B.C.	507 B.C.	490 B.C.	404 B.C.	338 B.C.
Greek city-states emerge	Athens expands citizenship	Sparta adopts constitution	Persian Wars begin	Sparta wins Peloponnesian War	Philip II conquers Greece

162 UNIT 4 THE GREEKS

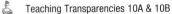

TEACHING RESOURCES

TEACHER PLANNING AND SUPPORT

- Reproducible Lesson Plan
- Block Scheduling Implementation Guide
- Videodisc Bar Code Correlation
- Presentation Plus!

REVIEW AND REINFORCEMENT

- Reading Essentials and Study Guide 10-1, 10-2, 10-3, 10-4
- Chapter 10 Vocabulary and Guided Reading Activity
- Vocabulary PuzzleMaker Software

- Teaching Transparencies 10A & 10B
- Chapter 10 Reteaching Activity
- Chapter 10 Cooperative Learning Activity
- Chapter 10 Activity Book Activity
- Chapter 10 Chart and Graph Skill Activity
- Interactive Tutor Self-Assessment Software

APPLICATION AND HANDS-ON ACTIVITIES

- Daily World History, Geography, and Culture Question
- Unit 4 Hands-On History Lab Activity

Chapter Focus

 Read to Discover

- Why the polis was the geographic and political center of Greek life.
- What life was like in the city-states of Sparta and Athens.
- How the Persian Wars affected Greece.
- How Athens controlled other city-states.
- Why the Greek city-states declined.

Terms to Learn	**People to Know**	**Places to Locate**
polis	Solon	Sparta
acropolis	Cleisthenes	Athens
agora	Darius	Ionia
aristocrats	Xerxes	Delos
oligarchy	Pericles	Thebes
constitution		
mercenaries		

Why It's Important   The geography of Greece—the mountains and the sea—separated communities from each other. Although these communities spoke the same language and shared many of the same customs, no single community had power over the others. Because of this, people developed a loyalty to the community in which they lived. These communities, known as city-states, became a feature of Greek civilization.

SECTION 1 The Polis

The **polis** (pah' lis), or city-state, was the geographic and political center of Greek life. At first, each polis was made up of farming villages, fields, and orchards grouped around a fortified hill called an **acropolis** (uh krop' uh lis). At the top of the acropolis stood the temple of the local god. At the foot was the **agora** (ag' uh ruh). This was an open area used as a marketplace. As time passed, artisans, traders, and members of the upper class settled near the agora. By 700 B.C., this inner part of the polis had become a city. Together with the villages and farmland around it, it formed a city-state.

Each city-state had its own government and laws. The average city-state contained between 5,000 and 10,000 citizens. Workers born outside Greece, as well as women, children, and to

✓ Reading Check
Why was the **polis** important? What was the **acropolis?** How did the Greeks use the **agora?**

 HISTORY *Online*

Chapter Overview
Visit the *Human Heritage* Web site at **humanheritage.glencoe.com** and click on *Chapter 10— Chapter Overviews* to preview this chapter.

HISTORY *Online*

Chapter Overview introduces students to chapter content and key terms. Have them access *Chapter 10 Overview* at **humanheritage.glencoe.com**

FOCUS

🎏 Bellringer

Ask each student to list two advantages and two disadvantages of living in a modern city.

Motivational Activity

Discuss students' lists of advantages and disadvantages of living in a modern city. Tell students that Greeks lived in city-states. Ask them to look for the advantages and disadvantages of life in the Greek city-states as they read the chapter.

GUIDE TO READING

Reading Strategy

Ask students to read "Why It's Important" and summarize the chapter's main theme. (*The geography of Greece encouraged the rise of independent city-states.*)

Vocabulary Precheck

Ask students to define each of the "Terms to Learn." Have a volunteer consult the dictionary for any unfamiliar words. **L1** **ELL**

📁 Use the Vocabulary PuzzleMaker for Chapter 10 to create a crossword puzzle. **L1**

📂 Assign Chapter 10 Vocabulary and Guided Reading Activity.

📂 Assign Reading Essentials and Study Guide 10-1.

✓ Reading Check Answer
The **polis** was the political center of Greek life.
The **acropolis** was a fortified hill.
The Greeks used the **agora** as a marketplace.

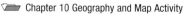

GEOGRAPHY ACTIVITIES
📂 Chapter 10 Geography and Map Activity
📂 Social Studies Outline Map Resource Book

INTERDISCIPLINARY CONNECTIONS
📂 Unit 4 World Literature Reading 2
📖 World History & Art Transparency 5, *Amphora from Vulci*
🎵 World Music Cultural Traditions

ENRICHMENT AND EXTENSION
📂 Chapter 10 Enrichment Activity
💿 World History Primary Source Document Library CD-ROM
ABCNEWS INTERACTIVE Turning Points in World History

📂 Foods Around the World

ASSESSMENT AND EVALUATION
📂 Chapter 10 Performance Assessment Activity
📂 Chapter 10 Section Quizzes 10-1, 10-2, 10-3, 10-4
📂 Chapter 10 Test
💿 Chapter 10 ExamView® Pro Testmaker Software
🎧 Chapter 10 Digests Audiocassettes Activities and Tests

SPANISH RESOURCES
📂 Chapter 10 Spanish Chapter Summary and Glossary
🎧 Chapter 10 Spanish Chapter Digests Audiocassettes Activities and Tests

Guided Practice

L2 **Critical Thinking** Ask students to name the characteristics of Sumerian city-states discussed in Chapter 3. Write student responses on the board. *(Each had its own god and government; included the city—surrounded by a brick wall—and farmland around it; houses surrounding courtyards; ziggurat surrounded by courts.)* Ask students how Greek city-states were similar to or different from Sumerian city-states.

💾 Use **Interactive Tutor Self-Assessment Software** to review Section 1.

✓ **Reading Check Answer**
The **aristocrats** were nobles who took over Spartan government.

✓ **Reading Check Answer**
The **helots** were enslaved people who were owned by the city-state and who did most of the farming.

💾 Use the **Vocabulary Puzzle-Maker** to create crossword and word search puzzles.

164

---

enslaved people, were not citizens. Only citizens could vote, own property, hold public office, and speak for themselves in court. In return, they were expected to take part in government and to defend their polis in time of war or conflict.

For Greek citizens in ancient times, civic and personal honor were one and the same. The polis gave them a sense of belonging. They put the good of the polis above everything else.

Two of the greatest Greek city-states were Sparta and Athens. Sparta had the strongest army in Greece, while Athens had the strongest navy. However, each developed differently with a different kind of government and a different way of life.

Section 1 Assessment

1. **Define:** polis, acropolis, agora.
2. What areas generally made up each city-state?
3. What rights and duties did Greek citizens have?

Critical Thinking

4. **Demonstrating Reasoned Judgment** Which of the requirements for citizenship in early Greece do you think were fair and which were not? Explain.

Graphic Organizer Activity

5. Draw a web like this one, and use it to show characteristics of most Greek city-states.

Greek City-States

SECTION 2 Sparta

✓ **Reading Check** Who were the **aristocrats?**

Sparta was in the south-central region of Greece, in an area known as the Peloponnesus (pel ō puh nē' sus). By 500 B.C., it had become the greatest military power in Greece.

At first, Sparta was ruled by a king. About 800 B.C., **aristocrats** (uh rist' ō kratz), or nobles, took over the government. From that time on, Sparta had two kings who ruled jointly. Although they kept the title of king, they had little power. Their only duties were to lead the army and conduct religious services.

Only aristocrats could be Spartan citizens. All citizens over 20 years old were members of the Assembly, which passed laws and decided questions of war and peace. Each year, the Assembly chose five managers, known as *ephors* (ef' uhrs), to take charge of public affairs and guide the education of young Spartans. The Council of Elders helped the ephors. The Council was made up of men over 60 years old who were chosen for life. It suggested laws to the Assembly and also served as a high court.

✓ **Reading Check** Who were the **helots?**

Aristocrats, Helots, and Perioeci The Spartans had little interest in farming. The land was worked by **helots** (hel' uhtz), or

---

Section 1 Assessment Answers

1. polis, city-state (p. 163); acropolis, fortified hill (p. 163); agora, open marketplace (p. 163)
2. Sample response: farming villages, fields and orchards grouped around an acropolis, an agora at the foot of the acropolis
3. rights—they could vote, own property, hold public office, and speak for themselves in court; duties—they were expected to take part in government and to defend their polis
4. Answers will vary but could include references to discrimination by birth.
5. Items in the graphic organizer might include any of the characteristics in this section such as: centered around an acropolis; had own governments and laws; contained an average of 5,000–10,000 citizens; included an open-air market; only citizens could vote, own property, speak for themselves, or hold office.

Assign Chapter 10 **Section 1 Quiz** in the TCR. Testmaker available.

Reading Physical Maps

Physical maps are used to show something about the surface of Earth. The colors used on physical maps may show the rainfall of a certain area. They may also be used to show an area's temperatures or elevations. In the physical map below, the colors indicate elevation. Colors ranging from green to brown are used. The meaning of each color is explained in the legend.

Look at the map "Elevation of Ancient Greece" shown below. The legend says that light brown means above 5,000 feet, or above 1,500 meters. This means that any area on the map that is shaded light brown is at least 5,000 feet, or 1,500 meters, above sea level. Remember that having an elevation of above 5,000 feet does not necessarily mean that an area is covered with mountains. The area may actually be a plateau.

Map Practice

1. What color shows an elevation of 1,000 to 2,000 feet, or 300 to 600 meters?
2. What elevation is shown by the color dark green?
3. What generalization can you make about the elevation of ancient Greece?

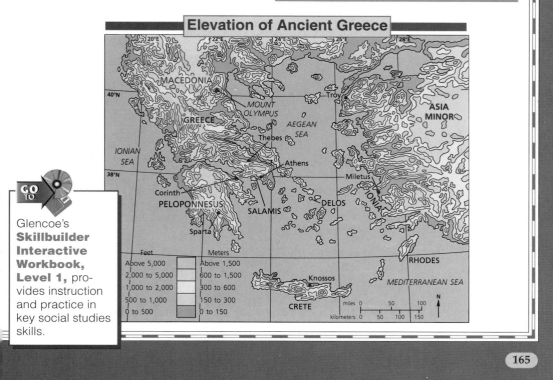

Elevation of Ancient Greece

Feet		Meters
Above 5,000		Above 1,500
2,000 to 5,000		600 to 1,500
1,000 to 2,000		300 to 600
500 to 1,000		150 to 300
0 to 500		0 to 150

GO TO

Glencoe's **Skillbuilder Interactive Workbook, Level 1,** provides instruction and practice in key social studies skills.

MAP SKILLS

TEACH

Reading physical maps

Have students read the introductory section of the skill on page 165. Ask what they think colors can be used to show on maps? *(rainfall, temperatures, or elevations)* What does light brown shading on the map "Elevation of Ancient Greece" mean? *(the area is at least 5,000 feet, or 1,500 m, above sea level)* Direct students' attention to the map on the skill page. Ask students at what elevation most of the city-states are located? *(Most range from 0 to 1,000 feet, or 0 to 300 m, above sea level.)*

Answers to Map Practice

1. yellow
2. dark green shows 0 to 500 feet, or 0 to 150 meters
3. It has steep mountains and small, narrow plains.

SPOTLIGHT ON: ANCIENT GREECE

The Mediterranean climate of ancient Greece made it an optimum place for growing olives, a crop that was as good as gold to the Greeks. Finding the olive growing wild, the Greeks cultivated it. Olive oil went into almost every dish prepared in Greek homes as well as in other ancient lands. Bread was dipped in oil as many people spread bread with butter today. Greek bathers used oil as soap and olive oil was burned for fuel.

Reading Check Answer
The **perioeci** worked as merchants or artisans while the aristocrats trained for the army and war.

MAKING CONNECTIONS

➤➤ **Civics** Young Spartan boys were trained to steal to survive. If they were caught, however, they were severely punished.

CAPTION ANSWER
They were left on a hillside to die.

Reading Check How did the **perioeci** differ from the aristocrats of Sparta?

enslaved people owned by the city-states. Helots had to turn over one half of their crops to the aristocrats who owned the land but lived in the center of the polis.

The Spartans were not interested in business or trade either. They left those to the **perioeci** (pār ē ē' sī), or merchants and artisans who lived in the villages. The perioeci were neither enslaved people nor citizens. Helots and perioeci worked, while aristocrats trained for the army and war.

By about 750 B.C., there were 20 times as many helots and perioeci as there were aristocrats. The aristocrats were now faced with a choice. They could make life better for their workers by letting them share in the government, or they could allow things to stay the way they were. To do that meant keeping the workers down by force. Since the aristocrats were afraid that any change would destroy their way of life, they chose to keep things the way they were.

Spartan Way of Life The Spartans tried to become the strongest people in Greece. Newborn babies were examined to see if they were healthy. If they were, they were allowed to live. If they were not, they were left on a hillside to die.

THE SPARTAN WAY OF LIFE The life of a Spartan male centered on military training and physical fitness from the time he was seven years old. Here, a group of young warriors performs exercises on a Spartan racecourse. **What happened to unhealthy Spartan babies?**

MULTICULTURAL PERSPECTIVES

Many of the words in the English language came from the Spartans. The word *spartan* means "avoiding luxury and comfort" and "being as simple and frugal as possible." Another English word that came from the Spartans is *laconic*. Laconia was the plain in the southwestern part of the Peloponnesus where Sparta was situated. The Spartans were not impressed by oratory. They trained their young men to walk in silence and to say only what was absolutely necessary. The English word *laconic* refers to a person whose speaking style is short, sharp, and to the point.

When Spartan boys turned seven, they were sent to live in military camps. There, they were trained in groups under teenage leaders. They learned to read, write, and use weapons. The boys received only small amounts of food. They had to go barefoot and were given only one cloak to wear. They walked in silence, with their eyes to the ground, and spoke only when necessary. They slept outdoors without cover. Every ten days they were lined up and examined to make sure they were not getting fat.

Spartan men were expected to marry at 20 years of age. However, they could not have a household of their own. They had to live and eat in military barracks, where they shared expenses with other soldiers. They could retire from the army when they were 60 years old.

Spartan women had more freedom than the women of other Greek city-states. In the other city-states, women spent most of their time at home performing household duties. They did not go out without a chaperone. Then, they went out only to visit other women or attend religious festivals. They never spoke to men on the street or entertained their husbands' friends.

Spartan women, on the other hand, mixed freely with men. They enjoyed sports such as wrestling and racing. When Spartan women sent their men into battle, they told the men to come home with their shields or on them. If the men brought their shields home with them, it meant they had won the battle. Dead warriors were carried home on their shields.

The Spartans believed new ideas would weaken their way of life. Because of this, they tried to prevent change. When people of other Greek city-states began to use coins as money, for example, the Spartans kept using iron rods. Other city-states developed literature and art. Other city-states built up business and trade and improved their standard of living. Sparta remained a poor farming society that depended on the labor of slaves.

From its beginnings until its defeat in 371 B.C., Sparta had only one goal—to be militarily strong.

Sculpture of Spartan Girl

Section 2 Assessment

1. **Define:** aristocrats, helots, perioeci.
2. How did the lifestyles of Spartan women differ from other Greek women?
3. Why did Sparta try to prevent change?

Critical Thinking

4. **Making Comparisons** How was Sparta similar to other Greek city-states? How was it different?

Graphic Organizer Activity

5. Draw a chart like this one, and use it to weigh the pros and cons of living in Sparta.

Pros	Cons

Section 2 Assessment Answers

1. aristocrats, Greek nobles (p. 164); helots, enslaved people (p. 164); perioeci, Greek merchants and artisans (p. 166)
2. Spartan women had more freedom, mixed freely with their husbands' friends, enjoyed sports, and encouraged their men in battle.
3. They believed new ideas would weaken their way of life.
4. Sample responses: *similarities*—made own government and laws, trained youth in sports; *differences*—more freedom for women, spent energy on war, little interest in trade and the arts, depended on slave labor
5. Answers will vary, but should accurately reflect features of Spartan life.

Assign the Chapter 10 **Section 2 Quiz** in the TCR. Testmaker available.

L1 **Daily Life** Divide the class into two groups, but have them work individually within their group. Assign one group to imagine they are Spartan teenagers and the other Athenian teenagers. Have students in each group write a letter to someone in the other group describing their schooling and how they feel about it. Have the groups exchange letters and have each student write a letter of response.

DID YOU KNOW ??

Women in Greek city-states could be prominent and influential in religion as priestesses.

NATIONAL GEOGRAPHIC SOCIETY

Use these materials to enrich student understanding of ancient Greek culture.

- **NGS PICTURESHOW CD-ROM**
  Greece and Rome

- **NGS PICTUREPACK TRANSPARENCY SET**
  Ancient Greece

- **ANCIENT CIVILIZATIONS POSTER SET**
  Ancient Greece

Use **Interactive Tutor Self-Assessment Software** to review Section 2.

L1 **Critical Thinking** Ask students why they think Solon ordered every father to teach his son a trade. *(Answers will vary but students may say that he wanted to strengthen industry in Athens.)*

DID YOU KNOW ??

Draco's laws were so strict that a person could be put to death for stealing an apple. The word *draconian* comes from *Draco* and means "extremely harsh or cruel."

CAPTION ANSWER

It was important to the town's economy and was a meeting place of the people.

 Use the **Vocabulary Puzzle-Maker** to create crossword and word search puzzles.

HISTORY *Online*

Student Web Activity objectives, goals, and answers can be found at the *Chapter 10 Web Activity Lesson Plan* at humanheritage.glencoe.com

SECTION 3 Athens

Northeast of Sparta, another city-state developed that had a very different philosophy about living than the Spartans. This polis located on the Aegean coast was Athens. Like Sparta, the location of Athens was strategic. Like all the other Greek city-states, Athens was first ruled by kings. However, about 750 B.C., some Athenian nobles, merchants, and manufacturers took over

ATHENS MARKET PLACE The agora of Athens was a favorite meeting place of the people. These ruins show archaeologists the importance of this community area. **Why would the agora be located near the center of Athens?**

 HISTORY *Online*

Student Web Activity
Visit the *Human Heritage* Web site at **humanheritage.glencoe.com** and click on *Chapter 10— Student Web Activities* to find out more about life in the Greek city-states.

MEETING SPECIAL NEEDS

Organize auditory learners into two groups. Direct one group to imagine they are Athenians defending the idea that a woman's place is in the home. Direct the other group to imagine they are Spartans defending the idea that women should be free to mix with their husband's friends and attend sporting events. Give each group time to research and develop its arguments. Hold a debate over the issues.

Refer to *Inclusion for the Middle School Social Studies Classroom: Strategies and Activities* for additional resources.

the government. They set up an **oligarchy** (ol' uh gahr kē), or form of government in which a few people have the ruling power. Fights broke out between them and the farmers and artisans over land ownership. The upper-class Athenians did not want these fights to turn into an uprising against the government, they agreed to make reforms. To do this, they had to change the government.

The first attempt to change the government was made by Draco (drā' kō), a noble. Draco, however, failed because his punishments were too harsh. Then, in 594 B.C., a rich merchant named Solon (sah' lon) was chosen to undertake the task.

Solon prepared a **constitution,** or a set of principles and rules for governing. This constitution broke the political power of the rich. Solon set a limit on how much land a person could own and gave landowners the right to vote in the Assembly. The Assembly was given the power to pass laws. Solon erased all debts. He freed all the people who had been forced into enslavement because of debt. Solon offered citizenship to artisans who were not Athenians, and he ordered every father to teach his son a trade.

Under Solon, more Athenians began to take part in government. Trade also increased. Still, many people were not happy. The rich thought Solon had gone too far, while the poor thought he had not gone far enough. By the time Solon had left office, he had lost much of his original popularity.

About 560 B.C., the government was taken over by another Athenian named Peisistratus (pī sis' trah tus). Peisistratus was supported by the lower classes. He divided large estates among farmers who owned no land. He stated that a person no longer had to own land to be a citizen. He also encouraged sculpture and other arts.

A Democratic Constitution

When Peisistratus died, his sons took over as leaders of the Athenian government. Not long after that, their government was overthrown by the Spartans.

In 508 B.C., the Spartans themselves were overthrown by a noble named Cleisthenes (klīs' thuh nēz). A year later, Cleisthenes put into effect the world's first constitution that was **democratic,** or favoring the equality of all people. For example, it gave Athenians the right of freedom of speech. The political reforms made by Cleisthenes lasted until the fall of Greece almost 300 years later.

Cleisthenes opened the Assembly to all males over 20 years old. Each year, the Assembly elected ten generals to run the Athenian army and navy and to serve as chief *magistrates* (maj' uh strātz), or judges. One of the generals was named commander-in-chief.

Reading Check
What type of government is an **oligarchy**?

Reading Check
What is a **constitution**?

Image of Solon

Reading Check
What idea does a **democratic** government uphold?

Reading Check Answer
An **oligarchy** is a government in which a few people have the power.

Reading Check Answer
A **constitution** is a set of principles and rules for governing.

Reading Check Answer
A **democratic** government upholds the equality of all people.

ABCNEWS INTERACTIVE™

Videodisc
Turning Points in World History

Side One
Chapter 5

Title: *Democracy in Greece*
Subject: Athenian democracy laid the foundation for the concept of democratic government in which the majority rules, but the minority still has rights.
Ask: What are the basic ideals behind democracy?
(individual equality and freedom)

COOPERATIVE LEARNING

Organize the class into groups of seven or eight. Have four or five in each group role-play residents of Athens and the remaining group members role-play newspaper reporters who interview the residents. Have the groups research to find out about an Athenian merchant, a member of the Council of Five Hundred, an upper-class woman, a priestess to Athena, or an enslaved person. Have each group write questions the reporter might ask and answers that might be given. Each group should hold their interviews for the class.

Assign Chapter 10 *Cooperative Learning Activity* in the TCR.

CRITICAL THINKING SKILLS

TEACH

Recognizing Bias

You might introduce this skill by requesting a volunteer to take the part of a well-known athlete. Ask the student actor to present the following lines to the class: "Hi. I'm [name of athlete], and I just want to tell you that there is no other sport in the world like [name of athlete's sport]. It's the best!" Encourage the student to present all the pluses of the sport.

When the student is done, ask the rest of the class how athletes in other sports might react to this speech. *(probably disagree)* Encourage students to explain why. *(It is a very one-sided view of sports.)* Have students suggest reasons it is important to detect bias, or one-sided opinions. *(Bias can prevent people from looking at a person, issue, idea, or situation in a reasonable or truthful light.)*

Next, assign the skills lesson and the accompanying questions.

Answers to Skill Practice

1. an anti-Athens bias
2. does not think they should be promoted to positions of honor
3. resents being tried by the people
4. dislikes democracy; believes the "better sort of people" should rule

CRITICAL THINKING SKILLS

Recognizing Bias

Cats make better pets than dogs. If you say this—without ever having owned a dog—then you are stating a bias. A bias is a prejudice. It can prevent one from looking at a situation in a reasonable or truthful way.

Learning the Skill Most people have feelings and ideas that affect their point of view. This viewpoint, or *bias*, influences the way they interpret events. For this reason, an idea that is stated as a fact may really be only an opinion. Recognizing bias will help you judge the accuracy of what you read.

To recognize bias, follow these steps:

• Identify the author of the statement and examine his or her views and possible reasons for writing the material.
• Look for language that reflects an emotion or opinion—words such as *all, never, best, worst, might,* or *should.*
• Examine the writing for imbalances—leaning only to one viewpoint and failing to provide equal coverage of other possible viewpoints.
• Identify statements of fact. Factual statements usually answer the *Who? What? Where?* and *When?* questions.
• Determine how the author's bias is reflected in the work.

Skill Practice

Read the following excerpt in which a supporter of oligarchy—government by the few—evaluates how Athens dealt with members of the Delian League. Then answer the questions that follow.

[R]epresentatives of Athens come out, and . . . vent their hatred upon the better sort of people. . . . [T]he better sort of people are punished, . . . robbed of their money, driven from their homes, and put to death, while the lower classes are promoted to honor. . . .

[E]very single individual among the allies is forced to flatter the People of Athens . . . because he knows he will be tried . . . by the . . . People themselves, for such is the law and custom in Athens. He is forced to behave like a beggar in the courts of justice. . . . For this reason . . . the allies find themselves more and more . . . slaves to the people of Athens.

1. **Is the writer expressing a pro-Athens or anti-Athens bias?**
2. **What prejudice does the writer hold toward the lower classes?**
3. **What bias does the writer have toward the system of justice in Athens?**
4. **What bias does the writer hold toward democracy?**

Glencoe's **Skillbuilder Interactive Workbook, Level 1,** provides instruction and practice in key social studies skills.

170

TEAM-TEACHING STRATEGY

Language Arts Work together with a language arts teacher to introduce the concept of "loaded words," or words that evoke some type of emotional reaction. Ask students in which of these two sources they would most expect to find loaded words—an encyclopedia article or a letter to the editor. *(letter to the editor)* Have them explain why. *(The letter to the editor is expressing an opinion and seeking to influence the opinions of others.)* Use this discussion to link loaded words to recognizing bias. Have small groups of students identify loaded words or phrases in the selection provided in the above skill lesson. **L2**

The Council of Five Hundred handled the daily business of Athens. Members were chosen each year by lot. The names of 500 citizens were drawn from a large pot. No one could serve on the Council for more than two terms. Thus, every citizen had a chance to be a Council member.

There were two reasons why the Athenians preferred choosing council members by lot rather than by voting. First, they believed that in an election, people who had money or who could speak well would have an unfair advantage. Second, the Athenians believed that every citizen was smart enough to hold public office. The only exception was in times of war. Then, a skillful general was needed on the Council.

Under Cleisthenes, citizens were required to educate their sons. Since there were no public schools, boys either had a tutor or attended a private school. Starting when they were seven years old, boys studied writing, mathematics, and music. They also practiced sports and memorized the works of Homer and other noted Greek poets.

When they turned 18 years old, Athenian males became citizens. They went to the temple of the god Zeus (zūs) and took an oath of citizenship in front of their family and friends. In the oath, they promised to help make Athens a better place in which to live. They also promised to be honorable in battle, follow the constitution, and respect their religion.

The Persian Wars About the time Athens was going through government changes, the Persians ruled the largest and most powerful empire in the western world. In 545 B.C., the Persians conquered Ionia—the Greek city-states in Asia Minor and on the Aegean islands. About 20 years later, the Ionians revolted. They asked the city-states on the Greek mainland for help. Athens and another polis responded by sending a few warships. After five years of fighting, however, the Persians put down the revolt. Although the Ionians were defeated, Darius, the Persian king, was not satisfied. He wanted to punish the mainland Greeks for helping the Ionians.

In 490 B.C., Darius sent a fleet of 600 ships and a well-equipped army to Greece. The Persians landed on the plain of Marathon about 26 miles, or 41 kilometers, northeast of Athens. After several days, the Persians decided to sail directly to Athens and attack it by sea. They began loading their ships. As soon as most of the Persian soldiers were aboard, Greek soldiers ran down in close order from the hills around Marathon. The remaining Persian troops were not prepared to meet this kind of attack and were defeated. A runner set off for Athens with news of the victory. Upon reaching Athens, he cried out *Nike!*, the Greek goddess of victory, and then died of exhaustion. Winning the Battle of Marathon gave the Greeks a great sense of confidence.

Greek Helmet

The Marathon The runner Pheidippides (fi dip' uh dez) carried the news of the victory at Marathon back to Athens, about 26 miles away. He delivered his message and fell dead of exhaustion. Today, a *marathon* is a footrace of 26 miles, 385 yards, or the term may describe any long-distance race.

L1 **Chronology** As a class, develop a time line depicting the historical events of Greece dating from 545 B.C., the defeat of the Ionians, to 404 B.C., the defeat of the Athenians. Lead the class in a discussion of the causes of the events listed on the time line and what effect each event had on the Greek city-states. **ELL**

LINKING PAST TO PRESENT

The present-day marathon is a race named after the Athenian victory over the Persians. The Greek runner who died bringing the victory news from Marathon to Athens was a well-known professional athlete named Phidippides. His run from Marathon to the agora in Athens—about 26 miles, or 42 km—was the inspiration for the modern marathon race. This race was part of the first modern Olympic Games in 1896.

PRIMARY SOURCES
Library

You might assign "Greek Society," from pages 680–681 of the Primary Sources Library.

MULTICULTURAL PERSPECTIVES

Have interested students research information about Greek city-states other than Athens and Sparta and report their findings to the class. The city-states of Argos, Corinth, Sicyon, Olympia, Delphi, Thessaly, Thebes, Miletus, and Ehesus are possible choices. Have students discuss the similarities and differences among the city-states.

Shortly after the Battle of Marathon, rich silver mines were found near Athens. The Athenians spent their new wealth on **triremes** (trī′ rēmz), or warships that had three levels of rowers on each side, one above the other. Soon, Athens had the largest navy in Greece. The Athenians planned to be prepared if the Persians returned.

The Persians did return. In 480 B.C., Darius's son Xerxes (zerk′ sēz) sent 250,000 soldiers across the Aegean and conquered northern Greece. In order to stop the Persians from taking all of Greece, 20 Greek city-states banded together. The Spartans led the army, while the Athenians led the navy.

First, 7,000 Greek soldiers headed for the narrow pass of Thermopylae (ther mop′ uh lē), about 100 miles, or 160 kilometers, from Athens. There, they held off the Persian army for three days. This gave the people of Athens time to flee to the island of Salamis (sal′ uh muhs). Meanwhile, all but 300 Spartans and 700 other Greeks withdrew from Thermopylae. The Persians, helped by a traitor, found a way around the pass. They killed every soldier guarding the pass and then marched on Athens. Finding the city almost deserted, they set it on fire.

BATTLE OF SALAMIS The Greek fleet, led by the Athenians, defeated the Persian navy in the Bay of Salamis. The faster Greek triremes were able to sail close to the Persian ships and attack with spears and arrows. **What happened to the Persians after the Battle of Salamis?**

SPOTLIGHT ON: LEONIDAS

King Leonidas of Sparta stayed with the 300 Spartans at the narrow pass of Thermopylae to stand against the Persian army. He wanted to remain obedient to the law of Sparta—never surrender on the battlefield but fight until victory or death.

Ancient Greece

Athenian Empire, c. 450 B.C.
■ Independent Greek City-States
✳ Battles

MAP STUDY

LOCATION The Persians wanted to extend their empire into Europe. **How did the location of Greece make it a likely place for a Persian attack?**

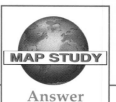

MAP STUDY

Answer

because Persia would have needed to conquer Greece in order to reach the European mainland

Then, the Greeks tricked the Persian fleet into sailing into the strait between Athens and Salamis. Since the strait was too narrow for all the Persian ships to enter at once, the Greeks could take them on a few at a time. Also, once the Persian ships were in the strait, their large size made them difficult to handle. With their lighter, faster ships, the Greeks defeated the Persian fleet.

Following the defeat, Xerxes returned to Asia. However, he left some troops behind. In 479 B.C., they were defeated by the Greeks in the Battle of Plataea (pluh tē′ uh). A few days later, Greek ships destroyed what was left of the Persian navy. The Persian Wars were over.

The Delian League and the Athenian Empire The Persians had been driven from Greece, but they still ruled Ionia. Because of this, the Athenians suggested that the Greek city-states form a *defensive league*, or protective group. Since the league had its headquarters on the island of Delos, it was called the Delian (dē′ lē uhn) League. Sparta was one of the few Greek city-states that did not join the League.

Once a city-state became a League member, it could not withdraw unless all the other members agreed. The League had a common navy. Its ships were usually built and crewed by Athenians, but the other city-states paid the costs.

✓ Reading Check
What is a **defensive league**?

GEOGRAPHY AND HISTORY
Direct the students to use the map on this page. Have them locate the battle sites of the Persian War. Ask students what the location of the battle sites suggests about the probable outcome of the Persian War? *(The battles were fought on territory of Greek city-states instead of territory on the Persian Empire; therefore, the Greek soldiers knew the geography of the area better than the Persian soldiers, which gave them a great advantage toward winning.)*

✓ Reading Check Answer
A **defensive league** is a group organized for the purpose of protection.

MULTICULTURAL PERSPECTIVES

Pericles expressed his ideas about the importance of democracy in a funeral speech when he said democracy must be controlled by many and not a few people. He also said:

When it is a question of putting one person before another in positions of public responsibility, what counts is not membership of a particular class, but the actual ability which the man possesses.

Male citizens were expected to participate in government and to defend the polis in time of war. As Pericles said, "We do not say that a man who takes no interest in politics minds his own business. We say he has no business here at all."

Many countries today expect the same participation from their citizens, both male and female.

➤➤ **Geography: Region** At the beginning of the Peloponnesian War, Pericles planned Athenian strategy. To avoid a direct battle with the well-trained Spartan troops, he moved the rural population of Athens behind the city walls. He ordered the Athenian navy to attack the Spartan coast and to keep the sea lanes open for supplies.

Linking Across Time

because olives were an important food and trade item for the Athenians

People in History

Pericles
c. 495 B.C.–429 B.C.

Athenian General

As leader of Athens, Pericles turned the city-state into a center of learning. His influence was so great that historians call the period of his power the "Age of Pericles."

The League worked well for a while. As time passed, though, Athens gained more and more power. Other city-states had to ask Athens for permission to sail or to trade. Criminal cases were brought to Athens for trial. Athenian coins replaced other Greek money. Athenian soldiers interfered in the politics of other Greek city-states. In short, the Delian League had turned into the Athenian Empire.

The main leader of Athens at the time was a general named Pericles (per' uh klēz). Pericles was known as the "first citizen" of Athens. He had a dream of Athens as the most beautiful and perfect city of the time. To help make this dream come true, he rebuilt the palaces and temples on the Acropolis. It took 11 years to build the Parthenon (par' thuh non), the temple of the goddess Athena. Much of this building was done with money that belonged to the Delian League.

Pericles also built the Long Walls. These were two parallel, fortified walls with tile roofs. The Long Walls connected Athens with its seaport of Piraeus (pī rē' uhs) some five miles, or eight kilometers, away. Having the Long Walls meant Athens could get supplies even in times of war.

Linking Across Time

The Olive Tree According to Greek legend, the goddess Athena created the olive tree as her gift to human beings. Greek farmers have harvested olives for food and oil (below) for thousands of years. The olive tree continues to play an important part in the Greek economy today (right). **Why do you think Sparta burned the olive groves around Athens when it declared war on the city-state in 434 B.C.?**

174

COOPERATIVE LEARNING

Organize the class into two groups. Assign one group the Persian Wars and the other group the Peloponnesian War. Each group should prepare an oral and visual presentation about their assigned war. Divide each group into subgroups to research facets of the topic, such as the impact of geography on the battles and the leaders involved. Visuals might include drawings of soldiers, weapons, battle formations, fortifications, and ships. Each group should prepare a large time line of the events.

Pericles led Athens for almost 30 years. During this period, art, philosophy, and literature reached new heights. Many people who came to Athens from other city-states settled there.

Sculpture of Pericles

Decline of Athens   The more powerful Athens became, the more resentful other Greek city-states grew. Anti-Athenian feelings soon spread throughout Greece. When the Athenians attacked one of Sparta's allies, a group of city-states led by Sparta declared war on Athens. The war, which was called the Peloponnesian (pel uh puh nē' zhuhn) War, lasted almost 30 years. It ended in 404 B.C. when Athens surrendered to Sparta.

Between the war and a plague that struck during the war, Athens also lost more than one quarter of its people. Much of its land was ruined. Thousands of young Athenian men left home and became **mercenaries** (mer' suh när ēz), or hired soldiers, in the Persian army.

When the Spartans took control of Athens in 404 B.C., they set up an oligarchy and chose 30 Athenian aristocrats to rule there. Not long after that, the Athenians successfully revolted and once more set up a democracy. However, Athens was never again as powerful as it had been before the Peloponnesian War.

> ✓ **Reading Check**
> What type of jobs did Greek **mercenaries** seek in Persia?

Section 3 Assessment

1. **Define:** oligarchy, constitution, democratic, triremes, mercenaries.
2. What political reforms did Cleisthenes introduce?
3. What changes did Pericles bring to Athens?

Critical Thinking

4. **Understanding Cause and Effect** What were some of the causes and effects of the Peloponnesian War?

Graphic Organizer Activity

5. Draw a diagram like this, and use it to show how the Delian League affected both Athens and other city-states.

Effects of the Delian League	
in Athens	in other City-States

SECTION 4 Decline of the City-States

After the Peloponnesian War, most Greeks began to lose their sense of community. The war had lasted a long time and had cost a great deal of money. People became more interested in making money and having a good time. Soon, bitterness developed between the upper and lower classes within each polis.

CHAPTER 10 THE CITY-STATES   **175**

Evaluate

Assign Chapter 10 **Performance Assessment Activity** in the TCR.

Administer **Chapter 10 Test** in the TCR. Testmaker available.

Reteach

Help students chart the main ideas and events described in the chapter.

Assign Chapter 10 **Reteaching Activity** in the TCR.

Enrich

Have students present to the class illustrations of Greek vase painting, and describe the details shown on the paintings.

Assign Chapter 10 **Enrichment Activity** in the TCR.

CLOSE

Ask students to compare the advantages and disadvantages of living in a Greek-city state with those they listed for modern city life in the Bellringer activity.

Use **Interactive Tutor Self-Assessment Software** to review Section 4.

Self-Check Quiz gives students an interactive chapter tutorial. Have them access **Chapter 10 Quiz** at **humanheritage.glencoe.com**

After the war, Sparta ruled Greece. The Spartans were harsh rulers who angered the other Greeks. As a result, in 371 B.C., a group of city-states led by Thebes (thēbz) overthrew Spartan rule. The rule of Thebes, however, was no better than that of Sparta. It weakened the city-states even more. The Greeks were no longer strong enough or united enough to fight off invaders. In 338 B.C., Philip II of Macedonia (mas uh dō′ nē uh) conquered Greece.

Section 4 Assessment

1. **Define:** How did the Peloponnesian War help destroy the sense of community in most Greek city-states?
2. What were some of the reasons for the decline of the Greek city-states?

Critical Thinking
3. **Drawing Conclusions** Why might the Greeks have become more interested in making money for themselves rather than for the city-state after the Peloponnesian War?

Graphic Organizer Activity

4. Draw a flow chart like this one, and use it to trace the decline of the Greek city-states after the Peloponnesian War.

Peloponnesian War

Chapter Summary & Study Guide

1. Around 700 B.C., city-states became the center of Greek life.
2. The two greatest city-states were Sparta and Athens.
3. Sparta spent most of its time training its citizens for war.
4. Spartan women had more freedom than women in other city-states.
5. Spartans believed new ideas would weaken their way of life, so they tried to prevent change.
6. Between 750 and 507 B.C., Athens went through a series of reforms to broaden democracy.
7. In 507 B.C., Cleisthenes put into effect the first democratic constitution.
8. After several wars with Persia, Athens became Greece's leading polis.
9. Sparta defeated Athens in the Peloponnesian War, which was fought between 431 and 404 B.C.
10. The Peloponnesian War weakened the Greek city-states, leading to the conquest of Greece by Philip II of Macedonia in 338 B.C.

Self-Check Quiz

Visit the *Human Heritage* Web site at **humanheritage.glencoe.com** and click on *Chapter 10—Self-Check Quiz* to assess your understanding of this chapter.

176 UNIT 4 THE GREEKS

Section 4 Assessment Answers

1. The war lasted a long time and was costly; people were discouraged and they began to lose interest in what was good for their city-state.
2. Bitterness developed between the upper and lower classes within each polis, the rule of Thebes weakened the city-states, and the Greeks could no longer fight off invaders.
3. Answers will vary but might include the idea that they were tired of being involved in war and decided to pay attention to themselves.
4. Sample responses: lost sense of community, increased interest in money-making, increased bitterness between upper and lower classes in each polis, harsh rule by Sparta, rebellion and rule by Thebes, lack of strength to resist invaders

Assign Chapter 10 **Section 4 Quiz** in the TCR. Testmaker available.

Using Key Terms

Imagine you are living in Greece during the time of the Persian Wars. Use the following words to write a letter to a friend describing the organization and government of Sparta and Athens at that time.

polis	acropolis	agora
aristocrats	perioeci	oligarchy
helots	democratic	constitution
triremes	mercenaries	defensive league

Understanding Main Ideas

1. Why did Greek communities have little contact with one another?
2. What did the citizens of a polis consider most important?
3. Why was it important for Spartan women to be physically fit?
4. Why did Sparta remain a poor farming society?
5. Why was the Battle of Marathon important for the Greeks?
6. How did Athenians use the Delian League to build an empire?

Critical Thinking

1. Do you think that the Spartan emphasis on military training benefited Sparta? Why or why not?
2. What method of choosing members of the Athenian Council of Five Hundred would you have suggested? Explain your answer.
3. Why do you think some people in Athens might have objected to the title of "first citizen" for Pericles? Explain your answer.

4. What may happen to a community as a result of a long war? Why?

Graphic Organizer Activity

Culture Draw a Venn diagram like this one, and use it to compare Sparta and Athens at their height of power.

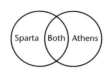

Geography in History

Place Note the location of the Greek city-states on the map on page 173. Why do you think these city-states developed in the places that they did, and what geographic features might have affected this development? Write a paragraph explaining the relationship between a city's location and the surrounding geographic features.

Using Your Journal

Review any details you may have noted about the ideas developed by the Greeks. Write a paragraph describing how the ideas of Solon and Cleisthenes affect you today.

Bonus Test Question

For Chapter 10 Test
What would Cleisthenes say about a city-state ruled by one woman who served for life, a council elected by voting, no organized army, and public schools for all citizens?

Using Your Journal

Paragraphs should include the idea that democratic constitutions are part of the U.S. and many local governments. The House of Representatives, like the Assembly, has the power to make laws.

Geography in History

Answers may vary but could include references to good farming land, optimum location for trade and/or sea access, the safety of highlands or islands, and heritage.

Using Key Terms

Letters will vary but should include several comparisons.

Understanding Main Ideas

1. because they were separated by mountains and by the sea
2. the good of the polis
3. so they would bear healthy male warriors
4. because it spent its time and energy only on the art of war
5. because it gave the Greeks a great sense of confidence
6. Athens gained more power, controlled sailing and trade, and interfered in the politics of other city-states.

Critical Thinking

1. Answers will vary.
2. Answers will vary but could include the blind drawing being more fair but less qualitative than an election.
3. Answers will vary but could include reference to his good and bad qualities.
4. Answers will vary but should include that people may become discouraged, fight among themselves, and lose their sense of community.

Graphic Organizer Activity

Venn diagrams should reflect unique features of each city-state. Shared characteristics might include such items as: spoke the Greek language, created its own government and laws, valued a strong military, worshiped same gods and goddesses, etc.

Chapter 11 Planning Guide

Objectives	Reproducible Resources	Multimedia Resources
Section 1 **Religious Practices** Describe how the Greeks honored their gods and goddesses, and summarize what contributions were made in athletics and the arts during the Golden Age of Greek culture.	Reproducible Lesson Plan Chapter 11 Vocabulary and Guided Reading Activity Reading Essentials and Study Guide 11-1 Chapter 11 Cooperative Learning Activity Unit 4 World Literature Reading 1 Section 1 Quiz	Teaching Transparency and Activity 11A Vocabulary PuzzleMaker Interactive Tutor Self-Assessment Software ExamView® Pro Testmaker Glencoe Skillbuilder Interactive Workbook, Level 1 Presentation Plus!
Section 2 **Science** Discuss how Socrates, Plato, Aristotle, and other Greek thinkers influenced the development of western civilization.	Reproducible Lesson Plan Reading Essentials and Study Guide 11-2 Chapter 11 Chart and Graph Skill Activity Chapter 11 Geography and Map Activity Chapter 11 Activity Book Activity Chapter 11 Enrichment Activity Section 2 Quiz	Teaching Transparency and Activity 11B Vocabulary PuzzleMaker Interactive Tutor Self-Assessment Software ExamView® Pro Testmaker Glencoe Skillbuilder Interactive Workbook, Level 1
Chapter 11 **Review and Evaluation**	Chapter 11 Reteaching Activity Chapter 11 Performance Assessment Activity Spanish Chapter Summary and Glossary Chapter 11 Test	Vocabulary PuzzleMaker Interactive Tutor Self-Assessment Software Glencoe Skillbuilder Interactive Workbook, Level 1 Audiocassettes* ExamView® Pro Testmaker

*Also available in Spanish.

Presentation Plus!
Use Glencoe's **Presentation Plus!** multimedia teacher tool to easily present dynamic lessons that visually excite your students. Using Microsoft® PowerPoint, you can customize the presentations to create your own personalized lessons.

Interactive Lesson Planner

Planning has never been easier! Using this CD-ROM, organize your week, month, semester, or year with all the help you need. The **Interactive Lesson Planner** gives you access to all of the blackline masters which accompany *Human Heritage*.

✓ PERFORMANCE ASSESSMENT ACTIVITIES

Time Capsules Have students contribute to a "Golden Age of Greece" time capsule. Ask each student to research and write about one of the following aspects of Greek culture: architecture, art, history, literature, science, mathematics, philosophy, or law. Encourage students to create a visual representation of their subject to post with their writing.

CHAPTER RESOURCES

LITERATURE ABOUT THE PERIOD

Hamilton, Edith, trans. *Three Greek Plays*. Norton, 1958. Included are the *Trojan Woman* of Euripedes, *Prometheus Bound*, and *Agamemnon* of Aeschylus.

Jowett, Benjamin, trans. *The Dialogues of Plato*. Random House, 1920. The definitive translation, including *The Republic*.

READINGS FOR THE STUDENT

Boyer, Sophia A., and Winifred Lubell. *Gifts from the Greeks, Alpha to Omega*. Rand McNally, 1970. Descriptions of areas of Greek life illustrated with drawings of Greek art.

READINGS FOR THE TEACHER

Grant, Michael. *The Classical Greeks*. Scribner, 1989. Connects culture with historical events. Spans art, architecture, philosophy, and drama.

KEY TO ABILITY LEVELS

Teaching strategies have been coded for varying learning styles and abilities.

L1 Level 1 activities are **basic** activities and should be within the ability range of all students.

L2 Level 2 activities are **average** activities and should be within the ability range of the average to above-average student.

L3 Level 3 activities are **challenging** activities designed for the ability range of above-average students.

ELL ELL activities should be within the ability range of English Language Learning students.

NATIONAL GEOGRAPHIC SOCIETY — Teacher's Corner

INDEX TO NATIONAL GEOGRAPHIC MAGAZINE

The following articles relate to this chapter:

- "Ancient Greece: Part II, "Ascent to Glory," by Caroline Alexander, February 2000.
- "Let the Games Begin," by Frank Deford, July 1996.

NATIONAL GEOGRAPHIC SOCIETY PRODUCTS AVAILABLE FROM GLENCOE

To order the following, call Glencoe at 1-800-334-7344:

- *PicturePack: Physical Geography of the World (Transparencies)*
- *PicturePack: Ancient Greece (Transparencies)*
- *PictureShow: Ancient Civilizations: Greece and Rome (CD-ROMs)*
- *Ancient Civilizations: Ancient Greece (Poster Set)*
- *PicturePack: Ancient Civilizations Library, Part I (Transparencies)*

Access *National Geographic*'s new dynamic MapMachine Web site and other geography resources at:
http://www.nationalgeographic.com/
http://www.nationalgeographic.com/maps

  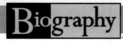

THE HISTORY CHANNEL.

The following videotape program is available from Glencoe:

- **Powerful Gods of Mount Olympus**
  1-56501-927-X

To order, call Glencoe at 1-800-334-7344. To find classroom resources to accompany many of these videos, check the following home pages:

A&E Television: http://www.aetv.com
The History Channel: http://www.historychannel.com

OVERVIEW

Chapter 11 describes the many cultural contributions made by the Greeks during the Golden Age.

➤ **Section 1** discusses Greek creativity and the people's attempt to honor their gods and goddesses especially in athletics and theater.

➤ **Section 2** identifies Socrates, Plato, and Aristotle and the development of Greek science.

CHAPTER OBJECTIVES

After reading Chapter 11, students will be able to:

1. describe how the Greeks honored their gods and goddesses.

2. summarize Greek contributions to athletics and the arts.

3. discuss how Greek thinkers influenced the development of world civilization.

EXAMINING ARTIFACTS

Refer students to the chapter title, and ask: What cultural contributions are represented by the artifacts on this page? *(Most students will probably say sculpture and pottery.)* Call student attention to the women runners on the vase. Then write the word "Olympics" on the board. Challenge students to name Olympic events that might be traced back to the Greeks.

PERFORMANCE ASSESSMENT ✓

Use the Performance Assessment activities on page 178B to help you evaluate students as they complete the chapter.

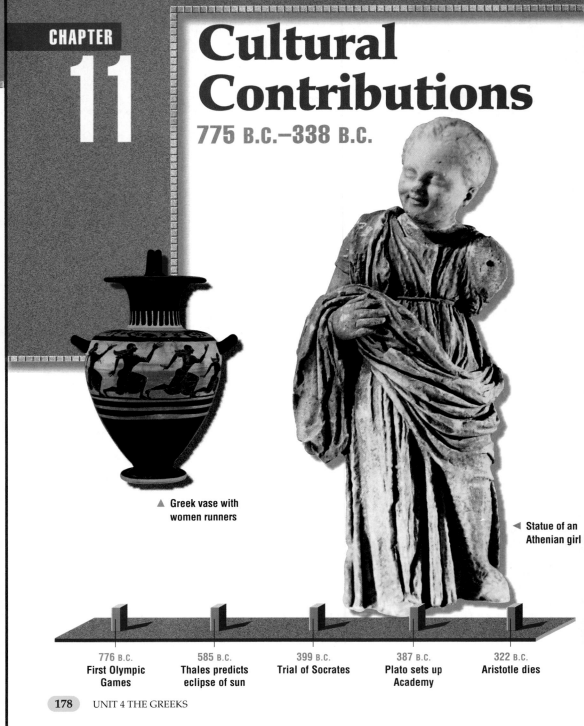

CHAPTER
11

Cultural Contributions
775 B.C.–338 B.C.

▲ Greek vase with women runners

◄ Statue of an Athenian girl

776 B.C. **First Olympic Games**	585 B.C. **Thales predicts eclipse of sun**	399 B.C. **Trial of Socrates**	387 B.C. **Plato sets up Academy**	322 B.C. **Aristotle dies**

178 UNIT 4 THE GREEKS

TEACHING RESOURCES

TEACHER PLANNING AND SUPPORT

🗁 Reproducible Lesson Plan
🗁 Block Scheduling Implementation Guide
🗁 Videodisc Bar Code Correlation
⊙ Presentation Plus!

REVIEW AND REINFORCEMENT

🗁 Reading Essentials and Study Guide 11-1, 11-2
🗁 Chapter 11 Vocabulary and Guided Reading Activity
💾 Vocabulary PuzzleMaker Software

✎ Teaching Transparencies 11A & 11B
🗁 Chapter 11 Reteaching Activity
🗁 Chapter 11 Cooperative Learning Activity
🗁 Chapter 11 Activity Book Activity
🗁 Chapter 11 Chart and Graph Skill Activity
💾 Interactive Tutor Self-Assessment Software

APPLICATION AND HANDS-ON ACTIVITIES

🗋 Daily World History, Geography, and Culture Question
🗁 Unit 4 Hands-On History Lab Activity

Chapter Focus

Read to Discover

- How the Greeks honored their gods and goddesses.
- What contributions in athletics and the arts were made during the "Golden Age" of Greek culture.
- How Greek thinkers influenced the development of world civilization.

Chapter Overview
Visit the *Human Heritage* Web site at **humanheritage.glencoe.com** and click on ***Chapter 11— Chapter Overviews*** to preview this chapter.

 Terms to Learn

oracles
prophecy
pancratium
pentathlon
philosophia
Socratic
   method
hypothesis
syllogism

 People to Know

Herodotus
Socrates
Plato
Aristotle

Places to Locate

Mount Olympus
Olympia

Why It's Important   The Greeks made many contributions to world civilization. Their accomplishments resulted, in part, because of an important religious belief. The Greeks felt their gods were honored if people tried to imitate them. The greater the skill the Greeks showed in thinking, athletic games, or the arts, the more the gods were honored. Greek efforts to do their best produced a "Golden Age" of learning. Many historians call this period the "Classical Age of Greece."

SECTION 1   Religious Practices

Although most Greeks held similar religious beliefs, there was no single Greek religion. Each city-state worshiped its own gods. Officials in each polis were in charge of public feasts and sacrifices. In their own homes, heads of families prayed and offered sacrifices to the gods.

Greek priests and priestesses often served as **oracles,** or persons who, it was believed, could speak with the gods. Many Greeks went to oracles for advice. The advice was generally given in the form of a **prophecy** (prof′ uh sē), or a statement of what might

Reading Check
Why did many Greeks go to the **oracles?**
What is a **prophecy?**

GEOGRAPHY ACTIVITIES

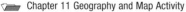

- Chapter 11 Geography and Map Activity
- Social Studies Outline Map Resource Book

INTERDISCIPLINARY CONNECTIONS

- Unit 4 World Literature Reading 1
- World Music: Cultural Traditions

ENRICHMENT AND EXTENSION

- Unit 4 Primary Sources Reading
- World History Primary Source Document Library CD-ROM
- Chapter 11 Enrichment Activity

- Foods Around the World

ASSESSMENT AND EVALUATION

- Chapter 11 Performance Assessment Activity
- Chapter 11 Section Quizzes 11-1, 11-2
- Chapter 11 Test
- Chapter 11 ExamView® Pro Testmaker Software
- Chapter 11 Digests Audiocassettes Activities and Tests

SPANISH RESOURCES

- Chapter 11 Spanish Chapter Summary and Glossary
- Chapter 11 Spanish Chapter Digests Audiocassettes Activities and Tests

---

Chapter Overview introduces students to chapter content and key terms. Have them access ***Chapter 11 Overview*** at **humanheritage.glencoe.com**

FOCUS

Bellringer

Write this quotation from John Keats on the board: *A thing of beauty is a joy forever.* Have students write a few sentences telling whether they agree.

Motivational Activity

Discuss students' opinions of Keats's quotation and what might constitute a "thing of beauty" in modern times. Ask students what things from more than 2,000 years ago might be considered "a joy forever."

GUIDE TO READING

Reading Strategy

Ask students to read "Why It's Important" and summarize the chapter's main theme. (*Greek accomplishments, growing out of efforts to honor the gods, helped shape world civilization.*)

Vocabulary Precheck

Ask students to define each of the "Terms to Learn." Have a volunteer consult the dictionary for any unfamiliar words. **L1** **ELL**

Use the Vocabulary PuzzleMaker for Chapter 11 to create a crossword puzzle. **L1**

Assign Chapter 11 Vocabulary and Guided Reading Activity.

Assign Reading Essentials and Study Guide 11-1.

Reading Check Answer

Greeks went to **oracles** to seek advice from the gods.
A **prophecy** is a statement of what might happen in the future.

179

Guided Practice

L2 **Religion** Write the following scenario on the board: *You are a scholar with an interest in religions, living across the sea from the Greeks during the Classical Age. Your society has heard rumors that the Greeks approach their gods and goddesses differently than people have in the past. Your superiors have expressed great interest in these new religious beliefs, and have sent you to gather information on the Greek gods and goddesses.* Then tell students to write an account of their findings to be presented to their superiors upon their return home.

CAPTION ANSWER

Often a prophecy could mean more than one thing. People seeking advice had to decide what they believed to be the true meaning of the prophecy.

The following videotape program is available from Glencoe to enrich Chapter 11:

- **Powerful Gods of Mount Olympus**

To find classroom resources to accompany this video, check the following home page:

A&E Television:
http://www.aetv.com

 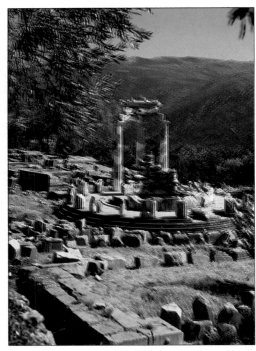

THE DELPHIC ORACLE   The most popular oracle was a priestess in the temple at Delphi. The Greeks believed that Delphi was the center of the world, and they built many temples and other public buildings there (right). The painting of the Delphic oracle (left) shows offering a prophecy to a Greek man. **Why was a prophecy from an oracle often confusing?**

The Oracle at Delphi
Pilgrims to the oracle at Delphi descended a staircase into an underground vault in the Temple of Apollo, where a priestess sat. Sulfurous gases bubbled up from the crack in the earth beneath her chair, swirling around her as the pilgrim asked a question. Priests then translated the answer into a verse for the pilgrim to recite and try to understand.

happen in the future. Often, a prophecy could mean more than one thing. The person seeking advice had to decide what he or she believed to be the true meaning of the prophecy.

Gods and Goddesses of Mount Olympus   During the Golden Age, the Greeks worshiped the gods of Mount Olympus (ō lim' puhs). There were 12 major gods and goddesses. Each had specific duties to carry out.

Most ancient peoples feared their gods. They believed that people were put on Earth only to obey and serve the gods. The Greeks were the first people to feel differently. They placed importance on the worth of the individual. Because they believed in their own value, the Greeks had a great deal of self-respect. This allowed them to approach their gods with dignity.

The Greeks built temples to honor their gods. Inside each temple stood a statue of the god being honored. In front of the

EXTENDING THE CONTENT

The architects of the Parthenon—the temple to Athena—understood perspective and optical illusions. Thus they made the temple's columns thicker in the middle and thinner at the top so that the columns appeared straight when viewed from a distance. The steps leading up to the Parthenon, actually lower in the center than at either end, likewise appear straight.

statue was an altar. Because the Greeks believed the temple was the god's home, they did not enter it. They worshiped outside, as a sign of respect.

Another way the Greeks honored their gods was with different kinds of festivals. Each showed the power of the god in whose honor it was given. Out of the festivals came two important contributions to western culture. These were the Olympic Games and the theater.

The Olympic Games Every four years, in the middle of summer, a festival was held in Olympia (ō lim′ pē uh) to honor the god Zeus. Olympia was not really a town. It was a group of

Student Web Activity
Visit the *Human Heritage* Web site at **humanheritage.glencoe.com** and click on *Chapter 11— Student Web Activities* to find out more about Greek contributions.

OLYMPIAN GODS AND GODDESSES

Name	Realm
Zeus	ruler of Mount Olympus, king of the gods, god of the weather
Aphrodite	goddess of love and beauty
Apollo	god of the sun; patron of truth, archery, music, medicine, and prophecy
Ares	god of war
Artemis	goddess of the moon; mighty huntress and "rainer of arrows"; guardian of cities, young animals, and women; twin sister of Apollo
Athena	goddess of wisdom; city god of Athens; patron of household crafts; protectress in war of those who worshipped her; daughter of Zeus
Demeter	goddess of crops, giver of grain and fruit
Dionysus	god of fertility, of joyous life and hospitality, and of wild things
Hephaestus	god of fire and artisans; maker of Pandora, the first mortal woman; husband of Aphrodite
Hera	protectress of marriage, children, and the home; wife of Zeus
Hermes	god of orators, writers, and commerce; protector of thieves and mischief-makers; guardian of wayfarers; messenger to mortals; son of Zeus
Poseidon	god of the sea and earthquakes, giver of horses to mortals

Student Web Activity objectives, goals, and answers can be found at the *Chapter 11 Web Activity Lesson Plan* at **humanheritage.glencoe.com**

L2 Language Arts Have students choose a god or goddess from the chart on this page and read a myth about them. Students might refer to *Book of Greek Myths* by Ingri and Edgar D'Aulaire. Then have students give oral-reading reviews of the myths and their opinion of the worthiness of their deity.

NATIONAL GEOGRAPHIC SOCIETY

Use these materials to enrich student understanding of ancient Greek culture.

NGS PICTURESHOW CD-ROM
Greece and Rome

NGS PICTUREPACK TRANSPARENCY SET
Ancient Greece

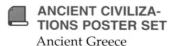

ANCIENT CIVILIZA-TIONS POSTER SET
Ancient Greece

MEETING SPECIAL NEEDS

Help students who need to review the vocabulary and concepts in this chapter by having them create a crossword puzzle on a large sheet of butcher paper or on the board. Have a volunteer find a word or term in the chapter and write it on the paper horizontally or vertically. Have another student write a clue that defines that word, and then add a word to the paper crossing the previous word in crossword puzzle fashion. Have students continue composing the puzzle as long as they can fit words, adding numbered clues as they go. After compiling 10 words or more, have students create a blank puzzle, using squares or blanks for each letter, and the list of numbered clues to challenge another class.

📁 Refer to *Inclusion for the Middle School Social Studies Classroom: Strategies and Activities* for additional resources.

The Olympics
According to legend, King Pelops founded the Olympics to repay Zeus for helping him win a chariot race and gain Hippodameia, a rival king's daughter. Hippodameia then began the Heraia, a festival honoring Zeus's wife Hera. The Heraia, held at the same time as the Olympics, gave women a chance to compete in foot races.

temples and arenas built in fields. A 40-foot, or 12-meter, gold and ivory statue of Zeus stood in one of the temples.

The festival was known as the Olympic Games. It was the most important sporting event in Greece. While the games were going on, the Greeks would stop fighting any war in which they were involved. When the Spartans refused to call a truce during the Peloponnesian War to compete in the games, they had to pay a fine.

Athletes came from all over Greece and from Greek colonies in Africa, Italy, and Asia Minor to take part in the games. Individuals, rather than teams, competed. Only men were allowed to take part. Women were not even allowed to watch. Each athlete had to swear on the sacred boar of Zeus that he would follow the rules of the games. Those who broke the rules were fined.

The Olympics were made up of many events. One of the most exciting was the chariot race. It was held in the Hippodrome (hip' uh drōm), which was an oval track with grandstands around it. The chariots had small wheels and were open in the back. At first, they were pulled by four horses. Later, only two horses were used. About 40 chariots started the race, but only a few could finish the 9 miles, or 14.4 kilometers. The driver of the winning chariot received a crown made from olive leaves.

WARRIOR'S RACE The first Olympic Games were mainly simple foot races. Later, other events were added. One of these additions was the warrior's race. In it, runners competed wearing full armor and carrying a shield. **What were some other events in the early Olympics?**

MULTICULTURAL PERSPECTIVES

Though the Olympic Games were the oldest and most prestigious athletic event in Greece, they were not unique. There were three other major sports festivals held at two- or four-year intervals: the Pythian Games honoring Apollo at Delphi, the Nemean Games for Zeus, and the Isthmian Games held at Corinth to honor Poseidon. Games alternated so there was at least one major event a year. All of these games were "Panhellenic," drawing from all of Greece and its colonies.

Another major event was boxing. Boxers did not use their fists. They wrapped their hands with strips of ox hide and slapped one another with the flat of the hand. There were no set rounds or points. A match between two boxers went on until one raised a finger in the air as a sign of defeat.

Another fighting event was the **pancratium** (pan krā' shē uhm). This was a combination of boxing and wrestling in which no holds were barred between the two fighters. The only two things a fighter could not do were gouge an opponent's eyes or bite.

The winner of the **pentathlon** (pen tath' luhn) was considered the best all-around athlete. The pentathlon itself was made up of five events. Those who took part had to run, jump, throw the discus (dis' kuhs), wrestle, and hurl the javelin (jav' luhn). Like other winners, the winner of the pentathlon was crowned with an olive-leaf wreath.

Olympic winners were heroes. Poets wrote about them. City-states held parades for them. Some city-states even gave them free meals for a year.

Between the different events at the games, poets read their works aloud. Herodotus (hi rahd' uh tuhs), the "Father of History," first read his account of the Persian Wars at the Olympics. Greek historians even dated events by Olympiads (ō lim' pē ads), or the four-year periods between games. The first recorded date in Greek history is the date of the first Olympic Games, which occurred in 776 B.C.

The Theater The theater grew out of festivals given in honor of the god Dionysus (dī uh nī' suhs). About 600 B.C., the Ionians began telling stories about Dionysus at festivals. A chorus chanted and danced each story to the music of a flute. At certain points, the chorus fell silent. The chorus leader then gave a *soliloquy* (suh lil' uh kwē), or talk in which personal thoughts and feelings are expressed to the audience.

In time, the chorus became shorter and the soliloquies longer. Stories were then told about other gods and heroes. About the time of the Persian Wars, a Greek poet named Aeschylus (es' kuh luhs) added an additional character to each story. Now, instead of singing or telling a story, it was acted out. Thus, Aeschylus created what came to be known as a play.

The first Greek plays were *tragedies* (traj' uh dēz), or stories about suffering. All dealt with the past and with the relationships between people and gods. Not all of them had unhappy endings. Still, they all pointed out that though people suffered, most individuals were able to carry on despite their suffering.

Three of the great writers of tragedy were Aeschylus, Sophocles (sahf' uh klēz), and Euripides (yū rip' uh dēz). All three lived in Athens during its Golden Age. Aeschylus wrote about power and its effect on people. Sophocles showed that people

CHAPTER 11 CULTURAL CONTRIBUTIONS 183

Reading Check

How did athletes compete in the **pancratium?** What five events made up the **pentathlon?**

Orchestra *Orchestra* is a Greek word from the verb "to dance." At first, it meant the space between the stage and the audience where the chorus performed. In modern times, the term designates both the area in front of the stage and the group of musicians who plays there.

Reading Check Answer

In the **pancratium,** athletes competed in a no-holds barred fighting event that combined wrestling and boxing. In a **pentathlon,** athletes had to run, jump, throw the discus, wrestle, and hurl the javelin.

MAKING CONNECTIONS

➤➤ **Drama** The Greek playwrights differed with each other on important issues. For example, Aeschylus, who had fought at Marathon and Salamis, was proud of Athens' military accomplishments and said so in his plays. Euripedes, on the other hand, condemned the suffering caused by war.

DID YOU KNOW

Sophocles's most famous play, *Oedipus Rex*, deals with the plight of Oedipus, a king who unknowingly kills his father and marries his mother. Oedipus uses all his powers to solve the crime of murder, only to discover that he is the murderer.

COOPERATIVE LEARNING

Have students plan and execute a Greek Heritage Day. Divide the class into groups. Assign each group an ancient Greek achievement to demonstrate to the class, such as drama, painting, sculpture, and architecture. The groups should decide what form their demonstration will take. Make sure that each member of the group has a specific assignment. The demonstrations could include a performance of part of a drama, a model of a vase, or a model of a building.

🗀 Assign Chapter 11 *Cooperative Learning Activity* in the TCR.

Comedy and Tragedy Masks

suffered because of their sins and mistakes and that suffering could make someone a better person. Euripides tried to show that people suffered because they did bad things.

Soon after the development of tragedy, a second kind of play came into being. It was *comedy*, or a play with a happy ending. Unlike tragedies, Greek comedies were about the present. At first, they poked fun at certain politicians and other polis leaders, who often were in the audience. Later, comedies did away with the chorus. They also stopped poking fun at specific people. Instead, they poked fun at a certain kind of person, such as a son who wastes money or an enslaved person who plots against a master. One of the greatest writers of Greek comedy was Aristophanes (ar uh stahf' uh nēz). He found something funny about everyone.

Greek plays were performed only at community festivals. They began at sunrise and went on all day. Tragedies were presented in the morning and comedies in the afternoon. All the performers were men. Women were allowed to watch plays but could not act in them.

Each actor wore a huge canvas and plaster mask that showed the sex, age, and mood of the character. The mouth of the mask was shaped like a funnel. This helped carry the sound of the actor's voice to the entire audience. Actors also wore heavy padding under their robes and boots with thick soles. This made them seem larger than they really were.

Linking Across Time

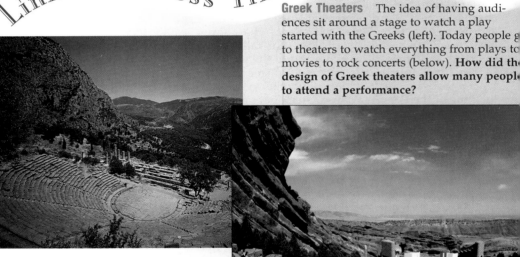

Greek Theaters The idea of having audiences sit around a stage to watch a play started with the Greeks (left). Today people g to theaters to watch everything from plays to movies to rock concerts (below). **How did the design of Greek theaters allow many people to attend a performance?**

184 UNIT 4 THE GREEKS

EXTENDING THE CONTENT

The earliest Greek plays took place around 600 B.C. at festivals honoring Dionysus, the Greek god of wine and fertility. The audience sat on a hillside around an open space, where a chorus chanted a story about Dionysus and danced to the sound of a flute. Eventually cities began building permanent amphitheaters, carving into a hillside, adding rows of stone seats, and paving the stage area. A low building erected behind the stage served as a dressing room and backstage area.

Plays were given in open-air theaters some large. Anyone who did not have enough money to buy a ticket was admitted free. The audience sat on rows of stone benches set on the side of a hill. The benches were arranged in a semicircle around a stage that was level with the ground.

The Greeks believed support of the theater was a public responsibility. An official of each polis chose the plays to be performed. This official then assigned each play to a wealthy citizen to stage. A panel of citizens judged the plays at each festival.

Section 1 Assessment

1. **Define:** oracles, prophecy, pancratium, pentathlon.
2. How did the Greeks honor their gods and goddesses?
3. Who took part in the Olympics?

Critical Thinking

4. **Demonstrating Reasoned Judgement** Do you think support of the theater should be the responsibility of government or private groups? Explain.

Graphic Organizer Activity

5. Draw a diagram like this one, and use it to list events at the Greek Olympics. (Add additional answer lines as needed.)

Olympics — Event / Event / Event

SECTION 2 Science

Among the things on which the Greeks placed great importance was *intellect* (in' tuh lekt), or the ability to learn and reason. The Greeks thought intellect should be used to its fullest. Because of this, they asked questions about many things and studied the laws of nature. To the Greeks, studying the laws of nature and loving wisdom were the same thing. They called it *philosophia* (fi la sō fē' ya). Today, people who search for such knowledge and wisdom are known as scientists and *philosophers.* Much of what they know is based on the thoughts of the Greeks.

Socrates   In 399 B.C., a trial was held in Athens. The person on trial was Socrates (sok' ruh tēz), a 70-year-old Athenian philosopher who was interested in the thinking process. Socrates gave up private business so he could spend his time searching for truth. He believed people could discover truth if they knew how to think.

In his search for truth, Socrates walked throughout Athens trying to teach people how to think. He did this by asking questions. Each question was designed to make a person arrive

✓ Reading Check
What did *philosophia* mean to the ancient Greeks?

L3 **Writing** Have students imagine they are playwrights who have a temporary writer's block. Suggest they look through the daily newspaper for an event or story that would make a good play. If time allows, suggest they outline the major characters and plot line of their play.

💾 Use **Interactive Tutor Self-Assessment Software** to review Section 1.

✓ Reading Check Answer
To the Greeks, **philosophia** meant a love of wisdom and studying the laws of nature.

DID YOU KNOW

Socrates's wife, Zantippe, was known to be a disgruntled person who was constantly nagging her husband for not earning more money. Socrates, instead of becoming upset, merely said that living with such a person was good training for learning how to get along with other people.

💾 Use the **Vocabulary Puzzle-Maker** to create crossword and word search puzzles.

Section 1 Assessment Answers

1. oracles, those able to speak to gods (p. 179); prophecy, a statement of what might happen in the future (p. 179); pancratium, boxing and wrestling contest (p. 183); pentathlon, five-event contest (p. 183)

2. They built temples, held festivals, and tried to imitate the gods by excelling in everything they did.

3. athletes from all over Greece and from Greek colonies in Africa, Italy, and Asia Minor

4. Answers will vary but issues of financing and control could be included.

5. Sample events: chariot racing, boxing, pancratium (boxing and wrestling), pentathlon (running, jumping, discus throwing, wrestling, hurling the javelin)

Assign Chapter 11 **Section 1 Quiz** in the TCR. Testmaker available.

Reading Check Answer
The **Socratic method** encouraged people to think by asking questions in an effort to reach a conclusion or to find the truth.

Independent Practice

L3 **Critical Thinking** Have students debate this resolution: *The trial of Socrates was not justified.* Have students draw folded slips of paper on which you have written "pro" or "con." Tell students they must defend whatever side of the question they draw. Have them research the background of the trial and the arguments presented. Conduct the debate so that students with opposing arguments alternate with each other. Have the audience decide the debate's winner.

CAPTION ANSWER

They regretted executing Socrates and put up a bronze statue in his honor.

DID YOU KNOW ??

Socrates could have easily escaped death with the help of friends, but he refused. He argued that a state is doomed when individuals start flouting the laws that do not suit them.

Reading Check
How did the **Socratic method** encourage people to think?

Rules for Life
Many quotes about ethical, or morally correct, living have been attributed to Socrates. These are two of the best known:
- "The unexamined life is not worth living."
- "I am a citizen, not of Athens or Greece, but of the world."

step-by-step at a final conclusion, or truth. This form of questioning is known as the **Socratic** (sō krat′ ik) **method.**

All Athenians did not react in the same way to Socrates's teachings. Some were pleased because they learned how to examine their own beliefs and to think things out. Others saw Socrates's ideas as dangerous. They did not like self-examination, particularly when it pointed out their own mistakes. In time, they began to consider Socrates a threat to Athens. Finally, they accused him of denying the gods, corrupting the young, and trying to overthrow the government.

Socrates was tried before a jury of some 500 citizens. He defended himself by speaking about truth and goodness. He said, "Wealth does not bring goodness. But goodness brings wealth and every blessing, both to the citizen and to the polis." He also said he would not change his beliefs even to save his life.

The jury found Socrates guilty and sentenced him to death. The sentence was carried out by making Socrates drink poisonous hemlock juice. Later, the Athenians regretted having executed Socrates, so they put up a bronze statue in his honor.

DEATH OF SOCRATES   Socrates faced death with self-control and dignity. Here, in an eighteenth-century painting, he is surrounded by his sorrowing friends as he prepares to drink poisonous hemlock juice. **How did the Athenians regard Socrates after his death?**

SPOTLIGHT ON: SOCRATES

An example of the Socratic method:
Socrates: Does falsehood then exist among men?
Euthydemus: It does assuredly.
Socrates: Under which head [justice or injustice] *shall we place it?*
Euthydemus: Under injustice, certainly.
Socrates: Well then . . . if a father, when his son requires medicine, and refuses to take it, should deceive him, and give him the medicine as ordinary food, and, by adopting such deception, should restore him to health, under which head must we place such an act of deceit?
Euthydemus: We must place it under [justice].
—Xenophon, from *Memorabilia*

GREEK PHILOSOPHERS The ideas of Greek thinkers influenced the development of world civilization. Here, in a sixteenth-century European painting, Plato and Aristotle discuss the meaning of human achievement with their pupils. **What was the subject of Plato's** *The Republic?*

Plato Socrates left no writings. All that is known about him comes from one of his pupils, an Athenian aristocrat named Plato (plā' tō). Plato recorded the speeches Socrates made at his trial and just before his death.

Plato was 30 years old when Socrates died. Until then, Plato had wanted to become a politician. In 399 B.C., he changed his mind. He left Greece and traveled in Egypt and Italy for the next 12 years. When he returned, he set up a school outside Athens in the sacred grove of the hero Academus (ak uh dē' muhs). The school, where Plato hoped to train government leaders, was called the Academy. Plato taught there almost 40 years. The Academy itself lasted almost 900 years after Plato's death.

Plato's beliefs were contrary to the ideas that had made Athens great. Plato believed in order. He thought political liberty was disorder and did not approve of it. He thought only the wise and good should rule.

Plato set down his ideas about an ideal state in a book called *The Republic.* It is the first book ever written on **political science,** or the study of government. In it, Plato examined different kinds of government and explained how to avoid political errors.

Like Socrates, Plato believed in truth. He thought it could be found only after a long, hard search. In a work called *The Dialogues*

Reading Check
What is the subject of **political science?**

CHAPTER 11 CULTURAL CONTRIBUTIONS **187**

SPOTLIGHT ON: PLATO

Plato distrusted the lower classes and wanted only the best-educated citizens to participate in government. As he explained in the *Republic,*

Until philosophers are kings, or the kings and princes of the world have the spirit and *power of philosophy, and those commoner natures who pursue either to the exclusion of the other are compelled to stand aside, cities will never have rest from their evils, no, nor the human race.*

Sculpture of Aristotle

☑ **Reading Check**
What is the purpose of the **scientific method**? What is a **hypothesis**? How does a **syllogism work**?

People in History

Aristotle
384 B.C.–322 B.C.

Greek Scientist

After studying in Greece, Aristotle returned to Macedonia to teach the son of King Philip II. This boy, later known as Alexander the Great, would one day conquer many lands, including Greece. Thus, Aristotle's ideas came to influence an entire empire.

(dī' uh logs), he showed how difficult it is to discover truth. *The Dialogues* consists of a series of discussions in which different people talk about such things as truth and loyalty. Socrates is the leading speaker in many discussions. Through these discussions, Plato brings out the self-questioning that goes on within a person troubled by such issues.

Aristotle   One of Plato's brightest pupils was Aristotle (ār' uh stot l). Aristotle came to the Academy when he was 17 years old and stayed for 20 years. Before he died in 322 B.C., he founded his own school in Athens and wrote more than 200 books.

Aristotle was known as "the master of them that know." He believed in using one's senses to discover the laws that govern the physical world. He was the first to *classify,* or group together, plants and animals that resemble each other. His system, with some changes, is still used today. It has helped scientists handle a great amount of information in an orderly way.

Aristotle also added to the ideas of an earlier Greek scientist named Thales (thā' lēz) of Miletus (mi let' uhs). Thales developed the first two steps of what is known today as the **scientific method.** This is the process used by scientists to study something. First, Thales collected information. Then, based on what he observed, he formed a **hypothesis** (hī poth' uh sis), or possible explanation. Aristotle provided a third step in the scientific method when he said that a hypothesis must be tested to see if it is correct.

Another important contribution Aristotle made was in *logic* (loj' ik), or the science of reasoning. He developed the **syllogism** (sil' uh jiz uhm). This is a method of reasoning that uses three related statements. The third statement is a conclusion based on the information given in the first two. For example:

Athenians are Greeks.
Socrates is an Athenian.
Therefore, Socrates is Greek.

Discoveries and Inventions   Greek scientists were not looking for ways to make life easier or better. They were trying to add to their store of knowledge. They had none of the tools scientists have today. There were no telescopes, microscopes, or scales that weigh small amounts. Even without these, however, the Greeks made important discoveries.

Their curiosity led Greek scientists to discover that natural events are not caused by the way gods behave. They also learned that the world is governed by natural laws that people can discover and understand.

There were many Greek scientists. The first was Thales of Miletus, who came from Ionia. Thales not only developed the first two steps of the scientific method, but he also correctly predicted

GREEK SCIENTISTS

Name	Field	Accomplishments
Archimedes	*Mathematics*	explained principle of lever
Aristarchus	*Astronomy*	concluded that Earth revolves around the sun
Anaximander	*Astronomy*	pioneered concept of Earth as a body suspended in space
Eratosthenes	*Geography*	figured Earth's circumference within 200 miles, or 320 kilometers; made map complete with longitude and latitude of Asia, Africa, and Europe that accurately showed the three continents forming single landmass
Euclid	*Mathematics*	collected and organized all existing knowledge about geometry; developed axioms, or fundamental rules, used in modern geometry
Hipparchus	*Astronomy*	created system of celestial mechanics to explain how heavenly bodies move
Hippocrates	*Medicine*	founder of scientific medicine
Ptolemy	*Astronomy*	developed mathematical model of Hipparchus' system of celestial mechanics
Pythagoras	*Mathematics*	sought to explain the nature of all things in mathematical terms
Thales of Miletus	*Science*	first known Greek scientist; using Chaldean observations of stars, planets, and moon, predicted solar eclipse of 585 B.C.; developed theory about basic substance common to matter; developed first two steps of scientific method

L2 **Science** Have students research the accomplishments of a Greek scientist listed in the chart. Then hold a science fair and have students role-play their chosen scientist and explain accomplishments or discoveries using visuals or other means.

DID YOU KNOW

Being a doctor in Greece was often an occupation that was passed from father to son. Many doctors ran clinics near the marketplace where they bandaged wounds or bled patients to draw out diseases.

ASSESS

Check for Understanding

Ask students to summarize orally or in writing the main points of the chapter. Discuss the answers to the Section and Chapter Assessment questions.

Evaluate

Assign Chapter 11 **Performance Assessment Activity** in the TCR.

Administer **Chapter 11 Test** in the TCR. Testmaker available.

EXTENDING THE CONTENT

The ancient Greeks were heir to all the mathematical knowledge of the Mesopotamian and Egyptian civilizations. They built upon that inheritance by using their sense of reason to pursue the "Why?" and "What does it mean?" questions of mathematics. Thales of Miletus began the mathematical revolution. He laid the foundation that is still part of introductory courses in geometry. The followers of Pythagoras advanced mathematics into a quasi-religion. Euclid simplified and organized the new knowledge. Apollonius explored the aspects of conic sections. Archimedes is the father of scientific notation.

Reteach

Divide the class into teams to try and guess a term defined in the chapter or the name of a person described in the chapter from clues given by other team members.

Assign Chapter 11 **Reteaching Activity** in the TCR.

Enrich

Have students write syllogisms and share them with one another.

Assign Chapter 11 **Enrichment Activity** in the TCR.

CLOSE

Ask students to compare the role religion played in the lives of ancient Greeks to the role it plays in modern American society. Encourage them to note both similarities and differences.

💾 Use **Interactive Tutor Self-Assessment Software** to review Section 2.

Self-Check Quiz gives students an interactive chapter tutorial. Have them access ***Chapter 11 Quiz*** at **humanheritage.glencoe.com**

---

an eclipse of the sun in 585 B.C. The contributions made by Thales and other Greek scientists were important to the growth of scientific thought.

Greek scientists also contributed to the field of medicine. The "Father of Scientific Medicine" was Hippocrates (hi pok' ruh tēz). Hippocrates was considered the perfect physician. He traveled throughout Greece diagnosing illnesses and curing sick people. He believed diseases came from natural causes. At the time, most other doctors thought diseases were caused by evil spirits entering the body.

Hippocrates drew up a list of rules about how doctors should use their skills to help their patients. His rules are known as the Hippocratic (hip uh krat' ik) Oath. The oath says that doctors should honor their teachers, do their best for the sick, never give poisons, and keep the secrets of their patients. Doctors all over the world still promise to honor the Hippocratic Oath.

Section 2 Assessment

1. **Define:** *philosophia*, Socratic method, political science, scientific method, hypothesis, syllogism.
2. What were Plato's beliefs about government?

Critical Thinking

3. **Drawing Conclusions**   Review the syllogism on page 188. Then write a syllogism to help you draw a conclusion about one of the Greek thinkers in this chapter.

Graphic Organizer Activity

4. Draw a diagram like this one, and use it to show the steps in the scientific method.

```
                              Step 3
                    Step 2 ┌────────
          Step 1 ┌────────┘
        ┌────────┘
```

Chapter Summary & Study Guide

1. During the "Golden Age," the Greeks made many contributions in thinking, athletics, and the arts.
2. The Olympic Games, held every four years in honor of the Greek god Zeus, was the most important sporting event in Greece.
3. The theater, and eventually the play, developed out of a festival given in honor of the Greek god Dionysus.
4. Socrates, in his search for truth, developed a form of questioning known as the Socratic method.
5. Plato, who was one of Socrates's pupils, founded a school and wrote the first book on political science.
6. Aristotle developed a system of classification and provided a third step in the scientific method.

Self-Check Quiz

Visit the *Human Heritage* Web site at **humanheritage.glencoe.com** and click on ***Chapter 11—Self-Check Quiz*** to assess your understanding of this chapter.

Section 2 Assessment Answers

1. *philosophia*, studying nature and loving wisdom (p. 185); Socratic method, way of questioning (p. 186); political science, study of government (p. 187); scientific method, studying science (p. 188); hypothesis, possible explanation (p. 188); syllogism, three-statement reasoning (p. 188)

2. order, no political liberty, and wise and good rulers

3. Syllogisms will vary but should show an understanding of the way in which a syllogism works. The conclusion reached in each syllogism should accurately reflect the thinking of the philosophers chosen.

4. Step 1: collect information; Step 2: form a hypothesis; Step 3: test the hypothesis

Assign Chapter 11 **Section 2 Quiz** in the TCR. Testmaker available.

Using Key Terms

Use the following words to make a chart that explains the ideas and contributions of the Greeks.

oracles
pancratium
philosophia
political science
hypothesis

prophecy
pentathlon
Socratic method
scientific method
syllogism

Understanding Main Ideas

1. What was the role of oracles in Greek religion?
2. What role did women play in the Olympic Games?
3. What was the relationship between Greek historians and the Olympic Games?
4. How did tragedies differ from comedies?
5. How did Athenians react to the teachings of Socrates?
6. Why did Plato set up the Academy?
7. How does the scientific method work?
8. In what subjects were Greek scientists most interested?
9. What was Euclid's most famous achievement?

Critical Thinking

1. What would you have done if it had been your decision whether or not to put Socrates on trial?
2. Why is the scientific method important to modern science?
3. How important was religion in ancient Greek civilization? Explain your answer.
4. Would you like being taught through the Socratic method? Why or why not?

Graphic Organizer Activity

History Draw a chart like this one, and use it to list four Greek ideas or inventions and to explain the effect each has had on your life.

Idea/Invention	Effect on My Life
1.	
2.	
3.	
4.	

Geography in History

Movement The Olympic Games drew contestants from all the areas under Greek control. What different methods of travel would athletes have used to reach Olympia where the games were held? Create a poster advertising transportation to the games.

Using Your Journal

Review any details you may have noted about the ideas developed by the Greeks. Imagine that you have a chance to interview an important Greek thinker. Write a list of questions you might like to ask this person.

Bonus Test Question

For Chapter 11 Test
The Greek oracles often spoke in riddles. Solve the following riddle: Your mother has received some sad news. Your mother's father's daughter has called to say your brother's grandfather's son's wife's son has died. Who called? (*your aunt*) Who died? (*your cousin*)

Using Your Journal

Questions will vary but should include major points significant to the person's achievement. You could have students role-play the interview, one assuming the part of the Greek historical figure.

Geography in History

Answers may vary but should include major forms of transportation such as by foot, cart, and horse, and the proximity of the sea.

Using Key Terms

Charts will vary but should explain the contributions made by ancient Greeks.

Understanding Main Ideas

1. They spoke to the gods and gave advice and prophecies to the Greek people.
2. They were not allowed to take part in or watch the games.
3. Historians read their works aloud at the games and dated historical events by the Olympiads.
4. Tragedies told about suffering and relationships between people and the gods. Comedies were humorous and poked fun at people.
5. Some were pleased but others saw Socrates' ideas as very dangerous.
6. because he hoped to train government leaders
7. collecting information and forming and testing a hypothesis
8. adding to their knowledge
9. advances in mathematics

Critical Thinking

1. Answers will vary but could include the reasons for and against this decision.
2. Answers will vary but include that it provides a consistent way for scientists to do research.
3. Answers will vary but should include that religion and the gods were very important.
4. Answers will vary.

Graphic Organizer Activity

Ideas or inventions will vary, but students should provide realistic examples of how each item chosen can be linked to their lives today. (As an extension, you might have students illustrate some of these connections in Linking Across Time features such as the one on page 184.)

Chapter 12 Planning Guide

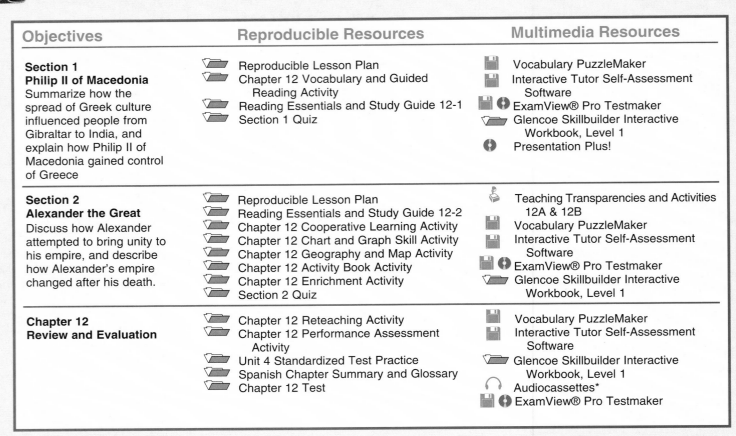

Objectives	Reproducible Resources	Multimedia Resources
Section 1 **Philip II of Macedonia** Summarize how the spread of Greek culture influenced people from Gibraltar to India, and explain how Philip II of Macedonia gained control of Greece	Reproducible Lesson Plan Chapter 12 Vocabulary and Guided Reading Activity Reading Essentials and Study Guide 12-1 Section 1 Quiz	Vocabulary PuzzleMaker Interactive Tutor Self-Assessment Software ExamView® Pro Testmaker Glencoe Skillbuilder Interactive Workbook, Level 1 Presentation Plus!
Section 2 **Alexander the Great** Discuss how Alexander attempted to bring unity to his empire, and describe how Alexander's empire changed after his death.	Reproducible Lesson Plan Reading Essentials and Study Guide 12-2 Chapter 12 Cooperative Learning Activity Chapter 12 Chart and Graph Skill Activity Chapter 12 Geography and Map Activity Chapter 12 Activity Book Activity Chapter 12 Enrichment Activity Section 2 Quiz	Teaching Transparencies and Activities 12A & 12B Vocabulary PuzzleMaker Interactive Tutor Self-Assessment Software ExamView® Pro Testmaker Glencoe Skillbuilder Interactive Workbook, Level 1
Chapter 12 **Review and Evaluation**	Chapter 12 Reteaching Activity Chapter 12 Performance Assessment Activity Unit 4 Standardized Test Practice Spanish Chapter Summary and Glossary Chapter 12 Test	Vocabulary PuzzleMaker Interactive Tutor Self-Assessment Software Glencoe Skillbuilder Interactive Workbook, Level 1 Audiocassettes* ExamView® Pro Testmaker

*Also available in Spanish.

Presentation Plus!

Use Glencoe's **Presentation Plus!** multimedia teacher tool to easily present dynamic lessons that visually excite your students. Using Microsoft® PowerPoint, you can customize the presentations to create your own personalized lessons.

Interactive Lesson Planner

Planning has never been easier! Using this CD-ROM, organize your week, month, semester, or year with all the help you need. The **Interactive Lesson Planner** gives you access to all of the blackline masters which accompany *Human Heritage*.

✔ PERFORMANCE ASSESSMENT ACTIVITIES

Geography Have students draw a base map showing the empire of Alexander the Great and the growth of the Greek influence. (See the map on page 196.) Then have students research to find the route of Alexander's conquest and add the route to the base map of the empire.

CHAPTER RESOURCES

LITERATURE ABOUT THE PERIOD

Easterling, P.E. and B. M. W. Knox, eds. *The Cambridge History of Classical Literature, Vol. 1, Greek Literature.* Cambridge, 1985. Collection of ancient Greek literature.

READINGS FOR THE STUDENT

Harris, Nathaniel. *Alexander the Great and the Greeks.* Bookwright Press, 1986. Details about the contributions Alexander made to the Greeks.

Renault, Mary. *The Persian Boy.* Bantam, 1988. The second of three novels about Alexander the Great.

READINGS FOR THE TEACHER

Editors of Time-Life Books. *Empires Ascendent.* Time-Life Books, 1987. Includes a chapter tracing Alexander's triumphant military campaign.

Nichols, Roger and Kenneth McLeish. *Through Greek Eyes.* Cambridge University Press, 1991. Integrates excerpts from primary sources in discussions of ancient Greek history.

KEY TO ABILITY LEVELS

Teaching strategies have been coded for varying learning styles and abilities.

L1 Level 1 activities are **basic** activities and should be within the ability range of all students.

L2 Level 2 activities are **average** activities and should be within the ability range of the average to above-average student.

L3 Level 3 activities are **challenging** activities designed for the ability range of above-average students.

ELL ELL activities should be within the ability range of English Language Learning students.

NATIONAL GEOGRAPHIC SOCIETY

Teacher's Corner

INDEX TO NATIONAL GEOGRAPHIC MAGAZINE

The following articles relate to this chapter:

- "Tale of Three Cities," by Joel L. Swerdlow, August 1999.
- "Yugoslavia: A House Much Divided," by Kenneth C. Danforth, August 1990.

NATIONAL GEOGRAPHIC SOCIETY PRODUCTS AVAILABLE FROM GLENCOE

To order the following products, call Glencoe at 1-800-334-7344:

- *PicturePack: Physical Geography of the World (Transparencies)*
- *Picture Atlas of the World (CD-ROM)*

ADDITIONAL NATIONAL GEOGRAPHIC SOCIETY PRODUCTS

To order the following, call National Geographic at 1-800-368-2728:

- *National Geographic Atlas of World History (Book)*
- *Wonders of the Ancient World: National Geographic Atlas of Archaeology (Book)*

Access *National Geographic*'s new dynamic MapMachine Web site and other geography resources at:
http://www.nationalgeographic.com/
http://www.nationalgeographic.com/maps/

  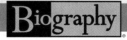

THE HISTORY CHANNEL. | **A&E HOME VIDEO.** | **Biography**

The following videotape program is available from Glencoe:

- **Mystical Monuments of Ancient Greece**
  0-7670-0012-9

To order, call Glencoe at 1-800-334-7344. To find classroom resources to accompany many of these, check:

A&E Television: http://www.aetv.com
The History Channel:
http://www.historychannel.com

OVERVIEW

Chapter 12 describes the accomplishments of Philip of Macedonia and Alexander the Great in spreading Greek civilization.

➤ **Section 1** analyzes the political and military strategies that enabled Philip to conquer the Greek city-states.

➤ **Section 2** describes the personality, military conquests, and political objectives of Alexander the Great.

CHAPTER OBJECTIVES

After reading Chapter 12, students will be able to:

1. summarize how the spread of Greek culture influenced people from Gibraltar to India.

2. explain how Philip II of Macedonia gained control of Greece.

3. discuss how Alexander tried to unify his empire.

4. describe how Alexander's empire changed after his death.

EXAMINING ARTIFACTS

Point out the relationship between the two figures in the artifacts—i.e., father and son. Ask students what they can infer from the fact that Alexander is known as Alexander the Great rather than his real name, which was Alexander III. Tell students that they will learn how Alexander greatly extended his father's empire.

PERFORMANCE ASSESSMENT ✓

Use the Performance Assessment Activities on page 192B to help you evaluate students as they complete the chapter.

The Hellenistic Period
335 B.C.–145 B.C.

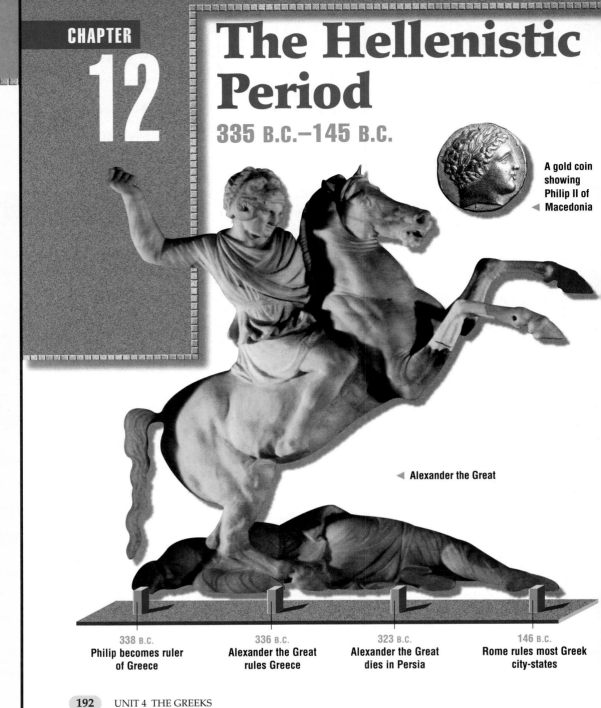

▲ A gold coin showing Philip II of Macedonia

◄ Alexander the Great

338 B.C.	336 B.C.	323 B.C.	146 B.C.
Philip becomes ruler of Greece	Alexander the Great rules Greece	Alexander the Great dies in Persia	Rome rules most Greek city-states

192   UNIT 4 THE GREEKS

TEACHING RESOURCES

TEACHER PLANNING AND SUPPORT
- Reproducible Lesson Plan
- Block Scheduling Implementation Guide
- Videodisc Bar Code Correlation
- Presentation Plus!

REVIEW AND REINFORCEMENT
- Reading Essentials and Study Guide 12-1, 12-2
- Chapter 12 Vocabulary and Guided Reading Activity
- Vocabulary PuzzleMaker Software
- Teaching Transparencies 12A & 12B

- Chapter 12 Reteaching Activity
- Chapter 12 Cooperative Learning Activity
- Chapter 12 Activity Book Activity
- Chapter 12 Chart and Graph Skill Activity
- Interactive Tutor Self-Assessment Software
- Unit 4 MindJogger VideoQuiz

APPLICATION AND HANDS-ON ACTIVITIES
- Daily World History, Geography, and Culture Question

Chapter Focus

Read to Discover

- How the spread of Greek culture influenced people from Gibraltar to India.
- How Philip II of Macedonia gained control of Greece.
- How Alexander attempted to bring unity to his empire.
- How Alexander's empire changed after his death.

 Terms to Learn
hostage
phalanx
alliances
orator
barbaroi
factories
emigrated

 People to Know
Philip of
   Macedonia
Demosthenes
Alexander the
   Great

 Places to Locate
Macedonia
Persia
Alexandria

Why It's Important   After the Greek city-states lost their independence, many changes took place. The new rulers of Greece built empires and increased trade. At the same time, they spread Greek culture and customs. Before long, Greek ideas were influencing people from Gibraltar (juh brol' tuhr) to India.

The Greek language came to be spoken by many people. Greek architecture was copied for new buildings. Students studied Greek literature in school. People used Greek furniture in their homes. Greek plays became a popular form of entertainment. Business people took up Greek ways of banking.

The period in which all this took place has come to be called the Hellenistic (hel uh nis' tik) Age. The term "Hellenistic" means "like the Hellenes, or the Greeks."

HISTORY Online

Chapter Overview

Visit the *Human Heritage* Web site at **humanheritage.glencoe.com** and click on *Chapter 12—Chapter Overviews* to preview this chapter.

SECTION 1 Phillip II of Macedonia

By 338 B.C., Greece had a new ruler, Philip II of Macedonia. Macedonia was a small, mountainous country north of Greece. Most Macedonians were farmers. They cared little for the Greeks and had fought them in the Persian Wars. Macedonian kings, however, were of Greek descent and admired Greek culture.

Philip became ruler of Macedonia in 359 B.C. During his youth, he was a **hostage** (hos' tij), or a person held by an enemy until certain promises are carried out, for three years in Thebes. In those

Reading Check
What is a **hostage**?

FOCUS

 Bellringer

Have each student list three accomplishments of the ancient Greeks they have studied so far.

Motivational Activity

Discuss students' lists and write accomplishments on the board. Have students copy the list and then survey the chapter to add Hellenistic accomplishments.

GUIDE TO READING

Reading Strategy

Ask students to read "Why It's Important" and summarize the chapter's main theme. (*The new Greek rulers built empires, increased trade, and spread Greek culture.*)

Vocabulary Precheck

Ask students to define each of the "Terms to Learn." Have a volunteer consult the dictionary for any unfamiliar words. **L1** **ELL**

Use the Vocabulary PuzzleMaker for Chapter 12 to create a crossword puzzle. **L1**

Assign Chapter 12 Vocabulary and Guided Reading Activity.

Assign Reading Essentials and Study Guide 12-1.

Reading Check Answer

A **hostage** is a person held by an enemy until certain promises are carried out.

Guided Practice

L2 **History** Have students work in pairs to create a dialogue for an interview between Philip of Macedonia and a newspaper reporter from the *Macedonian Times*. Tell students to focus the dialogue on Philip's campaign to unify the Greek city-states and spread the Greek culture. Have pairs read the dialogue to the class, with one student playing the role of the reporter and the other, the role of Philip.

✓ **Reading Check Answer**
A **phalanx** was powerful because soldiers charged as a group.

CAPTION ANSWER

He tried to warn them that Philip was dangerous.

---

years, he learned to love Greek culture. However, he learned to dislike the weaknesses of the Greek form of government.

Philip believed it was his destiny to unify the Greek city-states and spread Greek culture. As soon as he became ruler of Macedonia, he set out to fulfill that destiny. It took him a little over 20 years.

Philip went about reaching his goal in many ways. For example, until his time, the Macedonian army was made up of volunteers, who fought only in summer. Philip turned this part-time volunteer army into a year-round, well-organized, professional one.

Philip developed an infantry formation called a **phalanx** (fā' langks). Foot soldiers formed a solid body some 16 rows deep. Those in each line stayed so close together that their shields overlapped. This gave them added protection. The phalanx charged as a group, which gave it more striking power.

Philip also armed his soldiers with spears that were 14 feet, or over 4 meters, long. This was twice as long as ordinary spears. He

✓ **Reading Check**
Why was a **phalanx** powerful?

People in History

Demosthenes
383 B.C.–322 B.C.

Greek Orator

Demosthenes, born into a wealthy Athenian family, was a great speaker and politician. He is most famous for a series of speeches called "Philippics," in which he warned the Greek people about King Philip of Macedonia. By 338 B.C., however, Philip had conquered Greece, and the city-states had lost their independence.

DEMOSTHENES Demosthenes worked to preserve the freedom of the Greek city-states. He was known for his ability as a public speaker. It is said he trained himself by shouting above the roar of the ocean waves with his mouth full of pebbles. **What did Demosthenes try to tell the Greeks about Philip of Macedonia?**

SPOTLIGHT ON: DEMOSTHENES

To extend People in History, provide these additional details on Demosthenes.

Demosthenes, born in 384 B.C., was the son of the owner of a sword-making factory. He was orphaned at age 7, and his guardians squandered his inheritance so that he did not have a good education. At 22, he sued them and won, which encouraged his driving ambition to be a great orator. According to Plutarch, a first-century Greek biographer and essayist, Demosthenes studied with a well-known actor for help with gestures and expression. He practiced his gestures in front of a large mirror. Demosthenes' fervor and skill won admiration from Philip, even though Demosthenes angrily spoke against Philip.

added soldiers trained in the use of slingshots and bows and arrows. These soldiers could fight in hilly areas where the phalanx was not able to go.

Philip flattered local Greek officials and gave them gold. He found ways to cause disagreements among Greek city-states. Then, when city-states were weak from fighting each other, his army moved in and conquered them.

Philip made treaties with Greek leaders only to break them when the Greeks let down their guard. He saw marriage as a way of forming political **alliances** (uh lī' uhn siz), or partnerships. He married six or seven times for this reason.

Demosthenes (di mahs' thuh nēz), an Athenian **orator** (ōr' uh ter), or public speaker, tried to warn the Greeks that Philip was dangerous, but most would not listen. They were unhappy with their local governments and thought Philip would improve things.

When Philip led his soldiers into central Greece in 338 B.C., Thebes and Athens raised a small army to stop the invasion. The Greek army, however, was not strong enough and was defeated at the Battle of Chaeronea (ker uh nē' uh). Having gained control of Greece, Philip began preparing for a campaign against Persia. However, in 336 B.C., in the middle of his preparations, he was killed, and his son Alexander took over the throne.

 Reading Check
How did Philip II use **alliances?** What is an **orator?**

 Reading Check Answer
Philip used **alliances** to form political partnerships. An **orator** is a public speaker.

Section 1 Assessment

1. **Define:** hostage, phalanx, alliances, orator.
2. Why was Philip able to defeat the Greek city-states?
3. Who was Demosthenes?

Critical Thinking

4. **Making Inferences** How do you think a Greek citizen living under the rule of Philip II would describe him as a ruler?

Graphic Organizer Activity

5. Use a web like the one shown to list the achievements of Philip II.

Philip II

SECTION 2 Alexander the Great

Painting of Soldier

Alexander took over Philip's throne at the age of 20. He had been a commander in the army since he was 16. Upon becoming a commander he cut his shoulder-length hair and ordered his soldiers to shave their beards. This, he said, would keep enemy soldiers from grabbing them in close combat.

Alexander was physically strong and good-looking. He also had developed his mind. For three years, Aristotle had taught him literature, political science, geography, and biology. Because of this, Alexander included philosophers and scientists in his army.

Section 1 Assessment Answers

1. hostage, a person held by an enemy until promises are carried out (p. 193); phalanx, infantry formation of foot soldiers (p. 194); alliances, political partnerships (p. 195); orator, public speaker (p. 195)

2. because he encouraged them to fight each other until they became weak and disunited, and because the Greek army was small

3. an Athenian statesman and orator who warned the Greeks about Philip II

4. Answers will vary but could include a list of Philip's good and bad points as they related to the people.

5. Sample answers: turned part-time army into professional army, developed phalanx, armed soldiers with spears 14 feet (4 meters) long, trained soldiers with slingshots and bows and arrows, conquered Greek city-states, unified Greece

Assign Chapter 12 **Section 1 Quiz** in the TCR. Testmaker available.

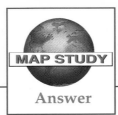

Alexander had his first major encounter with the Persians at the Granicus River in western Asia Minor. After his victory there, he sent 300 coats of Persian armor to Athens as a thanksgiving offering to the goddess Athena. Other conquests include the Battle of Issus, the seaports of Phoenicia, the port city of Tyre, Egypt, Babylon, and Persepolis.

MAP STUDY

Answer

because it was located in a rich area, on a river where trade was an important way of blending the cultures of Greece and Asia [trade routes were most likely established throughout the empire]

DID YOU KNOW ??

The Greeks thought the Macedonians were barbarians because they had produced no famous writers, philosophers, or artists.

The scientists collected plant and animal samples from newly conquered lands and sent them to Aristotle for examination.

Alexander was a great general who feared nothing. He crushed the Persian Empire and then marched as far east as northern India. He would have gone farther, but his troops refused. In the course of his conquests, Alexander covered more than 22,000 miles, or over 35,200 kilometers, from the Nile to the Indus rivers. Through all that territory, he never lost a battle.

Alexander's Empire   Alexander had a dream of a world-wide state in which all people would live together in peace. He wanted to bring unity and justice to his empire.

Alexander believed the only way to achieve his goal was to unite the Macedonians, the Greeks, and the Persians. He began by taking Persian soldiers into his army. Next, he married a Persian woman and had 80 of his leading army officers marry Persian women, too. Then, he began to dress in Persian fashion and to follow some Persian customs.

One custom was for rulers to claim they were gods. So, Alexander claimed he was a god and insisted that people treat him that way. The Macedonians and Greeks, however, refused to do so. The Greeks also objected to equal treatment for the Persians. They looked down on all people who did not speak Greek or

MAP STUDY

LOCATION At the time of his death, Alexander the Great ruled over much of the classical world. **Why do you think Alexander founded his capital where he did?**

The Empire of Alexander the Great

MULTICULTURAL PERSPECTIVES

Alexander the Great, like many ancient Greeks, spent much of his time reading books. According to Plutarch, a first-century Greek biographer, Alexander's favorite books were Homer's *Iliad* and *Anabasis* by Xenophon. Alexander had a copy of the *Iliad* that Aristotle had edited. It was one of the books that he took everywhere, keeping it with his dagger and pillow at night. According to Plutarch, as Alexander set off to lead his troops into Asia, he first went straight to the ruins of Troy as a kind of pilgrimage. He made a sacrifice to the goddess Athena and honored the grave of the hero Achilles.

LIGHTHOUSE OF ALEXANDRIA   The lighthouse of Alexandria was one of the Seven Wonders of the Ancient World. It towered over Alexandria's two excellent harbors. A fire on top provided light to guide ships into port. **Why was Alexandria also considered a center for learning?**

follow Greek customs. They called such people *barbaroi,* (bar' buh roi) from which the word "barbarians" comes. Because of such feelings, Alexander's attempt to achieve unity among the people in his empire was not successful.

Alexandria   During his rule, Alexander founded about 70 cities, 16 of which were named Alexandria (al ig zan' drē uh) after himself. He encouraged Greeks and Macedonians to settle in the new cities, which were scattered throughout the empire.

The most noted Alexandria was in Egypt. Within 70 years after its founding, it had become a center of trade and learning. Greeks from throughout the eastern Mediterranean came there. They wanted to make the most of its economic opportunities and to be a part of its intellectual and social life.

Alexandria had two great harbors. They were protected by *breakwaters,* or barriers that break the force of waves. A lighthouse 400 feet, or about 122 meters, tall dominated the harbors. It is considered one of the Seven Wonders of the Ancient World.

Looking out over the chief harbor was a palace and a school with a library. The school was known as the Museum. It became a center for poets, writers, philosophers, and scientists. The library had the largest collection of books in ancient times. There, Euclid (ū' kluhd) wrote his geometry book. There, Eratosthenes (er uh

 Reading Check What English word is derived from *barbaroi?*

HISTORY Online

Student Web Activity
Visit the *Human Heritage* Web site at **humanheritage.glencoe.com** and click on **Chapter 12— Student Web Activities** to find out more about Alexandria.

L1   **The Arts** Prepare the class to view the film *Alexander the Great & the Greeks.* (See Chapter Resources in the Chapter 12 Planning Guide.) After viewing the film ask: *What are some examples of how Alexander tried to bring unity to his empire? Was Alexander successful in achieving this goal? Was his goal realistic? Why or why not? Could such a goal be realized today? Is such a goal desirable?*

Reading Check Answer "Barbarians" comes from *barbaroi.*

 HISTORY Online
Student Web Activity objectives, goals, and answers can be found at the ***Chapter 12 Web Activity Lesson Plan*** at **humanheritage.glencoe.com**

L2   **Geography: Location** Have students research the other 15 cities named after Alexander the Great and locate them on a map. **ELL**

 DID YOU KNOW
Alexander probably built the world's first zoo. It featured lions, leopards, bears, and most of the other major species known to the world at the time.

COOPERATIVE LEARNING

Divide the class into groups to prepare a class book that illustrates the exploits of Alexander. Assign each group an area of conquest to work on including Thebes, Granicus River, Issus, Egypt, Guagamela, and Indus River valley. Each group's contribution should include a description of the geographic area, what happened there and when, and a map of the region. Groups could include drawings such as costumes, weapons, and buildings. Have members agree upon individual tasks and manner of presentation.

Assign Chapter 12 *Cooperative Learning Activity* in the TCR.

Independent Practice

L1 **Daily Life** Show students examples of advertisements for cities or regions from business or travel magazines. Have them write advertisement copy for a magazine to be distributed throughout the Hellenistic world that extols the virtues of living in Alexandria, Egypt.

L1 **History** Have students use the map on page 196 to identify and locate the three divisions of Alexander's empire following his death. **ELL**

CAPTION ANSWER

because his troops refused to go any farther

MAKING CONNECTIONS

➤➤ **The Arts** Arrian, a Roman general, used the eyewitness accounts of Alexander's generals to write a thorough, unbiased biography of Alexander the Great. In describing the retreat from India, Arrian told the story of Alexander that reveals his leadership qualities. Marching through the hot sands toward water, Alexander led his men on foot. A party he had sent ahead to search for water returned with a helmut full. Although thirsty, Alexander took the water and poured it on the ground. This action, and that of walking when he could ride, showed the soldiers that he did not expect them to endure hardships that he wasn't willing to endure himself.

Alexander's Hero
The mother of Alexander the Great told her son that Achilles, a hero of the Trojan War, was his ancestor. He learned Homer's *Iliad*—which tells Achilles' story—by heart and always carried a copy of it with him.

ALEXANDER THE GREAT   Alexander conquered tremendous amounts of territory. His empire stretched from Greece to northern India. This painting of Alexander shows him leading his army ashore in Asia Minor and claiming all lands to the east as his own. **Why was Alexander unable to continue his conquests beyond India?**

Greek Translation In about 250 B.C., Jewish scholars in Alexandria translated the Hebrew Bible into Greek, a version known as the Septuagint. The Eastern Orthodox Church still uses the Septuagint version of the Old Testament.

tahs' thuh nēz) reasoned that a ship could reach India by sailing west from Spain. There, Archimedes (ar kuh mēd' ēz) and Hero (hē' rō) invented several machines.

End of the Empire   In 323 B.C., when Alexander was in Babylon, he became ill and died. He was 33 years old and had ruled for 13 years. His body was wrapped in gold and placed in a glass coffin in the Royal Tombs of Alexandria, Egypt. After his death, Alexander became a romantic legend. More than 80 versions of his life have been written in more than 20 languages.

After Alexander's death, fights broke out over who was to rule the empire. The areas Alexander had conquered in India returned to their original rulers. Three of Alexander's generals divided the rest of the empire among themselves. Antigonus (an tig' uh nuhs) became king of Macedonia. Ptolemy (tahl' uh mē) established the dynasty of the Ptolemies in Egypt. Seleucus (suh lū' kuhs) formed the Seleucid Empire in Persia. Athens and

198   UNIT 4 THE GREEKS

EXTENDING THE CONTENT

People in the Hellenistic world admired the Hellenic style of art and architecture and enthusiastically imitated it in temples and other public buildings that adorned their thriving cities. Greek style inspired architects and sculptors in Roman times, and later, during the Renaissance, European humanists revived the Classical style of art and architecture. The Greek Revival, or neoclassical, style of architecture arose in the late 1700s and lasted into the early 1800s. Buildings in the Greek style are still being built.

198

Sparta again became independent city-states. Most other Greek city-states banded together into one of two leagues, but neither league had much power or importance.

Greek cultural influence, however, became stronger than ever after Alexander's death. The rulers who took Alexander's place adopted Greek as their language and used Alexander's titles. They even used his portrait on their coins.

Trade grew. From Africa and Asia came spices, ivory, incense, pearls, and rare woods. From Syria and Egypt came glass, metals, and linen. From Greece came olive oil, wine, and pottery. From Sicily and Egypt came wheat.

The cities that had been part of Alexander's empire now existed chiefly for trade and grew along with it. City officials made their law, language, calendar, and coins Greek. Teachers brought Greek customs and ideas into schools. Merchants and bankers used Greek methods to run their businesses.

Fun Facts....

Greek Discoveries
Greek scientists at Alexandria made several key discoveries. Eratosthenes calculated the earth's circumference to within 1 percent of its actual size. Archimedes invented a watering tool that Egyptian farmers used for nearly 2,000 years.

Linking Across Time

Hellenistic Influence   The columns of an ancient Greek temple (below) influenced the style of this United States government building (right). **Why do you think the Hellenistic style of art and architecture is often used on present-day government buildings?**

CHAPTER 12 THE HELLENISTIC PERIOD   **199**

Reading Check Answer
Factories are places
where goods are made.
Population fell when many
young Greeks **emigrated.**

Reteach

Have volunteers tell the main
ideas under each chapter heading.
Assign Chapter 12 **Reteaching Activity** in the TCR.

Enrich

Assign Chapter 12 **Enrichment Activity** in the TCR.

CLOSE

Ask students to discuss
whether they agree or disagree
with the following statement:
Might makes right.

Use **Interactive Tutor Self-
Assessment Software** to review
Section 2.

HISTORY Online

Self-Check Quiz gives students an
interactive chapter tutorial. Have
them access **Chapter 12 Quiz** at
humanheritage.glencoe.com

✓ **Reading Check**
What are
factories?
What happened to
city-states when
many young Greeks
emigrated?

The Greek city-states, however, were never the same again.
Although they kept their political independence, they could not
gain back the power of the past. In time, economic conditions
grew worse. Great **factories,** or places where goods are made, had
been built in the new Hellenistic cities. Greek manufacturers now
found they could not compete with these factories. Because of
this, more and more young Greeks **emigrated** (em' uh grāt ed), or
left one place to settle in another. Population in the Greek
city-states fell. There were not enough people to work the land,
and many farms once again became wilderness. By 146 B.C., most
of the Greek city-states were under Roman control.

Section 2 Assessment

1. **Define:** *barbaroi*, factories, emigrated.
2. Who was Alexander the Great?
3. What conquests did Alexander make?
4. How did Greek influence continue to
   grow and spread after Alexander's
   death?

Critical Thinking

5. **Forming Conclusions**   How successful would Alexander's dream of uniting the world in peace be today?
   Explain.

Graphic Organizer Activity

6. Draw a time line like this one, and use
   it to show the major events in the life
   of Alexander the Great.

   ☐——☐——☐——☐

Chapter Summary & Study Guide

1. Philip II believed it was his destiny to
   unify the Greek city-states and spread
   Greek culture.
2. Philip II was able to conquer Greece
   in 338 B.C.
3. When Philip II died in 336 B.C., his son
   Alexander took over power.
4. Alexander was a great general whose
   conquests stretched from the Nile to
   the Indus
5. Alexander tried without success to
   unite the Macedonians, the Greeks,
   and the Persians.
6. The most famous city founded by
   Alexander was Alexandria, Egypt.
7. After Alexander died in 323 B.C., his
   empire was divided among three of
   his generals.
8. Despite Alexander's death, Greek cultural influence became stronger.
9. Although the Greek city-states again
   became independent following
   Alexander's death, economic conditions in Greece grew worse.
10. Most Greek city-states were under
    Roman control by 146 B.C.

HISTORY Online

Self-Check Quiz

Visit the *Human Heritage* Web site at **humanheritage.
glencoe.com** and click on **Chapter 12—Self-Check Quiz**
to assess your understanding of this chapter.

Section 2 Assessment Answers

1. *barbaroi*, non-Greeks (p. 197); factories,
places where goods were made (p. 200);
emigrated, left one place to settle in another
(p. 200)
2. emperor who spread Greek culture
3. a union among the Macedonians, the
Greeks, and the Persians
4. later rulers adopted Greek language,
titles, law, language, calendar, and coins;
teachers used Greek ideas in schools; and
merchants used Greek methods.

5. Answers will vary but could include the
difficulty of ending world conflicts and
efforts by the United Nations.
6. Sample events: studies with Aristotle,
comes to throne at age 20, builds empire,
builds 70 cities, dies at age 33.

Assign Chapter 12 **Section 2 Quiz** in the
TCR. Testmaker available.

Using Key Terms

Use the following words to write a short paragraph about how Philip II gained control of Greece. Then write a paragraph about what helped cause the end of the city-states.

hostage	phalanx	alliances
orator	*barbaroi*	factories
emigrated		

Understanding Main Ideas

1. What changes did Philip II make in his army?
2. How did Philip II view marriage?
3. Why did the Greeks refuse to listen to Demosthenes' warnings?
4. What did Aristotle teach Alexander?
5. Why was Alexander unable to achieve unity among the people of his empire?
6. Why did many Greeks go to Alexandria, Egypt?
7. How did the physical features of Alexandria, Egypt, help trade?
8. What happened to the Greek city-states by 146 B.C.?

Critical Thinking

1. Why do you think many people did not listen to Demosthenes' warnings? Explain your answer.
2. What other names might historians have given Alexander besides "the Great"?
3. What do you think Alexander could have done differently to achieve unity among the people in his empire? Explain.
4. In what ways can customs be spread without conquest?

Graphic Organizer Activity

Economics Create a cause-and-effect chart like this one, and use it to show reasons the Greek city-states declined and the effects of their decline.

```
Causes
  ↓
Decline of the City-States
  ↓
Effects
```

 Geography in History

Human/Environmental Interaction What geographical features had an impact on the Greek economy? Note especially the development of manufacturing over farming and the Greeks' constant travel and trade.

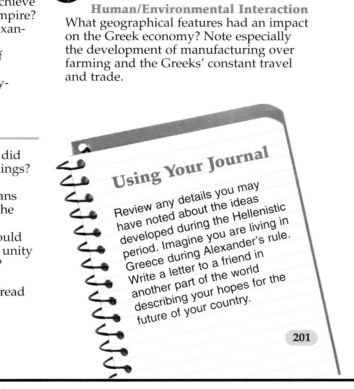

Using Your Journal

Review any details you may have noted about the ideas developed during the Hellenistic period. Imagine you are living in Greece during Alexander's rule. Write a letter to a friend in another part of the world describing your hopes for the future of your country.

201

 Bonus Test Question
For Chapter 12 Test
Alexander was a very practical, clear-thinking leader. If he were to write a handbook of rules on how to organize an army, what do you think would be the first three suggestions in his book? (*Answers will vary.*)

Using Your Journal
Letters will vary but might include the idea that Greek culture and people would flourish and leaders would settle disagreements among Greek city-states, and form political alliances.

 Geography in History
Answers will vary but should include the accessibility of the sea for trade and for obtaining raw materials, lack of good farmland, and mountains.

Using Key Terms

Paragraphs will vary but should include specific references to Philip's methods.

Understanding Main Ideas

1. armed a professional army with long spears, slingshots, and bows and arrows; developed the phalanx
2. to form political alliances
3. because they were unhappy with their local governments
4. literature, political science, geography, and biology
5. They refused to treat Alexander as a god; Greeks looked down on all non-Greeks.
6. its economic opportunities and intellectual and social life
7. It had two great harbors that were protected by breakwaters.
8. fell under Roman control

Critical Thinking

1. Answers will vary but should include the powers of a crowd mentality.
2. Answers will vary but could include aspects of Alexander's character.
3. Answers will vary. Students may say Alexander should not have tried to force a new way of life on the people.
4. Answers will vary but might include through trade, learning, traveling missionaries and merchants, marriage, and alliances.

Graphic Organizer Activity

Sample causes: rise of factories in new Hellenistic cities, emigration of Greek youth. Sample effects: declining population, land/farms became wilderness, fell to Romans.

UNIT 4 Around

FOCUS

Objectives

After reading the Around the World for Unit 4, your students will be able to:

1. locate Nubia and cite geographic factors that protected it from invasion.

2. cite some of Nubia's accomplishments.

3. compare the civilizations of Nubia and ancient Greece.

Bellringer

Ask students to name the earliest ancient African civilization that they can think of. *(Many students will probably say Egypt. If any students say Kush [Chapter 8], hold a class vote on which civilization students think is the oldest.)*

Motivational Activity

Refer students to the Around the World feature, pointing out that many archaeologists today think that Nubia preceded the development of Egypt. Ask: What works of art on pages 202–203 show contact between Nubia and Egypt? *(Sample responses: style of Nubian pendant, silver mask, figures from Egyptian grave, etc.)*

TEACH

Geography: Location Tell students that many Greek writers sang the praises of Egypt, which later led Europeans to speak of the "Glory of Egypt" rather than the "Glory of Nubia." Have students study the map on page 202. Ask: What geographic obstacles made it difficult for the ancient Greeks to reach Nubia? *(cataracts, deserts, and perhaps, depending upon political relations, passage through Egypt itself)*

THE NUBIANS

Tales of Nubia—the vast land south of Egypt—fascinated the Greeks. They learned of its existence from stories told by the Egyptians or by the Nubians who lived in Egypt. However, few non-Africans visited Nubia until the rule of the Ptolemies, the Greek rulers of Egypt from 332 B.C. to 30 B.C. Under the Ptolemies, the Greeks got a firsthand look at one of the oldest civilizations in the ancient world.

Today, many archaeologists believe the Nubians may have developed their first culture around 8000 B.C. The Nubians also established a series of kingdoms in the area, such as Kush, that challenged the power of Egypt, Greece, and Rome. By the time Kush fell in 350 A.D., the Greek city-states had been under Roman rule for almost 500 years.

Ancient Nubia

▲ Geographical features, such as strong rapids and blazing deserts, protected the Nubians from unwanted visitors.

◀ Nubian craftworkers excelled at creating fine works of art. This pendant is topped with a gold figure of a Nubian ruler.

SPOTLIGHT ON: NUBIA

European knowledge of Nubia came mostly from legend. No European knew whether or not cities such as Meroë actually existed. In 1772, Scottish explorer James Bruce rightly guessed that he had sighted the ruins of Meroë on his search for the source of the Blue Nile. Final proof came when a French expedition found the fabled city in the early 1800s. Read aloud this account from a diary written by one of the explorers, and ask students how the discovery might have changed European views of history.

Imagine my joy when I saw the tops of a crowd of pyramids raised a little on the horizon, and tipped by the rays of the sun. . . . Looking round, I saw a second group of pyramids to the west, and, not far from the river, a huge field of ruins . . . indicating the site of an ancient city.

the World

▲ The animals of inland Africa, such as lions, elephants, and giraffes, inspired Nubian artists. This bottle shows a bound oryx—a large African antelope prized by the Nubians for their beautiful long straight horns.

These figures of Nubian bowmen were found in the grave of a wealthy Egyptian buried around 2000 B.C. The Nubians were such skilled archers that the Egyptians called Nubia the "Land of the Bow." In times of peace, the Egyptians hired the Nubians as bodyguards. ▲

The Nubians learned to work in bronze thousands of years ago. This statue of a Nubian king shows the skullcap and headband worn by the rulers of Kush. ▼

This bronze statue of a ▶ Nubian king, dating from about 700 B.C., was found in Cairo, Egypt, in 1929.

Taking Another Look

1. Where was Nubia located?
2. How did Nubia's location prevent the ancient non-African world from knowing much about its accomplishments?

Hands-On Activity

Creating an Advertisement Create a newspaper advertisement announcing a tour of Nubian artworks around the United States.

203

ASSESS

Check for Understanding

Have students answer the questions in **Taking Another Look** on page 203.

Enrich

Have students imagine they are Greek geographers in the 400s B.C. After a long and dangerous journey, they have finally reached Meroë, the center of Nubian power at this time. Have students write an account of the journey and the wonderful sights that they have seen. (For more on Meroë, refer students to pages 130–131.)

CLOSE

Have students compare the geography of Greece with the geography of Nubia. Encourage them to suggest reasons Nubia was able to achieve greater unity than the Greek city-states. (*Sample response: Greek communities were separated by the mountains and the sea, while Nubians lived along the band of fertile soil that stretched along the banks of the Nile River south of the first cataract.*)

ANSWERS TO TAKING ANOTHER LOOK

1. Sample responses: At its height, Nubia stretched along both banks of the Nile from an area just above the first cataract to the area where the Nile River forks into the White Nile and the Blue Nile. It covered lands in southern Egypt and parts of the Sudan.
2. The cataracts and deserts served as obstacles to contact.

Hands-On Activity
The advertisements should accurately describe artworks shown in this feature and the uniqueness of the culture that created them.

Answers and Analyses

1B   Geography

According to the map, Athens is located at 24°E (24 degrees east) longitude.

2G   Civics

There is no provision in the American constitution for choosing by lot. Remind students to be very careful when they see the words NOT or EXCEPT in a question. Overlooking these words is a common source of error on multiple-choice tests.

TEST-TAKING TIP

Students can often answer EXCEPT and NOT questions by association. Choices F, H and J are all associated with the Constitution of the United States, but G is not. Therefore G is the best guess.

3C   History

The Delian League is discussed on pages 173–175. There it states that *Athens gained more and more power,* and eventually *Athenian soldiers interfered in the politics of other Greek city-states.* This power imbalance led to anti-Athenian sentiment.

TEST-TAKING TIP

Encourage students to use what they know, even if their knowledge is incomplete. Even if all they recall is that Athens was the driving force behind the Delian League, they will realize that choices A and D are unlikely.

THE PRINCETON REVIEW

Standardized Test Practice

Directions: Choose the *best* answer to each of the following multiple choice questions. If you have trouble answering a question, use the process of elimination to narrow your choices. Write your answers on a separate piece of paper.

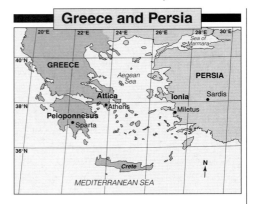

Greece and Persia

1. **Along which line of longitude is Athens located?**

   A   22°E

   B   24°E

   C   38°N

   D   36°N

> **Test-Taking Tip:**   *Lines of longitude,* or *meridians,* are used to measure distances <u>east</u> and <u>west</u>. They run from the North Pole to the South Pole. Be careful not to confuse *longitude* and *latitude.*

2. **The Constitution of the United States has much in common with the constitution of ancient Athens. Which of the following provisions of the Athenian constitution is NOT part of the United States Constitution?**

F   Freedom of speech

G   Choosing members of government by lottery

H   Limits on the terms of elected officials

J   Two separate bodies of government

> **Test-Taking Tip:**   Remember that the correct answer is true of the Athenian constitution but not true of the U.S. Constitution. Therefore, you can eliminate any answer that you know to be true of the U.S. Constitution. For instance, the United States Constitution *does* provide for freedom of speech, and so answer F cannot be the correct choice.

3. **To protect themselves from attacks by the Persians, many Greek city-states joined the Delian League. This alliance allowed them to work together to defend themselves. Why did the Delian League eventually fall apart?**

   A   The League suspended the voting rights of the Athenians.

   B   Most city-states decided that they would rather defend themselves alone.

   C   Athens took over the League, which made Athens too powerful.

   D   Athens stopped giving money to the League, so the League went bankrupt.

> **Test-Taking Tip:**   This question requires you to remember a *fact* about the Delian League. Make sure that you read the question and *all* of the answer choices carefully before selecting the *best* answer.

4. Socrates made several contributions to the fields of philosophy and science. Why was he sentenced to death in 399 B.C.?

F Many people thought that he gave the rulers of Athens bad advice.

G He designed a plan to overthrow the government of Greece.

H He encouraged all people to leave their jobs and go in search of truth.

J Many Athenians felt threatened by him because he pointed out their mistakes.

Test-Taking Tip: Eliminate answers that do not make sense. Socrates was not interested in overthrowing the government; therefore, you can eliminate answer G.

5. The goal of early Greek philosophers was

A to create new inventions to improve Greek society

B to look for truths by using logic

C to find ways to spread Christianity throughout the world

D to redesign the military to be more effective

Test-Taking Tip: It is important to remember what *philosophers* are. Although they are a type of scientist, their goal is not to *create new inventions* (answer A). The word *philosopher* means "lover of knowledge." Which answer choice fits best with this information?

6. Socrates' method of reaching a conclusion came to be called the Socratic method. However, this technique is not the only way to reach a conclusion. The scientific method is another way. How are the Socratic method and the scientific method similar?

F Both require performing experiments with chemicals in a laboratory.

G Both rely on following a step-by-step process to come to a conclusion.

H Both place an emphasis on trusting instincts and ideas over physical evidence.

J Both have been replaced by more advanced methods today.

Test-Taking Tip: This question requires you to make a *comparison*. That means you must choose the answer that is true for *both* methods. Since the Socratic method does *not* use chemicals, and the scientific method *does* rely on physical evidence, you can rule out answers F and H.

7. Which of the following contributed to the end of the Greek empire?

F Alexander the Great, a powerful and well-liked ruler, died.

G People started moving out of Greek city-states, creating a shortage of workers

H There were conflicts about who would rule over the empire.

J All of the above.

Test-Taking Tip: Do not choose the first answer that "makes sense." Always read *all* of the answer choices before choosing the *best* one, especially when one of your choices is "all of the above" or "none of the above."

4J History

Socrates is discussed on pages 185–186. There it states that some Athenians *did not like self-examination, particularly when it pointed out their own mistakes,* and that for this reason they began to see Socrates as a threat.

5B History

No mention is made of Christianity or of the military, so choices C and D can be eliminated. While choice A is tempting, since modern scientists often create new inventions, no inventions are discussed on the pages about philosophers. On page 185, Socrates is said to have been *searching for truth.*

6G History

At the top of page 186, the Socratic method is described as a step-by-step approach to arrive at a final conclusion. On page 188, the scientific method developed by Thales and completed by Aristotle is described as having three steps: collecting information, making a hypothesis, and testing the hypothesis.

7J History

The demise of the Greek empire is discussed on pages 198–200. Among the reasons cited were Alexander's death; a drop in population and subsequent shortage of workers; and fights over control of the empire.

Tested Objectives	
Questions	**Reading Objective**
1	Analyze information
2	Make comparisons
3	Draw conclusions
4, 7	Perceive relationships and recognize outcomes
5	Identify central issues
6	Make comparisons

OVERVIEW

Unit 5 surveys the history of Rome from its beginnings as a small city-state to the decline of its powerful empire.

➤ **Chapter 13** discusses the settlement of Italy, focusing on the Etruscans.

➤ **Chapter 14** analyzes the history of the Roman Republic from the sixth century B.C. to the establishment of the Roman Empire and its decline.

➤ **Chapter 15** explains the development of the Roman Empire from its founding in 31 B.C. to its fall in 476 A.D., focusing on the *Pax Romana*.

➤ **Chapter 16** summarizes the rise of Christianity to become a major influence on Western civilization.

UNIT OBJECTIVES

After reading Unit 5, students will be able to:

1. explain how the city of Rome became a great empire.

2. summarize what contributions the Romans made to Western civilization.

3. discuss the relationship between the Roman Empire and Christianity.

UNIT PROJECT

Organize students into three groups. Assign each group one of the following topics: Etruria, the Roman Republic, or the Roman Empire. Tell groups to create a chart about their topic using the following headings: *Government, Religion, Daily Life, Contributions, Famous Rulers.* Compile the three charts into a master chart titled *The Romans.*

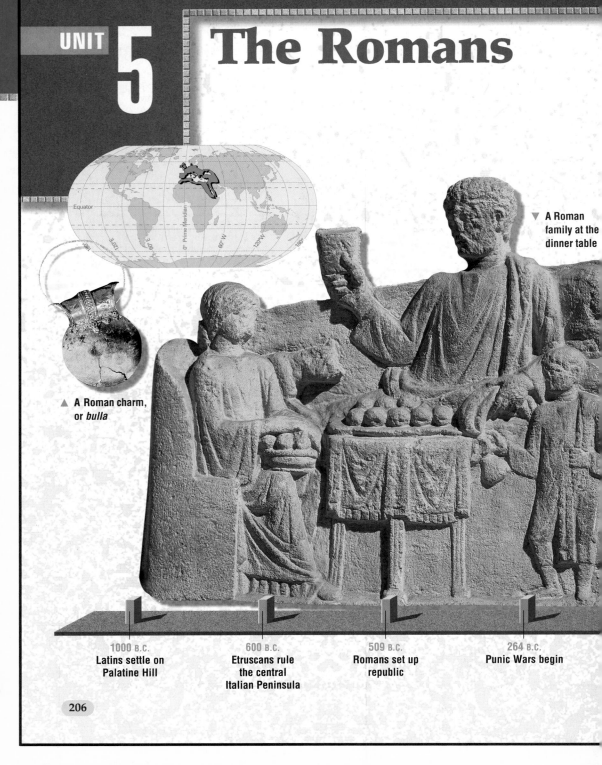

UNIT 5 — **The Romans**

▼ A Roman family at the dinner table

▲ A Roman charm, or *bulla*

1000 B.C.	600 B.C.	509 B.C.	264 B.C.
Latins settle on Palatine Hill	Etruscans rule the central Italian Peninsula	Romans set up republic	Punic Wars begin

206

ABOUT THE UNIT OPENING

Examining Artifacts

Tell students that a *bulla* was a good-luck charm commonly given to Roman children by adults. Based on this information and the scene of a Roman family, what can they infer about how the Romans viewed children? *(They valued children.)* Explain that Rome built one of the greatest empires in the ancient world. Ask: What do you think it would be like to grow up as a citizen of a huge empire?

Global Chronology

Ask students to explain what the time line covers. *(major events in the history of Rome)* Ask students to name the time line entry that indicates that Rome had an organized government. *(Romans set up republic)*

Multimedia Activity

Surfing the Net
Roman Achievements

The Romans excelled at practical achievements such as aqueducts, roads, and architectural innovations like the dome and the arch. To find out more about Roman achievements, visit the Internet.

Getting There

Follow these steps to gather information on practical Roman innovations, particularly engineering feats.
1. Pick a search engine, such as Excite, Lycos, WebCrawler, Yahoo, etc.
2. Type in the main search words *Roman culture*. Then add words to focus your research. Words might include *ancient, archaeology, buildings*, or *engineering*.
3. Explore links that the search engine brings up on the screen. (Links point the way to Web sites on the Internet.)
4. Click on links that provide information on the subject of your research.

Hands-On Activity

Create a gallery of Roman innovations. Organize pictures of the various inventions or achievements along one wall in the classroom. Then develop a written script to guide viewers through the gallery.

PRIMARY SOURCES
Library

See pages 682–683 for a primary source reading to accompany Unit 5.

46 B.C.
Julius Caesar is appointed dictator of Rome

27 B.C.
Pax Romana begins

392 A.D.
Christianity becomes official religion of Roman Empire

Journal Notes

What contributions did the Etruscans and Romans make to world civilization? Note details about these people as you read.

207

INTRODUCING THE UNIT

Write the following statements on the board: *"The people's good is the highest law."* (Cicero, c. 50 B.C.) *"Divine nature made the country, human art built the cities."* (Marcus Terentius Varro, c. 40 B.C.) *"It is sweet and beautiful to die for your country."* (Horace, 30 B.C.) Ask: How did the Romans view themselves? What was important to them, and how did they regard life?

RECORDING JOURNAL NOTES

Have students make a list of Roman contributions. Write responses on the board. Have students note in their journals details about the contributions of the Etruscans and Romans to the modern world.

PRIMARY SOURCES
Library

Items in the Primary Sources Library for this unit focus on the eruption of Mount Vesuvius. Elements include:

- An eyewitness account of the eruption by Pliny the Younger
- Artifact found at Pompeii

For additional primary source documents, have students use the **World History Primary Source Document CD-ROM.**

Geographic Location

At its peak, the Roman Empire extended into the following regions: the Mediterranean, North Africa, and the Middle East. Have students locate these places in their text Atlas and name the continents that this area includes. *(Europe, Africa, and Asia)* Ask students what problems might arise in governing such a vast area. *(delays in communication, need to provide defense against invaders and rebellions, tax collection, law enforcement)*

Chapter 13 Planning Guide

Objectives	Reproducible Resources	Multimedia Resources
Section 1 **Founding of Rome** Describe how Rome was founded.	Reproducible Lesson Plan Chapter 13 Vocabulary and Guided Reading Activity Reading Essentials and Study Guide 13-1 Section 1 Quiz Unit 5 Hands-On History Lab	Vocabulary PuzzleMaker Interactive Tutor Self-Assessment Software ExamView® Pro Testmaker Glencoe Skillbuilder Interactive Workbook, Level 1 Presentation Plus!
Section 2 **The Etruscans** Describe what daily life was like for the Etruscans and identify their religious beliefs.	Reproducible Lesson Plan Reading Essentials and Study Guide 13-2 Chapter 13 Cooperative Learning Activity Chapter 13 Geography and Map Activity Section 2 Quiz	Teaching Transparencies and Activities 13A & 13B Vocabulary PuzzleMaker Interactive Tutor Self-Assessment Software ExamView® Pro Testmaker Glencoe Skillbuilder Interactive Workbook, Level 1
Section 3 **Etruscans and Romans** Identify how the Etruscans contributed to Roman civilization.	Reproducible Lesson Plan Reading Essentials and Study Guide 13-3 Chapter 13 Chart and Graph Skill Activity Chapter 13 Activity Book Activity Section 3 Quiz	Vocabulary PuzzleMaker Interactive Tutor Self-Assessment Software ExamView® Pro Testmaker Glencoe Skillbuilder Interactive Workbook, Level 1
Chapter 13 **Review and Evaluation**	Chapter 13 Reteaching Activity Chapter 13 Performance Assessment Activity Spanish Chapter Summary and Glossary Chapter 13 Test	Vocabulary PuzzleMaker Interactive Tutor Self-Assessment Software Glencoe Skillbuilder Interactive Workbook, Level 1 Audiocassettes* ExamView® Pro Testmaker

*Also available in Spanish.

Presentation Plus!

Use Glencoe's **Presentation Plus!** multimedia teacher tool to easily present dynamic lessons that visually excite your students. Using Microsoft® PowerPoint, you can customize the presentations to create your own personalized lessons.

Interactive Lesson Planner

Planning has never been easier! Using this CD-ROM, organize your week, month, semester, or year with all the help you need. The **Interactive Lesson Planner** gives you access to all of the blackline masters which accompany *Human Heritage.*

Chapter 13 Planning Guide

✓ PERFORMANCE ASSESSMENT ACTIVITIES

Legends Have students create legends about the founding of their community. Students might use the name of their community, its geographic location, or its main economic activity as inspiration.

CHAPTER RESOURCES

LITERATURE ABOUT THE PERIOD
Virgil. *Aeneid.* Translated by John Dryden. Heritage, 1944. The national epic of Rome.

READINGS FOR THE STUDENT
Hamblin, Dora Jane. *The Etruscans* (Emergence of Man series). Time-Life Books, 1975. History of Etruscan people.

READINGS FOR THE TEACHER
Editors of Time-Life Books. *Lost Civilizations: Etruscans—Italy's Lovers of Life.* Time-Life Books, 1995. Provides a close-up look at a little-known people.

Sprenger, Maja and Gilda Bartolini. *The Etruscans: Their History, Art, and Architecture.* Abrams, 1983. Analyzes the history of the Etruscans through their art and architecture.

KEY TO ABILITY LEVELS

Teaching strategies have been coded for varying learning styles and abilities.

L1 Level 1 activities are **basic** activities and should be within the ability range of all students.

L2 Level 2 activities are **average** activities and should be within the ability range of the average to above-average student.

L3 Level 3 activities are **challenging** activities designed for the ability range of above-average students.

ELL ELL activities should be within the ability range of English Language Learning students.

NATIONAL GEOGRAPHIC SOCIETY — Teacher's Corner

INDEX TO NATIONAL GEOGRAPHIC MAGAZINE
The following articles relate to this chapter:
- "Roman Legacy," by T.R. Reid, August 1997.
- "Roman Empire," by T.R. Reid, July 1997.

NATIONAL GEOGRAPHIC SOCIETY PRODUCTS AVAILABLE FROM GLENCOE
To order the following, call Glencoe at 1-800-334-7344:
- *PicturePack: Physical Geography of the World (Transparencies)*
- *PicturePack: Ancient Rome (Transparencies)*
- *PictureShow: Ancient Civilizations: Greece and Rome (CD-ROM)*
- *Ancient Civilizations: Rome (Poster Set)*
- *PicturePack: World Geography Library (Transparencies)*

ADDITIONAL NATIONAL GEOGRAPHIC SOCIETY PRODUCTS
To order the following, call National Geographic at 1-800-368-2728:
- *National Geographic Atlas of World History (Book)*
- *Wonders of the Ancient World: National Geographic Atlas of Archaeology (Book)*
- *Romans (Map)*

Access *National Geographic*'s new dynamic MapMachine Web site and other geography resources at:
http://www.nationalgeographic.com/
http://www.nationalgeographic.com/maps/

  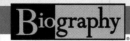

The following videotape program is available from Glencoe:
- **Hidden City of the Etruscans**
  1-56501-972-5

To order, call Glencoe at 1-800-334-7344. To find classroom resources to accompany many of these videos, check the following home pages:

A&E Television: http://www.aetv.com
The History Channel: http://www.historychannel.com

OVERVIEW

Chapter 13 describes the beginnings of civilization in Italy.
➤ **Section 1** describes the founding of Rome.
➤ **Section 2** discusses the rise of the Etruscans, their daily life, and their religious beliefs.
➤ **Section 3** summarizes the contributions the Etruscans made to Roman civilization.

CHAPTER OBJECTIVES

After reading Chapter 13, students will be able to:
1. explain how Rome was founded.
2. describe what daily life was like for the Etruscans.
3. identify the religious beliefs held by the Etruscans.
4. cite Etruscan contributions to Roman civilization.

EXAMINING ARTIFACTS

Refer students to the artifacts, and challenge them to brainstorm a list of skills that the Etruscans may have possessed. *(painting, dancing, pottery-making, use of an alphabet)* Encourage students to add to this list as they read the chapter.

PERFORMANCE ASSESSMENT ✓

Use the Performance Assessment Activities on page 208B to help you evaluate students as they complete the chapter.

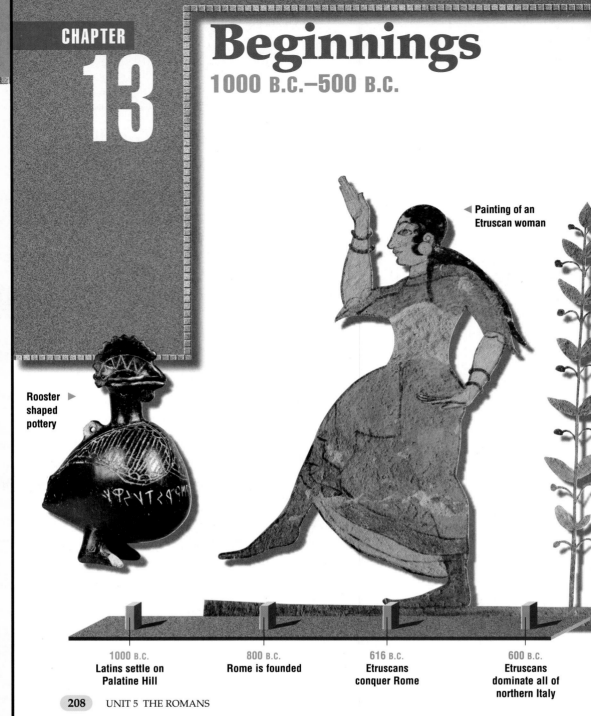

CHAPTER 13

Beginnings
1000 B.C.–500 B.C.

◀ **Painting of an Etruscan woman**

Rooster shaped pottery ▶

1000 B.C.	800 B.C.	616 B.C.	600 B.C.
Latins settle on Palatine Hill	**Rome is founded**	**Etruscans conquer Rome**	**Etruscans dominate all of northern Italy**

208 UNIT 5 THE ROMANS

TEACHING RESOURCES

TEACHER PLANNING AND SUPPORT

📂 Reproducible Lesson Plan
📂 Block Scheduling Implementation Guide
📂 Videodisc Bar Code Correlation
🔘 Presentation Plus!

REVIEW AND REINFORCEMENT

📂 Reading Essentials and Study Guide 13-1,13-2, 13-3
📂 Chapter 13 Vocabulary and Guided Reading Activity
💾 Vocabulary PuzzleMaker Software
🖨 Teaching Transparencies 13A & 13B

📂 Chapter 13 Reteaching Activity
📂 Chapter 13 Cooperative Learning Activity
📂 Chapter 13 Activity Book Activity
📂 Chapter 13 Chart and Graph Skill Activity
💾 Interactive Tutor Self-Assessment Software
📼 Unit 5 MindJogger VideoQuiz

APPLICATION AND HANDS-ON ACTIVITIES

📂 Daily World History, Geography, and Culture Question
📂 Unit 5 Hands-On History Lab Activity

Chapter Focus

 Read to Discover

- How Rome was founded.
- What daily life was like for the Etruscans.
- What religious beliefs were held by the Etruscans.
- How Etruscans contributed to Roman civilization.

Chapter Overview

Visit the *Human Heritage* Web site at **humanheritage.glencoe.com** and click on **Chapter 13— Chapter Overviews** to preview this chapter.

Terms to Learn	**People to Know**	**Places to Locate**
soothsayers	Aeneas	Rome
omens	Romulus	Palatine
catacombs	Remus	Etruria
Forum		Lydia
fasces		
mundus		

Why It's Important   Italy is a boot-shaped peninsula that extends south from Europe into the Mediterranean Sea. On the west coast of the peninsula is the mouth of the Tiber (tī´ buhr) River. Fifteen miles upstream is a group of seven hills. On the hill known as the Palatine (pal´ uh tīn), an early people called the Latins founded a settlement later known as Rome. This settlement would one day become the center of a great empire, whose achievements still influence life today.

SECTION 1   Founding of Rome

Romans have a legend about the founding of their city. After the fall of Troy, the gods ordered a Trojan prince called Aeneas (uh nē´ uhs) to lead his people to a promised land in the West. When Aeneas's group reached Italy, they joined forces with a people known as Latins (lat´ nz).

About 800 B.C., a Latin princess gave birth to twin sons fathered by the god Mars. The princess had taken an oath never to have children. Because she broke her word, she was punished. Her sons, Romulus (rom´ ū luhs) and Remus (rē´ muhs), were taken from her and left to die on the bank of the flooding Tiber.

Romulus and Remus were found by a she-wolf, which fed and cared for them. One day a shepherd killed the she-wolf and discovered the babies. He took them to his home.

When the boys grew older, they decided to build a city on the Tiber. The brothers, however, could not agree on which one should rule the city. They decided to let the gods choose between them.

CHAPTER 13 BEGINNINGS   **209**

GEOGRAPHY ACTIVITIES
 Chapter 13 Geography and Map Activity
Social Studies Outline Map Resource Book

INTERDISCIPLINARY CONNECTIONS
World Music: Cultural Traditions

ENRICHMENT AND EXTENSION
World History Primary Source Document Library CD-ROM
Chapter 13 Enrichment Activity
Foods Around the World

ASSESSMENT AND EVALUATION
Chapter 13 Performance Assessment Activity
Chapter 13 Section Quizzes 13-1, 13-2, 13-3
Chapter 13 Test
Chapter 13 ExamView® Pro Testmaker Software
Chapter 13 Digests Audiocassettes Activities and Tests

SPANISH RESOURCES
Chapter 13 Spanish Chapter Summary and Glossary
Chapter 13 Spanish Chapter Digests Audiocassettes Activities and Tests

---

Chapter Overview introduces students to chapter content and key terms. Have them access **Chapter 13 Overview** at **humanheritage.glencoe.com**

FOCUS

 Bellringer

Have students complete the following statement: *People made up legends to _____.*

Motivational Activity

Call on students to read their completed statements. *(Students' statements should include that legends often were created to explain mysterious or unknown happenings.)* Tell students that in this chapter they will learn about a legend that explains the founding of Rome.

GUIDE TO READING

Reading Strategy

Ask students to read "Why It's Important" and summarize the chapter's main theme. *(The Latin settlement of Rome would one day become the center of an empire that still influences life today.)*

Vocabulary Precheck

Ask students to define each of the "Terms to Learn." Have a volunteer consult the dictionary for any unfamiliar words. **L1** **ELL**

Use the Vocabulary PuzzleMaker for Chapter 13 to create a crossword puzzle. **L1**

Assign Chapter 13 Vocabulary and Guided Reading Activity.

Assign Reading Essentials and Study Guide 13-1.

Guided Practice

L2 Language Arts Have students work in small groups to write a script for the legend about the founding of Rome. Encourage them to include a list of characters and a setting description. Have groups present their scripts to the class.

L1 Geography: Location Have a student locate Italy on a wall map. Note its location in relation to the Mediterranean world. Discuss why Italy was a good place for an important civilization to develop. (*The country's central location helped the Romans assert their control over the Mediterranean world.*) **ELL**

LINKING PAST TO PRESENT

Scholars are still trying to translate the inscriptions found in Etruscan tombs and temple ruins.

💾 Use **Interactive Tutor Self-Assessment Software** to review Section 1.

NATIONAL GEOGRAPHIC SOCIETY

Use these materials to enrich student understanding of ancient Rome.

💿 **ANCIENT CIVILIZA-TIONS POSTER SET**
Rome

💾 Use the **Vocabulary Puzzle-Maker** to create crossword and word search puzzles.

Each brother climbed to the top of a different hill to watch for a sign from the gods. Then 12 vultures flew over the Palatine. Since Romulus stood atop the Palatine, he claimed to be king. He and Remus then fought, and Remus was killed. Romulus became king of the city, which he named Rome.

Experts have learned that about 1000 B.C, groups of people with iron weapons began invading the lands around the Mediterranean. One group invaded Egypt and brought down the New Kingdom. Another group moved into the Balkan Peninsula. A third group, the Latins, settled on the Palatine. Romans belonged to this group.

The area where the Latins settled had a pleasant climate and fertile soil. Nearby were dense forests that supplied the Latins with timber. They built gravel roads to bring salt and other items from the coast.

By 776 B.C., the settlement on the Palatine had become a village of about 1,000 people. Most of the people were farmers who lived in wooden huts and worked the land. Their main crops were wheat and barley.

Section 1 Assessment

1. According to legend, how was Rome founded?
2. What natural resources existed in the area settled by the Latins?
3. How did the Latins live?

Critical Thinking

4. **Evaluating Information** How true do you think the legend of Rome's founding is? Explain your answer.

Graphic Organizer Activity

5. Draw a diagram like this one, and use it to show the main events in the legend of Romulus and Remus. (Add more boxes, if necessary.)

Event 1 → Event 2 → Event 3 → Event 4

SECTION 2 The Etruscans

Etruscan Jewelry

Around 800 B.C., a people called Etruscans (ē truhs' kuhnz) settled in Etruria (ē trur' ē uh), the rolling hill country north of the Latin village on the Palatine. The Etruscans wrote in an alphabet borrowed from the Greeks. They spoke a language different from any other in the ancient world. Many historians believe they came from the kingdom of Lydia in Asia Minor.

The Etruscans dug tunnels and built dams to drain their marshy fields. High on hilltops, they built a number of cities, each surrounded by a thick wall.

The Etruscans were Italy's first highly civilized people. They were known as "the people of the sea." As pirates, they were

---

Section 1 Assessment Answers

1. About 800 B.C., a Latin princess gave birth to twin sons fathered by a god. As punishment, her sons, Romulus and Remus, were taken from her and raised by a she-wolf and then a shepherd and his wife. Later the brothers built a city on the Tiber and let the gods choose the city's ruler. The two fought, Remus was killed, and Romulus became king of Rome.

2. pleasant climate, fertile soil, dense forests, salt and fish carried from the coast

3. Most were farmers who lived in wooden huts.

4. Answers will vary. Students should give reasons why they think the legend does or does not have some validity.

5. Events should follow the chronological order in the story. You might expand on this activity by having students turn their graphic organizers into storyboards.

Assign Chapter 13 **Section 1 Quiz** in the TCR. Testmaker available.

Reading A Political Map

In all parts of the world, people have created governments in order to live together. Maps that show areas ruled by particular governments are called **political maps.** Most people use political maps to find cities and countries.

Political maps use symbols to show the location of capitals and other cities. A star is usually used to show the capital of a country or state, and a dot is used to show other cities. Boundary lines mark where a country or state begins and ends. Boundaries may be shown by solid, dashed, or dotted lines. Colors often show the size and shape of countries and states. All these symbols, lines, and colors are not really on Earth's surface, but what they show exists.

On the map of "Early Italy" below, the three colors show the particular areas ruled by three peoples.

Map Practice

1. **Who controlled the southermost part of Italy?**
2. **What two cities are shown?**
3. **What people controlled the smallest area?**

Early Italy

Etruscans
Greeks
Latins

miles 0 50 100 150
kilometers 0 50 100 150 200

Glencoe's **Skillbuilder Interactive Workbook, Level 1,** provides instruction and practice in key social studies skills.

211

TEACH

Reading a Political Map

Have students read the introductory section of the skill on page 211. Ask students what they think most people use political maps for. *(to find cities and countries)* What are three ways boundaries may be shown on maps? *(by solid, dashed, or dotted lines)* What are often used on political maps to show the size and shape of countries and states? *(colors)* Direct students' attention to the map on the skill page. Ask them what is used to show boundary lines on this map of early Italy. *(solid lines)* What people controlled the Arno River? *(Etruscans)* What city was ruled by the Etruscans? *(Caere)*

Answers to Map Practice

1. Greeks
2. Caere and Rome
3. Latins

GEOGRAPHY AND HISTORY

Why do you think the Etruscans became "the people of the sea"? *(Their extensive coastline would have encouraged the people to become dependent on the sea for their livelihood.)*

Assign Chapter 13 **Geography and Map Activity** in the TCR.

SPOTLIGHT ON: EARLY ITALY

The Tiber River was a dominant influence on Etruria. Some historians believe this 252-mile (405 km) river was known originally as Albulla—referring to the whiteness of its waters—and was later changed to the name Tiber for Tiberius, a king of Alba Lunga (an area south of Rome) who drowned in it.

HISTORY
Online

Student Web Activity objectives, goals, and answers can be found at the *Chapter 13 Web Activity Lesson Plan* at humanheritage.glencoe.com

HISTORY
Online

Student Web Activity

Visit the *Human Heritage* Web site at **humanheritage.glencoe.com** and click on **Chapter 13— Student Web Activities** to find out more about the historical roots of Rome.

Linking Across Time

Buildings might include one-story homes with central courtyards, temples, and so on. (Students might also name some of the public buildings in the Forum, described on page 215.)

L3 Critical Thinking Point out that most civilizations borrow from other culture groups. For example, the Etruscans borrowed the Greek alphabet and some Greek gods. Have students brainstorm a list of some things American culture has borrowed from other cultures. (*Examples: words from Latin, French, Greek, or Spanish; foods from Italy, China, or Mexico; holiday traditions such as the Christmas tree from Germany*)

feared and envied throughout the Mediterranean. As traders, they were admired and respected.

Etruscan farmers used mostly iron tools to grow barley, millet, wheat, grapes, and other fruits. They raised pigs, goats, sheep, ducks, chickens, and cattle. The farmers used cattle for food and to pull plows and wagons.

Etruscan miners dug copper, lead, iron, and tin. Etruscan metalworkers and sculptors turned these metals into weapons, utensils, and jewelry. Etruscan merchants exchanged both metals and finished goods for luxury items of gold, silver, and ivory from Syria, Greece, and other eastern Mediterranean countries.

The Etruscans had a strong army. The soldiers learned much about weapons and battle techniques from the Greeks. Their infantry formed a phalanx much like the one used by the Greeks. However, the Etruscans had one "weapon" no one else

Linking Across Time

Arches Etruscan engineers were among the first to use arches widely in their architecture. The semicircular stone arches could support great weight and allowed them to build gateways into fortified cities (below). Today the arch remains the symbol of a gateway, as illustrated by the stainless steel Gateway Arch at the entrance of St. Louis, Missouri (right). **What types of buildings might be found in an Etruscan city?**

212

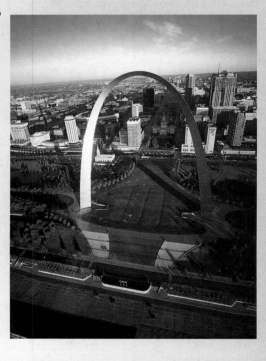

The Romans borrowed extensively from other cultures. Provide students with a wall-sized sheet of paper on which to show a composite of what Romans borrowed with a graphic organizer of their own design. Assign students to small groups. Have each group research one major topic and then complete one portion of the wall diagram. (*Romans adapted Etruscan rituals, Etr-uscan and Greek gods, Greek styles of architecture and sculpture, Greek medicine and science, and Egyptian astronomy.*) Each group should divide among its members the tasks of researching, obtaining pictures, drawing illustrations, and writing captions.

Assign Chapter 13 *Cooperative Learning Activity* in the TCR.

had—their shoes. They wore heavy leather shoes that laced firmly around the ankle. This gave them better footing than their enemies on rough or hilly ground.

Over time, the Etruscan cities grew in size and power. The Etruscans became rich. By 600 B.C., they dominated all of northern Italy, including the Latin village on the Palatine.

Daily Life

The Etruscans enjoyed bright colors, riches, and a good time. They gambled with ivory dice or played games similar to chess and backgammon. They often watched or took part in such sports as wrestling, running, boxing, and horse racing.

Most of all, the Etruscans loved music and dancing. Sounds from a double flute or a stringed lyre (līr) accompanied most of their activities. Much of their dancing was connected to religion. Dances were done to gain favor from the gods.

Both Etruscan men and women danced. Dancing was just one of the freedoms enjoyed by Etruscan women. Unlike Greek or Latin women, Etruscan women took part in public celebrations. They could also own property.

The Etruscans had a strong sense of **social order,** or the way groups of people are classed. At first, there were no great class differences among them. Only acrobats and enslaved people, who were captives of war, were thought inferior. Later, people were divided into three classes. The upper class consisted of wealthy landowners, nobles, and priests. The middle class had farmers, traders, and city workers. The lower class was enslaved people.

A few wealthy families owned most of the land. They also owned most of the enslaved people, who tended the land and did other work. The rich lived in rectangular, one-story homes made of sun-dried brick on a frame of heavy timbers. A pitched roof covered with clay tiles extended beyond the house. Stone-lined drains led from each house into the main drains that ran along the pebble-paved streets. Most homes also had broad, walled courtyards open to the sky. During the day, the center room was often used for talking about business. At night, it was the scene of entertainment.

Religious Beliefs

The Etruscans had many gods, most of whom were modeled after those of the Greeks. At first, the Etruscans worshiped their gods outdoors on platforms of stone or earth. Later, they built temples of wood, mud-brick, and clay on stone foundations. The temples had peaked, tiled roofs adorned with sculptures.

The Etruscans believed the universe was divided into provinces. Each province was ruled by different gods. Humans lived in the center of the universe, facing south towards the gods of nature and Earth. To the right lay the West, which was ruled by the gods of death and of the underworld. To the left lay the East,

People in History

Romulus
c. 800 B.C.–715 B.C.

Founder of Rome

Romulus and his twin brother Remus founded Rome around 753 B.C. Quarrels over the kingship of Rome led to the death of Remus. According to legend, Romulus populated Rome with people fleeing harsh rule elsewhere. After a long reign, he vanished in a thunderstorm. Romans later worshiped him as the war god Quirinus.

✔ **Reading Check**
What three classes made up the Etruscan **social order** during later years?

✔ **Reading Check Answer**
The Etruscan **social order** consisted of an upper class, middle class, and lower class.

DID YOU KNOW ??
Wealthy Etruscans wore a great many jewels, especially ornaments of gold.

MULTICULTURAL PERSPECTIVES

The Etruscans believed that a person was destined to live 70 years. By reading omens correctly and making the proper sacrifices to the gods, a person might live 84 years. Then, even if the body survived, the soul would be taken away.

Reading Check Answer
The Etruscans went to **soothsayers** to find out about the future.
Soothsayers read **omens** or signs that explained the will of the gods.

LINKING PAST TO PRESENT

The three main Etruscan gods were Tinia, ruler of the heavens and of the other gods; Uni, Tinia's wife and goddess of love and the well-being of women; and Minerva, goddess of wisdom and the arts. The names of these gods have become components of modern English.

Reading Check Answer
The Etruscans built **catacombs** as tombs for their dead.

Reading Check Answer
A **necropolis** was a cemetery made up of acres of Etruscan tombs.

Use **Interactive Tutor Self-Assessment Software** to review Section 2.

Use the **Vocabulary Puzzle-Maker** to create crossword and word search puzzles.

---

which was ruled by the gods of the heavens. Because of this, Etruscans planned their cities and built their temples to face east.

The Etruscans also believed humans were powerless before the gods. More than anything else, the Etruscans wanted to please their gods. First, however, they had to discover what their gods willed. They did this through a priestly group of aristocrats called **soothsayers** (sūth' sā uhrz), or people who can predict events.

Soothsayers read certain **omens** (ō' muhnz), or signs of what is to happen. One group of soothsayers read omens from the livers of sacrificed animals. Another group of soothsayers explained the will of the gods by studying the direction and sounds of thunder and lightning and the flights of birds.

Reading Check Why did the Etruscans go to **soothsayers?** What did **omens** reveal to the Etruscans?

Tombs of Gold   When an Etruscan noble died, a great banquet was held. At the banquet, two of the noble's slaves fought one another to the death. The spirit of the slave who was killed went with the noble's spirit to the underworld.

The dead were buried in tombs beneath the ground called **catacombs** (kat' uh kōmz). Much of what is known about Etruscan life comes from such tombs, whose inside walls were brightly painted with pictures of daily life. The tombs had chairs and beds. The bodies of the dead rested on the beds.

Reading Check Why did the Etruscans build **catacombs?**

The Etruscans believed that life after death lasted longer and was more important than life on Earth. So, they carved their tombs out of natural rock, which would last for a long time. They filled the tombs with works of art and treasures of gold, silver, bronze, and ivory. Because of this, Etruscan tombs are known as "tombs of gold."

Outside each Etruscan city was a **necropolis** (nek rop' uh luhs), or cemetery, made up of acres of these tombs. The necropolis outside the city of Caere (sir' ē) is one of the largest Etruscan cemeteries. There, great mounds of soil are piled in the shape of a dome on top of a base. Some of the mounds measure 100 feet, or 30 meters, across.

Reading Check What was a **necropolis?**

Section 2 Assessment

1. **Define:** social order, soothsayers, omens, catacombs, necropolis.
2. How did the Etruscan social order change over time?

Critical Thinking

3. **Making Comparisons**   What similarities are there between the way the Etruscans treated their dead and the way modern people do?

Graphic Organizer Activity

4. Draw a diagram like this one, and use it to show the members of the three main Etruscan social classes.

Upper Class
Middle Class
Lower Class

Section 2 Assessment Answers

1. social order, classes of people (p. 213); soothsayers, people who predict (p. 214); omens, signs of the future (p. 214); catacombs, underground tombs (p. 214); necropolis, cemetery (p. 214)
2. At first there were no great class differences. Only acrobats and enslaved people were thought of as inferior. Over time, however, three social classes emerged.

3. Answers will vary, but students could note Etruscan burial tombs, practices, and cemeteries.
4. *upper class*—wealthy landowners, nobles, priests; *middle class*—farmers, traders, city workers; *lower class*—enslaved people.

Assign the Chapter 13 **Section 2 Quiz** in the TCR. Testmaker available.

SECTION 3 Etruscans and Romans

In 616 B.C., Lucius Tarquinius (lū' shuhs tar kwin' ē uhs) became the first Etruscan ruler of Rome. No one is certain whether Tarquinius took the throne from the Latin king by force or by cleverness. Nevertheless, his dynasty ruled Rome for more than 100 years.

The Etruscans were more culturally advanced than the Latins. They made many contributions to Roman civilization. In the area of architecture, the Etruscans taught the Latins how to use the arch in building bridges. The Etruscans also laid the foundations of Rome's first sewer system. They drained the swamp at the foot of the Palatine. This later became the place where Rome's **Forum** (fōr' uhm), or the public square, was built. The Forum housed a palace, government buildings, and law courts.

The Etruscans made a contribution in the area of language as well. They borrowed the Greek alphabet and made some changes in it. The Romans, in turn, borrowed the Etruscan alphabet.

The Romans also borrowed some Etruscan customs. One was the fights of enslaved people held at Etruscan funerals. These were models for the **gladiatorial** (glad' ē uh tōr ē uhl) **games** with which the Romans amused themselves. These games were fights between armed men, between men and animals, between women and dwarfs, and between animals. Another custom borrowed from the Etruscans was the **triumph** (trī' uhmf), or the parade-like welcome given a Roman hero returning from battle.

In addition, the Romans borrowed Etruscan symbols of authority. One of these was the **fasces** (fas' ēz), or a bundle of rods bound around an ax. It became the symbol of a Roman ruler's power to beat or execute other people.

The Etruscans also introduced the Romans to certain religious beliefs. These included soothsayers and gods with human forms. The Etruscans built the first temple on the Capitoline (kap' uh tuh līn), one of the seven hills of Rome. Today, it is the center of Rome's **municipal** (myū nis' uh puhl), or city, government.

The Romans founded their cities according to a ritual borrowed from the Etruscans. Soothsayers read omens that told where the city's boundaries should be. A ditch was dug to mark the boundaries. The plow used to dig the ditch had a bronze blade and was pulled by a white bull and cow yoked together. Workers then dug a trench at the center of the city. After each of the city's founders had tossed a handful of earth into the trench, the priests took over. They laid out the main street and determined the principal cross street. The place where the two streets met was marked by a stone.

Etruscan Gold Clasp

Reading Check
What buildings were found at the Roman **Forum?**

Reading Check
What was the model for the Roman **gladiatorial games?** When did the Etruscans and the Romans hold a **triumph?**

Reading Check
What did the **fasces** symbolize during Roman times?

Reading Check
What is a **municipal** government?

EXTENDING THE CONTENT

Mussolini's Fascist party, organized after World War I with the goal of restoring Italy's national pride and prosperity, adopted symbols from ancient Rome that they admired. The party's name and symbol was an ancient Roman-Etruscan symbol—the fasces. This symbol of the power to punish was originally a bundle of elm or birch rods tied tightly around an ax with a red strap.

Evaluate

Assign Chapter 13 **Performance Assessment Activity** in the TCR.

Administer the **Chapter 13 Test** in the TCR. Testmaker available.

Reteach

Organize the class into three groups and assign each group a section. Have the groups write questions about the main concepts in the sections. Have groups exchange questions and answer them.

Assign Chapter 13 **Reteaching Activity** in the TCR.

Enrich

Have students research and report on the Roman poet Virgil, and on the influence of Homer's *Iliad* and *Odyssey* on Virgil's epic poem, the *Aeneid*.

Assign Chapter 13 **Enrichment Activity** in the TCR.

CLOSE

Ask students to discuss how the information historians know about Etruscan culture might be distorted since they are able only to find artifacts of the very wealthy Etruscans.

 Use **Interactive Tutor Self-Assessment Software** to review Section 3.

Self-Check Quiz gives students an interactive chapter tutorial. Have them access ***Chapter 13 Quiz*** at humanheritage.glencoe.com

---

Reading Check
What two worlds did the Romans think came together at the **mundus?**

The Etruscans believed that the stone covered a shaft leading to the underworld. Three times a year, an Etruscan priest lifted the stone to allow the souls of the dead to return to Earth. The Romans believed the place where the two streets met was the **mundus** (muhn′ duhs), or the meeting point for the worlds of the living and the dead.

Etruscans were not the first to develop or use many of the ideas and practices the Romans borrowed from them. They were, however, the people who brought these ideas to the notice of the Romans. Thus, they played an important role in the development of Roman civilization.

Section 3 Assessment

1. **Define:** Forum, gladiatorial games, triumph, fasces, municipal, mundus.
2. What contributions did the Etruscans make to the Roman language?
3. How did the Etruscans and Romans establish their cities?

Critical Thinking
4. **Distinguishing Fact From Opinion** "The Latins benefited from Etruscan rule." What facts support this opinion?

Graphic Organizer Activity

5. Draw this diagram, and use it to show Etruscan contributions to the Romans.

Chapter Summary & Study Guide

1. According to legend, Rome was founded by Romulus and Remus on the Palatine.
2. Some of the earliest farming settlements at Rome were built by the Latins.
3. The main occupation of the Latins was farming.
4. The Etruscans conquered Rome in 616 B.C. and took control of northern Italy.
5. The Etruscans enjoyed life and had a strong sense of social order.
6. The Etruscans were noted throughout the Mediterranean world as traders and pirates.
7. Religion was important to the Etruscans, and they went to soothsayers to find ways to please their many gods.
8. The Romans learned many things from the Etruscans, including use of the arch in building, an alphabet, and a ritual for establishing cities.

Self-Check Quiz

Visit the *Human Heritage* Web site at **humanheritage.glencoe.com** and click on ***Chapter 13—Self-Check Quiz*** to assess your understanding of this chapter.

Section 3 Assessment Answers

1. All terms are defined in the text glossary.
2. They borrowed the Greek alphabet, changed it, and passed it on to the Romans.
3. Soothsayers told where a city's boundaries should be, and a ditch was dug to mark them. Then the priests laid out the main street and cross streets and marked the intersection with a stone.
4. Facts should include specific skills, ideas, or customs that improved the quality of life for Latins, such as the construction of a sewer system or use of the arch to build bridges.
5. Sample contributions: the arch, the forum, gladiatorial games, customs like the triumph, symbols such as the fasces, certain religious beliefs, and so on.

Assign Chapter 13 **Section 3 Quiz** in TCR. Testmaker available.

Using Key Terms

Imagine you are an archaeologist studying the ruins of an Etruscan city for the first time. Use the following words to write a letter describing some of the exciting things that you have discovered.

social order	soothsayers	omens
catacombs	necropolis	Forum
gladiatorial games	triumph	fasces
municipal	mundus	

Understanding Main Ideas

1. What part of Italy did the Etruscans dominate?
2. How did the kind of shoes the Etruscans wore help them in battle?
3. What group of people owned most of the land in Etruria?
4. Why did the Etruscans build their temples to face east?
5. How have experts learned much of what they know about Etruscan life?
6. Who was the first Etruscan ruler of Rome?
7. What customs did the Romans borrow from the Etruscans?
8. What religious beliefs did the Etruscans intoduce to the Romans?

Critical Thinking

1. Compare the role of women in Etruria with their role in Greek civilization.
2. What role did religion play in Etruscan life? How did Etruscan religious ideas differ from the religious ideas of the Greeks?
3. What would you have enjoyed the most about living in Etruria? Explain.
4. Was the Etruscan conquest of Rome good for the Romans? Explain why or why not.

Graphic Organizer Activity

Culture Draw a diagram like the one shown, and use it to compare the role of women in Etruria with the role of women in most Greek city-states.

Greek Women — Both — Etruscan Women

 Geography in History

Location Look at the map on page 211. If the people of Etruria were attacked by another empire, from what direction and by what means would the attack come? What geographic feature might protect Etruria? Draw a map showing the most likely routes of a possible attack.

Using Your Journal

Review any details you may have noted about contributions made by the Etruscans to world civilization. Prepare an illustrated chart showing some of the contributions of Etruscan architecture in the area where you live.

Bonus Test Question

For Chapter 13 Test
You are a stranger leaving an Etruscan city with one of its citizens. Outside the city, the citizen tells you that you are looking at a *necropolis*. Describe what you see. *(rows of mounds of earth piled above tombs, wide streets that open into plazas)*

Using Your Journal

Charts will vary, but students might include the arch, bridges, sewer systems, and the public square.

 Geography in History

Answers will vary but should include attacks coming from the sea, down rivers, or overland from north or south. Protection came from two mountain ranges.

Using Key Terms

Letters will vary but should include all the key terms.

Understanding Main Ideas

1. Etruria and eventually all of northern Italy, including the Latin village on the Palatine
2. They gave them better footing on rough or hilly ground.
3. a few wealthy families
4. because the Etruscans believed the east and the left were lucky
5. from Etruscan tombs
6. Lucius Tarquinius
7. gladiatorial games, the triumph, and the fasces
8. soothsayers and gods with human forms

Critical Thinking

1. Etruscan women danced, took part in public celebrations, and could own property. Greek women could not attend the Olympic Games or go out without a chaperon.
2. Religion influenced Etruscan building of temples and cities, and ceremonies, songs, and dances. The Greeks were not afraid of their gods, as Etruscans were.
3. Answers will vary but students should provide reasons for their conclusions.
4. Answers will vary but Etruscans made contributions to many Roman achievements.

Graphic Organizer Activity

Answers will vary, but comparisons should reveal that Etruscan women had greater personal freedom than Greek women. As a variation, you might assign students to compare women in specific city-states (such as Sparta or Athens) with Etruscan women.

Chapter 14 Planning Guide

Objectives	Reproducible Resources	Multimedia Resources
Section 1 **The Government** Describe how the government of the Roman Republic was formed.	Reproducible Lesson Plan Chapter 14 Vocabulary and Guided Reading Activity Reading Essentials and Study Guide 14-1 Chapter 14 Chart and Graph Skill Activity Chapter 14 Enrichment Activity Section 1 Quiz	Vocabulary PuzzleMaker Interactive Tutor Self-Assessment Software ExamView® Pro Testmaker Glencoe Skillbuilder Interactive Workbook, Level 1 Presentation Plus!
Section 2 **Roman Expansion** Explain how the Roman Republic was able to expand and protect its territory.	Reproducible Lesson Plan Reading Essentials and Study Guide 14-2 Chapter 14 Cooperative Learning Activity Chapter 14 Geography and Map Activity Section 2 Quiz	Vocabulary PuzzleMaker Interactive Tutor Self-Assessment Software ExamView® Pro Testmaker Glencoe Skillbuilder Interactive Workbook, Level 1
Section 3 **The Punic Wars** Describe the Punic Wars and their effect on the Roman Republic.	Reproducible Lesson Plan Reading Essentials and Study Guide 14-3 Section 3 Quiz	Vocabulary PuzzleMaker Interactive Tutor Self-Assessment Software ExamView® Pro Testmaker Glencoe Skillbuilder Interactive Workbook, Level 1
Section 4 **Effects of Conquest** Discuss how the effects of conquest changed the Roman economy and government.	Reproducible Lesson Plan Reading Essentials and Study Guide 14-4 Section 4 Quiz	Vocabulary PuzzleMaker Interactive Tutor Self-Assessment Software ExamView® Pro Testmaker Glencoe Skillbuilder Interactive Workbook, Level 1
Section 5 **Roman Leadership** Analyze how reformers and generals attempted to save the Roman Republic.	Reproducible Lesson Plan Reading Essentials and Study Guide 14-5 Chapter 14 Activity Book Activity Unit 5 Primary Sources Reading Section 5 Quiz	Teaching Transparencies and Activities 14A & 14B Vocabulary PuzzleMaker ExamView® Pro Testmaker Glencoe Skillbuilder Interactive Workbook, Level 1
Chapter 14 **Review and Evaluation**	Chapter 14 Reteaching Activity Chapter 14 Performance Assessment Activity Spanish Chapter Summary and Glossary Chapter 14 Test	Vocabulary PuzzleMaker Interactive Tutor Self-Assessment Software Glencoe Skillbuilder Interactive Workbook, Level 1 Audiocassettes* ExamView® Pro Testmaker

*Also available in Spanish.

Presentation Plus!
Use Glencoe's **Presentation Plus!** multimedia teacher tool to easily present dynamic lessons that visually excite your students. Using Microsoft® PowerPoint, you can customize the presentations to create your own personalized lessons.

Interactive Lesson Planner

Planning has never been easier! Using this CD-ROM, organize your week, month, semester, or year with all the help you need. The **Interactive Lesson Planner** gives you access to all of the blackline masters which accompany *Human Heritage.*

✓ PERFORMANCE ASSESSMENT ACTIVITIES

The Arts Have students prepare a visual "tour" of modern Rome and the remnants of the ancient Roman civilization. They should present illustrations, diagrams, and pictures while providing information as "tour guides."

CHAPTER RESOURCES

READINGS FOR THE STUDENT

Burrell, Roy. *The Romans: Rebuilding the Past*. Oxford University Press, 1991. Historical outline of ancient Rome.

Tingay, Graham. *Julius Caesar*. Cambridge University Press, 1991. Account of the life and achievements of Julius Caesar.

Windrow, Martin. *The Roman Legionary*. Franklin Watts, 1984. Historical background and detailed information on the Roman soldier's training and duties, weapons, armor, equipment, and daily life.

READINGS FOR THE TEACHER

Asimov, Isaac. *The Roman Republic*. Houghton Mifflin, 1966. Focuses on Rome's rise to power from the founding of the city.

The following videotape programs are available from Glencoe to enrich Chapter 14:

- **Ancient Rome**
  0-7670-1263-1
- **Julius Caesar: Master of the Romans**
  0-7670-0572-4
- **The Lost Legions of Rome**
  1-56501-952-0

To order, call Glencoe at 1-800-334-7344. To find classroom resources to accompany many of these videos, check the following home pages:

A&E Television: http://www.aetv.com
The History Channel:
http://www.historychannel.com

 NATIONAL GEOGRAPHIC SOCIETY | **Teacher's Corner**

INDEX TO NATIONAL GEOGRAPHIC MAGAZINE

The following articles relate to this chapter:

- "Roman Shipwrecks," by Robert D. Ballard, April 1998.
- "Roman Legacy," by T.R. Reid, August 1997.
- "Roman Empire," by T.R. Reid, July 1997.
- "Brindisi Bronzes," by O. Louis Mazzatenta, April 1995.

NATIONAL GEOGRAPHIC SOCIETY PRODUCTS AVAILABLE FROM GLENCOE

To order the following, call Glencoe at 1-800-334-7344:

- *PicturePack: Ancient Rome (Transparencies)*
- *PictureShow: Ancient Civilizations: Greece and Rome (CD-ROM)*
- *Ancient Civilizations: Ancient Rome (Poster Set)*
- *PicturePack: Ancient Civilizations Library, Part I (Transparencies)*

ADDITIONAL NATIONAL GEOGRAPHIC SOCIETY PRODUCTS

To order the following, call National Geographic at 1-800-368-2728:

- *In the Shadow of Vesuvius (Video or Videodisc)*
- *Romans (Map)*

Access *National Geographic's* new dynamic MapMachine Web site and other geography resources at:
http://www.nationalgeographic.com/
http://www.nationalgeographic.com/maps/

KEY TO ABILITY LEVELS

Teaching strategies have been coded for varying learning styles and abilities.

L1 Level 1 activities are **basic** activities and should be within the ability range of all students.

L2 Level 2 activities are **average** activities and should be within the ability range of the average to above-average student.

L3 Level 3 activities are **challenging** activities designed for the ability range of above-average students.

ELL ELL activities should be within the ability range of English Language Learning students.

OVERVIEW

Chapter 14 traces Rome's development as a republic.

➤ **Section 1** summarizes the rise of Roman democracy.
➤ **Section 2** describes the army's role in the Roman Republic.
➤ **Section 3** discusses Rome's rise to power in the Mediterranean region.
➤ **Section 4** analyzes the effects of foreign conquests.
➤ **Section 5** examines the attempts to solve the Republic's problems.

CHAPTER OBJECTIVES

After reading Chapter 14, students will be able to:
1. describe how the Roman government was organized.
2. explain how the Roman Republic was able to expand.
3. summarize how the effects of conquest changed the Roman economy and government.
4. discuss efforts to save the Roman Republic.

EXAMINING ARTIFACTS

Have students study the artifacts. Then ask: What do you think was one of the reasons the Roman Republic grew so strong? *(the power and/or loyalty of legionaries)* Call on students to describe what the eagle symbolizes to them. Tell them to decide whether this was an accurate symbol for the Roman Republic, as they read through the chapter.

PERFORMANCE ASSESSMENT ✓

Use the Performance Assessment Activities on page 218B to help you evaluate students as they complete the chapter.

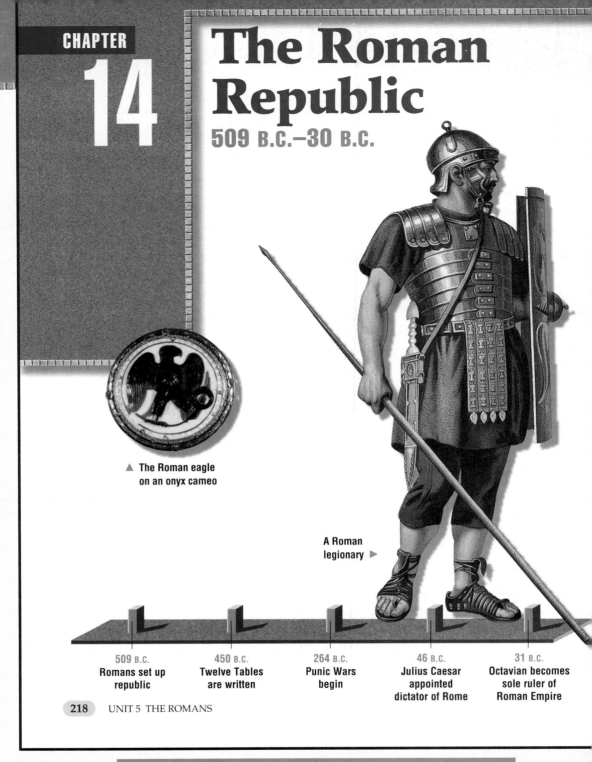

CHAPTER

14

The Roman Republic
509 B.C.–30 B.C.

▲ The Roman eagle on an onyx cameo

A Roman legionary ▶

509 B.C.	450 B.C.	264 B.C.	46 B.C.	31 B.C.
Romans set up republic	**Twelve Tables are written**	**Punic Wars begin**	**Julius Caesar appointed dictator of Rome**	**Octavian becomes sole ruler of Roman Empire**

218 UNIT 5 THE ROMANS

TEACHING RESOURCES

TEACHER PLANNING AND SUPPORT

▱ Reproducible Lesson Plan
▱ Block Scheduling Implementation Guide
▱ Videodisc Bar Code Correlation
💿 Presentation Plus!

REVIEW AND REINFORCEMENT

▱ Reading Essentials and Study Guide 14-1, 14-2, 14-3, 14-4, 14-5
▱ Chapter 14 Vocabulary and Guided Reading Activity
▯ Vocabulary PuzzleMaker Software

 Teaching Transparencies 14A & 14B
▱ Chapter 14 Reteaching Activity
▱ Chapter 14 Cooperative Learning Activity
▱ Chapter 14 Activity Book Activity
▱ Chapter 14 Chart and Graph Skill Activity
▯ Interactive Tutor Self-Assessment Software

APPLICATION AND HANDS-ON ACTIVITIES

▱ Daily World History, Geography, and Culture Question
▱ Unit 5 Hands-On History Lab Activity

Chapter Focus

 Read to Discover

- How the government of the Roman Republic was organized.
- How the Roman Republic was able to expand and protect its territory.
- How the effects of conquest changed the Roman economy and government.
- How reformers attempted to save the Roman Republic.

 Terms to Learn | **People to Know** | **Places to Locate**

Terms to Learn	People to Know	Places to Locate
republic	Tarquin the Proud	Carthage
patricians	Hannibal Barca	Sicily
plebeians	Tiberius	Gaul
consuls	Gracchus	Corinth
legionaries	Julius Caesar	
dictator	Mark Antony	
triumvirate	Octavian	

Why It's Important   In 509 B.C., the Romans overthrew Tarquin (tar' kwin) the Proud, their Etruscan king, and set up a **republic**. Under this form of government, people choose their rulers. However, not everyone had an equal say in the Roman Republic. The **patricians** (puh trish' uhnz)—members of the oldest and richest families—were the only ones who could hold public office or perform certain religious rituals. Poorer citizens, known as **plebeians** (pli bē' uhnz), paid taxes and served in the army. Yet they could not marry patricians or hold office. If they fell into debt, they could be sold into slavery.

In later years, reformers would take steps to make the Roman Republic more democratic. The idea of a government chosen by the people would serve as a model for future generations, including the founders of the United States.

SECTION 1 The Government

At the head of the Roman Republic were two **consuls** (kon' suhlz) who were chosen each year. They were administrators and military leaders. Each had the power to **veto,** or say no to, the acts of the other. Both had to agree before any law was passed.

Next in importance was the Senate. It was made up of 300 men called senators who were chosen for life. The Senate handled the daily problems of government. It advised the consuls.

 Chapter Overview
Visit the *Human Heritage* Web site at **humanheritage.glencoe.com** and click on *Chapter 14—Chapter Overviews* to preview this chapter.

☑ **Reading Check**
What is a **republic?**
Who were the **patricians** and the **plebeians?**

☑ **Reading Check**
How long did the **consuls** hold power?
How did the **veto** prevent a consul from becoming too powerful?

GEOGRAPHY ACTIVITIES
- Chapter 14 Geography and Map Activity
- Social Studies Outline Map Resource Book

INTERDISCIPLINARY CONNECTIONS
- Focus on World Art Print 9, *Girl with Writing Tablet*
- World Music: Cultural Traditions

ENRICHMENT AND EXTENSION
- World History Primary Source Document Library CD-ROM
- Chapter 14 Enrichment Activity
- Foods Around the World

ASSESSMENT AND EVALUATION
- Chapter 14 Performance Assessment Activity
- Chapter 14 Section Quizzes 14-1, 14-2, 14-3, 14-4, 14-5
- Chapter 14 Test
- Chapter 14 ExamView® Pro Testmaker Software
- Chapter 14 Digests Audiocassettes Activities and Tests

SPANISH RESOURCES
- Chapter 14 Spanish Chapter Summary and Glossary
- Chapter 14 Spanish Chapter Digests Audiocassettes Activities and Tests

---

 Chapter Overview introduces students to chapter content and key terms. Have them access **Chapter 14 Overview** at **humanheritage.glencoe.com**

FOCUS

🗺 **Bellringer**

Ask students to write what first comes to their minds when they hear this phrase: *fields upon fields of Roman legions.*

Motivational Activity

Call on students to read their responses. Ask: What are the implications of keeping a standing army? (*Students may mention the need for defense or the use of armies for conquest.*)

GUIDE TO READING

Reading Strategy

Ask students to read "Why It's Important" and summarize the chapter's main theme. (*Efforts to make the Roman Republic more democratic became the model for future generations.*)

Vocabulary Precheck

Ask students to define each of the "Terms to Learn." **L1** **ELL**

💾 Use the Vocabulary PuzzleMaker for Chapter 14. **L1**

📁 Assign Chapter 14 Vocabulary and Guided Reading Activity.

📁 Assign Reading Essentials and Study Guide 14-1.

☑ **Reading Check Answer**
In a **republic,** people choose their rulers. **Patricians** were members of the oldest and richest families and **plebeians** were poorer citizens.

☑ **Reading Check Answer**
The **consuls** held power for one year. The **veto** allowed one consul to negate the other.

TEACH

Guided Practice

L3 Language Arts Have students imagine they are well-educated plebeians in the early days of the Roman Republic. Have them write letters to the Roman Senate demanding representation and written laws.

☑ **Reading Check Answer**
Tribunes protected the rights of the plebeians.

🖫 Use **Interactive Tutor Self-Assessment Software** to review Section 1.

CAPTION ANSWER

The Senate handled the daily problems of government. It advised the consuls, discussed ways to deal with other countries, proposed laws, and approved public contracts for building roads and temples.

DID YOU KNOW ??

The consuls were in charge of the state treasury, were judges in all law cases, and were commanders in chief of the army during wars.

MAKING CONNECTIONS

➤➤ **Citizenship** The Twelve Tables outlined how Roman citizens were to act in public. The Roman people considered knowledge of the law so important that Roman schoolboys had to learn the laws of the Twelve Tables by heart.

ROMAN SENATE   This painting shows the famous orator Cicero making a speech attacking a political opponent. **What duties did the Senate perform in the Roman Republic?**

☑ **Reading Check**
What role did the **tribunes** play in Roman government?

It discussed ways to deal with other countries, proposed laws, and approved public contracts for building roads and temples.

Judges, assemblies, and **tribunes** (trib′ yūnz), or government officials who protected the rights of plebeians, were also part of the Roman government. All Roman citizens belonged to the assemblies, which could declare war or agree to peace terms.

Until about 450 B.C., Roman laws were not written down. In that year laws were carved on 12 bronze tablets known as the Twelve Tables. These were placed in the Forum. The laws applied to both patricians and plebeians. Most were about wills, property rights, and court actions. The laws on the Twelve Tables became the foundation for all future Roman law.

The election of tribunes and recording of laws were the first steps to a more democratic government. Later, more plebeian demands were met. By about 250 B.C., no one could be sold into slavery because of debt. Plebeians could hold public office.

Section 1 Assessment

1. **Define:** republic, patricians, plebeians, consuls, veto, tribunes.
2. What were some restrictions placed on the plebeians during the early years of the Roman Republic?

Critical Thinking

3. **Demonstrating Reasoned Judgment** Why do you think it was important for the Romans to have laws written down?

Graphic Organizer Activity

4. Draw this diagram, and use it to describe each part of Roman government.

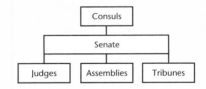

Section 1 Assessment Answers

1. republic, government where people choose their rulers (p. 219); patricians, the oldest and richest Roman families (p. 219); plebeians, poorer people of Rome (p. 219); consuls, heads of the Roman Republic (p. 219); veto, to say no to (p. 219); tribunes, Roman officials elected to protect the lower class (p. 220)

2. They could not marry patricians or serve in the government, and if they got into debt, they could be enslaved.

3. Answers will vary, but students could note that recording laws makes them enforceable.

4. Descriptions should match each of the parts of Roman government discussed in Section 1.

Assign the Chapter 14 **Section 1 Quiz** in the TCR. Testmaker available.

SECTION 2 Roman Expansion

Once the Romans had set up a republic, they worked to protect it. They were afraid that the Etruscans would try to get back control of Rome. To prevent this, the Romans crossed the Tiber River and conquered several Etruscan cities. Roman land now bordered that of other Italian people. To protect their new boundaries, the Romans either conquered their neighbors or made alliances with them. By 290 B.C., Rome was the leading power in central Italy. By 275 B.C., it ruled the whole peninsula. By 146 B.C., Rome ruled most of the Mediterranean world.

The Romans were able to gain territory because they had a strong army that was organized into **legions** (lē' juhnz). Each legion contained some 5,000 soldiers called **legionaries** (lē' juh ner ēz) and was divided into groups of 60 to 120 soldiers.

The legion had several advantages over the phalanx. The legion was smaller and could move faster. Soldiers in a phalanx fought as a group and attacked from only one direction. Each legionary depended on his own fighting ability. The groups within a legion could split off from the main body and attack from the sides and the rear as well as the front.

Then...&Now

Rank and File The basic unit of the Roman legion was the *maniple*—120 soldiers standing side by side in ranks of 10 and lined up one behind another in files of 12. The term *rank and file,* which refers to the ordinary members of an organization, comes from this military system.

Reading Check
How did Roman **legions** differ from the phalanx? How many **legionaries** were in each legion?

Linking Across Time

Citizen-Soldiers During the early years of the Roman republic, all male citizens were required to serve in the army (below). Today military service continues to be an important responsibility of citizenship in democratic nations such as the United States (right). **Why did the use of citizen-soldiers help ensure the loyalty of legionaries to Rome?**

CHAPTER 14 THE ROMAN REPUBLIC **221**

Reading Check Answer
Roman **legions** were smaller and could move faster than the phalanx. There were some 5,000 **legionaries** in each legion.

Use the **Vocabulary Puzzle-Maker** to create crossword and word search puzzles.

Linking Across Time

Answers will vary, but most students will focus on the desire of citizens to protect both their rights and their homeland.

GEOGRAPHY AND HISTORY

The Romans established military settlements—called *coloniae*—throughout Italy to defend strategic heights over river crossings. To link these *coloniae,* the legions forged a chain of roads up and down the Italian peninsula. As war yielded gradually to peace, some of these roads became major trade routes.

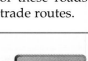

The following videotape programs are available from Glencoe to enrich Chapter 14:

- **Ancient Rome**
- **The Lost Legions of Rome**

To find classroom resources to accompany these videos, check the following home page:
A&E Television:
http://www.aetv.com

COOPERATIVE LEARNING

Review information on Roman legions in Section 2. Then divide the class into groups, and tell each group of students to imagine that they are army recruiters for the Roman republic. Their job is to enlist citizen-soldiers in the military. Assign them to design recruitment posters that might be hung in the Forum or other public place. You might ask volunteers to call a local recruitment office for one of the military services and request contemporary posters. These can be hung in the classroom as models. When students are done, have them present their posters to the class as a whole.

Assign Chapter 14 *Cooperative Learning Activity* in the TCR.

💾 Use **Interactive Tutor Self-Assessment Software** to review Section 2.

💾 Use the **Vocabulary Puzzle-Maker** to create crossword and word search puzzles.

Roman Bronze Lamp

Legionaries were well trained. They spent hours practicing with their double-edged iron swords. They went on long marches every day. Before going to sleep, they had to build complete fortified camps, even when the legion would stay in an area only one night. They built roads out of lava blocks so soldiers and supplies could move forward more rapidly.

The Romans were mild rulers. At first, they did not tax the people they conquered. They let the conquered people keep their own governments and take care of their own affairs. Some were even allowed to become Roman citizens. In return, the conquered people were expected to serve in the Roman army and to support Rome's foreign policy. As a result, many enemies of Rome became loyal Roman allies.

Section 2 Assessment

1. **Define:** legions, legionaries.
2. Why were the Romans able to gain territory?
3. What was life like for a Roman legionary?

Critical Thinking

4. **Drawing Conclusions** How would you describe the way the Romans treated people they conquered, and do you think this was wise? Explain.

Graphic Organizer Activity

5. Draw a chart like this one, and use it to show the cause and effects of Roman conquest of Etruscan cities.

| Cause | → | Conquest of Etruscan Cities | → | Effects |

SECTION 3 The Punic Wars

By 264 B.C., the Romans had conquered some Greek city-states in southern Italy. This brought them into contact with the Phoenician city of Carthage. Carthage controlled most of North and West Africa, most of what is now Spain, and some islands off the coast of Italy. Carthage also ruled the western half of Sicily (sis' uh lē), a large island at the toe of the Italian "boot." The Romans felt threatened by the Carthaginians (kar thuh jin' ē uhnz). They also wanted Sicily's granaries.

The First Punic War In 264 B.C., the Romans and Carthaginians clashed. The war that broke out lasted for 23 years. It was the first of three wars between Rome and Carthage that came to be known as the Punic (pyū' nik) Wars.

Carthage's military strength lay in its navy, while Rome's lay in its army. At first, the Romans had no navy. They built their first fleet to fight the Carthaginians. The Romans modeled their ships after a Carthaginian warship they found abandoned on a beach. They made one improvement on the Carthaginian model. They added a *corvus* (kor' vuhs), or a kind of movable bridge, to the front of each ship. The Romans knew they could not outsail the Carthaginians, but believed they could outfight them. The corvus allowed soldiers to board an enemy ship and fight hand-to-hand on its decks. In a sense, it changed a sea war into a land war.

The Romans lost many ships and men in storms during the First Punic War. Yet, in the end, they defeated the Carthaginians. In 241 B.C., the Carthaginians agreed to make peace and left Sicily.

Hannibal and the Second Punic War   In 218 B.C., the Second Punic War began. At that time, the Carthaginians, led by General Hannibal Barca (han' uh buhl bar' ka), attacked the Roman army by land from the north. Hannibal and his troops surprised the Roman army by marching from Spain through southern Gaul (gol), or present-day France, and then crossing the Alps into Italy. They brought elephants with them across the snow-covered mountains to help break through the Roman lines.

Winning victory after victory, Hannibal's army fought its way to the gates of Rome. When the Carthaginian army got to Rome, however, it did not have the heavy equipment needed to

HANNIBAL   Hannibal's army, with elephants, faced many dangers in its attack on Rome. The elephants had to be floated on barges across rivers and brought over the snow-capped Alps. **Why did Hannibal's attack on the city of Rome fail?**

HISTORY Online

Student Web Activity
Visit the *Human Heritage* Web site at **humanheritage.glencoe.com** and click on *Chapter 14— Student Web Activities* to find out more about the Punic Wars.

Fun Facts . . .

Carthage Marcus Portius Cato, a prominent statesman and writer, believed that Carthage posed a great threat to Rome. He reportedly ended every speech—no matter what the subject—with "Carthage must be destroyed!"

L1 Geography: Region Suggest students work together to develop a chart on the chalkboard or posterboard summarizing the three Punic Wars. For each war, include the dates, the areas where the war was fought, the locations of major battles, and the final outcome. **ELL**

MAKING CONNECTIONS

➤➤ **History** Hannibal's father was a Carthaginian general during the first Punic War. He made Hannibal take an oath to never be friends with the Romans. Hannibal was commander in chief of the Carthaginian army by age 26.

CAPTION ANSWER

because Hannibal's army did not have the heavy equipment needed to break down Rome's walls, and it was short on supplies and soldiers

HISTORY Online

Student Web Activity objectives, goals, and answers can be found at the *Chapter 14 Web Activity Lesson Plan* at **humanheritage.glencoe.com**

MEETING SPECIAL NEEDS

Have gifted learners debate the following topic: *The wars between Rome and Carthage were worth the short-term and long-term costs for Rome.* Half of the group should defend the statement, the other half should argue against the statement. The rest of the class can act as the audience and decide which side presented the most persuasive arguments.

📁 Refer to *Inclusion for the Middle School Social Studies Classroom: Strategies and Activities* for additional resources.

LINKING PAST TO PRESENT

Speakers of English are often speakers of Latin without knowing it. Everyday terms like "A.M." and "P.M." are short for the Latin *ante meridiem* and *post meridiem*—"before noon" and "after noon." The *Exit* sign over a door is Latin for "he (she, it) goes out." Anyone who has joined an *ad hoc* committee, gone to an *alumni* reunion, figured something *per capita*, or added *P.S. (post scriptum)* to a letter, has used Latin.

Use **Interactive Tutor Self-Assessment Software** to review Section 3.

MAKING CONNECTIONS

➤➤ **History** One of Rome's opponents, King Pyrrhus of Epirus, won two difficult victories over the Romans in 280 and 279 B.C. He sustained such great losses, however, that he reportedly exclaimed, "Another such victory and we are lost."

Use the **Vocabulary Puzzle-Maker** to create crossword and word search puzzles.

Hannibal's Strength
Hannibal began crossing the Alps with about 46,000 troops and 37 elephants. He emerged with 26,000 troops and almost no elephants. A Roman general proclaimed: "They are ghosts and shadows of men already half dead. All their strength has been crushed and beaten out of them by the Alpine crags." The general was wrong. The Gauls, who were enemies of the Romans, joined Hannibal and boosted his army to almost 50,000.

batter down the city's walls. It could not get more supplies because the Roman navy controlled the sea.

Unable to capture Rome, Hannibal and his troops roamed the countryside of southern Italy for 15 years. They raided and burned towns and destroyed crops. Then, the Romans attacked Carthage, and Hannibal was called home to defend it. Hannibal lost his first battle—and the war—at the town of Zama (zā' muh). The power of Carthage was broken.

In 201 B.C., Carthage agreed to pay Rome a huge sum of money and to give up all its territories, including Spain. The Spanish resources of copper, gold, lead, and iron now belonged to the Romans.

The Third Punic War   Following the Second Punic War, there was peace for about 50 years. Then, Carthage began to show signs of regaining power. To prevent this, the Romans attacked in 149 B.C., the Third Punic War. They burned Carthage and plowed salt into its fields so nothing would grow. They killed the Carthaginians or sold them into slavery.

That same year, 146 B.C., the Greek city-state of Corinth (kor' inth) and some of its allies refused to obey a Roman order. The Romans attacked Corinth and burned it to the ground. Rome already controlled Macedonia and Syria. Now, it added Greece to the areas under its rule. Thus, Rome became the leading power of the Mediterranean world.

Section 3 Assessment

1. What territory did Carthage control in 264 B.C.?
2. What happened to Carthage in the Third Punic War?
3. How did Rome become the leading power of the Mediterranean world?

Critical Thinking

4. **Predicting Consequences** What might have happened to Rome if it had lost the Punic Wars?

Graphic Organizer Activity

5. Draw a chart like this one, and use it to summarize the outcome of each of the Punic Wars.

Punic Wars	Outcome
First	
Second	
Third	

SECTION 4 Effects of Conquest

The conquests and the wealth that came with them changed Rome's economy and government. Among the changes were the replacement of small farms by large estates, the coming of slavery, a movement from farms to cities, and the decline of the Roman Republic.

Agricultural Changes

Rome's conquests brought changes in agriculture. One change was in the size and purpose of farms. Most Romans had been small farmers who believed in hard work and service to Rome. Now, the small farms were replaced by large estates called **latifundias** (lat uh fuhn' dē uhs). The small farms had grown wheat for food. Latifundias, on the other hand, produced crops, sheep, and cattle for sale at market. Some contained olive groves and vineyards. Because they no longer grew their own wheat, the Romans began to import wheat from such conquered areas as Sicily and North Africa.

The main reason for this change in Roman agriculture was Hannibal's invasion. While his soldiers were in Italy, they lived off the land. To prevent them from getting food, Roman farmers burned their fields and crops. By the time the Second Punic War was over, much of the land was ruined. Most Roman farmers did not have money to fix up their farms or restore the land. Only patricians and rich business people had that kind of money. They bought the small farms and combined them to make latifundias.

Another change in agriculture was in who worked the land. When Rome first began expanding, the Romans did not enslave the people they conquered. By 146 B.C., that was no longer true. The Romans were impressed by the wealth of Greece, Syria, and Carthage. Since those areas had widespread slavery, the Romans sent thousands of prisoners to Rome as enslaved people. Most lived and worked on latifundias.

From Farm to City

The farmers who had sold their land had little choice. They could stay and work the land for the new owners or move to the city. Almost all of them moved to Rome.

There the farmers crowded into wooden apartment buildings six or more stories high. Living conditions were terrible. The aqueducts that brought water to the city were not connected to apartment buildings. Neither were the sewers that carried away waste. Buildings often caught fire or collapsed. Such diseases as typhus (tī' fuhs) were common.

Most farmers could not earn a living in the city. Except for construction, Rome had almost no industry. Most businesses were staffed by enslaved people from Greece. About the only way the farmers could get money was by selling their votes to politicians.

Decline of the Roman Republic

As Rome's rule spread beyond Italy, the Romans began to demand taxes, as well as enslaved people, from the areas they conquered. Tax contracts were sold to people called **publicans** (pub' luh kuhnz). They paid Rome ahead of time for the contracts. Then, they collected taxes from the conquered people. The amount of taxes collected was supposed to be no more than 10 percent above the price paid for the contract. Most publicans, however, made extra money.

 Reading Check
What was the purpose of the **latifundias?**

Sculpture of Roman Consul

 Reading Check
Why did Rome sell tax contracts to the **publicans?**

 Reading Check Answer
The **latifundias** produced crops, sheep, and cattle for sale at market.

 GEOGRAPHY AND HISTORY

The technique of people buring their own fields and crops in the path of an invading army is known as a scorched-earth policy. It has been used for centuries by many societies.

DID YOU KNOW ??

In the ancient Roman apartment buildings, five or six people lived in one room.

 Reading Check Answer
Rome sold tax contacts because the **publicans** paid Rome ahead of time.

 NATIONAL GEOGRAPHIC SOCIETY

Use these materials to enrich student understanding of ancient Rome.

NGS PICTUREPACK TRANSPARENCY SET
Ancient Rome

EXTENDING THE CONTENT

Enslaved persons' lives varied dramatically in the Roman Republic.

Those who worked in mines or quarries, or who rowed in the galleys of the navy, lived under brutal conditions. In contrast, educated Greeks taken prisoner might become tutors or stewards in wealthy households, leading lives more comfortable than those of free peasants. One estimate places the number of enslaved persons at one-fourth of the Italian population during Augustus's time.

ROMAN APARTMENTS   Wealthy Romans built brick and stone apartments. They decorated the floors with mosaics and the walls with paintings. These apartment dwellers owned only a few pieces of furniture, most of which were simple in design. **What sort of buildings did poor Romans live in during the Republic?**

By about 135 B.C., Rome was in a great deal of trouble. Because farmers had lost their land, they had also lost their economic and political independence. Merchants had become poorer because rich Romans could get luxuries elsewhere. Artisans had lost business because rich Romans wanted goods from Greece and Syria. Government officials were too busy getting rich to worry about solving the republic's problems.

The gap between rich and poor grew greater. The poor hated the rich for what the rich had done to them. The rich hated and feared the poor. Rome was no longer politically stable.

Section 4 Assessment

1. **Define:** latifundias, publicans.
2. How was Roman agriculture influenced by Hannibal?
3. What was life like in Rome during the decline of the republic?

Critical Thinking

4. **Identifying Central Issues** Why might a large gap between rich and poor present problems for an empire?

Graphic Organizer Activity

5. Draw this diagram, and use it to compare Roman agriculture before and after the rise of the latifundias.

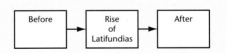

SECTION 5 Roman Leadership

Over the next 100 years, many different popular leaders tried to improve conditions in Rome. Some were reformers, while others were generals.

The Reformers   Tiberius Sempronius Gracchus (tī bir′ ē uhs sem prō nē uhs grak′ uhs) was the first reformer. He thought making small farmers leave their land had caused Rome's troubles.

When he became a tribune in 133 B.C., Tiberius Gracchus wanted to limit the amount of land a person could own. He wanted to divide up public lands and give them to the poor. Another tribune vetoed his idea. Tiberius Gracchus then talked the assembly into putting his idea into effect and getting rid of that tribune.

Tiberius Gracchus ran for a second term as tribune, although it was against the law. To stop him, the Senate staged a riot and had him and hundreds of his followers killed.

In 123 B.C., Tiberius Gracchus's younger brother Gaius (gī′ yuhs) Sempronius Gracchus was elected tribune. He thought moving the poor from the city back to the countryside was the answer to Rome's troubles.

Gaius Gracchus improved and extended the reforms of his brother. He had the government take over the sale of wheat and sell it to the poor below market price. Soon, however, wheat was being given away rather than sold. Nearly one out of every three Romans was receiving free wheat. Meanwhile, the Senate began to feel threatened by some of Gaius Gracchus's ideas and in 121 B.C. had him killed.

The Generals   After the reformers came the generals. In 107 B.C., General Gaius Marius (mar′ ē uhs), a military hero, became consul. The son of a day laborer, Marius was the first lower-class Roman to be elected to such a high office. He was supported by many ex-soldiers who felt the rich and the government had taken advantage of them. Many of the ex-soldiers had been farmers who had lost their farms when they left to serve in the army.

Marius thought he could end Rome's troubles by setting up a professional army. Until this time, only property owners could become legionaries. Marius opened the army to everyone. He convinced the poor to join by offering them pay, land, pensions, and *booty*, or things taken from the enemy in war. Marius's plan helped Rome by providing jobs for many out-of-work Romans. At the same time, it hurt the Roman Republic. Instead of giving loyalty to the government, the soldiers gave it to the general who hired and paid them.

Sculpture of Tiberius Gracchus

CHAPTER 14 THE ROMAN REPUBLIC   **227**

L1 **Critical Thinking** Help students create cause-event-effects graphic organizers on the chalkboard showing the attempts made by reformers and generals to improve conditions in Rome. Create an organizer for each reformer or general. **ELL**

DID YOU KNOW ??

During their terms of office, tribunes could not be away from the city for even one night. They also had to always keep their doors open so that citizens could come to them for help.

 Use the **Vocabulary Puzzle-Maker** to create crossword and word search puzzles.

COOPERATIVE LEARNING

Organize the class into eight groups. Assign each group one of the following Roman leaders: Tiberius Gracchus, Gaius Marius, Lucius Cornelius Sulla, Pompey, Julius Caesar, Mark Antony, and Octavian.

Tell each group to research its assigned leader and write a list of five or six questions, along with the leader's responses, to be used in an interview for a talk show titled "Roman Forum." Then have two members of each group role-play the part of their group's leader and the part of the talk show host of "Roman Forum."

Independent Practice

L2 **Critical Thinking** Have students write two problem-solving questions about the map "The Expansion of the Roman Empire." Then have students work in pairs to exchange and answer one another's questions.

Assign Chapter 14 **Geography and Map Activity** in the TCR.

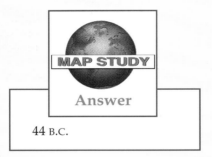

MAP STUDY
Answer

44 B.C.

HOME VIDEO.

The following videotape program is available from Glencoe to enrich Chapter 14:

• **Julius Caesar: Master of the Romans**

To find classroom resources to accompany this video, check the following home page:

A&E Television:
http://www.aetv.com

Reading Check What power does a **dictator** hold? What kind of government exists under a **triumvirate?**

MAP STUDY

REGION Rome gained control of the Italian Peninsula in 275 B.C. **By what year did the Roman Republic**

Marius was opposed by another general, Lucius Cornelius Sulla (kor nēl' yuhs suhl' uh). Sulla had been given a military command that Marius wanted. Marius tried to get the assembly to take the command away from Sulla and give it to him. An angry Sulla marched his army on Rome and seized the city. It was the first time a Roman commander had led his soldiers against the capital.

Civil war broke out. When it was over, Sulla made himself **dictator** (dik' tā tuhr), or absolute ruler, of Rome. Sulla believed the way to end Rome's troubles was to increase the power of the Senate. So, he doubled the Senate's size. He gave the senators more duties and weakened the power of the tribunes. At the same time, he stopped generals from holding the same army command for more than one year at a time.

Julius Caesar When Sulla retired, a new group of generals fought for control of Rome. In 60 B.C., political power passed to a **triumvirate** (trī um' vuhr it), or a group of three persons with equal power. This First Triumvirate was made up of Marcus

The Expansion of the Roman Republic

Rome, 500 B.C.
Start of 1st Punic War, 264 B.C.
End of 3rd Punic War, 146 B.C.
Death of Caesar, 44 B.C.
Hannibal's Route

MULTICULTURAL PERSPECTIVES

The writers of *The Federalists*, a series of articles published in the 1780s supporting the U.S. Constitution, admired Roman republican principles. They considered a single executive officer—a president—as preferable to the "instances of mischief to the republic" such as had been caused by disagreements between consuls and tribunes in ancient Rome.

Licinius Crassus (mar' kus luh sin' ē uhs kras' us), Gnaeus Pompeius (guh nā' uhs pom pē' uhs), and Julius Caesar (jūl' yuhs sē' zuhr). Pompeius, who was also known as Pompey (pom' pē), and Caesar had different ideas about how Rome should be ruled. Pompey believed in a republic that was ruled by upper-class senators. Caesar believed in one-man rule.

After Crassus's death, the two remaining rulers fought for power. Caesar finally gained control after Pompey was murdered in 48 B.C. Caesar was a well-educated politician who had become a soldier. He had both military strength and strong family alliances to back him.

In 58 B.C., Caesar was named governor of a Roman province. There, he built up a large, strong army that was loyal to him. Within seven years, he conquered what is now northern France and Belgium (bel' juhm) and invaded Britain. The Senate began to fear he was growing too strong. So, in 50 B.C., it ordered Caesar to break up his legions and return to Rome. Instead, Caesar entered the city at the head of his troops. By 46 B.C., he was dictator of Rome.

Caesar brought about many reforms. He redistributed state lands in Italy and founded new colonies overseas. This gave land to thousands of ex-soldiers who had none. He began such public works projects as building roads and buildings and draining the marshes around Rome. This gave jobs to thousands of Romans who had not been able to find work. He planned and paid for gladiatorial games that were free to the public. This kept the poor and the idle from turning into unhappy and angry mobs. He doubled the size of the Senate. Although this made each senator less powerful, it gave business people a chance to become senators. He cut back the activities of the publicans. He gave Roman citizenship to Greeks, Spaniards, and Gauls. He adopted a new calendar based on the Egyptian calendar. Called the Julian (jūl' yuhn) calendar, a form of it is still in use today.

Caesar did a great deal for Rome and its people. Still, some Romans were afraid that Caesar planned to make himself king. About 60 men, most of them senators, worked out a plan to kill him. As he entered the Senate on the Ides (ī dz) of March, or March 15, 44 B.C., Caesar was stabbed to death.

End of the Republic   Angered by Caesar's death, the Roman people turned against those who had killed him. Political power passed to another triumvirate. Marcus Antonius (an tō' nē uhs), or Mark Antony, Caesar's closest follower and a popular general, took command of Rome's territories in the East. Octavian (ok tā' vē uhn), Caesar's grand-nephew and adopted son, took charge of the West. Marcus Aemilius Lepidus (uh mēl' ē uhs lep'uhd uhs), one of Caesar's top officers, took over the rule of Africa. All three shared control of the Italian homeland.

People in History

Julius Caesar
102 B.C–44 B.C.

Roman General/ Statesman

Born into one of the oldest patrician families in Rome, Gaius Julius Caesar knew politics could be a dangerous job. Even so, he had a big advantage—the loyalty of the legions who served him. The legions helped Caesar become the reform-minded ruler of Rome, but they could not save him from murder by the senators who felt his popularity and power threatened the republic.

L3 **Language Arts** Have students research the meaning and significance of Caesar's remark, "Veni, vidi, vici," (I came, I saw, I conquered.) concerning one of his campaigns against Pompey. Then have them write a brief explanation of what this tells them about Caesar's personality.

MAKING CONNECTIONS

➤➤ **History** Caesar followed Pompey to Egypt where he met Cleopatra, the sister of the Egyptian king and co-ruler of Egypt. Caesar helped Cleopatra take full control of the Egyptian throne.

LINKING PAST TO PRESENT

Probably the most widely read Latin work in modern times is Julius Caesar's Commentaries on the Gallic Wars—*Commentarii de Bello Gallico.* Many first- or second-year Latin students today read at least part of this Latin classic.

ASSESS

Check for Understanding

Ask students to summarize the main points of the chapter, orally or in writing. Discuss the answers to the Section and Chapter Assessment questions.

Evaluate

Assign Chapter 14 **Performance Assessment Activity** in the TCR.

Administer **Chapter 14 Test** in the TCR. Testmaker available.

MEETING SPECIAL NEEDS

Read brief portions of Shakespeare's *Julius Caesar* to auditory learners. Have students work as individuals or in small groups to present dramatic readings of *Julius Caesar* to the class.

Refer to *Inclusion for the Middle School Social Studies Classroom: Strategies and Activities* for additional resources.

Reteach

Have students explain briefly, in their own words, the importance of each of the following: the government of the Roman Republic, the Punic Wars, Hannibal, latifundia, Gracchus, Marius, Sulla, Julius Caesar, and Octavian.

Assign Chapter 14 **Reteaching Activity** in the TCR.

Enrich

Have students prepare a report on the Roman legions. Encourage students to illustrate their reports. Display the reports in the classroom.

Assign Chapter 14 **Enrichment Activity** in the TCR.

CLOSE

Work with students to prepare a chronology of events and issues that led to the fall of the republic. Have students choose two or three events or issues that they think were the most significant and explain their choices.

Use **Interactive Tutor Self-Assessment Software** to review Section 5.

Self-Check Quiz gives students an interactive chapter tutorial. Have them access **Chapter 14 Quiz** at humanheritage.glencoe.com

For a while, the triumvirate worked. Then, fights broke out among the three leaders. When the fighting ended in 31 B.C., Octavian had won. Within four years, he became sole ruler of the Roman Empire.

Section 5 Assessment

1. **Define:** dictator, triumvirate.
2. Why did civil war break out in Rome?
3. Why did a group of Roman senators murder Julius Caesar?

Critical Thinking

4. **Demonstrating Reasoned Judgment** How effective do you think a triumvirate is as a form of government? Explain.

Graphic Organizer Activity

5. Draw this chart, and use it to summarize the reforms supported by popular leaders during the closing years of the Roman Republic.

Leader	Reform	Effect

Chapter Summary & Study Guide

1. In 509 B.C., the Romans overthrew the Etruscans and set up a republic.
2. About 450 B.C., leaders wrote down Roman laws in the Twelve Tables.
3. By 275 B.C., well-trained Roman legions had taken control of Italy.
4. Between 264 and 146 B.C., Rome and Carthage fought three wars known as the Punic Wars.
5. The organization of Roman lands into large estates forced many small farmers off the land and into the cities.
6. By 135 B.C., Rome faced many serious political and economic problems.
7. A series of reform-minded leaders tried various ways to improve conditions in Rome, but political rivalries prevented any leader from holding power for long.
8. After Julius Caesar was killed by Romans who feared he might become king, power was divided among three leaders.
9. Fights among the three-way rule of Mark Antony, Octavian, and Marcus Lepidus led to the collapse of the Roman Republic.
10. In 31 B.C., Octavian became the sole ruler of the Roman Empire.

Self-Check Quiz

Visit the *Human Heritage* Web site at **humanheritage.glencoe.com** and click on *Chapter 14—Self-Check Quiz* to assess your understanding of this chapter.

Section 5 Assessment Answers

1. dictator, absolute ruler (p. 228); triumvirate, three-person rule (p. 228)
2. Sample responses: conflicts between Marius and Sulla over a military command; rise of a professional army more loyal to its commanders than to Rome
3. because they feared Caesar planned to make himself king

4. Answers will vary. Some students might see a triumvirate as a way to check executive power. Others might see it as divisive and an invitation to conspiracy.
5. Charts should correctly show the changes brought about by each reform.

Assign Chapter 14 **Section 5 Quiz** in the TCR. Testmaker available.

Using Key Terms

Imagine that you are writing a "Citizenship Handbook" for the new Roman citizens of 46 B.C. Write one sentence explaining the importance of each of the following terms.

republic	patricians	plebeians
consuls	veto	tribunes
legions	legionaries	latifundias
publicans	dictator	triumvirate

Understanding Main Ideas

1. What changes were made in Rome's government as a result of demands by the plebeians?
2. Why was the Roman legion so effective in battle?
3. Why did Rome decide to fight three wars against Carthage?
4. How were the Romans able to overcome the navy of Carthage?
5. What effect did latifundias have on Rome's small farmers?
6. Who won the struggle for political power after the death of Julius Caesar?
7. What effect did Marius's reforms have on the loyalty of the legionaries?
8. Why did the Senate order Julius Caesar to break up his legions?

Critical Thinking

1. How wise do you think the Romans were to enslave the people they conquered? Explain.
2. Do you think the Romans were wise or foolish to start taxing the people they conquered? Explain.
3. If you had lived in Rome after 135 B.C., what would you have done to solve its problems?

4. If you had lived when Caesar was killed, how would you have felt about his murder? Explain.

Graphic Organizer Activity

History Create a chart like this one, and use it to show steps in the decline of the Roman Republic.

Height of Republic

End of Republic

Geography in History

Movement Refer to the map on page 228. Imagine you are a government representative who must travel from Rome to Cyprus. Describe how you would travel and what route you would take. Then draw a map showing your route.

Using Your Journal

Review any details you may have noted about the contributions made by Romans to world civilization. Write a paragraph explaining what part of the government of the Roman Republic can be seen in the United States government today.

231

 Bonus Test Question

For Chapter 14 Test
Predict what will happen: Julius Caesar was not murdered in 44 B.C. He continued as ruler of Rome, but was advised to share ruling with Mark Anthony. The Senate has resigned in protest against Caesar's laws. Caesar must do something—what?

Using Your Journal

Paragraphs will vary, but students might make their comparisons with the Roman Senate, tribunes, veto, and the Twelve Tables.

Geography in History

Answers will vary and may include a sea route by ship or a land-sea route involving horses, carts, and ships.

Using Key Terms

Handbooks will vary but students should use all the words and complete explanations.

Understanding Main Ideas

1. No one could be enslaved because of debt, and plebeians could marry patricians and hold public office.
2. because it was small and fast and could split off and attack from all sides
3. because Rome felt threatened by Carthage and wanted the Carthaginian granaries in Sicily
4. They added a corvus to the front of their ships, thus changing a sea war into a land war.
5. They forced many farmers to move to the city.
6. Octavian
7. shifted the loyalty of legionaries from the government to the general who hired them
8. because they feared he was growing too strong

Critical Thinking

1. Answers will vary, but students could note that enslaving conquered people caused dissension.
2. Answers will vary, but taxing coincided with the Republic's decline.
3. Answers will vary.
4. Answers will vary, but students should give reasons.

Graphic Organizer Activity

Steps chosen by students will vary somewhat but should include important factors in chronological order, such as Roman expansion and rise of latifundias, forced movement of small farmers into cities, enslavement of conquered peoples, sale of tax contracts to publicans, and so on.

Chapter 15 Planning Guide

Objectives	Reproducible Resources	Multimedia Resources
Section 1 **The Rule of Augustus** Explain how Augustus ruled the Roman Empire.	Reproducible Lesson Plan Chapter 15 Vocabulary and Guided Reading Activity Reading Essentials and Study Guide 15-1 Unit 5 World Literature Reading 2 Chapter 15 Enrichment Activity Section 1 Quiz	Teaching Transparency and Activity 15A Vocabulary PuzzleMaker Interactive Tutor Self-Assessment Software ExamView® Pro Testmaker Glencoe Skillbuilder Interactive Workbook, Level 1 Presentation Plus!
Section 2 ***Pax Romana*** Analyze what happened to trade and law during the *Pax Romana*.	Reproducible Lesson Plan Reading Essentials and Study Guide 15-2 Section 2 Quiz	Teaching Transparency and Activity 14B Vocabulary PuzzleMaker Interactive Tutor Self-Assessment Software ExamView® Pro Testmaker Glencoe Skillbuilder Interactive Workbook, Level 1
Section 3 **Daily Life** Describe what daily life was like during the *Pax Romana*.	Reproducible Lesson Plan Reading Essentials and Study Guide 15-3 Chapter 15 Cooperative Learning Activity Unit 5 World Literature Reading 1 Section 3 Quiz	Vocabulary PuzzleMaker Interactive Tutor Self-Assessment Software ExamView® Pro Testmaker Glencoe Skillbuilder Interactive Workbook, Level 1
Section 4 **Fall of the Empire** Summarize why the Roman Empire declined and what attempts were made to save the empire from collapse.	Reproducible Lesson Plan Reading Essentials and Study Guide 15-4 Chapter 15 Chart and Graph Skill Activity Chapter 15 Geography and Map Activity Chapter 15 Activity Book Activity Section 4 Quiz	Vocabulary PuzzleMaker Interactive Tutor Self-Assessment Software ExamView® Pro Testmaker Glencoe Skillbuilder Interactive Workbook, Level 1
Chapter 15 **Review and Evaluation**	Chapter 1 Reteaching Activity Chapter 1 Performance Assessment Activity Spanish Chapter Summary and Glossary Chapter 15 Test	Vocabulary PuzzleMaker Interactive Tutor Self-Assessment Software Glencoe Skillbuilder Interactive Workbook, Level 1 Audiocassettes* ExamView® Pro Testmaker

*Also available in Spanish.

Presentation Plus!

Use Glencoe's **Presentation Plus!** multimedia teacher tool to easily present dynamic lessons that visually excite your students. Using Microsoft® PowerPoint, you can customize the presentations to create your own personalized lessons.

Interactive Lesson Planner

Planning has never been easier! Using this CD-ROM, organize your week, month, semester, or year with all the help you need. The **Interactive Lesson Planner** gives you access to all of the blackline masters which accompany *Human Heritage.*

✓ PERFORMANCE ASSESSMENT ACTIVITIES

Mathematics Have students prepare a chart of Arabic numerals (1 through 15, then 20, 30, 40, 50, 60, 70, 80, 90, 100, 500, and 1,000), the corresponding Roman numerals, and the Latin names for the numerals. Ask them to research how Romans performed mathematical calculations and to write a few problems for other students to solve.

CHAPTER RESOURCES

LITERATURE ABOUT THE PERIOD

Grant, Michael. *Greek and Latin Authors, 800 B.C.-A.D. 1000.* H.W. Wilson Co., 1980. Sketches of Greek and Latin authors and their works.

READINGS FOR THE STUDENT

Dillon, Eilis. *Rome Under the Emperors.* Thomas Nelson, 1975. Views of Roman society and family life in the time of Trajan, as seen by young people of four different families and social classes.

Foster, Genevieve. *Augustus Caesar's World.* Scribner's Sons, 1947. Classic history of Augustus's time.

READINGS FOR THE TEACHER

Fagg, Christopher. *Ancient Rome.* Warwick Press, 1978. Examines the Roman Empire from its beginnings through its decline.

Gibbon, Edward. *The Portable Gibbon: The Decline and Fall of the Roman Empire.* Viking, 1965. Summary of the classic historical study.

KEY TO ABILITY LEVELS

Teaching strategies have been coded for varying learning styles and abilities.

L1 Level 1 activities are **basic** activities and should be within the ability range of all students.

L2 Level 2 activities are **average** activities and should be within the ability range of the average to above-average student.

L3 Level 3 activities are **challenging** activities designed for the ability range of above-average students.

ELL ELL activities should be within the ability range of English Language Learning students.

NATIONAL GEOGRAPHIC SOCIETY — Teacher's Corner

INDEX TO NATIONAL GEOGRAPHIC MAGAZINE

The following articles relate to this chapter:

- "Roman Shipwrecks" by Robert D. Ballard, April 1998.
- "Roman Legacy," by T.R. Reid, August 1997.
- "Roman Empire," by T.R. Reid, July 1997.
- "Brindisi Bronzes," by O. Louis Mazzatenta, April 1995.

NATIONAL GEOGRAPHIC SOCIETY PRODUCTS AVAILABLE FROM GLENCOE

To order the following, call Glencoe at 1-800-334-7344:

- *PicturePack: Ancient Rome (Transparencies)*
- *PictureShow: Greece and Rome (CD-ROM)*
- *Ancient Civilizations: Ancient Rome (Poster Set)*

ADDITIONAL NATIONAL GEOGRAPHIC SOCIETY PRODUCTS

To order the following, call National Geographic at 1-800-368-2728:

- *National Geographic Atlas of World History (Book)*
- *Wonders of the Ancient World: National Geographic Atlas of Archaeology (Book)*
- *The Builders: Marvels of Engineering (Book)*

Access *National Geographic's* new dynamic MapMachine Web site and other geography resources at:
http://www.nationalgeographic.com/
http://www.nationalgeographic.com/maps/

  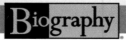

THE HISTORY CHANNEL.

The following videotape programs are available from Glencoe to enrich Chapter 15:

- **Augustus: First of the Emperors**
  0-7670-0573-2

- **The Incredible Monuments of Rome**
  1-56501-870-2

- **Rome's Glorious Cities**
  0-7670-0611-9

To order, call Glencoe at 1-800-334-7344. To find classroom resources to accompany many of these, check:

A&E Television: http://www.aetv.com
The History Channel:
http://www.historychannel.com

OVERVIEW

Chapter 15 traces the Roman Empire from the rule of Augustus to the fall of Rome.

➤ **Section 1** summarizes the rule of Augustus.
➤ **Section 2** describes Roman contributions to trade and law during the *Pax Romana*.
➤ **Section 3** discusses the daily life of Romans.
➤ **Section 4** analyzes the causes of the fall of the Roman Empire.

CHAPTER OBJECTIVES

After reading Chapter 15, your students will be able to:

1. explain how Augustus ruled the Roman Empire.
2. analyze what happened to trade and law during the *Pax Romana*.
3. describe daily life during the *Pax Romana*.
4. summarize why the Roman Empire declined.
5. discuss efforts to save the Roman Empire.

EXAMINING ARTIFACTS

Ask students to describe ways the education of Romans—and the tools for learning—differed from their own. *(Students may note the one-on-one instruction, the informal [home] setting, use of a scroll instead of a book, use of inkpot and pen instead of a ballpoint or computer.)* Call on students to guess some of the subjects a Roman student might study. Have them check their answers as they read Chapter 15.

PERFORMANCE ASSESSMENT ✔

Use the Performance Assessment Activities on page 232B to help you evaluate students as they complete the chapter.

232

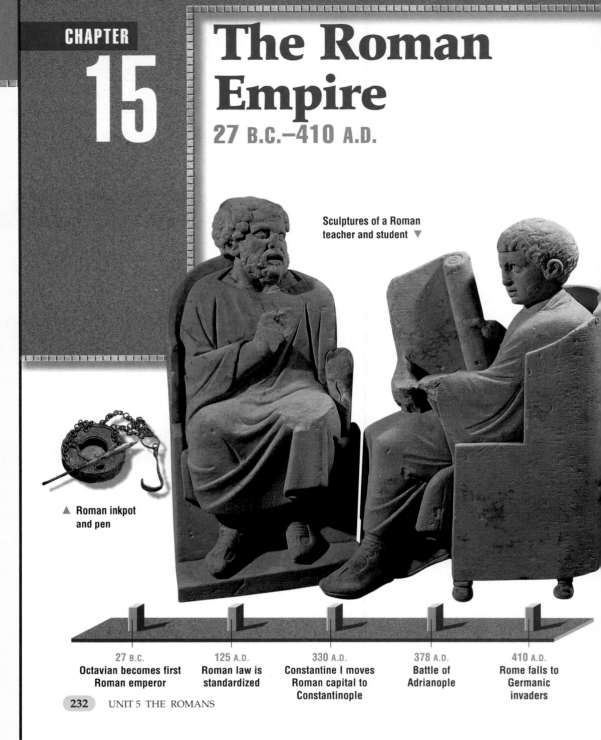

The Roman Empire
27 B.C.–410 A.D.

Sculptures of a Roman teacher and student ▼

▲ **Roman inkpot and pen**

27 B.C.	125 A.D.	330 A.D.	378 A.D.	410 A.D.
Octavian becomes first Roman emperor	Roman law is standardized	Constantine I moves Roman capital to Constantinople	Battle of Adrianople	Rome falls to Germanic invaders

232 UNIT 5 THE ROMANS

TEACHING RESOURCES

TEACHER PLANNING AND SUPPORT

- Reproducible Lesson Plan
- Block Scheduling Implementation Guide
- Videodisc Bar Code Correlation
- Presentation Plus!

REVIEW AND REINFORCEMENT

- Reading Essentials and Study Guide 15-1, 15-2, 15-3, 15-4
- Chapter 15 Vocabulary and Guided Reading Activity
- Vocabulary PuzzleMaker Software
- Teaching Transparencies 15A & 15B

- Chapter 15 Reteaching Activity
- Chapter 15 Cooperative Learning Activity
- Chapter 15 Activity Book Activity
- Chapter 15 Chart and Graph Skill Activity
- Interactive Tutor Self-Assessment Software

APPLICATION AND HANDS-ON ACTIVITIES

- Daily World History, Geography, and Culture Question
- Unit 5 Hands-On History Lab Activity

Chapter Focus

 Read to Discover

- How Augustus ruled the Roman Empire.
- What happened to trade and law during the *Pax Romana.*
- What daily life was like during the *Pax Romana.*
- Why the Roman Empire declined.

Chapter Overview
Visit the *Human Heritage* Web site at **humanheritage.glencoe.com** and click on *Chapter 15— Chapter Overviews* to preview this chapter.

Terms to Learn	People to Know	Places to Locate
emperor	Augustus	Circus Maximus
census	Marcus Aurelius	Constantinople
tariffs	Diocletian	Adrianople
gladiators	Constantine I	Danube River
	Alaric	

Why It's Important In 27 B.C., Octavian told the Senate that he had restored the republic, and he offered to resign as sole ruler of Rome. The Senate turned down the offer and gave him several titles. In the end, Octavian took for himself the title of Augustus (ah guhs' tuhs), or "revered one." That is what he is generally called in history books.

In practice, Octavian became the first Roman **emperor,** or absolute ruler of an empire. His policies paved the way for more than 200 years of peace. Even after the empire collapsed, Roman influence would survive in much of the world.

Reading Check
What is an **emperor?**

SECTION 1   The Rule of Augustus

Augustus was a clever politician. He held the offices of consul, tribune, high priest, and senator all at the same time. However, he refused to be crowned emperor. Augustus knew that most Romans would not accept one-person rule unless it took the form of a republic.

Augustus kept the assemblies and government officials of the republic. He was careful to make senators feel honored. He talked of tradition and the need to bring back "old Roman virtues."

At the same time, Augustus strengthened his authority in two ways. First, he had every soldier swear allegiance to him personally. This gave him control of the armies. Second, he built up his imperial household to take charge of the daily business of

CHAPTER 15 THE ROMAN EMPIRE   **233**

Guided Practice

L1 **Geography: Place** Display a wall map of Western Europe and North Africa to point out the natural barriers that Augustus used to round out the Roman Empire—the Rhine and Danube rivers, the Atlantic Ocean, and the Sahara. Discuss why these barriers made the empire easy to defend. **ELL**

✓ Reading Check Answer
The **freedmen** were former enslaved people.

✓ Reading Check Answer
Augustus ordered a **census** to make sure people were not paying too little or too much tax.

Use **Interactive Tutor Self Assessment Software** to review Section 1.

The following videotape programs are available from Glencoe to enrich Chapter 15:

- **Augustus: First of the Emperors**
- **Rome's Glorious Cities**

To find classroom resources to accompany these videos, check the following home page:

A&E Television:
http://www.aetv.com

234

✓ Reading Check
Who were the **freedmen?**

✓ Reading Check
Why did Augustus order a **census?**

government. He chose people because of their talent rather than their birth. This gave enslaved people and **freedmen**, or former enslaved people, a chance to be part of the government.

Augustus wanted boundaries that would be easy to defend. So, he rounded out the empire to natural frontiers—the Rhine (rīn) and Danube (dan' yūb) rivers in the north, the Atlantic Ocean in the west, and the Sahara in the south—and stationed soldiers there.

Augustus was not interested in gaining new territory for Rome. Instead, he worked on governing the existing empire. He gave provincial governors long terms of office. This allowed them to gain experience in their jobs. He also paid them large salaries. In this way, they would not feel the need to overtax the people or keep public money for themselves. To make sure that people did not pay too little or too much tax, Augustus ordered a **census** (sen' suhs), or population count, to be taken from time to time.

Augustus also made Rome more beautiful. He wrote strict laws to govern the way people behaved in public. He protected the city by setting up a fire brigade and a police force. He encouraged learning by building Rome's first library.

Augustus ruled for 41 years. During that time, he brought peace to Rome. He also gave the Romans a new sense of patriotism and pride. He made Roman citizenship available to people in the provinces. Most important, however, he reorganized the government of Rome so that it ran well for more than 200 years.

Section 1 Assessment

1. **Define:** emperor, freedmen, census.
2. Why did Augustus refuse to be crowned emperor?
3. How did Augustus try to make the Roman Empire like a republic?

Critical Thinking

4. **Demonstrating Reasoned Judgment** Which of Augustus's improvements do you think was the most important? Explain.

Graphic Organizer Activity

5. Draw this diagram, and use it to show the achievements of Augustus.

Augustus's Achievements

SECTION 2 Pax Romana

The peace that Augustus brought to Rome was called the *Pax Romana* (pahks rō mah' nah). It lasted for 200 years. Of course, revolts and other problems were not unknown during this time. For the most part, however, Rome and its people prospered. Civilization spread, and cultures mixed.

Section 1 Assessment Answers

1. emperor, absolute ruler (p. 233); freedmen, former enslaved people (p. 234); census, population count (p. 234)
2. He knew most Romans would not accept one-person rule unless it was in a republic.
3. He kept the assemblies and government officials, made senators feel honored, talked of tradition and the need to bring back "old Roman virtues," and made the official religion important again.
4. Answers will vary, but students should explain their choices.

5. Sample achievements: won the loyalty of soldiers, gave enslaved people and freedmen a chance to be part of government, rounded out the empire to its natural frontiers, reformed provincial government, ordered a census, wrote strict laws to control public behavior, set up a fire brigade and police force, built Rome's first library, and so on.

Assign Chapter 15 **Section 1 Quiz** in the TCR. Testmaker available.

Trade With peace came increased trade. The same coins were used throughout the empire. There were no **tariffs** (tar' ifz), or taxes placed on goods brought into the country. Goods and money moved freely along the trade routes. The Mediterranean was cleared of pirates, making it safe for trade and travel. Shipping became a big business. Every summer, hundreds of ships carried grain from North Africa to Italy. Other ships bound for Rome were loaded with cargoes of brick, marble, granite, and wood to be used for building. Luxury items, such as amber from the north and silk from China, passed overland across Roman roads.

Increased trade meant more business for Romans. The city hummed. Shopkeepers grew richer. Wine and olive oil were the main items bought by other countries. Italy became a manufacturing center for pottery, bronze, and woolen cloth.

Law During the *Pax Romana*, Roman law went through major changes. Because the times were different, the laws first set down

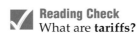

Reading Check
What are **tariffs**?

MAP STUDY

PLACE The Roman Empire had been divided into two parts. **What empire did Greece belong to?**

The Expansion of the Roman Empire

At Death of Caesar, 44 B.C.
To Death of Augustus, 14 A.D.
To Death of Marcus Aurelius, 180 A.D.

miles 0   300   600
kilometers 0   300   600   900

The map shows labels: Hadrian's Wall, NORTH SEA, BALTIC SEA, BRITAIN, GERMANY, Rhine River, ATLANTIC OCEAN, GAUL, PYRENEES, Po River, Danube River, BLACK SEA, SPAIN, CORSICA, Rome, Tiber River, ITALY, ADRIATIC SEA, APENNINES, MACEDONIA, Bosporus, Constantinople, ASIA MINOR, SARDINIA, GREECE, Carthage, SICILY, Athens, SYRIA, RHODES, CYPRUS, CRETE, MEDITERRANEAN SEA, AFRICA, Alexandria, PALESTINE, EGYPT, Nile River, SAHARA, WESTERN ROMAN EMPIRE, EASTERN ROMAN EMPIRE

Reading Check Answer
Tariffs are taxes placed on goods coming into a country.

Use the **Vocabulary Puzzle-Maker** to create crossword and word search puzzles.

L2 **Map Skills** Have students refer to the map on this page to identify the regions in which the empire expanded. *(Western Europe, Middle East, North Africa)* What sea did most Roman land border? *(Mediterranean)* Have students use the map scale to calculate the distance of the farthest point of the empire from the city of Rome. *(about 1,800 miles, or 2,896 km)*

Assign the Chapter 15 **Geography and Map Activity** in the TCR.

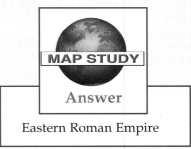

MAP STUDY

Answer

Eastern Roman Empire

NATIONAL GEOGRAPHIC SOCIETY

Use these materials to enrich student understanding of everyday life in ancient Rome.

NGS PICTURESHOW CD-ROM
Greece and Rome

COOPERATIVE LEARNING

Assign students to groups to research specific areas of culture during the *Pax Romana*. Divide each topic into smaller areas to be covered by individuals in each group. Groups should decide how to organize their reports into coordinated presentations. The following topics might be suggested: Roman daily life (food, housing, amusements, household duties, women's lives, education); philosophy (ideas of citizenship, justice, religion); language and literature (Romance languages, specific poets or historians); or architecture (Roman roads, the arch in architecture).

L1 Economics During the *Pax Romana* many changes took place in trade in the Roman Empire. This affected more people than those who actually carried goods to other markets. Using student volunteers, ask students to list on the board all people and/or occupations that were affected by the increase in Roman trade.

✓ **Reading Check Answer**
The *juris prudentes* were special lawyers and legal writers who helped Roman judges write new laws.

💾 Use **Interactive Tutor Self-Assessment Software** to review Section 1.

PRIMARY SOURCES
Library

You might assign "Eruption of Mount Vesuvius" from pages 682–683 of the Primary Sources Library.

✓ **Reading Check Answer**
A Roman **domus** had marble walls, colored stone floors, glass windows, a furnace to heat rooms, and pipes to carry water to upper floors.

💾 Use the **Vocabulary Puzzle-Maker** to create crossword and word search puzzles.

✓ **Reading Check**
Who were the *juris prudentes,* and what were they supposed to do?

on the Twelve Tables were changed. When Rome conquered a new territory, Roman merchants had to do business with non-Romans. Roman judges had to write new laws that would be as fair to non-Romans as to Romans. The Roman judges were helped by special lawyers and legal writers called *juris prudentes* (jū′ ruhs prū′ duhntz).

After a while, the judges and their helpers developed certain principles of law that were fair to everyone. A law was believed to be just because it was reasonable, not because the government had the power to make people obey it. Everyone was considered equal before the law. A person was innocent until proven guilty.

By about 125 A.D., Roman law was *standardized.* This meant that legal procedures were the same in all parts of the empire. This helped Rome govern a large area successfully. In later years, Roman legal principles formed the basis for the laws of most western countries and of the Christian church.

Section 2 Assessment

1. **Define:** tariffs, *juris prudentes*.
2. What happened to trade during the *Pax Romana*?
3. What happened to law during the *Pax Romana*?

Critical Thinking

4. **Evaluating Information** Do you think the term *Pax Romana* was a good term for this 200-year period in Roman history, or would you describe it with another term? Explain.

Graphic Organizer Activity

5. Draw this diagram, and use it to show the effects of the *Pax Romana*. (Add more lines as needed.)

Pax Romana	Effect
	Effect
	Effect
	Effect

SECTION 3 Daily Life

In the early years of the empire, about 1 million people lived in Rome. It suffered from many of the same problems as cities of today. There was too little housing. The air was polluted. There was crime in the streets. The cost of living was high. Many Romans could not find jobs and had to pay taxes on almost everything.

A rich person in Rome lived in a **domus** (dō′ muhs), or house, with marble walls, colored stone floors, and windows made of small panes of glass. A furnace heated the rooms, and pipes brought water even to the upper floors.

Most Romans, however, were not rich. They lived in apartment houses called *islands* that were six or more stories high. Each island covered an entire block. At one time, there were 26

✓ **Reading Check**
What were some of the features of a Roman **domus?**

Section 2 Assessment Answers

1. tariffs, taxes placed on goods brought into the country (p. 235), *juris prudentes*, special lawyers (p. 236)
2. It increased.
3. Certain principles of fairness were developed, including the ideas that everyone is equal before the law and that a person is considered innocent until proven guilty. By about 125 A.D. the law was standardized.
4. Answers will vary, but students could note because it was a time that Rome pros-

pered, few battles took place, civilization spread, and cultures mixed.
5. Sample effects: Rome prospered, civilization spread, cultures mixed, trade increased, pirates cleared from the Mediterranean, shipping became big business, Roman businesses grew, new laws were written and old ones revised, laws became standardized, and so on.

Assign Chapter 15 **Section 2 Quiz** in the TCR. Testmaker available.

ROMAN FLOOR PLAN   This is a typical floor plan of a *domus*. **What class of Romans would live in a house such as this?**

The Atrium Many shopping malls today have an atrium, a sky-lit central court. The idea for the atrium comes from ancient Rome. In a Roman house, the atrium was the central room. It was often open to the sky and had a pool to collect rainwater.

blocks of islands for every private house in Rome. The ground floor of most islands was given over to shops. These opened onto the street from large arched doorways.

Rents were high in Rome. They varied according to the apartment floor—the higher up the apartment, the lower the rent.

The Family   In Rome, the family was all-important. The father was head of the household. His word was law. He arranged the children's marriages to improve social position or to increase wealth. Cousins were expected to help one another politically.

Until they were 12 years old, most Roman boys and girls went to school together. Then, the sons of poor families went to work, while the sons of rich families began their formal education. They studied reading, grammar, writing, music, geometry, commercial arithmetic, and shorthand. When they were 15 years old, they entered a school of *rhetoric* (ret' uhr ik), or speech and writing, to prepare for a political career. Some went to schools in Athens or Alexandria for philosophy or medicine.

Girls received a different kind of education. When they were 12 years old, their formal education stopped. Instead of going to school, the daughters of the rich were given private lessons at

Painting of Roman Couple

CHAPTER 15 THE ROMAN EMPIRE   **237**

Linking Across Time

Under the republic, the games had generally been staged by politicians looking for votes. Under the empire, they were staged by the government.

✔ **Reading Check Answer**
Most **gladiators** were enslaved people, prisoners of war, criminals, or poor people.

Linking Across Time

Stadiums   During Roman times, people filled stadiums such as the Colosseum (left) to watch gladiator fights and other public games. Stadiums remain popular today but are usually used for team sports such as baseball, football, or soccer (right). **Who staged the public games held at stadiums in Rome?**

home. As a result, many Roman women were as well as or better informed than Roman men. Some women worked in or owned small shops. Wealthy women had enslaved people to do their housework. This left them free to study the arts, literature, and fashions, or to ride chariots in the countryside for a day's *pigsticking*, or a type of hunt.

At Leisure   At home, the Romans enjoyed gambling with dice. They met friends at public bathhouses where they could take warm, cold, or steam baths. The bathhouses of Rome, however, provided more than baths. Some had gymnasiums, sports stadiums, and libraries. There, the Romans could watch or play games. They also could listen to lectures, see musical shows, exercise, or just sit and talk.

The Romans had no team sports to watch. Instead, they flocked to see free public games, which often ran from dawn to dusk. Under the republic, the games had generally been staged by politicians who were looking for votes. Under the empire, the games were staged by the government. The games included circuses, chariot races, and gladiatorial games. The most exciting chariot races were held at the Circus Maximus, an oval arena that could seat more than 200,000 people.

The people who fought animals and one another in arenas were called **gladiators** (glad' ē ā tuhrz). Most were enslaved people, prisoners of war, criminals, or poor people. They were

✔ **Reading Check**
Which groups of people were trained as **gladiators?**

238   UNIT 5 THE ROMANS

MULTICULTURAL PERSPECTIVES

Most men in Rome had three names. The middle name told from which clan a man was descended. The last name told to which branch of the clan he belonged. The first name identified the person. Thus, Caius Julius Caesar was a member of the Caesarian branch of the Julian clan. His personal name was Caius. Unmarried women had two names—the feminine form of their father's middle name, and a last name that indicated chronological rank among the girls of the family. For example, if Caesar had fathered two daughters, the older would have been called Julia Prima and the other Julia Secunda. When a woman married, a form of her husband's last name was added to her other two names.

trained by managers who hired them out. A few gladiators were upper-class Romans who wanted excitement and public attention.

The night before they were to fight, gladiators would appear at a feast. There, they could be looked over by fans and gamblers who wanted to bet on the outcome of a match. When the gladiators entered the arena on the day of the games, they would walk past the emperor's box and say, "Hail Emperor, those who are about to die salute you."

Many gladiators did die. Those whose fighting pleased the crowd became idols of the people. A few won their freedom. Those who gave a poor performance were killed, even if they survived the fight.

All kinds of animals were used in the public games. Some animals pulled chariots or performed tricks. Most, however, fought one another or gladiators. Sometimes, as many as 5,000 wild animals were killed in a single day. In some cases, such as that of the Mesopotamian lion and the North African elephant, whole species were eventually wiped out.

HISTORY Online

Student Web Activity
Visit the *Human Heritage* Web site at humanheritage.glencoe.com and click on *Chapter 15—Student Web Activities* to find out more about early Roman life.

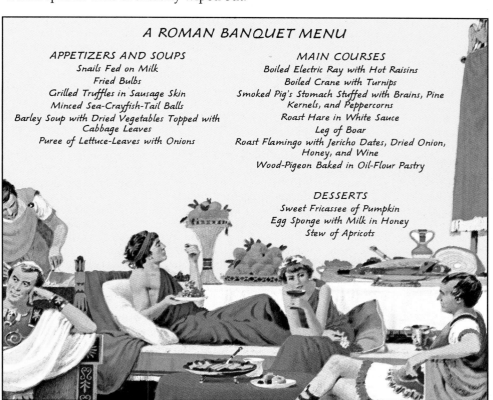

A ROMAN BANQUET MENU

APPETIZERS AND SOUPS
Snails Fed on Milk
Fried Bulbs
Grilled Truffles in Sausage Skin
Minced Sea-Crayfish-Tail Balls
Barley Soup with Dried Vegetables Topped with Cabbage Leaves
Puree of Lettuce-Leaves with Onions

MAIN COURSES
Boiled Electric Ray with Hot Raisins
Boiled Crane with Turnips
Smoked Pig's Stomach Stuffed with Brains, Pine Kernels, and Peppercorns
Roast Hare in White Sauce
Leg of Boar
Roast Flamingo with Jericho Dates, Dried Onion, Honey, and Wine
Wood-Pigeon Baked in Oil-Flour Pastry

DESSERTS
Sweet Fricassee of Pumpkin
Egg Sponge with Milk in Honey
Stew of Apricots

HISTORY Online
Student Web Activity objectives, goals, and answers can be found at the *Chapter 15 Web Activity Lesson Plan* at humanheritage.glencoe.com

DID YOU KNOW
Gladiators who were killed during combat were dragged from the arena by men wearing the mask of an Etruscan demon of the underworld.

MAKING CONNECTIONS

➤➤ **Culture** All Roman households had a central place to honor the spirits of the hearth and household. The hearth of the home was watched over by the goddess Vesta (or Hestia), spirit of the home fire. Family meals began and ended with thanks to her. A newborn child was carried around the hearth to symbolize becoming part of the family. Lares and Penates were the Roman spirits of everyday things. They came from ancient times when the Romans were mostly farmers. Each family had its own Lar, perhaps the spirit of an ancestor, to guide it. A household had several Penates representing prosperity.

MEETING SPECIAL NEEDS

Have interested students research and present an oral report on Hadrian's Wall built by Romans in northern Britain in the 120s A.D. Ask students to indicate the location of the wall on a map of Britain.

📖 Refer to *Inclusion for the Middle School Social Studies Classroom: Strategies and Activities* for additional resources.

L3 **Health** Have students work together in small groups to research Roman diets. Suggest they prepare a day's menu for a peasant family similar to the Patrician menu shown in the illustration on this page.

Critical Thinking Before students read the information about Diocletian and Constantine I, have them brainstorm ways in which a Roman emperor might have strengthened the empire to save it from collapse. Write their ideas on the board and revisit the lists after students have read Section 4.

💾 Use **Interactive Tutor Self-Assessment Software** to review Section 3.

DID YOU KNOW

Marcus Aurelius was so loved by the Romans that there was no mourning when he died. They were sure he had come from the gods and had now returned to heaven.

✔️ **Reading Check Answer**
Inflation is a period of ever-rising prices.

HOME VIDEO.

The following videotape program is available from Glencoe to enrich Chapter 15:

- **The Incredible Monuments of Rome**

To find classroom resources to accompany this video, check the following home page:

A&E Television:
http://www.aetv.com

💾 Use the **Vocabulary Puzzle-Maker** to create crossword and word search puzzles.

Section 3 Assessment

1. **Define:** *domus,* gladiators.
2. What kind of schooling did Roman children receive?
3. What did the Romans do for entertainment?

Critical Thinking

4. **Drawing Conclusions** What conclusions can you draw about Roman society based upon popular leisure activities?

Graphic Organizer Activity

5. Draw this diagram, and use it to compare family life in the United States with Roman family life during the *Pax Romana.*

Roman Families — Both — U.S. Families

SECTION 4 Fall of the Empire

The *Pax Romana* ended after about 200 years. From then on, conditions in the Roman Empire grew worse. By 476 A.D., there was no empire left. Instead, much of western Europe was a patchwork of Germanic kingdoms. The eastern part of the empire, however, lasted about 1,000 years longer as part of the Byzantine (biz′ n tēn) Empire.

There are many reasons the Roman Empire fell. The first was political. The emperors had no written rule about who was to inherit the throne upon an emperor's death. Sometimes, the title was inherited by a son. Sometimes, an emperor adopted an heir to the throne. Between 96 and 180 A.D., all the emperors were adopted. The system worked well until 180 A.D.

Marcus Aurelius (ah rē′ lē uhs) became emperor in 161 A.D. He was kind, intelligent, and devoted to duty. His son Commodus (kahm′ uh duhs), however, was the opposite. He became emperor when Marcus Aurelius died in 180 A.D. He was so cruel and hated that in 192 A.D. he was strangled by the Praetorian (prē tōr′ ē uhn) Guard, or the emperor's bodyguards. The Praetorian Guard then sold the throne to the highest bidder. This set a terrible example. For nearly 100 years, legion fought legion to put its own emperor on the throne. By 284 A.D., Rome had 37 different emperors. Most were murdered by the army or the Praetorian Guard.

The second reason for Rome's downfall was economic. To stay in office, an emperor had to keep the soldiers who supported him happy. He did this by giving them high wages. This meant more and more money was needed for the army payroll. As a result, the Romans had to pay higher taxes.

In addition to higher taxes, the Romans began to suffer from **inflation,** or a period of ever-increasing prices. Since there were

The Pantheon The "good emperor" Hadrian, built the Pantheon in Rome as a temple to honor all the gods. Today the beautiful building is a national shrine, a church, and the burial place of two kings of Italy.

✔️ **Reading Check**
What is **inflation?**

Section 3 Assessment Answers

1. *domus,* house (p. 236); gladiators, people who fought in Roman arenas (p. 238)

2. Until age 12, boys and girls went to school. Wealthy males continued their studies while girls did not. Wealthy females may have been taught at home.

3. They gambled with dice, met at public bathhouses, and watched public games.

4. Answers will vary, but students should be prepared to present evidence that supports their conclusions.

5. Diagrams will vary. To get students started, you might provide these examples. *Roman families*—fathers arranged children's marriages. *U.S. families*—Children usually select their own partners. *Both*—Education of young children is important.

Assign Chapter 15 **Section 3 Quiz** in the TCR. Testmaker available.

no new conquests, gold was no longer coming into Rome. Yet, much gold was going out to pay for luxury items. This meant there was less gold to use in coins. As the amount of gold used in coins decreased, money began to lose its value. Prices went up. Many people stopped using money altogether. Instead, they began to **barter**, or exchange goods without using money.

The third major reason Rome fell centered on foreign enemies. While the Romans fought each other over politics and money, they left Rome's frontiers open to attack. Germanic hunters and herders from northern and central Europe began to raid Greece and Gaul. Trade and farming in those areas declined. Cities again began to surround themselves with protecting walls.

Reading Check
Why did Romans begin to **barter?**

Diocletian and Constantine I

Two emperors, Diocletian (dī ō klē' shuhn) and Constantine I (kon stan tēn'), tried very hard to save the Roman Empire from collapse.

EMPERORS DURING THE *PAX ROMANA*

Emperor	Reign	Accomplishments
Augustus	27 B.C.–14 A.D.	first emperor of Roman Empire reorganized government of Rome; brought peace to Rome
Tiberius	14 A.D.–37 A.D.	reformed taxes and improved financial state of government
Caligula	37 A.D.–41 A.D.	repaired roads and began construction of two aqueducts
Claudius	41 A.D.–54 A.D.	conquered most of England extended citizenship to many people outside Rome set up ministries to handle government administration
Nero	54 A.D.–68 A.D.	rebuilt Rome after the fire of 64 A.D. and gave it a city plan
Flavian Emperors Vespasian Titus Domitian	69 A.D.–96 A.D.	brought people from the provinces into the Senate secured frontier regions brought Rome new prosperity built the Coliseum
Five Good Emperors Nerva Trajan Hadrian Antoninus Pius	96 A.D.–180 A.D.	built aqueducts, bridges, and harbors extended citizenship to more provinces cut dishonesty in business and government

Reading Check Answer
Romans began to **barter** because gold fell into short supply and money lost its value.

Independent Practice

L3 **Art** Ask students to research and present an oral report about the artifacts that have been found from the destruction of Pompeii, Italy, after the eruption of Mount Vesuvius in 79 A.D. Students' reports should include a variety of artifacts that have been found in excavations and what they explain about life in Pompeii.

L1 **History** Have students work in pairs to create five questions based on the chart of Roman emperors on this page. Collect the questions, ask for a volunteer moderator, and have students play a game of "Who Am I?" using their questions.

SPOTLIGHT ON: ZENOBIA

One of the most celebrated women in the Roman Empire was Zenobia, queen of Palmyra—located in central Syria—from 267 to 272 A.D. As queen she helped her husband lead the army and rule the lands entrusted to him. She became known for her leadership and bravery. In 267 A.D. she succeeded her husband who had died, as ruler. Most of the people of Palmyra supported her because she was a just ruler, selected competent advisers, and was tolerant of other's beliefs. In 269 A.D. she seized Egypt, conquered most of Asia Minor, and declared her country independent from Rome. From 270 to 272 A.D., she was ruler of the Eastern Roman Empire.

TEACH

Identifying the Main Ideas

Write this phrase on the board: *What's the big idea?* Ask students what this phrase means to them. *(What is this all about? What are you trying to do?)* Explain that people usually ask this question when they want an explanation for someone's behavior. Call on students to suggest reasons they should also ask this question of historians, reporters, or any other person providing information. *(To find out why they are writing or saying something.)*

Explain to students that they can discover the "big idea" even if the writer or speaker is not available to answer the question. To find out how, assign the skills lesson and the accompanying questions.

Answers to Skill Practice

1. to announce laws regulating the maximum price of goods
2. widespread high prices
3. Possible details: prices stay high even in good years or time of ample supply, some greedy merchants have enough wealth to satisfy entire nations, a single purchase might rob a soldier of his bonus or salary
4. He says, "the penalty for violating this law shall be death."

CRITICAL THINKING SKILLS
Identifying the Main Idea

As you read about world history, you come across historical dates, events, and names. These details are easier to understand and remember when they are connected to one main idea.

Understanding the main ideas allows you to grasp the whole picture or story. The details then become more easily understood.

Learning the Skill Follow these steps to identify a main idea:

- **Before you read the material, find out the setting of the article or document: the time, the place, and who the writer is.**
- **Read the material and ask, "What is the purpose of this information?"**
- **Study any photographs or illustrations that accompany the material.**
- **Ask, "What are the most forceful statements in this material?"**
- **Identify supporting details.**
- **Identify the main idea, or central issue.**

Glencoe's **Skillbuilder Interactive Workbook, Level 1,** provides instruction and practice in key social studies skills.

242

Skill Practice

The passage that follows comes from a document issued by Diocletian, the emperor of Rome from 284 to 305 B.C. In it, he describes a plan for ending Rome's economic problems. Read this passage and answer the questions that follow.

In the commerce carried on in the markets or involved in the daily life of cities, high prices are so widespread that they are not lowered even by abundant supplies or good years. . . . There are men who try . . . to profit in good as well as poor years even though they have enough wealth to satisfy entire nations. . . . Prices have been driven so high that sometimes in a single purchase a soldier is deprived of his bonus and salary. . . .

We have decreed that there be established . . . maximum prices. . . . It is our pleasure, therefore, that the prices . . . be observed in the whole of our empire and the penalty for violating this law shall be death. . . . We urge obedience to this law, since it provides . . . against those whose greed could not be satisfied.

1. **Why has Diocletian issued this document?**
2. **What main idea, or central issue, is discussed by the document?**
3. **What supporting details are used to support the main idea?**
4. **What forceful statement does Diocletian use to make sure people do not miss the seriousness of the central issue?**

TEAM TEACHING STRATEGIES

Art Work with an art teacher to present a lesson on identifying the main idea in a painting or other work of art. Tell students that artists (or photographers) can get across an idea through a number of techniques. They might emphasize certain details over others. They might draw a viewer's eyes to a key figure or event. They might also use familiar symbols to convey emotion or paint figures from an emotional standpoint.

Then refer students to the painting on page 238. Ask: What is the subject of the painting? *(a chariot race)* What main idea is the artist trying to convey? *(Sample response: That it was an exciting event.)* What techniques or details did the artist use to support this idea? *(Answers will vary but might include the cheering crowd, the speeding horses, the overturned chariot, and so on.)*

Diocletian, who was the son of a freedman, ruled from 284 to 305 A.D. He made many changes as emperor. He fortified the frontiers to stop invasions. He reorganized the state and provincial governments to make them work better. To keep prices from rising, he set maximum prices for wages and goods. To make sure goods were produced, he ordered workers to stay in the same jobs until they died. He also made city officials personally responsible for the taxes their communities had to pay.

One of the most important changes Diocletian made concerned the position of the emperor. Diocletian established the official policy of **rule by divine right.** This meant the emperor's powers and right to rule came not from the people but from the gods.

Diocletian realized the Roman Empire covered too much area for one person to rule well. So, he divided it into two parts. He allowed someone else to govern the western provinces, while he ruled the richer eastern provinces.

In 312 A.D., Constantine I became emperor. He ruled until 337 A.D. Constantine took even firmer control of the empire than Diocletian. To keep people from leaving their jobs when things got bad, he issued several orders. The sons of workers had to follow their fathers' trades. The sons of farmers had to stay and work the land their fathers worked. The sons of ex-soldiers had to serve in the army.

To escape government pressure and control, wealthy landowners moved to their *villas*, or country estates. Most villas were like small, independent cities or kingdoms. Each produced enough food and goods to meet the needs of everyone who lived on the estate.

Despite the changes made by Diocletian and Constantine, the Roman Empire continued to decline in the west. In 330 A.D., Constantine moved the capital from a dying Rome east to the newly built city of Constantinople (kon stan tuh nō' puhl) in present-day Turkey.

End of the Empire   Both Diocletian and Constantine I worked hard to save the Roman Empire. However, neither emperor succeeded in the end.

German attacks increased, especially in western Europe. There, the Germans crossed the Danube River in order to escape from the Huns, nomadic herders who had wandered west from Outer Mongolia in Asia. In 378 A.D., a Germanic group defeated Roman legions at the Battle of Adrianople (ā drē uh nō' puhl). One reason the Germans were able to defeat the Romans was because of an invention they borrowed from the Huns. This invention was the iron stirrup. Using iron stirrups made cavalry stronger than infantry, even the powerful Roman legions. This was because the force of the charging horse was added to the force of the weapon.

✓ **Reading Check**
What does **rule by divine right** mean?

People in History

Diocletian
245 A.D.–313 A.D.

Roman Emperor

Diocletian was born of humble parents in what is now Croatia, an area in eastern Europe ruled by the Romans. He rose to power as an officer in the Roman army, and it was his troops who proclaimed him emperor in 284 B.C. Diocletian's division of the empire into parts earned him the loyalty of powerful supporters such as Constantine I. In 305 A.D., he retired to a castle in present-day Split, Croatia.

CHAPTER 15 THE ROMAN EMPIRE   **243**

Evaluate

Assign Chapter 15 **Performance Assessment Activity** in the TCR.

Administer the **Chapter 15 Test** in the TCR. Testmaker available.

Reteach

Have students work in small groups to list the Roman emperors and their accomplishments.

Assign the Chapter 15 **Reteaching Activity** in the TCR.

Enrich

Have students imagine they are a friend of a Roman emperor and write a feature describing the most difficult problems that this emperor faced.

Assign Chapter 15 **Enrichment Activity** in the TCR.

CLOSE

Write these headings on the board: *Trade, Science, Literature, Government, Law, Religion, Entertainment, Military, Architecture.* Have students describe the characteristics of each of these aspects of the *Pax Romana.*

💾 Use **Interactive Tutor Self-Assessment Software** to review Section 4.

Self-Check Quiz gives students an interactive chapter tutorial. Have them access *Chapter 15 Quiz* at humanheritage.glencoe.com

---

By about 400 A.D., Rome had grown quite weak. In the winter of 406 A.D., the Rhine River froze. Groups of Germans crossed the frozen river and entered Gaul. The Romans were not able to force them back across the border.

In 410 A.D., the Germanic chief Alaric (al' uhr ik) and his soldiers invaded Rome. They burned records and looted the treasury. The Roman Senate told the people, "You can no longer rely on Rome for finance or direction. You are on your own."

Section 4 Assessment

1. **Define:** inflation, barter, rule by divine right.
2. How did wealthy landowners react to economic reforms by Diocletian and Constantine?
3. How did the Germans gain control of the Roman Empire?

Critical Thinking

4. **Identifying Alternatives** What do you think could have been done by either Diocletian or Constantine to save the Roman Empire?

Graphic Organizer Activity

5. Draw this diagram, and use it to summarize the causes for the fall of the Roman Empire.

Chapter Summary & Study Guide

1. Octavian, better known as Augustus, became the first Roman emperor in 27 B.C.
2. Reorganization of the empire by Augustus introduced a 200-year period of peace, called the *Pax Romana.*
3. During the *Pax Romana,* trade increased, and Roman law became standardized.
4. During the *Pax Romana,* about one million people lived in Rome, where they suffered from such problems as overcrowding, pollution, crime, and unemployment.
5. Whether rich or poor, most Roman children went to school until age 12.

6. The Roman government staged free public games to entertain the people.
7. Reasons for the fall of Rome include the lack of a formal rule for inheriting the throne, inflation, and attacks by Germanic invaders.
8. Despite efforts by Diocletian and Constantine I to save the empire, Rome fell to Germanic invaders in 410 A.D.

Self-Check Quiz

Visit the *Human Heritage* Web site at **humanheritage. glencoe.com** and click on *Chapter 15—Self-Check Quiz* to assess your understanding of this chapter.

Section 4 Assessment Answers

1. inflation, increasing prices (p. 240); barter, exchange goods without using money (p. 241); rule by divine right, emperor's right to rule from the gods (p. 243)
2. They opposed the economic reforms or tried to escape them.
3. They defeated Roman legions at the Battle of Adrianople with the help of the iron stirrup, crossed the frozen Rhine River and entered Gaul, and invaded Rome.
4. Answers will vary. Students should explain their ideas.

5. Sample responses: *political*—no written rules on inheriting the throne, influence of the Praetorian Guard; *economic*—high taxes to buy loyalty of soldiers, inflation, gold shortages and declining value of money; *foreign*—frontiers left open to invaders, attacks by German hunters and herders, pressure from the Huns.

Assign Chapter 15 **Section 4 Quiz** in the TCR. Testmaker available.

Using Key Terms

Imagine you are living in Rome around 400 A.D. Use the following words to write a letter to a friend explaining some of the reasons for the decline of the Roman Empire.

emperor   freedmen   census
juris prudentes tariffs   *domus*
gladiators   inflation   barter
rule by divine right

Understanding Main Ideas

1. How did Augustus make life safer for people living in Rome?
2. How did increased trade during the *Pax Romana* affect the Romans?
3. Why did the Romans change the laws set down in the Twelve Tables?
4. Why was it important to make Roman law standardized across the empire?
5. What happened to some animal species as a result of the public games?
6. How did the Praetorian Guard contribute to the empire's decline?
7. Why did Diocletian divide the Roman Empire in two?
8. What were the main reasons for the fall of the Roman Empire?

Critical Thinking

1. What were Augustus's strengths and weaknesses as a ruler?
2. Why would the absence of tariffs increase trade?
3. Would you have enjoyed living in Rome during the *Pax Romana*? Explain.
4. What happens to a government if it does not have rules for passing on power from leader to leader?

Graphic Organizer Activity

Culture Create this diagram, and use it to compare the education of Roman children with the education of children in the United States.

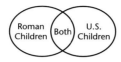

Roman Children — Both — U.S. Children

Geography in History

Location Refer to the map on page 235. Describe the general location of the Roman Empire according to its longitude and latitude. Also identify the location of the imaginary dividing line between the Western and Eastern Empires.

Using Your Journal

Review any details that you may have noted about the contributions of the Romans to world civilization. Write a newspaper article explaining the contributions of the Romans to the ideas about law in the United States today.

245

Using Key Terms

Letters will vary but should include all the words in explaining the end of the Roman Empire.

Understanding Main Ideas

1. by setting up a fire brigade and a police force
2. It brought more business and wealth, turning Italy into a manufacturing center.
3. because the times were different and the old laws did not apply to conquered territories
4. helped govern a large area
5. They were eventually wiped out.
6. They weakened Rome by murdering the emperor and selling the throne.
7. The Roman Empire was too big for one person to rule well.
8. the absence of a written rule for inheriting the throne, high taxes and inflation, and the Germanic invasions

Critical Thinking

1. Answers will vary but should be explained.
2. Answers will vary, but without tariffs, the prices of goods are lower.
3. Answers will vary, but students should provide reasons.
4. Answers will vary.

Graphic Organizer Activity

Review or repeat the discussion of the artifacts on page 232. Then have students complete this exercise, comparing things like subjects studied, length of education, place of schooling, and so on.

Bonus Test Question

For Chapter 15 Test
The Roman Empire's employment office has published a list of job openings, and all people are invited to apply. During the rule of which later Roman emperor, Marcus Aurelius or Diocletian, might this have occurred?

Using Your Journal

Articles will vary but might include making laws fair to everyone; considering a person innocent until proven guilty; requiring the accuser to have to prove a case; standardizing legal procedures.

Geography in History

The empire stretched from about 10° W to 45° E longitude, and north and south from 25° N to 40° N latitude. The division between empires approximately paralleled 20° E longitude.

Chapter 16 Planning Guide

Objectives	Reproducible Resources	Multimedia Resources
Section 1 **The Beginnings** Explain how Jesus' life and teachings formed the basis of Christianity.	Reproducible Lesson Plan Chapter 16 Vocabulary and Guided Reading Activity Reading Essentials and Study Guide 16-1 Chapter 16 Enrichment Activity Section 1 Quiz	ABCNEWS INTERACTIVE Turning Points in World History Vocabulary PuzzleMaker Interactive Tutor Self-Assessment Software ExamView® Pro Testmaker Glencoe Skillbuilder Interactive Workbook, Level 1 Presentation Plus!
Section 2 **Christianity and Rome** Summarize how Christianity spread throughout the Roman Empire.	Reproducible Lesson Plan Reading Essentials and Study Guide 16-2 Chapter 16 Geography and Map Activity Chapter 16 Cooperative Learning Activity Section 2 Quiz	Vocabulary PuzzleMaker Interactive Tutor Self-Assessment Software ExamView® Pro Testmaker Glencoe Skillbuilder Interactive Workbook, Level 1
Section 3 **The Church** Explain how the early Christian church was organized and what relationship existed between Christianity and Roman society before and after the time of Constantine I.	Reproducible Lesson Plan Reading Essentials and Study Guide 16-3 Chapter 16 Chart and Graph Skill Activity Section 3 Quiz	Teaching Transparencies and Activities 16A & 16B Vocabulary PuzzleMaker Interactive Tutor Self-Assessment Software ExamView® Pro Testmaker Glencoe Skillbuilder Interactive Workbook, Level 1
Chapter 16 **Review and Evaluation**	Chapter 16 Reteaching Activity Chapter 16 Performance Assessment Activity Unit 5 Standardized Test Practice Spanish Chapter Summary and Glossary Chapter 16 Test	Vocabulary PuzzleMaker Interactive Tutor Self-Assessment Software Glencoe Skillbuilder Interactive Workbook, Level 1 Audiocassettes* ExamView® Pro Testmaker

*Also available in Spanish.

Presentation Plus!

Use Glencoe's **Presentation Plus!** multimedia teacher tool to easily present dynamic lessons that visually excite your students. Using Microsoft® PowerPoint, you can customize the presentations to create your own personalized lessons.

Interactive Lesson Planner

Planning has never been easier! Using this CD-ROM, organize your week, month, semester, or year with all the help you need. The **Interactive Lesson Planner** gives you access to all of the blackline masters which accompany *Human Heritage.*

✓ PERFORMANCE ASSESSMENT ACTIVITIES

Religion Have students imagine that they are Constantine I. Tell them to write a speech in which Constantine explains to his soldiers that he has converted to Christianity. Call on students to read their speeches to the class.

CHAPTER RESOURCES

LITERATURE ABOUT THE PERIOD

Comte, Fernand. *Sacred Writings of World Religions.* Chambers, 1992. Examines the history, beliefs, and major figures of more than 20 religions, among them Judaism, Islam, and Christianity.

READINGS FOR THE STUDENT

Rice, Edward. *The Early Christians: A Young People's Pictorial History of the Church.* Farrar Straus, 1963. An adaptation of a well-known Roman Catholic scholar's history of the early Church.

READINGS FOR THE TEACHER

Chadwick, Henry and G. R. Evans, eds. *Atlas of the Christian Church.* Facts on File, 1987. Offers an authoritative survey of the impact of the Christian Church on world civilization.

Gibbon, Edward. *The Early Growth of Christianity & the History of the First Christians.* American Classical College Press, 1986. Discusses the history of the first Christians.

KEY TO ABILITY LEVELS

Teaching strategies have been coded for varying learning styles and abilities.

L1 Level 1 activities are **basic** activities and should be within the ability range of all students.

L2 Level 2 activities are **average** activities and should be within the ability range of the average to above-average student.

L3 Level 3 activities are **challenging** activities designed for the ability range of above-average students.

ELL ELL activities should be within the ability range of English Language Learning students.

NATIONAL GEOGRAPHIC SOCIETY — Teacher's Corner

INDEX TO NATIONAL GEOGRAPHIC MAGAZINE

The following articles relate to this chapter:

- "The Three Faces of Jerusalem," by Alan Mairson, April 1996.
- "New Views of the Holy Land," by Richard Cleave and Technion-Israel Institute of Technology, June 1995.

NATIONAL GEOGRAPHIC SOCIETY PRODUCTS AVAILABLE FROM GLENCOE

To order the following, call Glencoe at 1-800-334-7344:

- *PicturePack: Ancient Rome (Transparencies)*
- *PictureShow: Ancient Civilizations: Greece and Rome (CD-ROM)*
- *PicturePack: Ancient Civilizations Library, Part I (Transparencies)*

ADDITIONAL NATIONAL GEOGRAPHIC SOCIETY PRODUCTS

To order the following, call National Geographic at 1-800-368-2728:

- *Jerusalem: Within These Walls (Video)*

Access *National Geographic's* new dynamic MapMachine Web site and other geography resources at:
http://www.nationalgeographic.com/
http://www.nationalgeographic.com/maps/

  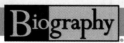

The following videotape programs are available from Glencoe:

- **Constantine: The Christian Emperor**
  0-7670-0577-5
- **Shroud of Turin**
  1-56501-557-6
- **Who Built the Catacombs?**
  1-56501-881-8

To order, call Glencoe at 1-800-334-7344. To find classroom resources to accompany many of these, check:

A&E Television: http://www.aetv.com
The History Channel:
http://www.historychannel.com

CHAPTER
16

Christianity
1 B.C.–1054 A.D.

OVERVIEW

Chapter 16 describes the rise of Christianity and its impact on the Roman Empire.

➤ **Section 1** discusses the origins of Christianity.

➤ **Section 2** describes the difficulties Christianity faced in a hostile Roman society.

➤ **Section 3** explains the organization of the Roman Catholic church.

CHAPTER OBJECTIVES

After reading Chapter 16, students will be able to:

1. explain how Jesus' life and teachings formed the basis of Christianity.

2. trace the spread of Christianity.

3. explain how the early Christian church was organized.

4. discuss the relationship between Christianity and Roman society before and after the time of Constantine I.

EXAMINING ARTIFACTS

Ask students why, based on the jeweled artifact, Roman officials might consider Jesus a threat. *(Students may note that he is seated on a throne, a symbol of royal power, and portrayed as a sacred figure, which challenged Roman gods.)* Tell students that in this chapter they will learn how Romans tried to stop Christianity and how it spread nonetheless.

◄ Early Christian symbol

Jesus on his throne ►

30 A.D.	64 A.D.	312 A.D.	392 A.D.	1054 A.D.
Jesus is crucified by Romans	**Romans ban Christianity**	**Constantine I accepts Christianity**	**Christianity becomes official religion of Roman Empire**	**Latin and Greek churches separate**

246 UNIT 5 THE ROMANS

PERFORMANCE ASSESSMENT ✓

Use the Performance Assessment Activities on page 246B to help you evaluate students as they complete the chapter.

TEACHING RESOURCES

TEACHER PLANNING AND SUPPORT

🗁 Reproducible Lesson Plan
🗁 Block Scheduling Implementation Guide
🗁 Videodisc Bar Code Correlation
💿 Presentation Plus!

REVIEW AND REINFORCEMENT

🗁 Reading Essentials and Study Guide 16-1, 16-2, 16-3
🗁 Chapter 16 Vocabulary and Guided Reading Activity
💾 Vocabulary PuzzleMaker Software
 Teaching Transparencies 16A & 16B
🗁 Chapter 16 Reteaching Activity

🗁 Chapter 16 Cooperative Learning Activity
🗁 Chapter 16 Activity Book Activity
🗁 Chapter 16 Chart and Graph Skill Activity
💾 Interactive Tutor Self-Assessment Software
💿📼 Unit 5 MindJogger VideoQuiz

APPLICATION AND HANDS-ON ACTIVITIES

🗁 Daily World History, Geography, and Culture Question

GEOGRAPHY ACTIVITIES

🗁 Chapter 16 Geography and Map Activity
🗁 Social Studies Outline Map Resource Book

Chapter Focus

 Read to Discover

- How Jesus' life and teachings formed the basis of Christianity.
- How Christianity spread throughout the Roman Empire.
- How the early Christian church was organized.
- What relationship existed between Christianity and Roman society before and after the time of Constantine I.
- What life was like for the early monks and nuns.

Terms to Learn	People to Know	Places to Locate
scriptures	Jesus	Bethlehem
messiah	Paul	Nazareth
gentiles	Constantine I	Jerusalem
missionary	Theodosius	
churches	Jerome	
apostles	Augustine	
priest		
bishop		
heresy		
monks		
nun		

Why It's Important   Just as the Romans influenced the lives of people they conquered, these people influenced the lives of the Romans. Among those who brought new ideas and important changes to the Roman Empire were the Christians. Their religion, Christianity, started in Palestine among the Jews and later spread throughout the empire and the world. Despite cruel treatment, the early Christians clung to their faith, and by 400 A.D. most Romans had come to accept the religion as their own.

Chapter Overview

Visit the *Human Heritage* Web site at **humanheritage.glencoe.com** and click on **Chapter 16— Chapter Overviews** to preview this chapter.

SECTION 1   The Beginnings

Christianity is based on the life and teachings of Jesus (jē' zuhs), who lived in Palestine during the reign of Augustus. After Jesus died, his teachings were spread by his followers. Christianity survived the fall of Rome and grew to be one of the major influences on western civilization.

The Life of Jesus   Jesus, born a Jew in the town of Bethlehem (beth' luh hem), grew up in Nazareth (naz' uhr uhth). There, he received a Jewish education. He studied the **scriptures**

✔ Reading Check
What are the **scriptures?**

INTERDISCIPLINARY CONNECTIONS

 World History & Art Transparency 15, *Cover of the Lindau Gospels*

Focus on World Art Print 15, *Saint George and the Dragon*

World Music: Cultural Traditions

ENRICHMENT AND EXTENSION

World History Primary Source Document Library CD-ROM

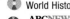 Turning Points in World History

 Chapter 16 Enrichment Activity

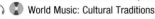 Foods Around the World

ASSESSMENT AND EVALUATION

Chapter 16 Performance Assessment Activity

Chapter 16 Section Quizzes 16-1, 16-2, 16-3

Chapter 16 Test

Unit 5 Standardized Test Practice

Chapter 16 ExamView® Pro Testmaker Software

Chapter 16 Digests Audiocassettes Activities and Tests

SPANISH RESOURCES

Chapter 16 Spanish Chapter Summary and Glossary

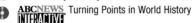 Chapter 16 Spanish Chapter Digests Audiocassettes Activities and Tests

---

Chapter Overview introduces students to chapter content and key terms. Have them access **Chapter 16 Overview** at **humanheritage.glencoe.com**

FOCUS

⚑ Bellringer

Write the following unfinished statement on the chalkboard. *"When I hear the word Christianity the first thing I think of is_____."* Ask students to fill in the blank.

Motivational Activity

Discuss student responses to the unfinished statement. Explain that in this chapter they will learn about the teachings of Jesus and the religion that eventually became Christianity.

GUIDE TO READING

Reading Strategy

Ask students to read "Why It's Important" and summarize the chapter's main theme. *(Despite early resistance, Romans came to accept Christianity—a religion that started in Palestine among the Jews.)*

Vocabulary Precheck

Ask students to define each of the "Terms to Learn." Have a volunteer consult the dictionary for any unfamiliar words. **L1** **ELL**

💾 Use the Vocabulary PuzzleMaker for Chapter 16 to create a crossword puzzle. **L1**

🗂 Assign Chapter 16 Vocabulary and Guided Reading Activity.

🗂 Assign Reading Essentials and Study Guide 16-1.

✔ Reading Check Answer
Scriptures are sacred writings.

TEACH

Guided Practice

Writing Ask the students to rewrite the parable of the man from Samaria (the Good Samaritan) as if the story took place in modern times. Have students read their parables to the class and explain any changes in the meaning from the original that occurred in modernizing it.

During the time that Jesus preached, there were about 2½ million Jews in Palestine and another 4 million elsewhere in the Roman Empire.

Reading Check Answer
Jews waited for the arrival of a **messiah** who would save them.

ABCNEWS INTERACTIVE™

Videodisc
Turning Points in World History

Side One
Chapter 6

Title: *Jerusalem: City of Three Faiths*
Subject: Christian, Muslim, and Jewish scholars discuss the importance of Jerusalem to their three faiths.
Ask: Why is the land of Israel significant to Christianity? *(The events of Jesus' life took place there.)*

Mosaic of Christian Symbol

(skrip' churz), or sacred writings, and learned prayers in the Hebrew language. Later, he went to work as a carpenter.

When he was about 30 years old, Jesus began to travel around Palestine preaching to people. Men and women came in large numbers from all over the country to see and hear him. Jesus taught that God created all people and loves them the way a father loves his children. Therefore, people should behave like God's children and love God and one another. Jesus said that God loves even people who have sinned. Jesus told people that if they were truly sorry and placed their trust in God, they would be forgiven.

Jesus spoke in the everyday language of the people. He presented his teachings in *parables* (par' uh buhlz), or stories, about persons and things that were familiar to his listeners. In this way, they could better understand the religious principles he was trying to teach. For example, in the parable of the Good Samaritan (suh mar' uh tuhn), Jesus told about a man from Jerusalem who was attacked by robbers. They beat the man severely and left him lying in the road. Two passers-by from Jerusalem saw him there but did nothing. Then came a man from the city of Samaria (suh mar' ē uh). He stopped, washed the man's wounds, and carried him to a nearby inn. The parable taught that people should not ignore wrong but should do something about it. The parable also taught that people should help everyone, not just those from their own community.

In 30 A.D., after about three years of preaching, Jesus and 12 of his disciples went to Jerusalem to celebrate Passover, the holiday that marks the exodus of the Jews from Egypt. At the time, there was much unrest in the city. Many Romans were angry because the Jews refused to worship statues of the Roman emperor. The Jews were tired of the high taxes they had to pay and of the pressure put on them by the Romans. They hoped and waited for a **messiah** (muh sī' uh), or someone who would save them.

When Jesus arrived in Jerusalem, many Jews greeted him as the messiah. This worried other Jews and Romans alike. Jesus was convicted of treason under Roman law and was *crucified* (krū' suh fīd), or executed on a cross, outside Jerusalem. Usually, only lower-class criminals were killed in this way.

The loss of their leader greatly saddened Jesus' disciples. Then, according to Christian tradition, Jesus rose from the dead. He remained on Earth for 40 days before going directly to heaven. His *resurrection* (rez uh rek' shuhn), or rising from the dead, convinced his disciples that Jesus was the Son of God who had become man. They believed that because Jesus had suffered death and had risen to life, he could forgive the sins of all people. They thought that anyone who believed in Jesus and lived by his teachings would know eternal life after death. From then on, the disciples called him Christ, after the Greek word *Christos* (khrēs tōs'), meaning "messiah."

Reading Check
Why did Jews await the arrival of a **messiah?**

Painting of Jesus' Disciples

MEETING SPECIAL NEEDS

Have auditory learners interview a Christian minister, a priest, or a Jewish rabbi about the Jewish roots of Christianity. Students should prepare a list of questions in advance of their interview, and then they should tape record their interviews. Have students report orally on their interviews.

Refer to *Inclusion for the Middle School Social Studies Classroom: Strategies and Activities* for additional resources.

THE LAST SUPPER   The night before he was crucified, Jesus met with his closest disciples for the meal that marks the start of Passover. At this meal, known as the Last Supper, Jesus set the guidelines for later Christian ceremonies. **Why did Jesus and his disciples go to Jerusalem?**

LINKING PAST TO PRESENT

About 1497, Italian Leonardo da Vinci painted the scene "The Last Supper" on a monastery wall. Soon after he finished the scene, the paint began to peel. Today the painting, although still greatly admired and considered a masterpiece, is in poor condition.

Reading Check Answer
The **gentiles** were non-Jews.

Paul   The disciples were among the first people to become Christians. After Jesus died, they tried to spread his *gospel,* or teachings, among the Jews in Palestine. They had little success, however. Most Palestinian Jews wanted a political messiah. They were not interested in a religious one. The disciples then began to spread their message to Jews who lived outside Palestine. Soon, small groups of people who believed in Christ were meeting in Antioch (ant' ē ahk), Corinth, Rome, and other trading cities of the Mediterranean area.

At about the same time, a Jew named Paul decided to teach Christianity to **gentiles** (jen' tīls), or non-Jews, as well as to Jews. Paul had once been a close follower of Judaism. Then, according to Christian tradition, while he was traveling on the road to Damascus (duh mas' kuhs), Paul was blinded by a bright light and heard Christ's voice. After he was able to see again, Paul became a Christian. He spent the rest of his life spreading the Christian message throughout the Roman world.

Reading Check
Who were the **gentiles?**

HOME VIDEO.

The following videotape program is available from Glencoe to enrich Chapter 16:

• **Shroud of Turin**

To find classroom resources to accompany this video, check the following home page:

A&E Television:
http://www.aetv.com

CHAPTER 16 CHRISTIANITY   **249**

MULTICULTURAL PERSPECTIVES

Messiah comes from a Hebrew word that means "the anointed one." The term derives from an ancient but widespread custom of using sacred oil in certain kinds of religious ceremonies. A priest might, for instance, place holy oil on the head of a new ruler to indicate God's approval. Anointing was also used in times of danger to give symbolic protection. Sometimes objects (even weapons) were anointed. The Greek word *Christos* also means "anointed one."

MAKING CONNECTIONS

➤➤ **History** The last Roman emperor to persecute large numbers of Christians was Diocletian. In A.D. 311, Galerius, ruler of the Eastern Roman Empire, permitted freedom of worship.

✓ **Reading Check Answer**
Paul is often considered the first **missionary** because of his work to spread religious beliefs to those who do not believe.

DID YOU KNOW ⁇

According to traditional legend, the emperor Nero sat in his palace and "fiddled" while Rome burned. In reality there were no fiddles at the time; Nero played a harp. One story hinted that Nero himself set fire to the city so he could admire the sight of Rome in flames.

💾 Use **Interactive Tutor Self-Assessment Software** to review Section 1.

HISTORY Online
Student Web Activity objectives, goals, and answers can be found at the *Chapter 16 Web Activity Lesson Plan* at humanheritage.glencoe.com

💾 Use the **Vocabulary Puzzle-Maker** to create crossword and word search puzzles.

In each city where Paul preached, new Christian communities formed. Paul wrote letters to these groups to help guide the members. In his letters, he stated that gentiles who became Christians did not have to follow Jewish rituals and laws. All they needed was to have faith in Jesus. This appealed to many people.

Paul was very important to the growth of Christianity. He was its first **missionary** (mish' uh ner ē), or person who spreads religious beliefs to those who do not believe. After Paul's death, other Christian missionaries continued his work.

✓ **Reading Check**
Why is Paul considered the first Christian **missionary**?

Section 1 Assessment

1. **Define:** scriptures, messiah, gentiles, missionary.
2. Why did the Romans charge Jesus with treason?
3. What changes did Paul make in the Christian religion?

Critical Thinking
4. **Demonstrating Reasoned Judgment** Of the people you know about today, who could be called a Good Samaritan? Give examples.

Graphic Organizer Activity
5. Draw this diagram, and use it to show some of the Christian beliefs taught by Jesus.

[Diagram: Jesus' Teachings]

SECTION 2 Christianity and Rome

The Roman Empire helped Christianity spread. The *Pax Romana* allowed missionaries to move across Roman lands in safety. The Roman system of roads helped them go from one place to another quickly. Since most people spoke either Latin or Greek, the missionaries could talk with them directly.

Political Conditions Political conditions did not favor the spread of Christianity, however. Although all people in the Roman Empire were generally allowed to worship freely, the Romans expected everyone to honor the emperor as a god. The Christians, like the Jews, refused to do this. They claimed that only God could be worshiped. This made the Romans angry.

The Romans also did not like other Christian ideas. For example, Christians did not want to serve in the army or hold public office. They often criticized Roman festivals and games. They taught that all people would be equal in heaven if they followed Jesus' teachings.

Because of these differences, the Romans blamed and punished Christians for all kinds of disasters, such as plagues and famines (fam' uhnz). In 64 A.D., the Romans accused the Chris-

HISTORY Online
Student Web Activity
Visit the *Human Heritage* Web site at humanheritage.glencoe.com and click on *Chapter 16—Student Web Activities* to find out more about early Christianity.

Section 1 Assessment Answers

1. scriptures, sacred writings (p. 247); messiah, Savior (p. 248); gentiles, non-Jews (p. 249); missionary, person who spreads religious beliefs to nonbelievers (p. 250)
2. because many Jews greeted him like the messiah, which threatened the power of the Roman emperor
3. that gentiles who became Christians did not have to follow Jewish rituals and laws but needed only to have faith in Jesus

4. Answers will vary but should be examples of situations in which a person came to the help of another person.
5. Sample beliefs: God created all people and loves them, people should behave like God's children and love one another, God loves even people who have sinned, anyone who puts trust in God will be forgiven, people should help each other.

Assign Chapter 16 **Section 1 Quiz** in the TCR. Testmaker available.

tians of starting a fire that burned much of Rome. Christianity was then made illegal, and many Christians were killed.

Some officials paid no attention to the law that made Christianity illegal. However, Christians still had a hard time in most areas. In Rome, they were not allowed to use Roman burial places. They had to bury their dead in crowded catacombs.

The Spread of Christianity   Even with all of the hardships, Christianity spread. It was of more interest to the poor workers and enslaved people in the cities. They led very hard lives. They liked a religion that promised a happier life after death.

Over time, however, Christianity began to draw people from all classes. After 250 A.D., many Romans grew tired of war and

MAP STUDY

MOVEMENT By 1100 Christianity had spread throughout most of Europe and parts of Asia and North Africa. **How did Paul's journeys help the spread of Christianity?**

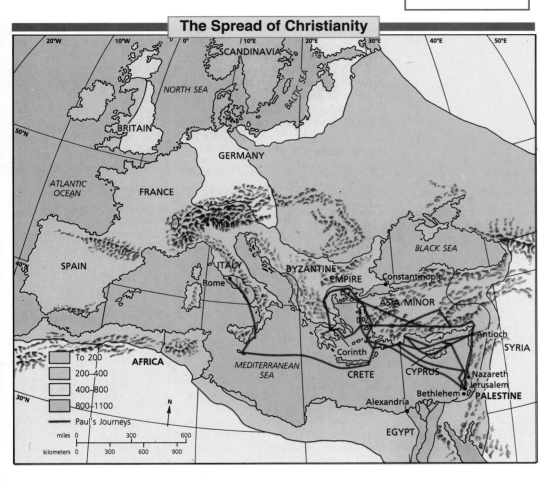

The Spread of Christianity

To 200
200–400
400–800
800–1100
— Paul's Journeys

L3 Geography: Region Have students refer to the map of the "Spread of Christianity." Have them discuss the difference in size of the religion's area of influence from 200 to 1100, and the pattern, if any, that it followed. Then have students use the map scale to calculate the approximate length of the empire, from west to east, by the year 1100.

L2 Critical Thinking Have students discuss the major differences in attitudes that existed between some Roman non-Christians and Christians. Have students list these differences in two columns under the headings *Christian* and *non-Christian.* *(Students should mention differences over army service, and who should be honored as a god, hold public office, and be blamed for disasters.)* **ELL**

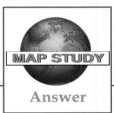

MAP STUDY

Answer

Paul traveled extensively throughout the Mediterranean region spreading the ideas of Christianity.

Assign Chapter 16 **Geography and Map Activity** in the TCR.

DID YOU KNOW

Early Christians tried to escape Roman persecution by worshiping in catacombs—underground passages dug by the Christians.

COOPERATIVE LEARNING

Divide students into several groups. Have each group research one of the various religions practiced in the Roman Empire. Make sure each group member is responsible for either research, compiling information, providing illustrations, preparing answers for possible questions, or presenting to the class. Religions to be researched include the official religion of Rome, Judaism, Christianity, and the Persian and Egyptian mystery religions, such as Mithraism and the cult of Isis. Have the groups act as a panel, answering questions from the class about the religion it studied.

Assign Chapter 16 *Cooperative Learning Activity* in the TCR.

feared the end of the empire. They began to admire the certainty and courage of the Christian missionaries. They wanted the love, kindness, and feeling of safety that Christianity offered. At the same time, many Christians started to accept the empire.

Constantine I and Theodosius In 312 A.D., Constantine I, who was a general at the time, accepted Christianity. Legend says that as he was about to go into battle, Constantine saw a flaming cross in the sky. Written beneath the cross were the Latin words *in hoc signo vinces* (in hok sig' nō win' kās). This means, "In this sign thou shalt conquer." Constantine won the battle and with it the throne of the Roman Empire. Constantine believed God had helped him gain his victory. Because of this, he ordered his soldiers to paint crosses on their shields.

The following year, the Edict (ē' dikt) of Milan (mi lan') was issued. It gave religious freedom to all people. It also made Christianity legal. Constantine I did many other things to help Christianity grow. He had churches built in Rome and Jerusalem. He used government money to pay for Christian schools. He let church leaders enter government service and excused them from paying taxes.

The emperor who followed Constantine I continued pro-Christian policies. In 392 A.D., Emperor Theodosius (thē uh dō' shē uhs) made Christianity the official religion of the Roman Empire. At the same time, he outlawed all other religions.

Section 2 Assessment

1. What factors brought about a change in attitude between Romans and Christians?

Critical Thinking

2. **Making Inferences** Why do you think the hardships put on Christians by the Romans could not stop the spread of Christianity?

Graphic Organizer Activity

3. Draw this diagram, and use it to show changes in the relationship between Christianity and Roman society before and after the time of Constantine I.

✔ **Reading Check**
Why did early Christians form **churches**?

SECTION 3 The Church

Early Christians thought the end of the world was near. At the time, they believed Jesus would return to set up God's kingdom on Earth. While they were waiting for this to happen, they lived together in small groups called **churches.** They shared their possessions and took turns leading worship services in

252

homes and outdoors. Each group was in charge of its own affairs. **Apostles** (uh pos' uhls), or those people Jesus chose to teach his gospel, visited the different groups. The apostles taught and gave advice. They also provided a sense of unity.

Church Structure

After the apostles died, Christians realized that Jesus was not going to return to Earth as quickly as they had expected. They looked for ways to hold their churches together. One way was by organizing the churches. They used the Roman Empire's structure of government as a model for this organization.

By 300 A.D., each church was called a **parish** (par' ish). Each had a leader known as a **priest.** Several parishes were put together into larger groups. Each group was called a **diocese** (dī' uh sis), a word that originally meant a Roman military district. A **bishop** headed each diocese. The most important bishops were called **archbishops.** They governed churches in larger cities. The five leading archbishops were called **patriarchs** (pā' trē arks).

As time went on, the archbishop of Rome began to claim power over the other archbishops. By 600 A.D., he was called Pope. This comes from a Latin word meaning "father." Christians who spoke Latin saw him as the head of all the churches. Christians who spoke Greek, however, would not accept him as the leader of their churches. They turned instead to the archbishop of Constantinople. In 1054 A.D., the two church groups separated. The Latin churches as a group became known as the Roman Catholic Church. The Greek churches became known as the Eastern Orthodox Church.

The New Testament

At the same time Christians were developing a church organization, they were deciding what writings to put into the New Testament, or Christian scriptures. Jesus had left no written records. However, after his death, others wrote about Jesus' life and teachings.

Toward the end of the 300s A.D., four accounts were accepted as part of the New Testament. The accounts were believed to have been written by Matthew, Mark, Luke, and John. These men were four of Jesus' early followers. A number of letters written by Paul and other disciples were also accepted as part of the New Testament.

At about the same time, bishops met to discuss questions about Christian thinking. Decisions they reached at these meetings came to be accepted as official *doctrine* (dok' truhn), or statements of faith. The points of view the bishops did not accept were declared to be **heresy** (her' uh sē), or false doctrines.

Fathers of the Church

Between 100 and 500 A.D., different scholars wrote works that greatly influenced later Christians. These scholars became known as the "Fathers of the Church."

CHAPTER 16 CHRISTIANITY   253

Reading Check
Who were the **apostles?**

Reading Check
What is a **parish?** What was the role of an early **priest?** What was the original meaning of **diocese?**

Reading Check
What was the role of the **bishop?** Who were the **archbishops** and **patriarchs?**

Reading Check
What did bishops consider as **heresy?**

Reading Check Answer
The **apostles** were the people Jesus chose to spread his teachings.

Reading Check Answer
A **parish** is a local church. A **priest** was the leader of a parish.
The word **diocese** originally meant a Roman military district.

MAKING CONNECTIONS

➤➤ **Language** The word *church* means "belonging to the Lord."

Reading Check Answer
A **bishop** headed each diocese. **Archbishops** were the most important bishops, and the five leading archbishops were called **patriarchs.**

Independent Practice

L3 **Critical Thinking** Ask students to write a brief description of everything they can remember that happened in class the day before. Have students read descriptions aloud to compare details. After students conclude that some differences are bound to appear, ask them why they think the same events are retold in different chapters of the New Testament.

Reading Check Answer
Bishops considered views contrary to official church teachings as **heresy**.

MULTICULTURAL PERSPECTIVES

The Bible is the most sacred book to Christians. They consider the Bible to be the word of God. The word *Bible* comes from a Greek word that means "books." The Bible is not one book but actually a collection of books, or sections. The number of books in the Bible depends on the Christian group. The Roman Catholic Bible includes 73 books, while most Protestant groups include 66 books in their Bible. It is the most-read book in history.

Followers of Benedict promised to give up all their possessions, wear simple clothes, and eat only certain foods. They agreed not to marry, obeyed abbots without question, and attended religious services day and night. They also worked in the fields and church and spent their lives serving Christ.

DID YOU KNOW

St. Augustine was born a Christian but left Christianity at age 17. In 387 A.D., he met St. Ambrose, the bishop of Milan, who influenced him to return to Christianity.

L1 **The Arts** Many movies have been made about the life of Jesus or the impact of Christianity on the people of ancient Rome. Have students view a videotape of *The Robe, Ben Hur, The Silver Chalice,* or *The Greatest Story Ever Told* and then write a review of the film. Tell them to include descriptions of details they learned about life under *Pax Romana* (for example, in *Ben Hur,* the chariot races; in *The Silver Chalice,* the Greek artisan and enslaved person; *The Robe,* the Roman legionaries). **ELL**

Religious Orders   The religious order that lived at the monastery at Monte Cassino (left) followed the teachings of Benedict and were known as Benedictines. In 1950, Mother Teresa, an eastern European nun, continued this tradition by founding the Missionaries of Charity, an order dedicated to helping the poor of India (right). **What rules did early members of the Benedictine order follow?**

People in History

Saint Augustine
354 A.D.–430 A.D.

Christian Scholar

Augustine was born in present-day Algeria. In 387 A.D., he embraced Christianity. As invaders poured into Rome, Augustine became one of the leading defenders of Christianity. After his death, church leaders declared him a saint.

One such scholar was Jerome (juh rōm'). He translated the Old and New Testaments into Latin. His translation was called the *Vulgate* (vul' gāt). It became the official Bible used by the Roman Catholic Church.

Augustine (o' guh stēn) was an important leader of Christian thought. His best-known work was *City of God.* In it, he defended Christianity against those who said that Rome would not have fallen if it had not accepted Christianity. Augustine said that Rome fell because it became rich and corrupt and persecuted Christians.

Monasteries   In the early years of Christianity, thousands of Christians left the cities to live and pray alone in isolated areas. Such people were known as *hermits.* In Egypt and Syria especially, thousands of hermits lived in the desert. They believed that this would help them grow closer to Christ.

A hermit was protected from the temptations of daily life. At the same time, however, such a person was not doing anything to improve the world. Near the end of the 300s A.D., a bishop named Basil (baz' uhl) suggested a different way of life. He said that Christians should form religious settlements near cities. In this way, they would be protected from the evils of the world. At the same time, they could help other people by doing good deeds and

EXTENDING THE CONTENT

The first significant translation of the scriptures was by St. Jerome, which he began in about 383 at the request of the Pope. Jerome first translated the Gospels. They came from several sources, mainly Greek. The scholarly Jerome then decided the standard Greek translation of the Old Testament would not do. He went back to Hebrew sources and made a new translation. His work completed in about 405, was called *Vulgate,* from the Latin word meaning popular.

by setting an example of Christian living. Many Christians took Basil's advice.

Christian men who did as Basil suggested were called **monks.** Their settlements, or communities, were known as **monasteries** (mon' uh ster ēz). Christian women who did the same were called **nuns.** They lived in quarters of their own called **convents** (kon' vents). Basil drew up a list of rules for these religious communities. This list, which is known as the Basilian (buh zil' ē uhn) Rule, became the model for Eastern Orthodox religious life.

In the West, another set of rules called the Benedictine (ben uh dik' tuhn) Rule was followed. It was drawn up about 529 A.D. by an Italian named Benedict (ben' uh dikt). The monks who followed Benedict's rule promised to give up all their possessions before entering a monastery. They agreed to wear simple clothes and eat only certain foods. They could not marry. They had to obey without question the orders of the **abbot** (ab' uht), or leader of the monastery. They had to attend religious services seven times during the day and once at midnight. They also were expected to work six or seven hours a day in the fields around the monastery. When they grew older, they did clerical work or worked as carpenters and weavers. They spent their whole lives serving Christ.

Reading Check
Why did **monks** build the first **monasteries?** Why did Christian women become **nuns** and live at **convents?**

Reading Check
What was the role of an **abbot?**

EARLY CHRISTIANS   Church leaders often dictated their thoughts as Pope Gregory is shown (left) doing. Those thoughts were studied by a church monk shown here (right) in order to improve his knowledge of Christianity. **Where did monks at this time live?**

CHAPTER 16 CHRISTIANITY   **255**

EXTENDING THE CONTENT

Many monks copied ancient manuscripts. Without their efforts many literature classics would have been lost. Monks also served as missionaries, sent by the monasteries to spread the religious message to neighboring people. Nuns taught needlework and the medicinal use of herbs to the daughters of nobles.

Reading Check Answer
Monks built the first **monasteries** to do good works and serve as an example of Christian living.
Christian women became **nuns** and lived at **convents** for much the same reason as monks.

Reading Check Answer
An **abbot** was the leader of a monastery.

ASSESS

Check for Understanding
Ask students to summarize the main points of the chapter, orally or in writing. Discuss the answers to the Section and Chapter Assessment questions.

Evaluate
Assign Chapter 16 **Performance Assessment Activity** in the TCR.
Administer **Chapter 16 Test** in the TCR. Testmaker available.

Reteach
Help students create an outline of the chapter on the board. Have students work in pairs to ask one another questions using the outline.
Assign Chapter 16 **Reteaching Activity** in the TCR.

Enrich
Have students research the parables told by Jesus. Have students retell a parable to the class and explain its meaning.
Assign Chapter 16 **Enrichment Activity** in the TCR.

CAPTION ANSWER
monasteries

CLOSE

Ask students to discuss what
Jesus meant when he said that
he would make his disciples
"fishers of men." *(He would
teach them to convert others to
Christianity.)* Ask students if
they think Jesus succeeded in
making his disciples "fishers of
men."

Use **Interactive Tutor Self-
Assessment Software** to review
Section 3.

Self-Check Quiz gives students
an interactive chapter tutorial. Have
them access *Chapter 16 Quiz* at
humanheritage.glencoe.com

By 800 A.D., monks were playing an important role in
spreading Christianity throughout Europe. By preserving old
Roman and Greek writings, they helped western civilization survive and progress.

Section 3 Assessment

1. **Define:** churches, apostles, parish,
   priest, diocese, bishop, archbishops,
   patriarchs, heresy, monks, monasteries,
   nuns, convents, abbot.
2. How was the early Christian church
   organized?
3. How did monks help western civilization survive?

Critical Thinking

4. **Making Generalizations** What general statement can you make about the
   main purpose of monastic life?

Graphic Organizer Activity

5. Draw this diagram, and use it to compare the lives of hermits with the lives
   of monks and nuns.

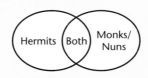

Chapter Summary & Study Guide

1. Jesus' teachings angered Roman officials, who arrested and executed him
   around 30 A.D.
2. Paul preached Christianity to Jews
   and non-Jews alike, helping to make
   Christianity a world religion.
3. Some Romans, particularly the emperors, tried unsuccessfully to stop the
   spread of Christianity.
4. In 313 A.D., Christianity became legal
   in Rome. In 392 A.D., it became the
   empire's official religion.
5. By the end of the 500s A.D., early
   Christians had organized a church
   and decided which writings should
   appear in the New Testament.
6. By 600 A.D., most Latin-speaking
   Christians looked on the Pope in
   Rome as the head of the Church.
7. In 1054 A.D., most Greek-speaking
   Christians split from the Latin Church
   to form the Eastern Orthodox Church.
8. Religious scholars and monks helped
   preserve Greek and Roman writings
   and wrote works that greatly influenced later Christian thinkers.

Self-Check Quiz

Visit the *Human Heritage* Web site at **humanheritage.
glencoe.com** and click on *Chapter 16—Self-Check Quiz*
to assess your understanding of this chapter.

Section 3 Assessment Answers

1. All terms are defined in the text Glossary.
2. It was modeled after the Roman government. Each church or parish was led by a
priest. Several parishes formed a diocese
headed by a bishop. The archbishops led
city churches.
3. by preserving old Roman and Greek
writings
4. Answers will vary, but most statements
will focus on a desire to do good deeds and

set an example for Christian living.
5. Comparisons will vary, but both hermits
and monks and nuns followed lives of religious devotion, and both tried to escape
worldly evils. Hermits, however, lived
apart from society, while monks and nuns
tried to help other people through example
and teaching.
Assign Chapter 16 **Section 3 Quiz** in the
TCR. Testmaker available.

Using Key Terms

Sort the following words into these categories: *people*, *places*, and *other*, as they apply to the beginning of Christianity. Then write one sentence explaining each term you classified as *other*.

scriptures   messiah   gentiles
missionary   churches   apostles
parish   priest   diocese
bishop   archbishops   patriarchs
heresy   monks   monasteries
nuns   convents   abbot

Understanding Main Ideas

1. Where did Christianity start?
2. Why did Jesus teach in parables?
3. Why did the Romans blame and punish the Christians for many disasters?
4. What groups of people were first attracted to Christianity?
5. What legend is told about Constantine I?
6. Why did Christians develop a church organization?
7. Why did the Latin and Greek churches split into two groups?
8. What kinds of work did the monks do?

Critical Thinking

1. Why do you think people seemed to remember Jesus' teachings more when he used parables?
2. Do you think citizens should have religious freedom or be required to follow one official religion? Explain.
3. What do you think could have been done to prevent the split between the Latin and Greek churches?
4. Would you have been interested in becoming a monk or nun in 600 A.D.? Explain.

Graphic Organizer Activity

Culture Create a chart like the one shown, and use it to show the organization of the early Church. Arrange these religious offices in order of authority: monks and nuns, patriarchs, bishops, pope, archbishops, priests.

Geography in History

Place Refer to the map on page 251, noting Paul's journeys. Describe what geographic features and landscape Paul would have seen as he traveled from Antioch to Corinth.

Using Your Journal

Review any details you may have noted about Roman contributions to world civilization. Write a short explanation of how Roman ideas about religion have affected present-day thoughts, beliefs, and ideas.

257

Bonus Test Question

For Chapter 16 Test Two Romans are talking. One states "If the winter of 406 had been milder, the empire would not have fallen." The other claims, "No. The winter had no effect. The empire was doomed." With whom do you agree? Why?

Using Your Journal

Essays will vary but should include the idea that Christianity is a strong religious force in Western civilization today.

Geography in History

As Paul traveled from Antioch to Corinth overland he would encounter arid land, seacoast, mountains, islands, and a peninsula. Traveling by sea, he would have viewed the same features.

Building Vocabulary

People
messiah
gentiles
missionary
apostles
priest
bishop
archbishop
patriarchs

Places
parish
diocese
monasteries
convents

Other
scriptures
heresy

Check For Understanding

1. in Palestine among the Jews
2. so listeners could better understand his religious principles
3. because the Romans did not like Christian ideas
4. the poor and enslaved
5. he saw a flaming cross in the sky with the words *in hoc signo vinces* written beneath it
6. to hold their churches together while they waited for Jesus to return to Earth
7. because the Greek Christians would not accept the Pope
8. They attended religious services, worked in the fields, and did clerical work, carpentry, and weaving.

Critical Thinking

1. Answers will vary, but students could note that stories are easy to remember.
2. Answers will vary, but students should explain.
3. Answers will vary, but students should give reasons.
4. Answers will vary, but students should explain.

Graphic Organizer Activity

From top to bottom: pope, patriarchs, archbishops, bishops, priests, monks and nuns

UNIT 5 Around

FOCUS

Objectives

Your students will be able to:
1. state where and when the Moche built their civilization.
2. link geography to the population boom among the Moche.
3. explain the archaeological and cultural importance of the Pyramid of the Sun.

Bellringer

Remind students that they have now studied ancient civilizations all over the world. Ask: If you were to choose a location for a civilization, what would be some ideal features? *(fertile soil, water for farming, waterways for trade, natural barriers to discourage invasion, rich natural resources)*

Motivational Activity

Compile and discuss a list of student responses to the Bellringer question. Then tell students that a people called the Moche built their civilization in the coastal deserts of present-day Peru—one of the driest areas on earth. Refer them to the map. Ask: What geographic advantages did this location possess? *(rivers to provide water for farming, mountains and deserts to protect from invasion, fish from the ocean, and minerals from the desert)*

TEACH

Geography: Human/Environmental Interaction Have students study the Around the World feature, looking for ways in which the Moche changed and adapted to their environment. (changes—*dug irrigation ditches, planted gardens, built*

258

THE MOCHE

As the Roman Empire reached its height, a people named the Moche rose to power in the coastal deserts of present-day Peru. The Moche civilization lasted from roughly 100 A.D. to 800 A.D.

Although the Moche did not develop a written language, the story of their culture is told through the buildings and artwork that they left behind.

Moche Civilization

▲ A series of rivers run out of the Andes Mountains and cut through the dry deserts of Peru's northern coast. The Moche dug irrigation ditches and used water from these rivers to turn the deserts into farmland. They produced so much food that the population boomed. One river valley may have supported more than 10,000 people.

258   UNIT 5

▲ One of the most powerful groups in Moche society were the warrior-priests—nobles who served as both military and religious leaders. A curved, gold headdress symbolized their power.

SPOTLIGHT ON: THE MOCHE

Nobody knows for sure why the Moche disappeared. Some experts suggest an earthquake, such as those that still occur along the Pacific Rim. Many others, however, trace the problem to El Niño—the name given to the periodic change in the temperatures of an ocean current off the coast of South America.

The Moche had mastered living in a nearly rainless area and knew how to sur-

vive droughts. However, they had little experience with the torrential downpours that an El Niño can bring. Scientists think that an El Niño of mammoth proportions hit the Moche somewhere around 750 A.D. The deluge washed out fields, overwhelmed irrigation systems, and melted clay-brick buildings. When the flood waters receded, so did the Moche civilization.

◄ When a warrior-priest died, the Moche filled his grave with a wealth of treasures to accompany him to the next life. Talented metal workers, Moche artists produced complicated designs. This gold-and-turquoise ear ornament shows what a Moche warrior-priest looked like.

The Moche built hundreds of flat-topped ► pyramids. Temples and platforms on the top of the pyramids made them religious and administrative centers. The biggest Moche pyramid—the Pyramid of the Sun—covered over 12.5 acres. It was the largest structure built in the ancient Americas.

Pottery often took the form of animals important ► to the Moche, such as the llama. The llama served as a pack animal for long-distance trips. It also provided meat for food and wool for weaving.

◄ The Moche crafted some of the most realistic pottery in the ancient world. They decorated jars and bottles with faces that bring the Moche back to life.

huge pyramids; adaptations— settled near rivers, used sand and stone as building materials, fashioned large jugs to hold water.)

DID YOU KNOW ??

The Pyramid of the Sun contains more than 140 million mud bricks, estimated to weigh over four million tons. It towered more than 135 feet above the coastal plain and covered an area almost as large as the Great Pyramid at Giza. As many as 10,000 people may have lived there.

ASSESS

Check for Understanding

Have students answer the questions in **Taking Another Look** on page 259.

Enrich

Share the information at the bottom of page 258. Then assign interested students to research articles on how El Niño affects weather patterns in the Americas today. Ask students to present their findings to the class.

CLOSE

Have students compare the Moche with one other ancient desert civilization and record their findings in the form of a Venn diagram.

Taking Another Look

1. Where and when did the Moche build their civilization?

2. Why did the Moche experience a population boom?

Hands-On Activity

Designing a Historical Marker Design a historical marker that might be placed at the Pyramid of the Sun. Include this fact: The Spanish word for pyramids made of mud bricks is *huacas*. Thus the Spanish name for this pyramid is *Huaca del Sol*.

259

ANSWERS TO TAKING ANOTHER LOOK

1. The Moche built their civilization roughly around 100 A.D. in the coastal deserts of present-day Peru.

2. The Moche population boomed when irrigation allowed farmers to coax large crops of food from the desert.

Hands-On Activity
The markers will vary, but students should include an explanation of the pyramid's name and its importance to the history of the Americas, and identification of the Moche.

Answers and Analyses

1B History

According to page 219, the plebeians paid taxes and served in the army, but they could not serve in the government.

2F History

According to pages 179–180, a Greek oracle gave advice about *what might happen in the future*. Of the choices given, this is the closest match to a soothsayer.

 TEST-TAKING TIP

Remind students to scrutinize the language of the question. Very often there is a word or phrase that is key to finding the best answer. In this case the question asks specifically for something or someone who can predict the future. This information should allow students to eliminate G, H, and J.

3A Geography

According to the map, most of the Roman Empire was on the Mediterranean Sea.

4J Geography

According to the map, Spain is the only country that is both west of the Prime Meridian and part of the Roman Empire in 146 B.C.

 TEST-TAKING TIP

Review with students the terms *longitude, latitude,* and *Prime Meridian.*

THE PRINCETON REVIEW

Standardized Test Practice

Directions: Choose the *best* answer to each of the following multiple choice questions. If you have trouble answering a question, use the process of elimination to narrow your choices. Write your answers on a separate piece of paper.

1. **Plebeians made up a majority of ancient Rome's total population. However, early Roman laws did not treat the plebeians fairly. Which of the following is an example of a law that was unfair to the plebeians?**

   A Senators in Rome held their positions for their whole lives.

   B Plebeians had to pay taxes but could not serve in the government.

   C There were only two consuls chosen to lead the Roman Republic each year.

   D Tribunes were set up to represent plebeians in Roman government.

   > *Test-Taking Tip:* The important phrase in this question is *unfair to the plebeians.* Answer A may seem unfair, but was it specifically *unfair to the plebeians?*

2. **Early Romans believed that certain people, called *soothsayers*, could predict the future. Roman soothsayers were most similar to**

   F Greek oracles

   G modern-day priests

   H philosophers like Socrates

   J Egyptian pharaohs

   > *Test-Taking Tip:* This question asks you to make a *comparison.* Although oracles, priests, philosophers, and pharaohs may have all been consulted for *advice,* they did not all *predict the future.*

Use the map on the top of the next page to answer questions 3 and 4.

3. **In 130 A.D., the Roman Empire surrounded which body of water?**

   A The Mediterranean Sea

   B The Atlantic Ocean

   C The North Sea

   D The Adriatic Sea

   > *Test-Taking Tip:* Make sure that your answer is supported by information *on the map.* Use the *map key,* or *legend,* to help you understand how the map is organized. Remember that all the different patterns and shades of gray in the key refer to the Roman Empire. They just help to differentiate it at different points during its expansion.

4. **In 146 B.C., which part of the Roman Empire was west of the Prime Meridian?**

   F Great Britain

   G Syria

   H Italy

   J Spain

   > *Test-Taking Tip:* This question requires you to remember the term *Prime Meridian.* The Prime Meridian is the line of longitude that divides *east* and *west.* What degree represents it?

Roman Expansion

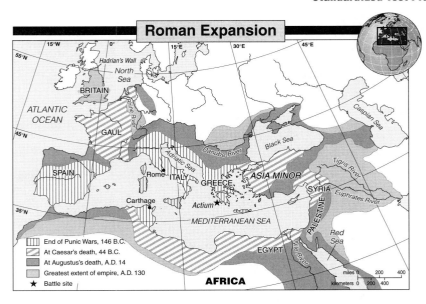

- ▦ End of Punic Wars, 146 B.C.
- ▨ At Caesar's death, 44 B.C.
- ▧ At Augustus's death, A.D. 14
- ▩ Greatest extent of empire, A.D. 130
- ★ Battle site

miles 0   200   400
kilometers 0 200 400

5. During the *Pax Romana*, when Rome was at peace for 200 years, Augustus

A established the principle that laws must be fair to everyone

B focused on conquering other lands to increase trade opportunities

C paid pirates to patrol the trade routes that Roman merchants used

D failed to maintain a strong army, leaving Rome open to foreign attacks

> **Test-Taking Tip:** Eliminate answers that do not make sense. For example, if Rome was *at peace*, then Romans were probably not *conquering other lands* (answer B) or *open to foreign attacks* (answer D).

6. Which of the following was NOT a factor that facilitated the spread of Christianity through the Roman Empire?

A Missionaries spread the religion along the trade routes established by the Romans.

B Many people in the Empire understood the same languages, so Christians could spread their ideas.

C Christianity appealed to poor people by saying that there was a better life after death.

D People who became Christians were still allowed to worship Roman gods.

> **Test-Taking Tip:** Be careful when a question says NOT or EXCEPT. Look for the answer choice that does NOT fit. For instance, answer B, that people spoke the same languages, would be very helpful in communicating any ideas. Therefore, it was probably helpful in spreading Christianity, and you can eliminate it as a possible correct answer. **STOP**

261

Answers and Analyses

5A   History

The *Pax Romana* is discussed on pages 234–236. There it states *that certain principles of law that were fair to everyone* were developed, and that Roman law was standardized. Therefore, A is the best choice.

6D   History

The ways in which the Roman Empire helped Christianity to spread are discussed on pages 250–251. There it states that the Roman system of roads facilitated the movement of missionaries, and the common languages of Latin and Greek made it easy for people to communicate. Therefore, choices A and B can be eliminated. The top of page 251 states that Christianity appealed to poor people, so choice C can be eliminated. Since page 250 states that Christians refused to worship Roman gods, choice D is the best answer.

THE PRINCETON REVIEW   **TEST-TAKING TIP**

Remind students to take enough time to understand the question thoroughly. If they scrutinize the language of the question, they will see that the question discusses the *spread* of Christianity. Both A and B mention spreading religion, so they can be eliminated.

Tested Objectives

Questions	Reading Objective
1	Evaluate information
2	Make comparisons
3, 4	Analyze information
5	Identify central issues
6	Make inferences and generalizations

OVERVIEW

Unit 6 discusses the early Middle Ages, which began in western Europe after the fall of Rome and lasted until about A.D. 1000.

➤ **Chapter 17** describes how Germanic peoples replaced the Roman Empire with their own kingdoms.

➤ **Chapter 18** analyzes the rise of the Franks.

➤ **Chapter 19** describes the civilizations that emerged in the British Isles after the fall of the Roman Empire.

➤ **Chapter 20** summarizes the Viking expansion and how they influenced other people.

UNIT OBJECTIVES

After reading Unit 6, students will be able to:

1. explain why the early Middle Ages is an important period in European history.

2. describe changes in government, economy, and learning in the early Middle Ages.

3. analyze what role religion played in the lives of the people during the early Middle Ages.

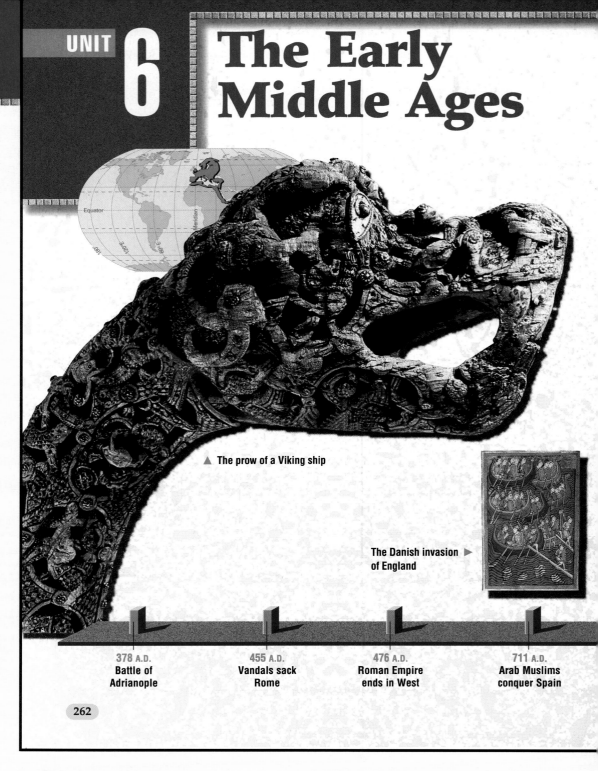

UNIT **6** # The Early Middle Ages

▲ The prow of a Viking ship

The Danish invasion ▶ of England

378 A.D.	455 A.D.	476 A.D.	711 A.D.
Battle of Adrianople	Vandals sack Rome	Roman Empire ends in West	Arab Muslims conquer Spain

262

ABOUT THE UNIT OPENING

Examining Artifacts

Ask students to study the artifacts on this page. What inferences can they make about life in the early Middle Ages? *(Lead students to understand that it was a period of fighting, invasion, and conquest.)* Have students determine what events in the time line support their inferences.

Global Chronology

Ask students to explain what the time line covers. *(major events during the early Middle Ages in Europe)* Have students explain the connection between the end of the Roman Empire in the West and conquest of Spain by Arab Muslims. *(After Rome fell, there was no strong government to stop invaders from marching into Europe.)*

Multimedia Activity

Surfing the Net
The Vikings

The Vikings earned a reputation as some of the most courageous sea-farers of their time. Viking ships prowled the inland rivers of Europe and headed far into the Atlantic Ocean. To find out more about Viking ships, search the Internet.

Getting There

Follow these steps to gather information on the ships built by the Vikings.
1. Pick a search engine, such as Excite, Lycos, WebCrawler, Yahoo, etc.
2. Type in the main search word *Viking*. Then add words to focus your research. Words might include *ships, history,* or *longboats.*
3. Explore links that the search engine brings up on the screen. (Links point the way to Web sites on the Internet.)
4. Click on links that provide information on the subject of your research.

Hands-On Activity

Create a model, or a scale drawing, of a Viking longboat. Include a short description of the various parts of the boat, including the decorated *prow*—the foremost part of the ship.

PRIMARY SOURCES
Library

See pages 684–685 for a primary source reading to accompany Unit 6.

732 A.D.
Battle of Tours

800 A.D.
Charlemagne is crowned emperor

911 A.D.
Normans settle in Normandy

Journal Notes

What was life like in Europe and other areas during the early Middle Ages? Note details about the changes taking place in government, the economy, and learning.

263

Geographic Location

Have students use their text Atlas to locate the places in this unit that are in western Europe. *(England, Ireland, France, Spain, Italy, Germany, Denmark, Sweden, and Norway)* Ask them to locate Paris, Cluny, Canossa, Worms, and other cities in which important events in this unit take place.

GLENCOE
TECHNOLOGY

Videodisc
Use the MindJogger to preview the unit content.

MindJogger Videoquiz

Unit 6
Disc 1 Side B

Also available in VHS.

INTRODUCING THE UNIT

Tell students that during the early Middle Ages, western Europe was developing a new civilization to which the Germans, Franks, Irish, Anglo-Saxons, and Vikings contributed. Ask students to name some things all civilizations have in common. *(government, religion, customs, leaders, achievements)* Tell students that in Unit 6 they will learn about the developing civilization in Europe and other areas during the early Middle Ages.

RECORDING JOURNAL NOTES

Have students list major changes that have taken place in the world in their lifetimes. As they read the text, have students note in their journal details about the changes that took place in government, the economy, and learning in Europe and other areas during the early Middle Ages.

PRIMARY SOURCES
Library

Items in the Primary Sources Library for this unit focus on:
- Monastery accounts of Viking raids.
- Viking metalwork.

 For additional primary source documents, use the **World History Primary Source Document CD-ROM.**

Chapter 17 Planning Guide

Objectives	Reproducible Resources	Multimedia Resources
Section 1 **Village Life** Characterize family life in German villages, and analyze Germans' love of battle and how their laws influenced their lives.	Reproducible Lesson Plan Chapter 17 Vocabulary and Guided Reading Activity Reading Essentials and Study Guide 17-1 Chapter 17 Cooperative Learning Activity Section 1 Quiz Unit 6 Hands-On History Lab	Teaching Transparency and Activity 17A Vocabulary PuzzleMaker Interactive Tutor Self-Assessment Software ExamView® Pro Testmaker Glencoe Skillbuilder Interactive Workbook, Level 1 Presentation Plus!
Section 2 **The Conquerors** Discuss what role the Goths and the Vandals played in the decline of the Roman Empire, and describe what replaced the Roman Empire in the West.	Reproducible Lesson Plan Reading Essentials and Study Guide 17-2 Chapter 17 Chart and Graph Skill Activity Chapter 17 Geography and Map Activity Chapter 17 Activity Book Activity Chapter 17 Enrichment Activity Section 2 Quiz	Teaching Transparency and Activity 17B Vocabulary PuzzleMaker Interactive Tutor Self-Assessment Software ExamView® Pro Testmaker Glencoe Skillbuilder Interactive Workbook, Level 1
Chapter 17 **Review and Evaluation**	Chapter 17 Reteaching Activity Chapter 17 Performance Assessment Activity Spanish Chapter Summary and Glossary Chapter 17 Test	Vocabulary PuzzleMaker Interactive Tutor Self-Assessment Software Glencoe Skillbuilder Interactive Workbook, Level 1 Audiocassettes* ExamView® Pro Testmaker

*Also available in Spanish.

Presentation Plus!

Use Glencoe's **Presentation Plus!** multimedia teacher tool to easily present dynamic lessons that visually excite your students. Using Microsoft® PowerPoint, you can customize the presentations to create your own personalized lessons.

 Interactive Lesson Planner

Planning has never been easier! Using this CD-ROM, organize your week, month, semester, or year with all the help you need. The **Interactive Lesson Planner** gives you access to all of the blackline masters which accompany *Human Heritage.*

✓ PERFORMANCE ASSESSMENT ACTIVITIES

Laws Remind students that German laws during the early Middle Ages were not written down, but instead were passed on by word of mouth. Have students imagine that they have been assigned the task of writing down the German laws. Have them write a German Law Book based on the information in the textbook and in other reference sources. Have students read their laws to the class.

CHAPTER RESOURCES

LITERATURE ABOUT THE PERIOD

Newark, Tim. *The Barbarians: Warriors and Wars of the Dark Ages.* Poole (Sterling), 1985. Account by a military historian of the medieval period.

READINGS FOR THE STUDENT

Lyttle, Richard B. *Land Beyond the River: Europe in the Age of Migration.* Atheneum, 1986. Overview of the second through ninth centuries and the customs and characters of the various peoples on the move in Europe, including Germans, Huns, Mongols, and Gypsies.

READINGS FOR THE TEACHER

Barbor, Richard. *The Penguin Guide to Medieval Europe.* Penguin Books, 1984. Describes the political and intellectual climate of Europe from a.d. 800 to a.d. 1400.

Burns, Thomas S. *A History of the Ostro-Goths.* Indiana University Press, 1984. Highlights the history of the Ostrogoths.

Simons, George E., gen. ed. *Barbarian Europe.* Time-Life Books, 1968. Surveys the history of Europe from a.d. 406 to a.d. 1200.

NATIONAL GEOGRAPHIC SOCIETY — Teacher's Corner

NATIONAL GEOGRAPHIC SOCIETY PRODUCTS AVAILABLE FROM GLENCOE

To order the following, call Glencoe at 1-800-334-7344:

- *MapPack: Europe (Transparency Maps)*
- *Europe (Laminated Desk Maps)*
- *PicturePack: Physical Geography of the World (Transparencies)*
- *PicturePack: The Middle Ages (Transparencies)*
- *PictureShow: The Middle Ages (CD-ROM)*
- *Picture Atlas of the World (CD-ROM)*
- *PicturePack: Physical Geography of the World (Transparencies)*

ADDITIONAL NATIONAL GEOGRAPHIC SOCIETY PRODUCTS

To order the following products for use with this chapter, call National Geographic Society at 1-800-368-2728:

- *Physical Geography of the Continents Series: Europe (Video)*
- *National Geographic Atlas of World History (Book))*
- *Wonders of the Ancient World: National Geographic Atlas of Archaeology (Book)*

Access *National Geographic*'s new dynamic MapMachine Web site and other geography resources at:

http://www.nationalgeographic.com/
http://www.nationalgeographic.com/maps/

KEY TO ABILITY LEVELS

Teaching strategies have been coded for varying learning styles and abilities.

L1 Level 1 activities are **basic** activities and should be within the ability range of all students.

L2 Level 2 activities are **average** activities and should be within the ability range of the average to above-average student.

L3 Level 3 activities are **challenging** activities designed for the ability range of above-average students.

ELL ELL activities should be within the ability range of English Language Learning students.

OVERVIEW

Chapter 17 discusses the Germanic impact on western Europe.

➤ **Section 1** compares the cultures of the Romans and the Germans.

➤ **Section 2** describes the Germanic invasions and the end of the Roman Empire.

CHAPTER OBJECTIVES

After reading Chapter 17, students will be able to:

1. describe family life in German villages.
2. analyze how the love of battle and their laws influenced the Germans.
3. discuss what role the Goths and the Vandals played in the decline of the Roman Empire.
4. describe what replaced the Roman Empire in the West.

EXAMINING ARTIFACTS

Tell students that the Romans often used the word "barbarian" to describe the Germans who moved into their empire from the north. Call on students to define this word. *(a person whose culture is considered uncivilized)* Ask students how these artifacts disprove this description.

PERFORMANCE ASSESSMENT ✓

Use the Performance Assessment Activities on page 264B to help you evaluate students as they complete the chapter.

264

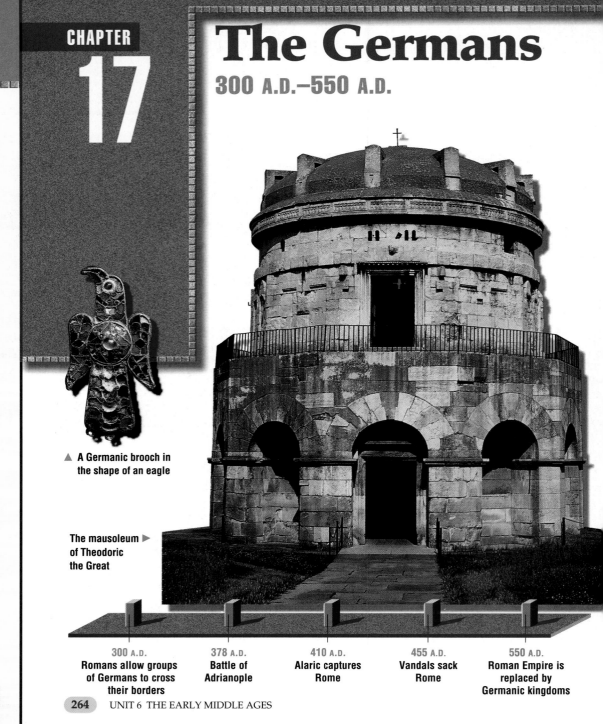

CHAPTER
17

The Germans
300 A.D.–550 A.D.

▲ **A Germanic brooch in the shape of an eagle**

The mausoleum ► of Theodoric the Great

300 A.D.	378 A.D.	410 A.D.	455 A.D.	550 A.D.
Romans allow groups of Germans to cross their borders	**Battle of Adrianople**	**Alaric captures Rome**	**Vandals sack Rome**	**Roman Empire is replaced by Germanic kingdoms**

TEACHING RESOURCES

TEACHER PLANNING AND SUPPORT

- 🗀 Reproducible Lesson Plan
- 🗀 Block Scheduling Implementation Guide
- 🗀 Videodisc Bar Code Correlation
- 💿 Presentation Plus!

REVIEW AND REINFORCEMENT

- 🗀 Reading Essentials and Study Guide 17-1, 17-2
- 🗀 Chapter 17 Vocabulary and Guided Reading Activity
- 💾 Vocabulary PuzzleMaker Software
- Teaching Transparencies 17A & 17B

- 🗀 Chapter 17 Reteaching Activity
- 🗀 Chapter 17 Cooperative Learning Activity
- 🗀 Chapter 17 Activity Book Activity
- 🗀 Chapter 17 Chart and Graph Skill Activity
- 💾 Interactive Tutor Self-Assessment Software
- 📼 Unit 6 MindJogger VideoQuiz

APPLICATION AND HANDS-ON ACTIVITIES

- 🗀 Daily World History, Geography, and Culture Question
- 🗀 Unit 6 Hands-On History Lab Activity

Chapter Focus

Read to Discover

- What life was like in German villages.
- How the Germans' laws and love of battle influenced them.
- What role the Goths and Vandals played in the decline of the Roman Empire.
- What replaced the Roman Empire in the West.

Chapter Overview

Visit the *Human Heritage* Web site at **humanheritage.glencoe.com** and click on ***Chapter 17— Chapter Overviews*** to preview this chapter.

✎ **Terms to Learn**	👥 **People to Know**	🌐 **Places to Locate**
clans	Wodan	Danube River
chieftain	Thor	valley
blood feuds	Atilla	Valhalla
oath-helpers	Alaric	
ordeal	Odoacer	
wergeld	Theodoric	

Why It's Important   During the first 400 years after the birth of Christ, the Germans left the forests and marshes of northern Europe in search of warmer climates and better grazing land for their cattle. They slowly drifted south toward the Roman Empire.

Attracted by Rome's wealth and culture, the Germans hoped to live peacefully within the empire's borders. However, the Romans considered them enemies and for many years fought to keep the Germans out of Rome. By 300 A.D., however, the empire had begun its long decline and could no longer turn back the Germans. So the Romans allowed groups of Germans to move into the Danube River valley, where a blending of German and Roman ways took place.

SECTION 1   Village Life

Although the Germans took part in Roman life, they also kept much of their own culture. They lived in villages surrounded by farmlands and pastures. Most of the homes were long thatched-roof huts with an open space around them. The family lived in one end of the hut and divided the other end into animal stalls.

CHAPTER 17 THE GERMANS   **265**

Chapter Overview introduces students to chapter content and key terms. Have them access ***Chapter 17 Overview*** at **humanheritage.glencoe.com**

FOCUS

🔖 Bellringer

Have students answer the following: *What caused the fall of the Roman Empire?*

Motivational Activity

Discuss students' responses. Then read the following quote written by a Christian bishop of the 400s A.D. as his province was being overrun by the Germans: *We have planted our crops only for the enemy to burn. All our resources are gone—the flocks of sheep, the herds of camels and horses. I am writing this behind walls, under siege.* Tell students that they will learn more about Germanic groups who helped cause the end of the Roman Empire.

GUIDE TO READING

Reading Strategy

Ask students to read "Why It's Important" and summarize the chapter's main theme. (*As the Roman Empire declined, the Germans and Romans influenced each other's way of life.*)

Vocabulary Precheck

Ask students to define each of the "Terms to Learn." **L1** **ELL**

💾 Use the Vocabulary PuzzleMaker for Chapter 17 to create a crossword puzzle. **L1**

📁 Assign Chapter 17 Vocabulary and Guided Reading Activity.

📁 Assign Reading Essentials and Study Guide 17-1.

GEOGRAPHY ACTIVITIES

- Chapter 17 Geography and Map Activity
- Social Studies Outline Map Resource Book

INTERDISCIPLINARY CONNECTIONS

- 🎧💿 World Music: Cultural Traditions

ENRICHMENT AND EXTENSION

- 💿 World History Primary Source Document Library CD-ROM
- Chapter 17 Enrichment Activity
- Foods Around the World

ASSESSMENT AND EVALUATION

- Chapter 17 Performance Assessment Activity
- Chapter 17 Section Quizzes 17-1, 17-2
- Chapter 17 Test
- 📀 Chapter 17 ExamView® Pro Testmaker Software
- 🎧 Chapter 17 Digests Audiocassettes Activities and Tests

SPANISH RESOURCES

- Chapter 17 Spanish Chapter Summary and Glossary
- 🎧 Chapter 17 Spanish Chapter Digests Audiocassettes Activities and Tests

Guided Practice

L1 **Daily Life** Ask the students to imagine they are teenagers living in a German village during the Roman Empire and have them write a diary entry describing a day in their lives. Ask students to share their entries with the class. **ELL**

CAPTION ANSWER

Most homes were long, thatched-roof huts with an open space around them. Families lived in one end of the hut and divided the other end into animal stalls. Wooden tables and benches were the only furniture.

DID YOU KNOW ??

The Germans were divided into groups that ranged in size from about 10,000 individuals to as many as 300,000.

HISTORY Online

Student Web Activity objectives, goals, and answers can be found at the **Chapter 17 Web Activity Lesson Plan** at <u>humanheritage.glencoe.com</u>

GERMAN VILLAGE   The Germans built their villages just within the borders of the Roman Empire. There they became farmers. They lived in family groups that included parents, children, grandparents, aunts, uncles, and cousins. **What was a German home like?**

HISTORY Online

Student Web Activity
Visit the *Human Heritage* Web site at <u>humanheritage.glencoe.com</u> and click on *Chapter 17— Student Web Activities* to find out more about Germanic tribes.

The body heat of the animals helped to warm the hut during the cold winters. Wooden tables and benches placed along the walls of the hut were the only furniture. A few wealthier villagers added wall hangings or carpets.

German villagers made their living herding cattle, which provided food and clothing. They also traded cattle for Roman glass vessels, table articles, and jewelry. The Germans farmed as well. They grew barley, rye, wheat, beans, and peas. Most farm work was done by women, children, and enslaved people. When the women were not working in the fields or cooking, they spun wool and wove cloth on upright looms.

German dress was simple. The women wore long skirts made of different yarns, or one-piece sack-like dresses that extended from the shoulders to the feet. Sometimes, they wore scarves or shawls fastened with a bone pin. The men wore short woolen *tunics*, or coat-like garments, and close-fitting trousers. They covered the tunics with cloaks fastened on the right shoulder with a brooch.

SPOTLIGHT ON: TACTICUS

Most of what modern historians know about the customs, appearance, and beliefs of the Germanic tribes comes from a Roman—not a Germanic—historian. Cornelius Tacticus, a Roman lawyer, official, and historian, wrote about people in two distant parts of the Roman Empire in the 100s A.D. and early 200s A.D. His book *Germania*, written in 98 A.D., describes the Germans along the Rhine River frontier of the empire. He uses the Germanic tribes as moral examples of upright, if primitive, people who still hold on to the simple virtues that many Romans have forgotten. He also writes about the laws, customs, and fighting methods of the Germans that developed from nearly 100 years of Roman wars and other contacts.

The Germans believed in hospitality. So strong was this belief that it was against the law to turn away anyone who came to the door. Invited guests and strangers alike were welcomed, fed, and entertained. Feasting, drinking, and dancing were favorite German pastimes. Men also enjoyed gambling with dice. Sometimes, they took part in such organized sports as boxing and wrestling. In winter, they skated on frozen ponds and lakes using skates made of flat bone.

The Germans spoke a language that later became modern German. At first, they could not read or write, because their language had no alphabet. However, some learned to speak and write Latin. Gradually, they began to use Roman letters to write their own language.

Warriors   German men were warriors. They spent most of their time fighting, hunting, or making weapons. They began training for war when they were young boys. When a male reached manhood, he was brought before a special gathering held in a sacred grove under a full moon. There, he received a shield and a spear, which he had to carry with him at all times. The loss of the shield and spear meant loss of honor.

The Germans were divided into **clans,** or groups based on family ties. At first, the Germans gave their greatest loyalty to their clan. After a while, however, they developed a strong feeling of loyalty toward a military leader called a **chieftain** (chēf' tuhn). A man had to fight well to become a chieftain. In the beginning, a chieftain was elected by a band of warriors. Later, this office became hereditary.

Chieftains gave their men leadership, weapons, and a chance for wealth and adventure. They also kept peace among their warriors. In some cases, they gave their warriors food and shelter. In return, warriors gave their chieftains complete loyalty. Some even gave their chieftains credit for the brave deeds they themselves did. In battle, chieftains fought for victory and warriors fought for their chieftains.

German warrior bands did not have fixed plans of fighting. Each band was small and usually fought on its own, apart from other bands. The bands made surprise raids against their enemies. Warriors on foot and on horseback would charge wildly, yelling in loud voices to frighten their foes. They fought with daggers, short swords, and heavy axes made of metal and stone. They carried light wooden shields and wore suits of leather. A successful attack provided warriors with enslaved people, cattle, and other treasures.

The Germans' love of battle was closely linked to their religion. Germans had many gods who liked to fight and to hunt. The chief god, Wodan (wōd' n), was the god of war, poetry, learning, and magic. Another god of war was Wodan's

People in History

Theodoric the Great
c. 454 A.D.–526 A.D.

Germanic King

Theodoric was king of the East Goths, a Germanic people from eastern Europe. When Rome fell in 476 A.D., he took part in the struggle. About 500 A.D., Theodoric declared himself king of Italy. As king, he encouraged the Roman and Germanic peoples to get along. He respected Roman customs, and during his reign peace and prosperity returned.

Reading Check
What are **clans?** How did a German leader become a **chieftain?**

L2 **Critical Thinking** Have students work in pairs to learn more about the German belief in hospitality. Have them create a presentation that compares and contrasts German hospitality in the 400s to that of today. Suggest they share their presentations with the class. **ELL**

MAKING CONNECTIONS

▸▸ **Religion** The warlike Wodan became the chief god of German warriors and chieftains. Earlier, these people held beliefs that centered on Mother Earth—Erce or Nerthus. Even after the Germans adopted Christianity, they kept some old beliefs in the spirits of the earth and forest. Customs such as the Yule log and the lighted Christmas tree, for instance, derive from rituals of the Germanic forest tribes.

Reading Check Answer
Clans are groups based on family ties.
A German leader became **chieftain** by fighting well. At first, he was elected by warriors, but later the office became hereditary.

COOPERATIVE LEARNING

Tell students that our seven-day week comes from the Babylonians, but the days of the week come mainly from the Germanic calendar. The Germans picked up Sun Day and Moon Day from the Greeks and Romans. They also kept Saturn's Day, in honor of the Roman god of agriculture. However, they gave the rest of the days to their own deities.

Divide the class into four groups, and assign students to research and design posters for each of the following days:

Tiu's Day (in honor of the Germanic god of war); **Wodan's Day** (in honor of the chief Germanic god); **Thor's Day** (in honor of the Germanic god of thunder); **Freya's Day** (in honor of the Germanic goddess of clouds, the sky, love and wife of Wodan). Have students present their posters when they are done.

▭ Assign Chapter 17 *Cooperative Learning Activity* in the TCR.

Linking Across Time

Public Assemblies Germanic people picked leaders and decided laws in public assemblies. All freemen—except "cowards"—took part in these meetings (left). The Germanic conquest of the Roman Empire helped spread this practice. It became the basis of later democratic assemblies, including modern-day town meetings (right). **How did the Germans record their laws?**

son Thor (thōr), who was also the god of thunder. The Germans believed that the sound of thunder came from Thor's chariot wheels.

The Germans admired bravery. Like the Spartans, they expected their warriors to win in battle or to die fighting. The only German shields left on a battlefield were those of dead warriors. The Germans believed that goddesses carried the spirits of warriors who died in battle into the afterlife. There, in the hall of Wodan called Valhalla (val hal' uh), the warriors would feast and fight forever.

German Shield

Law The Romans believed that law came from the emperor. The Germans believed it came from the people. German rulers could not change a law unless the people approved.

The Germans based their laws on the customs of their ancestors. Instead of writing down the laws, the Germans memorized them and passed them from parent to child.

Reckless fighting, often caused by too much drinking, caused problems in German villages. The Germans wanted to keep such

268   UNIT 6 THE EARLY MIDDLE AGES

fights from becoming **blood feuds** (fyūds), or quarrels in which the families of the original fighters seek revenge. Blood feuds could go on for generations. To keep this from happening, the Germans set up courts. Judges listened to each side and tried to find a settlement that would bring peace to the village.

The Germans decided who was guilty or innocent in different ways. One way was by oath-taking. People accused of crimes would declare their innocence by oath. Then, they would be defended by **oath-helpers.** These were people who swore that the accused was telling the truth. The Germans believed that anyone who lied when taking an oath would be punished by the gods.

People accused of crimes could not always find oath-helpers to come to their aid. In such cases, guilt or innocence was decided by **ordeal** (ōr dēl'), or a severe trial. Accused persons had to walk barefoot over red-hot coals or put an arm into boiling water. The burns of the innocent were supposed to heal within three days. There was also ordeal by water. A person was tied hand and foot and thrown into a lake or river. The Germans viewed water as a symbol of purity. If a person sank to the bottom, he or she was innocent. If a person floated, he or she was guilty.

A person who was judged guilty was not always punished physically. Courts could impose fines called *wergeld* (wuhr' geld). The exact amount of the payment varied. For example, the wergeld for harming a chieftain was higher than the one for harming a warrior. In the same way, a fine for killing a young girl was greater than one for killing a woman too old to have children. Although courts could set these fines, they did not have the power to collect them. They had to depend on public opinion to make a guilty person pay the fine.

The German legal system did not treat all people fairly. A person's wealth and importance, rather than the seriousness of the crime, determined the penalty. German laws did, however, keep the peace.

✓ **Reading Check**
How did Germans try to prevent **blood feuds?**

✓ **Reading Check**
How did **oath-helpers** take part in German trials?

✓ **Reading Check**
Why would an accused person be required to go through an **ordeal?**

✓ **Reading Check**
What was a *wergeld?*

✓ **Reading Check Answer**
The Germans tried to prevent **blood feuds** by setting up courts to settle the quarrels.

✓ **Reading Check Answer**
The **oath-helpers** swore the accused was telling the truth.

✓ **Reading Check Answer**
If oath-helpers did not come forward, an accused person went through an **ordeal** to decide guilt or innocence.

✓ **Reading Check Answer**
A *wergeld* was a fine imposed as punishment for a crime.

💾 Use **Interactive Tutor Self Assessment Software** to review Section 1.

Section 1 Assessment

1. **Define:** clans, chieftain, blood feuds, oath-helpers, ordeal, *wergeld.*
2. What were some of the duties of a German chieftain?
3. What were some features of German religion?

Critical Thinking

4. **Making Inferences** Why do you think hospitality was so important to the Germans?

Graphic Organizer Activity

5. Draw this diagram, and use it to compare strengths and weaknesses of German law.

Strengths	Weaknesses

MAKING CONNECTIONS

➤➤ **History** Most Germanic groups had an assembly made up of free men from the village that met once a year to discuss war, laws, and punishment for crimes. Before a cheiftan could go to war, he had to get the assembly's approval. To show approval, assembly members banged their weapons against their shields.

CHAPTER 17 THE GERMANS **269**

Section 1 Assessment Answers

1. clans, family groups (p. 267); chieftain, military leader (p. 267); blood feuds, quarrels between families (p. 269); oath-helpers, people who swore that the accused was telling the truth (p. 269); ordeal, severe trial (p. 269); *wergeld,* fines (p. 269)
2. Chieftains gave their men leadership, weapons, and a chance for wealth and adventure. They also kept peace among warriors and sometimes provided them with food and shelter.
3. It had many gods who fought and hunted; the chief gods were Wodan and Thor; and goddesses carried the spirits of warriors to Valhalla.
4. Answers will vary but should refer to German beliefs.
5. Sample responses: *strengths*—helped settle quarrels, kept the peace; *weaknesses*—did not treat people fairly since penalties were determined by a person's wealth and importance.

Assign the Chapter 17 **Section 1 Quiz** in the TCR. Testmaker available.

DID YOU KNOW ??

The value of a person—and therefore the amount of his or her *wergeld*—was tied directly to that person's importance in warfare.

SECTION 2 The Conquerors

The Goths (gahths) were a Germanic people who lived in the Balkan Peninsula of Europe. They were divided into two groups called Ostrogoths (ahs' truh gahths), or East Goths, and Visigoths (viz' uh gahths), or West Goths.

In the late 300s, both groups were attacked by the Huns led by Attila (at' uhl uh), or "Little Daddy." The Huns conquered the East Goths. The West Goths feared they would be next. So, they asked the Roman emperor for protection. He let them settle just inside the empire's frontier. In return, they gave up their weapons and promised to be loyal to Rome.

Before long, trouble broke out between the West Goths and Roman officials. The West Goths had to buy the empire's food at very high prices. The Romans also kidnapped many young West Goths and enslaved them.

Germanic Invasions

Western Roman Empire, 400
Eastern Roman Empire, 400
—— Routes of German Tribes
- - - Route of Huns

EXTENDING THE CONTENT

In 472 Germanic tribes controlled only about 20 percent of the territory that had belonged to the Roman Empire. The Huns so thoroughly devastated the western Roman Empire, however, that by 476 these Germanic tribes were able to take over the remaining 80 percent of the weakened empire.

The Germanic Kingdoms

- JUTES
- ANGLO-SAXONS
- SAXONS
- FRANKS
- LOMBARDS
- OSTROGOTHS
- VISIGOTHS
- VANDALS

NORTH SEA, BALTIC SEA, EUROPE, ATLANTIC OCEAN, Rhine River, Danube River, BLACK SEA, Rome, Constantinople, MEDITERRANEAN SEA, AFRICA

Eastern Roman Empire, 526

miles 0 200 400 600
kilometers 0 200 400 600 800

Finally, the West Goths rebelled against the Romans and defeated them at the Battle of Adrianople in 378. Then, in 410, led by the chieftain Alaric, they captured and looted Rome.

After the capture of Rome, the West Goths continued on to Gaul. Then, they moved into Spain, which was occupied by Romans and another Germanic group called Vandals (van' duhlz). The West Goths ended Roman rule in Spain, drove out the Vandals, and set up their own kingdom.

The Vandals in turn crossed the Mediterranean to North Africa. They became pirates and attacked cities along the Mediterranean coast. From these attacks came the English word *"vandalism,"* meaning the willful destruction of property.

In 455, the Vandals attacked and burned Rome. They did, however, spare the lives of the Romans. Afterwards, the Vandals returned to North Africa. Like Rome's capture in 410 by the West Goths, this event shook the Roman world.

MAP STUDY

REGIONS The Visigoths defeated the Vandals whom they forced to settle in North Africa. **What advantage did the Vandals have because of their new location in the region?**

COOPERATIVE LEARNING

Many people in the United States today are of German, other European, or non-European descent. Have the class do an "Ancestor Hunt" of your class. Have them devise a way to chart or graph the ancestral background of each student. Suggest they also display their information with charts and visual representations from the countries of heritage of your students. Interested students may want to read *The Great Ancestor Hunt* by Lila Perl.

Independent Practice

L1 Map Skills Have students work in pairs to write two questions based on the map on page 271. Collect the questions and ask the class to respond. **ELL**

L3 Critical Thinking Ask students why they think the German generals usually chose a Roman citizen to serve as emperor of the Roman Empire. Would the students have done the same? Why or why not?

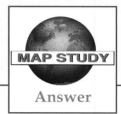

MAP STUDY

Answer

They were able to control large areas of the Mediterranean Sea.

DID YOU KNOW

Theodoric's kingdom included people of different races and religions, all of whom were allowed to live according to their own customs and to worship their own gods.

ASSESS

Check for Understanding

Ask students to summarize the main points of the chapter. Discuss the answers to the Section and Chapter Assessment questions.

Evaluate

Assign Chapter 17 **Performance Assessment Activity** in the TCR.

Administer **Chapter 17 Test** in the TCR. Testmaker available.

Reteach

Have students summarize factors that led to the fall of Rome and their importance.

Assign Chapter 17 **Reteaching Activity** in the TCR.

Enrich

Have students research Germanic mythology and report on the gods and goddesses that were worshiped in the early Middle Ages.

Assign the Chapter 17 **Enrichment Activity** in the TCR.

CLOSE

Ask students to discuss whether they think the Western Roman Empire would have fallen even if the Germanic tribes had not invaded the empire.

💾 Use **Interactive Tutor Self-Assessment Software** to review Section 2.

The Germanic invasions were one of the three main reasons the Roman Empire in the West began to fall. While the Roman Empire in the East prospered, generals in the West fought for control of Rome and Italy.

In 476, a German general named Odoacer (ŏd′ uh wā suhr) took control. He did not appoint an emperor. Instead, he ruled the western empire in his own name for almost 15 years. Then, a group of East Goths invaded Italy, killed Odoacer, and set up a kingdom under their leader Theodoric (thē ahd′ uh rik).

By 550, the Roman Empire in the West had faded away. In its place were six major and a great many minor Germanic kingdoms. Many Roman beliefs and practices remained to shape later civilizations.

Section 2 Assessment

1. What happened to the East Goths in the late 300s? What effect did this have on the West Goths?
2. What did the Vandals do after leaving Spain?
3. What replaced the Roman Empire in the West?

Critical Thinking

4. **Predicting Consequences** What do you think might have happened if Roman officials had treated the West Goths fairly? Explain.

Graphic Organizer Activity

5. Draw this diagram, and use it to describe important events in the fall of Rome. (Key dates are given.)

Chapter Summary & Study Guide

1. About 300 A.D., groups of Germans began settling in the Roman Empire.
2. German warriors were organized into bands, headed by military chieftains.
3. The Germans' love of battle was closely linked to their religion.
4. The Germans determined a person's guilt or innocence through use of oath-helpers and by ordeal.
5. The Germans believed that law came from the people and that a ruler could not change a law.
6. The Huns conquered the East Goths and forced the West Goths to turn to Rome for protection.
7. Harsh treatment of the West Goths by the Romans set off a chain of events leading to the capture of Rome in 410 A.D.
8. A Germanic chieftain took control of Rome in 476 A.D., and by 550 A.D., the Roman Empire had been replaced by a number of Germanic kingdoms.

Section 2 Assessment Answers

1. They were conquered by the Huns. It led them to ask the Roman emperor for protection.
2. They crossed the Mediterranean to North Africa, became pirates, and attacked and burned Rome.
3. six major and a great many minor Germanic kingdoms
4. Answers will vary but will probably mention that the West Goths might not have rebelled.

5. 378—Romans defeated at Battle of Adrianople; 410—West Goths capture Rome; 455—Vandals attack and burn Rome; 476—Odoacer takes control of the western empire; 550—six major and many minor Germanic kingdoms replace the western Roman empire

Assign Chapter 17 **Section 2 Quiz** in the TCR. Testmaker available.

Using Key Terms

Write a short story describing the daily life of a person in one of the early Germanic groups. Use the following words in your story.

clans   chieftain   blood feuds
oath-helpers   ordeal   *wergeld*

Understanding Main Ideas

1. Why did the Germans begin to move south toward the Roman Empire?
2. Why were the Germans allowed to cross the borders of the Roman Empire?
3. How did German warriors show their loyalty to their chieftain?
4. What did the Germans believe the afterlife would be like for warriors?
5. According to German beliefs, from what source did law come?
6. What was the reason for the German ordeal by water?
7. Why did the West Goths want to enter the Roman Empire?
8. What happened to Rome after its capture by Odoacer in 476 A.D.?

Critical Thinking

1. What parts of Roman culture did the Germans adopt? What parts of their own culture did they keep?
2. Imagine you will soon become a Germanic chieftain. Explain what you would provide for your band of warriors.
3. What would you have liked and disliked about living in a German village?
4. Do you believe the penalty for a crime should depend on a person's wealth or importance? If not, on what should it depend? Explain.

Graphic Organizer Activity

Citizenship Create a diagram like the one shown, and use it to show German contributions to Western ideas on law and government.

German Contributions	1.
	2.
	3.

Geography in History

Place Refer to the map on page 271. Access to the sea played an important role in the economy of each Germanic kingdom. Which kingdom had the longest seacoast? About how many miles (km) long was it?

Using Your Journal

Review any details you may have noted about the changes that took place during the early Middle Ages. Imagine you are in a German village at that time. Write a letter to a friend describing the important traits in a German leader. Compare these traits to the ones that you would look for in a leader today.

273

Bonus Test Question

For Chapter 17 Test

"If I may join your army I swear on our god of war, Zeus, I will fight hard. I have a letter from my chieftain saying I am a good warrior." Why would this warrior speaking to a Roman not be considered a true German?

Using Your Journal

Letters will vary but should compare and contrast the ideas of German law with ideas of law today.

Geography in History

Ostrogoth; about 2,000 miles (or 3,226 km)

CHAPTER 17
Assessment Answers

Using Key Terms

Short stories should include a description of daily activities and use all the words.

Understanding Main Ideas

1. looking for a warmer climate, grazing land, wealth, culture
2. because the Romans realized they were not strong enough to keep them out
3. They obeyed in battle and some gave their chieftains credit for their own brave deeds
4. spent in Valhalla, where they would feast and fight forever
5. from the people
6. They believed water would accept anyone who was pure and reject anyone who was not pure.
7. because they were afraid the Huns would conquer them.
8. Odoacer did not pick an emperor. Instead, he ruled the empire in his own name for 15 years, until the East Goths invaded and killed him.

Critical Thinking

1. They became farmers, traded with Romans, and joined the Roman army. Some became Christians. They lived in villages and spoke what later became modern German.
2. Answers will vary but should include some responsibilities of chieftains.
3. Answers will vary but should include specific details.
4. Answers will vary.

Graphic Organizer Activity

Contributions will vary, but might include: the use of public assemblies to pick leaders; the belief that law came from the people instead of the gods; the use of courts to settle quarrels.

Chapter 18 Planning Guide

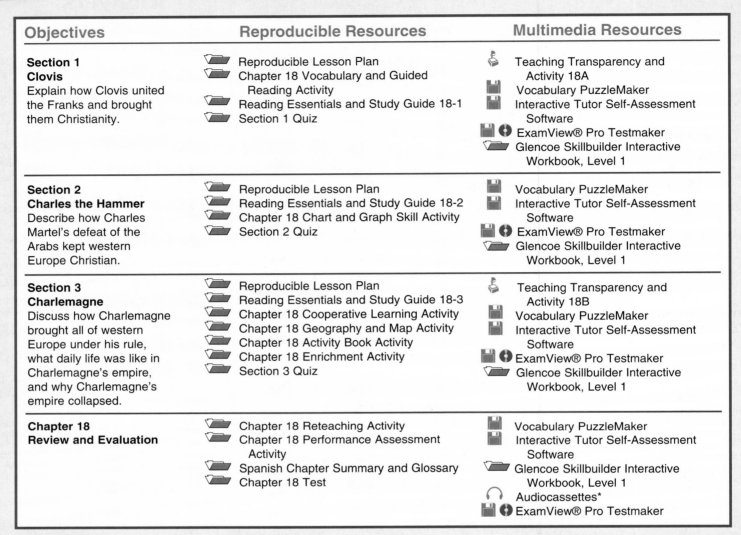

Objectives	Reproducible Resources	Multimedia Resources
Section 1 **Clovis** Explain how Clovis united the Franks and brought them Christianity.	Reproducible Lesson Plan Chapter 18 Vocabulary and Guided Reading Activity Reading Essentials and Study Guide 18-1 Section 1 Quiz	Teaching Transparency and Activity 18A Vocabulary PuzzleMaker Interactive Tutor Self-Assessment Software ExamView® Pro Testmaker Glencoe Skillbuilder Interactive Workbook, Level 1
Section 2 **Charles the Hammer** Describe how Charles Martel's defeat of the Arabs kept western Europe Christian.	Reproducible Lesson Plan Reading Essentials and Study Guide 18-2 Chapter 18 Chart and Graph Skill Activity Section 2 Quiz	Vocabulary PuzzleMaker Interactive Tutor Self-Assessment Software ExamView® Pro Testmaker Glencoe Skillbuilder Interactive Workbook, Level 1
Section 3 **Charlemagne** Discuss how Charlemagne brought all of western Europe under his rule, what daily life was like in Charlemagne's empire, and why Charlemagne's empire collapsed.	Reproducible Lesson Plan Reading Essentials and Study Guide 18-3 Chapter 18 Cooperative Learning Activity Chapter 18 Geography and Map Activity Chapter 18 Activity Book Activity Chapter 18 Enrichment Activity Section 3 Quiz	Teaching Transparency and Activity 18B Vocabulary PuzzleMaker Interactive Tutor Self-Assessment Software ExamView® Pro Testmaker Glencoe Skillbuilder Interactive Workbook, Level 1
Chapter 18 **Review and Evaluation**	Chapter 18 Reteaching Activity Chapter 18 Performance Assessment Activity Spanish Chapter Summary and Glossary Chapter 18 Test	Vocabulary PuzzleMaker Interactive Tutor Self-Assessment Software Glencoe Skillbuilder Interactive Workbook, Level 1 Audiocassettes* ExamView® Pro Testmaker

*Also available in Spanish.

Presentation Plus!

Use Glencoe's **Presentation Plus!** multimedia teacher tool to easily present dynamic lessons that visually excite your students. Using Microsoft® PowerPoint, you can customize the presentations to create your own personalized lessons.

Interactive Lesson Planner

Planning has never been easier! Using this CD-ROM, organize your week, month, semester, or year with all the help you need. The **Interactive Lesson Planner** gives you access to all of the blackline masters which accompany *Human Heritage.*

✓ PERFORMANCE ASSESSMENT ACTIVITIES

Writing   Have students research the many inventions from the Middle Ages. Then have them create advertisements for some of these inventions, using both text and drawings. Some possibilities are portable clocks (the first watches), pies, fireplaces for warming drafty castles, improved farming equipment such as wheelbarrows and plows, and buttons and buttonholes. Display the advertisements in the classroom.

CHAPTER RESOURCES

LITERATURE ABOUT THE PERIOD

Sayers, Dorothy, trans. *The Song of Roland.* Penguin, 1957. Chronicles the events and legends in Charlemagne's career and the career of his young nephew Roland.

READINGS FOR THE STUDENT

Heer, Friedrich. *Charlemagne and His World.* Macmillan, 1975. Large, lavishly illustrated description of the period.

READINGS FOR THE TEACHER

Editors of Time-Life. "The Changing Face of Europe," in *TimeFrame AD 600–800: The March of Islam.* Time-Life Books, 1988. Shows how Frankish kings helped preserve Christianity and usher in important cultural changes.

KEY TO ABILITY LEVELS

Teaching strategies have been coded for varying learning styles and abilities.

L1   Level 1 activities are **basic** activities and should be within the ability range of all students.

L2   Level 2 activities are **average** activities and should be within the ability range of the average to above-average student.

L3   Level 3 activities are **challenging** activities designed for the ability range of above-average students.

ELL   ELL activities should be within the ability range of English Language Learning students.

NATIONAL GEOGRAPHIC SOCIETY — Teacher's Corner

NATIONAL GEOGRAPHIC SOCIETY PRODUCTS AVAILABLE FROM GLENCOE

To order the following, call Glencoe at 1-800-334-7344:

- *MapPack: Europe (Transparency Maps)*
- *Europe (Laminated Desk Maps)*
- *PicturePack: Physical Geography of the World (Transparencies)*
- *PicturePack: The Middle Ages (Transparencies)*
- *PictureShow: The Middle Ages (CD-ROM)*
- *Picture Atlas of the World (CD-ROM)*

ADDITIONAL NATIONAL GEOGRAPHIC SOCIETY PRODUCTS

To order the following, call National Geographic at 1-800-368-2728:

- *PicturePack: Physical Geography of the World (Transparencies)*
- *Physical Geography of the Continents Series: Europe (Video)*
- *National Geographic Atlas of World History (Book)*
- *Wonders of the Ancient World: National Geographic Atlas of Archaeology (Book)*

Access *National Geographic's* new dynamic MapMachine Web site and other geography resources at:
http://www.nationalgeographic.com/
http://www.nationalgeographic.com/maps/

OVERVIEW

Chapter 18 discusses the Franks and the first strong kingdom in medieval Europe.

➤ **Section 1** discusses the goals of Clovis and the role of the Catholic Church in the political affairs of the Franks.

➤ **Section 2** describes the rule of Charles Martel and the Battle of Tours.

➤ **Section 3** explains important developments during the reign of Charlemagne.

CHAPTER OBJECTIVES

After reading Chapter 18, students will be able to:

1. explain how Clovis united the Franks under Christianity.

2. describe how Charles Martel's defeat of the Arabs kept western Europe Christian.

3. discuss how Charlemagne brought all of western Europe under his rule.

4. characterize what life was like in Charlemagne's empire.

5. summarize why Charlemagne's empire collapsed.

EXAMINING ARTIFACTS

Focus student attention on the artifacts, and ask them to describe how the artist who created the bronze statue wanted people to view Charlemagne. *(as a noble and perhaps holy warrior-king)* Tell students that in this chapter they will decide whether Charlemagne lived up to the artist's vision of him.

PERFORMANCE ASSESSMENT ✓

Use the Performance Assessment Activities on page 274B to help you evaluate students as they complete the chapter.

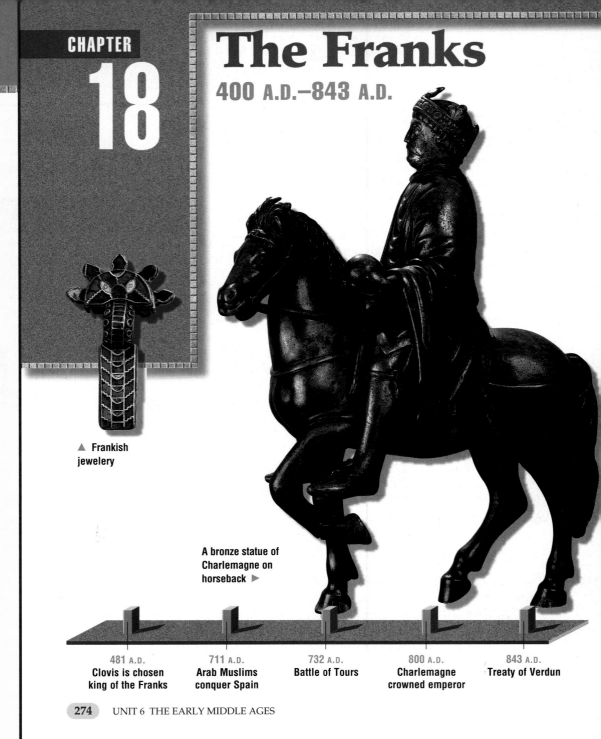

CHAPTER 18

The Franks
400 A.D.–843 A.D.

▲ Frankish jewelery

A bronze statue of Charlemagne on horseback ▶

481 A.D.	711 A.D.	732 A.D.	800 A.D.	843 A.D.
Clovis is chosen king of the Franks	Arab Muslims conquer Spain	Battle of Tours	Charlemagne crowned emperor	Treaty of Verdun

274 UNIT 6 THE EARLY MIDDLE AGES

TEACHING RESOURCES

TEACHER PLANNING AND SUPPORT

📁 Reproducible Lesson Plan
📁 Block Scheduling Implementation Guide
📁 Videodisc Bar Code Correlation
💿 Presentation Plus!

REVIEW AND REINFORCEMENT

📁 Reading Essentials and Study Guide 18-1, 18-2, 18-3
💾 Chapter 18 Vocabulary and Guided Reading Activity
💾 Vocabulary PuzzleMaker Software
🖨 Teaching Transparencies 18A & 18B

📁 Chapter 18 Reteaching Activity
📁 Chapter 18 Cooperative Learning Activity
📁 Chapter 18 Activity Book Activity
📁 Chapter 18 Chart and Graph Skill Activity
💾 Interactive Tutor Self-Assessment Software

APPLICATION AND HANDS-ON ACTIVITIES

📖 Daily World History, Geography, and Culture Question

Chapter Focus

 Read to Discover

- How Clovis united the Franks and brought them Christianity.
- How Charles Martel's defeat of the Arabs kept western Europe Christian.
- How Charlemagne brought all of western Europe under his rule.
- What life was like in Charlemagne's empire.
- Why Charlemagne's empire collapsed.

 Terms to Learn

converted
anointed
counts
lords
serfs
minstrels

 People to Know

Clovis
Charles Martel
Pepin
Charlemagne
Roland
Louis the Pious

🌐 **Places to Locate**

Paris
Tours
Aachen

Why It's Important The decline of the Roman Empire lead to disorder everywhere in western Europe. Many of the Germanic invaders were too weak to govern well. As a result, towns and villages fell into ruin. Roads and bridges were not repaired. Robbers roamed the countryside, making it unsafe for travelers. Trading and business slowed down, and there were shortages of food and other goods. People were no longer interested in learning, and many books and works of art were damaged or lost.

Chapter Overview
Visit the *Human Heritage* Web site at **humanheritage.glencoe.com** and click on **Chapter 18— Chapter Overviews** to preview this chapter.

SECTION 1 Clovis

During this period, a Germanic people called Franks became very important. They began to build a new civilization, one that later developed into modern France and Germany. The Franks lived along the Rhine River in what is now Germany. They were more successful in governing than other Germans. One reason for this was that the area in which they lived was close to their homeland, and they felt fairly secure. Also, unlike the Goths and Vandals, the Franks did more than just fight and rule. They became farmers.

At first, the Franks were divided into separate groups without a common ruler. In 481, one Frankish group chose a man named

---

GEOGRAPHY ACTIVITIES

- 📁 Chapter 18 Geography and Map Activity
- 📁 Social Studies Outline Map Resource Book

INTERDISCIPLINARY CONNECTIONS

- 🔵 World Music: Cultural Traditions

ENRICHMENT AND EXTENSION

- 💿 World History Primary Source Document Library CD-ROM
- 📁 Chapter 18 Enrichment Activity
- 📁 Foods Around the World

ASSESSMENT AND EVALUATION

- 📁 Chapter 18 Performance Assessment Activity
- 📁 Chapter 18 Section Quizzes 18-1, 18-2, 18-3
- 📁 Chapter 18 Test
- 💿 Chapter 18 ExamView® Pro Testmaker Software
- 🎧 Chapter 18 Digests Audiocassettes Activities and Tests

SPANISH RESOURCES

- 📁 Chapter 18 Spanish Chapter Summary and Glossary
- 🎧 Chapter 18 Spanish Chapter Digests Audiocassettes Activities and Tests

---

HISTORY Online

Chapter Overview introduces students to chapter content and key terms. Have them access **Chapter 18 Overview** at humanheritage.glencoe.com

FOCUS

📢 **Bellringer**

Ask students to respond in writing to the term *Dark Ages*.

Motivational Activity

Discuss students' responses to the term *Dark Ages*. Tell students that by 500 A.D. western Europe was so backward compared to other contemporary societies that scholars once called the early part of the Middle Ages the Dark Ages. Tell students that in this chapter they will learn about events that helped move western Europe out of the Dark Ages and into an age of enlightenment.

GUIDE TO READING

Reading Strategy

Ask students to read "Why It's Important" and summarize the chapter's main theme. *(The decline of the Roman Empire led to a decline of order and a loss of interest in learning.)*

Vocabulary Precheck

Ask students to define each of the "Terms to Learn." Have a volunteer consult the dictionary for any unfamiliar words. **L1 ELL**

💾 Use the Vocabulary PuzzleMaker for Chapter 18 to create a crossword puzzle. **L1**

📁 Assign Chapter 18 Vocabulary and Guided Reading Activity.

📁 Assign Reading Essentials and Study Guide 18-1.

TECHNOLOGY SKILLS

Developing Multimedia Presentations

TEACH

Developing Multimedia Presentations

You might introduce the lesson by writing this statement on the board: "Computers—More Than Just Typewriters." Ask students to brainstorm some of the things computers can do besides word processing. *(draw pictures, design tables and graphs, download/scan photos, create animation, record sound, etc.)*

Next, identify the "computer experts" in your class—those students who are comfortable with multimedia programs. Divide the class into groups, making sure each group has at least one technology advisor. Assign the skills lesson, which helps students plan a multimedia presentation on the Frankish empire.

Performance Assessment

To encourage self-assessment of the multimedia presentation, have each student complete this individual task management plan.

Self-Management Plan

Name: _____
Task: _____
Audience: _____
Steps to accomplish the task:

Problems to completing the task:

Solutions or attempted solutions:

Signed: _____

You want to present a research report to your class, and you want to really hold their attention. How do you do it? Your presentation can be exciting if you use various forms of media.

Learning the Skill At its most basic, a multimedia presentation involves using several types of media. To discuss life under the Frankish kings, for example, you might show photographs of historic paintings. You could also record selections from *The Song of Roland* or ballads sung by minstrels. Or you might present a video of Charlemagne's life.

You can also develop a multimedia presentation on a computer. Multimedia as it relates to computer technology is the combination of text, video, audio, and animation in an interactive computer program.

In order to create multimedia productions or presentations on a computer, you need to have certain tools. These may include traditional computer graphic tools and draw programs, animation programs that make still images move, and authoring systems that tie everything together. Your computer manual will tell you what tools your computer can support.

This chapter focuses on the growth of the Frankish empire in the early Middle Ages. Ask yourself questions like the following to create a multimedia presentation on the cultural and political developments of that era:

- Which forms of media do I want to include? Video? Sound? Animation? Photographs? Graphics? Other?
- Which of these media forms does my computer support?
- What kind of software programs or systems do I need? A paint program? A draw program? A program to create interactive, or two-way, communication? An authoring system that will allow me to change images, sound, and motion?
- Is there a "do-it-all" program I can use to develop the kind of presentation I want?

Skill Practice

Developing Multimedia Presentations

Keeping in mind the four guidelines given above, write a plan describing a multimedia presentation you would like to develop. Indicate what tools you will need and what steps you must take to make the presentation a reality.

276

TEAM TEACHING STRATEGIES

Art Work together with the art teacher in your school to develop visual materials and/or original drawings that students might scan into their computers. The visuals/drawings should focus on the political and cultural accomplishments of the Frankish empire. Students might also consult with the art teacher on the selection of computer fonts and styles to use with their presentations.

Clovis (klō' vis) as king. Although he was cruel and greedy, Clovis was a good general and an able king. He eventually brought all the Franks under one rule. Part of Clovis's kingdom later became France, which took its name from the Franks.

Clovis was the first Germanic king to accept the Catholic religion. Clovis was not happy with the Frankish gods. Although he prayed to them faithfully, they failed to help him win battles. Clovis decided that if he defeated the enemy, he would become a Christian. Clovis's army won its next battle. Clovis and some 3,000 Frankish soldiers, still in full battle dress, immediately **converted** (kuhn ver' tuhd), or changed religion, to Christianity. It was not long before all the Franks followed his example.

When Clovis became a Christian, he gained the support of the Romans in his kingdom. Before long, the Franks began speaking a form of Latin that later became the modern French language. Now, all the people in Clovis's kingdom practiced the same religion, spoke the same language, and felt united.

The Pope and other church officials gave Clovis their support. Priests served in his government. In return for the Church's help, Clovis was expected to protect the Church against all non-believers.

Clovis extended his rule over what is now France and western Germany and set up his capital in Paris. He admired the Roman Empire. He wore purple robes similar to those of the Roman emperors, and made Latin the official language of the court.

✔ **Reading Check**
What happened after Clovis **converted** to Christianity?

Section 1 Assessment

1. **Define:** converted.
2. What modern nations developed out of the civilization built by the Franks?
3. Why were the Franks more successful at governing than other Germanic peoples?

Critical Thinking

4. **Drawing a Conclusion** Why was it important for Clovis to have the Pope's blessing and the support of the Church?

Graphic Organizer Activity

5. Draw this diagram, and use it to show the cause and effects of Clovis's conversion to Christianity.

| Cause | → | Clovis Converts | → | Effects |

SECTION 2 Charles the Hammer

The Frankish kings who followed Clovis were weak rulers. Instead of keeping the kingdom united, they divided it among their sons. The sons often fought over their shares of land. They

L1 **Government** Write the following question on the chalkboard: *How was Clovis able to unify the Franks?* Lead a discussion in which students answer this question. Direct the discussion with the following questions: Why did Clovis's conversion to Christianity gain the support of the Romans in his kingdom? Do you think Clovis would have had a united kingdom if he had not become a Christian and adopted the Latin language? Why or why not?

✔ **Reading Check Answer**
After Clovis **converted** to Christianity, other Franks followed his example and the Frankish empire underwent many changes.

💾 Use **Interactive Tutor Self-Assessment Software** to review Section 1.

💾 Use the **Vocabulary PuzzleMaker** to create crossword and word search puzzles.

Section 1 Assessment Answers

1. converted, changed religion (p. 277)
2. France and western Germany
3. because the area in which they lived was close to their homeland, and they felt fairly secure; also, they became farmers instead of just fighting and ruling
4. Answers will vary but might include that through this, Clovis gained the support of the Romans in his kingdom.
5. Sample responses: *causes*—unhappy with Frankish gods, decided to convert if defeated enemy in next battle, won battle and converted; *effects*—gained support of Romans within kingdom, began speaking a form of Latin, promoted unity through use of same language and religion, won support of Pope and church officials, extended rule

Assign Chapter 18 **Section 1 Quiz** in the TCR. Testmaker available.

Fun Facts...

Mounted Knights
Charles Martel could not follow up his victory at Tours because he had too few mounted soldiers. From then on, he required every landowner to provide him with at least one fully outfitted knight. Over time, mounted knights became the core of the Frankish army.

spent so much time and energy fighting that they lost much of their power to local nobles.

It was not long before the Franks began to accept the leadership of a government official known as the "Mayor of the Palace." The Mayor was a noble and the most important official in the king's household. As the Frankish kings grew weaker, the Mayors took over many of their duties. In time, the Mayors were conducting wars, giving out land, and settling disputes. Of all the Mayors, the most powerful was Charles Martel (mahr tel'). He wanted to reunite all the Frankish nobles under his rule. Before long, Charles Martel had gained the support of the Church.

Charles Martel became known as "The Hammer" because of his strength in battle. In 732, he led the Franks in the Battle of

BATTLE OF TOURS Charles Martel (shown center in this painting) leads his army against the Muslims at the Battle of Tours. The Frankish victory halted the Muslim advance into western Europe. It also helped the Frankish rulers to build a strong kingdom. **Why were the Muslims invading western Europe?**

EXTENDING THE CONTENT

Charles Martel, who held power effectively from about 720 until his death in 741, depended in part on having the backing of the Church. In return, and to help unify the empire, he encouraged Christianity and protected missionaries from the pagan Germans across the Rhine River. The most famous missionary was St. Boniface, an Anglo-Saxon priest from England.

Tours (tūrz), one of the most important battles in European history. The Franks defeated an army of Arabs and Berbers who had conquered Spain in 711. The Arabs and Berbers were Muslims, who hoped to spread their religion of Islam everywhere. The Franks' victory at the Battle of Tours enabled Christianity to survive in western Europe.

When Charles Martel died, his son Pepin (pep' in) became Mayor of the Palace. With the help of the Pope and most Frankish nobles, Pepin removed the king and started a new dynasty. Pepin was the first Frankish king to be **anointed** (uh noin' tuhd), or blessed with holy oil, by the Pope. In return for the Church's support, Pepin helped the Pope when he was threatened by a group of Germans known as Lombards (lahm' bahrdz). Pepin led an army into Italy, defeated the Lombards, and gave the land they held in central Italy to the Pope. This gift made the Pope the political ruler of much of the Italian Peninsula.

 Reading Check
Who **anointed** Pepin, and why was this an important event?

Reading Check Answer
The Pope **anointed** Pepin, showing his approval of the new dynasty and strengthening ties between Pepin and the Roman Catholic Church.

💾 Use **Interactive Tutor Self-Assessment Software** to review Section 2.

Section 2 Assessment

1. **Define:** anointed.
2. Why was the Battle of Tours a turning point in history?
3. How did Pepin help the Pope?

Critical Thinking

4. **Predicting Consequences** What might western Europe have been like if the Arabs and Berbers had won the Battle of Tours?

Graphic Organizer Activity

5. Draw this diagram, and use it to compare the accomplishments of Charles Martel and his son Pepin.

Student Web Activity objectives, goals, and answers can be found at the **Chapter 18 Web Activity Lesson Plan** at humanheritage.glencoe.com

💾 Use the **Vocabulary Puzzle-Maker** to create crossword and word search puzzles.

SECTION 3 Charlemagne

When Pepin died in 768, his kingdom was divided between his two sons. His son Carloman died within a few years. Pepin's other son Charles then became king of the Franks. He is best known by his French name Charlemagne (shar' luh mān), which means "Charles the Great."

A powerful leader, Charlemagne wanted to bring all of western Europe under his rule. He also wanted all the Germanic people to become Christian. To achieve these goals, he waged a series of wars.

First, Charlemagne went to Italy and defeated the Lombards. Next, Charlemagne attacked Saxons (sak' suhnz), who lived in what is now northern Germany. For years, the Saxons had been raiding towns and monasteries inside the Frankish border. He

HISTORY Online

Student Web Activity
Visit the *Human Heritage* Web site at humanheritage.glencoe.com and click on *Chapter 18— Student Web Activities* to find out more about Charlemagne.

People in History

Charlemagne
C. 742 A.D.–814 A.D.

Christian Emperor

Charlemagne continued the German warrior tradition, spreading the Christian religion at the tip of a sword. In building his empire, he brought together the German, Roman, and Christian cultures that became the basis for European civilization.

sent thousands of captured Saxons into Frankish territory and then moved many Franks onto Saxon lands. Eventually, the Saxons accepted Christianity.

Charlemagne also led his armies in several campaigns across the Pyrenees (pēr' uh nēz) Mountains to fight the Muslims in Spain. A mountain people known as Basques (basks) did not want the Frankish armies to cross their territory. When Charlemagne was returning home from one of his Spanish campaigns, Basque warriors attacked the rear guard of his army in a narrow mountain pass. The rear guard was led by Roland, a fine warrior. Since Roland had far fewer soldiers than the Basques, he lost the battle. Even so, the fight was remembered, told, and retold throughout Europe. Over time, it became legend and was written down in French as a poem called *The Song of Roland*.

By 800, Charlemagne had created a large empire. It included most of the Germanic peoples who had settled in Europe since the early 400s. Charlemagne also fought against non-Germanic peoples in northern and eastern Europe. Although they managed to keep their freedom, they agreed to respect Charlemagne's power and not fight against his army.

CROWNING OF CHARLEMAGNE   In 800, Charlemagne became emperor of a new Christian Roman Empire. Here, Charlemagne is crowned "Emperor of the Romans" by the Pope. **How did Charlemagne aid the Church?**

SPOTLIGHT ON: CHARLEMAGNE

To extend People in History, provide these additional details on Charlemagne.

Charlemagne's secretary—a monk named Einhard—wrote the following description of Charlemagne: "Bodily Charles was well-built, strong and noble in height, measuring seven times his own foot. His head was round, his eyes large and lively, his nose a little larger than the mean, his hair in his later years a brilliant white, his expression calm and cheerful, his bearing full of majesty, his tread firm, his carriage erect, his voice high."

A Christian Empire   Charlemagne became the most powerful leader in western Europe. The people considered him as important as any Roman emperor. Charlemagne wanted to keep close ties between the Church and the government. Church officials kept records and helped Charlemagne run the country. In turn, he appointed the bishops and regarded any act against the Church as a sign of disloyalty to him.

Both Charlemagne and the Pope wanted a new Christian Roman Empire in western Europe. Charlemagne's conquests had brought him closer to their goal. On Christmas day in 800, Charlemagne was worshiping in St. Peter's Church in Rome. When the religious ceremony was over, the Pope placed a crown on Charlemagne's head. The Pope then declared that Charlemagne was the new Roman emperor. Although Charlemagne accepted the title, he was not pleased that the Pope had crowned him. This made it seem as if the emperor's right to rule came from the Pope rather than directly from God.

Charlemagne was a wise and just ruler who issued many laws. To make sure these laws were obeyed, he set up law courts all through the empire. Charlemagne chose officials called **counts** to run the courts. The counts took care of local problems, stopped feuds, protected the poor and weak, and raised armies for Charlemagne.

Charlemagne often had trouble keeping the counts under his control because of poor transportation and communication. So, he sent royal messengers all through the empire to check on them. These messengers reported to Charlemagne how well the counts were doing their jobs. Once a year, Charlemagne called his counts and warriors together. They reported troubles and talked over new laws for the empire. The final decision on what new laws to issue, however, was made by Charlemagne.

Charlemagne ruled his empire from Aachen (ah' kuhn), known today as Aix-la-Chapelle (āks' lah shah pel'). However, he did not always stay in the capital. He journeyed throughout the empire with his advisers and servants. The royal party would stop and rest at different palaces or homes. Wherever the king and his officials went, they were given food and entertained by the people. Such royal visits ensured the loyalty of local officials and people to Charlemagne's government.

Education   Most people in Charlemagne's empire could neither read nor write. Charlemagne, however, appreciated learning. Unlike earlier Frankish rulers, he believed in education and was proud of his own ability to read Latin. He kept a slate and copybook next to his bed so that he could practice writing.

Charlemagne wanted his people to be educated also. He worked hard to push back the darkness that had followed the fall of the Roman Empire. He encouraged churches and monasteries

Reading Check
What role did **counts** play in Charlemagne's government?

Fun Facts....

Frankish Officials
Officials in Charlemagne's court had specific duties. His *chaplain* advised the emperor on matters of conscience and supervised official documents. The *count of the palace* judged court cases not handled by Charlemagne and managed the palace in the emperor's absence. The *chamberlain* took care of the royal bedroom and treasury. The *seneschal* kept the palace supplied with food, wine, and servants. The *constable* cared for the horses.

CHAPTER 18 THE FRANKS   **281**

L1 **Education** Organize students into small groups. Tell students to imagine they are graduates of Charlemagne's school. The school's director, the monk Alcuin, has asked them to write a short catalog about the school that will be sent to prospective students. Each group should make a catalog that includes the following topics: the school's faculty, the courses offered, the achievements of the school, and the role of Charlemagne. Have each group present its catalog to the class. Then have the class vote on which catalog would most motivate them to enter Charlemagne's school.

Reading Check Answer
The **counts** ran the courts, took care of local problems, stopped feuds, protected the poor and weak, and raised armies.

DID YOU KNOW ??
Much of what is known about Charlemagne and the lands he ruled comes from a biography written by Einhard, his personal secretary.

MULTICULTURAL PERSPECTIVES

Charlemagne and his court seemed to have lived well and vigorously. The king liked good food, especially roast venison. He encouraged minstrels, jugglers, and other traveling entertainers, who would tell others about the comforts of the king's court. Sometimes there were lively discussions about theology, poetry, science, or military strategy. Charlemagne also liked to have someone read to him as he ate, preferring stories or works like St. Augustine's *City of God*.

CHARLEMAGNE'S SCHOOL   Charlemagne often visited his palace school, which was attended by children of the court. Directed by the monk Alcuin, the school also provided a place where scholars could gather to share their knowledge and to inspire one another. **Why was Charlemagne interested in learning?**

Deep Sleep Many legends spread about Charlemagne. According to one legend, he did not die but was only sleeping, and would awaken at the hour of his country's need.

to found schools. He had a scholar named Alcuin (al' kwin) start a school in one of the palaces to train the children of government officials to serve in the Church or in the royal household. The children studied such subjects as religion, Latin, music, literature, and arithmetic.

Scholars came from all over Europe to teach in Charlemagne's school. One of their many tasks was to copy manuscripts. This led to the development of a new form of writing. The Roman writing the scholars used contained only capital letters. These letters took up a lot of space on a page. So, the scholars began to write with small letters instead of capital ones. The new letters not only took up less space, but they were also easier to read. The new letters became the model for the lower-case letters used today.

Under Charlemagne, the arts began to flower again. Painters, sculptors, and metalworkers developed their talents. They built palaces and churches around a large courtyard as the Romans did. Artists covered palace and church walls with pictures showing stories from the Bible. They made book covers and ornamental weapons, and they decorated the manuscripts copied by scholars.

282   UNIT 6 THE EARLY MIDDLE AGES

Estate Life **Lords,** or nobles, were the most powerful people in Charlemagne's empire. They were the descendants of Frankish warriors and Roman landowners. Most of the lords' wealth came from goods grown or made on their estates. As there was little trade in Charlemagne's empire, each estate took care of its own needs. There were shoemakers, carpenters, and blacksmiths on each estate. There were also artisans who made weapons, cooking vessels, and jewelry.

Lords lived in stone farmhouses. Wooden *stockades* (stah kādz'), or fences, often were built around the houses. Each farmhouse had a banquet hall, sleeping quarters, cellars, stables, storage places, and a small chapel.

Farmers lived in simple wooden houses in small villages on the estates. They worked in the fields, vineyards, orchards, and forests around their villages. The fields were owned by the lords, but the farmers worked them three days a week. The rest of the time they worked small pieces of land the lords had given them.

Reading Check
Who were the **lords,** and from where did they get their wealth?

Reading Check Answer
The **lords** were nobles who got most of their wealth from goods grown or made on their estates.

GEOGRAPHY AND HISTORY

Long-distance trade with the near East improved during the reign of Charlemagne. Items traded consisted mostly of spices and silks. The trade was carried on by Jewish merchants, who were acceptable to both Christians and Muslims. Charlemagne's protection of the Jewish merchants led to the rise of the new middle class in the later Middle Ages.

Linking Across Time

Writing in Minuscule Today the word *minuscule* means "extremely small." However, during Charlemagne's times, it referred to the small letters that replaced the all-capital letters used by the Romans. This style of writing spread throughout Charlemagne's realm (below). It later developed into the capital and lowercase letters used in the writing of all Western languages (right).

COOPERATIVE LEARNING

Have students work in small groups to create diagrams, dioramas, or models of estates in Charlemagne's empire. Students can use the information in the textbook and in reference books to create their estates. Each member of the group should be assigned a particular task in order to complete the assignment. Display students' work in the classroom.

📁 Assign the Chapter 18 *Cooperative Learning Activity* in the TCR.

TEACH

Understanding Inset Maps

Have students read the instructional part of the feature to answer the following questions: What are inset maps? *(small maps that are set within larger ones)* What are two reasons that inset maps are used? *(to show parts of the main map enlarged and in greater detail; to show in a different way an area on the main map)* Direct students to study the map to answer the following questions: What kingdom did the Saxons become part of after the Treaty of Verdun? *(Kingdom of Louis)* What kingdom did most Lombards become part of after the Treaty of Verdun? *(Kingdom of Lothair)*

Assign the Chapter 18 **Geography and Map Activity** in the TCR.

Answers to Skill Practice

1. Paris and Tours
2. Lothair
3. Kingdom of Louis

Understanding Inset Maps

Sometimes, there is not enough space on a map for information to be shown clearly. Mapmakers have solved this problem by using **inset maps,** or small maps that are set within larger ones. Often placed in a corner of the main map, inset maps may have their own scales and legends.

Inset maps are used for two reasons. One is to show parts of the main map enlarged and in greater detail. Maps of countries or states often include inset maps showing individual cities.

Another reason inset maps are used is to show in a different way an area on the main map. For example, on the map below, the main map shows the Frankish Empire from Clovis through Charlemagne. The inset map in the upper right shows what happened to the same territory after the death of Charlemagne.

Map Practice

1. **What two cities were in the kingdom of Charles?**
2. **Who controlled Rome after the Treaty of Verdun?**
3. **Through which kingdom did the Danube River flow?**

The Frankish Empire

GO TO

Glencoe's **Skillbuilder Interactive Workbook, Level 1,** provides instruction and practice in key social studies skills.

284

The farmers divided the land into three sections. They let one section lie *fallow* (fal' ō), or not planted. On the other two sections, they used heavy metal plows to prepare the hard but fertile soil. In autumn, they planted wheat or rye in one section. In spring, they planted oats or barley in the other section. Each year, the farmers *rotated* (rō' tā tuhd), or changed by turns, the kind of crops they grew in each section. They also let a different section lie fallow. These changes helped them grow larger crops.

Besides working the land, the farmers had to give the nobles food and animals. The farmers had to perform many services for the nobles, too. Men repaired buildings on the estates, cut down trees, carried loads, gathered fruits, and served in the army. Women worked as hard as men. They looked after the children and small animals, wove cloth, and sewed clothing copied from earlier Roman styles. The farmers gradually did more for the nobles and less for themselves. They were becoming **serfs,** or people bound to the land.

Neither the nobles nor the farmers had much time to learn to read or write or to think about religion. Both groups accepted Christianity, but the new religion had little to do with their daily lives. However, on religious holidays, both rich and poor sang, danced, and feasted. They listened to traveling musicians called **minstrels** (min' struhlz). The minstrels journeyed from place to place singing the praises of Charlemagne and his empire.

The Collapse of the Empire   The glory of the empire did not last long after Charlemagne's death in 814. The empire needed a strong and able ruler. Charlemagne's heirs were neither. Many counts and lords became increasingly independent. They cared more about their own estates than about the good of the empire. They refused to obey Louis the Pious (pī' uhs), Charlemagne's son.

Louis the Pious unknowingly weakened the empire further when he divided it among his three sons. After he died, they began fighting among themselves over their shares. Lothair (lō thahr'), Louis's oldest son, received the title of emperor. His younger brothers, Charles and Louis, were jealous of Lothair.

In 843, the brothers agreed to a new and different division of the empire. Under the Treaty of Verdun (ver duhn'), Lothair kept the title of emperor, but he ruled only a narrow strip of land that stretched from the North Sea to the Italian Peninsula. Louis received the area to the east. Called the East Frankish Kingdom, it later became the nation of Germany. Charles received the area to the west. Called the West Frankish Kingdom, it later became France.

The brothers were weak rulers who allowed the counts and nobles to have most of the power. Once again, a united western Europe was divided into smaller territories.

Painting of Minstrel

✔ **Reading Check**
How did farmers gradually become **serfs?**

✔ **Reading Check**
How did **minstrels** increase Charlemagne's popularity?

L3 **Literature** Have students read *The Song of Roland* and write a report on the characters and personalities of Charlemagne and Roland as presented in the poem. Ask students to comment on their reports on the mythical and legendary quality given to historical figures in poems.

✔ **Reading Check Answer**
In exchange for a noble's protection, farmers became bound to the land as **serfs.**

✔ **Reading Check Answer**
The **minstrels** journeyed from place to place singing the praises of Charlemagne and his empire.

ASSESS

Check for Understanding
Ask students to summarize orally or in writing the main points of the chapter. Discuss the answers to the Section and Chapter Assessment questions.

Evaluate
Assign the Chapter 18 **Performance Assessment Activity** in the TCR.

Administer the **Chapter 18 Test**. Testmaker available.

MEETING SPECIAL NEEDS

Have auditory learners or gifted learners debate the following topic: *The collapse of Charlemagne's empire was inevitable.* Form two teams, one to defend the idea that the collapse of the empire was inevitable and one to defend the idea that the collapse of the empire could have been prevented. Allow each team enough time to research and develop its arguments before beginning the debate.

📁 Refer to **Inclusion for the Middle School Social Studies Classroom: Strategies and Activities** for additional resources.

Reteach

Ask students to explain how each of the following influenced the early Middle Ages: Germanic invasions, the donation of the land held by the Lombards to the Pope, and Charlemagne's dedication to education.

Assign the Chapter 18 **Reteaching Activity** in the TCR.

Enrich

Have students research and share with the class illustrations of Charlemagne's tomb and/or manuscripts of the period.

Assign the Chapter 18 **Enrichment Activity** in the TCR.

CLOSE

Ask students to explain how during the early Middle Ages, western Europe was in a dark age, and how it was moving toward an age of enlightenment—creating a bridge between an old world and a new one.

💾 Use **Interactive Tutor Self-Assessment Software** to review Section 3.

Self-Check Quiz gives students an interactive chapter tutorial. Have them access **Chapter 18 Quiz** at humanheritage.glencoe.com

---

Section 3 Assessment

1. **Define:** counts, lords, serfs, minstrels.
2. Why did Charlemagne object to the Pope crowning him emperor?
3. What did Charlemagne do to encourage learning?

Critical Thinking

4. **Identifying Alternatives** What might have prevented the collapse of Charlemagne's government?

Graphic Organizer Activity

5. Draw this diagram, and use it to summarize Charlemagne's political, educational, and cultural accomplishments.

```
        Charlemagne's Accomplishments
         ┌──────────┼──────────┐
     Political   Educational  Cultural
```

Chapter Summary & Study Guide

1. During the late 400s, the Franks began to build a civilization that would later develop into the modern nations of France and Germany.
2. Clovis united the Franks and was the first Germanic king to accept the Catholic religion.
3. Clovis gained the support of the Romans in his kingdom and made Latin the official language of the royal court.
4. A series of weak kings followed Clovis, and leadership gradually came into the hands of a government official known as the "Mayor of the Palace."
5. In 732, a Mayor of the Palace named Charles Martel defeated the Muslim army at the Battle of Tours. This kept western Europe Christian.
6. Charles Martel's son Pepin started a new dynasty and became the first Germanic king to be anointed by the Pope.
7. Pepin's son Charlemagne brought all of western Europe under his control.
8. In 800, the Pope crowned him the new Roman emperor.
9. Charlemagne was a wise and just ruler who wrote new laws.
10. Charlemagne was very interested in learning and encouraged the founding of schools in his empire.
11. During the rule of Charlemagne, powerful lords grew wealthy from goods grown or made on their estates.
12. Louis the Pious divided the Frankish Empire among his three sons, which led to its final collapse.

Self-Check Quiz

Visit the *Human Heritage* Web site at **humanheritage. glencoe.com** and click on **Chapter 18— Self-Check Quiz** to assess your understanding of this chapter.

Section 3 Assessment Answers

1. counts, court officials (p. 281); lords, nobles (p. 283); serfs, people bound to the land (p. 285); minstrels, traveling musicians (p. 285)

2. It seemed the emperor's right to rule came from the Pope rather than from God.

3. He encouraged churches and monasteries to found schools, and had Alcuin teach the children of government officials.

4. Answers will vary but could include that Charlemagne might have planned on who was to succeed him after his death.

5. Contributions will vary in wording, but should reflect high points in Charlemagne's rule, particularly the creation of courts and closely supervised counts to manage local affairs (political), spread of literacy through the establishment of schools (education), and flourishing of religious art and popular art such as minstrels (culture).

Assign the Chapter 18 **Section 3 Quiz** in the TCR. Testmaker available.

Using Key Terms

Write a paragraph about the Franks and their rule in western Europe. Highlight one of the people mentioned in the chapter in your paragraph. Use the following words.

converted   anointed   counts
lords   serfs   minstrels

Understanding Main Ideas

1. What happened to western Europe after the decline of the Roman Empire?
2. How did Clovis help people within his empire feel united?
3. What was the relationship between the Church and Clovis?
4. Why did the Mayor of the Palace become important?
5. What were Charlemagne's main goals when he became king of the Franks?
6. How did Frankish farmers become serfs?
7. What happened to western Europe after Charlemagne's heirs came to power?

Critical Thinking

1. Do you think that Charlemagne's traveling all over the empire was a wise idea? Why or why not?
2. Why was the title "the Great" good for Charlemagne? What other title might have been better? Why?
3. What parts of life in Charlemagne's empire would you have liked? What parts would you have disliked?
4. What do you think Louis the Pious could have done with the Frankish Empire instead of dividing it among his three sons?

Graphic Organizer Activity

Economics Create a diagram like the one shown, and use it to show details that support this main idea: "Life in the Frankish Empire centered around the estates of lords."

Geography in History

Place Refer to the map on p. 284 and compare the locations of Saragossa, Paris, and Rome. Each of these was an important city in the Frankish Empire. What geographic similarities and differences can you see in these places?

Using Your Journal

Review any details you may have noted about the changes that took place during Charlemagne's empire. Write a diary entry describing how some of these changes can still be seen today.

287

Bonus Test Question
For Chapter 18 Test
A historian has incorrectly reported several facts. What are they?—*Scholars from Europe and the Americas came to teach in Charlemagne's school. Most people could not read or write. Religion, however, was not taught.*

Using Your Journal

Diary entries will vary. Changes may include heads of government keeping in touch with the people they govern, the use of lowercase letters, and the importance of art in public buildings.

Geography in History

Paris and Saragossa are both located on rivers; all three cities lie on flat lands somewhat near a seacoast; Paris is centrally located while Saragossa and Rome are not.

Building Vocabulary

Paragraphs will vary but should include specific details and use all the words.

Understanding Main Ideas

1. There was disorder, towns and roads fell into ruin, the countryside was unsafe, trading slowed, and there were shortages of food.
2. They all had the same religion and language.
3. The Pope and other Church officials supported Clovis's government. In return, Clovis was expected to protect the Church.
4. because he took over many of the king's duties
5. to rule all of western Europe and to have all Germanic peoples become Christian
6. They began to work more for the nobles on estates.
7. It was divided into smaller territories.

Critical Thinking

1. Answers will vary but might include that it was wise because it made him appear strong and in control.
2. Answers will vary but might include that Charlemagne unified his empire.
3. Answers will vary but should include examples.
4. Answers will vary.

Graphic Organizer Activity

Details will vary, but might include: most goods were grown or made on estates, little trade existed so each estate had to take care of its own needs, farmers and artisans worked on estates in exchange for protection.

Chapter 19 Planning Guide

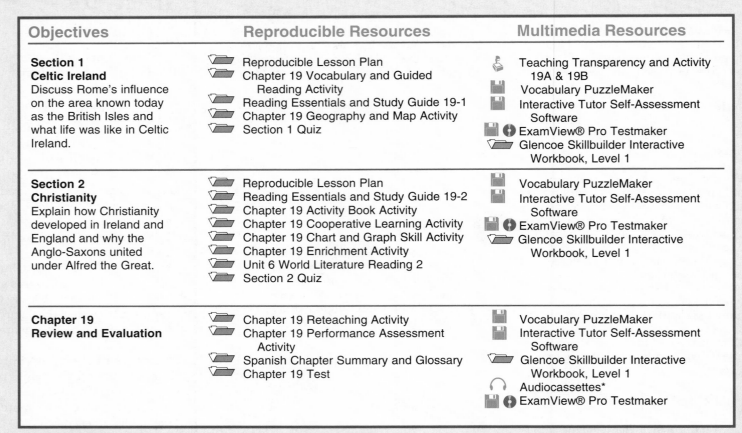

Objectives	Reproducible Resources	Multimedia Resources
Section 1 **Celtic Ireland** Discuss Rome's influence on the area known today as the British Isles and what life was like in Celtic Ireland.	Reproducible Lesson Plan Chapter 19 Vocabulary and Guided Reading Activity Reading Essentials and Study Guide 19-1 Chapter 19 Geography and Map Activity Section 1 Quiz	Teaching Transparency and Activity 19A & 19B Vocabulary PuzzleMaker Interactive Tutor Self-Assessment Software ExamView® Pro Testmaker Glencoe Skillbuilder Interactive Workbook, Level 1
Section 2 **Christianity** Explain how Christianity developed in Ireland and England and why the Anglo-Saxons united under Alfred the Great.	Reproducible Lesson Plan Reading Essentials and Study Guide 19-2 Chapter 19 Activity Book Activity Chapter 19 Cooperative Learning Activity Chapter 19 Chart and Graph Skill Activity Chapter 19 Enrichment Activity Unit 6 World Literature Reading 2 Section 2 Quiz	Vocabulary PuzzleMaker Interactive Tutor Self-Assessment Software ExamView® Pro Testmaker Glencoe Skillbuilder Interactive Workbook, Level 1
Chapter 19 **Review and Evaluation**	Chapter 19 Reteaching Activity Chapter 19 Performance Assessment Activity Spanish Chapter Summary and Glossary Chapter 19 Test	Vocabulary PuzzleMaker Interactive Tutor Self-Assessment Software Glencoe Skillbuilder Interactive Workbook, Level 1 Audiocassettes* ExamView® Pro Testmaker

*Also available in Spanish.

Presentation Plus!

Use Glencoe's **Presentation Plus!** multimedia teacher tool to easily present dynamic lessons that visually excite your students. Using Microsoft® PowerPoint, you can customize the presentations to create your own personalized lessons.

Interactive Lesson Planner

Planning has never been easier! Using this CD-ROM, organize your week, month, semester, or year with all the help you need. The **Interactive Lesson Planner** gives you access to all of the blackline masters which accompany *Human Heritage.*

✓ PERFORMANCE ASSESSMENT ACTIVITIES

Travel Journals Have students imagine they are Romans traveling through the British Isles in the year A.D. 250. On their trip, they see many sights and talk with many people. Tell students to write a travel journal describing the Roman influences they have noticed in the region and the different people they have encountered. Encourage volunteers to read their diary entries for the class.

CHAPTER RESOURCES

LITERATURE ABOUT THE PERIOD

Guerber, H.A., ed. *Middle Ages*. Avenel Books, 1985. From the *Myths and Legends Series*, covers Beowulf, Charlemagne, Arthur and his knights, and other tales of the Middle Ages.

READINGS FOR THE STUDENT

Corfe, Tom. *St. Patrick and Irish Christianity* (A Cambridge Topic Book). Lerner Publications, 1979. Brief overview with illustrations.

Crossley-Holland, Kevin. *Green Blades Rising: The Anglo-Saxons*. Seabury Press, 1976 (A Clarion Book). An introduction to Anglo-Saxon culture through artifacts and literature.

READINGS FOR THE TEACHER

Cunliffe, Barry. *The Celtic World*. McGraw-Hill, 1979. Portrays the civilization of the Celts from prehistoric Europe to present-day Ireland.

Thompson, E.A. *Who Was St. Patrick?* St. Martin's Press, 1985. Focuses on the writings of St. Patrick.

THE HISTORY CHANNEL.

The following videotape program is available from Glencoe:

• **A Celtic Journey Through Time**
  0-7670-0864-2

To order, call Glencoe at 1-800-334-7344. To find classroom resources to accompany many of these check:

A&E Television: http://www.aetv.com
The History Channel: http://www.historychannel.com

NATIONAL GEOGRAPHIC SOCIETY

Teacher's Corner

INDEX TO NATIONAL GEOGRAPHIC MAGAZINE

The following articles relate to this chapter:

• "The Celts," by Merle Severy, May 1977

NATIONAL GEOGRAPHIC SOCIETY PRODUCTS AVAILABLE FROM GLENCOE

To order the following, call Glencoe at 1-800-334-7344:

• *MapPack: Europe (Transparency Maps)*
• *Europe (Laminated Desk Maps)*
• *PicturePack: Physical Geography of the World (Transparencies)*
• *Picture Atlas of the World (CD-ROM)*
• *PicturePack: Physical Geography of the World (Transparencies)*

ADDITIONAL NATIONAL GEOGRAPHIC SOCIETY PRODUCTS

To order the following, call National Geographic at 1-800-368-2728:

• *Physical Geography of the Continents Series: Europe (Video)*
• *National Geographic Atlas of World History (Book)*
• *Wonders of the Ancient World: National Geographic Atlas of Archaeology (Book)*

Access *National Geographic's* new dynamic MapMachine Web site and other geography resources at:
http://www.nationalgeographic.com/
http://www.nationalgeographic.com/maps/

KEY TO ABILITY LEVELS

Teaching strategies have been coded for varying learning styles and abilities.

L1 Level 1 activities are **basic** activities and should be within the ability range of all students.

L2 Level 2 activities are **average** activities and should be within the ability range of the average to above-average student.

L3 Level 3 activities are **challenging** activities designed for the ability range of above-average students.

ELL ELL activities should be within the ability range of English Language Learning students.

OVERVIEW

Chapter 19 discusses the development of civilization in the British Isles.

➤ **Section 1** describes the development of an independent Celtic culture in Ireland.

➤ **Section 2** explains the development of English government and society under the Anglo-Saxon kings.

CHAPTER OBJECTIVES

After reading Chapter 19, students will be able to:

1. summarize what life was like in Celtic Ireland.

2. describe how Christianity developed in both Ireland and England.

3. explain why the Anglo-Saxons united under Alfred the Great.

4. describe what life was like in Anglo-Saxon England.

EXAMINING ARTIFACTS

Ask students who they think might wear a helmet such as the one pictured. *(soldier or warrior-leader)* Explain that this particular helmet belonged to the king that inspired the jewel on this page. Explain that in this chapter students will learn how leaders such as King Alfred helped shape the history of the British Isles.

PERFORMANCE ASSESSMENT ✓

Use the Performance Assessment Activities on page 288B to help you evaluate students as they complete the chapter.

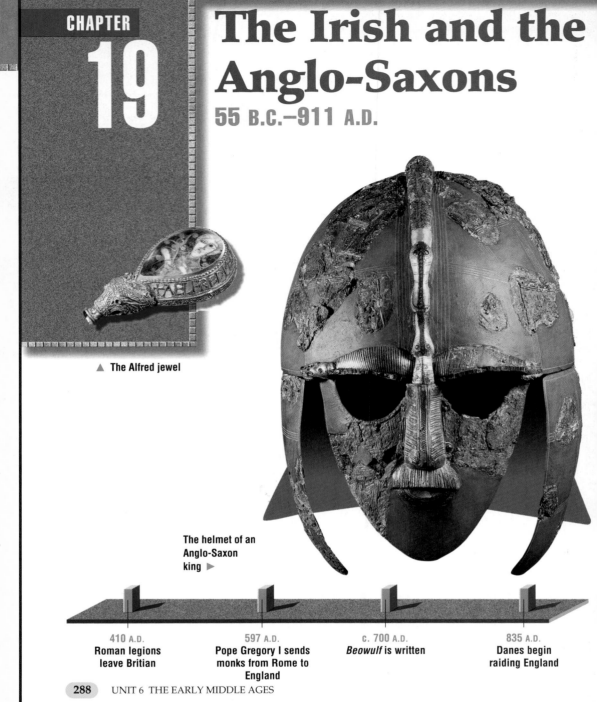

CHAPTER 19

The Irish and the Anglo-Saxons

55 B.C.–911 A.D.

▲ The Alfred jewel

The helmet of an Anglo-Saxon king ▶

410 A.D.	597 A.D.	c. 700 A.D.	835 A.D.
Roman legions leave Britian	**Pope Gregory I sends monks from Rome to England**	***Beowulf* is written**	**Danes begin raiding England**

288 UNIT 6 THE EARLY MIDDLE AGES

TEACHING RESOURCES

TEACHER PLANNING AND SUPPORT

- 🗀 Reproducible Lesson Plan
- 🗀 Block Scheduling Implementation Guide
- 🗀 Videodisc Bar Code Correlation
- 💿 Presentation Plus!

REVIEW AND REINFORCEMENT

- 🗀 Reading Essentials and Study Guide 19-1, 19-2,
- 🗀 Chapter 19 Vocabulary and Guided Reading Activity
- 💾 Vocabulary PuzzleMaker Software
- 🖨 Teaching Transparencies 19A & 19B

- 🗀 Chapter 19 Reteaching Activity
- 🗀 Chapter 19 Cooperative Learning Activity
- 🗀 Chapter 19 Activity Book Activity
- 🗀 Chapter 19 Chart and Graph Skill Activity
- 💾 Interactive Tutor Self-Assessment Software

APPLICATION AND HANDS-ON ACTIVITIES

- 🗀 Daily World History, Geography, and Culture Question
- 🗀 Unit 6 Hands-On History Lab Activity

Chapter Focus

Read to Discover

- How Rome influenced the area known today as the British Isles.
- What life was like in Celtic Ireland.
- How Christianity developed in Ireland and England.
- Why the Anglo-Saxons united under Alfred the Great.
- What life was like in Anglo-Saxon England.

 Terms to Learn
coracles
shires
sheriff
king's peace
witenagemot
witan

 People to Know
Saint Patrick
Saint Columba
Pope Gregory I
Ethelbert
Bede
Alfred the Great

 Places to Locate
British Isles
Kent
Wessex
Daneland

Why It's Important   Off the west coast of Europe lies a group of islands that never became part of Charlemagne's empire. Known today as the British Isles, they consist of Great Britain, Ireland, and many smaller islands.

Roman legions led by Julius Caesar invaded Britain in 55 B.C. The Romans eventually conquered much of the island and ruled it for almost 400 years. The Romans had difficulties ruling some of the area. A conquered people called Celts (kelts) were not interested in or influenced by Roman culture.

During the 300s A.D. Roman soldiers were called home to defend the empire's borders against the Germanic invasions. After 410 A.D., the island was overrun by groups from northern Germany and Denmark, called Angles, Saxons, and Jutes. These groups united to become The Anglo-Saxons. They built settlements and set up several small kingdoms. The southern part of Britain soon became known as Angleland, or England. The people became known as the English.

HISTORY Online

Chapter Overview
Visit the *Human Heritage* Web site at **humanheritage.glencoe.com** and click on *Chapter 19— Chapter Overviews* to preview this chapter.

SECTION 1 Celtic Ireland

With the coming of the Anglo-Saxons, most of the Celts who lived in Britain fled to Ireland. In time, Ireland became the major center of Celtic culture. Ireland had no cities. The people were divided into clans that lived in small villages. Most farmed and

---

Chapter Overview introduces students to chapter content and key terms. Have them access *Chapter 19 Overview* at **humanheritage.glencoe.com**

FOCUS

Bellringer

Ask students to write a sentence or two answering this question: *Who was Saint Patrick?*

Motivational Activity

Have students read their sentences about Saint Patrick. Explain that Saint Patrick brought Christianity to Ireland. Tell students that in this chapter they will learn more about Saint Patrick and the importance of Christianity in Ireland and England in the early Middle Ages.

GUIDE TO READING

Reading Strategy

Ask students to read "Why It's Important" and summarize the chapter's main theme. *(The northern part of the British Isles was shaped by the Celts, while the Anglo-Saxons strongly influenced the southern portion.)*

Vocabulary Precheck

Ask students to define each of the "Terms to Learn." Have a volunteer consult the dictionary for any unfamiliar words. **L1** **ELL**

Use the Vocabulary PuzzleMaker for Chapter 19 to create a crossword puzzle. **L1**

Assign Chapter 19 Vocabulary and Guided Reading Activity.

Assign Reading Essentials and Study Guide 19-1.

GEOGRAPHY ACTIVITIES

- Chapter 19 Geography and Map Activity
- Social Studies Outline Map Resource Book

INTERDISCIPLINARY CONNECTIONS

- Unit 6 World Literature Reading 1
- World Music: Cultural Traditions

ENRICHMENT AND EXTENSION

- Chapter 19 Enrichment Activity
- World History Primary Source Document Library CD-ROM
- Foods Around the World

ASSESSMENT AND EVALUATION

- Chapter 19 Performance Assessment Activity
- Chapter 19 Section Quizzes 19-1, 19-2
- Chapter 19 Test
- Chapter 19 ExamView® Pro Testmaker Software
- Chapter 19 Digests Audiocassettes Activities and Tests

SPANISH RESOURCES

- Chapter 19 Spanish Chapter Summary and Glossary
- Chapter 19 Spanish Chapter Digests Audiocassettes Activities and Tests

Guided Practice

L1 **Legends** Point out that many legends have grown up around St. Patrick. Have volunteers research some of these stories and share them with the class. **ELL**

Reading Check Answer
The Irish used **coracles** for travel, trade, and fishing.

GEOGRAPHY AND HISTORY

The Anglos, Saxons, and Jutes were seafaring peoples who traveled across the North Sea to Britain in long, open boats. They were strong warriors and controlled most of the land by the A.D. 600s.

HISTORY Online

Student Web Activity objectives, goals, and answers can be found at the **Chapter 19 Web Activity Lesson Plan** at humanheritage.glencoe.com

---

Reading Check
How did the Irish use boats called **coracles?**

The Book of Kells
Irish monks produced one of the masterpieces of early Christian art—the Book of Kells, a beautifully illustrated version of the four gospels. The illuminated manuscript was done in the late 700s.

HISTORY Online

Student Web Activity
Visit the *Human Heritage* Web site at humanheritage.glencoe.com and click on **Chapter 19— Student Web Activities** to find out more about the work of Irish monks.

---

raised cattle. The more cattle a person owned, the wealthier that person was considered to be.

The Irish were a seafaring people, too. They made boats called **coracles** (kor' uh kuhls) by stretching cow hides over a wooden frame. Some coracles were large enough to hold as many as 30 people. The boats handled well at sea and were used for travel, trade, and fishing.

The Irish were able to remain free of Germanic attacks because their island was located farther out in the Atlantic Ocean than Britain. Scholars, artists, merchants, and monks from many parts of Europe came to Ireland because of its peace and safety.

Irish scholars and artists were influenced by Christianity. The Irish Church was founded by Saint Patrick. Born in Britain in the 400s A.D., Saint Patrick was kidnapped when he was young and taken to Ireland by Irish pirates. Later, he escaped to Europe, where he studied to be a priest. After becoming a bishop, he returned to Ireland and converted the people to Christianity. He spread his message all through the island and set up many new churches.

Ireland lost contact with Rome during the Germanic invasions of the Roman Empire. This meant the Pope could no longer lead the Irish Church. So, the Church turned to its abbots. Many were related to the heads of the different clans. Each clan supported its own monastery.

The monasteries became centers of Irish life although many were in places that were not accessible—on rocky coasts or steep hills. Most monasteries were made up of a group of huts with a wooden stockade around them. Later, some monasteries were built of stone. Because of poor transportation and communication, church organization was weak. So, each monastery took charge of its own affairs. Irish monks soon began to follow practices different from those of the Roman Church. They wore their hair in a different way and celebrated Easter on a different day. Their rituals were not the same as those of the Romans.

Irish monasteries set down few rules. A monk was free to move from one monastery to another. Many monks chose to be hermits. Others set up schools to teach Christianity. Still others became missionaries. They sailed the North Atlantic and the Irish Sea seeking new converts and looking for islands on which to build new monasteries.

One of the best-known monks was Saint Columba (kuh luhm' buh). He set up a monastery on Iona (ī ō' nuh), an island off the west coast of Scotland. From his base on Iona, Saint Columba did missionary work among the many non-Christian Celts along the coast.

Monks from Iona went to northern England to preach to the Anglo-Saxons. Other Irish monks went to northern Europe,

---

EXTENDING THE CONTENT

In Celtic Britain and Ireland, distinctive styles of arts and crafts developed. Celtic bronzeworkers in southern Britain, for example, made mirrors engraved with intricate curving designs. Metalworkers also worked in gold and silver, making jewelry, armlets, and a neck ornament called a torc. Christian Celtic art developed using Christian symbols. The objects were mainly religious such as stone crosses, chalices, and intricately illuminated manuscripts.

IRISH MONASTERY   Irish Christian monks established monasteries throughout the British Isles and Europe. Many of their stone living quarters, like the ones shown here, still stand today along the rocky coast of western Ireland. **What attracted monks to Ireland?**

where they built monasteries and churches. Many Irish scholars became part of Charlemagne's palace school. They helped spread Christianity and learning throughout his empire.

Section 1 Assessment

1. **Define:** coracles.
2. How did the Irish earn a living?
3. Why did Irish monasteries take charge of their own affairs?

Critical Thinking

4. **Predicting Consequences** What might have happened in Britain if the Romans had not left in 410 A.D.?

Graphic Organizer Activity

Draw this diagram, and use it to show the cause and effects of Irish isolation from Germanic invasions.

| Cause | → | Irish Isolation | → | Effects |

DID YOU KNOW

The Celts, skilled warriors and metalworkers, created Europe's first civilization north of the Alps. The Celts had many gods and goddesses. Priests known as Druids offered sacrifices to the gods, settled disputes, and educated the young.

LINKING PAST TO PRESENT

The Celts of medieval England and Ireland were descendants of people from the eastern part of central Europe who migrated throughout Europe. The Celts settled in Gaul and northern Spain and then crossed over to the British Isles by about 800 B.C. Celtic culture still is part of the modern cultures and languages of Ireland, Scotland, Wales, and Cornwall.

Use **Interactive Tutor Self-Assessment Software** to review Section 1.

291

People in History

Alfred the Great
849 A.D.–899 A.D.

Anglo-Saxon King

Son of a Saxon king, Alfred led the resistance against Danish invaders. He made his kingdom the rallying point for other kingdoms, paving the way for the unification of England. In 886 A.D., he captured London and was soon recognized as king of all England. One of his greatest achievements was the creation of a navy—the basis of England's future strength as a nation.

SECTION 2 Christianity

Ireland was Christian, but the Anglo-Saxon kingdoms of Britain were not. They followed the Germanic religions. Then, Pope Gregory I decided to convert the Anglo-Saxons to Christianity. Legend has it that he saw some Anglo-Saxon boys waiting in the marketplace of Rome to be sold into slavery. Gregory noticed their light skin, handsome faces, and blonde hair and asked where their home was. When he learned that the boys were Angles, he said they had the faces of angels and should be Christians.

Therefore, in 597 A.D., Pope Gregory sent a mission of 41 monks from Rome to England under the leadership of Augustine. The missionaries landed in the small kingdom of Kent in southern England. Kent's queen, Bertha, was already a Christian, but its king, Ethelbert (eth' uhl bert), was not. At first, Ethelbert was very suspicious of Augustine and the other monks. He would meet with them only in the open air where their "magic" could not hurt him. Within a year, however, Ethelbert became a Christian. He allowed Augustine to build a church in the town of Canterbury (kant' uhr ber ē) and to teach the people about Christianity.

The Anglo-Saxons were quick to accept the new religion, and by 700 A.D. all England was Christian. The Pope was head of the Church. Monasteries were built throughout England. As in Ireland, they became centers of religion and culture.

One monk, Bede (bēd), was a great scholar. He wrote the first history of the English people. He also brought to England the Christian way of dating events from the year of Jesus' birth.

Although they accepted Christianity, the Anglo-Saxons kept much of their old culture. They told old legends about brave warriors fighting monsters and dragons. One such legend was about a warrior named Beowulf (bā' uh wulf). *Beowulf,* one of the earliest known tales, is an epic poem of almost 3,200 lines. Written by an unknown poet in about 700, it was passed along by oral tradition for two centuries. Finally, in the 900s, the work was written down. In colorful verses it describes how the hero warrior Beowulf goes from place to place fighting wicked people and ferocious animals. His greatest battle is when he defeats a horrible monster named Grindel. The language in which *Beowulf* was written is a form of English called Old English. This poem is one of the most important works of Anglo-Saxon literature.

During this time, stories, tales, and historical events were told orally, sung or recited. *Beowulf* and other early literature became the source of later Anglo-Saxon poetry and music. With the increased influence of the Christian Church in western

MULTICULTURAL PERSPECTIVES

Many legends developed about the saints. A legend about Saint Patrick stated that his fervent preaching drove the snakes out of Ireland. A legend about a seafaring monk, Saint Brendan, claimed that he sailed a coracle to new lands across the ocean, perhaps to America.

Europe, religion would also provide the subjects for much early literature. This literature reflected the lives of the people of the time and their culture.

Alfred the Great   About 835 A.D., bands of Danes began attacking the coast of England. Before long, they were making permanent settlements in conquered areas. The English kingdoms decided to resist the invaders. They chose as their leader Alfred, King of Wessex (wes' iks). Alfred later became known as Alfred the Great, one of England's best-loved rulers.

Alfred knew the Anglo-Saxons were not yet strong enough to drive out the Danes. To gain time to build a stronger army, he paid the Danes a sum of money each year to leave England alone. When he felt his army was strong enough, he refused to make any more payments. The Danes invaded England and defeated the

Fun Facts . . . .

Early History The *Anglo-Saxon Chronicle,* begun in the reign of Alfred the Great, records events in England from the beginning of the Christian era to the middle of the 12th century. It is the earliest known history of a European people written in the vernacular, or everyday spoken language.

L3 **Writing** Remind students that a common element in Anglo-Saxon folklore is the slaying of a monster or dragon, such as in *Beowulf*. Ask students to write their own folktale that involves a similar situation of a hero or heroine destroying a monster or evil force. Encourage students to share their folktales.

Linking Across Time

The central government was too weak to govern the whole country. Some students may also mention the inability of the king to drive out invaders, especially the Danes.

DID YOU KNOW ??

Alfred the Great's united kingdom became known as "Angleland" or England.

Linking Across Time

Keeping the Peace   In Anglo-Saxon times, the job of peace keeping fell to local nobles known as sheriffs (below). In the United States, the job of sheriff now belongs to a paid public official (right). **What conditions in England made it necessary for nobles to enforce the law?**

CHAPTER 19 THE IRISH AND THE ANGLO-SAXONS **293**

SPOTLIGHT ON: ALFRED THE GREAT

Alfred the Great encouraged a revival of English culture and learning. He wrote, "So completely had learning decayed in the English nation that there were very few from here to the Humber [River] who could understand their mass-books in English . . . and I think there were not many beyond the Humber." Alfred learned Latin so he could make his own Old English translations, including comments, of classic works that he thought people ought to be able to read in their own language.

L3 **Religion** Have students research one of the following saints: Saint Patrick, Saint Augustine, or Saint Columba. Students should investigate why the saint was important and how he contributed to the spread of Christianity in Ireland or England.

MAKING CONNECTIONS

➤➤ **History** Alfred risked his life many times for his country. Legend states that he once disguised himself as a minstrel to go into the Danes' camp to find out their plan of attack. The next day, he and his army ambushed and defeated them.

MAP STUDY
Answers

the North Sea and the Irish Sea; London, Canterbury
Assign the Chapter 19 **Geography and Map Activity** in the TCR.

Anglo-Saxons. The next year, Alfred again gathered his army and met the Danes in battle. This time, the Danes were defeated.

Alfred continued to strengthen his army. He built the first English fighting ships and constructed fortresses throughout England. The entire country rallied behind him. He was no longer just King of Wessex but King of England.

Alfred never became strong enough to drive the Danes completely out of England. So, he signed a treaty with them. The treaty recognized the right of the Danes to rule the northeast part of England, an area that became known as the Danelaw (dăn' lah). In return, the Danes promised to remain inside the Danelaw and not try to conquer more English land. In later years, the English took control of the Danelaw and made it part of their kingdom.

The Danes had destroyed part of the English city of London. Alfred had it rebuilt. Before long, it became the country's leading city. To gain the continued loyalty and obedience of the people, Alfred set forth new laws based on old Anglo-Saxon customs. These customs protected the weak against the strong and stressed honesty in making agreements.

LOCATION The Danes had conquered an area north of the Thames River and established permanent settlements there. **What bodies of water border Danelaw? What two cities were located south of Danelaw?**

England and the Danelaw

MEETING SPECIAL NEEDS

Have visual learners create murals or wall hangings to illustrate what life was like in Anglo-Saxon England. Divide the group in two. Have one group illustrate what life was like for nobles, and the other group illustrate what life was like for the peasants. The murals should feature the dress, housing, and activities of the nobles or peasants.

📁 Refer to *Inclusion for the Middle School Social Studies Classroom: Strategies and Activities* for additional resources.

Alfred was well-educated and interested in learning. He did much to educate the English. Like Charlemagne, Alfred started a palace school to train nobles' sons for government posts. At that time, books were generally written in Latin, a language most English church and government officials did not know. Alfred's scholars translated the books into English. So that the people would become familiar with their history, Alfred had monks begin a record of English history starting with Roman times.

The Government

The government of Anglo-Saxon England centered on the king. A council of lords generally elected kings from among members of the royal family. After 700 A.D., the Church usually crowned the new rulers. The king directed the central government, which was made up of royal servants and advisers. They handled the king's needs and wishes.

The central government, however, was too weak to govern the whole country. So, the king set up local governments. England was divided into districts called **shires** (shīrz). Each was run by a **sheriff,** who was a local noble chosen by the king. The sheriff collected money, enforced the law, called out soldiers when needed, and told the king what was happening in the shire.

The king and his household moved around instead of remaining in a capital city. Whatever area the royal household was in was under the **king's peace,** or royal protection. Lawless acts were not allowed. Anyone who committed a crime was punished under the king's laws rather than local laws. In time, the king's peace spread to all areas of the kingdom, whether the king was there or not. This helped unite Anglo-Saxon England.

Nobles and church officials gave the king advice on how to run the country. They could not, however, order a king to act against his will. A group of nobles and church leaders, known as the **witenagemot** (wit uhn uh' guh mōt), met with the king to talk over problems. Each member of the group was known as a **witan** (wi' tuhn), or wiseman. The group approved laws drawn up by the king and his household. It also acted as a court.

The People

The people in Anglo-Saxon England were generally divided into two classes. One was the nobles. An Anglo-Saxon became a noble by birth or as a reward for special service to the king. Nobles had to attend the witenagemot, keep peace in local areas, and serve the king in war. Noblemen wore pants and tunics covered by silk or fur cloaks. Noblewomen wore tunics and long cloaks held in place on each shoulder by a brooch.

The king rewarded many nobles with gifts of gold, silver, horses, and weapons. He also gave them estates throughout the kingdom. As a result, nobles spent a great deal of time moving from place to place with their families and servants. A noble's house had a large hall where meals were served and guests

Reading Check
Why did early English kings divide the country into **shires?** What were some of the jobs of the **sheriff?**

Reading Check
How did the **king's peace** help unite England?

Reading Check
What was the purpose of the **witenagemot?** Who might become a **witan?**

L1 **Writing** Have students imagine that they are monks assigned the task of recording English history. Have them choose an event from early English history and write an account for the *Anglo-Saxon Chronicle.*

Reading Check Answer
Early English kings divided the country into **shires** because the government was too weak to govern the entire country.
The **sheriff** collected money, enforced the law, called out soldiers when needed, and told the king what was happening in the shire.

Reading Check Answer
The **king's peace** spread to all areas of the kingdom, and people followed it whether the king was there or not.

Reading Check Answer
The **witenagemot** advised the king on how to handle problems.
A **witan** was one of the nobles or church leaders who served on the witenagemot.

ASSESS

Check for Understanding

Ask students to summarize orally or in writing the main points of the chapter. Discuss the answers to the Section and Chapter Assessment questions.

Evaluate

Assign Chapter 19 **Performance Assessment Activity** in the TCR.

Administer **Chapter 19 Test** in the TCR. Testmaker available.

COOPERATIVE LEARNING

Have students choose a historical event presented in this chapter and plan the presentation of a pictorial record. Divide the class into three groups. One group will determine the style and nature of the record and how it will be produced, choose particular scenes to present, and make recommendations during its execution. Another group will be responsible for the actual production. The third group will be responsible for creating a narrative to accompany the record. Have a class presentation when the record is finished.

Assign Chapter 19 *Cooperative Learning Activity* in the TCR.

Reteach

Have students work in small groups to write a sentence that summarizes each subsection in the chapter.

Assign the Chapter 19 **Reteaching Activity** in the TCR.

Enrich

Have students role-play a scene from one of the many legends of King Arthur and the Knights of the Round Table.

Assign the Chapter 19 **Enrichment Activity** in the TCR.

CLOSE

Have students discuss how the settlements in the British Isles during the early Middle Ages might have been different if Christianity had not been an important part of everyday life.

💾 Use **Interactive Tutor Self-Assessment Software** to review Section 2.

Self-Check Quiz gives students an interactive chapter tutorial. Have them access **Chapter 19 Quiz** at **humanheritage.glencoe.com**

---

entertained. Its walls were covered with *tapestries* (tap' uh strēz), or woven hangings with pictures on them. Tables and benches were the hall's only furniture. The bedrooms of nobles and their families were next to the hall or in a separate building.

The other class of people in Anglo-Saxon England was the peasants. They lived in small villages on or near a noble's estate and led a hard life. Most did not own their own land but worked fields belonging to the noble. Every year, the noble redivided the land, and each peasant received different strips. This was done to make sure that peasants would be treated equally. They helped each other farm the land by sharing tools and oxen. The peasants kept part of the crop for food and gave part to the noble. In return, the noble protected his peasants from enemy attacks.

Peasants lived in one-room wood and plaster huts. Both the family and the animals shared the same room. An open fireplace, which provided heat during winter, stood in the center. Smoke from the fire escaped through a hole in the straw roof.

Section 2 Assessment

1. **Define:** shires, sheriff, king's peace, witenagemot, witan.
2. How did Christianity come to the Anglo-Saxon kingdoms of England?
3. What did Alfred do to unite Anglo-Saxon England?

Critical Thinking

4. **Drawing Conclusions** Why do you think Alfred was given the title of "the Great"?

Graphic Organizer Activity

5. Draw this diagram, and use it to record the things that nobles and peasants gave to each other.

Chapter Summary & Study Guide

1. After Roman legions left Britain in 410 A.D., it was overrun by the Angles, Saxons, and Jutes, who united to become the Anglo-Saxons.
2. After the Anglo-Saxons drove most of the Celts from Britain, Ireland became a center of Celtic culture.
3. Monasteries became centers of Irish life.
4. In 597 A.D., Pope Gregory I sent monks to England, and by 700 A.D. England had become Christian.
5. When bands of Danes began raiding England in the 800s, the Anglo-Saxons united behind Alfred the Great.
6. English kings directed the central government, but they relied on help from local governments, nobles, and church leaders.

Self-Check Quiz

Visit the *Human Heritage* Web site at **humanheritage.glencoe.com** and click on **Chapter 19—Self-Check Quiz** to assess your understanding of this chapter.

Section 2 Assessment Answers

1. shires, districts (p. 295); sheriff, noble who ran a district (p. 295); king's peace, royal protection (p. 295); witenagemot, group of nobles and Church leaders (p. 295); witan, wise man (p. 295)
2. Pope Gregory I sent Augustine and other monks to England to convert the Anglo-Saxons. After King Ethelbert converted, other people quickly accepted the religion.

3. He defeated the Danes, built ships, constructed fortresses, and set forth new laws.
4. Answers will vary, but students will most likely point to his achievements.
5. Sample response: *nobles gave*—land and protection; *peasants gave*—their labor and part of their crops.

Assign the Chapter 19 **Section 2 Quiz** in the TCR. Testmaker available.

Using Key Terms

Write a paragraph to be used in a book on the Celts and Anglo-Saxons describing one part of their lives. Use the following words in your paragraph.

coracles   shires   sheriff
king's peace   witenagemot   witan

Understanding Main Ideas

1. Why did the Romans have trouble ruling Britain?
2. Why did Roman rule in Britain crumble during the 300s A.D.?
3. What happened to Britain when the Roman legions left?
4. What country became the major center of Celtic culture?
5. Why did the Irish church turn to its abbots for leadership?
6. Why did Alfred the Great pay the Danes to leave England alone?
7. Why did the king set up local governments in England?
8. What were the duties of nobles?

Critical Thinking

1. What effect did the Germanic invasions of the Roman Empire have on the history of England?
2. How did Ireland's location affect the development of Celtic culture? Explain your answer.
3. Would you agree or disagree that the king had too much power in Anglo-Saxon England? Explain.
4. What parts of an Anglo-Saxon noble's life would you have liked? What parts would you not have liked?

Graphic Organizer Activity

Culture Create a diagram like this one, and use it to compare the development of Christianity in Ireland and in the Frankish Empire.

Ireland   Both   Frankish Empire

Geography in History

Movement Refer to the map on page 294, and determine the most direct route from Edinburgh to London. How far would a person using this route have to travel? How much farther would that person have to travel to meet with priests of the church in Canterbury?

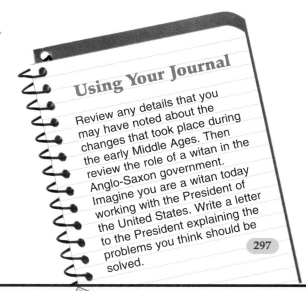

Using Your Journal

Review any details that you may have noted about the changes that took place during the early Middle Ages. Then review the role of a witan in the Anglo-Saxon government. Imagine you are a witan today working with the President of the United States. Write a letter to the President explaining the problems you think should be solved.

297

Bonus Test Question

For Chapter 19 Test
Two Anglo-Saxon people were arguing. One said, "My family has been here since the Romans left the British Isles. That makes my family the oldest." The other replied, "My family has been here since the Celts fled to Ireland." Whose family history is the oldest?
(neither—both began at about the same time)

Using Your Journal

Letters will vary but should include specific problems. You might call on volunteers to read their letters to the class.

Geography in History

About 310 miles (or 500 km); about 55 miles (or 85 km)

Using Key Terms

Paragraphs describing the lives of the Celts and Saxons will vary but should include all the vocabulary words.

Understanding Main Ideas

1. They could not win over the Celts.
2. because Roman soldiers were called home to defend the empire's borders against the Germanic invasions
3. It was gradually overrun by Angles, Saxons, and Jutes.
4. Ireland
5. because Ireland lost contact with Rome and the Pope during the Germanic invasions
6. to gain time to build a stronger army
7. because the central government was too weak to govern the whole country
8. They had to attend the witenagemot, keep peace, and serve the king in war.

Critical Thinking

1. They forced Roman soldiers to be called home, which allowed Angles, Saxons, and Jutes to overrun the island.
2. Its isolation allowed it to remain free of Germanic attacks. This allowed Celtic culture to develop.
3. Answers will vary, but students should support their reaction with examples.
4. Answers will vary but should include specific examples.

Graphic Organizer Activity

Diagrams will vary, but should show that the Frankish Empire had close ties with Rome while Ireland did not. Similarities might include practices such as the use of monasteries, activities of monks, and so on.

Chapter 20 Planning Guide

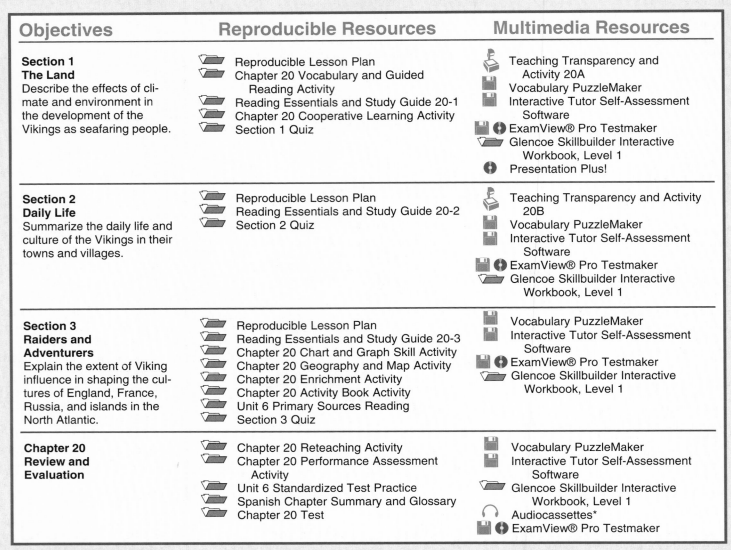

Objectives	Reproducible Resources	Multimedia Resources
Section 1 **The Land** Describe the effects of climate and environment in the development of the Vikings as seafaring people.	Reproducible Lesson Plan Chapter 20 Vocabulary and Guided Reading Activity Reading Essentials and Study Guide 20-1 Chapter 20 Cooperative Learning Activity Section 1 Quiz	Teaching Transparency and Activity 20A Vocabulary PuzzleMaker Interactive Tutor Self-Assessment Software ExamView® Pro Testmaker Glencoe Skillbuilder Interactive Workbook, Level 1 Presentation Plus!
Section 2 **Daily Life** Summarize the daily life and culture of the Vikings in their towns and villages.	Reproducible Lesson Plan Reading Essentials and Study Guide 20-2 Section 2 Quiz	Teaching Transparency and Activity 20B Vocabulary PuzzleMaker Interactive Tutor Self-Assessment Software ExamView® Pro Testmaker Glencoe Skillbuilder Interactive Workbook, Level 1
Section 3 **Raiders and Adventurers** Explain the extent of Viking influence in shaping the cultures of England, France, Russia, and islands in the North Atlantic.	Reproducible Lesson Plan Reading Essentials and Study Guide 20-3 Chapter 20 Chart and Graph Skill Activity Chapter 20 Geography and Map Activity Chapter 20 Enrichment Activity Chapter 20 Activity Book Activity Unit 6 Primary Sources Reading Section 3 Quiz	Vocabulary PuzzleMaker Interactive Tutor Self-Assessment Software ExamView® Pro Testmaker Glencoe Skillbuilder Interactive Workbook, Level 1
Chapter 20 **Review and Evaluation**	Chapter 20 Reteaching Activity Chapter 20 Performance Assessment Activity Unit 6 Standardized Test Practice Spanish Chapter Summary and Glossary Chapter 20 Test	Vocabulary PuzzleMaker Interactive Tutor Self-Assessment Software Glencoe Skillbuilder Interactive Workbook, Level 1 Audiocassettes* ExamView® Pro Testmaker

*Also available in Spanish.

Presentation Plus!

Use Glencoe's **Presentation Plus!** multimedia teacher tool to easily present dynamic lessons that visually excite your students. Using Microsoft® PowerPoint, you can customize the presentations to create your own personalized lessons.

Interactive Lesson Planner

Planning has never been easier! Using this CD-ROM, organize your week, month, semester, or year with all the help you need. The **Interactive Lesson Planner** gives you access to all of the blackline masters which accompany *Human Heritage*.

Chapter 20 Planning Guide

✓ PERFORMANCE ASSESSMENT ACTIVITIES

Re-creations   Have students research and draw illustrations of Viking ships or make models of them. These creations should be accompanied by explanations of ship construction and parts.

CHAPTER RESOURCES

LITERATURE ABOUT THE PERIOD
Treece, Henry. *The Invaders*. Crowell, 1972. Three stories about the Vikings.

READINGS FOR THE STUDENT
Wernick, Robert. *The Vikings: The Seafarers*. Time-Life Books, 1979. An in-depth look at the Viking traders, raiders, and conquerors.

READINGS FOR THE TEACHER
Jones, Gwyn. *A History of the Vikings*. Oxford University Press, 1984. Surveys the Viking world, including archaeological findings.

KEY TO ABILITY LEVELS
Teaching strategies have been coded for varying learning styles and abilities.

L1 Level 1 activities are **basic** activities and should be within the ability range of all students.

L2 Level 2 activities are **average** activities and should be within the ability range of the average to above-average student.

L3 Level 3 activities are **challenging** designed for the ability range of above-average students.

ELL ELL activities should be within the ability range of English Language Learning students.

Teacher's Corner

INDEX TO NATIONAL GEOGRAPHIC MAGAZINE
The following articles relate to this chapter:

- "Viking Trail East," by Robert Paul Jordan, March 1985.
- "Eskimo and Viking Finds in the High Arctic: Ellesmere Island," by Peter Schledermann, May 1981.

NATIONAL GEOGRAPHIC SOCIETY PRODUCTS AVAILABLE FROM GLENCOE
To order the following, call Glencoe at 1-800-334-7344:

- MapPack: Europe (Transparency Maps)
- Europe (Laminated Desk Maps)
- *PicturePack: Physical Geography of the World (Transparencies)*

ADDITIONAL NATIONAL GEOGRAPHIC SOCIETY PRODUCTS
To order the following, call National Geographic at 1-800-368-2728:

- *Physical Geography of the Continents Series: Europe (Video)*
- *National Geographic Atlas of World History (Book)*

Access *National Geographic's* new dynamic MapMachine Web site and other geography resources at:
http://www.nationalgeographic.com/
http://www.nationalgeographic.com/maps/

 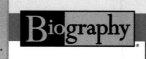

THE HISTORY CHANNEL.

The following videotape programs are available from Glencoe:

- **The Vikings in North America**
  1-56501-663-7

- **Leif Ericson: Voyages of a Viking**
  1-56501-673-4

To order, call Glencoe at 1-800-334-7344. To find classroom resources to accompany many of these, check:

A&E Television: http://www.aetv.com
The History Channel: http://www.historychannel.com

OVERVIEW

Chapter 20 discusses the development of Scandinavia and the Vikings' impact upon world civilization.

➤ **Section 1** describes the effects of geography on the development of the Vikings as seafaring people.

➤ **Section 2** describes the culture of the Viking people.

➤ **Section 3** discusses Viking influence in England, France, Russia, and the North Atlantic.

CHAPTER OBJECTIVES

After reading Chapter 20, students will be able to:

1. explain how the Vikings earned their living.

2. summarize what daily life was like for the Vikings.

3. describe how Viking warriors traded and raided.

4. explain what role the Danish Vikings played in the histories of England and France.

EXAMINING ARTIFACTS

Refer students to the artifacts. Ask: What does the ice skate tell you about the Viking homeland? *(that it was cold enough for ice at least part of the year)* What does the picture of the dragon slayer reveal? *(that the Vikings were warriors and/or valued stories about warriors)* Direct students to find events in the time line that confirm their answers.

PERFORMANCE ASSESSMENT ✓

Use the Performance Assessment activities on page 298B to help you evaluate students as they complete the chapter.

CHAPTER 20

The Vikings
900 A.D.–1035 A.D.

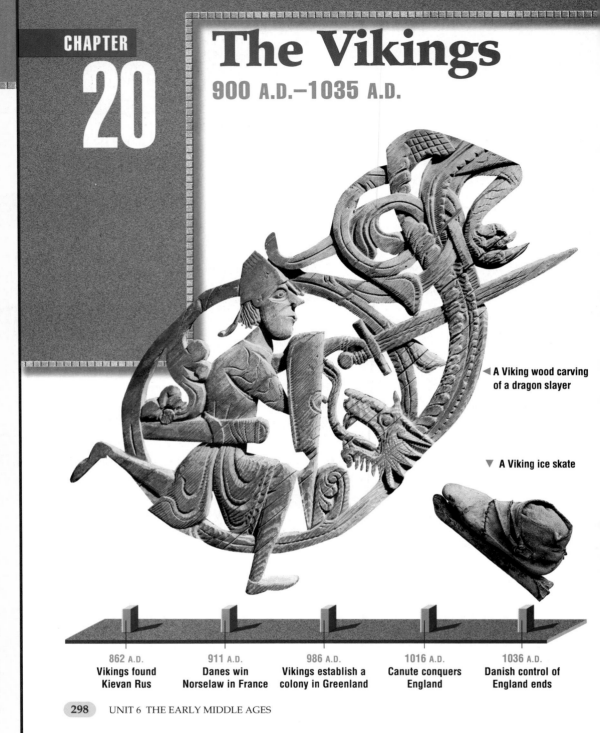

◄ A Viking wood carving of a dragon slayer

▼ A Viking ice skate

862 A.D.	911 A.D.	986 A.D.	1016 A.D.	1036 A.D.
Vikings found Kievan Rus	**Danes win Norselaw in France**	**Vikings establish a colony in Greenland**	**Canute conquers England**	**Danish control of England ends**

TEACHING RESOURCES

TEACHER PLANNING AND SUPPORT

📁 Reproducible Lesson Plan
📁 Block Scheduling Implementation Guide
📁 Videodisc Bar Code Correlation
💿 Presentation Plus!

REVIEW AND REINFORCEMENT

📁 Reading Essentials and Study Guide 20–1, 20–2, 20–3
📁 Chapter 20 Vocabulary and Guided Reading Activity
💾 Vocabulary PuzzleMaker Software
🖨 Teaching Transparencies 20A & 20B

📁 Chapter 20 Reteaching Activity
📁 Chapter 20 Cooperative Learning Activity
📁 Chapter 20 Activity Book Activity
📁 Chapter 20 Chart and Graph Skill Activity
💾 Interactive Tutor Self-Assessment Software
💿 Unit 6 MindJogger VideoQuiz

APPLICATION AND HANDS-ON ACTIVITIES

📁 Daily World History, Geography, and Culture Question
📁 World History Game Card 5

Chapter Focus

Read to Discover
- How the Vikings earned a living.
- What daily life was like for the Vikings.
- How Viking warriors and adventurers traded and raided.
- What role the Danish Vikings played in the histories of England and France.

Chapter Overview
Visit the *Human Heritage* Web site at **humanheritage.glencoe.com** and click on *Chapter 20—Chapter Overviews* to preview this chapter.

Terms to Learn	People to Know	Places to Locate
jarls	Rurik	Scandinavia
berserkers	Erik the Red	Jutland
Eddas	Leif Eriksson	Vinland
runes	Canute	Norselaw
	Rollo	

Why It's Important   During the 900s, Charlemagnes's empire and Anglo-Saxon England were attacked by new invaders known as Norseman, or Vikings (vī′ kēngs). They came from the far northern part of Europe in an area now called Scandinavia (skan duh nā′vē uh). The tall, fair-skinned Vikings were brutal fighters and robbers. They spread fear and destruction throughout western Europe for several hundred years. However, they opened up new trade routes and taught seafaring skills to other Europeans.

The Vikings captured parts of Britain and France. They ruled cities in Russia and set up colonies on islands in the North Atlantic. They even paid a visit to North America. Those who went abroad married the people they conquered and accepted a new religion and new customs. Others stayed in Scandinavia and set up the kingdoms of Norway, Sweden, and Denmark.

SECTION 1   The Land

The Viking homeland of Scandinavia was an area mostly of forests and long, rugged coastlines. The southern part, known as Jutland (juht′ luhnd), or Denmark, had many natural harbors and was well suited for farming. It had large plains where the Vikings grew grains and pastured their cattle, sheep, and pigs.

The rest of Scandinavia was not as well suited to farming. The soil was rocky, and the growing season was short. The coastline, however, had many *fjords* (fē yōrdz′), or narrow bays. Because of this, the people turned to the sea to make a living.

CHAPTER 20 THE VIKINGS   **299**

Chapter Overview introduces students to chapter content and key terms. Have them access **Chapter 20 Overview** at **humanheritage.glencoe.com**

FOCUS

Bellringer
Ask students to write down the first three ideas that occur to them when they think of the word *Viking*.

Motivational Activity
Have students read their responses to the word Viking. Explain that much of what we know about the Vikings comes from church records. Clerics and monks, who were often victims of Viking raids, portray a predominantly negative picture of the Vikings. Tell students that they will read more about the Vikings and what they were really like in this chapter.

GUIDE TO READING

Reading Strategy
Ask students to read "Why It's Important" and summarize the chapter's main theme. *(The Vikings were fearless conquerors and explorers who influenced European cultures and were in turn influenced by those they conquered.)*

Vocabulary Precheck
Ask students to define each of the "Terms to Learn." Have a volunteer consult the dictionary for any unfamiliar words. **L1** **ELL**

💾 Use the Vocabulary PuzzleMaker for Chapter 20 to create a crossword puzzle. **L1**

📁 Assign Chapter 20 Vocabulary and Guided Reading Activity.

📁 Assign Reading Essentials and Study Guide 20-1.

GEOGRAPHY ACTIVITIES
- 📁 Chapter 20 Geography and Map Activity
- 📁 Social Studies Outline Map Resource Book

INTERDISCIPLINARY CONNECTIONS
- 💿 World Music: Cultural Traditions

EXTENSION AND ENRICHMENT
- 📁 Unit 6 Primary Sources Reading
- 💿 World History Primary Source Document Library CD-ROM
- 📁 Chapter 20 Enrichment Activity
- 📁 Foods Around the World

ASSESSMENT AND EVALUATION
- 📁 Chapter 20 Performance Assessment Activity
- 📁 Chapter 20 Section Quizzes 20–1, 20–2, 20–3
- 📁 Chapter 20 Test
- 📁 Unit 6 Standardized Test Practice
- 💾🎧 Chapter 20 ExamView® Pro Testmaker Software
- 🎧 Chapter 20 Digests Audiocassettes Activities and Tests

SPANISH RESOURCES
- 📁 Chapter 20 Spanish Chapter Summary and Glossary
- 🎧 Chapter 20 Spanish Chapter Digests Audiocassettes Activities and Tests

TEACH

Guided Practice

L1 **Daily Life** Have students help complete an informational bulletin board about the daily life of the Vikings. Ask them to make illustrations about one of the following areas of Viking life: family life, occupations, or religion. Have them write captions to explain their illustrations. Display the illustrations and captions on the bulletin board. **ELL**

MAKING CONNECTIONS

➤➤ **Language** The word *Viking* comes from the word *vik* which means "creek" in all the Scandinavian languages. *Vik* was also the name of a pirate lair in southern Norway. The phrase *to go a Viking* meant "to fight as a pirate."

CAPTION ANSWER

silk, wine, and wheat

Ships and Trade

The Vikings built ships with timber from the dense forests. These ships were large and well suited for long voyages. The bodies were long and narrow. The sides, where a single row of 16 oars was placed, were usually decorated with black or yellow shields. The tall bows were carved in the shape of a dragon's head. This was supposed to frighten both enemies and the evil spirits of the ocean. The strongly sewn sails were square and often striped red and yellow. The ships bore names like "Snake of the Sea," "Raven of the Wind," and "Lion of the Waves."

An awning in the forepart of the ship protected sailors from bad weather. They slept in leather sleeping bags and carried bronze pots in which to cook meals. Whenever possible, they cooked meals ashore to avoid the danger of a fire on board ship.

The Vikings plotted their courses by the positions of the sun and the stars. They sailed far out into the North Sea and the Atlantic Ocean in search of good fishing areas and trade. They did most of their traveling and trading in spring after their fields were sown or in fall after their crops were harvested. They spent the long winters repairing their boats and weapons.

The Vikings were as successful in trade as the Phoenicians. Viking traders carried furs, hides, fish, and enslaved people to western Europe and the Mediterranean. They returned from these areas with silk, wine, wheat, and silver.

VIKING TRADE   The Vikings traveled very far in order to trade. They sailed to the Mediterranean and traded for Arabic silver coins. The Vikings then melted down the coins and used the silver to make jewelry. **What other items did the Vikings trade for?**

Then...&Now

Berserk Of the many words that entered English from Old Norse, one of the most threatening is *berserk*. It comes from the Viking warriors known as *berserkers*, who rushed headlong into battle shrieking, leaping, and seemingly unaware of pain.

MULTICULTURAL PERSPECTIVES

Perhaps one of the best indications of how important the ship was in Viking life is the custom of ship burials. Sometimes the body of a dead chief or hero was set adrift on his boat. Sometimes the entire ship was buried on land, richly equipped for the afterlife much as an Egyptian pyramid was.

Archaeologists have discovered many interesting and beautiful Viking artifacts in ship burials, including solid gold jewelry and ornaments. Two of the most famous ship burials are at Sutton Hoo in England and Gokstad in Norway.

Towns, Villages, and Jarls   Trade led to the growth of market towns in Scandinavia. These towns generally had two main streets that ran along the water's edge. Buyers and sellers set up booths along these streets where they showed their wares. The towns were protected on their land side by mounds of earth surrounded by wooden walls with towers.

Most Vikings lived in villages scattered all through the country. Their houses were made of logs or boards. The roofs, which were made of sod-covered wood, slanted deeply to shed the heavy winter snows. Carved dragons decorated the roofs at either end. Each house had a small porch at its front that was held up by carved pillars.

Distance and the cold winters isolated the people of one village from those of another. Because of this, there was no central government. The people were divided into groups ruled by military chiefs called *jarls* (yahrlz). Some jarls were elected, while others inherited their position. Sometimes, a jarl became strong enough to take over neighboring lands. When a jarl had enough land under his rule, he was looked upon as a king.

> **Reading Check**
> Who were the *jarls*, and how were they selected?

Section 1 Assessment

1. **Define:** *jarls*.
2. How did people in Scandinavia make a living?
3. What were some of the features of Viking towns?

Critical Thinking

4. **Making Generalizations** How did the Vikings use their natural resources?

Graphic Organizer Activity

5. Draw this diagram, and use it to describe geographic features of the Viking homeland.

SECTION 2   Daily Life

Family life was important to the Vikings. Most households had 20 to 30 members, including parents, grandparents, married children, and grandchildren. Families often fought bloody feuds to defend their honor. The payment of fines later ended such feuds.

The People   Viking warriors were called *berserkers* (ber zerk' erz). They believed in a life of action and valued deeds that called for strength and courage. They fought to gain wealth, honor, and fame. They believed that a liking for war brought special honors from the gods.

To call their warriors to battle, the Vikings lit bonfires on the tops of mountains. Those who saw a fire would light a new one to

> **Reading Check**
> Who were the Viking *berserkers*, and why did they fight?

GEOGRAPHY AND HISTORY

Viking boats were sturdy enough to cross the Atlantic Ocean, shallow enough to navigate Europe's rivers, and light enough to be carried past fortified bridges. The Vikings became known for surprise attacks and speedy retreats. What they could not steal, they burned.

> **Reading Check Answer**
> Viking *jarls* were military chiefs. Some were elected; others inherited their position.

💾 Use **Interactive Tutor Self-Assessment Software** to review Section 1.

> **Reading Check Answer**
> Viking *berserkers* were warriors who fought to gain wealth, honor, and fame.

💾 Use the **Vocabulary Puzzle-Maker** to create crossword and word search puzzles.

Section 1 Assessment Answers

1. *jarls*, Viking military chiefs (p. 301)
2. by farming, fishing, and trading
3. They generally had two main streets that ran along the water's edge and were lined with booths. They were protected on their land side by mounds of earth surrounded by wooden walls with towers.
4. The Vikings built ships and houses with timber from the dense forests, turned to the sea to make a living, and grew herbs that

were used as medicines.
5. Sample responses: mostly forests; long, rugged coastlines; many natural harbors in southern part (Jutland); large plains suitable for farming in south; region north of harbor area not well suited to farming; rocky soil and short growing season.

Assign the Chapter 20 **Section 1 Quiz** in the TCR. Testmaker available.

Viking Sword Hilt

spread the message. Warriors fought with battle axes, swords, and spears. Metal helmets decorated with animal figures protected their heads. Shirts made of iron rings and covered by a large cloth protected their bodies. Warriors preferred to die by their own hand rather than give their enemies the satisfaction of capturing or killing them.

The women encouraged their men to fight. A Viking groom bought his wife from her family on their wedding day. If he was not pleased with her, he could sell her. Yet, the position of Viking women was quite high. They took complete charge of the home. They could attend public meetings and talk with men other than their husbands. They could own property and get a divorce. Many Viking women grew herbs that were used as medicine.

Both men and women liked fine clothes. Men usually dressed in trousers and woolen shirts covered by knee-length tunics. Broad leather belts held the clothing in place. Sheepskin hoods and caps kept their heads warm. For special events, men wore red cloaks with brooches and carried decorated swords and daggers. Women also wore tunics held in place by a belt. They covered their heads with woolen or linen caps and wore large brooches, pins, and bracelets. Both men and women wore their hair long. The men took great pride in their mustaches and beards. Calling a

VIKING ADVENTURES This painting of Leif Eriksson, one of the most adventuresome Vikings, shows the detail and decoration these north people put into their ships. The bows of their ships were usually elaborately carved. **Why did many Viking ships display the head of a dragon on the bow?**

Viking man "beardless" was an insult that could be wiped out only by death.

The Vikings had no schools. Girls were taught household skills, such as spinning, weaving, and sewing, by their mothers. Boys were taught to use the bow and arrow and to be good fighters by their fathers. Boys also memorized tales of heroes and gods and competed in games that tested their strength and endurance.

Religion

The Vikings worshiped many gods that at first were similar to the Germanic gods. Over time, they changed their gods to suit the hard life of Scandinavia. The Vikings believed that the gods were responsible for the weather and for the growth of crops. Since the gods liked to hunt, fish, and play tricks on one another, the Vikings viewed them as extra-powerful humans.

The Vikings bargained with their gods to get what they wanted. Priests offered sacrifices of crops and animals for the whole village. Most Vikings also had small shrines in their homes where they could pray or offer sacrifices.

The Vikings were proud of their gods and told stories of the gods' great deeds. These stories later became written poems called *Eddas* (ed' uhz). The Vikings also made up *sagas* (sah' guhz), or long tales. At first, storytellers used to recite them at special feasts. One such tale took 12 days to recite. After 1100, the Vikings wrote down their sagas. With the coming of Christianity, however, the people lost interest in them. Many were forgotten or were forbidden by the Church. Only the people on the isolated island of Iceland passed on the old tales.

Early on, the Vikings spoke a language similar to that of the Germans. In time, the one language developed into four—Danish, Norwegian (nor wē' juhn), Swedish, and Icelandic. These languages were written with letters called *runes* (rūnz), which few people except priests could understand or use. The Vikings used the runes as magic charms. They wrote the runes in metal and carved them in bone in the hope that they would bring good luck. When the Vikings accepted Christianity, they began to write their languages with Roman letters.

Viking Rune Stone

✓ **Reading Check**
What were the *Eddas?*

✓ **Reading Check**
What were some of the ways that the Vikings used *runes?*

MAKING CONNECTIONS

➤➤ **History** The Vikings believed in a heaven called Asgard, which contained 12 great halls. Warriors wanted to go to the Hall of the slain, called Valhalla. There, the chief Viking god, Odin, held court.

✓ **Reading Check Answer**
The *Eddas* were written poems about the deeds of Viking gods.

✓ **Reading Check Answer**
The Vikings used *runes* as letters to write their language and as magic charms.

💾 Use **Interactive Tutor Self Assessment Software** to review Section 2.

Section 2 Assessment

1. **Define:** *berserkers, Eddas, runes.*
2. What kind of education did Viking children receive?
3. How did the Vikings view their gods?

Critical Thinking

4. **Demonstrating Reasoned Judgment** What might have been some of the advantages and disadvantages of living in the large Viking households?

Graphic Organizer Activity

5. Draw this diagram, and use it to compare the role of Viking women with the role of women in the United States today.

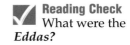

Section 2 Assessment Answers

1. berserkers, Viking warriors (p. 301); *Eddas*, Viking poems (p. 303); *runes*, Viking letters (p. 303)

2. Girls were taught household skills. Boys were taught to use the bow and arrow and to be good fighters, and they memorized tales of heroes and gods and competed in games.

3. as extra-powerful humans

4. Sample responses: *advantages*—a lot of people to help with the work, protection and care for the sick; *disadvantages*—blood feuds between large families, lack of privacy, payment of the fines charged to the family.

5. Answers will vary, but might point out that women today have equal rights and cannot be sold by their husbands. Both Viking and modern women can take charge of the home, attend public meetings, talk to men, own property, and get a divorce.

Assign the Chapter 20 **Section 2 Quiz** in the TCR. Testmaker available.

304

L2 **Myths and Legends** Have students write a list of the Norse gods and goddesses and their realms. Then have them brainstorm a list of where these names are used in modern times. For example, names are used as calendar items, in advertising, in city names, and so on. **ELL**

LINKING PAST TO PRESENT

In 1991, 3 authentically built Viking ships retraced early Norse exploration routes, sailing from Norway to L'Anse aux Meadows, Newfoundland, Canada. The trip, lasting 3 months, was made to honor the Vikings who sailed to America 1,000 years before.

L1 **Geography: Movement** Refer students to the map of "Viking Trade and Expansion" on page 306 to trace the routes that the Vikings traveled to raid places. **ELL**

THE HISTORY CHANNEL®

The following videotape program is available from Glencoe to enrich Chapter 20::

• **The Vikings in North America**

To find classroom resources to accompany this video, check the following home page:

A&E Television:
http://www.aetv.com

 Use the **Vocabulary Puzzle-Maker** to create crossword and word search puzzles.

304

NORSE GODS

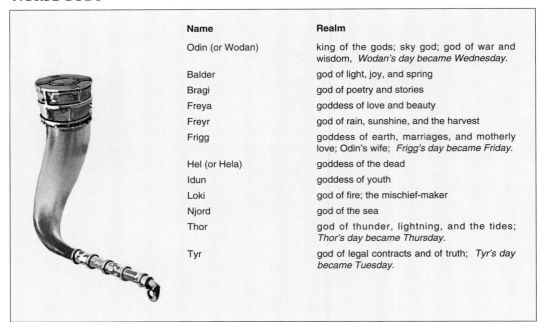

Name	Realm
Odin (or Wodan)	king of the gods; sky god; god of war and wisdom, *Wodan's day became Wednesday.*
Balder	god of light, joy, and spring
Bragi	god of poetry and stories
Freya	goddess of love and beauty
Freyr	god of rain, sunshine, and the harvest
Frigg	goddess of earth, marriages, and motherly love; Odin's wife; *Frigg's day became Friday.*
Hel (or Hela)	goddess of the dead
Idun	goddess of youth
Loki	god of fire; the mischief-maker
Njord	god of the sea
Thor	god of thunder, lightning, and the tides; *Thor's day became Thursday.*
Tyr	god of legal contracts and of truth; *Tyr's day became Tuesday.*

SECTION 3 Raiders and Adventurers

Scandinavia's population kept increasing. By the end of the 800s, many Viking villages were overcrowded, and there was not enough food for everyone. Since there was no central government, the kings constantly fought one another and made life difficult for their enemies. Before long, many Viking warriors began to seek their fortunes in other lands. They set sail on their long, deckless ships that were propelled through the water with oars. On them, the Vikings could safely sail the deep water of the Atlantic Ocean or the shallow rivers of Europe.

From East Europe to North America Viking adventurers traveled to and raided areas from east Europe to North America. Swedish Vikings crossed the Baltic Sea and traveled down the rivers toward what is now Belarus, Ukraine, and Russia. They established a trade water route from the Baltic to the

MEETING SPECIAL NEEDS

Help students who are having difficulty accessing the information in the chapter by creating cause-and-effect graphic organizers of the major events in the chapter on the chalkboard.

Refer to *Inclusion for the Middle School Social Studies Classroom: Strategies and Activities* for additional resources.

Black Sea and on to the wealthy city of Byzantium (bi zan' tē uhm). This water route became known as the Varangian (vah rahng ē'uhn) Route. In 862, a Swedish chief named Rurik (rū' rik) founded a Viking settlement that became the Kievan Rus state.

Norwegian Vikings set up trading towns in Ireland, explored the North Atlantic, and founded a colony on Iceland. Led by an adventurer named Erik the Red, they founded a colony on the island of Greenland in 986. Then, Erik's son, Leif Eriksson (lēf er' ik suhn), landed on the northeast coast of North America. He and his followers named the spot where they landed Vinland because of the wild grapes they found growing there. Today, the area is called Newfoundland (nū' fuhn luhnd). The Vikings did not set up a colony in Vinland because it was so far away from home and because they were repeatedly attacked by Native Americans.

Most Viking adventurers, however, went to western and southern Europe in search of food and valuables. They disguised their ships to look like wooded islands by covering them with tree

Linking Across Time

Iceland   Viking settlers braved frozen seas to settle in Iceland during the late 800s and early 900s. Around 930, they drew up a constitution that provided for a legislative assembly called the Althing (left). The Althing still meets today (right), making it the oldest practicing legislative assembly in the world. **What conditions in Scandinavia led the Vikings to settle in Iceland?**

GEOGRAPHY AND HISTORY

Some historians believe that Viking sailors first spotted the North American continent in 986 when Bjarni Herjulfsson was blown off course on a trip to the Greenland settlement. Leif Eriksson's voyage included stops at what he called "Helluland" (perhaps Baffin Island), "Markland" (Labrador), and "Vinland" (Newfoundland), so called because of the grapes that grew there.

Linking Across Time

Overcrowding in Scandinavia and a lack of food led the Vikings to settle in Iceland.

PRIMARY SOURCES
Library

You might assign "The Age of Viking Conquest" on pages 684–685 of the Primary Sources Library.

SPOTLIGHT ON: VIKINGS

Viking adventurers made many voyages across the Northern Atlantic. One such Viking believed the first to set eyes on North America was Bjarni Herjulfsson. Bjarni, living in Iceland, set sail for Greenland in search of his father. Following the North Star, he reached the coast of Labrador, Canada, instead. According to Norse sagas, it was his course that Leif Eriksson and his men followed years later to reach Vinland.

MAP SKILLS

Tracing Historical Routes

TEACH

Tracing Historical Routes

Have students read the introductory section of the skill on page 306. Ask: Why are historical routes often colored? *(to show information more clearly and to make the map easier to read)* Why do historical routes on maps often have arrows at their beginning or several arrows along its length? *(to point out the directions taken by people or goods)* Where should you look to find out the meaning of the different lines and colors on a map? *(in the legend or key)* Direct students' attention to the map on the skills page. Ask: What rivers and seas did the Viking invasion routes follow? *(Volga River, Dnieper River, Caspian Sea)* What bodies of water did the Vikings cross on their trade routes? *(North Sea, Baltic Sea, Mediterranean Sea, Atlantic Ocean)*

Assign the Chapter 20 **Geography and Map Activity** in the TCR.

Answers to Map Practice

1. England, Ireland, Iceland, Greenland, Vinland, France, Spain, Italy, Norway, Sweden, and Denmark

2. invasion routes and the Varangian Route

3. Kiev and Baghdad

Lines on maps generally show boundaries or rivers. On some maps, however, lines may show other things, such as **historical routes.** These are roads or courses over which people or goods have traveled all through history.

Such routes are often colored to make the map easier to read. A colored line may have arrows to point out the direction taken by people or goods. If there is a legend on the map, it may provide clues to the meaning of the different lines and colors.

For example, on the map of "Viking Trade and Expansion" below, the legend shows that the brown line is the Varangian Route. The two arrows along the line point out that the route began in Sweden and ended in Byzantium.

Map Practice

1. **What were some places visited by Vikings along their trade routes?**
2. **Which routes ran through the largest area of Viking settlement?**
3. **What two cities lay along Viking invasion routes?**

Glencoe's **Skillbuilder Interactive Workbook, Level 1,** provides instruction and practice in key social studies skills.

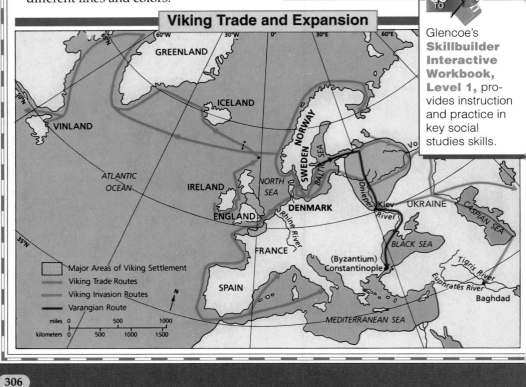

Viking Trade and Expansion

Major Areas of Viking Settlement
Viking Trade Routes
Viking Invasion Routes
Varangian Route

306

COOPERATIVE LEARNING

Divide the class into five groups. Have each group do research and prepare a report on one of the following Viking leaders: Eric the Red, Leif Eriksson, Rurik, Canute, or Rollo. Each report should describe the Viking leader's life and achievements. Have students illustrate their reports. Each member of the group should be assigned a specific task in preparing the report. Have a spokesperson from each group read its report to the class.

VIKING SHIPS The Vikings were among the best shipbuilders of their time. At sea, the Vikings depended on the wind and sails for power. On a river, rowers powered the ship. The Viking ships in this painting pursue enemy trading ships. **How did Vikings disguise their ships on rivers?**

attacks. They stole goods, destroyed homes, burned churches, and killed or enslaved people they captured. All Europe feared the Vikings. In their churches, the people prayed, "From the fury of the Norsemen, Good Lord, deliver us!"

The Danes The Danes were among those Vikings who raided western and southern Europe. One group invaded England and set up settlements there in the Danelaw. Their right to rule this area had been recognized by Alfred the Great. In 954, an heir of Alfred the Great forced the Danes to leave. In 978, Ethelred (eth' uhl red), nicknamed the Unready, became king of England. The Danes saw their chance and began raiding England again. At first, Ethelred was able to buy them off with silver. In 1016, however, a Danish king called Knut, or Canute (kuh nūt'), conquered England and made it part of his North Sea Empire. Canute was a powerful and just ruler. He converted to Christianity and brought peace and prosperity to England. Soon after his death in 1035, however, Danish control of the country came to an end. Some Danes left England. Those who remained became a part of the English people and culture.

Another group of Danes tried to take the city of Paris in France, but the French managed to fight them off. In 885, the

People in History

Canute
c. 995–1035

Danish King
Canute followed in the footsteps of his father, who conquered England in 1013. When his father died, the Anglo-Saxons refused to make Canute king, so he led the Danes in a second war of conquest. In 1016, he became the sole king of England. In 1018 he inherited the Danish throne, and in 1028 he seized the throne of Norway. Although Canute's sons lost England, a distant kinsman from Normandy—William the Conqueror— would reclaim it in 1066.

SPOTLIGHT ON: CANUTE

To extend People in History, provide these additional details on Canute.

Canute was the first Danish king of England. Legend states that he wanted to end the flattery of his nobles, who declared that he was all-powerful. To teach the nobles a lesson, he took them to the edge of the sea, where he commanded the incoming tide to come no further. His failure to stop the water proved to his nobles that a king's power was limited.

Independent Practice

L2 Time Line Have students make a time line of events in the chapter. Have students draw conclusions about the possible similarities among events on their time lines; explain the causes and effects of the events; and summarize the Vikings by describing them with no more than two adjectives. **ELL**

L3 Critical Thinking Ask students to write a paragraph comparing the importance of Christianity in the everyday lives of the Celts and the Anglo-Saxons during the Middle Ages with the importance of Christianity in the everyday life of the Vikings.

LINKING PAST TO PRESENT

A Viking settlement called *L'Anse aux Meadows* on the northern tip of Newfoundland has been carefully studied and is believed to be the probable site of Vinland. Archaeologists have excavated the remains of several houses with turf walls. One was a Norse "longhouse" with a great hall and other rooms. This and other houses resembled those in Greenland. A soapstone spindle that was found is believed to be evidence that the settlers included both women and men.

ASSESS

Check for Understanding

Ask students to summarize the main points of the chapter. Discuss answers to the Section and Chapter Assessment questions.

Evaluate

Assign the Chapter 20 **Performance Assessment Activity** in the TCR.

Administer the **Chapter 20 Test** in the TCR. Testmaker available.

Reteach

Assign Chapter 20 **Reteaching Activity** in the TCR.

Enrich

Assign the Chapter 20 **Enrichment Activity** in the TCR.

CLOSE

Have students discuss the importance of poems, myths, legends, and sagas in the everyday life of the Vikings.

Use **Interactive Tutor Self Assessment Software** to review Section 3.

308

Danes tried again. The people of Paris held them off for ten months. Finally, the French king paid the Danes gold to abandon their attack.

Led by a warrior named Rollo (rahl′ ō), the Danes began settling along the French coast opposite England. In 911, the French king signed a treaty with Rollo. He gave the Danes this land. In return, the Danes became Christians and promised to be loyal to the French king. The region in which the Danes settled became known first as the Norselaw and then as Normandy (nōr′ muhn dē). The people became known as Normans.

Section 3 Assessment

1. Why did many Vikings leave Scandinavia?
2. Why did Europeans fear the Vikings?
3. What happened to the Danes who settled in England?

Critical Thinking

4. **Predicting Consequences** How might life have been different for the Vikings if there had been a central government in Scandinavia?

Graphic Organizer Activity

5. Draw the following diagram, and use it to summarize key dates in Viking history.

Chapter Summary & Study Guide

1. The Vikings lived in northern Europe in an area called Scandinavia.
2. The geography of the Viking homeland led people to become excellent sailors who earned their living through fishing, trading, and raiding.
3. The Vikings worshiped many gods and often told stories about them.
4. When the Vikings accepted Christianity, they stopped writing their languages in runes and began using Roman letters.
5. Overpopulation in Scandinavia in the 800s led many Vikings to establish settlements elsewhere, including Kievan Rus and Greenland.
6. In 1016, a Danish king called Canute conquered England, but after his death, Danish control of the country came to an end.
7. After besieging Paris, Danish Vikings settled along the French coast in an area known as Norselaw.

Section 3 Assessment Answers

1. Viking villages were overcrowded and had food shortages, and the kings constantly fought one another
2. because they stole, destroyed homes, and killed or enslaved people
3. Danes in England lost control of England after Canute died. Danes in France settled in Normandy and became Christians.
4. Answers will vary but could include that life might have been more stable.
5. 911—Danes win Norselaw in France; 954—heir to Alfred the Great forces the Danes to leave England; 978—Ethelred the Unready becomes king of England and Danes resume raids; 1016—Canute conquers England; 1035—Danish control of England ends.

Assign the Chapter 20 **Section 3 Quiz** in the TCR. Testmaker available.

Using Key Terms

Imagine you are a journalist writing a magazine article about Scandinavia. Use the following words to write a paragraph describing the Viking way of life.

jarls   *Eddas*
runes   *berserkers*

Understanding Main Ideas

1. Why did many Vikings turn to the sea to make a living?
2. How did the Vikings plot the courses of their voyages?
3. How were Viking houses protected from the winter?
4. Why was there no central government in Scandinavia?
5. How did a *jarl* bacome a king?
6. What role did women play in Viking society?
7. What were Viking stories about?
8. How did the Vikings use *runes*?
9. What effect did the Vikings have on Kievan Rus?
10. Why did the Vikings decide not to set up a colony in North America?

Critical Thinking

1. What effect did Christianity have on Viking life?
2. What would you have liked about being a Viking? What would you have disliked?
3. What do you think might have happened in Scandinavia if many Viking warriors had not left the area during the 800s?
4. What effect did Vikings have on the development of Europe during the Middle Ages?

Graphic Organizer Activity

Culture Create a diagram like the one shown, and use it to compare Viking culture before and after the arrival of Christianity in Scandinavia.

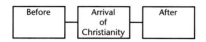

| Before | → | Arrival of Christianity | → | After |

Geography in History

Region Look at the map on page 306. The Vikings settled in areas beyond the Scandinavian region. What geographic features of Scandinavia may have contributed to the Vikings' expansion and movement? Write a paragraph showing how geographic features affected the Vikings' movement. Then draw a map showing the Vikings' routes.

Using Your Journal

Review any details you may have noted about Viking explorations that took place in Europe during the early Middle Ages. Imagine you are a Viking adventurer landing on the northeast coast of North America. Write a diary entry describing your first impression of North America.

309

Bonus Test Question

For Chapter 20 Test

If the Vikings had sailed directly from Norway to Newfoundland, they could have covered the approximate 2,500-mile distance in under 20 days. About how many miles per hour would their speed have to be to make the trip in under 20 days? *(slightly over 5 miles [3 km] per hour)*

Using Your Journal

Diary entries will vary but could include a description of their emotional reactions. You might ask volunteers to read their entries to the class.

Geography in History

Viking expansion was caused by limited space and mountains on their peninsula, and their access to the Baltic Sea and the Atlantic Ocean.

Understanding Key Terms

Paragraphs will vary but should use all the key terms.

Understanding Main Ideas

1. because the land was not suited to farming
2. by the positions of the sun and the stars
3. Their roofs slanted deeply to shed the heavy winter snows.
4. because distance and the cold winters isolated the people
5. seizing neighboring lands
6. They took charge of the home and could attend public meetings, talk with all men, own property, and get a divorce.
7. the gods' great deeds
8. as magic charms
9. They founded a settlement that became the Russian nation.
10. It was too far from home, and Native Americans attacked them.

Critical Thinking

1. It caused the people to lose interest in their sagas and to write with Roman letters.
2. Answers will vary but should include examples.
3. Answers will vary but could include that there might not have been any explorations to North America.
4. They spread fear but also opened up new trade routes and taught seafaring skills.

Graphic Organizer Activity

Sample responses: *before*—worshiped many gods, viewed gods as extra-powerful humans who could influence weather and other phenomena, bargained with gods and built shrines, told stories and wrote poems about the feats of gods; *after*—lost interest in the sagas and *Eddas,* adopted use of Roman letters to write their languages, abandoned most old religious practices

FOCUS

OBJECTIVES

After reading the Around the World for Unit 6, your students will be able to:

1. identify the years that the Gupta culture reached its peak and flourished.
2. cite features of the Gupta empire.
3. appreciate the importance of Gupta achievements in mathematics and other areas.

📹 Bellringer

Instruct students to write the following information on a sheet of paper: their age in years, the age of their best friend, and the number of years they expect to be in school.

Motivational Activity

Call on volunteers to write their answers on the board. Then tell students they have just used symbols invented more than 1,500 years ago by a people from India. Have students quickly scan the photos in the Around the World feature. Ask: What are some of the other things accomplished by the people known as the Guptas? *(Students will probably note the architectural and artistic achievements, such as painting and sculpture. Use this as a springboard to examine the Gupta more closely.)*

TEACH

Geography: Region Remind students that a geographic region shares certain common characteristics. Based on the map on this page, ask: What were some of the landforms that defined northern India as a region? *(the Himalayan and Hindu Kush mountains that formed a natural border and barrier, the rivers that flowed out of*

THE GUPTAS

As the Roman Empire crumbled, the Gupta (gup' tuh) Empire in what is now northern India entered a Golden Age. Beginning around 310 A.D., the Guptas began a period of great achievement and expansion.

Among the Gupta's contributions are many folktales and stories. In mathematics, the Gupta invented the concept of zero and developed symbols for the numbers 1 through 9. These symbols were carried to the West by traders and came to be called "Arabic numerals."

The empire lasted until about 600 A.D., when it dissolved into a collection of small states much like Europe.

Gupta Empire

▲ The Gupta Empire covered much of India and reached into parts of southwest Asia.

▶ The Guptas practiced Hinduism, but they tolerated other religions, especially Buddhism. Buddhism was founded about 563 B.C. by Siddartha Gautama (si dahr' tuh gow' tuh muh), who later became known as the Budda. The Budda, meaning the "Enlightened One," became the subject of many huge Gupta sculptures.

SPOTLIGHT ON: THE GUPTAS

Share these extra facts about the Guptas:
• The Gupta period is known as the "Golden Age" of ancient India.
• Rulers gave money to artists, writers, and scholars to encourage their work.
• People in the Gupta empire received free medical care, including simple surgery.
• Villages were protected by local military squads made up of one elephant, one chariot, three cavalrymen, and five foot soldiers.

• In times of war, all the squads were brought together to form the royal army.
• The Guptas did not believe in capital punishment. They issued fines instead.
• With the coming of Buddhism and the reform of Hinduism, most Guptas lived as vegetarians.
• In a popular marriage practice called the Swayamvara, suitors met at a bride's house and the bride picked her own groom.

◄ Despite the continued influence of Buddhism, Hinduism became the dominant religion of the Gupta Empire. During this period, rulers ordered the construction of stone or brick temples to honor Hindu gods and goddesses.

The great Gupta conqueror Samudra Gupta (suh mu' druh gup' tuh) minted his own coins. Ruling from about 335 A.D. to 375 A.D., he took over much of northern India and expanded trade as far south as islands in the Indian Ocean. The Sanskrit inscription on this coin describes Samudra Gupta as "the unconquered one, whose victory was spread in hundreds of battles, having conquered his enemies, conquers heaven." ▶

◄ Under the Guptas, Buddist monks decorated the inside of caves, which were used as temples and monasteries, with paintings, statues, and carved pillars. Most paintings illustrated stories from the life of Budda. Some paintings, however, show Gupta rulers and scenes from daily life, such as this woman.

Taking Another Look

1. During what years did the Gupta Empire flourish?
2. How did Gupta rulers try to unify their empire?

Hands-On Activity

Writing a Speech Write a one-minute speech in which you recommend that the phrase "Arabic numerals" be changed to "Gupta numerals."

311

---

the mountains, the location on the Indian subcontinent, and so on)

Next, direct students, working individually or in small groups, to use information in the Around the World feature to find other features that distinguished the Gupta empire as a region. *(Encourage students to identify such things as religion, shared history, common government, and so on.)*

DID YOU KNOW ??

Hindu legend holds that a curse lays over the Buddhist caves at Ajanta. The story claims that some deities angered Indra, the king of gods, by overstaying a visit on earth. As punishment, Indra turned them into pictures on the Buddhist walls of Ajanta, frozen there for all time. The gods, say the legend, retaliate against any mortal who tries to copy or destroy their beauty.

ASSESS

Check for Understanding

Have students answer the questions in Taking Another Look on page 311.

Enrich

Build on the Technology Skill lesson on page 276 of this unit, and assign interested students to prepare a multimedia presentation on the artwork at the Ajanta and Ellora caves. Encourage students to include maps, photos, sound clips, and more.

CLOSE

Review the attitude of the Gupta toward other religions. *(They practiced tolerance.)* Ask: How did religious tolerance help explain the success of Gupta rule? *(reduced religious dissention, promoting peace and unity)*

ANSWERS TO TAKING ANOTHER LOOK

1. The Gupta empire flourished from roughly 310 A.D. to 600 A.D.
2. Sample response: The Guptas promoted unity in their empire through religious tolerance, trade, and spread of the Hindu religion.

Hands-On Activity
Speeches will vary, but most students will credit the Guptas with inventing the concept of zero and symbols for the numbers 1 through 9. Some students may suggest the need to "set the record straight" or the importance of historical inaccuracies.

Standardized Test Practice

Answers and Analyses

1A   Geography

Since this map shows the boundaries of kingdoms, it is a political map.

 TEST-TAKING TIP

Review with students the characteristics of various kinds of maps and the different purposes they serve.

2B   Culture/Environment

A table of Norse gods, including Thor, "the god of thunder, lightning, and the tides," is on page 304. According to page 268, the Germans also believed *that the sound of thunder came from Thor's chariot wheels.*

 TEST-TAKING TIP

Encourage students to use the process of elimination and to guess aggressively, even if their knowledge is incomplete. Even if all they recall is that Thor was a powerful god, they can probably eliminate C and D.

Directions: Choose the *best* answer to each of the following multiple choice questions. If you have trouble answering a question, use the process of elimination to narrow your choices. Write your answers on a separate piece of paper.

Use the map below to answer question 1.

The Germanic Kingdoms

1. **This type of map is called a**

   A   political map

   B   physical map

   C   military map

   D   demographic map

   Test-Taking Tip: Even though this map does show some landforms, such as rivers, it is *not* primarily a physical map (answer B). What is the map's *main purpose?* A map's title—or legend (if there is one)—can give you clues.

2. **The legend of the Norse god Thor was used to explain**

   A   why the Vikings were such good warriors

   B   the sound of thunder

   C   the story of Adam and Eve

   D   the origins of language

   Test-Taking Tip: Eliminate answers that you know are incorrect. For example, the story of Adam and Eve (answer C) is a Bible story, and it is not related to the Vikings' religion.

312

3. The early Dark Ages were characterized by

F the development of strong trade routes in eastern Europe

G the failure of Christianity to spread to most parts of Europe

H a darkening of the sky due to air pollution around Europe

J an emphasis on war and conquest over education and trade

Test-Taking Tip: This question asks you to make a *generalization* about the Dark Ages. A generalization is a type of conclusion based on facts. Which of the answer choices *best* summarizes the Dark Ages? If you cannot remember any specific facts about the Dark Ages, ask yourself if it sounds like it was a positive or a negative time. In other words, what does the word *dark* suggest? Are there any answer choices you can eliminate as a result?

4. The battles waged by Charlemagne were different from earlier battles because

A for the first time, the purpose of war was to convert people to Christianity

B for the first time, wars were fought primarily on the water

C legends were written about the battles and Charlemagne's military leaders

D Charlemagne was the first to fight a war against the Pope

Test-Taking Tip: Always read the question and *all* the answer choices carefully. For example, Charlemagne fought *for* the Pope, not *against* the Pope, so you can eliminate answer D.

5. The Roman Catholic Church lost control of the Irish Church during the Germanic wars. What do you think was the reason for this?

F Ireland was far away, isolated, and relatively unimportant to Rome.

G Irish monks refused to follow the laws set by the Pope.

H Irish nobles refused to pay the taxes demanded by the Pope.

J The Irish refused to accept Christianity and kept worshiping their Celtic gods.

Test-Taking Tip: Make sure that you know where the major European countries are located on a map. How far was Ireland from Rome? Eliminate answer choices that do not make sense. If the Irish were already part of the Church, they must have accepted Christianity. Therefore, you can eliminate answer J.

6. After their encounters with the Germanic people in Europe, the Vikings stopped writing down their *sagas*, or long stories, about their gods. Why?

A They decided that they no longer had time to recite the long sagas.

B The Germanic people convinced the Vikings that stories were only for children.

C The Vikings were no longer interested in tales of warriors and exciting battles.

D The Vikings accepted Christianity, which outlawed stories about other gods.

Test-Taking Tip: For this question, you will have to think about the *influence* of the Germans on the Vikings. Since it is unlikely that the Vikings simply lost interest in these stories, you can get rid of answer C. **STOP**

313

3J History

Pages 270–272 discuss the invasions that marked the end of the Roman Empire and the beginning of the Dark Ages. According to the introduction to Chapter 18 (page 275), *The decline of the Roman Empire led to disorder everywhere in western Europe. . . . People were no longer interested in learning, and many books and works of art were damaged or lost.*

4A History

No mention is made of battles on water, so choice B can be eliminated. Charlemagne fought *for* the Pope, so choice D can be eliminated. There were earlier war legends, such as the *Iliad*, so choice C can be eliminated. According to page 279, Charlemagne waged wars because he wanted *all the Germanic people to become Christian.*

5F History

No mention is made of taxes or laws demanded by the Pope in the discussion of Ireland on pages 289–291, so choices G and H can be eliminated. According to page 290, Ireland was not a target for Germanic attacks because it was farther out than Britain. Likewise, it might have been too far away for the Roman Catholic Church to remain in contact.

6D History

The Viking sagas are discussed on page 303. There it states that after meeting Christians, the sagas were forgotten or were forbidden by the Church.

Tested Objectives	
Questions	**Reading Objective**
1	Analyze information
2	Identify supporting ideas
3	Identify central issues
4	Make comparisons
5, 6	Draw conclusions

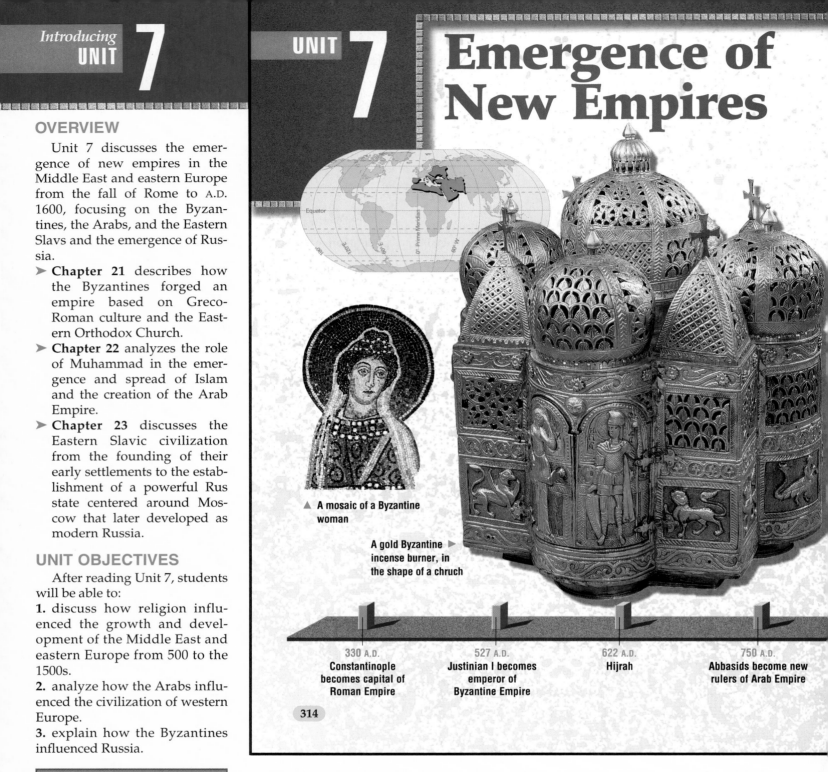

Emergence of New Empires

OVERVIEW

Unit 7 discusses the emergence of new empires in the Middle East and eastern Europe from the fall of Rome to A.D. 1600, focusing on the Byzantines, the Arabs, and the Eastern Slavs and the emergence of Russia.

➤ **Chapter 21** describes how the Byzantines forged an empire based on Greco-Roman culture and the Eastern Orthodox Church.

➤ **Chapter 22** analyzes the role of Muhammad in the emergence and spread of Islam and the creation of the Arab Empire.

➤ **Chapter 23** discusses the Eastern Slavic civilization from the founding of their early settlements to the establishment of a powerful Rus state centered around Moscow that later developed as modern Russia.

UNIT OBJECTIVES

After reading Unit 7, students will be able to:

1. discuss how religion influenced the growth and development of the Middle East and eastern Europe from 500 to the 1500s.

2. analyze how the Arabs influenced the civilization of western Europe.

3. explain how the Byzantines influenced Russia.

▲ A mosaic of a Byzantine woman

A gold Byzantine ▶ incense burner, in the shape of a chruch

330 A.D.
Constantinople becomes capital of Roman Empire

527 A.D.
Justinian I becomes emperor of Byzantine Empire

622 A.D.
Hijrah

750 A.D.
Abbasids become new rulers of Arab Empire

314

UNIT PROJECT

Divide the class into three groups. Assign each group one of the following leaders: Justinian, Muhammad, or Ivan the Great. Tell each group that it will be responsible for writing and performing a short play based on the life of their assigned leader.

ᴀBOUT THE UNIT OPENING

Examining Artifacts

Based on the artifacts, what can students infer about the role of religion in the Byzantine Empire? *(It was important.)* Ask: How do you know this? *(the use of a church as the subject of art, the intricate detail of the church, the use of gold to depict the church, etc.)* What other inferences can students make about the Byzantine Empire?

Global Chronology

Ask students to explain what time period the time line covers. *(330 to 1500)* According to the time line, what empires existed during this time period? *(Roman, Byzantine, Arab empires)*

Multimedia Activity

Turning Points in World History
Jerusalem: City of Three Faiths

ABCNEWS INTERACTIVE™

Setting up the Video

Work with a group of your classmates to view "Jerusalem: City of Three Faiths" on the videodisc *Turning Points in World History*.

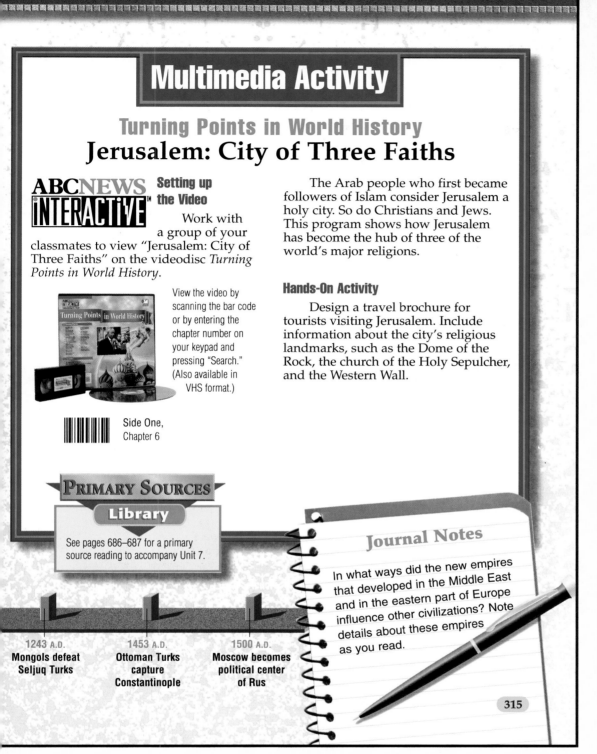

View the video by scanning the bar code or by entering the chapter number on your keypad and pressing "Search." (Also available in VHS format.)

Side One, Chapter 6

The Arab people who first became followers of Islam consider Jerusalem a holy city. So do Christians and Jews. This program shows how Jerusalem has become the hub of three of the world's major religions.

Hands-On Activity

Design a travel brochure for tourists visiting Jerusalem. Include information about the city's religious landmarks, such as the Dome of the Rock, the church of the Holy Sepulcher, and the Western Wall.

PRIMARY SOURCES Library

See pages 686–687 for a primary source reading to accompany Unit 7.

1243 A.D.
Mongols defeat Seljuq Turks

1453 A.D.
Ottoman Turks capture Constantinople

1500 A.D.
Moscow becomes political center of Rus

Journal Notes

In what ways did the new empires that developed in the Middle East and in the eastern part of Europe influence other civilizations? Note details about these empires as you read.

315

INTRODUCING THE UNIT

Ask students to consider the cultural changes they have witnessed during their lives. (*Answers can include technological advances, medical breakthroughs, etc.*) Point out that each civilization in this unit changed throughout history and that many of these changes had a far-reaching impact.

RECORDING JOURNAL NOTES

Ask students to list ways in which other cultures have influenced the culture of the United States in their lifetimes. Have students note in their journal details about the ways the empires that developed in the Middle East and in eastern Europe influenced other civilizations.

PRIMARY SOURCES Library

Items in the Primary Sources Library for this unit focus on Byzantine women. Elements include:
• Selection from the *Alexiad*, by Anna Commena
• Gold coin showing Empress Irene

For additional primary source documents, use the World History Primary Source Document CD-ROM.

Geographic Location

Have students use their text Atlas to locate the places in this unit that are in the Mediterranean area, identifying the Balkan Peninsula and the waterways from the Mediterranean Sea to the Black Sea and up to Russia. Then have students locate the Arabian Peninsula—the area where Islam originated—and identify the areas to its north, west, and east where Islam spread.

Chapter 21 Planning Guide

Objectives	Reproducible Resources	Multimedia Resources
Section 1 **Constantinople** Explain why the Byzantine Empire survived and prospered for 1,000 years.	Reproducible Lesson Plan Chapter 21 Vocabulary and Guided Reading Activity Reading Essentials and Study Guide 21-1 Section 1 Quiz Unit 7 Hands-On History Lab	Vocabulary PuzzleMaker Interactive Tutor Self-Assessment Software ExamView® Pro Testmaker Glencoe Skillbuilder Interactive Workbook, Level 1 Presentation Plus!
Section 2 **Justinian I** Discuss why Constantinople was important to the empire.	Reproducible Lesson Plan Reading Essentials and Study Guide 21-2 Chapter 21 Cooperative Learning Activity Chapter 21 Chart and Graph Skill Activity Chapter 21 Geography and Map Activity Chapter 21 Enrichment Activity Unit 7 Primary Sources Reading Section 2 Quiz	Teaching Transparency and Activity 1B Vocabulary PuzzleMaker Interactive Tutor Self-Assessment Software ExamView® Pro Testmaker Glencoe Skillbuilder Interactive Workbook, Level 1
Section 3 **The Church** Analyze practices of the Eastern Orthodox Church and the role these practices played in the Byzantine Empire.	Reproducible Lesson Plan Reading Essentials and Study Guide 21-3 Section 3 Quiz	Vocabulary PuzzleMaker Interactive Tutor Self-Assessment Software ExamView® Pro Testmaker Glencoe Skillbuilder Interactive Workbook, Level 1
Section 4 **Decline of the Empire** Summarize reasons the Byzantine Empire declined.	Reproducible Lesson Plan Reading Essentials and Study Guide 21-4 Chapter 21 Activity Book Activity Section 4 Quiz	Vocabulary PuzzleMaker Interactive Tutor Self-Assessment Software ExamView® Pro Testmaker Glencoe Skillbuilder Interactive Workbook, Level 1
Chapter 21 **Review and Evaluation**	Chapter 21 Reteaching Activity Chapter 21 Performance Assessment Activity Spanish Chapter Summary and Glossary Chapter 21 Test	Vocabulary PuzzleMaker Interactive Tutor Self-Assessment Software Glencoe Skillbuilder Interactive Workbook, Level 1 Audiocassettes* ExamView® Pro Testmaker

*Also available in Spanish.

Presentation Plus!

Use Glencoe's **Presentation Plus!** multimedia teacher tool to easily present dynamic lessons that visually excite your students. Using Microsoft® PowerPoint, you can customize the presentations to create your own personalized lessons.

 Interactive Lesson Planner

Planning has never been easier! Using this CD-ROM, organize your week, month, semester, or year with all the help you need. The **Interactive Lesson Planner** gives you access to all of the blackline masters which accompany *Human Heritage.*

✓ PERFORMANCE ASSESSMENT ACTIVITIES

Word Puzzles Have students create a list of important people, places, buildings, or religious terms mentioned in this chapter. Tell them to use these lists to create crossword puzzles.

CHAPTER RESOURCES

LITERATURE ABOUT THE PERIOD

Dickinson, Peter. *The Dancing Bear*. Dell, 1972. Tells an adventure story that takes place during the time of the Byzantine Empire.

READINGS FOR THE STUDENT

Browning, Robert. *The Byzantine Empire*. Charles Scribner's Sons, 1980. Byzantine world from A.D. 500 to fall of Constantinople in 1453.

READINGS FOR THE TEACHER

Browning, Robert. *Justinian and Theodora: The Byzantine Recovery*. Thames & Hudson, 1987. Explores the relationship between Justinian and Theodora and their attempt to recreate the Christian Roman Empire of Constantine.

Mango, Cyril. *Byzantium: The Empire of New Rome*. Charles Scribner's Sons, 1980. Considers Byzantine life from a thematic perspective.

KEY TO ABILITY LEVELS

Teaching strategies have been coded for varying learning styles and abilities.

L1 Level 1 activities are **basic** activities and should be within the ability range of all students.

L2 Level 2 activities are **average** activities and should be within the ability range of the average to above-average student.

L3 Level 3 activities are **challenging** activities designed for the ability range of above-average students.

ELL ELL activities should be within the ability range of English Language Learning students.

NATIONAL GEOGRAPHIC SOCIETY — Teacher's Corner

INDEX TO NATIONAL GEOGRAPHIC MAGAZINE

The following article relates to this chapter:

• "The Byzantine Empire," by Merle Severy, December 1983.

NATIONAL GEOGRAPHIC SOCIETY PRODUCTS AVAILABLE FROM GLENCOE

To order the following, call Glencoe at 1-800-334-7344:

• *PicturePack: Physical Geography of the World (Transparencies)*
• *PicturePack: The Middle Ages (Transparencies)*
• *Picture Show: The Middle Ages (CD-ROM)*
• *Picture Atlas of the World (CD-ROM)*
• *Picture Pack: World Geography Library (Transparencies)*

ADDITIONAL NATIONAL GEOGRAPHIC SOCIETY PRODUCTS

To order the following, call National Geographic at 1-800-368-2728:

• *National Geographic Atlas of World History (Book)*
• *Wonders of the Ancient World: National Geographic Atlas of Archaeology (Book)*

Access *National Geographic's* new dynamic MapMachine Web site and other geography resources at:
http://www.nationalgeographic.com
http://www.nationalgeographic.com/maps/

OVERVIEW

Chapter 21 describes the Byzantine Empire from the founding of Constantinople to the Turkish conquest.

➤ **Section 1** describes Constantinople as the "New Rome."
➤ **Section 2** discusses the Byzantine contributions to government and law.
➤ **Section 3** discusses the effects of Orthodox Christianity on Byzantine and eastern European culture.
➤ **Section 4** traces the decline of the Byzantine Empire.

CHAPTER OBJECTIVES

After reading Chapter 21, students will be able to:

1. explain why the Byzantine Empire survived and prospered for 1,000 years.
2. discuss why Constantinople was important to the empire.
3. describe the Eastern Orthodox Church and the role it played in the Byzantine Empire.
4. summarize causes of the decline of the Byzantine Empire.

EXAMINING ARTIFACTS

Have students examine the Byzantine crown, and ask: What does this artifact tell you about the relationship between church and government in the Byzantine Empire? *(They were closely tied.)* Call on to students to explain how they reached their answer. *(the cross, icons, etc., on the crown)* Tell students to use the time line to figure out how long the empire prospered.

PERFORMANCE ASSESSMENT ✓

Use the Performance Assessment Activities on page 316B to help you evaluate students as they complete the chapter.

316

The Byzantine Empire
330 A.D.–1455 A.D.

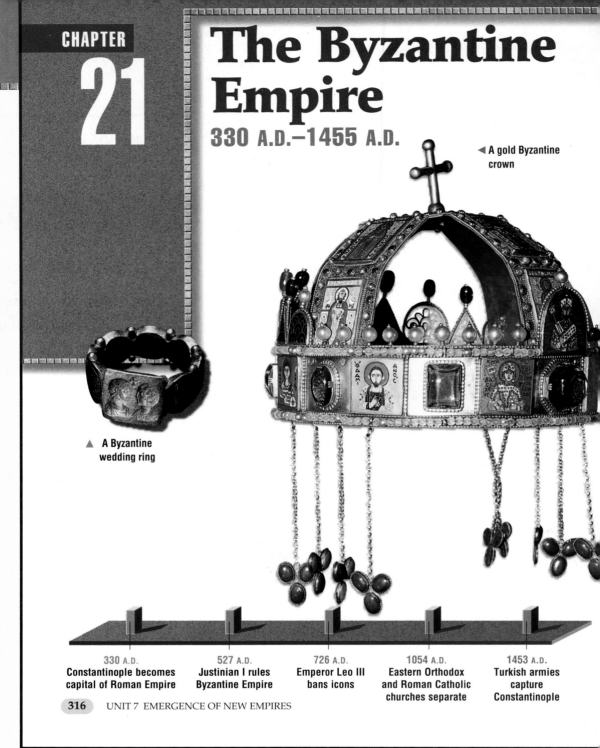

◀ A gold Byzantine crown

▲ A Byzantine wedding ring

330 A.D.	527 A.D.	726 A.D.	1054 A.D.	1453 A.D.
Constantinople becomes capital of Roman Empire	Justinian I rules Byzantine Empire	Emperor Leo III bans icons	Eastern Orthodox and Roman Catholic churches separate	Turkish armies capture Constantinople

316   UNIT 7 EMERGENCE OF NEW EMPIRES

TEACHING RESOURCES

TEACHER PLANNING AND SUPPORT

- 🗀 Reproducible Lesson Plan
- 🗀 Block Scheduling Implementation Guide
- 🗀 Videodisc Bar Code Correlation
- 💿 Presentation Plus!

REVIEW AND REINFORCEMENT

- 🗀 Reading Essentials and Study Guide 21-1, 21-2, 21-3, 21-4
- 🗀 Chapter 21 Vocabulary and Guided Reading Activity
- 💾 Vocabulary PuzzleMaker Software
- 🖨 Teaching Transparencies 21A & 21B

- 🗀 Chapter 21 Reteaching Activity
- 🗀 Chapter 21 Cooperative Learning Activity
- 🗀 Chapter 21 Activity Book Activity
- 🗀 Chapter 21 Chart and Graph Skill Activity
- 💾 Interactive Tutor Self-Assessment Software
- ⏺📼 Unit 7 MindJogger VideoQuiz

APPLICATION AND HANDS-ON ACTIVITIES

- 🗀 Daily World History, Geography, and Culture Question
- 🗀 Unit 7 Hands-On History Lab Activity

Chapter Focus

Read to Discover

- Why the Byzantine Empire survived and prospered for 1,000 years.
- Why Constantinople was important to the empire.
- What role the Eastern Orthodox Church played in the Byzantine Empire.
- What forces helped bring about the decline of the Byzantine Empire.

 Terms to Learn **People to Know** **Places to Locate**

Terms to Learn	People to Know	Places to Locate
relics	Constantine I	Constantinople
theology	Justinian	Byzantium
Greek fire	Theodora	Hagia Sophia
icons	Leo III	

Why It's Important Emperor Constantine I moved the capital of the Roman Empire from Rome to Constantinople about 330. About 100 years later, the Roman Empire in the West fell. The Roman Empire in the East, however, survived and prospered. It became known as the Byzantine Empire. Its people were called Byzantines. The Byzantines built a civilization based on a blend of Greek, Roman, and Christian ideas.

The empire in the East survived for several reasons. Constantinople was a mighty fortress that needed few soldiers to defend it. This freed soldiers to protect other areas of the empire. The empire's wealth supported a large army and was used to pay invaders to move farther and farther west.

Chapter Overview
Visit the *Human Heritage* Web site at **humanheritage.glencoe.com** and click on **Chapter 21— Chapter Overviews** to preview this chapter.

SECTION 1 Constantinople

When Constantine first chose the old Greek city of Byzantium as the place for his new capital, he was aware of its advantages. The Roman Empire depended on trade, and the great centers of trade lay to the east. Byzantium was on the waterway between the Black and Aegean seas. Its harbor offered a safe haven for fishing boats, merchant ships, and warships. The city sat at the crossroads of the trading routes between Europe and Asia. Its location gave it control of the sea trade between Kievan Rus and the Mediterranean area. One of the most important east-west land routes passed through the city, too.

GEOGRAPHY ACTIVITIES
- Chapter 21 Geography and Map Activity
- Social Studies Outline Map Resource Book

INTERDISCIPLINARY CONNECTIONS
- World History & Art Transparency 12, *Theodora and Attendants*
- World Music Cultural Traditions

ENRICHMENT AND EXTENSION
- Unit 7 Primary Sources Reading
- World History Primary Source Document Library CD-ROM
- Chapter 21 Enrichment Activity
- Foods Around the World

ASSESSMENT AND EVALUATION
- Chapter 21 Performance Assessment Activity
- Chapter 21 Section Quizzes 21-1, 21-2, 21-3, 21-4
- Chapter 21 Test
- Chapter 21 ExamView® Pro Testmaker Software
- Chapter 21 Digests Audiocassettes Activities and Tests

SPANISH RESOURCES
- Chapter 21 Spanish Chapter Summary and Glossary
- Chapter 21 Spanish Chapter Digests Audiocassettes Activities and Tests

---

Chapter Overview introduces students to chapter content and key terms. Have them access **Chapter 21 Overview** at **humanheritage.glencoe.com**

FOCUS

Bellringer

Write the following on the board: *Make a list of some things you know about the country of Turkey.*

Motivational Activity

Discuss students' lists of what they know about Turkey. Ask them if they realize that Istanbul is the ancient city of Constantinople. Explain that they will learn about the importance of this city in history.

GUIDE TO READING

Reading Strategy

Ask students to read "Why It's Important" and summarize the chapter's main theme. *(The Byzantine Empire survived and prospered, creating a civilization that blended Greek, Roman, and Christian ideas.)*

Vocabulary Precheck

Ask students to define each of the "Terms to Learn." Have a volunteer consult the dictionary for any unfamiliar words. **L1** **ELL**

Use the Vocabulary PuzzleMaker for Chapter 21 to create a crossword puzzle. **L1**

Assign Chapter 21 Vocabulary and Guided Reading Activity.

Assign Reading Essentials and Study Guide 21-1.

Guided Practice

L1 **Geography: Location** Ask students to make an outline map of Europe, the Middle East, and North Africa similar to the one on page 323. Have them locate and label Rome, Constantinople, Athens, the Mediterranean and Black seas, the Bosphorus, Asia Minor, Syria, Egypt, Italy, Greece, and the Balkan Peninsula. Explain that the boundaries of the Byzantine Empire varied over time, but that it remained a geographic crossroads of sea and land travel. **ELL**

DID YOU KNOW ??

Constantinople's oval arena was called the Hippodrome.

CAPTION ANSWER

because it was modeled after Rome

NATIONAL GEOGRAPHIC SOCIETY

CD-ROM
Picture Atlas of the World
You and your students can see the present-day skyline of Istanbul and the beautiful Hagia Sophia by clicking the "Photos" button of Istanbul, Turkey.

People in History

Constantine I
C. 288 A.D.–337 A.D.

Roman Emperor

Born in what is now Serbia, Constantine grew up the son of a Roman army officer. In 305 A.D., he became the co-emperor of Rome, but he continued to fight alongside the troops. During one battle, he saw a vision that convinced him to become the first Roman Emperor to accept Christianity. In 324 A.D., he triumphed as sole ruler of Rome and ordered a new capital city built at Byzantium. His rule helped ensure the eastward spread of Christianity.

The location also favored the city's defense. The sea protected it on three sides, and a huge wall protected it on the fourth side. Later, a huge chain was even strung across the city's north harbor for greater protection. Invaders would not easily take the new capital, which was renamed Constantinople.

It took more than four years to build Constantinople. Constantine modeled it after Rome. The city stood on seven hills. Government buildings and palaces were designed in the Roman style. Streets were narrow and apartment houses crowded. Constantinople even had an oval arena like the Circus Maximus where races and other events were held.

The city's political and social life was patterned on that of Rome, too. The emperor operated under Roman laws and ruled with the help of highly trained officials, who took charge of building roads, bridges, wells, and caravan shelters. The army followed Roman military customs. The poor people of Constantinople received free bread and enjoyed circuses and chariot races put on by the government. The wealthy people lived in town or on large farming estates. In fact, Constantine convinced many of the wealthy Romans to move to Constantinople by offering to build them palaces.

CONSTANTINOPLE Constantinople's location made it an important center for trade. The wealth from this trade was used to make Constantinople an ornate and beautiful city. Citizens shown in this painting gather to watch a royal procession. **Why was Constantinople called the "new Rome"?**

MULTICULTURAL PERSPECTIVES

A contemporary historian points out that a modern-day time traveler would feel more at home in the Byzantine world of Constantinople than in any of the depressed, dangerous countries of the early medieval western Europe. The city had shops, factories, and banking houses. It had a well-educated population who were curious and informed about current events, politics, and literature. The Byzantines were enthusiastic sports fans at games and chariot races. They loved ornamentation and rich colors especially in their illuminated manuscripts and stained-glass windows.

The family was the center of social life for most Byzantines. The majority of them made their living through farming, herding, or working as laborers. There was, however, one important difference between Constantinople and Rome. From the beginning, Constantinople was a Christian city. It had been dedicated to God by Constantine, who viewed it as the center of a great Christian empire. Church leaders were consulted about all important events of everyday life and had great influence over the people. For a young man of Constantinople, a career in the church was considered a very high goal.

Constantinople had many Christian churches. Constantine saw to it that they were the most magnificent buildings in the city. Government and church leaders gathered relics (rel' iks), or valued holy objects from the past, from throughout the Christian world. These were placed in public monuments, palaces, and churches. The bodies of saints rested in beautiful shrines. Thousands of people came to these shrines to pray to God for cures for their ills.

The city's Christian values could be seen in the way needy people were treated. The Byzantines believed that each Christian was responsible for the well-being of other Christians. Wealthy Byzantines formed organizations to care for the poor, the aged, and the blind. Even members of the emperor's household took great pride in founding and supporting good causes.

About 600,000 people lived in Constantinople during Constantine's rule. There were Greeks, Turks, Italians, Slavs, Persians, Armenians, and Jews. They spoke Greek among themselves but used Latin, the official language, for government business. Most people became Christians, and all called themselves Romans. Byzantine nobles and rulers continued to boast of their ties to Rome for the next 1,100 years.

Byzantine Coins

Reading Check
What are **relics**, and why did they lure thousands of people to Constantinople?

Student Web Activity
Visit the *Human Heritage* Web site at **humanheritage.glencoe.com** and click on *Chapter 21—Student Web Activities* to find out more about the city of Constantinople.

Section 1 Assessment

1. **Define:** relics.
2. Why did Constantine choose Byzantium as the site for the empire's new capital?
3. How could the influence of Christianity be seen in the city?

Critical Thinking

4. **Demonstrating Reasoned Judgment** In your opinion, what were some of the good things about living in Constantinople?

Graphic Organizer Activity

5. Draw this diagram, and use it to compare the cities of Rome and Constantinople.

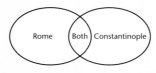

Rome   Both   Constantinople

Reading Check
What is **theology?**

Theodora Although Theodora was the daughter of a bear-keeper with a traveling circus, her strong will took her as far as the royal court. Justinian's court historian commented: "She never did anything at any time as the result of persuasion. . . . She claimed the right to govern the whole Roman Empire."

SECTION 2 Justinian I

After Constantine died, his sons ruled the empire. They were followed first by a general named Julian and then by a series of other emperors. Finally, in 527, a Macedonian named Justinian (juh stin' ē uhn) came to the throne. He was a strong ruler who came to be considered the greatest Byzantine emperor.

Justinian had served in the army and was a good general. He was well trained in law, music, architecture, and **theology** (thē ol' uh jē), or the study of religion. The people who served him were chosen for their ability rather than wealth or social position.

As emperor, Justinian controlled the army and navy, made the laws, headed the Church and the government, and was supreme judge. He could declare war or make peace. The Church taught that the emperor's acts were inspired by God. Therefore, what Justinian did could not be questioned. Those who came into contact with him were expected to bow down before him and kiss his feet and hands.

Theodora Justinian's wife, the empress Theodora (thē uh dor' uh), was a great help to him. Theodora's family had been poor, and she had worked as an actress before meeting Justinian.

JUSTINIAN AND THEODORA Theodora had a much greater influence on Byzantine government than other empresses. In this painting she urges Justinian to take action against a revolt. **What problems did Justinian face in marrying Theodora?**

320

Making Generalizations

If you say, "We have a good soccer team," you are making a generalization, or general statement, about your team. If you go on to say that the team has not lost a game this season and is the top-rated team, you are providing evidence to support your generalization. When studying history, it is often necessary to put together pieces of information—supporting statements—to arrive at a full picture.

Learning the Skill In some cases, authors provide only supporting statements, and you will need to make generalizations on your own. To make generalizations, follow these steps:

- Identify the subject matter and gather facts and examples related to it.

- Identify similarities or patterns among these facts.

- Use these similarities or patterns to form general ideas about the subject.

Read the passage about Hagia Sophia, a cathedral built by Justinian, and study the picture on this page. Then answer the questions that follow.

Hagia Sophia is the fourth largest cathedral in the world. Only St. Paul's Cathedral in England and St. Peter's Cathedral and Milan Cathedral in Italy are larger.

The building's huge round dome can be seen from everywhere in the church. The dome rests on four arches and four gigantic piers. It measures 102 feet (31 m) in diameter and stands 184 feet (56 m) high. A series of 40 arching windows flood the interior with light and draw the visitor's eyes upward.

GENERALIZATIONS:

a. It took great engineering skills to build Hagia Sophia.
b. Hagia Sophia made Constantinople the center of the Christian world.
c. Hagia Sophia is one of the world's greatest churches.
d. The arching windows are Hagia Sophia's most impressive feature.

Skill Practice

1. **Which of the generalizations above are supported by details in the passage?**
2. **Which of the generalizations are not supported by the passage? Explain.**
3. **Go to pages 322–323. Write three generalizations.**

Glencoe's **Skillbuilder Interactive Workbook, Level 1,** provides instruction and practice in key social studies skills.

TEACH

Making Generalizations

You might introduce this lesson by writing this information from a survey conducted in the late 1990s on the board.

- Some 89 percent of all teenagers report using the Internet at least once.
- On average, teens surf the Internet 5.1 hours per week.
- More than 75 percent of teenagers say they would rather look something up on the Internet than in a book.

Ask students to form a statement that summarizes these facts in some way. (*An example might be: Teenagers feel comfortable using the Internet.*) Have students share their responses. Then introduce the definition of a generalization—a statement that ties together facts in a general but accurate way.

Next, assign the skills lesson and accompanying questions on this page.

Answers to Skill Practice

1. a, c
2. b, because there are no facts to support this statement; d, because it is an opinion (someone else may think other features are more impressive)
3. Generalizations will vary, but should take into account all facts.

TEAM-TEACHING STRATEGY

Art Work with an art teacher to help students design a brochure on Hagia Sophia that might be given to tourists visiting the famous structure. Encourage students to use the Internet to locate such things as street maps, photographs, and other items that might be included in the brochure.

After collecting information, assign students to plan the brochure's design by drawing storyboards. Have them review their storyboards with the art teacher, making any necessary improvements. When students have written their rough drafts, direct them to exchange the copy with each other for editing. Urge students to watch for any faulty or unsupported generalizations. When students have edited each other's work, have them produce their final version for display on a bulletin board and/or inclusion in their portfolios.

✓ **Reading Check Answer**
A **dowry** is the wealth a bride brings with her when she marries. Theodora said that the dowry should be used to measure the amount of land a woman could own.

PRIMARY SOURCES
Library

You might assign "Byzantine Women" on pages 686–687 of the Primary Sources Library.

The people of the empire had a low opinion of actresses. There was even a law forbidding marriages between them and high government officials. Justinian, however, wanted to marry Theodora. After he became emperor, he abolished the law and made Theodora his empress.

At first, Theodora only entertained guests and attended palace ceremonies. Gradually, however, she began to take an interest in politics. Soon she was helping Justinian fill government and church offices. She also convinced Justinian to allow women more rights. For the first time, a Byzantine wife could own land equal in value to her **dowry** (dow' rē), or the wealth she brought with her when she married. A widow could raise and support her young children without government interference.

In 532, Theodora made her most important contribution. A group of senators had organized a revolt to protest high taxes. They were able to gain much support from both the poor and the rich. The poor were angry because they were receiving less free food and entertainment. The rich were angry because, for the first time, they had to pay taxes. The leaders of the revolt were prepared to crown a new emperor. Justinian's advisers urged him to leave the city. Theodora, however, urged him to stay and fight. Justinian and his supporters took Theodora's advice. They stayed in Constantinople, trapped the rebels, killed 300,000 of them, and crushed the uprising. As a result, Justinian kept control of the government and became an even stronger ruler.

✓ **Reading Check**
What is a **dowry**, and what did Theodora say it should be used to measure?

Hagia Sophia Hagia Sophia, first built in the reign of Constantine, was twice destroyed by fire. When Justinian rebuilt the church, he ordered it be made fireproof. Earthquakes caused the dome to collapse in 559, but it too was rebuilt. The building became a mosque in 1453 and today is a museum.

Law and Public Works Justinian was very interested in law and spent much time reading the laws made by other emperors. He decided that the old legal system was too complicated and disorganized. He chose ten men to work out a simpler and better system. This group was headed by a legal scholar named Tribonian (tri bō' nē ahn).

Tribonian and the others studied the existing laws. They did away with those that were no longer needed. They organized and rewrote those laws that remained. In six years, they had developed a legal code that became the law of the land.

This code came to be known as the Justinian Code. It is considered one of Justinian's greatest achievements. It provided a summary of Roman legal thinking. It also gave later generations insight into the basic ideas of Roman law. It has had a great influence on the legal systems of almost every western country.

Justinian was as interested in public works as he was in law. He was almost always busy with some building program. He built churches, bridges, monasteries, and forums. He also built a system of forts connected by a large network of roads. When an earthquake destroyed Antioch, he had the whole city rebuilt.

One of Justinian's greatest accomplishments was the church called Hagia Sophia (hag'ē ī sō fē' uh), or "Holy Wisdom."

EXTENDING THE CONTENT

In May 542 a plague struck Constantinople and raged for four months. The Greek historian Procopius witnessed the epidemic and wrote detailed accounts. At its height, the disease killed 10,000 people a day. By the end of that summer 300,000 people had died. Justinian contracted the plague, which caused serious political concern because he and Theodora had no children and a successor had yet to be named. Theodora called a secret meeting with her ministers to plan for her husband's nephew to succeed him. Justinian survived the plague. During the months when he was sick, Theodora was in charge and dealt with the plague's devastation.

Nearly 10,000 workers, watched over by 200 supervisors, labored in shifts to build the church. It was built exactly as Justinian planned. The church had a gold altar and walls of polished marble. Gold and silver ornaments, woven cloth, and colorful **mosaics** (mō zā' iks), or pictures made up of many bits of colored glass or stone, were everywhere. Figures of Justinian and Theodora were among the angels and saints that lined the walls.

Most impressive was the huge dome that rose high over the central part of the church. It was the first time such a huge circular dome had been set atop a rectangular opening. During the day, sunlight poured through the many windows in the dome. At night, thousands of oil lamps turned the building into a beacon that could be seen for miles.

Hagia Sophia was later called St. Sophia. For more than 900 years, it served as the religious center of the Byzantine Empire. It still stands today.

Conquest   Justinian wanted to reunite the eastern and western parts of the empire and restore the glory and power that was Rome's. To do this, he needed to conquer the German kingdoms in western Europe and North Africa. He appointed an officer named Belisarius (bel uh sar' ē uhs) to reorganize and lead the Byzantine army.

Reading Check
What are **mosaics**?

MAP STUDY

PLACE Justinian conquered parts of Italy, North Africa, and Spain. **About how many miles (km) did the Byzantine Empire under Justinian extend from its most eastern to its most western points?**

Reading Check Answer
Mosaics are pictures made up of many bits of colored glass or stone.

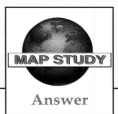

MAP STUDY

Answer

2,850 miles (or 4,585 km)
Assign the Chapter 21 **Geography and Map Activity** in the TCR.

The Byzantine Empire Under Justinian

Byzantine Empire Before Justinian

Justinian's Conquests to 565

miles 0   300   600
kilometers 0   300   600   900

SPOTLIGHT ON: THEODORA

Theodora was considered a feminist in her time. She was determined to improve the status of women in the Byzantine patriarchal society. Changes and improvements for which Theodora is credited include equal inheritance rights for daughters and sons. Another social reform provided that children of female slaves did not automatically become slaves. Theodora also converted a palace on the Bosporus into a convent where young girls could begin a new life.

Reading Check Answer

Greek fire was the Byzantine's secret weapon because nobody knew its formula or how to put it out once it came in contact with water.

🖫 Use **Interactive Tutor Self-Assessment Software** to review Section 2.

🖫 Use the **Vocabulary Puzzle-Maker** to create crossword and word search puzzles.

Until that time, the cavalry had been divided into groups of private soldiers hired by landowning nobles. Each group had its own commanders. Foot soldiers, who made up the largest part of the army, were called up when needed and then sent back to their homes. As a result, they felt little loyalty toward their officers.

When Belisarius took command, he set up a basic group of loyal and heavily armed cavalry soldiers. The group was so strong that the other soldiers willingly obeyed its orders. Then, Belisarius developed a series of battle moves that greatly strengthened the army's striking power.

During this time, the Byzantine navy was also improved and the first secret weapon in history was developed. It was called **Greek fire,** a chemical mixture that ignited when it came into contact with water. Greek fire burned a person's skin and was hard to put out. The Byzantines guarded their secret so carefully that its exact formula is still unknown.

✓ **Reading Check** Why was **Greek fire** the Byzantines' "secret weapon"?

With these improvements, the Byzantines were able to control more of the Mediterranean. They were also able to win back much of Italy and North Africa. They defeated the Persians, and ensured the security of the empire's eastern borders. Most of the western provinces Justinian regained, however, were lost again a generation or so after his death.

Section 2 Assessment

1. **Define:** theology, dowry, mosaics, Greek fire.
2. How did Justinian feel about the old system of Roman laws? What did he do about it?
3. What was Justinian's goal for the Byzantine Empire?

Critical Thinking

4. **Making Inferences** What do you think Justinian would say about the state of the American legal system today? Explain.

Graphic Organizer Activity

5. Draw this diagram, and use it to write and support a generalization about Theodora's role as empress.

SECTION 3 The Church

Church and government worked closely together in the Byzantine Empire. Christianity was the official religion, which meant that everyone in the empire was supposed to be a Christian. The Byzantines believed the emperor represented Christ on Earth. Thus, the emperor was not only the head of the government but also of the Church.

324 UNIT 7 EMERGENCE OF NEW EMPIRES

Linking Across Time

Mosaics Byzantine artists excelled in the use of glass mosaics, especially in the design of icons (right). Today mosaics are still an important art form in Mexico (far right), continuing a tradition started by ancient peoples such as the Maya and Aztec. **Why did the Byzantines argue over the use of icons?**

The leader of the Church in Constantinople was called the Patriarch. He was chosen by the emperor. Under him were the **metropolitans** (met ruh pol' uh tuhns), or church officials in charge of the empire's important areas. Under them were the bishops and priests. Most priests were married. All higher Church officials, however, came from monasteries and were not married.

The monasteries played an important role in the Byzantine Empire. They helped the poor and ran hospitals and schools for needy children. They sent missionaries to neighboring lands to help keep the peace. These missionaries translated parts of the Bible and some religious services into several eastern European languages. They believed more people would become Christians if the Bible and Church ceremonies were in their own language.

Some missionaries, including a man named Cyril (sir' uhl), traveled among the Slavs, a people who had settled in eastern Europe. These missionaries gave the Slavs a new alphabet. It was based on the Greek alphabet and was called the Cyrillic (suh ril' ik) alphabet in honor of the man who had helped create it.

Religion was very important to the Byzantines. They often argued about religious matters. One point divided the Byzantines for more than 100 years. It centered on whether or not **icons** (ī' konz), or religious images, should be used in worship.

Many Byzantines honored icons. They covered the walls of their churches with them. Monasteries owned icons that were

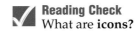
Reading Check
What was the role of the **metropolitans** in the Byzantine Church?

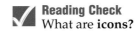
Reading Check
What are **icons**?

Linking Across Time

Some Byzantines thought that honoring icons was a form of idol worship forbidden by God.

Reading Check Answer
The **metropolitans** were church officials who were in charge of the empire's important areas.

MAKING CONNECTIONS

➤➤ **Language** The Cyrillic alphabet has 33 letters and is based largely on the Greek alphabet.

Reading Check Answer
Icons are religious images.

MEETING SPECIAL NEEDS

To help auditory learners understand the role of the Eastern Orthodox Church in the Byzantine Empire, invite a resource person to speak to the students. The speaker might be a member of the Eastern Orthodox Church, a professor of theology or history, or someone else well versed in Byzantine history. Ask the speaker to examine the role of the emperor and the importance of monasteries and to show illustrations or examples of Byzantine art and architecture. Ask the speaker to explain that much of what we know about the early Eastern Orthodox Church is the result of the striking artwork that has survived from that period.

📂 Refer to *Inclusion for the Middle School Social Studies Classroom: Strategies and Activities* for additional resources.

Painting of Cyril

believed to work miracles. Some Byzantines, however, wanted an end to the use of icons. They thought honoring them was a form of idol worship forbidden by God.

In 726, Emperor Leo III ordered a stop to the use of icons in religious worship. He did not approve of icons and he wanted to keep church officials who favored them from gaining too much power. Leo and the church leaders argued over this. Most people refused to give up their icons. In 843, the emperor realized the cause was lost and once again allowed their use.

The fight over icons damaged the empire's relations with western Europe. Because so few people in the West could read, church leaders there used images instead of the written word to explain Christian teachings. When Leo decided to do away with icons, the Pope called a council of bishops. The council declared that Leo and his supporters were no longer Church members.

An argument also developed between the Pope and the Patriarch. The Patriarch would not recognize the Pope as head of the Church. The Pope broke his ties with the Byzantine emperor and turned to the Frankish kings for military protection. When the Pope crowned Charlemagne "Emperor of the Romans" in 800, the Byzantines were very angry. They believed this title belonged only to their emperor. These disputes helped pave the way for the break between Western and Eastern Christianity in 1054.

Section 3 Assessment

1. **Define:** metropolitans, icons.
2. What role did Christianity play in the Byzantine Empire?
3. What were some of the contributions of monasteries to Byzantine society and culture?

Critical Thinking

4. **Making Inferences** Why do you think the Slavs needed an alphabet that was different from the one used in the Byzantine Empire?

Graphic Organizer Activity

5. Draw this diagram, and use it to show the causes and effects of conflicts between the Pope in Rome and the Patriarch of Constantinople.

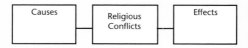

| Causes | | Religious Conflicts | | Effects |

SECTION 3 Decline of the Empire

The Byzantine Empire lasted for about 1,100 years. Its capital was the largest, richest, and most beautiful city in Europe. Its people were among the most educated and creative of that time. They preserved Greek culture and Roman law for other civilizations. They also spread Christianity to peoples in the East. The empire did much to help the growth of trade. It also gave the world new techniques in the fine arts. Even with all of these achievements, however, forces from both inside and outside the empire weakened it and led to its downfall.

Early Byzantine emperors had counted on farmers to make up the army. In return for their services, these farmers were given land. By the 1100s, however, the empire's borders were safe, and not as many soldiers were needed. The emperor decided to cut costs by changing the policy toward the farmers. Once they had lost their land, the farmers found little reason to remain loyal to the empire.

The empire also began to have problems with trade. When the Vikings conquered Byzantine lands in southern Italy in 1080, they threatened to attack Constantinople. The Byzantines no longer had enough soldiers to fight them. So, they turned for help to the Italian city-state of Venice. The Venetians defeated the Vikings. In return, the Byzantine emperor gave them the right to do business tax-free in all the empire's cities. Venetian ships and merchants soon controlled most of the empire's trade. This meant a great loss of income for the Byzantines.

Meanwhile, Christians from the West and Muslims from the East attacked the empire. Asia Minor was lost to these invaders. This greatly weakened the empire, which had depended on Asia Minor for food and materials as well as soldiers. One by one, the invaders took over more lands. Before long, the Byzantine Empire was reduced to a small area around Constantinople.

The End of the Byzantine Empire

Lands of Ottoman Turks, 1453

MAP STUDY

REGION The Byzantine Empire was frequently attacked by invading armies. Compare this map with the map on page 323. **What territory did the Byzantine Empire lose between 565 and 1453?**

MAKING CONNECTIONS

➤➤ **History** The Byzantine court became so poor as the empire declined that at the marriage feast of Emperor John V, food was served in clay vessels. No gold or silver items appeared on the table.

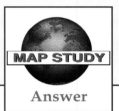

MAP STUDY

Answer

parts of Spain, North Africa, Italy, Macedonia, and Egypt

GEOGRAPHY AND HISTORY

By A.D. 700 the Byzantine Empire was reduced to the territories that were primarily Greek. The loss of the non-Greek lands actually helped strengthen the empire because it now had one religion, one language, and one culture.

EXTENDING THE CONTENT

The Church of Holy Wisdom, or Hagia Sophia, was such a miracle of architecture that legend said an angel had given Justinian directions for building it. Its architects were actually two Greeks from Asia Minor. The remarkable engineering of the broad central dome and the brilliant reds, blues, and greens of the interior are still amazing nearly 1,500 years after their construction. The floor mosaics are rich marble and the wall mosaics are glittering glass.

Check for Understanding

Ask students to summarize the main points of the chapter. Discuss the answers to the Section and Chapter Assessment questions.

Evaluate

Assign Chapter 21 **Performance Assessment Activity** in the TCR.

Administer **Chapter 21 Test** in the TCR. Testmaker available.

Reteach

Ask students to make lists of the key elements of Byzantine culture during Emperor Justinian's rule.

Assign Chapter 21 **Reteaching Activity** in the TCR.

Enrich

Have students prepare a report about the Turkish attack on Constantinople in 1453.

Assign Chapter 21 **Enrichment Activity** in the TCR.

Have students list the achievements of the Byzantine Empire and rank them in order of importance. Have students explain their rankings.

💾 Use **Interactive Tutor Self-Assessment Software** to review Section 4.

Self-Check Quiz gives students an interactive chapter tutorial. Have them access *Chapter 21 Quiz* at humanheritage.glencoe.com

---

The population dropped to less than 100,000. Docks and marketplaces stood empty. Even the emperors were poor. When Turkish armies with guns and gunpowder attacked Constantinople in 1453, they easily conquered the Byzantines.

Section 4 Assessment

1. What problems within the Byzantine Empire helped bring about its decline?
2. What outside forces helped cause the empire's downfall?

Critical Thinking

3. **Demonstrating Reasoned Judgment** Do you think the Byzantine emperor was wise in asking Venice for help against the Vikings? Why or why not?

Graphic Organizer Activity

4. Draw this diagram, and use it to show Byzantine contributions to world civilization.

Byzantine Contributions

Chapter Summary & Study Guide

1. Around 330, Constantine moved the capital of the Roman Empire to Constantinople, the site of the old Greek city of Byzantium.
2. After the fall of Rome, the Roman Empire in the East became known as the Byzantine Empire.
3. Although Constantine patterned much of life in Constantinople after Rome, his acceptance of Christianity also helped shape the city.
4. When Justinian became emperor in 527, he was influenced in some of his decisions by the empress Theodora, who favored increased women's rights.
5. Two of Justinian's greatest achievements were development of a system of law known as the Justinian Code and construction of Hagia Sophia.
6. Under Justinian, Belisarius reorganized the Byzantine army and expanded the empire's borders.
7. Relations between the Pope and the Patriarch were weakened by the argument over icons, by the Patriarch's refusal to recognize the Pope as the head of the Church, and by the Pope's crowning of Charlemagne as emperor.
8. Both internal problems and outside forces weakened the Byzantine Empire, which was conquered by Turkish armies in 1453.

Self-Check Quiz

Visit the *Human Heritage* Web site at **humanheritage.glencoe.com** and click on *Chapter 21—Self-Check Quiz* to assess your understanding of this chapter.

Section 4 Assessment Answers

1. The emperor stopped protecting farmers from rich landlords; aristocrats then took over the farmers' properties, and the farmers lost their loyalty.

2. Venetian merchants gained control of most of the empire's trade, and the empire was attacked by Christians and Muslims.

3. Answers will vary but could include that it was wise because the Byzantine Empire could not defend itself against the Vikings; or that it was unwise because it led to the Venetian control of most of the empire's trade.

4. Sample contributions: established Constantinople, preserved Greek culture, preserved Roman law, spread Christianity to peoples in the East, spurred the growth of trade, developed new techniques in art

Assign Chapter 21 **Section 4 Quiz** in the TCR. Testmaker available.

Using Key Terms

You live in ancient Byzantium and are asked to write a paragraph describing your culture. Your paragraph is to be put in a time capsule to be opened by a future generation. Write your paragraph, including the following words.

relics   theology   dowry
mosaics   Greek fire   metropolitans
icons

Understanding Main Ideas

1. Why did the Roman Empire in the East survive the fall of Rome?
2. How did Constantinople's location help it become a great trading center?
3. How did Christianity affect Byzantine attitudes toward the care of needy people?
4. How did Theodora help women within the Byzantine Empire?
5. What led to the separation of the Eastern Orthodox Church and the Roman Catholic Church in 1054?
6. Why did Byzantine farmers gradually lose their loyalty to the empire?

Critical Thinking

1. What is your opinion of the following statement: "Constantine was wise to model Constantinople after Rome"?
2. What are the advantages for a government to have an offical religion? What are the disadvantages?
3. What do you think had the most to do with the decline of the Byzantine Empire? Explain.
4. What contribution made by the Byzantines do you think was the most important? Explain.

Graphic Organizer Activity

Citizenship Create a chart like the one shown, and use it to show the causes and effects of Justinian's decision to draw up a new code of laws.

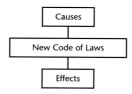

Geography in History

Movement Justinian expanded his empire greatly. Refer to the map on page 323. If you had been Justinian, in which direction would you have sent troops next to gain new territory? Why?

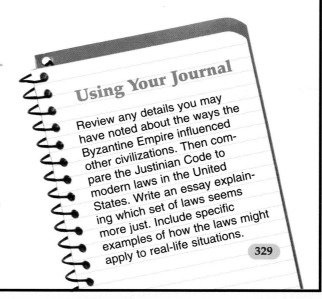

Using Your Journal

Review any details you may have noted about the ways the Byzantine Empire influenced other civilizations. Then compare the Justinian Code to modern laws in the United States. Write an essay explaining which set of laws seems more just. Include specific examples of how the laws might apply to real-life situations.

329

Bonus Test Question

For Chapter 21 Test
Imagine you were a citizen of Constantinople during the Byzantine Empire and you met a man named Cyril, about whom everyone was talking. What were people saying about this man?

Using Your Journal

Essays will vary but should include references to specific laws. You might call on volunteers to read their essays to the class and have the class weigh the comparison.

Geography in History

Answers will vary but should reflect a logical plan for avoiding geographical features that might make an invasion difficult.

Assessment Answers

Using Key Terms

Paragraphs will vary, but should use descriptive phrases and all the key terms.

Understanding Main Ideas

1. Most Christians were united; Constantinople was strong and supported a large army and paid invaders.
2. gave Constantinople control of the sea trade to the Mediterranean and a key land route
3. The Byzantines formed organizations to care for the poor.
4. She convinced Justinian to allow a wife to own land and widows to raise children.
5. disputes over icons and the power of the Pope
6. because the emperor no longer helped protect them

Critical Thinking

1. Answers will vary but students should support opinions.
2. Answers will vary. An advantage might be that it would end conflict. A disadvantage is that it would end freedom of religion.
3. Answers will vary but could include loss of trade and invasions.
4. Answers will vary.

Graphic Organizer Activity

Sample responses: *causes*—Justinian's interest in law, disorganization and complication of old laws; *effects*—summarized Roman legal thinking, provided later generations with an insight into the basic ideas of Roman law, had an impact on the legal systems of almost every western country

Chapter 22 Planning Guide

Objectives	Reproducible Resources	Multimedia Resources
Section 1 **Islam** Explain how Islam developed around the teachings of Muhammad and the religious beliefs held by Muslims.	Reproducible Lesson Plan Chapter 22 Vocabulary and Guided Reading Activity Reading Essentials and Study Guide 22-1 Chapter 22 Enrichment Activity Section 1 Quiz	**ABCNEWS INTERACTIVE** Turning Points in World History Teaching Transparency and Activity 22A Vocabulary PuzzleMaker Interactive Tutor Self-Assessment Software ExamView® Pro Testmaker Glencoe Skillbuilder Interactive Workbook, Level 1 Presentation Plus !
Section 2 **The Arab Empire** Describe how Islam spread beyond the Arabian Peninsula and what Islamic life was like.	Reproducible Lesson Plan Reading Essentials and Study Guide 22-2 Chapter 22 Cooperative Learning Activity Chapter 22 Chart and Graph Skill Activity Chapter 22 Geography and Map Activity Section 2 Quiz	Teaching Transparency and Activity 22B Vocabulary PuzzleMaker Interactive Tutor Self-Assessment Software ExamView® Pro Testmaker Glencoe Skillbuilder Interactive Workbook, Level 1
Section 3 **Arab Contributions** Discuss what ideas and inventions the Arab Empire contributed to science, mathematics, medicine, and the arts.	Reproducible Lesson Plan Reading Essentials and Study Guide 22-3 Chapter 22 Activity Book Activity Unit 7 World Literature Reading 1 Section 3 Quiz	Vocabulary PuzzleMaker Interactive Tutor Self-Assessment Software ExamView® Pro Testmaker Glencoe Skillbuilder Interactive Workbook, Level 1
Chapter 22 **Review and Evaluation**	Chapter 22 Reteaching Activity Chapter 22 Performance Assessment Activity Spanish Chapter Summary and Glossary Chapter 22 Test	Vocabulary PuzzleMaker Interactive Tutor Self-Assessment Software Glencoe Skillbuilder Interactive Workbook, Level 1 Audiocassettes* ExamView® Pro Testmaker

*Also available in Spanish.

Presentation Plus!

Use Glencoe's **Presentation Plus!** multimedia teacher tool to easily present dynamic lessons that visually excite your students. Using Microsoft® PowerPoint, you can customize the presentations to create your own personalized lessons.

 Interactive Lesson Planner

Planning has never been easier! Using this CD-ROM, organize your week, month, semester, or year with all the help you need. The **Interactive Lesson Planner** gives you access to all of the blackline masters which accompany *Human Heritage.*

✓ PERFORMANCE ASSESSMENT ACTIVITIES

Sharing Religion   Have students research Muslim celebrations other than Ramadan. Suggest they choose either a religious or national holiday to describe in an oral presentation. Encourage students to include visuals displays.

CHAPTER RESOURCES

LITERATURE ABOUT THE PERIOD

Arnold, T.W. and A. Guillame. *The Legacy of Islam.* Gordon Press, 1976.

READINGS FOR THE STUDENT

Powell, Anton. *The Rise of Islam.* Warwick Press, 1980. An overview of Islamic culture.

READINGS FOR THE TEACHER

Editors of Time-Life Books. *What Life Was Like in the Land of the Prophet: Islamic World* A.D. *570–1405.* Time-Life Books, 1999. Richly illustrated story of life in the medieval Islamic world.

Mahmud, S.F. *A Short History of Islam.* Oxford University Press, 1989. A study of Islamic civilization and a history of the Islamic Empire.

KEY TO ABILITY LEVELS

Teaching strategies have been coded for varying learning styles and abilities.

L1 Level 1 activities are **basic** activities and should be within the ability range of all students.

L2 Level 2 activities are **average** activities and should be within the ability range of the average to above-average student.

L3 Level 3 activities are **challenging** activities designed for the ability range of above-average students.

ELL ELL activities should be within the ability range of English Language Learning students.

NATIONAL GEOGRAPHIC SOCIETY   Teacher's Corner

INDEX TO NATIONAL GEOGRAPHIC MAGAZINE

The following articles relate to this chapter:

- "Tale of Three Cities," by Joel Swerdlow, August 1999.
- "Petra, Ancient City of Stone," by Don Belt, December 1998.
- "The Promise of Pakistan," by John McCarry, October 1997.
- "India," by Geoffrey C. Ward, May 1997.
- "Morocco," by Erla Zwingle, October 1996.
- "Syria Behind the Mask," by Peter Theroux, July 1996.
- "The Fractured Caucasus," by Mike Edwards, February 1996.

NATIONAL GEOGRAPHIC SOCIETY PRODUCTS AVAILABLE FROM GLENCOE

To order the following, call Glencoe at 1-800-334-7344:

- *MapPack: Asia (Transparency Maps)*
- *PicturePack: Physical Geography of the World (Transparencies)*

ADDITIONAL NATIONAL GEOGRAPHIC SOCIETY PRODUCTS

To order the following, call National Geographic at 1-800-368-2728:

- *Arabia: Sand, Sea, and Sky (Video)*
- *Asia (Laminated Desk Maps)*
- *The Soul of Spain (Video)*
- *National Geographic Atlas of World History (Book)*
- *Wonders of the Ancient World: National Geographic Atlas of Archaeology (Book)*

Access *National Geographic's* new dynamic MapMachine Web site and other geography resources at:
http://www.nationalgeographic.com/
http://www.nationalgeographic.com/maps

The following videotape program is available from Glencoe:

- **Legends of the Arabian Knights**
  0-7670-0232-6

To order, call Glencoe at 1-800-334-7344. To find classroom resources to accompany many of these videos, check the following home pages:

A&E Television: http://www.aetv.com
The History Channel: http://www.historychannel.com

OVERVIEW

Chapter 22 discusses the rise of Islam and its central role in the creation of the Arab Empire.

➤ **Section 1** describes the rise of Islam.

➤ **Section 2** discusses the formation of the Arab Empire and the spread of Islam.

➤ **Section 3** describes the Arab contributions to world civilizations.

CHAPTER OBJECTIVES

After reading Chapter 22, students will be able to:

1. explain the teachings of Muhammad.

2. discuss the religious beliefs held by Muslims.

3. describe how Islam spread beyond the Arabian Peninsula.

4. describe Arab contributions to science, mathematics, medicine, and the arts.

EXAMINING ARTIFACTS

Point out that Islamic beliefs forbade artists from trying to capture living creatures in their work. Nobody, said Muslim Arabs, could recreate the work of God. Call on students to describe the artistic techniques developed to replace representational art. *(Students should note the use of geometric patterns, bright color, beautiful calligraphy, and so on.)* Tell students that they will learn more about the beliefs and accomplishments of Muslim Arabs in this chapter.

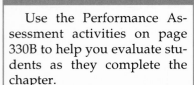

PERFORMANCE ASSESSMENT ✓

Use the Performance Assessment activities on page 330B to help you evaluate students as they complete the chapter.

CHAPTER 22

The Spread of Islam
500 A.D.–1300 A.D.

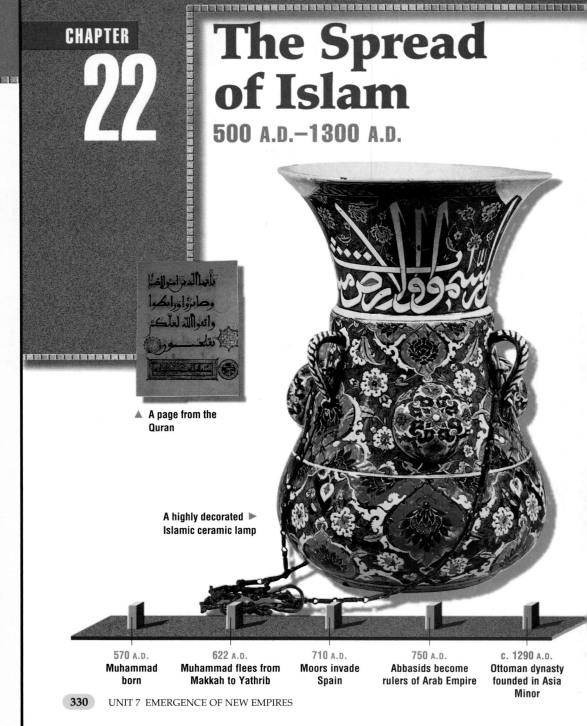

▲ **A page from the Quran**

A highly decorated ▶ Islamic ceramic lamp

| 570 A.D.
Muhammad born | 622 A.D.
Muhammad flees from Makkah to Yathrib | 710 A.D.
Moors invade Spain | 750 A.D.
Abbasids become rulers of Arab Empire | c. 1290 A.D.
Ottoman dynasty founded in Asia Minor |

TEACHING RESOURCES

TEACHER PLANNING AND SUPPORT

🗁 Reproducible Lesson Plan
🗁 Block Scheduling Implementation Guide
🗁 Videodisc Bar Code Correlation
💿 Presentation Plus!

REVIEW AND REINFORCEMENT

🗁 Reading Essentials and Study Guide 22-1, 22-2, 22-3
🗁 Chapter 22 Vocabulary and Guided Reading Activity
💾 Vocabulary PuzzleMaker Software
📖 Teaching Transparencies 22A & 22B
🗁 Chapter 22 Reteaching Activity

🗁 Chapter 22 Cooperative Learning Activity
🗁 Chapter 22 Activity Book Activity
🗁 Chapter 22 Chart and Graph Skill Activity
💾 Interactive Tutor Self-Assessment Software

APPLICATION AND HANDS-ON ACTIVITIES

🗂 Daily World History, Geography, and Culture Question
🗂 World History Game Card 9

GEOGRAPHY ACTIVITIES

🗁 Chapter 22 Geography and Map Activity
🗁 Social Studies Outline Map Resource Book

Chapter Focus

Read to Discover

- How Islam developed around the teachings of Muhammad.
- What religious beliefs are held by Muslims.
- How Islam spread beyond the Arabian Peninsula.
- What early Islamic life was like.
- What the Arab Empire contributed to science, mathematics, medicine, and the arts.

Terms to Learn	People to Know	Places to Locate
pillars of faith	Muhammad	Makkah
mosque	al-Idrisi	Madina (Yathrib)
imam	ar-Rāzi	Damascus
hajj	Omar Khayyám	Baghdad
alchemists	Ibn Khaldum	

Why It's Important Between the northeast coast of Africa and central Asia lies the Arabian Peninsula. The people who live there are known as Arabs. At one time, most were Bedouins (bed' uh wuhnz). They were herders who roamed the desert in search of grass and water for their camels, goats, and sheep. They lived in tents woven from camel or goat hair.

Bedouin warriors during the 600s raided other peoples and fought one another over pastures and springs. They valued their camels and swords above all else. They enjoyed poetry and music. They believed in many gods.

In the 600s, a religion called Islam (is' luhm) began in the mountainous area of western Arabia known as the Hejaz (hej az'). Within 100 years, an Arab empire based on Islamic beliefs had developed. It controlled an area larger than that of the Roman Empire.

HISTORY Online

Chapter Overview

Visit the *Human Heritage* Web site at <u>humanheritage.glencoe.com</u> and click on ***Chapter 22— Chapter Overviews*** to preview this chapter.

SECTION 1   Islam

The word "Islam" is an Arabic word. It means "the act of submitting, or giving oneself over, to the will of God." The Islamic faith was founded by an Arab merchant named Muhammad (mō ham' id). Muhammad came to be known as the prophet of Allah (ahl' uh). The word "Allah" is an Arabic word meaning

---

INTERDISCIPLINARY CONNECTIONS

- Unit 7 World Literature Reading 1
- World History and Art Transparency 47, *Mihrab*
- World Music: Cultural Traditions

ENRICHMENT AND EXTENSION

- Chapter 22 Enrichment Activity
- World History Primary Source Document Library CD-ROM
- ABCNEWS INTERACTIVE Turning Points in World History
- Foods Around the World

ASSESSMENT AND EVALUATION

- Chapter 22 Performance Assessment Activity
- Chapter 22 Section Quizzes 22-1, 22-2, 22-3
- Chapter 22 Test
- Chapter 22 ExamView® Pro Testmaker Software
- Chapter 22 Digests Audiocassettes Activities and Tests

SPANISH RESOURCES

- Chapter 22 Spanish Chapter Summary and Glossary
- Chapter 22 Spanish Chapter Digests Audiocassettes Activities and Tests

---

HISTORY Online

Chapter Overview introduces students to chapter content and key terms. Have them access ***Chapter 22 Overview*** at <u>humanheritage.glencoe.com</u>

FOCUS

Bellringer

Write this sentence on the board: *The Islamic civilization of 600 to 1300 A.D. has had a great influence on present-day civilizations.* Have students respond by writing *true* or *false* and giving a reason for their choice.

Motivational Activity

Have students read their responses to the sentence regarding whether the Islamic civilization of 600 to 1300 A.D. influenced present-day civilizations. Tell students that Chapter 22 describes how the Muslim Arabs developed ideas and inventions that eventually spread around the world.

GUIDE TO READING

Reading Strategy

Ask students to read "Why It's Important" and summarize the chapter's main theme. *(The Islamic religion started on the Arab Peninsula and eventually spread over an area larger than the Roman Empire.)*

Vocabulary Precheck

Ask students to define each of the "Terms to Learn." Have a volunteer consult the dictionary for any unfamiliar words. **L1** **ELL**

Use the Vocabulary PuzzleMaker for Chapter 22 to create a crossword puzzle. **L1**

Assign Chapter 22 Vocabulary and Guided Reading Activity.

Assign Reading Essentials and Study Guide 22-1.

Guided Practice

L1 **Geography: Place** On a physical wall map of the world point out the Arabian Peninsula to the students. Explain that it is the largest peninsula in the world. Ask students to name the physical features on the Arabian Peninsula. *(deserts and mountains)* Explain that although this peninsula is part of Asia it is usually referred to as part of a region called the Middle East. **ELL**

✓ Reading Check Answer
Arab **pilgrims** traveled to Makkah to worship at the *Ka'bah.*

MAKING CONNECTIONS

➤➤ **Religion** Muslims believe that Arabs are descendants of Abraham's son Ishmael and that Jews are descendants of Abraham's son Isaac.

DID YOU KNOW ??
It was not unusual during Muhammad's time for a person to retreat somewhere to solve problems. Both Moses and Jesus had done the same thing many hundreds of years earlier.

✓ Reading Check
Why did Arab **pilgrims** travel to Makkah?

People in History

Muhammad
570 A.D.–632 A.D.

Prophet of Islam

Muhammad is one of the great figures in world history. His revelations and teachings form the basis of Islam, a faith that now claims more than one billion followers. While living in Yathrib (Madina), he established a model for future Islamic states in which religious leaders oversee government. His appeal for Islamic unity helped Muhammad to extend his Islamic state to the entire Arabian Peninsula.

"the God." Muhammad called those who followed his faith Muslims, which means "followers of Islam."

Islam shook the foundations of Byzantium and Persia, the two most powerful civilizations of the time. It brought into its fold people from different races and continents. It came to shape a way of life for one of every seven persons on Earth.

Makkah (Mecca) By the middle of the 500s, three major towns had developed in the Hejaz. They were Yathrib (yath' ruhb), Ta' if (tah' if), and Makkah (mak' uh). Of the three, Makkah was the largest and the richest.

Makkah was supported by trade and religion. Traders stopped there for food and water on their way north to Constantinople. Arab **pilgrims,** or travelers to a religious shrine, came there to worship. Arabia's holiest shrine, the *Ka'bah* (kah' buh), stood in the center of Makkah. It was a low, cube-shaped building surrounded by 360 idols. A black stone believed to have fallen from paradise was set in one of its walls. Nearby was a holy well.

Muslims believe that the Ka'bah was first built by Adam. Later, Abraham and his son, Ishmael, together rebuilt it. They had dedicated it to the worship of the one God. Later, however, people filled it with idols that represented the gods and goddesses of different tribes.

Muhammad In 570, Muhammad was born to a widow of a respectable clan in Makkah. When he was six years old, his mother died, and he went to live with an uncle. When he reached his teens, he began working as a business person. At the age of 25, he married a rich 40-year-old widow named Khad'juh (kahd' yuh).

Muhammad was very successful in the caravan business. He was troubled, however, by the drinking, gambling, and corruption in Makkah. He began spending much time alone in a cave on a hillside outside the city. There, he thought and fasted. He decided that the people of Makkah had been led into evil by their belief in false gods. He concluded that there was only one God, Allah, the same god as the God of the Jews and the Christians.

In 610, Muhammad had a *revelation,* or vision. It is said that, when he was meditating in the cave, an angel appeared and ordered him to read some writing. According to Muslim tradition, he heard the voice of the angel Gabriel (gā' brē uhl) telling him to preach about God. Muhammad told Khad'juh what had happened. She went to see a holy man, hoping he could explain the meaning of Muhammad's story. The holy man told her that the heavenly visitor was the same one who had visited Moses and other prophets and that Muhammad was to be the prophet of his people.

MULTICULTURAL PERSPECTIVES

Before the founding of Islam, some Arabs followed the two earlier monotheistic religions, Judaism and Christianity. Most, however, carried idols of wood or stone with them and also traveled to worship at holy places or caves or wells.

Makkah, a crossroads for caravans from Egypt, Palestine, and the Persian Gulf, had holy places and many idols. Traders stopped there to pray for safe journey or to give thanks for having reached the city safe from robbers or desert storms.

Student Web Activity
Visit the *Human Heritage* Web site at
humanheritage.glencoe.com
and click on **Chapter 22—**
Student Web Activities to find
out more about the Islamic faith.

KA' BAH SHRINE   Modern Muslim pilgrims travel to Makkah to pray facing the shrine called the Ka' bah. It is considered a very holy place. **Who do Muslims believe first built the Ka' bah?**

In 613, Muhammad began to preach to the people of Makkah. He told them that there is only one God, Allah, before whom all believers are equal. He urged the rich to share with the poor. Muhammad saw life as a preparation for the Day of Judgment, or the day on which people would rise from the dead to be judged for their actions on Earth.

At first, the rich leaders of Makkah laughed at Muhammad. As he continued to preach, however, they began to feel threatened. They were afraid that people would stop coming to Makkah to worship at the Ka'bah. When pilgrims visited Makkah, they spent money on meals and clothing. The leaders thought that if fewer pilgrims came to Makkah, the city's economy would be ruined. Then, the leaders would no longer be rich. Because of this fear, they started persecuting Muhammad and his followers.

In 620, Muhammad preached to a group of pilgrims from Yathrib. They invited him to come there and be their leader. During the summer of 622, he and several hundred of his followers fled from Makkah to Yathrib. The year 622, called *Anno Hijrah* (an' ō hi jī' ruh), or "Year of the Migration," became the first year of the Muslim calendar. The city of Yathrib was renamed Madinat al-Nabi, "the city of the prophet," or Madina.

In Madina, Muhammad proved himself an able leader. He gave the people a government that united them and made them

Calendars The Islamic calendar, started in 622, is a lunar calendar with 354 days divided into 12 months. The Muslim Era, which counts years from the *Hijrah,* is used officially in Saudi Arabia, Yemen, and the Persian Gulf states. Even in Muslim countries that officially use the Gregorian calendar, many people follow the Muslim calendar at home.

EXTENDING THE CONTENT

The black rock housed in the *Ka'bah* was, most likely, a meteorite. Arabs believed that Abraham had built the first temple around the rock. Similarly, Makkah's holy spring or well, called Zamzam, was associated with the flight into the desert of Hagar, Abraham's handmaiden, and their son Ishmael. The well's miraculous appearance (perhaps with the aid of the angel Gabriel) saved their lives and allowed Ishmael to find the Arabic peoples. These legends gave the Arabs and the Jews a common ancestor, Abraham.

CAPTION ANSWER

It was built by Adam and then rebuilt by Abraham and Ishmael.

LINKING PAST TO PRESENT

A *Kiswah* is the black cloth that covers *Ka'bah*. It is embroidered in gold thread with verses from the Quran and is replaced each year. Formerly made in Egypt and carried by pilgrims to Makkah, the *Kiswah* is now made in a special Saudi Arabian government factory in Makkah.

ABCNEWS INTERACTIVE™

VIDEODISC
Turning Points in World History

Side One
Chapter 9

Title: *Ted Koppel: Three Religions*
Subject: Introduction to Islam, Christianity, and Judaism
Ask: What is the hajj?
(annual pilgrimage to Makkah)

Geography: Human/Environmental Interaction Have students locate the cities of Makkah, Yathrib, and Ta'if on the map of Muhammad's Arabia. Have them use the map scale to calculate the approximate distances between these cities. **ELL**

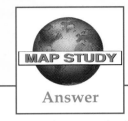

MAP STUDY

Answer

50 miles (or 80.45 km)

DID YOU KNOW ??

Muhammad's tomb is located in the Prophet's Mosque in Madina.

MAKING CONNECTIONS

➤➤ **Language** *Quran* means the reading, or that which is to be read. Its final version, put together in 655, contains 144 suras, or chapters.

MAP STUDY

LOCATION Yathrib was an oasis of farms, Ta'if was a mountain refuge, and Makkah was a crossroads for trade. **About how many miles (km) inland from the Red Sea was Makkah located?**

Then... & Now

The Quran As Muhammad preached, his followers wrote down or memorized his teachings. After Muhammad's death, his successor Abu Bakr ordered Muslims to retrieve those teachings wherever they could be found. It took 20 years to compile the teachings into the Quran, the Muslim scriptures followed today.

Muhammad's Arabia

proud of their new faith. The people of Makkah were very angry with Muhammad's success in Madina. With far superior armies they invaded Madina several times to crush the newly established Muslim community. The Muslims defended their city with great courage every time. In 628, Muhammad signed a peace treaty with the people of Makkah, which they violated in 630. It was in that year that Muhammad and his companions triumphantly entered their home city, Makkah. Their conquest was peaceful. Muhammad issued general forgiveness to all who had persecuted and opposed him. Within two years, all the tribes of Arabia declared their faith in Islam and their loyalty to Muhammad. In 632 Muhammad died.

The Quran At the heart of Islam is the Quran (ko ran'), or Muslim scriptures. Muslims believe it is the direct word of God as revealed to Muhammad. For this reason, they feel they should follow it exactly.

The Quran is written in Arabic. It tells how good Muslims should live. They should not eat pork, drink liquor, or gamble. The Quran also gives advice on marriage, divorce, inheritance, and business.

334 UNIT 7 EMERGENCE OF NEW EMPIRES

EXTENDING THE CONTENT

According to Muslim tradition, the angel Gabriel revealed divine messages to Muhammad over a 22-year period. Faithful Muslims wrote down or memorized these messages, but they were not compiled into one written collection until after Muhammad died. Then his successor, Abu Bakr, ordered Muslims to retrieve these messages from wherever they could be found, from the "ribs of palm-leaves and tablets of white stone and from the breasts of men." It took 20 years before the messages were compiled into the Quran.

The Quran describes the **pillars of faith,** or the five duties all Muslims must fulfill. The first duty is the confession of faith. All Muslims must recite the Islamic creed that states, "There is no God but Allah, and Muhammad is his prophet."

The second duty deals with prayer. Muslims must pray five times a day, facing Makkah each time. The prayers are said at dawn, noon, late afternoon, sunset, and evening. The prayers can be said anywhere. The only exception is the Friday noon prayer. It is usually recited at a **mosque** (mosk), or Muslim house of worship. There, believers are led by an **imam** (i mam'), or prayer leader.

The third duty has to do with the giving of *zakah,* or charity. This is a donation that every Muslim has to give at the rate of 2.5 percent of his or her annual savings. It can be given to needy people or to institutions that are involved in education and social services.

Reading Check
What are the **pillars of faith?**

Reading Check
What is a **mosque,** and what does an **imam** do there? What action is called for in the giving of *zakah?*

ISLAMIC FAITH Muslims learn the teachings of the Quran at an early age. A child in the photograph (left) studies passages from the Quran. From the prayer tower (right) of each mosque, announcers call the people to prayer. **What are the five duties that all Muslims must fulfill, called?**

Reading Check Answer
The **pillars of faith** are five duties that all Muslims must fulfill.

Reading Check Answer
A **mosque** is a Muslim house of worship, and an **imam** is the prayer leader at a mosque.
The *zakah* calls upon Muslims to give donations at a rate of 2.5 percent of his or her annual savings.

MAKING CONNECTIONS

➤➤ **Religion** Until the Muslims took Makkah and made it their holy city, prayers were said facing Jerusalem. To offer a prayer, a Muslim kneels, bows, and touches the forehead to the ground as a symbol of submitting to God.

CAPTION ANSWER

the pillars of faith

DID YOU KNOW

Arabic, the language of the Quran, belongs to the Semitic language group. Although no one knows for sure when the language developed, it is known from poets writing before the time of Muhammad that it had reached its present stage 100 years before the prophet was born.

MULTICULTURAL PERSPECTIVES

Up until the 1800s, there were three main caravans to Makkah. One caravan formed in Damascus, Syria, and moved south by way of Madina, and reached Makkah in about 30 days. When Constantinople was captured by the Ottoman Turks in 1453, this caravan started in Constantinople and then went through Damascus to Makkah. Along the way, pilgrims throughout Asia Minor joined the caravan. A second caravan assembled in Cairo and crossed the Sinai Peninsula following the coastal plain of western Arabia to Makkah. This journey took from 30 to 45 days and included pilgrims from North Africa. A third much more sizable caravan crossed the peninsula from Baghdad.

Reading Check Answer
In a *hajj*, a Muslim must travel to Makkah, where Muslims from all over the world go to gather two months after Ramadan.

💾 Use **Interactive Tutor Self-Assessment Software** to review Section 1.

L2 **Geography: Movement** Discuss the spread of Islamic influence beyond the Arabian Peninsula. Have students use the map on page 337 and a map of the world to identify the modern countries that were partially or totally included in the Arab Empire. **ELL**

Reading Check Answer
A **caliph** is one of the successors of Muhammad who leads Muslims in the practice of their faith. The first caliph was Abu Bakr, Muhammad's father-in-law.

💾 Use the **Vocabulary Puzzle-Maker** to create crossword and word search puzzles.

The fourth duty deals with fasting. The young, sick people, pregnant women, and travelers do not have to fast. Everyone else, however, must fast each year during the daylight hours of the holy month of Ramadan (ram' uh dahn).

The fifth duty involves a pilgrimage. Each able Muslim, at least once in his or her lifetime, must travel to Makkah two months after Ramadan. The journey is called the *hajj* (haj). For three days, Muslims from all over the world come together for ceremonies and sacrifice.

The Quran promises that all believers who fulfill their duties will go to Paradise, which has shade, fruit trees, beautiful flower gardens, cold springs, and singing birds. Hell is a flame-filled pit where drinking water comes from a salty well and where food is a strong-smelling plant that causes hunger.

✔ **Reading Check** What religious duty is performed in the *hajj*?

Section 1 Assessment

1. **Define:** pilgrims, pillars of faith, mosque, imam, *zakah*, hajj.
2. According to Muslim tradition, what caused Muhammad to begin his preachings?
3. What does the Quran say will happen after death?

Critical Thinking

4. **Identifying Cause and Effect** What effect did the rise of Islam have on Byzantium and Persia?

Graphic Organizer Activity

5. Draw this diagram, and use it to summarize the five pillars of faith.

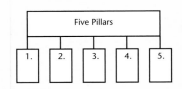

SECTION 2 The Arab Empire

When Muhammad died in 632, his followers needed a new leader. Without someone to guide them, the community could have broken up, and the faith could have been lost. A group of Muslims chose a new leader whom they called *khalifa*, or **caliph** (kā'lif), which means "successor."

✔ **Reading Check** What is a **caliph**, and who was the first caliph chosen?

The Rightly Guided Caliphs   The first caliph was Abu Bakr (uh bū' bak' uhr), Muhammad's father-in-law and close friend. Bakr and the next three caliphs were elected for life. These caliphs ruled from Madina. They kept in close touch with the people and asked advice of their most trusted friends. For this reason, they were called the Rightly Guided Caliphs.

The Rightly Guided Caliphs honored Muhammad's wish to carry Islam to other peoples. They sent warriors into Palestine, Syria, Iraq, Persia, Egypt, and North Africa. Throughout all these places, the Arabs were victorious.

The Arabs were successful for many reasons. Islam held them together. They were united in striving for a common goal which they considered holy—to carry Islam to other people. This helped them to fight against tyranny and oppression. It also helped them earn an eternal place in Paradise after death. It helped them to fight against tyranny and oppression. Arab leaders were mentally and physically tough. They planned and carried out attacks. They also handled their camels and horses with great skill.

The Arab way of treating the people they conquered also contributed to their success. Those who gave in without a fight had to pay taxes. In return, the Arabs protected them and allowed them to keep their land. Those who fought and were defeated not only had to pay taxes, but also lost their land.

The Umayyads   Ali, Muhammad's son-in-law and the last of the Rightly Guided Caliphs, was killed in 661. Mu'awiya (mū uh' wi yuh), the new caliph, moved the capital from Madina to Damascus and founded the Umayyad (ū mī' yuhd) Dynasty. From that time on, the title of caliph was hereditary.

MAP STUDY

LOCATION By 750 the Muslims ruled a vast empire that extended from the Atlantic Ocean to the Indus River. **Which caliphs added most of the territory in Asia?**

LINKING PAST TO PRESENT

The schism that developed in Islam in the A.D. 600s persists today. It was seen in the war between Iran and Iraq that began in 1980. Then many Westerners heard the term *jihad* for the first time.

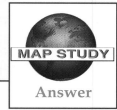

MAP STUDY

Answer

the Rightly Guided Caliphs

Assign Chapter 22 **Geography and Map Activity** in the TCR.

The Expansion of Islam

At Death of Muhammad, 632

Under Rightly Guided Caliphs, 632–661

Under Umayad Caliphs, 661–750

Byzantine Empire, 750

miles 0   500   1000
kilometers 0   500   1000   1500

MEETING SPECIAL NEEDS

Ask students with strong organizational skills to work in small groups with students who are having difficulty tracking the expansion of Islam. Ask the groups to create descriptive outlines that show the spread of this religion. Remind students to include the succession of leaders of the Arab Empire that coincided with major events.

⬭ Refer to *Inclusion for the Middle School Social Studies Classroom: Strategies and Activities* for additional resources.

LINKING PAST TO PRESENT

Shi'ite means party or faction in Arabic. The Shi'ites form the largest sect of the Islamic religion, numbering about 20 million. Most of them live in Iran.

L1 **Language Arts** Tell students that many words of Arabic origin have become part of the English language. Have students look up definitions of the following words in the dictionary and write the Arabic word from which each was derived: orange *(naranj)*, giraffe *(zirafah)*, syrup *(sharab)*, sofa *(suffah)*, and muslin *(mawsiliy)*.

✓ Reading Check Answer

As chief advisor to the Abbasid emperor, the **vizier** stood between the throne and the people, taking charge of the administration of the empire and the selection of governors for the provinces.

The Bazaar Muslim merchants traded their wares in the *bazaar*, originally the term for Persian public markets. The name came to be used for colorful outdoor marketplaces throughout the Middle East and North Africa. In English today, *bazaar* means a store that sells many kinds of goods.

✓ Reading Check

What was the role of the **vizier?**

The Umayyads ruled more like kings than religious leaders. They reorganized the government and made Arabic the official language. They minted the first Arab money. They set up horseback postal routes. They repaired and maintained irrigation canals. They also built beautiful mosques and encouraged the arts.

Many of these changes helped the people of the empire. However, the Umayyads had social and economic troubles that, in the end, led to their downfall. The conquered people who became Muslim complained that they were not treated the same as those who were born Muslim. They received less money for serving in the army. They also had to pay higher taxes.

The Muslims themselves divided into two groups. The smaller group was called the Shi'ah (shē' ah). Its followers, called Shi'ites (shē' īts), believed the office of caliph should be held only by descendants of Ali. The larger group, called the Sunni (sun' nē), followed the Rightly Guided Caliphs and the caliphs after them. After a while, war broke out between the Umayyads and a group of Muslims called Abbasids (uh' bas uhdz). In 750, the Abbasids defeated the Umayyads. They then became the new rulers of the Arab Empire.

The Abbasids The Abbasids ruled the Arab Empire from 750 to 1258. Their first 100 years in power was known as the Golden Age of Islam.

The Abbasids built a new capital called Baghdad (bag' dad) on the east bank of the Tigris River. The city was designed by a Jewish astronomer and a Persian engineer. Over 100,000 people worked four years to build it.

Baghdad was built in the shape of a circle. Around it were three huge, sloping brick walls and a deep *moat*, or wide ditch filled with water. Each wall had four large gates linked together by two highways that crossed in the center of the city. At that point stood the great mosque and the caliph's magnificent palace. A number of public officials had luxurious homes there also. The highways divided Baghdad into four pie-shaped sections. From the gates, each highway led to a different part of the empire.

Under the Abbasids, all that remained of Arab influence was the Arabic language and the Islamic religion. The name Arab no longer meant only a person from Arabia. It meant any subject of the empire who spoke Arabic.

The Abbasids created the government post of **vizier** (vi zir'), or chief adviser. The person serving as vizier stood between the throne and the people. He took charge of running the empire and chose the governors of the provinces.

The Abbasids did not try to conquer new lands. Instead, they made Baghdad one of the major trading centers of the world. Improved trade between countries led to a fresh

EXTENDING THE CONTENT

Once a part of ancient Babylon, the area known as Baghdad has been inhabited since 4000 B.C. In A.D. 762 Baghdad was a small village when the headquarters of the Arab Empire were located nearby. Thereafter, Baghdad experienced rapid growth under Abbasid rule, with a population of more than one million people by the A.D. 800s. The Abbasid Empire declined, however, from the A.D. 800s to the A.D. 1200s. In ending the empire, Mongols from Central Asia nearly destroyed Baghdad. In 1638 it became part of the Ottoman Empire. Baghdad's population was reduced to only 15,000 people by the 1700s as a result of wars, floods, and fires.

Linking Across Time

Carpets Arab carpets were among the most sought-after items in the markets of the Islamic Empire. Carpets adorned the floors of mosques, palaces, and the tents of shepherds (below). Today, skilled Islamic weavers (right) continue to make some of the world's most prized carpets, including the prayer rugs used for kneeling in daily prayers. **What effect did the growth of trade have upon daily life in the Islamic Empire?**

exchange of ideas. Many writers and philosophers flocked to Baghdad. The Syrian Christians and Jews were instructed by the caliph to translate Greek writings into Arabic. Other scholars translated Indian literature into Arabic. The world's store of knowledge advanced greatly. Mathematical and scientific achievements were recorded. Mathematicians adapted numeric systems developed by the Guptas of India which are still in use today. Practical applications of this mathematics were used.

Life in the empire changed. Advanced farming methods were used to produce wheat, rice, beans, melons, cucumbers, celery, and mint. Orchards provided almonds and olives. Trade made many Arabs rich. They desired so many luxury goods that Arab artisans began producing some themselves. As trade

Sample response: As trade grew, more records had to be kept. This led to the opening of banks. People had time for leisure activities and adopted new customs and clothing.

MAKING CONNECTIONS

➤➤ **Government** The Arabs got their idea for the office of vizier from the Persians. Many of the government officials under the Abbasids were Persians.

DID YOU KNOW

The Arabs also developed a variety of business practices such as the use of checks, receipts, and letters of credit.

COOPERATIVE LEARNING

Have students research and organize an informational presentation of Arab contributions. Suggest students work in groups to decide what areas they will research such as: science, mathematics, medicine, philosophy, or the arts. Students should decide what form their presentation will take and what role each student will take.

Other topics might be education, religion, or business activities. Ask students to include the impact of these contributions on their own lives.

🗁 Assign Chapter 22 *Cooperative Learning Activity* in the TCR.

CAPTION ANSWER

the Moors

MAKING CONNECTIONS

➤➤ **Science** The Jewish physician Moses Maimonides fled from Spain after the Berber conquest in 1145, and became court physician to Saladin. He wrote extensively on diet and personal hygiene. He also wrote *Guide for the Perplexed*, showing how religion and Aristotle's scientific thinking could work together.

grew, more records had to be kept. This led to the opening of banks. People had time to play games like polo and chess. Men stopped wearing the traditional Arab robe and began wearing pants. Meals were now served on tables instead of on the floor.

The empire soon became too large for one caliph to control. It began to break up into independent kingdoms. In 836, the caliph moved to a new capital city called Samarra. He returned to Baghdad in 892 and tried to regain power. By then, however, it was too late. In 945, the Persians took control of Baghdad.

Cordoba By the 900s, Cordoba, the capital of Muslim Spain, was the largest city in Europe and a cultural center for scholars, musicians, and artisans. Cordoba was known especially for its fine leatherwork, woven silk and brocades, and gold and silver jewelry. Visitors to Cordoba today can still see the Great Mosque, completed about 976.

The Golden Age of Muslim Spain The Muslim Arabs who conquered North Africa intermarried with the Berbers and became known as Moors (mūrz). In 710, they invaded Spain. With the help of Spanish Jews, they defeated the West Goths, who had taken the country from the Romans. Then, the Moors set up a kingdom that allowed religious freedom.

For the next 400 years, a rich culture flourished in Spain. Many beautiful buildings, such as the Alhambra (al ham' bruh) in Granada, were built all through the country. Schools were founded in which Muslims, Jews, and Christians studied medicine and philosophy together.

During this time, Jews traveled to and traded in every part of the Arab Empire and beyond. In southeastern Rus, they met the Khazars (kuh zarz'), a half-Mongolian people who had converted to Judaism. From India and China, they brought back spices and silks to Spain.

THE ALHAMBRA Under Islamic rule, many beautiful buildings were built in Spain. The Alhambra, a palace in Granada, is considered the finest example of Islamic architecture in Europe. **What Islamic group invaded Spain in 710?**

MULTICULTURAL PERSPECTIVES

During Abbasid rule, Islamic philosophers translated Aristotle from Greek to Arabic. Since Islamic philosophers had no philosophical system of their own, they turned to the system that was within their reach, classical Greek. Their goal, like that of early Christian thinkers, was to solve the apparent contradiction between a perfect God and an imperfect world.

EASTERN CONQUERORS

Seljuq Turks *c. 900-1258*

Seljuq *c. 900*	chief from central Asia; settled with a group of followers near city of Bokhara and became Muslim
Toghril *c. 1055*	grandson of Seljuq, conquered Baghdad; took title al-sultan, meaning "he with authority"; set up Muslim kingdom in western Asia

Mongols *c. 1206-1300*

Genghis Khan *c. 1220*	united central Asian nomads; conquered Arab territory and created empire that covered most of Asia and eastern Europe
Hulagu *c. 1258*	grandson of Genghis Khan; led attack on Baghdad in 1258; became first khan, or overlord, of a kingdom that stretched from Syria to India

Mamelukes *c. 1250-1517*

Shajar *c. 1250*	freed slave who became first Mameluke ruler of Egypt; only Muslim woman to rule a country
Baybars *c. 1260*	seized throne of Egypt; restored caliphate in Cairo; created Mameluke dynasty

Ottoman Turks *c. 1290-1922*

Osman *c. 1290-1326*	founded Ottoman dynasty in Asia Minor
Muhammad II *c. 1451-1481*	captured Constantinople in 1453; established Ottoman Empire

Genghis Khan

Muhammad II

L2 History Have students make a crossword puzzle by using the Eastern Conquerors on this page. Students should construct a grid for their puzzle and write short clues for the conquerors. Have students exchange and solve each others' puzzles. **ELL**

Independent Practice

L1 Religion Ask students to imagine that they are followers of Muhammad in Madina during his lifetime. Have them write what they would say on a flier or poster to be put in the town to announce the next time Muhammad would be speaking. Remind them to include all necessary information and encouragement for people to attend. **ELL**

MEETING SPECIAL NEEDS

Have students who are having difficulty understanding the main concepts in the chapter and students who are visual learners, create charts showing the Arab contributions to modern civilization.

📂 Refer to *Inclusion for the Middle School Social Studies Classroom: Strategies and Activities* for additional resources.

Islamic Jug

Islamic Life   Islam was born in a society where men could have unlimited numbers of wives and the killing of female children was common. Islam attempted to correct this situation.

Muhammad taught that raising a female child guaranteed a reward in Paradise for her parents. Before Islam, women could not inherit property from their parents. Islam, however, entitled them to half the share of their husband's wealth. Islam recognized a woman's right to an inheritance. In Islam only under extreme circumstances is a man allowed to have up to four wives. One condition of this is the man could afford and could deal fairly with more than one wife.

Both men and women were obligated to seek knowledge. Islamic society produced some women of great knowledge and power. At the time of the birth of a Muslim baby, the call for prayer was recited into the baby's ears. By doing this, the child was brought into a life of Islamic culture. Reciting and memorizing the Quran was an important requirement in education. The mosques served as neighborhood schools. The boys were sent for higher education to institutions in major cities. People would travel from country to country within the Muslim world seeking more knowledge. There was tremendous interest in traveling and exploration.

Section 2 Assessment

1. **Define:** caliph, vizier.
2. What were some of the accomplishments of the Umayyads?
3. How did the Arab Empire change under the Abbasids?

Critical Thinking

4. **Drawing a Conclusion** Why were the years from 710 to around 300 called the Golden Age of Muslim Spain?

Graphic Organizer Activity

5. Draw this diagram, and use it to show how the teachings of Islam tried to improve the treatment of women in Arab society.

| Before | Rise of Islam | After |

SECTION 3 Arab Contributions

Between the 770s and the 1300s, Arab scholars helped preserve much of the learning of the ancient world that otherwise would have been lost. They also made many other contributions to the modern world. The use of Arabic as a common language helped unite scholars and promote the sharing of knowledge. The Quran being written in Arabic contributed to this advancement.

Many Arab scientists tried to turn base metals, such as tin, iron, and lead, into gold and silver. These scientists, called **alchemists** (al' kuh mists), used both chemistry and magic in their work. The word "chemistry" comes from the Arabic word "Al-Chemist." Alchemists never were able to turn base metals into gold and silver. However, their work led to the practice of making experiments and keeping records of the results. The Arabs are considered the founders of modern chemistry.

Arab astronomers studied the heavens. They gave many stars the names they still carry today. They correctly described the eclipses of the sun. They also proved that the moon affects the *tides,* or the rise and fall of the oceans. The astronomers worked with Arab geographers to determine the size of Earth and the distance around it. From their studies, they decided that Earth might be round. The astronomer-geographer al-Idrisi (al i drē' si) drew the first accurate map of the world.

Arab mathematicians invented algebra and taught it to Europeans. Arab mathematicians also borrowed the numerals 0-9 from Gupta mathematicians and passed them to Europeans.

The Arabs gave much to the field of medicine. Unlike doctors in most other countries, Arab doctors had to pass a test before they could practice medicine. The Arabs set up the world's first school of pharmacy. They also opened the world's first drugstores. They organized medical clinics that traveled all through the empire giving care and medicines to the sick.

Arab doctors were the first to discover that blood *circulates,* or moves, to and from the heart. They were the first to diagnose certain diseases. The Persian doctor ar-Razi (al rā sē') discovered differences between measles and smallpox. Another Persian, Avicenna (ä vä sēn ä), was the first to understand that tuberculosis is *contagious,* or could be passed from person to person.

Arab doctors informed the scientific community about their discoveries by publishing their findings. Avicenna's *Canon of Medicine,* an encyclopedia of medicine, was used in European medical schools for 500 years.

The Arabs also made many contributions to the arts. One of their best known writings is *The Arabian Nights,* a collection of tales put together from Persian stories. The tales paint an exciting picture of Islamic life at the height of the empire. The Persian poet Omar Khayyám's (ō' mahr kī yahm') *Rubáiyát* (rū' bē aht) has been translated into many languages. It is considered one of the finest poems ever written.

Islamic art is distinct and full of color. It is used on walls, books, rugs, and buildings. It differs from most other art because of the Muslim belief that Allah created all living creatures. Islamic artists think it is a sin to make pictures of Allah's creations. As a result, most of their art is made up of geometric designs entwined with flowers, leaves, and stars.

Reading Check
Why are Arab **alchemists** considered the founders of modern chemistry?

Arabic Numerals
Europeans resisted the use of Arabic numerals well into the 1400s. An Italian bookkeeping manual insisted that Roman numerals "cannot be falsified as easily as those of the new art of computation, of which one can, with ease, make one out of another, such as turning the zero into a 6 or a 9."

Islamic Medical Diagram

Reading Check Answer
Arab **alchemists** made experiments and kept records of their results, laying the foundation for modern chemistry.

DID YOU KNOW ??
The symbol of Islam, the crescent and star, appears on the flags of several nations whose population has a Muslim majority.

The following videotape program is available from Glencoe to enrich Chapter 22:

• **Legends of the Arabian Knights**

To find classroom resources to accompany this video, check the following home page:

A&E Television:
http://www.aetv.com

ASSESS

Check for Understanding

Ask students to summarize orally or in writing the main points of the chapter. Discuss the answers to the Section and Chapter Assessment questions.

Evaluate

Assign Chapter 22 **Performance Assessment Activity** in the TCR.

Administer the **Chapter 22 Test** in the TCR. Testmaker available.

EXTENDING THE CONTENT

Carpets made by craftspeople in the Islamic world are famous for their glowing colors and intricate designs of interwoven leaves and flowers, geometric figures, and in some rugs, animal figures. From the silk rugs that adorned the caliph's palaces to the carpets of sheep's wool that served as walls between different sections of a tent, carpets have always been far more than floor coverings in this culture. Most Muslims owned small rugs that they used in daily prayer. Today, carpets from Iran, Afghanistan, and other parts of the Islamic world are prized.

Reteach

Have students review the chapter sections and list the main ideas in each part. Discuss the lists in class.

Assign Chapter 22 **Reteaching Activity** in the TCR.

Enrich

Have students research caravans in the Middle East during this time period. Have them write a description of a typical caravan and the importance of oases to the caravans.

Assign the Chapter 22 **Enrichment Activity** in the TCR.

CLOSE

Write these names on the board: *Abu Bakr, Ali, Umayyads,* and *Abbasids*. Have students identify the names and explain the importance of each in the history of Islam and the expansion of the Arab Empire.

Use **Interactive Tutor Self-Assessment Software** to review Section 3.

Self-Check Quiz gives students an interactive chapter tutorial. Have them access *Chapter 22 Quiz* at **humanheritage.glencoe.com**

Much of what is known about this time comes from Arabs who wrote down the history of Islam. They began to write about events centered around rulers and peoples. This is how most historians present history today. The Muslim historian Ibn Khaldun (ib' uhn kal dun') wrote about the Arabs, the Berbers, and the Persians. His writings were the first to take into account the influence of geography and climate on people.

Section 3 Assessment

1. **Define:** alchemists.
2. How did the use of the Arabic language promote learning?
3. What are two of the best-known Arab writings?

Critical Thinking

4. **Drawing Conclusions** Do you think the numerals 0 through 9 should be called Arabic or Gupta numerals? Explain.

Graphic Organizer Activity

5. Draw this diagram, and use it to show Arab contributions to science, math, and the arts.

```
        Arab Contributions
     ┌───────┼───────┐
   Math   Science   Arts
```

Chapter Summary & Study Guide

1. Muhammad was born in Makkah in 570.
2. In 613, Muhammad began to preach that the only god is Allah. This was the start of the Islamic religion.
3. In 622, Muhammad and his followers went from Makkah to Yathrib, where they organized a new government and army.
4. In 630, Muhammad led his followers into Makkah and dedicated the Ka'bah to Allah.
5. In 631, delegates throughout Arabia declared their loyalty to Muhammad and their belief in teachings such as the five pillars.
6. After Muhammad's death in 632, his followers chose a new leader, known as a caliph, and began building a huge empire.
7. In 661, the capital of the Arab Empire was moved to Damascus and the Umayyad Dynasty began.
8. In 750, the Abbasids took control of the Arab Empire and concentrated on trade rather than war.
9. The Moors in Spain combined Arab and Jewish cultures and allowed religious freedom.
10. The Arabs made many contributions to modern civilization, especially in science, math, and the arts.

Self-Check Quiz

Visit the *Human Heritage* Web site at **humanheritage. glencoe.com** and click on *Chapter 22—Self-Check Quiz* to assess your understanding of this chapter.

Section 3 Assessment Answers

1. alchemists, Arab scientists (p. 343)
2. It helped unite scholars throughout the Arab Empire.
3 *The Arabian Nights* and *Rubáiyát*
4. Answers will vary, but students should support their opinions about the development of numbering systems with reasons.

5. Completed charts should include the many accomplishments cited on pages 343–344. In a follow-up activity, you might challenge students to vote on the top five Arab ideas or inventions.

Assign Chapter 22 **Section 3 Quiz** in the TCR. Testmaker available.

Using Key Terms

Imagine you are a traveler in the Arab Empire. Use the following words to write a journal entry describing your impressions of the empire.

pilgrims   pillars of faith   mosque
Imam   *zakah*   *hajj*
caliph   vizier   alchemists

Understanding Main Ideas

1. How did Bedouins earn a living?
2. Why did Muhammad begin to spend time alone in a cave outside Makkah?
3. Why did Makkah's leaders persecute Muhammad and his followers?
4. What is the Islamic Creed?
5. In what direction do Muslims face when they pray?
6. What does the Quran promise all believers who fulfill their duties?
7. What brought about the downfall of the Umayyad Dynasty?
8. What did the name "Arab" mean under the Abbasids?
9. What discoveries did Arab doctors make?

Critical Thinking

1. What role did religion play in Arab life?
2. How did the Moorish kingdom in Spain show it had been influenced by different cultures?
3. Which Arab contribution do you think has most affected other civilizations? Explain your choice.
4. What parts of life in the Arab Empire would you have liked? What parts would you have disliked?

Graphic Organizer Activity

History Create a time line like the one shown, and use it to summarize the main events in Muhammad's life. (Dates have been provided to help you get started.)

565 — 570 610 620 628 632 — 635
           595 613 622 630

Geography in History

Location Islam spread across a wide area, as seen on the map on page 337. It included most of the area from the western edge of the Mediterranean Sea to the eastern shores of the Arabian Sea. What longitude and latitude lines mark the approximate location of this area?

Using Your Journal

Review any details you may have noted about the ways the Arabs influenced other civilizations. Then choose three contributions made by the Arabs that you see in your everyday life. Write a paragraph explaining how these contributions affect you.

345

Bonus Test Question

For Chapter 22 Test
What is false about the following: A man and woman move to Madina in 613, the year Muhammad began preaching. That year, called the *Anno Hijrah,* they joined the thousands who supported Muhammad.

Using Your Journal

Paragraphs will vary but should include three specific examples. You might ask volunteers to read their paragraphs to the class.

Geography in History

The area spanned from about 45° N to 25° N and 5° W to 65° E.

CHAPTER **22**

Assessment Answers

Using Key Terms

Journal entries will vary.

Understanding Main Ideas

1. as herders and traders
2. because he was troubled by the corruption in Makkah
3. They were afraid of losing money because fewer pilgrims would come to Makkah.
4. a confession of faith stating "There is no God but Allah, and Muhammad is His prophet."
5. toward Makkah
6. They will go to Paradise.
7. conquered people who became Muslim felt unfairly treated; the division of Muslims into the Shi'ah and the Sunni
8. any subject who spoke Arabic
9. the circulation of the blood, the differences between measles and smallpox, and that tuberculosis is contagious

Critical Thinking

1. brought pilgrims to Makkah, which helped its economy; united Muslims; set guidelines for the way Muslims lived
2. Many groups lived there; and Muslims, Jews, and Christians studied medicine and philosophy together.
3. Answers will vary.
4. Answers will vary, but students should cite specific examples of likes and dislikes.

Graphic Organizer Activity

570—birth; 595—marriage; 610—vision of Gabriel; 613—starting of preaching in Makkah; 620—invitation to come to Yathrib; 622—flight from Makkah to Yathrib; 628—peace treaty with people of Makkah; 630—violation of treaty and conquest of Makkah by Muhammad and his followers; 632—death

Chapter 23 Planning Guide

Objectives	Reproducible Resources	Multimedia Resources
Section 1 **Early Eastern Slavs** Describe what life and economic development was like for the earliest Eastern Slavs.	Reproducible Lesson Plan Chapter 23 Vocabulary and Guided Reading Activity Reading Essentials and Study Guide 23-1 Chapter 23 Chart and Graph Skill Activity Section 1 Quiz	Vocabulary PuzzleMaker Interactive Tutor Self-Assessment Software ExamView® Pro Testmaker Glencoe Skillbuilder Interactive Workbook, Level 1
Section 2 **Kievan Rus** Summarize how early Rus states developed around Kiev.	Reproducible Lesson Plan Reading Essentials and Study Guide 23-2 Chapter 23 Cooperative Learning Activity Chapter 23 Enrichment Activity Section 2 Quiz	Teaching Transparencies and Activities 23A & 23B Vocabulary PuzzleMaker Interactive Tutor Self-Assessment Software ExamView® Pro Testmaker Glencoe Skillbuilder Interactive Workbook, Level 1
Section 3 **The Mongol Conquest** Analyze how the Mongol invasion influenced internal development and foreign relations of Rus states.	Reproducible Lesson Plan Reading Essentials and Study Guide 23-3 Section 3 Quiz	Vocabulary PuzzleMaker Interactive Tutor Self-Assessment Software ExamView® Pro Testmaker Glencoe Skillbuilder Interactive Workbook, Level 1
Section 4 **The Rise of Moscow** Discuss how Moscow became powerful and how the czars affected life in Rus states.	Reproducible Lesson Plan Reading Essentials and Study Guide 23-4 Chapter 23 Activity Book Activity Chapter 23 Geography and Map Activity Unit 7 World Literature Reading 2 Section 4 Quiz	Vocabulary PuzzleMaker Interactive Tutor Self-Assessment Software ExamView® Pro Testmaker Glencoe Skillbuilder Interactive Workbook, Level 1
Chapter 23 **Review and Evaluation**	Chapter 23 Reteaching Activity Chapter 23 Performance Assessment Activity Unit 7 Standardized Test Practice Spanish Chapter Summary and Glossary Chapter 23 Test	Vocabulary PuzzleMaker Interactive Tutor Self-Assessment Software ExamView® Pro Testmaker Glencoe Skillbuilder Interactive Workbook, Level 1 Audiocassettes*

*Also available in Spanish.

Presentation Plus!

Use Glencoe's **Presentation Plus!** multimedia teacher tool to easily present dynamic lessons that visually excite your students. Using Microsoft® PowerPoint, you can customize the presentations to create your own personalized lessons.

 ## Interactive Lesson Planner

Planning has never been easier! Using this CD-ROM, organize your week, month, semester, or year with all the help you need. The **Interactive Lesson Planner** gives you access to all of the blackline masters which accompany *Human Heritage.*

✓ PERFORMANCE ASSESSMENT ACTIVITIES

Newspaper Articles Have students write five newspaper headlines about major events in the life of Ivan the Great or one of the other czars of the early Rus states. Then have the students choose one of the headlines and write a newspaper article explaining the details of the headline.

CHAPTER RESOURCES

LITERATURE ABOUT THE PERIOD

Kimmel, Eric A. *Mishka, Pishka, and Fishka.* Coward, McCann & Geoghan, 1976. English translations of folktales from Ukraine.

READINGS FOR THE STUDENT

Sutcliff, Rosemary. *Blood Feud.* E.P. Dutton, 1977. Young adult novel about an English boy sold as an enslaved person to Varangian traders.

READINGS FOR THE TEACHER

Chambers, John. *The Devil's Horsemen: The Mongol Invasion of Europe.* Atheneum, 1985. Traces the westward push of the Mongols, beginning with the invasion of Russia.

Klein, Mina C. *The Kremlin: Citadel of History.* Macmillan, 1973. Describes the origin and growth of the Kremlin from the ninth century to modern times.

KEY TO ABILITY LEVELS

Teaching strategies have been coded for varying learning styles and abilities.

L1 Level 1 activities are **basic** activities and should be within the ability range of all students.

L2 Level 2 activities are **average** activities and should be within the ability range of the average to above-average student.

L3 Level 3 activities are **challenging** activities designed for the ability range of above-average students.

ELL ELL activities should be within the ability range of English Language Learning students.

Teacher's Corner

INDEX TO NATIONAL GEOGRAPHIC MAGAZINE

The following articles relate to this chapter:

- "Hunting with Eagles" by Candice S. Millard, September 1999.
- "A Comeback for the Cossacks," by Mike Edwards, November 1998.
- "Moscow: The New Revolution," by David Remnick, April 1997.
- "Sons of Genghis Khan," by Mike Edwards, February 1997.
- "Genghis Khan," by Mike Edwards, December 1996.
- "Past Becomes Future for Mongolian Nomads," by Cynthia Beall and Melvyn Goldstein, May 1993.
- "Mother Russia on a New Course," by Mike Edwards, February 1991.

NATIONAL GEOGRAPHIC SOCIETY PRODUCTS AVAILABLE FROM GLENCOE

To order the following, call Glencoe at 1-800-334-7344:

- *PicturePack: Physical Geography of the World (Transparencies)*
- *PicturePack: World Geography Library (Transparencies)*

ADDITIONAL NATIONAL GEOGRAPHIC SOCIETY PRODUCTS

To order the following, call National Geographic at 1-800-368-2728:

- *The Mongols (Maps)*
- *Physical Geography of the Continents Series: Asia (Video)*

Access *National Geographic*'s MapMachine Web site and other geography resources at:
http://www.nationalgeographic.com/
http://www.nationalgeographic.com/maps/

  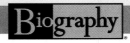

The following videotape program is available from Glencoe:

- **Genghis Khan: Terror and Conquest**
  1-56501-578-9

To order, call Glencoe at 1-800-334-7344. To find classroom resources to accompany many of these, check:

A&E Television: http://www.aetv.com
The History Channel: http://www.historychannel.com

OVERVIEW

Chapter 23 discusses the Eastern Slav civilization.

➤ **Section 1** describes the influences that transformed the early Slav agricultural settlements into trading centers.

➤ **Section 2** discusses the emergence of a Rus state.

➤ **Section 3** describes the effects of the Mongol invasions on the Rus states.

➤ **Section 4** discusses the reigns of Ivan the Great and Ivan the Terrible.

CHAPTER OBJECTIVES

After reading Chapter 23, students will be able to:

1. describe what life was like for the earliest Eastern Slavs.

2. summarize how early Rus states developed around Kiev.

3. analyze how Eastern Christianity influenced the Rus.

4. explain changes the Mongols brought about in Rus life.

5. examine how the czars affected life in Rus states.

EXAMINING ARTIFACTS

Direct students to study the artifacts for evidence of contact between the Eastern Slavs and the Byzantines. *(Students may note the influence of Christianity, the use of icons, and so on.)* Tell students to study the time line on this page. Ask: What other people influenced the civilization developed by the Eastern Slavs? *(Mongols)*

PERFORMANCE ASSESSMENT ✓

Use the Performance Assessment activities on page 346B to help you evaluate students as they complete the chapter.

346

CHAPTER 23

The Eastern Slavs

500 A.D.–1035 A.D.

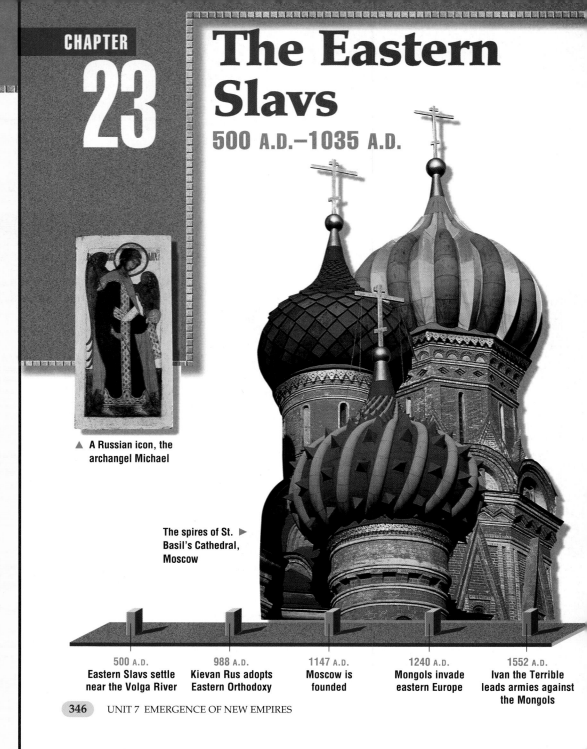

▲ A Russian icon, the archangel Michael

The spires of St. ▶ Basil's Cathedral, Moscow

500 A.D.	988 A.D.	1147 A.D.	1240 A.D.	1552 A.D.
Eastern Slavs settle near the Volga River	**Kievan Rus adopts Eastern Orthodoxy**	**Moscow is founded**	**Mongols invade eastern Europe**	**Ivan the Terrible leads armies against the Mongols**

346 UNIT 7 EMERGENCE OF NEW EMPIRES

TEACHING RESOURCES

TEACHER PLANNING AND SUPPORT

- Reproducible Lesson Plan
- Block Scheduling Implementation Guide
- Videodisc Bar Code Correlation
- Presentation Plus!

REVIEW AND REINFORCEMENT

- Reading Essentials and Study Guide 23-1, 23-2, 23-3, 23-4
- Chapter 23 Vocabulary and Guided Reading Activity
- Vocabulary PuzzleMaker Software
- Teaching Transparencies 23A & 23B

- Chapter 23 Reteaching Activity
- Chapter 23 Cooperative Learning Activity
- Chapter 23 Activity Book Activity
- Chapter 23 Chart and Graph Skill Activity
- Interactive Tutor Self-Assessment Software
- Unit 7 MindJogger VideoQuiz

APPLICATION AND HANDS-ON ACTIVITIES

- Unit 7 Hands-On History Lab Activity
- World History Game Card 7
- World History Craft Card 8

Chapter Focus

Read to Discover
- What life was like for the earliest Eastern Slavs.
- How early Rus states developed around Kiev.
- How Eastern Christianity influenced the people of Rus.
- What changes the Mongols brought about in Rus life.
- How Moscow became powerful.
- How the czars affected life in Muscovy.

Terms to Learn
izbas
boyars
veche
khan
kremlin
czar

People to Know
Rurik
Vladimir I
Ivan the Great
Ivan the Terrible

Places to Locate
Volga River
Kiev
Dnieper River
Moscow

Why It's Important   North of the Byzantine Empire lived a people that historians today call Slavs. All that is known about their origins is that they were Indo-Europeans, like the Aryans who entered the Indus Valley and the Dorians who conquered the Mycenaeans. About 500 B.C., the Slavs began to develop well-organized settlements in eastern Europe in the areas now known as eastern Poland and western Ukraine.

HISTORY Online
Chapter Overview
Visit the *Human Heritage* Web site at **humanheritage.glencoe.com** and click on **Chapter 23—Chapter Overviews** to preview this chapter.

SECTION 1   Early Eastern Slavs

About 500 A.D., a group of Eastern Slavs began to move eastward toward the Volga (vol' guh) River. They were hunters and farmers who were the ancestors of Ukrainians, Belarussians, and Russians. They settled in villages made up of about 25 related families. Each family owned a house that was built partly underground to provide warmth during the cold winter months. The house had low walls and an earth-covered roof. The land, animals, tools, and seed belonged to the village. Around each village was a wall of earth and a wooden stockade.

The oldest male governed the village with the help of a council. He assigned villagers different farming tasks and judged quarrels. During attacks, he acted as military leader.

By the 600s, the Eastern Slavs controlled all the land as far east as the Volga River. To clear this heavily forested land for farming, farmers used a method called *slash-and-burn.* They cut

---

HISTORY Online
Chapter Overview introduces students to chapter content and key terms. Have them access **Chapter 23 Overview** at **humanheritage.glencoe.com**

FOCUS

Bellringer
Write this direction on the board: *List as many cities in Russia as you can.*

Motivational Activity
Have students share their lists of Russian cities. One city likely to be on their lists is Moscow. Tell students that they will learn about the early history of Moscow and other Russian cities in this chapter.

GUIDE TO READING

Reading Strategy
Ask students to read "Why It's Important" and summarize the chapter's main theme. *(The Slavs developed well-organized settlements and spread their influence through part of what is now eastern Europe.)*

Vocabulary Precheck
Ask students to define each of the "Terms to Learn." Have a volunteer consult the dictionary for any unfamiliar words. **L1 ELL**

💾 Use the Vocabulary PuzzleMaker for Chapter 23 to create a crossword puzzle. **L1**

📁 Assign Chapter 23 Vocabulary and Guided Reading Activity.

📁 Assign Reading Essentials and Study Guide 23-1.

TEACH

Guided Practice

L1 **Daily Life** Have students imagine they are members of the early Eastern Slavs and they are to write an entry in their diaries describing a day in their lives. Have students share their entries with the class. **ELL**

Reading Check Answer

Izbas were one-room cabins with gabled roofs and wooden window frames.

GEOGRAPHY AND HISTORY

Russia's rivers form a unique network of navigable waterways. Although all the major rivers run north-south, their lateral branches provide east-west access to land. This helped increase trade for the early Eastern Slavs.

CAPTION ANSWER

It was only one room. Although each *izba* had a fireplace, some did not have chimneys, and smoke had to escape through the shutters that covered the windows.

---

down trees, which they burned for fertilizer. On the cleared land, they planted such crops as barley, rye, and flax. After a few years, when the wood fertilizer in the soil had been used up, the farmers moved to a new place. There, they repeated the process.

The forests provided the East Slavs with all the timber they needed. The East Slavs soon became skilled in building with wood. They made musical instruments out of wood and used logs to make boats and *izbas* (uhz bahs'). An izba was a one-room log cabin with a gabled roof and wooden window frames. The whole family lived, worked, ate, and slept in the single room. Although each izba had a fireplace, some did not have a chimney. Smoke from fires had to escape through shutters that covered the windows.

The villagers worshipped many gods and honored nature, spirits, and ancestors. The most popular gods were Volos (vō' lōs), who protected cattle and sheep; Perun (pār' uhn), the god of thunder and lightning; and the Great Mother, the goddess of the land and harvest. The people built wooden images of their favorite gods on the highest ground outside the villages.

There were many slow-moving rivers in the area west of the Volga. At first, the East Slavs used them as roads between their villages. Before long, they began using them for trade as well. They set up a trade route that ran from the Baltic Sea in the north to the Caspian in the south.

Reading Check What did Eastern Slavic *izbas* look like?

Then & Now

Slavic Peoples Descendants of the West Slavs include the people of Poland, the Czech Republic, and Slovakia. Descendants of the South Slavs include Serbs, Croats, Slovenes, and Bosnians. Most West Slavs follow the Roman Catholic Church. South Slavs generally follow Eastern Orthodox Christianity, except for those Bosnians who follow Islam.

RUS CABIN Houses in early Rus towns and villages were made of wood from the surrounding thick forests. Here, a modern Russian cabin is shown that is a good example of decorative styles passed on from early Rus artisans. **What was the inside of an izba, or Rus log cabin, like?**

MEETING SPECIAL NEEDS

Have students who are tactile/kinesthetic learners make models or dioramas of early Russian towns or villages. Students can use the information in the textbook and in other resources. Display the models or dioramas in the classroom.

📁 Refer to *Inclusion for the Middle School Social Studies Classroom: Strategies and Activities* for additional resources.

By the end of the 800s, the East Slavs had built many trading towns along the riverbanks. During the five months of winter, merchants who lived in the towns gathered furs, honey, and other forest products from the people in neighboring villages. In spring, when the ice on the rivers had melted, the merchants loaded their goods on boats and floated south to Byzantium. There, they traded their goods for cloth, wine, weapons, and jewelry. Trade helped the East Slavs to live more comfortably and to develop their civilization.

The Eastern Slavs, to protect their trade route, relied on Viking warriors from Scandinavia. These men were known as Varangians, and the route was called the Varangian Route or the route from the Varangians to the Greeks. Eventually, the Varangians became part of the larger Slav population.

Drawing of Rus Sled

Section 1 Assessment

1. **Define:** *izbas.*
2. How were early Eastern Slavic villages governed?
3. Why were rivers important to the Eastern Slavs?

Critical Thinking

4. **Making Inferences** Why do you think the Eastern Slavs chose the Vikings to protect their trade routes?

Graphic Organizer Activity

5. Draw this diagram, and use it to show details about early Eastern Slavic life.

Eastern Slavic Life

SECTION 2 Kievan Rus

In 862, a Varangian named Rurik became the prince of Novgorod (nahv′ guh rahd), a northern town on the East Slav trading route. About 20 years later, Rurik's Varangian friend Oleg (ō′ leg) established the state of Kievan Rus. The term "Rus" meant "warrior band." He set up his capital at Kiev (kē ev′).

Kiev stood on a group of hills overlooking the main bend in the Dnieper (nē′ puhr) River. It was the southernmost town on the Varangian trading route. Whoever ruled Kiev controlled trade with Byzantium. Kiev also lay close to where the Ukraine forest turned into a *steppe* (step), or grassland. For hundreds of years, this steppe had served central Asian warriors as a highway into Europe. Because of this, Kiev was in a good location to protect merchant ships from attack.

The Kievan Rus state that Oleg established was really a group of small territories. The main ruler was the Grand Prince of Kiev. He was helped by local princes, rich merchants, and

Painting of Eastern Slav Warriors

CHAPTER 23 THE EASTERN SLAVS **349**

L2 **Culture** Discuss the influences from the Byzantines on early Slav people *(trade items such as silk, jewels, food; the Cyrillic alphabet; and Christianity).* Ask students to consider how they think the early Eastern Slavs might have felt about these influences on their traditional culture and practices. Suggest they write a description of what their feelings might be as if they were an Eastern Slav.

MAKING CONNECTIONS

➤➤ **History** Around A.D. 1100 Slavic traditions were written down in the *Primary Chronicle,* a record that combines legends and facts. According to the *Primary Chronicle,* in about A.D. 860 the Slavic people from the northern forest village of Novgorod asked Vikings from Scandinavia for aid: "Our land is great and rich, but there is no order in it. Come to rule and reign over us." The Viking leader Rurik accepted the invitation.

Use **Interactive Tutor Self-Assessment Software** to review Section 1.

Use the **Vocabulary Puzzle-Maker** to create crossword and word search puzzles.

Section 1 Assessment Answers

1. *izbas,* one-room log cabins (p. 348)
2. by the oldest male with the help of a council
3. because they were used as roads between the Rus villages and for trade
4. Answers will vary but might include that they needed people to protect their trade route.
5. Sample details: lived in villages made up of about 25 related families; built houses partly underground; land, tools, animals, and seed belonged to village; oldest male, with help of a council, governed village; used slash-and-burn farming; skilled at building and making things out of wood; worshiped many gods, nature spirits, and ancestors.

Assign Chapter 23 **Section 1 Quiz** in the TCR. Testmaker available.

L1 Geography: Movement

Have students trace an outline map of eastern Europe and draw and label the following on the map: Dnieper, Don, and Volga rivers; Novgorod, Smolensk, Moscow, Kiev, and Constantinople; the Black and Baltic seas. Then have students draw and label the Varangian Route. Point out the openness of the land to attackers. **ELL**

L2 Geography: Movement

Refer students to the map, "Kievan Rus" on page 350, and have them trace the Varangian Route. Ask students to identify the part of the route that did not follow a river or body of water. *(the north central part of Kievan Rus)*

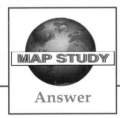

MAP STUDY

Answer

Baltic Sea, Dnieper River, Black Sea (to Mediterranean Sea)

Assign the Chapter 23 **Geography and Map Activity** in the TCR.

Reading Check Answer

The **boyars** were landowning nobles.

The *veche* did everything from settling business disputes to accepting or removing a prince.

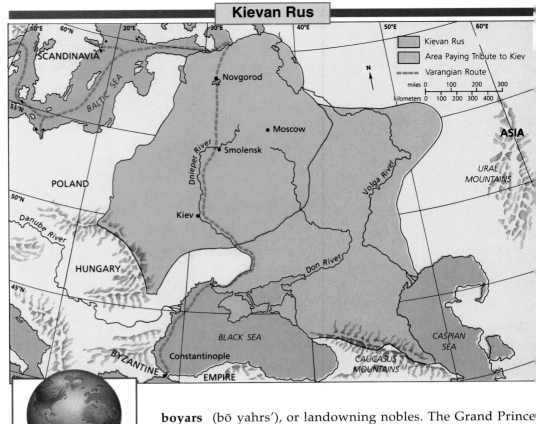

Kievan Rus
Area Paying Tribute to Kiev
Varangian Route

MAP STUDY

PLACE Rivers that flow north to south provided an easy means of transportation. **Along what bodies of water did the Varangian Route extend?**

Reading Check
Who were the **boyars?** What daily matters were handled by the *veche?*

boyars (bō yahrs'), or landowning nobles. The Grand Prince collected tribute from the local princes who in turn collected it from the people in their territory.

A *veche* (ve' chuh), or assembly, handled the daily matters of the towns. It did everything from settling business differences to accepting or removing a prince. Any free man could call a meeting of the veche by ringing the town bell.

Vladimir I and the Eastern Orthodox Church
One of the most important princes of Kiev was Vladimir I (vlad' uh mēr), a good soldier and a strong ruler. He spent the early years of his reign expanding Kievan Rus territory. His armies pushed the country's borders west into Poland and north along the stormy Baltic coast.

In 988, Vladimir chose Eastern or Byzantine Christianity as the country's official religion. The story is told about Vladimir's long search for a new faith that would unite the people. Vladimir sent a number of people to other countries to observe different

MEETING SPECIAL NEEDS

Students with any hearing impairment will need extra visual help with learning the material in this chapter. Select an advanced student to prepare a simple graphic organizer of key events of the chapter. Have students list key terms under appropriate events once organizers are complete. Encourage students to share organizers with the class as a whole, since this is an effective study method for all students.

Refer to *Inclusion for the Middle School Social Studies Classroom: Strategies and Activities* for additional resources.

religions. Those sent were not impressed with what they saw in Islamic, Jewish, or Roman Catholic worship. Then, in Byzantium's Hagia Sophia, they saw Eastern Orthodox worship. They were stunned by its beauty. When they returned to Kievan Rus, Vladimir accepted Eastern Orthodoxy as the official religion.

The Eastern Orthodox Church brought Byzantine culture to Kievan Rus. Priests from Byzantium taught the people religious rituals and the art of painting icons. They learned to write their language in the Cyrillic alphabet. Sons of boyars and priests were sent to newly built schools. The look of Kievan Rus towns changed as stone churches with domes and arches rose among the wooden buildings. Monasteries appeared.

Eastern Orthodoxy gave the Kievan Rus people a sense of belonging to the civilized world. However, it separated them

RELIGIOUS LIFE   Eastern Orthodoxy inspired art and architecture in Kievan Rus. These later Russian icons (left) closely resembled Byzantine examples. Stone churches with ornate, tiled domes (right) were built in Rus towns. **How did Eastern Orthodoxy separate Kievan Rus from the culture of western Europe?**

MAKING CONNECTIONS

➤➤ **Language** The Kievan Rus people told stories about Vladimir and the *bogatyrs*, or knights, that are similar to western European tales about King Arthur and his Knights of the Round Table.

CAPTION ANSWER

Since Russian scholars had books in their own language, they developed their own body of learning separate from that of the West.

COOPERATIVE LEARNING

Tell students that Russian artists excelled at painted lacquer boxes. One of their favorite themes was scenes from traditional Russian fairy tales. Request several students to locate some of these tales for reading or retelling to the class as a whole. Many of these tales can be located on the Internet or in children's collections at the library. Possible stories include: "Prince Ivan and the Firebird," "The Little Humpbacked Pony," "The Magic Golden Fish,"

"The Tale of the Dead Princess," "Old Man Winter," and "The Snow Maiden."

After students have heard the stories, show some samples or pictures of lacquered boxes to the class as a whole. Then divide the class into groups, and have them design sketches for lacquered boxes based on the fairy tales told in class.

🗀 Assign Chapter 23 *Cooperative Learning Activity* in the TCR.

Fur-lined Crown

from western Europe. Since Kievan scholars had books in their own language, they had developed their own body of learning separate from that of the West.

Yaroslav the Wise   Another important ruler of early Rus was Yaroslav (yuh ruh slahf'), son of Vladimir I. Yaroslav became the Grand Prince of Kiev in 1019, after a long struggle with his brothers. Yaroslav was very interested in learning. He invited scholars from Byzantium to live in Kiev and he was called Yaroslav the Wise.

Yaroslav encouraged artisans to practice their skills. The artisans built magnificent brick churches covered with white plaster and decorated with gold. Artists covered the walls of Yaroslav's palace in Kiev with scenes of music and hunting.

Under Yaroslav's rule, Kievan Rus enjoyed a golden age of peace and prosperity. Kiev grew until the city was larger than either Paris or London. Yaroslav developed closer ties with western Europe by family marriages.

Yaroslav also organized Kievan Rus laws based on old Slavic customs and Byzantine law. Under Yaroslav's code, crimes against property were thought to be more serious than those against people. There was no death penalty. In fact, criminals usually were not punished physically but had to pay a fine.

Decline of Kievan Rus   Kievan Rus began to decline around 1054. After Yaroslav's death, the princes of Kiev began to fight over the throne. People from the steppe took advantage of this fighting and attacked Kievan Rus's frontiers. This upset the trade flow which meant the loss of Kiev's major source of wealth. Kievan Rus became more isolated. In 1169 Kiev was attacked and plundered by Andrei Bogoliubsky who wanted Kiev destroyed. The area never recovered.

Gradually, Kievan Rus changed from a trading land of towns into a farming land of peasants. To escape the invaders from the steppe, many of its people fled to the north and settled in the dense forests along the upper Volga.

Pravda The Russian word *pravda* means "truth," but during Yaroslav's reign it also meant "justice." The Kievan legal system that Yaroslav organized was called *Russkaya Pravda.* In modern times, the word became familiar to the West as the name of a Moscow newspaper.

Section 2 Assessment

1. **Define:** boyars, *veche*.
2. Why was Kiev a good location to build a city?
3. How did the decline of Kiev affect the area and people?

Critical Thinking

4. **Demonstrating Reasoned Judgment** How would you have felt about Yaroslav's code of laws and his ways to punish criminals? Explain.

Graphic Organizer Activity

5. Draw this diagram, and use it to show the causes and effects of Vladimir I's acceptance of Eastern Orthodoxy as the official religion of Kievan Rus.

Causes	Acceptance of Eastern Orthodoxy	Effects

SECTION 3 The Mongol Conquest

About 1240, a group of different but united tribes known as Mongols (mon' guhls) swept out of central Asia and took control of Rus principalities, or states. They destroyed villages and towns and killed many people. They made the Rus people pay tribute to the **khan** (kahn), or Mongol leader. They also made the Rus citizens serve in the Mongol armies.

The Church   The Eastern Orthodox Church remained strong during the Mongol invasion. Priests continued to preach and to write. They encouraged the people to love their land and their religion.

During this time, monks began to found monasteries deep in the northern forests. They were followed by Rus farmers searching for new land. Soon, towns and villages began to grow up around the monasteries. Although the Mongol rule caused Rus people to cling more to their religion, it also made them distrustful of ideas and practices from other countries.

Reading Check
What duties did the Rus people have to perform for the **khan?**

Fun Facts....

A Lone Cathedral Mongol invaders completely destroyed Kiev. The only building left standing was the cathedral of Saint Sophia, which contains the tomb of Yaroslav.

Linking Across Time

Easter Eggs   The Eastern Orthodoxy practiced by the Rus people included elements of early Eastern Slavic religions. Painted clay eggs (below) associated with springtime became the models for the eggs associated with the Christian festival of Easter. In the late 1800s and early 1900s, Russian goldsmith Carl Faberge elevated these eggs into what are now priceless works of art (right) housed in museums around the world. **How did the Mongol conquest strengthen the Rus Church?**

Reading Check Answer
Under the **khan,** the Rus people paid tribute and served in Mongol armies.

Linking Across Time

Mongol conquest led monks to establish monasteries deep in the northern forests. The Rus farmers who followed them built villages and clung more deeply to their religious beliefs.

Biography

The following videotape program is available from Glencoe to enrich chapter 23:

- **Genghis Khan: Terror and Conquest**

To find classroom resources to accompany this video, check the following home page:

A&E Television:
http://www.aetv.com

Use the **Vocabulary Puzzle-Maker** to create crossword and word search puzzles.

EXTENDING THE CONTENT

Mongols were not the only invaders of the Rus states in the thirteenth century. Although the northerly town of Novgorod was out of the direct wave of Mongol destruction, it still had to contend with invaders from the west. Its leader, Prince Alexander, was an outstanding military leader who became one of the great heroes of Rus history.

L2 **Daily Life** Have students prepare a report with illustrations or a fashion show on some traditional Russian dress for both the wealthy and the peasants. Encourage students to include what influence this dress has had on modern fashion styles. **ELL**

LINKING PAST TO PRESENT

From a small unimportant town on the Moskva River, Muscovy grew to be a center of an empire. Troikas, or sleighs, guided by horses, still glide over snowy trails on the city's outskirts. Today the golden-domed Kremlin has walls of brick and stone instead of the wooden ones of the thirteenth century.

💾 Use **Interactive Tutor Self-Assessment Software** to review Section 3.

💾 Use the **Vocabulary Puzzle-Maker** to create crossword and word search puzzles.

✅ **Reading Check Answer**
The **kremlin** was a fortress located at Moscow.

Church Vestment

The Mongol conquest somewhat isolated the Rus Church from other Christian churches. Because of this, the Church developed local rituals and practices. This united the people and made them proud of their own culture.

Daily Life Even under Mongol rule, differences between the lives of the rich in Rus and the lives of peasants remained. The wealthy sometimes entertained guests with feasts of deer and wild pig. Peasants, on the other hand, rarely ate meat. Instead, they ate dark rye bread, cabbage, salted fish, and mushrooms.

The few pleasures the peasants had were visiting one another. They told stories that praised the brave deeds of their warriors and other heroes. The stories were passed from old to young and became part of the Rus heritage.

Common dress for peasant men was white tunics, wide linen trousers, and heavy shoes woven from long strips of tree bark. They tied rags around their legs and feet instead of stockings to keep out the cold. Rich merchants and boyars wore tall fur hats and *caftans* (kaf' tanz), or long robes tied at the waist with a sash.

Rus women of all classes wore blouses or smocks, skirts, and long shawls. On holidays, they added headdresses with decorations that indicated the region from which a woman came and if she was married.

Section 3 Assessment

1. **Define:** khan.
2. Where did the Mongols come from?
3. What did the Mongols do to the Rus people when they invaded Rus lands?

Critical Thinking

4. **Predicting Consequences** How might life have been different in the Rus states if the Mongols had not conquered these lands?

Graphic Organizer Activity

5. Draw this diagram, and use it to compare the lives of the rich and the lives of the peasants in Rus during Mongol rule.

Rich | Both | Peasants

✅ **Reading Check**
What was the **kremlin?**

SECTION 4 The Rise of Moscow

At the time of the Mongol conquest, Moscow (mos' kō), or Muscovy, founded in 1147, was a small trading post on the road from Kiev to the forests in the north. As more Rus people moved north to escape the Mongols, many artisans settled in or near Moscow's **kremlin** (krem' luhn), or fortress.

Section 3 Assessment Answers

1. khan, Mongol leader (p. 353)
2. central Asia
3. They murdered people, destroyed villages, and made Rus people pay tribute and serve in the Mongol armies.
4. Answers will vary but could include that if the Mongols had not conquered Rus, these states might have been less isolated.
5. Sample responses: *rich*—sometimes entertained guests with large feasts of deer and other meat, wore tall fur hats and caftans; *poor*—rarely ate meat, entertainment consisted of visits to friends and storytelling, wore linen clothes, wrapped rags around their legs for warmth, wore shoes made of woven tree bark

Assign Chapter 23 **Section 3 Quiz** in the TCR. Testmaker available.

The princes of Moscow were bold and ambitious. They learned to cooperate with the Mongols and even recruited Muscovy soldiers for the Mongol army. In return, the Mongols gave the princes of Moscow the power to collect taxes throughout the country. If a Rus territory could not provide soldiers or tax money for the Mongols, Moscow's princes took it over. In this way, Moscow, the principality of Muscovy, began to expand.

As Moscow grew in size, it became stronger. The princes passed their thrones from father to son. Thus, there was no fighting over who the next ruler would be, and the people remained united.

The Muscovite metropolitan lived in Moscow. This created a second center for the Eastern Orthodox Church outside of Kiev. The metropolitan blessed the princes for their efforts to make Moscow a great city. The people obeyed the prince as a ruler chosen and protected by God.

Meanwhile, Mongol chiefs started fighting among themselves. As a result, they grew weaker, while Moscow grew stronger. In 1380, an army formed by Dmitry (duh mē′ trē), the prince of Moscow, attacked and defeated the Mongols. The Mongols still remained powerful but no longer were feared or obeyed as they had been in the past.

Ivan the Great

In 1462, Ivan III (ī′ vuhn), known as Ivan the Great, became prince of Moscow. In 1480, he ended Mongol control of Muscovy. He also expanded its boundaries to the north and west.

A few years before Mongol rule ended, Ivan married Sophia, a niece of the last Byzantine emperor. The Muscovite people felt this marriage gave Ivan all the glory of past Byzantine emperors. The Church believed it meant that Moscow had taken Byzantium's place as the center of Christianity.

Ivan began living in the style of the Byzantine emperors. He used the two-headed eagle of Byzantium on his royal seal. He brought Italian architects to Moscow to build fine palaces and large cathedrals in the kremlin. He raised the huge walls that still guard the kremlin. He called himself **czar** (zahr), or emperor. This later became the official title of the emperor.

Ivan died in 1505. By then, the people were convinced that their ruler should have full and unquestioned power over both Church and state.

Ivan the Terrible

In 1533, Ivan IV, the three-year-old grandson of Ivan III, became czar of Muscovy. He was not crowned until 1547, however. While he was growing up, a council of boyars governed the country for him. The boyars, however, wanted more power. To frighten Ivan into obeying

Painting of Ivan the Great

Student Web Activity
Visit the *Human Heritage* Web site at humanheritage.glencoe.com and click on *Chapter 23—Student Web Activities* to find out more about the history of Moscow.

Reading Check
What did the official title of **czar** mean?

L3 **Editorial Cartoons** Have the students write an editorial cartoon concerning one of the following events: Ivan the Great's marriage to Sophia, Ivan the Great's end of Mongol control of Rus, Ivan the Terrible's order to peasants not to leave their land, Ivan the Terrible's move to a monastery, Ivan the Terrible's takeover of boyar lands. Display cartoons on a bulletin board.

HISTORY Online
Student Web Activity objectives, goals, and answers can be found at the *Chapter 23 Web Activity Lesson Plan* at humanheritage.glencoe.com

Reading Check Answer
The title of **czar** meant emperor.

EXTENDING THE CONTENT

Moscow was first settled on a trail by a river where people built a blockhouse as a place to stop on the way to Kiev. The site—a hill of pines—was chosen because it offered protection and provided a good observation point. Around A.D. 1155, a log stockade was built to protect against raiders. Huts and storehouses were later added, and eventually the area became known as the *kremlin,* or fort. The heart of today's Moscow is still the Kremlin, although Moscow has spread and grown since then. The "new" Kremlin has a massive red brick wall surrounding a medieval fortress that was built in the fifteenth century.

MAP SKILLS

Analyzing Historical Maps

Have students read the introductory section of the skill on page 356. Ask: What do historical maps show? *(boundary changes over time)* Direct students' attention to the map on the skill page. Ask: In what year was Muscovy smallest? *(1300)* In what year did Moscow first acquire part of the Volga River? *(1462)* Under which czar did Moscow gain control of Novgorod? *(Ivan III)*

Next, have students refer to a current map of the area shown on the map "The Growth of Moscow" and name the countries that were once controlled by Moscow.

Answers to Map Practice

1. 1462
2. 1505
3. Ivan IV

Analyzing Historical Maps

Some maps show how a certain country expanded and changed its boundaries over time. Maps that show boundary changes are called **historical maps.**

The map of "The Growth of Moscow" below shows the changes in Moscow's borders from 1300 to 1584. The color used to shade a certain area shows when that land became part of Moscow. It also shows the exact location of the land that was added. For example, green is the color used to show the land acquired by the time of Ivan IV's death. The shading on the map indicates that this land extended to the Caspian Sea in the southeast and to the Black Sea in the southwest.

Map Practice

1. By what year did Moscow include part of the Don River?
2. By what year had Moscow acquired territory bordering on the Arctic Ocean?
3. Under which czar did Moscow control the largest amount of territory?

The Growth of Moscow

Glencoe's **Skillbuilder Interactive Workbook, Level 1,** provides instruction and practice in key social studies skills.

356

SPOTLIGHT ON: MOSCOW

The area around Moscow was dependent on both the Don and Volga rivers. The Volga is Europe's largest river, being comprised of 151,000 rivers, streams, and temporary streams, and having a length of 357,000 miles (or 574,000 km). The Volga River basin occupies a huge area stretching from the Valdi and Central Russian hills on the west to the Ural Mountains in the east, to the Caspian Sea in the south. Snow accounts for 60 percent of the river's annual drainage.

them, they began to mistreat him. Ivan came to hate the boyars. He did, however, adopt their cruel habits. By the time he was a teenager, he was killing people just for going against his wishes.

When Ivan IV was 16 years old, he was crowned czar and began to rule in his own right. He ignored the boyars and turned to merchants and close friends for advice. He gave his advisers gifts of land and jobs as officials. To make sure that the officials' country estates were farmed while the officials themselves were in Moscow with him, Ivan ordered peasants not to leave their land. In this way, he took the first step in turning free peasants into serfs.

In 1552, Ivan led his armies against Mongol territories on the Volga. By this time, the Muscovites had learned the use of gunpowder from western Europe. The Mongols, however, still depended on bows and arrows. Within six years, Ivan conquered most of the Mongol territories. Muscovites settlers began to move east. Some, called Cossacks (kos' aks), began to farm along the Volga.

In 1558, Muscovite armies attacked Livonia (luh vō' nē uh), a land on the Baltic Sea. Livonia's neighbors sent troops to fight the Muscovite armies. In 1562, these troops defeated the Muscovite soldiers and took over much of their Baltic territory. Ivan blamed the boyars for his terrible defeat.

In 1564, Ivan suddenly left Moscow and went to live in a small monastery in the country. A month later, he announced that he was giving up the throne because of the boyars. Afraid that without Ivan the empire would fall, the people begged him to change his mind. They told Ivan that if he came back, he could have full authority to punish traitors and to take over their lands.

Ivan returned to Moscow, took over boyar lands, and gave the land to 5,000 of his most loyal supporters. In return, they formed the *Oprichnina* (ah prich' nē nuh), or secret police or soldiers of terror. Members of the Oprichnina dressed in black and rode black horses through the countryside. They scared the czar's enemies and carried a broom to show their desire to sweep treason from the land. They killed thousands of people. Finally, when the Oprichnina had defeated the boyars and returned control of the empire to Ivan, he broke up the group.

Ivan came to be called Ivan the Terrible. This is because the English translated the word meaning "awesome" as "terrible." To the Muscovites, however, Ivan was a great ruler who protected their country from enemies.

Ivan encouraged art and learning. He brought artists, scholars, and engineers from western Europe to teach the Muscovites new skills. He established a link between Moscow and England and Holland. He also increased the czar's power.

Painting of Ivan the Terrible

People in History

Ivan the Terrible
1530–1584

Russian Czar

Ivan was the first Russian ruler to be officially crowned as czar. He built a strong central government and was the first ruler to ever call a national assembly. He began Russian expansion eastward, conquering Siberia, and he began trade with England. His undoing was his fearful temper, which fell on enemies and friends alike.

GEOGRAPHY AND HISTORY

Under Ivan's rule, the first Rus settlers began to move eastward into Siberia.

MAKING CONNECTIONS

➤➤ **History** Ivan introduced printing in Russia and allowed English traders to enter the country. He was so fascinated with the West and its culture that he considered marrying one of the ladies of Queen Elizabeth's court.

DID YOU KNOW

The Cossacks were rebellious pioneers against medieval Rus's established order. They generally included bands of runaway peasants, serfs, farmers, and adventurers who moved to the frontier, along the Dnieper and Don rivers in the sixteenth century.

ASSESS

Check for Understanding

Ask students to summarize orally or in writing the main points of the chapter. Discuss the answers to the Section and Chapter Assessment questions.

Evaluate

Assign the Chapter 23 **Performance Assessment Activity** in the TCR.

Administer **Chapter 23 Test** in the TCR. Testmaker available.

COOPERATIVE LEARNING

Divide the class into six groups. Assign each group one of the following characters: Rus peasant, prince of Moscow, Rus soldier, Rus church leader, the khan, or Ivan the Great. Inform students that they will role-play these characters in a panel discussion based on the question, "Is Mongol rule good for Moscow?" Ask each group to decide how Mongol rule affected their assigned character and prepare a note card containing approximately five points to be brought out in the discussion. Have each group select a representative to role-play their character.

Reteach

Assign Chapter 23 **Reteaching Activity** in the TCR.

Enrich

Assign Chapter 23 **Enrichment Activity** in the TCR.

CLOSE

Have students evaluate the declaration by Ivan the Terrible that Rus was the third Rome.

💾 Use **Interactive Tutor Self-Assessment Software** to review Section 4.

When he died in 1584, however, Ivan left no suitable heir. He had killed the oldest of his three sons in a fit of rage. His middle son was feeble-minded, and his youngest son was still a baby. As a result, for some 25 years after Ivan's death, the Muscovy was in confusion and disorder.

Section 2 Assessment

1. **Define:** kremlin, czar.
2. Why did Moscow become powerful?
3. What happened to Muscovy after Ivan the Terrible's death?

Critical Thinking

4. **Drawing a Conclusion** Which name do you think most accurately describes Ivan IV—Ivan the Awesome or Ivan the Terrible? Explain.

Graphic Organizer Activity

5. Draw this chart, and use it to compare the accomplishments of Dmitry, Ivan the Great, and Ivan the Terrible.

Dmitry	Ivan the Great	Ivan the Terrible

Chapter Summary & Study Guide

1. Between 500 and 800 A.D., groups of Eastern Slavs settled in lands west of the Volga River.
2. The early Eastern Slavs relied on Viking warriors known as the Varangians to protect a trade route running from the Baltic Sea in the north to the Caspian Sea in the south.
3. In 882, a Viking warrior named Oleg built the first Kievan Rus state.
4. In 988, Eastern Orthodoxy became the official religion of Kievan Rus.
5. The Eastern Orthodox Church brought Byzantine culture, including the Cyrillic alphabet, to Kievan Rus.
6. After 1054, Rus trade declined and people shifted to farming.
7. Around 1240, the Mongols conquered Rus, forcing many Rus people to flee. Many settled near Moscow in the north.
8. Moscow gradually became the center of economic and religious life.
9. In the late 1400s, Ivan the Great ended Mongol control of Muscovy and took the title of czar.
10. Beginning in 1552, Ivan the Terrible conquered most of the Mongol territories, and many Muscovites began moving eastward.
11. In 1584, Ivan the Terrible died without leaving a capable heir. Muscovy then entered a 25-year period of disorder.

Section 4 Assessment Answers

1. kremlin, fortress (p. 354); czar, emperor (p. 355)
2. because its princes cooperated with the Mongols who took over territories that were not wealthy; and because the princes passed their thrones from father to son, which eliminated fighting
3. It was in a state of confusion and disorder because he left no suitable heir.
4. Answers will vary, but students should give reasons for their choice of names.
5. *Dmitry*—attacked and defeated Mongols; *Ivan the Great*—ended Mongol control of Muscovy, expanded its boundaries to the north and west, tried to revive glory of Byzantine Empire, built beautiful churches in Moscow, took title of czar; *Ivan the Terrible*—undermined power of boyars, conquered Mongol territories, encouraged art and learning, established a link between Moscow and England and Holland, increased the czar's power

Assign Chapter 23 **Section 4 Quiz** in the TCR. Testmaker available.

Using Key Terms

Imagine what a photograph illustrating each of the following words might look like. Write a sentence describing each picture, using the vocabulary word.

zbas   boyars   *veche*
khan   kremlin   czar

Understanding Main Ideas

1. How did the houses of the Eastern Slavs provide warmth?
2. Why did the early Eastern Slavs invite the Vikings into their lands?
3. How was the Rus state established by Oleg organized?
4. Why did Vladimir choose the Eastern Orthodox Church as the offical church of the state?
5. How did Yaroslav develop closer ties with western Europe?
6. How did the Muscovites view the princes of Moscow?
7. What did Ivan III do for Muscovy?
8. Why did many Muscovites think Ivan the Terrible was a great ruler?
9. Between what European countries and Moscow did Ivan IV develop a link?

Critical Thinking

1. Why do you think trade with other cities is one of the first activities of successful cities such as Kiev?
2. What do you think are the advantages and disadvantages of passing power from father to son, such as the czars did?
3. Do you think the word "terrible" describes Ivan IV? What other word or term might describe him better? Explain your answer.

Graphic Organizer Activity

History Create a diagram like this one, and use it to summarize reasons for the rise and decline of Kievan Rus.

Geography in History

Location Refer to the map on page 356. Imagine the czar has asked you to choose the location of a new settlement in the area acquired by the death of Ivan IV. Where would you locate the settlement and why? What geographic features affected your decision?

Using Your Journal

Review any details you may have noted about the ways the people of the Rus states were influenced by other civilizations. Then write a short newspaper article explaining how the Eastern Orthodox Church affected the culture of the area.

359

Bonus Test Question

For the Chapter 23 Test
The distance between Novgorod and Kiev along the Varangian Route was about 600 miles. The town of Smolensk was halfway between them. Traveling at 3 miles per hour, how many days would it take to go from Kiev to Smolensk, traveling by day? *(about 10 days)*

Using Your Journal

Articles should indicate that the Eastern Orthodox Church brought Byzantine culture to Rus states, the Cyrillic alphabet to Russia, and unity to the people of Rus during the Mongol invasion.

Geography in History

Answers will vary but should include an explanation of why they would locate the settlement where they did.

Using Key Terms

Sentences will vary.

Understanding Main Ideas

1. built partly underground
2. to protect their trade route to Byzantium
3. as a group of small territories ruled by the Grand Prince of Kiev
4. because observers had been stunned by the beauty of Eastern Orthodox worship
5. by having family members marry European royalty
6. as rulers protected by God
7. He ended Mongol rule, expanded Muscovy, built palaces and cathedrals, and built walls around the Kremlin.
8. because he protected their country, encouraged art and learning, and created a Rus empire
9. England and Holland

Critical Thinking

1. Answers will vary but might include that successful cities needed industries, and isolated cities do not grow.
2. Answers will vary.
3. Answers will vary, but students should refer to the ruler's deeds and explain their choices.

Graphic Organizer Activity

Answers will vary. Reasons for rise might include: geographic location ideal for trade and defense; support of local princes and rich merchants and boyars; role of *veche* in settling disputes; unity provided by Eastern Orthodoxy; leadership of early rulers, etc. Reasons for decline might include: quarrels over throne, attacks on Kievan Rus's frontiers, disrupted trade, attack by Andrei Bogoliubsky.

UNIT 7 Around

FOCUS

Objectives

After reading the Around the World for Unit 7, your students will be able to:

1. Locate the Anasazi homeland.
2. Explain the purpose of a kiva.
3. Identify Anasazi economic activities.
4. Describe features of the Anasazi ruins.

Bellringer

Conduct a brainstorming session in which students name Native American people who live in the present-day Southwest. *(Possibilities include: Zuñi, Hopi, Pima, Navajo, Pueblo, Apache, Acoma.)*

Motivational Activity

Review the results of student brainstorming, correcting or adding to their lists. Then refer students to the map on page 360. Ask: Where was the Anasazi homeland located? *(throughout much of the Southwest, especially the present-day Four Corners area)* Ask students to speculate on how many Native American people who live in this area might view the Anasazi. *(as their ancestors)*

TEACH

Geography: Place Remind students that each place on the earth has its own unique physical and human features. Working in small groups, have students list the unique features of the Anasazi. You might have them organize information in a chart, such as the one on page 361.

360

THE ANASAZI

The Anasazi (a' na sa' zē) built one of the most advanced cultures in North America outside of Mexico. From roughly 200 A.D. to 1300 A.D., they established thousands of settlements throughout the present-day southwestern United States. A network of trails and roads—some more than 30 feet wide—connected many of these settlements. Artifacts found at Anasazi sites show that these people traded far and wide, including with the ancient civilizations of Mexico and Central America. Today many Native Americans who live in this region, such as the Pueblo (pweb' lō), trace their roots to the Anasazi.

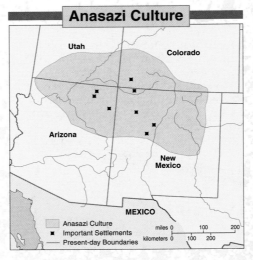

Anasazi Culture

Utah
Colorado
Arizona
New Mexico
MEXICO

▢ Anasazi Culture
■ Important Settlements
— Present-day Boundaries

miles 0 / 100 / 200
kilometers 0 / 100 / 200

▲ The Anasazi lived in the area known as the Four Corners—the meeting place of the present-day states of Utah, Colorado, Arizona, and New Mexico. Like other desert cultures, they learned to farm the land by digging irrigation ditches to catch the rain and to channel water from rivers.

▲ The Anasazi never developed a written language. However, archaeologists think they may have left messages in the form of pictures painted or scratched into rocks throughout the Four Corners area. The meanings of many of these pictures remain unknown to this day.

SPOTLIGHT ON: ANASAZI

The Anasazi irrigation ditches allowed them to produce enough corn, squash, and beans—or what their descendants call the "three sisters"—to fuel a population explosion. Archaeological remains attest to their success as a people. More than 25,000 Anasazi sites can be found in New Mexico alone.

In areas where the Anasazi could not rely on the rivers for water, they learned to collect runoff from the cliff tops during heavy rains. As water ran through flumes from the cliff, they channeled it into a system of dams, canals, ditches and floodgates until it reached fields on the canyon floor.

Nobody knows for sure why the Anasazi left their cliff homes—perhaps drought, perhaps overpopulation. Nor do they know where they went. For some Native Americans, however, they never left at all. Instead, people such as the Pueblo and Hopi believe the Anasazi resettled in the area to form the basis of their own cultures.

The Anasazi used turquoise as a trade item. At Chaco (cha' kō) Canyon, New Mexico, over 100,000 pieces of turquoise have been found. The Anasazi fashioned turquoise into beads for necklaces or used to decorate everyday objects.

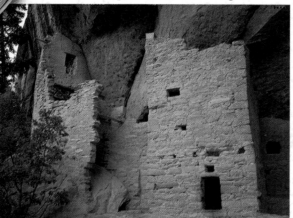

The Anasazi moved into the cliffs and canyons of the Southwest and built houses made of mud bricks. Perhaps 1,000 people lived in what is known as the Cliff Palace. Located in Mesa Verde, Colorado, the Cliff Palace had about 200 rooms and looked something like a modern apartment complex. When Spanish explorers first saw these houses, they called them *pueblos*—the Spanish word for "villages." ▼

Features of the Anasazi Homeland	
Physical Features	**Human Features**

Nearly all Anasazi villages included large circular underground chambers known as *kivas* (kē' əs). Scholars believe that the Anasazi used the kivas as religious centers and as clubhouses. They also believe that the kivas were restricted to men, with women entering the kivas only on special occasions. ▼

ASSESS

Check for Understanding

Have students answer the questions in Taking Another Look on page 361.

Enrich

Request interested students to research important Anasazi landmarks in the Four Corners area. Have them display their findings in an illustrated map of the region. A possible source of information is *North American Indian Landmarks: A Traveler's Guide,* by George Cantor, Gale Research Inc., 1993.

Taking Another Look

1. What was the purpose of the kivas?
2. What were the main economic activities of the Anasazi?

Hands-on Activity

Designing a Postcard Design a postcard that you might send from the Four Corners area to a friend in another part of the United States. The front of the card should show a picture of an Anasazi ruin or artifact, while the back should include a description of your experiences.

361

CLOSE

Have students compare economic activities in medieval Europe with those conducted by the Anasazi. Ask: What is one of the biggest differences that you notice? *(Help students to understand that while trade collapsed in most of western Europe, the Anasazi built a trading network that reached far and wide.)*

ANSWERS TO TAKING ANOTHER LOOK

1. Scholars believe the kivas were used for religious purposes and as clubhouses.
2. The Anasazi farmed and traded with people as far away as Central America.

Hands-On Activity
Postcards will vary but should accurately reflect the geographic conditions in the Anasazi homeland as well as the significance of the ruins. You might give extra credit to those students who do additional research on a site not shown in the feature, such as Chaco Canyon or Canyon de Chelly.

Answers and Analyses

1D History

Theodora is discussed on page 322. She never served as emperor, nor in the army, so choices B and C can be eliminated. Page 322 states, however, that she helped Justinian *fill government and church offices,* and that she was an important advisor to him.

 TEST-TAKING TIP

As with any specific question, students should begin by eliminating the implausible. Choices A and C are unlikely.

2H History

Page 326 discussed the split between the Orthodox and Catholic churches. There it states that *An argument also developed between the Pope and the Patriarch. The Patriarch would not recognize the Pope as head of the Church.*

3B History

Muhammad was born in Makkah, not Palestine, and had nothing to do with the Pope. Therefore, choices A and D can be eliminated. According to page 333, the leaders of Makkah began to fear Muhammad and began to persecute him and his followers. According to page 248, the same was true of Jesus.

4F History

The split between the Sunni and the Shiites is discussed on page 338. There it states that the Shiites believed that *the office of caliph should be held only by descendants of Ali.* This information makes F the best choice.

Standardized Test Practice

Directions: Choose the *best* answer to each of the following multiple choice questions. If you have trouble answering a question, use the process of elimination to narrow your choices. Write your answers on a separate piece of paper.

1. **How was Justinian's wife, Theodora, different from the wives of previous emperors?**

   A She bore a male heir to the emperor's throne.

   B She was the first female to serve as emperor.

   C She fought as a member of the army to defend her husband.

   D She played a large role in shaping law and public policy.

   > *Test-Taking Tip:* Eliminate answers that do not make sense. Since it is unlikely that Justinian was the first emperor's wife to give birth to a son (answer A), you can easily eliminate this answer choice.

2. **The Eastern Orthodox Church split from the Roman Catholic Church because of a disagreement over**

   F the content of the Old and New Testaments

   G what kinds of work missionaries should perform

   H who the leader of the Christian church should be

   J the role of women in the church

   > *Test-Taking Tip:* This question requires you to remember a *fact* about the Eastern Orthodox Church. Make sure that you read the question and *all* of the answer choices carefully before selecting the *best* answer.

3. **In which of the following ways were Muhammad and Jesus similar?**

   A Both were born in Palestine.

   B Both were seen as threats to the existing governments.

   C Both stopped gaining followers after their deaths.

   D Both required their followers to accept the power of the Pope.

   > *Test-Taking Tip:* This question asks you to make a *comparison* between these two leaders. Since Islam and Christianity are still gaining followers today, answer C is an unlikely choice.

4. **Like the Catholic Church, the Muslims split into two groups. How were the Sunni different from the Shiites?**

   F They believed that Islamic rulers did not have to be descendents of Ali.

   G They wanted the religious center of Islam to be Constantinople.

   H They were opposed to the use of religious icons as a part of ceremonies.

   J They wanted to recognize the Pope as their religious leader.

   > *Test-Taking Tip:* This question also asks you to make a comparison, but this time it asks for a *difference* rather than a *similarity.* Be careful: even though the question mentions the split in the Catholic church, it is *not* asking for a comparison between Catholicism and Islam. Therefore, you can eliminate any answers that have to do with the Catholic Church, like answer J.

The Growth of Moscow

Legend:
- Grand Principality of Moscow, 1300
- Acquired by 1462
- Acquired by Death of Ivan III, 1505
- Acquired by Death of Ivan IV, 1584

miles 0 — 200 — 400
kilometers 0 — 200 — 400

5. Based on the map above, what important contribution to Moscow's potential for trade was made by the time of Ivan IV's death?

F Moscow gained access to the Ottoman Empire through the Volga and Don rivers.

G Moscow gained access to trade routes to Norway and Sweden through the Baltic Sea.

H Moscow gained access to western Europe through the Danube River.

J Moscow gained control of land reaching to the Arctic Ocean.

Test-Taking Tip: Use the *map key*, or *legend*, to help you understand how the map is organized. Make sure that your answer is supported by information *on the map*.

6. The distance between Moscow and Novgorod is approximately

A 200 kilometers

B 400 kilometers

C 600 kilometers

D 700 kilometers

Test-Taking Tip: The map's *scale* will help you answer this question. If you do not have a ruler, you can copy the scale onto a small piece of paper to measure the distance. Notice that the answer choices are given in *kilometers*, not miles. The scale shows both: miles on the top, and kilometers below.

STOP

363

5F Geography

According to the map, only the Volga and Don rivers, as well as the Arctic Ocean, fell within the area acquired by the time of Ivan IV's death. The Arctic Ocean, however, did not have great potential for trade.

THE PRINCETON REVIEW | **TEST-TAKING TIP**

Students need to understand how to read the legend and to determine what areas were under Moscow's control at this time. The Volga and Don rivers are the only choices listed that were both under Moscow's control *and* valuable for trade.

6C Geography

The scale on the map indicates that the distance between Moscow and Novgorod is about 600 kilometers.

THE PRINCETON REVIEW | **TEST-TAKING TIP**

All of the information needed to answer the question is on the map, but students need to read very carefully to avoid mistakes. In this case, students need to make sure that they do not confuse miles and kilometers on the scale.

Tested Objectives	
Questions	**Reading Objective**
1	Make generalizations
2	Determine cause and effect
3, 4	Make comparisons
5	Analyze information

OVERVIEW

Unit 8 discusses the changes that took place in western Europe during the late Middle Ages.

➤ **Chapter 24** describes feudalism.

➤ **Chapter 25** discusses the role of the Roman Catholic Church in medieval life.

➤ **Chapter 26** describes how the growth of trade during the Middle Ages led to the rise of towns in western Europe.

➤ **Chapter 27** examines the development of strong national governments under monarchs in France, England, Germany, and Spain.

UNIT OBJECTIVES

After reading Unit 8, students will be able to:

1. discuss what roles the clergy, nobles, and peasants played during the late Middle Ages.

2. explain what led to the growth of trade and towns in western Europe.

3. describe how kings in western Europe built strong nations during the late Middle Ages.

UNIT PROJECT

Organize the class into four teams to play "The Late Middle Ages Quiz Bowl." Assign each team one chapter from this unit. Have the teams each prepare strips of paper with the names of important people, places, events, and themes discussed in their chapter, and place them in a large container. Have a moderator select a paper and read it aloud. The first team member must explain, define, or give information about the topic. If the team member is unable to do so, the question passes to the next team.

364

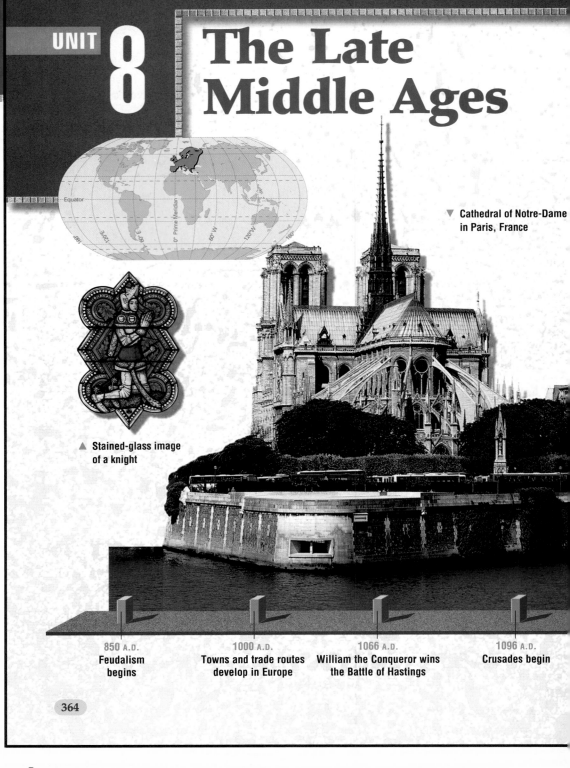

UNIT 8 The Late Middle Ages

▼ Cathedral of Notre-Dame in Paris, France

▲ Stained-glass image of a knight

850 A.D.
Feudalism begins

1000 A.D.
Towns and trade routes develop in Europe

1066 A.D.
William the Conqueror wins the Battle of Hastings

1096 A.D.
Crusades begin

364

ABOUT THE UNIT OPENING

Examining Artifacts

Based on these two artifacts, what can students infer about the role of religion in the late Middle Ages. *(It was very important.)* Ask students how they reached this answer. *(Sample responses: complexity and grandeur of the cathedral, the knight kneeling in prayer, etc.)* Tell students that this unit examines the influence of the Roman Catholic Church and its relationship with emerging national governments.

Global Chronology

Ask students to explain what time period the time line covers. *(850 to 1337)* How many years passed between the beginning of feudalism and the development of towns and trade routes? *(150 years)* When did the Hundred Years' War begin? *(1337)* Who were some important people during this time? *(William the Conqueror, Frederick I)*

Multimedia Activity

Turning Points in World History
The Crusades

Setting up the Video

Work with a group of your classmates to view "The Crusades" on the videodisc *Turning Points in World History*.

View the video by scanning the bar code or by entering the chapter number on your keypad and pressing "Search." (Also available in VHS format.)

Side One,
Chapter 7

The Crusades started out as a Christian military campaign to free Jerusalem from Muslim control. These campaigns, however, helped end the Middle Ages in Europe. This program highlights the modern institutions, such as banks and increased trade, which came about as a result of the Crusades.

Hands-On Activity

Create a cause-and-effect chart about the Crusades, showing how the actions of the Europeans and the Muslims caused changes in Europe. Illustrate the chart with pictures.

PRIMARY SOURCES
Library

See pages 688–689 for a primary source reading to accompany Unit 8.

1152 A.D.
derick I becomes y Roman Emperor

1215 A.D.
Magna Carta is signed

1337 A.D.
Hundred Years' War begins

Journal Notes

What was life like during the late Middle Ages? Note details about it as you read.

365

INTRODUCING THE UNIT

Help students create a list of topics they associate with the Middle Ages such as the Crusades, the Black Death, feudalism, cathedrals, etc. Ask students what it might have been like in the Middle Ages—exciting, frightening, dangerous, dull. Point out that the late Middle Ages was a time of turbulent change, and that many of the institutions in existence today had their origins in the late Middle Ages.

RECORDING JOURNAL NOTES

Set aside time for the students to record details about life in the late Middle Ages after reading each chapter in the unit. Have students read their journal entries after each recording.

PRIMARY SOURCES
Library

Items in the Primary Sources Library for this unit focus on life on a medieval manor. Elements include:
- Description of a noble's household
- Selection from *The Vision of Piers Plowman*

For additional primary source documents, use the **World History Primary Source Document CD-ROM.**

Geographic Location

Have students look at their text Atlas to find the city of Jerusalem. *(located in the present state of Israel)* Discuss some of the difficulties an army in the Middle Ages might encounter traveling from Europe to Jerusalem. *(crossing mountains, crossing or going around the Black Sea, or crossing the Mediterranean Sea)*

Chapter 24 Planning Guide

Objectives	Reproducible Resources	Multimedia Resources
Section 1 **Land and Government** Explain why feudalism developed in western Europe.	Reproducible Lesson Plan Chapter 24 Vocabulary and Guided Reading Activity Reading Essentials and Study Guide 24-1 Chapter 24 Chart and Graph Skill Activity Unit 8 World Literature Reading 2 Section 1 Quiz Unit 8 Hands-On History Lab	Teaching Transparencies and Activities 24A & 24B Vocabulary PuzzleMaker Interactive Tutor Self-Assessment Software ExamView® Pro Testmaker Glencoe Skillbuilder Interactive Workbook, Level 1 Presentation Plus!
Section 2 **The Nobility** Describe the roles played by lords and vassals.	Reproducible Lesson Plan Reading Essentials and Study Guide 24-2 Chapter 24 Cooperative Learning Activity Section 2 Quiz	Vocabulary PuzzleMaker Interactive Tutor Self-Assessment Software ExamView® Pro Testmaker Glencoe Skillbuilder Interactive Workbook, Level 1
Section 3 **Knighthood** Discuss the training and duties of a knight.	Reproducible Lesson Plan Reading Essentials and Study Guide 24-3 Chapter 24 Enrichment Activity Section 3 Quiz	Vocabulary PuzzleMaker Interactive Tutor Self-Assessment Software ExamView® Pro Testmaker Glencoe Skillbuilder Interactive Workbook, Level 1
Section 4 **The Manor** Characterize manor life, identifying the relationship between nobles and serfs.	Reproducible Lesson Plan Reading Essentials and Study Guide 24-4 Chapter 24 Activity Book Activity Chapter 24 Geography and Map Activity Unit 8 Primary Sources Reading Section 4 Quiz	Vocabulary PuzzleMaker Interactive Tutor Self-Assessment Software ExamView® Pro Testmaker Glencoe Skillbuilder Interactive Workbook, Level 1
Chapter 24 **Review and Evaluation**	Chapter 24 Reteaching Activity Chapter 24 Performance Assessment Activity Spanish Chapter Summary and Glossary Chapter 24 Test	Vocabulary PuzzleMaker Interactive Tutor Self-Assessment Software Glencoe Skillbuilder Interactive Workbook, Level 1 Audiocassettes* ExamView® Pro Testmaker

*Also available in Spanish.

Presentation Plus!

Use Glencoe's **Presentation Plus!** multimedia teacher tool to easily present dynamic lessons that visually excite your students. Using Microsoft® PowerPoint, you can customize the presentations to create your own personalized lessons.

 Interactive Lesson Planner

Planning has never been easier! Using this CD-ROM, organize your week, month, semester, or year with all the help you need. The **Interactive Lesson Planner** gives you access to all of the blackline masters which accompany *Human Heritage.*

✓ PERFORMANCE ASSESSMENT ACTIVITIES

Tapestry Mural Have students create murals modeled after tapestry made during the Middle Ages such as the Bayeux Tapestry. (This tapestry included 72 embroidered scenes depicting the Norman Conquest of England by William I in 1066.) Have them include portraits of people from the chapter, showing details of their dress and objects that symbolize their station in life. For instance, students might depict a knight in full armor with a shield displaying his coat of arms.

CHAPTER RESOURCES

LITERATURE ABOUT THE PERIOD

Scott, Sir Walter. *Ivanhoe.* Longmans, Green, and Co., 1897. Twelfth-century story of hidden identity, intrigue, and romance among the English nobility.

READINGS FOR THE STUDENT

Gies, Frances and Joseph. *Life in a Medieval Village.* Harper Perennial, 1990. An illustrated look at the way most medieval people passed their lives.

McEvedy, Colin. *The New Penguin Atlas of Medieval History.* Penguin, 1992. Details the medieval history of the Mediterranean, Europe, and the nomad steppelands. Details enhanced with 45 maps.

READINGS FOR THE TEACHER

Gies, Frances, and Joseph Gies. *Marriage and the Family in the Middle Ages.* Harper and Row, 1987. Summarizes family history during the medieval period.

  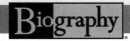

THE HISTORY CHANNEL

The following videotape programs are available from Glencoe:

- **Knights and Armor**
  1-56501-443-X

- **King Arthur: His Life and Legends**
  1-56501-644-0

To order, call Glencoe at 1-800-334-7344. To find classroom resources to accompany many of these, check:
A&E Television: http://www.aetv.com
The History Channel: http://www.historychannel.com

NATIONAL GEOGRAPHIC SOCIETY — Teacher's Corner

INDEX TO NATIONAL GEOGRAPHIC MAGAZINE

The following articles relate to this chapter:

- "The Basques," by Thomas J. Abercrombie, November 1995.
- "Oxford," by Bill Bryson, November 1995.

NATIONAL GEOGRAPHIC SOCIETY PRODUCTS AVAILABLE FROM GLENCOE

To order the following, call Glencoe at 1-800-334-7344:

- *PicturePack: Europe (Transparencies)*
- *PicturePack: The Middle Ages (Transparencies)*
- *PictureShow: The Middle Ages (CD-ROM)*

Access *National Geographic*'s new dynamic MapMachine Web site and other geography resources at:
http://www.nationalgeographic.com/
http://www.nationalgeographic.com/maps/

KEY TO ABILITY LEVELS

Teaching strategies have been coded for varying learning styles and abilities.

L1 Level 1 activities are **basic** activities and should be within the ability range of all students.

L2 Level 2 activities are **average** activities and should be within the ability range of the average to above-average student.

L3 Level 3 activities are **challenging** activities designed for the ability range of above-average students.

ELL ELL activities should be within the ability range of English Language Learning students.

OVERVIEW

Chapter 24 discusses the development of feudal society in western Europe after the collapse of Charlemagne's empire.

➤ **Section 1** describes the origins of feudalism.
➤ **Section 2** discusses the feudal social hierarchy.
➤ **Section 3** describes the duties of feudal knights.
➤ **Section 4** explains the lifestyles of the people in feudal society and the organization of the manors.

CHAPTER OBJECTIVES

After reading Chapter 24, students will be able to:
1. explain why feudalism developed in western Europe.
2. describe what roles were played by lords and vassals.
3. discuss a knight's duties.
4. describe manor life.

EXAMINING ARTIFACTS

Ask students what these artifacts tell them about the daily life of peasants. *(milled their own grain, used simple tools, worked as farmers, etc.)* Next, have students examine the time line for other clues about life during the years 700–1000 A.D. Tell them that in this chapter they will learn about the relationship that developed between peasants and nobles as they struggled to survive.

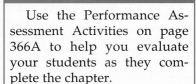

PERFORMANCE ASSESSMENT ✓

Use the Performance Assessment Activities on page 366A to help you evaluate your students as they complete the chapter.

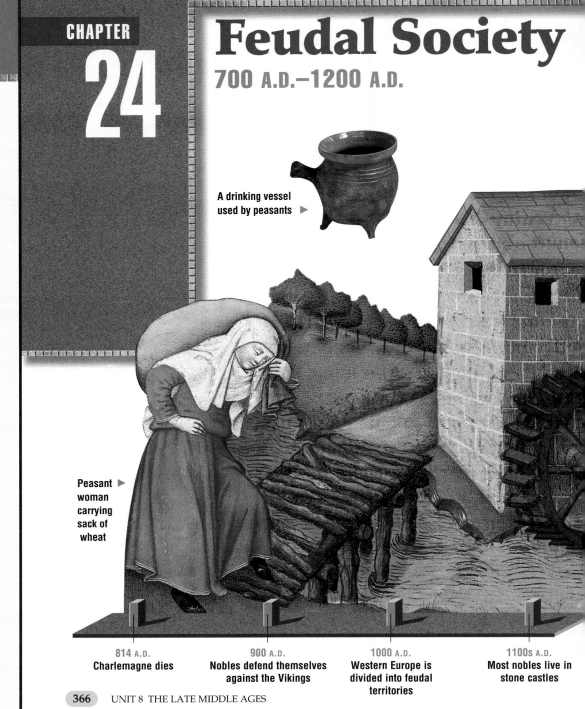

CHAPTER 24

Feudal Society
700 A.D.–1200 A.D.

◀ A drinking vessel used by peasants ▶

Peasant ▶ woman carrying sack of wheat

814 A.D.
Charlemagne dies

900 A.D.
Nobles defend themselves against the Vikings

1000 A.D.
Western Europe is divided into feudal territories

1100s A.D.
Most nobles live in stone castles

TEACHING RESOURCES

TEACHER PLANNING AND SUPPORT

📁 Reproducible Lesson Plan
📁 Block Scheduling Implementation Guide
📁 Videodisc Bar Code Correlation
💿 Presentation Plus!

REVIEW AND REINFORCEMENT

📁 Reading Essentials and Study Guide 24-1, 24-2, 24-3, 24-4
📁 Chapter 24 Vocabulary and Guided Reading Activity
💾 Vocabulary PuzzleMaker Software
🖐 Teaching Transparencies 24A & 24B
📁 Chapter 24 Reteaching Activity

📁 Chapter 24 Cooperative Learning Activity
📁 Chapter 24 Activity Book Activity
📁 Chapter 24 Chart and Graph Skills Activity
💾 Interactive Tutor Self-Assessment Software
📼 Unit 8 MindJogger VideoQuiz

APPLICATION AND HANDS-ON ACTIVITIES

📁 Daily World History, Geography, and Culture Question
📁 Unit 8 Hands-On History Lab Activity

Chapter Focus

Read to Discover
- Why feudalism developed in western Europe.
- What roles were played by lords and vassals.
- What the duties of a knight were.
- What life was like on a manor.

Terms to Learn

feudalism	castles	tournaments
clergy	keep	joust
fiefs	ladies	manors
vassal	code of chivalry	seneschal
act of homage	page	bailiff
knight	squire	freemen
	dubbing	

Why It's Important Central government collapsed after the death of King Charlemagne. As the Vikings invaded western European kingdoms, local nobles took over the duty of raising armies and protecting their property. Power passed from kings to local lords, giving rise to a system known as **feudalism** (fyoo' dul ih zum). Under feudalism, landowning nobles governed and protected the people in exchange for services, such as fighting in a noble's army or farming the land.

The **clergy,** or religious leaders, also owned land and held power. Members of the clergy taught Christianity, helped the poor and sick, and advised the nobles who belonged to the Church. With western Europe divided into thousands of feudal territories, the Church served as a unifying force and exerted a strong influence over the culture of the Middle Ages.

Chapter Overview
Visit the *Human Heritage* Web site at **humanheritage.glencoe.com** and click on *Chapter 24— Chapter Overviews* to preview this chapter.

✓ **Reading Check**
What was **feudalism?**

✓ **Reading Check**
Who were the **clergy?**

SECTION 1 Land and Government

During feudal times, power was based on the ownership of land. Before feudalism, kings owned all the land within their territories. Then Charles Martel the Frankish leader began giving his soldiers **fiefs** (fēfs), or estates, as a reward for their service and loyalty. From their fiefs, the soldiers got the income they needed to buy horses and battle equipment. After 800, the kings of Europe followed Martel's example. From that time on, land ownership was tied to military service. With land ownership went power and wealth, giving soldiers a base from which to rule Europe.

✓ **Reading Check**
Why did soldiers receive **fiefs** during the Middle Ages?

CHAPTER 24 FEUDAL SOCIETY **367**

Chapter Overview introduces students to chapter content and key terms. Have them access *Chapter 24 Overview* at **humanheritage.glencoe.com**

FOCUS

🖾 Bellringer
Ask students to write a one-sentence description of the following: a knight, a squire, a page, a noblewoman, and a serf.

Motivational Activity
Have students read their sentences, and discuss their ideas about people in the Middle Ages.

✓ **Reading Check Answer**
Under **feudalism,** landowning nobles governed and protected the people in exchange for services.
The **clergy** were religious leaders.
Soldiers received **fiefs** as a reward for service and loyalty.

GUIDE TO READING

Reading Strategy
Ask students to read "Why It's Important" and summarize the chapter's main theme. *(Collapse of central government and Viking invasions gave rise to feudalism— a time when the Church served as the main unifying force in Europe.)*

Vocabulary Precheck
Ask students to define each of the "Terms to Learn." **L1 ELL**

💾 Use the Vocabulary PuzzleMaker for Chapter 24 to create a crossword puzzle. **L1**

📁 Assign Chapter 24 Vocabulary and Guided Reading Activity.

📁 Assign Reading Essentials and Study Guide 24-1.

Guided Practice

L1 **Daily Life** Draw a simple figure to represent the human body on the chalkboard and label its parts as you explain the following comparison made by one medieval scholar who compared feudal society to the human body. He saw: priests and clerks, as spiritual guides, or the head and eyes; nobles, as protectors and defenders, or the arms and hands; and peasants, the workers on whose labor all society was based, as the legs and feet. **ELL**

L2 **Critical Thinking** Ask: *Was feudalism an effective system of government? Why or why not?* Have students write a list of recommendations of changes they would submit to improve government.

Reading Check Answer
A **vassal** served a lord of a higher rank and gave him loyalty.
During an **act of homage,** the vassal and lord took part in a ceremony in which their tie became official.

NATIONAL GEOGRAPHIC SOCIETY

Use these materials to enrich student understanding of the Middle Ages.

NGS PICTUREPACK TRANSPARENCIES
The Middle Ages

NGS PICTURESHOW CD-ROM
The Middle Ages

The Rise of Feudal Territories After Charlemagne's death in 814, Europe had no central government. The kings who followed Charlemagne were so weak they could not even rule their own kingdoms well. They ignored their responsibilities and spent most of their time traveling from one royal estate to another. Before long, they began to depend on the nobles for food, horses, and soldiers. Some nobles grew more powerful than the king and became independent rulers. They gained the right to collect taxes and to enforce the law in their areas. Many nobles raised armies and coined their own money.

Around 900, the nobles took on the duty of protecting their lands and people from the Vikings. They built fortresses on hilltops and fenced their lands. The peasants asked these powerful nobles to protect them. In return, the peasants gave their lands to nobles and promised to work for them in the fields. However, most peasants ended up giving the nobles not only their land but also their freedom.

By 1000, the kingdoms of western Europe were divided into thousands of feudal territories. Each was about the size of an ancient Greek city-state. Unlike the polis, however, a feudal territory had no central city. The noble who owned the land also had the political power. He made the laws for his fief, and the people obeyed them. Peasants, unlike Greek citizens, had no say in the government.

Although the peasants and townspeople made up the largest group, they had fewer rights than the clergy and nobles. Almost everyone believed that God wanted it that way. As a result, few people tried to improve society or change their own way of life. Most people remained in the group into which they were born.

Lord and Vassal Feudalism was based on ties of loyalty and duty among nobles. Nobles were both lords and vassals. A **vassal** (vas′ uhl) was a noble who served a lord of higher rank and gave him loyalty. In return, the lord protected the vassal. All nobles were ultimately vassals of the king, who might even be the vassal of another king.

The tie between lord and vassal was made official in a special ceremony known as the **act of homage** (om′ ij). The vassal, his head bare to show respect, knelt on one knee and placed his hands between those of the lord. He promised to serve the lord and to help him in battle. The lord accepted the promise, helped the vassal to his feet, and kissed him.

In return for the promise of loyalty and service, the lord gave his vassal a fief. Since there were few written agreements in the Middle Ages, the lord gave his vassal a glove, a stick, or a stone. This was to show that the lord's word could be trusted. He also gave the vassal the right to govern the people who lived on the

Reading Check
What were the duties of a **vassal?** What took place during an **act of homage?**

EXTENDING THE CONTENT

The basic structure of feudalism looks like a simple pyramid, but in fact sometimes grew very complicated. Many lords, of course, simply had peasants or very minor knights as their vassals. On the other hand, in the higher ranks of feudalism, lords and vassals often were social equals.

Even a poor knight with a rundown manor house might come from a family as proud as that of his overlord. At several times in history, the kings of England were vassals of the kings of France for territories such as Anjou and Aquitaine.

ef. The lord promised to protect his vassal from enemy attacks. f the lord failed in this, the vassal no longer owed him loyalty.

Vassals had certain duties to perform. Their most important uty was to help the lord in battle. Vassals had to bring their own nights with them. They themselves were expected to take part n military service 40 to 60 days a year.

Vassals had to make payments to their lord. When a lord's aughter married, or his son became a **knight,** or warrior on orseback, his vassals had to give the lord money. If a lord were aptured in battle, his vassals either became prisoners in his place r paid his *ransom.* This is a sum of money given in exchange for person's release.

Another duty of vassals was to attend the lord's court. Vasals were also expected to provide food and entertainment when neir lord visited them. If a vassal failed in his duties to his lord, ne lord had the right to take away the vassal's fief. When a vasal died, his fief usually passed on to his oldest son. The son then erformed the act of homage.

Reading Check
What was a **knight?**

L1 **Critical Thinking** Ask students to create lists of the responsibilities of lords and vassals. Then create two columns on the chalkboard headed, "Lords" and "Vassals." Have students write their ideas in the appropriate column. Then ask students to explain why the relationship between the lords and vassals developed and whether they think it was a fair one. **ELL**

💾 Use **Interactive Tutor Self-Assessment Software** to review Section 1.

Section 1 Assessment

. **Define:** feudalism, clergy, fiefs, vassal, act of homage, knight
. How did land ownership become tied to military service?
. How did nobles become so powerful?
. What were some duties of a vassal?

ritical Thinking

. **Demonstrating Reasoned Judgment** What were the advantages of being a vassal? What were the disadvantages?

Graphic Organizer Activity

6. Draw this diagram, and use it to show some of the causes of feudalism.

Causes

Feudalism

SECTION 2 The Nobility

Life was not always easy or pleasant for nobles during eudal times. They did, however, enjoy more benefits than the ommon people.

From the 800s to the 1000s, nobles and their families lived in vooden houses surrounded by *palisades* (pal uh sāds'), or high vooden fences built for protection. In case of attack, people from earby villages sought shelter inside the palisade.

The house consisted of one room with a high ceiling and a traw-covered floor. All activity took place in that one room. 'here, nobles met with vassals, carried out the laws, and said neir prayers. The nobles, their families, servants, and warriors

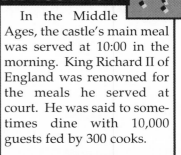
DID YOU KNOW ⁇

In the Middle Ages, the castle's main meal was served at 10:00 in the morning. King Richard II of England was renowned for the meals he served at court. He was said to sometimes dine with 10,000 guests fed by 300 cooks.

💾 Use the **Vocabulary Puzzle-Maker** to create crossword and word search puzzles.

CHAPTER 24 FEUDAL SOCIETY **369**

Section 1 Assessment Answers

1. feudalism, government by land-owning nobles (p. 367); clergy, religious leaders (p. 367); fiefs, estates (p. 367); vassal, a noble who served a lord (p. 368); act of homage, ceremony tying a lord and his vassal (p. 368); knight, warrior on horseback (p. 369)
2. Fiefs were given to soldiers as a reward.
3. Kings depended on nobles for food, horses, soldiers, and taxes.
4. to serve the lord in battle, make payments to the lord, become a prisoner in his

place or pay his ransom, and entertain him
5. Answers will vary but should show an understanding of feudal relationships.
6. Sample causes: lack of a central government, the weak kings who followed Charlemagne, the increasing power of nobles, the willingness of peasants to give their land to nobles for protection against the Vikings

Assign the Chapter 24 **Section 1 Quiz** in the TCR. Testmaker available.

Too much! Guests at a noble's banquet consumed huge amounts of food. In the 1340s, Pope Clement VI gave a feast that included 13,000 birds, 1,000 sheep, 50,000 fruit pies, and 200 casks of wine. At the 1403 wedding of Henry IV of England and Joan of Navarre, the royal couple tasted about 100 separate dishes.

NOBLE'S FEAST Nobles celebrated special occasions with elaborate feasts. Such meals often included many courses of meats, fruits, and vegetables. In this painting a noble sits down to dinner while his many servants bring out more food. **Where were meals for nobles held?**

also ate and slept in that room. At mealtime, wooden tables were set up and piled high with meat, fish, vegetables, fruits, and honey. People ate with their fingers and threw scraps of food on the floor for the dogs. The straw got so dirty with mud, bones, and food that every few months it had to be swept outdoors and burned.

The fires that cooked the meals were also used to heat the house. Actually, the fires did little to keep out the cold. Smoke from them often stung the eyes and darkened the walls and ceiling.

The Castle By the 1100s, nobles were living in stone houses called **castles.** Because they were designed as fortresses, the castles made nobles secure and independent. Castles had thick stone walls, one within another. Each corner had its own lookout tower with archers in it. Some castles were further protected by moat with a soft and muddy bottom that stopped attackers from using ladders to climb over the outer walls. To cross the moat,

MULTICULTURAL PERSPECTIVES

During the Middle Ages, several books on courtesy were written to teach the nobility table manners. Since fingers were used to transport food from large platters to individual trenchers, and from there to one's mouth, the cleanliness of one's fingers was a matter of concern for all the diners. One author wrote, "Thou must not put thy fingers into thine ears." Other writers asked their readers not to blow their noses with their fingers or scratch their heads, especially since fleas and lice were common.

person had to use the castle's drawbridge, which could be raised to prevent entry. The drawbridge led to the *portcullis* (pōrt kul' is), an iron gate that often served as the entrance to the castle.

Within the castle walls was a large open area. In the middle of this area was a **keep,** or tall tower with thick walls. It contained a great hall, many rooms, and a dungeon. The people of the household lived in the keep, which could be defended even if the rest of the castle fell to attackers. Shops, kitchens, stables, and rooms for troops and guests were also built inside the castle walls.

Many people, including the noble's servants and officials, lived in the castle. Since the noble was away fighting most of the time, the servants and officials were responsible for the castle's care and defense. Most castles had enough space to store a large supply of food and drink. As a result, people inside a castle could hold out against attackers for as long as six months.

Reading Check
Why did the people of a household live inside the **keep?**

Student Web Activity
Visit the *Human Heritage* Web site at **humanheritage.glencoe.com** and click on *Chapter 24— Student Web Activities* to find out more about castles.

CASTLE A castle was both a noble's home and a military fortress. During enemy attack, people from the surrounding area sought protection within the castle walls. Here, the moat and entrance of an English castle are shown. **Who was responsible for a castle's care and defense?**

Reading Check Answer
People of a household lived inside the **keep** because they could defend it even if the rest of the castle fell.

Student Web Activity objectives, goals, and answers can be found at the *Chapter 24 Web Activity Lesson Plan* at **humanheritage.glencoe.com**

CAPTION ANSWER

servants and officials

GEOGRAPHY AND HISTORY

Castles were often built on top of hills or mounds so sentries could easily spot attackers. Castles had their own wells so that defenders would have water if the castle came under attack.

DID YOU KNOW

Early stone castles had square towers that were easily damaged by large siege-cannons. The towers were later rounded off so they could withstand a direct hit from the cannons.

COOPERATIVE LEARNING

Have the class work in small groups to create plans for a medieval castle like the one described in this section. Refer to David Macaulay's book *Castle* and the videocassette that accompanies it. Tasks may be divided in several ways: researching medieval architecture, organizing data, writing plans, and illustrating the finished design by blueprint and sketch on poster board. Another group can present the finished project, describing various aspects of the castle and explaining the rationale.

Assign Chapter 24 *Cooperative Learning Activity* in the TCR.

Reading Check Answer
The marriages of most **ladies** were planned to unite families.

Linking Across Time

Other popular activities included: hunting and fishing, listening to wandering minstrels.

DID YOU KNOW ???
Some knights attacked and robbed passersby, especially traveling merchants, and raided their neighbors' lands for sheep and cattle.

MAKING CONNECTIONS

➤➤ **The Arts** Many ladies of the Middle Ages could read and were interested in music and poetry. They also spent time riding, hunting, and doing hard exercise.

Reading Check What was the main purpose of marriage for most **ladies** in the Middle Ages?

Castle Life   When nobles were at home, they looked after their estates, went hunting and fishing, and held court. During long winter evenings, they often played chess with family members. Wandering minstrels sometimes came to entertain the nobles and their guests by singing songs and playing stringed instruments.

Noblewomen were called **ladies.** Once they married, their husbands had complete authority over them. Most marriages were planned to unite important families, and a woman had little say about who was chosen for her. The bride's family gave the groom a dowry. Most nobles looked for wives with large dowries. Women were often married by the time they were 12 years old. Those who were not married by the time they were 21 could expect to stay single for the rest of their lives.

Wives helped their husbands run their estates. When the men were away, the women had to defend the castle. The main duties of a wife, however, were to have and raise children and to

Linking Across Time

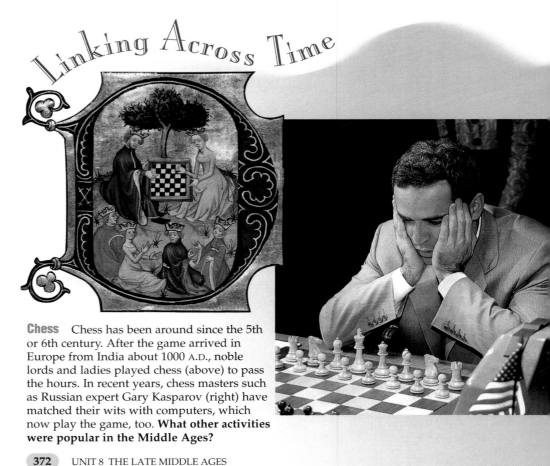

Chess   Chess has been around since the 5th or 6th century. After the game arrived in Europe from India about 1000 A.D., noble lords and ladies played chess (above) to pass the hours. In recent years, chess masters such as Russian expert Gary Kasparov (right) have matched their wits with computers, which now play the game, too. **What other activities were popular in the Middle Ages?**

372   UNIT 8 THE LATE MIDDLE AGES

SPOTLIGHT ON: NOBLEWOMEN

The noblewoman was technically under her husband's control, although she could exert power both inside and outside of the castle. If her dowry included lands and manors or abbeys, they remained under her control. When the lord was away or at war—sometimes a matter of many years—the lady was in charge of the castle. If necessary, she organized its defenses. Some women actually led the castle troops into battle.

ake care of the household. She was also expected to train young
irls from other castles in household duties and to supervise the
naking of cloth and fine embroidery. Another duty was to use her
nowledge of plants and herbs to care for the poor and sick on her
usband's fief.

Section 2 Assessment

1. **Define:** castles, keep, ladies.
2. What activities took place in the noble's house?
3. How did the design of a castle protect people?
4. What were the duties of a feudal noble-woman?

Critical Thinking

5. **Drawing Conclusions** What parts of castle life would you have liked? What parts would you have disliked?

Graphic Organizer Activity

6. Draw this diagram, and use it to compare the living conditions of nobles before and after the rise of castles.

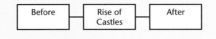

| Before | | Rise of Castles | | After |

SECTION 3 Knighthood

Almost all nobles were knights. However, knighthood had
o be earned. Knights were expected to follow certain rules
nown as the **code of chivalry** (kōd of shiv' uhl rē). These rules
tated that a knight was to obey his lord, show bravery, respect
vomen of noble birth, honor the Church, and help people. A
night was also expected to be honest and to fight fairly against
is enemies. The code of chivalry became the guide to behavior
rom which the western idea of good manners developed.

Training   A noble began training to be a knight when he was
even years old. He was sent away from his family to the castle of
nother lord. There, he learned to be a **page,** or a person who
elped the knights of the castle care for their *destriers* (dā trē'
hrs), or war-horses. Pages also polished the knights' armor,
ome of which weighed up to 80 pounds, or 36 kilograms.

A page learned good manners and ran errands for the ladies.
Ie was taught to ride and fight. By the age of 14, he could handle
 lance and sword while on horseback.

When he was 15 years old, a page became a **squire.** Each
quire was put under the care and training of one knight. The
quire's duty was to go into battle with his knight. He was
xpected to rescue the knight if he was wounded or fell off his
orse.

If the squire proved to be a good fighter, he was rewarded
y being made a knight. This was done in a special ceremony

✓ **Reading Check** What was the **code of chivalry?**

✓ **Reading Check** What did a **page** hope to become?

✓ **Reading Check** What were the duties of a **squire?**

CHAPTER 24 FEUDAL SOCIETY   **373**

💾 Use **Interactive Tutor Self-Assessment Software** to review Section 2.

✓ **Reading Check Answer** The **code of chivalry** was a set of rules that a knight was expected to follow.

✓ **Reading Check Answer** A **page** hoped to become a knight.

💾 Use the **Vocabulary Puzzle-Maker** to create crossword and word search puzzles.

✓ **Reading Check Answer** The duties of a **squire** including going into battle with a knight and rescuing him if he was wounded or fell off his horse.

Section 1 Assessment Answers

1. castles, stone houses of nobles (p. 370); keep, tall tower (p. 371); ladies, noblewomen (p. 372)
2. Nobles met with vassals, carried out laws, and said their prayers; people slept there; meals were cooked and eaten there.
3. Student answers should reflect the description of a castle on pp. 370–371.
4. She helped her husband run their estates, defended the castle when the men were away, raised children, took care of the household, and cared for the poor and sick.
5. Answers will vary, but students should provide specific examples of castle life.
6. Sample response: *Before*—lived in one-room wooden houses surrounded by palisades; *After*—lived in stone fortresses.

Assign the Chapter 24 **Section 2 Quiz** in the TCR. Testmaker available.

L1 Language Arts Divide students into teams of two. Have each team write an interview between a squire and a knight on how nobles achieved knighthood and what a knight's duties were. Then have each team read the dialogue to the rest of the class, with one student playing the role of the knight and the other, the role of the squire.

CAPTION ANSWER

because men and horses might be killed, equipment damaged, and all the people who attended had to be fed

☑ Reading Check Answer At a **dubbing** ceremony, a squire officially became a knight.

☑ Reading Check Answer At medieval **tournaments,** knights trained for war.

☑ Reading Check Answer In a **joust,** two armed knights with dull lances galloped toward each other from opposite ends of a field in an effort to knock one or the other to the ground.

DID YOU KNOW ??

There were two types of medieval jousts. One was held for pleasure or exercise, and the knights used lances with blunt tips and swords that were not pointed. The other was a fight to the death in which sharp weapons were used. The arms of a defeated man belonged to the victor and could be ransomed for money. Because of this, tournaments were a way for poor but powerful fighters to earn a living.

Fun Facts....

Coats of Arms To identify themselves in battle, knights had individual designs, or "coats of arms," painted on their shields and tunics. In noble families, the coat of arms passed down through the generations. The flags of some modern European nations are based on medieval coats of arms.

MEDIEVAL TOURNAMENT In this painting knights on horseback joust during a tournament. Even the king is attending this match. **Why were medieval tournaments costly events?**

☑ Reading Check What took place during the ceremony known as **dubbing?**

☑ Reading Check What was the purpose of medieval **tournaments?**

☑ Reading Check What was the event known as the **joust?**

known as **dubbing.** The squire knelt before his lord with his sword suspended from his neck. He then promised to defend the Church, his lord, and to protect the weak. Then, the lord tapped the squire on his shoulder with the blade of a sword and pronounced him a knight. The knight's sword was placed in a *scabbard,* or sword holder, at the knight's side. This showed that the knight would fight by the side of his lord.

Tournaments Knights trained for war by fighting each other in **tournaments,** or special contests that test strength, skill, and endurance. Tournaments were held in large fields. They were exciting gatherings that brought in lords, ladies, and knights who watched the events from stands. The most popular event was the **joust** (jowst). Two armored knights on horseback carrying dull lances galloped towards each other from opposite ends of the field. Each tried with all his strength and skill to knock the other to the ground with his lance.

The cost of tournaments was high. Men and horses were killed and wounded. Lances, swords, and suits of armor were damaged. The noble who gave the tournament had to feed hundreds of people. In spite of the cost, however, tournaments remained popular. In fact, it was believed that a knight who had not learned to fight in one could not fight well in battle.

374 UNIT 8 THE LATE MIDDLE AGES

MEETING SPECIAL NEEDS

Have tactile/kinesthetic or gifted learners research the styles of armor worn by knights in the various regions of western Europe. Then have students make armor and model it or draw pictures of its various styles and designs. Students may wish to write a report explaining their findings.

Refer to *Inclusion for the Middle School Social Studies Classroom: Strategies and Activities* for additional resources.

1. **Define:** code of chivalry, page, squire, dubbing, tournaments, joust.
2. Why did noble families send their sons to other castles to work as pages?
3. How did knights train for war?

Critical Thinking

4. **Making Comparisons** How were tournaments similar to the Olympic games in ancient Greece? How were they different?

Graphic Organizer Activity

5. Draw this diagram, and use it to show the steps leading to knighthood.

Step 1 · Step 2 · Step 3 · Knighthood

SECTION 3 The Manor

Nobles, knights, and peasants all depended on the land for everything they needed. The land was divided into **manors,** or farming communities. Manors were found on fiefs and were owned by nobles.

Daily Life   The noble chose a number of officials to run his manor. They were loyal to the noble and made sure his orders were carried out. One official was the **seneschal** (sen' uh shuhl).

✔ **Reading Check**
What were **manors?**

✔ **Reading Check**
Who was the **seneschal?**

TOLL GATE

NORTH FIELD

COMMON PASTURE

STABLE

PORTCULLIS

GATEHOUSE

MOAT

EAST FIELD

DRAWBRIDGE

WEST FIELD

CHURCH AND RECTORY

STREAM

SOUTH FIELD

TOLL GATE

SERFS' HUTS

CHAPTER 24 FEUDAL SOCIETY   **375**

Independent Practice

L3 **Science** There were many diseases and medical problems during the Middle Ages. Ask students to research and present information about the following to the class: Who would treat peasants' diseases? Who did a king go to for medical problems? What kinds of treatments were commonly used?

✔ **Reading Check Answer**
Manors were the farming communities found on all fiefs.

✔ **Reading Check Answer**
The **seneschal** looked after the noble's fiefs, visiting them regularly.

💾 Use **Interactive Tutor Self-Assessment Software** to review Section 3.

💾 Use the **Vocabulary Puzzle-Maker** to create crossword and word search puzzles.

MAKING CONNECTIONS

▶▶ **History** Manors formed the basis of the medieval agricultural system known as manorialism. While feudalism involved ties among nobles, manorialism concerned agreements between the nobles and peasants.

PRIMARY SOURCES
Library

You might assign "The Medieval Manor" on pages 688–689 of the Primary Sources Library.

Section 3 Assessment Answers

1. code of chivalry, rules for knights (p. 373); page, person who helped the knights (p. 373); squire, second step in becoming a knight (p. 373); dubbing, ceremony in which a squire became a knight (p. 373); tournament, contests for knights (p. 374); joust, an event in a tournament (p. 374)
2. so that they could receive training to become a knight
3. by taking part in tournaments with events such as the joust
4. Like the Olympics, the tournaments had many events watched by many people outside. The tournaments were designed to prepare knights for war. The Olympic Games, however, were held to honor the gods. Unlike the Olympic Games, women were allowed to view the tournaments.
5. Step 1—receive training as a page; Step 2—serve as squire to a knight; Step 3—take part in the dubbing ceremony

Assign the Chapter 24 **Section 3 Quiz** in the TCR. Testmaker available.

Reading Check
What was the main job of a **bailiff**?

Fun Facts....

Peasant Life A typical peasant's cottage had one door that opened into a central room with a pressed dirt floor. Often a number of animals— piglets, ducklings, cats, and hens—shared the space with a married couple and their children. In cold weather, a cow might be brought inside to the warmth of the fire.

He looked after the noble's fiefs by visiting each fief regularly. Another official was the **bailiff** (bā′ lif). He made sure the peasants worked hard in the fields. Every manor had its own court of law. The court settled differences, gave out fines and punishments, and discussed manor business.

Poor transportation and frequent fighting isolated manors from one another. The men and women of each manor produced food, clothing, and shelter for themselves and the noble. They raised sheep for wool and cattle for meat and milk. They also grew grain and vegetables, made cloth, built homes, and fashioned tools.

The noble of each manor lived in a wooden house or a castle. Nearby stood a small village of cottages in which the peasants lived. Most villages also had a church, a mill, a bread oven, and a wine press. Around the village were forests, meadows, pastures, and fields.

The cottages were crowded around an open area called the village green. They were made of wood and earth and had thatched roofs. Most had only one room. At night, family members slept there on piles of straw or on the dirt floor. Three-legged stools and a table were the only furniture. Diseases and fleas from the animals that also slept in the cottage often sickened the people.

PEASANTS AT WORK Peasants spent long hours working in the fields of a manor. In this painting, a group of peasants is shown mowing and binding sheaves of wheat (left). Another group of peasants is shown shearing sheep (right). **What other work did the peasants do?**

MULTICULTURAL PERSPECTIVES

Commercial fairs served as centers of trade for medieval Europe. These fairs were great annual events that attracted merchants from all over Europe, and brought many people from different cultures together.

PEASANT CELEBRATION Although peasants' lives were mostly long hours of hard work, there were times for celebration. Peasants celebrated special occasions with music, dancing, and feasting. Here, the festivities at a peasant wedding are shown. **What sports did peasants enjoy?**

Freemen and Serfs Two groups of peasants worked on a manor. One was the **freemen,** or peasants who paid the noble for the right to farm land. They worked only on their own strips of land and had rights under the law. They moved wherever and whenever they wished. The noble, however, had the right to throw them off the manor without warning.

The other group was the serfs. Serfs and their descendants were a noble's property. They could not move to another area, own their own property, or marry without the noble's permission. Serfs, however, could not be driven off the land and did not have to serve in the army.

It was not easy for serfs to gain their freedom. One way was to escape to the towns. If a serf was not caught and remained in town for more than a year, he or she was considered free. By the end of the Middle Ages, serfs were allowed to buy their freedom.

As in Charlemagne's time, the serfs worked long hours in the fields and performed many services for the nobles. Serfs spent three days of the week working the lord's strips of land and the rest of the week caring for their own strips. However, they had to give part of their own crops to the noble. They also paid him for the use of the village's mill, bread oven, and wine press.

In spite of the difficulties, a serf's life had some bright moments. Sunday was a day of rest from work. At Christmas, the

People in History

Trotula of Salerno
C.1097 A.D.

Doctor

Both noble and peasant women took care of the sick, but Trotula broke with tradition by becoming a trained doctor. She studied and taught at the medical school at Salerno, Italy. Trotula specialized in the health of women and wrote a book called *The Diseases of Women.* Her book influenced doctors for centuries to come. Today she is considered one of Europe's early women of science.

Reading Check
How did **freemen** differ from serfs?

Serf Work A monk at Canterbury recorded an English serf's account of his day: "I work very hard. I go out at dawn, driving the oxen to the field, and I yoke them to the plough. However hard the winter, I dare not stay home for fear of my master."

Reading Check Answer
Unlike serfs, **freemen** paid a noble for the right to farm the land and could move about freely.

LINKING PAST TO PRESENT

A serf and his family could be sold as part of the property on which they lived and worked. This made the serf different from an enslaved person, whose family could be sold separately to anyone. The idea of enslavement, originally started by Greeks and Romans, prepared people's minds for the eventual enslavement of other peoples, such as Africans, when Europe later expanded its empires.

ASSESS

Check for Understanding

Ask students to summarize the main points of the chapter, orally or in writing. Discuss the answers to the Section and Chapter Assessment questions.

EXTENDING THE CONTENT

Peasant meals varied from country to country, just as basic cuisines do today. Bread—whole wheat, rye, or barley—was basic, along with several kinds of pasta in Italy. Porridges and oatmeal made of grain with peas or beans were common everywhere. In France, peasants ate hearty soups, stews, and vegetables and drank wine or cider. They grew apples and grapes and stored them over the winter by drying or cooking them in honey. The English had several kinds of cheese and curds. They made ale, cider, and mead—a fermented honey drink. Germans made lentils, sauerkraut, cabbage, peas, and turnips.

Evaluate

Assign the Chapter 24 **Performance Assessment Activity** in the TCR. Administer the **Chapter 24 Test**. Testmaker available.

Reteach

Divide the class into small groups. Have each group summarize a particular part of the chapter.

Assign the Chapter 24 **Reteaching Activity** in the TCR.

Enrich

Have students research the kinds of "mystery plays" that serfs attended for amusement. Students may perform a skit similar to one of the plays.

Assign the Chapter 24 **Enrichment Activity** in the TCR.

CLOSE

Ask students to share their opinions of people in the Middle Ages. If students had to travel back in time to medieval England, what kind of life would they choose? Why?

💾 Use **Interactive Tutor Self Assessment Software** to review Section 4.

Self-Check Quiz gives students an interactive chapter tutorial. Have them access **Chapter 24 Quiz** at humanheritage.glencoe.com

---

lord paid for a great feast and entertainment. Certain holidays were celebrated with singing and dancing on the village green. When they could, serfs took part in such sports as wrestling, archery, and soccer.

By the 1200s, peasants began to learn better farming methods. They used the three-field system of farming and started to use a heavy iron plow. The horse collar was invented, allowing horses instead of slow-moving oxen to plow fields. All of this enabled the peasants to grow more food.

Section 4 Assessment

1. **Define:** manors, seneschal, bailiff, freemen.
2. What were some features of a manor village?
3. What rights did freemen have?
4. What did serfs contribute to a manor?

Critical Thinking

5. **Making Comparisons** What interests did nobles and serfs have in common?

Graphic Organizer Activity

6. Draw this diagram, and use it to show technological improvements in farming in the 1200s.

Improved Farming Methods		

Chapter Summary & Study Guide

1. Following Charlemagne's death, kings began to depend on nobles for food, horses, and soldiers.
2. Some nobles began to collect their own taxes, run their own courts, coin their own money, and raise their own armies.
3. As the power of kings declined, the nobles took on the duty of defending their land and people from Viking attacks.
4. By 1000, the kingdoms of western Europe were divided into thousands of feudal territories.
5. Under feudalism, landowning nobles gave vassals land in exchange for loyalty and military service.
6. Knights followed the code of chivalry and trained for war by fighting in tournaments.
7. Fiefs were owned by nobles and worked by peasants.
8. Peasants included freemen and serfs. While freemen could leave the land if they wished, serfs were considered a noble's property.
9. By the 1200s, improvements in farming methods helped the peasants to grow more food.

Self-Check Quiz

Visit the *Human Heritage* Web site at **humanheritage. glencoe.com** and click on *Chapter 24—Self-Check Quiz* to assess your understanding of this chapter.

378 UNIT 8 THE LATE MIDDLE AGES

Section 4 Assessment Answers

1. manors, farming communities (p. 375); seneschal, overseer of a noble's fief (p. 375); bailiff, official who supervised peasants (p. 376); freemen, peasants who paid for the right to farm land (p. 377)
2. peasant cottages surrounded by forests, meadows, pastures, and fields; usually with a church, mill, bread oven, and wine press
3. to move about freely
4. They worked long hours in the fields,

obeyed nobles' wishes, and had to give the noble part of their crops.
5. Answers will vary but might indicate that nobles and serfs depended upon each other to survive.
6. Sample improvements: three-field system, use of iron plow, invention of horse collar

Assign the Chapter 24 **Section 4 Quiz** in the TCR. Testmaker available.

Using Key Terms

Imagine you are living in the late Middle Ages. Write an interview with a noble and a serf in which they describe their lives. Use the following words in your interview.

feudalism	clergy	fiefs
vassal	act of homage	knight
castles	keep	ladies
code of chivalry	page	squire
dubbing	tournaments	joust
manors	seneschal	bailiff
freemen		

Understanding Main Ideas

1. Into what three groups were people divided under feudalism?
2. Who held the political power within a feudal territory?
3. Who usually received a vassal's fief when the vassal died?
4. What was expected of a knight?
5. Why was it necessary for the people on a manor to produce everything they needed?
6. In what two ways could serfs obtain their freedom?
7. What changes had taken place in farming by the 1200s?

Critical Thinking

1. What advantages would there be to being a vassal rather than a lord?
2. Why do you think women provided the medical care in a fief?
3. What would you have enjoyed about being a knight? What would you have disliked?
4. How do you think a serf's life would be affected by the improved farming methods of the thirteenth century?

Graphic Organizer Activity

Citizenship Create a diagram like this one, and use it to show the organization of government under feudalism. Each of these groups should appear on the chart: serfs, landowning nobles, freemen, knights.

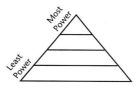

Geography in History

Human/Environmental Interaction
The people of the manor made good use of their natural resources to support themselves. Predict and describe how you think manor life would have changed if a plant disease had killed all the trees in an area.

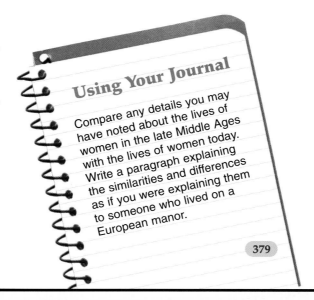

Using Your Journal

Compare any details you may have noted about the lives of women in the late Middle Ages with the lives of women today. Write a paragraph explaining the similarities and differences as if you were explaining them to someone who lived on a European manor.

379

Bonus Test Question

For Chapter 24 Test
Who is not telling the truth here? *Noble 1*: "The king gave this manor to my mother. Here is the paper to prove it." *Noble 2*: "This is my land. I served the king in battle, was held hostage in his place, and he awarded it to me."

Using Your Journal

Paragraphs will vary but may include issues of basic human freedoms. You might ask volunteers to read their paragraphs to the class.

Geography in History

Answers will vary but should reflect the uses of wood in the lives of serfs and the impact of the loss of trees. Students may also suggest other plants may have been affected by the same disease.

CHAPTER 24

Assessment Answers

Using Key Terms

Interviews will vary, but students should use all the terms.

Understanding Main Ideas

1. the clergy, the nobles, and the peasants and townspeople
2. the noble who owned the land
3. his oldest son
4. to follow the code of chivalry
5. because the manors were isolated from one another
6. by escaping to the towns for more than a year or by buying their freedom
7. Peasants began to learn better farming methods, used the heavy iron plow, and used horses instead of slow-moving oxen to plow their fields.

Critical Thinking

1. Answers will vary but should include the ideas that vassals had fewer responsibilities, received a fief, and had the protection of a noble.
2. Answers will vary but might include that she was usually there, and medical care was considered a domestic concern.
3. Answers will vary, but students should give some specific examples.
4. Answers will vary but might include that serfs would have more time for themselves. With more food grown, they would be healthier.

Graphic Organizer Activity

From top to bottom, groups should appear in this order: landowning nobles, knights, freemen, serfs.

Chapter 25 Planning Guide

Objectives	Reproducible Resources	Multimedia Resources
Section 1 **Catholic Influence** Discuss how the Roman Catholic Church influenced life during the Middle Ages.	Reproducible Lesson Plan Chapter 25 Vocabulary and Guided Reading Activity Reading Essentials and Study Guide 25-1 Section 1 Quiz	Teaching Transparency and Activity 25A Vocabulary PuzzleMaker Interactive Tutor Self-Assessment Software ExamView® Pro Testmaker Glencoe Skillbuilder Interactive Workbook, Level 1 Presentation Plus!
Section 2 **Attempts to Reform** Summarize attempts made to reform the Church and Church practices during the Middle Ages.	Reproducible Lesson Plan Chapter 25 Reading Essentials and Study Guide 25-2 Chapter 25 Enrichment Activity Section 2 Quiz	Vocabulary PuzzleMaker Interactive Tutor Self-Assessment Software ExamView® Pro Testmaker Glencoe Skillbuilder Interactive Workbook, Level 1
Section 3 **Learning** Describe what learning was like during the Middle Ages.	Reproducible Lesson Plan Reading Essentials and Study Guide 25-3 Section 3 Quiz	Teaching Transparency and Activity 25B Vocabulary PuzzleMaker Interactive Tutor Self-Assessment Software ExamView® Pro Testmaker Glencoe Skillbuilder Interactive Workbook, Level 1
Section 4 **The Crusades** Explain why the Crusades took place, and analyze the effect of the Crusades upon the Middle Ages.	Reproducible Lesson Plan Reading Essentials and Study Guide 25-4 Chapter 25 Cooperative Learning Activity Chapter 25 Geography and Map Activity Chapter 25 Chart and Graph Skill Activity Chapter 25 Activity Book Activity Section 4 Quiz	ABCNEWS INTERACTIVE Turning Points in World History Vocabulary PuzzleMaker Interactive Tutor Self-Assessment Software ExamView® Pro Testmaker Glencoe Skillbuilder Interactive Workbook, Level 1
Chapter 25 **Review and Evaluation**	Chapter 25 Reteaching Activity Chapter 25 Performance Assessment Activity Spanish Chapter Summary and Glossary Chapter 25 Test	Vocabulary PuzzleMaker Interactive Tutor Self-Assessment Software Glencoe Skillbuilder Interactive Workbook, Level 1 Audiocassettes* ExamView® Pro Testmaker

*Also available in Spanish.

Presentation Plus!

Use Glencoe's **Presentation Plus!** multimedia teacher tool to easily present dynamic lessons that visually excite your students. Using Microsoft® PowerPoint, you can customize the presentations to create your own personalized lessons.

 Interactive Lesson Planner

Planning has never been easier! Using this CD-ROM, organize your week, month, semester, or year with all the help you need. The **Interactive Lesson Planner** gives you access to all of the blackline masters which accompany *Human Heritage.*

✓ PERFORMANCE ASSESSMENT ACTIVITIES

Historic Imagination Have students imagine they are a member of the Children's Crusade. Tell students to each prepare these trip materials: a list of supplies and a map showing their planned route. Have students share their plans with the rest of the class.

CHAPTER RESOURCES

LITERATURE ABOUT THE PERIOD

Konisburg, E. L. *A Proud Taste for Scarlet and Miniver.* Atheneum, 1973. A biography of Eleanor of Aquitaine.

READINGS FOR THE STUDENT

Boyd, Anne. *Life in a 15th-Century Monastery* (A Cambridge Topic Book). Lerner Publications, 1979. An account of the daily life of monks in the monastery at Durham, England.

READINGS FOR THE TEACHER

Gies, Frances, and Joseph Gies. *Women in the Middle Ages: The Lives of Real Women in a Vibrant Age of Transition.* Barnes and Noble, 1978. Highlights women's lives in the Middle Ages.

KEY TO ABILITY LEVELS

Teaching strategies have been coded for varying learning styles and abilities.

L1 Level 1 activities are **basic** activities and should be within the ability range of all students.

L2 Level 2 activities are **average** activities and should be within the ability range of the average to above-average student.

L3 Level 3 activities are **challenging** activities designed for the ability range of above-average students.

ELL ELL activities should be within the ability range of English Language Learning students.

NATIONAL GEOGRAPHIC SOCIETY — Teacher's Corner

INDEX TO NATIONAL GEOGRAPHIC MAGAZINE

The following articles relate to this chapter:

- "The Gothic Revolution," by James L. Stanfield and Victor R. Boswell, Jr., July 1989.
- "A Renaissance for Michelangelo," by David Jeffery, December 1989.

NATIONAL GEOGRAPHIC SOCIETY PRODUCTS AVAILABLE FROM GLENCOE

To order the following, call Glencoe at 1-800-334-7344:

- *PicturePack: Europe (Transparencies)*
- *PicturePack: The Middle Ages (Transparencies)*
- *PictureShow: The Middle Ages (CD-ROM)*

Access *National Geographic*'s new dynamic MapMachine Web site and other geography resources at:
http://www.nationalgeographic.com/
http://www.nationalgeographic.com/maps/

  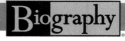

The following videotape programs are available from Glencoe:

- **The Crusades**
  1-56501-505-3

- **Gothic Cathedrals**
  1-56501-639-4

- **Richard the Lionheart**
  1-56501-916-4

To order, call Glencoe at 1-800-334-7344. To find classroom resources to accompany many of these, check:

A&E Television: http://www.aetv.com
The History Channel:
http://www.historychannel.com

OVERVIEW

Chapter 25 discusses the role of the Roman Catholic Church during the Middle Ages.

➤ **Section 1** describes the influence of the Church in daily life in western Europe.

➤ **Section 2** discusses Church reforms.

➤ **Section 3** explains the spread of Christian teachings in western Europe.

➤ **Section 4** describes reasons for the Crusades.

CHAPTER OBJECTIVES

After reading Chapter 25, students will be able to:

1. discuss how the Roman Catholic Church influenced life during the Middle Ages.

2. summarize attempts to reform the Church.

3. describe education during the Middle Ages.

4. explain why the Crusades took place.

5. list effects of the Crusades.

EXAMINING ARTIFACTS

Link these two works of art by pointing out the cross worn by the crusader. Ask: What do you think the crusader would be willing to do for the Church? *(to fight for it)* Bridge chapters 24 and 25 by having students name groups in medieval society who they think might go on a crusade. Save their responses to review as students read this chapter.

PERFORMANCE ASSESSMENT ✔

Use the Performance Assessment Activities on page 380B to help you evaluate students as they complete the chapter.

380

CHAPTER
25

The Church
1000 A.D.–1300 A.D.

◄ Christian crusader and his wife

◄ Enameled cross

1071 A.D.	1096 A.D.	1129 A.D.	1212 A.D.	1291 A.D.
Seljuq Turks conquer Jerusalem	Start of the Crusades	Inquisition begins	Children's Crusade	Muslims win the Crusades

380   UNIT 8 THE LATE MIDDLE AGES

TEACHING RESOURCES

TEACHER PLANNING AND SUPPORT

- Reproducible Lesson Plan
- Block Scheduling Implementation Guide
- Videodisc Bar Code Correlation
- Presentation Plus!

REVIEW AND REINFORCEMENT

- Reading Essentials and Study Guide 25-1, 25-2, 25-3, 25-4
- Chapter 25 Vocabulary and Guided Reading Activity
- Vocabulary PuzzleMaker Software
- Teaching Transparencies 25A & 25B

- Chapter 25 Reteaching Activity
- Chapter 25 Cooperative Learning Activity
- Chapter 25 Activity Book Activity
- Chapter 25 Chart and Graph Skill Activity
- Interactive Tutor Self-Assessment Software

APPLICATION AND HANDS-ON ACTIVITIES

- Daily World History, Geography, and Culture Question
- World History Craft Card 5

GEOGRAPHY ACTIVITIES

- Chapter 25 Geography and Map Activity
- Social Studies Outline Map Resource Book

Chapter Focus

 Read to Discover

- How the Roman Catholic Church influenced life during the Middle Ages.
- What attempts were made to reform the Church during the Middle Ages.
- What learning was like during the Middle Ages.
- Why the Crusades took place during the Middle Ages.
- What the effects of the Crusades were.

Terms to Learn	People to Know	Places to Locate
mass	Gregory VII	Cluny
tithes	Francis of Assisi	Palestine
cathedrals	Thomas Aquinas	Outremer
unions	Urban II	Venice
chancellor	Saladin	Acre
crusades	Richard the	
emirs	Lionheart	

Why It's Important Leaders in the Roman Catholic Church wanted to develop a civilization in western Europe that was based on Christian ideals. By 1000, missionary monks had brought the Church's teachings to most of Europe. They converted people and built new churches and monasteries. The Roman Catholic Church united western Europeans and took the lead in government, law, art, and learning for hundreds of years. The Church helped pass on the heritage of the Roman Empire. Latin became the official language of the Church.

SECTION 1 Catholic Influence

The Roman Catholic Church had great influence during the Middle Ages. It was the center of every village and town. It played an important part in the political life of the period. At times, it even had the power of life or death over people.

Daily Life In every village and town, daily life revolved around the Church. To become a king, vassal, or knight, a man had to take part in a religious ceremony. Most holidays were in honor of saints or religious events. On Fridays, the people obeyed the Church's rule not to eat meat. On Sundays, they went to

CHAPTER 25 THE CHURCH   **381**

Guided Practice

L1 **Discussion** Lead students in a discussion about the influence of the Catholic Church on all aspects of life in western Europe during the Middle Ages. Ask: *How was the Church a force that brought people together in western Europe during the Middle Ages? How did the Church influence daily life?*

Reading Check Answer
The parish priest usually held **mass** in medieval villages and towns.

CAPTION ANSWER
Priests recorded births, performed marriages, and conducted burials.

Reading Check Answer
Canon laws were laws set up by the Church.
People who were **excommunicated** lost their membership in the Church as well as their political rights.

MAKING CONNECTIONS
▶▶ **Religion** The religion of most people in the Middle Ages was a mixture of Christian and pagan beliefs. Prayer was viewed as a way of working magic, and the saints were believed to have the same miracle-working powers as the gods and goddesses.

VILLAGE CHURCH   During the Middle Ages, the church was the religious and social center of the village. Both the local noble and the peasants contributed to the building of the church and its upkeep. **What were some daily tasks performed by the parish priest?**

Reading Check
Who usually held **mass** in medieval villages and towns?

Reading Check
What were **canon laws?** What happened to people who were **excommunicated?**

mass, or a worship service, held by the parish priest. Church leaders ran schools and hospitals. Monks and nuns provided food and shelter for travelers. Priests recorded births, performed marriages, and conducted burials.

Political Life   The Church played an important role in the political life of the Middle Ages. Together with kings and nobles, Church officials helped govern western Europe. As large landowners, high Church leaders were both lords and vassals of other lords. They served as advisers to kings and other nobles, keeping records for the kings who could not read or write. Parish priests also played a part in government. They were chosen by local nobles and were expected to tell the people to respect the king, the nobles, and other government officials.

The Church told people to obey the king's laws unless they went against **canon laws,** or laws set up by the Church. People who disobeyed the Pope or canon laws were **excommunicated** (ek skuh myū′ nuh kā ted), or lost their membership in the Church. They also lost their political rights.

The Inquisition   Despite its power, the Church faced the problem of heresy. At first, it tried to stop the spread of heresy by preaching. Then, in 1129, a council of bishops set up the Inquisition (in kwuh zish′ uhn), or Church court, to end heresy by force.

The Church gave people it suspected of heresy one month to confess. Those who appeared in front of the Inquisition before the month ended were whipped or sent to prison for a short time. Those who did not appear were seized and brought to trial.

EXTENDING THE CONTENT

Nobles thought little of hurting or killing peasants, serfs, and villagers, burning their crops and barns, or killing their livestock. Within the Church there were those who tried to stop the bloodshed. Late in the 900s a movement within the Church called the Peace of God tried to protect certain persons or places from violence. For instance, there was to be no fighting in church. Knights were not to attack people on their way to church. In 1017 the Church tried putting a further ban on casual fighting called the Truce of God. This forbade fighting from early Saturday until Monday.

The reason for the trial was to get a confession. The court called only two witnesses. Based on what they said, the court decided whether or not a person was a heretic. Heretics who confessed were punished. Then, they were allowed to become Church members again. Heretics who refused to confess were often tortured. A number of people were burned at the stake.

Section 1 Assessment

1. **Define:** mass, canon laws, excommunicated.
2. What part did parish priests play in government?

Critical Thinking

3. **Making Inferences** How do you think a king might have felt about being excommunicated from the Church?

Graphic Organizer Activity

4. Draw this diagram, and use it to show examples of Church powers during the Middle Ages.

Church Powers
- Example
- Example
- Example

THE INQUISITION   The Inquisition was established to strengthen the beliefs of the Church in France, Germany, Italy, and Spain. In this painting, a heretic under trial confesses. **What punishment came to those who confessed to heresy?**

LINKING PAST TO PRESENT

Unlike American courts, which hold that a defendant is innocent until proven guilty, the Inquisition assumed that a defendant was guilty. Also, during the Middle Ages, Church leaders sought to maintain their authority and to limit state influence. Today in the United States, the state usually favors separation of church and state so that neither religious beliefs nor government infringe on one another.

DID YOU KNOW

Monks and nuns worked hard to make monastery lands productive. They became known as the best farmers of western Europe.

CAPTION ANSWER

They were whipped or sent to prison for a short time.

Section 1 Assessment Answers

1. mass, a worship service (p. 382); canon laws, laws set up by the Church (p. 382); excommunicated, lost membership in the Church (p. 382)

2. They were expected to tell the people to respect the kings, the nobles, and other government officials.

3. Answers will vary but might include that it would not be desirable for a king to be excommunicated because then the king would lose his political rights.

4. Student answers should reflect the many Church powers identified on pages 381–382. You might adapt the graphic organizer to display examples by category, such as political powers, legal powers, social powers, and so on.

Assign the Chapter 25 **Section 1 Quiz** in the TCR. Testmaker available.

SECTION 2 Attempts at Reform

✓ **Reading Check**
What were **tithes?**

The Church became rich during the Middle Ages. Church members supported it by giving **tithes** (tīthz), or offerings equal to 10 percent of their income. Rich nobles donated money to build large churches and gave land to monasteries. The wealthier the monasteries became, however, the more careless many monks grew about carrying out their religious duties.

Monks were not the only ones to grow careless about religious duties. When a bishop died, his office and lands were taken over by the local noble. The noble often chose a close relative as the new bishop or sold the office for money or favors.

Linking Across Time

Stained-Glass Windows During the time of Charlemagne, Europeans started designing windows made from individual pieces of colored glass and held together by lead. The art form reached its peak in the church windows of the late Middle Ages (below). In the late 1800s and early 1900s, artists such as Louis Comfort Tiffany revived this art form in stained-glass windows and lamps (right). **How did church leaders raise money to pay for works of art like stained-glass windows?**

384

MULTICULTURAL PERSPECTIVES

Inquisition officials often accused people of heresy without sufficient proof; sometimes they even used torture to obtain confessions. The Church welcomed back those who repented, but those who did not were punished with imprisonment, loss of property, or execution. According to Church teachings, these punishments were necessary to save the souls of the heretics.

Because of this, men who were not very religious often held important Church posts. They did not keep Church rules or bother with the needs of the poor.

Before long, some western Europeans became worried about the direction in which the Church was headed. During the late 900s and early 1000s, they worked to return the Church to Christian ideals.

The Monks of Cluny

To fight corruption in the Church, *devout*, or deeply religious, nobles founded new monasteries that strictly followed the Benedictine Rule. One of the most important of these was Cluny (klū' nē) in eastern France. The monks there led simple lives, spending much time in prayer. They soon won the respect of the people. The monks of Cluny recognized only the authority of the Pope and said that the Church, not kings or nobles, should choose all Church leaders. Over time, a number of new monasteries connected with Cluny spread across Europe.

Pope Gregory VII

The reforms begun by the monks of Cluny were continued by Pope Gregory VII. By Gregory's time, the Pope had become a powerful political as well as religious leader. He had his own courts of justice and government offices. He ruled from Rome with the help of a group of bishops known as the College of Cardinals.

Gregory had two goals as Pope. He wanted to rid the Church of control by kings and nobles. He also wanted to increase the Pope's power over the Church officials. To reach these goals, Gregory made many changes in the Church. Church leaders who bought or sold Church offices were removed from their posts. Bishops and priests were forbidden to marry.

In a document issued in 1075, Gregory stated that the Pope was above all kings and nobles. Only the Pope had the power to choose bishops and other Church leaders. Government officials who did not obey the Pope could be removed from office. People did not have to obey officials who went against the Pope.

Some kings viewed Gregory's reforms as attacks on their power. So, they resisted his changes. In the end, however, they lost some of their power to him.

Friars

During the early 1200s, Church reforms were carried out by preachers called **friars.** Since they sold all their belongings before becoming friars, they depended on gifts of food and money from the people.

Friars were different from other monks. They followed many monastic rules, including the one about not marrying. However, they did not shut themselves off from the rest of the world. Instead, they lived in towns and worked to bring Christianity directly to the people.

Painting of Pope Gregory VII

✓ Reading Check
How did **friars** differ from monks?

✓ Reading Check Answer
Friars followed many of the same rules as monks, but they did not shut themselves off from the rest of the world.

MEETING SPECIAL NEEDS

Have gifted learners research and prepare a report on one of the following reformers: the monks of Cluny, Pope Gregory VII, and the friars. The reports should include the answers to the following questions: How did the reformers attempt to change the Church? How successful were the reformers in achieving their desired goal? Have students read their reports to the class.

📂 Refer to *Inclusion for the Middle School Social Studies Classroom: Strategies and Activities* for additional resources.

L2 **The Arts** Explain to students that in the Middle Ages stained glass might be one of the few means of communication some people would understand. Have students create posters in the style of stained glass windows to tell a story of something they have learned about people or events in this chapter. **ELL**

Use **Interactive Tutor Self-Assessment Software** to review Section 2.

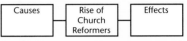

NATIONAL GEOGRAPHIC SOCIETY

Use these materials to enrich student understanding of the culture of the Middle Ages.

NGS PICTURESHOW CD-ROM
The Middle Ages

NGS PICTUREPACK TRANSPARENCY SET
The Middle Ages

Use the **Vocabulary Puzzle-Maker** to create crossword and word search puzzles.

Reading Check
What were two well-known **orders** of friars in the Middle Ages?

Two well-known **orders,** or groups of friars, were the Franciscans (fran sis′ kuhns) and Dominicans (duh min′ uh kuhns). The Franciscan order was founded in 1200 by Francis of Assisi (uh sē′ zē), the son of a rich Italian merchant. Franciscans were known for their cheerfulness and confidence that God would take care of them. They had a deep love of nature. They believed it was a gift of God and should be respected.

The Dominican order was started in 1216 by a Spanish monk named Dominic. Like the Franciscans, the Dominicans lived a life of poverty. They studied different languages so they could preach everywhere. Through their words and deeds, they kept many people loyal to Church teachings.

Section 2 Assessment

1. **Define:** tithes, friars, orders.
2. What reforms did Gregory VII introduce?
3. How did the Franciscans and Dominicans try to bring Christianity directly to the people?

Critical Thinking

4. **Drawing Conclusions** Why do you think the monks of Cluny gained the people's respect?

Graphic Organizer Activity

5. Draw this diagram, and use it to show the causes and effects of the rise of Church reformers in the 900s and 1000s.

| Causes | → | Rise of Church Reformers | → | Effects |

SECTION 3 Learning

During the late Middle Ages, the rise of governments brought more security, and the economy grew stronger. There was more time for learning and learning was in the hands of the Church.

Reading Check
What were **cathedrals?**

Cathedral Schools   The parish clergy set up schools in **cathedrals,** or churches headed by bishops. The schools were to prepare the sons of nobles for service in the Church. Not every boy who went to school, however, wanted to be a priest or monk. So, the schools also trained students to be government workers, lawyers, and teachers. Seven subjects were taught at cathedral schools. They were grammar, rhetoric, logic, arithmetic, geometry, astronomy, and music.

Students paid a fee to attend classes held in a cold, dark hall rented by the teacher. Books were few and costly. So, students memorized the teacher's explanation.

Section 2 Assessment Answers

1. tithes, Church offerings equal to 10 percent of income (p. 384); friars, preachers (p. 385); orders, groups of friars (p. 386)

2. continued reforms started by the monks of Cluny, removed Church leaders who bought or sold Church offices, forbade bishops and priests from marrying, increased power of the Pope

3. lived in towns among the people; learned many languages so they could preach everywhere

4. because they led simple lives, spending much of their time in prayer

5. *Causes:* Some monks neglected their religious duties. Church offices were bought and sold. Some officials did not keep Church rules or bother with the needs of the poor. *Effects:* New monasteries and religious orders emerged. The power of kings to appoint Church officials decreased, while the power of the Pope increased.

Assign the Chapter 25 **Section 2 Quiz** in the TCR. Testmaker available.

Universities   After a while, students began to complain that teachers held few classes and did not cover enough subjects. Teachers began to complain that too many untrained people were teaching. So, students and teachers decided to make some changes by forming **unions,** or groups of people joined together for a common cause. These unions became **universities,** or groups of teachers and students devoted to learning. By the 1200s, universities had spread all through Europe.

Universities were alike in many ways. A Church official called a **chancellor** (chan' suh luhr) headed each. No one could teach without his permission. All universities had well-organized classes held at set times each day. In class, students listened to lectures on a specific subject. All students had to pass special tests. Lecturers had to be at least 21 years old and had to have studied for at least 6 years.

Students from all over Europe came to the universities. At first, they lived in boarding houses. Later, rich sponsors built special buildings in which they could live. Those who missed daily mass, disturbed the peace, or took part in gambling or sword practice were punished.

MEDIEVAL CLASSROOM   Dissatisfied with earlier forms of schools, teachers and students joined together to create universities as places for serious study. In this painting a teacher at the University of Paris holds a discussion with students. **What did a scholar have to do in order to become a teacher?**

Fun Facts....

Universities In Medieval Latin, the word *universitas* meant "corporation." The earliest universities were given charters to do business by popes or emperors. Because teachers depended on their students' fees, they had to attract enough students to earn a living.

✓ **Reading Check**
What led students and teachers to form **unions** in the Middle Ages? What are **universities?**

✓ **Reading Check**
What was the role of a **chancellor?**

✓ **Reading Check Answer**
Teachers and students formed **unions** because they wanted more classes taught by better trained teachers. Medieval **universities** were groups of teachers and students devoted to learning.

✓ **Reading Check Answer**
A **chancellor** was the church official who headed each university.

LINKING PAST TO PRESENT

The crisscross-shaped pretzels that we enjoy today were the creation of an Italian monk who baked treats for children as an incentive for memorizing their prayers. He shaped his prize to resemble the folded arms of children in prayer.

CAPTION ANSWER

Each had to pass special tests, be at least 21 years old, and have studied for at least six years.

THE HISTORY CHANNEL.

The following videotape program is available from Glencoe to enrich Chapter 25:

• **Gothic Cathedrals**

To find classroom resources to accompany this video, check the following home page:
A&E Television:
http://www.aetv.com

COOPERATIVE LEARNING

Have students research and then represent a person from a particular sect of the medieval clergy: Benedictine monks, abbesses and nuns, missionaries, or Franciscan or Dominican friars. Have students work in groups to present a day in the life of someone in their order, complete with fictitious names and background history. Have them relate, for instance, how they came to enter a certain order and what their family background might have been.

L3 **Music** Have students research the type of music fostered by the Church during the Middle Ages—the Gregorian Chant. Encourage students to obtain records or tapes of this type of music and learn how and why it was created.

Use **Interactive Tutor Self-Assessment Software** to review Section 3.

MAKING CONNECTIONS

➤➤ **History** The first European universities offered the seven liberal arts—Latin grammar and rhetoric, logic, arithmetic, geometry, astronomy, and music—along with natural science taught according to Aristotle.

✓ **Reading Check Answer**
The capture of Jerusalem by the Seljuq Turks led to a series of **crusades.**

VIDEODISC
Turning Points in
World History

Side One
Chapter 6

Title: *Jerusalem: City of Three Faiths*
Subject: Discussion of the importance of the Holy City to three faiths
Ask: Why is Jerusalem important to Muslims?
(because Muhammad ascended from Jerusalem to heaven)

Thomas Aquinas One noted scholar of the Middle Ages was Thomas Aquinas (uh kwī′ nuhs). Aquinas believed that both faith and reason were gifts of God. He saw no conflict between the two and tried to bring them together. He thought reason helped people know what the world was really like. It helped them lead a good life. He thought faith revealed religious truths to people. It helped them find life after death.

Aquinas wrote a book called *Summa Theologica* (sū′ muh tā ō lō′ ji kuh), or *A Summary of Religious Thought*. In it, he asked questions and presented different opinions. He then gave answers to the questions. Aquinas's teachings were later accepted and promoted by the Church.

Section 3 Assessment

1. **Define:** cathedrals, unions, universities, chancellor.
2. Why were cathedral schools started?
3. In what ways were universities alike?

Critical Thinking

4. **Demonstrating Reasoned Judgment** Why do you think that only specific subjects were taught at cathedral schools?

Graphic Organizer Activity

5. Draw this diagram, and use it to compare universities in the Middle Ages with universities today.

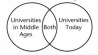

SECTION 4 The Crusades

For hundreds of years, Christians from western Europe had visited shrines in Jerusalem. Then, in 1071, a people called Seljuq (sel′ juk) Turks conquered Jerusalem and took control of the Christian shrines. Traveling in Palestine became difficult for the Christians because of the trouble there.

When news of what was happening in the Holy Land reached Christians in western Europe, they were shocked and angered. The result was a series of holy wars called **crusades** (krū sāds′), which went on for about 200 years.

✓ **Reading Check**
What event led to a series of **crusades?**

A Call to War Even after they had taken Palestine, Turkish armies continued to threaten the Byzantine Empire. The Byzantine emperor asked the Pope for military aid. Pope Urban II (er′ buhn) agreed to help the Byzantines. He hoped that in return, the Eastern Orthodox Church would again unite with the Roman Catholic Church and accept him as its religious leader.

In 1095, Urban spoke before a large crowd in the town of Clermont in eastern France. He told the people that Europe's

Section 3 Assessment Answers

1. cathedrals, churches headed by bishops (p. 386); unions, groups of people joined by a common cause (p. 387); universities, groups of teachers and students devoted to learning (p. 387); chancellor, a church official (p. 387)
2. to prepare the sons of nobles for service in the Church
3. A chancellor headed each, all had well-organized courses of study, all students had to pass special tests, and lecturers had to be 21 years old and have studied six years.
4. Answers will vary but might include that these subjects were considered ones that would provide people with a balanced and well-rounded education.
5. Diagrams will vary, but should reflect an accurate understanding of medieval universities.

Assign the Chapter 25 **Section 3 Quiz** in the TCR. Testmaker available.

lords should stop fighting among themselves. Instead, they should fight in a crusade against the Turks.

Urban reminded the people that Europe was not producing enough food to feed its growing population. Palestine, on the other hand, had rich, fertile land on which any knight could live in comfort. The Pope promised that those who went on a crusade would be free of debts and taxes. He also promised that God would forgive the sins of those who died in battle. He encouraged soldiers to go to Palestine wearing a red cross on their tunics as a symbol of obedience to God.

The Peasants' Crusade   Urban II spent nine months journeying from one European city to another calling for a crusade. The people of Europe responded eagerly to his call. As a sign of their religious devotion, they adopted the war cry *"Deus vult"* (dā' uhs wūlt'), which means "It is the will of God." The people felt it was their duty as Christians to win back the Holy Land. They had other reasons for being willing to fight, too. Nobles hoped to gain more land for themselves in Palestine. They also wanted the fame a crusade could bring. Peasants wanted to escape from their hard work on the land.

Urban II wanted the nobles to plan and lead the crusade. While they were drawing up their plans, however, the peasants

---

CALL FOR A CRUSADE   The conquest of Palestine and persecution of Christians by the Seljuq Turks angered western Europeans. A call went up to free the Holy Land from the Muslims. A church leader in this painting urges local knights to join the crusade. **What symbol did the crusaders wear?**

CAPTION ANSWER

They wore a red cross on their tunics as a symbol of obedience to God.

ABCNEWS INTERACTIVE™

VIDEODISC
Turning Points in World History

Side One
Chapter 7

Title: *The Crusades*
Subject: Western Europeans warred against the Muslim Turks to secure Jerusalem.
Ask: How did the Crusades encourage Europeans to increase trade? *(increased knowledge of Asia's civilizations increased the demand for imported goods)*

COOPERATIVE LEARNING

Request three teams to preview the ABCNEWS InterActive™ Videodisc entitled *The Crusades*. Instruct one team to create a poster advertising the video for display in the classroom. Direct another team to write a review of the video, much like those seen in newsmagazines. Have the third team design a guide for viewing the film, identifying important people, places, and events to look for. Display or distribute these materials and then present the video to the rest of the class.

After students have watched the video, have them complete the following statement: "The most important thing that this video taught me about the Crusades is _____." Call on students to read their completed statements aloud.

📁 Assign Chapter 25 *Cooperative Learning Activity* in the TCR.

TECHNOLOGY SKILLS

TEACH

Using the Internet

You might introduce this lesson by writing the following emoticons on the board:

:-) :-D ;-) :-O :-X

See how many of your students know what they mean. *(From left to right, "smiling," "laughing," "just kidding," "Wow!" and "my lips are sealed.")* Then explore the purpose of emoticons, or "smileys." *(to liven up "conversation" over the Net)*

Use this activity to discuss the many ways in which people use the Internet today—to communicate, to shop, to check the weather, and more. Next, assign the skills lesson, which helps students use the Internet to prepare an account of the Crusades from either a Christian or Muslim perspective.

PERFORMANCE ASSESSMENT ✓

To encourage self-assessment of use of the Internet to write an account of the Crusades, have each student complete this individual task management plan.

Self-Management Plan

Name: _____

Task: _____

Audience: _____

Steps to accomplish the task:

Problems to completing the task:

Solutions or attempted solutions:

Signed: _____

TECHNOLOGY SKILLS   Using the Internet

Are you one of the many people worldwide who have learned—or plan to learn—how to surf the Net? Using the Internet can help you to locate information on many subjects from many different sources.

Learning the Skill The Internet is a global computer network that offers many features, including electronic mail (E-mail), magazine articles, and on-line shopping. Before you can connect to the Internet, however, you must have three things: a computer, a modem (a device that lets your computer send and receive data over telephone lines), and a service provider. A service provider is a company that, for a fee, gives you entry to the Internet.

Once you are connected, the easiest and fastest way to access sites and information is to use a "Web browser," a program that lets you view and explore information on the World Wide Web. The Web consists of many documents called "Web pages," each of which has its own address, or Uniform Resource Locator (URL). Many URLs start with the keystrokes *http://*.

This chapter talks about the series of Crusades that took place in the late Middle Ages. Surf the Internet to learn about these religious wars from the point of view of both the Christians and the Muslims.

Skill Practice

1. Log on to the Internet and access one of the "search engines" provided by your Web browser, such as Yahoo, Lycos, or WebCrawler. (For information designed by or written for students your own age, check out this Web site: *http://www.Yahooligans.com*)
2. Type in your search words, such as *Crusades, Children's Crusade, Peasant's Crusade*, and so on.
3. Scroll down the list of Web pages that appears when the search is complete. Select a page to bring up, and read or print the page. Repeat the process until you have enough information to write an account of the Crusades as they might have been described by either a Christian or a Muslim.

Remains of a medieval fortress in Jerusalem

TEAM-TEACHING STRATEGY

Language Arts Work with a language arts teacher to introduce the following literary terms:

• **Diary**: Informal record of daily happenings, written for personal use.

• **Journal**: Formal record of daily happenings, often written to share with others.

• **Essay**: A brief piece of nonfiction presenting a personal view on a subject.

• **Dialogue**: Conversation between two or more people.

• **Monologue**: Extended speech by one person.

When students understand the terms, assign them to pick one of these styles for presenting their account of the Crusades. Have students read their accounts aloud, and ask other students to identify the form in which each account is presented.

grew impatient and formed their own armies. Although they lacked training in warfare, they believed God would help them.

In the spring of 1096, about 12,000 French peasants began the long journey to Palestine. At the same time, two other groups of peasants set out from Germany. As the peasant armies marched through Europe, they attacked farmers, looted cottages, and burned wheat fields. They *massacred*, or killed, all the Jews they could find. The peasants thought that since Jews were not Christians, they were enemies. Frightened villagers tried to keep the armies away from their homes. At night, the villagers often poisoned wells and attacked crusader camps.

By the time the peasant armies reached Constantinople, they had lost about one third of their number. Their clothes were in rags, and they had no money. They wandered through the streets of the city attacking passersby and stealing from markets and homes.

The Byzantine emperor had expected the Pope to send trained soldiers, not unskilled peasants. The actions of the western Europeans worried him, and he wanted to get them out of his capital. So, he gave them supplies and ships and sent them to fight the Turks in Asia Minor. There, the peasant armies were almost completely wiped out by Turkish bowmen.

The Nobles' Crusade   In 1097, the nobles set out on their crusade. Great lords led each army. They brought with them their vassals, wives, children, clerks, cooks, and blacksmiths. The crusade was very costly. Each lord had to provide his own battle gear, wagons, supplies, and horses. Nobles often had to borrow money or sell their land or jewelry to cover the costs.

About 30,000 **crusaders** arrived in Asia Minor and defeated the Turks. From there, they moved south through the desert to Syria. However, they were not prepared for the heat and did not have enough food or water. Many died of starvation or thirst. Those who survived pushed on to Palestine, capturing Syrian cities along the way.

In 1099, the 12,000 surviving crusaders reached Jerusalem. They captured the Holy City, killing Turks, Jews, and Christians alike. Then, they looted it, taking gold, silver, horses, mules, and all kinds of goods.

The Kingdom Beyond the Sea   After the crusaders captured Jerusalem, they lost much of their religious enthusiasm. Many returned to their homes in western Europe. Those who remained set up four feudal kingdoms called Outremer (ū truh mār'), or "the kingdom beyond the sea," in the areas they won.

The crusaders took over the estates of rich Turkish and Arab Muslims and divided them among themselves and their best knights. Arab peasants worked the land for them and cared for

Fun Facts....

Women in the Crusades Women responded to the call to recapture Jerusalem. A Greek historian wrote of "women dressed as men, mounted on horses and armed with lance and battle-axe." The Pope banned women from fighting in the Third Crusade (1189–1192), a decision that the kings of Europe approved. Women continued to join the crusades, however, both as soldiers and as nurses.

Reading Check What hardships did **crusaders** in the Nobles' Crusade face?

HISTORY Online

Student Activity
Visit the *Human Heritage* Web site at **humanheritage.glencoe.com** and click on *Chapter 25— Student Web Activities* to find out more about the Crusades.

Reading Check Answer During the Nobles Crusade, **crusaders** endured starvation, thirst, and constant battle.

HISTORY Online
Student Web Activity objectives, goals, and answers can be found at the *Chapter 25 Web Activity Lesson Plan* at **humanheritage.glencoe.com**

THE HISTORY CHANNEL.

The following videotape program is available from Glencoe to enrich Chapter 25:

• **The Crusades**

To find classroom resources to accompany this video, check the following home page:

A&E Television:
http://www.aetv.com

L2 **Geography: Human/Environmental Interaction** Ask students to report on how the European lifestyle of a knight differed from the lifestyle he had in the Middle East. Have students report on such things as housing, food, and clothing, and what adjustments the knight had to make in his new home. Ask students to read their reports aloud in class.

CAPTION ANSWER

They were not prepared for the desert's heat and did not have enough food or water. Many died.

GEOGRAPHY AND HISTORY

The city of Jerusalem became historically important about 1000 B.C. when King David united the Israelite tribes and made Jerusalem the capital. Although Jerusalem has been under the control of many nations and groups through the centuries, today Jerusalem is once again the capital city of Israel.

DID YOU KNOW ??

Outremer consisted of the kingdom of Jerusalem and the counties of Tripoli, Antioch, and Edessa.

People in History

Eleanor of Aquitaine
c. 1122–1204

French Queen

At age 15, Eleanor inherited Aquitaine, a region in southern France. As one of the largest land owners in Europe, she married a French king, Louis VII, and accompanied him on a crusade. She later married King Henry II of England and had nine children. One of them included Richard the Lionheart. While Richard headed off on a crusade, Eleanor ruled England in his absence. When Richard died, she helped put her son John on the throne. Few doubted Eleanor's power when she died at age 82.

CRUSADERS' ATTACK ON JERUSALEM   After weeks of siege warfare, the crusaders were finally able to mount a successful attack on Jerusalem. The Christians, using towers and catapults, broke through the city's walls and defeated the Muslim defenders. **What hardships did the crusaders face on their way to Jerusalem?**

the orchards and vineyards. Other Arabs served as advisers and helped them manage their estates. Friendships developed between the crusaders and the Muslims. The Muslims admired the crusaders' bravery. The crusaders discovered that many Arab scholars knew more than Europeans did about medicine, science, and mathematics.

When the crusaders were not fighting Turks, they ran their estates, went hunting, and attended the local court. Each noble built a castle in Outremer more magnificent than the one he had in Europe. This castle was more than a fortress. It was a comfortable place in which to live, with a large dining hall, living room, and bedchambers. All the rooms had marble walls and painted ceilings and were decorated with silk hangings, carpets, silver and gold objects, and beautiful furnishings.

The crusaders found that their old way of living did not suit their new surroundings. It was too hot in Palestine to wear fur and woolen clothes. Men began to wear turbans and loose, flowing silk or linen robes. However, they continued to fight in armor. Women wore jeweled tunics and gowns made with gold thread. They adopted the Muslim custom of wearing veils when they were outdoors and learned to use makeup and perfume. The heat also led the westerners to develop the habit of bathing.

EXTENDING THE CONTENT

During the Crusades several military orders of monks developed. Some are still in existence. The Knights Hospitallers first formed to care for pilgrims in Jerusalem and for the sick. They were dedicated to Saint John the Baptist and were sometimes known as the Knights of Saint John. They followed Benedictine rule. In 1291 they moved to Cyprus when the Muslims took over Jerusalem. Another group, the Knights of Templars took their name from the Dome of the Rock in Jerusalem. They helped guide and protect pilgrims as well as keeping order among crusaders and Saracens. The Templars became a wealthy secret army. King Philip the Fair of France, fearing their influence, tried to destroy the group.

The crusaders changed their eating habits, too. It was too hot to eat the heavy, solid foods they were used to. They learned to have light meals with less meat and more fruit and vegetables. They also ate new foods, such as rice, oranges, figs, and melons.

The crusaders led an easier life in Palestine than they had at home. Still, they had trouble adjusting. Many died in battle against the Turks or in fights among themselves over rights and lands. Others could not survive the hot climate.

Saladin and the Crusade of Kings In 1174, a Muslim military leader named Saladin (sal' uhd uhn) became the ruler of Egypt. He united the Muslims throughout the Near East and started a war against the Christian occupation of Palestine by western Crusaders. Saladin's armies were well organized and devoted to Islam. Groups of soldiers headed by leaders called **emirs** (i miuhrs') made up the armies. Many emirs were known for their honesty and for the consideration they showed their captives. The emirs often were shocked by the cruelty and greed of the Christian soldiers.

Saladin's soldiers rode into battle on swift ponies. Their weapons were short bows. The crusaders found it hard to fight them. The crusaders' armor was heavy, their swords were too long to handle easily, and their horses were not protected. They had to learn to depend on a new weapon called the *crossbow,* which fired an arrow with great force and speed. In 1187, Saladin's armies took Jerusalem. When he refused to massacre the city's Christians, he won the respect of many of the crusaders.

After Saladin's victory, the Church urged another crusade. This time the western armies were led by King Richard I of England, Emperor Frederick Barbarossa (bahr buh ros' uh) of Germany, and King Philip II Augustus of France. They were the three most powerful rulers in Europe.

This Crusade of Kings, as it was called, was a failure. Frederick died in Asia Minor, and many of his troops returned home without ever having fought a battle. Richard and Philip were enemies and were always quarreling. They did take a few coastal cities in Palestine together. Then, Philip returned home. Richard and his armies had to continue the crusade alone.

Richard was a brave warrior. Because of this, he was called "the Lionheart." Nevertheless, he could not defeat Saladin. After three years, he gave up and signed a truce with the Muslim leader. Although the crusaders still controlled large areas of Palestine, Jerusalem remained in Muslim hands.

The Loss of an Ideal In 1202, Pope Innocent III called for yet another crusade. Knights from all over Europe answered the call. They decided not to take a land route to Palestine but to go by ship from the Italian port of Venice. Rich merchants there wanted

Painting of Arab Scholars

✔ **Reading Check**
What were **emirs** known for?

Painting of Saladin

✔ **Reading Check Answer**
Emirs were known for their honesty and for the consideration they showed their captives.

DID YOU KNOW ??

The medieval practice of making a pilgrimage to Jerusalem began during Constantine's time and was common among all classes of people including the aristocracy. Some people made the pilgrimage as an act of piety; others went to ask for forgiveness for their sins.

Biography

The following videotape program is available from Glencoe to enrich Chapter 25:

• **Richard the Lionheart**

To find classroom resources to accompany this video, check the following home page:

A&E Television:
http://www.aetv.com

SPOTLIGHT ON: SALADIN

Saladin made the following reply to King Richard I of England after Richard wrote Saladin that he and his men would continue to fight for Jerusalem: *To us Jerusalem is as precious, aye and more precious than it is to you, in that it was the place whence our Prophet made his journey by night and is destined to be the gathering place of our nation at the last day. Do not dream that we shall give it up to you. . . . It belonged to us originally, and it is you who are the aggressors.*

MAP SKILLS

TEACH

Determining Exact Location

Have students read the introductory section of the skill on page 394. Ask: Why do most maps have grids? *(to help find different points on a map)* What do you need to find in order to know the exact location of a place? *(the line of latitude and the line of longitude that cross at that exact location)* Direct students to the map on this page. Ask: What are the coordinates of Constantinople? *(41° N, 29° E)*

Next, have students write five questions about the Crusades based on the information on the map. Then collect the questions and quiz the class on the map using the questions written by the students.

Assign the Chapter 25 **Geography and Map Activity** in the TCR.

Answers to Map Practice

1. Jerusalem
2. 45° N, 12° E

Determining Exact Location

Most maps have **grids,** or patterns of horizontal and vertical lines that cross each other. Generally, the horizontal lines are lines of latitude, and the vertical ones are lines of longitude. Grids make it easier to determine the exact location of a place on Earth.

To find a place exactly, it is necessary to find where lines of latitude and longitude cross at that place. The point at which they cross is the exact location.

Exact location may be shown by a set of numbers that list latitude first and then longitude (30°N, 60°E). Such sets are called **coordinates** (kō ōr' din uhts).

Look at the map of "The Crusades" below. Locate the city of Marseilles on the southern coast of France. The line of latitude that passes through the city is 43°N. The line of longitude that passes through it is 5°E. This means that the exact location of Marseilles is 43°N, 5°E.

Map Practice

1. **What city is located at 32°N, 35°E?**
2. **What are the coordinates of Venice's location?**

Glencoe's **Skillbuilder Interactive Workbook, Level 1,** provides instruction and practice in key social studies skills.

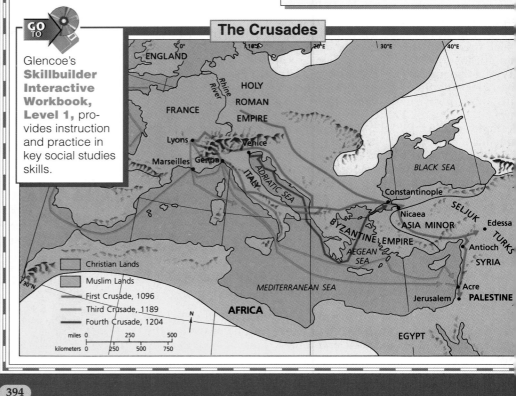

The Crusades

SPOTLIGHT ON: THE CRUSADES

The general climate of the area through which the crusaders travelled was not unlike that of the western United States and Mexico—a combination of semi-desert and mediterranean climates. The average annual temperature fell in the range of 60°–70° F (16°–21° C), which is similar to the temperatures felt throughout the southern half of the United States.

Venice to replace Constantinople as the trading center of the eastern Mediterranean. The crusaders agreed to pay these merchants a large sum of money and to share one half of all their conquests with the Venetians. In return, the Venetians agreed to supply the crusaders with ships and equipment.

When the soldiers found they could not pay all they owed, they agreed to conquer the city of Zara for the Venetians. Then, the Venetians convinced them to capture Constantinople. For three days, the crusaders and the Venetians burned and looted Constantinople. Many priceless manuscripts and works of art were either taken to Venice, lost, or destroyed.

Jeweled Box

The crusaders finally decided not to go to Palestine. Instead, they stayed in Constantinople and divided the city with the Venetians. Their conduct shocked many western Europeans, who lost respect for the crusader ideal.

Several other crusades were fought during the 1200s, but the Europeans did not win any of them. The saddest of all was the Children's Crusade. A group of French children, led by a peasant boy named Stephen of Cloyes, set sail from Marseilles (mahr sā'), France, in 1212. Most of the children never reached Palestine. Along the way they were sold into slavery by captains of the ships on which they sailed. At the same time, another group of children set forth on foot from Germany, intending to march toward Italy. Most of them, however, starved to death or died from disease.

In 1291, the Muslims took over the city of Acre (ah' kuhr), the last Christian stronghold. The Muslims had won the Crusades. They also gained back all the land in Palestine that the crusaders had taken earlier.

Effects of the Crusades   The Crusades affected both the Near East and western Europe. The Byzantines were so angry at the actions of western Europeans that the split between eastern and western Christianity became permanent. At the same time, the Byzantine Empire was so weakened by the Crusades that it could no longer defend itself. This left Europe open to Turkish attack.

The Crusades helped to break down feudalism in western Europe. While feudal lords were fighting in Palestine, kings at home increased their authority. The desire for wealth, power, and land grew and began to cloud the religious ideals of many western Europeans.

The crusaders' contact with the cultured Byzantines and Muslims led western Europeans to again become interested in learning. At the same time, Europeans began to demand such luxuries as spices, sugar, lemons, rugs, tapestries, and richly woven cloth. To meet these demands, European merchants opened up new trade routes. As trade grew, so did the towns of western Europe.

CHAPTER 25 THE CHURCH   395

L3 **Culture** Have students research and report on some of the ideas brought back by the crusaders, especially new knowledge in mathematics and the sciences, that have impacted modern society. How were medieval universities like universities today? How have medieval mathematics impacted modern mathematics?

DID YOU KNOW

The children were not going to the Holy Land to fight but to convert the Muslims to Christianity.

ASSESS

Check for Understanding

Ask students to summarize the main points of the chapter, orally or in writing. Discuss the answers to the Section and Chapter Assessment questions.

Evaluate

Assign the Chapter 25 **Performance Assessment Activity** in the TCR.

Administer the **Chapter 25 Test.** Testmaker available.

Reteach

Have students work in small groups to list the important features of each crusade. Have the groups compare and discuss their lists.

Assign the Chapter 25 **Reteaching Activity** in the TCR.

MULTICULTURAL PERSPECTIVES

Have students debate the following topic: *The Crusades took place only for religious reasons and purposes.* Divide students into two groups, one group to defend the idea that the motivations of the crusaders were solely religious and the other to defend the idea that the crusaders had other reasons for going to the Holy Land. Allow each group time to research and develop their arguments. Then have each group present its views.

Enrich

Have students investigate accounts of Saladin and King Richard I of England during the Crusade of Kings. Ask students to give a brief oral report on the character of these two men, their motives for fighting, and how they regarded each other.

Assign the Chapter 25 **Enrichment Activity** in the TCR.

CLOSE

Discuss how the Crusades changed western civilization. Ask: *Did the crusaders help or hurt western civilization?* Have students debate the gains and losses.

 HISTORY *Online*

Use **Interactive Tutor Self-Assessment Software** to review Section 4.

Self-Check Quiz gives students an interactive chapter tutorial. Have them access *Chapter 25 Quiz* at **humanheritage.glencoe.com**

Section 4 Assessment

1. **Define:** crusades, crusaders, emirs.
2. Why were western Europeans of all classes of society eager to go on a crusade?
3. What effect did the Crusades have on trade?

Critical Thinking

4. **Understanding Cause and Effect** What do you think was the most important effect of the Crusades on the entire civilized world (not just on western Europe)? Explain.

Graphic Organizer Activity

5. Draw this diagram, and use it to support a generalization about the effect of the Crusades on feudalism.

Chapter Summary & Study Guide

1. The Roman Catholic Church was the center of life in Europe during the Middle Ages.
2. Increased wealth led many members of the clergy to grow careless about their religious duties, sparking a spirit of reform.
3. During the Middle Ages, monks and friars worked to win the respect of the people.
4. In 1075, Pope Gregory VII issued a document placing the power of the Pope above all kings and feudal lords.
5. By the 1200s, students and teachers at cathedral schools had helped form universities, which soon spread throughout Europe.
6. Scholars such as Thomas Aquinas tried to bring faith and reason together.
7. In 1071, the Seljuq Turks conquered the Holy Land and took control of the Christian shrines there.
8. In 1095, Pope Urban II agreed to help the Byzantines against the Turks and called on the people of western Europe to join in a crusade.
9. The Nobles' Crusade of 1097 succeeded in capturing Jerusalem, but the Christians could not hold on to the city.
10. Richard the Lionheart, who set out on a crusade with two other kings, could not defeat Saladin and signed a truce with him.
11. In 1202, crusaders, with the help of the Venetians, burned and looted Constantinople. This event badly damaged the crusading ideal.
12. Even though the Muslims regained all of Palestine in 1291, the Crusades brought lasting changes to Europe, including the end of feudalism.

 HISTORY *Online*

Self-Check Quiz

Visit the *Human Heritage* Web site at **humanheritage. glencoe.com** and click on *Chapter 25—Self-Check Quiz* to assess your understanding of this chapter.

Section 4 Assessment Answers

1. crusades, a series of holy wars (p. 388); *emirs*, Muslim military leaders (p. 393)
2. They felt it was their duty as Christians to win back the Holy Land; nobles hoped to acquire more land and gain glory; and peasants wanted to escape hard work.
3. They led to the opening up of new trade routes and an increase in trade.
4. Answers will vary, but students should provide reasons for their choices.
5. Supporting details will vary with the generalization written by students. If you need to provide an example of a generalization, offer this statement from page 395: "The Crusades helped to break down feudalism in western Europe."

Assign the Chapter 25 **Section 4 Quiz** in the TCR. Testmaker available.

Using Key Terms

Imagine that you are a traveler in Europe during the Middle Ages. Write an article for a travel magazine describing the influence of the Roman Catholic Church. Use the following words.

mass	canon laws	excommunicated
tithes	friars	orders
cathedrals	unions	universities
chancellor	crusades	crusaders
emirs		

Understanding Main Ideas

1. What role did Church officials play in the political life of the Middle Ages?
2. Why did many monks grow careless about carrying out their religious duties?
3. Why were universities started?
4. Why did Urban II encourage people to go on a crusade?
5. What effect did the climate in Palestine have on the crusaders?
6. What happened during the Children's Crusade?
7. Why did the split in the Roman Catholic Church become permanent?
8. How did the Crusades affect the power of western Europe's kings?

Critical Thinking

1. What were the advantages and disadvantages of having Church leaders run the government during the Middle Ages?
2. What would have been enjoyable about being a student in a medieval university?

3. How would you have responded to Urban II's call for a crusade?
4. How do you think crusaders felt about settling in Palestine? Explain your answer.

Graphic Organizer Activity

Economics Create a diagram like the one below, and use it to show the economic changes that the Crusades brought to western Europe.

Geography in History

Movement Soldiers in the Fourth Crusade sailed from Venice to Constantinople. About how many miles long was their voyage? Was their voyage longer or shorter than it would have been if they had sailed to Jerusalem as planned?

Using Your Journal

Review any details you may have noted about how the Church influenced daily life, government, and education during the late Middle Ages. Write a paragraph comparing the role of the Church then with the role of churches in the lives of people today.

397

Bonus Test Question
For Chapter 25 Test
You are a Monk of Cluny faced by an angry bishop who resents your activities. Explain your beliefs and convince the bishop to work with you. *(Answers may vary, but students should indicate that the Cluny monks were trying to reform the Church.)*

Using Your Journal
Paragraphs will vary but might indicate that churches have a more personal effect on people today rather than the all-encompassing effect the Church had in the Middle Ages.

Geography in History
about 1,400 miles (or 2,250 km); shorter

Using Key Terms

Articles will vary but should describe highlights of the area and dominance of the Church.

Understanding Main Ideas

1. They served as advisers and kept records for illiterate kings.
2. because they became wealthy
3. because students complained that teachers were poor and held few classes, and untrained people were teaching
4. to free Jerusalem from the Seljuq Turks; to win a chance to regain control of the Eastern Orthodox Church
5. They were not accustomed to the heat and lack of water. Many died of thirst.
6. Many of the children were sold into enslavement, starved to death, or died from disease.
7. because the Byzantines were so angry at the actions of western Europeans in burning and looting Constantinople
8. They increased the kings' authority.

Critical Thinking

1. Answers will vary, but one advantage was that the Church was a unifying force. The disadvantage was that Church officials became wealthy and corrupt.
2. Answers will vary but should include examples.
3. Answers will vary.
4. Answers will vary, but students should indicate why they would or would not have liked to settle there.

Graphic Organizer Activity

Graphic organizers will vary but should contrast the largely self-sufficient manors prior to the Crusades with the revival of trade and cities after the Crusades.

Chapter 26 Planning Guide

Objectives	Reproducible Resources	Multimedia Resources
Section 1 **Trading Centers** Analyze how the growth of trade led to the rise of towns in the Middle Ages.	Reproducible Lesson Plan Chapter 26 Vocabulary and Guided Reading Activity Reading Essentials and Study Guide 26-1 Chapter 26 Geography and Map Activity Section 1 Quiz	Vocabulary PuzzleMaker Interactive Tutor Self-Assessment Software ExamView® Pro Testmaker Glencoe Skillbuilder Interactive Workbook, Level 1
Section 2 **Merchants** Summarize how merchants became an important part of European life.	Reproducible Lesson Plan Reading Essentials and Study Guide 26-2 Section 2 Quiz	Vocabulary PuzzleMaker Interactive Tutor Self-Assessment Software ExamView® Pro Testmaker Glencoe Skillbuilder Interactive Workbook, Level 1
Section 3 **Living Conditions** Describe what living conditions were like in medieval towns.	Reproducible Lesson Plan Reading Essentials and Study Guide 26-3 Section 3 Quiz	Vocabulary PuzzleMaker Interactive Tutor Self-Assessment Software ExamView® Pro Testmaker Glencoe Skillbuilder Interactive Workbook, Level 1
Section 4 **The Rise of Guilds** Explain why guilds were formed and why they were later opposed.	Reproducible Lesson Plan Reading Essentials and Study Guide 26-4 Chapter 26 Cooperative Learning Activity Chapter 26 Enrichment Activity Section 4 Quiz	Vocabulary PuzzleMaker Interactive Tutor Self-Assessment Software ExamView® Pro Testmaker Glencoe Skillbuilder Interactive Workbook, Level 1
Section 5 **Cultural Changes** Summarize the cultural changes that took place in Europe during the 1400s.	Reproducible Lesson Plan Reading Essentials and Study Guide 26-5 Chapter 26 Activity Book Activity Chapter 26 Chart and Graph Skill Activity Unit 8 World Literature Reading 1 Section 5 Quiz	Vocabulary PuzzleMaker ExamView® Pro Testmaker Glencoe Skillbuilder Interactive Workbook, Level 1
Chapter 26 **Review and Evaluation**	Chapter 26 Reteaching Activity Chapter 26 Performance Assessment Activity Spanish Chapter Summary and Glossary Chapter 26 Test	Vocabulary PuzzleMaker Interactive Tutor Self-Assessment Software Glencoe Skillbuilder Interactive Workbook, Level 1 Audiocassettes* ExamView® Pro Testmaker

*Also available in Spanish.

Presentation Plus!

Use Glencoe's **Presentation Plus!** multimedia teacher tool to easily present dynamic lessons that visually excite your students. Using Microsoft® PowerPoint, you can customize the presentations to create your own personalized lessons.

 Interactive Lesson Planner

Planning has never been easier! Using this CD-ROM, organize your week, month, semester, or year with all the help you need. The **Interactive Lesson Planner** gives you access to all of the blackline masters which accompany *Human Heritage.*

✓ PERFORMANCE ASSESSMENT ACTIVITIES

Literature Collages As students learn about people in the Middle Ages , read the following portraits from Chaucer's Prologue to *The Canterbury Tales* aloud to them: the Knight, the Wife of Bath, the Squire, the Monk, the Friar, the Parson, the Prioress. Have students create collages to represent the people as described by Chaucer.

CHAPTER RESOURCES

LITERATURE ABOUT THE PERIOD

Chaucer, Geoffrey. *The Canterbury Tales.* In *The Complete Poetry and Prose of Geoffrey Chaucer.* Holt, Rhinehart and Winston, 1977. This English classic gives insight into the character of the Middle Ages.

READINGS FOR THE STUDENT

Clarke, Charles Cowden. *Tales from Chaucer.* The Heritage Press, 1947. A selection of nine tales (and the Prologue) retold in prose for young readers.

READINGS FOR THE TEACHER

Editors of Time-Life Books. *What Life was Like in the Age of Chivalry.* Time-Life Books, 1997. Illustrated look at daily life in the period 800–1500.

Tuchman, Barbara W. *A Distant Mirror.* Ballantine Books, 1978. Examines problems of the fourteenth century.

KEY TO ABILITY LEVELS

Teaching strategies have been coded for varying learning styles and abilities.

L1 Level 1 activities are **basic** activities and should be within the ability range of all students.

L2 Level 2 activities are **average** activities and should be within the ability range of the average to above-average student.

L3 Level 3 activities are **challenging** activities designed for the ability range of above-average students.

ELL ELL activities should be within the ability range of English Language Learning students.

NATIONAL GEOGRAPHIC SOCIETY — **Teacher's Corner**

INDEX TO NATIONAL GEOGRAPHIC MAGAZINE

The following articles relate to this chapter:

- "A World Together," by Erla Zwingle, August 1999.
- "The Hanseatic League," by Edward Von der Porten, October 1994.
- "The Power of Money," by Peter T. White, January 1993.

NATIONAL GEOGRAPHIC SOCIETY PRODUCTS AVAILABLE FROM GLENCOE

To order the following, call Glencoe at 1-800-334-7344:

- *PicturePack: Europe (Transparencies)*
- *PicturePack: The Middle Ages (Transparencies)*
- *PictureShow: The Middle Ages (CD-ROM)*

ADDITIONAL NATIONAL GEOGRAPHIC SOCIETY PRODUCTS

To order the following, call National Geographic at 1-800-368-2728:

- *National Geographic Atlas of World History (Book)*
- *The Builders: Marvels of Engineering (Book)*

Access *National Geographic*'s new dynamic MapMaker Web site and other geography resources at:
http://www.nationalgeographic.com/
http://www.nationalgeographic.com/maps/

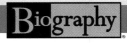

THE HISTORY CHANNEL   A&E HOME VIDEO   Biography

The following videotape programs are available from Glencoe:

- **Marco Polo: Journey to the East**
  1-56501-668-8

- **Scourge of the Black Death**
  0-7670-0534-1

To order, call Glencoe at 1-800-334-7344. To find classroom resources to accompany many of these, check:

A&E Television: http://www.aetv.com
The History Channel:
http://www.historychannel.com

OVERVIEW

Chapter 26 examines the rise of towns in western Europe during the Middle Ages.

➤ **Section 1** explains the growth of trade and rise of towns.
➤ **Section 2** discusses the medieval merchant class.
➤ **Section 3** identifies living conditions in the towns.
➤ **Section 4** describes the guilds.
➤ **Section 5** summarizes the cultural developments in medieval towns.

CHAPTER OBJECTIVES

After reading Chapter 26, students will be able to:

1. link the growth of trade to the rise of medieval towns.
2. tell how merchants became a key part of European life.
3. describe medieval town life.
4. explain why guilds were formed and later opposed.
5. summarize the cultural changes that took place in Europe during the 1400s.

EXAMINING ARTIFACTS

Have students compare these artifacts to the ones on page 380. How do these artifacts differ? *(Craftsmen and guilds are the subjects rather than crusaders and the Church.)* Focus on the fact that medieval craftsmen now appear in stained-glass windows—a place once reserved for religious figures and nobles. Ask: What does this suggest to you? *(that craftsmen have become more influential)*

PERFORMANCE ASSESSMENT ✓

Use the Performance Assessment activities on page 398B to help you evaluate students as they complete the chapter.

Rise of Trade and Towns

500 A.D.–1400 A.D.

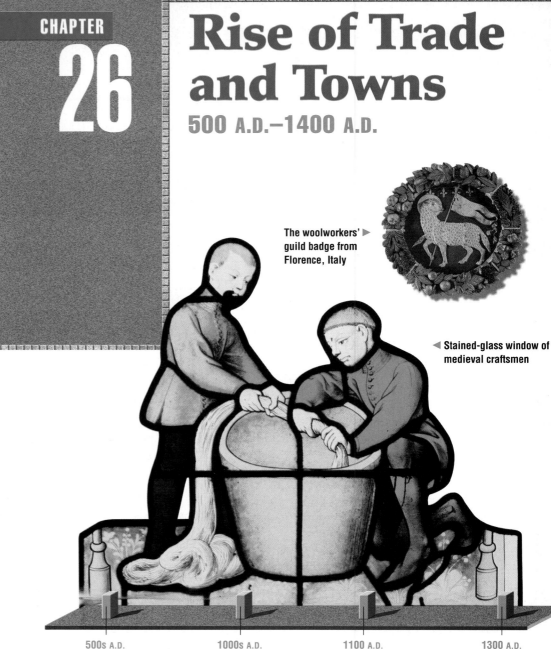

The woolworkers' ▶ guild badge from Florence, Italy

◀ Stained-glass window of medieval craftsmen

500s A.D.	1000s A.D.	1100 A.D.	1300 A.D.
Venice founded	Trade increases between Europe and the Near East	Italian trading towns drive Muslims from the Mediterranean	Flemish develop thriving trade with England

398 UNIT 8 THE LATE MIDDLE AGES

TEACHING RESOURCES

TEACHER PLANNING AND SUPPORT

🗀 Reproducible Lesson Plan
🗀 Block Scheduling Implementation Guide
🗀 Videodisc Bar Code Correlation
💿 Presentation Plus!

REVIEW AND REINFORCEMENT

🗀 Reading Essentials and Study Guide 26-1, 26-2, 26-3, 26-4, 26-5
💾 Chapter 26 Vocabulary and Guided Reading Activity
💾 Vocabulary PuzzleMaker Software
🗀 Chapter 26 Reteaching Activity

🗀 Chapter 26 Cooperative Learning Activity
🗀 Chapter 26 Activity Book Activity
🗀 Chapter 26 Chart and Graph Skill Activity
💾 Interactive Tutor Self-Assessment Software

APPLICATION AND HANDS-ON ACTIVITIES

🗀 Daily World History, Geography, and Culture Question

GEOGRAPHY ACTIVITIES

🗀 Chapter 26 Geography and Map Activity
🗀 Social Studies Outline Map Resource Book

Chapter Focus

Read to Discover

- How the growth of trade led to the rise of towns in the Middle Ages.
- What living conditions were like in medieval towns.
- Why guilds were formed and why they were later opposed.
- What cultural changes to civilization took place in Europe during the 1400s.

 Terms to Learn
guilds
apprentice
masters
journeyman

 People to Know
Dante
Geoffrey
  Chaucer

Places to Locate
Venice
Flanders

Why It's Important Beginning in the 1000s, the population of western Europe grew for the first time since the fall of Rome. Better ways of farming helped farmers grow more food. Many peasants left the fields to work in villages. They began to turn out cloth and metal products.

Western nobles, however, wanted such luxury items as sugar, spices, silks, and dyes. These goods came from the East. So, European merchants carried western products to the East to exchange for luxury goods.

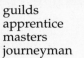

HISTORY *Online*

Chapter Overview
Visit the *Human Heritage* Web site at **humanheritage.glencoe.com** and click on ***Chapter 26— Chapter Overviews*** to preview this chapter.

SECTION 1 Trading Centers

The growth of trade led to the rise of the first large trading centers of the later Middle Ages. They were located on the important sea routes that connected western Europe with the Mediterranean Sea, Russia, and Scandinavia. Two of the earliest and most important trading centers were Venice and Flanders.

Venice Venice was an island port in the Adriatic (ā drē t′ ik) Sea close to the coast of Italy. It was founded in the 500s by people fleeing from the Germans.

INTERDISCIPLINARY CONNECTIONS
- Unit 8 World Literature Reading 1
- World History & Art Transparency 16, *May*
- World Music Cultural Traditions

ENRICHMENT AND EXTENSION
- Chapter 26 Enrichment Activity
- World History Primary Source Document Library CD-ROM
- Foods Around the World

ASSESSMENT AND EVALUATION
- Chapter 26 Performance Assessment Activity
- Chapter 26 Section Quizzes 26-1, 26-2, 26-3, 26-4, 26-5
- Chapter 26 Test
- Chapter 26 ExamView® Pro Testmaker Software
- Chapter 26 Digests Audiocassettes Activities and Tests

SPANISH RESOURCES
- Chapter 26 Spanish Chapter Summary and Glossary
- Chapter 26 Spanish Chapter Digests Audiocassettes Activities and Tests

---

HISTORY *Online*

Chapter Overview introduces students to chapter content and key terms. Have them access ***Chapter 26 Overview*** at **humanheritage.glencoe.com**

FOCUS

Bellringer
Ask students this question: *What if there were no place to take the garbage?*

Motivational Activity
Review student responses. Then explain that during the Middle Ages, peasants began moving to towns from manorial estates. Although the towns were safer, they were also dirty, noisy, and crowded. Garbage as well as raw sewage was thrown into the streets, and wooden houses with thatched roofs were fire hazards. Tell students that in this chapter they will learn about the advantages and disadvantages of living in towns in the Middle Ages.

GUIDE TO READING

Reading Strategy
Ask students to read "Why It's Important" and summarize the chapter's main theme. (*Better farming methods and the Crusades helped give rise to a class of artisans and an interest in trade.*)

Vocabulary Precheck
Ask students to define each of the "Terms to Learn." Have a volunteer consult the dictionary for any unfamiliar words. **L1** **ELL**

Use the Vocabulary PuzzleMaker for Chapter 26 to create a crossword puzzle. **L1**

Assign Chapter 26 Vocabulary and Guided Reading Activity.

Assign Reading Essentials and Study Guide 26-1.

Guided Practice

L1 **Discussion** Lead a discussion on how the growth of trade led to the rise of towns in western Europe during the Middle Ages. Ask: *What effect did increased trade have on western European life? Where were some of the most important trading centers located? What did these centers have in common?* **ELL**

GEOGRAPHY AND HISTORY

Two reasons for the population growth during the 1000s and 1100s were the decline of foreign invasions and good weather, caused by a retreat of polar ice.

MAKING CONNECTIONS

➤➤ **Economics** Italian merchants loaned money to the kings of France and England. In return, the merchants were allowed to conduct trade and collect taxes there. As a result, French and English townspeople often disliked the merchants.

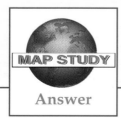

MAP STUDY

Answer

a land route to Genoa and then a water route to Alexandria

Assign the Chapter 26 **Geography and Map** Activity in the TCR.

MAP STUDY

MOVEMENT Trade routes tied all parts of western Europe together. **What was the most direct route merchants could take from Milan to Alexandria?**

Since the land was not very fertile, the early Venetians had to depend on the sea for a living. They fished in the Adriatic and produced salt from the seawater. They exchanged their products for wheat from towns on the mainland of Italy. They also traded wheat, wine, and slaves to the Byzantines for fabrics and spices.

During the 1100s, Venice became a leading port and many of its citizens became fulltime merchants. Venetian merchants learned to read and write, use money, and keep records. In time they developed an effective banking system.

Venice's prosperity soon spread to other parts of Italy. Towns on the Italian mainland began to make cloth, which they sent to Venice to be shipped to other areas. Before long, other Italian towns along the seacoast became shipping centers.

The navies of the Italian trading towns drove the Muslims from the Mediterranean, making it safe for Italian seafarers. As a result, the Italians opened the Near East to Europeans.

However, the Italian trading towns quarreled among themselves over profits and trade routes. While they were quarreling

Medieval Towns and Trade Routes

EXTENDING THE CONTENT

The most famous Venetian traveler is Marco Polo who wrote a colorful journal of his adventures in Mongol China. Marco's father and uncle were wealthy jewel merchants and the first Polos to trade in Asia. In about 1260, they traded in central Asia with the Khan of the Golden Horde and then went on to the court of Kublai Khan, emperor of China. On their second trip in 1271, the Polos took Marco, then about 17. They traveled overland through Tibet on the Silk Road. Marco had a flair for languages and a gift for diplomacy, which allowed him to become a trusted official for the Khan.

towns along Europe's Atlantic coast developed trade routes. By 1500, these towns had become more powerful than those in Italy.

Flanders Flanders, which today is part of Belgium, was an area of small towns on the northwest coast of Europe. The Flemish (flem' ish) people raised sheep and used the wool to develop a weaving industry. The cloth they produced became famous for its quality and soon was in heavy demand.

Flanders became the earliest Atlantic trading center. Its rivers joined together before they emptied into the North Sea. Where the rivers met, the Flemish built harbors. From these harbors, they shipped their valuable woolen cloth to other lands.

Flanders became an important stopping place for ships traveling along the Atlantic coast from Scandinavia to the Mediterranean. It also became an important link in the trade route between Constantinople and the North Sea.

By 1300, the most important trading partner of Flanders was England. Flemish traders set up shop in the dockyards of London. They relied on English shepherds to supply them with wool to be made into cloth. The finished cloth was then shipped back to England. In this way, the Flemish developed an international industry.

Painting of Money Changers

Section 1 Assessment

1. What led to the growth and development of Venice's trade?
2. How did the location of Flanders help it become an important trading center?
3. How did the Flemish develop an international industry?

Critical Thinking

4. **Identifying Alternatives** What do you think would be attractive about living in a trading town during the Middle Ages?

Graphic Organizer Activity

5. Draw this diagram, and use it to compare the trading towns of Italy and Flanders.

	Italy	Flanders
Location		
Trade Items		
Key Trade Routes		

SECTION 2 Merchants

Painting of Medieval Merchant

As sea trade grew, so did overland trade. Italian towns began sending goods across the Alps to areas in the north. Soon, an overland trade route connected Italy and Flanders. From this route, other routes developed and spread across Europe.

Merchants became an important part of European life during the late Middle Ages. The first merchants were mostly adventurers who traveled from place to place. As protection

 Use **Interactive Tutor Self-Assessment Software** to review Section 1.

DID YOU KNOW

Medieval fairs were much more than a chance to buy goods from faraway places, though that was rare and exciting. They also broadened the world of the medieval townspeople. Though they might never have traveled more than a few miles from home, the fair drew travelers with exciting stories and visitors from distant places.

NATIONAL GEOGRAPHIC SOCIETY

Use these materials to enrich student understanding of the Middle Ages.

NGS PICTURESHOW CD-ROM The Middle Ages

NGS PICTUREPACK TRANSPARENCY SET The Middle Ages

Biography

The following videotape program is available from Glencoe to enrich Chapter 26:

• **Marco Polo: Journey to the East**

To find classroom resources to accompany this video, check the following home page:

A&E Television: http://www.aetv.com

Use the **Vocabulary Puzzle-Maker** to create crossword and word search puzzles.

Reading Check
Who sponsored most medieval **fairs?**

Wandering Musicians
In southern France, wandering poet-musicians called troubadours visited towns and nobles' courts, composing songs about love and the brave deeds of heroes. Some troubadours also traveled parts of southern Spain, singing lyrics in Arabic, Hebrew, and Spanish.

against robbers, they traveled in armed groups. They carried their goods in open wagons pulled by horses.

Fairs   Merchants traveling along the chief route through eastern France stopped to trade with each other at special gatherings called **fairs.** The fairs were sponsored by nobles who collected taxes on sales. Fairs were held once a year for a few weeks at selected places. Over time, they attracted merchants from as far away as England and Egypt.

At the fairs, merchants could buy and sell goods or settle debts. They set up booths to show such *wares,* or things for sale, as pots, swords, armor, and clothing. Before long, merchants began to pay for goods with precious metals instead of bartering. Italian money changers tested and weighed coins from many different lands to determine their value. From the *banc,* or bench, at which the money changers sat comes the English word "bank."

The Growth of Towns   After awhile, merchants grew tired of moving around. They began to look for places where they could settle permanently and store their goods. They generally chose places along a trade route near waterways or road crossings. They also tried to settle close to a castle or monastery. This helped protect them from robbers and fights between nobles. The merchants surrounded their settlements with pal-

MEDIEVAL MARKETPLACE   During the Middle Ages merchants set up permanent shops that eventually developed into towns. Medieval merchants in this painting sell shoes, cloth, and tableware. **Why did merchants try to settle near castles or monasteries?**

isades and moats. Most towns of the Middle Ages developed from these merchant settlements.

The towns came to be called **burgs** (bergs) because they were often near castles, which the Germans called *burgs*. The new towns grew steadily and attracted people from the surrounding countryside. Markets became centers of business and social life. Once a week, nobles and peasants sold food for goods they could not make on the manor. Artisans came from the villages to find work. Often they brought their families with them. Over time, the towns became more than just centers of trade. They became communities in which people lived.

 Reading Check
How did **burgs** get their name?

 Reading Check Answer
Towns came to be called **burgs** because they often lay near castles, which the Germans called *burgs*.

L2 **Environment** Have students discuss the garbage problem that faced medieval towns. Encourage them to brainstorm solutions to the problem. Then have them devise the best way to inform the people of what they must do to achieve "garbage control." **ELL**

💾 Use **Interactive Tutor Self-Assessment Software** to review Section 2.

Section 2 Assessment

1. **Define:** fairs, burgs
2. Why did nobles sponsor fairs?
3. Where did merchants set up their marketplaces?

Critical Thinking

4. **Making Generalizations** How did merchants contribute to the growth of towns?

Graphic Organizer Activity

5. Draw the diagram below, and use it to compare the activities at medieval fairs with the activities at fairs today.

SECTION 3 Living Conditions

By the 1200s, many towns were wealthy and large enough to have their palisades replaced by walls and towers. Inside the walls, public buildings of stone and houses of wood were jammed close together. To save even more space, the houses had extra stories that extended over crooked narrow alleys.

The crowded conditions often made towns unhealthy places in which to live. Sewers were open, and there was little concern for cleanliness. People threw garbage out of windows onto the streets below. Rats were everywhere.

During the 1300s, diseased rats came to Europe on trading ships from the Middle East. They carried with them a plague called the "Black Death." This disease swept through Europe, killing millions of people. Experts think that one out of three Europeans died in the plague. To escape it, people fled from the towns and settled in the countryside. Trading, farming, and war came to a temporary halt.

Burgher Life Merchants and artisans controlled a town's business and trade. They hired workers from the countryside to

Between 1348 and 1350, the Black Death claimed nearly 25 million lives. The epidemic stopped wars and slowed trade. Officials sealed off infected homes, suspended religious services, and made it illegal to meet in groups. It took almost 200 years for Europe to regain its pre-1348 level of population.

THE HISTORY CHANNEL.

The following videotape program is available from Glencoe to enrich Chapter 26:

• **Scourge of the Black Death**

To find classroom resources to accompany this video, check the following home page:

A&E Television
http://www.aetv.com

🌐 **GEOGRAPHY AND HISTORY**

In Switzerland and western Germany, the Jews were blamed for the Black Death, and thousands were burned to death or hanged. As a result, there was a movement of Jews into eastern Germany and Poland.

💾 Use the **Vocabulary Puzzle-Maker** to create crossword and word search puzzles.

Section 2 Assessment Answers

1. fairs, special gatherings for trade (p. 402); burgs, medieval towns (p. 403)
2. because they collected taxes on sales
3. along a trade route near waterways or road crossings, and close to a castle or monastery
4. Sample generalization: Most of the towns developed from merchant settlements.
5. Diagrams will vary but should show an accurate understanding of medieval fairs, especially in promoting trade and the use of money. Shared features of both fairs might be such things as: largely an annual event, draw people from all over, and so on. Differences might include the kinds of technological entertainment at modern fairs or the use of credit to purchase goods.

Assign the Chapter 26 **Section 2 Quiz** in the TCR. Testmaker available.

Reading Check Answer
At first, the merchants, artisans, and workers who lived in towns were all called **burghers.**

LINKING PAST TO PRESENT

The term *burg* originally meant a fortified town or castle. As part of town names, it appeared in the Germanic *-burg*, the French *-bourg*, and the English *-borough* and *-bury*. Today, in Europe, we find Hamburg, Strasbourg, Edinburgh, and Canterbury; in the United States, Pittsburgh, Harrisburg, and Salisbury.

DID YOU KNOW

Peasants ate dark bread, broth, cheese, and curds. Other dishes of the burghers and manor nobility included miniature cod liver pastries, beef marrow fritters, a sauce of pounded crayfish tails, and other types of fish. Aristocrats ate many of the foods that the burghers ate, but in larger quantities.

Reading Check
At first, what groups were called **burghers?**

Manners Robert of Blois, a French poet, listed rules of correct conduct for daughters of burghers. They included:
• A lady must walk straight and not trot or run.
• Take care: glances are messengers of love; men are prompt to deceive themselves by them.

make goods for them. At first, the merchants, artisans, and workers who lived in towns were all called **burghers** (ber' guhrz). Later the title was used to mean rich merchants.

The daily life of burghers and their families started with prayers at dawn. The burgher hurried off to the docks and market to see how his products were selling. Then, he met with his business partners.

The burgher's wife kept house, managed servants, and cared for children. The family ate two large meals a day—one at ten o'clock in the morning and another at six o'clock in the evening. A typical meal consisted of eel, roast beef, lark pastry, and curded milk. About nine o'clock in the evening, the family went to bed.

Changing Ways   Under the feudal system, the land on which towns were built was owned by kings, nobles, and bishops. They taxed the people in the towns and charged them

Linking Across Time

Health Care   The unhealthy, overcrowded conditions of medieval cities encouraged the rapid spread of diseases such as measles, smallpox, polio, flu, and the "Black Death" (below). Today doctors know that most diseases are caused by bacteria and viruses. Many diseases common in medieval times have been wiped out or curbed through good health practices such as washing hands or receiving vaccinations like the polio shot (right).

MULTICULTURAL PERSPECTIVES

Town life in the Middle Ages gave middle-class women many new opportunities. They not only worked with their husbands or sons in family shops and businesses, but they also had the freedom to operate their own enterprises in what became known as *femme sole*. It is true that women were kept out of certain crafts and guilds unless they were a master's wife, widow, or daughter. In other guilds, however, women had equal status with men, and in some trades and businesses they had a near monopoly. Women dominated the silk-making industry in Paris and London and were important in the cloth trades such as spinning, weaving, dyeing, tailoring, and glove making. Women also worked in the medieval food industry as bakers, fishmongers, and poultry sellers.

fees to use the marketplace. The burghers did not like this or the other restrictions placed on them. They resented having to get a noble's permission to marry, move around, or own land and serving in the noble's army.

Many nobles viewed the rise of towns as a threat to their power. They resented the wealth of the burghers and began to use feudal laws to keep them in their place. The Church was also against the rise of towns. Its leaders feared that the making of profit would interfere with religion.

The burghers, however, resented feudal laws. They thought these laws were not suited to business. The burghers now had wealth and power. Thus, they began to depend less on nobles and bishops. Instead, they developed a sense of loyalty toward their town. They worked together to build schools, hospitals, and churches. They began to demand changes.

Communes and Charters   In the 1100s, townspeople in northern Italy formed political groups called **communes** (kom' yūnz). Their purpose was to work against the nobles and bishops and for the people by establishing local self-government. The Italian communes were successful. Soon, the idea of communes spread to the towns of northern Europe. Some kings and nobles gave the townspeople **charters,** or documents allowing towns to run their own affairs.

The charters gave the townspeople the right to elect officials to run their towns. A council collected taxes and set charges for merchants who bought and sold goods in the town market. It also repaired streets, formed citizen armies, and ran hospitals, orphanages, and special homes for the poor.

The towns enforced their own laws and special courts were set up. To reduce crime, the towns severely punished those who broke the law. Murderers were hanged. Robbers lost a hand or an arm. Those who committed minor crimes, such as disturbing the peace, were whipped or put in the *stocks,* or a wooden frame with holes in which the feet and hands were locked.

Student Web Activity
Visit the *Human Heritage* Web site at **humanheritage.glencoe.com** and click on **Chapter 28— Student Web Activities** to find out more about the towns of the Middle Ages.

✓ **Reading Check**
What was the purpose of **communes?**

✓ **Reading Check**
What did **charters** allow townspeople to do?

Section 2 Assessment

1. **Define:** burghers, communes, charters.
2. What were some of the problems faced by medieval towns?
3. What changes did burghers want to make in feudal laws?

Critical Thinking

4. **Demonstrating Reasoned Judgment** What laws or regulations would you have written to further improve conditions in medieval towns?

Graphic Organizer Activity

5. Draw this diagram, and use it to show characteristics of towns in the late Middle Ages.

Medieval Towns

L2 **Critical Thinking** Ask students to compare the forms of punishment for crimes committed during the Middle Ages with the forms of punishment for crimes committed today. Ask them to create a chart showing each. Then ask students to vote on which society seems more humane.

✓ **Reading Check Answer**
Communes worked against nobles and bishops and helped the people set up local self-government.

✓ **Reading Check Answer**
Medieval **charters** allowed townspeople to run their own affairs.

MAKING CONNECTIONS

➤➤ **Economics** Burghers got around the Church's opposition to interest in two ways. First, they used Jews as moneylenders. Second, they lent money at no interest but charged "damages" if the loan was not repaid at once. By the 1200s, the Church changed its position, and interest became acceptable.

💾 Use **Interactive Tutor Self-Assessment Software** to review Section 3.

Section 3 Assessment Answers

1. burghers, rich merchants (p. 404); communes, political groups (p. 405); charters, documents allowing towns to run their own affairs (p. 405)
2. They were overcrowded, unhealthy, and dirty.
3. They wanted to run their own affairs and to have their own courts and laws.
4. Answers will vary, but students might suggest regulations to relieve overcrowd-ing, to plan for growth, and to determine disposal of sewage.
5. Sample characteristics: crowded conditions, open sewers, lack of sanitation, crooked narrow streets, large population of merchants and artisans, enforced own laws, etc.

Assign the Chapter 26 **Section 3 Quiz** in the TCR. Testmaker available.

Use the **Vocabulary Puzzle-Maker** to create crossword and word search puzzles.

✓ **Reading Check Answer**
Merchants, artisans, and workers formed **guilds** to ensure that members were treated equally.

L3 **Critical Thinking** Ask students to discuss how well the guild system would work in present-day society. Suggest they write a case study of its application in modern times.

LINKING PAST TO PRESENT

Medieval guilds controlled all the business in a town, establishing rules on prices, wages, and unemployment. In the United States today, laws prohibit price fixing and monopolies. In addition, the Taft-Hartley Act outlaws both hiring only union members and forcing employees to join unions.

✓ **Reading Check Answer**
An **apprentice** was a trainee in a trade, usually for two to seven years.
The **masters** were the experts in a guild.

✓ **Reading Check Answer**
Unlike an apprentice, a **journeyman** worked under a master for a daily wage until ready to take a test for guild membership.

MAKING CONNECTIONS

➤➤ **History** Often, masters were required to teach their apprentices to read and write and to provide them with clothing and a salary. Masters were also responsible for their behavior.

✓ **Reading Check** Why did merchants, artisans, and workers form **guilds?**

Geoffrey Chaucer

✓ **Reading Check** What was an **apprentice?** Who were the **masters** in a guild?

✓ **Reading Check** How did a **journeyman** differ from a apprentice?

Around the 1100s, merchants, artisans, and workers formed **guilds** (gildz). These were business groups whose purpose was to make sure that their members were treated equally. Each craft had its own guild, whose members lived and worked in the same area of town.

Craft guilds controlled the work of artisans such as carpenters, shoemakers, blacksmiths, masons, tailors, and weavers. Women working as laundresses, seamstresses, embroiderers, and maidservants had their own trade association. Guild members were not allowed to compete with one another or to advertise. Each member had to work the same number of hours, hire the same number of workers, and pay the same wages.

Guilds controlled all business and trade in a town. Only members could buy, sell, or make goods there. Outsiders who wanted to sell their goods in the town market had to get permission from the guilds. The guild decided the fair price for a product or service, and all members had to charge that price. Guild members who sold poorly made goods or cheated in business dealings had to pay large fines. They could also be expelled from the guild.

Guilds were more than business or trade groups. If members became ill, other members took care of them. If members were out of work, the guild gave them food. When members died, the other members prayed for their souls, paid for funerals, and supported the families. Guilds were also centers of social life. Holy day celebrations, processions, and outdoor plays were sponsored by the guild. Close friendships often developed among guild members.

It was not easy to become a member of a guild. A person had to be an **apprentice** (uh pren' tis), or trainee, in a trade for two to seven years. Apprentices were taught their trade by **masters,** or experts. They had to live with and obey their masters until their training was finished.

The next step was becoming a **journeyman** (jer' nē muhn), or a person who worked under a master for a daily wage. After a certain amount of time, journeymen took a test to become masters. The test was given by guild officials. Journeymen had to make and present a "masterpiece" to prove they had learned their craft. Those who passed the test were considered masters and could make their own goods. Often, they worked in the back of their houses and sold their goods in a shop in the front of the house.

By 1400, many merchants and artisans had begun challenging the control of the guilds. They felt the guilds kept them from

COOPERATIVE LEARNING

Have students work in groups to write and present a brief skit showing daily life in a medieval town. Assign small groups to research the daily work, clothing, food, and homes of townspeople. Assign each student a specific task such as selecting an event and characters, outlining and writing parts of the script, and obtaining or making props. Students can choose to portray such characters as apprentices, journeymen, masters of various guilds, university students, clergy, moneychangers, or troubadours.

◤ Assign Chapter 26 *Cooperative Learning Activity* in the TCR.

increasing their trade and profits. Then, too, apprentices disliked the strict rules set by guilds. It was getting harder and harder for apprentices to become masters. Many masters were grouping together and hiring unskilled workers instead of apprentices.

Section 4 Assessment

1. **Define:** guilds, apprentice, masters, journeyman.
2. What rules did guild members have to obey?
3. Why did people begin to challenge guilds in the 1400s?

Critical Thinking

4. **Analyzing Information** "The steps taken to become a master were too diffi-cult." Do you agree or disagree with this statement? Give reasons for your opinion.

Graphic Organizer Activity

5. Draw this diagram, and use it to show the steps in joining a guild.

Step 1 — Step 2 — Step 3 — Step 4 — Guild Membership

SECTION 5 Cultural Changes

During the 1400s, merchants, artisans, and bankers became more important than they had been in the past. Their growing power led to the decline of feudalism.

Many townspeople were as rich as, or richer than, the nobles. Bankers lent money to kings, nobles, and church officials for wars, building repairs, and entertainment. With their new wealth, merchants turned their homes into mansions. Some even bought castles from nobles who had lost their money. They began to set fashions. Women wore furs and gowns made of *brocade* (bro kād'), or a cloth woven with raised designs on it. Men dressed in colorful jackets, stockings, and feathered caps.

The townspeople had more leisure time and money to spend on their interests. Many hired private teachers to educate their sons. The sons later went to universities to study law, religion, and medicine. There was time to enjoy art and books, so townspeople began to support the work of painters and writers.

Most townspeople used such languages as German, French, and English. A scholar named Dante (dahn' tā) wrote the *Divine Comedy* in Italian. It is one of the most famous poems of the Middle Ages. Geoffrey Chaucer (jef' rē cho' suhr) wrote the *Canterbury Tales* in English. These tales are still popular today.

Townspeople began to think differently from nobles and peasants. The townspeople came to believe that they should be free to develop their talents and to improve their way of life. They wanted a strong central government. They began to look toward kings to provide leadership.

People in History

Geoffrey Chaucer
c. 1340–1400

English Poet

Chaucer's poems include the *Legend of Good Women*, an unfinished work about heroines from the past. His most famous poem is the *Canterbury Tales*, which tells the tales told by a group of travelers on their way to a shrine.

Section 4 Assessment Answers

1. guilds, business groups organized to protect members (p. 406); apprentice, trainee (p. 406); masters, experts (p. 406); journeyman, person who worked under a master (p. 406)
2. were not allowed to compete with one another or to advertise; had to work the same number of hours, hire the same number of workers, and pay the same wages
3. because they felt the guilds kept them from increasing their trade and profits, and

because apprentices found it hard to become masters
4. Answers will vary, but students should provide evidence to support their opinions.
5. Step 1—apprentice; Step 2—journeyman; Step 3—presentation of masterpiece; Step 4—approval of masterpiece by guild officials

Assign the Chapter 26 **Section 4 Quiz** in the TCR. Testmaker available.

Independent Practice

L3 **Writing** Have students imagine that they are editors of a newspaper during the Middle Ages. Tell them to write two editorials, one written about 1220 titled, "Why We Need to Establish Guilds," the other one written about 1400, titled, "Why We Need to Abolish Guilds."

💾 Use **Interactive Tutor Self-Assessment Software** to review Section 4.

MAKING CONNECTIONS

➤➤ **Literature** Dante's *Divine Comedy* is divided into three parts—*Inferno* (Hell), *Purgatio* (Purgatory), and *Paradiso* (Paradise). The epic's main theme is life after death.

💾 Use the **Vocabulary Puzzle-Maker** to create crossword and word search puzzles.

DID YOU KNOW

Chaucer was a government official who wrote poetry as an avocation. His *Canterbury Tales* is a collection of stories told by a group of pilgrims on a journey to Thomas á Becket's shrine in Canterbury.

ASSESS

Check for Understanding

Ask students to summarize the main points of the chapter. Discuss the answers to the Section and Chapter Assessment questions.

Evaluate

Assign the Chapter 26 **Performance Assessment Activity** in the TCR.

Administer the **Chapter 26 Test**. Testmaker available.

Reteach

Have students in groups prepare charts of significant medieval innovations in economics, trade, literature, and art.

Assign the Chapter 26 **Reteaching Activity** in the TCR.

Enrich

Have students investigate the death rates of western European countries during the Black Death and graph their findings.

Assign the Chapter 26 **Enrichment Activity** in the TCR.

CLOSE

Have students summarize how medieval life shifted from the feudal manor to the towns.

💾 Use **Interactive Tutor Self-Assessment Software** to review Section 5.

Self-Check Quiz gives students an interactive chapter tutorial. Have them access **Chapter 26 Quiz** at humanheritage.glencoe.com

---

Section 5 Assessment

1. In what ways did the cultural life of townspeople change during the 1400s?
2. What did townspeople want government to do?

Critical Thinking

3. **Making Inferences** Why might nobles have disliked the success of merchants during the Middle Ages?

Graphic Organizer Activity

4. Draw this diagram, and use it to show details that support the following main idea: "The growing power of merchants, artisans, and bankers led to the decline of feudalism."

Chapter Summary & Study Guide

1. During the 1000s and 1100, increased trade between Europe and the Near East led to the rise of trading centers, such as Venice and Flanders.
2. Venetian traders developed an effective banking system and, with the help of other Italian trading towns, drove the Muslims from the Mediterranean.
3. Flanders was the earliest Atlantic trading center and, by 1300, had developed a flourishing international trade with England.
4. The first medieval merchants traveled overland in armed groups and traded with each other at fairs.
5. After a while, merchants began to settle in towns known as burgs.
6. Most medieval towns were overcrowded, unhealthy places to live.
7. Artisans and rich merchants controlled the business and trade of towns.
8. Nobles and church officials viewed the rise of towns as a threat to their power and wealth.
9. Burghers resented feudal laws, and they resisted nobles and demanded charters for greater self-government.
10. Guilds set wages, prices, and working conditions, and helped members who were sick or out of work.
11. By the 1400s, many masters and artisans resented the control of guilds over profits, and they began to hire untrained workers instead of apprentices.
12. As townspeople grew richer and more powerful, they looked to kings for leadership, and feudalism declined.

Self-Check Quiz

Visit the *Human Heritage* Web site at **humanheritage.glencoe.com** and click on *Chapter 26—Self-Check Quiz* to assess your understanding of this chapter.

408 UNIT 8 THE LATE MIDDLE AGES

Using Key Terms

Imagine you are living in a town in western Europe during the late Middle Ages. Write a diary entry describing your life there. Use the following words in your diary.

fairs	burgs	burghers
communes	charters	guilds
apprentice	masters	journeyman

Understanding Main Ideas

1. What led to the development of trade between Europe and the Near East during the 1000s and 1100s?
2. What led to the decline of Italian trading centers?
3. How did fairs affect the development of banking?
4. What effects did the "Black Death" have on Europe?
5. How did a person become a master in a guild?
6. Why were nobles and church officials against the rise of towns?
7. How were the ideas of townspeople different from those of the nobles and peasants?

Critical Thinking

1. What would you have liked about being a merchant in the Middle Ages? Explain.
2. Would you have supported or opposed the position taken by Italian communes during the 1100s? Explain.
3. Would you have preferred to be a burgher or a noble during the Middle Ages? Explain.

4. Do you approve or disapprove of the rules established by the guilds? Explain.

Graphic Organizer Activity

Culture Create a diagram like the one below, and use it to compare life on a medieval manor with life in a medieval trading town.

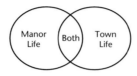

Geography in History

Place Refer to the map on page 400. Imagine you are a pirate hoping to rob European trading ships. At what place would you wait for ships to attack? What geographic features of this place affected your choice? Explain.

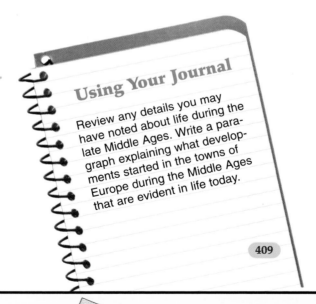

Using Your Journal

Review any details you may have noted about life during the late Middle Ages. Write a paragraph explaining what developments started in the towns of Europe during the Middle Ages that are evident in life today.

Bonus Test Question

For Chapter 26 Test
How did the Flemish become one of the first to develop an international industry?
(They were able to create an economic bridge between the supply source, production source, and customer; became merchants of products people needed and wanted.)

Using Your Journal

Paragraphs will vary but students might indicate commerce, fairs, banks, towns, town charters, business associations, fashion, and literature.

Geography in History

Answers will vary but should include reference to the trade routes crossing the Mediterranean Sea. Likely spots for pirates were the passage between Spain and Africa, or near Constantinople.

Using Key Terms

Entries will vary, but students should use all the terms.

Understanding Main Ideas

1. Nobles wanted luxury goods from the Near East.
2. They quarreled among themselves over profits and routes.
3. Merchants began to pay for goods with precious metals and coins from many different lands.
4. It killed millions of people and halted trading, farming, and war.
5. by becoming an apprentice first, then a journeyman, then passing a master's test, and finally creating a masterpiece
6. They viewed towns and burghers as a threat to their power.
7. Townspeople believed they should be free to improve their way of life.

Critical Thinking

1. Answers will vary, but students should include specific examples.
2. Answers will vary, but students should support their opinion with reasons.
3. Answers will vary, but students should explain their preference of burgher or noble.
4. Answers will vary.

Graphic Organizer Activity

Diagrams will vary. Some sample responses might include: *manors*—largely self-sufficient, ruled by the noble or lord, little freedom for peasants; *both*—large class differences, poor health conditions; *towns*—enriched by trade, greater freedom, strongly influenced by merchants and artisans.

Chapter 27 Planning Guide

Objectives	Reproducible Resources	Multimedia Resources
Section 1 **France** Describe how the Capetian kings strengthened the French monarchy.	Reproducible Lesson Plan Chapter 27 Vocabulary and Guided Reading Activity Reading Essentials and Study Guide 27-1 Section 1 Quiz	Vocabulary PuzzleMaker Interactive Tutor Self-Assessment Software ExamView® Pro Testmaker Glencoe Skillbuilder Interactive Workbook, Level 1
Section 2 **England** Explain what changes took place in the English monarchy during the Middle Ages.	Reproducible Lesson Plan Reading Essentials and Study Guide 27-2 Section 2 Quiz	Vocabulary PuzzleMaker Interactive Tutor Self-Assessment Software ExamView® Pro Testmaker Glencoe Skillbuilder Interactive Workbook, Level 1
Section 3 **The Hundred Years' War** Analyze the causes and results of the Hundred Years' War.	Reproducible Lesson Plan Reading Essentials and Study Guide 27-3 Chapter 27 Cooperative Learning Activity Chapter 27 Chart and Graph Skill Activity Section 3 Quiz	Teaching Transparencies and Activities 27A & 27B Vocabulary PuzzleMaker Interactive Tutor Self-Assessment Software ExamView® Pro Testmaker Glencoe Skillbuilder Interactive Workbook, Level 1
Section 4 **Germany** Trace the start of the Holy Roman Empire, and describe how it was ruled.	Reproducible Lesson Plan Reading Essentials and Study Guide 27-4 Chapter 27 Geography and Map Activity Section 4 Quiz	Vocabulary PuzzleMaker Interactive Tutor Self-Assessment Software ExamView® Pro Testmaker Glencoe Skillbuilder Interactive Workbook, Level 1
Section 5 **Spain** Summarize how the Catholic monarchs governed Spain.	Reproducible Lesson Plan Reading Essentials and Study Guide 27-5 Chapter 27 Activity Book Activity Section 5 Quiz	Vocabulary PuzzleMaker ExamView® Pro Testmaker Glencoe Skillbuilder Interactive Workbook, Level 1
Chapter 27 **Review and Evaluation**	Chapter 27 Reteaching Activity Chapter 27 Performance Assessment Activity Unit 8 Standardized Test Practice Spanish Summary and Glossary Chapter 27 Test	Vocabulary PuzzleMaker Interactive Tutor Self-Assessment Software Glencoe Skillbuilder Interactive Workbook, Level 1 Audiocassettes* ExamView® Pro Testmaker

*Also available in Spanish.

Presentation Plus!

Use Glencoe's **Presentation Plus!** multimedia teacher tool to easily present dynamic lessons that visually excite your students. Using Microsoft® PowerPoint, you can customize the presentations to create your own personalized lessons.

 Interactive Lesson Planner

Planning has never been easier! Using this CD-ROM, organize your week, month, semester, or year with all the help you need. The **Interactive Lesson Planner** gives you access to all of the blackline masters which accompany *Human Heritage*.

✓ PERFORMANCE ASSESSMENT ACTIVITIES

News Account Have students imagine that they are English newspaper reporters who have just witnessed the 1066 Battle of Hastings. Assign them to create headlines and accounts of the battle. Some students may also choose to illustrate their stories.

CHAPTER RESOURCES

LITERATURE ABOUT THE PERIOD

Warner, Marina. *Joan of Arc: The Image of Female Heroism.* Random House, 1982. Account of Joan of Arc.

READINGS FOR THE STUDENT

McKendrick, Melveena. *Ferdinand and Isabella.* American Heritage, 1968. Photographs and contemporary paintings help recreate the period.

READINGS FOR THE TEACHER

Brown, R. Allen. *The Normans.* St. Martin's Press, 1984. Concentrates on Norman influence on the western world.

Hallam, Elizabeth, ed. *The Plantagenet Chronicles.* Weidenfeld and Nicholson, 1986. Examines the reigns of Henry II, Richard I, and King John and discusses the Magna Carta, the Crusades, and life in England during the 1100s.

NATIONAL GEOGRAPHIC SOCIETY
Teacher's Corner

INDEX TO NATIONAL GEOGRAPHIC MAGAZINE

The following articles relate to this chapter:

- "The Tale of the *San Diego,*" by Franck Goddio, July 1994.
- "The Living Tower of London," by William R. Newcott, October 1993.
- "Legacy from the Deep: Henry VIII's Lost Warship," by Margaret Rule, May 1983.

NATIONAL GEOGRAPHIC SOCIETY PRODUCTS AVAILABLE FROM GLENCOE

To order the following, call Glencoe at 1-800-334-7344:

- *PicturePack: Europe (Transparencies)*
- *PicturePack: Physical Geography of the World (Transparencies)*
- *STV: World Geography (Videodisc)*

ADDITIONAL NATIONAL GEOGRAPHIC SOCIETY PRODUCTS

To order the following, call National Geographic at 1-800-368-2728:

- *Atocha: Quest for Treasure (Video)*
- *National Geographic Atlas of World History (Book)*

Access *National Geographic*'s new dynamic MapMachine Web site and other geography resources at:
http://www.nationalgeographic.com/
http://www.nationalgeographic.com/maps/

KEY TO ABILITY LEVELS

Teaching strategies have been coded for varying learning styles and abilities.

L1 Level 1 activities are **basic** activities and should be within the ability range of all students.

L2 Level 2 activities are **average** activities and should be within the ability range of the average to above-average student.

L3 Level 3 activities are **challenging** activities designed for the ability range of above-average students.

ELL ELL activities should be within the ability range of English Language Learning students.

OVERVIEW

Chapter 27 describes the growth of central governments in France, Germany, and Spain.

➤ **Section 1** discusses the powers of the French monarchy.
➤ **Section 2** describes the English monarchy, the Magna Carta, and the Parliament.
➤ **Section 3** analyzes the Hundred Years' War.
➤ **Section 4** explains the role of the Holy Roman Empire.
➤ **Section 5** summarizes the unification of Spain.

CHAPTER OBJECTIVES

After reading Chapter 27, students will be able to:

1. describe how the Capetian kings strengthened the French monarchy.
2. discuss limits placed on the English monarchy.
3. analyze the causes and results of the Hundred Years' War.
4. explain how the Holy Roman Empire was created and ruled.
5. summarize how the Catholic monarchs united Spain.

EXAMINING ARTIFACTS

Direct students to study both the artifacts and the time line. Ask: What groups of people seem to be shaping history? *(kings, soldiers, and conquerors)* What effect do students think this trend might have on western Europe? Save student responses for review as they read the chapter.

PERFORMANCE ASSESSMENT ✓

Use the Performance Assessment activities on page 410B to help you evaluate students as they complete the chapter.

410

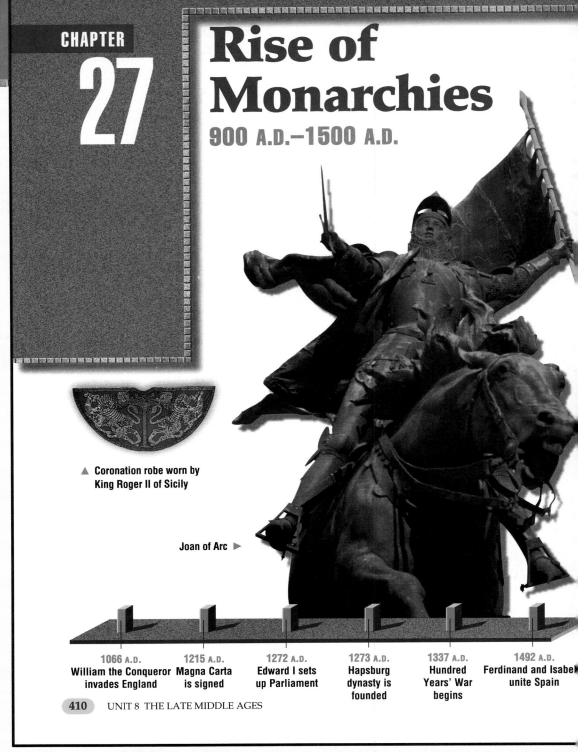

Rise of Monarchies
900 A.D.–1500 A.D.

▲ **Coronation robe worn by King Roger II of Sicily**

Joan of Arc ▶

1066 A.D.	1215 A.D.	1272 A.D.	1273 A.D.	1337 A.D.	1492 A.D.
William the Conqueror invades England	Magna Carta is signed	Edward I sets up Parliament	Hapsburg dynasty is founded	Hundred Years' War begins	Ferdinand and Isabel unite Spain

410 UNIT 8 THE LATE MIDDLE AGES

Chapter Focus

 Read to Discover

- How the Capetian kings strengthened the French monarchy.
- What changes took place in the English monarchy during the Middle Ages.
- What the main causes and results were of the Hundred Years' War.
- How the Holy Roman Empire was created and ruled.
- How the Catholic monarchs united Spain.

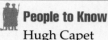

Terms to Learn	**People to Know**	**Places to Locate**
monarchies	Hugh Capet	Hastings
circuit judges	William the	Orleans
grand jury	Conqueror	Sicily
trial jury	Joan of Arc	Holy Roman
dauphin	Frederick II	Empire
diet	Ferdinand and	Granada
corregidores	Isabella	

Why It's Important The growth of trade and towns during the late Middle Ages led to many changes in western Europe. Some of these changes were political. The rise of **monarchies** ('mon' uhr kēz), or countries governed by one ruler, led to the decline of feudalism.

HISTORY Online

Chapter Overview
Visit the *Human Heritage* Web site at **humanheritage.glencoe.com** and click on **Chapter 27— Chapter Overviews** to preview this chapter.

✓ **Reading Check**
What are **monarchies?**

 SECTION 1 **France**

In 987, Hugh Capet (ka pā'), a French noble, was chosen as the new king of France. At the time, France consisted of many feudal territories. As king, Capet ruled only a small area between the Seine (sān) and Loire (lwahr) rivers. Capet, who died in 996, was the first of a line of Capetian (kuh pē' shuhn) kings who ruled France for some 300 years. For 100 years after his death, however, these kings were weak and did little to increase royal power.

In 1108, Louis VI, known as "Louis the Fat," became king and increased the power of the monarchy. He got rid of disloyal nobles and put loyal persons of lower birth in their place. He stopped the raids of lawless vassals and granted charters to many towns, thus winning the loyalty of the townspeople.

The king's power was further increased under Philip II, also known as Philip Augustus. Philip, who ruled from 1179 to 1223,

---

GEOGRAPHY ACTIVITIES
- Chapter 27 Geography and Map Activity
- Social Studies Outline Map Resource Book

INTERDISCIPLINARY CONNECTIONS
- World Music: Cultural Traditions

ENRICHMENT AND EXTENSION
- World History Primary Source Document Library CD-ROM
- Foods Around the World

ASSESSMENT AND EVALUATION
- Chapter 27 Performance Assessment Activity
- Chapter 27 Section Quizzes 27-1, 27-2, 27-3, 27-4, 27-5
- Chapter 27 Test
- Unit 8 Standardized Test Practice
- Chapter 27 ExamView® Pro Testmaker Software
- Chapter 27 Digests Audiocassettes Activities and Tests

SPANISH RESOURCES
- Chapter 27 Spanish Chapter Summary and Glossary
- Chapter 27 Spanish Chapter Digests Audiocassettes Activities and Tests

---

HISTORY Online

Chapter Overview introduces students to chapter content and key terms. Have them access **Chapter 27 Overview** at **humanheritage.glencoe.com**

FOCUS

📩 **Bellringer**

Have students reply to this question: *What do you think it means to be a king?*

Motivational Activity

Discuss student responses. Then explain that over time the power of kings has varied dramatically. Sometimes they were absolute rulers, and sometimes they were nothing more than figureheads. Ask students to discuss what problems might arise for our federal government if our leaders collected their own taxes and raised their own armies.

✓ **Reading Check Answer**
Monarchies are countries governed by one ruler.

GUIDE TO READING

Reading Strategy

Ask students to read "Why It's Important" and summarize the chapter's main theme. *(As the power of monarchs increased, feudalism declined and the influence of the Church over political affairs decreased.)*

Vocabulary Precheck

Ask students to define each of the "Terms to Learn." Have a volunteer consult the dictionary for any unfamiliar words. **L1** **ELL**

💾 Use the Vocabulary PuzzleMaker for Chapter 27 to create a crossword puzzle. **L1**

📂 Assign Chapter 27 Vocabulary and Guided Reading Activity.

📂 Assign Reading Essentials and Study Guide 27-1.

TEACH

Guided Practice

L2 **Panel Discussion** Organize the class into five groups. Assign each group one of the following Capetian monarchs: Hugh Capet, Louis VI, Philip Augustus, Louis IX, and Philip the Fair. Tell the students to decide how their monarch strengthened the French monarchy and prepare an index card containing at least three points to be brought out in a panel discussion of the Capetian kings.

MAKING CONNECTIONS

➤➤ **Architecture** Philip Augustus built a fortress called the Louvre, which is now France's national museum. He was also responsible for the construction of the great Cathedral of Notre Dame.

CAPTION ANSWER

the Capetians

DID YOU KNOW

Hugh Capet always wore beautiful capes. At first, he had no last name. He was given the name *Capet* from the French word meaning "cape."

LOUIS IX   King Louis IX of France was known for his honesty and just dealings. After his death, he was made a saint of the Roman Catholic Church. Louis's support of the Church is expressed in this painting of the king feeding a church official. **To what line of French kings did Louis IX belong?**

Painting of Philip the Fair

made Paris the center of government. He increased the size of his kingdom through marriage and by winning back French lands held by the English. To make sure the nobles did not become too powerful while he was fighting in the Crusades, Philip II appointed royal agents to keep a close watch on them.

In 1226, Philip's grandson became King Louis IX. He brought peace to France and helped unite the French people. He ordered the nobles to stop feuding and forbade them to settle disputes by fighting duels. Most nobles minted their own money. Louis IX made it illegal to use coins made anywhere else but the royal mint. He set up a royal court to which anyone could bring disputes.

Philip IV, Louis's grandson, ruled from 1285 to 1314. Known as "Philip the Fair," Philip IV believed the interests of the state came first. So, he seized the English fortresses in France that he felt were necessary for his kingdom's security. He also went to war with the Flemish when they refused to let France control their cloth trade. Philip believed a kingdom could not exist without taxes. So, he made sure that taxes were collected regularly. He also taxed the clergy, who had not been taxed before. To help him run the country, Philip IV formed the Estates-General, an assembly of nobles, clergy, and townspeople. This marked the beginning of a national government in France. By the time Philip IV died in 1314, France was united under one ruler.

MULTICULTURAL PERSPECTIVES

The structure of the Estates-General reflected medieval French society (and did so until the French Revolution). The First Estate was the clergy. The Second Estate was the nobility. The Third Estate was the townspeople, the *bourgeoisie*. Philip IV had the support of all three estates, including the French clergy, in his struggle for power with the Pope. Philip IV had a French Pope elected in 1305 and installed at Avignon, France, not Rome. This papacy lasted until 1378. There was a period of time in which there were two popes—one in Rome and one in Avignon.

Section 1 Assessment

1. **Define:** monarchies.
2. How did Louis VI increase the power of the monarchy?
3. What did Louis IX and Philip the Fair do to help unite France?

Critical Thinking

4. **Drawing Conclusions** Why do you think Louis IX made it illegal for nobles to coin their own money?

Graphic Organizer Activity

5. Draw this diagram, and use it to summarize the accomplishments of these French kings: Hugh Capet, Louis VI, Philip II, Louis IX, and Philip IV.

Accomplishments

Hugh Capet	Louis VI	Philip II	Louis IX	Philip IV

SECTION 2 England

In 1042, the witenagemot made Edward the Confessor, an Anglo-Saxon prince, king of England. Edward gave money to the poor and sponsored the building in London of Westminster Abbey, the church in which later English kings and queens were crowned. He spent so much time in religious work, however, that he failed to carry out his royal duties. As a result, the nobles increased their hold on the country. The most powerful noble was Harold Godwinson. When Edward died in 1066 without an heir, Harold became the new king.

William the Conqueror   Harold Godwinson did not remain king for long. William, Duke of Normandy, a cousin of Edward the Confessor, claimed that before Edward died, he had promised him the English throne.

In 1066, William led an army of between 4,000 and 7,000 Norman knights across the channel to England. They met Harold's army in battle near Hastings, a town just south of London. To stop the Norman charge, English foot soldiers armed with axes formed a wall of shields on the edge of a low hill. William knew he could not break through the wall. So, he had his soldiers pretend to retreat. When the English broke formation to follow them, the Normans turned on the English. By nightfall, King Harold was dead, and the English were defeated. William the Conqueror, was crowned King William I of England.

At first, the English resisted William's rule. To crush English revolts—and to keep the Normans in line—William introduced feudalism. He seized the lands of English nobles and divided them among Norman nobles. In return, they became his vassals. They promised to be loyal and to provide him with soldiers.

Language For years after the Norman Conquest, the upper classes in England spoke Norman French, the lower classes Anglo-Saxon English. Modern English preserves this double heritage. Words for farm animals are mainly Anglo-Saxon: *ox* and *cow, pig, sheep*. Words for cooked meat, once served mainly to the upper classes, come from French: *beef, pork, mutton* (from *boeuf, porc, mouton*).

L1 Government Each of the French kings detailed in Section 1 made reforms that made life easier for peasants. Help students make a chart that lists the kings and at least one beneficial reform they instigated. Have students decide what information should be included in the chart, and have several students put the information on a large poster board. **ELL**

💾 Use **Interactive Tutor Self-Assessment Software** to review Section 1.

DID YOU KNOW

The witenagemot was a group of church officials and nobles that advised the king.

MAKING CONNECTIONS

➤➤ **History** William's and Harold's armies were very different. William's soldiers were knights and full-time fighters. Harold's were farmers who left their fields when called to battle.

💾 Use the **Vocabulary Puzzle-Maker** to create crossword and word search puzzles.

Section 1 Assessment Answers

1. monarchies, countries governed by one ruler (p. 411)
2. He got rid of nobles who did not fulfill their feudal duties and put loyal persons of lower birth in their place; stopped raids of lawless vassals; and granted charters of freedom to many towns.
3. Louis IX ordered the nobles to stop feuding and fighting duels, required use of royal coins, and set up a royal court. Philip the Fair seized the English fortresses in France, went to war with the Flemish, set up a tax system, and formed the Estates-General.
4. Sample conclusions: to increase his power; to promote unity
5. Accomplishments should reflect information in the text and show efforts to increase royal power. As an extension, you might ask students to vote on which of these kings they think did the most to strengthen France.

Assign the Chapter 27 **Section 1 Quiz** in the TCR. Testmaker available.

The Final Say The *Domesday Book* got this popular name because people said there was no chance of arguing with its records. That is, its determinations were as final as those of God on doomsday—the Day of Judgment.

William kept many English laws and government practices. He received advice from the witenagemot, now called the Great Council. He depended on such local officials as the sheriff. William also made many changes. In 1086, he took a census and a survey of the land in order to tax the people properly. This information was recorded in two huge volumes called the *Domesday Book.* The title comes from the Anglo-Saxon word *doom,* meaning "judgment."

William brought *continental,* or European mainland, ways to England. Under his rule, the English learned Norman customs and the French language. The wealthy built castles, cathedrals, and monasteries in the French style. The people learned new skills from Norman weavers and other artisans.

Henry II   After William died in 1087, there was confusion in England until 1154 when William's great-grandson became King Henry II. Henry ruled England, most of Ireland, Scotland, and Wales. He was also a feudal lord in France, where he owned more land than he did in England. Some of the French lands belonged to his wife, Eleanor of Aquitaine.

BATTLE OF HASTINGS   William the Conqueror took the throne of England after his army defeated the English army at the Battle of Hastings in 1066. This painting shows Norman knights on horseback attacking the English soldiers. **What title did William the Conqueror take after his victory at Hastings?**

COOPERATIVE LEARNING

Divide the class into four groups. Assign each group one of the following topics: William the Conqueror, Henry II, Magna Carta, and Parliament. Each group is responsible for researching and preparing a report explaining how these rulers and institutions brought about changes in the English monarchy during the Middle Ages. Have a spokesperson from each group present their group's report to the class.

Henry II restored order and forced the nobles to give him their loyalty. He also used the law to gain more power, and he worked to reform English courts. A central royal court was set up in London with trained lawyers as judges. **Circuit judges,** or judges who travel throughout the country, brought the king's law to all parts of England. They made it the common law of the land, thus helping to unite the country.

Henry also set up juries to settle quarrels about land. After a while, two kinds of juries came into being. One was the **grand jury,** or a group of people who present to judges the names of people suspected of crimes. The other was the **trial jury,** or a group of people who decide whether a person accused of a crime is innocent or guilty. The trial jury took the place of the medieval trial by ordeal.

Henry II believed that everyone, even church officials, should be tried in the king's courts. Thomas à Becket, Henry's close friend and the Archbishop of Canterbury, did not agree. Becket wanted Church officials to be free of royal control. The quarrel between the king and the archbishop ultimately led to the murder of Becket by four of Henry's knights. After the murder, Henry II made peace with the Church by allowing some of the clergy to be tried in church courts.

Magna Carta and Parliament

When Henry II died in 1189, his oldest son Richard became king. Richard, however, was more interested in his French lands than in ruling England. He spent most of his time fighting in the Near East on the Crusades.

When Richard died in 1199, his brother John became king of England. John lost most of his lands in France to the French king. When he increased England's taxes and began to ignore the law, the country's nobles became angry. They refused to obey him unless he agreed to give them certain rights. In 1215, John met the nobles in the meadow of Runnymede (ruhn' ē mēd), where they forced him to sign the *Magna Carta* (mag' nuh kar' tuh), or Great Charter.

The Magna Carta took away some of the king's power and increased that of the nobles. A king could no longer collect taxes unless the Great Council agreed. Freemen accused of crimes had the right to a trial by their *peers,* or equals. The Magna Carta was viewed as an important step toward democracy. It brought to government the new idea that even a king is not above the law.

John died in 1216, and his son became King Henry III. Henry, however, was a weak ruler who allowed the feudal lords in the Great Council to rule England. In 1264, Simon de Montfort (mahnt' fuhrt), Henry's brother-in-law, came to power. He gave the people a voice in government by letting them have representatives in the Great Council.

✔ **Reading Check**
How did **circuit judges** spread English law?

✔ **Reading Check**
What was the difference between a **grand jury** and a **trial jury?**

✔ **Reading Check Answer**
Circuit judges traveled throughout the country, making the king's law the common law of the land.

✔ **Reading Check Answer**
A **grand jury** presented judges with the names of people suspected of crimes, while the **trial jury** decided a person's guilt or innocence.

L2 **Language Arts** Discuss the word *conflict* as it applies to the conflicts between the English monarch and the Church. Ask students for other words that could be used in place of *conflict.* List these on the chalkboard and have volunteers research their origins and meanings for comparison. **ELL**

DID YOU KNOW ??
Thomas à Becket was murdered in his own cathedral during Christmastime. He became an instant medieval celebrity. Within months, miracles were reported at Becket's tomb and pilgrims flocked to the site.

MAKING CONNECTIONS

➤➤ **History** During the 10 years of his rule, Richard spent less than a year in England. Most of his time was spent on the Crusades. On his way home from the Third Crusade, he was shipwrecked in the Adriatic Sea. While trying to make his way home by land, the Duke of Austria took him prisoner. He was released after the English people collected and paid a large ransom.

MEETING SPECIAL NEEDS

Have auditory learners hold a debate between representatives of the English monarchy and the Church of Rome. Divide the class into three groups. One group should gather information from the text and from other references. The second group should prepare arguments, questions and possible answers to be used during the debate. The third group should form a committee to hear the arguments from each side, weigh the merits of each argument, and determine the winning position.

📁 Refer to *Inclusion for the Middle School Social Studies Classroom: Strategies and Activities* for additional resources.

L3 **Debate** Have students learn more about the importance of the Magna Carta. Form two groups of students, one to represent King John and the other to represent the nobles. Have students prepare their arguments to debate the need for the Magna Carta. Students should hold their debate, and the other students, as audience, can judge who presents the most convincing arguments.

MAKING CONNECTIONS

➤➤ **Language** The word *parliament* introduced by Simon de Montfort, comes from *parler,* the French word meaning "to talk or discuss." Because it set the precedent for the holding of future parliaments, Edward I's gathering was later called the Model Parliament.

L2 **History** Ask students to imagine that they were newspaper reporters living during the Middle Ages. They have been asked to write two articles on the Hundred Years' War. One article should discuss the causes of the war between France and England in 1339. The other should deal with the end of the war in 1453 and emphasize the results of the war. Students should write appropriate headlines for the two articles. Have students read their articles to the class.

💾 Use **Interactive Tutor Self-Assessment Software** to review Section 2.

Then... &Now

Constitutions Unlike the United States, the United Kingdom does not have a single written document called a "constitution." Instead, British leaders govern according to a series of laws and charters. The oldest of those is the Magna Carta.

MAGNA CARTA The Archbishop of Canterbury and merchants joined the nobles at Runnymede to force King John to sign the Magna Carta. In this painting, as the Archbishop looks on, a noble shows King John where to sign the document. **What new idea did the Magna Carta bring to government?**

Eight years later, the new king, Edward I, went even furthe He called for a meeting of representatives to advise him and t help him make laws. This gathering, known as Parliament (pal luh muhnt), gave the people a greater share in the ruling of Eng land. Parliament later broke into two separate groups. Noble and clergy met as the House of Lords, while knights and towns people met as the House of Commons.

Section 2 Assessment

1. **Define:** circuit judges, grand jury, trial jury.
2. How did the Normans win the Battle of Hastings?
3. Why was King John forced to sign the Magna Carta?

Critical Thinking

4. **Predicting Consequences** How might the history of English government have been different if nobles had not forced King John to sign the Magna Carta?

Graphic Organizer Activity

5. Draw this diagram, and use it to show some of the milestones in democracy that took place in medieval England.

Milestones in English Democracy	1.
	2.
	3.
	4.

Section 2 Assessment Answers

1. circuit judges, judges who travel (p. 415); grand jury, people who judge others suspected of crimes (p. 415); trial jury, group who decides innocence or guilt (p. 415)
2. William's soldiers pretended to retreat and attacked when the English broke formation to follow after them.
3. because he had increased taxes and had begun to ignore the law
4. Answers will vary, but most students will probably indicate that England would not have developed a system of government in which the people have a share in ruling.
5. Sample milestones: invasion of William the Conqueror and his efforts to end feudalism; William's use of the Great Council; 1086 census to determine fair taxation; use of circuit judges, grand jury, and trial by jury under Henry II, signing of Magna Carta, creation of Parliament.

Assign the Chapter 27 **Section 2 Quiz** in the TCR. Testmaker available.

SECTION 3 The Hundred Years' War

In the early 1300s, the English still held a small part of southwest France. The kings of France, who were growing more powerful, wanted to drive the English out. In 1337, the English king, Edward III, declared himself king of France. This angered the French even more. In 1337, England and France fought the first in a long series of battles known as the Hundred Years' War.

The Hundred Years' War began when the English defeated the French fleet and won control of the sea. The English then invaded France. They defeated the French at the Battle of Crécy (krā sē') in 1346 and again at the Battle of Agincourt (aj' uhn kōrt) in 1415.

The English owed their success on land mostly to a new weapon called the *longbow,* which shot steel-tipped arrows. The French still used the shorter crossbow. The crossbow could not send arrows as far as the longbow, and the French arrows were not as sharp as the steel-tipped English arrows.

At Crécy the English forces also used the first portable firearm in European warfare—a very crude cannon. This early weapon was made of a long iron tube mounted on a pole. The weapon was difficult to carry and use, but led to the development of a more refined cannon that was a major weapon in many later wars.

Joan of Arc   By 1429, much of France was in English hands. Charles, the French *dauphin* (do' fuhn), or eldest son of the king, was fighting the English for the French throne. Then, a 17-year-old French peasant named Jeanne d'Arc (zhahn dark'), or Joan of Arc, appeared. She said that while praying, she had heard heavenly voices telling her she must save France. She went to see Charles and told him that God had sent her to help him. She said that if she had an army she would free Orleans (or lā ahn'), a city the English had been besieging for seven months. Charles gave Joan an army, a suit of armor, and a white linen banner.

Joan led an attack against the English army at Orleans. Within ten days, the city was free, and Joan became known as the "Maid of Orleans." Shortly after, with Joan at his side, the dauphin was crowned King Charles VII of France. Joan wanted to return home, but Charles convinced her to stay with the army. A few months later, a French traitor captured her and sold her to the English. After spending a year in prison, she was tried as a witch and burned at the stake. Joan died at the age of 18, a girl who could neither read nor write but who had led an army. A trial twenty-four years later proclaimed her innocence.

People in History

Joan of Arc
c. 1412–1431

French Heroine

Born a peasant, Joan began to hear heavenly voices as a child. They urged her to drive the English from France. At age 17, Joan convinced the king's son to give her an army. She battled the English for seven months before she was captured. The English turned her over to Church officials sympathetic to their cause. They demanded that Joan deny that she was guided by heaven. When she refused, they burned her at the stake. A later court found Joan innocent, and in 1920 the Catholic Church declared her a saint.

✔ **Reading Check**
Who was the French *dauphin?*

L2 **Religion** Ask students why Joan of Arc was successful and why French soldiers accepted her reports of hearing heavenly voices. List the reasons on the chalkboard. Remind students that religion played an important role during the Middle Ages. **ELL**

L3 **Research** Ask students to research and report on the life of Joan of Arc. With their report, have students prepare a scenario of what might happen if she appeared in modern times in the same kind of situation. How do students think people today would react to her and her "messages"?

MAKING CONNECTIONS

➤➤ **History** It is believed that gunpowder, invented in China, was used for the first time in European warfare at the Battle of Crécy. Its use helped bring the Middle Ages to an end by destroying the ability of castles to withstand an attack.

✔ **Reading Check Answer**
The French *dauphin* was the eldest son of the king.

💾 Use the **Vocabulary Puzzle-Maker** to create crossword and word search puzzles.

COOPERATIVE LEARNING

Have groups of students prepare and present readings from the play *Saint Joan* by George Bernard Shaw, choosing suitable passages for presentation, assigning and reading the roles, preparing and presenting a summary of the play, and explaining scenes being presented.

📁 Assign Chapter 27 *Cooperative Learning Activity* in the TCR.

LINKING PAST TO PRESENT

Today, Joan of Arc is the second patron saint of France.

CAPTION ANSWER

She led an attack against the English army at Orleans and freed the city.

MAKING CONNECTIONS

➤➤ **Government** During the Hundred Years' War, English kings depended increasingly on Parliament to raise funds in order to support the war. This reliance on Parliament by England's monarchy strengthened Parliament's power. The arrangement strengthened the king as well, giving him power to work with Parliament to raise funds and change laws. In France, the Estates-General was the king's council. Because the king retained the right to raise money and make laws, the Estates-General never assumed the same powers as the English Parliament and eventually was disbanded. Without the Estates-General, the French king was an absolute monarch.

The French continued to fight after Joan's death. By 1453, they had driven the English from all of France except the seaport of Calais (ka lā'), and the war came to an end.

Results of the War Both France and England were changed by the Hundred Years' War. By 1500, the last French feudal territories were under the king's rule, and France was unified. England, too, was unified by the war, but its monarchy was weakened. Not until 1485, when a Welshman named Henry Tudor (tū' duhr) became king, did it become strong again.

Because of the Hundred Years' War, the common people in both England and France became more important. Many peasants had died during the war from disease or fighting. Those who remained were greatly needed as workers. The peasants knew this and began to make demands. They forced the nobles to pay them wages and allow them to move outside the manors. When the nobles tried to force them back to the old ways, they revolted. Most became farmers who rented land from the nobles.

JOAN OF ARC Claiming that heavenly voices had instructed her to do so, Joan of Arc led a French army against the invading English and helped return the French king to the throne. She became a national heroine and a saint of the Roman Catholic Church. **How did Joan earn her nickname "Maid of Orleans"?**

EXTENDING THE CONTENT

One of the most famous uprisings was the 1381 Peasant's Revolt in England, led by Wat Tyler and a priest, John Ball. Three ragged peasant armies marched on London in the summer of 1381. They kidnapped several high royal officials, including the Archbishop of Canterbury, and beheaded them. They demanded freedom and an end to all class distinctions or feudal duties. King Richard II began to bargain with the rioters. His army seized and punished the leaders, and the rebellion came to an end.

Section 3 Assessment

1. **Define:** *dauphin.*
2. Why did France and England go to war?
3. How did the Hundred Years' War affect French and English peasants?

Critical Thinking

4. **Understanding Cause and Effect**
   What was the connection between the Hundred Years' War and the end of feudalism?

Graphic Organizer Activity

5. Draw this diagram, and use it to show facts about Joan of Arc's life. (Add more answer circles as necessary.)

Germany

During the 900s, Germany was the most important country in western Europe. Over time, though, German kings lost much of their authority to powerful nobles who wanted to rule their own territories. The king, however, still had the right to remove lords who would not obey him.

Otto I In 936, Otto I became king of Germany. He wanted to unite the country and rule without nobles. He removed lords who would not obey him and gave their estates to his family. Then, he turned to the Roman Catholic Church for help. Its leaders wanted him to set up a Christian Roman Empire in western Europe. So, Otto made many of his loyal followers bishops and abbots and gave them government posts. In return, they supplied him with money and soldiers.

Otto began expanding Germany. In 951, he marched south into Italy, where he took over the northern Italian trading cities. In 962, he led an army to Rome to free the Pope from the control of Roman nobles. In return, the Pope crowned Otto I emperor of the Holy Roman Empire, a large new state made up of Germany and northern Italy. Otto saw himself as the heir of the Roman emperors. For the next 90 years, Otto and the emperors who followed him controlled the office of Pope.

Frederick I In 1152, Frederick I became emperor. Because of his full red beard, he was called Barbarossa, or "red beard." Frederick forced the powerful lords to promise him loyalty and to work for his government.

Frederick's attempts to control the nobles and unify the empire worked against him. The nobles grew rich from their government posts. At the same time, the Italian city-states, aided

German Crown

💾 Use **Interactive Tutor Self-Assessment Software** to review Section 3.

L1 **Discussion** Lead a discussion of the following questions as students build a cause-and-effect graphic organizer on the chalkboard. Encourage volunteers to add to the graphics as the questions are answered. Ask: *How was the Holy Roman Empire created and ruled? What was the relationship between Otto I and the Roman Catholic Church? How did Otto I become emperor of the Holy Roman Empire? What caused the Holy Roman Empire to become weaker during the rule of Frederick I? Why did the Pope call for a crusade against Frederick II? What happened as a result of Hapsburg rule?* **ELL**

MAKING CONNECTIONS

>> **History** Otto was the son of Henry I, or Henry the Fowler, powerful German Duke of Saxony who was elected king of Germany in 919. Henry's bravery and ability won the respect of the nobles and paved the way for the rule of his son.

💾 Use the **Vocabulary Puzzle-Maker** to create crossword and word search puzzles.

Section 3 Assessment Answers

1. *dauphin,* eldest son of the French king (p. 417)
2. The kings of France wanted to drive the English out, and Edward III of England declared himself king of France.
3. They became more important.
4. Answers will vary but could include that kings took control of feudal territories, England and France were unified, and peasants became more important.
5. In selecting their sample facts, remind students to use the People in History on page 417, including the declaration of Joan's innocence in 1920.

   Assign the Chapter 27 **Section 3 Quiz** in the TCR. Testmaker available.

by the Pope, banded together and defeated Frederick's armies. Frederick had to accept a peace that recognized the independence of the city-states.

While leading the Third Crusade in 1190, Frederick drowned in a river in Asia Minor. Later, a legend about him spread among the Germans. It stated that he was not dead but under a magic spell that had put him to sleep somewhere high in the mountains. The people believed that one day he would awake and restore the glory of Germany.

Frederick II   In 1220, Frederick II, Frederick I's grandson, became emperor. Frederick II was raised in Palermo (puh luhr mō), Sicily, which his father had made part of the Holy Roman Empire. So, he ignored Germany and concentrated on ruling the people of Sicily.

Frederick was known as the best-educated monarch of his time. He spoke several languages and enjoyed doing scientific experiments. He supported many artists and scholars. He

FREDERICK II   Frederick II was greatly interested in the sciences and medicine and encouraged their study during his reign. He had a special interest in the study of birds and wrote a book on the subject. This painting of Frederick is showing him with his falcon handler. **How did Frederick II aid medieval learning?**

EXTENDING THE CONTENT

Today the Catholic Pope is elected by the College of Cardinals without interference from any political groups. The Popes have been traditionally Italian, however, in 1978 the college elected the Polish Pope John Paul II.

Universities Scholarship was important to the Hapsburg family, which included Maximilian I. The Hapsburgs encouraged the growth of universities throughout the Holy Roman Empire (left). Universities spread throughout Europe and the rest of the world (below). **Why are universities important today?**

founded a university in Palermo so young men could study at home rather than in other countries. Although the Church was against it, Frederick even adopted many Muslim customs.

When Frederick began conquering land in Italy, the Pope became afraid that he would take over church lands around Rome. To stop Frederick, the Pope excommunicated him in 1227. He also called for a crusade against Frederick. This gave the German princes the chance for which they had been waiting. They broke away from Frederick's rule and made Germany a loose grouping of states under their control.

The Hapsburgs Whenever an emperor of the Holy Roman Empire died, the German princes met in a **diet,** or assembly. There, they elected a new emperor. In 1273, the princes elected as emperor a member of the Hapsburg (haps' berg) family named Rudolf. He and members of his family served as Holy Roman emperors for about the next 650 years.

One important Hapsburg was Maximilian I (mak suh mil' yuhn), who became emperor in 1493. He worked to extend the empire's power all through Europe. When he married Mary of Burgundy, he gained control of Flanders and other areas of what are now the Low Countries, or Belgium, the Netherlands, and Luxembourg. By marrying his children into other European

Reading Check
What was the purpose of the German **diet?**

Answers will vary, but students should mention the importance of universities as centers of learning.

L2 **Culture** One of the favorite pastimes of nobles was falconry. Suggest students research this sport, and report their findings to the rest of the class.

GEOGRAPHY AND HISTORY

Maximilian's older son Philip I, married Joanna, the daughter of Ferdinand and Isabella of Spain. His second son, Ferdinand, married Anna of Bohemia and Hungary. By 1520, the Hapsburgs ruled half of Europe and most of the settled areas in the Americas.

Reading Check Answer
The German **diet** elected a new emperor whenever an emperor of the Holy Roman Empire died.

SPOTLIGHT ON: THE HAPSBURGS

Emperor Charles V retired to a monastery in 1556 after ruling much of Europe for 37 years. The resulting division of Hapsburg lands gave the family power in parts of Europe for hundreds of years, outlasting the Holy Roman Empire. Charles' son became king of Spain as Philip II, who ruled a vast empire in the Americas. The Spanish line continued until 1700. A lack of an heir caused the War of the Spanish Succession. The Austrian Hapsburg dynasty continued under Charles' brother Ferdinand. Hapsburg emperors and an empress ruled the Holy Roman Empire until the empire was ended in the early 1800s. They then ruled Austria-Hungary. The last Hapsburg emperor of Austria had to abdicate after World War I.

L1 **History** Have students work in pairs to prepare a list of questions that a news reporter might ask one of the people mentioned in this chapter. Have them role-play the interview for the class.

L2 **Geography: Region** Have the students create five geography-based questions based on the map of "Europe in the Late Middle Ages." Collect the questions and use them to quiz the students. **ELL**

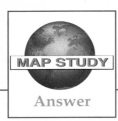

MAP STUDY

Answer

The Holy Roman Empire was larger than the other regions.

Assign the Chapter 27 **Geography and Map Activity** in the TCR.

Use **Interactive Tutor Self-Assessment Software** to review Section 4.

royal families, he brought still more countries under Hapsburg control. He could not gain complete control, however, in Germany where the princes continued to have authority over their own lands.

Section 4 Assessment

1. **Define:** diet.
2. How were the German emperors able to control the office of Pope in the late 900s and early 1000s?
3. How did the Hapsburgs come to power?

Critical Thinking

4. **Drawing Conclusions** Why do you think a strong rule by a king or queen did not develop in Germany?

Graphic Organizer Activity

5. Draw this diagram, and use it to show the achievements of German rulers in the Middle Ages.

Ruler	Achievements

MAP STUDY

REGIONS Strong kings and queens appeared in England, France, Spain, and Portugal in the late Middle Ages. **How did the size of the Holy Roman Empire compare to other regions of western Europe during the late Middle Ages?**

Europe in the Late Middle Ages

Section 4 Assessment Answers

1. diet, assembly (p. 421)
2. Otto had freed the Pope from the control of Roman nobles. In return, the Pope crowned him Emperor of the Holy Roman Empire.
3. through election in a diet, or assembly, of German princes
4. Answers will vary but might include the idea that Germany was a loose grouping of states under the control of German princes.

Also, emperors were elected by German princes rather than by inheriting the position.
5. Charts should show the accomplishments of Otto I, Frederick I, Frederick II, Rudolf, and Maximilian I. Completed charts will review efforts to promote unity and expand German power.

Assign the Chapter 27 **Section 4 Quiz** in the TCR. Testmaker available.

SECTION 5 Spain

While the western European monarchies were increasing their power, Spain was under the control of the Moors. When the Moors conquered Spain in 711, they brought with them learning and luxury. Most Spaniards, however, were Christians and opposed Muslim rule. They banded together to drive the Moors out of the country. By the 1200s, the Moors controlled only the small southern kingdom of Granada (gruh nahd' uh).

The rest of Spain was made up of several kingdoms, the most powerful of which were Castile (kas tēl') and Aragon (ar' uh gahn). In 1469, Prince Ferdinand of Aragon married Princess Isabella of Castile. Within ten years, they became king and queen and united their kingdoms into one country.

Ferdinand and Isabella accomplished this in different ways. To control the nobles, the king and queen took away some of their privileges. To keep order in the land, they sent royal officials called *corregidores* (kō rā hē dō' rās) to govern the towns. They also set up special courts in the countryside.

The most important way in which they unified Spain, however, was through religion. Ferdinand and Isabella were known as the "Catholic Monarchs." They believed that to be truly united, all Spaniards should be Catholic. They turned their attention first to the Jews. The Jews had lived freely under the Moors. However, as Christians took over more of Spain, they killed thousands of Jews. To save themselves, many Jews converted.

Ferdinand and Isabella believed these new Christians were practicing their old religion in secret. So, they set up the Spanish Inquisition. The Spanish Inquisition tried and tortured thousands of people charged with heresy. More than 2,000 people were burned to death. Still, most Jews refused to change their faith. So, in 1492, Ferdinand and Isabella told the remaining Jews to convert or leave the country. Most left the country.

Next, the king and queen turned their attention to the Moors. In 1492, the last of the Moors had surrendered Granada to armies of Ferdinand and Isabella. The treaty signed at the time promised the Moors freedom of religion. Nevertheless, in 1502 the Catholic Monarchs ordered the remaining Moors to convert or leave. Most left Spain for northern Africa.

Although now a united Catholic monarchy, Spain was weaker than it had been before. This was because most of its artisans, merchants, bankers, doctors, and educators had been either Jews or Moors. After these people left, there were few trained Spaniards to take their place.

Painting of Spanish Hero El Cid

☑ Reading Check
What was the role of the *corregidores*?

Equal Footing In 1990 Spain finally overturned the 1492 order calling for the expulsion or conversion of the Jews. Now both Judaism and Protestantism are on an equal basis with Roman Catholicism, giving all three religions the same tax breaks and privileges.

SPOTLIGHT ON: EL CID

Spain's national epic, which created a hero like England's King Arthur or France's Roland, comes out of the long period of wars between Moors and Christians known as the *Reconquista.* The Christians of the old Visigothic kingdoms had been pushed back into the Pyrenees. From there they moved southward city by city. Spanish rulers also warred against each other. In addition, Muslim kingdoms were resisting takeover by fanatic Almoravids from North Africa. The hero of the battle of Valencia in 1094 was El Cid. This was the name given to the military leader Rodrigo Díaz de Vivar who later became ruler of Valencia. More legends than facts are known about El Cid.

💾 Use the **Vocabulary Puzzle-Maker** to create crossword and word search puzzles.

L2 **The Arts** When Ferdinand and Isabella captured the Moorish province of Granada, they gained some remarkable examples of Moorish art and architecture, such as the Alhambra. Have students research and report on the art and architecture of the Spanish Moors. Have them give oral summaries of their reports including pictures of the art and architecture.

☑ Reading Check Answer
The *corregidores* governed towns and also set up special courts in the countryside.

ASSESS

Check for Understanding

Ask students to summarize the main points of the chapter, orally or in writing. Discuss the answers to the Section and Chapter Assessment questions.

Evaluate

Assign the Chapter 27 **Performance Assessment Activity** in the TCR.

Administer the **Chapter 27 Test.** Testmaker available.

Reteach

Have the students create a time line of events covered in this chapter.

Assign the Chapter 27 **Reteaching Activity** in the TCR.

Enrich

The son of the English King Edward III was known as the Black Prince because he wore black armor. Have students research the Black Prince and his role in the Hundred Years' War and write a first-person account of his career.

Assign the Chapter 27 **Enrichment Activity** in the TCR.

CLOSE

Have students debate the advantages and disadvantages of a strong monarchy during the Middle Ages.

💾 Use **Interactive Tutor Self-Assessment Software** to review Section 5.

Section 5 Assessment

1. **Define:** *corregidores.*
2. How did Ferdinand and Isabella control the nobles and keep order in Spain?
3. How did Ferdinand and Isabella use religion to unite Spain?

Critical Thinking

4. **Predicting Consequences** How might Spain have been different if the Spanish king and queen had allowed freedom of religion?

Graphic Organizer Activity

5. Draw this diagram, and use it to show the causes and effects of Ferdinand and Isabella's united Catholic monarchy.

| Causes | → | United Catholic Monarchy | → | Effects |

Chapter Summary & Study Guide

1. The rise of trade and towns in western Europe led to the rise of strong monarchies.
2. The Capetian dynasty strengthened the French monarchy by granting town charters and by setting up a national court, a national currency, a tax system, and the Estates-General.
3. William the Conqueror defeated the English at the Battle of Hastings in 1066 and brought the system of feudalism to England.
4. Henry II strengthened England by imposing his law on the land and by reforming courts.
5. In 1215, English nobles forced King John to sign the Magna Carta, which established the idea that a king was not above the law.
6. In 1272, Edward I set up Parliament to advise him.
7. During the Hundred Years' War, fought between 1337 and 1453, Joan of Arc led armies to force the English from France.
8. Because of the Hundred Years' War, both France and England were unified and the common people became more important.
9. The Pope crowned Otto I emperor of the Holy Roman Empire in 962. However, future German emperors had a hard time uniting unruly German princes.
10. The Hapsburg family ruled the Holy Roman Empire from 1273 until the early 1900s.
11. By 1492, Ferdinand and Isabella had conquered the Moors and made Spain a united Catholic country.

Section 5 Assessment Answers

1. *corregidores,* Spanish royal officials (p. 423)
2. They took away some of their privileges, sent *corregidores* to govern the towns, and set up special courts in the countryside.
3. They forced the Jews and the Moors to convert to Christianity or leave the country.
4. Answers will vary but might include that the artisans, merchants, bankers, doctors, and educators who were needed to keep the nation strong would not have left Spain.

5. *Sample causes*—opposition to Moorish control, marriage of Ferdinand and Isabella *Sample effects*—decreased privileges for nobles; use of *corregidores*; persecution of non-Catholics and establishment of Inquisition; defeat of Moors at Granada; loss of most of Spain's artisans, merchants, bankers, doctors, and educators who had been Jews or Moors

Assign the Chapter 27 **Section 5 Quiz** in the TCR. Testmaker available.

Using Key Terms

Imagine that you are a news reporter who has a chance to interview one of the kings or queens you have read about in his chapter. Identify whom you will interview and write five questions you would like to ask that person. Use the following words in your questions.

monarchies   circuit judges   grand jury
trial jury   *dauphin*   diet
corregidores

Understanding Main Ideas

- How did the Estates-General help strengthen the French monarchy?
- What changes did the Magna Carta bring about in English government?
- Why did the position of the common people in England and France improve as a result of the Hundred Years' War?
- How did Otto I set up a Christian Roman Empire in western Europe?
- What did the Moors bring to Spain?
- What was the purpose of the Spanish Inquisition?

Critical Thinking

- If you had been King John, how would you have reacted to the demand that you sign the Magna Carta? Explain your answer.
- If you had been Joan of Arc, what decision would you have made about attacking the English at Orleans? Explain your answer.
- How did the Hundred Years' War both help and hurt England and France?

4. Would you have agreed or disagreed with Ferdinand and Isabella that all people in a country should follow the same religion? Explain.

Graphic Organizer Activity

Citizenship Create a diagram like the one below, and use it to compare English government in 1275 with government in the United States today.

Geography in History

Place Refer to the map on page 422. There were several places outside the control of either the English or the Holy Roman Empire. What geographic features do these places have in common?

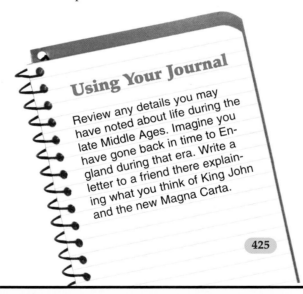

Using Your Journal

Review any details you may have noted about life during the late Middle Ages. Imagine you have gone back in time to England during that era. Write a letter to a friend there explaining what you think of King John and the new Magna Carta.

425

For Chapter 27 Test

Bonus Test Question

If medieval monarchs had been able to access modern technology, they might have avoided some of their problems. Assume the role of one of these monarchs and name a modern invention you could have used and what problem it would have solved.

Using Your Journal

Letters will vary but students might include the idea of grand juries, trial juries, right to a trial by peers, and Parliament.

Geography in History

They are on the outer fringes of Europe and are widely spaced and most often surrounded by water.

Using Key Terms

Questions will vary according to the king or queen selected but should use all the terms.

Understanding Main Ideas

1. It united the nobles, clergy, and townspeople.
2. It increased the nobles' power, gave freemen the right to a trial, and said that the king had to obey laws.
3. because many had died, and those who remained were greatly needed as workers
4. He made his loyal followers bishops and abbots and gave them government posts.
5. learning and luxury
6. to deal with heresy

Critical Thinking

1. Answers will vary, but students might disagree with King John's acceptance.
2. Answers will vary.
3. Answers will vary, but might include that it helped by unifying them but hurt the countries by resulting in the deaths of many peasants.
4. Answers will vary, but students should explain why they agree or disagree.

Graphic Organizer Activity

Diagrams will vary but should show the roots of United States government in English law as well as the increased rights of United States citizens and additional curbs on executive power such as the system of checks and balances. Some features of both governments might include: a two-house assembly, trial by jury, written document setting limits on government, and so on.

UNIT 8 **Around**

FOCUS

Objectives

After reading the Around the World for Unit 8, your students will be able to:

1. explain how Japan's geography helped shape life during feudal times.
2. identify the Noh theater and other feudal Japanese accomplishments.
3. appreciate the meaning of a Zen garden to Japanese Buddhists.

Bellringer

Instruct students to write down the geographic features that can isolate a people or a culture.

Motivational Activity

Call on students to share their responses, compiling a list of geographic features that can promote cultural isolation. Then refer students to the map of Japan on page 426. Ask: Which of these features did Japan possess? *(Sample responses: its island location—i.e., surrounding oceans and seas.)*

TEACH

Geography: Place Tell students to look closely at the map. Is Japan one island or several islands? *(several)* What is the most common landform on these islands? *(mountains)* Challenge students to suggest how Japan's islands and mountains might encourage the rise of feudalism. *(It would divide people from one another, encouraging the growth of small independent kingdoms.)*

FEUDAL JAPAN

From about 1000 A.D.–1600 A.D., Japan went through its own feudal age. Like the feudal age in Europe, this was a time when power belonged to military leaders, known as *samurai*, and the soldiers who served them. The most powerful samurai became *daimyo*, or local lords. The samurai, like medieval knights, pledged their loyalty and military service to the daimyo. Individual states controlled by the daimyo battled for control of Japan and the right to claim the title of *shogun*—the head of Japan's military government. The principle of *bushido*, which means "the way of the warrior," shaped life in much of feudal Japan.

Japan

SEA OF JAPAN

JAPAN

miles 0   150   300
kilometers 0 150 300

▲ Japan's island location helped isolate it from unwanted intruders. Its rugged terrain limited the amount of available land and increased the power of the land-owning daimyo and the samurai who served them.

▶ The Japanese considered a samurai's armor a work of art. The armor was made of horizontal rows of lacquered iron or leather held together by braided silk cords. The artisans who fashioned the armor—and the swords that went with it—were held in high regard.

SPOTLIGHT ON: FEUDAL JAPAN

Courtship and marriage in feudal Japan followed fixed rituals. Usually a bridegroom's family chose a suitable match from an equal or higher class. An exception was made for the daughters of emperors, where the royal family chose the husband.

Courtship often began with a sentimental poem sent to the woman by the prospective bridegroom. Her reply was examined closely for its calligraphy and style. If the woman was willing and the man impressed, the two might then go through a series of meetings set by custom. A third meeting was considered a sign of commitment.

Marriages generally took place while the bride and groom were in their early teens. Since children this young could not manage their own affairs, they went to live with the wife's family. Houses and other property frequently passed from mothers to daughters, ensuring security for a woman in case she lost her husband to death or divorce.

the World

Japanese nobles tried to include beauty and poetry in every aspect of their lives. Even everyday objects such as this tea pot were crafted with an artist's care.

Swordsmiths produced such beautiful —and sharp—swords.

The Japanese imported Zen Buddhism from China. Zen holds that enlightenment can be achieved by anyone who experiences a revelation, or vision, following meditation. To encourage meditation, the Japanese built Zen gardens where monks, samurai, and others came to meditate. ▼

The tales of ancient warriors and the bravery and suffering of women were told in the Noh theaters of medieval Japan. Noh theater combined music, dance, poetry, and elaborate customs. The Noh actors—all male—often wore wooden masks such as this one. ►

▼ The samurai received land for their loyal service. They built castles to protect themselves against attack from rival states. This castle is called the White Heron, for its white plaster walls and because it perches high on a hill like a bird protecting its nest. The castle originally belonged to samurai Toyotomi Hideyoshi.

Taking Another Look

1. How did Japan's geography help shape life in feudal Japan?
2. What was Noh theater?

Hands-On Activity

Designing a Garden Design a plan for a Zen garden. It should be simple, with wandering paths and private spots for meditation.

427

Answers and Analyses

1B   History

The rise of feudalism is discussed on the top of page 368. There it states that *The kings who followed Charlemagne were so weak they could not even rule their own kingdoms well . . . . Before long they began to depend on the nobles.*

2J   History

Page 385 describes the reforms begun by the monks of Cluny and continued by Pope Gregory VII. There it states that Gregory wanted to *rid the Church of control by kings and nobles.*

 TEST-TAKING TIP

Students probably recall the struggles for power between the monarchy and the Church, and this information is enough to make J a good guess. Choices F and H are unlikely, since these attempts have only been made in modern times.

3B   History

The rise of universities is discussed on page 387. On the top of the page it states that universities arose in part because *students began to complain that teachers held few classes and did not cover enough subjects.*

Standardized Test Practice

Directions: Choose the *best* answer to each of the following multiple choice questions. If you have trouble answering a question, use the process of elimination to narrow your choices. Write your answers on a separate piece of paper.

1. One reason for the growth of feudalism in western Europe was

  A an increase in the population of lords and nobles

  B the failure of kings to develop a centralized government

  C the need for many more people to work farmland

  D the desire of peasants to have a more secure future

Test-Taking Tip: The key to being able to answer this question correctly is knowing what *feudalism* is. Always consult the **glossary** in the back of your book when you come across a word you are unsure of. In this case, *feudalism* was a medieval system of government by landowning nobles. Which answer choice *best* fits with this information?

2. During the Middle Ages, the Church attempted to institute reforms aimed at

  F reuniting the Roman Catholic and the Eastern Orthodox churches

  G obtaining more land and wealth for the Church

  H expanding the role of women in the Church

  J reducing the influence of kings, lords, and nobles in the Church

Test-Taking Tip: Think about the meaning of the word *reform*. It means "change that leads to improvement." Usually, reforms are needed when an institution strays from its original purpose. In the Middle Ages, Church officials were often wealthy nobles who were more concerned with money than with religious ideals. Which answer choice do you think would *best* help the Church *improve*, so that it could fulfill its original *religious purposes*?

3. During the Middle Ages, universities arose

  A because there was no more classroom space in the cathedrals

  B to teach subjects not covered in cathedral schools

  C as preparation to become a ruler or a nobleman

  D to provide the underprivileged with educational opportunity

Test-Taking Tip: This question is looking for a *cause and effect* relationship. During the Middle Ages, governments were more secure, and the economy was stronger. Therefore, people had more time for—and more interest in—learning new things. Therefore, which of the answer choices would most likely have been the cause of the rise of universities?

428

4. What was one important result of the Crusades?

F   Muslim and Byzantine culture was introduced to western Europe.

G   The Eastern Orthodox Church accepted the Pope as its leader.

H   Jerusalem came under control of the Roman Catholic Church.

J   The Byzantine Empire was at last safe from the Turks.

> *Test-Taking Tip:*   Always read *carefully.* Although the Crusades began as an attempt to help the Byzantine Empire, they were ultimately unsuccessful. Therefore, answer J is incorrect.

5. Why were craft guilds created?

A   To help royalty regain control over the price of goods

B   To protect the rights of people who bought goods and services

C   To protect the rights of people working in these trades

D   To make it easier for apprentices to become masters

> *Test-Taking Tip:*   This question requires you to remember the meaning of the word *guild.* Craft guilds, like present-day unions, were business associations of artisans, such as carpenters, shoemakers, and weavers. What is the purpose of unions today?

Read the passage below, which is an excerpt from the Magna Carta, and answer the question that follows.

> We . . . have granted to all the freemen of our kingdom, for us and for our heirs forever, all the underwritten liberties, to be had and holden by them and their heirs . . .
>
> No freeman shall be taken or imprisoned, or diseased, or outlawed, or banished, or in any way destroyed, nor will we pass upon him, nor will we send upon him, unless by the lawful judgement of his peers, or by the law of the land.
>
> All merchants shall have safe and secure conduct to go out of, and to come into, England . . . without any unjust tolls. . . .

6. The main idea of the Magna Carta was

F   to help the king further centralize his power

G   to secure certain rights and liberties for noblemen

H   to entitle people accused of crimes to a trial by jury

J   for the Church to take on a greater role in England's government

> *Test-Taking Tip:*   This question asks for the *main idea.* Remember, the main idea is a generalization about the *entire passage,* not just one detail. For example, the second paragraph does mention *the lawful judgement of peers* (a reference to trial by jury), but this is not the main idea of the *entire passage.*

4F   History

The Eastern Orthodox Church did not accept the Pope as its leader, so choice G can be eliminated. While Jerusalem was temporarily in the hands of Christians, it was retaken by the Muslims, so choice H can be eliminated. After the Crusades, the Byzantine Empire was weaker than ever, and so choice J can be eliminated. According to the bottom of page 395, the crusaders' contact with the Byzantine and Muslim cultures led to a taste for eastern luxuries and for the knowledge that the Muslims had.

5C   History

The rise of guilds is discussed on pages 406–407. There it states that guilds *were business groups whose purpose was to make sure that their members were treated equally.* This information best supports choice C.

Encourage students to use their common sense about political positions of individuals and groups. Since guilds were made up of artists, the guilds naturally protected the interests of the artists. Therefore, students can eliminate choices A and B.

6G   History

According to page 415, *the Magna Carta took away some of the king's power and increased that of the nobles.*

Tested Objectives

Questions	Reading Objective
1, 4	Determine cause and effect
2, 6	Identify central issues
3	Identify supporting ideas
5	Perceive relationships and recognize outcomes

OVERVIEW

Unit 9 discusses the changes that took place in western Europe from the 1300s to the 1600s as the Middle Ages came to an end.

➤ **Chapter 28** describes the Renaissance, when western Europeans experienced new attitudes about themselves and the world around them.

➤ **Chapter 29** discusses the Reformation and how differences in religions led to religious wars.

➤ **Chapter 30** summarizes the principal European voyages of discovery from the 1400s to the 1600s.

UNIT OBJECTIVES

After reading Unit 9, students will be able to:

1. describe what changes took place in learning in western Europe during the 1300s and 1400s.

2. summarize what changes took place in religion during the 1400s and 1500s.

3. discuss what western Europeans learned about the world during the Age of Discovery.

UNIT PROJECT

Tell the students to imagine they are on an explorer's ship in the middle 1600s. Their ship has landed in an overseas port. The local ruler expresses interest in hearing about the Renaissance, the Reformation, and the Age of Discovery in western Europe. The students are asked by the captain to give a historical sketch of important events and people during this time. Have them prepare their presentations.

UNIT 9 Beginning of Modern Times

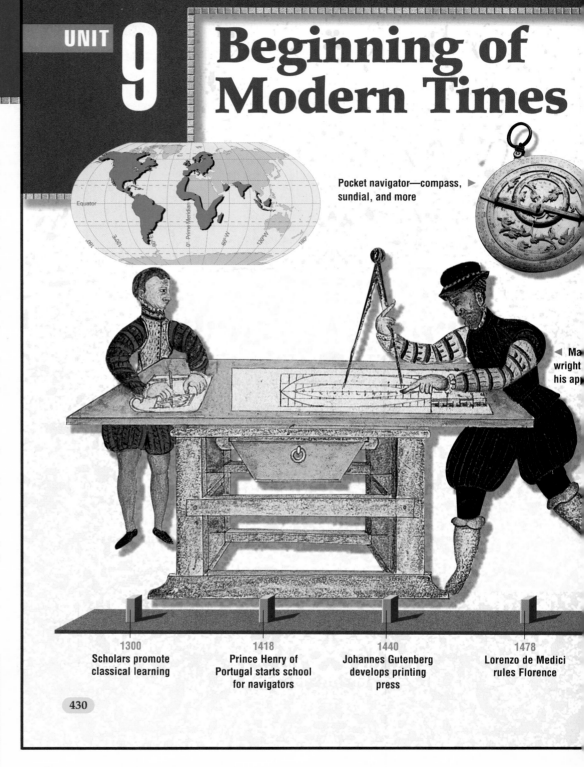

Pocket navigator—compass, ► sundial, and more

◄ Ma wright his ap

1300	1418	1440	1478
Scholars promote classical learning	Prince Henry of Portugal starts school for navigators	Johannes Gutenberg develops printing press	Lorenzo de Medici rules Florence

430

ABOUT THE UNIT OPENING

Examining Artifacts

Ask students what the two artifacts have in common. *(Both are related to ships or sailing.)* Explore reasons these artifacts might be used to illustrate a unit on the start of modern times. Lead students to understand the importance of exploration and trade to ushering in a new era.

Global Chronology

Ask students to explain what time period the time line covers. *(1300 to 1519)* How do they know learning was important? *(scholars promote learning, school for navigators started, printing press invented)* What entries indicate exploration? *(Prince Henry starts school for navigators; Columbus lands at San Salvador; Magellan begins voyage to Pacific)*

Multimedia Activity

Turning Points in World History
Age of Exploration

ABC NEWS INTERACTIVE™

Setting up the Video

Work with a group of your classmates to view "Age of Exploration" on the videodisc *Turning Points in World History*.

View the video by scanning the bar code or by entering the chapter number on your keypad and pressing "Search." (Also available in VHS format.)

Side One, Chapter 9

Until around 1500, most of the world's great civilizations existed in isolation from each other. Exploration by Portugal and Spain ended the isolation forever. This program shows how the Age of Exploration opened the door of new global contacts and paved the way for future exploration.

Hands-On Activity

Many scientists believe the last frontier on Earth lies beneath the world's oceans. Research the underwater explorations that are currently underway. Share your findings in an oral report called "Into the Depths." Mention equipment needed for underwater exploration, strange creatures discovered, world depth records, and so on.

PRIMARY SOURCES
Library

See pages 690–691 for a primary source reading to accompany Unit 9.

1492
Columbus lands at San Salvador

1517
Martin Luther posts 95 theses

1519
Magellan begins voyage to Pacific

Journal Notes

What changes took place in western Europe between 1300 and 1600? Note details about these changes as you read.

431

Glencoe Literature Library

The following novels from the **Glencoe Literature Library** may be used to enrich this unit:
- *Hamlet*, by William Shakespeare
- *A Midsummer Night's Dream*, by William Shakespeare
- *The Tempest*, by William Shakespeare

Geographic Location

Using a world map or globe, have students locate the countries of western Europe and North and South America, the islands of the Caribbean, Africa, and the East Indies. Discuss the dangers involved in sailing from western Europe to unknown lands during the 1400s–1600.

INTRODUCING THE UNIT

Write the word *CHANGES* on the chalkboard. Ask students to make a list of innovations in a particular area such as communications that have occurred in recent times. *(Student lists might include CDs, cellular phones, personal computers, FAX machines, etc.)* Inform students that in this unit they will learn about the changes and, innovations that took place in western Europe in the 1300s and 1400s.

RECORDING JOURNAL NOTES

Help students begin writing in their journals by asking them to name the changes described in the unit introduction. Explain that these are the kinds of changes they should detail in their journals.

PRIMARY SOURCES
Library

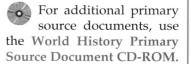

Items in the Primary Sources Library for this unit focus on the fall of the Aztec empire. Elements include:
- Aztec description of the arrival of Cortés
- Aztec "song of sorrow" on Spanish conquest

For additional primary source documents, use the **World History Primary Source Document CD-ROM.**

Chapter 28 Planning Guide

Objectives	Reproducible Resources	Multimedia Resources
Section 1 **The Italian Renaissance** Explain how the Renaissance began and flourished in the Italian city-states.	Reproducible Lesson Plan Chapter 28 Vocabulary and Guided Reading Activity Reading Essentials and Study Guide 28-1 Chapter 28 Cooperative Learning Activity Chapter 28 Chart and Graph Skill Activity Unit 9 Primary Sources Reading Chapter 28 Enrichment Activity Section 1 Quiz Unit 9 Hands-On History Lab	Teaching Transparencies and Activities 28A & 28B Vocabulary PuzzleMaker Interactive Tutor Self-Assessment Software ExamView® Pro Testmaker Glencoe Skillbuilder Interactive Workbook, Level 1
Section 2 **France** Identify ways in which France was influenced by the Italian Renaissance.	Reproducible Lesson Plan Reading Essentials and Study Guide 28-2 Section 2 Quiz	Teaching Transparency and Activity 28B Vocabulary PuzzleMaker ExamView® Pro Testmaker Glencoe Skillbuilder Interactive Workbook, Level 1
Section 3 **Germany and Flanders** Describe how the Renaissance spread to Germany and Flanders.	Reproducible Lesson Plan Reading Essentials and Study Guide 28-3 Chapter 28 Geography and Map Activity Section 3 Quiz	Vocabulary PuzzleMaker Interactive Tutor Self-Assessment Software ExamView® Pro Testmaker
Section 4 **Spain** Discuss the influence of the Roman Catholic Church and government on the Renaissance in Spain.	Reproducible Lesson Plan Reading Essentials and Study Guide 28-4 Unit 9 World Literature Reading 2 Section 4 Quiz	Vocabulary PuzzleMaker Interactive Tutor Self-Assessment Software ExamView® Pro Testmaker Glencoe Skillbuilder Interactive Workbook, Level 1
Section 5 **England** Summarize how the English monarchy promoted the Renaissance in England.	Reproducible Lesson Plan Reading Essentials and Study Guide 28-5 Chapter 28 Activity Book Activity Unit 9 World Literature Reading 1 Section 5 Quiz	Teaching Transparencies and Activities 28A & 28B Vocabulary PuzzleMaker ExamView® Pro Testmaker Glencoe Skillbuilder Interactive Workbook, Level 1
Chapter 28 **Review and Evaluation**	Chapter 28 Reteaching Activity Chapter 28 Performance Assessment Activity Unit 9 Standardized Test Practice Spanish Chapter Summary and Glossary Chapter 28 Test	Vocabulary PuzzleMaker Interactive Tutor Self-Assessment Software Glencoe Skillbuilder Interactive Workbook, Level 1 Audiocassettes* ExamView® Pro Testmaker

*Also available in Spanish.

Presentation Plus!

Use Glencoe's **Presentation Plus!** multimedia teacher tool to easily present dynamic lessons that visually excite your students. Using Microsoft® PowerPoint, you can customize the presentations to create your own personalized lessons.

 ## Interactive Lesson Planner

Planning has never been easier! Using this CD-ROM, organize your week, month, semester, or year with all the help you need. The **Interactive Lesson Planner** gives you access to all of the blackline masters which accompany *Human Heritage.*

✓ PERFORMANCE ASSESSMENT ACTIVITIES

Art Museum Have students bring to class books with examples of Renaissance art and architecture to be used to set up their own Renaissance museum. Encourage students to tape an audio description for each art piece as many museums do.

CHAPTER RESOURCES

LITERATURE ABOUT THE PERIOD

Castiglione, Baldassare. *The Book of the Courtier.* Translated by George Bull. Penguin, 1976. Contemporary handbook of courtly etiquette.

READINGS FOR THE STUDENT

Mee, Charles L. *Daily Life in the Renaissance.* American Heritage, 1975. Illustrated with works of art showing people in their daily lives.

READINGS FOR THE TEACHER

Editors of Time-Life. *What Life Was Like In Europe's Golden Age.* Time-Life, Inc., 1999. A vividly illustrated study of northern Europe during the years 1500 to 1675.

Editors of Time-Life. *What Life Was Like at the Rebirth of Genius.* Time-Life, Inc., 1999. A look at the outburst of creativity that characterized Renaissance Italy.

KEY TO ABILITY LEVELS

Teaching strategies have been coded for varying learning styles and abilities.

L1 Level 1 activities are **basic** activities and should be within the ability range of all students.

L2 Level 2 activities are **average** activities and should be within the ability range of the average to above-average student.

L3 Level 3 activities are **challenging** activities designed for the ability range of above-average students.

ELL ELL activities should be within the ability range of English Language Learning students.

NATIONAL GEOGRAPHIC SOCIETY

Teacher's Corner

INDEX TO NATIONAL GEOGRAPHIC MAGAZINE

The following articles relate to this chapter:

• "Italy's Endangered Art," by Erla Zwingle, August 1999.
• "Venice," by Erla Zwingle, February 1995.

NATIONAL GEOGRAPHIC SOCIETY PRODUCTS AVAILABLE FROM GLENCOE

To order the following, call Glencoe at 1-800-334-7344:

• *MapPack: Europe (Transparency Maps)*
• *PicturePack: The Renaissance (Transparencies)*
• *PictureShow: The Renaissance (CD-ROM)*

Access *National Geographic*'s new dynamic MapMaker Web site and other geography resources at:
http://www.nationalgeographic.com/
http://www.nationalgeographic.com/maps/

The following videotape programs are available from Glencoe:

• **Henry VIII**
  1-56501-917-2

• **Michelangelo: Artist and Man**
  1-56501-425-1

• **The Miraculous Canals of Venice**
  1-56501-840-0

To order, call Glencoe at 1-800-334-7344. To find classroom resources to accompany many of these, check:

A&E Television: http://www.aetv.com
The History Channel:
http://www.historychannel.com

OVERVIEW

Chapter 28 describes the Renaissance and the changes it brought to western Europe.

➤ **Section 1** discusses the start of the Renaissance in Italy.

➤ **Section 2** describes the Renaissance in France.

➤ **Section 3** analyzes the Renaissance in Germany and Flanders.

➤ **Section 4** explains the Renaissance in Spain.

➤ **Section 5** summarizes the Renaissance in England.

CHAPTER OBJECTIVES

After reading Chapter 28, students will be able to:

1. explain how the Renaissance flourished in Italy.

2. identify how France was influenced by the Renaissance.

3. describe how the Renaissance spread to Germany and Flanders.

4. discuss how the Church and the government influenced the Renaissance in Spain.

5. cite features of the Renaissance in England.

EXAMINING ARTIFACTS

Ask students what these artifacts reveal about Renaissance interests. *(People took an interest in music and invention.)* Based on the time line, have students identify other pursuits or pastimes. *(printing/reading; theater)* Encourage students to add to their lists of Renaissance activities as they read the chapter.

PERFORMANCE ASSESSMENT ✔

Use the Performance Assessment activities on page 432B to help you evaluate students as they complete the chapter.

432

The Renaissanc
1300 A.D.–1600 A.D.

A replica of a bicycle designed by Leonardo da Vinci ▼

◄ Renaissance musicians

c. 1440	1478	1485	1494	1580
Johannes Gutenberg develops printing press	Lorenzo de Medici becomes ruler of Florence	Tudors take over the English throne	The Renaissance spreads to France	First English theaters built

432 UNIT 9 BEGINNING OF MODERN TIMES

TEACHING RESOURCES

TEACHER PLANNING AND SUPPORT

📁 Reproducible Lesson Plan
📁 Block Scheduling Implementation Guide
📁 Videodisc Bar Code Correlation
💿 Presentation Plus!

REVIEW AND REINFORCEMENT

📁 Reading Essentials and Study Guide 28-1, 28-2, 28-3, 28-4, 28-5
📁 Chapter 28 Vocabulary and Guided Reading Activity
💾 Vocabulary PuzzleMaker Software
🖨 Teaching Transparencies 28A & 28B

📁 Chapter 28 Reteaching Activity
📁 Chapter 28 Cooperative Learning Activity
📁 Chapter 28 Activity Book Activity
📁 Chapter 28 Chart and Graph Skill Activity
💾 Interactive Tutor Self-Assessment Software
💿📺 Unit 9 MindJogger VideoQuiz

APPLICATION AND HANDS-ON ACTIVITIES

📁 Daily World History, Geography, and Culture Question
📁 Unit 9 Hands-On History Lab Activity
📁 World History Craft Card 5

Chapter Focus

 Read to Discover

- How the Renaissance flourished in the Italian city-states.
- How France was influenced by the Italian Renaissance.
- How the Renaissance spread to Germany and Flanders.
- How the Roman Catholic Church and the government influenced the Renaissance in Spain.
- How the English monarchy promoted the Renaissance in England.

Terms to Learn	People to Know	Places to Locate
classical writings	Leonardo da Vinci	Florence
humanists	Michelangelo	Venice
piazza	Johannes Gutenberg	Papal States
doge	El Greco	Toledo
chateaux	Henry VIII	
printing press	Elizabeth I	
	William Shakespeare	

Why It's Important   Around 1300, scholars in western Europe developed a new interest in **classical writings**, or the writings of the ancient Greeks and Romans. The scholars improved their knowledge of Greek and Latin. They also began to accept some Greek and Roman ideas.

One idea that the scholars accepted was a belief in the importance of people. Because of this, the scholars were called **humanists** (hyū muh nists). Their work caused a break with the thinking of the Middle Ages and led to a new age called the Renaissance (ren' uh sahns), a French word meaning "rebirth." During this age, people became less concerned with the mysteries of heaven and more interested in the world around them.

Chapter Overview
Visit the *Human Heritage* Web site at **humanheritage.glencoe.com** and click on **Chapter 28— Chapter Overviews** to preview this chapter.

Reading Check
Where did **classical writings** come from?

Reading Check
What was the main belief of the **humanists?**

SECTION 1   The Italian City-States

The first and leading center of the Renaissance was Italy, which consisted of small, independent city-states. The most important were Florence, Venice, and the Papal (pā' puhl) States. The Papal States in central Italy included Rome and were ruled by the Pope. All these city-states had grown wealthy from trade.

CHAPTER 28 THE RENAISSANCE   **433**

Guided Practice

L1 **The Arts** Divide students into small groups. Have each group write brief descriptions of the visuals in this chapter. How does this art look different from the medieval art shown in Chapters 24–27? Discuss the groups' descriptions as a class. *(Students' responses might include three dimensional, less likely to have religious themes, more emotional expression.)* **ELL**

MAKING CONNECTIONS

➤➤ **Daily Life** In their workshops, artists worked on dozens of projects at a time. In addition to painting and sculpting, Renaissance artists designed and carved furniture, made jewelry, painted festival cloaks and carnival masks, planned scenery for plays, molded candlesticks and chandeliers, and decorated cakes.

Student Web Activity objectives, goals, and answers can be found at the *Chapter 28 Web Activity Lesson Plan* at humanheritage.glencoe.com

---

Use these materials to enrich student understanding of the Renaissance.

NGS PICTURESHOW CD-ROM
The Renaissance

NGS PICTUREPACK TRANSPARENCY SET
The Renaissance

Painting of Leonardo da Vinci

Student Web Activity

Visit the *Human Heritage* Web site at **humanheritage.glencoe.com** and click on *Chapter 28— Student Web Activities* to find out more about Leonardo da Vinci.

At first, each city-state was ruled by guilds. Later, powerfu[l] individuals or families took control. They often fought each othe[r] for land and wealth. At times, they had difficulty gaining th[e] people's loyalty and had to govern by force.

The leaders of the Italian city-states, however, wer[e] interested in more than power. They wanted to be remembered a[s] wise, generous rulers. To be sure this would happen, they spen[t] money on ceremonies and parades to impress and entertain th[e] people. They ordered the building of churches and palaces. The[y] also encouraged scholars, poets, and philosophers to set u[p] palace schools to educate the sons of the rich. In these school[s] pupils learned to develop their minds and make their bodie[s] stronger. They spent part of the day studying classical writing[s] and learning good manners. They spent the rest of the da[y] wrestling, fencing, and swimming.

Art Art was an important part of life in Renaissance Ital[y]. City-states were proud of their artists. In fact, the city-states ofte[n] competed for the services of certain painters and sculptors. Th[e] artists knew they were important and began to seek individua[l] honor and attention. They worked hard to develop their own dis[-]tinctive style.

Renaissance artists carefully studied ancient Greek an[d] Roman art, science, and mathematics. They began to pay clos[e] attention to the details of nature. They became interested i[n] *perspective* (puhr spek' tiv), or a way of showing objects as the[y] appear at different distances. Above all, the artists studied th[e] structure of the human body to learn how to draw it accuratel[y]. They began to experiment with light, color, and shade. As [a] result, they painted and sculpted works that were true to life an[d] full of color and action.

Good artists were given money by the rulers of the city[-] states. In return, they were expected to make paintings an[d] sculptures for the rulers' palaces and gardens. Artists often ha[d] workshops where they trained apprentices. The apprentice[s] added backgrounds, costumes, or hands to the artists' paintings.

Many artists painted portraits for the rich. The artists tried t[o] paint people's facial features so they showed what the peopl[e] were really like. At first, portraits were painted only to hono[r] dead or famous people. Later, any merchant with money coul[d] have a portrait painted.

One of the greatest Renaissance artists was Leonardo da Vinc[i] (lē uh nahr' dō dah vin' chē). He is known for the *Mona Lisa,* [a] portrait of an Italian noblewoman. He also painted a fresc[o] called *The Last Supper* on the wall of an Italian monastery's dinin[g] room. It shows Christ and his disciples at their last meal befor[e] Christ's death. In these works, da Vinci tried to reveal people's feel[-]ings as well as their outward appearance.

COOPERATIVE LEARNING

Divide students into groups with each group taking on the role of Da Vinci, the inventor. Tell each group they are to look around them and come up with an invention that would be helpful to them all, as Da Vinci did. Within the group, have them choose an illustrator, planner, supply man-ager, builder, and whatever else they need to plan and create their invention. Have groups present their inventions, with explanations, to the class.

📁 Assign Chapter 28 *Cooperative Learning Activity* in the TCR.

Da Vinci was a scientist as well as an artist. He filled notebooks with drawings of inventions far ahead of the times. Da Vinci designed the first parachute and made drawings of flying machines and mechanical diggers.

Another outstanding artist was Michelangelo Buonarroti (mī kuh lan' juh lō bwah nah rō' tē). He is known for his paintings on the ceiling and altar wall of Rome's Sistine (sis' tēn) Chapel. He also sculpted the *Pietà* (pē ā' tah), which shows the dead Christ in his mother's arms. Michelangelo went farther than the ancient Greeks and Romans in presenting the human body. His figures are large and muscular, and show a sense of motion.

City Life   Most Italian Renaissance cities had narrow paved streets with open sewers in the middle. Merchants and shop-keepers lived on the top floors of the buildings that housed their

RENAISSANCE ARTISTS   Michelangelo Buonarroti and Leonardo da Vinci were two leading artists of the Italian Renaissance. Michelangelo carved a very large statue of Christ and his mother known as the *Pietà* (left). Da Vinci tried to capture the personality of an Italian noblewoman in the painting known as the *Mona Lisa* (right). **What did da Vinci try to reveal in his works of art?**

SPOTLIGHT ON: MICHELANGELO

Michelangelo was working on the sculpture of Moses for Pope Julius's tomb when the Pope asked him to paint the ceiling of the Sistine Chapel instead. Michelangelo painted scenes from the Bible on the ceiling while lying on his back on scaffolding 70 feet (or 21 m) above the floor. The Renaissance biographer Giorgio Vasari described the completion of Michelangelo's ceiling of the Sistine Chapel in the following way: *"When the work was thrown open, the whole world came running to see what Michelangelo had done; and certainly it was such as to make everyone speechless with astonishment."*

Reading Check Answer
People gathered in the **piazza** to talk to friends, carry out business dealings, and watch or take part in parades and celebrations on holidays.

L1 **Geography: Place** Have students locate the various Italian city-states on the map on page 438 as they are mentioned in the chapter narrative. Have volunteers keep a running list of city-states on the chalkboard. Have students add one adjective to the list that describes each city. **ELL**

L2 **Daily Life** Ask students to create a list of manners that might appear in a modern book on etiquette. Have them compare their lists with the list on page 436. What conclusions about Renaissance manners can students draw? **ELL**

LINKING PAST TO PRESENT

The Renaissance revived the Greek ideal of the balanced individual who participated in a variety of activities, such as politics, art, sports, and music. Today we still admire this ideal, and we apply the term *Renaissance man* or *Renaissance woman* to someone who has wide interests and many different talents. Ask students to think of someone today whom they would describe this way.

Reading Check
What activities went on in the **piazza?**

shops. The rich built homes in the classical style, with rooms that were large and had high ceilings. In the center of the homes stood courtyards filled with statues, fountains, and gardens. Most people in the cities, however, were poor. They worked for low wages and lived in run-down areas.

The center of city life was the **piazza** (pē aht′ suh), or central square. There, markets were set up, and merchants traded goods. People gathered to talk to friends and to carry out business dealings. On holidays, the people often watched or took part in parades and ceremonies there.

Families were close-knit. Most family members lived and worked together in the same neighborhood. Marriages were arranged as if they were business deals. Women stayed at home, ran the household, and raised children. Men spent their days at work and talking with friends on the streets and in taverns.

Most men dressed in tights and tunics. Some also wore cloaks and caps. Women dressed in simply cut, flowing dresses with tight bodices. The rich often wore brightly colored clothing made from expensive silks and velvets and trimmed with fur.

Florence The Italian Renaissance began in Florence, which was ruled by the Medici (med′ uh chē) family. One of its most

RENAISSANCE MANNERS

Do not blow your nose and then open and look inside your handkerchief, as if pearls or rubies had dropped out of your head.

Do not offer anyone a fruit from which you have already taken a bite.

Do not tell sad stories at parties or mealtimes. If someone starts talking this way, gently and politely change the subject and talk about something more cheerful.

Do not brag about honors, wealth, or intelligence.

Do not speak while yawning.

Do not clean your teeth with your napkin or your finger.

Do not lie all over the dinner table or fill both sides of your mouth with so much food that your cheeks stick out widely.

Do not undress, comb, or wash your hair in front of others.

Do not stick out your tongue, rub hands together, or groan out loud.

Do not talk too much, especially if your knowledge is small.

MULTICULTURAL PERSPECTIVES

The Renaissance revived the Greek notion that an ideal person participated in a variety of activities, including sports. Games and sports that were popular at this time included javelin hurling, chess, archery, fencing, boxing, snowfights, and gambling. Women as well as men participated in many sports, including *giuco della palla*—a game that led to the modern game of tennis.

Linking Across Time

Banking Moneylenders in Florence carried out their transactions on work areas covered with brightly embroidered cloth (below). Known as *bianchi* in Italian, these countertops gave their name to present-day banks (right), which trace their roots to the financial institutions of Florence. **Why did the Renaissance begin in Florence?**

famous members was Lorenzo de Medici, who became the ruler of Florence in 1478. He made the city a center of art and learning. Artists, poets, and philosophers flocked there to benefit from his generous support. Because of the city's prosperity and fame, Lorenzo became known as "the Magnificent."

About 1490, Florence's trade started to decline. Merchants began to complain that Lorenzo was too strict and spent too much money. The poor in Florence began to grumble about their housing and the shortages of food.

People looked for an escape from their problems. They thought they found it in a monk named Savonarola (sav uh nuh rō' luh). Savonarola accused the Medicis of not ruling justly. He gained the people's support and overthrew the Medicis in 1494.

Savonarola did not like the gaiety and loose life of the Renaissance. He thought Renaissance ideas were hurting Florence. On his advice, the new government did away with parties, gambling, swearing, and horse-racing. Savonarola's supporters also burned paintings, fancy clothes, musical instruments, and classical books.

By 1498, the people of Florence had tired of Savonarola's strict ways, and he was hanged for heresy. The Medicis returned to power. Florence's greatness, however, had passed.

The Papal States During the 1300s and 1400s, the power of the Popes declined. However, they wanted to show Europe's

Guidelines for Rulers
Niccolò Machiavelli wrote a handbook for rulers called *The Prince*. Here are some of Machiavelli's ideas:
• It is much safer to be feared than loved, if one must choose.
• There cannot be good laws where the state is not well armed.
• A wise leader cannot and should not keep his word when keeping it is not to his advantage.

L3 **Economics** The Medicis, who dominated the politics and culture of Florence, obtained their wealth from international banking. Have students research the Medici family and write a brief report on their role in the origins of modern banking.

Linking Across Time

The Renaissance began in Florence because of the city's great wealth from trade and the support of artists and scholars by rulers such as Lorenzo de Medici.

DID YOU KNOW
The Medici family ruled Florence from the 1400s to the 1700s.

MAKING CONNECTIONS

➤➤ **History** Under Savonarola, children were organized into Bands of Hope. They watched for gamblers and swore to help stamp out dancing, pageants, love poems, and music schools. During Carnival Week, the bands went from house to house seeking such forbidden objects as playing cards and musical instruments to throw into a large bonfire.

MEETING SPECIAL NEEDS

To help students with Limited English Proficiency, divide students into small heterogeneous groups and ask each group to discuss one section of the chapter. Have group members work together to prepare a list of the important points. Discuss each group's list in class and write major points on the chalkboard. Have students who are visual learners illustrate important events discussed in this chapter. After they present all the drawings, ask the class to identify what event was illustrated in each drawing.

Refer to *Inclusion for the Middle School Social Studies Classroom: Strategies and Activities* for additional resources.

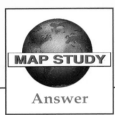

L1 **Geography: Place** Have students study the map of Renaissance Italy to answer the following questions: Which Italian city-state was the largest in land size? *(Naples)* In which city-state was Rome located? *(Papal States)* Which city-states had access to both the Adriatic Sea and the Tyrrhenian Sea? *(Naples, Papal States)* **ELL**

MAP STUDY
Answer

Venice had easier access to the Byzantine Empire by both land and water.

Assign the Chapter 28 **Geography and Map Activity** in the TCR.

MAKING CONNECTIONS

➤➤ **Religion** Unlike today, earlier Popes had children. The actions of such church leaders as Pope Alexander VI caused many devout Catholics to favor reform of the Church.

kings that the Church was still powerful. In Rome they built large churches and palaces. Piazzas and wide streets were built in areas that had been in ruins.

Most Popes were not very religious. They acted more like political rulers than church leaders. They sent representatives to other states and countries, collected taxes, minted money, raised armies, and fought wars.

In 1492, Rodrigo Borgia (rōd rē′gō bōr′ jah) became Pope Alexander VI. He did this by bribing cardinals to vote for him. Pope Alexander's goal was to make central Italy a kingdom ruled by the Borgia family. His daughter Lucretia (lū krā′ shuh) married a noble and became known for her lively parties and for poisoning her enemies.

Alexander spent a great deal of money building an army for his favorite son, Cesare (chā′ sah rā). The army marched through Italy and took control of many towns. All of this territory was lost, however, after Alexander's death in 1503. By this time, Rome had replaced Florence as the center of the Renaissance.

MAP STUDY

PLACE The Renaissance began in Italy partly because Italian towns were important centers of trade during the late Middle Ages. **Why did Venice trade more with the areas outside of Italy than other Italian city-states?**

Renaissance Italy

COOPERATIVE LEARNING

Have students compare the Renaissance in Florence, the Papal States, and Venice. Assign students to three teams, each of which will study one city. Team members can choose topics such as architecture, government, and painting. Split teams into subgroups. The subgroups will research their topics together and bring their findings back to their whole team. Have the team then prepare a panel report on their city to be presented to the rest of the class.

VENICE The city of Venice is famous for being built on 117 islands. About 150 canals, rather than streets, carry most of the city's traffic. Here, some of Venice's many bridges and grand palaces are shown. **Who ruled Renaissance Venice?**

L2 **Government** Create three columns on the chalkboard, headed *Florence, Papal States,* and *Venice.* Ask students to compare the governments of these three Renaissance city-states. What did they have in common? How did they differ? **ELL**

Venice The Renaissance did not reach Venice until the late 1500s. This was because the Venetians had looked to Constantinople rather than to western Europe for art and literature.

Venice was different from most Italian city-states in other ways, too. The city, including its palaces and churches, was built on 117 islands linked by nearly 400 bridges. Instead of streets, Venice had canals. The largest and busiest was the Grand Canal, which was lined with brightly colored stone and marble palaces. The Rialto (rē ahl' tō), or the business area of Venice, also lay along a stretch of the Grand Canal. There, traders from Europe and the East crowded the docks to buy and sell goods.

Venice was ruled by a few merchant aristocrats. They controlled the Senate and the Council of Ten. The Council passed laws and chose the **doge** (dōj), or official ruler. The doge had little power and had to obey the Council of Ten.

The Venetians were expected to place loyalty to their city above anything else. If a neighbor did something suspicious, a Venetian was expected to report it to the Council of Ten. Citizens who wanted to accuse someone of treason placed a letter stating the charges in special boxes located all through the city. Those charged were quickly arrested and brought before the Council. Council members then met in secret to study the evidence, listen to witnesses, and decide guilt or innocence.

Then . . .
& Now

Venice Located on the Adriatic Sea between the Po and Piave rivers, Venice is known as the "Queen of the Adriatic." Flooding, sinking land, pollution, and age have threatened the city and its many landmarks. In recent times, the United Nations has worked to preserve the city as a world historic site.

✓ **Reading Check** Why did the **doge** have little power?

CHAPTER 28 THE RENAISSANCE **439**

CAPTION ANSWER
a few merchant aristocrats

DID YOU KNOW
During the 1400s the penknife was just that—a knife for trimming quill pens, which lost their points quickly. After steel pens were invented, the term came to mean any small blade that can be carried in a pocket.

✓ **Reading Check Answer**
The **doge** had little power because merchant aristocrats controlled the Council of Ten, which picked the doge and forced him to obey.

The following videotape program is available from Glencoe to enrich Chapter 28:

• **The Miraculous Canals of Venice**

To find classroom resources to accompany this video, check the following home page:

A&E Television:
http://www.aetv.com

MEETING SPECIAL NEEDS

Have auditory learners bring recordings of Renaissance music to class or perform a piece themselves. Before playing the piece, each student should give background information. Students who are studying foreign languages could help with translation and pronunciation of songs.

📁 Refer to *Inclusion for the Middle School Social Studies Classroom: Strategies and Activities* for additional resources.

✔ **Reading Check Answer**
Francis I built his *chateaux* along the Loire River.

💾 Use **Interactive Tutor Self-Assessment Software** to review Sections 1 and 2.

Section 1 Assessment

1. **Define:** classical writings, humanists, piazza, doge.
2. How important was art during the Renaissance? Explain.
3. What made Venice different from other Italian city-states?

Critical Thinking

4. **Demonstrating Reasoned Judgment** Do you approve or disapprove of the system of justice in Renaissance Venice? Explain.

Graphic Organizer Activity

5. Draw this diagram, and use it to show characteristics of life in Renaissance Italy. (Add more answer circles as needed.)

Life in Renaissance Italy

SECTION 2 France

In 1494, the French began invading Italy. French kings became fascinated by Italian architecture, art, and fashions. In the 1500s, King Francis I arranged for Italian artisans to work for him in France. He and many of his nobles hired Italian architects to design **chateaux** (sha tōz'), or castles, which were then built along the Loire River.

Francis I also encouraged French authors to model their works on those of Italian authors. Every evening, Francis and his family listened to readings of the latest books. Many were written by Rabelais (rahb' uh lā), a physician-monk. He believed that humans were not tied down by their past and could do whatever they wished. In his most popular book, *The Adventures of Gargantua and Pantagruel,* Rabelais's main characters were two comical giants.

✔ **Reading Check**
Where did King Francis I build his first **chateaux?**

Section 2 Assessment

1. **Define:** *chateaux.*
2. What did Francis I do to encourage Renaissance thought in French literature?
3. What did Rabelais believe?

Critical Thinking

4. **Making Inferences** How do you think people of the time reacted to Rabelais's ideas? Explain.

Graphic Organizer Activity

5. Draw this diagram, and use it to show the cause and effects of the arrival of the Renaissance in France.

Cause → French Renaissance → Effects

SECTION 3 Germany and Flanders

The Renaissance also spread to the rich trading centers of Germany and Flanders. There, religious scholars learned Greek and Hebrew so they could understand the earliest versions of the Bible. The German and Flemish scholars decided that over the years many church leaders had interpreted the Bible to suit their own needs. The scholars wanted changes that would make church teachings simpler. One outspoken scholar, a Dutchman named Erasmus (i raz' muhs), made a new Latin translation of the New Testament. He also wrote *Praise of Folly*, a book that attacked corrupt church leaders and practices.

At the same time, Italian traders living in the north set an example for merchants. The German merchants began to appreciate wealth, beauty, personal improvement, and other Renaissance values. This was the beginning of a new, privileged middle class.

Northern European artisans made many discoveries during the Renaissance. About 1440, a German named Johannes Gutenberg (yō' hahn gūt' n berg) developed a **printing press.** It used carved letters that could be moved around to form words and then could be used again. As a result, books could be quickly printed by machine rather than slowly written by hand. This made many more books available to people. Since printing came at a time when many townspeople were learning to read and think for themselves, new ideas spread rapidly.

Northern European artists studied Italian works of art and then developed their own styles. They painted scenes from the Bible and daily life in sharp detail. Hubert and Jan Van Eyck (van īk'), two brothers from Flanders, discovered how to paint in oils. The colors of the oil paintings were deep and rich. Soon, other artists began to use oils also.

Moveable Type The Chinese knew how to make moveable type long before European printers did. The large number of Chinese characters, however, made it difficult to use. The Roman alphabet has just 26 letters, making interchangeable type quick and efficient.

Reading Check
Who developed a **printing press** in Germany?

Reading Check Answer
Johannes Gutenberg developed a **printing press** in Germany.

MAKING CONNECTIONS

➤➤ **History** Printing was invented by the Chinese. The oldest-known printed book in the world is a Buddhist scripture dated A.D. 868.

L2 **Science** Have students research the development of paper and the different materials from which it has been made. Divide students into groups and have each group outline a presentation of a different paper-making process to share with the class. If possible, encourage students to demonstrate how each process was completed.

Use **Interactive Tutor Self-Assessment Software** to review Section 3.

Use the **Vocabulary Puzzle-Maker** to create crossword and word search puzzles.

Section 3 Assessment

1. **Define:** printing press.
2. What church reforms did German and Flemish scholars want to make?
3. How did the printing press change European life?

Critical Thinking

4. **Predicting Consequences** How might life in Europe have been different without the development of Gutenberg's printing press?

Graphic Organizer Activity

5. Draw this diagram, and use it to support a generalization about the role of religion in spreading the Renaissance to Germany and Flanders.

Section 3 Assessment Answers

1. printing press, machine that used carved letters that could be reused to print (p. 441)
2. They wanted changes that would make church teachings simpler.
3. It made many more books available to people and also made them cheaper to buy.
4. Answers will vary but could include that Renaissance ideas might not have spread as quickly throughout Europe.
5. Supporting details will vary with the generalization written by students. A sample generalization might be: "Religion played an important role in spreading Renaissance ideas to Germany and Flanders." Supporting details will center on the efforts of German and Flemish scholars to translate the Bible for themselves.

Assign the Chapter 28 **Section 3 Quiz** in the TCR. Testmaker available.

L2 **History** Have students choose someone from the chart of Renaissance people on this page to write a biographical report about, using outside sources as well as the text. Tell students to focus on the impact this person made on the modern world and to include important dates and events of this person's life. Have them conclude by explaining how they think their own lives would be different if this person had not lived.

MAKING CONNECTIONS

➤➤ **History** Known as the Prudent King, Philip II was cautious, hardworking, and suspicious of others. The Spanish Armada was built and defeated during Philip's reign.

DID YOU KNOW ???

During the Renaissance, both men and women used cosmetics. "Face painting" was done with white lead and a red pigment called vermilion.

Use the **Vocabulary Puzzle-Maker** to create crossword and word search puzzles.

SECTION 4 Spain

The Renaissance took root in Spain in the late 1400s and early 1500s. It was influenced by the close ties between the Roman Catholic Church and the government. The leading Church official, Cardinal Jiménez (hē mā′ nuhs), was a loyal supporter of the monarchy. He was also a strong believer in the value of learning. He founded universities and welcomed students from other countries. He helped scholars produce a new translation of the Bible that had three columns of text side-by-side. One column was in Greek, one was in Latin, and one was in Hebrew.

In 1555, Philip II became king. He was very religious and did not trust the work of scholars. Many were charged with heresy by the Spanish Inquisition, and some were burned at the stake.

RENAISSANCE PEOPLE

Baldassare Castiglione	1478–1529	Italian writer; wrote book on rules of behavior for ladies and gentlemen
Benvenuto Cellini	1500–1571	Italian goldsmith; sculptor; wrote about his life and times
Vittoria Colonna	1492–1547	Italian author; wrote religious and love poems
Nicolaus Copernicus	1473–1543	Polish astronomer; stated that Earth moves around the sun
Albrecht Dürer	1471–1528	German artist; painted and made woodcuts of religious and classical subjects
Beatrice d'Este	1475–1497	Italian noblewomen; sisters; honored for their learning; supported writers and artists
Isabella d'Este	1474–1539	
Galileo	1564–1642	Italian scientist; did experiments on the motion of objects; used telescope to discover new facts about universe
Niccolò Machiavelli	1469–1527	Italian politician; writer; wrote advice to rulers on how to keep power
Thomas More	1477–1535	English scholar; saint; government official; refused to accept king as Church head
Petrarch	1304–1374	Italian poet; scholar; restored study of classics; collected manuscripts; wrote letters and poems
Raphael	1483–1520	Italian religious painter and architect
Andreas Vesalius	1514–1564	Flemish surgeon; founder of modern medicine; wrote first full description of human body

SPOTLIGHT ON: PHILIP II

In person, Philip II was very reserved, devoutly religious, and ready to act ruthlessly to safeguard Spain and the Roman Catholic Church. He made no effort to be liked by his people. One court historian wrote, "His smile and his dagger were very close." Other historians picture him working alone in a small private office in the "gloomy magnificence" of El Escorial. Philip, however, loved books and paintings and collected both.

Philip had a new granite palace built just outside Madrid. Called El Escorial (el es kō rē ahl'), it served as a royal court, art gallery, monastery, church, and tomb for Spanish royalty. El Escorial soon became a symbol of the power and religious devotion of Spanish rulers.

Despite strong Church and government controls, the arts flowered. The city of Toledo (tō lā' dō) became a center for painters and poets. One artist who settled there was a Greek whom the Spanish called El Greco (el grek' ō). He painted figures with very long bodies, parts of which stretched beyond normal size. Some art experts believe that El Greco copied his style from Byzantine artists. Others insist he painted as he did because of an eye problem that distorted his vision.

The theater was also popular in Renaissance Spain. Miguel de Cervantes Saavedra (suh vē druh) (mē gel' dā suhr van' tēs) was one of the most noted authors of the time. He wrote many plays, short stories, and other works. His novel, *Don Quixote* (don ki hō' tā), about the adventures of a comical knight and his peasant squire, is still read today.

Painting of Don Quixote

L2 **The Arts** Have students choose a Northern Renaissance painting (one by Brueghal or Van Eyck, for example) and compare it to one by an Italian Renaissance artist (such as Masaccio or Michelangelo). Ask students to compare how "real" the people look and tell what effect the paintings have on them. **ELL**

Use **Interactive Tutor Self-Assessment Software** to review Section 4.

Section 4 Assessment

1. What factors influenced the Renaissance in Spain?
2. Why did Philip II mistreat Spanish scholars?

Critical Thinking

3. **Making Comparisons** How did Cardinal Jiménez and Philip II differ in their attitudes toward learning?

Graphic Organizer Activity

4. Draw this diagram, and use it to summarize the contributions of Jiménez, El Greco, and Cervantes to the Spanish Renaissance.

SECTION 5 England

Peace did not come to England after the Hundred Years' War. In 1455, two noble families, York and Lancaster, began a fight for the throne. The Yorkist symbol was a white rose, and the Lancastrian symbol was a red rose. For this reason, the struggle between the House of York and the House of Lancaster was called the Wars of the Roses.

When the wars ended in 1485, a family called the Tudors, who fought on the Lancastrian side, took over the English throne. The first Tudor king, Henry VII, prepared the way for the Renaissance. He made the monarchy stronger and built up trade, which made England both peaceful and rich.

Painting of English Singers

MAKING CONNECTIONS

➤➤ **Architecture** It took 21 years to build El Escorial, which was finished in 1586. Philip often sat on a rock throne set on a nearby hilltop and supervised the workers. Lit by 200,000 oil lamps, the building was dedicated on the eve of the Feast of Saint Lorenzo, the saint for whom El Escorial was named.

LINKING PAST TO PRESENT

El Greco's real name was Doménikos Theotokópoulos. One of his most famous paintings, "View of Toledo," hangs in New York's Metropolitan Museum of Art.

Use the **Vocabulary Puzzle-Maker** to create crossword and word search puzzles.

Section 4 Assessment Answers

1. the close ties between the Roman Catholic Church and the government
2. He did not trust their work and considered much of it to be heretical.
3. Cardinal Jiménez believed in the value of learning and helped spread education. Philip II distrusted the work of scholars and charged many of them with heresy.
4. Sample contributions: Jiménez—founded universities, welcomed scholars from other countries, helped scholars produce a new version of the Bible in three languages; El Greco—spread new painting styles; Cervantes—wrote many plays, short stories, and other works, including the novel *Don Quixote*.

Assign the Chapter 28 **Section 4 Quiz** in the TCR. Testmaker available.

THE TUDORS These paintings of King Henry VIII of England (left) and his daughter Queen Elizabeth I (right) show members of the Tudor family, who ruled England from 1485 to 1603. Henry and Elizabeth both were strong and forceful rulers, and they were able to gain the respect and love of the English people. **How did the first Tudor king, Henry VII, pave the way for the English Renaissance?**

People in History

Henry VIII
1491–1547

English King

Henry VIII was a typical Renaissance ruler. He played tennis, liked to joust, and wrote music. He also built up the English navy and changed the course of history by convincing Parliament to declare him the head of the Church of England, splitting with the Roman Catholic Church (see Chapter 29).

Henry VII's work was continued by his son, Henry VIII, who became king in 1509. He enjoyed and encouraged art, literature, hunting, and parties. He played several musical instruments and even composed his own music. Under his rule, English nobles and merchants began to look to Renaissance Italy for guidance in politics, diplomacy, and behavior.

The English Renaissance reached its height, however, during the reign of Henry VIII's daughter Elizabeth I. She became queen in 1558 when she was 25 years old. She was shrewd, and well-educated. Although she had a sharp tongue and iron will, she won the loyalty and confidence of her people.

Elizabeth often made journeys through the kingdom so that the people could see her. During her travels, she stayed at the homes of nobles who entertained her with banquets, parades, and dances. Poets and writers praised her in their writings. The sons of merchants, lawyers, and landowners copied Italian clothes and manners and came to court to capture her attention and favor.

Poetry, music, and the theater became a part of daily life. Most nobles wrote poetry. People of all classes enjoyed singing ballads and folk songs. Many played violins, guitars, and lutes.

444 UNIT 9 BEGINNING OF MODERN TIMES

EXTENDING THE CONTENT

Henry V died in France in 1422 leaving an infant son, Henry VI. Nobles from rival branches of the Plantagenet family (Henry II's line) began maneuvering for power, and Henry VI never gained control. When rivalry erupted into war in 1455, two parties formed around Richard, Duke of York, and Cardinal Beaufort, who backed King Henry VI. Shifting loyalties, intermittent fighting, and treachery marked the war. Over the next 30 years, four men became king of England and were deposed, murdered, or killed in battle. The young sons of Edward IV (York) were sent to the Tower of London and never seen again. The deaths of hundreds of nobles seriously weakened the English nobility.

The people of Renaissance England were especially fond of plays. Not since the days of ancient Greece had so many plays been written and performed. About 1580, the first theaters in England were built. Their stages stood in the open air. Most of the audience, however, sat under a roof or some sort of covering. Those who could not afford to pay for seats stood in the *pit*, or an open area in the front of the theater, and on the sides of the stage. Since there were no lights, plays were performed in the afternoon. They attracted large crowds.

One of the best known English *playwrights*, or authors of plays, was William Shakespeare (shāk′ spir). He drew ideas for his tragedies and comedies from the histories of England and ancient Rome. He often used Italian scenes, characters, and tales in his plays. Some of his most famous works are *Romeo and Juliet*, *Macbeth*, *Hamlet*, *Julius Caesar*, and *A Midsummer Night's Dream*. Many experts consider Shakespeare the greatest playwright in the English language.

ENGLISH THEATER The Globe Theater (left) stood near the south bank of the Thames River in the London suburb of Southwark. The Globe Theater became the home of William Shakespeare's (right) acting company in 1599. **What kind of reputation have the plays of William Shakespeare earned for him?**

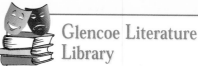

Glencoe Literature Library

You might assign the following titles from the **Glencoe Literature Library**:
• *Hamlet*, by William Shakespeare
• *A Midsummer Night's Dream*, by William Shakespeare
• *The Tempest*, by William Shakespeare

DID YOU KNOW ??

Audiences that disliked a play would hurl insults and toss ripe fruit at the actors to drive them from the stage. Since women were not permitted on the stage, boys whose voices had not yet changed played the female roles, which were usually smaller and less important than the male roles.

CAPTION ANSWER

He is considered the greatest playwright in the English language.

ASSESS

Check for Understanding

Ask students to summarize the main points of the chapter, orally or in writing. Discuss the answers to the Section and Chapter Assessment questions.

Evaluate

Assign the Chapter 28 **Performance Assessment Activity** in the TCR.

Administer the **Chapter 28 Test** in the TCR. Testmaker available.

COOPERATIVE LEARNING

Assign students to small groups to develop a set of TV quiz-show-style questions about a Renaissance artist of their choice. Students should consult art history books and, as a group, analyze the artist's style, subjects of art, and also the facts of their lives. Each panel can present their questions in a class competition. Each member of the group should be responsible for a task: research, recording group discussion, developing questions, or acting as panel moderator in presenting the questions.

Reteach

Ask students to suggest the ways in which Italian Renaissance ideas spread to other areas of western Europe. Have volunteers write responses on the chalkboard.

Assign the Chapter 28 **Reteaching Activity** in the TCR.

Enrich

Have students choose an influential social critic who lived during the Renaissance, such as Erasmus or Rabelais, and report on the person's criticisms of the Catholic Church or Renaissance society.

Assign the Chapter 28 **Enrichment Activity** in the TCR.

CLOSE

Have students write an essay that summarizes major characteristics of the arts of the Renaissance—painting, literature, drama, and architecture.

💾 Use **Interactive Tutor Self-Assessment Software** to review Section 5.

Self-Check Quiz gives students an interactive chapter tutorial. Have them access **Chapter 28 Quiz** at humanheritage.glencoe.com

Section 5 Assessment

1. What did the Tudors do to encourage the Renaissance in England?
2. What were English theaters like?
3. From where did Shakespeare draw ideas for his plays?

Critical Thinking

4. **Understanding Cause and Effect** What was the cause of the Wars of the Roses? How did this war affect English history?

Graphic Organizer Activity

5. Draw this diagram, and use it to write four facts about the English Renaissance.

Chapter Summary & Study Guide

1. Around 1300, western European scholars showed a growing interest in classical writings, which in turn led to the Renaissance.
2. The Renaissance began in the Italian city-states, where the wealth from trade help fuel a burst of artistic achievement.
3. Leading figures in the Italian Renaissance included rulers such as the Medicis of Florence and artists like Michelangelo Buonarroti and Leonardo da Vinci.
4. The Renaissance moved from Florence to Rome when the Popes rebuilt the city to prove their power to the rulers of Europe.
5. In the late 1500s, the Renaissance spread from Rome to Venice.
6. After 1494, King Francis I helped bring the Renaissance to France.
7. An interest in religious reform and trading contacts with Italy helped bring the Renaissance to Germany and Flanders.
8. Development of a printing press by Johannes Gutenberg helped new Renaissance ideas to reach more people.
9. In the late 1400s and early 1500s the Renaissance spread to Spain, where it was influenced by strong ties with the Roman Catholic Church and strict government policies.
10. The Tudors paved the way for the arrival of the Renaissance in England, where it reached its peak under Elizabeth I.
11. The people of Renaissance England were very fond of plays, especially those by William Shakespeare.

Self-Check Quiz

Visit the *Human Heritage* Web site at **humanheritage.glencoe.com** and click on *Chapter 28—Self-Check Quiz* to assess your understanding of this chapter.

Section 5 Assessment Answers

1. They made the monarchy stronger, built up trade, and encouraged the arts.
2. open-air stages where the audience sat under a roof or stood in the pit to see afternoon plays
3. from the histories of England and ancient Rome and also from Italian tales
4. Sample responses: *cause*—struggle for the throne waged by the York and Lancaster families; *effects*—the Tudors, who fought for the Lancasters, took the throne and paved the way for the English Renaissance.
5. Facts will vary but should reflect the achievements of the Elizabethan era.

Assign the Chapter 28 **Section 5 Quiz** in the TCR. Testmaker available.

Using Key Terms

Imagine you are a drama critic writing about the literature of the Renaissance. Write a short magazine article explaining the kinds of plays being written and how they reflect the life of the times. Use the following words in your article.

classical writings   humanists   *piazza*
printing press   *chateaux*   *doge*

Understanding Main Ideas

1. Whose writings did the scholars of western Europe study during the Renaissance?
2. Why were the Renaissance scholars called humanists?
3. What did the rulers of the Italian city-states do to encourage learning and development of art?
4. Why did the people of Florence turn to Savonarola in 1494?
5. How was France introduced to the Renaissance?
6. What did Germany, Flanders, Spain, and England contribute to the Renaissance?
7. Of what did El Escorial become a well-known symbol?
8. How did the Wars of the Roses get their name?

Critical Thinking

1. How did the Renaissance differ from the Middle Ages?
2. What was the connection between trade and the start of the Renaissance?
3. Why was Lorenzo de Medici called "the Magnificent"?

4. If you could go back in time and talk with a Renaissance artist or ruler, whom would you choose? What questions would you ask? Explain your answer.

Graphic Organizer Activity

Culture Create a diagram like the one below, and use it to compare the Renaissance to the Middle Ages.

 ## Geography in History

Location Refer to the map of Renaissance Italy on page 438. This country is often compared to the shape of a boot. Describe the location of this country by giving its latitude and longitude. Then describe its relative location.

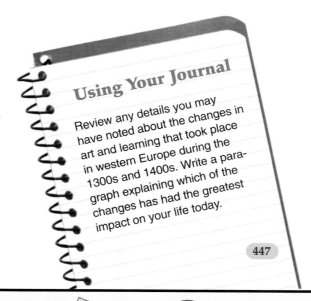

Using Your Journal

Review any details you may have noted about the changes in art and learning that took place in western Europe during the 1300s and 1400s. Write a paragraph explaining which of the graph changes has had the greatest changes has had the greatest impact on your life today.

447

Using Key Terms

Magazine articles will vary, but students should use all the key terms.

Understanding Main Ideas

1. those of the ancient Greeks and Romans
2. because they believed in the importance of people
3. They spent money and encouraged scholars, poets, and philosophers, and set up palace schools.
4. They thought he would stop too much government spending, and food and housing shortages.
5. through French invasions of Italy
6. Answers will vary, but should reflect the achievements of each nation.
7. the power and religious devotion of Spanish rulers
8. from the symbols of the two noble families who fought

Critical Thinking

1. During the Renaissance, people became more interested in art, learning, and the world around them.
2. The Italian city-states had grown wealthy from trade and spent their wealth on the arts.
3. Answers will vary but might include that he made Florence prosper.
4. Answers will vary but students should write specific questions.

Graphic Organizer Activity

Diagrams will vary, but entries on the Middle Ages should reflect the influence of feudalism and the Church, while entries on the Renaissance should show the effects of trade and an increased interest in human potential. Entries for both periods might include: concern with religious topics, education at universities, creation of beautiful cathedrals, etc.

 Bonus Test Question

For Chapter 28 Test
Is the man charged with theft innocent or guilty? His alibi: "During the theft, at 3:00 P.M., I was at the Globe Theater watching Shakespeare's *Romeo and Juliet.* Afterward, it was so crowded along the Thames River that I didn't leave the area until after dark." *(innocent—facts are accurate)*

Using Your Journal

Paragraphs will vary, but students should explain that learning and art do have an impact on their lives. You might call on volunteers to read their paragraphs to the class.

 Geography in History

Italy stretched from about 48°–38° N latitude, and from about 5°–18° E longitude.

Chapter 29 Planning Guide

Objectives	Reproducible Resources	Multimedia Resources
Section 1 **Martin Luther** Explain why Martin Luther's beliefs brought him into conflict with the Roman Catholic Church.	Reproducible Lesson Plan Chapter 29 Vocabulary and Guided Reading Activity Reading Essentials and Study Guide 29-1 Chapter 29 Cooperative Learning Activity Section 1 Quiz	Teaching Transparency and Activity 29A ABCNEWS INTERACTIVE Turning Points in World History Interactive Tutor Self-Assessment Software ExamView® Pro Testmaker
Section 2 **A New Religion** Describe how Protestantism developed.	Reproducible Lesson Plan Reading Essentials and Study Guide 29-2 Section 2 Quiz	Vocabulary PuzzleMaker Interactive Tutor Self-Assessment Software Glencoe Skillbuilder Interactive Workbook, Level 1
Section 3 **Catholic Reform** Identify how Catholic reformers worked to improve their Church.	Reproducible Lesson Plan Reading Essentials and Study Guide 29-3 Chapter 29 Chart and Graph Skill Activity Chapter 29 Enrichment Activity Section 3 Quiz	Interactive Tutor Self-Assessment Software ExamView® Pro Testmaker Glencoe Skillbuilder Interactive Workbook, Level 1
Section 4 **A Middle Way** Discuss how the reformation of the Church of England came about.	Reproducible Lesson Plan Chapter 29 Reading Essentials and Study Guide 29-4 Section 4 Quiz	Teaching Transparency and Activity 29B Vocabulary PuzzleMaker Interactive Tutor Self-Assessment Software
Section 5 **Wars of Religion** Explain why Europeans became involved in religious wars.	Reproducible Lesson Plan Reading Essentials and Study Guide 29-5 Chapter 29 Geography and Map Activity Section 5 Quiz	Vocabulary PuzzleMaker ExamView® Pro Testmaker Glencoe Skillbuilder Interactive Workbook, Level 1
Section 6 **The Thirty Years' War** Discuss how the Thirty Years' War affected Europe.	Reproducible Lesson Plan Reading Essentials and Study Guide 29-6 Chapter 29 Activity Book Activity Section 6 Quiz	Vocabulary PuzzleMaker ExamView® Pro Testmaker Glencoe Skillbuilder Interactive Workbook, Level 1
Chapter 29 **Review and Evaluation**	Chapter 29 Reteaching Activity Chapter 29 Performance Assessment Activity Unit 9 Standardized Test Practice Spanish Chapter Summary and Glossary Chapter 29 Test	Interactive Tutor Self-Assessment Software Glencoe Skillbuilder Interactive Workbook, Level 1 Audiocassettes* ExamView® Pro Testmaker

*Also available in Spanish.

Presentation Plus!

Use Glencoe's **Presentation Plus!** multimedia teacher tool to easily present dynamic lessons that visually excite your students. Using Microsoft® PowerPoint, you can customize the presentations to create your own personalized lessons.

Interactive Lesson Planner

Planning has never been easier! Using this CD-ROM, organize your week, month, semester, or year with all the help you need. The **Interactive Lesson Planner** gives you access to all of the blackline masters which accompany *Human Heritage.*

✓ PERFORMANCE ASSESSMENT ACTIVITIES

Comparing Reformers Have students choose one of the following reformers to compare to a modern reformer of their choice: Teresa of Avila, William Tyndale, Charles Borromeo, John Knox, Jan Hus, or John Wycliffe. Tell students to create a poster that parallels the achievements of both reformers.

CHAPTER RESOURCES

LITERATURE ABOUT THE PERIOD

Dumas, Alexandre. *The Three Musketeers.* Translated by Henry L. Williams. Street and Smith, 1919. Exaggerated tale of four swashbucklers in France during the reign of Louis XIII.

READINGS FOR THE STUDENT

Cowie, Leonard W. *Martin Luther: Leader of the Reformation* (A Pathfinder Biography). Frederick Praeger, 1969. Detailed biography of Luther.

O'Dell, Scott. *The Hawk that Dare Not Hunt by Day.* Houghton Mifflin, 1975. Novel about a boy who helps the reformer Tyndale smuggle his translation of the Bible into England.

READINGS FOR THE TEACHER

Bainton, Roland H. *The Age of Reformation.* Van Nostrand Reinhold Company, 1956. Shows how the Christian faith shaped history during the Reformation.

KEY TO ABILITY LEVELS

Teaching strategies have been coded for varying learning styles and abilities.

L1 Level 1 activities are **basic** activities and should be within the ability range of all students.

L2 Level 2 activities are **average** activities and should be within the ability range of the average to above-average student.

L3 Level 3 activities are **challenging** activities designed for the ability range of above-average students.

ELL ELL activities should be within the ability range of English Language Learning students.

NATIONAL GEOGRAPHIC SOCIETY

Teacher's Corner

INDEX TO NATIONAL GEOGRAPHIC MAGAZINE

The following article relates to this chapter:

• "The World of Martin Luther," by Merle Severy, October 1983.

NATIONAL GEOGRAPHIC SOCIETY PRODUCTS AVAILABLE FROM GLENCOE

To order the following, call Glencoe at 1-800-334-7344:

• *PicturePack: Europe (Transparencies)*
• *STV: World Geography (Videodisc)*
• *Picture Atlas of the World (CD-ROM)*

ADDITIONAL NATIONAL GEOGRAPHIC SOCIETY PRODUCTS

To order the following, call National Geographic at 1-800-368-2728:

• *National Geographic Atlas of World History (Book)*
Access *National Geographic's* new dynamic MapMachine Web site and other geography resources at:
http://www.nationalgeographic.com
http://www.nationalgeographic.com/maps/

THE HISTORY CHANNEL® | **A&E HOME VIDEO®** | **Biography®**

The following videotape program is available from Glencoe:

• **Elizabeth I: The Virgin Queen**
  0-7670-0209-1

To order, call Glencoe at 1-800-334-7344. To find classroom resources to accompany many of these, check:

A&E Television: http://www.aetv.com
The History Channel: http://www.historychannel.com

OVERVIEW

Chapter 29 examines the Protestant and Catholic reformations.

➤ **Section 1** discusses Martin Luther's excommunication.
➤ **Section 2** describes the founding of Protestantism.
➤ **Section 3** explains the work of Catholic reformers.
➤ **Section 4** examines the Reformation in England.
➤ **Section 5** summarizes the religious wars in Europe in the late 1500s and the 1600s.
➤ **Section 6** discusses the Thirty Years' War.

CHAPTER OBJECTIVES

After reading Chapter 29, students will be able to:

1. explain why Luther's beliefs brought him into conflict with the Roman Catholic Church.
2. describe how Protestantism developed.
3. identify how Catholic reformers changed their Church.
4. discuss the English Reformation.
5. explain why Europeans became involved in religious wars.
6. trace the Thirty Years' War.

EXAMINING ARTIFACTS

Have students state the connection between the two artifacts. *(Luther opposed indulgence boxes.)* Explain that the boxes were used for documents (indulgences) sold to free people from their sins. Ask: Why might Luther object to this practice? Record student responses for review.

PERFORMANCE ASSESSMENT ✓

Use the Performance Assessment activities on page 448B to help you evaluate students as they complete the chapter.

448

The Reformatio
1475 A.D.–1650 A.D.

▲ **Indulgence box—an item Luther opposed**

Martin Luther, Church reformer ▶

1517	1534	1545	1588	1598	1618
Luther posts 95 theses	**Henry VIII heads Church of England**	**Council of Trent meets**	**England defeats the Armada**	**Edict of Nantes is signed**	**Thirty Years' War begins**

448   UNIT 9 BEGINNING OF MODERN TIMES

TEACHING RESOURCES

TEACHER PLANNING AND SUPPORT

- 📁 Reproducible Lesson Plan
- 📁 Block Scheduling Implementation Guide
- 📁 Videodisc Bar Code Correlation
- 💿 Presentation Plus!

REVIEW AND REINFORCEMENT

- 📁 Reading Essentials and Study Guide 29-1, 29-2, 29-3, 29-4, 29-5, 29-6
- 📁 Chapter 29 Vocabulary and Guided Reading Activity
- 💾 Vocabulary PuzzleMaker Software
- 🖨 Teaching Transparencies 29A & 29B

- 📁 Chapter 29 Reteaching Activity
- 📁 Chapter 29 Cooperative Learning Activity
- 📁 Chapter 29 Activity Book Activity
- 📁 Chapter 29 Chart and Graph Skill Activity
- 💾 Interactive Tutor Self-Assessment Software

APPLICATION AND HANDS-ON ACTIVITIES

- 📁 Daily World History, Geography, and Culture Question
- 📁 Unit 9 Hands-On History Lab Activity

Chapter Focus

▷ Read to Discover

Why Martin Luther's beliefs brought him into conflict with the Roman Catholic Church.

How Protestantism developed.

How Catholic reformers worked to improve their Church.

How and why the reformation of the Church of England came about.

How the Thirty Years' War affected Europe.

Terms to Learn	People to Know	Places to Locate
reformation	Martin Luther	Wittenberg
indulgences	Pope Leo X	Geneva
theses	John Calvin	
heretic	Henry VIII	
armada	Mary Tudor	
galleons	Elizabeth I	

Why It's Important   The Roman Catholic Church did not adjust to the many changes taking place in western Europe during the 1400s and 1500s. Many Europeans began to call for a **reformation** (ref uhr mā' shuhn), or a change, in the way the Church taught and practiced Christianity.

Church leaders, however, were too busy with their own and government affairs to make changes. They did not like the reformers' ideas, especially those that could affect their power. Because of this, the unity of the Church was threatened.

HISTORY Online

Chapter Overview
Visit the *Human Heritage* Web site at **humanheritage.glencoe.com** and click on **Chapter 29— Chapter Overviews** to preview this chapter.

✓ Reading Check
Why did many Europeans call for a **reformation?**

SECTION 1   Martin Luther

One reformer who challenged the Church was a German monk named Martin Luther. Luther, born in 1483, was the son of peasants. His family wanted him to be a lawyer, but he decided to become a monk. As a monk, Luther faithfully followed Church teachings and practices. However, he could find no peace of mind. He wondered how God would judge his actions.

While studying the New Testament, Luther found the answer to the questions that had been troubling him. He decided that trusting in Jesus, rather than doing good works, would save people from their sins. Luther's ideas soon brought him into conflict with the Church. In 1517, Pope Leo X wanted money to

---

HISTORY Online

Chapter Overview introduces students to chapter content and key terms. Have them access **Chapter 29 Overview** at **humanheritage.glencoe.com**

FOCUS

📧 Bellringer

Write the following quotation on the board, "*It is neither safe nor prudent to do aught against conscience. Here I stand—I cannot do otherwise. God help me.*" Ask students to write down their first impressions of the speaker.

Motivational Activity

Have students share their impressions of the quotation above. Explain that the person quoted was Martin Luther, the reformer who shattered Christian unity in western Europe.

✓ Reading Check Answer

Many Europeans called for a **reformation** so that the Church would adjust its teachings and practices to the changing times.

GUIDE TO READING

Reading Strategy

Ask students to read "Why It's Important" and summarize the chapter's main theme. *(The unity of the Church was threatened; the unwillingness of Church officials to make changes or listen to the ideas of reformers).*

Vocabulary Precheck

Ask students to define each of the "Terms to Learn." **L1** **ELL**

📁 Assign Chapter 29 Vocabulary and Guided Reading Activity.

📁 Assign Reading Essentials and Study Guide 29-1.

Guided Practice

L1 **History** Have students create a time line of major events during the Reformation of western Europe as they read this chapter. **ELL**

✓ **Reading Check Answer**
Indulgences were documents that freed their owners from the punishment they were due to receive for their sins.

✓ **Reading Check Answer**
In his list of 95 **theses**, Luther stated that only God could forgive sins and challenged anyone who disagreed to debate with him.

CAPTION ANSWER

Pope Leo X wanted money to rebuild Peter's Church in Rome.

VIDEODISC
Turning Points in World History

Side One
Chapter 8

Title: *The Reformation*
Subject: Martin Luther's questioning led to the founding of numerous Protestant sects.
Ask: Who was Martin Luther? *(a professor and priest who founded Lutheranism)*

450

✓ **Reading Check**
What were **indulgences**?

✓ **Reading Check**
What did Luther state in his list of 95 **theses**?

rebuild St. Peter's Church in Rome. He sent out monks to sell **indulgences** (in dul' juhnt sez), or documents that freed their owners from the punishment they were due to receive for their sins. Luther believed the sale of indulgences led people to think they could buy God's forgiveness for their sins.

One night Luther posted a list of 95 **theses** (thē' sēz), or statements of beliefs, on the door of the castle church in Wittenberg (wit' uhn buhrg), Germany. In the list, Luther stated that only God could forgive sins. He challenged anyone who disagreed to debate with him.

Luther began to attack other Catholic beliefs openly. He said that Popes could make mistakes; that the only true guide to religious truth was the Bible, which every Christian had the right to read; and that every Christian had the right to pray to God without the aid of a priest.

In 1520, Pope Leo condemned Luther's teachings and excommunicated him. Leo insisted that the German emperor,

SALE OF INDULGENCES Hoping to lessen God's punishment upon them, many Christians bought the indulgences offered by the Church. Here, indulgences are sold at the village marketplace. **Why was the Church selling indulgences?**

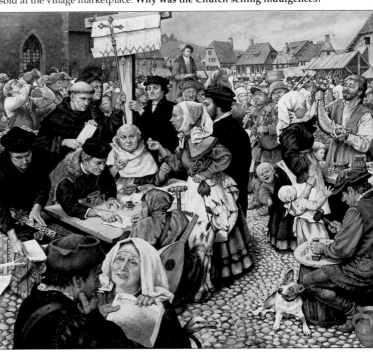

COOPERATIVE LEARNING

Divide students into two teams: one representing John Tetzel, the Church's agent for selling indulgences in northern Germany, and the other representing Martin Luther. Have students research the practice of selling indulgences and prepare arguments from the point of view of the person they represent. Have each team choose its representative to debate this proposition:

The sale of indulgences is justified by the beauty of the rebuilt St. Peter's Basilica that it helps to finance. One student should serve as moderator. Conclude by having the entire class analyze the arguments.

📁 Assign the Chapter 29 *Cooperative Learning Activity* in the TCR.

Charles V, try Luther as a **heretic** (her' uh tik), or person who holds a belief that is different from the accepted belief of the Church. Charles was loyal to the Church, but he relied on German princes who supported Luther. To keep their loyalty, Charles agreed to give Luther a fair trial. At the same time, he secretly promised the Pope that Luther would be condemned. In 1521, Luther was tried by the German Diet of Worms. When he refused to give up his ideas, he was condemned for heresy.

✓ **Reading Check** Why did the Pope want to try Luther as a **heretic?**

✓ **Reading Check Answer** The Pope wanted to try Luther as a **heretic** because he disagreed with accepted Church beliefs.

L2 Critical Thinking Have students imagine they are the editor of the Worms newspaper. Tell them to write an editorial—from the Church's point of view—about Luther's appearance before the diet.

💾 Use **Interactive Tutor Self-Assessment Software** to review Section 1.

Section 1 Assessment

1. **Define:** reformation, indulgences, theses, heretic.
2. Why did Luther come into conflict with the Church?
3. What happened to Luther at Worms?

Critical Thinking

4. **Identifying the Central Issue** What was the central or underlying issue in the debate between Luther and Pope Leo X?

Graphic Organizer Activity

5. Draw this diagram, and use it to summarize Luther's beliefs on indulgences, the Bible, the Pope, and prayer.

MAKING CONNECTIONS

➤➤ **History** After the Diet of Worms, Luther was "kidnapped" by his protector, Prince Frederick of Saxony, and hidden in his castle for a year. In 1525, Luther married Katherina con Bora, a former nun, thus emphasizing his rejection of monastic rules. He died in 1546 and was buried in the castle church in Wittenberg.

SECTION 2 A New Religion

By 1524, most people in northern Germany supported Luther. They left the Roman Catholic Church and formed the Lutheran (lū' thuhr uhn) Church.

The Lutheran princes of Germany had strong armies, which Charles V could not defeat. In 1555, Charles realized he could not force the people to return to the Roman Catholic Church. He then agreed to sign a treaty known as the Peace of Augsburg (ogz' buhrg). There could be both Catholic and Lutheran churches in Germany. The Peace of Augsburg kept German Lutherans and Catholics from fighting each other for nearly 50 years.

Protestant Groups   Luther's ideas soon spread to other areas of Europe. People in Scandinavia founded Lutheran churches. Preachers and merchants in Switzerland (swit' suhr uhnd) also left the Roman Catholic Church. They set up Reformed churches. Because they protested against Catholic ideas, Lutheran and Reformed churches were called Protestant (prot' uh stuhnt). Protestant church leaders were called **ministers.** They spent more time teaching from the Bible. They conducted services in the language of the area instead of in Latin. This made services easier for people to understand.

✓ **Reading Check** How did Protestant **ministers** differ from Catholic priests?

✓ **Reading Check Answer** **Ministers** spent more time teaching from the Bible, conducted services in the language of the area instead of in Latin, and made services easier for people to understand.

💾 Use the **Vocabulary Puzzle-Maker** to create crossword and word search puzzles.

CHAPTER 29 THE REFORMATION   **451**

Section 1 Assessment Answers

1. reformation, a change (p. 449); indulgences, documents that freed owners from punishment for their sins (p. 450); theses, statements of beliefs (p. 450); heretic, person who holds a belief different from accepted Church beliefs (p. 451)
2. believed that trusting in Jesus, rather than doing good works, would save people from their sins
3. He was condemned for heresy.
4. that the purchase of indulgences would free people from punishment for their sins
5. Sample responses: *indulgences*—that people could not buy forgiveness for their sins; *Bible*—that it was the only guide to religious truth; *Pope*—that the Pope could make mistakes; *prayer*—that every Christian had the right to pray to God without the aid of a priest

Assign the Chapter 29 **Section 1 Quiz** in the TCR. Testmaker available.

Painting of John Calvin

Ulrich Zwingli was important in leading the Protestant movement in Switzerland. Zwingli lived from 1484 to 1531. Unlike Luther, however, he wanted to break completely from Catholic rituals. He ordered the removal of images from churches, and he wanted to close monasteries. Zwingli led a group of Protestants from Zurich, Switzerland, in a battle against Catholic forces in 1531 and was killed. After Zwingli's death the Protestant church was firmly established in Switzerland.

John Calvin The most powerful Reformed group was in the Swiss city of Geneva (juh nē' vuh). There, John Calvin set up the first Protestant church governed by a council of ministers and elected church members. Calvin also wrote books that became a guide for Protestants throughout Europe.

Calvin believed that there was nothing in the past, present, or future that God did not know about or control. He also held that from the beginning of time, God decided who would be saved and who would not. Calvin used the scriptures to support his ideas. He believed that God's will was written in the Bible, which ministers had the right to interpret. The ministers also had the right to make sure everyone obeyed God's will. Calvin had the Geneva town council pass laws to force people to follow strict rules of behavior. They could not dance, play cards, go to the theater, or take part in drinking parties. Those who refused to obey these laws were put in prison, executed, or banished.

Calvinism taught people to work hard and to save money. For this reason, many rich merchants supported Calvin. With their help, Calvin worked to improve Geneva. Streets and buildings were kept clean. New workshops opened, providing more jobs for people. Persecuted Protestants from all over Europe found safety in Geneva. Young men came to study at the school Calvin founded to train Reformed ministers. Many of them later returned to their own countries to set up Reformed churches.

Section 2 Assessment

1. **Define:** ministers.
2. What was the Peace of Augsburg?
3. Why were Lutheran and Reformed churches called Protestant?

Critical Thinking

4. **Analyzing Information** What ideas of Calvinism do you agree with? What ideas do you disagree with?

Graphic Organizer Activity

5. Draw this diagram, and use it to compare Protestant and Catholic practices.

Protestant Practices	Catholic Practices

SECTION 3 Catholic Reform

While Protestants formed new churches, Catholic reformers worked to improve their church. Many came from Spain and Italy, the leading countries of the Catholic reform movement.

One of the best known Catholic reformers was Ignatius (ig nā' shē uhs) of Loyola (loi ō' luh). In 1521, he gave up his life as a Spanish noble to serve God and the Roman Catholic Church. In 1540, he founded the Society of Jesus. Its members were called Jesuits (jezh' ū its). This group was formed to spread Roman Catholic ideas to all parts of the world. Jesuits also worked to help the people strengthen their faith. They wore black robes and lived simple lives. They set up schools, helped the poor, and preached to the people. They also taught in universities, served as advisers in royal courts. Jesuit missionaries were the first to carry Catholic ideas to India, China, and Japan.

Linking Across Time

St. Peter's Basilica   In 1506, Donato Bramante proposed a bold design for the rebuilding of St. Peter's Basilica. Instead of medieval spires, he revived the Roman dome, as captured in a medal issued by Pope Julius II (left). Work progressed slowly, and in 1546 71-year-old Michelangelo took over the project. Today the inner dome, built to Michelangelo's specifications, is considered one of the world's great architectural feats (right). **What other steps did Catholic reformers take to revive the Church's influences?**

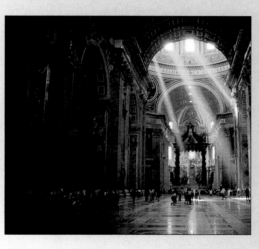

CHAPTER 29 THE REFORMATION   **453**

Then... & Now

Church Membership
Worldwide, the Roman Catholic Church is still the largest Christian church, with about 968 million people. About 466 million follow some of the many varieties of Protestantism. The next largest Christian community, with nearly 218 million, includes the different congregations of the Eastern Orthodox Church, which was once centered in Constantinople.

🖫 Use the **Vocabulary PuzzleMaker** to create crossword and word search puzzles.

MAKING CONNECTIONS

➤➤ **Geography: Region** In 1549, Jesuit missionaries began preaching in Japan. They were expelled in 1638. In 1600, Jesuit missionaries established themselves at Beijing, China, where they served for 200 years as advisers to the emperor in astronomy, mathematics, translation, and other areas. Encourage students to locate this city on a map.

Linking Across Time

Catholic reformers worked to improve their church by forming societies such as the Jesuits, acting as missionaries, living simple lives, helping people to strengthen their faith, setting up schools, helping the poor, and using reason and good deeds to defend the Church.

LINKING PAST TO PRESENT

The Catholic Reformation renewed religious enthusiasm in the arts, sparking a new style of art and music called *baroque*. Renaissance art had demonstrated symmetry, order, and restraint, but baroque art employed asymmetry and exaggeration for dramatic effect. This art style had great influence on later generations of artists.

EXTENDING THE CONTENT

In addition to Loyola, the movement for Catholic reform (or the Counter-Reformation) produced other outstanding and unforgettable figures. Francis Xavier, an early follower of Loyola, was perhaps the most indefatigable missionary since Paul. Following closely behind Portuguese explorers who reached India, Francis Xavier brought Catholic Christianity to Asia, establishing Jesuit communities in India, Goa, Ceylon (Sri Lanka), and Hong Kong. He was one of the first Europeans in Japan (1549).

453

L3 **Critical Thinking** Ask: Why do you think another name for the Catholic Reformation is the Counter-Reformation? *(The Catholic Church was reacting to the Protestant Reformation.)*

GEOGRAPHY AND HISTORY

The reason masses were spoken in Latin only was to insure religious uniformity regardless of what country or area in which the service was to be held.

CAPTION ANSWER

to discuss changes in the Church and to defend Catholic teachings

LINKING PAST TO PRESENT

The Catholic Church published the *Index Librorum Prohibitorum*—Index of Prohibited Books—until 1966.

Reading Check Answer

A **seminary** was a school for training priests.

COUNCIL OF TRENT   Meeting three times between 1545 and 1563, the Council of Trent helped to renew Catholic life and worship. In this painting bishops and other church leaders from throughout Europe debate an issue at a session of the Council. **Why did the Pope call for the Council of Trent?**

The Jesuits used reason and good deeds to defend the Roman Catholic Church against criticisms. They also tried to bring Protestants back to the Church. Because of their work, people in eastern European countries such as Poland, Bohemia (bō hē mē uh), and Hungary once again became loyal to the Roman Catholic Church.

During this time, the Pope also took steps to strengthen the Roman Catholic Church. He called a council of bishops to discuss reforms and to defend Catholic teachings. The council met at different times between 1545 and 1563 at Trent, Italy. The Council of Trent ended many Church practices that had been criticized for hundreds of years such as the sale of indulgences. Church leaders were ordered to follow strict rules. Each diocese was told to build a **seminary** (sem' uh ner ē), or a school to train priests.

The Council of Trent also explained Catholic doctrine. It said that good works, as well as faith, helped people get to heaven. It also held that the Church alone decided how the Bible was to be interpreted and that mass would be said in Latin only. Together, the Council of Trent and the Jesuit missionaries helped the Pope reclaim Protestant areas.

Reading Check What was the purpose of a **seminary?**

SPOTLIGHT ON: HENRY VIII

Henry VIII was typical of Renaissance rulers—a king who tried to excel in many areas. As a youth he had a lean, athletic physique and a keen mind. He enjoyed tennis, jousting, music, and discussions about astronomy and geometry. He composed several pieces of music and may have even written the song "Greensleeves." He also wrote the book called *Assertions of the Seven Sacraments,* in which as a devout Catholic he attacked the views of Martin Luther.

Section 3 Assessment

1. **Define:** seminary.
2. What were the leading countries involved in the Catholic reform movement?
3. What did the Council of Trent do?

Critical Thinking

4. **Evaluating Information** "The Council of Trent was important in strengthening the Roman Catholic Church." What is your opinion of this statement? Explain.

Graphic Organizer Activity

5. Draw this diagram, and use it to describe the Jesuits founded by Ignatius of Loyola.

Jesuits

SECTION 4 | A Middle Way

Reformation of the Church in England was led by a monarch, not by church leaders. It started as a political quarrel between the Tudor king Henry VIII and Pope Clement VII. Religious beliefs did not play a part in the struggle until later.

HENRY VIII AND ANNE BOLEYN   Henry's hopes for a son made him determined to marry Anne Boleyn and led to a political break with the Pope. In this painting Henry and Anne are shown at the home of Thomas Wolsey, the king's chief adviser. **How was Henry eventually able to marry Anne Boleyn?**

Independent Practice

L2 **Critical Thinking** Have students watch a film portraying people from the time period discussed in this chapter, such as *Anne of a Thousand Days* (Anne Boleyn) or *A Man for All Seasons* (Thomas More). Have them write notes about the presentation and decide from what point of view these people are represented. **ELL**

CAPTION ANSWER

Henry set up the Anglican Church and received permission from the Archbishop of Canterbury to end his marriage to Catherine of Aragon.

DID YOU KNOW

Henry's desire for an heir and a happy marriage led him to marry six times.

💾 Use the **Vocabulary Puzzle-Maker** to create crossword and word search puzzles.

Painting of Thomas Cranmer

The Break With Rome

The trouble between Henry VIII and the Pope began in 1527. At that time, Henry was married to Catherine of Aragon, the daughter of Ferdinand and Isabella of Spain and the aunt of German emperor Charles V. Henry and Catherine had only one living child, Mary. As Catherine grew older, Henry feared she could not have any more children. This was very important to Henry because he wanted a son to succeed to the throne.

At the same time, Henry had fallen in love with Anne Boleyn (bu lin') a young woman of the court. He wanted Pope Clement to end his marriage to Catherine so that he could marry Anne, by whom he hoped to have a son. When the Pope refused, Henry declared that the Pope no longer had power over the Church in England. Henry was then excommunicated.

In 1534, the English Parliament passed a law stating that the king was head of the Church of England. Any English church leader who did not accept the law would stand trial as a heretic. Thomas Cranmer (kran' muhr), the Archbishop of Canterbury and the most important church leader in England, supported Henry. Cranmer helped Henry end his marriage to Catherine. Henry then married Anne Boleyn, who gave him one child, a daughter named Elizabeth. A few years later, Henry had Anne executed for treason. He then married Jane Seymour (sē' mōuhr) who died shortly after giving Henry the son he wanted.

Edward and Mary

When Henry VIII died, his nine-year-old son became King Edward VI. Since Edward was too young and sick to rule, a council of nobles governed England for him. Most of the council members were Protestants, and they brought Protestant doctrines into the English Church. Thomas Cranmer supported the council. He wanted the people to have an orderly form of Protestant worship. To help achieve this, he wrote a worship service in English called the *Book of Common Prayer*. It was used in all the churches in England.

Painting of Edward VI

When Edward died in 1553, the council of nobles tried to bring a Protestant noblewoman to the throne. Their attempt failed, however, because the people of England refused to accept any ruler who was not a Tudor. They wanted Henry's daughter Mary as their monarch.

Mary was Catholic. As soon as she became queen, she accepted the Pope as head of the English Church. She then insisted that all English men and women return to the Roman Catholic Church. Many Protestants refused and were persecuted. More than 300 of them, including Cranmer, were burned at the stake for heresy. The people turned against their queen, calling her "Bloody Mary."

Mary was married to King Philip II of Spain. The English were unhappy about the marriage because Spain was England's

MULTICULTURAL PERSPECTIVES

Anabaptists, Protestant sects in western Europe who admitted only adult members, denied the authority of local governments to direct their lives. They refused to hold office, bear arms, or swear oaths, and many lived separate from a society they saw as sinful. As a result, they were often perse-cuted by government officials, forcing many Anabaptists to wander from country to country seeking refuge. Many Anabaptist groups left Europe for North America during the 1600s. There they promoted the ideas of religious liberty and separation of church and state.

PHILIP II AND MARY TUDOR   Queen of England from 1553 to 1558, Mary I shown in this painting (right) longed to bring England back to the Roman Catholic Church. Mary married Philip II (left) of Spain, shown here, who considered himself the champion of the Roman Catholic faith. **Why did the English people object to the marriage of Mary and Philip?**

enemy and the leading Catholic power in Europe. They feared that Philip and the Pope would become the real rulers of England. The people decided that England would remain free only if it became a Protestant country. For this reason, they wanted a Protestant ruler.

Elizabeth's Church   Mary died in 1558 without a child to succeed her. Thus, her half-sister, Elizabeth, became queen. Elizabeth I was Protestant. With the help of Parliament, she ended the Pope's authority in the English Church.

Elizabeth was very popular with her subjects. She worked to set up the Church in a form that would appeal to as many people as possible. Elizabeth and Parliament decided that the Church should be Protestant. However, the Church would keep some Catholic features. The monarch would be head of the Church, which would use Cranmer's prayer book and teach Protestant beliefs.

How did the religious turmoil in England influence the colonization of America? Encourage students to brainstorm ideas, and then research to find how valid their ideas were. Encourage them to make a graphic organizer of their ideas.

CAPTION ANSWER

Spain was England's enemy and the leading Catholic power in Europe. The English people feared that Philip and the Pope would become the real rulers of England.

MAKING CONNECTIONS

➤➤ **Religion** The combination of Protestant beliefs and Catholic rituals devised by Elizabeth and Parliament became known as the beliefs of Anglicanism.

Biography

The following videotape program is available from Glencoe to enrich Chapter 29:

- **Elizabeth I: The Virgin Queen**

To find classroom resources to accompany this video, check the following home page:

A&E Television:
http://www.aetv.com

MEETING SPECIAL NEEDS

Help visual learners create an outline of Section 4 on the chalkboard. Place the following brief outline on the chalkboard. Then have students give details to complete the outline.

How the Reformation of the Church of England Came About:
  I. Henry VIII
  II. Edward VI
  III. Mary Tudor
  IV. Elizabeth I

📂 Refer to *Inclusion for the Middle School Social Studies Classroom: Strategies and Activities* for additional resources.

HISTORY Online

Student Web Activity objectives, goals, and answers can be found at the **Chapter 29 Web Activity Lesson Plan** at humanheritage.glencoe.com

LINKING PAST TO PRESENT

Several new Protestant sects in western Europe, called Anabaptists, initiated the practice of baptizing only adult members. They based this practice on the belief that only people who could make a free and informed choice to become Christians should be allowed to do so. The Mennonite church originated among Anabaptists in Europe in the 1500s under the leadership of Menno Simons. Many of the Mennonites who migrated to the United States settled in Lancaster County, Pennsylvania.

CAPTION ANSWER

Italy

Use **Interactive Tutor Self-Assessment Software** to review Section 4.

HISTORY Online

Student Web Activity
Visit the *Human Heritage* Web site at **humanheritage.glencoe.com** and click on **Chapter 29— Student Web Activities** to find out more about English monarchs of the Reformation.

ST. TERESA OF AVILA   Another church reformer, St. Teresa of Avila, Spain lived from 1515–1582. As a nun she reformed convent life and wrote about religious life. **What other country besides Spain had many Roman Catholic reformers?**

Most of the English people were pleased with the mix of Protestant belief and Catholic practice since many Catholic rituals remained. Those who were not pleased stayed outside the church. Some Protestants also did not like Elizabeth's Church, but they did not leave it. Because these people wanted to purify the English Church of Catholic ways, they became known as Puritans (pyur' uh tuhnz).

Section 4 Assessment

1. What happened when Pope Clement refused to end Henry VIII's marriage?
2. What did Mary Tudor expect the people to do as soon as she became queen? How did the people feel about this?
3. What was the Church of England like under Elizabeth I?

Critical Thinking

4. **Demonstrating Reasoned Judgment** How effective do you think Elizabeth I was in establishing a new national church?

Graphic Organizer Activity

5. Draw this diagram, and use it to compare the reigns of Mary Tudor and Elizabeth I.

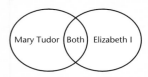

Mary Tudor   Both   Elizabeth I

Section 4 Assessment Answers

1. Henry said he controlled the Church in England and was excommunicated.
2. return to the Roman Catholic Church; many refused and were persecuted
3. led by the monarch, used Cranmer's prayer book, and taught Protestant beliefs
4. Answers will vary, but most students will conclude that Elizabeth successfully defended the new church. Students should be prepared to support their position.

5. Diagrams will vary, but should contrast Mary Tudor's efforts to restore Catholicism with Elizabeth's efforts to protect the Church of England. Both were Tudors— strong-willed daughters of Henry VIII. Both also inherited a religious conflict started in part by their father.

Assign the Chapter 29 **Section 4 Quiz** in the TCR. Testmaker available.

SECTION 2 Wars of Religion

By the middle 1500s, most northern Europeans were Protestants, while most southern Europeans were Catholics. European monarchs had used religion to help unite their people and to build powerful nations. The ruler and people of each country were expected to belong to the same church. Those who refused were persecuted. This led to much bitterness between people of different faiths. Differences in religion also led to wars between countries. Toward the end of the 1500s, Europe entered a period of religious wars that lasted until 1648.

The Armada Under Elizabeth I, England became the leading Protestant power in Europe. Spain, under Philip II, remained the leading Catholic power. Philip knew that if he could defeat England, Protestant Europe would be open to Catholic control. Therefore, he ordered the building of an **armada** (ar mah' duh), or a large group of warships.

After two years, the Spanish Armada, with its 130 ships, was ready. Its strength lay in its **galleons** (gal' ēuhns), or heavy ships with square-rigged sails and long, raised decks. In 1588, the Armada sailed toward England. Its main purpose was to help the Spanish armies on the continent cross over to the English shore.

☑ **Reading Check**
Why did Philip II order the building of an **armada?**

☑ **Reading Check**
What did Spanish **galleons** look like?

SPANISH ARMADA In 1588, the English fleet faced the Spanish Armada in the English Channel. Here, English fire ships move toward the Armada. This action broke the curved formation of the Spanish ships and made possible a successful English attack. **What was the main strength of the Spanish Armada?**

DID YOU KNOW

When the Spanish Armada faced the English ships, the Spanish ships carried 1,100 cannons and about 27,000 men, half of whom were soldiers. The English ships carried about 2,000 cannons and 16,000 sailors.

☑ **Reading Check Answer**
Philip II ordered the building of the **armada** so that he could launch an invasion of Protestant England.

☑ **Reading Check Answer**
Spanish **galleons** were heavy ships with square-rigged sails and long, raised decks.

CAPTION ANSWER

its galleons, or heavy ships with square-rigged sails and long, raised decks

MAKING CONNECTIONS

➤➤ **History** People expected that Elizabeth would marry and that her husband would rule. The common attitude of the time was that only men were fit to rule and that government matters were beyond a woman's ability. Elizabeth, however, feared that marrying a foreign prince would endanger England and that marrying an Englishman would cause jealousy among the English nobility.

COOPERATIVE LEARNING

Divide students into three research groups. Ask them to do research and write a report about one of the Spanish minorities during Philip's reign—Protestants, Marranos, and Moriscos. Reports should include information about daily life, professions, reasons for conversion or defiance in the face of danger, persecution during the Spanish Inquisition, and decisions people made to flee Spain or stay in spite of persecutions. Students should delegate tasks of finding information, organizing ideas, making outlines and note cards, and writing the drafts.

GEOGRAPHY AND HISTORY

Spain and France posed the greatest naval threats to England. The attack of the Spanish Armada made England realize the dangers of an alliance between Spain and France. As a result England relied on diplomacy as well as sea power to protect its interests. During Elizabeth's reign, England worked to balance the power of European nations.

People in History

Elizabeth I
1533–1603

English Queen

Elizabeth came to the throne at age 25. She faced a nation deeply in debt, caught up in European wars, and torn apart by religious conflicts at home. King Philip II offered to marry her, but Elizabeth rejected him— and all other suitors as well. Instead, she led England through one of its greatest eras, producing a united country, a strong navy, and a powerful European nation.

Elizabeth knew the Spanish forces were coming and prepared England for war. She had a naval commander, John Hawkins, reorganize the English fleet. He remodeled old ships and built new ones. He formed a new navy of 134 fighting ships and merchant vessels. Most of the ships were smaller than the Spanish ships, but they had larger guns and more ammunition. Expert sailors handled the English ships with much skill. One naval captain, Sir Francis Drake, was known for his overseas voyages and his capture of Spanish merchant ships.

The English knew they had to make the Spanish ships break their curved formation. Their chance came when the Spanish fleet anchored off the coast of Europe to wait for the Spanish armies to meet it. That night, the English set fire to eight small ships and sent them into the Spanish fleet. As the burning ships reached the Armada, the Spanish ships broke formation and began to drift. The English were then able to fight the Spanish ships one by one.

The Spanish naval command soon realized that the Armada was defeated. Short of food and water, it decided to return to Spain. A great storm came up, however, causing the voyage to be long and difficult. Only half the Armada reached home.

The English celebrated their victory with bonfires and parades. Although Spain was still a powerful enemy, England had shown it could defend itself. The English gained respect throughout Europe as champions of the Protestant cause. The defeat of the Armada allowed northern Europe to remain a Protestant stronghold.

The Huguenots Most people in France during the 1500s were Catholics. Many nobles, lawyers, doctors, and merchants, however, were Protestants. These French Protestants, who were called Huguenots (hyū' guh nots), followed Calvin's teachings.

In 1534, King Francis I, who was Catholic, forbade the Huguenots to worship freely. He wanted all French people to support the Roman Catholic Church. Catholics began to persecute Huguenots, and by 1562 a civil war broke out. By then, Charles IX had become king. Since he was too young to rule, his mother, Catherine de Medici, ruled for him.

Catherine tried to keep peace by showing favor first to one group and then to the other. She finally decided to support the Roman Catholic Church. In 1572, she allowed Catholic nobles to kill the leading Huguenots in Paris. Catholic mobs in other parts of France began to kill Protestants and burn their homes. Many Protestants left the country. The few who remained to carry on the fight were led by Henry of Navarre (nuh var'), a Huguenot prince.

In 1589, the king of France was killed. Henry of Navarre, who was next in line for the throne, became Henry IV. He wanted to gain the loyalty of the people. Since most French people were still

EXTENDING THE CONTENT

Ruling France as regent for her sons, Catherine de Medici balanced Catholic and Huguenot rivalries for many years. The leader of the Huguenots was Henry of Navarre, who was in line for the throne after Catherine's sons. On August 24, 1572—St. Bartholomew's Day—the queen's daughter Margaret of Valois was to marry Henry of Navarre in Paris. Most Protestant nobles came to the wedding, where hired assassins attacked and murdered them all except Henry and another heir to the throne. At the same time, mobs of Catholic Parisians turned on their Protestant neighbors and slaughtered thousands of them. As the killing spread to the countryside, more than 10,000 Huguenots were killed in the next six weeks.

Drawing Conclusions

"Elementary, my dear Watson." Detective Sherlock Holmes often said these words to his assistant when he solved yet another mystery. Holmes would examine all the available evidence, or facts, and draw conclusions to solve the case.

Learning the Skill Drawing conclusions allows you to understand ideas that are not stated directly. Follow these steps in learning to draw conclusions:

- Review the facts that are stated directly.
- Use your knowledge and insight to develop some new conclusions about these facts.
- Look for information to check the accuracy of your conclusions.

Glencoe's **Skillbuilder Interactive Workbook, Level 1,** provides instruction and practice in key social studies skills.

CRITICAL THINKING SKILLS

Skill Practice

The excerpt on this page comes from a speech delivered to Parliament by Queen Elizabeth in 1601, just two years before her death. In it, she reviews her reign as queen. Read this excerpt, and then answer the questions that follow.

To be a king and wear a crown is a thing more glorious to them that see it than it is pleasing to them that bear it. For myself, I was never so much enticed with the glorious name of a king, or royal authority of a queen, as delighted . . . to defend this kingdom (as I said) from peril, dishonour, tyranny, and oppression.

There will never [be a] queen sit in my seat with more zeal to my country . . . and that sooner . . . will venture her life for your good and safety than myself. . . . And though you have had, and may have many princes, more mighty and wise sitting in this state; yet you never had, or shall have, any more careful and loving.

1. How does Elizabeth say she views the title of queen?
2. What aspect of being England's ruler has "delighted" her the most?
3. What conclusion can you draw from this speech about how Elizabeth would like to be remembered?
4. What evidence from the speech supports your conclusion?

461

TEAM-TEACHING STRATEGY

Language Arts Work with a language arts teacher to describe some of the features of a mystery—a novel, play, or story centering on efforts to solve a crime. Explain to students that a mystery—a form of popular fiction—is sometimes called a "whodunit." Ask students how they think mysteries got this nickname. *(because stories center on efforts to figure out who committed a crime)*

Next, divide students into groups, and assign each group to create a mystery set in Elizabethan England. Somebody has kidnapped the queen, and the main character has the job of figuring out "whodunit." Tell students to fill their stories with clues and possible suspects. Each group should end their story with the question: Whodunit?

Call on students to read their mysteries aloud. Challenge the rest of the class to draw conclusion, based on clues, about who kidnapped the queen.

L1 **Religion** Before beginning the section on the Thirty Years' War, refer students to the map "Religions of Europe" on page 463 and have them familiarize themselves with the religions of the areas involved in the war.

ELL

L2 **History** Divide the class into two groups. Have students in one group imagine they are living in France in 1648 and students in the other group imagine they are living in Germany during the same year. Tell students that the Thirty Years' War has just ended. Ask students to write an eyewitness account of how life in their country has changed since the war ended. The account should include any changes that have occurred in religion. Have volunteers read their accounts to the class.

💾 Use **Interactive Tutor Self-Assessment Software** to review Section 5.

💾 Use the **Vocabulary Puzzle-Maker** to create crossword and word search puzzles.

Catholic, he decided to convert. Nevertheless, Henry ended the fighting between Protestants and Catholics. Although he made Catholicism the national religion, he also made life easier for Protestants. In 1598, he signed the Edict of Nantes (nahnts), which gave Huguenots freedom of worship. France thus became the first European country to allow two Christian religions.

The Low Countries   The Low Countries were part of the Spanish Empire. The people of the Low Countries were divided into Protestants and Catholics. Neither group liked Philip II's harsh rule. They did not like the heavy taxes imposed by Spain or the Spanish laws. Philip, however, made money from the wealth and trade of the Low Countries. He wanted to keep them under Spanish control.

Philip also wanted all his subjects to be Catholic. To achieve this, he set up an Inquisition in the Low Countries to stamp out Protestantism. In 1567, Protestants in the northern provinces revolted. Philip sent soldiers to restore order. They were joined by French Catholics from the southern provinces.

The fighting did not end until 1648. At that time, it was decided that the southern provinces, known today as Belgium, were to remain Catholic and continue under the rule of Spain. The northern provinces, known today as the Netherlands, were to be an independent Protestant country.

Section 5 Assessment

1. **Define:** armada, galleons.
2. How did the English defeat the Spanish Armada?
3. What led to civil war in France in 1562?

Critical Thinking

4. **Identifying Alternatives**   How do you think the religious wars in Europe in the 1500s and 1600s might have been avoided?

Graphic Organizer Activity

5. Draw this diagram, and use it to show the causes and effects of the Edict of Nantes.

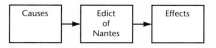

SECTION 6 **The Thirty Years' War**

During the 1590s and early 1600s, the German states began to quarrel over the terms of the Peace of Augsburg. They formed alliances based on religion. The Catholic alliance was led by the German emperor Ferdinand II.

Section 5 Assessment Answers

1. armada, group of warships (p. 459); galleons, ships with square-rigged sails (p. 459)
2. by causing the Spanish ships to break formation and fighting the Spanish ships one by one
3. King Francis I forbade Huguenots to worship freely, and Catholics began to persecute Huguenots.
4. Answers will vary, but could say by allowing different religions to exist in their countries.

5. Sample responses: *causes*—conflicts between Catholics and Protestants in France, desire of Henry IV to win people's loyalty; *effects*—gave Huguenots freedom of worship; made France first European country to allow two Christian religions

Assign the Chapter 29 **Section 5 Quiz** in the TCR. Testmaker available.

One Protestant state that resisted Ferdinand was Bohemia. In 1618, the Protestant nobles of Bohemia revolted. They chose a German Protestant prince as their new king. Ferdinand's armies crushed the Bohemians in a fierce battle, and Ferdinand proclaimed himself king of Bohemia. He did not allow Protestant worship. He sent Jesuits throughout the country to win the people back to the Roman Catholic Church.

The revolt in Bohemia soon grew into the Thirty Years' War. During the war, half the armies of Europe fought in Germany. First Denmark and then Sweden invaded Germany. Their kings were Protestants who wanted to stop the spread of Catholicism. They also hoped to conquer German territory. When the Swedes were finally defeated in 1634, the French became involved. Although France was a Catholic country, it entered the war on the Protestant side. This changed the nature of the war. It became

MAP STUDY

REGIONS By 1560 many Europeans were either Protestants or Catholic. **In which European countries did Calvinism take hold?**

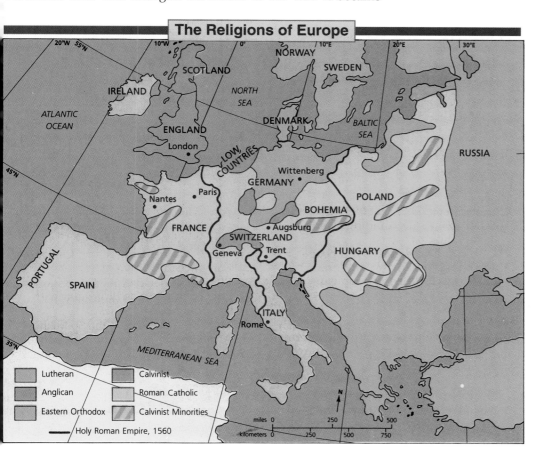

The Religions of Europe

Lutheran
Anglican
Eastern Orthodox
Calvinist
Roman Catholic
Calvinist Minorities
——— Holy Roman Empire, 1560

L1 **Geography: Location** Most of the Thirty Years' War took place in Germany, but soon other powers became involved. Have students list all the powers involved in the Thirty Years' War and locate them on the map on page 463.

DID YOU KNOW

In the midst of the brutal Thirty Years' War, traders brought tulip bulbs into Europe from Turkey. Public demand for tulips reached a peak in the 1630s. Frenzied buyers bid increasingly large sums for the flowers. Investing in tulips became big business.

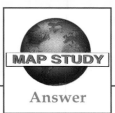

MAP STUDY

Answer

Scotland, Low Countries, Germany, Switzerland
Assign the Chapter 29 **Geography and Map Activity** in the TCR.

GEOGRAPHY AND HISTORY

The splitting of the northern and southern provinces, as discussed in the section on Low Countries, was also part of the Peace of Westphalia.

ASSESS

Check for Understanding

Ask students to summarize the main points of the chapter. Discuss answers to the Section and Chapter Assessment questions.

EXTENDING THE CONTENT

The Thirty Years' War ended as a struggle over the balance of power in Europe. The huge landholdings and family ties between the Spanish and Austrian Hapsburgs combined to make the German Hapsburg emperors dominant, thereby upsetting the balance. France under the Bourbon kings was the only serious political rival. Sweden, Denmark, and the Netherlands entered the war for religious and political reasons. Cardinal Richelieu, Louis XIII's adviser, then brought Catholic France into the war to resist the alarming growth in Hapsburg power. The peace treaty changed the balance of power. German princes were autonomous; Bourbon France dominated western Europe; and Sweden was locally powerful in the north.

Evaluate

Assign the **Chapter 29 Performance Assessment Activity** in the TCR.

Administer the **Chapter 29 Test** in the TCR. Testmaker available.

Reteach

Divide students into six groups. Assign each group a section from this chapter. Have the students write questions about the main ideas of their assigned section and quiz other groups.

Assign the Chapter 29 **Reteaching Activity** in the TCR.

Enrich

Ask students to summarize the main reasons Luther felt he must break away from the Roman Catholic Church.

Assign the Chapter 29 **Enrichment Activity** in the TCR.

CLOSE

Have students discuss how religious wars during this time seemed to have been started by one or two people, but ended up involving whole nations.

💾 Use **Interactive Tutor Self-Assessment Software** to review Section 6.

Self-Check Quiz gives students an interactive chapter tutorial. Have them access **Chapter 29 Quiz** at <u>humanheritage.glencoe.com</u>

---

less a war over religion and more a struggle for territory and wealth.

The German people suffered great hardships during the war. Finally, in 1643, after a serious defeat, the German emperor asked for peace. In 1648, representatives of European nations signed the Peace of Westphalia (west fāl' yuh), which ended the war. The German emperor lost much of his power and France emerged as a strong nation. After this war, Europeans no longer fought over religion. Instead, nations tried to gain power through trade and expansion overseas.

Section 6 Assessment

1. What led to the Thirty Years' War?
2. What effect did the Thirty Years' War have on Europe?

Critical Thinking

3. **Drawing Conclusions** Based on the Thirty Years' War, what conclusions can you draw about the reasons nations go to war?

Graphic Organizer Activity

4. Draw this diagram, and use it to show the main events in the Thirty Years' War. (Add answer boxes as needed.)

| Thirty Years' War | → | Event 1 | → | Event 2 | → | Event 3 | → | Event 4 |

Chapter Summary & Study Guide

1. Luther posted his list of 95 theses to object to the sale of indulgences and other Church practices.
2. Luther's ideas spread, with people in northern Germany forming the Lutheran Church and people in Switzerland and elsewhere adopting what became known as Protestantism.
3. While Protestant reformers established new churches, Catholic reformers worked to improve their Church.
4. Between 1545 and 1563, the Council of Trent reformed many Catholic practices.
5. The reformation came to England when Parliament declared Henry VIII the head of the Church of England.
6. After Henry's death, advisers to his young son Edward introduced Protestant practices to the English Church.
7. Mary Tudor tried to return England to Catholicism, but failed.
8. Elizabeth I decided the Church of England should be Protestant with some Catholic features.
9. The English defeat of the Spanish Armada in 1588 kept northern Europe Protestant, but it did not prevent other religious wars.

Self-Check Quiz

Visit the *Human Heritage* Web site at <u>humanheritage.glencoe.com</u> and click on *Chapter 29—Self-Check Quiz* to assess your understanding of this chapter.

464   UNIT 9 BEGINNING OF MODERN TIMES

Section 6 Assessment Answers

1. the revolt in Bohemia against the German emperor Ferdinand II

2. The German emperor lost much of his power, France emerged as a strong nation, and nations tried to gain power through trade and expansion.

3. Sample conclusion: for religion, land, wealth, and political power. Students should be prepared to support their conclusions.

4. Events may vary, but should be in chronological order. For example: Denmark and Sweden invade Germany, Swedes defeated, France enters the war on Protestant side, Germans suffer serious defeat, German emperor asks for peace, warring nations sign Peace of Westphalia.

Assign the Chapter 29 **Section 6 Quiz** in the TCR. Testmaker available.

Using Key Terms

Use the following words to write a paragraph explaining the conflicts over religion among European countries during the 1500s and 1600s.

reformation   indulgences   theses
heretic   ministers   seminary
armada   galleons

Understanding Main Ideas

1. How did Protestantism get its name, and what were some of the churches that belonged to this faith?
2. What rules of behavior did John Calvin propose for his followers?
3. What organization did Ignatius of Loyola form?
4. Why did Mary Tudor become known as "Bloody Mary"?
5. How did the defeat of the Spanish Armada help the Protestant cause?
6. What was the basis of alliances formed by German states in the 1590s and early 1600s?

Critical Thinking

1. What would you have liked about living in Geneva at the time of John Calvin? What would you have disliked? Explain your answer.
2. Do you approve or disapprove of the way Elizabeth I organized the Church of England? Explain your answer.
3. Explain whether you would or would not have converted to Catholicism if you had been Henry IV.
4. If you had been a Catholic in the mid-1500s, in which European country would you have preferred to live? Why?

Graphic Organizer Activity

History Create a diagram like the one below, and use it to summarize the causes and effects of the reformation on the history of western Europe.

Geography in History

Location Refer to the location of Calvinist minorities on the map of western European religions on p. 463. What connection might there be between their locations and the fact that they are minority groups (groups with fewer members than other religions)?

Using Your Journal

Review any details you may have noted about changes in religion that took place in western Europe during the 1500s and 1600s. Review the Edict of Nantes and the importance it had at the time. Write an editorial explaining why the idea in that edict continues to be important today.

465

Bonus Test Question

For Chapter 29 Test
How would Akbar have treated a non-Muslim farmer in his district whose crops had failed? (*Answers will vary but should include the idea that the treatment would be fair.*)

Using Your Journal

Editorials will vary but might include the idea that the Edict of Nantes had the beginnings of religious freedom, which is guaranteed in the U.S. today.

 Geography in History

The minorities were spread all over Europe in small pockets, while other religious groups lived in larger areas. Smaller groups are more apt to remain minorities if cut off from others of their beliefs.

Using Key Terms

Paragraphs will vary but students should use all the terms.

Understanding Main Ideas

1. Protestants got their name because they protested teaching of the Roman Catholic Church. Some of their churches included the Lutheran and Reformed churches.
2. They could not dance, play cards, go to the theater, or take part in drinking parties.
3. the Society of Jesus
4. because under her rule, many Protestants were persecuted or burned at the stake for heresy
5. It allowed northern Europe to remain a Protestant stronghold.
6. religion

Critical Thinking

1. Answers will vary but should make reference to the agreement or disagreement with Calvinism.
2. Answers will vary but students should explain why they approve or disapprove.
3. Answers will vary but students should provide reasons for their choices.
4. Answers will vary but students should choose a specific location and explain the reasons for their choices.

Graphic Organizer Activity

Sample responses: *causes*— sale of indulgences by the Church, posting of the 95 theses, excommunication of Luther; *effects*—formation of Lutheran and Reformed churches, start of a new form of Christianity known as Protestantism, reforms by the Roman Catholic Church to stop the spread of Protestantism, religious wars, and so on.

Chapter 30 Planning Guide

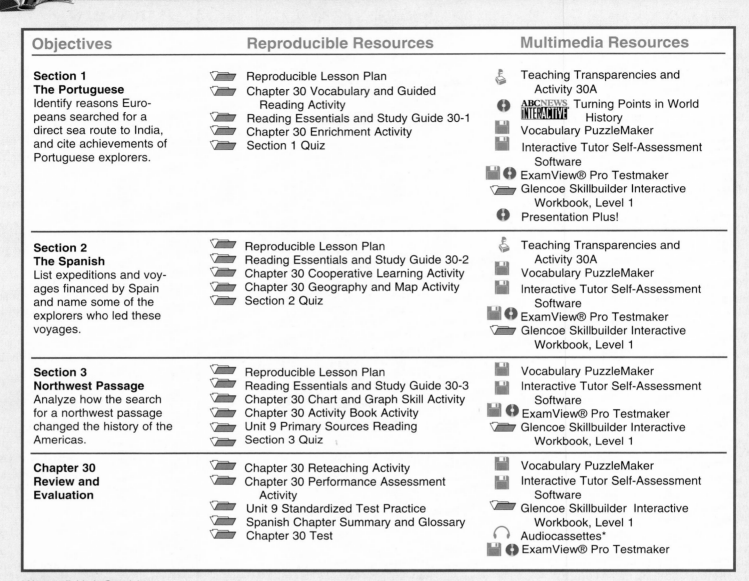

Objectives	Reproducible Resources	Multimedia Resources
Section 1 **The Portuguese** Identify reasons Europeans searched for a direct sea route to India, and cite achievements of Portuguese explorers.	Reproducible Lesson Plan Chapter 30 Vocabulary and Guided Reading Activity Reading Essentials and Study Guide 30-1 Chapter 30 Enrichment Activity Section 1 Quiz	Teaching Transparencies and Activity 30A **ABCNEWS INTERACTIVE** Turning Points in World History Vocabulary PuzzleMaker Interactive Tutor Self-Assessment Software ExamView® Pro Testmaker Glencoe Skillbuilder Interactive Workbook, Level 1 Presentation Plus!
Section 2 **The Spanish** List expeditions and voyages financed by Spain and name some of the explorers who led these voyages.	Reproducible Lesson Plan Reading Essentials and Study Guide 30-2 Chapter 30 Cooperative Learning Activity Chapter 30 Geography and Map Activity Section 2 Quiz	Teaching Transparencies and Activity 30A Vocabulary PuzzleMaker Interactive Tutor Self-Assessment Software ExamView® Pro Testmaker Glencoe Skillbuilder Interactive Workbook, Level 1
Section 3 **Northwest Passage** Analyze how the search for a northwest passage changed the history of the Americas.	Reproducible Lesson Plan Reading Essentials and Study Guide 30-3 Chapter 30 Chart and Graph Skill Activity Chapter 30 Activity Book Activity Unit 9 Primary Sources Reading Section 3 Quiz	Vocabulary PuzzleMaker Interactive Tutor Self-Assessment Software ExamView® Pro Testmaker Glencoe Skillbuilder Interactive Workbook, Level 1
Chapter 30 **Review and Evaluation**	Chapter 30 Reteaching Activity Chapter 30 Performance Assessment Activity Unit 9 Standardized Test Practice Spanish Chapter Summary and Glossary Chapter 30 Test	Vocabulary PuzzleMaker Interactive Tutor Self-Assessment Software Glencoe Skillbuilder Interactive Workbook, Level 1 Audiocassettes* ExamView® Pro Testmaker

*Also available in Spanish.

Presentation Plus!

Use Glencoe's **Presentation Plus!** multimedia teacher tool to easily present dynamic lessons that visually excite your students. Using Microsoft® PowerPoint, you can customize the presentations to create your own personalized lessons.

 Interactive Lesson Planner

Planning has never been easier! Using this CD-ROM, organize your week, month, semester, or year with all the help you need. The **Interactive Lesson Planner** gives you access to all of the blackline masters which accompany *Human Heritage.*

✓ PERFORMANCE ASSESSMENT ACTIVITIES

Drama   Have students write scripts for a class presentation of the first voyage of Christopher Columbus. Encourage students to include at least these scenes: (1) Columbus at the court of Ferdinand and Isabella; (2) Columbus at sea on October 12, 1492; (3) Columbus landing in the Americas.

CHAPTER RESOURCES

LITERATURE ABOUT THE PERIOD

Cervantes, Miguel de. *The Ingenious Gentleman Don Quixote de la Mancha* in *The Portable Cervantes*. Modern Library, 1949. Translation of the adventures of Don Quixote.

READINGS FOR THE STUDENT

Bilaug, Karla (trans. by Neil Jones). *Voyages of Discovery: Through Artists' Eyes*. St. Martin's Press, 1976. Intriguing introduction, for young readers, to art styles as they reflect world discoveries.

Lomask, Milton. *Exploration: Great Lives*. Scribners, 1988. Biographies of explorers.

READINGS FOR THE TEACHER

Fuson, Robert H., translator. *The Log of Christopher Columbus*. International Marine Publishing, 1987. Illustrated translation of Columbus' journal.

Morison, Samuel E. *The European Discovery of America: The Northern Voyages*. Oxford University Press, 1971. Focuses on the discoveries of North America.

KEY TO ABILITY LEVELS

Teaching strategies have been coded for varying learning styles and abilities.

L1 Level 1 activities are **basic** activities and should be within the ability range of all students.

L2 Level 2 activities are **average** activities and should be within the ability range of the average to above-average student.

L3 Level 3 activities are **challenging** activities designed for the ability range of above-average students.

ELL ELL activities should be within the ability range of English Language Learning students.

Teacher's Corner

INDEX TO NATIONAL GEOGRAPHIC MAGAZINE

The following articles relate to this chapter:

- "Why Explore?" by Priit J. Vesilind, February 1998.
- "Treasure From the Silver Bank," by Tracy Bowden, July 1996.
- "Portugal's Sea Road to the East," by Merle Severy, November 1992.

NATIONAL GEOGRAPHIC SOCIETY PRODUCTS AVAILABLE FROM GLENCOE

To order the following, call Glencoe at 1-800-334-7344:

- *Picture Atlas of the World* (CD-ROM)
- *PicturePack: Age of Exploration, Parts 1 & 2* (Transparencies)
- *PictureShow: Age of Exploration, Parts 1 & 2* (CD-ROMs)

ADDITIONAL NATIONAL GEOGRAPHIC SOCIETY PRODUCTS

To order the following, call National Geographic at 1-800-368-2728:

- *Latitude and Longitude* (Video)

Access *National Geographic's* new dynamic MapMachine Web site and other geography resources at:

http://www.nationalgeographic.com/
http://www.nationalgeographic.com/maps/

The following videotape programs are available from Glencoe:

- **The Aztec Empire**
  0-7670-0542-2

- **Christopher Columbus: Explorer of the New World**
  1-56501-667-X

- **Ponce de Leon: The First Conquistador**
  1-56501-669-6

To order, call Glencoe at 1-800-334-7344. To find classroom resources to accompany many of these check:

A&E Television: http://www.aetv.com
The History Channel:
http://www.historychannel.com

OVERVIEW

Chapter 30 discusses European trade and exploration from the 15th to the 17th centuries.

➤ **Section 1** discusses Portuguese explorations and discoveries.

➤ **Section 2** describes the Spanish race for new trade routes and overseas claims.

➤ **Section 3** explains how England, France, and the Netherlands established claims in the Americas.

CHAPTER OBJECTIVES

After reading Chapter 30, students will be able to:

1. explain why Europeans searched for a sea route to India.

2. list Portuguese discoveries.

3. cite discoveries financed by Spain.

4. discuss how the search for a northwest passage affected the Americas.

EXAMINING ARTIFACTS

Point to the Portuguese bowl, and explain that ships such as these were like present-day space ships. They carried explorers into uncharted seas and lands. Ask: Based on the bronze casting, how did West Africans view the explorers? *(as invaders or conquerors)* Using the time line, have students suggest some of the regions affected by European voyages of discovery.

PERFORMANCE ASSESSMENT ✓

Use the Performance Assessment activities on page 466B to help you evaluate students as they complete the chapter.

CHAPTER 30

The Age of Discovery
1300 A.D.–1620 A.D.

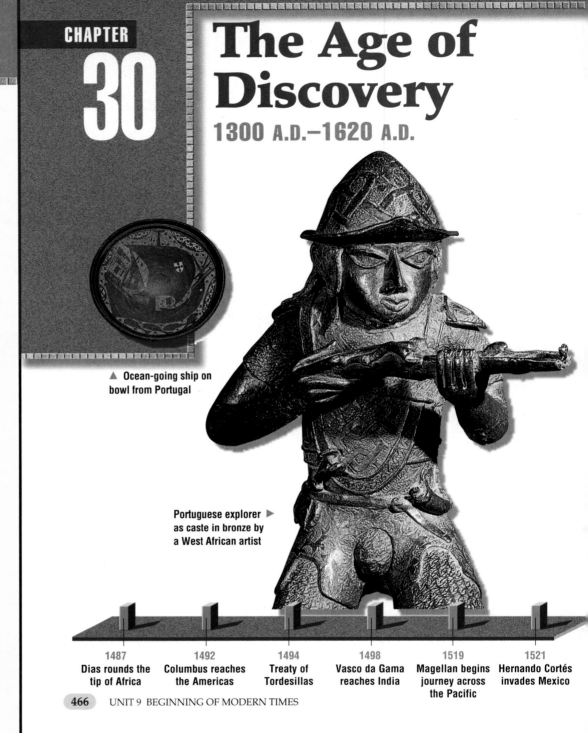

▲ **Ocean-going ship on bowl from Portugal**

Portuguese explorer ▶ as caste in bronze by a West African artist

1487	1492	1494	1498	1519	1521
Dias rounds the tip of Africa	**Columbus reaches the Americas**	**Treaty of Tordesillas**	**Vasco da Gama reaches India**	**Magellan begins journey across the Pacific**	**Hernando Cortés invades Mexico**

466   UNIT 9 BEGINNING OF MODERN TIMES

TEACHING RESOURCES

TEACHER PLANNING AND SUPPORT

- Reproducible Lesson Plan
- Block Scheduling Implementation Guide
- Videodisc Bar Code Correlation
- Presentation Plus!

REVIEW AND REINFORCEMENT

- Reading Essentials and Study Guide 30-1, 30-2, 30-3
- Chapter 30 Vocabulary and Guided Reading Activity
- Vocabulary PuzzleMaker Software
- Teaching Transparencies 30A & 30B
- Chapter 30 Reteaching Activity

- Chapter 30 Cooperative Learning Activity
- Chapter 30 Activity Book Activity
- Chapter 3 Chart and Graph Skill Activity
- Interactive Tutor Self-Assessment Software
- Unit 9 MindJogger VideoQuiz

APPLICATION AND HANDS-ON ACTIVITIES

- Daily World History, Geography, and Culture Question

GEOGRAPHY ACTIVITIES

- Chapter 30 Geography and Map Activity
- Social Studies Outline Map Resource Book

Chapter Focus

 Read to Discover

- Why the Europeans searched for a direct sea route to Asia.
- What Portuguese explorers accomplished.
- How explorers financed by Spain sailed to the Americas and beyond.
- How the search for a northwest passage affected the history of the Americas.

 Terms to Learn | **People to Know** | **Places to Locate**

Terms to Learn	People to Know	Places to Locate
compass	Henry the	Cape of Good
astrolabe	Navigator	Hope
caravel	Vasco da Gama	St. Lawrence
mutiny	Christopher	River
papal line of	Columbus	Hudson River
demarcation	Ponce de León	
conquistadores	Ferdinand	
sea dogs	Magellan	

Why It's Important By the 1500s, Italy controlled Europe's trade with India and other parts of Asia. To break the Italian hold on trade, other European nations began to search for an all-water route to the east. They hoped their journeys would enrich their countries and spread Christianity.

A number of developments—such as more accurate maps, improved ships, and better navigation instruments—aided European explorers. One instrument was the **compass,** which has a magnetic needle that always points north. Another was the **astrolabe** (as' trō lāb), which measures the angle of the stars and helps sailors find latitude. These journeys changed world history forever.

HISTORY Online

Chapter Overview
Visit the *Human Heritage* Web site at **humanheritage.glencoe.com** and click on **Chapter 30— Chapter Overviews** to preview this chapter.

Reading Check
How did the **compass** and the **astrolabe** help explorers chart direction?

SECTION 1 The Portuguese

The desire for new trade routes led to a great age of exploration in the 1400s. Information from such early explorers as Marco Polo was very helpful. The Portuguese were among the first to travel beyond the Mediterranean Sea. The accomplishments of Prince Henry the Navigator and the discoveries of Bartolomeu Dias (bahr thol' uh myū dē ahs) and Vasco da Gama (vas' kō duh gah' muh) opened the way for later explorations.

CHAPTER 30 THE AGE OF DISCOVERY **467**

HISTORY Online

Chapter Overview introduces students to chapter content and key terms. Have them access **Chapter 30 Overview** at **humanheritage.glencoe.com**

FOCUS

Bellringer
Write these words on the board: *cinnamon, cloves, nutmeg, pepper*. Ask students what the words have in common.

Motivational Activity
Discuss student responses. Then link these spices with Christopher Columbus's voyages to the Americas.

Reading Check Answer
The **compass** has a magnetic needle that points north. The **astrolabe** measures the angle of the stars and helps determine latitude.

GUIDE TO READING

Reading Strategy
Ask students to read "Why It's Important" and summarize the chapter's main theme. (*The desire for trade, an interest in spreading Christianity, and new inventions led Europeans to search for new all-water routes to Asia.*)

Vocabulary Precheck
Ask students to define each of the "Terms to Learn." Have a volunteer consult the dictionary for any unfamiliar words. **L1** **ELL**

Use the Vocabulary PuzzleMaker for Chapter 30 to create a crossword puzzle. **L1**

Assign Chapter 30 Vocabulary and Guided Reading Activity.

Assign Reading Essentials and Study Guide 30-1.

TEACH

Guided Practice

L2 **Science** Have students discuss the design innovations of the caravel that contributed to successful voyages by the Portuguese and the Spanish and the scientific principles involved in its buoyancy. Ask students to conclude why explorers could not have ventured very far into the Atlantic or Pacific without the use of caravels. **ELL**

Linking Across Time

Portugal took the lead in exploration.

GEOGRAPHY AND HISTORY

The compass was invented by the Chinese and came to Europe over the Old Silk Road.

Reading Check Answer

The **caravel** combined the heavy, squared-rigged European ship with the light, slim Arab ship to produce a vessel that was faster and easier to handle.

Linking Across Time

Maps Mapmakers often went on voyages of exploration so they could draw more accurate maps of the world, such as this map of Africa (below). In 1972 the United States launched its first Landsat, or land satellite, to beam back even more accurate maps of the earth, such as this image of Africa and the Indian Ocean (right). **What country took the lead in exploration in the early 1400s?**

Prince Henry

Prince Henry the Navigator, son of the king of Portugal, had heard from African merchants about discoveries of gold there. Europe's supplies of *bullion* (būl' yuhn), or gold and silver for making coins, were running out. Prince Henry became eager for Portuguese sailors to explore the west coast of Africa. He also hoped they would find a new route to the Far East. He saw this as a way to extend Portugal's trade and power. The demand for spices such as ginger, cloves, and pepper, which he could obtain there, was great.

In the early 1400s, Henry set up the first European school for navigators in Sagres (sag' rēsh), Portugal. Prince Henry was fascinated by all information concerning sailing, navigation, and astronomy. Although he never sailed on a single ocean voyage himself, Henry organized a way for others to learn the most skilled way to sail. He gathered together Portuguese, Spanish, Jewish, Arab, and Italian mathematicians, chartmakers, astronomers, and sea captains. They taught Portuguese sailors all they knew and helped Henry make better charts, improve navigational instruments, and put together more detailed astronomical tables.

At the same time, Henry worked with others to design and build better ships. The result was the Portuguese **caravel** (kar' uh vel). It combined the heavy, square-rigged European ship

Reading Check

What improvements did the **caravel** bring to sailing?

MEETING SPECIAL NEEDS

Have tactile/kinesthetic learners role play the following roles: East Indian farmer, Muslim trader, Italian trader, Italian merchant, French merchant, French shopkeeper, and French noble to show the trading process. Explain that these characters are to simulate the process by which Chinese spices might have reached a French customer during the 1300s by role-playing each exchange. Tell participants that in the simulation they should identify their role, point out their location on a large wall map, explain their part in the process, and sell the spices to the next character at a profit.

Refer to *Inclusion for the Middle School Social Studies Classroom: Strategies and Activities* for additional resources.

with the light, slim Arab one to produce a ship that was faster and easier to handle.

Henry sent parties of explorers south along Africa's west coast. There, they discovered the Gold Coast and Cape Verde (vuhr' dē), as well as the Azores (ā' zōrz), Madeira (muh dir' uh), and Canary islands. These islands were used as supply stations for further explorations.

In Africa, the Portuguese explorers found gold dust, ivory, and people whom they enslaved. Some explorers soon began to take more interest in trade than in discovery. Trading forts were set up along the west coast of Africa and contacts were established with African leaders. This trade brought new wealth to Portugal, and Henry saw his country become powerful. When he died in 1460, however, Portuguese caravels had gone only part of the way down the west coast of Africa.

Bartolomeu Dias   Exploration went on after Prince Henry's death, but more slowly. In 1473, the Equator was crossed. Europeans discovered that the sea did not boil and was not the

Student Web Activity
Visit the *Human Heritage* Web site at **humanheritage.glencoe.com** and click on *Chapter 30— Student Web Activities* to find out more about Prince Henry the Navigator.

PRINCE HENRY THE NAVIGATOR   Prince Henry's school for navigators helped make possible the great new discoveries of lands and water routes in the 1400s. In this painting Henry watches for his ships to return. **Why did Prince Henry hope to find a new route to the Far East?**

EXTENDING THE CONTENT

Cartographer's skills gradually improved. About 1300, coastal charts showed the Mediterranean coastline with a great degree of accuracy. During the Renaissance, works by the Egyptian Ptolemy reappeared in Europe. His maps, improved over the centuries by Byzantine and Arab scholars, gave Europeans a new picture of the world. Ptolemy also introduced the grid system of map references based on the coordinates of latitude and longitude that is still in use today all over the world.

Student Web Activity objectives, goals, and answers can be found at the *Chapter 30 Web Activity Lesson Plan* at **humanheritage.glencoe.com**

L2 **Geography: Location** Have students demonstrate the use of a compass and a map for orienteering. Suggest volunteers change positions in the room, hold the compass, and check the direction in which the needle is pointing. Explain that a compass needle always points north. Have students refer to the text Atlas and prepare several directional route or location problems for other students to solve.

L2 **Critical Thinking** Ask students to consider the Portuguese exploration of Africa in the context of the development of trade of enslaved Africans. Have them write an essay that discusses whether they think such trade would have developed without Prince Henry's continued interest in African explorations.

CAPTION ANSWER

because he wanted to extend Portugal's trade and power

GEOGRAPHY AND HISTORY

Henry insisted that the logs, charts, and maps from each voyage be carefully guarded. This tight security helped the Portuguese keep their advantage over foreign competitors in the area.

Painting of Vasco da Gama

Goa Goa, on the southwest coast of India, was a Portuguese colony from 1510 until 1961, when it became part of India. Catholic and Hindu traditions blended there. Today the people of Goa celebrate festivals such as Carnival in much the same way as people in Brazil, also once a Portuguese colony.

home of great monsters as had once been believed. Gradually and carefully, Portuguese explorers made their way south along the African coast.

In 1487, Bartolomeu Dias readied ships for a long, hard voyage. Included for the first time was a supply ship with enough water and food for an extended trip. Dias touched at several points on Africa's west coast before strong winds blew him southward. After the storm ended, Dias went on to reach Africa's east coast, without knowing his ships had been blown around the tip of the continent. On the return home, Dias named what he now knew to be the southern tip of Africa the Cape of Storms. The king of Portugal later renamed it the Cape of Good Hope because the Portuguese now knew they could reach the Far East by sailing around Africa.

Vasco da Gama In the summer of 1497, a Portuguese noble named Vasco da Gama led a *convoy* (kon' voi), or group, of four ships down the Tagus (tā' guhs) River from Lisbon, Portugal. The ships had been designed by Bartolomeu Dias. Dias, in fact, accompanied da Gama as far as Cape Verde. Da Gama had orders from the king to "proclaim the Christian faith" and to "wrest kingdoms and new states from the hands of the barbarians."

After four months at sea, da Gama's convoy rounded the Cape of Good Hope. By then, many of the crew were sick. Their water smelled, and their food was spoiling. Still, the convoy continued on, sailing north along the east coast of Africa toward the island of Mozambique (mō zam bēk'). This island was a Muslim trading center. There, the Portuguese sailors saw ships loaded with cargoes of cloves, pepper, gold, silver, pearls, and precious stones. For the first time, they saw a coconut, which they described as "fruit as large as a melon, of which the kernel is eaten." When the Muslims found out that da Gama and his party were Christians, they forced the Europeans to leave.

The next stop was Malindi (mahl in' dē) in present-day Kenya. There, the crew took on supplies and learned to make rope from coconut fiber. The king of Malindi sent da Gama an Arab pilot to lead him to his final destination of Calicut (kal' i kuht), a port and trading center on the southwest coast of India.

On May 20, 1498, da Gama's ships landed at Calicut. His arrival alarmed the Arab and Persian merchants there. They feared that Portugal would take over the trade between Africa and India. An attempt was made to kill da Gama. In August, da Gama decided to leave. He and his crew loaded what spices they could and started home.

The trip back to Lisbon took 11 months for one ship and 13 months for the ship that da Gama was sailing. During that time, the convoy was threatened by storms, and many of the men died of *scurvy* (sker' vē), a disease caused by the lack of vitamin C.

MULTICULTURAL PERSPECTIVES

The *Kilwa Chronicle*, the written history of that city, briefly mentions Vasco da Gama's voyage, which had been reported from Mozambique and from Malindi, farther up the coast: *There came news from the land of Mozambique that men had come from the land of the Franks* [Christian Europe] . . . *After a few days there came word that the ships had passed Kilwa and had gone to Mafia* [another island]. *The lord of Mafia rejoiced, for they thought they were good and honest men. But those who knew the truth confirmed that they* [the Portuguese] *were corrupt and dishonest persons who had only come to spy out the land in order to seize it.*

When the ships finally reached Lisbon in 1499, da Gama was greeted with great rejoicing and rewards. His voyage opened the way for later explorations and for an era of increased trade. Before long, Lisbon became one of the major trading centers of Europe.

Section 1 Assessment

1. **Define:** compass, astrolabe, caravel.
2. Why was Dias's trip important?
3. What were the results of da Gama's voyage to India?

Critical Thinking

4. **Predicting Consequences** How do you think the lives of African Americans today might be different if Prince Henry the Navigator had not sent explorers to West Africa?

Graphic Organizer Activity

5. Draw this diagram, and use it the show the accomplishments of Portuguese leaders in exploration.

Accomplishments		
Prince Henry	Dias	da Gama

💾 Use **Interactive Tutor Self-Assessment Software** to review Section 1.

L1 **Geography: Movement** Have students trace da Gama's route on the map "European Voyages of Discovery" on page 475.

💾 Use the **Vocabulary Puzzle-Maker** to create crossword and word search puzzles.

MAKING CONNECTIONS

➤➤ **Medicine** Scurvy causes bleeding of the gums, loss of teeth, and anemia as well as death in severe cases. In 1795, the British navy began giving out regular rations of lime juice during the long sea voyages to prevent scurvy, a practice that led to the nickname *limeys* for British sailors.

SECTION 2 — The Spanish

The Spanish were as interested as the Portuguese in the wealth that could be obtained from India and the Far East. Until the late 1400s, however, they were too busy trying to gain their freedom from the Moors. By 1492, Spain had become a Christian country united under King Ferdinand and Queen Isabella. It was now ready to enter the race for new trade routes.

Christopher Columbus Christopher Columbus, the son of a weaver, was a skilled navigator from Genoa (jen' uh wuh), Italy. Like most educated people of his time, Columbus believed the world was round, not flat. Therefore, he believed he could reach Asia by sailing west. He tried for eight years to convince rulers from different nations to finance an expedition. The Portuguese, French, and English monarchs all turned him down. Finally, in 1492, Queen Isabella of Spain agreed to support his plan, the enterprise (en' tuhr prīz) of the Indies.

Columbus set sail from Spain in August, 1492, with three small ships—the *Niña*, the *Pinta*, and the *Santa Maria*—and a crew of about 90 sailors. At first, the voyage went well. The longer they were at sea, however, the more afraid Columbus's crew became. They urged their captain to turn back. When he refused,

Painting of Santa Maria

Biography

The following videotape program is available from Glencoe to enrich Chapter 30:

- **Christopher Columbus: Explorer of the New World**

To find classroom resources to accompany this video, check the following home page:

A&E Television:
http://www.aetv.com

Section 1 Assessment Answers

1. compass, instrument with a magnetic needle that always points north (p. 467); astrolabe, instrument that measures the angle of stars (p. 467); caravel, Portuguese ship (p. 468)

2. the Portuguese now knew they could reach the Far East by sailing around Africa

3. It opened the way for later explorations and for a new era of increased trade, and made Lisbon a major trading center.

4. Answers will vary but could include that the enslavement trade might not have begun at that time, if at all.

5. Accomplishments should reflect achievements mentioned in this section.

Assign the Chapter 30 **Section 1 Quiz** in the TCR. Testmaker available.

L3 **Critical Thinking** Ask: Why do you think Columbus kept two separate logs—in one record he recorded the actual distance covered, and in the other he recorded a much shorter distance. *(He reported the shorter distance to his crew so they would not know how far they had gone.)*

GEOGRAPHY AND HISTORY

Although Columbus was one of the first to reach the Americas, it was named after the Florentine geographer Amerigo Vespucci. In 1504, Vespucci was quoted as saying that the lands across the ocean made up a new continent which "it is proper to call the new world." Martin Waldseemüller, a German publisher, was so taken with the remark that in 1507, he issued a world map that labeled the southern land "America."

CAPTION ANSWER

that the world was round, not flat, and that he could find the shortest route to Asia

Reading Check
Why did Columbus's crew threaten **mutiny?**

Looking to the Sea
Columbus's interest in seafaring may have been shaped by the geography of his birthplace, the Republic of Genoa. As the city lacked fertile land and was surrounded by powerful rival cities like Milan and Florence, many Genoans looked to the Mediterranean Sea to find their fortune.

they threatened **mutiny** (myūt' nē), or an overthrow of officers. Columbus then promised to turn back if land was not sighted within three days. The night of the second day, a lookout on the *Pinta* spotted land. In the morning, Columbus landed at an outer island in the Bahamas (buh hah' muhs), probably Watling Island. Because he thought he had reached the Indies, Columbus called the people living on the islands Indians. For this reason, Native Americans are sometimes referred to as Indians.

Columbus spent several months sailing around the Bahamas, Cuba, and Hispaniola (his puhn yō' luh), an island that today consists of Haiti (hā' tē) and the Dominican Republic. In Cuba, he found Native Americans smoking cigars. This was the first European contact with tobacco.

On Christmas Eve, the *Santa Maria* ran aground on a reef and was wrecked. Columbus had his crew use the wood from the *Santa Maria* to build a fort. This was the first European settlement in the Americas.

In January 1493, Columbus boarded the *Niña* and headed back to Spain. He took with him gold, parrots, cotton, other plants and animals, and a few Native Americans. In Spain, he was

CHRISTOPHER COLUMBUS   Upon his return from the Americas, Columbus was greeted as a hero. In this painting he is being received by King Ferdinand and Queen Isabella. At the bottom of the steps are Native Americans and riches from the Americas. **What did Columbus hope to prove by sailing westward to Asia?**

472   UNIT 9 BEGINNING OF MODERN TIMES

MULTICULTURAL PERSPECTIVES

Columbus wrote the following impression of the inhabitants of the Bahamas: *The islanders came to the ships' boats, swimming and bringing us parrots and balls of cotton thread...which they exchanged for...glass beads and bawk bells...they took and gave of what they had very willingly, but it seemed to me that they were poor in every way. They bore no weapons, nor were they acquainted with them, because when I showed them swords they seized them by the edge and so cut themselves from ignorance.*

received with great honors. Six months later, he was leading a fleet of 17 ships and 1,500 men on another search for Asia.

Columbus made four voyages in all. He explored the coasts of Venezuela and Central America. He returned from his last voyage in 1504. Two years later, he died still convinced he had found the way to Asia. He never realized he had discovered the Americas.

The Treaty of Tordesillas

The Spanish monarchs were worried that Portugal might try to take from Spain the riches Columbus had discovered. So, they asked Pope Alexander VI for help.

In 1493, the Pope drew a **papal line of demarcation** (dē mahr kā' shuhn), or an imaginary line from the North Pole to the South Pole, some 300 miles, or 480 kilometers, west of the Azores Islands. Spain was to have the non-Christian lands west of the line, and Portugal the non-Christian lands east of the line.

The Portuguese, however, did not like the way the lands were divided. They protested and called for a meeting. In 1494, the Treaty of Tordesillas (tord uh sē' yuhs) was drawn up. It moved the line about 500 miles, or 800 kilometers, farther west. Because of this, Portugal was able to claim Brazil.

Other countries, like England, France, and the Netherlands, paid no attention to the Pope's rulings. They explored and claimed land where they wished.

The Conquistadores

The Spanish were eager to learn more about their new possessions. Over the next few years, Spanish *conquistadores* (kon kē stuh dōr' āz), or conquerors, set out to find the gold Columbus had talked about and to explore new lands.

In 1513, Ponce de León (pahn' suh de lē on') sailed north from the island of Puerto Rico (pwer' tō rē' kō) to explore Florida. That same year, Vasco Núñez de Balboa (vas' kō nū' nyāth dā bal bō' uh) crossed the isthmus of Panama and became the first European to see the Great South Sea. Between 1519 and 1521, Hernando Cortés (her nan' dō kōr tes') invaded Mexico. With the help of guns and the spread of smallpox, he destroyed the Native American empire ruled by the Aztec king Montezuma. Cortés and his troops took large amounts of gold from the Native Americans to send back to Spain.

In 1532, Francisco Pizarro (fran sis' kō puh zahr' ō) invaded Peru. Within five years, he conquered the Inca Empire. Like Cortés, Pizarro took great treasures of gold and silver from the Native Americans. Pizarro and his men then headed for the coast, where they built Lima (lē' muh), the "City of Kings."

In 1539, Hernando de Soto (duh sō' tō) sailed from Cuba to Florida and explored westward from there. He found no gold but explored the Mississippi River. In 1540, Francisco Coronado

---

✓ **Reading Check**
What was the **papal line of demarcation?**

✓ **Reading Check**
Who were the *conquistadors*?

Seeds Across the Sea
Did you have orange juice for breakfast? If you did, it may be because of Columbus's second voyage to the Americas in 1493. The citrus seeds that he brought to the West Indies took root in the islands and later were grown in Mexico and Florida.

✓ **Reading Check Answer**
The **papal line of demarcation** was an imaginary line from the North Pole to the South Pole that divided non-Christian lands between Spain and Portugal.

✓ **Reading Check Answer**
The *conquistadores* were conquerors who set out to find the gold Columbus had talked about and to explore new lands.

PRIMARY SOURCES
Library

You might assign "The Fall of the Aztec Empire," from pages 690–691 of the Primary Sources Library.

Independent Practice

L1 Language Arts Students may enjoy reading the diary written by Fernando, Columbus's 13-year-old son, in *The High Voyage: The Final Crossing of Christopher Columbus*, by Olga Litowinsky (Delacorte, 1991). Encourage students to share their impressions of the book with the class.

SPOTLIGHT ON: CORONADO

Francisco Vasquez de Coronado was a younger son who had not inherited his family estate. He went to the Americas as an aide to the viceroy of New Spain in order to seek his fortune. In 1540 he was sent on an expedition in search of the fabled Cíbola—seven cities of gold. Coronado took along about 250 horsemen, 70 Spanish foot soldiers, about 1,000 Native American allies, and numerous priests, along with baggage animals and sheep, goats, and cattle for food. According to the myth, Cíbola—located somewhere near what is now New Mexico—had rich pastures, cities with jewel-studded temples, and people riding on camels and elephants. Coronado only found barren land and pueblos of Zuni Indians.

L1 **Geography: Movement** After tracing Magellan's voyage on the map on page 475, have students locate the Strait of Magellan and notice that it is a narrow waterway that separates the islands of Tierra del Fuego from the mainland of South America.

L2 **Culture** Explain to students that common ship supplies for voyages to the Americas were: sea biscuits, salted meat, cheese, raisins, beans, honey, water, and wine. Ask students to choose an explorer they would like to travel with and create a supply list for what they would take along if their exploratory voyage were made today. Have them share their lists with the rest of the class.

L3 **Language Arts** Have students select an explorer that is discussed in this chapter and write five entries in a ship's log that describes the discoveries of these explorers and the difficulties of the journeys.

People in History

Ferdinand Magellan
c. 1480–1521

Portuguese Navigator

Born a noble, Magellan sailed on early Portuguese voyages to India. However, when he sought permission to look for a new western route to this region, Portuguese rulers turned him down. He moved to Spain, where he received funding for his voyage. Sailing as a Spanish citizen, Magellan charted a journey that proved what the Greeks had guessed—that the world was round and that the continents of the earth were linked by bodies of water.

PONCE DE LEÓN   While governing Puerto Rico, Ponce de León heard stories of an island to the north that held great riches. Setting out to find this island, Ponce de León discovered Florida instead. He is shown in this painting landing on the Florida coast. **From which two Native American civilizations did the Spaniards acquire much gold?**

(kōr uh nahd' ō) led an army overland from Mexico into the present-day United States. He reached the Grand Canyon but returned without finding any treasure. Thus, between 1492 and 1550, Spain explored an area from North America through Central America and the West Indies to South America.

Ferdinand Magellan   In 1517, Portugal controlled the eastern route to the Indies. As a result, Portugal was growing rich. This angered the Spanish king. So, when a Portuguese explorer named Ferdinand Magellan (muh jel' uhn) offered to find Spain a western route to the Indies, the king accepted the offer. He wanted Spain to become as wealthy as Portugal.

In 1519, Magellan set sail from Spain. He commanded a fleet of five ships and a crew of 256. In October of the following year, he sailed through a stormy strait at the tip of South America. The trip took one month. Today, the strait bears Magellan's name.

From the strait, Magellan sailed on into the Great South Sea. He renamed it the Pacific Ocean from the Spanish word *pacifico*, meaning peaceful. By this time, Magellan had lost two of his ships. He continued on, however. Conditions were terrible. The drinking water was spoiled, and the biscuits were full of worms. The crew was forced to eat rats, sawdust from ship boards, and leather soaked in the sea and grilled on wood coals. By the time the fleet reached the Mariana (mar ē an' uh) Islands three months

474   UNIT 9 BEGINNING OF MODERN TIMES

COOPERATIVE LEARNING

Early Spanish and Portuguese explorers encountered many groups in the Americas (the Arawak, Carib, Maya, Aztec, Inca), each culture slightly different from the others. Divide the class into small groups and have each group research and report on one of these Native American groups. Each student should be assigned one of the following areas to research: geographic location and method of subsistence, art and decorations, religious beliefs, customs, and effect of European contact on the inhabitants.

Assign the Chapter 30 *Cooperative Learning Activity* in the TCR.

Reviewing Map Legends

Legends, as explained in the map skill on page 75, are used to identify information shown on maps. Legends provide the key to the meaning of an unlimited number of symbols and colors that can be used on maps.

Sometimes, however, one legend may be used in several ways. For example, on the "European Voyages of Discovery" map below, five colors are used in the legend. On this particular map, these colors are used to show two different things. First, they point out the five European countries that took part in the voyages of discovery. Second, the colors show the different routes taken by explorers from these countries. For example, Portugal is shown in yellow. The routes that the Portuguese explorers took are also shown in yellow.

Map Practice

1. **What two countries had explorers sail around the world?**
2. **What country did not send any explorers south of 25°N latitude?**

European Voyages of Discovery

Glencoe's **Skillbuilder Interactive Workbook, Level 1,** provides instruction and practice in key social studies skills.

Legend: Portuguese, Spanish, English, Dutch, French

miles 0 / 2000 / 4000
kilometers 0 / 2000 / 4000 / 6000

Reviewing Map Legends

Have the students read the instructional part of the feature and answer the following questions: What are used to identify information shown on maps? *(legends)* In what two ways are colors used on the map on this page? *(to point out the five European countries that took part in the voyages of discovery and to show the routes taken by explorers from these countries)* Next, direct the students to study the map to answer the following questions: What countries explored the coastline of South America? *(Portugal, Spain, England)* What countries explored North America? *(Spain, England, France, the Netherlands)* What countries explored the Philippine Islands and the East Indies? *(England, Spain)*

Assign the Chapter 30 **Geography and Map Activity** in the TCR.

Answers to Map Practice

1. Spain and England
2. France

SPOTLIGHT ON: WORLD VOYAGES

After Spanish soldiers and explorers followed Columbus to the Americas, they returned to Europe with fantastic stories of the Seven Cities of Gold. One Spaniard, Estevanico, a black sailor shipwrecked in the Gulf of Mexico, spent many years wandering the deserts of southwest North America in search of these cities. He eventually died, unsuccessful in his quest, and the rumors of the existence of these golden cities persisted.

476

Painting of Ferdinand Magellan

later, it was almost helpless. The crew was suffering from scurvy and had no food of any kind.

After they had eaten and rested, Magellan and his crew set a southwest course for the Philippine (fil uh pēn') Islands. There Magellan became involved in a local war and was killed. Shortly after, more crew members were killed, and two more ships were lost. The one remaining ship continued on into the Indian Ocean and around Africa. It finally arrived in Seville (suh vil'), Spain, in 1522 with 18 men and a load of spices.

The voyage was a great accomplishment. By *circumnavigating*, or sailing completely around the world, it proved that Earth is indeed round. The voyage opened the Pacific Ocean to European ships. It also proved that Columbus did not land in Asia but in the Americas.

Section 2 Assessment

1. **Define:** mutiny, papal line of demarcation, *conquistadores*.
2. What were some discoveries made by the Spanish between 1513 and 1540?
3. What did Magellan's voyage prove?

Critical Thinking

4. **Making Comparisons** Which of Spain's explorers do you think advanced knowledge of the world the most? Explain.

Graphic Organizer Activity

5. Draw this diagram, and use it to show some of the effects of Columbus's voyages.

	Effect
Columbus's Voyages	Effect
	Effect

SECTION 3 Northwest Passage

Even after the Americas were reached, the English, French, and Dutch continued to look for another route to the Far East. Since the Portuguese and the Spanish controlled the southern sea lanes, the others looked for a northwest passage.

English merchants persuaded their king to send John Cabot (kab' uht), an Italian navigator, to the Far East by a northwest route. In 1497, Cabot set sail with a handful of men. He explored the coasts of Newfoundland and Nova Scotia (nō' vuh skō' shuh) and established claims for England in the Americas.

In 1523, the French hired Giovanni da Verrazano (jē uh vahn' ē dah ver rah tsah' nō), another Italian navigator, to find a northwest passage. He sailed along the Atlantic coast from North Carolina to New York. Eleven years later, Jacques Cartier (zhahk kahr tyā'), a French navigator, sailed up the St. Lawrence River as far as present-day Montreal (mahn trē ahl'). This gave the French a claim to eastern Canada.

In 1576, Sir Martin Frobisher (frō' bi shuhr), an English **sea dog,** or sea captain, sailed the coast of Greenland and fought a storm that almost wrecked one of his three ships. Frobisher finally discovered the bay that today bears his name.

In 1609, the Dutch sent Henry Hudson an English navigator to locate the passage. He explored the Hudson River and sailed to what is today Albany, New York. In 1610 he set out on a second voyage. He became lost in a storm and was never seen again. Nevertheless, his first voyage gave the Dutch their claim in the Americas.

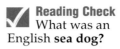
Reading Check
What was an English **sea dog?**

EXPLORERS

Name	Country	Achievements
Amerigo Vespucci	*Spain Portugal*	explored Atlantic coast of South America, 1497–1504; one of first to believe he had reached a new world
Pedro Alváres Cabral	*Portugal*	discovered Brazil and sailed east to India, 1500–1501
Vasco Núñez de Balboa	*Spain*	first European to sight eastern shore of Pacific Ocean, 1513
Alvar Núñez Cabeza de Vaca	*Spain*	explored Florida and Gulf region from Texas to Mexico, 1528–36
Juan Rodríguez Cabrillo	*Spain*	explored Pacific coast to Drake's Bay near San Francisco, 1542
Richard Chancellor	*England*	reached Moscow in search of northeast passage to Asia; opened trade with Russia, 1553–54
John Davis	*England*	explored west coast of Greenland in search of northwest passage to Asia, 1585
Sir Francis Drake	*England*	first Englishman to sail around the world, 1577–80
Father Jacques Marquette Louis Jolliet	*France*	explored Mississippi Valley to mouth of Arkansas River, 1673
Vitus Bering	*Russia*	explored coasts of Alaska and northeast Asia; discovered Bering Strait and Bering Sea, 1728, 1741

Vasco Núñez de Balboa led an expedition of soldiers and guides across the Isthmus of Panama in 1513 to search for a region rumored to be "flowing with golde," and to find "another sea, where they sayle with shippes as bigge as yours." Balboa's company fought rain forest undergrowth, poisonous snakes, and angry inhabitants for about 25 days as they crossed the isthmus. Today, people travel by ship through the Panama Canal completed in 1914.

Reading Check Answer
An English **sea dog** was the name given to the sea captains who sailed for England.

ASSESS

Check for Understanding

Ask students to summarize the main points of the chapter, orally or in writing. Discuss the answers to the Section and Chapter Assessment questions.

Evaluate

Assign the Chapter 30 **Performance Assessment Activity** in the TCR.

Administer the **Chapter 30 Test** in the TCR. Testmaker available.

EXTENDING THE CONTENT

In 1522, French pirates captured a Spanish treasure ship filled with gold, silver, and jade mosaics sent home from Mexico by Cortés. Amazed and covetous, King Francis I decided to send his own expedition to bring home wealth from the Americas. Francis chose the Italian navigator Giovanni da Verrazano to head the expedition in 1524. It was paid for by silk merchants of France who also had an interest in finding a route to China. Verrazano worked his way gradually up the coast from North Carolina to Nova Scotia. His ships sailed in and around Chesapeake Bay, the Hudson River, Cape Cod, and the Maine coast.

DID YOU KNOW ??

It was not until 1906 that the northwest passage was successfully navigated by Roald Amundsen, a Norwegian explorer. His voyage took three years, part of which was spent at a standstill because of ice.

Reteach

Assign the Chapter 30
Reteaching Activity in the TCR.

Enrich

Assign the Chapter 30 **Enrichment Activity** in the TCR.

CLOSE

Ask students to discuss the discoveries made by the explorers discussed in this chapter. Ask them to rank the discoveries in the order of importance. Then ask students to explain their rankings.

Use **Interactive Tutor Self-Assessment Software** to review Section 3.

Self-Check Quiz gives students an interactive chapter tutorial. Have them access **Chapter 30 Quiz** at humanheritage.glencoe.com

---

All of these voyages failed in their search to find a northwest passage to the Far East. They did, however, establish claims in the Americas for England, France, and the Netherlands.

Section 3 Assessment

1. **Define:** sea dog.
2. How did English, French, and Dutch explorers plan to reach Asia?
3. What lands in the Americas were claimed by England? By France? By the Netherlands?

Critical Thinking

4. **Demonstrating Reasoned Judgment** What characteristics or kinds of personalities do you think the English, French, and Dutch explorers had to have to achieve what they did?

Graphic Organizer Activity

5. Draw this diagram, and use it to show the causes and effects of the search for a northwest passage.

Causes		Search for Northwest Passage		Effects

Chapter Summary & Study Guide

1. By the 1300s, Europeans tried to break the Italian hold on trade by searching for an all-water route to India and beyond.
2. The development of better maps, ships, and navigation instruments helped Europeans in their search.
3. In the early 1400s, Prince Henry of Portugal opened the first school in Europe for navigators.
4. By 1473, Portuguese ships had crossed the equator. By 1498, they had reached India.
5. Between 1492 and 1504, Columbus made four voyages to what he thought was Asia but was really the Americas.
6. In 1494, the Treaty of Tordesillas divided non-Christian lands between Spain and Portugal, but other nations ignored the agreement.
7. In the first half of the 1500s, Cortés and Pizarro conquered the Aztec and Inca empires, encouraging other explorers to search for other empires in the Americas.
8. Between 1519 and 1522, Magellan's expedition sailed around the world, proving that Columbus did not land in Asia.
9. Between 1497 and 1609, England, France, and the Netherlands sent explorers to find a northwest passage through the Americas.
10. Early English, French, and Dutch voyages paved the way for future claims in North America.

Self-Check Quiz

Visit the *Human Heritage* Web site at **humanheritage. glencoe.com** and click on *Chapter 30—Self-Check Quiz* to assess your understanding of this chapter.

Section 3 Assessment Answers

1. sea dog, sea captain (p. 477)
2. by a northwest passage
3. Newfoundland, Nova Scotia; lands along the St. Lawrence River; lands along the Hudson River
4. Answers will vary but might include that these explorers were brave, adventurous, or greedy, or that they liked traveling.

5. Sample responses: *causes*—Spanish and Portuguese control of southern sea lanes, desire of other European nations for sea routes to the Far East; *effects*—exploration of North America's Atlantic coast; land claims by England, France, and the Netherlands

Assign the Chapter 30 **Section 3 Quiz** in the TCR. Testmaker available.

Using Key Terms

Imagine you are writing a newspaper column entitled "Great Explorer Achievements." Use each of the following words in a description of what you think some of these achievements were.

compass   astrolabe   caravel
mutiny   papal line of   *conquistadores*
sea dog   demarcation

Understanding Main Ideas

1. What were some of the problems that European explorers faced on their voyages of discovery?
2. What was the first European settlement in the Americas?
3. What are three bodies of water named after European explorers?
4. How long did it take Magellan's ship to sail around the world?
5. What did voyages in search of a northwest passage to Asia accomplish?

Critical Thinking

1. Why do you think Queen Isabella of Spain agreed to support Columbus when others had turned him down?
2. How do you think Native Americans felt about the *conquistadores?*
3. How did competition between nations affect European voyages of exploration?

Graphic Organizer Activity

History Create a chart like the one on this page, and use it to write a headline for an important event that occurred in each of the years shown.

Year	Headline
1473	
1487	
1492	
1494	
1497	
1499	
1521	
1522	
1532	
1609	

 ## Geography in History

Movement The lengths of voyages made by explorers were very different. Whose voyage from Portugal to India was longer in miles (or kilometers)—da Gama's or Cabral's? How many miles (or kilometers) longer was it?

Using Your Journal

Review any details you may have noted about the changes that took place in western Europe between 1300 and 1600. Imagine you are a peasant living in London, England, in 1550. Write a diary entry describing what you have learned about the world in recent years.

479

 Bonus Test Question

For Chapter 30 Test
How did discoveries by non-Europeans help Europeans begin their voyages of exploration? Make a cause-and-effect chart showing these relationships. Add a summary statement to explain your chart. (*Charts will vary.*)

Using Your Journal

Diary entries will vary but should include major events that affected England. You might ask volunteers to read their entries to the class.

Geography in History

da Gama's; about 2,900 miles (or 4,666 km) longer

Using Key Terms

Columns will vary, but students should include some achievements and use all the key terms.

Understanding Main Ideas

1. storms, scurvy, spoiled food and water, and starvation
2. a fort built with wood from the Santa Maria
3. Strait of Magellan, Frobisher Bay, and Hudson River
4. three years
5. claims in the Americas for England, France, and the Netherlands

Critical Thinking

1. Answers will vary but might include that she thought finding a new route to Asia would make Spain richer.
2. Answers will vary but might include fear, dread, and sadness.
3. Each nation wanted to extend its trade and power, and to be richer than other nations. They thought they could do this by finding a new route to the Far East. The search led to the discovery of the Americas.

Graphic Organizer Activity

Headlines will vary but should show the importance of the event chosen for each date. To get students started, you might use this example for 1522: "Ragged Crew Completes Magellan's Voyage—The World Is Round!"

FOCUS

Objectives

After reading the Around the World for Unit 9, your students will be able to:

1. locate the region influenced by the Swahili culture, and name some of the nations or people that contributed to its development.

2. cite evidence proving that Swahili merchants traded throughout the Arab world and with China.

3. predict how Portuguese explorers might have reacted when they first arrived in one of the Swahili towns.

📧 Bellringer

Ask students to write down what they think the word "simba" means.

Motivational Activity

Most students will probably correctly guess "lion." Tell them that they have just learned a Swahili word. If any of your students speak Swahili, have them share other words with the class. Then refer students to the Around the World feature, pointing out that today Swahili is the most widely spoken language on the African continent. Ask: From looking at the works of art on pages 480–481, what cultures do you think influenced the Swahili culture? *(Sample answers: Chinese, Arabic, and African cultures.)*

TEACH

Geography: Location Focus student attention on the map on page 480. Ask: How does the location of the East African harbor towns explain the region's cultural diversity? To help students with their answer, have a volunteer trace the Swahili coast on a wall map of the world.

480

THE SWAHILI CULTURE

Between 1000 and 1700 A.D., the harbor towns of East Africa blossomed. Like other trading centers, they attracted a variety of influences. More than 1,200 years ago, Arab traders came to the area, bringing the Muslim religion with them. Other influences came from Persia, India, and China. Later, Portuguese explorers edging their way along the East African coast brought yet another influence to the area.

By far the strongest influence, however, was that of the African peoples who already lived in the region. The blending of their cultures with the cultures of other regions produced the Swahili culture, which is still alive and vibrant today.

Swahili Culture

 In the early 1400s, Chinese explorer Zheng He made several voyages to East Africa. On his fourth voyage, the sultan of Malindi presented him with a giraffe—a gift to the Chinese emperor. The Chinese called the giraffe a "celestial unicorn" and saw it as a sign of good luck.

▲ The term *Swahili* comes from an Arab word meaning "coastal people." The Swahili culture includes African Muslims who live on African islands and lands bordering the Indian Ocean.

480 UNIT 9

SPOTLIGHT ON: SWAHILI CULTURE

Swahili, the language spoken along the Swahili coast and in much of East Africa, reflects the region's far-flung contacts. Classified as a Bantu language, Swahili has borrowed words from many other languages, including Portuguese, Persian, Arabic, German, and English. Some Swahili words taken from English include: *basikeli* (bicycle), *pensili* (pencil), *mashine* (machine), and *komputya* (computer).

Millions of non-Africans learned Swahili when they watched the movie *The Lion King* and met the characters Simba (the Swahili word for "lion") and Rafiki (the Swahili word for "friend"). People who watched the original *Star Trek* learned yet another word when they met Lieutenant Uhura. In Swahili, *uhura* means "freedom," a rallying cry for East Africans during their struggle for independence.

From the 100s to the early 1900s, Swahili merchants used a ship known as the *mtepe* to sail the coastal waters. Built without nails, the timbers of the boats were held together by rope woven from coconut husks and powered by sails made from the leaves of coconut trees. The Arabs introduced the *dhow* and its triangular cotton sail to the region around the 800s. Arab *dhows* can still be seen along the Swahili coast today. ▼

▲ Trade goods from China made their way to the Swahili coast as early as the 800s A.D. Pottery, such as this bowl made during the Ming dynasty, has been uncovered up and down the coast.

This present-day market shows the blend of people that make up the Swahili culture and the many goods, particularly spices, that have made the region famous.

Gold coins found on Pemba, an island off the coast of Kenya, prove that Swahili merchants traded all over the Arab world in the 1000s. These coins come from Tunisia, Egypt, and Syria. The Swahili towns also minted their own coins, made of gold, silver, and copper. ▶

Taking Another Look

1. Where are the Swahili peoples located?

2. What evidence proves that Swahili merchants traded with the Arab world? With China?

Hands-On Activity

Writing Diary Entries Imagine you are a Portuguese ship captain visiting one of the Swahili towns for the first time. Write several entries in the ship's log describing the experience.

481

Direct the student to use a pointer or ruler to point out nations along the northern rim of the Indian Ocean with which the Swahili harbor towns may have traded.

LINKING PAST TO PRESENT

European explorers hoped to reach the spice islands of Asia, but in Zanzibar they found spices that far exceeded their dreams. Although the island's main exports are cloves and coconuts, more than 50 different kinds of spices and fruits can still be found there: cinnamon, cardamon, nutmeg, pepper, pimentos, ginger, tamarind, vanilla, figs, lemons, litchi, bananas, pineapples, passion fruit, breadfruit, ten kinds of mangos, and more.

ASSESS

Check for Understanding

Have students answer the questions in Taking Another Look on page 481.

Enrich

Assign the Chapter 30 **Enrichment Activity** in the TCR. Have students compare the account from *The Kilwa Chronicle* with the journal entries that they wrote in the Hands-On Activity.

CLOSE

Ask students why the Swahili harbor towns might have been the envy of almost any European merchant during the period covered by this unit. *(Sample responses: their location on an all-water route to the Far East, their direct contact with India and China, and so on.)*

ANSWERS TO TAKING ANOTHER LOOK

1. Swahili peoples are located on the African islands and lands bordering the Indian Ocean. The culture reaches from present-day Somalia in the north to Mozambique in the south.

2. Coins found on Pemba come from all over the Arab world. Chinese prints record a picture of a giraffe that the Sultan of Malindi gave to the emperor of China. Pieces of Chinese pottery and other trade goods have been found up and down the Swahili coast.

Hands-On Activity

The log entries will vary, but will probably reflect surprise at the level of development or perhaps concern over the spread of Muslim influence. Some entries might express greed or an interest in claiming the coastal towns for Portugal.

Answers and Analyses

1C History

While each of these contributions occurred during the Renaissance, the most important element was the printing press. The Renaissance was essentially the rediscovery of Greek and Roman ideas. According to page 441, the printing press made books available to people, and therefore, *new ideas spread rapidly.*

2G History

Pages 434–435 state that da Vinci was an artist, scientist, and inventor. This information makes G the best choice.

THE PRINCETON REVIEW **TEST-TAKING TIP**

Students can probably answer this question by association: da Vinci was definitely an artist, so the word *artist* must figure into the correct answer. Only G then qualifies.

3D History

Luther is discussed on pages 449–451. There it states that he posted his theses, which brought him into conflict with Catholic doctrine, on the church in Wittenberg. For this action, he was condemned and excommunicated by the Pope.

4F History

According to page 451, Protestant church leaders *conducted services in the language of the area instead of in Latin.* This information makes F the best choice. No mention is made of improving the conditions of women or recognition by the Catholic Church.

THE PRINCETON REVIEW

Standardized Test Practice

Directions: Choose the *best* answer to each of the following multiple choice questions. If you have trouble answering a question, use the process of elimination to narrow your choices. Write your answers on a separate piece of paper.

1. Which of the following Renaissance contributions was most helpful in spreading new ideas?

  A The creation of piazzas in the center of cities

  B The use of perspective in artists' work

  C The invention of the printing press

  D The generosity of Lorenzo de Medici toward artists, poets, and philosphers

> *Test-Taking Tip:* Always read the question and *all* the answer choices carefully. Notice that all of the answer choices are examples of Renaissance contributions to European culture. Although Lorenzo de Medici's generosity (answer D) probably helped people *create* new ideas, there is another choice that was more helpful in *spreading* these ideas to many people.

2. Leonardo da Vinci was

  F a scholar and a church leader

  G an artist, scientist, and inventor

  H the founder of modern medicine

  J a philosopher and historian

> *Test-Taking Tip:* Eliminate answers that are incorrect. Leonardo da Vinci was not a church leader, so answer F can be eliminated.

3. Why was Martin Luther charged with heresy?

  A He worshiped more than one god.

  B He worked to secure rights for Spanish Jews.

  C He declared himself the one true voice of God.

  D His theses challenged the Pope and the Catholic Church.

> *Test-Taking Tip:* This question requires you to remember a *fact* about Martin Luther. Reading all the answer choices carefully may help you remember information about this important religious leader.

4. Which of the following was most responsible for the spread of the Protestant church through Europe?

  F Services were not conducted in Latin, but rather in local languages.

  G Women were given a greater role in the Protestant church.

  H Church members could buy indulgences to free themselves from punishment.

  J The Protestant church was recognized by the Roman Catholic Church.

> *Test-Taking Tip:* Again, read carefully. Lutheran and Reformed churches were known as *Protestant* because they *protested* against Catholic ideas, such as the sale of indulgences. Therefore, answer H can be eliminated.

European Voyages of Discovery

5. **According to the map above, which nations' explorers sailed around the Cape of Good Hope?**

   A Portugal and Spain

   B Portugal, France, and England

   C Spain, England, and France

   D Portugal, Spain, and England

   > **Test-Taking Tip:** Use the *map legend*, or *key*, to help you understand how the map is organized. How does this map show the routes of different countries' explorers?

6. **Which countries had explorers whose routes crossed the equator?**

   F England, Spain, and Portugal

   G England, Spain, and France

   H Spain, France, and Portugal

   J Spain, Portugal, and Holland

   > **Test-Taking Tip:** Make sure that you do not confuse the *equator* with the *Prime Meridian*. Although both are indicated by 0°, the equator is a line of latitude, and the Prime Meridian is a line of longitude. Do you remember which is which?

5D Geography

According to the map, Drake (English), Magellan (Spanish) and Da Gama and Cabral (Portuguese) sailed around the Cape of Good Hope.

All of the information needed to answer the question is on the map itself. Make sure that students understand how to read the legend, and remind them to work carefully to avoid making simple errors.

6F Geography

According to the map, Drake (English), Magellan (Spanish), and Da Gama, Cabral, and Dias (Portuguese) crossed the equator.

Be sure to help students understand lines of longitude and latitude, and how to identify the line that represents the equator.

483

Tested Objectives

Questions	Reading Objective
1	Evaluate information
2	Identify supporting ideas
3	Determine cause and effect
4	Identify central issues
5, 6	Analyze information

OVERVIEW

Unit 10 discusses the changes that took place in the world from the time the Europeans discovered the Americas to the 1800s.

➤ **Chapter 31** describes the colonizing efforts of Portugal, Spain, England, the Netherlands, and France from the early 1500s to 1763.

➤ **Chapter 32** outlines the revolutions in England, the American colonies, and France during the 1600s and the 1700s.

➤ **Chapter 33** summarizes the Industrial Revolution of the 1700s and 1800s, highlighting key developments in textiles, agriculture, mining, and transportation.

UNIT OBJECTIVES

After reading Unit 10, students will be able to:

1. describe how the Americas changed during the 1500s and 1600s.

2. discuss what changes in government took place in the West during the 1600s and 1700s.

3. analyze economic changes that took place in the West during the 1700s and early 1800s.

UNIT PROJECT

Tell students to create an advertising campaign that does one of the following: encourages Europeans in the 1500s to help colonize the Americas; supports a political uprising against a monarchy in the 1700s; promotes the latest inventions and their uses and benefits. Encourage students to use whatever advertising media are available today. Have them share their campaigns with the rest of the class.

UNIT 10 The Changing World

◀ **Early microscope, which revolutionized science**

Model of the *Rocket*, one of England's first steam locomotives ▼

1500	1607	1619	1688
Cabral claims Brazil for Portugal	**First permanent English settlement at Jamestown**	**Virginia House of Burgesses meets**	**Glorious Revolution in England**

484

ABOUT THE UNIT OPENING

Examining Artifacts

Have students suggest the areas of life that these two artifacts may have changed. *(science, medical research, transportation, etc.)* Point out that the microscope opened a whole new world invisible to the naked eye and that the train carried people and goods faster than ever before. Tell students they will explore other far-reaching changes in this unit.

Global Chronology

Ask students to explain what time period the time line covers. *(1500 to 1847)* What entries indicate new ideas about government were taking place? *(Virginia House of Burgesses meets, Glorious Revolution in England, Declaration of Independence)*

Multimedia Activity

Turning Points in World History
The Industrial Revolution

Setting up the Video

Work with a group of your classmates to view "The Industrial Revolution" on the videodisc *Turning Points in World History.*

View the video by scanning the bar code or by entering the chapter number on your keypad and pressing "Search." (Also available in VHS format.)

Side Two,
Chapter 3

The Industrial Revolution of the late 1700s forever changed the way that people lived and worked. This program shows the far-reaching effects that factories and machines brought to the world.

Hands-On Activity

Interview adults in your community and ask them to name inventions that have come into widespread use since they were children. Compare your findings with those collected by your classmates. What is the most commonly mentioned invention? Debate whether this invention can be described as "revolutionary."

PRIMARY SOURCES
Library

See pages 692–693 for a primary source reading to accompany Unit 10.

Journal Notes

What changes took place in the world between the 1500s and the 1800s? Note details about these changes as you read.

1769	**1776**	**1847**
James Watt perfects steam engine	U.S. Declaration of Independence	Samuel Colt develops the assembly line

485

INTRODUCING THE UNIT

Ask students what would happen if explorers today suddenly discovered a nearby planet inhabited by intelligent life. Discuss how our civilization might react.

RECORDING JOURNAL NOTES

Help students begin writing in their journals by asking them to name time line entries and data in the unit introduction that indicate the kinds of changes taking place in the world between the 1500s and the 1700s. Tell students that these are the kinds of changes they should detail in their journals as they read Unit 10.

PRIMARY SOURCES
Library

Items in the Primary Sources Library for this unit focus on invention of the railroad. Elements include:
- account of a journey by railroad
- report of a race between a locomotive and a horse

For additional primary source documents, use the **World History Primary Source Document CD-ROM.**

Geographic Location

Using their text Atlas, have students locate the countries of western Europe and North and South America, the islands of the Caribbean, Africa, the Philippines, and the East Indies. Have students calculate the approximate distances from the countries in western Europe to the other continents or islands listed above. Discuss the length of time that it might have taken colonists to get to these foreign lands in the 1500s–1700s.

Chapter 31 Planning Guide

Objectives	Reproducible Resources	Multimedia Resources
Section 1 **Portugal** Summarize the development and decline of Portugal's empire in the Americas.	Reproducible Lesson Plan Chapter 31 Vocabulary and Guided Reading Activity Reading Essentials and Study Guide 31-1 Section 1 Quiz Unit 10 Hands-On History Lab	Vocabulary PuzzleMaker Interactive Tutor Self-Assessment Software ExamView® Pro Testmaker Glencoe Skillbuilder Interactive Workbook, Level 1
Section 2 **Spain** Discuss the rise and decline of Spain's colonial empire in the Americas.	Reproducible Lesson Plan Reading Essentials and Study Guide 31-2 Chapter 31 Cooperative Learning Activity Section 2 Quiz	Teaching Transparency and Activity 31A Vocabulary PuzzleMaker Interactive Tutor Self-Assessment Software ExamView® Pro Testmaker
Section 3 **England** Describe the colonies established by the English in the Americas.	Reproducible Lesson Plan Reading Essentials and Study Guide 31-3 Chapter 31 Chart and Graph Skill Activity Chapter 31 Geography and Map Activity Section 3 Quiz	Teaching Transparency and Activity 31B Vocabulary PuzzleMaker ExamView® Pro Testmaker Glencoe Skillbuilder Interactive Workbook, Level 1
Section 4 **The Netherlands** Discuss how the Dutch established colonies in the Americas.	Reproducible Lesson Plan Reading Essentials and Study Guide 31-4 Section 4 Quiz	Vocabulary PuzzleMaker Interactive Tutor Self-Assessment Software Glencoe Skillbuilder Interactive Workbook, Level 1
Section 5 **France** Explain how and where the French established settlements in the Americas.	Reproducible Lesson Plan Reading Essentials and Study Guide 31-5 Section 5 Quiz	Vocabulary PuzzleMaker ExamView® Pro Testmaker Glencoe Skillbuilder Interactive Workbook, Level 1
Section 6 **The Influence of Empires** Describe how empires in the Americas influenced Europe.	Reproducible Lesson Plan Reading Essentials and Study Guide 31-6 Chapter 31 Activity Book Activity Section 6 Quiz Chapter 31 Reteaching Activity	Vocabulary PuzzleMaker ExamView® Pro Testmaker Glencoe Skillbuilder Interactive Workbook, Level 1
Chapter 31 **Review and Evaluation**	Chapter 31 Performance Assessment Activity Spanish Chapter Summary and Glossary Chapter 31 Test	Interactive Tutor Self-Assessment Software Glencoe Skillbuilder Interactive Workbook, Level 1 Audiocassettes* ExamView® Pro Testmaker

*Also available in Spanish.

Presentation Plus!
Use Glencoe's **Presentation Plus!** multimedia teacher tool to easily present dynamic lessons that visually excite your students. Using Microsoft® PowerPoint, you can customize the presentations to create your own personalized lessons.

Interactive Lesson Planner

Planning has never been easier! Using this CD-ROM, organize your week, month, semester, or year with all the help you need. The **Interactive Lesson Planner** gives you access to all of the blackline masters which accompany *Human Heritage.*

✓ PERFORMANCE ASSESSMENT ACTIVITIES

Mapmaking   Have students research in historical atlases and create two maps of European claims in the Americas. One map should show the claims in 1650, the other map should show the claims in 1753. Assign students to write five questions about the two maps and exchange them with each other.

CHAPTER RESOURCES

READINGS FOR THE STUDENT

Davis, James E. and Sharryl Davis Hawke. *Seeds of Change: The Story of Cultural Exchange After 1492.* Addison-Wesley, 1992. An account of the exchanges made between Europe and the Americas and their effects on each region.

Hooks, William H. *The Legend of White Doe.* Macmillan, 1988. A tale about Virginia Dare, the first child of English settlers born in the Americas.

READINGS FOR THE TEACHER

Scott, John Anthony. *Settlers on the Eastern Shore: The British Colonies in North America 1607-1750.* Facts on File, 1991. Eyewitness accounts and primary sources describe the first years of British settlement in the Americas.

KEY TO ABILITY LEVELS

Teaching strategies have been coded for varying learning styles and abilities.

L1 Level 1 activities are **basic** activities and should be within the ability range of all students.

L2 Level 2 activities are **average** activities and should be within the ability range of the average to above-average student.

L3 Level 3 activities are **challenging** activities designed for the ability range of above-average students.

ELL ELL activities should be within the ability range of English Language Learning students.

NATIONAL GEOGRAPHIC SOCIETY — Teacher's Corner

INDEX TO NATIONAL GEOGRAPHIC MAGAZINE

The following articles relate to this chapter:

- "LaSalle's Last Voyage," by Lisa Moore LaRoe, May 1997.
- "Treasure From the Silver Bank," by Tracy Bowden, July 1996.
- "David Thompson," by Priit J. Vesilind, May 1996.

NATIONAL GEOGRAPHIC SOCIETY PRODUCTS AVAILABLE FROM GLENCOE

To order the following, call Glencoe at 1-800-334-7344:

- *STV: North America (Videodisc)*
- *GTV: The American People: Fabric of a Nation (Videodisc)*
- *GTV: A Geographic Perspective on American History (Videodisc)*
- *PicturePack: The Age of Exploration, Parts 1 & 2 (Transparencies)*
- *PictureShow: The Age of Exploration, Parts 1 & 2 (CD-ROMs)*

ADDITIONAL NATIONAL GEOGRAPHIC SOCIETY PRODUCTS

To order the following, call National Geographic at 1-800-368-2728:

- *National Geographic Atlas of World History (Book)*

Access *National Geographic*'s new dynamic MapMachine Web site and other geography resources at:

http://nationalgeographic.com/
http://nationalgeographic.com/maps/

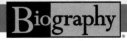

The following videotape program is available from Glencoe:

- **Pocahontas: Her True Story**

  1-56501-555-X

To order, call Glencoe at 1-800-334-7344. To find classroom resources to accompany many of these, check:

A&E Television: http://www.aetv.com
The History Channel:
http://www.historychannel.com

OVERVIEW

Chapter 31 outlines European expansion into the Americas.

➤ **Section 1** discusses Portugal's empire in the Americas.
➤ **Section 2** describes Spanish expansion and the role of the Church.
➤ **Section 3** summarizes English settlement of the Americas.
➤ **Section 4** examines the Dutch colonies in the Americas.
➤ **Section 5** describes French settlements in the Americas.
➤ **Section 6** discusses the effects of colonization on Europe.

CHAPTER OBJECTIVES

After reading Chapter 31, students will be able to:

1. summarize why Europeans colonized the Americas.
2. discuss what European empires were established in the Americas.
3. explain why many colonial empires declined.
4. describe how the empires in the Americas influenced Europe.

EXAMINING ARTIFACTS

Explain that these artifacts come from Spanish settlements in North America. Ask: What aspects of European culture did Spanish settlers bring to the Americas? *(the idea of a university education, the practice of Christianity).* Tell students that in this chapter they will learn more about the changes that European expansion brought both to the Americas and to Europe.

PERFORMANCE ASSESSMENT ✓

Use the Performance Assessment activities on page 486B to help you evaluate students as they complete the chapter.

486

Expansion Into the Americas

1500 A.D.–1700 A.D.

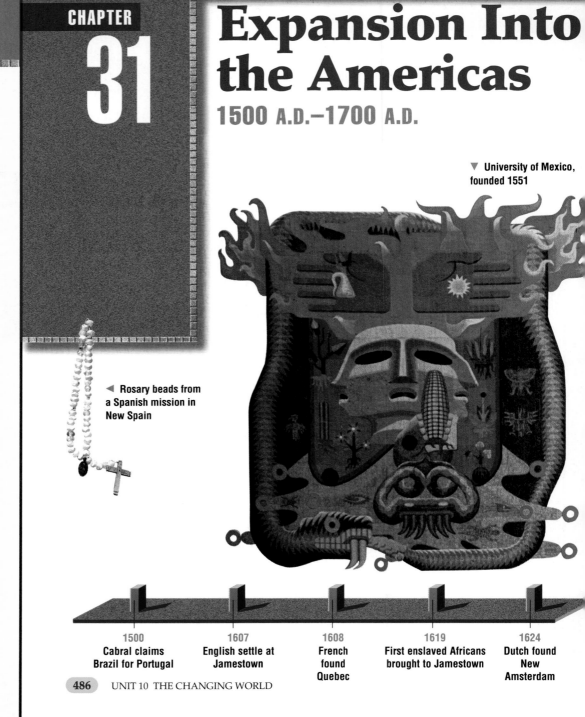

▼ **University of Mexico, founded 1551**

◄ **Rosary beads from a Spanish mission in New Spain**

1500	1607	1608	1619	1624
Cabral claims Brazil for Portugal	**English settle at Jamestown**	**French found Quebec**	**First enslaved Africans brought to Jamestown**	**Dutch found New Amsterdam**

486 UNIT 10 THE CHANGING WORLD

TEACHING RESOURCES

TEACHER PLANNING AND SUPPORT

- Reproducible Lesson Plan
- Block Scheduling Implementation Guide
- Videodisc Bar Code Correlation
- Presentation Plus!

REVIEW AND REINFORCEMENT

- Reading Essentials and Study Guide 31-1, 31-2, 31-3, 31-4, 31-5, 31-6
- Chapter 31 Vocabulary and Guided Reading Activity
- Vocabulary PuzzleMaker Software
- Teaching Transparencies 31A & 31B

- Chapter 31 Reteaching Activity
- Chapter 31 Cooperative Learning Activity
- Chapter 31 Activity Book Activity
- Chapter 31 Chart and Graph Skill Activity
- Interactive Tutor Self-Assessment Software
- Unit 10 MindJogger VideoQuiz

APPLICATION AND HANDS-ON ACTIVITIES

- Daily World History, Geography, and Culture Question
- Unit 10 Hands-On History Lab Activity
- World History Craft Card 2

Chapter Focus

 Read to Discover

- Why Europeans colonized the Americas.
- What European empires were established in the Americas.
- Why many colonial empires declined.
- How empires in the Americas influenced Europe.

HISTORY *Online*

Chapter Overview
Visit the *Human Heritage* Web site at **humanheritage.glencoe.com** and click on **Chapter 31— Chapter Overviews** to preview this chapter.

 Terms to Learn

colonize
viceroy
peninsulares
mestizos
indentured
  servants

 People to Know

Cabral
Sir Francis Drake
Sir Walter Raleigh
John Smith
John Rolfe
William Penn

🌐 **Places to Locate**

Brazil
Peru
Roanoke Island
Jamestown
Plymouth
New France

Why It's Important From the early 1500s to the 1700s, several western European countries set out to **colonize**, or build permanent settlements in, the Americas. Europeans wanted the riches of the Americas, which they thought would bring them power. They also wanted to spread Christianity.

✅ **Reading Check**
How did western Europeans **colonize** the Americas?

SECTION 1 Portugal

By 1512, the Portuguese had claimed all of Brazil. They had also established trading posts in Africa, India, Southeast Asia, and the Moluccas (muh luhk′ uhz), or Spice Islands. They took most of the Asian coastal cities by force. First, Portuguese warships bombarded the coast. Then soldiers went ashore.

Portugal found it difficult to rule its new territories. One reason was that it did not have a large enough population to send settlers to all its territories. Also, most of Portugal's territories already had large populations. Then, too, the hot, wet climate of the trading posts was too uncomfortable for most Portuguese. As a result, Portugal had to depend on sea power and the cooperation of defeated leaders to protect its interests.

Brazil In 1500, the Portuguese explorer Pedro Alváres Cabral (pā′ dr ō al vah′ rez kah brahl′) claimed Brazil for Portugal. Since no precious metals were found, Portugal paid little attention to the discovery. Then, other countries started to take *brazilwood*, or a red wood used to make dyes. When the Portuguese realized the value of the wood, they became more interested in Brazil.

CHAPTER 31 EXPANSION INTO THE AMERICAS 487

GEOGRAPHY ACTIVITIES

- 📂 Chapter 31 Geography and Map Activity
- 📂 Social Studies Outline Map Resource Book

INTERDISCIPLINARY CONNECTIONS

- 🖼 World History & Art Transparency 19, *Quilled Buckskin Robe*
- 🎵 World Music: Cultural Traditions

ENRICHMENT AND EXTENSION

- 📂 Chapter 31 Enrichment Activity
- 📀 World History Primary Source Document Library CD-ROM
- 📂 Foods Around the World

ASSESSMENT AND EVALUATION

- 📂 Chapter 31 Performance Assessment Activity
- 📂 Chapter 31 Section Quizzes 31-1, 31-2, 31-3, 31-4, 31-5, 31-6
- 📂 Chapter 31 Test
- 💾🖥 Chapter 31 ExamView® Pro Testmaker Software
- 🎧 Chapter 31 Digests Audiocassettes Activities and Tests

SPANISH RESOURCES

- 📂 Chapter 31 Spanish Chapter Summary and Glossary
- 🎧 Chapter 31 Spanish Chapter Digests Audiocassettes Activities and Tests

---

HISTORY *Online*

Chapter Overview introduces students to chapter content and key terms. Have them access **Chapter 31 Overview** at **humanheritage.glencoe.com**

FOCUS

📝 **Bellringer**

Write the following quotation on the board: *Of gold is treasure made, and with it he who has it does as he wills in the world and it even sends souls to Paradise.* Have students interpret this quote from Christopher Columbus.

Motivational Activity

Link students' interpretations of the quote with the establishment of empires in the Americas. Tell students that the desire for wealth, as well as the desire to spread Christianity, inspired European colonization.

✅ **Reading Check Answer**
The Europeans set out to **colonize** the Americas by building permanent settlements.

GUIDE TO READING

Reading Strategy

Ask students to read "Why It's Important" and summarize the chapter's main theme. (*In colonizing the Americas, European nations hoped to increase their wealth and power and to spread Christianity.*)

Vocabulary Precheck

Ask students to define each of the "Terms to Learn." **L1 ELL**

💾 Use the Vocabulary PuzzleMaker for Chapter 31 to create a crossword puzzle. **L1**

📂 Assign Chapter 31 Vocabulary and Guided Reading Activity.

📂 Assign Reading Essentials and Study Guide 31-1.

Guided Practice

L1 **History** Show students on a wall map of the world the city of Calicut, India, located in southwestern India. Tell them that Calicut was one of the world's five great harbors in the 1500s. The city reflected elements of Muslim and Asian culture because of its location at the junction of the Arabian-Indian sea trade. Ask students why they think Portugal wanted control of this seaport. (*The Portuguese wanted control of the spice trade.*)

✔ **Reading Check Answer**
Captaincies were given to families who would establish towns, give out land, and raise armies.

✔ **Reading Check Answer**
The *bandeirantes* were fortune hunters who expanded Portuguese land claims as they searched for precious stones and escaped enslaved people.

Glencoe Literature Library

The following novel from the **Glencoe Literature Library** may be used to enrich this chapter:
• *The Slave Dancer*, by Paula Fox. (Forced journey of Africans to the Americas.)

GEOGRAPHY AND HISTORY

Cabral wanted to sail around Africa but traveled too far west and accidentally landed in Brazil. The question of when Brazil was first discovered by Europeans is still argued by scholars.

✔ **Reading Check**
How did the Portuguese use **captaincies** to colonize Brazil?

✔ **Reading Check**
Who were the *bandeirantes*, and how did they increase Portuguese land claims?

Early Map of Brazil

In 1532, the Portuguese established their first permanent settlement in Brazil. The king of Portugal divided the area into 15 territorial strips called **captaincies** (kap' tuhn sēz). Each strip was given to a different Portuguese family who could establish towns, give out land, and raise armies. In return, they promised to colonize and protect their captaincies.

Portugal sent large numbers of settlers to Brazil. Portuguese sailors landed there and decided to stay. Criminals were sent to work off their sentences. Soldiers and officials came to protect royal interests. Ranchers arrived with herds of cattle. Missionaries came looking for converts to Christianity.

The Portuguese set up plantations in Brazil. Most plantations grew sugarcane, which was used to make sugar, molasses, and rum. About 2 million Native Americans were living in Brazil when Portugal claimed the land. The Portuguese settlers enslaved them to work the land. Most of the Native Americans, however, either ran away or died from diseases brought by the Europeans.

Before long, the Portuguese settlers began bringing over enslaved Africans. The number of Africans grew until, in some places, there were at least 20 enslaved Africans for each Portuguese settler. The Africans brought their religions with them. They also brought African music and dance to Brazil. They told folktales about their African history and carved wooden figures for churches. They also added many new words to the Portuguese language.

By the end of the 1600s, there was less demand for sugar. *Bandeirantes* (ban duh ran' tās), or fortune-hunters, looking for precious stones and escaped enslaved people, began to appear. Bandeirantes were the frontiersmen of Brazil. Traveling in bands of fifty to several thousand men, they followed the rivers into the jungle. They established Portugal's claim to the far western and southern areas of Brazil.

Royal interest in Brazil grew when gold was discovered in the 1690s. The king sent government clerks to check the mineral resources and make sure the monarchy received one fifth of each miner's gold. Gold brought still more people to Brazil and more wealth to Portugal. So did the growing of coffee, which was introduced in the early 1700s.

In many ways, Brazil was a tolerant society. It welcomed people of different countries and religions. Many men of part-African ancestry rose to high positions in the Church and the government. Women, however, were allowed little freedom or power, and hardly anyone knew how to read and write.

The Loss of Empire   By the middle of the 1500s, Portugal began losing its empire. The colonial government was not well

---

MULTICULTURAL PERSPECTIVES

Jesuit missionaries to Brazil set up mission villages in remote areas along the Amazon River. There, thousands of Native Americans were baptized, gathered into fortified settlements, and taught farming. These missions provided a place of safety for the Native Americans against raiders who enslaved people. They also became outposts of Portuguese political and economic influence. At the same time, however, they disrupted the hunting and gathering life of the Native Americans.

organized and the economy was in poor shape. Another reason was that the conquered peoples of Southeast Asia disliked the Portuguese for forcing Christianity on them. By the time the Portuguese king died in 1580, Portugal was very weak. The king left no heirs, and the throne was claimed by Philip II of Spain. Portugal was ruled by Spain until 1640. Then, Portugal regained its independence. During that time, the English and the Dutch took over most of the Portuguese trading centers in Southeast Asia.

Section 1 Assessment

1. **Define:** colonize, captaincies, *bandeirantes*.
2. What kept Portugal from colonizing settlements?
3. What happened to the Native Americans who lived in Brazil when the Portuguese claimed the land?

Critical Thinking

4. **Making Inferences**   How do you think the Native Americans felt about the Portuguese settlement of Brazil?

Graphic Organizer Activity

5. Draw this diagram, and use it to show the causes of the decline of the Portuguese empire.

Causes
1.
2.
3.

Decline of Empire

BRAZILIAN PLANTATION   Early Portuguese settlers established plantations in Brazil. At first, Native American populations were enslaved to provide the needed labor. Most of the Native Americans, however, proved too rebellious or too sickly to perform the hard work required. Enslaved Africans were then brought to work on the plantations. **For what was the sugarcane grown on plantations used?**

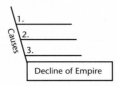

Carnival The Brazilian capital of Rio de Janeiro is known for its annual Carnival. Celebrated just before the beginning of Lent, the Christian holy season that comes before Easter, Carnival runs for four days.

LINKING PAST TO PRESENT

The culture of modern Brazil, like its people, is a blend of Portuguese, African, and Native American influences. Although major elements—the Portuguese language, the Roman Catholic religion, and many customs—came from Portugal, a unique Brazilian blend has developed since colonial times. The Native American language Tupi is still spoken in the northern interior of Brazil. The words *cashew* and *tapioca* are Tupi words. African influences are strongest on the coast north of Rio de Janeiro. Foods and dances such as the samba and bossa nova have African influences.

CAPTION ANSWER

to make sugar, molasses, and rum

Use **Interactive Tutor Self-Assessment Software** to review Section 1.

Section 1 Assessment Answers

1. colonize, to build permanent settlements (p. 487); captaincies, territorial strips into which the Portuguese divided Brazil (p. 488); *bandeirantes*, fortune-hunters (p. 488)
2. Portugal did not have a large enough population to send settlers to all its territories; most territories already had large populations; and the Portuguese were not accustomed to the hot, wet climate of the new colonies.
3. They were enslaved by the Portuguese.

4. Answers will vary but might include the idea that they were angry and overwhelmed.
5. Sample causes: government not well organized, economy in poor shape, resentment of Portuguese among conquered peoples in Southeast Asia, no direct heirs to the throne

Assign the Chapter 31 **Section 1 Quiz** in the TCR. Testmaker available.

490

L1 **Geography: Location** Have students locate the Spanish colonies on the map "European Colonies in the Americas" on page 498. Ask them why the Spanish colonies were difficult to govern.

L2 **Economics** Discuss the use of enslaved people in the colonies by explaining how enslaved Africans contributed to colonial economic prosperity. Ask students why enslaved people were used on sugarcane and coffee plantations. *(Growing these crops required a great deal of manual labor.)* Ask why large numbers of Africans were not imported to Europe. *(Europe did not have large plantations requiring a great deal of manual labor.)*

✓ **Reading Check Answer**
The **viceroyalties** were districts in New Spain.
The **viceroy** ruled each viceroyalty as a representative of the king of Spain.

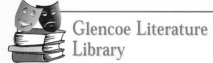
Glencoe Literature Library

The following novel from the **Glencoe Literature Library** may be used to enrich this chapter:
• *I, Juan de Pareja,* by Elizabeth Trevino. (Enslaved artist forced by Spanish law to hide his talent.)

💾 Use the **Vocabulary Puzzle-Maker** to create crossword and word search puzzles.

✓ **Reading Check Answer**
The *peninsulares* were Spaniards born in Spain, while the *mestizos* were of mixed European and Native American ancestry.

Colonial Vase

✓ **Reading Check**
What were the **viceroyalties?** What was the role of the **viceroy?**

✓ **Reading Check**
How did the *peninsulares* and *mestizos* differ from each other?

SECTION 2 Spain

By 1535, Spain had established the largest colonial empire i the Americas. Spain's colonies reached from southern Nort America through Central America and the West Indies to Sout America. Spain also had trade interests in the Philippines.

Unlike Portugal, Spain had a fairly large population. Th allowed it to send thousands of people to its colonies in the Amer cas. Spain also had a strong, centralized colonial government.

Mexico and Peru In the early 1500s, Spain conquered th Native American empires of Mexico and Peru. They set the exam ple for other Spanish colonies. They were governed by the Counc of the Indies, which met at the Spanish court. This council mad laws, acted as a court of final appeal, and chose officials to send the Americas. It even took charge of religious matters.

The colonies were divided into two **viceroyalties** (vīs' r uhl tēz), or districts—New Spain, or Mexico, and New Castile, o Peru. Each viceroyalty was ruled by a **viceroy** (vīs' roi), o person who represented the king.

The colonists in the viceroyalties sent large amounts of gol and silver back to Spain. They also ran plantations that produce cocoa, coffee, tobacco, tea, and sugar. They forced Nativ Americans to do all of the heavy work in mines and on plantation Most of the Native Americans were badly treated. Many died o overwork, starvation, or such diseases as measles and smallpox.

After a time, the Spanish, like the Portuguese, brough enslaved Africans to the Americas. Most of these enslaved peopl worked on sugar plantations located on the islands of th Caribbean. There were still far more Portuguese-owned enslave people in Brazil, however, than Spanish-owned peopl in the Caribbean.

By the middle 1500s, colonists in the Americas were divide into clear-cut social groups. At the top were *peninsulares* (pu nin sū la' rās), or Spaniards born in Spain. Then came Creole (krē' ōlz), or those of Spanish descent born in the Americas. Nex were *mestizos* (me stē' zōz), or people of mixed European an Native American ancestry. They were followed by Native Amer cans. At the lowest level were blacks. Each group held certai jobs. Peninsulares served as viceroys or important church lead ers. Mestizos were mostly artisans and merchants.

The way in which colonial cities grew up also reflected thi social structure. Most cities centered on a square. On one side o the square was the cathedral. On the other three sides stood th government headquarters and the houses of peninsulares Farther out were the houses of Creoles and mestizos.

COOPERATIVE LEARNING

Divide the class into small groups and assign an oral report on the advantages and disadvantages of the introduction of the profit motive during the age of exploration. Each student is responsible for a specific task or area of research. Have students address these questions: *What effect did the profit motive have on European countries? What effect did the profit motive have on the* *inhabitants of the Americas and Africa?* One or more students in each group should compile the research and prepare the report, gather necessary supplies and visuals, and another student should present the report to the class.

Assign the Chapter 31 *Cooperative Learning Activity* in the TCR.

The Roman Catholic Church played a large role in Spanish colonization. It controlled most of the best land in the Spanish colonies. Although the Church itself did not pay taxes, it charged the people who rented or farmed its land a 10 percent income tax.

The Church worked to better conditions in the colonies. Leaders, such as Bartholomé de Las Casas (bar tol uh mā' dā lahs kah' sahs), tried to improve life for the Native Americans. The Church built schools, hospitals, and *asylums* (uh sī' luhms), or places for the mentally ill, and staffed them mostly with nuns. It established the first two universities, in the Americas. One was the University of Mexico. The other was San Marcos (mar' kuhs) University at Lima.

The Decline of an Empire   Spain received a great deal of wealth from the colonies, but it did not hold on to that wealth. The Spanish Inquisition had driven out most of the Jews and Muslims who had been the backbone of Spanish industry. As a result, much of the gold and silver sent to Spain ended up going to northern Europe to pay for goods made there.

Laziness In Inca times, anyone entering the city of Cuzco was greeted by the phrase *Ama Sua, Ama Quella, Ama Lulla*—Don't Lie, Don't Steal, Don't Be Lazy. To the Incas, laziness was such a serious offense that it was punishable by death.

Linking Across Time

Music   The enslaved Africans carried to the Americas contributed to the development of the region's culture. They crafted drums (below) and other instruments similar to those in their homeland and shaped our musical heritage. Today the rhythms of Africa can be heard in the music of the steel drummers in the Caribbean (right) and in the sounds of reggae, calypso, salsa, rap, and other types of music. **What cultural contributions did Spanish settlers make?**

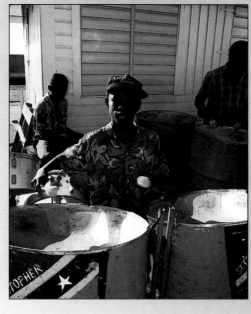

CHAPTER 31 EXPANSION INTO THE AMERICAS   **491**

EXTENDING THE CONTENT

Even the huge amounts of silver and gold from Mexico and Peru paid only about a quarter of the war costs that Philip II and his successors accrued. Their leaders saw themselves as the defenders of the Roman Catholic Church and went to war against Muslims, Turks, Huguenots, Calvinists, and Protestants. Little revenue from trade or industry could be had in the country because of the lack of middle class and the expulsion of non-Catholics. The Spanish people were heavily taxed, and still the government ran out of money. The high taxes caused rebellions.

✓ **Reading Check Answer**
The English hoped the raw materials and gold and silver supplied by colonies would allow them to establish a favorable **balance of trade** in which they sold more goods than they bought.

The Spanish also had trouble getting gold and silver from their colonies to Spain. Ships loaded with the precious metals were robbed at sea by English, French, and Dutch pirates. English sea dogs attacked Spanish treasure ships with the blessing of their queen, Elizabeth I. One of the most successful sea dogs was Sir Francis Drake. When the Spanish Armada was defeated by the English in 1588, Spain lost its power in the Atlantic. This opened the Americas to colonization by England, the Netherlands, and France.

Section 2 Assessment

1. **Define:** viceroyalties, viceroy, *peninsulares, mestizos.*
2. What role did the Roman Catholic Church play in the Spanish colonies?
3. Why did the Spanish have trouble transporting gold and silver from the Americas to Spain?

Critical Thinking

4. **Predicting Consequences** What do you think might have happened if Spain had used the gold and silver to develop industries in the Americas?

Graphic Organizer Activity

5. Draw this diagram, and use it to show the structure of Spanish society from the most powerful to the least powerful groups.

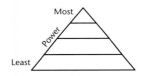

SECTION 3 England

✓ **Reading Check**
How did the English try to establish a favorable **balance of trade?**

Like Portugal and Spain, England looked to the Americas for wealth. English nobles and merchants saw it as a place to get raw materials as well as gold and silver. With enough gold, silver, and raw materials, the English could establish a favorable **balance of trade.** This meant England would be able to sell more products to other countries than it would have to buy from them. The English would no longer have to depend on other countries for their needs.

The English had other reasons for wanting colonies in the Americas. England had such a large population that jobs were becoming hard to find. New colonies meant more jobs. Then, too, the Anglican (ang' gluh kuhn) Church had become England's official church and the English people were expected to follow Anglican beliefs. Because of this, Catholics and groups of Protestants called Separatists (sep' uhr uh tists) were looking for a place where they could have religious freedom. They believed that in the Americas they would be able to worship freely.

In 1585, a group of colonists financed by Sir Walter Raleigh (rahl' ē) sailed for North America. There, they founded a colony on Roanoke (rō' uh nōk) Island off the coast of North Carolina. After six years, however, the colonists disappeared. No one knows for certain what happened to them. For this reason, Roanoke Island became known as the "Lost Colony."

The English did not try again to found colonies in the Americas for more than 20 years. However, in 1600 English merchants formed the East India Company to trade with the East Indies. The company set up trading posts in India, Malaya (muh lā' uh), and some islands in both the East and West Indies.

HISTORY Online
Student Web Activity
Visit the *Human Heritage* Web site at
humanheritage.glencoe.com
and click on ***Chapter 31—
Student Web Activities*** to find
out more about Jamestown.

HISTORY Online
Student Web Activity objectives,
goals, and answers can be found at the
Chapter 31 Web Activity Lesson Plan
at **humanheritage.glencoe.com**

Jamestown   In 1607, a group of English nobles and merchants formed the Virginia Company of London. The following year the company sent about 100 settlers to the Americas to search for gold and silver. They founded the first permanent English settlement in America. It was located near the mouth of Chesapeake (ches' uh pēk) Bay. The settlers named it Jamestown after their king, James I.

The area in which the colony was founded had long been home to Native Americans. By the time Christopher Columbus arrived in the Americas, there were more than 1 million Native Americans scattered across the North American continent. They were divided into some 500 different groups.

Each group of Native Americans had its own language, religion, and way of life. Some, like the Pima (pē' muh), Papago (pap' uh gō), Creeks, and Cherokee (cher' uh kē), were farmers. Others, like the Comanche (kuh man' chē), Blackfoot, Sioux (sū), Apache (uh pach' ē), and Navaho (nav' uh hō), were hunters and warriors who traveled in bands.

The Native Americans who lived in the area near Jamestown were the Powhatan (pau uh tan'). Their chief, whom the settlers called Powhatan, controlled 128 Native American villages.

Life in Jamestown was hard. The land was swampy and filled with mosquitoes that carried disease. Winters were colder in Jamestown than in England. The colonists burned parts of their houses as fuel. Many became sick and died.

Captain John Smith kept the settlement from total failure. He made it clear that those who did not work would not eat. He also convinced the Powhatan to supply the colonists with corn and beans. When Smith returned to England in 1609, however, many of the colonists starved to death. Those still alive a year later were ready to go back to England. When an English fleet arrived with supplies, the colonists decided to stay.

The settlers worked the land, but they did not own it. It belonged to the Virginia Company. Then, in 1618 the company began granting land to individuals. All colonists who paid their own way to America were given 50 acres, or about 20 hectares, of

L1 **Geography: Location** Ask students to locate Jamestown on the map of "European Colonies in the Americas" on page 498. Ask them to describe its location in reference to later British colonies. **ELL**

DID YOU KNOW ??
On August 18, 1587, Virginia Dare was born on Roanoke Island. She was the granddaughter of the governor of the island and the first child born in America of English parents.

Painting of John Smith

Biography

The following videotape program is available from Glencoe to enrich Chapter 31:

• **Pocahontas: Her True Story**

To find classroom resources to accompany this video, check the following home page:

A&E Television:
http://www.aetv.com

MEETING SPECIAL NEEDS

Help students having difficulty accessing chapter information use a kind of rapid "reading" or scanning to locate specific information in the text. Show students how to scan by sliding a finger down the middle of the column rapidly. Demonstrate finding the date 1585 on page 493. Read the event that occurred on that date. Then have students use this method to find the following dates and the events in Section 3: 1600, 1606, 1609, 1618, 1612, 1619, 1630, 1634, 1681, 1691, 1733. Create a time line of events on the chalkboard as students respond.

📁 Refer to *Inclusion for the Middle School Social Studies Classroom: Strategies and Activities.*

Geography: Region Provide students with an outline map of North America. Help them make a map of the regions where each of the Native American culture groups listed in the chart on page 494 lived in North America. Then have them compare their maps of the Native American culture groups with a climate map of North America. Discuss how the climate where each group lived affected their way of life. **ELL**

MAKING CONNECTIONS

➤➤ **Culture** In 1619, 20 enslaved African Americans were brought to Jamestown colony, the first of many such shipments. This important event changed the culture and social structure of the Americas from then on.

L3 **Science** John White, a Roanoke colonist and artist, painted pictures of the animals and vegetation that he encountered in the Americas. Ask students to research and write a report explaining how these paintings affected 16th-century science. Students might share examples of White's paintings with the class. **ELL**

NATIVE AMERICANS

REGION	WAY OF LIFE
Arctic	fished and hunted whales, seals, walruses, and caribou; lived in wood and stone houses or igloos in winter and animal skin tents in summer
Subarctic	hunted and gathered food; built wood-frame houses; traveled by snowshoes, canoe, and toboggan
Northwest Coast	fished and hunted; built cedar wood houses and sea-going canoes; carved totem poles to honor ancestors; held potlatches, or ceremonial feasts
Plateau	hunted bison, fished, and gathered food; lived in multifamily lodges; bred the Appaloosa horse
Great Basin	hunted and gathered food; wandered over territory; wove reed baskets decorated with beads, feathers, and shells
California	hunted, fished, and gathered food; settled in communities; used acorns to make bread
Southwest	farmed corn, beans, and squash; built pueblos of stone and adobe; wove straw and reed baskets and cotton cloth
Great Plains	farmed and hunted; lived in log houses or cone-shaped tipis; communicated with other tribes by hand signals
Eastern Woodlands	fished and hunted; lived in longhouses and birch lodges; women owned property, chose chief, and passed on family name
Southeast	farmed and hunted; built towns with open squares; women owned houses and land; counted descent through mothers

EXTENDING THE CONTENT

Many historians think that American settlers were influenced in their development of a new government by the confederations they observed among the Native Americans on the east coast. According to legend, a holy man in the 1500s tried to end the constant warfare among the related Iroquois-speaking peoples of the Five Nations. A Mohawk leader, Hiawatha, brought the tribes together in a political and military alliance that came to be known as the Iroquois League. In the confederation, each tribe continued to manage its internal affairs, but they cooperated against outside enemies. The Iroquois League served as a model for the Albany Plan of Union and the Articles of Confederation.

land. In order to attract more colonists, the company began giving each settler an additional 50 acres, or 20 hectares, for each person that settler brought to the Americas. Soon, the number of people coming to the Americas increased tremendously.

Most of the newcomers were **indentured** (in den' chuhrd) **servants.** These were people who agreed to work for four to seven years after their arrival to pay for their passage. At the end of that time, they were free and could obtain land of their own.

The settlers saw the Native Americans using tobacco and began to use it themselves. People in Europe also started using tobacco. At first, they used it as a medicine. Later, they smoked it in clay pipes. About 1612, a settler named John Rolfe (rahlf) began planting tobacco. It soon became Virginia's most important crop. Most of the tobacco grown was exported to England, because people there were willing to pay a good price for it.

The settlers brought English laws and government with them to the Americas. They were far from England, however, and travel was slow. Soon, it became necessary for them to make their own laws. In 1619, they elected 22 **burgesses** (ber' jis ez), or representatives, from among landowning males over 17 years old. The burgesses met to decide laws for the colony. This House of Burgesses set an important example of self-government.

Plymouth   Another company, the Virginia Company of Plymouth (plim' uhth), was formed in England in 1606. In 1620, it was reorganized as the Council for New England. It gained the right to grant land to settlers for colonies in New England.

That same year, a group of Separatists called Pilgrims sailed for Virginia on the *Mayflower*. They had received grants of land from the Virginia Company. Strong winds blew the *Mayflower* off course, causing the Pilgrims to land in New England just north of Cape Cod in present-day Massachusetts.

The lands in New England belonged to the Council for New England, and the Pilgrims had not been given the right to govern in them. Therefore, they signed an agreement to set up a civil government. This agreement was called the Mayflower Compact. The majority of free men would govern. Neither women nor indentured servants could vote.

The Pilgrims named their settlement Plymouth after the English town from which they had sailed. Their first winter in the Americas was hard. About one half of the settlers died. In the spring, those who remained cleared the fields for farming. The Native Americans taught them how to fertilize their crops, and how to hunt and fish in the wilderness.

The people of Plymouth governed themselves for 70 years with almost no outside control. Then, in 1691, Plymouth became part of the Massachusetts Bay Colony.

Reading Check
How did **indentured servants** pay for their passage to the Americas?

Reading Check
Who were the **burgesses,** and how did they encourage self-government?

Fun Facts....

Baptized Indentured Servants The first Africans in Virginia, who arrived at Jamestown in 1619, were indentured servants. Among them were a couple named Antoney and Isabella, who had probably been baptized by Spanish traders. In 1623 or 1624, Isabella gave birth to a son, the first African American born in the English colonies. The baby was named William and was baptized in the Church of England.

Reading Check Answer
To pay for their passage, **indentured servants** agreed to work for four to seven years after their arrival.

DID YOU KNOW ??
John Smith claimed he escaped death at the hands of Native Americans as a result of the pleas of Pocahontas, the daughter of a Native American chief. Pocahontas later married John Rolfe and settled in England.

Reading Check Answer
The **burgesses** were representatives from among landowning males over 17 years old who met to decide laws for the Virginia colony.

MAKING CONNECTIONS

➤➤ **History** Originally, the Pilgrims set sail in two ships—the *Mayflower* and the *Speedwell*. The *Speedwell*, however, was not seaworthy and had to turn back. Many of its passengers transferred to the already overcrowded *Mayflower*.

Glencoe Literature Library

The following novels from the **Glencoe Literature Library** may be used to enrich this chapter:
• *The Scarlet Letter*, by Nathaniel Hawthorne. (Boston in the mid-1600s.)
• *The Witch of Blackbird Pond*, by Elizabeth George. (Settler from Barbados in Puritan Connecticut.)

EXTENDING THE CONTENT

France and Great Britain fought three wars in Canada and the American frontier—King William's War, 1689-1697; Queen Anne's War, 1702-1713; and King George's War 1744-1748. In America, the French had more territory, the British more people. What is called the French and Indian War broke out in 1754. This war between France and England was a struggle for control of North America. Quebec, center of New France, fell to the British in 1759. So did the island possessions of France and Spain (which had joined France's side). The 1763 Treaty of Paris ended France's empire in the Americas and was the virtual end of its empire in India.

LINKING PAST TO PRESENT

The plentiful harvest in the fall of 1621 led Governor William Bradford to declare a festival. The Pilgrims invited their Native American friends to a three-day feast that is now known as Thanksgiving.

💾 Use **Interactive Tutor Self-Assessment Software** to review Section 3.

💾 Use the **Vocabulary Puzzle-Maker** to create crossword and word search puzzles.

Painting of Lord Baltimore

The Growth of Empire Jamestown and Plymouth were not the only English settlements in the Americas. In fact, by 1733 Great Britain had 13 colonies along the Atlantic coast of America. One of these colonies was founded in 1630, when a group of Puritans seeking religious freedom sailed to New England. There, they formed several settlements of the Massachusetts Bay Colony in the area around present-day Boston.

In 1634, the English settled in Maryland. King Charles I had granted the land to his friend Cecilius Calvert (se sēl′ yuhs kal′ vuhrt), the second Lord Baltimore. Calvert wanted a place in America where English Catholics could live in peace.

In 1681, William Penn, the leader of a religious group called the Quakers (kwā′ kuhrz), founded a colony in Pennsylvania. King Charles II had granted Penn the land in payment for a debt he owed Penn's father.

Section 3 Assessment

1. **Define:** balance of trade, indentured servants, burgesses.
2. Why did colonists set up the House of Burgesses?
3. What group founded the Massachusetts Bay Colony? Why did they establish it?

Critical Thinking

4. **Making Inferences** Why would the Americas be a likely place for people to settle who were unhappy in their own countries?

Graphic Organizer Activity

5. Draw this diagram, and use it to compare the English colonies at Jamestown and Plymouth.

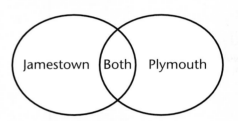

Jamestown | Both | Plymouth

SECTION 4 The Netherlands

The Dutch also established colonies in the Americas. In 1602, Dutch merchants founded the Dutch East India Company to trade in Africa and the East Indies. The Dutch had a fleet of more than 10,000 merchant ships. One by one, they seized Portuguese trading posts in the East Indies and soon controlled most of the East Indies. In addition, they became the first Europeans to reach Australia and New Zealand. They also founded a

496 UNIT 10 THE CHANGING WORLD

Section 3 Assessment Answers

1. balance of trade, balance of imports and exports (p. 492); indentured servants, pledged labor for passage (p. 495); burgesses, representatives (p. 495)
2. to make their own laws
3. the Puritans; for religious freedom
4. Answers will vary, but students should support their responses with examples of opportunities or freedoms that could be found in the Americas.

5. Distinctive information on each colony might include features such as geographic location, purpose for founding, groups that settled the colony, date founded, etc. Shared features might include ties to England, the practice of self-government, difficult early years, etc.

Assign the Chapter 31 **Section 3 Quiz** in the TCR. Testmaker available.

colony named Capetown at the southern tip of Africa. Many Dutch colonists, called Boers (borz), settled there.

In 1621, the Dutch formed another company called the Dutch West India Company to establish colonies in the Americas. Colonists were sent first to islands in the West Indies and along the coast of South America. In 1624, the Dutch founded the city of New Amsterdam (am' stuhr dam) on the island of Manhattan (man hat' n). They bought the island from the Native Americans for goods worth about $24. The Dutch called the colonies they established in North America "New Netherlands." New Amsterdam was the capital.

Later in the 1600s, rivalry between the Dutch and the English led to a series of wars, which the Dutch lost. The English took over most of the Dutch colonies, including New Amsterdam, which they renamed New York.

Section 4 Assessment

1. Why were the Dutch East India Company and the Dutch West India Company formed?
2. To what nation did the Dutch lose most of their colonies?

Critical Thinking

3. **Drawing Conclusions** Do you think the Dutch purchase of Manhattan was fair or unfair to the Native Americans? Explain.

Graphic Organizer Activity

4. Draw this diagram, and use it to show some of the areas that the Dutch explored or colonized.

SECTION 5 France

In 1608, Samuel de Champlain (sham plān'), a French explorer, founded the first permanent French colony in the Americas at Quebec (kwi bek'). Soon after, the French established other settlements around the Great Lakes. They also established settlements at the northern end of the Mississippi River and along the rivers and streams that flowed into it.

Most of these settlements resembled villages in France. Houses stood side by side along a lake or river bank. Behind each house stretched a long, narrow farm. The settlements were small, because few people wanted to leave France.

Most of the French in the Americas were fur traders. On foot or by canoe, they visited various Native American tribes. They gave the Native Americans blankets, guns, knives, and wine in

Painting of Robert de La Salle

Section 4 Assessment Answers

1. Dutch East India Company—to organize trade in Africa and the East Indies; Dutch West India Company—to establish colonies in the Americas
2. England
3. Answers will vary, but students should explain how they reached their conclusion.

4. Sample areas: East Indies, Australia, New Zealand, Capetown, West Indies, coast of South America, Manhattan Island (New Amsterdam)

Assign the Chapter 31 **Section 4 Quiz** in the TCR. Testmaker available.

Independent Practice

L2 **Critical Thinking** Have students make charts titled "Colonial Empires in the Americas," and use these headings to sort information: "Country," "Location of Empire," "Reason for Settlement," "Major Resources and Goods Received from Colonies," "Reasons for the Empire's Decline." Have volunteers write their charts on the chalkboard or large poster board.

GEOGRAPHY AND HISTORY

European politics and worldwide rivalry for trade and colonies were interconnected in the wars between France and Great Britain in the 18th century. By the 1750s, both had colonies in India, the West Indies, and the Americas. The general name given to the final encounter between these two European countries is the Seven Years' War (1756-1763.) Ask students to describe the British empire in the Americas after the Treaty of Paris. *(The British empire in the Americas after the Treaty of Paris included much of the eastern half of North America from the Great Plains east to the Atlantic Ocean and several Caribbean islands.)*

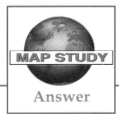

MAP STUDY

Answer

in the northern part of North America

Assign the Chapter 31 **Geography and Map Activity** in the TCR.

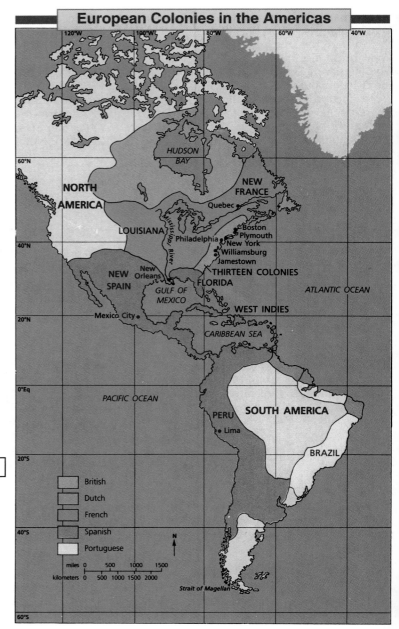

European Colonies in the Americas

MAP STUDY

LOCATION By the mid-1700s, France, England, Portugal, and the Netherlands had extended their American claims. **In what parts of the Americas were the British claims located?**

498 UNIT 10 THE CHANGING WORLD

EXTENDING THE CONTENT

Less than 50 years of Dutch occupation left some lasting reminders in the Middle Atlantic states. Besides the main settlement at New Amsterdam, the Dutch also had Fort Orange, near present-day Albany, and Fort Nassau, across the river from Philadelphia. Settlement in the Dutch colonies was slow, partly because the Dutch West India Company had strict rules for settlers and partly because life in Holland was peaceful and prosperous. To boost immigration, the Dutch tried the patron system—a semi-feudal arrangement in which large estate owners found settlers for their land and then oversaw their settlements.

498

exchange for beaver and other animal skins. Beaver hats for gentlemen became very fashionable in Europe, and the fur trade brought France much wealth.

In 1682, René-Robert Cavelier (ka ve lyā'), Sieur de La Salle (sjoer dā la sal), claimed the Mississippi River valley for France. He named the area Louisiana in honor of the French king, Louis XIV. The French called Louisiana and their other lands in the Americas "New France."

The French also established settlements in the West Indies and in India. In time, the French and the English became great rivals. They clashed in Europe, the Americas, and India. After a series of four wars, the French finally were defeated. In 1763, they signed the Treaty of Paris. Under the treaty, the French lost their North American colonial empire and almost all of their settlements in India.

People in History

Robert de La Salle
1643–1687
French Explorer
Robert de La Salle moved in 1666 to what is now Canada. His explorations in the Mississippi River Valley led to French claims in North America.

Section 5 Assessment

1. What was the first permanent French colony founded in the Americas?
2. Why did France's established settlements in the Americas remain small?
3. How did the French lose their lands in North America?

Critical Thinking
4. **Making Inferences** Why do you think so few French people wanted to settle in the Americas?

Graphic Organizer Activity
5. Draw this diagram, and use it to write at least three facts about French settlements in North America.

French Settlements — Fact 1 / Fact 2 / Fact 3

SECTION 6 The Influence of Empires

Empires in the Americas helped make the nations of western Europe richer and more powerful. These empires also introduced western Europeans to many new foods. Among them were avocados, lima beans, peanuts, pineapples, tomatoes, and turkeys. Farmers in Spain, Portugal, and Italy began to grow corn, while farmers in Germany and Ireland started to specialize in potatoes. Both corn and potatoes were nourishing and easy to grow. As a result, fewer western Europeans died because of famine, and Europe's population increased.

Another popular product from the Americas was a drink made by roasting dry cocoa beans over a fire and pounding them into a paste. The chocolate paste was then mixed with water,

Fun Facts . . . .

Chocolate Hernando Cortés may have been the first European to taste chocolate. At Montezuma's court in Mexico, he had sampled a bitter drink made from cocoa beans. He then brought the drink back to Spain. There people drank it hot, sweetened, and flavored with vanilla or cinnamon. The Spanish tried to keep the new drink a secret.

CHAPTER 31 EXPANSION INTO THE AMERICAS **499**

L1 **Role Play** Encourage students to learn more about the foods that were introduced to Europe by the empires. Have student pairs role-play a sea captain returning from the Americas who tries to sell some of these foods to the people of London and Paris. Have the rest of the class act as an audience, judging whether they would be willing to try the new foods from the sales pitch they hear.

MAKING CONNECTIONS

➤➤ **Religion** All the French settlers were Roman Catholic since Huguenots, or French Protestants, were not allowed in France's colonies.

Use **Interactive Tutor Self-Assessment Software** to review Section 5.

Use the **Vocabulary Puzzle-Maker** to create crossword and word search puzzles.

DID YOU KNOW ???

The Americas provided western Europeans with tobacco. People either smoked it in clay pipes or inhaled it in a powdered form called snuff.

ASSESS

Check for Understanding

Ask students to summarize the main points of the chapter, orally or in writing. Discuss the answers to the Section and Chapter Assessment questions.

Evaluate

Assign the Chapter 31 **Performance Assessment Activity** in the TCR.

Administer the **Chapter 31 Test**. Testmaker available.

Section 5 Assessment Answers

1. Quebec
2. because few people wanted to leave France
3. They were defeated by the English in a series of four wars.
4. Answers will vary but might include the idea that the French were satisfied and did not see opportunities in America.
5. Sample facts should reflect information in the textbook such as: first settlement founded at Quebec in 1608 by Samuel de Champlain, other settlements founded around the Great Lakes and northern end of the Mississippi River, settlements resembled villages in France, most settlers worked at the fur trade, and so on.

Assign the Chapter 31 **Section 5 Quiz** in the TCR. Testmaker available.

Reteach

Divide the class into five groups. Each group will represent one country: Spain, Portugal, France, England, or the Netherlands. Have the groups summarize their colonial actions.

Assign the Chapter 31 **Reteaching Activity** in the TCR.

Enrich

Have students investigate Portuguese exploration and colonization in Asia and Africa—the trading kingdoms on Africa's east coast, Native American trading posts, and Asian cities such as Macao. Ask them to write a report describing the history of each of these settlements.

Assign the Chapter 31 **Enrichment Activity** in the TCR.

CLOSE

Ask students to discuss the empires of the five European countries in the Americas and decide which of them most influenced the histories of the following places: Canada, the United States, the Caribbean islands, Central America, South America.

💾 Use **Interactive Tutor Self-Assessment Software** to review Section 6.

---

sugar, vanilla, and cinnamon, and shaken up and down until it bubbled. The people in London, Paris, and other cities in western Europe became so fond of the chocolate drink that they opened cafes where they could sip the drink and talk about events of the day.

Section 6 Assessment

1. What did the empires in the Americas do for the nations of western Europe?
2. What were some of the new foods the empires introduced to western Europeans?
3. What crops did Germany and Ireland specialize in raising?

Critical Thinking

4. **Synthesizing Information** Which of the foods introduced to western Europeans from the Americas are part of your diet today?

Graphic Organizer Activity

5. Draw this diagram, and use it to support this generalization: Contact with the Americas improved life for western Europeans.

Chapter Summary & Study Guide

1. By 1532, Portugal had a colony in Brazil and trading posts in Africa, India, and Southeast Asia.
2. A poorly organized government and a weak economy allowed Spain and other nations to take over many Portuguese lands.
3. English defeat of the Spanish Armada in 1588 weakened Spain's grip on the Americas and opened the door to colonization by other nations.
4. In 1607, the English founded their first successful settlement in the Americas at Jamestown.
5. Settlers at Jamestown established the House of Burgesses, which set the example of self-government in the English colonies.
6. In 1620, the Pilgrims established England's second permanent settlement at Plymouth in New England.
7. The Dutch and French also established settlements in North America, but the English seized most Dutch holdings.
8. Empires in the Americas gave western European nations wealth and power and introduced people to many new foods.

Section 6 Assessment Answers

1. They helped make the nations richer and more powerful.
2. avocados, lima beans, peanuts, pineapples, tomatoes, turkeys, corn, potatoes, and chocolate
3. corn and potatoes
4. Answers will vary but should include more than one food.

5. Sample supporting details: nations of western Europe became richer and more powerful; farmers learned to grow new crops; fewer western Europeans died of famine; western European population increased

Assign the Chapter 31 **Section 6 Quiz** in the TCR. Testmaker available.

Assessment

Using Key Terms

Write a paragraph as if you were a Spanish person of the 1500s who has decided to go to the Americas. Explain what you have heard that has influenced your decision. Use the following words in your paragraph.

colonize
bandeirantes
viceroy
mestizos
indentured servants

captaincies
viceroyalties
peninsulares
balance of trade
burgesses

Understanding Main Ideas

1. Why did western European nations want to colonize the Americas?
2. Why did the Portuguese settlers in Brazil bring over enslaved Africans?
3. What happened to most of the gold and silver Spain received from its colonies?
4. In what ways did Native Americans help the settlers at Jamestown? At Plymouth?
5. What kind of trade did the French establish with the Native Americans?

Critical Thinking

1. What changes did European colonization cause in the lives of Native Americans? Explain.
2. "Working as an indentured servant for several years to pay for a trip to the Americas was fair." What is your opinion of this statement? Explain.
3. What was the most difficult problem Europeans faced in the Americas?

4. What would you have liked about being a Jamestown settler? What would you have disliked?

Graphic Organizer Activity

Culture Create a chart like the one below, and use it to compare the colonies established by Portugal, Spain, England, the Netherlands, and France.

Geography in History

Place Refer to the map on page 498. The European colonies stretched from Hudson Bay in the north to the Strait of Magellan in the south. What is similar about the places where most colonial cities were established? Write a paragraph explaining the reasons for this similarity.

Using Your Journal

Review any details you may have noted about the changes that took place in the Americas in the 1500s and 1600s. Imagine you are a news reporter in the Americas at that time. Write an editorial in which you give your impression of the effects of your impression of the Americas on the land and its people.

Bonus Test Question

If you were the ruler of a viceroyalty in the early 1500s, what would your title be, where might you be living, and what major problems would you face? *(viceroy; Mexico or Peru; controlling Native Americans, making plantations profitable, and sending gold and silver back to Spain)*

Using Your Journal

Editorials will vary. You might call on volunteers to read their editorials to the class and discuss.

Geography in History

Colonial cities were located on seacoasts, often clumped in regions; the British established the most cities.

Using Key Terms

Paragraphs will vary but students should have reasons to support emigration from Spain.

Understanding Main Ideas

1. because they wanted its riches and to spread Christianity
2. because most of the Native Americans they had enslaved ran away or died from diseases
3. It ended up going to northern Europe to pay for goods made there.
4. They taught the colonists how to plant corn and beans, and how to hunt and fish.
5. fur trade

Critical Thinking

1. Many died from diseases and doing heavy work; many were moved and introduced to guns and wine.
2. Answers will vary, but students could mention that indentured servants were often treated badly.
3. Answers will vary but should present difficulties, such as disease, wars, and starvation.
4. Answers will vary but should give specific examples.

Graphic Organizer Activity

Charts will vary but should show main features of colonies as described in the chapter, such as geographic location, types of government, social organization, and methods of sustenance.

Chapter 32 Planning Guide

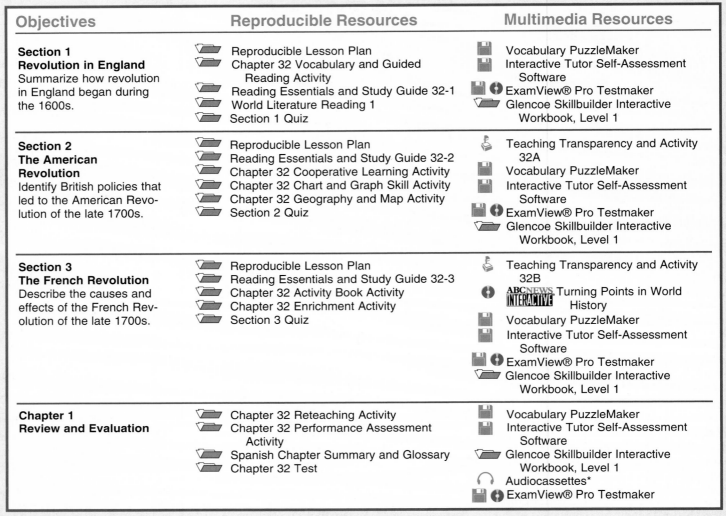

Objectives	Reproducible Resources	Multimedia Resources
Section 1 **Revolution in England** Summarize how revolution in England began during the 1600s.	Reproducible Lesson Plan Chapter 32 Vocabulary and Guided Reading Activity Reading Essentials and Study Guide 32-1 World Literature Reading 1 Section 1 Quiz	Vocabulary PuzzleMaker Interactive Tutor Self-Assessment Software ExamView® Pro Testmaker Glencoe Skillbuilder Interactive Workbook, Level 1
Section 2 **The American Revolution** Identify British policies that led to the American Revolution of the late 1700s.	Reproducible Lesson Plan Reading Essentials and Study Guide 32-2 Chapter 32 Cooperative Learning Activity Chapter 32 Chart and Graph Skill Activity Chapter 32 Geography and Map Activity Section 2 Quiz	Teaching Transparency and Activity 32A Vocabulary PuzzleMaker Interactive Tutor Self-Assessment Software ExamView® Pro Testmaker Glencoe Skillbuilder Interactive Workbook, Level 1
Section 3 **The French Revolution** Describe the causes and effects of the French Revolution of the late 1700s.	Reproducible Lesson Plan Reading Essentials and Study Guide 32-3 Chapter 32 Activity Book Activity Chapter 32 Enrichment Activity Section 3 Quiz	Teaching Transparency and Activity 32B ABCNEWS INTERACTIVE Turning Points in World History Vocabulary PuzzleMaker Interactive Tutor Self-Assessment Software ExamView® Pro Testmaker Glencoe Skillbuilder Interactive Workbook, Level 1
Chapter 1 **Review and Evaluation**	Chapter 32 Reteaching Activity Chapter 32 Performance Assessment Activity Spanish Chapter Summary and Glossary Chapter 32 Test	Vocabulary PuzzleMaker Interactive Tutor Self-Assessment Software Glencoe Skillbuilder Interactive Workbook, Level 1 Audiocassettes* ExamView® Pro Testmaker

*Also available in Spanish.

Presentation Plus!

Use Glencoe's **Presentation Plus!** multimedia teacher tool to easily present dynamic lessons that visually excite your students. Using Microsoft® PowerPoint, you can customize the presentations to create your own personalized lessons.

Interactive Lesson Planner

Planning has never been easier! Using this CD-ROM, organize your week, month, semester, or year with all the help you need. The **Interactive Lesson Planner** gives you access to all of the blackline masters which accompany *Human Heritage*.

✓ PERFORMANCE ASSESSMENT ACTIVITIES

Pictorial History Have students develop a pictorial history of one of the revolutions covered in this chapter. Tell them to illustrate the major events before, during, and after the revolution. Have students include written information that explains the events. Display the projects in the classroom.

CHAPTER RESOURCES

READINGS FOR THE STUDENT

Burton, Hester. *Kate Ryder* T.Y. Crowell, 1975. Novel focusing on a family's divided loyalties in the English Civil War.

Davis, Burke. *Black Heroes of the American Revolution.* Harcourt, Brace and Jovanovich, 1991. Highlights achievements of African Americans during the Revolution.

READINGS FOR THE TEACHER

Banfield, Susan. *The Rights of Man, The Reign of Terror: The Story of the French Revolution.* Lippincott, 1989. Explores the French Revolution and the French society in turmoil.

Lancaster, Bruce. *The American Revolution: American Heritage Library.* Houghton Mifflin, 1987. Details the American Revolution.

KEY TO ABILITY LEVELS

Teaching strategies have been coded for varying learning styles and abilities.

L1 Level 1 activities are **basic** activities and should be within the ability range of all students.

L2 Level 2 activities are **average** activities and should be within the ability range of the average to above-average student.

L3 Level 3 activities are **challenging** activities designed for the ability range of above-average students.

ELL ELL activities should be within the ability range of English Language Learning students.

Teacher's Corner

INDEX TO NATIONAL GEOGRAPHIC MAGAZINE

The following articles relate to this chapter:

* *France: Bicentennial of the Great Revolution, Special Issue,* July 1989.
* "Two Revolutions," by Charles McCarry, July 1989.

NATIONAL GEOGRAPHIC SOCIETY PRODUCTS AVAILABLE FROM GLENCOE

To order the following, call Glencoe at 1-800-334-7344:

* *PicturePack: The American Revolution (Transparencies)*
* *PictureShow: The American Revolution (CD-ROM)*
* *PicturePack: Geography of North America (Transparencies)*
* *PictureShow: Story of America Library, 1 (CD-ROMs)*

Access *National Geographic's* new dynamic MapMachine Web site and other geography resources at:
http://www.nationalgeographic.com/
http://www.nationalgeographic.com/maps/

The following videotape programs are available from Glencoe:

* **The American Revolution**
  1-56501-436-7

* **Benjamin Franklin: Citizen of the World**
  1-56501-426-X

* **King George III: Mad or Maligned?**
  1-56501-595-9

* **Marie Antoinette: Tragic Queen**
  1-56501-915-6

To order, call Glencoe at 1-800-334-7344. To find classroom resources to accompany many of these check:
A&E Television: http://www.aetv.com
The History Channel:
http://www.historychannel.com

OVERVIEW

Chapter 32 examines the political revolutions that took place in Europe and the American colonies during the 1600s and 1700s.

➤ **Section 1** discusses the reasons why revolution occurred in England in the 1600s.

➤ **Section 2** describes causes of the American Revolution.

➤ **Section 3** summarizes the causes and effects of the French Revolution.

CHAPTER OBJECTIVES

After reading Chapter 32, students will be able to:

1. summarize why revolutions erupted in England.

2. summarize causes of the American Revolution.

3. list the causes and effects of the French Revolution.

EXAMINING ARTIFACTS

Explain that these artifacts come from the French Revolution. Based on the badge, what do students think the revolutionaries were seeking? *(liberty and equality)* What evidence proves that this was a "people's revolution"? *(the presence of women, non-aristocratic clothing styles, use of farm implements as weapons, etc.)* Tell students the French Revolution took place in 1789. Using the time line, have them name events that might have influenced this revolt.

PERFORMANCE ASSESSMENT ✓

Use the Performance Assessment activities on page 502B to help you evaluate students as they complete the chapter.

502

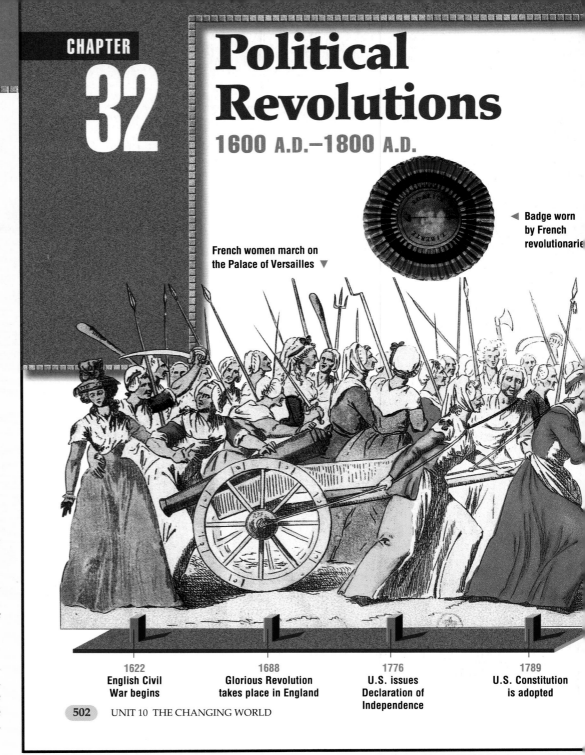

CHAPTER
32

Political Revolutions

1600 A.D.–1800 A.D.

◄ **Badge worn by French revolutionarie**

French women march on the Palace of Versailles ▼

1622	1688	1776	1789
English Civil War begins	**Glorious Revolution takes place in England**	**U.S. issues Declaration of Independence**	**U.S. Constitution is adopted**

502   UNIT 10 THE CHANGING WORLD

TEACHING RESOURCES

TEACHER PLANNING AND SUPPORT
- Reproducible Lesson Plan
- Block Scheduling Implementation Guide
- Videodisc Bar Code Correlation
- Presentation Plus!

REVIEW AND REINFORCEMENT
- Reading Essentials and Study Guide 32-1, 32-2, 32-3
- Chapter 32 Vocabulary and Guided Reading Activity
- Vocabulary PuzzleMaker Software
- Teaching Transparencies 32A & 32B

- Chapter 32 Reteaching Activity
- Chapter 32 Cooperative Learning Activity
- Chapter 32 Activity Book Activity
- Chapter 32 Chart and Graph Skill Activity
- Interactive Tutor Self-Assessment Software

APPLICATION AND HANDS-ON ACTIVITIES
- Daily World History, Geography, and Culture Question
- Unit 10 Hands-On History Lab Activity

Chapter Focus

Read to Discover

- How revolution in England began during the 1600s.
- What British policies led to the American Revolution of the late 1700s.
- How the French Revolution came about in the late 1700s and what its results were.

Chapter Overview

Visit the *Human Heritage* Web site at **humanheritage.glencoe.com** and click on **Chapter 32— Chapter Overviews** to preview this chapter.

Terms to Learn	People to Know	Places to Locate
revolution	James I	Concord
mercantilism	Charles I	Lexington
monopoly	Oliver Cromwell	Yorktown
direct tax	Charles II	Bastille
boycott	John Locke	
estates	Voltaire	

Why It's Important   By the 1700s, people in the western world had new ideas about government. They were less willing to be ruled without having a voice in politics. They also wanted equal justice under the law. They did not believe that monarchs or the Church had the right to tell them what to do. Thinkers and writers began spreading ideas about freedom and the right of people to change the government to meet their needs. For these reasons, the 1700s came to be known in Europe and the Americas as the Age of Enlightenment, or a time of increased knowledge.

SECTION 1   Revolution in England

In England, there was a struggle for power between the king and Parliament. After a civil war and a **revolution,** or an attempt to overthrow or change the government, Parliament won. From that point on, the monarch ruled in the name of the people.

Conflict with Parliament   In 1603, the last Tudor monarch, Queen Elizabeth I, died. Since she had never married, the Crown, or royal power, passed to a distant relative. This was James VI of Scotland, a member of the Stuart family. He became James I of England.

The Tudors had enjoyed great power. They had been careful, however, to get Parliament's opinion on their actions. James I, on the other hand, believed in rule by divine right. When Parliament

Reading Check
What is the goal of a political **revolution?**

GEOGRAPHY ACTIVITIES
- Chapter 32 Geography and Map Activity
- Social Studies Outline Map Resource Book

INTERDISCIPLINARY CONNECTIONS
- Unit 10 World Literature Reading 1
- World Music: Cultural Traditions

ENRICHMENT AND EXTENSION
- **ABCNEWS INTERACTIVE** Turning Points in World History
- World History Primary Source Document Library CD-ROM
- Foods Around the World

ASSESSMENT AND EVALUATION
- Chapter 32 Performance Assessment Activity
- Chapter 32 Section Quizzes 32-1, 32-2, 32-3
- Chapter 32 Test
- Chapter 32 ExamView® Pro Testmaker Software
- Chapter 32 Digests Audiocassettes Activities and Tests

SPANISH RESOURCES
- Chapter 32 Spanish Chapter Summary and Glossary
- Chapter 32 Spanish Chapter Digests Audiocassettes Activities and Tests

---

Chapter Overview introduces students to chapter content and key terms. Have them access **Chapter 32 Overview** at **humanheritage.glencoe.com**

FOCUS

Bellringer

Write this question on the chalkboard: *Do you think that the destruction of another person's property can ever be justified? If yes, under what circumstances?*

Motivational Activity

Discuss student responses. Then tell them that in this chapter they will learn about incidents such as the Boston Tea Party in which people destroyed property in order to get their point across. Ask students if they feel this justifies the protestors' actions.

Reading Check Answer

A political **revolution** seeks to overthrow or change a government.

GUIDE TO READING

Reading Strategy

Ask students to read "Why It's Important" and summarize the chapter's main theme. (*During the Age of Enlightenment, people were less willing to be ruled without a voice in politics and began to demand that governments change to meet their needs.*)

Vocabulary Precheck

Ask students to define each of the "Terms to Learn." **L1 ELL**

Use the Vocabulary PuzzleMaker for Chapter 32 to create a crossword puzzle. **L1**

Assign Chapter 32 Vocabulary and Guided Reading Activity.

Assign Reading Essentials and Study Guide 32-1.

Guided Practice

L1 Civics Point out that the English civil war was the outcome of the deep conflict between the king and Parliament. Ask students to identify the source of that conflict. (*the king's belief in the divine rights of kings and Parliament's desire to have a voice in government*)

ELL

L2 Critical Thinking Ask students to create a list of Parliament's grievances against the king. Putting themselves in the place of members of Parliament, have students rank the grievances from most to least important.

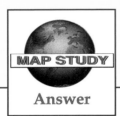

DID YOU KNOW ??

The mother of James I was Mary Queen of Scots, who had been put to death by Elizabeth I.

MAP STUDY

Answer

from the southern and eastern part of England; from the northern and western part of England

---

objected to some of his actions, he dismissed it and ruled without a legislature for ten years.

Religious differences also caused trouble between the king and Parliament. James I wanted to force the Anglican Church on the people. Many members of Parliament, however, were Puritans. They wanted to be able to worship as they pleased. They believed in hard work and plain living, and did not like the Crown's free-spending ways. They wanted a say in how the government raised and spent taxes. With the help of other groups, they worked against what they felt was the king's unjust power.

Although James I did not agree with many of his subjects about religion, it was his idea to have a new translation of the Bible. He appointed a committee of church officials who put together the King James version. Its style has greatly influenced English speech and literature. Many English-speaking Protestant churches today still use the King James version.

When James I died in 1625, his son became King Charles I. He held the same beliefs about the monarchy as his father.

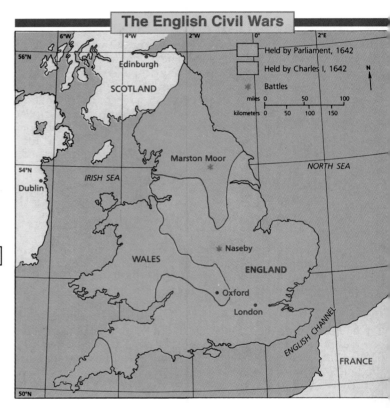

The English Civil Wars

- Held by Parliament, 1642
- Held by Charles I, 1642
- ★ Battles

MAP STUDY

LOCATION The English civil war was both a religious and a political war. **From what part of Englnd did Parliament draw its support? From what part did Charles I draw his support?**

MULTICULTURAL PERSPECTIVES

Many supporters of the Parliamentary cause were Puritans. Like other Protestants, Puritans believed that the Bible was the only source of religious authority. The Puritans were different from other Protestants, such as those belonging to the Church of England, in that Puritans were extremists in their religious discipline and the militancy of their beliefs. They wanted to "purify" the Church of England, which they felt retained too many vestiges of the Roman Catholic Church, and to purify the rest of society as well. Puritans considered themselves the spiritual elite, separate from the wickedness of the world.

In 1628, Charles I was forced to call a meeting of Parliament to approve new taxes to pay for wars with France and Spain. Parliament saw a chance to limit the Crown's power and gain more for itself. It drew up the Petition of Right. This said that the king could not declare **martial** (mar' shuhl) **law,** or rule by the army instead of by law. It also said that the Crown could not pass tax laws without Parliament's consent. In addition, people could not be put in prison just because the king wanted them out of the way. At first, Charles I agreed to the petition. Then, in 1629, he broke his word and dismissed Parliament.

In 1640, however, Charles I needed money to build a larger army to fight the Scots. He had tried to force the Anglican Church on the Presbyterian Scots, and they had revolted, taking over part of northern England. So, he called a meeting of Parliament.

Parliament again saw a chance to limit Charles' power. It passed a law abolishing taxes collected by the Crown without Parliament's consent. It also passed a law to set up regular meetings of Parliament and to do away with the Star Chamber. This was a royal court that tried people without a jury.

Civil War

Once again, Charles I at first accepted the laws Parliament passed and then disregarded them. In 1642, civil war broke out between the Crown and Parliament.

Those who backed the Crown were called Cavaliers (kav uh lirz'). They wore their hair shoulder length, often in curls. They were mostly rich Roman Catholics and Anglicans. Those who backed Parliament were called Roundheads because they wore their hair short. They were mostly middle- and lower-class Puritans and other Calvinists.

Oliver Cromwell (krahm' wel), a Puritan leader who backed Parliament, formed a New Model Army. It drilled hard and followed strict rules against drinking, swearing, and robbing. It chose its officers because they were good fighters and leaders, not because they were of high birth. In 1646, the New Model Army defeated the king's forces and ended the war.

Most English leaders still believed that monarchy was the best form of government. They did not, however, trust Charles I and were afraid to allow him to return to the throne. Cromwell and his supporters put Charles I on trial for treason. The court found him guilty, and he was beheaded in 1649.

Oliver Cromwell

After the king's death, Cromwell took over the rule of England, now called the Commonwealth. The Commonwealth was overwhelmed with troubles from the start. The Irish and the Scots both looked to Charles I's son as the true ruler of England. Cromwell had to put down their rebellion. He also had trouble balancing the English who felt enough changes had been made with those who wanted more. He finally did away

✓ **Reading Check**
What is **martial law?**

Religion Persecution of the Puritans under Charles I led to the Great Migration—the exodus of thousands of Puritans to America between 1630 to 1640. The Puritans founded the Massachusetts Bay Colony and later became known as the Congregationalist Church.

✓ **Reading Check Answer**
Martial law is rule by the military instead of by law.

L3 History Have students draw a political cartoon about the English civil war. For example, students might draw a cartoon that lampoons King Charles or Cromwell that expresses the ideas of the Parliamentarians or the Cavaliers, or that shows the tragedy of the civil war. **ELL**

DID YOU KNOW ??
The region that became the state of Maryland was named for Queen Henrietta Maria, the Catholic French wife of Charles I.

MAKING CONNECTIONS
➤➤ **History** Cromwell's New Model Army also became known for its religious devotion. Soldiers listened to sermons during their free time and often marched into battles singing psalms.

COOPERATIVE LEARNING

Divide students into three groups to stage the trial of King Charles. Explain that one group is to prosecute the king and one group is to defend the king. The third group is to act as witnesses for the prosecution and the defense. Make sure each student has a task to perform. Students should choose one student to role-play Charles and one to role-play Cromwell. Assign other students to research arguments for the prosecution and arguments used by the defense, and prepare dialogue for the role play. Then stage the trial.

OLIVER CROMWELL AND KING CHARLES I Oliver Cromwell shown in this painting (left) organized the New Model Army that defeated the army of King Charles I shown in the painting above (right) in 1646. This ended the four-year civil war between the Crown and Parliament. After Charles was beheaded, Cromwell took over the rule of England, which was then called the Commonwealth. **What problems did Cromwell face as he came to power?**

with Parliament and governed as a military dictator for the Puritan minority.

Many Puritans were very strict. They disapproved of dancing, theater-going, sports, and other popular amusements. They believed people should spend their free time praying and reading the Bible. Despite this, Puritan rule was not completely gloomy. Cromwell himself was fond of music and horses, and allowed women to act on stage for the first time. After Cromwell died, his son Richard took over. By 1660, however, Parliament decided that England again needed a monarch.

The Return of the Stuarts Parliament's choice was Charles I's son, who became Charles II. Charles II had spent most of the previous 15 years in France. He brought French dances, food, and clothing styles with him to London. Soon, the English court was a center of gaiety and fashion. Men copied the fashions of Paris and wore silks and velvets and huge wigs. The wealthy ate large meals. One meal might include rabbit and chicken stew, a leg of mutton, a side of lamb, roasted pigeons, lobsters, tarts, anchovies, and wine. The English nobility was ready for this kind of living, and Charles II became very popular.

506 UNIT 10 THE CHANGING WORLD

SPOTLIGHT ON: CHARLES II

Under the rule of Charles II, the Restoration period (1660-1685) was a brilliant time for literature, drama, music, architecture, and science. In 1662 Charles chartered the Royal Society to encourage investigations in science. The king had his own laboratory, where he performed experiments in chemistry. Charles also established the Royal Observatory at Greenwich. He hoped that discoveries in astronomy would produce better navigational instruments.

In September 1666, a great fire destroyed two-thirds of London's buildings. Charles II put Sir Christopher Wren, an architect, in charge of rebuilding the city. Wren designed St. Paul's Cathedral and 52 other churches. He also had most new houses and shops built of brick and stone instead of wood.

As king, Charles II tried to work with Parliament and not anger it. He refused, however, to consult with it about **foreign policy,** or relations with other countries. Parliament was worried by his friendship with the Roman Catholic king of France.

The Glorious Revolution

In 1685, Charles II died and his brother James became king. Openly Roman Catholic, James II named many Roman Catholics to high posts in the army and the government. This went against a law passed by Parliament under Charles II. James II also tried to have the Act of Habeas Corpus (hā' bē uhs kōr' puhs) **repealed,** or abolished. That act had also been passed under Charles II. It stated that a person could not be put in jail unless charged with a specific crime.

The leaders of Parliament did not like James II. They did not move against him, however, until 1688 when his second wife, who was Roman Catholic, had a son. Fearing the ultimate establishment of Roman Catholic rule, they offered the throne to Mary, James's Protestant daughter by his first wife. William landed in England in 1688 with a large army, and James II fled to France. William and Mary were then named joint rulers. Because the change in monarchs took place without a shot being fired, it came to be called the "Glorious Revolution."

After becoming the new rulers of England in 1689, William and Mary accepted Parliament's Declaration of Rights. This made Parliament stronger and protected the rights of the English people. The declaration stated that the Crown could not tax people or keep an army in peacetime without Parliament's consent. Parliament had the right to debate openly, meet often, and be freely elected. People had the right to a fair and speedy trial by a jury of their peers. People could also petition the Crown without fear of being punished.

The Writings of John Locke

Many of the ideas behind the Glorious Revolution were explained in a book called *Two Treatises of Government.* It was written in 1690 by an English philosopher named John Locke. He believed that people are born with certain natural rights. Among them are the right to life, liberty, and property. Locke believed that the purpose of government is to protect these rights. If it fails to do so, then the people can revolt and set up a new government. Locke thought the best kind of government was a representative one. His writings were widely read, and his ideas became a basis for the American Revolution and, later, the French Revolution.

✓ **Reading Check** Why did Parliament worry about the **foreign policy** of Charles II?

✓ **Reading Check** What would have happened if James II had **repealed** the Act of Habeas Corpus?

Painting of Queen Mary II

L2 Architecture Ask students to present a report on the life and works of Sir Christopher Wren, architect to Charles II. The report should include illustrations of some of the buildings Wren designed.

✓ **Reading Check Answer** Parliament worried about the **foreign policy** of Charles II because of his friendship with the Roman Catholic king of France.

✓ **Reading Check Answer** If James II had **repealed** the Act of Habeas Corpus, he could have put people in jail without charging them with a specific crime.

MAKING CONNECTIONS

➤➤ **Daily Life** In 1665, London was hit by the plague. It was carried by rats, who flourished in the filthy streets and old buildings. As many as 7,000 persons died in one week. They had to be buried in great pits because the churchyards were full. Business came to a standstill, and the royal court fled to the countryside.

MEETING SPECIAL NEEDS

Have tactile/kinesthetic or gifted learners produce a "documentary" about the London fire of 1666. Make sure each student is assigned a specific task. Assign, or have students choose, a "producer" to coordinate the class effort. Some teams should be responsible for researching, writing, and presenting "news desk" reports about the fire. Other teams should prepare on-the-scene skits about the fire, such as interviews with local residents, fire fighters, or government officials. If possible, have students videotape their documentaries. Have students present their documentaries for the class.

📁 Refer to *Inclusion for the Middle School Social Studies Classroom: Strategies and Activities* for additional resources.

Reading Check Answer
Under the system of **mercantilism,** colonies served as a source of raw materials and as a market for finished products.

Reading Check Answer
A **monopoly** is the sole right over the production and sale of an item.

MAKING CONNECTIONS

➤➤ **Economics** Mercantilists believed that a nation's strength depended on how much gold and silver it had. So, they emphasized foreign trade rather than the production of goods. Mercantilists also emphasized the role of the government in a nation's economy.

Section 2 Assessment

1. **Define:** revolution, martial law, foreign policy, repealed.
2. Why did civil war finally break out between the Crown and Parliament in 1642?
3. Why did Parliament remove James II from the throne?

Critical Thinking

4. **Identifying the Central Issue** What was the central issue addressed by England's Declaration of Rights?

Graphic Organizer Activity

5. Draw this diagram, and use it to summarize the key ideas of John Locke's *Two Treatises of Government.*

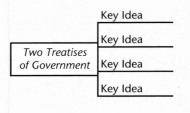

Two Treatises of Government	Key Idea
	Key Idea
	Key Idea
	Key Idea

SECTION 2 · The American Revolution

At first, England and its American colonies got along well. Over time, however, things changed. The colonists became angry over English controls. This led to revolution and the forming of a new country.

Reading Check
How did the system of **mercantilism** work?

Mercantilism In 1660, when Charles II became king of England, most European leaders believed in an economic system called **mercantilism** (mer′ kuhn tēl iz uhm). Under it, colonies served as a source of raw materials and as a market for finished products. England's colonies in America were supposed to send goods to England that were scarce or could not be grown there, such as furs, lumber, tobacco, and cotton. The colonists were supposed to buy only goods made in England so that English merchants could make money. These goods could be carried only in ships built in England or in the colonies. The ships also had to be sailed by English crews. This was to make the shipbuilding industry and merchant marine stronger in case of war.

Mercantilism worked well until the 1700s. There were not enough skilled people in the American colonies to produce many goods. The colonists also enjoyed a **monopoly** (muh nop′ uh lē), or sole right, on the sale of several major crops. In addition, their ships were protected against pirates by the English navy.

Reading Check
What is a **monopoly?**

Then, things changed. With the population in the colonies growing, the colonists wanted to make their own manufactured goods, such as iron products and beaver hats. Also, people in northern colonies were not able to sell as much to England as

Section 1 Assessment Answers

1. revolution, attempt to overthrow and change the government (p. 503); martial law, rule by the army instead of by the law (p. 505); foreign policy, relations with other countries (p. 507); repealed, abolished (p. 507)
2. because Charles accepted the laws Parliament passed and then disregarded them
3. because Parliament was afraid of control by the Roman Catholic Church

4. the power of the king vs. the power of Parliament
5. Key ideas: people are born with certain rights; the purpose of government is to protect those rights; if a government fails to do so, people can revolt and set up a new government; the best kind of government is a representative one.

Assign the Chapter 32 **Section 1 Quiz** in the TCR. Testmaker available.

eople in southern colonies did. Yet, they needed money to buy
nglish goods. So, they began smuggling goods to and from the
Vest Indies. Soon, a triangular, or three-way, trade grew up. The
olonists shipped in sugar and molasses from the West Indies.
hey made rum and traded it for enslaved Africans. Then, they
rought the enslaved Africans to the West Indies, where they
aded them for sugar and molasses.

Changes in British Policy   Although England, now
nown as Great Britain, regulated colonial trade, the colonists
andled local affairs. Their legislatures generally passed tax
ws. Since colonial officials were paid out of taxes, they had to
o as the colonial legislatures wished. This gave the legislatures
great deal of power.

In the middle of the 1700s, this changed. The French, who
so had colonies in America, built a fort on the site of present-
ay Pittsburgh, Pennsylvania. The French and their Native
merican allies wanted to keep the British out of northern and
estern America. Great Britain, however, had already claimed
e area for itself. The dispute led to the French and Indian War.
y the time it ended in 1763, the British controlled nearly all of
orth America east of the Mississippi River.

The war left the British government deeply in debt. It wanted
e colonies to pay a large share of the money owed. After all, the
ar had been fought partly to protect their western frontier. So,
reat Britain moved to raise money by tightening its control over
e colonies.

In 1765, Parliament passed the Stamp Act. It called for a tax
n all newspapers, legal documents, calendars, and playing
rds. All these items had to bear a stamp showing that the tax
ad been paid. This was the first **direct tax** Parliament placed on
e colonies. That is, it was a tax paid directly to the government,
ot included in the price of the goods.

The Stamp Act hurt merchants, lawyers, and people in the
ewspaper business. These groups were among the most able to
ad the colonists in a fight against British control. Angry mobs
rmed in many cities. Tax officials were threatened, and stamps
ere destroyed. People throughout the colonies decided to
oycott, or refuse to buy, British goods.

In October 1765, delegates from 9 of the 13 colonies met in
ew York to discuss the Stamp Act. They sent a letter to the
ritish government. It stated that the colonies had not been taxed
efore by anyone except their own legislatures. It also said that
arliament had no right to tax them because they did not have
presentatives in Parliament.

In March 1766, Parliament finally voted to repeal the Stamp
ct. At the same time, however, it passed the Declaratory Act,
hich stated that Parliament had the right to make laws on all

Stamp

Reading Check
Why was the
Stamp Act considered
a **direct tax?**

Reading Check
What action did
the colonists take
when they organized
a **boycott?**

L2 **History** Have students
write a report about the lasting
impact of the French on North
America, stating when the
French first came. Have them
note French influences that
remain, such as in the names of
cities, states, and other geographical features; French customs; French foods; and so on.

GEOGRAPHY
AND HISTORY

In 1707, England and Scotland united to become Great
Britain. After 1707, England
was referred to as Great
Britain.

Reading Check Answer
The Stamp Act was a
direct tax because it was a tax
paid directly to the government
instead of a tax included in the
price of goods.

Reading Check Answer
When the colonists orga-
nized a **boycott**, they refused to
buy British goods.

THE HISTORY CHANNEL®

*The following videotape program is
available from Glencoe to enrich
Chapter 32:*

• **The American Revolution**

To find classroom resources to
accompany this video, check the
following home page:

A&E Television:
http://www.aetv.com

MEETING SPECIAL NEEDS

Show students some current political
cartoons from the daily newspaper or magazines. Have students who are visual learners or who have Limited English
Proficiency draw a series of political cartoons depicting some of the events that led
to the Revolution and how the colonists felt
about the British. For example, students
might draw cartoons depicting the Stamp

Act, the Boston Tea Party, and the Boston
Massacre. Have them write dialogue for
their cartoons that explains what is being
expressed.

Refer to *Inclusion for the Middle
School Social Studies Classroom:
Strategies and Activities* for additional
resources.

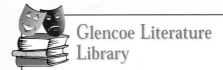

Glencoe Literature Library

The following novels from the **Glencoe Literature Library** may be used to enrich this chapter:

• *The Autobiography of Benjamin Franklin,* by Benjamin Franklin. (Rags-to-riches tale of one of the nation's founders.)

• *Johnny Tremain,* by Esther Forbes. (Events leading up to the American Revolution.)

MAKING CONNECTIONS

➤➤ **History** The song "Yankee Doodle" began as a song that mocked the colonists. *Macaroni* was a term used for British men who thought they were dressed in the latest styles but who actually looked ridiculous. British troops sang it as a song of ridicule. The colonists, however, loved the song and added their own verses to it. Ironically, it was to this tune that the British surrendered at Yorktown.

Painting of Boston Tea Party

matters concerning the colonies. This showed that Parliament was not going to give in completely to the demands of the American colonists.

The Road to Revolution In 1767, Parliament passed a series of laws known as the Townshend Acts. These acts placed a tax on such goods as paper, paint, glass, lead, and tea that were shipped to the colonies. Part of the tax money was to be used to pay colonial officials. This took away the colonial legislatures' main source of power. The following year, the British sent soldiers to Boston to make sure the colonists obeyed the new laws. The colonists called the soldiers "redcoats" because of their bright red uniforms.

The Townshend Acts made the colonists angry. Soon, there were incidents of violence. One of the worst of these took place in Boston in 1770. A crowd of colonists began insulting British soldiers and throwing stones at them. The soldiers fired into the crowd. Five people were killed. This incident came to be called the Boston Massacre. Shortly after, all the Townshend taxes were repealed except the one on tea. The Boston Massacre itself would probably have been forgotten had not some colonists used it to stir up feelings against British rule.

Three years later, Parliament passed the Tea Act. It allowed the British East India Company to sell tea directly to the colonists rather than to colonial merchants, who took part of the profits. This hurt the merchants. The act also further angered those colonists already tired of British tax policies. In Massachusetts, a group of colonists dressed as Native Americans boarded a British ship in Boston harbor and dumped its cargo of tea into the water. This event is known as the Boston Tea Party.

To punish the colonists, Parliament, in 1774, passed the Coercive (kō er' siv) Acts. These acts closed Boston harbor and put the government of Massachusetts under military rule. These acts also said that British troops in the colonies should be *quartered*, or given a place to live, in private homes. Next, Parliament passed the Quebec Act, which extended the boundaries of Quebec west of the Appalachians and north of the Ohio River. This took in land that Massachusetts, Connecticut, and Virginia claimed as their own. The colonists called these laws the Intolerable Acts, or laws they could not bear.

The Coercive Acts only made the colonists more determined than ever to fight for their liberties. In September 1774, delegates from 12 of the colonies met in Philadelphia. They called themselves the First Continental Congress. The Congress spoke out against the Coercive Acts and called for their repeal.

Colonial leaders, however, were divided about what to do. Some, like George Washington of Virginia, hoped to settle the differences with Great Britain. Others, like Samuel Adams of

510 UNIT 10 THE CHANGING WORLD

MULTICULTURAL PERSPECTIVES

As the struggle for control of the colonies began, colonial leader John Adams wrote in his diary: *The people have become more attentive to their liberties, . . . and more determined to defend them. . . . Our presses have groaned, our pulpits have thundered, our legislatures have resolved, our towns have voted; the crown officers have everywhere trembled, and all their little tools and creatures been afraid to speak and ashamed to be seen.*

Reading a Military Map

Maps that contain information about wars are called **military maps.** They show troop movements, battle sites and dates, and battle victories.

Look at the legend for the two maps below. Notice that different symbols and colors stand for American and British advances, retreats, and battle victories.

For example, the map has a solid red line to show that the British advanced to New York City, where they won a battle in August 1776. This victory is indicated by a red star. The Americans then retreated to Trenton, New Jersey, as shown by a dashed blue line.

Map Practice

1. Which army won the battle at Saratoga, New York?
2. Which army advanced to Camden, South Carolina, after the Battle of Charleston?
3. Where did the British retreat to after the Battle of Guilford Courthouse?

GO TO

Glencoe's **Skillbuilder Interactive Workbook, Level 1,** provides instruction and practice in key social studies skills.

American Revolution: North

- SARATOGA (October, 1777)
- ORISKANY (August, 1777)
- Albany
- BENNINGTON (August, 1777)
- LEXINGTON (April, 1775)
- BUNKER HILL (June, 1775)
- CONCORD (April, 1775)
- NEW YORK
- MASS.
- Boston
- CONN.
- R.I.
- PENNSYLVANIA
- GERMANTOWN (October, 1777)
- N.J.
- New York
- LONG ISLAND (August, 1776)
- BRANDYWINE (September, 1777)
- TRENTON (December, 1776)
- Philadelphia
- ATLANTIC OCEAN
- 76°W 74°W 72°W 70°W
- 43°N 41°N
- N
- miles 0 50 100
- kilometers 0 50 100 150

American Revolution: South

- VIRGINIA
- Richmond
- GUILFORD COURTHOUSE (March, 1781)
- YORKTOWN (October, 1781)
- COWPENS (January, 1781)
- NORTH CAROLINA
- KINGS MOUNTAIN (October, 1780)
- CAMDEN (August, 1780)
- Wilmington
- SOUTH CAROLINA
- ATLANTIC OCEAN
- CHARLESTON (May, 1780)
- GEORGIA
- SAVANNAH (December, 1778)
- 82°W 80°W 78°W 76°W
- 38°N 36°N 34°N 32°N
- N
- miles 0 50 100
- kilometers 0 50 100 150

Legend:
- —— American Advance
- —— British Advance
- ---- American Retreat
- ---- British Retreat
- ★ American Victory
- ★ British Victory

SPOTLIGHT ON: AMERICAN REVOLUTION

African Americans played an important role in the military successes that the American army was able to achieve against the British during the Revolutionary War. In 1776, Congress recruited only free African Americans. By the winter of 1777, however, General George Washington welcomed all African Americans, free or enslaved. At the time the war ended, 5,000 African Americans from all 13 states except North Carolina had served in the Continental Army. Another 2,000 had served in the colonial navy.

MAP SKILLS

TEACH

Reading a Military Map

Have the students read the instructional section of the feature. Ask: What kind of information is generally shown on a military map? *(information about wars such as troop movement, battle sites and dates, and battle victories)* Direct students to study the map. Ask: Who won most of the battles along the Atlantic coast? *(the British)* According to the maps, where did most of the fighting during the American Revolution take place, North or South? *(North)*

Next, have students use the information on the maps to create charts about the battles of the American Revolution. The charts might include the following headings: "Battles," "Dates," "Victories."

Assign the Chapter 32 **Geography and Map Activity** in the TCR.

Answers to Skill Practice

1. the American army
2. the British army
3. Wilmington

MAKING CONNECTIONS

➤➤ **History** Thomas Paine had come to the American colonies from Great Britain shortly before he wrote the following thoughts in his pamphlet *Common Sense* in January 1776: *Everything that is right begs for separation from Britain. The Americans who have been killed seem to say, 'TIS TIME TO PART. England and America are located a great distance apart. That is itself strong and natural proof that God never expected one to rule over the other.*

DID YOU KNOW ???

When the Second Continental Congress met, Georgia was the only colony without delegates.

CAPTION ANSWER

popular sovereignty and limited government

Massachusetts and Patrick Henry of Virginia, wanted the colonies to become independent.

The Outcome Before anything was decided, fighting broke out in Massachusetts between the colonists and British soldiers. The British set out to destroy a store of weapons at Concord. On the way there, they met the colonists at Lexington and fought the first battle of the American Revolution.

In May 1775, the Second Continental Congress met. George Washington was named head of the colonial army. The colonists then tried again to settle their differences with Great Britain. They appealed to King George III, who refused to listen.

On July 4, 1776, Congress issued the Declaration of Independence. Written mostly by Thomas Jefferson of Virginia, it stated that all men are created equal and have certain God-given rights. In the Declaration, the colonies broke away from Great Britain and declared themselves the United States of America.

War between the British and Americans dragged on. In 1778 the French, who were old enemies of Great Britain, agreed to help the Americans. In 1781, the Americans and French forced the British to surrender at Yorktown, Virginia. This ended the fighting. Two years later, the Treaty of Paris ended the war.

Peace Treaties Many peace treaties have been signed in Paris, France. In addition to the treaty ending the American Revolution, they include those that ended the French and Indian War (1763), the European allies' war with Napoleon (1814), and U.S. involvement in the Vietnam War (1973).

UNITED STATES CONSTITUTION In 1787, representatives from 12 states met in Philadelphia and drew up a constitution for the United States. George Washington is shown in this painting addressing the delegates. In 1789, Washington became the first President of the United States. **What are some principles of American government expressed in the Constitution?**

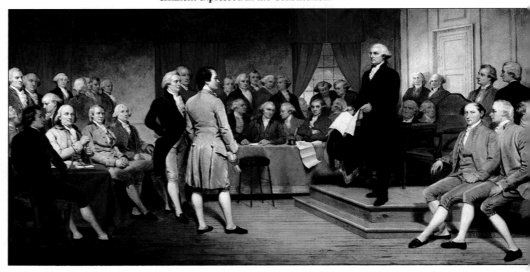

COOPERATIVE LEARNING

Tell students to imagine it is the eve of the American Revolution. Their village has just called a town meeting to decide the issue of independence. Next, divide the class into three teams. Tell one team to research arguments in support of independence, another team to research arguments in opposition of independence, and the final team to research the events leading up to the current crisis.

When students have completed their research, have the pro and con teams state their cases. Instruct the third team to listen carefully to all of the arguments—their votes will decide the position that the village takes. After they have listened to the arguments, allow them to meet in a caucus for no more than ten minutes. Call on each member of the group to vote "yea" or "nay," explaining why in two or three sentences.

📂 Assign Chapter 32 *Cooperative Learning Activity* in the TCR.

In 1789, the United States adopted a constitution that set up a new form of government. The Constitution set forth certain principles of government. One of these is **popular sovereignty** (sov' ruhn tē), or the idea that a government receives its powers from the people. Another is **limited government,** or the idea that a government may use only powers given to it by the people.

Later, ten **amendments,** or formal changes, known as the Bill of Rights, were added. The Bill of Rights guarantees all American citizens such rights as freedom of speech, press, and religion; the right to trial by jury; and freedom from unreasonable searches and seizures.

✔ **Reading Check**
What is the principle of **popular sovereignty?**
What is the principle of **limited government?**
What are the first ten **amendments** to the U.S. Constitution called?

✔ **Reading Check Answer**
Popular sovereignty is the idea that government gets its power from the people. The principle of **limited government** holds that a government may only use those powers given to it by the people. The first ten **amendments** are called the Bill of Rights.

Section 2 Assessment

1. **Define:** mercantilism, monopoly, direct tax, boycott, popular sovereignty, limited government, amendments.
2. Why were colonial legislatures powerful?
3. How did the Townshend Acts affect the power of the colonial legislatures?

Critical Thinking
4. **Evaluating Information**   "The Bill of Rights is an important addition to the U.S. Constitution." What is your opinion of this statement? Explain.

Graphic Organizer Activity
5. Draw this diagram, and use it to show the causes and effects of the American Revolution.

LINKING PAST TO PRESENT

The six fundamental principles on which the U.S. Constitution was based—popular sovereignty; separation of powers among legislative, executive, and judicial branches; checks and balances; federalism; supremacy of national law; and civilian control of government—were mostly derived from English political tradition. The U.S. Constitution became a model for other later democratic constitutions.

💾 Use **Interactive Tutor Self-Assessment Software** to review Section 2.

✔ **Reading Check Answer**
French society was divided into three **estates**, or classes.

💾 Use the **Vocabulary Puzzle-Maker** to create crossword and word search puzzles.

SECTION 3   The French Revolution

What happened in America influenced people in France. The American example pointed up the need for political change and helped bring about a revolution.

Old Regime   During the 1600s and early 1700s—the time of the Old Regime (ri zhēm′)—France was a divine-right monarchy. French society was divided into three **estates** (e stāts′), or classes. The First Estate was the clergy. Although they made up less than 1 percent of the people, they owned 10 percent of the land. They were not only *exempt,* or free, from taxes. They also received income from church lands. Church income was not divided evenly, however. Most went to high church officials, who were generally nobles. They wore robes of purple and scarlet velvet

✔ **Reading Check**
Into how many **estates** was French society divided?

Glencoe Literature Library

The following novel from the **Glencoe Literature Library** may be used to enrich this chapter.
• *A Tale of Two Cities,* by Charles Dickens. (Years leading up to the French Revolution of 1789.)

Section 2 Assessment Answers

1. mercantilism, system under which colonies served as a source of raw materials and a market for finished goods (p. 508); monopoly, sole right (p. 508); direct tax, tax paid directly to the government (p. 509); boycott, refusal to buy (p. 509); popular sovereignty, idea that the government receives its power from the people (p. 513); limited government, idea that a government may only use the powers given to it by the people (p. 513); amendments, formal changes (p. 513)

2. because they passed tax laws and controlled officials
3. took away the legislatures' main power
4. Answers will vary, but students should defend their position.
5. *causes*—growing colonial population, conflict over colonial manufacturing, triangular trades, conflict over taxation and representation; *effects*—colonial independence, new constitution, Bill of Rights

Assign the Chapter 32 **Section 2 Quiz** in the TCR. Testmaker available.

L2 **Language Arts** Ask students to brainstorm definitions of the term *revolution*. Stimulate the discussion by asking, "When are people justified in choosing revolution as a solution to political problems?" Have students write a case study of a situation they feel would justify a revolution or people taking the government into their own hands.

Reading Check Answer
The **bourgeoisie** was made up of bankers, merchants, lawyers, doctors, manufacturers, and teachers.

Reading Check Answer
The *philosophes* were French writers and thinkers who wrote articles pointing out France's political problems.

MAKING CONNECTIONS

➤➤ **History** From 1642 to 1715, France was ruled by Louis XIV. His was the longest rule in modern European history. Under Louis, France led Europe in the arts and had the most powerful army on the continent. After Louis, French power and influence began to decline.

trimmed with lace. Parish priests lived simply and served people's religious needs.

The Second Estate was the nobility. They made up about 2 percent of the people and also owned large areas of land. Nobles, too, were free from taxes. They lived off grants from the royal treasury and rents paid by the peasants. Some nobles spent their time at the royal court, dancing, hunting, and gambling. Others filled the highest posts in the government and the army.

The Third Estate was everyone else in France. At the top of this class was the **bourgeoisie** (bur zhwah zē')—bankers, merchants, lawyers, doctors, manufacturers, and teachers. They controlled much of France's wealth and trade. Next were the city workers—artisans, day laborers, and servants. At the bottom were the peasants, who made up more than 80 percent of the French people.

Members of the Third Estate had no power in the government. Yet, they paid the country's taxes. They paid taxes on income, personal property, land, and crops. They paid sales taxes on salt, tobacco, and wine. Parents even paid a tax when a child was born. In addition, the peasants still paid feudal dues.

Reading Check
What groups made up the French **bourgeoisie?**

The Estates-General By the 1780s, the French government was in trouble. Educated French writers and thinkers called *philosophes* (fē luh zofs'), or philosophers, wrote articles pointing out the country's political problems. One of the most widely read philosophes was Francois Marie Arouet (fran' swah muh rē' ah rwe'), known as Voltaire (vōl ter'). Voltaire favored free speech, a free press, freedom of religion, and equal justice for everyone. One of his favorite sayings was: "I do not agree with a word you say, but I will defend to the death your right to say it."

The major problem facing the French government, however, was a lack of money. The French government had given so much help to the colonies during the American Revolution that it was almost bankrupt. King Louis XVI and his wife added to the problem by spending money on jewels, hunting parties, horse races, and balls. In fact, Queen Marie-Antoinette (muh rē an twuh net') spent so much that France's *deficit,* or shortage of money, increased. For this reason, the French people called her Madame Deficit. The king wanted the clergy and nobles to give him money. They, however, had never paid taxes and saw no reason to start.

Finally, Louis XVI called a meeting of the French legislature to help decide how to raise money. It was the first time that this body, known as the Estates-General, had met since 1614. In the past, each of the estates had met separately, with each casting one vote. This meant the nobles and clergy together could outvote the Third Estate and protect themselves from change.

Reading Check
Who were the *philosophes?*

Painting of Louis XVI and Family

MULTICULTURAL PERSPECTIVES

Men and women were equally instrumental in spreading the Enlightenment ideas that helped to spark the French Revolution. Influential Parisian intellectuals such as Madame de Pompadour, Madame Geoffrin, and Madame du Deffand sponsored evenings of long political discussions in gatherings called salons—where writers, artists, and educated people of the middle class mingled with men and women of nobility.

Now the Third Estate wanted a bigger voice in government. What is the Third Estate?" one of their leaders wrote in a pamphlet. "Everything. What has it been until now? Nothing. What does it demand? To become something." The members of the Third Estate wanted the Estates-General to meet as a single body with each representative having a vote. They also wanted to have the same number of representatives as the other two estates together.

In May 1789, the Estates-General met. The Third Estate was granted more representatives, but the other two estates refused to meet with it. So, the Third Estate and a small number of parish priests and nobles met as a separate body. They called themselves the National Assembly. When Louis XVI threatened to break up the National Assembly, its members swore not to do so until they had written a constitution for France. At last, the king gave in and ordered the First and Second Estates to meet with the National Assembly.

Uprisings in City and Country   Meanwhile, a series of uprisings took place throughout most of France. When the Estates-General was called to meet, most French people had high hopes for change. Before long, however, they began to fear that nothing would improve. The fall harvests had been poor, and

People in History

Marie-Antoinette
1755–1793

French Queen

Born in Vienna, Austria, Marie-Antoinette grew up the daughter of the Holy Roman Emperor Francis I. At age 15, she married Louis XVI in an effort to strengthen ties between France and Austria. Disliked as a foreigner, the queen was mistakenly accused of pushing France into debt with her luxurious lifestyle. During the Reign of Terror, she was charged with treason and executed.

TENNIS COURT OATH   Members of the Third Estate met on a tennis court to write a new French constitution. **What was the Third Estate?**

CHAPTER 32 POLITICAL REVOLUTIONS   **515**

Independent Practice

L2 **Critical Thinking** Ask students to imagine they are members of the Third Estate and to write a letter to a friend in another country expressing their thoughts in the summer of 1789.

CAPTION ANSWER

the common people of France

DID YOU KNOW

Francis Bacon once described philosophers as ants who are diligent but only gather useless facts. Philosophers should be like bees, he said, not ants. They should find raw materials, absorb nature's lessons, and transform these lessons into theories.

ABCNEWS
INTERACTIVE™

VIDEODISC
Turning Points in World History

Side One
Chapter 11

Title: *French Revolution*
Subject: French Revolution
Ask: What great changes in the way people thought about political rights and freedoms took place in this period? *(The idea of divine right of monarchs to rule gave way to individual rights and rule by popular consent.)*

COOPERATIVE LEARNING

Explain that during the social unrest in the United States during the 1960s, a popular slogan was "Power to the People." Ask students to debate this phrase as it might have applied to pre-revolutionary France. Organize students into two groups: one group representing the common people of the Third Estate, the other group representing the nobility and clergy of the First and Second Estates. Each group should address the statement: "More power should be given to the common people of France." Each student should have a role in preparing for or taking part in the debate.

TEACH

Building a Database

You might introduce this lesson by proposing this situation to the class: *A newspaper reporter wants to do an article on kids your age. However, the reporter is not sure about what categories of information to collect. What things would you suggest that the reporter study?*

Record student answers on the board. When they are done, tell students that they have just created the start of a database—a collection of related information organized for quick access. Ask: Why might the reporter want to put the database on a computer instead of in a notebook? *(easier to edit, easier to retrieve, etc.)* Then assign the skills lesson, which helps students learn how to create an electronic database of their own.

Performance Assessment

To encourage self-assessment of the database on documents from the three revolutions in this chapter, have each student complete this individual task management plan.

Self-Management Plan

Name: _____

Task: _____

Audience: _____

Steps to accomplish the task:

Problems to completing the task:

Solutions, or attempted solutions:

Signed: _____

TECHNOLOGY SKILLS

Building a Database

Have you ever collected baseball cards or cataloged the CDs in your collection? Have you ever kept a list of the names and addresses of your friends and relatives? If you have collected information and kept some sort of list or file, then you have created a database.

Learning the Skill An electronic database is a collection of facts that are stored in files on a computer. The information is organized in fields.

A database can be organized and reorganized in any way that is useful to you. By using a database management system (DBMS)—special software developed for record keeping—you can easily add, delete, change, or update information. You give commands to the computer telling it what to do with the information, and it follows your commands. When you want to retrieve information, your computer searches through the files, finds the information, and displays it on the screen.

Practicing the Skill

A number of democratic documents are discussed in this chapter. Follow these steps to build a database of democratic documents written during the English, American, and French revolutions.

1. Determine what facts you want to include in your database.
2. Follow instructions in the DBMS you are using to set up fields. Then enter each item of data in its assigned field.
3. Determine how you want to organize the facts in your data base—in this case, alphabetically by the name of the document.
4. Follow the instructions in your computer program to place the information in order of importance.
5. Check that all the information in your database is correct. If necessary, add, delete, or change information or fields.

516

TEAM-TEACHING STRATEGIES

Language Arts You might work with the language arts teacher to help students set up a literature database for books that they read to enrich their study of world history. You might begin with the three books from **Glencoe's Literature Library** suggested for this chapter: *The Autobiography of Benjamin Franklin, Johnny Tremain,* and *A Tale of Two Cities.* The databases might be organized by title, period in history, or unit in *Human Heritage.* Students can then record information such as author, date published, main subject, and so on.

Students should be encouraged to add books of their own choosing to the database. You might have them print out the databases at regular intervals to provide an ongoing record for their portfolios.

food was scarce and expensive. A loaf of bread cost more than a day's pay. The winter was so cold that water froze in front of fireplaces. Hundreds of thousands of city workers were unemployed.

In Paris, mobs began to form. On July 14, 1789, a mob in search of weapons attacked and captured the Bastille (ba stēl'). This was an old fort used as a prison. To the mob, it was a symbol of the **tyranny** (tir' uh nē), or unjust use of power, of the monarchy. The mob then killed the mayor of Paris and set up a new city government.

News of what happened in Paris spread. In the countryside, there were rumors that the nobles were planning to hire *brigands* (brig' uhndz), or roving bandits, to destroy the peasants' homes and crops. So, the peasants attacked and burned the houses of the nobles, and destroyed all records of feudal dues.

The National Assembly   The uprisings caused the National Assembly to act. To calm the people, it did away with the privileges of the clergy and nobles.

On August 27, 1789, the Assembly issued the Declaration of the Rights of Man and the Citizen. It said that people "are born equal and remain free and equal in rights." It said that the government's right to rule came from the people, not from the

Reading Check
What is **tyranny**?

FRENCH PEASANTS   Farmers of the French countryside worked hard to raise their crops. They were tired of paying most of their earnings to the nobles. **What did peasants in the countryside do to show their unhappiness when they heard about the riots in Paris?**

Fun Facts....

The March of Women
In October 1789, a mob of women walked to Versailles, a few miles outside Paris. Armed with sticks and farm tools, the "March of Women" stopped first at the National Assembly and demanded lower prices for bread. They then burst into the royal palace and forced Louis XVI, Marie-Antoinette, and their son—whom they called "the baker, the baker's wife, and the baker's little boy"—to return to Paris as prisoners of the people.

MAKING CONNECTIONS

➤➤ **History** One famous French philosopher was François Marie Arouet, whose pen name was Voltaire. He wrote poetry, plays, essays, and books in a style that was entertaining and often satirical. He served time in the Bastille for his writings that mocked the Church and the royal court of France.

CAPTION ANSWER

Peasants attacked and burned the houses of nobles.

LINKING PAST TO PRESENT

Bastille Day, July 14, is celebrated as a national holiday in France every year with speeches, parades, and dancing in the streets.

MULTICULTURAL PERSPECTIVES

During the late 1700s the people of the Third Estate in France grew increasingly unhappy with their country's social structure. An Englishman, Arthur Young, traveling in France in 1789, recorded the following conversation with a French peasant woman in *Travels: Walking up a long hill . . . I was joined by a poor woman who com-* *plained of the times, and that it was a sad country; . . . she said her husband had but a morsel of land, one cow, and a poor little horse, yet they had [42 lbs.] of wheat and three chickens to pay as rent to one [lord], and [four lbs.] of oats, one chicken and 1s. [shilling] to pay another, besides very heavy tailles and other taxes.*

L2 **The Arts** The Enlightenment played a great role in shaping French political thought before and during the Revolution. Have students research and write a brief biography on an artist, philosopher, or writer of the Enlightenment and that person's ideas about the French Revolution.

Reading Check Answer
Under a **constitutional monarchy,** the ruler's power is limited by written law.

Reading Check Answer
The *sans-culottes* were city workers kept from voting because they did not have enough money.

Reading Check Answer
The French *émigrés* were political exiles who urged other rulers to march into France and help Louis XVI regain power.

Reading Check Answer
The **guillotine** was a machine with a heavy blade held between two wooden posts that was used to cut off a victim's head.

LINKING PAST TO PRESENT

The card game solitaire is said to have been invented by a French nobleman sentenced to solitary confinement in the Bastille.

The Tricolor The French revolutionaries adopted a red, white, and blue flag called the tricolor. France still uses this flag.

Reading Check
What kind of government is established under a **constitutional monarchy?**

Reading Check
Who were the *sans-culottes,* and how were they kept from voting?

Reading Check
Who were the French *émigrés,* and what did they want other rulers to do?

Reading Check
What was the **guillotine?**

Crown. It gave everyone freedom of speech and the right to share in government. The ideas of equal rights and individual freedoms came mostly from the philosophes and from the English and American revolutions.

For the next two years, the National Assembly worked to write a constitution. At the same time, to pay off what the government owed, it began selling church lands to peasants. Although many peasants now owned land for the first time, the Roman Catholic Church was angered. It was further angered when the National Assembly declared that the clergy should be elected and should swear an oath to the government. The Church did not like being brought under state authority.

In 1791, a constitution was finished. It established freedom of religion and made France a **constitutional monarchy.** Under this kind of government, the ruler's power is limited by written law. The Crown and the legislature would govern together. Both representatives and voters had to have a certain amount of wealth. This pleased the bourgeoisie because it gave them the power they wanted. It did not please most peasants and the *sans-culottes* (san skū lahts'), or city workers, because they did not have enough money to vote. (The word "sans-culottes" means "without knee breeches." Wealthy men wore knee breeches and silk stockings. Workers wore long pants.)

The End of the Monarchy   Many of the ideas of the French Revolution spread to other countries. Rulers throughout Europe were afraid that these ideas would weaken their own power. French *émigrés* (em' uh grāz), or political exiles, encouraged the rulers to march into France and help Louis XVI take back control of the government. Many of the French revolutionary leaders also wanted war because it would unite the French people. Before any country could act, in the spring of 1792 France declared war on Austria, where the queen's brother ruled.

At first, the war did not go well for France. By August 1792 Austrian and Prussian armies were marching toward Paris. Meanwhile, in the city, the sans-culottes took over. They set up a new government called the National Convention. It made France a republic. The following year, Louis XVI and Marie Antoinette were executed. As a result, more European countries joined the war against France.

Threats from outside and inside the country made the new French government take drastic action. Although another constitution was written, it never was put into force. Instead, the Committee of Public Safety, led by a lawyer named Maximilien de Robespierre (mak suh mil' yuhn duh rōbz' piuhr), took over the government. Thousands of people, suspected of being against the Revolution, lost their lives to the **guillotine** (gil' uh tēn). This was a machine with a heavy blade that fit between two wooden

COOPERATIVE LEARNING

Have the class work together to plan the front page of the *Revolutionary Times,* a newspaper chronicling the events of the French Revolution. The newspaper should have headlines, articles, and visuals. Divide the class into groups and have each group list the stories and visuals they would put on the front page. As a group they can decide which event gets the top headline and where the other lead articles and visuals should go. Then, as a class, the groups can decide on the final placement of stories and visuals.

posts. When it was released, the blade came crashing down and cut off the victim's head. The wave of killing came to be known as the "Reign of Terror." Because of it, the people began to turn against Robespierre. In 1794, government leaders had him executed.

The following year, a third constitution was written. It set up a government known as the Directory. Besides the legislature, there was an executive branch with five directors. Only people who owned land could vote.

Under the new government, most reforms of the Revolution came to an end. The people of France had grown more conservative. The Directory spent its time trying to handle food shortages, rising prices, government bankruptcy, and attacks by other countries.

One reform that did remain was the idea that all French people had the right to choose their government. Another was a standard system of weights and measures known as the metric

Linking Across Time

The Metric System After France adopted use of the metric system in 1791, the government attempted to educate people about its many uses (below). Today the metric system is followed in most technological nations in the world, except the United States. It is so widespread that the metric system is used for measurement at the Olympics. **What other lasting reform grew out of the French Revolution?**

CHAPTER 32 POLITICAL REVOLUTIONS **519**

MAKING CONNECTIONS

➤➤ **History** Historians estimate that about 40,000 people were executed during the Reign of Terror.

DID YOU KNOW

The guillotine was considered a "humane" way of execution at the time. Beheading was quick and merciful. It was the official instrument of execution in 1792 and was used until capital punishment was officially abolished in France in 1981.

Linking Across Time

A lasting reform that came out of the French Revolution was the idea that all French people had the right to choose their own government.

Biography

The following videotape program is available from Glencoe to enrich Chapter 32:

- **Marie Antoinette: Tragic Queen**

To find classroom resources to accompany this video, check the following home page:

A&E Television:

http://www.aetv.com

MULTICULTURAL PERSPECTIVES

The French Revolution destroyed an entire society and began a new era in France. Since France led European and colonial fashion, the styles of the revolutionary period influenced the rest of Europe and America. The revolutionary fashions were simplistic, at least in comparison to the brocade gowns, embroidered waistcoats, and large powdered wigs of the previous social system of France. During the Reign of Terror, wearing the old styles became dangerous. Anyone whose clothes suggested luxury was likely to be seized as an aristocrat and sent to the guillotine. Because England represented political freedom, the new fashions imitated English country styles, with muslin and broadcloth in place of silks and satins.

Check for Understanding

Ask students to summarize the main points of the chapter, orally or in writing. Discuss the answers to the Section and Chapter Assessment questions.

Evaluate

Assign the Chapter 32 **Performance Assessment Activity** in the TCR.

Administer the **Chapter 32 Test**. Testmaker available.

Reteach

Have students make time lines of the major events in the chapter.

Assign the Chapter 32 **Reteaching Activity** in the TCR.

Enrich

Have students read a book—fiction or nonfiction—related to events of this chapter, and deliver an oral report about the book to the class.

Assign the Chapter 32 **Enrichment Activity** in the TCR.

CLOSE

Have students discuss how the following slogan would have applied in each of the revolutions in this chapter: "No taxation without representation."

💾 Use **Interactive Tutor Self-Assessment Software** to review Section 3.

Self-Check Quiz gives students an interactive chapter tutorial. Have them access **Chapter 32 Quiz** at **humanheritage.glencoe.com**

system, which the National Assembly adopted in 1791. Metrics, a system of numbers that is based on powers of ten, helped scientists carry out experiments and made international trade easier. Today, metrics are used by all major countries in the world except the United States.

Section 3 Assessment

1. **Define:** estates, bourgeoisie, *philosophes*, tyranny, constitutional monarchy, *sans-culottes*, *émigrés*, guillotine.
2. What groups made up the three French estates?
3. What did the National Assembly do about the uprisings in 1789?
4. Why did most reforms of the French Revolution come to an end under the Directory?

Critical Thinking

5. **Understanding Cause and Effect** How did the storming of the Bastille help trigger the French Revolution?

Graphic Organizer Activity

6. Draw this diagram, and use it to compare the French Declaration of the Rights of Man and the Citizen to the U.S. Declaration of Independence.

Chapter Summary & Study Guide

1. As a result of new ideas about freedom and government, the 1700s are known as the Age of Enlightenment.
2. England's political revolution began in the 1600s when the Crown and Parliament disagreed over issues of divine right and religion.
3. In 1689, Parliament passed the Declaration of Rights, which made Parliament stronger and protected the rights of the people.
4. In 1776, disagreements between the American colonies and Great Britain led to the Declaration of Independence, which defended the right to self-government.

5. In 1789, the United States adopted a new constitution based on the principles of popular sovereignty and limited government.
6. The French Revolution, which began in 1789, was ended by reaction against the Reign of Terror. However, two lasting reforms survived—use of the metric system and the idea of popular government.

Self-Check Quiz

Visit the *Human Heritage* Web site at **humanheritage. glencoe.com** and click on *Chapter 32—Self-Check Quiz* to assess your understanding of this chapter.

Section 3 Assessment Answers

1. All terms are defined in the text Glossary.
2. the clergy, the nobility, and the bourgeoisie, city workers, and peasants
3. It ended the privileges of the clergy and nobles.
4. because the people of France had grown more conservative
5. Sample response: News of the Bastille spurred peasant uprising throughout France and caused the National Assembly to take steps that would end the French monarchy.

6. Sample responses: Both documents stressed equality and the idea that power came from the people rather than the crown. The French Declaration included specific individual freedoms, such as freedom of speech, that Americans later included in the Bill of Rights. The U.S. Declaration asserted independence from Great Britain.

Assign the Chapter 32 **Section 3 Quiz** in the TCR. Testmaker available.

Using Key Terms

Sort these words describing the revolutions in England, America, and France by the country to which each applies. (Words may be used more than once.) Use the words in each group to write a sentence or two about each country's revolution.

revolution
mercantilism
direct tax
boycott
bourgeoisie
martial law
guillotine

constitutional
  monarchy
monopoly
popular sovereignty
estates
tyranny

Understanding Main Ideas

1. What were some Puritan beliefs?
2. Why was the Glorious Revolution called "glorious"?
3. How did Great Britain tighten its control over the American colonies?
4. How did the British colonists respond to the Stamp Act?
5. Who had the most power in the French government before the French Revolution? After the Revolution?
6. Why were European rulers afraid of the ideas of the French Revolution?

Critical Thinking

1. What economic questions played a part in the American Revolution? In the French Revolution?
2. What were the most important political issues that played a part in England's Glorious Revolution? Explain your answer.
3. Do you agree with the idea that people have the right to rule themselves? Explain.

4. Why are the 1700s known as the Age of Enlightenment?

Graphic Organizer Activity

Citizenship Create a diagram like the one on this page, and use it to compare the reforms and rights sought by the leaders of the English, American, and French revolutions.

Geography in History

Movement Look at the maps of the American Revolution on page 511. The advances and retreats of both armies are shown. About how many miles (or kilometers) did the British advance from the battle at Long Island, New York, to the battle at Brandywine, Pennsylvania?

Using Your Journal

Review any details you may have noted about the changes in government that took place during the 1700s. Imagine you are setting up your own country with its own government. Using ideas you have noted, write a description of what you think would be the perfect government.

 Bonus Test Question

For Chapter 32 Test
Choose one of the revolutions you have read about and identify one thing that could have been done to avoid that revolution. Explain. *(Answers will vary.)*

Using Your Journal

Descriptions will vary but should include some of the governmental principles discussed. You might call on volunteers to read their letters to the class.

 Geography in History

about 575 miles (or 925 km)

Using Key Terms

England: revolution, martial law, mercantilism, tyranny, direct tax; America: revolution, foreign policy, monopoly, boycott, popular sovereignty; France: revolution, *sans-culottes*, mercantilism, tyranny, estates, bourgeoisie, constitutional monarchy. Sentences will vary.

Understanding Main Ideas

1. freedom of worship, hard work, and having a say in government
2. because the change in monarchs took place without gunfire
3. by passing new tax laws and taking steps to enforce them
4. Angry mobs threatened tax officials, and British goods were boycotted.
5. the king; the Directory
6. because these ideas would weaken their own power

Critical Thinking

1. mercantilism, direct taxes, and a boycott of British goods; exemption of a few from taxes, the nation's deficit, and high food prices
2. the conflict between Parliament and the king
3. Answers will vary but students should provide reasons.
4. Answers will vary.

Graphic Organizer Activity

Answers will vary, but should show that leaders of all three revolutions sought to protect the basic rights of individuals and to give the people an increased voice in political affairs. The United States differed from the other two revolutions because it sought complete independence from another nation rather than a change in the balance of power.

Chapter 33 Planning Guide

Objectives	Reproducible Resources	Multimedia Resources
Section 1 **Scientific Revolution** Summarize the inventions and discoveries that marked the Scientific Revolution.	Reproducible Lesson Plan Chapter 33 Vocabulary and Guided Reading Activity Reading Essentials and Study Guide 33-1 Section 1 Quiz	**ABCNEWS INTERACTIVE** Turning Points in World History Vocabulary PuzzleMaker Interactive Tutor Self-Assessment Software ExamView® Pro Testmaker Glencoe Skillbuilder Interactive Workbook, Level 1
Section 2 **Agricultural Revolution** Explain what the Agricultural Revolution was and how it contributed to the Industrial Revolution.	Reproducible Lesson Plan Reading Essentials and Study Guide 33-2 Section 2 Quiz	Vocabulary PuzzleMaker Interactive Tutor Self-Assessment Software ExamView® Pro Testmaker Glencoe Skillbuilder Interactive Workbook, Level 1
Section 3 **Industrial Revolution** Discuss the development of the Industrial Revolution.	Reproducible Lesson Plan Reading Essentials and Study Guide 33-3 Chapter 33 Cooperative Learning Activity Chapter 33 Chart and Graph Skill Activity Chapter 33 Geography and Map Activity Section 3 Quiz	Vocabulary PuzzleMaker Interactive Tutor Self-Assessment Software ExamView® Pro Testmaker Glencoe Skillbuilder Interactive Workbook, Level 1
Section 4 **Industrial Impact** Identify and describe the effects of industrialization.	Reproducible Lesson Plan Reading Essentials and Study Guide 33-4 Unit 10 Primary Sources Reading Section 4 Quiz	Teaching Transparency and Activity 33A Vocabulary PuzzleMaker Interactive Tutor Self-Assessment Software ExamView® Pro Testmaker Glencoe Skillbuilder Interactive Workbook, Level 1
Section 5 **Spread of Industry** Analyze how industrialization continued and spread.	Reproducible Lesson Plan Reading Essentials and Study Guide 33-5 Chapter 33 Activity Book Activity Chapter 33 Enrichment Activity World Literature Reading 2 Section 5 Quiz	Teaching Transparency and Activity 33B Vocabulary PuzzleMaker ExamView® Pro Testmaker Glencoe Skillbuilder Interactive Workbook, Level 1
Chapter 33 **Review and Evaluation**	Chapter 33 Reteaching Activity Chapter 33 Performance Assessment Activity Unit 10 Standardized Test Practice Spanish Chapter Summary and Glossary Chapter 33 Test	Vocabulary PuzzleMaker Interactive Tutor Self-Assessment Software Glencoe Skillbuilder Interactive Workbook, Level 1 Audiocassettes* ExamView® Pro Testmaker

*Also available in Spanish.

Presentation Plus!

Use Glencoe's **Presentation Plus!** multimedia teacher tool to easily present dynamic lessons that visually excite your students. Using Microsoft® PowerPoint, you can customize the presentations to create your own personalized lessons.

Interactive Lesson Planner

Planning has never been easier! Using this CD-ROM, organize your week, month, semester, or year with all the help you need. The **Interactive Lesson Planner** gives you access to all of the blackline masters which accompany *Human Heritage.*

✓ PERFORMANCE ASSESSMENT ACTIVITIES

Writing Commercials   Ask each student to select an invention or discovery of the 1400s-1800s and write a promotional flyer or commercial promoting the product. Have students present their commercials to the class.

CHAPTER RESOURCES

LITERATURE ABOUT THE PERIOD

Dickens, Charles. *Oliver Twist.* Bantam Books, 1982. The saga of an orphan's adventures in industrial London.

READINGS FOR THE STUDENT

Macaulay, David. *Mill.* Houghton Mifflin, 1983. Detailed drawings and clear descriptions of the history and construction of a typical New England mill.

READINGS FOR THE TEACHER

Smith, Page. *The Rise of Industrial America.* Facts on File, 1980. Examines the industrialization of the United States between the years 1876 and 1901.

Thompson, Paul. *The Edwardians: The Remaking of British Society.* Indiana University Press, 1975. Focuses on social change and class differences in Great Britain in the late 1800s.

THE HISTORY CHANNEL.

The following videotape programs are available from Glencoe:

- **Alexander Graham Bell: Voice of Invention**
  1-56501-946-6
- **The Electric Light**
  1-56501-892-3
- **Marconi: Whisper in the Air**
  1-56501-551-7
- **Sir Isaac Newton: The Gravity of Genius**
  1-56501-982-2

To order, call Glencoe at 1-800-334-7344. To find classroom resources to accompany many of these check:

A&E Television: http://www.aetv.com
The History Channel:
http://www.historychannel.com

NATIONAL GEOGRAPHIC SOCIETY — Teacher's Corner

INDEX TO NATIONAL GEOGRAPHIC MAGAZINE

The following articles relate to this chapter:

- "Robot Revolution," by Curt Suplee, July 1997.
- "Sir Joseph Banks," by T.H. Watkins, November 1996.
- "A Farming Revolution," by Verlyn Klinkenborg, December 1995.
- "Information Revolution," by Joel L. Swerdlow, October 1995.

NATIONAL GEOGRAPHIC SOCIETY PRODUCTS AVAILABLE FROM GLENCOE

To order the following, call Glencoe at 1-800-334-7344:

- *Picture Atlas of the World (CD-ROM)*
- *PicturePack: Europe (Transparencies)*

ADDITIONAL NATIONAL GEOGRAPHIC SOCIETY PRODUCTS

To order the following, call National Geographic at 1-800-368-2728:

- *Physical Geography of the Continents Series: Europe (Video)*
- *Wired World (Video)*
- *Inventors and Inventions (Video)*
- *Technology's Price (Video)*

Access *National Geographic's* new dynamic MapMachine Web site and other geography resources at:
http://www.nationalgeographic.com/
http://www.nationalgeographic.com/maps/

KEY TO ABILITY LEVELS

Teaching strategies have been coded for varying learning styles and abilities.

L1 Level 1 activities are **basic** activities and should be within the ability range of all students.

L2 Level 2 activities are **average** activities and should be within the ability range of the average to above-average student.

L3 Level 3 activities are **challenging** activities designed for the ability range of above-average students.

ELL ELL activities should be within the ability range of English Language Learning students.

OVERVIEW

Chapter 33 traces the rise of science and industry in Europe and North America during the 1700s and 1800s.

➤ **Section 1** traces the Scientific Revolution.

➤ **Section 2** describes developments in farming that led to the Agricultural Revolution.

➤ **Section 3** summarizes the major developments that led to the Industrial Revolution.

➤ **Section 4** examines the effects of industrialization.

➤ **Section 5** describes how industrialization spread.

CHAPTER OBJECTIVES

After reading Chapter 33, students will be able to:

1. summarize the inventions of the Scientific Revolution.

2. identify features of the Agricultural Revolution.

3. trace the rise of industry.

4. describe the social effects of industrialization.

5. analyze how industrialization spread.

EXAMINING ARTIFACTS

Ask students to speculate on the impact of the phonograph and steam engine. *(advanced communication; expanded the growth of industry and promoted mechanization)* Call on students to suggest effects of other ideas and inventions in the time line.

PERFORMANCE ASSESSMENT ✓

Use the Performance Assessment activities on page 522B to help you evaluate students as they complete the chapter.

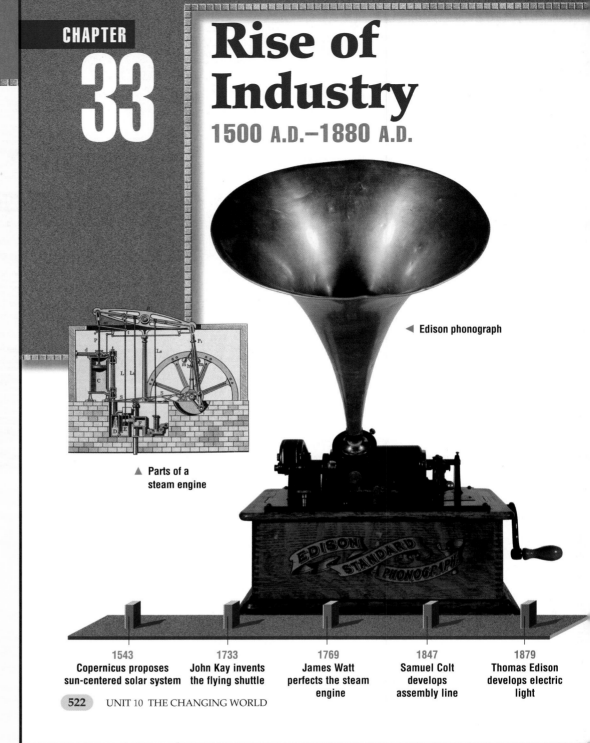

CHAPTER
33

Rise of Industry

1500 A.D.–1880 A.D.

◀ Edison phonograph

▲ Parts of a steam engine

1543	1733	1769	1847	1879
Copernicus proposes sun-centered solar system	**John Kay invents the flying shuttle**	**James Watt perfects the steam engine**	**Samuel Colt develops assembly line**	**Thomas Edison develops electric light**

TEACHING RESOURCES

TEACHER PLANNING AND SUPPORT

📂 Reproducible Lesson Plan
📂 Block Scheduling Implementation Guide
📂 Videodisc Bar Code Correlation
🔘 Presentation Plus!

REVIEW AND REINFORCEMENT

📂 Reading Essentials and Study Guide 33-1, 33-2, 33-3, 33-4, 33-5
📂 Chapter 33 Vocabulary and Guided Reading Activity
💾 Vocabulary PuzzleMaker Software
✏️ Teaching Transparencies 33A & 33B

📂 Chapter 33 Reteaching Activity
📂 Chapter 33 Cooperative Learning Activity
📂 Chapter 33 Activity Book Activity
📂 Chapter 33 Chart and Graph Skill Activity
💾 Interactive Tutor Self-Assessment Software
 Unit 10 MindJogger VideoQuiz

APPLICATION AND HANDS-ON ACTIVITIES

🔖 Daily World History, Geography, and Culture Question

Chapter Focus

 Read to Discover

- What inventions and discoveries marked the Scientific Revolution.
- How the Agricultural Revolution contributed to the Industrial Revolution.
- How the Industrial Revolution developed.
- What the effects of industrialization were.
- How industrialization continued and spread.

Terms to Learn	**People to Know**
enclosure	Galileo Galilei
textile	Sir Isaac Newton
factory system	Robert Fulton
cotton gin	Samuel F.B. Morse

Why It's Important By the 1700s, people in the western world also had new ideas about science. These led to new forms of power and ways of making goods. Industry and ways of living changed so much that historians call these changes the Industrial Revolution.

The Industrial Revolution involved the shift from animal and human power to machine power. This meant that society became less agricultural and more industrial. During the early years of the Industrial Revolution, Great Britain took the lead. Later, other countries rose to challenge Great Britain.

Chapter Overview
Visit the *Human Heritage* Web site at **humanheritage.glencoe.com** and click on ***Chapter 33—Chapter Overviews*** to preview this chapter.

SECTION 1 Scientific Revolution

Many of the changes that occurred during the Industrial Revolution grew out of changes in scientific thinking. Beginning in the 1400s, scientists started to break away from old ideas. They used the scientific method to form and test their own hypotheses. This became known as the Scientific Revolution.

Nicolaus Copernicus (kuh per' nuh kuhs) was one of the first people to use the scientific method. Copernicus was a Polish astronomer who studied the motion of the planets. What he saw proved to him that Ptolemy was wrong and that Earth was not the center of the universe. In 1543, Copernicus published a book explaining his idea that planets revolve around the sun rather

---

HISTORY *Online*

Chapter Overview introduces students to chapter content and key terms. Have them access **Chapter 33 Overview** at **humanheritage.glencoe.com**

FOCUS

Bellringer

Hold a two-minute brainstorming session in which students name devices, equipment, or machines powered by steam, gas, oil, or electricity. Record the results on the board.

Motivational Activity

Note the many items on the board. Then quickly erase everything. Tell students that none of these things would be available without the Industrial Revolution—the subject of this chapter.

GUIDE TO READING

Reading Strategy

Ask students to read "Why It's Important" and summarize the chapter's main theme. (*New scientific ideas and new forms of energy produced such far-reaching changes in society and industry during the 1700s that historians call these changes the Industrial Revolution.*)

Vocabulary Precheck

Ask students to define each of the "Terms to Learn." Have a volunteer consult the dictionary for any unfamiliar words. **L1 ELL**

Use the Vocabulary PuzzleMaker for Chapter 33 to create a crossword puzzle. **L1**

Assign Chapter 33 Vocabulary and Guided Reading Activity.

Assign Reading Essentials and Study Guide 33-1.

TEACH

Guided Practice

L1 **Critical Thinking** New interest in science led to discoveries and philosophies based on reason. Lead students in defining reason. *(the logical and systematic way of proving a case by supporting it with facts)*

L2 **Science** Have students choose one of the scientists discussed in the chart on this page. Have them research the inventions or discoveries of their chosen scientists, including lesser-known inventions. Then have students create a visual presentation of their inventor's achievements.

MAKING CONNECTIONS

➤➤ **History** Great Britain pioneered in the Industrial Revolution because it possessed the factors of industrialization, including (1) capital, (2) a mobile labor force, (3) natural resources, (4) entrepreneurs, (5) a new technology, (6) markets, (7) a supportive government.

SCIENTISTS

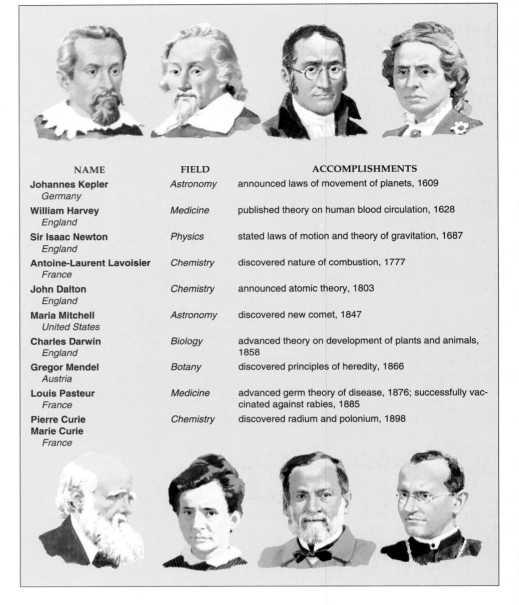

NAME	FIELD	ACCOMPLISHMENTS
Johannes Kepler Germany	Astronomy	announced laws of movement of planets, 1609
William Harvey England	Medicine	published theory on human blood circulation, 1628
Sir Isaac Newton England	Physics	stated laws of motion and theory of gravitation, 1687
Antoine-Laurent Lavoisier France	Chemistry	discovered nature of combustion, 1777
John Dalton England	Chemistry	announced atomic theory, 1803
Maria Mitchell United States	Astronomy	discovered new comet, 1847
Charles Darwin England	Biology	advanced theory on development of plants and animals, 1858
Gregor Mendel Austria	Botany	discovered principles of heredity, 1866
Louis Pasteur France	Medicine	advanced germ theory of disease, 1876; successfully vaccinated against rabies, 1885
Pierre Curie **Marie Curie** France	Chemistry	discovered radium and polonium, 1898

COOPERATIVE LEARNING

Divide the class into two groups to role-play a presentation on the solar system by Galileo before a group consisting of opposing academic and Church leaders. Have the first group plan Galileo's presentation in a manner that is convincing and tactful. The second group should prepare the academic and Church leaders' rebuttal. Within each group, have students assume tasks such as conducting research, listing arguments, anticipating responses, and taking part in the role play. After the presentation and rebuttal, have the class evaluate the statements and identify which group had the most convincing argument and why.

than around Earth. This book began a complete change in scientific thinking.

Another important scientist was the Italian astronomer Galileo Galilei (gal uh lē' ō gal uh lā' ē). He invented a telescope and began to study the stars and planets. He learned that the moon's surface is not smooth but has mountains and craters. He learned that the Milky Way holds a vast number of stars and that the sun rotates on its axis. Galileo was strongly criticized by the Roman Catholic Church for teaching that Earth revolves around the sun. Even so, Galileo's ideas spread throughout Europe.

In 1642, the same year Galileo died, another important scientist, Sir Isaac Newton (ī' zuhk nūt' n), was born in England. It was Newton who explained the theory of gravitation and how objects move through space. The technology for today's rockets and space satellites is based on his work.

It was at this time that scientists in Great Britain and France formed organizations in which they could discuss their ideas and research. In this way, scientific information began to spread more quickly. Soon, thousands of people were using the scientific method to add to their knowledge and improve their lives.

Painting of Copernicus

Section 1 Assessment

1. What scientific discoveries were made by Galileo Galilei?
2. Why were Sir Isaac Newton's theories important?

Critical Thinking

3. **Making Generalizations** Why was the time beginning in the 1400s known as the Scientific Revolution?

Graphic Organizer Activity

4. Draw this diagram, and use it to show some of the new ideas developed during the Scientific Revolution. (Add circles as needed.)

Ideas From Scientific Revolution

SECTION 2 Agricultural Revolution

As changes were taking place in science, there were new developments in farming. These changes were called the Agricultural Revolution. It set the stage for the Industrial Revolution.

By the 1700s, a system of land division called **enclosure** (en klō' zhuhr) was in use in Great Britain. Landowners combined the many small strips of land worked by tenant farmers into large areas closed in by fences, hedges, or ditches. Enclosure allowed landowners to make more money. Now, whole areas could grow the same crop. This meant larger harvests and greater profits. Landowners also needed fewer workers.

✓ **Reading Check**
How did the system of **enclosure** work?

Section 1 Assessment Answers

1. that the planets revolve around the sun
2. because his work formed the basis for today's rockets
3. This was a time when scientists broke away from old theories and used the scientific method.
4. Sample ideas: idea of a sun-centered solar system, discovery of moon's topo-graphic features, discovery of stars in the Milky Way, principle of gravity, any of the ideas or discoveries in the table on p. 524.

Assign the Chapter 33 **Section 1 Quiz** in the TCR. Testmaker available.

💾 Use **Interactive Tutor Self-Assessment Software** to review Section 1.

MAKING CONNECTIONS

➤➤ **Science** Changes also took place in medicine. In 1628, Dr. William Harvey discovered that blood circulates in one direction through the body. In 1718, Lady Mary Wortley Montague brought the Chinese practice of inoculation against smallpox from Turkey to England.

✓ **Reading Check Answer**
Under **enclosure,** landowners combined small strips of land worked by tenant farmers into large areas enclosed by fences, hedges, or ditches.

Biography

The following videotape program is available from Glencoe to enrich Chapter 33:

• **Sir Isaac Newton: The Gravity of Genius**

To find classroom resources to accompany this video, check the following home page:

A&E Television:
http://www.aetv.com

💾 Use the **Vocabulary Puzzle-Maker** to create crossword and word search puzzles.

L1 **Critical Thinking** Ask students to analyze the term *revolution*. What revolutions have they studied besides the Industrial Revolution? *(English, American, French political revolutions)* What changes occurred? *(changes in government and in society)* Ask if they think these changes were positive or negative. **ELL**

GEOGRAPHY AND HISTORY

In farming developments, Viscount Charles Townshend introduced the system of rotating crops. Instead of letting a field lie fallow for one year, Townshend planted such crops as alfalfa and clover, which restore nitrogen to the soil and make it more fertile. Townshend was nicknamed "Turnip" because he encouraged farmers to grow root crops.

💾 Use **Interactive Tutor Self-Assessment Software** to review Section 2.

✔️ **Reading Check Answer**
The **textile** industry produced cotton cloth. Under the **domestic system,** work was done in workers' cottages.

💾 Use the **Vocabulary Puzzle-Maker** to create crossword and word search puzzles.

DID YOU KNOW
The 1800s saw many innovations in Great Britain's textile industry. In 1807 the die-stamped metal button was invented. In 1820 T. Hancock invented the first elastic fabric. Called webbing, it replaced the ribbons that secured women's shoes.

The tenant farmers had two choices. They could stay on as paid workers, or they could look elsewhere for jobs. Most left to find work in other places. They moved to cities and became industrial workers.

Enclosure was just part of the revolution in agriculture. New ways of growing crops and breeding animals were also developed. These changes led to greater production of food. More food meant better health and longer life spans. Population increased, and the demand for manufactured goods grew.

Section 2 Assessment

1. **Define:** enclosure.
2. How did landowners use the enclosure system?
3. How did the growth of population influence the Industrial Revolution?

Critical Thinking

4. **Making Comparisons** Do you think agriculture was more or less important in the 1700s than it is today in Great Britain?

Graphic Organizer Activity

5. Draw this diagram, and use it to show some of the effects of the enclosure system.

Enclosure System	Effect
	Effect
	Effect

SECTION 3 Industrial Revolution

The Industrial Revolution began in the early 1700s. It was a long, slow process at first. However, as one development led to another, the revolution moved faster and faster. Much of the world changed. By the 1850s, the changes had become so widespread that people realized they were entering a new age.

The Textile Industry The Industrial Revolution began in Great Britain in the **textile** (tek' stuhl), or woven cloth, industry. In the 1600s and early 1700s, cloth was made by the **domestic system.** Under this system, most work was done in workers' cottages, where families worked together. Merchants went from cottage to cottage, bringing the workers raw wool and cotton. Using hand-powered spinning wheels and looms, the workers would spin the thread and weave it into wool and cotton cloth. The merchants then picked up the finished cloth to sell.

The domestic system could not meet the strong growing demand for cloth. Before long, people started looking for ways to make more cloth in less time. The first major breakthrough came in 1733 when a British inventor named John Kay invented the

✔️ **Reading Check**
What did the **textile** industry produce? What was the **domestic system?**

Section 2 Assessment Answers

1. enclosure, land division (p. 525)
2. They could grow the same crop over a large area with fewer workers.
3. As the population increased, the demand for manufactured goods grew.
4. Answers will vary but might include growing organic crops and hybrid crops.

5. Sample effects: allowed landowners to make more money; resulted in larger harvests, at greater profits, with fewer workers; forced many tenant farmers into cities; swelled the industrial labor force

Assign the Chapter 33 **Section 2 Quiz** in the TCR. Testmaker available.

flying shuttle. It was mounted on rollers, and one weaver could send it rapidly from one side of a loom to the other. It cut in half the time needed to weave cloth. Now, however, spinners could not keep up with the weavers. Then, in 1764, James Hargreaves (hahr′ grēvz), a British carpenter, invented the **spinning jenny.** It had a number of spindles fastened to a single wheel. The jenny made it possible for one person to spin many threads at the same time.

More progress was made when ways were found to use the power of falling water instead of hand power to run textile machines. This meant, however, that the machines had to be near a large water supply. Accordingly, factories were built next to rivers that could supply the necessary water power. This was the beginning of the **factory system,** which brought workers and machines together in one place to make goods. Workers still lived in their cottages, but they came to factories to work. In time, towns grew up around these factories.

Water power did not work very well with heavy machinery. So, people began looking for still another source of power. In 1769, a Scottish mechanic named James Watt perfected the steam engine. Steam soon replaced water as the major source of power. Factories of all kinds could now be set up near raw materials and town markets.

Cotton farmers in America and in India could not supply enough raw cotton to meet the needs of British textile factories. Eli Whitney (ē′ lī hwit′ nē), an American inventor, found a way to solve this problem. While visiting a cotton plantation in Georgia, he learned that it took a great deal of time to clean the seeds out of cotton by hand. In 1793, with the help of Catherine Littlefield Greene, he invented the **cotton gin,** or cotton-cleaning machine. It could clean cotton 50 times faster than a person working by hand. If it were driven by water power, it could clean cotton 1,000 times faster.

Organizing Production   About five years later, Whitney developed a new way of organizing production. This was the system of **interchangeable parts,** which means that a certain part of a product is the same size and shape as that same part in another product. Whitney first used interchangeable parts in the making of guns. Until that time, each gun was made individually, and no two guns were alike. Broken parts had to be specially made by a skilled worker in order to fit a specific gun. Whitney's use of parts of identical size and shape made it possible for less-skilled workers to make or fix guns much faster.

Other Americans also developed new ways of organizing production. In the late 1700s, a shopkeeper-mechanic named Oliver Evans was the first to use **automation,** or the process in which machines instead of people do much of the labor. Evans'

✓ Reading Check
Why was the **flying shuttle** important? Who invented the **spinning jenny?**

✓ Reading Check
How did the **factory system** differ from the domestic system?

✓ Reading Check
Who invented the **cotton gin,** and what did this machine do?

✓ Reading Check
What changes did the use of **interchangeable parts** bring to production?

✓ Reading Check
What is **automation?**

✓ Reading Check Answer
The **flying shuttle** cut in half the time needed to weave cloth. James Hargreaves invented the **spinning jenny.**

✓ Reading Check Answer
Under the **factory system,** workers left their cottages to work at machines located in buildings away from their cottages.

MAKING CONNECTIONS

➤➤ **History** The invention of the cotton gin brought about social changes as well as economic ones. Enslavment in the southern states of the United States increased partly because of it.

✓ Reading Check Answer
Eli Whitney invented the **cotton gin,** which cleaned seeds from cotton.

✓ Reading Check Answer
The use of **interchangeable parts** made it possible for less-skilled workers to make or fix guns and other products much faster.

✓ Reading Check Answer
Automation is the process in which machines, instead of people, do much of the labor.

MEETING SPECIAL NEEDS

To help students of Limited English Proficiency organize and remember information about the people in this chapter, have them make a graphic organizer of the names of these people and their achievements. Have the students work in pairs to classify and then quiz each other; for example, "Who was Galileo Galilei?" "He was an astronomer." After the students know these facts, have pairs add another fact about each person; then have them quiz each other again.

📁 Refer to *Inclusion for the Middle School Social Studies Classroom: Strategies and Activities* for additional resources.

Reading Check
How does an **assembly line** work?

Robert Fulton
1765–1815

American Inventor

Born near Lancaster, Pennsylvania, Robert Fulton had many talents. He was an expert gunsmith and an accomplished landscape painter. He also designed torpedoes and early submarines. Fulton is best known for launching the *Clermont,* the first commercially successful steamboat in America.

---

automated flour mill was water-powered, and cut by four-fifths the number of workers needed to run it.

In 1847, Samuel Colt used Whitney's idea of interchangeable parts to develop the **assembly line.** On an assembly line, each worker adds a part of the product and passes it on to the next worker, who also adds a part, until the entire product has been put together. Colt used the assembly line to produce the Colt revolver. Before assembly lines, a skilled worker had to make one product at a time from start to finish. With the assembly line, work could be divided, and many products could be put together at one time by unskilled workers. All of these discoveries and new techniques greatly increased production.

Iron, Coal, and Steel To build machine parts, iron was needed. To fire steam engines, coal was needed. Without iron, coal, and steel, which replaced iron, the Industrial Revolution could not have continued.

By the early 1700s, ironmaking had become expensive. To smelt iron, the British used *charcoal,* a fuel that is made by burning wood. The British, however, were running out of

SEWING MACHINE Issac Singer oversees a demonstration of his first sewing machine. **What industry did Singer's machine help the most?**

SPOTLIGHT ON: JOSIAH WEDGWOOD

When china clay, used for pottery and chinaware, was found in nearby Cornwall, Josiah Wedgwood took the lead in establishing the famous potteries in 18th-century Great Britain. Wedgwood learned the craft of making pottery from his family and other famous potters and opened his own factory in Etruria. His first success was a cream-colored earthenware he called Queen's ware. Wedgwood's dishes became quite popular with the prosperous middle class. Wedgwood was the first pottery maker to use steam-powered engines.

forests, which made wood scarce and costly. In 1753, a way was found to use coal instead of charcoal for smelting. As a result, iron became cheaper, iron production grew, and coal mining became a major industry.

Iron, however, was too brittle for rails, bridge supports, and heavy equipment. In 1856, a British inventor named Henry Bessemer (bes' uh muhr) found a cheap way of removing the impurities from iron to make steel, which was harder and stronger than iron. The Bessemer Process lowered the cost of making steel from $200 a ton to $4 a ton. Seven years later, in 1863, Pierre-Emile Martin of France and William Siemens of England invented the **open-hearth process,** which used a special kind of furnace to make steel. It was even cheaper than the Bessemer Process and could turn out many different kinds of steel. Soon, mining towns and steel centers grew up in areas with supplies of iron ore and coal.

Transportation   Raw materials and finished products had to be moved quickly and cheaply. Before this could happen, transportation had to be improved. Until the 1700s, the chief means of transportation over land was by horse or horse-drawn wagon. Roads were no more than rough and narrow dirt paths. Travel was slow and uncomfortable. It was even worse when rain made the roads muddy.

Late in the 1700s, the British began to improve their roads. A Scottish engineer named Thomas Telford (tel' fuhrd) designed roadbeds so that water would drain off the roads. Another Scottish engineer, John L. McAdam, developed what became known as the **macadam** (muh kad' uhm) **road.** It had a surface made of layers of crushed stone. This surface allowed horse-drawn wagons to use the roads in all kinds of weather and to travel faster.

The British also made their rivers wider and deeper and built canals to connect navigable rivers to factory and mining centers. Horses walked beside canals and pulled barges. The barges were slow but could carry 50 times the amount of goods that horse-drawn wagons could. By 1830, Great Britain had a complete system of inland waterways.

The biggest improvement in land transportation was the railroad. For years, donkeys had pulled carts over wooden rails inside coal mines. Then, the production of iron grew. The wooden rails were replaced by iron ones that could carry heavier loads. Inventors began to build locomotives to run on iron rails. In 1829, George Stephenson (stē' vuhn suhn), a British mining engineer, won a contest to see who could build the best locomotive. Stephenson's locomotive, the *Rocket,* could pull a train about 36 miles, or 58 kilometers, an hour. The *Rocket* started a railroad-building boom in Great Britain and around the world.

☑ **Reading Check**
What was the **open-hearth process?**

☑ **Reading Check**
How did the **macadam road** improve transportation?

A High Railway In 1870, an American engineer named Henry Meiggs built what is still the world's highest railroad—the Central Railway—across the Andes Mountains in Peru. At it's highest point, the Central Railway reaches an altitude of nearly 16,000 feet, or 4880 meters, higher than the tallest peak in the Alps.

la

Henry Bessemer established his steel works at Sheffield, England, a city that is still noted for its fine steel products.

☑ **Reading Check Answer**
The **open-hearth process** used a special kind of furnace to make steel cheaper than the Bessemer process.

PRIMARY SOURCES
Library

You might assign "The Iron Horse," from pages 692–693 of the Primary Sources Library.

☑ **Reading Check Answer**
The **macadam road** allowed horse-drawn carriages to use the roads in all kinds of weather and to move much faster.

LINKING PAST TO PRESENT

The use of tin cans for preserving food started in 1812. Originally these tin-plated containers were called *canisters.* The term *can* was used for the first time at Boston's Underwood Cannery in 1839 by bookkeepers who apparently tired of writing the longer word again and again.

COOPERATIVE LEARNING

Divide students into groups. Have each group research innovations in one of these areas: farming, transportation, power sources, textiles, factories. Each team member should be assigned a specific topic; students examining "power sources" could research the use of waterwheels or coal, for example. After researching, have groups share their findings. Have one member of each group orally present the group's findings.

📂 Assign Chapter 33 *Cooperative Learning Activity* in the TCR.

DID YOU KNOW

In 1825, the first locomotive in the United States was built by John Stevens, but it only ran in circles around Steven's estate. The first practical locomotive, the Tom Thumb, was built five years later by Peter Cooper.

GEOGRAPHY AND HISTORY

It took sailing ships about two months to cross the Atlantic. Steamboats made the trip in ten days.

Independent Practice

L2 **Literature** Have students read parts of *Life on the Mississippi* by Mark Twain, an account of the author's years as a steamboat pilot. Have students consider what functions steamboats served and how they affected life and commerce in that area. Have students conclude by discussing what the book tells about society in the Mississippi River valley at that time.

💾 Use **Interactive Tutor Self-Assessment Software** to review Section 3.

Student Web Activity objectives, goals, and answers can be found at the *Chapter 33 Web Activity Lesson Plan* at humanheritage.glencoe.com

💾 Use the **Vocabulary Puzzle-Maker** to create crossword and word search puzzles.

Railroads changed daily life as well as transportation. People started using such phrases as "keeping on track" and "tooting your own whistle." They also collected autographs of railway engineers. When American railroads adopted standard time zones in 1883, everyone else in the United States did too. The next year, time zones were established all over the world.

The biggest improvement in water transportation was the steamboat. The first practical one was developed by Robert Fulton (fūhl′ tuhn), an American inventor. In 1807, Fulton's *Clermont*, powered by a British steam engine, set a record by making the trip from Albany to New York City in 32 hours. Soon, steamboats were carrying passengers and goods along the inland waterways of the United States and Europe. Steamboats, however, did not replace sailing ships in trans-oceanic travel until the late 1800s, when fuel-efficient engines were developed.

Section 3 Assessment

1. **Define:** textile, domestic system, flying shuttle, spinning jenny, factory system, cotton gin, interchangeable parts, automation, assembly line, open-hearth process, macadam road.
2. What effect did the assembly line have on the type of workers needed for production?
3. Why did transportation have to be improved during the Industrial Revolution?

Critical Thinking

4. **Predicting Consequences** Suppose the steam engine was never invented.

Do you think the Industrial Revolution would have still occurred? Why or why not?

Graphic Organizer Activity

5. Draw this diagram, and use it to weigh the pros and cons of using an assembly line to produce goods.

Use of Assembly Line	
Pros	Cons

Student Web Activity
Visit the *Human Heritage* Web site at humanheritage.glencoe.com and click on *Chapter 33— Student Web Activity* to find out more about inventors who lived during the Industrial Revolution.

SECTION 4 Industrial Impact

The Industrial Revolution brought many changes in people's lives. These changes showed up first in Great Britain. They spread from there to other countries.

Changes in Society In England, until the Middle Ages, there had been two major social classes—the nobles, who were the upper class, and the peasants, who were the lower class. Then, a middle class of rich merchants developed.

Section 3 Assessment Answers

1. All terms are defined in the text Glossary.
2. It made it possible for less-skilled workers to make or fix products much faster.
3. to move raw materials and finished products quickly and cheaply
4. Answers will vary, but students should understand the importance of the steam engine in the expansion of the factory system and growth of a market economy.

Some students may suggest alternative inventions that could have had a similar impact as the steam engine.
5. Charts will vary, but may indicate the advantage of increased productivity and the disadvantage of monotonous work.

Assign the Chapter 33 **Section 3 Quiz** in the TCR. Testmaker available.

During the Industrial Revolution, the middle class increased in numbers and grew richer. Many factory, railroad, and mine owners became as wealthy as the nobles. They began to keep servants and to dress like members of the upper class. Women wore lacy petticoats and hooped skirts with stiff linings. Men wore dark suits, with top hats in winter and *boaters,* or stiff straw hats, in summer. Members of the middle class had iron ranges for cooking and gave huge dinner parties. Middle-class families began spending their weekends at seaside resorts, which were easy to reach now that railroads were common. Middle-class children went to upper-class schools.

In time, the middle class gained political power. In Great Britain, its male members gained the right to vote and to be represented in Parliament.

The Industrial Revolution also created an industrial working class. Most members of this class were peasants who could no longer support themselves by farming. Since they had no property of their own to sell, they had to sell their labor in order to live.

Members of the working class did not benefit from the Industrial Revolution in its early years. They worked 12 to 16 hours a day, six days a week, for low wages. They had to work at the pace set by machines and factory owners and were fined or

Linking Across Time

Automation The development of automation reduced the number of workers needed to produce goods. One person, for example, could run a machine that spun rows and rows of spindles of thread (below). Today the use of robots has eliminated the use of humans entirely on some jobs (right). **How did the use of machines affect the lives of workers in the Industrial Revolution?**

CHAPTER 33 RISE OF INDUSTRY **531**

SPOTLIGHT ON: ROBERT OWEN

Robert Owen tried to turn his mill town in New Lanark, Scotland, into an ideal community. He was a reformer who believed that better conditions would create better people and reduce crime and undesirable habits. Working hours were shortened and pay was increased at his mill. Owen built cottages for the workers. The town's stores offered affordable clothing and food. Children under ten did not work in the mill but attended free schools. Classes for older children were provided as well. By 1815, visitors from other parts of Great Britain and other countries came to observe the "ideal" town.

Glencoe Literature Library

The following novels from the **Glencoe Literature Library** may be used to enrich this chapter:
- *Jane Eyre,* by Charlotte Brontë. (Orphaned girl in 19th-century England.)
- *Pride and Prejudice,* by Jane Austen. (Rigid English social classes in the early 1800s.)
- *Frankenstein,* by Mary Shelley. (Moral responsibility of scientific invention.)
- *Great Expectations,* by Charles Dickens. (Rapid wealth and the meaning of friendship.)

Linking Across Time

Workers labored long hours for low wages, often under dangerous conditions. They had no job security and could be fined for falling behind.

ABCNEWS INTERACTIVE™

 VIDEODISC
Turning Points in World History

 Side Two Chapter 3

Title: *The Industrial Revolution*
Ask: What were working conditions like for children? *(Children worked long hours for low pay in terrible conditions.)*
How did workers express their opposition to work conditions? *(They formed unions and lobbied for government regulations to protect workers.)*

➤➤ **Daily Life** In 1841 an anonymous woman who worked in the textile mill in Lowell, Massachusetts, wrote about the poor working conditions in the workers' magazine *The Lowell Offering: I am going home, where I shall not be obliged to rise so early in the morning, . . . Up before day, at the clang of the bell—and out of the mill by the clang of the bell—into the mill, and at work in obedience to that ding-dong of a bell—just as though we were so many living machines.*

L2 Economics Have students research and present an in-class report on the early railroad industry. Students should use the following questions to focus their reports: *How did this new means of transportation affect the economies of countries such as Great Britain and the United States? How did railroads affect markets for goods, opportunities for travel, and communication?*

L3 Critical Thinking Have students investigate reform movements to outlaw child labor in the United States. Who headed these movements? Were they successful?

CAPTION ANSWER

because workers had little economic power; it was against the law to form trade unions, and workers could not vote.

---

beaten if they did not keep up. Working conditions were difficult, dirty, and dangerous. Many people were killed or injured by unsafe machinery. The working class did not have job security. Factory and mine owners hired and fired whenever they wanted.

Most children of the working class did not have time to go to school or to play. Instead, they worked in factories and mines along with men and women. Employers often preferred to hire children. One reason was that children were paid even less than adults. Another reason was that in mines, they could crawl through narrow tunnels into which adults could not fit. Children sometimes were crippled by this difficult work.

The Growth of Cities

The Growth of Cities Another change brought by the Industrial Revolution was the growth of cities. Before the Industrial Revolution, less than 10 percent of the people in Great Britain lived in cities. By 1900, the number had reached 75 percent. Indeed, 10 percent of the people in the whole country lived in the city of London.

Some cities grew up around factories or mines that had been built in rural areas. Most factories, however, were built in existing cities, which grew rapidly as people moved there to find jobs. Soon, the cities became overcrowded. Houses could not be built fast enough. Sometimes, a dozen people had to live in one room. Many moved into damp basements or rooms with no windows. Garbage floated in the streets because sewers had not yet been built. Water supplies became polluted. Epidemics of cholera (kol' uhr uh), typhoid, and tuberculosis were common. The death rate

Then . . . & Now

A Growing Population In 1800, less than 3 percent of the world's people lived in cities with 20,000 or more people. By the year 2000, however, as many as 50 percent will live in urban areas.

INDUSTRIAL CITIES The development of industry in England led to the growth of large cities. English industrial cities were located near coal or iron deposits. This painting shows a nineteenth-century steel factory in the city of Sheffield. **Why could workers in the city do nothing about their working or living conditions?**

EXTENDING THE CONTENT

The city of Manchester, England, had many geographic factors that an industrial city needed for growth, such as the availability of raw materials and accessible transportation routes. Manchester lies within 25 miles (or 40 km) of two coal fields, at the meeting point of three rivers, and has a canal that connects the city to the Irish Sea. During the 1800s, Manchester grew into one of the world's centers for the production of cotton textiles. Mills and warehouses replaced private homes in many areas.

among the working class was more than twice that of the middle and upper classes.

Workers had little economic or political power. It was against the law to form **trade unions,** or workers' associations. Workers did not have the right to vote. For these reasons, they could do nothing about their working or living conditions.

Reading Check
What were **trade unions?**

Reform   Most people in the middle and upper classes paid little attention to the suffering of the workers. Factory owners, for example, felt that raising wages and improving working conditions would raise the cost of goods and lower profits. Some, however, believed that higher wages and better working conditions could produce good profits. They began to work for reform.

The reformers started schools, orphanages, and hospitals for the poor. They also worked to change laws. In 1824, trade unions were made legal. During the 1830s and 1840s, children under ten years old and women were prohibited from working underground in mines. The workday was cut to ten hours.

The reformers also worked to improve living conditions. New laws required public sewer systems and the building of better houses. Every room had to have at least one window, and every house had to have piped-in water. Over time, life became better for the working class. There were fewer epidemics. Clothing, food, and other products became cheap enough for the workers to buy.

Section 4 Assessment

1. **Define:** trade unions.
2. What problems were caused by the rapid growth of cities?
3. Why were some people against reform?

Critical Thinking

4. **Demonstrating Reasoned Judgment** What reforms would you have worked for if you had lived during the Industrial Revolution?

Graphic Organizer Activity

5. Draw this diagram, and use it to support this generalization: The Industrial Revolution brought many changes to people's lives. (Add answer lines as needed.)

Generalization

Supporting Details
1.
2.
3.
4.
5.

SECTION 5   Spread of Industry

Meanwhile, the Industrial Revolution spread from Great Britain to other countries. These countries, aided by technology, soon **industrialized,** or built up industry. The expansion of railroads and transportation were also important factors.

Reading Check
What happened when countries **industrialized?**

Reading Check Answer
Trade unions were worker associations.

MAKING CONNECTIONS

➤➤ **History** The British laws against child labor were called the Factory Acts of 1833 and 1844. In the United States, the child labor problem was not settled until 1938, when the Fair Labor Standards Act was passed.

L1 History Have students investigate and present an oral report on child labor in the United States during the 1800s. Students should research the type of work young children performed, the length of their working day, and the amount they were paid. Suggest they create a list or daily schedule of what a day in the life of one of these children might have been like. What modern counterparts to these movements remain today? Have students report on their findings to the class.

💾 Use **Interactive Tutor Self-Assessment Software** to review Section 4.

Reading Check Answer
When countries **industrialized,** they built up industry.

💾 Use the **Vocabulary Puzzle-Maker** to create crossword and word search puzzles.

Section 4 Assessment Answers

1. trade unions, workers' associations (p. 533)
2. Overcrowding; disposing of garbage; obtaining fresh water supplies; and epidemics of cholera, typhoid, and tuberculosis were problems.
3. because they felt that raising wages and improving working conditions would raise the cost of goods and lower profits
4. Answers will vary, but students should give reasons for their answers.

5. Sample supporting details: middle class grew in size, wealth, and political power; an industrial working class appeared; industrial workers labored long hours for low wages; machines and factory owners set the pace of work; children went to work in factories and mines; cities expanded and the poor often lived in unhealthy conditions.

Assign Chapter 33 **Section 4 Quiz** in the TCR. Testmaker available.

Reading Check Answer
Other countries welcomed skilled British **immigrants** because they brought British industrial secrets to their new homelands.

MAKING CONNECTIONS

➤➤ **History** In 1789, a young British mechanic named Samuel Slater arrived in New York, bringing with him the secrets of new spinning and weaving machines built by British inventors. Slater was soon operating the first factory in the United States.

CAPTION ANSWER

British immigrants brought industrial secrets to their new homelands.

DID YOU KNOW ??

Crusader for workers' rights, especially those of African Americans, William Lloyd Garrison published his successful newspaper, *The Liberator*, in the early 1800s.

Reading Check
Why did other nations welcome skilled British **immigrants?**

Weights and Measures As industrialization spread, people needed a common system of weights and measures. Most countries adopted the metric system, first developed in France in the 1790s. Its basic measurement, the meter, equals one ten-millionth of the distance along a meridian from the North Pole to the Equator.

Other Countries At the beginning of the Industrial Revolution, Great Britain tried to keep its inventions secret. Machines or plans for machines were forbidden to be taken out of Great Britain. Skilled workers were forbidden to leave the country. By the 1800s, however, many workers had ignored the law and left. Other nations welcomed these **immigrants,** or people who settle permanently in a different country, because they brought British industrial secrets to their new homelands.

These countries used what they learned to build their own industries. Belgium, with its rich deposits of iron and coal, was the first country after Great Britain to industrialize. The next country was France. There, the process began in the 1700s but was slowed by war and revolution. The United States, with its many natural resources, soon followed France.

Then came Germany. Although Germany was well supplied with coal and iron, it was divided into more than 30 separate states. These states were not willing to cooperate in economic matters. Germany, therefore, did not make much industrial progress until after its unification in 1871. It then matched the others as a leading industrial power.

WORLD'S FAIR In 1851, Great Britain held the first World's Fair in London to celebrate its industrial achievements. Other countries then began to hold similar fairs. This painting shows the royal family attending opening day. **How did the Industrial Revolution spread from Great Britain to other countries?**

SPOTLIGHT ON: SAMUEL SLATER

Samuel Slater was working as an engineer overseeing the machines in a British cotton mill when he heard about the rewards for textile-machine designs in the United States. Disguising himself as an apprentice, he sailed to New York. There Moses Brown, a Quaker merchant from Rhode Island, hired him. Slater re-created from memory the Arkwright-designed spinning machines that he had worked with in England. His water-powered mill was built next to the falls of the Blackstone River. Slater later built other mills in New England. The Old Slater Mill in Pawtucket, Rhode Island, has been restored as a museum.

THOMAS EDISON Although best known for the electric light, Thomas Edison had numerous other important inventions. These include the first successful phonograph, an electric railroad, and an electric battery. This photograph shows Edison in his laboratory. **What advances in communications were powered by electricity?**

Technological Advances The development of new kinds of power helped continue the Industrial Revolution. One of these was electricity. In 1837, two Americans, Samuel F. B. Morse and Alfred Vail, built the first successful electric telegraph. It made quick communication possible. Some years later, Alexander Graham Bell, also an American, invented the telephone. Communications took another step forward. In 1895, an Italian physicist, Guglielmo Marconi (gū yel' mō mahr kō' nē), built the wireless telegraph, or radio. Six years later, he was able to send a message across the Atlantic Ocean.

Meanwhile, there were other advances in electricity. By 1879, Thomas Alva Edison, an American, developed the electric light. It would soon illuminate factories and homes all over the world.

Another new source of power was the **internal combustion engine,** or an engine that is fueled by gasoline. It was invented around 1885 by German engineer Gottlieb Daimler (gōt' lēb dīm' luhr). Daimler's engine was used to drive the first automobile as well as other machines. Another German engineer, Rudolf Diesel, developed an oil-burning internal combustion engine that could run large industrial plants, locomotives, and ocean liners. These developments helped open a whole new era in transportation.

Fun Facts...

Inspiration Guglielmo Marconi, inventor of the wireless telegraph, was inspired to experiment with science after reading a biography of Benjamin Franklin.

☑ **Reading Check**
What fueled the **internal combustion engine?**

EXTENDING THE CONTENT

The invention of the gasoline-powered engines carried aviation technology to new levels. In the 1890s Ferdinand von Zepplin streamlined the dirigible—a balloonlike craft that could carry passengers. Wilbur and Orville Wright achieved success in 1903 with the first flight of a motorized airplane. Airplanes and other vehicles needed a steady supply of fuel for power and rubber for tires and other parts. As a result, the worldwide petroleum and rubber industries skyrocketed.

CAPTION ANSWER
the electric telegraph, the telephone, and the wireless telegraph, or radio

☑ **Reading Check Answer**
The first **internal combustion engine** was fueled by gas. Later ones were also fueled by oil.

ASSESS

Check for Understanding

Ask students to summarize the main points of the chapter, orally or in writing. Discuss the answers to the Section and Chapter Assessment questions.

Evaluate

Assign the Chapter 33 **Performance Assessment Activity** in the TCR.

Administer the **Chapter 33 Test.** Testmaker available.

Reteach

Have students create time lines that list important inventions that contributed to the Industrial Revolution.

Assign the **Chapter 33 Reteaching Activity** in the TCR.

Enrich

Have students write scripts and perform skits showing working-class life during the Industrial Revolution.

Assign the **Chapter 33 Enrichment Activity** in the TCR.

CLOSE

Remind students that people often use the phrase, "the good old days," out of nostalgia for the past. Have them discuss what people living in the United States during the Industrial Revolution might have meant when they used this phrase.

Use **Interactive Tutor Self-Assessment Software** to review Section 5.

Section 5 Assessment

1. **Define:** industrialized, immigrants, internal combustion engine.
2. How did the Industrial Revolution spread?
3. What were the first countries to industrialize after Great Britain?

Critical Thinking

4. **Drawing Conclusions** Which of the advances in technology made during the Industrial Revolution do you consider the most important? Explain.

Graphic Organizer Activity

5. Draw this diagram, and use it to show inventions that advanced communication and the use of new forms of energy or power.

New Inventions	
Communication	Energy/Power

Chapter Summary & Study Guide

1. In 1543, Copernicus triggered the Scientific Revolution with his idea of a sun-centered solar system.
2. The Scientific Revolution helped lead to the Agricultural Revolution—a new system of land division, animal breeding, and growing crops.
3. The invention of new machines helped workers produce more goods in less time.
4. Perfection of the steam engine replaced the use of water power and allowed factories to be built near sources of raw materials.
5. Eli Whitney and Catherine Littlefield Greene invented the cotton gin in 1793. Whitney also developed the principle of interchangeable parts.
6. Automation and the assembly line increased production and reduced the need for skilled workers.
7. The development of inexpensive ways to smelt iron and make steel provided cheaper building materials for industry.
8. Improvements in transportation—better roads, canal systems, railroads, and steam boats—helped speed industrialization.
9. The Industrial Revolution increased the size of the middle class and created a new industrial working class, many of whom suffered poor living conditions in industrial cities.
10. During the 1800s, the Industrial Revolution spread from Great Britain to other countries, where inventors developed even more new ideas such as electricity and the internal combustion engine.

Section 5 Assessment Answers

1. industrialized, built up industry (p. 533); immigrants, people who settle in a different country (p. 534); internal combustion engine, engine fueled by gasoline (p. 535)
2. Workers who left England brought British industrial secrets to their new homelands.
3. Belgium, France, Germany, and the United States

4. Answers will vary but students should give reasons for their choices.
5. Sample responses: *communication*—telegraph, telephone, wireless telegraph (radio); *energy/power*—electricity, internal combustion engines run by gas, internal combustion engine run by oil

Assign the Chapter 33 **Section 5 Quiz** in the TCR. Testmaker available.

Using Key Terms

Imagine that you are having a conversation with Thomas Jefferson about the most important ideas and innovations of the Industrial Revolution. Write out the dialogue, using the following words.

enclosure   textile
domestic system   flying shuttle
spinning jenny   factory system
cotton gin   interchangeable parts
automation   assembly line
open-hearth process   macadam road
trade unions   industrialized
immigrants   internal combustion engine

Understanding Main Ideas

- In what ways did ideas about science change in the 1400s, 1500s, and 1600s?
- What effect did the Agricultural Revolution have on population growth?
- How did the development of the macadam road affect transportation?
- What benefits did people in the working class eventually receive from the Industrial Revolution?
- What new sources of power helped spread the Industrial Revolution?

Critical Thinking

- What did changes in agriculture have to do with the beginning of the Industrial Revolution?
- Why did Great Britian want to keep its inventions secret from the rest of the world?
- What things are necessary for a country to be able to industrialize?

4. Do you believe the Industrial Revolution was good or bad for most workers? Explain.

Graphic Organizer Activity

Economics Create a diagram such as the one shown, and use it to compare economic activities before and after the Industrial Revolution. (Tip: Think back to how people earned a living in the Renaissance and Middle Ages.)

Before the Industrial Revolution — Both — After the Industrial Revolution

Geography in History

Human/Environmental Interaction
Progress that came about during the Industrial Revolution was caused by people interacting with their environment. What geographic features were involved in this progress? Explain.

Using Your Journal

Review any details you may have noted about the changes that took place in the world between the 1400s and the 1800s. Write a newspaper editorial in which you give your opinion about how developments during the Industrial Revolution might cause problems for people in the future.

537

Key to Understanding

Paragraphs will vary but students should use all the terms.

Understanding Main Ideas

1. Scientists used the scientific method to test their hypotheses.
2. More food meant better health and longer life spans.
3. It allowed horse-drawn wagons to travel faster in all kinds of weather.
4. There were fewer epidemics, and products were cheaper.
5. electricity and the internal combustion engine

Critical Thinking

1. Farmers moved to cities; population grew and demand increased for manufactured goods.
2. because it wanted to monopolize profits
3. natural resources, technology, power sources, production, transportation, and workers
4. Answers will vary but students should explain their reasons.

Graphic Organizer Activity

Diagrams will vary, but economic activities prior to the Industrial Revolution will probably focus on farming and skilled crafts while economic activities after the Industrial Revolution will include factory work, mining and so on. Economic activities both before and after the Industrial Revolution might include trade, shipbuilding, and perhaps banking (starting in the Renaissance).

Bonus Test Question

For Chapter 33 Test
How did the invention of the electric light change American society forever? Explain. *(Answers will vary.)*

Using Your Journal

Editorials will vary. You might call on volunteers to read their editorials to the class and discuss them.

Geography in History

Factories were built next to rivers for water power and steam power, and near raw materials and markets. Transportation systems were improved.

FOCUS

Objectives

After reading the Around the World for Unit 10, students will be able to:

1. identify the size and location of the Russian empire at its height.

2. link Russian expansion to the diversity of its population

3. describe efforts to westernize Russia.

Bellringer

Ask students to write down what images come to mind when they hear the word "empire."

Motivational Activity

Discuss student responses. Then refer them to the Around the World feature on pages 538–539. In what ways did Russia fulfill students' expectations of what an empire should look like? *(Students might note the empire's huge size, the grandeur of objects such as the crown, the existence of a noble class, and so on.)*

TEACH

Geography: Location Tell students to study the map and map caption. Ask: On what continents was the Russian empire located at its height? *(parts of Europe, Asia, and North America)* Where were the two great Russian cities—St. Petersburg and Moscow—located? *(west of the Ural Mountains, in Europe)* Have students speculate on reasons Russian rulers might have found it hard to modernize their empire. *(sheer size of the empire, great distance of the government from lands east of the Urals, existence of many traditional cultures, and so on)*

538

RUSSIA

While western European nations pushed into the Americas, Russian czars expanded their borders both in the east and in the west. By the 1800s, Russia covered one-sixth of the earth's surface. It extended from the Baltic Sea in the west to Alaska in the east and from the Arctic Ocean in the north to central Asia in the south. The greatest czars—rulers like Peter the Great and Catherine the Great—worked tirelessly to modernize Russia. No matter how hard they tried, however, Russia remained a mostly rural nation, with nearly all of its vast population working as serfs or living in remote villages.

Russian Empire

ARCTIC OCEAN

Siberia

RUSSIA

Alaska

St. Petersburg

Moscow

URAL MOUNTAINS

Bering Strait

Kiev

OTTOMAN EMPIRE

PACIFIC OCEAN

CHINA

☐ Russian Empire at Its Height

miles 0 · 1250 · 2500

kilometers 0 · 1250 · 2500

▼ Both nobles and serfs loved the folktales that formed part of Russia's oral history. These tales drew an audience everywhere, whether it be in a peasant's cottag or a czar's palace. Russian artists captured scenes from these storie on beautiful lacquered boxes suc as this one.

▲ Most of the Russian empire stretched east of the Ural Mountains—the traditional boundary between Europe and Asia. Even so, the heart of the empire always lay west of the Urals—the place where the states of Rus and Muscovy were born. It was here that Russian rulers built their greatest cities and set up governments to rule their sprawling lands.

538 UNIT 10

SPOTLIGHT ON: RUSSIA

The revolutions of the late 1700s did not escape Russian notice. Inspired by the American and French revolutions, some 3,000 army officers from the Russian aristocracy took part in the Decembrist uprising of 1825. On December 26, the so-called "Decembrists" gathered at a statue of Peter the Great located in St. Petersburg's Senate Square. There, leaders of the uprising demanded a constitution and an immediate end to serfdom, which they called "our national disgrace."

The Decembrists expected the peasants to join them in revolt. What they got instead was the wrath of Czar Nicolas I, who ordered out the imperial guard. The czar's troops crushed the uprising—and hopes for democratic reform. After a quick trial, the leaders were hanged and the remaining officers sent into exile in Siberia.

the World

▶ Peter the Great founded St. Petersburg on the Baltic Sea in the early 1700s. Peter tried to "westernize" Russia. He even worked to ban beards on Russian men.

By the end of the 1700s, Russia reached some 6,000 miles from east to west. The larger it grew, the more diverse its population became. Peoples ranged from the hunters of the Tungus region in eastern Siberia (right) to the peasant women of the St. Petersburg area (left). ▶

◀ The skill of Russian artisans is shown in this fur-lined gold crown set with precious jewels. Crafted in the mid-sixteenth century, the crown is in a museum in the Kremlin today.

▲ Russian serfs farmed the land, worked as servants, and generally served the nobles who owned the land on which they lived. In this painting, serfs escort a noble family through the winter countryside in a carriage.

Taking Another Look

1. What was the size and location of the Russian empire at its height?
2. How did expansion affect the population makeup of Russia?

Hands-On Activity

Writing a Letter to the Editor Write a letter to the editor of a Russian newspaper commenting on Peter the Great's decision to ban all old-fashioned beards.

539

Biography

The following videotape program is available from Glencoe to enrich the Around the World feature.

- **Faberge: Imperial Jeweler**

  1-56501-878-8

To find classroom resources to accompany this video, check the following home page:

A&E Television:

http://www.aetv.com/

ASSESS

Check for Understanding

Have students answer the questions in Taking Another Look on page 539.

Enrich

Assign interested students to trace the Romanov dynasty that ruled imperial Russia. Have students present their findings in the form of an illustrated time line.

CLOSE

Have students compare Russia with western Europe in the late 1700s and early 1800s. Ask: What political and economic differences can you note between the two regions? *(the lack of democratic revolutions in Russia, the continued presence of a large population of serfs, lack of industry, etc.)*

ANSWERS TO TAKING ANOTHER LOOK

1. At its height, the Russian empire covered one-sixth of the earth's surface. It extended from the Baltic Sea in the west to Alaska in the east and from the Arctic Ocean in the north to central Asia in the south.
2. The larger the empire grew, the more diverse its population became.

Hand-On Activity

Letters will vary, but should reflect an understanding that the central issue is Peter's efforts to westernize Russia, rather than simply his ban on old-fashioned beards.

Standardized Test Practice

Answers and Analyses

1C Geography

According to the map, St. Augustine is located next to the 30°N (30 degrees north) line and is just to the east of the 90° W (90 degrees west) line.

2F Geography

According to the graph, the largest population belonged to Virginia, with close to 60,000 people; the smallest belonged to Pennsylvania, with about 18,000 people.

3D Culture/Environment

Since Native Americans had established ways of life before the arrival of colonists, choice A can be eliminated. Choice B is unlikely, and since Native Americans did not believe in land ownership, choice C can also be eliminated.

THE PRINCETON REVIEW TEST-TAKING TIP

Students should always begin by eliminating the unreasonable, and then take their best guess from among the remaining choices. Choices A and C are limited to the encounter between the Native Americans and the American settlers. They are not likely the cause of the different lifestyles.

Directions: Choose the *best* answer to each of the following multiple choice questions. If you have trouble answering a question, use the process of elimination to narrow your choices. Write your answers on a separate piece of paper.

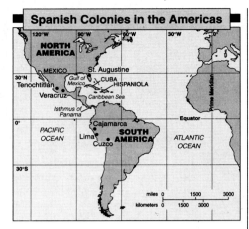

Spanish Colonies in the Americas

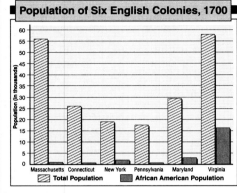

Population of Six English Colonies, 1700

1. **According to the map above, what colony was located at approximately 29°N and 82°W?**

   A Cuba
   B Gulf of Mexico
   C St. Augustine
   D Cajamarca

   Test-Taking Tip: Look at the map's labels carefully. How does it show which labels belong to *continents*? To *islands*? To *colonies*?

2. **According to the graph above, which colonies had the largest and smallest total populations in 1700?**

   F Virginia and Pennsylvania
   G Massachusetts and New York
   H New York and Pennsylvania
   J Connecticut and Maryland

   Test-Taking Tip: Notice that the question asks for *total population*. This graph shows two different bars for each colony. Do you need to add the bars together to get the total population? Why or why not?

3. **Native Americans in the Subarctic, Great Basin, and California areas relied on hunting, fishing, and gathering food. Native Americans in the Eastern Woodlands, Southwest, and Southeast became farmers. What might explain this difference?**

A Native Americans in the Eastern Woodlands, Southwest, and Southeast learned how to farm from the colonists.

B Native Americans in the Subarctic, Great Basin, and California did not have farming tools.

C Native Americans in the Eastern Woodlands, Southwest, and Southeast were allowed to own land, so they could establish permanent farms.

D The climate and soil in the Subarctic, Great Basin, and California areas were not good for farming.

Test-Taking Tip: Since the "hunters" and the "farmers" came from different geographic regions, it is likely that the answer has something to do with geography. Which answer choice fits *best* with this information?

4. The Civil War in England was fought between

F the government and serfs

G the monarchy and the feudal lords

H the king and Parliament

J England and France

Test-Taking Tip: Eliminate answers that do not make sense. A *civil war* is a type of war fought *within one country*. Therefore, answer J can be eliminated.

5. In *Two Treatises of Government*, John Locke wrote about certain natural rights with which all people are born. These rights did NOT include

A life

B liberty

C education

D property

Test-Taking Tip: It may be helpful to remember that Locke's ideas helped form the basis for the Declaration of Independence. What rights did the colonists *most* want to protect?

6. Like the English and American revolutions, the French Revolution was fought over

F the power of the monarchy

G the role of the Church

H the right to own property

J the rights of taxpaying citizens

Test-Taking Tip: This question asks you to make a *comparison*. What did *all three* revolutions have in common? For instance, did the American Revolution have anything to do with the role of the Church? No. Therefore, you can eliminate choice G.

7. The Agricultural Revolution led to

A a decrease in farm productivity

B more people moving to farms to work

C better farming technologies

D many bloody wars between farmers and the government

Test-Taking Tip: This question asks about a *different* type of revolution. Remember that the Agricultural Revolution set the stage for the Industrial Revolution a hundred years later. However, neither of these revolutions involved warfare. In this case, the word *revolution* refers to a change in the predominate system of farming. Therefore, you can eliminate choice D.

STOP

Tested Objectives

Questions	Reading Objective
1, 2	Analyze information
3	Make inferences and generalizations
4, 5	Identify central issues
6	Make comparisons
7	Draw conclusions

STANDARDIZED TEST PRACTICE

4H History

The English Civil War is discussed on page 505. There it states that *civil war broke out between the Crown and Parliament.*

5C Civics

Locke's *Two Treatises* is discussed on the bottom of page 507. There it states that Locke believed in the rights of *life, liberty, and property.* Therefore, the best choice is C.

6F History

While the American Revolution was fought, in part, over the rights of taxpayers, the English Revolution was not. Therefore, choice J can be eliminated. None of these revolutions was concerned with the role of the Church, so choice G can be eliminated. They were all concerned with the power of the monarchy, so choice F is the best answer.

THE PRINCETON REVIEW **TEST-TAKING TIP**

Since the question asks for something in common to all three revolutions, any choice that does not apply to even one revolution can be eliminated.

7C Culture/Environment

The top of page 526 states that the Agricultural Revolution led to *New ways of growing crops and breeding animals,* which resulted in *greater production of food.* This information makes C the best choice.

OVERVIEW

Unit 11 discusses the changes in the world during the 1800s, focusing on the emergence of new nations and the building of empires in Africa and Asia.

➤ **Chapter 34** describes how the United States and Latin American countries developed different forms of governments and economies.

➤ **Chapter 35** discusses how the ideas of the French Revolution spread.

➤ **Chapter 36** summarizes the move toward imperialism by western European powers, the United States, and Japan.

UNIT OBJECTIVES

After reading Unit 11, students will be able to:

1. discuss how nationalism influenced the western world during the 1800s.

2. identify what economic ideas developed in Europe.

3. describe changes in Africa and Asia during the 1800s.

UNIT PROJECT

Have students choose one of the following topics: the Americas during the early 1800s; or the Americas, Europe, Africa, Asia and the Pacific, during the late 1800s. Have students write newspaper headlines and articles that characterize the assigned region's economic ideas, nationalism, and imperialism during that time. Ask volunteers to compile all the articles into a newspaper.

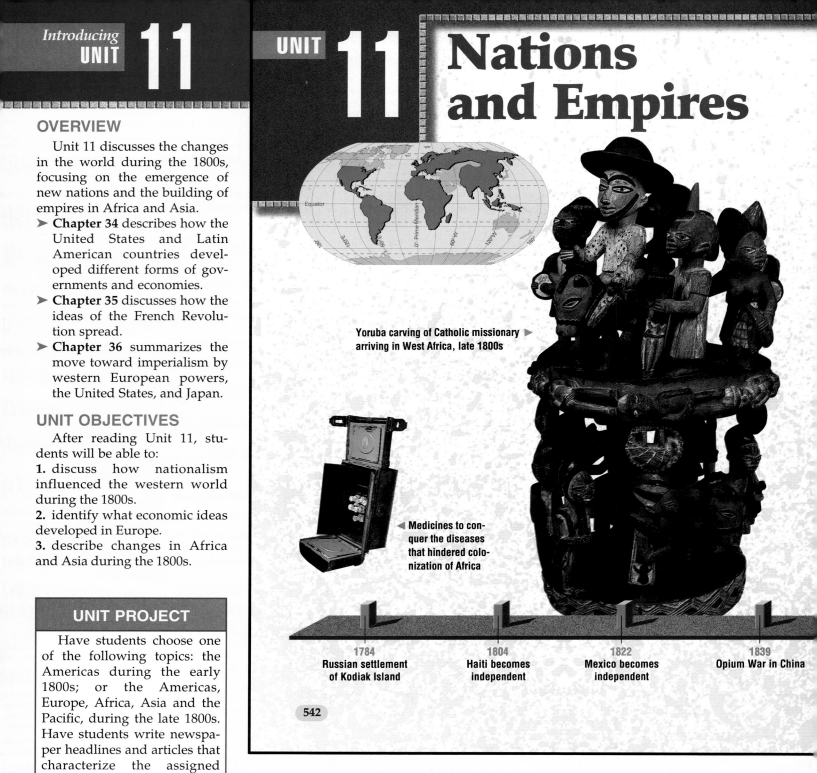

UNIT **11** # Nations and Empires

Yoruba carving of Catholic missionary ▶ arriving in West Africa, late 1800s

◀ Medicines to conquer the diseases that hindered colonization of Africa

1784	1804	1822	1839
Russian settlement of Kodiak Island	**Haiti becomes independent**	**Mexico becomes independent**	**Opium War in China**

542

ABOUT THE UNIT OPENING

Examining Artifacts

Based on these artifacts, ask students these questions: Where did European nations seek to build empires in the 1800s? *(Africa)* What was at least one of the motives behind expansion into Africa? *(to spread Christianity)* What was the link between European medicines and colonization? *(allowed Europeans to conquer African diseases)* Why might industrial nations have wanted to colonize Africa? *(for raw materials and markets)*

Global Chronology

Ask students to explain what time period the time line covers. *(1784 to 1910)* What countries are mentioned? *(Russia, Haiti, Mexico, China, United States, Mexico, South Africa)* What do the entries in 1804 and 1822 indicate? *(Latin American countries became independent.)* What dates and events indicate that this time period was turbulent? *(the wars and rebellions in 1839, 1846, and 1900)*

Multimedia Activity

Surfing the Net
Imperialism

During the Age of Imperialism, world powers carved out empires throughout the world, including Latin America. To look at how imperialism reached into the western hemisphere, search the Internet.

Getting There

Follow these steps to gather information about the effect of imperialism on a nation in Latin America.
1. Pick a search engine such as Excite, Lycos, WebCrawler, Yahoo, etc.
2. Type in the main search word—in this case, the name of a Latin American nation that interests you. Then add words to focus your research. Words might include *history, colonial, imperialism,* or *independence*.
3. Explore links that the search engine brings up on the screen. (Links point the way to Web sites on the Internet.)
4. Click on links that provide information on the subject of your research.

Hands-On Activity

Examine the reasons why an independence movement took shape in the Latin American nation that you have chosen. Present your findings in the form of a special two-minute news broadcast announcing the outbreak of revolution. The broadcast should name the nation against which the rebellion is directed, any actions taken by the United States, and the reasons for the rebellion. Deliver your broadcast aloud to the class.

PRIMARY SOURCES
Library

See pages 694–695 for a primary source reading to accompany Unit 11.

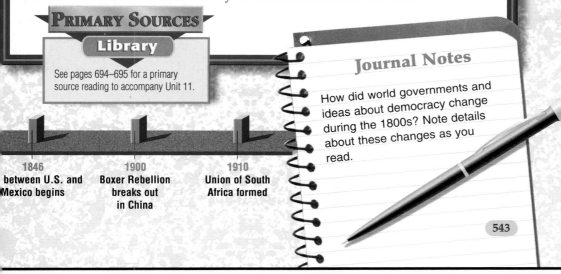

1846	1900	1910
between U.S. and Mexico begins	Boxer Rebellion breaks out in China	Union of South Africa formed

Journal Notes

How did world governments and ideas about democracy change during the 1800s? Note details about these changes as you read.

543

Geographic Location

Ask students to name the continents that will be discussed in this unit. *(all except Antarctic)* Tell students that in this unit they will learn how nationalism caused independence movements in countries and how industrialization increased the interest of some nations in building empires in nonindustrialized countries.

GLENCOE
TECHNOLOGY

VIDEODISC

Use the MindJogger to preview the unit content.
MindJogger Videoquiz

Unit 11
Disc 2 Side A

   Also available in VHS.

INTRODUCING THE UNIT

Have students name some national symbols of the United States. *(U.S. flag, Uncle Sam, bald eagle, etc.)* Ask students what feelings these symbols evoke. Use student answers to discuss the pros and cons of nationalism. Explain that in this unit they will learn about the rise of nationalism as a world force in the 1800s.

RECORDING JOURNAL NOTES

Help students begin writing in their journals by asking them to name changes, described in Unit 10 that advanced democracy. Record responses on the board. Tell the students that these are the kinds of changes they should detail in their journals as they read Unit 11.

PRIMARY SOURCES
Library

Items in the Primary Sources Library for this unit focus on British imperialism in India. Elements include:
- A memo from an Indian civil servant
- Postcard from India
- Photo of the Victoria Memorial in Calcutta

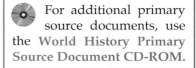 For additional primary source documents, use the **World History Primary Source Document CD-ROM.**

Chapter 34 Planning Guide

Objectives	Reproducible Resources	Multimedia Resources
Section 1 **The United States** Describe the development of government in the United States, westward expansion in the 1800s, and the causes of the Civil War.	Reproducible Lesson Plan Chapter 34 Vocabulary and Guided Reading Activity Reading Essentials and Study Guide 34-1 World Literature Reading 1 Chapter 34 Enrichment Activity Section 1 Quiz Unit 11 Hands-On History Lab	Teaching Transparency and Activity 34A Vocabulary PuzzleMaker Interactive Tutor Self-Assessment Software ExamView® Pro Testmaker Glencoe Skillbuilder Interactive Workbook, Level 1
Section 2 **Latin America** Describe the independence movements in Latin America and governments that were established in Latin America in the late 1800s	Reproducible Lesson Plan Reading Essentials and Study Guide 34-2 Chapter 34 Cooperative Learning Activity Chapter 34 Chart and Graph Skill Activity Chapter 34 Geography and Map Activity Chapter 34 Activity Book Activity Unit 11 Primary Sources Reading Section 2 Quiz	Teaching Transparency and Activity 34B Vocabulary PuzzleMaker Interactive Tutor Self-Assessment Software ExamView® Pro Testmaker Glencoe Skillbuilder Interactive Workbook, Level 1
Chapter 34 **Review and Evaluation**	Chapter 34 Reteaching Activity Chapter 34 Performance Assessment Activity Spanish Chapter Summary and Glossary Chapter 34 Test	Vocabulary PuzzleMaker Interactive Tutor Self-Assessment Software Glencoe Skillbuilder Interactive Workbook, Level 1 Audiocassettes* ExamView® Pro Testmaker

*Also available in Spanish.

Presentation Plus!

Use Glencoe's **Presentation Plus!** multimedia teacher tool to easily present dynamic lessons that visually excite your students. Using Microsoft® PowerPoint, you can customize the presentations to create your own personalized lessons.

Interactive Lesson Planner

Planning has never been easier! Using this CD-ROM, organize your week, month, semester, or year with all the help you need. The **Interactive Lesson Planner** gives you access to all of the blackline masters which accompany *Human Heritage.*

✓ PERFORMANCE ASSESSMENT ACTIVITIES

Role Play Have students research the 19th-century leaders of voting-rights movements in some of the countries discussed in this chapter. After students complete their research, have them prepare scripts in which they role-play a leader of their choice, explaining their philosophies and methods.

CHAPTER RESOURCES

LITERATURE ABOUT THE PERIOD

Keith, Harold. *Rifles for Watie.* T.Y. Crowell, 1957. Story of a teenage soldier in the West during the American Civil War.

READINGS FOR THE STUDENT

Freedman, Russell. *Lincoln: A Photobiography.* Clarion Books, 1987. Newbery Award winner that offers a photo essay of the life of Abraham Lincoln.

Lester, Julius. *To Be A Slave.* Scholastic, 1968. A primary source of the feelings and experiences of African Americans from colonial times through the Civil War.

READINGS FOR THE TEACHER

Prago, Albert. *The Revolutions in Spanish America: The Independence Movements of 1808-1825.* Macmillan, 1970. Surveys the history of the independence movements in Latin America during the early 1800s.

KEY TO ABILITY LEVELS

Teaching strategies have been coded for varying learning styles and abilities.

L1 Level 1 activities are **basic** activities and should be within the ability range of all students.

L2 Level 2 activities are **average** activities and should be within the ability range of the average to above-average student.

L3 Level 3 activities are **challenging** activities designed for the ability range of above-average students.

ELL ELL activities should be within the ability range of English Language Learning students.

Teacher's Corner

NATIONAL GEOGRAPHIC SOCIETY PRODUCTS AVAILABLE FROM GLENCOE

The following articles relate to this chapter:
- *PictureShow: The Civil War (CD-ROM)*
- *PicturePack: The Civil War (Transparencies)*
- *PictureShow: Story of America Library, 1 & 2 (CD-ROMs)*
- *PictureShow: The Westward Movement (CD-ROM)*
- *PicturePack: The Westward Movement (Transparencies)*
- *Native Americans (Poster Set)*

ADDITIONAL NATIONAL GEOGRAPHIC SOCIETY PRODUCTS

To order the following, call National Geographic at 1-800-368-2728:

- *American Indians: A Brief History (Video)*
- *American West (Classroom Library)*
- *Steal Away: The Harriet Tubman Story (Video)*

Access *National Geographic*'s new dynamic MapMachine Web site and other geography resources at:
http://www.nationalgeographic.com/
http://www.nationalgeographic.com/maps/

  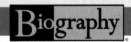

The following videotape programs are available from Glencoe:

- **The Alamo**
  1-56501-784-6
- **Civil War Journal (Set 1 and 2)**
  1-56501-200-3 (set 1)   1-56501-326-3 (set 2)
- **Lewis & Clark**
  1-56501-592-4
- **Mexico: A Story of Courage and Conquest**
  0-7670-1622-X
- **Tecumseh: The Dream of Confederacy**
  0-7670-1247-X
- **Underground Railroad**
  0-7670-1679-3

To order, call Glencoe at 1-800-334-7344. To find classroom resources to accompany many of these, check:

A&E Television: http://www.aetv.com
The History Channel:
http://www.historychannel.com

OVERVIEW

Chapter 34 examines the political, economic, and cultural developments in the Western Hemisphere during the 1800s.

➤ **Section 1** discusses changes in United States government, westward expansion, and the Civil War.

➤ **Section 2** describes the independence movements in Latin America.

CHAPTER OBJECTIVES

After reading Chapter 34, students will be able to:

1. describe the growth of democracy in the United States.

2. trace the expansion of the United States during the 1800s.

3. analyze causes of the Civil War.

4. identify cultural changes in the United States during the late 1800s and early 1900s.

5. discuss how colonies in Latin America won independence, and examine the types of governments they developed.

EXAMINING ARTIFACTS

Have students identify each of the artifacts. Then ask: How are these two items linked? *(Settlers pushed into Native American homelands. Items represent the groups that clashed in the West.)* Explain that this chapter traces the causes and effects of the expansion of the United States.

PERFORMANCE ASSESSMENT ✓

Use the Performance Assessment Activities on page 544B to help you evaluate students as they complete the chapter.

The Americas
1800 A.D.—1875 A.D.

◄ **Native American dress**

Covered wagons carrying U.S. settlers westward ▼

1803	1804	1822	1861
U.S. buys the Louisiana Territory	**Haiti becomes first independent country in Latin America**	**Mexico wins independence**	**U.S. Civil War begins**

544   UNIT 11 NATIONS AND EMPIRES

TEACHING RESOURCES

TEACHER PLANNING AND SUPPORT

- 🗀 Reproducible Lesson Plan
- 🗀 Block Scheduling Implementation Guide
- 🗀 Videodisc Bar Code Correlation
- Presentation Plus!

REVIEW AND REINFORCEMENT

- 🗀 Reading Essentials and Study Guide 34-1, 34-2
- 🗀 Chapter 34 Vocabulary and Guided Reading Activity
- Vocabulary PuzzleMaker Software
- Teaching Transparencies 34A & 34B

- 🗀 Chapter 34 Reteaching Activity
- 🗀 Chapter 34 Cooperative Learning Activity
- 🗀 Chapter 34 Activity Book Activity
- 🗀 Chapter 34 Chart and Graph Skill Activity
- Interactive Tutor Self-Assessment Software
- Unit 11 MindJogger VideoQuiz

APPLICATION AND HANDS-ON ACTIVITIES

- Daily World History, Geography, and Culture Question
- Unit 11 Hands-On History Lab Activity
- World History Game Cards 1 & 2

Chapter Focus

⤷ Read to Discover

- What kind of government developed in the newly formed United States.
- How and why the United States expanded its boundaries during the 1800s.
- What led to the Civil War in the United States.
- What cultural changes took place in the United States during the late 1800s and early 1900s.
- How colonies in Latin America won their independence.
- Why democracy did not develop in Latin America.

Terms to Learn	People to Know	🌐 Places to Locate
federal	Abraham	Alamo
manifest	Lincoln	Rio Grande
destiny	Simón Bolívar	Haiti

Why It's Important Many changes took place in the Americas from 1800 to the early 1900s. The United States more than doubled in size, and its government was set on a firm base. This allowed the country to grow industrially and to become a world power. Latin America, which is made up of Mexico, Central America, the Caribbean islands, and South America, won independence from European rule. However, colonial traditions remained strong. So, despite many efforts, democracy did not develop in most of Latin America.

HISTORY Online

Chapter Overview

Visit the *Human Heritage* Web site at **humanheritage.glencoe.com** and click on ***Chapter 34— Chapter Overviews*** to preview this chapter.

SECTION 1 The United States

In the years after winning independence, the Americans set up a democratic government and expanded the boundaries of their country. They fought each other in a civil war and then worked to reunite the nation after the war ended. Industry grew and brought about many changes in daily life. By 1900, the United States had become a powerful country.

Government One thing that helped the United States become powerful was its government. Americans developed a tradition of **stable government,** or a government that rules from year to year without great changes.

✔️ **Reading Check**
Why was a **stable government** important to the future of the United States?

FOCUS

🗝️ Bellringer

Tell students that in the 1800s many settlers wanted to expand the United States across the continent. Have students write three reasons Native Americans or Mexicans might be hostile to this attitude.

Motivational Activity

Discuss student responses. Then tell them that in this chapter they will learn how U.S. expansion changed the lives of Native Americans and Mexicans.

GUIDE TO READING

Reading Strategy

Ask students to read "Why It's Important" and summarize the chapter's main theme. *(The 1800s saw the rise of the United States as a world power and the independence of Latin American nations from European rule.)*

Vocabulary Precheck

Ask students to define each of the "Terms to Learn." Have a volunteer consult the dictionary for any unfamiliar words. **L1** **ELL**

💾 Use the **Vocabulary PuzzleMaker** for Chapter 34 to create a crossword puzzle. **L1**

🗀 Assign Chapter 34 Vocabulary and Guided Reading Activity.

🗀 Assign Reading Essentials and Study Guide 34-1.

✔️ **Reading Check Answer**
A **stable government** prevented major upheavals and encouraged the country to grow.

Guided Practice

L1 **History** To help students understand the swiftness of the expansion of the United States, guide them in developing a time line showing the acquisition of territory. **ELL**

 Reading Check Answer
The two **political parties** were the Federalist party and the Democrat-Republican party. The **federal** government is the national government.

 Reading Check Answer
In a **representative government,** officials are elected by the people.

NATIONAL GEOGRAPHIC SOCIETY

Use these materials to enrich student understanding of U.S. expansion.

GTV VIDEODISC:
The American People
Close-Up U.S.A.

Side 2
Chapter 5

GTV VIDEODISC:
A Geographic Perspective on American History
Going to Extremes: The Far West

Side 2
Chapter 11

✔ **Reading Check**
What two **political parties** had formed by 1800? What is the **federal** government?

✔ **Reading Check**
How are officials chosen in a **representative government?**

By 1800, two **political parties,** or groups with different ideas about government, had come into being. One was the Federalist (fed' uhr uh list) party. It favored a strong **federal,** or national, government. Most Federalists believed that only people of wealth and education should hold office. They thought the economy should be based more on industry than on trade or agriculture. The other political party was the Democrat-Republican party. It favored more power for the states. Most Democrat-Republicans believed that average people should lead the country. They thought the economy should be based more on agriculture than on industry or trade.

Although in other countries wars were often fought when political power changed hands, in the United States the government changed hands through peaceful elections. For example, in 1800 Thomas Jefferson, who was a Democrat-Republican, was elected President. He took the place of John Adams, who was a Federalist. This was the first peaceful passing of power from one political group to another.

The United States also had a tradition of **representative government.** This is a government in which officials are elected by the people. In 1800, however, only white males who owned property could vote. This changed over the next 30 years. New states in the West began to allow all adult white males to vote. Other states soon followed. By 1830, the number of voters had greatly increased. Although women, enslaved people, and Native Americans were not allowed to vote, the United States government was one of the most democratic in the world at the time.

With the growing number of voters, election campaigns changed. They became filled with entertainment and advertising. People sang songs and wore ribbons to show which candidates they backed. Political parties held parades, rallies, and dinners. Presidential races in particular were noted for slogans and symbols. For example, Andrew Jackson, who became President in 1829, was known as "Old Hickory." So, during his campaign, the newly formed Democratic party planted hickory trees in town squares and gave out hickory brooms and canes.

The Westward Movement At the end of the American Revolution, the United States claimed most of the land east of the Mississippi River. Soon, thousands of Americans were putting their belongings into farm wagons and traveling across the Appalachian Mountains to find new homes. When they came to the Ohio River and other water routes, they loaded their goods and animals on flatboats and floated downstream.

The settlers were careful about choosing a spot for their new home. It had to be near a stream for water. It also had to be near a large settlement or fort for safety. After choosing a place, the settlers would clear the land of trees and build a log cabin. It

---

EXTENDING THE CONTENT

In the election of 1800 there was no distinction on the electoral ballot between President and vice president. Thomas Jefferson and Aaron Burr of the Democratic-Republican party ran against John Adams and Charles C. Pinckney of the Federalist party. During this election, the candidate who received the most electoral votes became President. The person who won the second-largest number of votes became vice president. Since both Jefferson and Burr received the same number of electoral votes, the House of Representatives had to vote to break the tie. They voted to make Jefferson president and Burr vice president. The Twelfth Amendment was passed in 1804 to assure that an electoral tie could not happen again.

usually had one room, with a dirt-packed floor and a door made of wood planks. Each cabin had one or two tiny windows covered with deerskin. There was a fireplace that supplied heat for warmth and cooking.

The settlers' way of life was generally different from that of the Native Americans in the area. The settlers were farmers, while most Native Americans were hunters. The settlers claimed land for themselves. The Native Americans believed land belonged to everyone.

The Native Americans and the settlers did learn from one another, however. Many of the settlers wore Native American clothing, such as moccasins and deerskin leggings. They used Native American herbs as medicine and paddled Native American canoes. Many of the Native Americans used rifles, iron pots and woolen blankets that were made in Great Britain.

The Native Americans tried to defend their lands against the settlers. However, there were many more settlers than Native Americans. Also, many Native Americans died from such diseases as measles and smallpox brought by the whites. Over time, the Native Americans were slowly pushed farther and farther west. In the 1830s, the United States government forced the Native Americans to live on reservations.

Territorial Expansion   Many settlers chose land newly acquired by the United States. In 1803, the United States doubled its size by buying the Louisiana Territory from France for $15 million. The Louisiana Purchase, as it was called, provided an

---

NATIVE AMERICAN LIFE   Many Native Americans west of the Mississippi were nomadic and hunted the great migrating herds of buffalo. The Native Americans depended on the buffalo meat for food and its hide for clothing and shelter. **Why were the Native Americans unable to stop the movement of the settlers?**

Ask students to research and map the changing center of population of the United States. (The Statistical Abstract of the United States *contains this data.*) Have students lead a class discussion that covers what the center of population is, why it moves, and speculate what its next move, if any, will be. Display student maps.

CAPTION ANSWER

There were more settlers than Native Americans, many Native Americans died from diseases, and the settlers were better armed and had an army.

Glencoe Literature Library

The following novels from the **Glencoe Literature Library** may be used to enrich this chapter:
- *Bearstone,* by Will Hobbs. (Troubled Native American youth rediscovers his heritage.)
- *Island of the Blue Dolphins,* by Scott O'Dell. (Native American woman on California island in the mid-19th century.)

Biography

The following videotape programs are available from Glencoe to enrich Chapter 34:

- **Tecumseh: The Dream of Confederacy**
- **Lewis and Clark**

To find classroom resources to accompany these videos, check the following home page:
A&E Television:
http://www.aetv.com

MEETING SPECIAL NEEDS

Obtain a copy of David S. Lavender's book, *The Way to the Western Sea: Lewis and Clark Across the Continent.* Harper, 1988. Read excerpts from the book to auditory learners. Ask students to describe the journal entries of Lewis and Clark in their own words. Have students find the places described in the journal on a map of the United States.

📁 Refer to *Inclusion for the Middle School Social Studies Classroom: Strategies and Activities* for additional resources.

MAKING CONNECTIONS

➤➤ **Geography: Movement**
The Spaniards had originally colonized California by establishing a series of 21 missions along the coast from San Diego to San Francisco. Each mission consisted of a central church, outlying buildings, and a fort. Father Junípero Serra was responsible for establishing the first of these missions.

Reading Check Answer
Manifest destiny held that it was the fate of the United States to stretch from the Atlantic Ocean to the Pacific Ocean.

THE ALAMO   The Alamo was a Catholic mission in San Antonio, Texas. In 1836, during the war for Texan independence, 187 Texans used the Alamo as a fortress and held out for several days against nearly 4,000 Mexican soldiers before being defeated. **What conditions had the Mexicans placed on Americans settling in Texas?**

Manifest Destiny The spirit of manifest destiny was captured in this 1821 speech by Francis Baylies, a Massachusetts Congressman. "Our natural boundary is the Pacific Ocean. The swelling tide of our population must and will roll on until that mighty ocean . . . limits our territorial empire."

Reading Check
What was the principle of **manifest destiny?**

area rich in farmland, minerals, and forests. It also gave the United States control of the Mississippi River and the important seaport of New Orleans.

In 1819, the United States and Spain signed a treaty. This treaty, called the Adams-Onís Treaty, gave Florida to the United States and set the boundary between the Louisiana Purchase and the Spanish lands to the south and west.

One of the Spanish lands was Mexico. It became independent in 1821. The Mexicans wanted more people to settle in their territory, especially in Texas. So, they offered people from the United States large areas of free land if they would swear loyalty to Mexico and become Catholic. By the early 1830s, there were 30,000 Americans living in Texas. Most were from the South, and many owned enslaved people.

Enslavement and other issues soon led to quarrels between the Americans who moved to Texas and the Mexican government. Mexico had outlawed enslavement in 1824, and it objected to Texans enslaving people. It also began wondering whether American settlers were loyal to Mexico or to the United States. So, the Mexican government tried to stop more Americans from entering Texas. The Texans then asked for more control over their local affairs. Finally, in 1835, the Texans revolted. The following year, they declared their independence.

Many Americans believed in the **manifest destiny** (man' uh fest des' tuh nē) of the United States, or the idea that it was the fate of the United States to stretch from the Atlantic Ocean to the Pacific Ocean. They wanted the federal government to allow the

EXTENDING THE CONTENT

Have interested students imagine the year is 1845 and many people want the United States to annex land from Mexico. Have students take the roles of Mexican peasants and landowners, southern plantation owners, northern industrialists, Native Americans, or others. Have students investigate the concerns of their choice of people and write speeches, articles, or posters promoting their view. Have students role-play their chosen person and share their information with the class.

annexation of Texas. **Annexation** (an ek sā' shuhn) is the act of taking over a territory and combining it with an existing country or state. In 1845, the United States did annex Texas. This greatly angered Mexico. A dispute over the Texas-Mexico boundary caused more trouble. By the following year, the two countries were at war. American soldiers invaded California, which was part of Mexico. They also marched into Mexico City.

In 1848, Mexico signed the Treaty of Guadalupe Hidalgo (gwah dl ū' pā huh duhl' gō). It gave the United States almost one half of Mexico's land. It also set the Rio Grande (rē' ō gran' dā) as the boundary between Texas and Mexico.

Five years after the treaty, in 1853, the United States bought a piece of land from Mexico in order to build a railroad to the Pacific. This was called the Gadsden (gadz' duhn) Purchase after James Gadsden, the American who arranged the purchase.

Meanwhile, the United States acquired the Oregon Territory. During the 1840s, thousands of American settlers made the long, hard trip over the Rocky Mountains to Oregon, which both the United States and Great Britain claimed. The presence of these settlers gave the United States control of much of the area. In 1846, the two countries agreed to divide the Oregon Territory at the 49th parallel.

Reading Check
How did the **annexation** of Texas affect U.S. relations with Mexico?

MAP STUDY

LOCATION The Louisiana Purchase eventually formed parts of 13 states. **What geographic features marked the western and eastern boundaries of the Louisiana Purchase?**

Reading Check Answer
The **annexation** of Texas by the United States greatly angered Mexico.

L1 **Geography: Human/Environmental Interaction** Have students use the map "The Growth of the United States" to locate the areas of territorial expansion discussed in this subsection. Have them name present states that were part of each territory. In particular, have them locate their own state and determine where it fit into U.S. expansion. **ELL**

DID YOU KNOW ??

The locations of the first Spanish missions in California was decided according to how far and fast a priest could walk. Each mission was one week's travel time apart.

The Growth of the United States

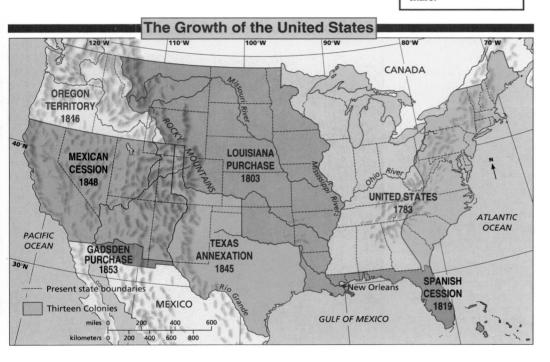

MAP STUDY

Answer

Rocky Mountains and Mississippi River

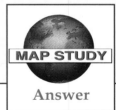

EXTENDING THE CONTENT

Explain to students that the term *Manifest Destiny* was first used in a magazine in 1845 supporting the view that the United States was given the divine right to conquer and settle new land in North America and elsewhere. The phrase soon became popular. Ask the students which acquisitions allowed the United States to reach its "Manifest Destiny" of spreading from sea to sea. *(Oregon Territory, 1846; Mexican Cession, 1848)*

Glencoe Literature Library

The following novels from the **Glencoe Literature Library** may be used to enrich this chapter:
- *My Antonia*, by Willa Cather. (Immigrants who helped settle the Plains.)
- *Call of the Wild*, by Jack London. (Tale of the Yukon gold rush.)

Later, another large area of land, Alaska, was added to the United States. In 1784, Russian fur hunters had established a permanent settlement at Kodiak (kōd' ē ak) Island off the Alaskan coast. From there, they set up hunting and trading settlements as far south as California. After a time, however, Russia lost interest in Alaska and sold the territory to the United States in 1867.

Civil War and Reunion   As the United States expanded westward, different ways of life developed in the northern and southern states. The northern states were industrialized. They had most of the nation's factories, railroads, and canals. Labor in the North was done by hired workers. About 20 percent of the people lived in cities. Education was widespread, and immigration brought in all different kinds of people. Northern leaders wanted a strong national government. They also wanted the government to aid industry and improve transportation. They believed that enslavement should not be allowed in new areas of the country.

The southern states depended on agriculture. Tobacco, rice, sugar cane, and especially cotton were important. These crops

ABRAHAM LINCOLN   As President during the Civil War, Abraham Lincoln led the United States through one of the most critical periods in the nation's history. Lincoln was assassinated by a southern sympathizer shortly after the North and South were reunited. **What did the southern states that seceded call their new government?**

were grown on large plantations that used enslaved labor. Enslaved people made up about one third of the South's population. Only 10 percent of the people lived in cities. There were few immigrants. Southern leaders believed that the rights of the states were more important than those of the federal government. They also believed that as the country grew, enslavement should be allowed in new areas.

In 1860, Abraham Lincoln was elected President. Southerners feared he would try to do away with enslavement and destroy their way of life. Seven southern states announced that they were **seceding** (si sēd' ē ng), or withdrawing, from the nation. They formed a new government called the Confederate States of America or the Confederacy (kuhn fed' uhr uh sē). Soon, four more states seceded and joined the Confederacy. Northerners did not think the southern states had a right to secede. By 1861, the North and the South were fighting a civil war. In 1865, the North won, and the country was once more politically united.

The Civil War settled the question of whether or not states have the right to secede. It also led to freedom for nearly 4 million enslaved African Americans. The country began to build itself up again. By 1870, it was on its way to becoming a strong industrial country and a world power.

Cultural Changes
As the United States expanded and industrialized, many cultural changes took place. The rise of industry led to **urbanization,** or the growth of cities. During the late 1800s and early 1900s, many Americans left the farm and moved to the city. At the same time, a large number of immigrants came to America. Most settled in cities. City life provided jobs, education, and new ways for people to enjoy themselves.

Not everyone lived in the same way in the cities. The lives of the lower, middle, and upper classes differed greatly from one another. One way in which people's lives differed was in housing. The lower class, which included most immigrants, lived in old houses or commercial buildings that had been made into apartments. These were called **tenements** and were generally run-down. Areas with large numbers of tenements were called **slums.**

The middle class lived in various types of housing. One was the apartment house. It was often six to eight stories high, with at least two apartments on each story. Another kind of house was the row house. It was a private house that shared its side walls with its neighbors. Some members of the middle class lived in homes built for two families or in single-family residences. The upper class generally lived in huge homes staffed with servants.

Another way in which people's lives differed was in jobs. Lower-class men, women, and children worked in factories. Middle- and upper-class men held business and professional jobs, and their wives rarely worked outside the home.

Reading Check
Why did seven southern states announce that they were **seceding** from the nation in 1861?

Reading Check
What were some of the reasons for **urbanization** in the United States?

Reading Check
Which groups of people generally lived in **tenements?** What were **slums?**

Glencoe Literature Library

The following novels from the **Glencoe Literature Library** may be used to enrich this chapter:
- *The Autobiography of Miss Jane Pittman,* by Ernest Gaines. (Journey from slavery to freedom.)
- *The Glory Field,* by Walter Meyers. (Saga of an African American family.)
- *The House of Dies Drear,* by Virginia Hamilton. (Underground Railroad.)
- *Red Badge of Courage,* by Stephen Crane. (Horror of the Civil War.)

Reading Check Answer
Seven southern states announced that they were **seceding** because they feared Lincoln would end slavery and destroy their way of life.

MAKING CONNECTIONS

➤➤ **History** On September 22, 1862, President Lincoln issued the Emancipation Proclamation. As of January 1, 1863, if the Confederate states had not surrendered, all enslaved persons held in states that were still in rebellion would be declared free.

Reading Check Answer
The growth of industry and immigration helped lead to the **urbanization** of the United States.

Reading Check Answer
The lower class, made up mostly of immigrants, lived in **tenements.**
Slums were areas with large numbers of tenements.

EXTENDING THE CONTENT

Although enslavement was one main moral issue dividing the North and the South, most white Northerners did not agree with abolitionism and viewed their efforts as a struggle to preserve the Union. In fact, many Northern Republicans supported a proposed amendment to the U.S. Constitution prohibiting the federal government from ending enslavement in any state that wanted it. Most white southerners saw the Confederate States of America as a way to keep states' rights intact.

MAKING CONNECTIONS

➤➤ **History** In towns and cities across the United States after 1890, racial segregation in housing continued. This was promoted in the South because of Jim Crow legislation, which called for separate facilities for whites and blacks. In northern cities, however, segregation was based on custom and economics rather than law.

💾 Use **Interactive Tutor Self-Assessment Software** to review Section 1.

L1 **Geography: Location** Have students use the map "Independence in Latin America" on page 555 to locate the areas of Latin America as they are discussed in this section. Have students name the present-day countries of the areas as they are discussed. **ELL**

💾 Use the **Vocabulary Puzzle-Maker** to create crossword and word search puzzles.

People's lives also differed in education. By the late 1800s, there were tax-supported public schools that all children could attend. However, it was generally middle- and upper-class children who benefited. Lower-class children, who had to work, rarely went past elementary school.

Technological advances changed daily life during the late 1800s and early 1900s. For example, the invention of the refrigerator ended the need for daily shopping. Labor-saving machines gave many Americans time to read books, newspapers, and magazines. They also enjoyed music and the theater. City governments began to set aside land for parks.

Section 1 Assessment

1. **Define:** stable government, political parties, federal, representative government, manifest destiny, annexation, seceding, urbanization, tenements, slums.
2. How did election campaigns change by the 1830s?
3. What were two results of the Civil War?

Critical Thinking

4. **Demonstrating Reasoned Judgment** Do you agree with the settlers' or the Native Americans' ideas about land ownership? Explain.

Graphic Organizer Activity

5. Draw this diagram, and use it to show the causes and effects of the war between Mexico and the United States.

Causes	War Between Mexico and the United States	Effects

Painting of Toussaint-L'Ouverture

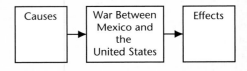

SECTION 2 Latin America

While the United States was expanding and settling its internal differences, the European-ruled colonies of Latin America were moving toward independence. The American and French Revolutions stirred the people of Latin America to action. Everywhere, colonists tried to take charge of their own affairs.

The First Revolt The first major successful revolt against European rule took place in the French West Indies on Saint Domingue (san duh manj'), the western part of the island of Hispaniola. There, a few French plantation owners used the labor of 500,000 enslaved African Americans to grow sugarcane, coffee, cotton, and *indigo* (in' duh gō), or a kind of plant that yields a blue dye.

Then, Pierre Dominique Toussaint-L'Ouverture (pē auhr' dom uh nēk' tū san' lū vuh tyuhr') appeared on the scene. The grandson of an African chief, Toussaint was born enslaved in 1743. His white master, however, taught Toussaint to read and write and, in 1777, gave him his freedom. When news of the French Revolution reached Saint Domingue, Toussaint was inspired. In 1791, he led a revolt of enslaved people. In 1794, the French government agreed to abolish enslavement. Toussaint became governor-general of Saint Domingue in 1801. Two years later, he issued a constitution. The French then tried to regain control of Saint Domingue but were unsuccessful. In 1804, Saint Domingue became the first free country in Latin America. It changed its name to Haiti, a Native American word meaning "mountainous."

Revolution Spreads

The fight for independence in South America was led by the Creoles. They were well educated and had enough power to change things. The Creoles resented the peninsulares, who held the most important government posts.

Soon after the French Revolution began, a Creole named Antonio Nariño (ahn tō' nē ō nah rēn' yō), translated into Spanish the Declaration of the Rights of Man and the Citizen. This helped spread French democratic ideas throughout the Spanish colonies. Before long, the people there began to revolt.

In the northern part of South America, Simón Bolívar (sē mōn' bō lē' vahr), another Creole, led the fight for freedom. Known as "the Liberator," Bolívar was the son of a rich family in New Granada, or what is today Columbia and Venezuela. In 1805, he went to Europe. There, he learned about the French Revolution and its ideas. He then returned home, vowing to free his people.

In 1810, Bolívar and other leaders of New Granada organized a **junta** (hun' tuh), or political committee, to take over the government. Spanish officials soon crushed the movement, however. Bolívar then went into exile where he formed and trained an army. In 1817, he successfully invaded what is today Venezuela. In August 1819, he defeated the Spanish in what is today Colombia (kuh lum' bē uh). Later that year, he became the first president of Gran Colombia, Ecuador (ek' wuh dor), and Panama. In 1824, Bolívar freed Peru from Spanish rule. He also sent one of his generals to free a Spanish colony called Upper Peru. After declaring its independence in 1825, the new nation was named Bolivia (buh liv' ē uh).

While Bolívar was fighting for freedom in the north, another Creole, José de San Martín (hō sā' dā san mahr tēn'), was fighting for freedom in the south. In 1810, Creole leaders in La Plata (luh plaht' uh) organized a junta to take over the government. In 1812, San Martín joined the struggle for independence. A professional

People in History

Toussaint-L'Ouverture
c. 1774–1803

Haitian Patriot

A self-educated grandson of an African chief, Toussaint-L'Ouverture led the battle to free enslaved people in what is now Haiti. With the help of generals Jean Jacques Dessalines and Henri Christophe, he forced the British to withdraw from the island, and he also resisted a French invasion. He later was seized by the French and died in a prison in 1803. His battle for freedom made Toussaint a symbol for the fight for liberty.

Reading Check
Why did Simón Bolívar form a **junta** in 1810?

L1 **Government** Review with the students the contents of the Declaration of the Rights of Man and the Citizen on pages 517–518 of Chapter 32. Ask which French democratic ideas spread throughout the Spanish colonies. **ELL**

L2 **Critical Thinking** Explain to students that Simón Bolívar is often called "the George Washington of South America." Ask students to give their opinions concerning the appropriateness of this name.

MAKING CONNECTIONS

➤➤ **Medicine** Thousands of French soldiers sent to Saint Dominque died from yellow fever, which was not eradicated from Hispaniola until the early 1900s.

Reading Check Answer
Bolívar formed a **junta** in 1810 to take over the government of New Granada.

DID YOU KNOW ???

Haiti was the second republic in the Western Hemisphere. The United States was the first. Its first leader, Touissant-L'Ouverture, fought for the Americans during the American Revolution.

MULTICULTURAL PERSPECTIVES

The class structure of Latin America was complex. In addition to peninsulares, Creoles, mestizos, and mulattoes, there were about 20 other classes including Native Americans and African Americans. With independence, this structure changed only slightly, although there was some shifting of power. African Americans gained some influence, although enslavement continued for many years in some countries. The Creoles were harsh judges of the Native American people. The Native Americans lost both power and security. For decades, the system prevailed, as Creoles ruled.

Glencoe Literature Library

The following novel from the **Glencoe Literature Library** may be used to enrich this chapter:

• *Dragonwings,* by Laurence Yep. (Chinese community in San Francisco in the early 1900s.)

soldier, San Martín organized an army. He was aided by his wife, who persuaded the women of Buenos Aires (bwā′ nuhs er′ ēz) to give their jewels to help buy supplies for her husband's troops. He was also aided by Father Luís Beltrán (lū ēs′ bel trahn′), who melted down church bells to make guns and bullets. In 1816, the part of La Plata that is now Argentina (ahr juhn tē′ nuh) won its independence.

In 1817, San Martín led his army across the Andes Mountains into what is now Chile. The crossing was difficult, and many soldiers died from the cold and the lack of oxygen. Most of their horses and pack mules also died. However, San Martín was able to take the Spanish forces in Chile by surprise. He and another soldier, Bernardo O'Higgins (ber nahrd′ ō ō hig′ enz), defeated the Spanish. Chile became independent a year later.

Mexico, Central America, and Brazil A fight for independence went on in Mexico as well. Father Miguel Hidalgo y Costilla (mē gel′ ē dahl′ gō ē kahs tē′ yuh) played an important part in this struggle. He had long been upset about the way the Native Americans were treated. Now, he urged his congregation not to submit any longer to Spanish rule.

Led by Hidalgo, the Native Americans revolted in 1810. Frightened by the Native Americans, the Creoles joined with the peninsulares to crush the revolt. Hidalgo himself was caught and put to death. Three years later, another priest, Father José María Morelos y Pavón (hō sā′ mah rē′ ah mō rā′ lōs ē pah vōn′), led a second revolt. It was no more successful than the first. Morelos, like Hidalgo, was caught and put to death.

In 1820, there was a revolt in Spain. The rebels there wanted to stop forced labor in Mexico and divide the land among the peasants. This greatly upset the Creoles, church leaders, and army officers. So, they joined together and revolted against Spanish rule in Mexico. Two years later, Mexico was declared to be independent. It was ruled by Agustín de Iturbide (ah gūs tēn′ dā ē tur bē′ thā), a Creole army officer, who served as emperor. Iturbide, however, refused to share power with the Mexican legislature. He was also a poor administrator. The Mexicans soon tired of his rule and in 1823, they overthrew him. In 1824, after a new constitution was written, Mexico became a republic.

Moved by what had happened in Mexico, the people of Central America also revolted. In 1821, they declared their independence and two years later joined together to form the United Provinces of Central America. Not long after, the United Provinces split into the present-day countries of Costa Rica (kos′ tuh rē′ kuh), El Salvador (el sal′ vuh dor), Guatemala, Honduras (hon dūr′ uhs), and Nicaragua (nik uh rah′ gwuh).

A struggle for independence also took place in Brazil. Many Brazilians could see no reason to remain a part of the Portuguese

Painting of Father Hidalgo

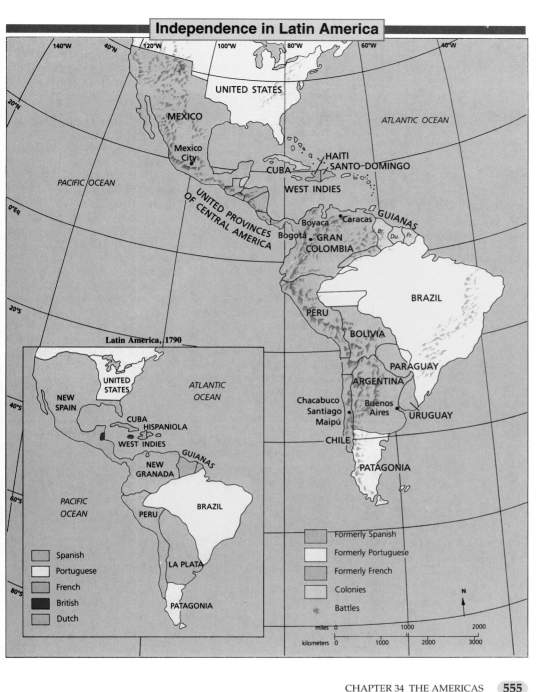

Independence in Latin America

Latin America, 1790

Spanish
Portuguese
French
British
Dutch

Formerly Spanish
Formerly Portuguese
Formerly French
Colonies
Battles

miles 0   1000   2000
kilometers 0   1000   2000   3000

Independent Practice

L2 **Geography: Region** Have students study the map on this page and draw conclusions about the difficulties early Latin Americans, especially those living in present-day Central and South America, may have had in communicating, trading, and transporting goods. Have students list their conclusions and rank them from most to least troublesome.

Assign the Chapter 34 **Geography and Map Activity** in the TCR.

L2 **History** Have students investigate the dictatorships of Santa Anna and Benito Juárez to compare and contrast their histories and styles of ruling. Ask students to act as historians, charting the information and writing a paragraph that summarizes what subsequent rulers could have learned from these two dictators.

MEETING SPECIAL NEEDS

Remind students that the main reason the European powers wanted colonies in the Americas was to obtain raw materials. Ask visual learners to research the natural resources of Latin America. Using a simple outline map, have them make natural resource maps of Latin America. Display the maps in the classroom.

Refer to *Inclusion for the Middle School Social Studies Classroom: Strategies and Activities* for additional resources.

LINKING PAST TO PRESENT

Caudillos ruled in Latin America well into the 1900s. Two latter-day examples are Rafael Trujillo of the Dominican Republic (1930-1961) and Juan Perón of Argentina (1943-1955).

✓ Reading Check Answer

Caudillos were backed by the army and by large landowners and church leaders who did not want their lands given to peasants.

CAPTION ANSWER

Brazil was the only country in South America to become a monarchy after gaining its independence.

L3 **Religion** The Roman Catholic Church was powerful in Latin America in the nineteenth century. Have students investigate the role of the Church in Latin America today and how its role has changed there in the past 150 years. Have students write a summary paragraph that tells how the Church's influence evolved and what they expect to happen concerning the Church in the future.

Then... & Now

Brazil In land area, Brazil is now the fifth-largest nation in the world. It covers an area greater than that of the 48 contiguous states of the United States.

✓ Reading Check
Which groups of people generally backed a Latin American **caudillo?**

Empire. They were angry that Portugal tried to control their trade. They also did not like the way the Portuguese parliament treated Brazilian representatives. In 1822, the Brazilians declared their independence from Portugal. Pedro (pā' drō), their Portuguese ruler, agreed to accept a constitution and became their emperor. Brazil was the only country in South America to become a monarchy after independence.

Rule by Caudillos   Most people in Latin America hoped the newly independent countries would become democratic. Spanish rule had given the people little training in self-government, however. The mestizos, Native Americans, and African Americans had received no opportunity for education. Also, the Creoles were not willing to share power with other groups.

A new kind of leader called a **caudillo** (kau thē' yō), or strong man, rose to power. Caudillos were backed by the army. Most were also backed by large landowners and church leaders, who did not want their lands divided among the peasants.

Generally, a caudillo took over a government by force. He ruled until he was overthrown by another caudillo. With each change in government, there was a violent revolution and much bloodshed. Because of this, most Latin American countries did not have a stable government.

Most caudillos ruled as dictators. They did not care about improving the lot of the people. One such caudillo was Antonio López de Santa Anna (ahn tō' nyō lō' pās da san' tuh an' uh) of Mexico, who had been a commander in Iturbide's army. One historian described Santa Anna as "a fortune hunter and a glory

BRAZILIAN INDEPENDENCE   Brazil gained its independence from Portugal in 1822. Here, Pedro I, Brazil's first emperor, is shown raising his sword and crying out "Independence or death." **What was unusual about Brazil's independence?**

556   UNIT 11 NATIONS AND EMPIRES

EXTENDING THE CONTENT

In 1808 Napoleon's French army had invaded Portugal, causing the Portuguese royal family to flee to Brazil. King João transferred his monarchy to Brazil, declaring Rio de Janiero capital of the Portuguese empire. João immediately introduced governmental reforms in Brazil. He reinstated more favorable trade laws by opening Brazil's ports to the world. João also worked to make the agriculture and mining industries more profitable. He funded public education including military academies, art school, and medical schools. João returned to Portugal in 1820 to save his throne and left Brazil to his son Pedro to rule.

hound." In 1833, Santa Anna led his troops into Mexico City and had himself elected president. He ruled Mexico six times between 1833 and 1855. During his rule Mexico lost almost one half of its land to the United States through the Treaty of Guadalupe Hidalgo.

A different type of caudillo eventually took Santa Anna's place. Benito Juárez (ba nē' tō hwahr' ez) proved that a caudillo could care about the people. A lawyer, Juárez was the first Native American to rule Mexico since the fall of the Aztec. Juárez was officially elected president in 1861, after several years of civil war. At the time, Mexico owed money to several countries, including France. Juárez asked these countries to wait two years for their money. France refused. Instead, it sent troops and made a European prince named Maximilian emperor. Juárez refused to give up, and finally defeated the French.

Juárez was again elected president in 1867. He held office until his death in 1872. As president, he worked to hold democratic elections. He reduced the power of the Roman Catholic Church by selling its land to the peasants. He started free schools to educate Native American children.

Benito Juárez
Orphaned as an infant, Benito Juárez spent his childhood tending sheep for an uncle. At age 12, Juárez walked to the city of Oaxaca, intent on getting an education. For a while, he worked for a priest who urged Juárez to enter the clergy, but Juárez chose law school. In 1853 Santa Anna exiled Juárez, who then worked for two years rolling cigars in a tobacco factory in New Orleans.

Linking Across Time

Juárez worked to hold democratic elections, reduced the power of the Roman Catholic Church by selling its land to the peasants, started free schools to educate Native American children, and reduced the size of the army.

MAKING CONNECTIONS

➤➤ **History** Mexican conservatives in exile prompted Napoleon III of France to send Maximilian of Hapsburg to restore a "Latin" empire in Mexico. In 1866 Napoleon yielded to international pressure and withdrew his support from Maximilian. Stranded and outnumbered, Maximilian tried to engineer an honorable defeat for himself. However, Juárez had Maximilian executed as a warning to European leaders. A month later the republic was restored.

ASSESS

Check for Understanding

Ask students to summarize the main points of the chapter, orally or in writing. Discuss the answers to the Section and Chapter Assessment questions.

Evaluate

Assign the Chapter 34 **Performance Assessment Activity** in the TCR.

Administer the **Chapter 34 Test.** Testmaker available.

Linking Across Time

Symbol of Mexico According to legend, the Aztec were to settle where they saw an eagle perched on a cactus. The eagle and cactus symbol appeared on the coat of arms adopted by the first ruler of an independent Mexico (left). It also appears on the flag of Mexico today (right). **What reforms did Benito Juárez bring to Mexico?**

CHAPTER 34 THE AMERICAS 557

SPOTLIGHT ON: BENITO JUÁREZ

Benito Juárez was born in 1806 to a Zapotec Native American family. He studied law and entered politics in Oaxaca in 1831. In a political system known for its corruption, Juárez gained a reputation for unshakable honesty. He served as a legislator, a judge, then governor of the state of Oaxaca. Land reform was one of Juárez's main goals, for most of Mexico's land belonged to the Church and a few aristocratic landowners. He believed that to prosper the country needed a middle class who owned small farms and businesses.

Reteach

Have students work in pairs. Assign each pair a subsection to summarize. Have a student from each pair read their summary to the class.

Assign the Chapter 34 **Reteaching Activity** in the TCR.

Enrich

Have students write an essay comparing the English, American, or French revolutions with revolutions that took place in Latin America.

Assign the Chapter 34 **Enrichment Activity** in the TCR.

CLOSE

Have students discuss the possible meanings of the following quotation by Simón Bolívar, "Those who have toiled for liberty in South America have plowed the sea."

💾 Use **Interactive Tutor Self-Assessment Software** to review Section 2.

Self-Check Quiz gives students an interactive chapter tutorial. Have them access **Chapter 34 Quiz** at **humanheritage.glencoe.com**

Section 2 Assessment

1. **Define:** junta, caudillo.
2. What inspired the people of Latin America to move toward independence?
3. Why did caudillos rule most of the newly independent nations of Latin America?

Critical Thinking

4. **Making Inferences** Why do you think Simón Bolívar was known as "The Liberator"?

Graphic Organizer Activity

5. Draw this diagram, and use it to show the accomplishments of key leaders in the Latin American struggle for independence.

Independence Leader	Accomplishment

Chapter Summary & Study Guide

1. A stable, independent government helped the United States grow in power.
2. In 1800, political power in the United States passed from one party to another through a peaceful election, rather than through war.
3. In 1830, most adult white males in the United States were able to vote, making it one of the world's most democratic governments at the time.
4. As settlers moved westward, they came into conflict with the Native Americans, who eventually were forced to live on reservations.
5. By 1867, the United States had tripled its size by acquiring the Louisiana Territory, Florida, the Oregon Territory, almost half of Mexico's land, and Alaska.
6. Different ways of life in the northern and southern states led to the Civil War in the United States between 1861 and 1865.
7. The Civil War resulted in freedom for enslaved African Americans and the preservation of the Union.
8. Urbanization changed life in the United States in the late 1800s and early 1900s.
9. The American and French revolutions inspired the people of Latin America to fight for independence.
10. In 1804, Haiti became the first independent nation in Latin America. Other Spanish colonies and Brazil soon followed its example.
11. The newly independent Latin American nations lacked a tradition of self-government. As a result, most were ruled by caudillos.

Self-Check Quiz

Visit the *Human Heritage* Web site at **humanheritage. glencoe.com** and click on **Chapter 34—Self-Check Quiz** to assess your understanding of this chapter.

Section 2 Assessment Answers

1. junta, political committee (p. 553); caudillo, strong man (p. 556)
2. the American and French revolutions
3. because Spanish rule had given the people little training in self-government, and because the Creoles were aggressive
4. because he freed so many countries in Latin America
5. Charts will vary, but should include accomplishments by the following leaders of Latin American independence: Pierre Dominique Toussaint-L'Ouverture, Antonio Nariño, Simón Bolívar, José de San Martín, Father Luís Beltrán, Bernardo O'Higgins, Miguel Hidalgo y Costilla, José Maria Morelos y Pavón, Benito Juárez.

Assign the Chapter 34 **Section 2 Quiz** in the TCR. Testmaker available.

Using Key Terms

Write a newspaper article that gives an overview or summary of the major changes in government that took place in the United States and Latin America during the 1800s. Use the following words in your article.

stable government
political parties
federal
representative government
manifest destiny
annexation

seceding
urbanization
tenements
slums
junta
caudillo

Understanding Main Ideas

1. What was important about the American election of 1800?
2. What did the United States gain by the Louisiana Purchase?
3. What happened to Native Americans as the United States expanded its borders?
4. How did city life differ for lower-, middle-, and upper-class Americans?
5. How did Antonio Nariño help spread French democratic ideas throughout the Spanish colonies?
6. Why did Father Hidalgo revolt against Spanish rule?

Critical Thinking

1. What do you think are some ways the creation of public schools changed American life?
2. If you lived in Brazil in 1822, would you have supported the Portuguese government or the monarchy? Explain your answer.

3. How did the revolution in Brazil compare to the revolution in Mexico? Explain your answer.

Graphic Organizer Activity

Citizenship Create a diagram like the one shown, and use it to compare voting rights in the United States in 1830 with voting rights today. (Think of the groups who can vote today but could not vote in 1830.)

Geography in History

Place Refer to the map of Latin America on page 555. The three battle sites marked show that they were all fought near large cities. What other things do these battle sites have in common? Describe them in a paragraph.

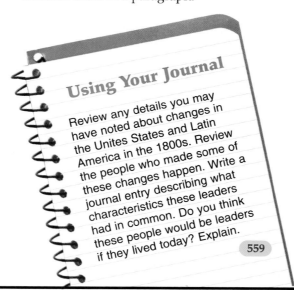

Using Your Journal

Review any details you may have noted about changes in the Unites States and Latin America in the 1800s. Review some of the people who made some of these changes happen. Write a journal entry describing what characteristics these leaders had in common. Do you think these people would be leaders if they lived today? Explain.

559

Bonus Test Question
For Chapter 34 Test
Imagine that in Latin America around 1800, no one could translate French. How would this have changed the history of the region? Explain. *(Answers should refer to the Declaration of the Rights of Man and the Citizen.)*

Using Your Journal
Journal entries will vary but students should describe some characteristics of good and bad leaders. If negatives are not stated, discuss how corruption in leadership can develop.

Geography in History
Answers could include that the three sites are in mountainous regions and located centrally but are at opposite ends of the continent.

CHAPTER 34

Assessment Answers

Using Key Terms

Newspaper articles will vary but students should include major points and all the terms.

Understanding Main Ideas

1. It was the first peaceful passing of power from one political group to another.
2. It doubled its size; gained rich farmland, minerals, and forests; and gained control of the Mississippi River.
3. The government began forcing them to live on reservations west of the Mississippi.
4. in housing, in jobs, and in education
5. He translated into Spanish the *Declaration of the Rights of Man and the Citizen.*
6. because he was upset about the way the Native Americans were treated

Critical Thinking

1. Answers will vary but should indicate that it gave people a chance for a better life.
2. Answers will vary, but students should support their opinions.
3. Answers will vary, but revolution in Brazil came about more peacefully than in Mexico.

Graphic Organizer Activity

Diagrams will vary, but should show the expansion of voting rights to go beyond all adult white males and include all U.S. citizens age 18 and over.

Chapter 35 Planning Guide

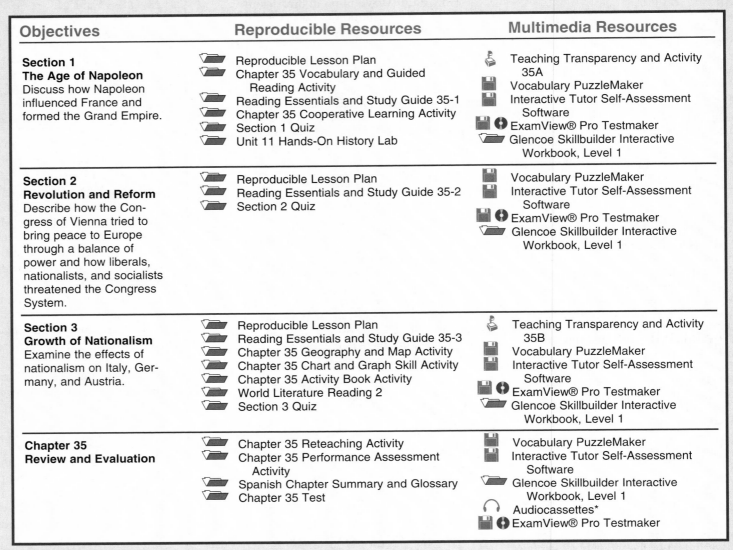

Objectives	Reproducible Resources	Multimedia Resources
Section 1 **The Age of Napoleon** Discuss how Napoleon influenced France and formed the Grand Empire.	Reproducible Lesson Plan Chapter 35 Vocabulary and Guided Reading Activity Reading Essentials and Study Guide 35-1 Chapter 35 Cooperative Learning Activity Section 1 Quiz Unit 11 Hands-On History Lab	Teaching Transparency and Activity 35A Vocabulary PuzzleMaker Interactive Tutor Self-Assessment Software ExamView® Pro Testmaker Glencoe Skillbuilder Interactive Workbook, Level 1
Section 2 **Revolution and Reform** Describe how the Congress of Vienna tried to bring peace to Europe through a balance of power and how liberals, nationalists, and socialists threatened the Congress System.	Reproducible Lesson Plan Reading Essentials and Study Guide 35-2 Section 2 Quiz	Vocabulary PuzzleMaker Interactive Tutor Self-Assessment Software ExamView® Pro Testmaker Glencoe Skillbuilder Interactive Workbook, Level 1
Section 3 **Growth of Nationalism** Examine the effects of nationalism on Italy, Germany, and Austria.	Reproducible Lesson Plan Reading Essentials and Study Guide 35-3 Chapter 35 Geography and Map Activity Chapter 35 Chart and Graph Skill Activity Chapter 35 Activity Book Activity World Literature Reading 2 Section 3 Quiz	Teaching Transparency and Activity 35B Vocabulary PuzzleMaker Interactive Tutor Self-Assessment Software ExamView® Pro Testmaker Glencoe Skillbuilder Interactive Workbook, Level 1
Chapter 35 **Review and Evaluation**	Chapter 35 Reteaching Activity Chapter 35 Performance Assessment Activity Spanish Chapter Summary and Glossary Chapter 35 Test	Vocabulary PuzzleMaker Interactive Tutor Self-Assessment Software Glencoe Skillbuilder Interactive Workbook, Level 1 Audiocassettes* ExamView® Pro Testmaker

*Also available in Spanish.

Presentation Plus!

Use Glencoe's **Presentation Plus!** multimedia teacher tool to easily present dynamic lessons that visually excite your students. Using Microsoft® PowerPoint, you can customize the presentations to create your own personalized lessons.

 Interactive Lesson Planner

Planning has never been easier! Using this CD-ROM, organize your week, month, semester, or year with all the help you need. The **Interactive Lesson Planner** gives you access to all of the blackline masters which accompany *Human Heritage.*

Chapter 35 Planning Guide

✓ PERFORMANCE ASSESSMENT ACTIVITIES

Flow Charts Have students create a flow chart or graphic organizer that shows the major events in Napoleon's career from beginning to end. Ask students to then imagine they could change history and intervene in Napoleon's career, having it end in a different way. Have them write an explanation that tells what the outcome would be.

CHAPTER RESOURCES

LITERATURE ABOUT THE PERIOD

Hugo, Victor. *Les Misérables.* New American Library, 1987. Novel about the conflicts in France in the early 1800s.

READINGS FOR THE STUDENT

Lengyel, Emil. *The Congress of Vienna.* Franklin Watts, 1974. Account of the Congress and its participants.

Marrin, Albert. *Napoleon and the Napoleonic Wars.* Viking, 1991. Biography of Napoleon.

READINGS FOR THE TEACHER

Cate, Curtis. *The War of the Two Emperors: The Duel Between Napoleon and Alexander, Russia, 1812.* Random House, 1985. Discusses Napoleon's invasion of Russia.

Cloarec, Yann, editor. *How to Make War.* Ediciones La Calavera, 1998. Napoleon's thoughts and sayings on war, as translated by Keith Sanborn.

  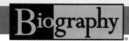

The following videotape program is available from Glencoe:

• **Napoleon Bonaparte: The Glory of France**
0-7670-1211-9

To order, call Glencoe at 1-800-334-7344. To find classroom resources to accompany many of these check:

A&E Television: http://www.aetv.com
The History Channel:
http://www.historychannel.com

 Teacher's Corner

INDEX TO NATIONAL GEOGRAPHIC MAGAZINE

The following articles relate to this chapter:

• "Reinventing Berlin," by Peter Ross Range, December 1996.
• "The Morning After: Germany Reunited," by William S. Ellis, September 1991.
• "Berlin's Ode to Joy," Priit J. Vesilind, April 1990.
• "Napoleon," by John J. Putnam, February 1982.

NATIONAL GEOGRAPHIC SOCIETY PRODUCTS AVAILABLE FROM GLENCOE

To order the following, call Glencoe at 1-800-334-7344:

• *PicturePack: Europe (Transparencies)*
• *PicturePack: Physical Geography of the World (Transparencies)*
• *Picture Atlas of the World (CD-ROM)*

ADDITIONAL NATIONAL GEOGRAPHIC SOCIETY PRODUCTS

To order the following, call National Geographic at 1-800-368-2728:

• *Europe (Laminated desk maps)*
• *Physical Geography of the Continents Series: Europe (Video)*
• *National Geographic Atlas of World History (Book)*

Access *National Geographic's* new dynamic MapMachine Web site and other geography resources at:
http://www.nationalgeographic.com/
http://www.nationalgeographic.com/maps/

KEY TO ABILITY LEVELS

Teaching strategies have been coded for varying learning styles and abilities.

L1 Level 1 activities are **basic** activities and should be within the ability range of all students.

L2 Level 2 activities are **average** activities and should be within the ability range of the average to above-average student.

L3 Level 3 activities are **challenging** activities designed for the ability range of above-average students.

ELL ELL activities should be within the ability range of English Language Learning students.

OVERVIEW

Chapter 35 discusses the political conflicts that transformed Europe during the 1800s.

➤ **Section 1** analyzes how reforms and military conquests by Napoleon helped spread French revolutionary ideas.

➤ **Section 2** describes the political movements that challenged the traditional European political order.

➤ **Section 3** discusses how each European country accepted or resisted change.

CHAPTER OBJECTIVES

After reading Chapter 35, students will be able to:

1. discuss how Napoleon influenced France.
2. describe how the Congress of Vienna brought peace to Europe.
3. analyze how revolutions in the 1800s threatened the Congress System.
4. examine the effects of nationalism on Italy, Germany, and Austria.

EXAMINING ARTIFACTS

Based on the statue, what can students infer about Napoleon's greatest strength? *(his military leadership)* Explain that the urn is an example of the Empire style of art favored by Napoleon. What does that tell students about how he saw himself? *(as emperor of France)* Ask students how Napoleon might have built his empire. *(by conquering European nations)*

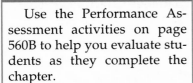

PERFORMANCE ASSESSMENT ✓

Use the Performance Assessment activities on page 560B to help you evaluate students as they complete the chapter.

560

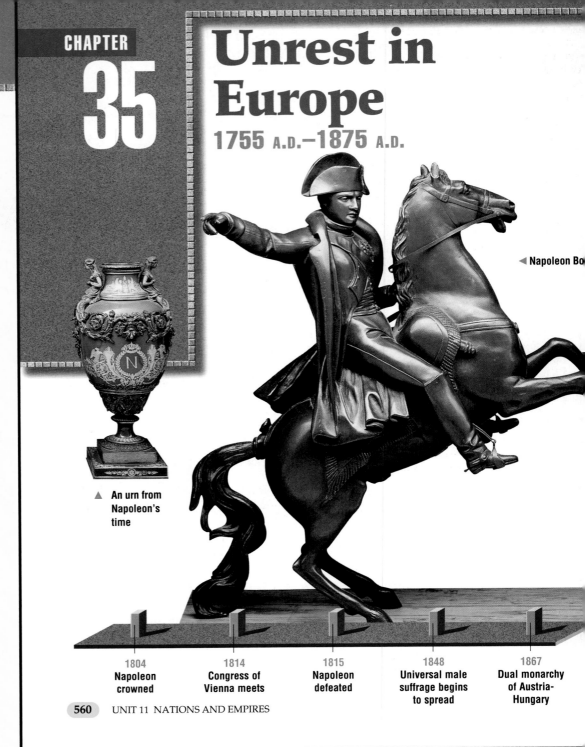

Unrest in Europe
1755 A.D.–1875 A.D.

◀ Napoleon Bo

▲ An urn from Napoleon's time

1804	1814	1815	1848	1867
Napoleon crowned	**Congress of Vienna meets**	**Napoleon defeated**	**Universal male suffrage begins to spread**	**Dual monarchy of Austria-Hungary**

560 UNIT 11 NATIONS AND EMPIRES

TEACHING RESOURCES

TEACHER PLANNING AND SUPPORT

- 🗂 Reproducible Lesson Plan
- 🗂 Block Scheduling Implementation Guide
- 🗂 Videodisc Bar Code Correlation
- 💿 Presentation Plus!

REVIEW AND REINFORCEMENT

- 🗂 Reading Essentials and Study Guide 35-1, 35-2, 35-3
- 🗂 Chapter 35 Vocabulary and Guided Reading
- 💾 Vocabulary PuzzleMaker Software
- 🖨 Teaching Transparencies 35A & 35B

- 🗂 Chapter 35 Reteaching Activity
- 🗂 Chapter 35 Cooperative Learning Activity
- 🗂 Chapter 35 Activity Book Activity
- 🗂 Chapter 35 Chart and Graph Skill Activity
- 💾 Interactive Tutor Self-Assessment Software

APPLICATION AND HANDS-ON ACTIVITIES

- 📇 Daily World History, Geography, and Culture Question
- 📇 World History Craft Card 6

560

Chapter Focus

Read to Discover

- How Napoleon influenced France and formed the Grand Empire.
- How the Congress of Vienna established a balance of power and brought peace to Europe.
- How liberals, nationalists, and socialists led revolutions that threatened the Congress System.
- What effects nationalism had on Italy, Germany, and Austria.

 Terms to Learn
plebiscite
abdicate
proletariat

 People to Know
Napoleon
Bonaparte
Karl Marx

Places to Locate
Waterloo
Vienna
Sardinia

Why It's Important   In the early 1800s, Napoleon occupied the center of the European stage. He came closer than anyone else to unifying Europe politically. In so doing, he spread revolutionary ideas. After his downfall, there was a return to the old order. However, the ideas of the Napoleonic (nuh pō lē ahn' ik) era had taken hold, and from 1820 to 1848, revolutions took place in country after country. The years after 1848 saw the breakup of the old order and the formation of new nations.

Chapter Overview
Visit the *Human Heritage* Web site at **humanheritage.glencoe.com** and click on *Chapter 35— Chapter Overviews* to preview this chapter.

SECTION 1   The Age of Napoleon

By 1799, France had experienced ten years of revolution and war. The people longed for a return to peace and order. They were ready for a strong leader to take charge. It was during this time that Napoleon rose to power. His rule started a chain of events that affected not only France, but all of Europe.

Napoleon   When the French Revolution began, Napoleon Bonaparte, who had come to France from Corsica (kōr' si kuh), was a lieutenant in the French army. By the time he was 24 years old, he had become a general. He was not satisfied, however. He wanted more.

In 1796, Napoleon was chosen to lead French troops into Italy. There, the French defeated the Austrians, who ruled Italy at

---

Chapter Overview introduces students to chapter content and key terms. Have them access **Chapter 35 Overview** at **humanheritage.glencoe.com**

FOCUS

Bellringer

Take a vote on this statement: *People have the right to overthrow a government with which they disagree.*

Motivational Activity

Discuss the vote with students. Then read the following quotation: "The world is always childish, and with each new gewgaw of a revolution or new constitution that it finds, thinks it shall never cry any more." Explain that Ralph Waldo Emerson wrote these words in 1847. Ask students if they agree or disagree. Tell them to keep the quote in mind as they read the chapter.

GUIDE TO READING

Reading Strategy

Ask students to read "Why It's Important" and summarize the chapter's main theme. *(Napoleonic rule spread ideas from the French revolution, leading to the breakup of the old order and formation of new nations.)*

Vocabulary Precheck

Ask students to define each of the "Terms to Learn." **L1** **ELL**

Use the **Vocabulary PuzzleMaker** for Chapter 35 to create a crossword puzzle. **L1**

Assign Chapter 35 Vocabulary and Guided Reading Activity.

Assign Reading Essentials and Study Guide 35-1.

GEOGRAPHY ACTIVITIES
- Chapter 35 Geography and Map Activity
- Social Studies Outline Map Resource Book

INTERDISCIPLINARY CONNECTIONS
- Unit 11 World Literature Reading 2
- World History & Art Transparency 29, *Napoleon Crossing the Alps*
- World Music: Cultural Traditions

ENRICHMENT AND EXTENSION
- World History Primary Source Document Library CD-ROM
- Chapter 35 Enrichment Activity
- Foods Around the World

ASSESSMENT AND EVALUATION
- Chapter 35 Performance Assessment Activity
- Chapter 35 Section Quizzes 35-1, 35-2, 35-3
- Chapter 35 Test
- Chapter 35 ExamView® Pro Testmaker Software
- Chapter 35 Digests Audiocassettes Activities and Tests

SPANISH RESOURCES
- Chapter 35 Spanish Chapter Summary and Glossary
- Chapter 35 Spanish Chapter Digests Audiocassettes Activities and Tests

Guided Practice

L1 **Chronology** Help students keep the events in this chapter in perspective by creating on the chalkboard or bulletin board a time line from 1775 to 1875. Have students record dates and events as they occur while reading the chapter. **ELL**

HISTORY *Online*

Student Web Activity objectives, goals, and answers can be found at the **Chapter 35 Web Activity Lesson Plan** at **humanheritage.glencoe.com**

DID YOU KNOW

Napoleon Bonaparte was known as "the little Corsican" because he was only 5 feet, 2 inches tall. He was a very hard worker who slept only three hours a night and often ate his meals while dictating to his secretaries.

MAKING CONNECTIONS

➤➤ **Medicine** The first ambulance was designed by Napoleon's personal surgeon, Baron Larrey, in 1792. The horse-drawn carts had special springs meant to smooth the ride over rough terrain. An ambulance division was first used in Napoleon's campaign against Italy in 1796.

Then... & Now

French Law France enforced the Napoleonic Code in its European empire and its North American colonies. Today Louisiana, once part of France's lands in America, is the only state with laws based on the Napoleonic Code.

HISTORY *Online*

Student Web Activity

Visit the *Human Heritage* Web site at **humanheritage.glencoe.com** and click on **Chapter 35— Student Web Activities** to find out more about Napoleon.

Example of Napoleonic Dress

that time. As a result of this victory, France acquired Belgium from Austria. France also acquired hundreds of art treasures from Italy, which were placed in the Louvre (lūv), the French national museum.

Two years later, Napoleon sailed for Egypt, where British forces were stationed. He won a great land victory there, but the British fleet destroyed the French fleet. Nevertheless, the French succeeded in establishing their influence in Egypt. Another important outcome of the French campaign was that soldiers accompanying Napoleon discovered the Rosetta Stone.

Meanwhile, Austria, Russia, and Great Britain defeated French forces in Europe. When Napoleon learned of this, he saw his chance to gain more power. He left his troops in Egypt and returned to Paris. There, he and two members of the Directory plotted to take over the government. On November 9, 1799, they put their plan into effect and met with success.

Napoleon set up a new government called the Consulate (kon' suh luht). He placed himself at its head and took the title of First Consul. By this time, Russia was no longer at war with France. However, Austria and Great Britain were. In 1801, Napoleon led French forces to victory over Austria. In 1802, he arranged a peace treaty with Great Britain.

Affairs at Home   Once France was at peace, Napoleon turned his attention to affairs at home. The Directory had been weak and in debt. Napoleon set out to make the Consulate strong and rich. He took away the people's right to choose their own local officials and gave that power to the national government. He prohibited local governments from collecting taxes and assigned all tax collection to the national government. Because Napoleon's system was better organized, the French government was able to collect more taxes. In a few years, France's debt was paid, and its economy had improved. Napoleon also used some of the tax money to set up a system of public education.

Napoleon also set to work to bring order to the French legal system. The French Revolution had swept away most laws and the different revolutionary governments had never been able to agree on new ones. As a result, different laws were followed in different parts of the country. To correct this, Napoleon appointed a committee of lawyers and told them to write a new code of law for the whole country. The laws they wrote were divided into five parts and were called the Napoleonic Code.

The Napoleonic Code preserved the most important rights won in the French Revolution. Serfdom was ended. People were made equal before the law. Anyone charged with a crime was guaranteed a public trial by jury. Freedom of religion was also guaranteed. However, some rights the people had won in the revolution were taken away. No one was allowed to criticize the

SPOTLIGHT ON: NAPOLEON

Napoleon was born in 1769 to a noble Italian family. He studied French for a few months and at 10 entered a French military school. Napoleon wasn't a brilliant student, but he was good in mathematics and history, was extremely persistent, and believed in himself. The French Revolution began in 1789. The fall of Toulon was credited to Napoleon. Here Napoleon developed a brilliant strategy that formed the basis for all his future battles. He learned to seek an enemy's weakest point, put all his effort into breaking through, and then overwhelm the enemy.

national government. There was no freedom of speech or of the press. A large police force kept watch on anyone suspected of being against Napoleon. Many people were put in jail.

Napoleon tried to make both Paris and France more beautiful. He had a huge marble arch, called the Arc de Triomphe (ahrk deh trē ahmf'), built as a monument to his campaigns. He named Jacques-Louis David as court painter. David designed furniture that looked like that of ancient Greece and Rome. Soon, the "Empire" style spread throughout Europe. This style affected clothes as well as furniture. Women wore narrow white cotton or muslin dresses with low square necklines and short puffed sleeves. They also fixed their hair like the women of ancient Rome.

Napoleon also worked to improve transportation. Under his direction, French workers dug canals and improved roads. Fourteen new bridges were built across the Seine River, which runs through Paris.

Because Napoleon brought peace and order, he was very popular. In 1802, he asked the people to elect him First Consul for life. They did so in a **plebiscite** (pleb' uh sīt), or popular vote. Two years later, the French made Napoleon emperor of France. His coronation was held in the Cathedral of Notre Dame (nō' truh dahm). The Pope came from Rome for the crowning but did not have a chance to place the crown on Napoleon's head. Instead, Napoleon took the crown from the Pope's hands and crowned himself.

The Grand Empire

Being emperor of France was not enough for Napoleon. He wanted to built a Grand Empire that would take the place of the Holy Roman Empire. He had the advantage of an army whose soldiers worshiped their emperor and whose officers were chosen because they were able in battle, not just because they were aristocrats.

In 1803, Great Britain, threatened by Napoleon's actions, declared war on France. Great Britain and its allies, however, were not able to stop Napoleon and his soldiers. In 1805, Napoleon had himself crowned king of Italy. In 1806, he formed the Confederation (kuhn fed uhr ā' shuhn) of the Rhine, which consisted of a group of conquered German states. In 1808, he invaded Spain and Portugal. The following year, he made the Papal States part of France and put the Pope in prison. France's boundaries now included much of Europe.

The countries in Napoleon's Grand Empire were strongly influenced by France. French citizens, including relatives of Napoleon, took over the government of many conquered areas. The French rulers made the Napoleonic Code law. Thus, Napoleon's conquests helped spread the ideas of the French Revolution all through Europe.

Photograph of Arc de Triomphe

Reading Check
What is a **plebiscite?**

Painting of Napoleonic Officer

L3 Critical Thinking Read aloud Napoleon's words: "I knew that I was superior to other men." Have students summarize Napoleon's strengths, and rank them from most to least important. Ask students whether Napoleon's beliefs about himself had any truth.

Reading Check Answer
A **plebiscite** is a popular vote.

MAKING CONNECTIONS

➤➤ **Culture** Some features of the Napoleonic Code were unfavorable to women. For example, a husband had complete control over his wife's money and property, and a wife was expected to obey her husband.

Bio**graphy**

The following videotape program is available from Glencoe to enrich Chapter 35:

• **Napoleon Bonaparte: The Glory of France**

To find classroom resources to accompany this video, check the following home page:

A&E Television:
http://www.aetv.com

COOPERATIVE LEARNING

Explain to students that most historians consider Napoleon a master military strategist. Then read or provide copies of these military sayings by Napoleon.
• "The art of war is a simple art and all in the execution; there is nothing vague in it, everything in it is common sense."
• "Never hold a council of war, but take the advice of each [person] in private."
• "Do not make a frontal attack on positions you can obtain by turning."
• "War is not the police."

Discuss what Napoleon may have meant by these sayings. Then divide the class into groups, and assign them to create sayings that Napoleon might have devised for each of these topics: art, leadership, taxes, debts, law, public education, elections, and conquest.

Assign the Chapter 35 *Cooperative Learning Activity* in the TCR.

L1 **Geography: Location**
Have students study the map "Napoleonic Europe" on this page to reinforce their awareness of the size and importance of Napoleon's empire in Europe. **ELL**

L2 **Role Play** Have students create a short skit about Napoleon's decision to march into Moscow. Students should include the invasion, the fire, the peace proposals sent to the Russians by Napoleon, and the French army's withdrawal from Moscow. **ELL**

DID YOU KNOW

The scorched-earth policy used by the Russians was the same policy the Romans had used against Hannibal and the Cartheginians.

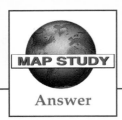

MAP STUDY

Answer

the North Sea and Atlantic Ocean

✓ **Reading Check Answer**
The Russians used a **scorched-earth policy** to burn their villages and food supplies so the advancing French army would have nothing to help them survive.

MAP STUDY

PLACE Napoleon had power over most of the European continent in 1812. **What geographic features helped to protect Great Britain from Napoleon's armies?**

Only Great Britain and Russia remained undefeated by Napoleon. Since the French could not defeat the British navy, Napoleon tried to obtain victory in a different way. He forbade the countries in his empire to trade with Great Britain, which he called a "nation of shopkeepers." His order, however, was hard to enforce, and it proved unsuccessful.

Napoleon then decided to take on Russia. He organized a Grand Army of about 600,000 soldiers of different nationalities. It was the largest army the world had yet seen. In the summer of 1812, the Grand Army invaded Russia. Except for one battle, though, the Russians did not fight. Instead, they retreated, drawing the French deeper into Russia. As the Russians retreated, they burned their villages and food supplies, leaving nothing for the advancing French. This tactic is called a **scorched-earth policy.**

Napoleonic Europe

[Map of Napoleonic Europe showing: UNITED KINGDOM OF GREAT BRITAIN AND IRELAND, NORTH SEA, KINGDOM OF DENMARK AND NORWAY, SWEDEN, BALTIC SEA, Moscow, RUSSIA, PRUSSIA, GRAND DUCHY OF WARSAW, WESTPHALIA, CONFEDERATION OF THE RHINE, Austerlitz, AUSTRIAN EMPIRE, Waterloo, Paris, FRENCH EMPIRE, SWITZERLAND, ITALY, BLACK SEA, OTTOMAN EMPIRE, ATLANTIC OCEAN, PORTUGAL, SPAIN, ELBA, CORSICA, Rome, NAPLES, SARDINIA, Trafalgar, MEDITERRANEAN SEA, SICILY. Legend: French Empire, Allied with Napoleon, Subject to Napoleon, Independent, Battles. Scale in miles and kilometers.]

564 UNIT 11 NATIONS AND EMPIRES

EXTENDING THE CONTENT

When Great Britain declared war on France in 1803, Napoleon had many different plans to invade England (including a fleet of hot air balloons to cross the Channel). In 1805 a combined French and Spanish navy set sail. At Trafalgar off the southern coast of Spain, they encountered the British fleet under Lord Horatio Nelson. Although Nelson was killed at Trafalgar, nearly two-thirds of the French fleet was destroyed. The British victory ended the threat of invasion. Later that same year, Napoleon recovered to win two famous battles. Splitting the Austrian and Russian forces, he beat one at Ulm, the other at Austerlitz.

In September, Napoleon reached Moscow, which had been abandoned by the Russians. Shortly after the French arrived, the city caught fire and three fourths of it was destroyed. The French army now had neither food nor shelter. Napoleon sent several peace proposals to the Russians, which they ignored. He finally gave the order to withdraw. By then the bitter Russian winter had started. Hundreds of thousands of French soldiers froze to death as temperatures fell to 40 degrees below zero. Thousands more died from disease and lack of food. In the end, fewer than 100,000 soldiers made it back to France.

Napoleon quickly raised another army, but the new soldiers were not well trained. They were defeated by the allied forces of Austria, Prussia, Russia, and Great Britain. This was the first time the four countries had joined together to fight Napoleon.

In 1814, the allies took Paris, and Napoleon was forced to **abdicate** (ab' duh kāt), or give up the throne. He was sent into exile to the small island of Elba off the coast of Italy. He managed to escape, however, and gathered together enough troops to invade France. For 100 days, Napoleon again reigned as emperor. The allies, under the British leadership of the Duke of Wellington, finally defeated him in 1815 at the Battle of Waterloo. This time, Napoleon was sent to the island of St. Helena (huh lē' nuh) off the west coast of Africa, where he died in 1821.

✓ **Reading Check**
How did the Russians use a **scorched-earth policy** to defeat the French?

✓ **Reading Check**
Where did Napoleon go when he was forced to **abdicate** his throne?

Section 1 Assessment

1. **Define:** plebiscite, scorched-earth policy, abdicate.
2. What was the Grand Empire?
3. Why did Napoleon's invasion of Russia fail?

Critical Thinking

4. **Understanding Cause and Effect** How did weaknesses of government under the Directory help pave the way for the rise of Napoleon?

Graphic Organizer Activity

5. Draw this diagram, and use it to summarize Napoleon's accomplishments in the areas of government, education, law, transportation, and the arts.

SECTION 2 Revolution and Reform

After Napoleon's defeat, representatives from Austria, Prussia, Russia, and Great Britain met in Vienna (vē en' uh) to decide what to do about France and the rest of Europe. Although the settlement they agreed upon brought peace to Europe for a time, it also set the stage for revolution in many countries and reform in some.

Painting of Metternich

L2 **Government** Help students make a chart on the chalkboard of the groups who were against the Congress System. The chart should explain the grievances of each group. Then suggest students put themselves in each group and choose the grievance they would *most* like to correct. **ELL**

✓ **Reading Check Answer**
The Congress of Vienna hoped a **balance of power** would prevent any single nation from starting another war.

DID YOU KNOW ???

The French representative, Prince Charles Maurice de Talleyrand, served under Louis XVI, the various revolutionary governments, Napoleon, and the restored French king, Louis XVIII.

✓ **Reading Check Answer**
Liberals supported individual freedom, equal rights under the law, freedom of thought and religion, voting rights for landowners, and protection of private property.

✓ **Reading Check Answer**
Nationalists opposed the Congress System because they wanted independence for areas where people shared the same language, customs, and history.

GEOGRAPHY AND HISTORY
The peace treaty had a significant effect on the German state of Prussia. Because its territories were divided, it became more interested in uniting the German states into a single nation.

566

The Congress of Vienna

The Congress of Vienna was sometimes called the "Waltzing Congress." This was because the representatives spent much of their time at dinners, dances, and fox hunts. However, decisions were made by a few leaders. They included Prince Klemens von Metternich (met' uhr nik), the Austrian foreign minister; Czar Alexander I of Russia; King Frederick William III of Prussia; and Viscount Castlereagh (vī' kownt kas' uhl rā), the British foreign secretary. Charles-Maurice de Talleyrand (tal' ē ran) decided matters for France.

The leaders did not want to punish France too harshly. At the same time, they wanted to build a peaceful and stable Europe. They believed the best way to do this was by establishing a **balance of power,** or equal strength among countries. They hoped that a balance of power would prevent any single country from starting another war.

To accomplish this, the leaders divided Napoleon's Grand Empire. Russia got Finland and most of Poland. Sweden got Norway. Austria got part of northern Italy. Great Britain got the islands of Malta (mahl' tuh) and Ceylon (sā lahn'), as well as the Dutch Cape Colony in South Africa. Belgium and Holland were made into a single nation. In addition, the 39 German states were combined into a loose confederation headed by Austria.

The leaders of the Congress of Vienna were against democracy. Hoping to crush revolutionary ideas, they brought back divine-right monarchy. They had already put Louis XVIII, younger brother of Louis XVI, on the French throne. Now, they brought back the monarchy in Spain and Portugal. The Pope was again made ruler of the Papal States.

✓ **Reading Check**
Why did the Congress of Vienna want to achieve a **balance of power?**

Political Movements

The balance of power in Europe was maintained for a number of years. However, the revolutionary ideas that had been spread by Napoleon's Grand Empire did not die. Several groups were against the Congress System, or the political plan and division of Europe set up by the Congress of Vienna.

One group was the **liberals.** They wanted political reform based on the ideals of the French Revolution. These included individual freedom, equal rights under the law, and freedom of thought and religion. Most liberals were members of the middle class. They also wanted changes that would improve their own lives. Among these changes were voting rights for landowners and the protection of private property. Some liberals wanted a constitutional monarchy. Others wanted a republic. The liberals were strongest in Great Britain and France.

Another group that was against the Congress System was the **nationalists** (nash' uh nuh lists). They wanted political independence for areas where people shared the same language, customs, and history. The Congress of Vienna had paid no

✓ **Reading Check**
What changes did the **liberals** support?

✓ **Reading Check**
Why did the **nationalists** oppose the Congress System?

EXTENDING THE CONTENT

Prince Klemmens von Metternich was the dominant figure at the Congress of Vienna. As an Austrian aristocrat, he disliked and feared nationalism, for the Austrian Empire included many minorities—Magyars, Czechs, Slavs, and others. Metternich believed that any upset in the established order might bring down the whole structure. To follow up the decisions made at the Congress of Vienna, Metternich put together a series of treaties aimed at involving all monarchs in preserving the status quo against liberalism and nationalism. The treaties called for periodic conferences and for settling international crises by diplomacy, if possible.

Comparing Historical Maps

A comparison of historical maps can reveal the changes that occur in the political features of an area over time.

Look at the map on page 564. Now, look at the map below. Note that both show about the same area, but at different times. The map on page 564 shows Europe's political aspects during Napoleon's rule. The map below shows Europe after the Congress of Vienna.

To compare historical maps, first look at both maps to make sure the same region is being illustrated. Then, study the boundaries and note any changes. Study also the names of the countries to see if they have changed.

For example, note that the Grand Duchy of Warsaw was subject to Napoleon. After the Congress of Vienna, however, both its boundaries and its name changed.

Compare both maps and answer the following questions.

Map Practice

1. How was the French Empire divided after the Congress of Vienna?
2. What countries were not directly affected by either Napoleon's rule or the Congress of Vienna?

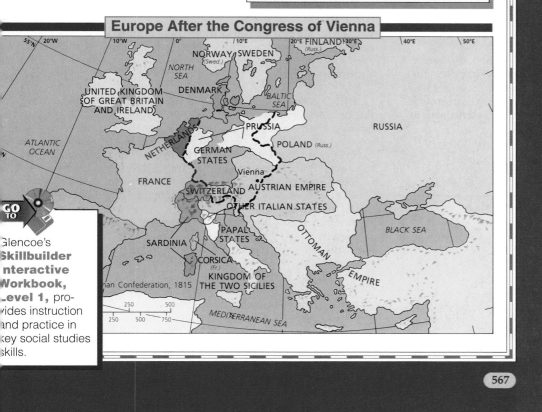

Europe After the Congress of Vienna

Glencoe's **Skillbuilder Interactive Workbook, Level 1,** provides instruction and practice in key social studies skills.

567

TEACH

Comparing Historical Maps

Have students read the instructional part of the feature. Ask: What can a comparison of historical maps of the same region show? *(the changes that occur in the political features of an area over time)* What are two things to study when comparing historical maps of the same region? *(boundaries, names of countries)*

Next, have students use the skills they have learned in this feature to compare the historical map "Europe After the Congress of Vienna" on this page with the map "Europe in the Late Middle Ages" on page 422. Ask them to write five questions that compare both maps. Then call on students to ask their questions of the class.

Answers to Map Practice

1. into France; the Netherlands; Sardinia; the Papal States; and parts of Italy, Austria-Hungary, and Prussia
2. Portugal, the United Kingdom of Great Britain and Ireland, Sweden, and the Ottoman Empire were not directly affected.

SPOTLIGHT ON: EUROPE

Several European leaders met at the Congress of Vienna to reorganize the Napoleonic lands. One leader, Alexander I of Russia, called a Holy Alliance that would let God guide the Congress and their relations. Most countries agreed to join his alliance although they doubted it could be successful. Alexander later died mysteriously in a remote part of Russia with many doubting he was really dead. He was sighted alive all over Europe.

Independent Practice

L3 **Debate** Have students discuss the part of Marx's philosophy that states: "In a worker's revolution all people would be equal and government would not be needed." In a blind drawing, assign students to a team, either agreeing or disagreeing with Marx's philosophy. Have students conduct a debate with the rest of the class deciding who presents the best arguments.

Reading Check Answer
The **socialists** wanted to end private property so the people as a whole could own it.

Reading Check Answer
The **utopian socialists** wanted to set up ideal communities based on economic cooperation. Karl Marx expected the **proletariat** to rise up and take power.

Reading Check Answer
Marx believed government would no longer be needed under **communism.**

GEOGRAPHY AND HISTORY

The delegates to the Congress of Vienna redrew national boundaries in Europe based on the desires of the rulers rather than those of the people they governed. The new boundaries ended the hopes of many groups. For example, the boundaries crushed the Polish people's hopes for a united nation. Instead their land was divided among Austria, Vienna, Prussia, and Russia.

Assign the Chapter 35 **Geography and Map Activity** in the TCR.

Reading Check How did the **socialists** feel about private property?

Reading Check Who were the **utopian socialists?** What did Karl Marx expect the **proletariat** to do?

Reading Check What did Marx believe would happen to government under **communism?**

Painting of Karl Marx

attention to nationalist feelings when it divided the Grand Empire. For example, the Belgians did not want to be part of Holland. The northern Italians did not want to be ruled by Austria.

A third group that was against the Congress System was the **socialists.** They wanted to end private ownership of land and factories. They believed the state, or the people as a whole, should own all means of production. In this way, the socialists believed, everyone would be treated fairly and the workers' lot would improve.

Some socialists tried to set up ideal communities based on economic cooperation. They thought these communities would show that theirs was a better way of life. Such socialists were known as **utopian socialists** (yū tō′ pē uhn sō′shuh lists).

Other socialists believed the only way to bring about reform was by revolution. One such socialist was Karl Marx, a German. He believed the **proletariat** (prō luh tār′ ē uht), or industrial working class, would rise up and take power. "The workers have nothing to lose . . . but their chains," he wrote in his book *The Communist Manifesto* (kahm′ yū nist man uh fes′ tō). "They have a world to gain. Workers of the world, unite!"

Marx believed that after the workers' revolution, there would be no hunger or poverty. Everyone would become equal. Governments would not even be needed. People would work because they wanted to give something to society. In return, they would be able to develop their own interests and talents. Marx called his kind of socialism **communism** (kahm′ yū niz uhm). He believed the workers' revolution would be led by his new Communist party.

An Era of Revolution Beginning in 1820, liberals, nationalists, and socialists led revolutions against the Congress System. The earliest of these took place in Spain, Portugal, Italy, and Russia. They all failed. However, Greek nationalists were given hope by these attempts. In 1821, they rebelled against the Ottoman Empire. After eight years of fighting, Greece gained its independence.

In 1830, there was another revolution in France. After Louis XVIII died, his brother Charles X had taken the throne. He wanted to bring back the Old Regime. Just a few weeks after being crowned, Charles did away with the National Assembly. He took the right to vote away from the middle class and returned control of the schools to the Roman Catholic Church. In response to Charles' actions, middle-class liberals, helped by students and unemployed workers, overthrew the government. After three days of fighting, Charles X fled.

The July Revolution, as it was called, was a victory for the middle class. Members of this class, unlike members of the working class, wanted a constitutional monarchy rather than a

---

EXTENDING THE CONTENT

Karl Marx believed that capitalism was only a temporary phase. A crisis in one of the advanced industrial countries would cause the workers, or the proletariat, to seize control from the bourgeoisie, or middle class. The proletariat would build a society in which the people owned everything. Without private property, class distinctions would disappear, and the government would wither away. He felt that this last stage would be genuine communism. He wrote *The Communist Manifesto* along with Friedrich Engels. Marx expanded his views in *Das Kapital* written in 1867.

Linking Across Time

Universal Suffrage   English author and teacher Mary Wollstonecraft (left) believed all people should vote, regardless of gender. In 1792, she published a widely read book defending the rights of women. Her book helped spark the start of the women's suffrage movement, which eventually made it possible for Margaret Thatcher (right) to become Great Britain's first woman Prime Minister. She held the office from 1979 to 1990. **What reforms helped increase suffrage in Great Britain in the 1830s?**

republic. So, they gave the throne to Charles X's cousin, Louis-Philippe (lū′ ē fi lēp′). Under Louis-Philippe's rule, the number of people who could vote increased. However, of the middle class, only its richest members could vote. This angered other members of the middle class. Working-class people were also angry. They had wanted not only a republic but also **universal male suffrage** (suhf′ rij), or the right of all adult males to vote.

News of the July Revolution touched off rebellions in other countries. In 1831, Belgian nationalists won independence from Holland. The Poles fought against Russia, but were defeated. Uprisings in several German and Italian states also were put down and ended quickly.

In Great Britain, however, liberal reforms were made by gradual change instead of revolution. In 1832, the British government passed a law that lowered the amount of land a man had to own in order to vote. This increased by one half the number of voters. It also gave the new industrial towns more representation in Parliament. As a result, the British middle class had more say in the government.

Reforms also helped the working class. Labor unions gained the right to **strike,** or stop work, in order to obtain shorter hours,

> ✓ **Reading Check**
> What group fought for **universal male suffrage** in France?

> ✓ **Reading Check**
> Why did workers want the right to **strike?**

MEETING SPECIAL NEEDS

Allow time for students with learning difficulties to make charts, diagrams, time lines, or other graphic organizers for each section. These organizers will help them retain a grasp of the relationships among people, dates, and events and will help them quickly review important data.

📁 Refer to *Inclusion for the Middle School Social Studies Classroom: Strategies and Activities* for additional resources.

L2 Government Organize the class into three groups, and assign each one of the following political groups: the liberals, the nationalists, and the socialists. Have students write a speech, the purpose of which is to gain support for his or her assigned political group in response to the Congress System. The speeches should outline the basic goals of the group's philosophy and indicate how they plan to achieve them. Have students read their speeches.

Linking Across Time

In 1832, the British government passed a law that lowered the amount of land a man had to own in order to vote. It also gave new industrial towns more representation in Parliament.

> ✓ **Reading Check Answer**
> The working class fought for **universal male suffrage** in France.

DID YOU KNOW

Only 3 percent of the French citizens could vote, even after the July Revolution.

> ✓ **Reading Check Answer**
> Workers wanted the right to **strike** in order to win shorter hours, higher wages, and better working conditions.

L2 **Critical Thinking** Ask students how the events described in this section can be called a continuation of the French Revolution of 1789. Encourage students to refer to pages 513–520 to refresh their memories. Then have them write a paragraph explaining the connections, if any, that they see.

MAKING CONNECTIONS

➤➤ **History** Although workers had done most of the fighting in the 1830 revolution that put Louis-Philippe on the throne, he ignored their demands for economic reforms. Labor unions were declared illegal, and police were used to break up strikes. Napoleon III was aware of the problems of the industrial age. He favored aid for industries, banks, railroads, and the poor. He also favored nationalism and supported international conferences to settle disputes.

✓ Reading Check Answer
National workshops provided jobs, but the number of people out of work grew faster than jobs could be created.

LINKING PAST TO PRESENT

In 1844 Antoine Joseph Sax performed in Paris on a new instrument he had invented—the saxophone—which still pleases audiences today.

higher wages, and better working conditions. By 1890, working class males also obtained the right to vote.

The Revolutions of 1848

In 1848, another series of revolutions broke out. All over Europe, governments were overthrown. Once again, the rebellion started in France.

Louis-Philippe had tried to be a "citizen-king." He walked through the streets of Paris without any servants to show that he was a bourgeois rather than an aristocrat. He wore a frock coat and trousers like the men of the middle class. He was very rich himself, however, and his government served only the rich. Industrial workers and middle-class liberals became increasingly unhappy. At the same time, the economy was bad throughout Europe, including France. Many people did not have jobs. Then in 1845 and 1846, the potato and wheat crops failed. There was not enough food to feed everyone.

In February of 1848, riots broke out in the streets of Paris. Louis-Philippe fled, and the revolutionary leaders declared the Second French Republic. They set up a temporary government to rule until a new National Assembly could be elected. Louis Blanc (lū ē blahnk), a socialist, was one of the leaders. He persuaded the other leaders to set up **national workshops**, or factories run by the workers but paid for by the government. The national workshops provided jobs for thousands of people. However, the number of people out of work grew faster than jobs could be created. Before long, the French government was supporting over 100,000 people.

When the new National Assembly was finally elected in April, it did away with the workshops. The workers revolted, fighting violently for three days. They were defeated by the army but not before over 10,000 people were killed.

The National Assembly then drew up a constitution. It called for a strong president to be elected by universal male suffrage. Napoleon's nephew, Louis-Napoleon Bonaparte, was elected president of the Second French Republic. He believed, however, that he had inherited his uncle's destiny. So, in 1851 he did away with the constitution. A year later, the people voted him Emperor Napoleon III. At the same time, the Second French Republic was renamed the Second French Empire. Louis-Napoleon remained on the throne until 1870.

The revolution in France was followed by revolutions in other parts of Europe. The Hungarians (hung ger' ē uhns), the Italians, and the Germans all rebelled. Their revolts failed. Even so, the revolutions of 1848 led to some important changes. In time, universal male suffrage spread to most northern and western European countries. Workers, who felt they had been cheated, began to form political parties. Soon, there was a socialist party in almost every European country.

✓ Reading Check
What was the purpose of the **national workshops,** and why did they fail?

Painting of Louis-Napoleon

COOPERATIVE LEARNING

Divide students into broadcast teams to provide coverage of the revolutions in France. Each team should divide up responsibility to research and prepare stories that provide a rounded picture of events in one of the revolutions. Each team member should have a role as a news anchor, on-the-scene reporter, or subject of an interview. Have teams report on events, reactions of royalists, republicans, leaders, and the person-in-the-street. Remind students to base their reports on actual events and actual people when possible. Have students write scripts and present their broadcasts to the class.

Predicting Consequences

Did you ever wish you could see into the future? Predicting future events is very difficult. You can, however, develop skills that will help you identify the logical consequences of decisions or actions.

Learning the Skill Follow these steps to help you accurately predict consequences.

- Review what you already know about a situation by listing facts, events, and people's responses. The list will help you recall events and how they affected people.

- Analyze patterns. Try to determine what the patterns show.

- Use your knowledge and observations of similar situations. In other words, ask yourself, "What were the consequences of a similar decision or action that occurred in the past?"

- Analyze each of the potential consequences by asking, "How likely is it that this will occur?"

- Make a prediction.

Louis-Philippe fled France in 1848

GO TO Glencoe's **Skillbuilder Interactive Workbook, Level 1,** provides instruction and practice in key social studies skills.

Skill Practice

Historians often make predictions about the future based on patterns from the past. Imagine you are a historian at the start of 1849. Use the information in the chart below to make predictions about what lies ahead for the 1850s and 1860s.

Events of the Early 1800s	Results and Reactions
Napoleon is defeated at the Battle of Waterloo.	The Congress of Vienna seeks to restore divine-right monarchy to Europe.
The July Revolution of 1830 returns constitutional monarchy to France.	Rebellions erupt in other European nations.
Worker riots in France lead to revolution and the Second French Republic.	The revolution in France is followed by revolutions in other parts of Europe.
The revolutions of 1848 fail to overturn the Congress System.	?

The following questions will serve as a guide.

1. Review the information on the chart. What patterns do you notice? What do the facts tell you about political affairs in Europe during the early 1800s?

2. Suppose one of the leaders who took part in the Congress of Vienna asked you to predict what to expect in the mid-1800s. What would you say? Was the Congress System safe from future threats? Explain.

571

CRITICAL THINKING SKILLS

TEACH

Predicting Consequences

You might open this lesson by asking students what would happen if they chose to watch a movie instead of handing in a homework assignment on time. Call on volunteers to explain how they are able to make these predictions. (*Students will probably cite past experiences.*)

Explore how the ability to predict consequences helps people to reach decisions—i.e., the importance of weighing alternative outcomes. Use this discussion to introduce the skills lesson and accompanying questions.

Answers to Skill Practice

1. Answers will vary, but most students will notice the pattern of revolution that spread across Europe. They will probably also indicate that the facts suggest a period of turbulent political affairs, filled with rebellions and efforts to restore order.

2. Answers will vary, but past patterns indicate a potential for future upheavals. As a result, the Congress System would probably face threats in the years ahead.

TEAM TEACHING STRATEGY

Math Along with the political turmoil of the 1800s came the turmoil of a population explosion. Invite a math teacher to develop word problems to help students interpret patterns on this table. Then ask these questions: (1) What population patterns do you notice? (2) What are some of the possible consequences of these patterns? (3) If you were a leader of one of these nations, what predictions or plans would you make for the future?

Population Growth (in millions)			
Country	1800	1850	1880
British Isles	16.1	27.5	35.1
France	27.3	35.8	37.7
Russia	37.0	60.2	88.0
Germany	24.6	35.9	45.2
Italy	18.1	24.3	28.5

W. S. Woytinsky and E. S. Woytinsky, *World Population and Production: Trends and Outlooks.* New York. Twentieth Century Fund, 1953, 44, 46.

Section 2 Assessment

1. **Define:** balance of power, liberals, nationalists, socialists, utopian socialists, proletariat, communism, universal male suffrage, strike, national workshops.
2. What were two goals of the Congress of Vienna?
3. What were some of the results of the revolutions of 1848?

Critical Thinking

4. **Making Comparisons** Which one of the three groups—liberals, nationalists, or socialists—would you have supported in the 1800s? Why?

Graphic Organizer Activity

5. Draw this diagram, and use it to show predictions made by Karl Marx.

Marx's Predictions

SECTION 3 Growth of Nationalism

After the revolutions of 1848 failed, the Congress System seemed stronger than ever. However, this was not the case. Before long, the growth of nationalism would destroy the balance of power that had been established at Vienna. Three countries that were affected by the growth of nationalism were Italy, Germany, and Austria.

Italy   In 1848, eight of the nine Italian states were under Austrian control. Only Sardinia (sahr din' ē uh) was independent. Ever since Napoleon's time, the Italians had been unhappy about this state of affairs. They remembered that Rome had once ruled the ancient world and that Italian city-states had led the Renaissance. They wanted to become a unified nation.

Many nationalists in Italy looked to Sardinia to take the lead. This was because of Sardinia's prime minister, Count Camillo di Cavour (kont kuh mē' lō dē kuh vuhr'). Cavour believed in industrialization and favored a constitutional monarchy. He also realized that Sardinia needed help to drive the Austrians out of Italy. To this end, he made an agreement with Napoleon III. It stated that if the Austrians attacked Sardinia, the French would help the Sardinians. When Austria declared war on Sardinia in 1859, Napoleon III kept his word. Austria was defeated, and the Italian state of Lombardy (lahm' bahr dē) was united with Sardinia. By 1860, the other northern Italian states also revolted against Austria and united with Sardinia.

That same year, an Italian nationalist named Giuseppe Garibaldi (jū zep' ā gār uh bahl' dē) led another revolution in

Fun Facts...

Charcoal and Freedom *Carbonari*, which means "charcoal burners" in Italian, was the name of one of the first secret societies formed to overthrow foreign rule in Italy. Charcoal is black, but it glows brightly when burning. Italian rebels associated the glow with the light of freedom and liberty.

Section 2 Assessment Answers

1. All terms are defined in the text Glossary.
2. to build a peaceful and stable Europe and to crush revolutionary ideas
3. In time, universal male suffrage spread to most northern and western European countries, and workers began to form political parties.
4. Answers will vary, but students should give reasons for their choices of one of the three groups.

5. Predictions include: the working class would rise up and take power; there would be no hunger or poverty; everybody would become equal; governments would not be needed; people would work because they wanted to give something to society; in return, they would be free to develop their talents and interests.

Assign the Chapter 35 **Section 2 Quiz** in the TCR. Testmaker available.

GIUSEPPE GARIBALDI Giuseppe Garibaldi led the fight for Italian unification in southern Italy. He was skilled in guerilla warfare, having fought in other revolutionary wars. In this painting, Garibaldi leads his Red Shirts in an attack on troops from Naples. **Who became king of the united Italy?**

southern Italy. Garibaldi had spent much of his life in exile in Brazil and Uruguay (yūr' uh gwī). There, he had learned how to lead small bands of soldiers behind enemy lines. The bands would hide in forests and on hillsides. They would make surprise attacks on the enemy and then go back into hiding. This kind of fighting is called **guerrilla warfare** (guh ril' uh wōr fār). In guerrilla warfare, a small group of soldiers can often defeat a much larger army.

Garibaldi taught guerrilla warfare to his followers. They were called "Red Shirts" because, like their leader, most of them wore red shirts. They also wore loose grey trousers, silk handkerchiefs around their necks, grey cloaks, and black felt hats. In 1860, Garibaldi's Red Shirts conquered Sicily within three months. Then, they sailed to the Italian mainland and conquered the state of Naples.

In 1861, the northern and southern nationalist groups combined. The Kingdom of Italy was formed as a constitutional monarchy. Victor Emmanuel II (ē man' yū el) of Sardinia became king. The Pope, who wanted to keep control over the Papal

Reading Check
Why might rebels such as the "Red Shirts" engage in **guerrilla warfare?**

LINKING PAST TO PRESENT

Major wars are not generally won exclusively through guerrilla warfare, which has been used since the eighteenth century to wear down the enemy and keep opponents from winning. During the American Revolutionary War, Francis Marion, the "Swamp Fox," effectively led guerrilla groups in South Carolina against the British. Guerrilla warfare has proven effective in rough terrain, as in the rain forests of Latin America and Southeast Asia.

Reading Check Answer
Rebels like the "Red Shirts" might engage in **guerrilla warfare** because in this type of warfare a small group can often defeat a much larger army.

MAKING CONNECTIONS

➤➤ **Biography** Garibaldi's military skills were recognized worldwide. In 1861, the United States offered him command of a Union force at the outbreak of the American Civil War. Garibaldi refused the offer.

MEETING SPECIAL NEEDS

Organize students who are auditory learners into small groups. Ask the students in each group to discuss all the examples they can think of—both historical and current—where regional differences have been a source of tension within a nation. Have students also include any examples of such tensions that exist in their own state. Bring the students back together and make a list on the chalkboard of each

group's examples. After discussing the kinds of factors that create regional differences, ask students if they can make any generalizations about the examples they have generated.

📂 Refer to *Inclusion for the Middle School Social Studies Classroom: Strategies and Activities* for additional resources.

MAKING CONNECTIONS

➤➤ **History** After Paris surrendered, a civil war broke out between the city's municipal government, called the Commune, and the national Assembly at Versailles. More people were killed in the civil war than during the entire French Revolution. After the Commune was defeated, some 20,000 persons were executed and another 7,000 were exiled to a penal colony on an island in the Pacific.

✓ Reading Check Answer
A **junker** was a rich landowner in Prussia.

✓ Reading Check Answer
William I of Prussia was the **kaiser** of the new German empire.

Germany Bismarck fought three wars to unify Germany, but another war—World War II— left Germany divided for 45 years. In 1990, West Germany and East Germany were reunited as one country.

✓ Reading Check
What was a **junker?**

✓ Reading Check
Who was the **kaiser** of the new German Empire?

States, fought against Italian unity and lost. In 1870, the Papal States became part of Italy, and Italian unification was complete. The balance of power in Europe, however, was weakened.

Germany   Nationalist feelings were also strong in the 39 German states. German poets and writers, like Johann Wolfgang von Goethe (ger' tuh) and Friedrich von Schiller (shil' uhr), wrote about German nationalism. German composer Richard Wagner (vahg' nuhr) wrote operas based on German folk tales. In 1834, many of the German states signed a trade agreement. In it, they promised not to tax goods coming from other German states. Soon, the economy of these states improved. However, many of the rulers of the smaller states were not willing to give up their political power. Austria was also against any attempt to unify Germany.

These obstacles were overcome by the Kingdom of Prussia. In 1862, King William I named Count Otto von Bismarck (biz' mahrk) prime minister of Prussia. Bismarck was a **junker** (yung' kuhr), or rich landowner, who believed in divine-right monarchy. He said that he would unite Germany, not "by speeches and majority votes—but by blood and iron." He also believed that war against a common enemy would bring the German states closer together.

In 1864, Bismarck joined with Austria to defeat Denmark and to gain territory. Two years later, he used a dispute over this territory as an excuse to go to war against Austria. Prussia won the war in seven weeks. It had superior weapons, as well as an excellent railroad system that moved troops quickly from one battlefield to another. The resulting peace treaty ended the loose German Confederation. The North German Confederation, led by Prussia, was set up in its place.

In 1870, Bismarck found an excuse to go to war against France, Germany's oldest enemy. As Bismarck had hoped, the southern German states joined the northern German states in the struggle. Well-trained and well-equipped, the German army easily defeated the French army. Bismarck then laid siege to Paris. The city held out for four months. Food became so scarce that the people were forced to eat the animals in the zoo. The trees that Napoleon III had planted along the streets of Paris were cut down and used for fuel. At last, on January 28, 1871, the city surrendered.

Meanwhile, at Versailles (vuhr sī'), William I of Prussia was named **kaiser** (kī' zuhr), or emperor, of the new German Empire. This included both the northern and the southern German states, as well as the rich mining and manufacturing lands of Alsace (al' sas) and Lorraine (luh rān'), which had been won from France. A unified Germany, however, meant a further weakening of the balance of power.

574   UNIT 11 NATIONS AND EMPIRES

EXTENDING THE CONTENT

Nationalism deeply influenced European music and literature during the 1800s. It inspired widespread interest in folktales, myths, and national history. In Germany, for instance, the Brothers Grimm (Jakob and Wilhelm) collected folktales in their famous collection, first printed in 1812–1815. Following the Grimm's example, Asbjornsen and Moe made a similar collection of Norwegian folktales, including stories like "East of the Sun and West of the Moon." Romantic novelists, playwrights, and poets found themes in national history. Sir Walter Scott collected Scottish ballads and wrote about medieval England in *Ivanhoe*. In Germany, Friedrich von Schiller wrote plays based on historical fighters for liberty, such as William Tell and Joan of Arc.

THE GERMAN EMPIRE The struggle for a united Germany was led by Count Otto von Bismarck, prime minister of Prussia. In this painting, Bismarck (center) proclaims King William I of Prussia (on platform) the emperor of a new German empire. **What effect did a unified Germany have on Europe?**

Austria Nationalists in Italy and Germany wanted to unify their nations. Nationalists in Austria, on the other hand, threatened the unity of the Austrian Empire.

The Austrian Empire was made up of many nationalities. Although its emperor, Francis Joseph, was German, four out of five people were not. Other nationalities included the Czechs, the Slovaks, the Poles, the Croats, the Slovenes, and the Magyars (mag' yahrs), the largest group in Hungary. Each had its own language and history and wanted to rule itself.

By 1866, Austria had been defeated by both Sardinia and Prussia. Magyar nationalists saw their chance to become independent. They revolted. In 1867, a weakened Austria agreed to create a dual monarchy. Now, the emperor ruled over two separate kingdoms—Austria and Hungary. Each had its own official language, parliament, and laws. Although they were separate politically, the two countries needed each other economically. Austria supplied manufactured goods to Hungary. In return, Hungary supplied Austria with food products.

People in History

Otto von Bismarck
1815-1898

German Prime Minister

Otto von Bismarck grew up the son of a wealthy landowner, whose noble ancestry stretched back more than five centuries. He was only an average student and showed little promise until his 30s, when he married and entered politics. For the rest of his life, Bismarck demonstrated the discipline he had lacked as a youth. He was the architect of German unification and served as the first *chancellor*, or prime minister, of unified Germany. People called him the "Iron Chancellor."

CAPTION ANSWER

The balance of power was weakened further.

DID YOU KNOW

In 1874 in Budapest, Hungary, Ehrich Weiss (later known as Harry Houdini, the world's greatest escape artist) was born.

LINKING PAST TO PRESENT

In addition to having a common ruler, Austria and Hungary had a single army and a common postal system. Systems today were modeled on these early examples.

ASSESS

Check for Understanding

Ask students to summarize the main points of the chapter, orally or in writing. Discuss the answers to the Section and Chapter Assessment questions.

MULTICULTURAL PERSPECTIVES

European composers in the 1800s were influenced by nationalism and drew on folk ballads or patriotic themes. Chopin, Liszt, and Smetana used traditional Polish, Hungarian, and Czech melodies. Folk songs came from German and Austrian composers including Beethoven, Schubert, and Schumann. In Italy, a patriotic chorus from Giuseppe Verdi's opera *Nabucco* became virtually the national anthem of the movement for unification. In 1874, Verdi wrote his "Requiem Mass" to honor the poet and nationalist patriot Alessandro Manzoni.

Evaluate

Assign the Chapter 35 **Performance Assessment Activity**

Administer the **Chapter 35 Test.** Testmaker available.

Reteach

Have students work in small groups. Assign each group a section to outline. Ask a student from each group to write their outline on the chalkboard.

Assign the Chapter 35 **Reteaching Activity** in the TCR.

Enrich

Have students choose one of the people mentioned in this chapter and write a short biographical sketch of the person.

Assign the Chapter 35 **Enrichment Activity** in the TCR.

CLOSE

Have students compare the map "Europe After the Congress of Vienna" on page 567 with a present-day map of Europe in the text Atlas. Discuss boundary and country name changes.

 Use **Interactive Tutor Self-Assessment Software** to review Section 3.

The Magyars were satisfied with the situation of having separate countries, but other nationalities in Austria-Hungary were not. Their unhappiness presented a continuing threat to the dual monarchy and the peace of Europe.

Section 3 Assessment

1. **Define:** guerrilla warfare, junker, kaiser.
2. What did Garibaldi do to further nationalism in Italy?
3. How was Austria-Hungary formed? How did most of its citizens feel about this?

Critical Thinking

4. **Drawing Conclusions** Why do you think the Italian city-states wanted to be a unified nation? Explain.

Graphic Organizer Activity

5. Draw this diagram, and use it to describe the importance of these dates in the drive for German unification: 1832, 1862, 1864, 1870.

| 1832 | → | 1862 | → | 1864 | → | 1870 |

Chapter Summary & Study Guide

1. In 1804, Napoleon became emperor of France. He then set out to conquer the rest of Europe—a plan that nearly succeeded.
2. Although Napoleon created a strong central government and a new code of laws, the people of France still lost certain rights.
3. After Napoleon's defeat, the Congress of Vienna tried to establish a balance of power in Europe and to restore divine-right monarchy.
4. Liberals, nationalists, and socialists opposed the Congress System.
5. A series of revolutions broke out in many European countries in 1820, 1830, and 1848.
6. Liberal reforms were made in Great Britain without a revolution.

7. The revolutions of 1848 failed to overthrow the Congress System, but they still had lasting results, including the spread of universal male suffrage and the rise of socialism among workers.
8. The rise of nationalism led to the unification of Italy between 1859 and 1870 and the unification of Germany between 1862 and 1871.
9. In the Austrian Empire, nationalism led to the Empire's division into two separate kingdoms—Austria and Hungary—each of which had many different national groups that wanted independence.

Section 3 Assessment Answers

1. guerrilla warfare, a kind of fighting (p. 573); junker, rich landowner (p. 574); kaiser, emperor of German Empire (p. 574)
2. He led a revolution in southern Italy. Soon after, the northern and southern nationalist groups combined.
3. Magyar nationalists in Hungary revolted, and Austria agreed to create a dual monarchy with a common emperor but separate language, parliament, and laws.

4. They remembered ancient Rome's strength and that of Italian city-states. They wanted to be strong and dominant again.
5. 1834—many German states sign trade agreement; 1862—Otto von Bismarck becomes prime minister of Prussia; 1864—Bismarck joins Austria to defeat Denmark; 1870—Bismarck goes to war against France

Assign the Chapter 35 **Section 3 Quiz** in the TCR. Testmaker available.

Assessment

Using Key Terms

Imagine you are a writer in Europe in the 1800s. You have been asked to prepare a brief introduction to a revolutionary handbook—a book telling people how to bring about change or to resist unfair governments. Use the following words in your introduction.

plebiscite	scorched-earth policy
abdicate	balance of power
liberals	proletariat
communism	strike
guerrilla warfare	kaiser

Understanding Main Ideas

1. Why did the representatives at the Congress of Vienna try to bring back divine-right monarchy?
2. Why did the temporary French government of 1848 set up national workshops?
3. How did Napoleon III help Italian nationalists?
4. How did the German states become unified?
5. What were some of the results of the war between Prussia and France?
6. Why were national groups in Austria-Hungary unhappy in the 1860s?

Critical Thinking

1. What did Napolean reveal about himself at his crowning as emperor?
2. Do you think Napoleon's conquests were good or bad for Europe? Explain your answer.
3. How important was nationalism in Europe during the second half of the 1800s? Explain.

4. "Liberal reforms can only be made with a revolution." Do you agree or disagree with this statement? Explain.

Graphic Organizer Activity

History Create a diagram like the one shown, and use it to give details that support the following generalization: The Congress of Vienna failed in its goal to return Europe to the old order.

Generalization
Supporting Details
1.
2.
3.
4.

Geography in History

Location Refer to the map on page 564. During Napoleon's time, as during other historical eras, Paris was an important city. What is the latitude of Paris? What is the longitude? Describe its relative location.

Using Your Journal

Review any details you may have noted about changes in government in European countries in the 1800s. Review the reasons the different revolutions took place. Write a brief editorial in which you give your opinion about one of these revolutions and whether the people had good reason to revolt. Be sure to support your opinions.

577

Bonus Test Question

For Chapter 35 Test
Think about the following group of words and tell what they have in common with one another in the context of this chapter: *liberals nationalists socialists* How are they different? *(Answers will vary.)*

Using Your Journal

Editorials will vary but students should support their choices with reasons. They might point to the conflict in the former Yugoslavia and other modern revolutions as comparisons.

Geography in History

about 49° N, 2° E

CHAPTER 35

Assessment Answers

Using Key Terms

Introductions will vary but should use all the terms.

Understanding Main Ideas

1. because they wanted to crush revolutionary ideas
2. to provide jobs for unemployed workers
3. He helped the Sardinians when Austria declared war on Sardinia.
4. by joining together to fight Denmark, Austria, and France
5. Prussia won from France the rich mining and manufacturing lands of Alsace and Lorraine.
6. because each had its own language and history and wanted to rule itself

Critical Thinking

1. He thought he was above the Church.
2. Answers will vary, but students should provide reasons for their answers.
3. very important because it led to important governmental changes in Italy, Austria, Germany, and France
4. Answers will vary but should include the idea that Great Britain adopted reforms without a revolution.

Graphic Organizer Activity

Sample responses: liberals, nationalists, and socialists led revolutions against the Congress System; Greece won its independence; July Revolution limited power of the French monarch; voters and labor unions increased their power in England; revolutions of 1848 helped spread universal male suffrage; worker parties formed; nationalism in Italy, Germany, and Austria upset the balance of power.

Chapter 36 Planning Guide

Objectives	Reproducible Resources	Multimedia Resources
Section 1 **Growth of Imperialism** Cite causes for the rise of imperialism.	Reproducible Lesson Plan Chapter 36 Vocabulary and Guided Reading Activity Reading Essentials and Study Guide 36-1 Section 1 Quiz	Vocabulary PuzzleMaker Interactive Tutor Self-Assessment Software ExamView® Pro Testmaker Glencoe Skillbuilder Interactive Workbook, Level 1
Section 2 **Africa** Discuss how Great Britain and other European powers established colonies in Africa.	Reproducible Lesson Plan Reading Essentials and Study Guide 36-2 Chapter 36 Geography and Map Activity Unit 11 Primary Sources Reading Chapter 36 Enrichment Activity Section 2 Quiz	Vocabulary PuzzleMaker Interactive Tutor Self-Assessment Software ExamView® Pro Testmaker Glencoe Skillbuilder Interactive Workbook, Level 1
Section 3 **Asia** Describe how Asian countries were affected by imperialism.	Reproducible Lesson Plan Reading Essentials and Study Guide 36-3 Chapter 36 Chart and Graph Skill Activity Section 3 Quiz	Teaching Transparencies and Activities 36A & 36B Vocabulary PuzzleMaker Interactive Tutor Self-Assessment Software ExamView® Pro Testmaker Glencoe Skillbuilder Interactive Workbook, Level 1
Section 4 **Latin America** Explain why the United States became involved in the affairs of Latin America.	Reproducible Lesson Plan Reading Essentials and Study Guide 36-4 Chapter 36 Cooperative Learning Activity Section 4 Quiz	Vocabulary PuzzleMaker Interactive Tutor Self-Assessment Software ExamView® Pro Testmaker Glencoe Skillbuilder Interactive Workbook, Level 1
Section 5 **Effects of Imperialism** Analyze the effects of imperialism on global politics.	Reproducible Lesson Plan Reading Essentials and Study Guide 36-5 Chapter 36 Activity Book Activity Section 5 Quiz	Vocabulary PuzzleMaker ExamView® Pro Testmaker Glencoe Skillbuilder Interactive Workbook, Level 1
Chapter 36 **Review and Evaluation**	Chapter 36 Reteaching Activity Chapter 36 Performance Assessment Activity Unit 11 Standardized Test Practice Spanish Chapter Summary and Glossary Chapter 36 Test	Vocabulary PuzzleMaker Interactive Tutor Self-Assessment Software Glencoe Skillbuilder Interactive Workbook, Level 1 Audiocassettes* ExamView® Pro Testmaker

*Also available in Spanish.

Presentation Plus!

Use Glencoe's **Presentation Plus!** multimedia teacher tool to easily present dynamic lessons that visually excite your students. Using Microsoft® PowerPoint, you can customize the presentations to create your own personalized lessons.

 Interactive Lesson Planner

Planning has never been easier! Using this CD-ROM, organize your week, month, semester, or year with all the help you need. The **Interactive Lesson Planner** gives you access to all of the blackline masters which accompany *Human Heritage.*

✓ PERFORMANCE ASSESSMENT ACTIVITIES

Making Maps   Provide the students with an outline map of the world. Have them label countries discussed in the chapter and create a key using different colors to indicate the European power that ruled each country. Then have students color their maps accordingly, creating a map titled, "Age of Imperialism."

CHAPTER RESOURCES

LITERATURE ABOUT THE PERIOD

Conrad, Joseph. *Heart of Darkness.* In *Joseph Conrad, Tales of Land and Sea.* Hanover House, 1916. Story of one man's journey up the Congo River in the 1800s.

Forster, E.M. *A Passage to India.* Harcourt Brace, 1989. A novel about life in India under British rule.

READINGS FOR THE STUDENT

Clark, Leon E. *Through African Eyes.* Center for International Training & Education, 1981. Collection of material about Africans from before the growth of enslavement to the present.

READINGS FOR THE TEACHER

Editors of Time-Life. *What Life Was Like: In the Jewel in the Crown.* Time-Life, Inc. 1999. A richly illustrated look at British India from 1600–1905.

Hsu, Immanuel C. *The Rise of Modern China.* Oxford Press, 1990. Focuses on major historical events in China from 1600 to present.

KEY TO ABILITY LEVELS

Teaching strategies have been coded for varying learning styles and abilities.

L1   Level 1 activities are **basic** activities and should be within the ability range of all students.

L2   Level 2 activities are **average** activities and should be within the ability range of the average to above-average student.

L3   Level 3 activities are **challenging** activities designed for the ability range of above-average students.

ELL   ELL activities should be within the ability range of English Language Learning students.

Teacher's Corner

INDEX TO NATIONAL GEOGRAPHIC MAGAZINE

The following articles relate to this chapter:

• "Malaysia," by T.R. Reid, August 1997.
• "French Polynesia," by Peter Benchley, June 1997.
• "India," by Geoffrey C. Ward, May 1997.
• "Hong Kong," by Mike Edwards, March 1997.

NATIONAL GEOGRAPHIC SOCIETY PRODUCTS AVAILABLE FROM GLENCOE

To order the following, call Glencoe at 1-800-334-7344:

• *PictureShow: Story of America Library, Part 2 (CD-ROMs)*

ADDITIONAL NATIONAL GEOGRAPHIC SOCIETY PRODUCTS

To order the following, call National Geographic at 1-800-368-2728:

• *China: Beyond the Clouds (Video)*
• *Great Indian Railway (Video)*
• *National Geographic Atlas of World History (Book)*

Access *National Geographic's* new dynamic MapMachine Web site and other geography resources at:
http://www.nationalgeographic.com/
http://www.nationalgeographic.com/maps/

 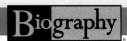

THE HISTORY CHANNEL.

The following videotape programs are available from Glencoe:

• **Theodore Roosevelt: From Roughrider to Rushmore**
  1-56501-806-0

• **The Panama Canal**
  1-56501-243-7

• **Pancho Villa: Outlaw Hero**
  0-7670-0315-2

• **The US in Latin America: Yankee Go Home**
  0-7670-0816-2

To order, call Glencoe at 1-800-334-7344. To find classroom resources to accompany many of these check:

A&E Television: http://www.aetv.com
The History Channel:
http://www.historychannel.com

Rise of Imperialism

1840 A.D.–1916 A.D.

OVERVIEW

Chapter 36 examines the rise of global imperialism during the late 1800s and early 1900s.

➤ **Section 1** analyzes the economic, religious, and political motivations of imperialism.
➤ **Section 2** describes European colonization of Africa.
➤ **Section 3** discusses imperialism in Asian countries.
➤ **Section 4** explores U.S. intervention in Latin America.
➤ **Section 5** discusses the effects of imperialism.

CHAPTER OBJECTIVES

After reading Chapter 36, students will be able to:
1. cite causes for the rise of imperialism.
2. discuss the division of Africa by European powers.
3. describe how Asian countries were affected by imperialism.
4. explain U.S. involvement in Latin America.
5. summarize the effects of imperialism.

EXAMINING ARTIFACTS

Ask students what they can infer about the relationship between the British and Indians. *(that it was unequal; that the Indians served the British)* Have students point to specific details to support their inferences. Then call on them to name one of the things England imported from India. *(tea)* Tell students to write down other reasons Britain wanted India as they read this chapter.

PERFORMANCE ASSESSMENT ✓

Use the Performance Assessment activities on page 578B to help you evaluate students as they complete the chapter.

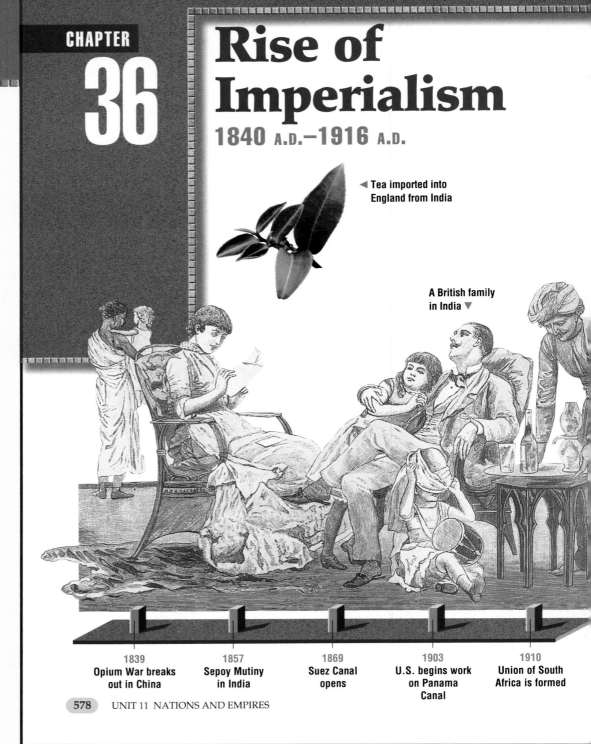

◄ Tea imported into England from India

A British family in India ▼

1839	1857	1869	1903	1910
Opium War breaks out in China	Sepoy Mutiny in India	Suez Canal opens	U.S. begins work on Panama Canal	Union of South Africa is formed

578   UNIT 11 NATIONS AND EMPIRES

TEACHING RESOURCES

TEACHER PLANNING AND SUPPORT

- Reproducible Lesson Plan
- Block Scheduling Implementation Guide
- Videodisc Bar Code Correlation
- Presentation Plus!

REVIEW AND REINFORCEMENT

- Reading Essentials and Study Guide 36-1, 36-2, 36-3, 36-4, 36-5
- Chapter 36 Vocabulary and Guided Reading Activity
- Vocabulary PuzzleMaker Software
- Teaching Transparencies 36A & 36B

- Chapter 36 Reteaching Activity
- Chapter 36 Cooperative Learning Activity
- Chapter 36 Activity Book Activity
- Chapter 36 Chart and Graph Skill Activity
- Interactive Tutor Self-Assessment Software
- Unit 11 MindJogger VideoQuiz

APPLICATION AND HANDS-ON ACTIVITIES

- Daily World History, Geography, and Culture Question
- World History Game Card 11
- World History Craft Card 11 & 12

Chapter Focus

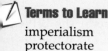

Read to Discover

- What caused the move toward imperialism.
- How Great Britain and other European powers established colonies in Africa.
- How Asian countries were affected by imperialism.
- Why the United States became involved in Latin America.
- What the effects of imperialism were.

 Terms to Learn
imperialism
protectorate

 People to Know
Leopold II
Cecil Rhodes
Matthew Perry

🌐 **Places to Locate**
Suez Canal
Indochina
Panama Canal

Why It's Important   In the late 1800s, an interest in colonies rose again. Many countries rushed to take over parts of the world that had not been claimed during the Age of Discovery and the Expansion of the Americas. New colonial powers were added. Among these new powers were Belgium, Germany, Italy, Japan, and the United States. Those countries in Africa, Asia, and Latin America who were colonized had little choice in how their nations developed.

HISTORY Online

Chapter Overview
Visit the *Human Heritage* Web site at **humanheritage.glencoe.com** and click on **Chapter 36— Chapter Overviews** to preview this chapter.

SECTION 1 Growth of Imperialism

There were many reasons for the rise of **imperialism** (im pir′ ē uh liz uhm), or the policy of setting up colonies and building empires. One was the Industrial Revolution. Factories in the industrialized countries needed such raw materials as rubber, cotton, oil, tin, and copper. There was also a growing demand for tea, sugar, and cocoa. Both the raw materials and the food could be found in areas that were not industrially developed, such as Africa, Asia, and Latin America.

Then, too, industries needed new markets for their products. Factories were turning out more goods than people at home could afford to buy. Many leaders believed new markets could be found in areas that were not industrially developed.

Also, many factory owners had grown rich during the Industrial Revolution. They could not find enough places in their

 Reading Check
What was **imperialism**?

GEOGRAPHY ACTIVITIES

- Chapter 36 Geography and Map Activity
- Social Studies Outline Map Resource Book

INTERDISCIPLINARY CONNECTIONS

- Focus on World Art Print 4, *Forever Free*
- World Music: Cultural Traditions

ENRICHMENT AND EXTENSION

- Unit 11 Primary Sources Reading
- Chapter 36 Enrichment Activity
- World History Primary Source Document Library CD-ROM
- Foods Around the World

ASSESSMENT AND EVALUATION

- Chapter 36 Performance Assessment Activity
- Chapter 36 Section Quizzes 36-1, 36-2, 36-3, 36-4, 36-5
- Chapter 36 Test
- Unit 11 Standardized Test Practice
- Chapter 36 ExamView® ProTestmaker Software
- Chapter 36 Digests Audiocassettes Activities and Tests

SPANISH RESOURCES

- Chapter 36 Spanish Chapter Summary and Glossary
- Chapter 36 Spanish Chapter Digests Audiocassettes Activities and Tests

---

Chapter Overview introduces students to chapter content and key terms. Have them access **Chapter 36 Overview** at **humanheritage.glencoe.com**

FOCUS

🏹 Bellringer

Ask students to explain this statement in writing: *The sun never sets on the British Empire.*

Motivational Activity

Have students share their sentences. Then explain that in 1900 the British Empire included one-fifth of the world's land and one-fourth of its population. Tell students that in this chapter they will learn how Great Britain and other world powers established colonies in Africa, Asia, Latin America, and Pacific Islands.

GUIDE TO READING

Reading Strategy

Ask students to read "Why It's Important" and summarize the chapter's main theme. *(Industrial nations built colonies in Africa, Asia, and Latin America and tried to control development in each of these regions.)*

Vocabulary Precheck

Ask students to define each of the "Terms to Learn."

L1 ELL

💾 Use the Vocabulary PuzzleMaker for Chapter 36 to create a crossword puzzle. **L1**

📁 Assign Chapter 36 Vocabulary and Guided Reading Activity.

📁 Assign Reading Essentials and Study Guide 36-1.

✓ Reading Check Answer

Imperialism was the policy of setting up colonies and building empires.

Guided Practice

L1 **Culture** Have students discuss travel during the late 1800s and early 1900s in relation to their own personal travels. How has traveling to new places changed their views of the world, of other people, and of themselves? **ELL**

L2 **Geography: Location** For an overall introductory view of the depth and spread of imperialism, have students note the nations and areas involved on the map "Imperialism" on page 590. **ELL**

💾 Use **Interactive Tutor Self Assessment Software** to review Section 1.

💾 Use the **Vocabulary Puzzle-Maker** to create crossword and word search puzzles.

Photo of Cocoa Pods

own countries in which to invest. Even when they did invest, they thought the profits were too small. Investments in undeveloped areas, however, generally brought large profits.

Another reason for imperialism was nationalism. Many people thought colonies would add to their country's power. The newly formed countries of Italy and Germany wanted to catch up with Great Britain, France, and other established colonial powers. Japan and the United States wanted to become as important as the colonial powers of western Europe.

Still another reason for imperialism was the belief that western countries had a duty to "civilize" the "backward" peoples of the world. To many westerners, any people whose way of life and religion were different from their own were "backward." These westerners believed they had a mission to spread Christianity and the Industrial Revolution everywhere. The British author Rudyard Kipling (ruhd' yuhrd kip' leng) called this mission "the white man's burden."

Section 1 Assessment

1. **Define:** imperialism.
2. How did the Industrial Revolution lead to imperialism?
3. How did nationalism lead to imperialism?

Critical Thinking

4. **Demonstrating Reasoned Judgment** If you had lived during the late 1800s, would you have supported or opposed imperialism? Why?

Graphic Organizer Activity

5. Draw this diagram, and use it to show characteristics of imperialist nations.

Imperialist Nations

SECTION 2 Africa

Painting of Rudyard Kipling

Before 1870, European powers had few holdings in Africa. Those they did have were mostly seaports and trading stations along the coast. The only major exceptions were the Cape Colony at Africa's southern tip and Algeria in northern Africa. Great Britain had received the Cape Colony from the Dutch at the Congress of Vienna. Algeria was held by France. Before long, however, most of Africa belonged to European powers.

The Opening of Africa At first, most Europeans stayed along the African coast because they were safer there from tropical diseases and other dangers. Little was known about Africa's interior. Then, missionaries and explorers opened up these areas.

Section 1 Assessment Answers

1. imperialism, having colonies and building empires (p. 579)
2. Industrialized countries needed raw materials and food such as tea, sugar, and cocoa, and new markets for their products.
3. Many people thought colonies would add to their country's power.
4. Answers will vary, but students should give reasons for their opinions about imperialism.

5. Sample characteristics: industrially developed, possessed a class of wealthy factory owners with money to invest, influenced by nationalism, viewed the cultures of undeveloped nations as "backward," felt they had a duty to spread Christianity and the Industrial Revolution

Assign the Chapter 36 **Section 1 Quiz** in the TCR. Testmaker available.

In 1840, a Scottish medical missionary named David Livingstone (liv' ing stuhn) went to Africa to convert the people to Christianity. During his years in Africa, Dr. Livingstone worked hard to end the Arab trade of enslaved Africans and explored much of the continent's interior. He wrote about his journeys in letters that appeared in newspapers in Great Britain and the United States. These letters aroused a great deal of interest in Africa.

Suddenly, the letters stopped. A New York newspaper decided to find out what had happened to Dr. Livingstone. It assigned reporter Henry Stanley to the story. After two years of searching, Stanley found Dr. Livingstone in a small Arab village on the shores of Lake Tanganyika (tan guhn yē' kuh). Stanley then became an explorer himself. Between 1874 and 1889, he explored the Congo and wrote about his adventures.

In 1879, Stanley was hired by King Leopold II of Belgium to obtain African lands for him. Stanley signed many treaties with African chiefs in the Congo Basin. Most of the chiefs could not

STANLEY AND LIVINGSTONE   This painting shows Henry Stanley (center left) who found David Livingstone (center right) living in the tiny village of Ujiji on Lake Tanganyika. Stanley greeted him with the now famous words, "Dr. Livingstone, I presume?" **Why had Dr. Livingstone gone to Africa?**

581

L2 Religion Have students read more about Dr. David Livingstone and other missionaries who went to Africa. To what areas did they go? What religious groups sent missionaries to these areas? How successful were they in achieving their goals?

L3 Economics Discuss the close connection between the Industrial Revolution in Europe and America and the rise of imperialism. Include the idea that the colonies that provided raw materials also became new markets for mass-produced goods. **ELL**

CAPTION ANSWER

to convert Africans to Christianity

MEETING SPECIAL NEEDS

Have students with learning problems divide into five groups and have each group concentrate on one area of Africa covered in this section: North Africa, West Africa, central Africa, East Africa, and southern Africa. Have the students in each group use the material in the chapter and an encyclopedia to prepare a brief oral or written report on the history of their region of Africa. Then ask one person in each group to present that group's oral report to the other groups.

Refer to *Inclusion for the Middle School Social Studies Classroom: Strategies and Activities* for additional resources.

Then... & Now

Reading Check
Why did Great Britain make Egypt a British **protectorate?**

Painting of Charles G. Gordon, Military Governor of the Sudan

read or write English and did not realize what they were signing away. In return for their lands, many of which were rich in minerals and rubber, the chiefs received cloth, beads, and sometimes guns. The signing of such treaties became a common way of gaining colonial territory.

Leopold II wanted to make a lot of money as quickly as possible. He had his soldiers force the Africans to collect rubber for him. Anyone who resisted was shot. However, missionaries and other Europeans protested so much that the king finally turned the Congo over to the Belgian government. The government did away with forced labor.

In northern Africa, the Suez (sū ez´) Canal was opened in 1869. Built by Egyptian workers and paid for with French funds, it connected the Mediterranean and Red seas. The Suez Canal made possible a shorter all-water route to India and the Far East. In 1875, however, the Egyptian ruler needed money. So, he sold his shares in the canal to Great Britain. Great Britain and France then took over Egypt's finances. This made many Egyptians angry. When they rebelled in 1882, British troops moved in. Egypt became a British **protectorate** (pruh tek´ tuhr it), or a country under the control and protection of a larger, stronger nation.

From the Cape to Cairo Soon after Great Britain made Egypt a protectorate, the British began moving south. After several years of fighting, they conquered the Sudan. There, Great Britain set up a joint government with Egypt.

At the same time, the British began moving north from the Cape Colony. The Boers, or Dutch farmers in South Africa, did not like British rule. They did not want to speak English, and they disagreed with Great Britain's doing away with enslavement. In 1836, many Boers decided to leave the Cape Colony. They traveled northward and finally settled in the grasslands of the interior. There, they set up two independent states, the Transvaal (trans vahl´) and the Orange Free State.

In the late 1800s, gold and diamonds were discovered in the Boer states. Thousands of adventurers began pouring into the area. The Boers were soon outnumbered. Afraid of losing control of their government, the Boers would not allow the newcomers, who were mostly British, to vote. However, the newcomers had to pay heavy taxes.

This angered Cecil Rhodes (rōdz), the prime minister of the Cape Colony. Rhodes had a dream of an English-speaking empire that would stretch from the Cape to Cairo (kī rō), the capital of Egypt. The British already controlled land to the south and west of the Boer states. So, Rhodes built a railway line into land to the north of the Boer states. As soon as the railroad was completed, British settlers began moving into this area, which was called Rhodesia (rō dē´ zhuh).

582 UNIT 11 NATIONS AND EMPIRES

South Africa The labor of black South Africans, such as these 1906 diamond miners (left), helped make South Africa rich. Even so, they lost their rights to the Afrikaners, a minority who dominated government. The Afrikaners held on to power until 1994, when South Africa held its first all-race election (right) and selected Nelson Mandela as president. **How did South Africa come under British control?**

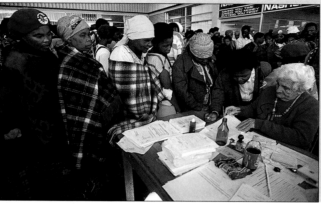

South Africa came under British control as a result of the Boer War.

LINKING PAST TO PRESENT

Cecil Rhodes came to Africa at the age of 18 and made a fortune in gold and diamonds. He used his wealth to support students by setting up Rhodes scholarships at England's Oxford University. Students may be interested in discovering what requirements must be fulfilled today to obtain a Rhodes scholarship.

At this point, Germany, jealous of Great Britain's growing power, offered the Boers its best artillery. The Boers promptly attacked British outposts, and the Boer War began. At first the Boers defeated the British. Then, the British captured the Boer capital. The Boers, however, refused to surrender and carried on guerrilla warfare for more than two years. Finally, the British destroyed Boer farms and imprisoned Boer women and children. When that happened, the Boers gave up. In 1910, the Transvaal and the Orange Free State were joined with the Cape Colony and one other British colony to form the Union of South Africa.

The British gained other African possessions besides Egypt, the Sudan, Rhodesia, and the Union of South Africa. Between 1890 and 1914, Zanzibar (zan' zuh bahr), Uganda (yū gan' duh), British East Africa, and Nigeria all came under British control. Except for one German colony, Cecil Rhodes's plan of an English-speaking empire in Africa came true.

CHAPTER 36 RISE OF IMPERIALISM   **583**

MEETING SPECIAL NEEDS

Have students who are visual learners work in pairs to create posters depicting the many opportunities awaiting the bold adventurer in the far-off colonies in the 1800s. Tell them to be detailed in their designs and add a title in the style of a headline. Some examples might include: gold mining in southern Africa; exchanging Western goods for tea and silk with traders in China. Display the posters in the classroom.

☞ Refer to *Inclusion for the Middle School Social Studies Classroom: Strategies and Activities* for additional resources.

Painting of King Menelik II

Other European Empires Leopold's actions in the Congo and the British takeover of Egypt spurred other European powers into action. Over the next few years, they divided the African continent among themselves.

Spain and Portugal kept their original possessions. Angola (an gō' luh), founded in 1648 by the Portuguese, was the oldest colony in Africa. In 1885, Portugal also made Portuguese East Africa, or Mozambique, a protectorate.

The French moved out from Algeria to establish the largest European empire in Africa. This empire included Tunisia, Morocco, French West Africa, French Equatorial Africa, and Madagascar (mad uh gas' kuhr).

The Italians conquered Eritrea (er uh trē' uh), an area on the east coast, and took over part of Somaliland (sō mahl' ē land). However, when they tried to take Ethiopia in 1896, they were defeated by the troops of King Menelik II. In 1911, the Italians acquired two Turkish provinces from the Ottomans. The Italians combined the two and renamed the area Libya. The Germans set up protectorates over Togoland and the Cameroons (kam uh rūnz') in 1884. They later added German Southwest Africa and German East Africa.

By 1914, only two areas in Africa remained independent. One was Ethiopia. The other was Liberia (lī bir' ē uh), which had been founded in the 1830s by former enslaved African Americans from the United States.

Section 2 Assessment

1. **Define:** protectorate.
2. Why did many Boers leave the Cape Colony?
3. What plan did Cecil Rhodes have for Africa? How successful was he in helping Great Britain achieve this plan?

Critical Thinking
4. **Making Inferences** Why do you think the Suez Canal was so valuable to Egypt?

Graphic Organizer Activity
5. Draw this diagram, and use it to show the causes and effects of what is known as the Boer War.

SECTION 3 Asia

The British and the Dutch started trading with Asia in the 1600s. However, Chinese and Japanese rulers allowed only limited contact with the West. So, western European countries turned their attention to India.

Section 2 Assessment Answers

1. protectorate, country under the control and protection of a larger nation (p. 582)
2. because they did not like British rule, abolition and enslavement, and did not want to speak English
3. He wanted an English-speaking empire that would stretch from the Cape to Cairo. Except for one German colony, it was achieved.
4. Answers will vary. Students might indicate that the canal made trade easier by providing a shorter all-water route to India and the Far East.
5. Answers will vary. Causes should reflect rivalries between the Boers and the British over control of southern Africa and imperialist competition between the British and Germans. Effects include British defeat of the Boers and the formation of the Union of South Africa.

Assign the Chapter 36 **Section 2 Quiz** in the TCR. Testmaker available.

India   By the middle 1700s, the Mogul Empire of India was breaking up. This allowed Great Britain and France to set up trading stations along the Indian coast. Then, in 1763, France lost the Seven Years' War, also known in the Americas as the French and Indian War. As a result, the French left India, and the British East India Company took over.

The British East India Company stayed in power for almost 100 years. During that time, it brought many changes to India.

Not everyone was happy with British rule, however. Many Indians felt the British were trying to change their culture. In 1857, the **sepoys** (sē' pois), or Indian soldiers in the British army, mutinied. The immediate cause was a new rifle. Its cartridges were greased, and one end had to be bitten off before loading. The Hindus thought the grease was beef fat. The Muslims thought it was pork fat. Hindus are not allowed by their religion to eat beef, while Muslims are not allowed to eat pork.

Although the Sepoy Mutiny failed, the British government realized that changes were needed. It took control of India away from the British East India Company and gave it to the Crown.

Great Britain wanted to protect its Indian empire from other countries, especially Russia. From 1865 to 1884, most of the central Asian centers of Muslim civilization fell to Russia. To guard India's northwest frontier, the British made Afghanistan (af gan' uh stan) a protectorate. In Persia, both Great Britain and Russia set up **spheres of influence,** or areas within a country in which another country has special rights.

☑ **Reading Check**
Who were the **sepoys,** and why did they mutiny?

☑ **Reading Check**
What were **spheres of influence?**

THE BRITISH IN INDIA   British settlers in India kept many Indian servants. In this painting, Indians unload a newly arrived British family and their luggage. **How did Great Britain try to protect its Indian Empire from Russia?**

☑ **Reading Check Answer**
The **sepoys** were Indian soldiers in the British army. They rebelled because they thought the British were trying to change their culture and because of a misunderstanding over the grease used on a new kind of cartridge. Hindus thought it was beef fat; Muslims thought it was pork fat.

MAKING CONNECTIONS

➤➤ **History** Local British garrisons were unprepared for the mutiny of the sepoys. Many British regulars had been sent to duty in the Crimean War before the rebellion began.

☑ **Reading Check Answer**
Spheres of influence were areas within a country in which another country had special rights.

DID YOU KNOW

The British allowed Indian princes to remain in power in many parts of India because it was easier to use them to help run the country than it was to conquer them all.

CAPTION ANSWER

To guard India's northwest frontier, the British made Afghanistan a protectorate and set up a sphere of influence in Persia.

MULTICULTURAL PERSPECTIVES

The incident that led to the Sepoy Rebellion reveals how Great Britain, like many of the imperialist powers in the 1800s, imposed its own culture and values on its colonies. Imperialists were often contemptuous of the sacred beliefs and rituals of the colonial people, often to the point of wiping out other cultures in the name of progress. Where Africans and Asians tried to resist imperialist pressures to discard traditional ways of life, as in the Sepoy Rebellion, tension—and sometimes fighting—occurred.

China From the early 1500s, all trade between China and the West was limited to the city of Guangzhou (gwong jō'). The Chinese looked upon westerners as barbarians.

The Chinese people were divided into two classes. The upper class were mostly government officials, scholars, and landowners. They knew how to read and write, and looked down upon people who worked with their hands. The lower class were usually farmers and artisans who did not know how to read and write.

Both classes, however, had certain things in common. They followed the teachings of Confucius and believed that the family was most important. Marriages were arranged to benefit families. When a son married, he and his wife lived with his parents. The Chinese greatly respected their ancestors. On New Year's Day they would burn incense and place an offering of food on the family altar. Then they would tell the ancestors what had happened to the family in the past year.

The Chinese followed their way of life until the 1800s. Then came the Industrial Revolution. Western factory owners and merchants became interested in increasing overseas trade. They were no longer satisfied with the amount of business the Chinese allowed them.

CHINESE SOCIETY Here an upper-class Chinese family is shown receiving gifts for a wedding. **Where will the new husband and wife probably live?**

OPIUM WAR   The British and Chinese battled over the selling of opium in China. **From what natural source did opium come?**

About this time, British traders discovered that they could make large profits selling *opium* (ō pē uhm), or a drug made from the dried juice of certain poppies, to the Chinese. The traders took cotton cloth made in Great Britain to India, where they traded it for opium. They then took the opium to China, where it was exchanged for tea and silk to be shipped to Great Britain.

At first, the Chinese government paid little attention to the opium trade. When it saw how much damage the drug was doing, the government declared the trade illegal. When a government official in Guangzhou seized and publicly burned a large shipment of opium, British traders became angry. In 1839, what became known as the Opium War broke out between the British and the Chinese.

Although they greatly outnumbered the British, the Chinese had neither cannon nor steam-driven warships. In 1842, they were defeated and forced to sign a treaty that opened more ports and gave Great Britain the island of Hong Kong. The treaty also gave British citizens in China the **right of extraterritoriality** (rīt of ek struh ter uh tōr ē al' uh tē). This meant that British citizens accused of breaking Chinese laws could be tried only in British courts.

> ☑ **Reading Check**
> How did the **right of extra-territoriality** weaken the power of the Chinese government?

L2 **Critical Thinking** Have students brainstorm a list of laws or rules they do not like to see broken, such as laws against theft or murder, or rules against destroying school property. Ask students how they would feel about students coming into their school, breaking rules, and not being punished for it by school officials. Have them write an explanation of how that situation relates to extraterritoriality, including a statement of their opinion of that practice in China.

LINKING PAST TO PRESENT

Hong Kong was a British colony from 1842 until 1997, when it was returned to Chinese rule. It is still one of the busiest trade and banking centers in Asia.

CAPTION ANSWER

the dried juice of certain poppies

☑ **Reading Check Answer**
The **right of extraterritoriality** said that British citizens accused of breaking Chinese laws could only be tried in British courts.

MULTICULTURAL PERSPECTIVES

The spirit of revolt, like that of western Europe, also swept through China during the 1800s. The Taiping Rebellion (1851-1864) tore the country apart. A group trying to combine Christian and ancient Chinese beliefs attempted to create a perfect society with an equal division of land among the people. Other goals of the Taipings included ridding China of both the Westerners and the Qing dynasty. Although the rebellion was a failure, it seriously weakened the Qing dynasty and the country. The cost in lives was between 20 million and 30 million. Ironically, the term *taiping* means "great peace."

China lost even more power in the late 1800s. In 1894, Japan and China went to war over Korea. The Japanese won easily and took Chinese territory. Great Britain, France, Germany, and Russia rushed to get *concessions* (kuhn sesh' uhns), or special rights, from the Chinese government. These included the rights to develop mineral resources and build railroads and naval bases. Several countries also got leases on Chinese port cities.

The United States did not want China divided up by foreign powers or kept from trading with American merchants. In 1899, the American government asked countries to approve the Open Door policy. This gave everyone equal trading rights in China.

The Open Door Policy did not please the Chinese because it meant that foreign powers were still trying to control them. So, the Chinese began a movement to drive all foreigners from their country. The movement was called the Boxer Rebellion because it had been started by a Chinese secret society called Boxers. In the spring of 1900, the Boxers began attacking foreigners, including

THE BOXER REBELLION The Boxers were a secret society dedicated to removing all foreign influences from China. British, French, Russian, American, German, and Japanese troops were sent to put down the revolt. In this painting foreign troops attacked the rebels in Beijing. **What was the outcome of the Boxer Rebellion?**

EXTENDING THE CONTENT

In signing the Open Door policy, China opened its ports to western trade. The U.S. business community profited greatly from this agreement. In the 1930s, as tensions leading to World War II escalated, Japan invaded China and threatened to close the open door of trade with the West. The American business community became harsh critics of Japan's aggressive expansionism, adding even more tension to a situation that would soon explode into a world war.

the diplomats at Beijing (bā jing'), the capital of China. The foreign powers joined forces and sent an army to China. In 1901, the rebellion was put down. China had to pay heavy penalties, and foreign powers gained almost total control of the country.

Japan Like China, Japan allowed only limited trade with the West at first. The Japanese government even refused to provide shelter to shipwrecked sailors. In the middle 1800s, however, this changed.

In 1853, the American government sent a naval force under Commodore Matthew Perry to Japan. Perry was able to negotiate a treaty to open up trade and to protect shipwrecked American sailors. Soon after, Japan signed similar treaties with Great Britain, France, Russia, and the Netherlands.

The military strength and industrial accomplishments of the West impressed most Japanese leaders. They felt that in order to survive, Japan must modernize. To this end, in 1868, several Japanese lords overthrew the shogun and restored the power of the emperor. The new emperor moved the capital of Japan from Kyoto (kyō' tō) to Tokyo. He called his rule Meiji (mā' jē), which means "enlightened peace." The changes that came about during this time are known as the Meiji Restoration.

The new government did away with feudalism. Common people were now allowed to take a family name. They also could live and work where they wished. The government ordered all Japanese males to cut off the topknots worn in their hair. Western-style clothing and a new calendar were introduced.

The Meiji government took away the special position of the samurai. Instead, all Japanese men were expected to serve for a certain amount of time in the armed forces. The government also set up a modern army and navy.

In 1889, Japanese leaders wrote Japan's first constitution. Public schools were opened, and education was required for all. Japanese leaders also began a push to industrialize. To help reach this goal, they gave certain privileges and protection to the *zaibatsu* (zī' bah tsū'), or the rich and powerful families who controlled many industries.

By the end of the 1800s, Japan was fully industrialized. However, Japan needed raw materials and markets for its manufactured goods. In addition, because of modern sanitation and medicine, its population was growing rapidly. Japan did not have enough fertile land to grow food for all its people.

To help find answers to these problems, the Japanese began a program of imperialism. Japan gained control of the island of Formosa (for mō' suh), or present-day Taiwan (tī wahn'), and part of Manchuria (man chūr' ē uh) after a war with China. Ten years later, Japan went to war with Russia and got control of the

Painting of Matthew Perry

✓ **Reading Check**
Why did Japanese leaders feel they needed the help of the *zaibatsu?*

Independent Practice

L1 **History** Have students research Matthew Perry's dealings with the Japanese and prepare a television interview with questions and answers for Perry and the Japanese shoguns who signed treaties with him. Have students prepare and present a news interview for U.S. citizens eager to know the outcome of Perry's dealings with the Japanese. Some students can take the role of reporters, and others can represent Perry, his crew, and the Japanese. **ELL**

L3 **Critical Thinking** Have students choose a topic dealing with European-Japanese or European-Chinese relations, and create a political cartoon that depicts the situation. In doing so, remind students that their opinion of the relationship also could enter into their cartoon.

✓ **Reading Check Answer**
Japanese leaders felt they needed the help of the *zaibatsu* because these families controlled many of Japan's industries.

DID YOU KNOW **??**
Topknots were symbolic to the Japanese because the samurai had worn their hair that way. The topknots had to be cut off because western military hats could not be worn over them.

SPOTLIGHT ON: PERRY

Matthew Calbraith Perry was born April 10, 1794, in Newport, Rhode Island. He began his naval career early at age 15 as a midshipman on the *Revenge,* under the command of his brother, Oliver Hazard Perry. In his dealings with the Japanese, Matthew Perry arranged for the protection of American seamen and property in Japanese waters. It is said that he impressed the Japanese who were suspicious of other countries, by his forcefulness and insistence on formality. His meetings with the Japanese were conducted with elaborate ceremony, and he and his officers always wore their finest uniforms and were always accompanied by a full honor guard.

MAKING CONNECTIONS

➤➤ **History** Under Japanese rule, the Koreans lost many of their liberties and began to resist the Japanese. However, the Japanese easily crushed Korean opposition.

L1 Geography: Human/Environmental Interaction Have students study the map "Imperialism" and make charts showing which countries were controlled by Japan and the European countries that are listed in the map legend.

Assign the Chapter 36 **Geography and Map Activity** in the TCR.

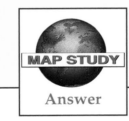

MAP STUDY

Answer

Great Britain

MAP STUDY

REGIONS By the early 1900s, Europeans had spread their rule throughout the world. **Which country's empire included territories in the greatest number of continents?**

southern half of the island of Sakhalin (sak' uh lēn). It also won a sphere of influence in Korea. Five years later, Japan annexed Korea.

Southeast Asia and the Pacific   Europeans first entered Southeast Asia in the 1500s in search of spices. By the 1600s, Portugal, Spain, and the Netherlands all had colonies there. Although there was an active trade with the islands in the area, no one paid much attention to the mainland.

In the late 1800s, the European powers changed their minds. The mainland of Southeast Asia was a source of cash crops, such as coffee and tea. It also had raw materials, such as petroleum, rubber, and tin.

Great Britain and France competed in Southeast Asia. The British took control of Burma, Ceylon, the Malay States, and Singapore. The French set up protectorates in Cochin-China

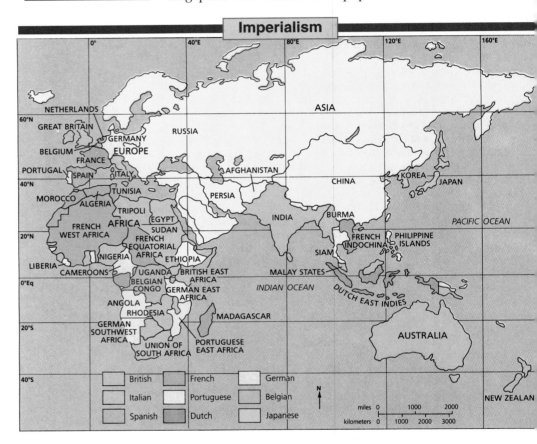

Imperialism

Legend: British, French, German, Italian, Portuguese, Belgian, Spanish, Dutch, Japanese

---

EXTENDING THE CONTENT

Liberia and Ethiopia were the only two countries in Africa that were never colonized. South Africa (1910) and Egypt (1922) gained their independence long before most other African colonies. Between 1951 and 1991, more than 50 African colonies achieved independence. Since the beginning of colonial rule, nationalist groups in Africa had resisted European control, often violently. But following World War II, these relatively small efforts for freedom swelled into powerful mass movements. Africans, many of whom served in the Allied armies, were inspired by the democratic ideals for which the Allies fought in the war—self-rule and freedom from tyranny.

(kō' chuhn chī nuh), Kampuchea, and Annam (a nam'). They then took over Laos (lah' ōs) and combined the four colonies into Indochina. Only Siam, or present-day Thailand, remained independent.

During this period, Great Britain, France, Germany, and the United States were also trying to win control of islands in the Pacific. Some of the islands had rich soil that could be used for sugar and pineapple plantations. Others had minerals. Still others could be used as bases for refueling and repairing ships.

Great Britain, which had the largest navy in the world, already held Australia and New Zealand. Now, it took the Fiji, Solomon, and Gilbert islands, along with parts of New Guinea (gin' ē) and Borneo (bor' nē ō). France claimed Tahiti, the Marquesas (mahr kā' zuhz), and several other islands. Germany took part of New Guinea and the Marshall, Caroline, and Mariana islands. Later, Germany divided the Samoan (suh mō' uhn) Islands with the United States. The United States also controlled the Hawaiian and Philippine islands and Guam (gwahm).

People in History

Liliuokalani
1838–1917

Hawaiian Queen

Born in Honolulu, Liliuokalani came to power in 1891. She tried to restore the power of the monarchy, which had been weakened by the mostly American sugar planters, but was forced to step down in 1895.

GEOGRAPHY AND HISTORY

The Pacific Islands are divided into three groups: Melanesia, Micronesia, and Polynesia. Encourage students to locate these groups in their text Atlas.

Section 3 Assessment

1. **Define:** sepoys, spheres of influence, right of extraterritoriality, *zaibatsu*.
2. Why did the Japanese start a program of imperialism?
3. Why did many European countries in the 1800s want to control territory in Southeast Asia?

Critical Thinking

4. **Identifying the Central Issue** What was the central issue in the Boxer Rebellion?

Graphic Organizer Activity

5. Draw this diagram, and use it to show the steps leading to the takeover of India by the British Crown.

Step 1 | Step 2 | Step 3 | Control by Crown

MAKING CONNECTIONS

➤➤ **Literature** The influences of various Asian cultures began to find their way into the works of Western writers and artists as a result of the increased contact brought about by imperialism. Joseph Conrad's stories, and Paul Gauguin's paintings reflect the influence of several of the cultures of Southeast Asia and the Pacific Islands.

💾 Use **Interactive Tutor Self Assessment Software** to review Section 3.

💾 Use the **Vocabulary Puzzle-Maker** to create crossword and word search puzzles.

SECTION 4 Latin America

The imperialist powers were also interested in Latin America. The countries there that had gained their independence in the early 1800s faced many problems. Most Latin Americans were poor and had no land of their own. The new leaders had little government experience. There were many revolutions. These shaky conditions seemed to invite outside interference.

Painting of Hawaiian Queen Liliuokalani

CHAPTER 36 RISE OF IMPERIALISM **591**

L2 **Geography: Location** Ask students to find North America and South America in the text Atlas. Have students consider the closeness of one land mass to the other. Have students write an explanation of how location explains why the United States issued the Monroe Doctrine. **ELL**

LINKING PAST TO PRESENT

Puerto Rico is now a commonwealth of the United States. Puerto Ricans can enter the United States without a passport. They serve in America's armed forces but do not pay federal taxes and cannot vote in national elections. The U.S. government handles Puerto Rico's foreign affairs. Guam is still a U.S. territory. Cuba became an independent republic in 1902.

CAPTION ANSWER

The United States supported a successful revolution by the people of Panama against Colombia and then signed a treaty with Panama.

THE HISTORY CHANNEL.

The following videotape programs are available from Glencoe to enrich Chapter 36:

- **The Panama Canal**
- **The U.S. in Latin America: Yankee Go Home**

To find classroom resources to accompany these videos, check the following home page:

A&E Television:
http://www.aetv.com

Fun Facts....

The Canal and Disease After the Spanish-American War, Colonel William C. Gorgas, a U.S. army physician, wiped out yellow fever in Havana, Cuba. In 1904, Gorgas began an effort to eliminate the disease from the Isthmus of Panama. Scientists had just found that mosquitoes transmit both yellow fever and malaria. By controlling mosquitoes, Gorgas greatly lowered the death toll among workers on the Panama Canal.

To stop this, President James Monroe issued the Monroe Doctrine in 1823. It said that any attempt to gain colonies in Latin America would be considered an unfriendly act toward the United States. Most of the European powers went along with the Monroe Doctrine, largely because the British navy supported the American position. The French made Prince Maximilian of Austria the emperor of Mexico.

By the late 1800s, Spain had colonies in Cuba and Puerto Rico. The Cubans, eager to be independent, had revolted in 1868 and again in 1895. Some Americans, who had large amounts of money invested there, wanted the rebels to win. In 1898, an American battleship, the U.S.S. *Maine,* blew up in the harbor of Havana, Cuba. People in the United States blamed the Spanish. Before long, Congress declared war on Spain.

In less than a year, the United States won the Spanish-American War. The resulting peace treaty gave the United States Puerto Rico, Guam, and the Philippine Islands. Cuba became an American protectorate.

The United States was now a world power. As such, it became even more involved in Latin America.

The United States needed a way to protect its new territories. Its fleet had to be able to sail quickly between American islands in the Caribbean Sea and those in the Pacific Ocean. President

PANAMA CANAL The building of the Panama Canal took over eight years and the labor of more than 40,000 persons. About 5,600 workers died from accidents and disease. Here, the digging of the Gaillard Cut is shown. **How was the United States able to gain rights to the land for a canal?**

COOPERATIVE LEARNING

Organize students into several small groups. Have each group research U.S. relations with the Philippines during one of these time periods: immediately after the Spanish-American War; during World War I; during World War II; during the Cold War; and today. Have each group divide the tasks of gathering data, preparing summaries of the materials, providing a time line to accompany the summaries, and exhibiting the material in a class presentation.

Assign Chapter 36 *Cooperative Learning Activity* in the TCR.

Theodore Roosevelt wanted to build a canal across Panama, a province of Colombia. The United States, however, could not come to terms with Colombia.

In 1903, the United States supported a revolution by people in Panama against Colombia. The revolution was a success. The United States and Panama then signed a treaty in which Panama leased land to the United States to be used for building a canal. In 1914, the Panama Canal was opened. It shortened the route between the two oceans by nearly 7,000 miles, or 11,200 kilometers. The Colombians, however, were angry that the United States had interfered in their affairs.

The United States' interest in Latin America continued. Some countries there had financial and political troubles that led to riots. The United States wanted to protect its business investments. So, between 1912 and 1916, the government sent American soldiers to Nicaragua, the Dominican Republic, and Haiti to restore order.

Student Web Activity
Visit the *Human Heritage* Web site at **humanheritage.glencoe.com** and click on *Chapter 36— Student Web Activities* to find out more about U.S. colonies.

Section 4 Assessment

1. Why did President Monroe issue the Monroe Doctrine?
2. Why did the United States want a canal through Panama?

Critical Thinking

3. **Predicting Consequences** What might have happened if most European powers had not gone along with the Monroe Doctrine?

Graphic Organizer Activity

4. Draw this diagram, and use it to show some of the effects of the Spanish-American War.

SECTION 5 Effects of Imperialism

By 1914, European colonial powers, Japan, and the United States had brought about 85 percent of the world under their control. This had many benefits. Orderly governments were set up. Many local wars were stopped. Industry, agriculture, and transportation were developed. Hospitals and schools were built, and sanitation was improved. Western ideas about democracy and individual rights spread.

At the same time, however, imperialism brought about major problems. One was bitter feelings between colonists and colonizers. Most Europeans, North Americans, and Japanese thought they were better than the people in the colonies. Colonists were seldom allowed to hold high jobs in government, industry, or the armed forces. Often, they were not even allowed in city areas where Europeans and North Americans lived.

CHAPTER 36 RISE OF IMPERIALISM 593

Student Web Activity objectives, goals, and answers can be found at the *Chapter 36 Web Activity Lesson Plan* at **humanheritage.glencoe.com**

💾 Use **Interactive Tutor Self Assessment Software** to review Section 4.

Biography

The following videotape program is available from Glencoe to enrich Chapter 36:

- **Theodore Roosevelt: From Roughrider to Rushmore**

To find classroom resources to accompany this video, check the following home page:

A&E Television:
http://www.aetv.com

💾 Use the **Vocabulary Puzzle-Maker** to create crossword and word search puzzles.

ASSESS

Check for Understanding

Ask students to summarize the main points of the chapter, orally or in writing. Discuss the answers to the Section and Chapter Assessment questions.

Evaluate

Assign the Chapter 36 **Performance Assessment Activity** in the TCR.

Administer the **Chapter 36 Test** in the TCR. Testmaker available.

Section 4 Assessment Answers

1. to stop outside interference in Latin American countries
2. to enable its fleet to sail quickly between the Caribbean Sea and the Pacific Ocean
3. Answers will vary, but students could indicate that these nations might have waged war to gain control of certain Latin American countries.

4. Sample effects: U.S. acquisition of Puerto Rico, Guam, and the Philippine Islands; establishment of Cuba as a U.S. protectorate; recognition of the U.S. as a world power; construction of Panama Canal

Assign the Chapter 36 **Section 4 Quiz** in the TCR. Testmaker available.

Reteach

Assign the Chapter 36 **Reteaching Activity** in the TCR.

Enrich

Assign the Chapter 36 **Enrichment Activity** in the TCR.

CLOSE

Have students comment on the meaning of the following quotation by Theodore Roosevelt in terms of imperialism: "No nation can claim rights without acknowledging the duties that go with the rights."

Use **Interactive Tutor Self Assessment Software** to review Section 5.

The colonists resented this. They blamed the colonial powers for the loss of their land and for being forced to work on plantations and in factories. They disliked the colonial power for trying to change their customs, languages, and religions. These feelings helped nationalism to grow.

There was yet another problem. The scramble for colonies led to a great deal of competition among colonial powers. This, in turn, led to disputes that caused future wars.

Section 5 Assessment

1. What percent of the world was colonized by 1914?
2. What problems did the scramble for empires create for the colonial powers?

Critical Thinking

3. **Identifying Alternatives** If you were a colonist in the early 1900s, would you have tried to get a job in the colonial government or would you have tried to rebel? Explain.

Graphic Organizer Activity

4. Draw this diagram, and use it to weigh the benefits and drawbacks of imperialism.

Benefits	Drawbacks

Chapter Summary & Study Guide

1. Imperialism developed in the 1800s because of the growth of nationalism; the need for raw materials, new markets, and investment opportunities; and the belief among Europeans that they should spread their way of life.
2. By the early 1900s, European nations had carved up Africa, with only Ethiopia and Liberia remaining independent.
3. By the late 1800s, Great Britain controlled India, Russia was moving into central Asia, and foreign powers were competing for control of China.
4. By the early 1900s, Japan had become industrialized and was a powerful imperialist nation.
5. By 1900, Great Britain, France, Germany, and the United States controlled most of Southeast Asia and many islands in the Pacific.
6. In 1823, the United States issued the Monroe Doctrine to keep European nations from expanding their control into Latin America.
7. The United States became an imperialist power after winning Puerto Rico, Guam, and the Philippines from Spain in 1898 and building the Panama Canal in 1903.
8. While imperialism led to the development of orderly governments, industry, and social reforms, it also increased nationalism and dangerous competition for empires.

Self-Check Quiz
Visit the *Human Heritage* Web site at **humanheritage. glencoe.com** and click on *Chapter 36—Self-Check Quiz* to assess your understanding of this chapter.

594   UNIT 11 NATIONS AND EMPIRES

Section 5 Assessment Answers

1. about 85 percent
2. Sample problems: bitter feelings between colonists and colonizers, competition for empires, disputes paving the way to future wars
3. Answers will vary, but students should provide reasons for their feelings.

4. Answers will vary but should reflect the points listed in the text. You might ask students to decide whether the benefits of imperialism outweighed the drawbacks or vice versa.

    Assign the Chapter 36 **Section 5 Quiz** in the TCR. Testmaker available.

Using Key Terms

Imagine it is the late 1800s. Write a newspaper advertisement to encourage more British citizens to settle in colonies in Africa or Asia. Use the following words in your ad.

imperialism
sepoys
right of extraterritoriality

protectorate
spheres of influence
zaibatsu

Understanding Main Ideas

1. What were the main reasons for the rise of imperialism?
2. How did some Europeans get colonial territory from African chiefs?
3. What caused settlers to move into Transvaal after 1885?
4. How did the British gain control over India?
5. What was the purpose of the Open Door Policy?
6. Why did Commodore Perry go to Japan in 1853?
7. Why was the United States interested in Latin American countries in the early 1900s?
8. How did imperialism increase nationalism in the colonies?

Critical Thinking

1. Do you think nations would be as interested or less interested today in gaining control of the Suez Canal? Why?
2. If you had lived in the United States in 1823, how would you have felt about the Monroe Doctrine? Explain your answer.

3. Do you think attitudes about imperialism have changed from the 1800s to today? Explain.

Graphic Organizer Activity

Economics Create a diagram such as the one shown, and use it to demonstrate the pattern of trade that developed between imperialist nations and their colonies.

Geography in History

Human/Environmental Interaction
Changes took place in nations when colonial powers took them over. What specific changes in the growing of crops took place in India and China when they were colonized? Draw a poster showing how the growing of typical crops likely changed.

Using Your Journal

Review any details you may have noted about changes that happened in Africa and Asia in the late 1800s. Imagine you are living in a European colony in one of these regions. Write a diary entry explaining how you feel about colonization.

Bonus Test Question

In which era and country would this be true: Your new emperor has called for an "enlightened peace." He has forbidden certain hairstyles, called for all men to join the new army or navy, and told peasants they can live and work where they wish. (*the Meiji Restoration; Japan*)

Using Your Journal

Diary entries will vary. You might call on volunteers to share their diary entries with the class.

Geography in History

Answers will vary but could include the increase in opium and resulting conflicts, and other crops grown to meet foreign demand.

Assessment Answers

Using Key Terms

Advertisements will vary, but students should use all the key terms.

Understanding Main Ideas

1. the Industrial Revolution, nationalism, and the idea that western countries had a duty to "civilize" the world
2. African chiefs signed treaties they could not read.
3. Gold and diamonds were discovered there.
4. The British East India Company took over from the French.
5. to give all countries equal trading rights in China
6. to negotiate a treaty to open up trade and to protect shipwrecked American sailors
7. because it needed a way to protect its new territories and American business investments
8. The colonists disliked the colonial powers for trying to change their countries.

Critical Thinking

1. Answers will vary but students might say countries would be less interested because of other means of transportation.
2. Answers will vary.
3. Answers will vary, but students should give reasons.

Graphic Organizer Activity

Diagrams will vary, but should show that imperialist nations sent their manufactured goods to colonies while the colonies supplied the imperialist nations with raw materials and cash crops such as tea.

FOCUS

After reading the Around the World for Unit 11, your students will be able to:

1. cite geographic features that protected Tibetan independence until the 1900s.
2. explain how imperialism changed Tibetan history.
3. describe Tibetan resistance to Chinese rule.

Bellringer

Ask students to suggest an answer to this question: What is the world's highest plateau?

Motivational Activity

Refer students to the Around the World feature, and point out that Tibet is nicknamed "Rooftop of the World" because of its high elevations. Ask: What other unique features of Tibet can you identify in the pictures on pages 596–597? *(Sample responses: widespread practice of Buddhism, rugged landscape, presence of a nomadic culture, and so on.)*

TEACH

Geography: Location Tell students that for much of its history Tibet remained isolated from the world. Based on the map on page 596, have students name geographic features that prevented people from reaching Tibet. *(Himalayas, high elevations, etc.)*

TIBET

Bordered by towering mountains and dry plains, the Tibetan Plateau is the highest and one of the most isolated regions on earth. With an average elevation of 12,000 feet, people sometimes call it the "Rooftop of the World." For much of its 2,000-year history, Tibet's geography helped protect its independence. In the late 1800s and early 1900s, however, it became the target of Russian, British, and Chinese imperialism. To block Russian expansion, Great Britain recognized Chinese rights in Tibet. The agreement, signed in 1906, began a long struggle for Tibetan freedom. Tibetans resisted Chinese rule from the start and continue to resist it today.

Tibet covers an area roughly the size of western Europe. For China, it has long represented a land of untapped natural resources and a thinly populated region where some of China's huge population might settle.

Outside of Lhasa, nomads have occupied Tibet for much of its history. In remote areas, many Tibetans still live as their ancestors did, herding livestock such as horses, sheep, and goats. They load trade goods—salt, cheese, rugs, and other items—onto horses or yaks and travel along caravan routes as old as Tibet itself.

SPOTLIGHT ON: TIBET

Today the Tibetan people number about 6 million. The Chinese who have migrated into the region number about 7.5 million. Despite the strong Chinese presence, Tibetans still regard the 14th Dalai Lama, Tenzin Gyatso, as their head of state and spiritual leader.

Born to a peasant family on July 6, 1935, Tenzin Gyatso was recognized as the reincarnation of the 13th Dalai Lama at age two and was enthroned at age five. Since going into exile after the failed 1959 Tibet Revolution, the Dalai Lama has led a protest of Chinese rule based on the UN's Declaration of Human Rights.

In 1989, the Nobel Committee awarded the Dalai Lama the Peace Prize. When asked the source of his inspiration, he cited these verses from an 8th century Buddhist saint: *For as long as space endures/And for as long as living beings remain, Until then I may too abide/To dispel the misery of the world.*

the World

▼ Until 1959, the Dalai Lama, the religious and political leader of Tibet, lived in the Potala. Begun in the 1600s, this huge palace continues to dominate Lhasa with its size and beauty.

ommunist troops took over
1949, the new government
d its control of Tibet. When
tans rebelled in 1959, Chi-
ops brutally put down the
n. More than 100,000
s fled into Bhutan, Nepal,
ia. The present-day Dalai
ves in Dharamsala, India,
e leads
t for
inde-
ce. ▶

ne, Tibet developed into a *theocracy*, or
nent run by religious leaders. In the early
n estimated 500,000 Buddhist *lamas*, or
lived in Tibet. When the last Chinese
fell in 1911, monks such as the ones in
oto led the fight to push the Chinese from
an effort that succeeded
ort time. Today monks
e their religious studies. ▶

◀ Missionaries from India introduced Buddhism to Tibet around 620 A.D. and developed an alphabet for the Tibetan language. Legend says this Buddhist statue was brought to Lhasa, the capital of Tibet, in the early 600s by the bride of a Tibetan king.

Taking Another Look

1. How did Tibet's geography help protect its independence?
2. How did imperialism change the history of Tibet?

Hands-On Activity

Creating a Poster Design a poster that a group of Tibetan children living in Nepal might create in defense of Tibetan freedom.

597

ANSWERS TO TAKING ANOTHER LOOK

1. The mountains and dry plains that border Tibet hindered invasion while the high elevations and harsh weather of the Tibetan Plateau discouraged settlement.
2. Russia, China, and Britain all sought to add Tibet to their empires. To block Russian expansion, Great Britain recognized Chinese rights in Tibet. China then seized control of Tibet, triggering the start of a long struggle for Tibetan freedom.

Hands-On Activity

Posters will vary, but should show evidence of the way of life that Tibet refugees want to reclaim and protect. Posters might also include pictures of the Dalai Lama and/or quotes that he has made in defense of Tibetan freedom.

Answers and Analyses

1G   Geography

According to the map, the territory that became Utah was acquired in 1848 as part of the Mexican cession.

TEST-TAKING TIP

Remind students to identify the features of a map, using such aids as the legend, lines of latitude and longitude, and scales if they exist. In this case, the map identifies the outlines of present-day states, including that of Utah.

2B   History

Page 547 describes the relocation of Native Americans to reservations. Pages 548–549 describe the acquisition of new land and the establishment of new states, and pages 550–551 discuss the tensions that arose between the states. Therefore, through the process of elimination, B is the best answer.

TEST-TAKING TIP

Students can usually answer NOT and EXCEPT questions by association. A and C were definitely associated with western expansion, so they can be eliminated.

Standardized Test Practice

Directions: Choose the *best* answer to each of the following multiple choice questions. If you have trouble answering a question, use the process of elimination to narrow your choices. Write your answers on a separate piece of paper.

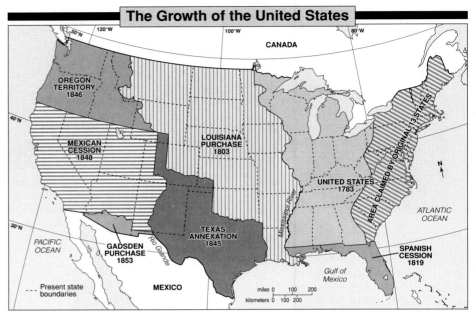

The Growth of the United States

1. According to the map above, in what year was the territory that includes present-day Utah acquired by the United States?

   F   1846
   G   1848
   H   1803
   J   1845

   Test-Taking Tip: This map uses *labels* as well as *symbols* to show the United States during different time periods. How are present state boundaries shown? (Make sure that you can identify all the state names on a map.)

2. The western movement of people in the United States after the American Revolution led to all of the following EXCEPT

   A   new states being added to the Union

   B   declining populations in east coast cities

   C   the relocation of Native Americans to reservations

   D   more tension between slave and non-slave states

   Test-Taking Tip: Be careful— overlooking the words NOT or EXCEPT on a multiple choice test is a common error. Look for the answer that is *not* true.

3. A difference between the American Revolution and the fight for independence in Haiti was that

- **A** Haiti's revolution was led by slaves
- **B** the revolution in Haiti did not involve fighting
- **C** Haiti was not seeking freedom from a European nation
- **D** the Haitian revolution was not successful

> **Test-Taking Tip:** Eliminate answers that you know are incorrect. For example, Haiti *was* seeking freedom from a European nation and the revolution *was* successful, so you can eliminate answers C and D.

4. Even though Napoleon took away many rights from the French citizens, they made him emperor of France. Why?

- **F** The citizens of France feared Napoleon.
- **G** The French no longer wanted a monarch.
- **H** The Pope approved of making Napoleon emperor.
- **J** Napoleon brought peace and order to France.

> **Test-Taking Tip:** This question requires you to remember a *fact* about Napoleon. Napoleon was a strong leader who preserved some rights (trial by jury, freedom of religion) but took away others (freedom of speech and the press). Remember, more than one answer may seem correct. Choose the answer that *best* fits the question. For instance, although Napoleon jailed many people whom he considered to be his enemies, he was still a very popular figure in France. He was not made emperor out of fear. Therefore, you can eliminate choice F.

5. Socialists believe that equality among people can only be achieved by

- **A** giving all adults the right to vote
- **B** letting the poor own land
- **C** making all land and factories publicly owned
- **D** electing a strong monarch

> **Test-Taking Tip:** *Socialism* is one of the many political movements that arose in Europe after the end of Napoleon's Grand Empire. As you study this time period, you may want to make a chart to compare these movements. They include: *liberalism, nationalism, socialism, utopian socialism,* and *communism.*

6. In the late 1800s, European nations began to set up colonies in foreign lands again. All of the following were reasons for imperialism EXCEPT the

- **F** need for more raw materials
- **G** desire of nations to gain more power
- **H** supposed duty to spread Christianity
- **J** need to bring more workers to Europe

> **Test-Taking Tip:** Remember, three of the answer choices for this question will be *true.* Look for the *exception.* For instance, would setting up colonies probably increase or decrease a nation's power? Most likely it would increase it. Therefore, you can eliminate choice G.

3A History

Since the revolt did involve fighting, was successful, and sought freedom from a European nation, choices B, C, and D can be eliminated. The top of page 553 states that Toussaint-L'Ouverture *led a revolt of enslaved people.*

4J History

According to page 563, *Because Napoleon brought peace and order, he was very popular.*

5C Economics

According to page 568, the socialists *wanted to end private ownership of land and factories. They believed the state, or the people as a whole, should own all means of production.* This information best supports choice C.

THE PRINCETON REVIEW | TEST-TAKING TIP

Important terms such as the names of political movements are often tested on standardized exams. Help your students to learn them by keeping a running glossary of new terms on the side of the board.

6J Economics

Page 579 mentions the need for raw materials. Page 580 discusses the desire to increase the country's power and to spread Christianity and civilization. Therefore, choices F, G, and H can be eliminated. The best answer is J.

Tested Objectives	
Questions	**Reading Objective**
1, 2	Analyze information
3	Make comparisons
4	Make inferences and generalizations
5	Identify supporting ideas
6	Determine cause and effect

OVERVIEW

Unit 12 discusses the major developments of the twentieth century—generally a period of turmoil marked by two global wars and the new world order.

➤ **Chapter 37** focuses on World War I and II, and the period between these wars.

➤ **Chapter 38** deals with the relationship between western countries and Communist powers after World War II and struggles in South Asia, Africa, Latin America, and the Middle East.

➤ **Chapter 39** describes the collapse of communism in Eastern Europe, the breakup of the Soviet Union, and the challenges facing the world today.

UNIT OBJECTIVES

After reading Unit 12, your students will be able to:

1. explain how World Wars I and II changed Western Europe.

2. explain how communism came into power in Russia and China.

3. describe world events during the cold war era.

4. discuss the end of communism in major areas.

5. summarize the problems facing the world in the twenty-first century.

UNIT PROJECT

Have students contact recent immigrants to their community and ask them to attend a "Cultural Exchange Day" program at school. Ask guests to discuss the cultures of their home countries, emphasizing their customs, music, food, and occupations. In preparation, have students develop questions for visitors.

Have students write a summary of what they learn.

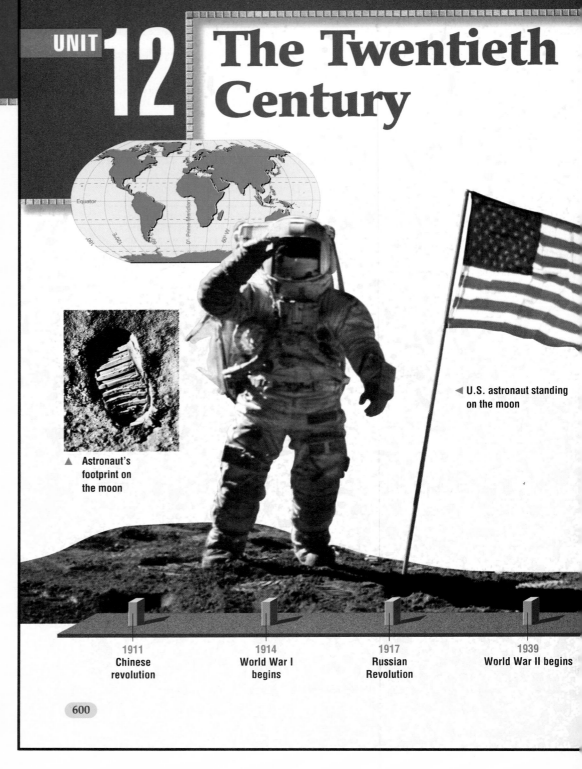

UNIT **12** The Twentieth Century

◄ **U.S. astronaut standing on the moon**

▲ **Astronaut's footprint on the moon**

| 1911 Chinese revolution | 1914 World War I begins | 1917 Russian Revolution | 1939 World War II begins |

600

ABOUT THE UNIT OPENING

Examining Artifacts

Ask students what revolutionary scientific event these artifacts depict. *(landing of humans on the moon)* Discuss with students what they might infer about the role of the United States in the 20th century. *(that it was a leading power)* Explain that this unit covers the sweeping changes that took place during the 1900s and shaped the 21st century world in which students live.

Global Chronology

Ask students what the events on the time line suggest about the world's state during the twentieth century. *(Answers will vary but should indicate that it was a time of conflict and change.)* According to the time line, how many years after the Chinese revolution was the People's Republic of China established? *(38 years)* Ask students which year was the "Year of Africa." *(1960)*

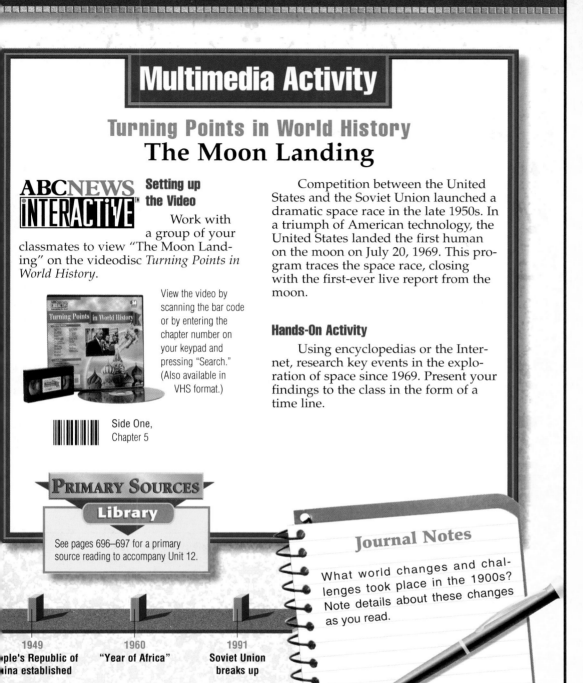

Multimedia Activity

Turning Points in World History
The Moon Landing

Setting up the Video

Work with a group of your classmates to view "The Moon Landing" on the videodisc *Turning Points in World History*.

View the video by scanning the bar code or by entering the chapter number on your keypad and pressing "Search." (Also available in VHS format.)

Side One, Chapter 5

Competition between the United States and the Soviet Union launched a dramatic space race in the late 1950s. In a triumph of American technology, the United States landed the first human on the moon on July 20, 1969. This program traces the space race, closing with the first-ever live report from the moon.

Hands-On Activity

Using encyclopedias or the Internet, research key events in the exploration of space since 1969. Present your findings to the class in the form of a time line.

PRIMARY SOURCES
Library

See pages 696–697 for a primary source reading to accompany Unit 12.

1949
ple's Republic of ina established

1960
"Year of Africa"

1991
Soviet Union breaks up

Journal Notes

What world changes and challenges took place in the 1900s? Note details about these changes as you read.

601

GLENCOE
TECHNOLOGY

VIDEODISC
Use the MindJogger to preview the unit content.

MindJogger Videoquiz

Unit 12
Disc 2 Side A

Also available in VHS.

INTRODUCING THE UNIT

Write these headings on the board and ask students to list changes that have occurred since 1900: Technology *(cars, airplanes, computers)*, Economics *(international trade)*, Environment *(acid rain, greenhouse effect, ozone depletion, toxic waste)*, Culture *(cross-cultural movies and music, human-rights movements)*. Write student responses on the board. Explain that in Unit 12 students will learn how these and other changes have helped create a new world order in an increasingly interdependent world.

RECORDING JOURNAL NOTES

Ask students to name major changes and challenges that have occurred in the world since they were born. Write their responses on the board. Explain that these are the types of things students should note in their journals as they read Unit 12.

PRIMARY SOURCES
Library

Items in the Primary Sources Library for this unit focus on the end of apartheid in South Africa.

For additional primary source documents, use the **World History Primary Source Document CD-ROM**.

Geographic Location

Have students note that the geographic location of this unit encompasses all parts of the earth but will focus on the Eastern Hemisphere. Explain that the technological and economic changes that have taken place and common environmental problems that face us in the twentieth century have affected all places in the world. The world has become a global village.

Chapter 37 Planning Guide

Objectives	Reproducible Resources	Multimedia Resources
Section 1 **World War I** Discuss the causes, events, and results of World War I.	📁 Reproducible Lesson Plan 📁 Chapter 37 Vocabulary and Guided Reading Activity 📁 Reading Essentials and Study Guide 37-1 📁 Chapter 37 Geography and Map Activity 📁 Section 1 Quiz 📁 Unit 12 Hands-On History Lab	💾 Vocabulary PuzzleMaker 💾 Interactive Tutor Self-Assessment Software 💾 ExamView® Pro Testmaker 📁 Glencoe Skillbuilder Interactive Workbook, Level 1
Section 2 **Between the Wars** Describe how communism developed in Russia.	📁 Reproducible Lesson Plan 📁 Reading Essentials and Study Guide 37-2 📁 Chapter 37 Enrichment Activity 📁 Section 2 Quiz	🖥 Teaching Transparency and Activity 37B 💾 Vocabulary PuzzleMaker 💾 Interactive Tutor Self-Assessment Software 💾 ExamView® Pro Testmaker 📁 Glencoe Skillbuilder Interactive Workbook, Level 1
Section 3 **World War II** Examine why Italy and Germany became dictatorships, and identify the causes and effects of World War II.	📁 Reproducible Lesson Plan 📁 Reading Essentials and Study Guide 37-3 📁 Chapter 37 Cooperative Learning Activity 📁 Chapter 37 Activity Book Activity 📁 Chapter 37 Chart and Graph Skill Activity 📁 Unit 12 World Literature Reading 1 📁 Section 3 Quiz	🔗 ABCNEWS INTERACTIVE Turning Points in World History 🖥 Teaching Transparency and Activity 37A 💾 Vocabulary PuzzleMaker 💾 Interactive Tutor Self-Assessment Software 💾 ExamView® Pro Testmaker 📁 Glencoe Skillbuilder Interactive Workbook, Level 1
Chapter 37 **Review and Evaluation**	📁 Chapter 37 Reteaching Activity 📁 Chapter 37 Performance Assessment Activity 📁 Spanish Chapter Summary and Glossary 📁 Chapter 37 Test	💾 Vocabulary PuzzleMaker 💾 Interactive Tutor Self-Assessment Software 📁 Glencoe Skillbuilder Interactive Workbook, Level 1 🎧 Audiocassettes* 💾 ExamView® Pro Testmaker

*Also available in Spanish.

Presentation Plus!

Use Glencoe's **Presentation Plus!** multimedia teacher tool to easily present dynamic lessons that visually excite your students. Using Microsoft® PowerPoint, you can customize the presentations to create your own personalized lessons.

 Interactive Lesson Planner

Planning has never been easier! Using this CD-ROM, organize your week, month, semester, or year with all the help you need. The **Interactive Lesson Planner** gives you access to all of the blackline masters which accompany *Human Heritage*.

✓ PERFORMANCE ASSESSMENT ACTIVITIES

Letters to the Editor   Ask students to imagine they live in one of these countries after World War I: Italy, Germany, the Soviet Union, France, or Great Britain. Have them write a letter to a newspaper editor expressing their opinions about their country's post-war situation. In their letters, students should describe their identity, such as "I am a young, unmarried woman who wants a university education," or "I am a middle-aged, male farmer." Collect the letters and read them aloud.

CHAPTER RESOURCES

LITERATURE ABOUT THE PERIOD

Hemingway, Ernest. *The Sun Also Rises.* Scribner's, 1926. A novel about English and American expatriates in France and Spain after World War I.

READINGS FOR THE STUDENT

Frank, Anne. *The Diary of a Young Girl.* Doubleday, 1972. First-person account of a young Jewish girl and her family who spent years during World War II hiding from the Nazis.

Ryan, Cornelius. *The Longest Day.* Simon & Schuster Pocket Books, 1984. Detailed account of D-Day and the Normandy invasion.

READINGS FOR THE TEACHER

Tuchman, Barbara W. *The Guns of August.* Macmillan, 1962. Account of the crucial first six weeks of World War I.

KEY TO ABILITY LEVELS

Teaching strategies have been coded for varying learning styles and abilities.

L1 Level 1 activities are **basic** activities and should be within the ability range of all students.

L2 Level 2 activities are **average** activities and should be within the ability range of the average to above-average student.

L3 Level 3 activities are **challenging** activities designed for the ability range of above-average students.

ELL ELL activities should be within the ability range of English Language Learning students.

NATIONAL GEOGRAPHIC SOCIETY

Teacher's Corner

INDEX TO NATIONAL GEOGRAPHIC MAGAZINE

The following articles relate to this chapter:

- "The Last Dive," by Priit J. Vesilind, October 1999.
- "The Battle of Midway," by Thomas B. Allen, April 1999.
- "Catherine the Great," by Erla Zwingle, September 1998.
- "Our Man in China," by Mike Edwards, January 1997.
- "Hiroshima," by Ted Gup, August 1995.
- "Blueprints for Victory," by John F. Shupe, May 1995.

ADDITIONAL NATIONAL GEOGRAPHIC SOCIETY PRODUCTS

To order the following, call National Geographic at 1-800-368-2728:
- *PicturePack: World War I Era (Transparencies)*
- *PictureShow: World War I Era (CD-ROM)*
- *PicturePack: World War II Era (Transparencies)*
- *PictureShow: World War II Era (CD-ROM)*
- *Russia's Last Tsar (Video)*
- *20th-Century History Series (3 videos)*

Access *National Geographic*'s new dynamic MapMachine Web site and other geography resources at:

http://www.nationalgeographic.com
http://www.nationalgeographic.com/maps/

  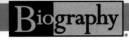

THE HISTORY CHANNEL.

The following videotape programs are available from Glencoe:

- **Biography: Anne Frank**
  0-7670-1409-X
- **The Decision to Drop the Bomb**
  1-56501-600-9
- **Joseph Stalin**
  1-56501-820-6
- **The Last Days of World War II**
  1-56501-536-3
- **V-J Day: The Day That Changed the World**
  0-7670-0202-4
- **World War II: The War Chronicles**
  1-56501-484-7

To order, call Glencoe at 1-800-334-7344. To find classroom resources to accompany many of these, check:

A&E Television: http://www.aetv.com
The History Channel: http://www.historychannel.com

OVERVIEW

Chapter 37 discusses international affairs during the twentieth century from World War I through World War II.

➤ **Section 1** discusses World War I, focusing on its underlying causes, significant campaigns, and impact.

➤ **Section 2** describes the origins and impact of communism, and traces the rise of dictatorships in Italy and Germany.

➤ **Section 3** analyzes the causes, events, and results of World War II.

CHAPTER OBJECTIVES

After reading Chapter 37, students will be able to:

1. discuss the causes, events, and results of World War I.

2. describe how communism developed in Russia.

3. explain reasons Italy and Germany became dictatorships.

4. trace the course and outcome of World War II.

EXAMINING ARTIFACTS

Ask students what these artifacts tell them about World War I. *(Students might mention the weapons, the faceless soldiers, the involvement of women in war plants, etc.)* Then refer students to the time line. Have them name other events that shook the first half of the 20th century.

PERFORMANCE ASSESSMENT ✓

Use the Performance Assessment activities on page 602B to help you to evaluate students as they complete the chapter.

602

CHAPTER
37

Conflict and Change
1900 A.D.–1945 A.D.

▲English poster

◄ Allied sol▶
from Worl▶

1914	1917	1929	1939	1945
World War I begins	**Russian Revolution**	**Worldwide depression**	**World War II begins**	**First atomic bomb dropped on Japan**

602 UNIT 12 THE TWENTIETH CENTURY

TEACHING RESOURCES

TEACHER PLANNING AND SUPPORT

- Reproducible Lesson Plan
- Block Scheduling Implementation Guide
- Videodisc Bar Code Correlation
- Presentation Plus!

REVIEW AND REINFORCEMENT

- Reading Essentials and Study Guide 37-1, 37-2, 37-3
- Chapter 37 Vocabulary and Guided Reading Activity
- Vocabulary PuzzleMaker Software
- Teaching Transparencies 37A & 37B

- Chapter 37 Reteaching Activity
- Chapter 37 Cooperative Learning Activity
- Chapter 37 Activity Book Activity
- Chapter 37 Chart and Graph Skill Activity
- Interactive Tutor Self-Assessment Software
- Unit 12 MindJogger VideoQuiz

APPLICATION AND HANDS-ON ACTIVITIES

- Daily World History, Geography, and Culture Question
- Unit 12 Hands-On History Lab Activity

Chapter Focus

Read to Discover

- What the causes, events, and results of World War I were.
- How communism developed in Russia.
- Why Italy and Germany became dictatorships.
- What the causes, events, and results of World War II were.

Chapter Overview

Visit the *Human Heritage* Web site at **humanheritage.glencoe.com** and click on **Chapter 37— Chapter Overviews** to preview this chapter.

Terms to Learn	People to Know	Places to Locate
mobilize	Franz Ferdinand	Sarajevo
armistice	Woodrow Wilson	Pearl Harbor
soviets	Nicholas II	Hiroshima
dictatorship	Vladimir Lenin	Nagasaki
appeasement	Joseph Stalin	
genocide	Adolf Hitler	
Holocaust	Winston Churchill	

Why It's Important The first half of the 1900s was a period of turmoil throughout the world. In 1914, a war broke out in Europe that soon grew to be World War I. Although it ended in 1918, anger over the peace settlement and poor economic conditions following the war led to World War II. The same period also saw the rise of communism in Russia and neighboring countries.

SECTION 1 World War I

For almost 100 years after Napoleon's defeat, no long, general European war developed. By the early 1900s, however, rivalries among the countries of Europe were causing trouble.

Background By the early 1900s, tension grew between several countries. France was jealous of Germany because it was industrializing rapidly. Great Britain did not like Germany expanding its navy. Russia involved itself with the problems of the Slavic peoples in Austria-Hungary.

Each European country built up its armed forces and made alliances with other nations. They each promised to help the others in their alliance if they were attacked. Thus, trouble between any two nations of different alliances could draw in many countries. A small war could easily grow into a large one. All that was needed was a spark.

CHAPTER 37 CONFLICT AND CHANGE   **603**

HISTORY
Online

Chapter Overview introduces students to chapter content and key terms. Have them access **Chapter 37 Overview** at **humanheritage.glencoe.com**

FOCUS

📶 Bellringer

Write the following on the board: *List two good things and two bad things about nationalism.*

Motivational Activity

Have students share their responses about nationalism. Point out that in the early 1900s nationalism created an atmosphere in which a simple incident could have serious consequences. Explain that the direct cause of World War I was the tension created by strong nationalist feelings in Austria-Hungary and Serbia. Tell students that in this chapter they will learn about other causes of conflicts in the first half of the 1900s.

GUIDE TO READING

Reading Strategy

Ask students to read "Why It's Important" and summarize the chapter's main theme. (*The first half of the 1900s was shaped by two world wars and the rise of communism.*)

Vocabulary Precheck

Ask students to define each of the "Terms to Learn." Have a volunteer consult the dictionary for any unfamiliar words. **L1** **ELL**

💾 Use the Vocabulary PuzzleMaker for Chapter 37 to create a crossword puzzle. **L1**

📁 Assign Chapter 37 Vocabulary and Guided Reading Activity.

📁 Assign Reading Essentials and Study Guide 37-1.

GEOGRAPHY ACTIVITIES

📁 Chapter 37 Geography and Map Activity
📁 Social Studies Outline Map Resource Book

INTERDISCIPLINARY CONNECTIONS

📖 Unit 12 World Literature Reading 1
🎨 World History & Art Transparency 37, *I Want You for the U.S. Army*
📗 Focus on World Art Print 23, *The Human Condition 1*
🎵 World Music: Cultural Traditions

ENRICHMENT AND EXTENSION

 Turning Points in World History
World History Primary Source Document Library CD-ROM

📁 Chapter 37 Enrichment Activity
📁 Foods Around the World

ASSESSMENT AND EVALUATION

📁 Chapter 37 Performance Assessment Activity
📁 Chapter 37 Section Quizzes 37-1, 37-2, 37-3
📁 Chapter 37 Test
💿 Chapter 37 ExamView® Testmaker Pro Software
🎧 Chapter 37 Digests Audiocassettes Activities and Tests

SPANISH RESOURCES

📁 Chapter 37 Spanish Chapter Summary and Glossary
🎧 Chapter 37 Spanish Chapter Digests Audiocassettes Activities and Tests

Guided Practice

L1 **Geography: Location** On an outline map of the world, have students show the locations of the Central and the Allied Powers. Then ask: How did the Central Powers get their name? *(They were located between Allied countries.)* What problem did the Central Powers' location pose? *(They had to fight on two fronts: east and west.)* **ELL**

☑ **Reading Check Answer**
Russia began to **mobilize** for war because Austria declared war on Serbia.

☑ **Reading Check Answer**
World War I was the first war in which **civilians** were attacked.

☑ **Reading Check Answer**
In **trench warfare,** opposing armies fight from trenches dug in the ground.
To get at the enemy, soldiers had to climb out of trenches and run across open land under heavy **artillery** fire.

ABCNEWS INTERACTIVE™

VIDEODISC
Turning Points in World History

Side Two
Chapter 4

Title: *Assassination Ignites World War I*
Ask: Why did the assassination of the archduke plunge Europe into war? *(A web of European alliances caused most major nations to declare war.)*

☑ **Reading Check**
Why did Russia **mobilize** for war?

☑ **Reading Check**
Why was World War I different from other wars for **civilians?**

☑ **Reading Check**
What is **trench warfare?**
Why did **artillery** fire claim so many lives?

The spark for World War I was provided at Sarajevo (sahr uh yē vō), a small town in Austria-Hungary. There, in June 1914, a teenager named Gavrilo Princip shot and killed Archduke Franz Ferdinand, heir to the throne of Austria-Hungary. Princip belonged to a secret nationalist group called the Black Hand. This group wanted the Serbs ruled by Austria-Hungary to be ruled by Serbia (ser' bē uh).

Austria-Hungary blamed the Serbian government for the Archduke's death and declared war on Serbia. Russia, an ally of Serbia, began to **mobilize,** or call up its troops, to go to Serbia's aid. Germany then showed its support of Austria-Hungary by declaring war on Russia. Shortly after, France and Great Britain entered the war on the side of Russia. So did Japan and, later, Italy and China. The Ottoman Empire, on the other hand, decided to support Germany and Austria-Hungary. Together, Germany, Austria-Hungary, the Ottoman Empire, and Bulgaria were called the Central Powers. Russia, Serbia, France, Great Britain, Japan, Italy, and China were called the Allied Powers.

From 1914 to 1918 World War I, also called the Great War, was different from any earlier war. It was the first war where **civilians** (suh vil' yuhnz), or people who are not soldiers, were also attacked. The war grew so large that 31 countries, with 65 million soldiers, took part. Although most land fighting took place in Europe, the Middle East, and Africa, naval warfare took place all over the world.

There was also a new technology of frightening weapons. Machine guns fired bullets one after another at a rapid speed. Huge guns fired shells more than 75 miles, or 120 kilometers. Some airplanes carried bombs behind enemy lines and dropped them on enemy cities. Submarines attacked ships at sea. Poison gases were used. Tanks and flame throwers were introduced.

Much of the fighting took place on the western front, the zone between France and Germany. There, opposing armies dug themselves into the ground in trenches protected by barbed wire. This kind of fighting is called **trench warfare.** To get at the enemy, each side had to climb out of its trenches and cross open land under **artillery** (ar til' uhr ē), or mounted gun, fire. The casualties were enormous. One battle alone cost 900,000 lives. In another area, French and German soldiers engaged in trench warfare for ten months.

On the eastern front, the Russian Empire suffered heavy losses. Some 3.8 million soldiers were killed in just the first ten months of the war. In 1918, after two revolutions, Russia withdrew and signed a separate peace treaty with Germany having recognized Ukraine as an independent country. The Russians gave up huge areas of land previously conquered by them. Located

604 UNIT 12 THE TWENTIETH CENTURY

COOPERATIVE LEARNING

Have students research and report on the first six weeks of World War I. Assign each of five groups one of the following: invasion of Belgium, German sweep through France to Paris, retreat of the Allies, Russian mobilization and early victories ending at Tannenberg, and the Battle of the Marne. Students should work in pairs, each student gathering specific information on a specific topic. Then have each group present its report to create a composite picture.

Student Web Activity

Visit the *Human Heritage* Web site at **humanheritage.glencoe.com** and click on *Chapter 37— Student Web Activities* to find out more about World War I.

TRENCH WARFARE   Much of the fighting of the First World War was carried out from trenches. Men had to charge across "no man's land," the open area in front of the enemy's trenches, in order to attack. Machine guns made these attacks especially dangerous. **Where was the western front located?**

to the west of Russia, these lands included one third of their farmland, one third of their population, and almost all of their resources of coal, iron, and oil.

In the meantime, German submarines tried to stop supply ships to Great Britain and France. In 1917, after the submarines sank American ships with civilians on board, the United States declared war on Germany. Until then, the United States had tried to stay out of the conflict.

The United States sent 2 million fresh troops to Europe to aid the tired Allied forces. The Americans helped to bring a quick end to the war, in favor of the Allied Powers. On November 11, 1918, Germany and its allies agreed to an **armistice** (ar′ muh stis), or a stop in the fighting.

The Great War was over. It had cost the lives of over 13 million soldiers and 17 million civilians. Another 20 million soldiers had been wounded, and billions of dollars in damage to property had been done.

Making the Peace   Woodrow Wilson, the President of the United States, had drawn up a peace plan called the Fourteen Points. Wilson believed that national groups in Europe should have the right to form their own countries. He wanted to reduce **armaments** (ar′ muh muhnts), or equipment for war. Above all,

Reading Check How did the arrival of American troops help bring about an **armistice?**

Reading Check What did Woodrow Wilson want nations to do with their **armaments?**

CAPTION ANSWER

between France and Germany

Reading Check Answer American troops relieved Allied forces, forcing Germany to agree to an **armistice.**

Reading Check Answer Woodrow Wilson wanted nations to reduce their **armaments.**

 VIDEODISC Lessons of War

 Side One Chapter 5

Frames: 11214-15727
Title: *How Wars Begin— World War I*
Subject: Exploration of the reasons behind war, specifically World War I.
Ask: What did Austria-Hungary want to acquire? Who helped them accomplish this? *(Serbian territory; Germany)*

EXTENDING THE CONTENT

On the eastern front, Russia was ill-equipped and badly led. Before Lenin's new government signed the Treaty of Brest-Litovsk, more than two million Russians had been killed. In Turkey, the failing Ottoman Empire still controlled the Dardanelles. Mines in the water and on-shore artillery kept the Russians blockaded in their Black Sea ports. At Gallipoli in 1915, an Allied force failed in its attempt to land on the Turkish coast and march to Constantinople. British, New Zealand, Australian, and French troops suffered terrible losses against the Turks and Germans.

Then... & Now

Remembering Veterans November 11, 1918—the day World War I ended—is a time when members of the armed services are honored in many of the former Allied countries. Once called Armistice Day, since 1954 it has been called Veterans Day in the United States. It is Remembrance Day in Canada and Armistice Day in Britain.

he wanted a world association of nations to keep the peace. The British, French, and Italian leaders, however, had other plans. They wanted repayment for their losses during the war from the defeated countries.

The peace treaty that Germany signed after World War I was called the Treaty of Versailles (vuhr sī'). This treaty put most of the blame for the war and the financial repayment on Germany, for which the Germans were very angry. Under this treaty, Germany lost land in Europe and overseas. Alsace and Lorraine, which Germany had taken from France in 1870, were returned to France. Some of Germany's eastern territory became part of the reestablished nation of Poland. Germany's African colonies were divided between France and Great Britain, while its Pacific colonies were given to Japan.

Under the Treaty of Versailles, Russia lost even more territory than Germany did. Part of the Russian territory was lost to Poland and Romania, and part of it became the new nations of Finland, Estonia, Latvia, and Lithuania. Ukraine's desire for independence, however, was ignored.

The treaty did not deal with the needs of some other countries, however. India and people in Southeast Asia who had supported the Allied Powers wanted independence from Great Britain and France. Their wishes were ignored. Over the next 30 years, serious troubles developed in all these areas.

The other Central Powers were dealt with in separate treaties. Austria-Hungary was broken up, and four new countries—Austria,

TREATY OF VERSAILLES The Treaty of Versailles was signed in June, 1919, at the palace of Versailles outside Paris. Only the Allied Powers took part in the negotiations. Germany was not allowed to participate. Here, the Allied leaders meet in the Hall of Mirrors. **How was Germany affected by the Treaty of Versailles?**

Reading Check What is a **mandate?** What type of policy does an **isolationist** country follow?

Hungary, Czechoslovakia, and Yugoslavia—were created. France received a **mandate** (man'dāt), or right to rule, in Syria and Lebanon. Great Britain received mandates in Iraq and Palestine.

For the most part, President Wilson's peace plan was not followed. However, one point was kept. An organization called the League of Nations was established so the countries of the world could come together to talk over their troubles. Most hoped the League could help prevent future wars. But the League had a serious weakness—it had no army of its own. If a country did not want to obey the League, it could not be forced to do so. The League was also weak because the United States refused to become a member. Many Americans disagreed with the World War I treaties. After 1919, the United States became an **isolationist** country. It decided to stay out of European affairs and world problems.

MAP STUDY

REGIONS The map of Europe changed a great deal after World War I. Some countries disappeared, while several new ones appeared. **Which part of Europe was most changed?**

DID YOU KNOW

After World War I, Germany's economy was especially hard-hit. High inflation caused the country's paper currency to be worthless and many people used it to light their stoves.

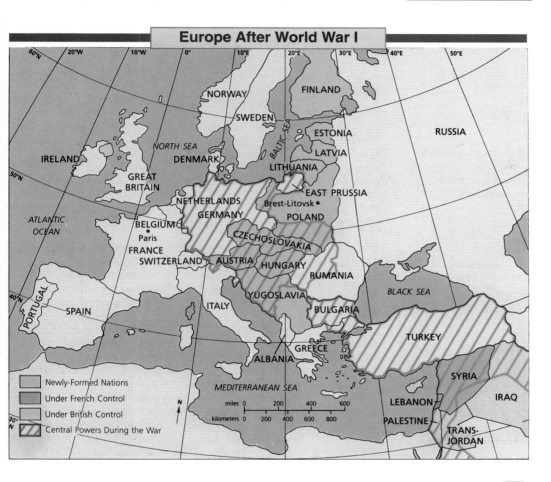

Europe After World War I

- Newly-Formed Nations
- Under French Control
- Under British Control
- Central Powers During the War

NORWAY, SWEDEN, FINLAND, ESTONIA, LATVIA, LITHUANIA, RUSSIA, NORTH SEA, IRELAND, DENMARK, GREAT BRITAIN, NETHERLANDS, EAST PRUSSIA, Brest-Litovsk, GERMANY, POLAND, BELGIUM, Paris, FRANCE, CZECHOSLOVAKIA, SWITZERLAND, AUSTRIA, HUNGARY, RUMANIA, ATLANTIC OCEAN, PORTUGAL, SPAIN, ITALY, YUGOSLAVIA, BULGARIA, BLACK SEA, ALBANIA, GREECE, TURKEY, MEDITERRANEAN SEA, SYRIA, LEBANON, IRAQ, PALESTINE, TRANS-JORDAN, BALTIC SEA

miles 0 200 400 600
kilometers 0 200 400 600 800

CHAPTER 37 CONFLICT AND CHANGE **607**

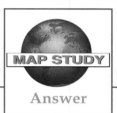

MAP STUDY

Answer

the eastern part

Assign the Chapter 37 **Geography and Map Activity** in the TCR.

Glencoe Literature Library

The following novel from the **Glencoe Literature Library** may be used to enrich this chapter:
• *All Quiet on the Western Front,* by Erich Maria Remarque (Disillusionment after WWI.)

MEETING SPECIAL NEEDS

For those students needing extra reinforcement, encourage oral summaries of each section of the chapter. Students may be divided into small groups. Each group would then assign different sections of the chapter to pairs of students who would prepare the summaries. Have groups meet again to present the summaries.

📂 Refer to *Inclusion for the Middle School Social Studies Classroom: Strategies and Activities* for additional resources.

Section 1 Assessment

1. **Define:** mobilize, civilians, trench warfare, artillery, armistice, armaments, mandate, isolationist.
2. What made World War I different from earlier wars?
3. Why did the United States refuse to join the League of Nations?

Critical Thinking
4. **Identifying the Central Issue** Why do you think many Americans opposed United States membership in the League of Nations?

Graphic Organizer Activity
5. Draw this diagram, and use it to show the new nations created by the treaties ending World War I. (Add more answer circles as needed.)

✓ **Reading Check**
What happens to business during a **depression?**

Painting of Peter the Great

<SECTION 2> **Between the Wars**

The 1920s and 1930s were a difficult time for people everywhere. Most were trying to recover from the damage caused by World War I. Then, in 1929, a **depression,** or a sudden slowdown in business, began. People in many countries started to question their forms of government. In Germany, the people turned to a leader who would soon threaten world peace. People in Russia had overthrown their government and set up the world's first Communist nation.

Emerging Russia In Muscovy, the years following the death of Ivan the Terrible in 1584 were called the "Time of Troubles." There was much disorder in the country. The troubles ended in 1613 with the crowning of seventeen-year-old Michael Romanov (rō′ muh nahf) as czar. The Romanov dynasty ruled Russia until 1917.

The first great Romanov ruler was a grandson of Michael's, Peter the Great, who came to the throne in 1682. Determined to make Muscovy strong and modern, Peter disguised himself as a sailor and visited the capitals of various European countries. There he learned all he could of western ways.

When Peter returned home, he began reforming the country he named Russia. He started textile factories, built canals, and encouraged mining. He ordered a new capital, St. Petersburg, built on the Baltic Sea. Since St. Petersburg was an ice-free port, the country's trade by water with western Europe continued even in winter. Peter revised the alphabet and set up schools for the upper class. He trained a powerful army and also built the country's first navy. He even changed people's appearance. He ordered men to shave their beards and to wear European-style short jackets instead of long coats.

The next great Romanov ruler was Catherine the Great, who came to the throne in 1762. At first Catherine wanted to improve the condition of the peasants. She even considered abolishing serfdom. Then peasants in a newly conquered area of Ukraine rebelled. Soon after, the French Revolution broke out. These two events so frightened Catherine that she gave up her ideas of reform.

Catherine did not help the peasants, but she did make Russia much larger. In a number of wars, the country's borders were pushed farther east, west, and south.

Painting of Catherine the Great

The Road to Revolution

During the 1800s, there was a great deal of discontent in the Russian Empire. About 30 million serfs, one half of whom were owned by the czar, labored to support about one-half million nobles and clergy. The czar controlled what industry there was. All society suffered and students protested, peasants revolted, and workers staged strikes. In 1825 a group of army officers, inspired by the ideas of the French Revolution, rose up against the czar. The rebellion, however, was put down.

A period of strong government controls followed. Writers who ridiculed government leaders were not published. Some writers were exiled. Even so, ideas about freedom and reform spread.

In 1861 Czar Alexander II, who was trying to modernize the country and appear to be a fair ruler, freed the serfs. However, he did not give them land of their own. As a result, most became tenant farmers.

In 1905 another uprising took place. It began when thousands of workers appeared in the square before the czar's palace. They carried petitions asking for a national assembly, freedom of speech and religion, and better conditions for workers and peasants. Government soldiers fired on the crowd, killing hundreds of unarmed people. A general strike then broke out. Finally, Czar Nicholas II agreed to some of the workers' demands. He ignored the national assembly, however, and its plans for reform.

World War I only made Russia's problems worse. The country did not have enough factories to produce guns and ammunition or enough railroads to carry supplies to the front. As a result, it suffered higher casualties than any other country. Nearly 9 million soldiers were killed or wounded in battle. Civilians suffered from lack of food and fuel.

Photograph of Nicholas II

CHAPTER 37 CONFLICT AND CHANGE **609**

L1 **Government** Have students work in small groups to chart the major leaders of Russia and their achievements and/or their acts of oppression as described in this chapter. Guide a class discussion based on their charts. **ELL**

MAKING CONNECTIONS

➤➤ **Economics** Russia began industrializing in the 1890s. Among its achievements was the building of the Trans-Siberian Railroad. Its 5,500 miles (or 8,800 km) make this the longest railroad in the world.

DID YOU KNOW ??

In autumn of 1917, the Bolsheviks seized Nicholas II and his family. They were reported to have been shot on July 16, 1918, although some unconfirmed reports claim that he or members of his family escaped from Russia.

Biography

The following videotape program is available from Glencoe to enrich Chapter 37:

• **Nicholas & Alexandra**

To find classroom resources to accompany this video, check the following home page:

A&E Television:
http://www.aetv.com

COOPERATIVE LEARNING

Have students work in small groups to research and compare and contrast the daily lives of women who lived in Russia during the time of Peter the Great and Catherine the Great, and women who live in Russia today. Russian feminism of the past and feminism of the present reports could include topics such as type of work, family responsibilities, intellectual interests, and political concerns. Have groups plan how to conduct the research and report on the findings.

L3 **Language Arts** More adept readers may be interested in being exposed to the rich heritage of Russian literature. Poets such as Pushkin and novelists such as Tolstoy, Turgenev, and Dostoyevsky created works displaying a revolutionary style long before the Russian overthrow in 1917.

Glencoe Literature Library

The following novel from the **Glencoe Literature Library** may be used to enrich this chapter:
• *The Brothers Karamazov,* by Fyodor Dostoyevsky. (Russian life in the late 19th century.)

VIDEODISC
Turning Points in World History

Side Two
Chapter 5

Title: *The Russian Revolution*
Ask: Why was the Russian Revolution a turning point in history? *(It established a communist government.)*

LENIN   Lenin was a powerful speaker and was able to rally much support for the Communist cause. He ruled the Soviet Union until his death in 1924. **What did the Bolsheviks promise in order to gain support?**

At last the Russian people could stand no more. In March 1917, they revolted. Striking workers, led by women textile laborers, jammed the streets of St. Petersburg, which had been renamed Petrograd (pet' ruh grad). They demanded bread and peace. The workers were soon joined by the city's **garrison** (gar' uh suhn), or military group stationed in the area. Within a few days, the revolt spread throughout the country. Peasants took over the lands of nobles. Soldiers left the front and began walking home. The czar was forced to abdicate, and a temporary government was set up.

Reading Check
What action did the military **garrison** in St. Petersburg take toward striking workers?

Lenin   There was much confusion in the months following the overthrow of Nicholas II. A revolutionary group called Bolsheviks (bol' shuh viks) took advantage of this. Led by Vladimir Lenin (len' in), they gained the support of the **soviets,** or committees that represent workers and soldiers. The Bolsheviks promised land to the peasants and bread to the workers. They also promised to get Russia out of the war.

In November 1917, the Bolsheviks seized power from the temporary government. Lenin was chosen to lead the new government. Soon after, he signed a peace treaty with Germany that ended Russia's part in World War I. The treaty, however, did not end the troubles at home.

Reading Check
What were the **soviets?**

EXTENDING THE CONTENT

In their struggle for survival during the civil war in Russia in 1918, Lenin and the Bolsheviks had introduced an economic policy called war communism. Under war communism, the government carried out a policy of nationalization in which it brought under state control all major industries. Applying the principle that those who would eat must work, the government required everyone between the ages of 16 and 50 to hold a job. It also erected a huge bureaucratic administration that wielded tremendous power but was shown to be extremely inefficient.

From 1918 to 1920, Russia was divided by a civil war between the majority Bolsheviks—now known as Communists—and the minority Mensheviks (men' chuh viks), or non-Communists. The Communists were also called Reds, because red had been the color of revolution since the French Revolution. The non-Communists were called Whites.

The Whites received soldiers and supplies from other countries, including the United States. These countries were afraid that if the Reds won, communism would spread throughout Europe. The Russian people as a whole did not like the Communists. However, because they did not want to return to old ways, most of them supported the Reds and by 1921 the Whites had been defeated.

In 1922 the Union of Soviet Socialist Republics, or the Soviet Union, was formed. It was made up of four republics, the largest of which was Russia. By 1924 the Soviet Union was completely under the control of the Communist party.

Lenin died that same year. His body was embalmed and placed in a glass coffin inside a red marble tomb near the wall of Moscow's Kremlin. In his honor, Petrograd was renamed Leningrad.

Stalin After Lenin died, there was a struggle for power in the Soviet Union which lasted until 1928. In that year, Joseph Stalin (stah'lin) took control of the government. He also controlled the Communist party, which was the only political party allowed in the country.

Stalin wanted the Soviet Union to industrialize as quickly as possible. So he set up a series of Five-Year Plans. Their major goal was to build up **heavy industry,** or the manufacture of basic materials and machines. Under these plans, steel mills, power plants, oil refineries, and chemical plants were built and kept under government control. Workers were paid according to how much they produced. Factory managers had to turn out a certain quantity of goods. By 1939 the Soviet Union was a major industrial power. The people paid a price for industrialization. Workers labored long hours for low wages. Consumer goods, such as clothing and household goods, were poorly made and hard to find, and housing shortages were common.

Another goal of the Five-Year Plans was **collectivization** (kuh lek ti vuh zā' shuhn), or uniting small farms into large ones controlled by the government. On a collective, farmers were paid according to the number of days they worked. Collectivization allowed them to share tractors and other farm machinery. The government bought their crops at fixed prices and sold them abroad to buy machinery for factories.

Many peasants wanted to keep working on their own farms. They resisted collectivization by killing their horses, cows, and

People in History

Joseph Stalin
1879–1953

SOVIET DICTATOR

A shoemaker's son, Joseph Stalin spent his childhood in Georgia, a region south of Russia. He attended a religious school, where he was punished for reading about revolution. Stalin later adopted the ideas of Karl Marx. However, instead of doing away with government, as Marx had hoped, Stalin built an all-powerful state in which workers had little say.

☑ **Reading Check**
How did Stalin try to promote the growth of **heavy industry?** How did peasants react to **collectivization?**

L1 Critical Thinking Have students create cause-event-effect graphic organizers to help them understand how communism developed in Russia. Start with the events in the subsection "The Road to Revolution" and end with events in the subsection "Lenin." **ELL**

L2 Government Have students list the changes that occurred in farming and industry in the Soviet Union under Stalin's Communist rule. Ask students to compare the benefits and costs of such government rule. **ELL**

GEOGRAPHY AND HISTORY

In 1922, the four republics that made up the Union of Soviet Socialist Republics included Russia, Belorussia, Transcaucasia, and Ukraine. The Russian Republic was the largest and most powerful.

☑ **Reading Check Answer**
Stalin used a series of Five-Year Plans to promote the growth of **heavy industry.** Peasants resisted **collectivization** by killing their horses, cows, and pigs.

Biography

The following videotape program is available from Glencoe to enrich Chapter 37:

• **Joseph Stalin**

To find classroom resources to accompany this video, check the following home page:

A&E Television:
http://www.aetv.com

COOPERATIVE LEARNING

Organize the class into small groups. Have the groups create advertising campaigns to promote the Five-Year Plans set up by Stalin to bring industrial and agricultural production under government control. Have each group research its topic, create a campaign, and then select a spokesperson to present the campaign.

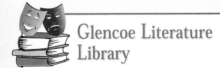
Answers will vary, but students should focus on the sweeping issues of the depression—unemployment, failed banks, homelessness, devalued money, skyrocketing prices—and their impact on people around the world.

L1 **Daily Life** Ask students to imagine that they are Soviet citizens under Stalin's rule. Have them write journal entries for a week, describing their everyday life in the Soviet Union. Encourage them to assume roles other than being a young person, for their writing. Have students share their journal entries. **ELL**

MAKING CONNECTIONS

➤➤ **Economics** More than half the farm animals in the Soviet Union were killed between 1929 and 1930. The unrest among the peasants kept them from working the land. The loss of crops led to a famine in which millions of people died.

Glencoe Literature Library

The following novels from the **Glencoe Literature Library** may be used to enrich this chapter:
- *And the Earth Did Not Devour Him,* by Tomás Rivera. (Migrant workers in the 1940s and 1950s.)
- *Where the Red Fern Grows,* by Wilson Rawls. (Ozarks in the Depression.)
- *Animal Farm,* by George Orwell. (Implications of totalitarianism.)

pigs. Those who refused to move were either shot or sent to labor camps in Siberia (sī bir′ ē uh), a frozen wilderness in the northeast. In Ukraine, Stalin caused famine to control the people. By 1936 most farms in the Soviet Union were collectivized.

The World Economy The worldwide depression that began in 1929 did not affect the Soviet Union. However, it affected most of the other industrialized countries. For this reason it was called the Great Depression. Factories closed and millions of people lost their jobs. By 1932 one out of four Americans and British and two out of five Germans were out of work. Banks failed and people lost their savings. People who had been put out of their homes lived in shacks built out of cardboard or tin. In Germany, prices skyrocketed. Money bought so little that people lit their stoves with it instead of using firewood.

Democracy or Dictatorship Some western countries, such as the United States and Great Britain, had a long tradition of stable, democratic government. Voters in these countries wanted to keep their government but felt it should do more to help the people.

Linking Across Time

News Media The invention of motion pictures with sound brought the news into the movie theaters of the 1930s and 1940s (below). Before the start of each "picture show," as movies were called, many theaters played *news reels*—short movies showing current events from around the world. Today, thanks to communication satellites, live coverage of the news can be sent directly into people's homes via television (right). **How did the Depression shape economic news in the 1930s?**

MULTICULTURAL PERSPECTIVES

Stalin insisted that Russian artists and writers create only works that glorified communism and Russian nationalism. For example, painters were to paint only portraits of Communist leaders or scenes from the Russian Revolution. Plays and books were supposed to encourage people to work harder. This style became known as Socialist realism. Artists and writers who violated these rules faced exile or imprisonment in labor camps. The Soviet government also banned foreign publications and jammed foreign radio broadcasts.

In the United States, President Franklin D. Roosevelt (roo' zuh velt) set up a program known as the New Deal. Two of its chief aims were relief and reform. To provide relief and put people back to work, the federal government set up several different agencies. One of these, the Civilian Conservation Corps (CCC), gave jobs mostly to young people. They planted trees and built small dams all over the United States. The Works Progress Administration (WPA) paid unemployed people to build roads, airports, bridges, and hospitals. It also provided work for artists and writers. The Tennessee Valley Authority (TVA) built dams that provided cheap electric power.

The federal government also planned long-range reform. Congress passed **social security laws** that provided money for elderly people and orphaned children. Many people, however, were not covered by these laws and did not receive help.

Other western countries, such as Germany and Italy, did not have a long tradition of stable, democratic government. Germany had only had an elected government since World War I. Many Germans thought their elected representatives spent too much time debating issues. They wondered if it might not be better to have one strong leader who could act quickly.

Italy was the first nation to become a **dictatorship** (dik tā' tuhr ship), or a country ruled by a single person with absolute authority. In 1922 Benito Mussolini (buh nēt' ō moo suh lē' nē), leader of the Fascist (fash'ist) Party, took over the Italian government.

Reading Check
What groups were helped by passage of **social security laws?**

Reading Check
What type of government is set up under a **dictatorship?**

UNEMPLOYMENT   The Great Depression caused many people who had lost their jobs to wait in long lines, hoping to get another. **What programs did the U.S. government offer to help the unemployed?**

Then... **& Now**

A Party Theme When Franklin D. Roosevelt ran for president in 1932, he adopted the song "Happy Days Are Here Again" as his campaign theme. The Democrats still play the song at their party's national convention.

L3 **Critical Thinking** The economic chaos created by World War I and the Great Depression caused nations such as Germany, Italy, Russia, and Japan to turn to dictators. Ask students how western democracies such as the United States, Great Britain, and France resisted such political change and solved their economic problems.

Reading Check Answer
Social security laws provided money for elderly people and orphaned children.

Reading Check Answer
A **dictatorship** sets up a government ruled by a single person with absolute authority.

CAPTION ANSWER

programs such as the Civilian Conservation Corps (CCC) and the Works Progress Administration (WPA)

MAKING CONNECTIONS

➤➤ **History** Mussolini was called *Il Duce*, meaning "the leader," by his followers. In 1945, he was court-martialed and shot. His body remained in an unmarked grave until 1957, when it was placed in his family's vault.

MEETING SPECIAL NEEDS

Have students who are visual learners investigate the artwork in Russia before communism and after Socialist realism took effect. Have them compare the themes, styles, and mediums of the artwork in the two periods. Have them write a brief report and, if possible, show examples of artwork from both time periods.

Refer to *Inclusion for the Middle School Social Studies Classroom: Strategies and Activities* for additional resources.

GEOGRAPHY AND HISTORY

The First Reich was the Holy Roman Empire in the Middle Ages. The Second Reich was the German Empire from 1871 to 1918.

ABCNEWS INTERACTIVE

VIDEODISC
Lessons of War

Side Two Chapter 11
Title: *The Enemy*
Subject: A discussion of the process of "demonization," which causes people to see their enemies as not being human.
Ask: Why is it important for governments to "dehumanize" the enemy?
(When the enemy is dehumanized, soldiers and others are justified in their killing of "monsters.")

614

Anne Frank Anne Frank, a Jewish teenager, kept a diary during the two years she and her family spent hiding from the Nazis in an attic room in Amsterdam. She was arrested in 1944 and sent to the Nazi death camp at Bergen-Belsen, where she died at age 15. Millions of people have read her account, *The Diary of a Young Girl,* first published in 1952.

NAZI RALLY   Adolf Hitler was an excellent speaker, and he used this skill to unite and gather support from the German people. The Nazis made impressive spectacles of huge rallies at which thousands of Germans would gather to listen to Hitler speak. **What political steps did Hitler take once he was in power in Germany?**

Reading Check
How did Hitler change German government once he became **chancellor?**

Reading Check
What did the **swastika** symbolize?

In 1933 Adolf Hitler became **chancellor,** or prime minister, of Germany. Before long, he did away with the German republic and set himself up as dictator. He called himself *Der Fuhrer* (dār fyū′ uhr), which means "the leader." He called Germany the Third Reich (rīk), which means the third empire. Hitler was supported by a violent political group called the National Socialist Party, or Nazis (nah′ tsēz). The Nazi symbol of identity was the **swastika** (swos′ tuh kuh), or hooked black cross. Many citizens of Germany were angry over the Treaty of Versailles. They saw Hitler as a leader who would make their country economically and politically strong.

Once Hitler was in power, he did away with all political parties except the Nazis. He had books about democracy burned. He took over the courts and set up a secret police. He took over the radio, the press, and abolished trade unions. He fought against the Christian churches.

Hitler blamed many of Germany's troubles on the Jews and others. The Nazis believed the Germans were a "master race." Jews were not part of the "master race." So the Nazis took away the Jews' businesses and jobs. Jews could not go to school or get medical care. They were no longer allowed to vote or to walk along the streets after eight o'clock. They had to wear a yellow six-pointed star on their clothing. This was only the beginning. Worse treatment was to come later.

614   UNIT 12 THE TWENTIETH CENTURY

EXTENDING THE CONTENT

German Jews had full rights of citizenship until the Nazis came to power. They were leaders in government, law, finance, medicine, and the arts. On November 9, 1938, however, the demonstrations against the Jews began. This night became known as *Kristallnacht,* translated "Crystal Night" or the "Night of Broken Glass." Mobs—and police—damaged Jewish shops and synagogues and sent 20,000 Jews to concentration camps. Hitler's goal was to eliminate all Jewish people in Europe. When Germany invaded the Soviet Union in 1941, the orders were to kill every Jew they could find. By the end of 1942, 2.5 million Jews had been brought to various camps and killed.

The Road to War   Soon Germany and its allies, Italy and Japan, began to threaten world peace. In 1935, the Italians, bitter about not getting enough land after World War I, invaded Ethiopia. The League of Nations was not able to stop them. Hitler announced that his goal was to unite all the German people. He sent German troops into the Rhineland, a disputed area, in 1936. Then, in March 1938 his army marched into Austria. Then he demanded that the Germans living in Czechoslovakia come under German rule. The British and the French were afraid of another war. So they decided to follow a policy of **appeasement,** or giving in to demands. They did nothing while Czechoslovakia was first divided and then made a part of Hitler's Germany in March 1939.

In Japan, the military who ran the country felt that Japan needed more land and natural resources to make its economy stronger. In 1931 Japan invaded Manchuria, in northern China. In 1937 Japanese troops invaded the main part of China. That same year, Japan signed a friendship treaty with Germany and Italy.

In August 1939, Germany and the Soviet Union signed a treaty agreeing not to attack each other. Now Hitler felt safe to take more land. On September 1, 1939, the German army attacked Poland. German troops overran the western part of the country, while the Soviets occupied the rest. The British and the French realized they had made a mistake in not resisting Hitler's aggression, or attacks, earlier. Both France and Great Britain declared war on Germany.

☑ Reading Check
What is a policy of **appeasement?**

Photograph of Adolf Hitler

Section 2 Assessment

1. **Define:** depression, garrison, soviets, heavy industry, collectivization, social security laws, dictatorship, chancellor, swastika, appeasement.
2. How did Peter the Great reform Russia?
3. What were the goals of Stalin's Five-Year Plans?
4. Why did Great Britain and France declare war on Germany?

Critical Thinking

5. **Understanding Cause and Effect**
   How did the policy of appeasement contribute to the start of World War II?

Graphic Organizer Activity

6. Draw this diagram, and use it to write a headline showing the importance of each of these dates in Russian history: 1613, 1682, 1762, 1825, 1861, 1905, 1917, 1921.

Date	Headline
1613	
1682	
1762	
1825	
1861	
1905	
1917	
1921	

CHAPTER 37 CONFLICT AND CHANGE   **615**

Section 2 Assessment Answers

1. All terms are defined in the text Glossary.
2. He learned modern western ways.
3. to build up heavy industry
4. The German army attacked Poland.
5. Answers will vary.
6. Headlines will vary, but should address the significance of the following events: 1613—crowning of Michael Romanov/start of Romanov dynasty; 1682—Peter the Great comes to the throne; 1762—Catherine the Great comes to the throne; 1825—reform-minded army officers rebel against the czar; 1861—Alexander II frees the serfs; 1905—workers uprising; 1917—revolt of Russian people/Bolsheviks seize power; 1921—defeat of non-communist Whites

Assign the Chapter 37 **Section 2 Quiz** in the TCR. Testmaker available.

L1 Economics Discuss specific examples of the role economics played in the events leading up to World War II. Ask students to identify any possible economic solutions that could have averted the war. **ELL**

L2 Geography: Movement Ask several students to demonstrate on a wall map of the world how Japan, Italy, and Germany moved into other countries to take them over. *(Italy: Ethiopia; Germany: Rhineland, Austria, Czechoslovakia, Poland; Japan: Manchuria, main part of China)*

☑ Reading Check Answer
A policy of **appeasement** gives into the demands of an aggression in hopes of avoiding war.

💾 Use **Interactive Tutor Self-Assessment Software** to review Section 2.

SECTION 3 World War II

For the second time during the 1900s, the world was at war. World War II caught the Allied Powers—including Great Britain, France, and, later, the Soviet Union and the United States—unprepared. The Axis Powers—Germany, Italy, and, later, Japan—were prepared. The war would end with the Allied Powers victorious, but not before a terrible cost was paid.

Early Axis Victories   Germany had developed a new way of fighting called **blitzkrieg** (blits′ krēg), or "lightning war." German airplanes would first bomb enemy cities, roads, and airfields. Then soldiers and civilians alike would be machine-gunned from the air. Finally armored tanks would roll through the countryside, wiping out all defenses.

Using the blitzkrieg, Germany crushed Poland in three weeks. In 1940 German forces overran most of western Europe except for Great Britain. Hitler tried to bomb the British into surrendering. The British, however, under the leadership of Prime Minister Winston Churchill, fought back for 10 months. Finally, British pilots and anti-aircraft guns shot down so many German planes that Hitler gave up the idea of invading Great Britain. In the meantime, however, German and Italian troops overran much of southeastern Europe and North Africa.

BLITZKRIEG   Germany's bombing of European cities was a devastating new attack in World War II. Many parts of London, as shown here, were destroyed. **Why was Germany's blitzkrieg of Great Britain unsuccessful in allowing Germany to invade that country?**

SPOTLIGHT ON: CHURCHILL

Winston Churchill became Prime Minister of Great Britain in 1940, when the country was on the brink of defeat. His eloquence and strength gave the British a renewed morale. A famous quote of Churchill's rallied his people: "We shall defend our island, whatever the cost may be. We shall fight on the beaches, we shall fight on the landing-grounds, we shall fight in the fields and in the streets, we shall fight in the hills. We shall never surrender."

At the same time, the Japanese made conquests in Asia. They took over much of China and Southeast Asia. Then they turned their attention to the United States who had military forces in the Pacific. On December 7, 1941, the Japanese made a surprise air attack on Pearl Harbor, the American naval base in the Hawaiian Islands. The United States, followed by most of Latin America, immediately entered the war on the side of the Allied Powers.

War in Europe   The entry of the United States helped the Allies win the war in Europe. The United States was the greatest

Then...&Now

Blitz As bombs rained down on London, Britons shortened the German word *blitzkrieg* to *blitz*. Today the word *blitz* is used for a defensive maneuver in American football, in which one or more defensive linebackers charge through the offensive line and try to tackle the quarterback before the ball can be passed.

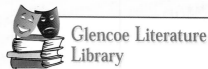

Glencoe Literature Library

The following novel from the **Glencoe Literature Library** may be used to enrich this chapter:
• *Picture Bride*, by Yoshiko Uchida. (Japanese American community in the early 1900s through internment.)

MAP STUDY

Answer

Portugal, Spain, Switzerland, Ireland, Sweden

Axis Expansion in Europe and Africa

(Map showing Axis Expansion in Europe and Africa)

Axis Powers
Area Controlled by Axis Powers, 1942
Allied Territory
Neutral Territory

miles 0 400 800 1200
kilometers 0 400 800 1200 1600

MAP STUDY

REGIONS By 1942 the Axis Powers had seized control of much of Europe and part of Africa. **Which European nations chose to be neutral during the war?**

ABCNEWS INTERACTIVE™

VIDEODISC
Lessons of War

Side Two
Chapter 8

Frames: 25814-28652
Title: *At the Front*
Subject: Contributions of minorities in World War II
Ask: How did the Japanese American 442nd Regimental Combat Team of World War II prove themselves during the war? *(This regiment was even more successful than other units.)*

EXTENDING THE CONTENT

World War II created an urgent need to control the infections of thousands of wounded soldiers. In 1928 Sir Alexander Fleming had discovered an antibiotic substance in certain strains of a mold grown in glass jars. Sir H. W. Florey, E. B. Chain, and other scientists and technicians had established that this substance had antibacterial powers and was nontoxic to humans. The substance, whose name *penicillin* was taken from the name of the mold, was first used on a human in 1940. Soon the War Production Board took over the production and allocation of the drug, which was used to treat a wide range of infections in wounded soldiers.

industrial power in the world. Soon its factories were turning out thousands of planes and tanks. Ships were built in large numbers. Other supplies the Allies were lacking were provided by the United States.

Earlier, Hitler had decided that Germany needed the resources of the Soviet Union. He ignored the treaty he had signed and attacked the Soviet Union in 1941. However, Hitler had underestimated the size of the Soviet Union, the bitterness of its winters, and the Russian people's fighting spirit.

In defense, Soviet troops used a scorched-earth policy. They burned cities, destroyed their own crops, and blew up dams that produced electric power. Though the Russians sustained great losses, the tide of battle turned in 1943. The Red Army surrounded German forces at Stalingrad (stah' lin grad) and forced them to surrender. From then on, Soviet forces kept pushing the Germans back all along the eastern front. That same year, American and British armies drove the Axis forces out of North Africa and invaded Italy.

In 1944, under the command of American General Dwight D. Eisenhower, Allied troops crossed the English Channel from Great Britain and landed on the beaches of Normandy in France. About 155,000 Allied soldiers landed on the first day, June 6, known as D-day. Another 2 million landed later. By August the Allied forces had retaken Paris and were moving eastward.

German armies were now caught between the Soviets in the east and the Americans, British, French, and Canadians in the west. In April 1945, the Allied forces joined together at the Elbe

NORMANDY Landing craft and supply ships crowded the Normandy coast when Allied troops landed on June 6, 1944. **What name was given to this date?**

618

(el' buh) River in Germany. Hitler and the Germans realized they could not win. Hitler killed himself, and on May 7 Germany surrendered. The next day, the war in Europe was officially over.

War in Asia and the Pacific   The war in Asia and the Pacific was fought at the same time as the one in Europe. At first the Japanese were victorious everywhere. They captured the Philippines and various other islands in the Pacific, including three islands off the coast of Alaska. They also captured Indochina (now Laos, Vietnam, and Cambodia), Malaya, Singapore, Hong Kong, Burma, Thailand, and the Dutch East Indies (now Indonesia). Then, in June 1942, a great sea and air battle took place at Midway Island. The battle changed the course

MAP STUDY

MOVEMENT
Between 1931 and 1942, Japan took over large areas of Southeast Asia and the Pacific. **How far east, in degrees longitude, did the Japanese extend their territory by 1942?**

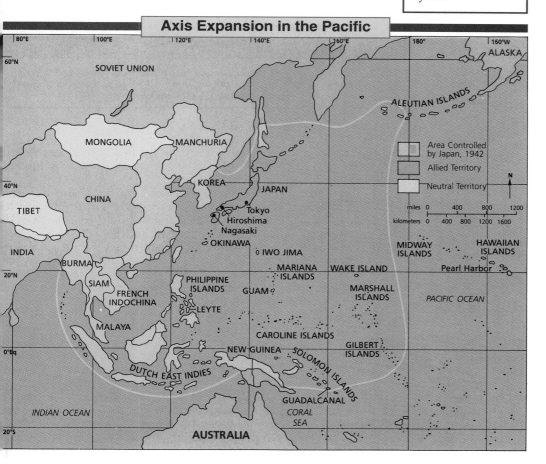

Axis Expansion in the Pacific

L2 Geography: Region Have students write five questions about the map, "Axis Expansion in the Pacific." Use the questions to lead a discussion about the war in the Pacific. **ELL**

MAKING CONNECTIONS

➤➤ **History** Despite a lack of weapons, some Jews resisted the Germans. The most famous holdout took place in the Warsaw Ghetto. For nearly a month, about 1,000 Jews with homemade bombs held off 5,000 armed German soldiers.

MAP STUDY

Answer

to 180º longitude

VIDEODISC
Lessons of War

Side One
Chapter 6

Frames 15755-18472
Title: *Can a Battle Change History?*
Subject: The Battle of Midway
Ask: Why was the Battle of Midway considered a turning point in World War II? *(Japan was winning, and Midway was a strategic attempt to shut off U.S. supply lines. Stopping the Japanese at Midway changed the direction of the war.)*

SPOTLIGHT ON: PHOTOJOURNALISTS

Robert Capa, born in 1913, was a famous combat photographer from the United States. Capa first achieved fame as a photojournalist in the Spanish Civil War. During World War II Capa covered much of the heaviest fighting in North Africa and Italy. Capa also covered the Normandy Invasion in June 1944. Margaret Bourke-White became one of the premier photojournalists in the United States during the Great Depression and after. At the end of World War II she traveled to Buchenwald, Germany, the location of a Nazi Concentration Camp and photographed the horrors faced by the Jews that had been held there.

ATOMIC BOMB   The United States dropped the atomic bomb on Japan in 1945. The huge mushroom cloud from it formed over the destruction of much of Nagasaki, shown here. **Why did President Truman allow the bombing?**

of the war in favor of the Allies. Over the next three years, Allied forces moved from island to island, pushing their way toward Japan.

President Harry S Truman (tru' muhn), who became President after Roosevelt died in April 1945, did not want to invade Japan. He knew that an invasion would cost the lives of hundreds of thousands of American and British soldiers. So, hoping for a Japanese surrender, he approved the use of a new weapon — the atomic bomb.

On August 6, 1945, the bomb was dropped on Hiroshima (hir ō she' muh), Japan. It destroyed most of the city and killed about 100,000 people. Thousands more died later from radiation poisoning. When the Japanese refused to surrender, a second atomic bomb was dropped on Nagasaki (nah guh sah' kē), Japan. About 75,000 people were killed. On August 14 Japan surrendered. The peace treaty was signed on September 2 aboard the USS *Missouri* in Tokyo Bay. World War II was over.

The Aftermath of War   After the war ended, Allied armies in Europe found German **concentration camps,** or camps where Germans had kept those they thought were enemies. There the Nazis had carried out a program of **genocide** (jen' uh sīd), or the mass murder of a people, against the Jews and others. This pro-

Reading Check
What did Allied armies discover when they entered German **concentration camps?** How does **genocide** violate the most basic rights of human beings?

620   UNIT 12 THE TWENTIETH CENTURY

gram became known as the **Holocaust** (hol' uh kahst). At the start of World War II, German forces shot hundreds of thousands of Jews in Poland and the Soviet Union. However, Hitler felt that Jews were not being killed fast enough. So he ordered six concentration camps to be equipped with poison gas chambers and **cremation** (kri mā' shuhn) **ovens,** or places to burn dead bodies. The Nazis then rounded up all the Jews in the areas of Europe they controlled and shipped them in sealed cattle cars to the camps. There, most of the Jews were gassed to death. By the end of World War II, the Nazis had killed more than 6 million Jews. About 1.5 million of them were children under the age of six.

The Jews were not the only ones who died at the hands of the Nazis. The Nazis used the people they conquered as slave laborers in German factories and on German farms. Poles, Ukrainians, and Russians, gypsies, and those people considered mentally ill or whom the Germans thought were inferior, were treated worst of all. By the end of the war, about 6 million had died from starvation, overwork, and torture. More than 3 million of these were Soviet prisoners of war.

The Japanese, too, had killed men, women, and children in the countries they conquered. Many Allied prisoners of war both soldiers and civilians died because of poor treatment from the Japanese army.

The Allied governments felt that the cruel acts of the Nazis and the Japanese could not be excused as normal occurrences of war. So the Allied governments put German and Japanese leaders on trial for war crimes.

Making the Peace   One result of World War II was the formation of the United Nations (UN); an organization like the League of Nations. In 1945, the United Nations was approved by 50 countries. UN responsibilities were to prevent war, lend money to poor countries, and provide them with medical care and better education.

Following the war, Germany was divided into four zones. Each was occupied by one of the major Allied powers—the United States, Great Britain, France, and the Soviet Union. The German capital of Berlin, located in the Russian zone, was also divided. In addition, German territory in the east was given to Poland. This was in exchange for the Soviet Union's acquiring western Ukraine which had been occupied by Poland since 1923. In fact, the Soviet Union acquired most of the land it had lost after World War I, including Estonia, Latvia, and Lithuania.

Japan was occupied by the United States for nearly seven years. Under American General Douglas MacArthur, the Japanese military lost power in the government and Japan became a democracy. Laws were passed giving women the right to vote and allowing trade unions. The secret police was abolished.

 Reading Check
What was the **Holocaust?**

 Reading Check
What did the **cremation ovens** reveal about the horror of Nazi Germany?

Photograph of Holocaust Victim

 Reading Check Answer
The **Holocaust** was the planned program of mass murder designed to wipe out the Jews and others.

Reading Check Answer
The **cremation ovens** revealed the vast number of people of all ages methodically murdered by the Nazis.

Biography

The following videotape program is available from Glencoe to enrich Chapter 37:

• **Biography: Anne Frank**

To find classroom resources to accompany this video, check the following home page:

A&E Television:
http://www.aetv.com

ABCNEWS INTERACTIVE™

VIDEODISC
Turning Points in World History

Side Two
Chapter 7

Title: *Dropping the Atomic Bomb*
Ask: What cities were bombed? *(Hiroshima and Nagasaki)*

Turning Points in World History

Side Two
Chapter 6

Title: *The Holocaust*
Ask: What lessons can we learn from the Holocaust? *(Ethnic and racial prejudices have no foundation; genocide must be prevented.)*

COOPERATIVE LEARNING

Have students hold a mock United Nations meeting with representatives from the five permanent members: the United States, France, Great Britain, the Commonwealth of Independent States, and China. Divide the class into five teams, one for each of these member nations. Select a current world problem for the teams to debate. First, have teams research the issue from the perspective of their nation. One member of each team will present their nation's view of the issue. The whole UN will then discuss the issue and vote on an appropriate resolution.

Assign Chapter 37 *Cooperative Learning Activity* in the TCR.

Check for Understanding

Ask students to summarize the main points of the chapter. Discuss the answers to the Section and Chapter Assessment questions.

Evaluate

Assign the Chapter 37 **Performance Assessment Activity** in the TCR.

Administer the **Chapter 37 Test** in the TCR. Testmaker available.

Reteach

Ask students to compile a list of leaders mentioned in this chapter. Have groups of students summarize the role of that leader in the two world wars.

Assign the Chapter 37 **Reteaching Activity** in the TCR.

Enrich

Assign the Chapter 37 **Enrichment Activity** in the TCR.

CLOSE

Ask students what leader during World War II might have said: *I cannot bear to see my innocent people suffer any longer.* (*Emperor Hirohito of Japan*)

📼 Use **Interactive Tutor Self-Assessment Software** to review Section 3.

Self-Check Quiz gives students an interactive chapter tutorial. Have them access **Chapter 37 Quiz** at **humanheritage.glencoe.com**

622

Large farms were divided and sold to farm workers at low prices. Loans were made to help rebuild the economy. Japan turned its efforts to building a strong economy rather than a strong military.

Section 3 Assessment

1. **Define:** blitzkrieg, concentration camps, genocide, Holocaust, cremation ovens.
2. Why did Germany attack the Soviet Union in 1941?
3. Why did the United States decide to drop atomic bombs on Hiroshima and Nagasaki?

Critical Thinking

4. **Demonstrating Reasoned Judgment** If you were living in 1945, would you have supported or opposed the use of the atomic bomb against Japan? Why?

Graphic Organizer Activity

5. Draw this diagram, and use it to show some of the results of World War II for Germany, Japan, and the Soviet Union.

Results of WWII
- for Germany
- for Japan
- for Soviet Union

Chapter Summary & Study Guide

1. In 1914, a conflict between Serbia and Austria-Hungary began World War I.
2. World War I involved more nations, used more technological weapons, and resulted in more deaths than any other earlier war.
3. The United States entered the war in 1917 and helped defeat Germany and its allies.
4. President Woodrow Wilson was unable to prevent the passage of treaties aimed at punishing Germany.
5. Despite efforts by Peter the Great and Catherine the Great to modernize Russia, Russian serfs and workers continued to suffer, leading to a series of revolts against the czars and the final overthrow of the government in 1917.
6. Under the leadership of Lenin and then Stalin, Russia became a Communist nation known as the Soviet Union.
7. A worldwide depression aided the rise of dictatorships and paved the way for a second world war.
8. World War II began in 1939 when Germany broke an agreement and invaded Poland. The United States entered the war in 1941 after Japan bombed naval bases at Pearl Harbor, Hawaii.
9. World War II ended a short time after the United States dropped two atomic bombs on Japan.
10. After World War II, the United Nations was formed, Germany was divided into four zones, and the United States occupied Japan.

Self-Check Quiz

Visit the *Human Heritage* Web site at **humanheritage. glencoe.com** and click on **Chapter 37—Self-Check Quiz** to assess your understanding of this chapter.

Section 3 Assessment Answers

1. blitzkrieg, lightning war (p. 616); concentration camps, for enemies of the Third Reich (p. 620); genocide, mass murder (p. 620); Holocaust, Nazi genocide (p. 621); cremation ovens, places to burn dead bodies (p. 621)
2. because Germany needed the resources of the Soviet Union
3. Truman did not want to invade Japan.
4. Answers will vary.
5. Sample responses: *Germany*—divided into four zones and occupied by Allied armies; capital of Berlin divided; territory given to Poland; Nazi leaders tried for war crimes; *Japan*—military government ousted; leaders tried for war crimes; democratic government formed; passage of voting rights for women; recognition of labor unions; secret police abolished; large farms broken up and sold to farm workers at low prices; loans granted to help rebuild the economy; *Soviet Union*—occupied part of Germany and Berlin; reacquired lands lost after World War I

Assign the Chapter 37 **Section 3 Quiz** in the TCR. Testmaker available.

Using Key Terms

Sort the following list of words into three columns under one of the following headings: World War I, Between Wars, or World War II. Then write a descriptive paragraph about something in each period using all the words under that heading.

mobilize
artillery
mandate
collectivization
appeasement
Holocaust

trench warfare
armistice
soviets
dictatorship
genocide

Understanding Main Ideas

- How did nationalism contribute to World War I?
- How was the Treaty of Versailles different from Wilson's Fourteen Points?
- What happened to the world economy in 1929?
- Why did the British and French give in to Hitler's demands at first?
- What major events led to the defeat of Germany in World War II? To the defeat of Japan?
- Why was the United Nations formed?

Critical Thinking

- What do you think might have happened if the United States had not entered World War I?
- Why do you think so many Soviet peasants resisted collectivization?
- What do you think could have been done to stop Hitler from invading neighboring countries?

4. Do you think the United States would have entered World War II if Japan had not bombed Pearl Harbor? Explain.

Graphic Organizer Activity

Citizenship Create a diagram like the one on this page, and use it to compare President Wilson's Fourteen Points with the Treaty of Versailles.

Fourteen Points — Both — Treaty of Versailles

 ## Geography in History

Location Refer to the map on page 619. Several small island groups in the Pacific Ocean were the sites of battles between the United States and Japan. Why do you think the battles occurred on these islands rather than on the Japanese mainland?

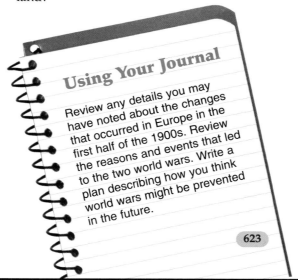

Using Your Journal

Review any details you may have noted about the changes that occurred in Europe in the first half of the 1900s. Review the reasons and events that led to the two world wars. Write a plan describing how you think world wars might be prevented in the future.

 ### Bonus Test Question

For Chapter 37 Test
Evaluate this 1945 plan: WWII is dragging on. President Truman orders a full invasion of Japan to be launched from California by American land, sea, and air forces. *(poor plan; Japan too far away; troops will be intercepted)*

Using Your Journal

Plans will vary. You might call on volunteers to read their plans to the class and discuss them. A review of world peace organizations and their current activities might also be appropriate.

 ### Geography in History

They were closer and easier to capture.

Using Key Terms

World War I: mobilize, artillery, trench warfare, armistice, mandate; *Between Wars*: garrison, soviets, collectivization, social security laws, dictatorship; *World War II*: appeasement, blitzkrieg, genocide, Holocaust; Paragraphs will vary, but students should include all key terms.

Understanding Main Ideas

1. Sample response: Nationalism fueled the growth of rival alliances and the desire of groups in eastern Europe, such as the Serbs, for independence from Austria-Hungary.
2. The treaty punished the nations that had lost the war.
3. A depression set in, factories closed, and banks failed.
4. They feared another war.
5. Allied forces crossed the English Channel, and the Germans were caught between them and the Soviets. Atomic bombs were dropped on Japan.
6. to prevent war

Critical Thinking

1. Answers will vary.
2. Answers will vary but might indicate that the peasants feared losing their lands.
3. Answers will vary, but students might indicate earlier counter-aggression.
4. Answers will vary.

Graphic Organizer Activity

Diagrams will vary but should include the main points listed in each document as stated on pp. 605–606. Both documents included plans for an international peacekeeping organization, but the Treaty of Versailles was far more punitive than Wilson's Fourteen Points.

Chapter 38 Planning Guide

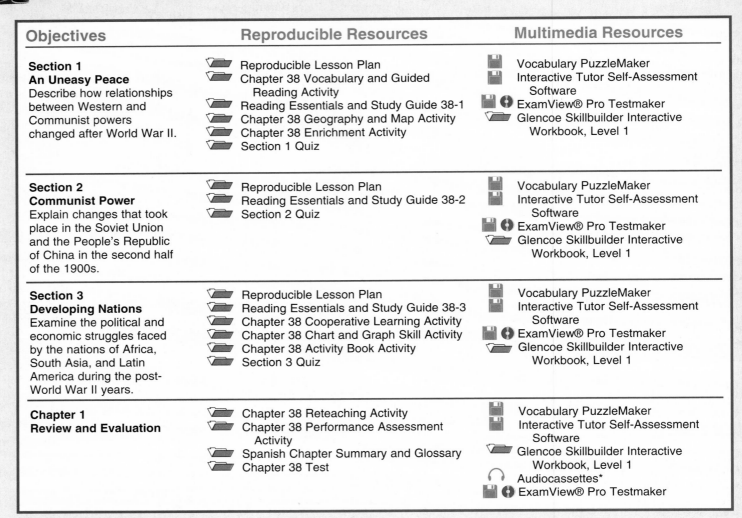

Objectives	Reproducible Resources	Multimedia Resources
Section 1 **An Uneasy Peace** Describe how relationships between Western and Communist powers changed after World War II.	Reproducible Lesson Plan Chapter 38 Vocabulary and Guided Reading Activity Reading Essentials and Study Guide 38-1 Chapter 38 Geography and Map Activity Chapter 38 Enrichment Activity Section 1 Quiz	Vocabulary PuzzleMaker Interactive Tutor Self-Assessment Software ExamView® Pro Testmaker Glencoe Skillbuilder Interactive Workbook, Level 1
Section 2 **Communist Power** Explain changes that took place in the Soviet Union and the People's Republic of China in the second half of the 1900s.	Reproducible Lesson Plan Reading Essentials and Study Guide 38-2 Section 2 Quiz	Vocabulary PuzzleMaker Interactive Tutor Self-Assessment Software ExamView® Pro Testmaker Glencoe Skillbuilder Interactive Workbook, Level 1
Section 3 **Developing Nations** Examine the political and economic struggles faced by the nations of Africa, South Asia, and Latin America during the post-World War II years.	Reproducible Lesson Plan Reading Essentials and Study Guide 38-3 Chapter 38 Cooperative Learning Activity Chapter 38 Chart and Graph Skill Activity Chapter 38 Activity Book Activity Section 3 Quiz	Vocabulary PuzzleMaker Interactive Tutor Self-Assessment Software ExamView® Pro Testmaker Glencoe Skillbuilder Interactive Workbook, Level 1
Chapter 1 **Review and Evaluation**	Chapter 38 Reteaching Activity Chapter 38 Performance Assessment Activity Spanish Chapter Summary and Glossary Chapter 38 Test	Vocabulary PuzzleMaker Interactive Tutor Self-Assessment Software Glencoe Skillbuilder Interactive Workbook, Level 1 Audiocassettes* ExamView® Pro Testmaker

*Also available in Spanish.

Presentation Plus!
Use Glencoe's **Presentation Plus!** multimedia teacher tool to easily present dynamic lessons that visually excite your students. Using Microsoft® PowerPoint, you can customize the presentations to create your own personalized lessons.

 Interactive Lesson Planner

Planning has never been easier! Using this CD-ROM, organize your week, month, semester, or year with all the help you need. The **Interactive Lesson Planner** gives you access to all of the blackline masters which accompany *Human Heritage.*

✓ PERFORMANCE ASSESSMENT ACTIVITIES

Time Lines Have students choose a country mentioned in the chapter and create a time line of important events in the country's history between World War II and the present. Tell students to include political, religious, economic, and cultural events. Encourage them to include illustrations or newsphotos on their time lines.

CHAPTER RESOURCES

LITERATURE ABOUT THE PERIOD

Soyinka, Wole. *Aké: The Years of Childhood.* Vintage Books, 1983. Autobiography by Nigerian Nobel Prize-winner.

READINGS FOR THE STUDENT

Bachelis, Faren. *The Central Americans.* Chelsea House, 1990. History and culture of Central Americans and reasons for their flight north.

READINGS FOR THE TEACHER

Cheng, Mien. *Life and Death in Shanghai.* Grove Press, 1987. Personal account of her trials during the Cultural Revolution by an "aristocratic" Chinese woman.

KEY TO ABILITY LEVELS

Teaching strategies have been coded for varying learning styles and abilities.

L1 Level 1 activities are **basic** activities and should be within the ability range of all students.

L2 Level 2 activities are **average** activities and should be within the ability range of the average to above-average student.

L3 Level 3 activities are **challenging** activities designed for the ability range of above-average students.

ELL ELL activities should be within the ability range of English Language Learning students.

Teacher's Corner

INDEX TO NATIONAL GEOGRAPHIC MAGAZINE

The following articles relate to this chapter:

- "Kashmir: Trapped in Conflict," by Lewis M. Simmons, September 1999.
- "Cuba," by John J. Putnam, June 1999.
- "India," by Geoffrey C. Ward, May 1997.
- "Hong Kong," by Mike Edwards, March 1997.
- "African Gold," by Carole Beckwith and Angela Fisher, October 1996.

ADDITIONAL NATIONAL GEOGRAPHIC SOCIETY PRODUCTS

To order the following, call National Geographic at 1-800-368-2728:

- *PicturePack: Civil Rights (Transparencies)*
- *PictureShow: Civil Rights (CD-ROM)*
- *1945-1989: The Cold War (Video)*
- *Capitalism, Socialism, Communism Series: (Video)*

Access *National Geographic's* new dynamic MapMachine Web site and other geography resources at:
http://www.nationalgeographic.com/
http://www.nationalgeographic.com/maps/

The following videotape programs are available from Glencoe:

- **Cuba and Castro**
  0-7670-1426-X

- **Democracy Crushed: Tiananmen Square**
  0-7670-1459-6

- **Mahatma Gandhi: Pilgrim of Peace**
  0-7670-0668-2

- **Vietnam: A Soldier's Diary**
  0-7670-0772-7

To order, call Glencoe at 1-800-334-7344. To find classroom resources to accompany many of these videos check:

A&E Television: http://www.aetv.com
The History Channel:
http://www.historychannel.com

OVERVIEW

Chapter 38 discusses the cold war (1945–1989) and its effect on world affairs.

➤ **Section 1** traces the growth of tensions between the United States and Soviet Union.

➤ **Section 2** describes changes in communism as practiced by the Soviet Union and China.

➤ **Section 3** summarizes the history of developing nations after World War II.

CHAPTER OBJECTIVES

After reading Chapter 38, students will be able to:

1. describe reasons for the cold war and cite examples of cold war crises.

2. discuss political and economic changes in the Soviet Union and China, especially in the 1980s.

3. examine how developing nations in Africa, South Asia, and Latin America have struggled for political and economic independence.

EXAMINING ARTIFACTS

Based on these artifacts, what do students think was one of the biggest popular concerns during the post-World War II era? *(use of nuclear weapons)* What actions did fears of nuclear war cause some people to do? *(take part in protests, build fallout shelters)* Call on students to use the time line to identify some of the crises during the cold war era.

PERFORMANCE ASSESSMENT ✓

Use the Performance Assessment activities on page 624B to help you to evaluate students as they complete the chapter.

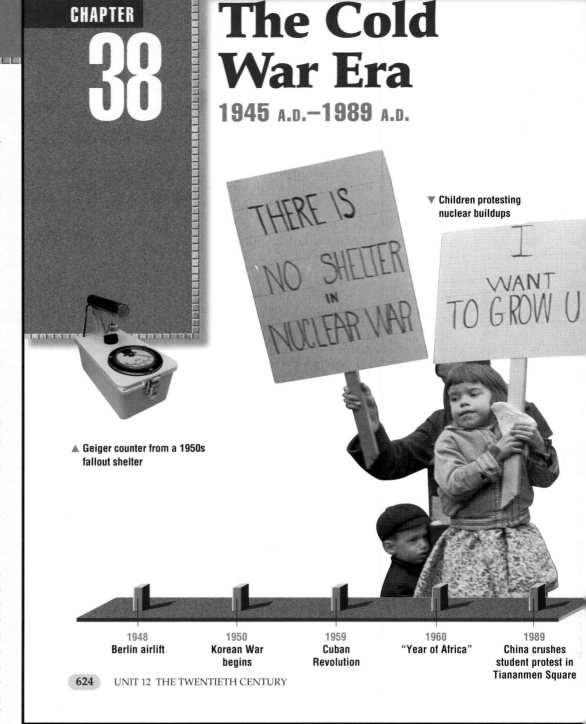

The Cold War Era

1945 A.D.–1989 A.D.

▲ Geiger counter from a 1950s fallout shelter

▼ Children protesting nuclear buildups

THERE IS NO SHELTER IN NUCLEAR WAR

I WANT TO GROW U

1948	1950	1959	1960	1989
Berlin airlift	Korean War begins	Cuban Revolution	"Year of Africa"	China crushes student protest in Tiananmen Square

624 UNIT 12 THE TWENTIETH CENTURY

TEACHING RESOURCES

TEACHER PLANNING AND SUPPORT

- Reproducible Lesson Plan
- Block Scheduling Implementation Guide
- Videodisc Bar Code Correlation
- Presentation Plus!

REVIEW AND REINFORCEMENT

- Reading Essentials and Study Guide 38-1, 38-2, 38-3
- Chapter 38 Vocabulary and Guided Reading Activity
- Vocabulary PuzzleMaker Software
- Teaching Transparencies 38A & 38B

- Chapter 38 Reteaching Activity
- Chapter 38 Cooperative Learning Activity
- Chapter 38 Activity Book Activity
- Chapter 38 Chart and Graph Skill Activity
- Interactive Tutor Self-Assessment Software

APPLICATION AND HANDS-ON ACTIVITIES

 Daily World History, Geography, and Culture Question

Chapter Focus

Read to Discover

- How relationships between Western and Communist powers have changed since World War II.
- What changes have occurred in the Soviet Union.
- What life has been like in the People's Republic of China.
- How countries in Africa, South Asia, and Latin America have struggled with political and economic problems.

 Terms to Learn

cold war
satellite nations
glasnost
perestroika

 People to Know

Fidel Castro
Ho Chi Minh
Mao Zedong

Places to Locate

Berlin
Tiananmen
Square

Why It's Important   Soon after World War II ended, a split occurred between the Soviet Union and other Allied Powers. At issue was the Soviet threat to spread communism beyond its borders. Gradually, a **cold war**, or state of hostility without fighting, developed. Tensions were so high that people feared the outbreak of the world's first all-out nuclear war.

Chapter Overview

Visit the *Human Heritage* Web site at **humanheritage.glencoe.com** and click on *Chapter 38— Chapter Overviews* to preview this chapter.

SECTION 1   An Uneasy Peace

After World War II Europe began its recovery. Tension between the United States and the Soviet Union grew over problems in Berlin, Korea, Cuba, and Vietnam (vē et nahm').

Western Europe   When World War II ended, most of Western Europe was in ruins. To help rebuild areas, the United States started a loan program in 1948. It was named the Marshall Plan after George Marshall, the U.S. Secretary of State. Under the Marshall Plan, factories were rebuilt, coal mines were reopened, and roads were repaired or replaced. The economies of Western Europe soon began to grow.

In 1957 six Western European nations formed an economic union called the European Common Market. The six nations were Belgium, France, Italy, Luxembourg (luk' suhm borg), the Netherlands, and West Germany. They agreed to remove all trade barriers among them. That meant that manufacturers could sell their goods in other member nations without paying tariffs.

✓ **Reading Check**
Why did a **cold war** develop?

CHAPTER 38 THE COLD WAR ERA   **625**

Chapter Overview introduces students to chapter content and key terms. Have them access *Chapter 38 Overview* at **humanheritage.glencoe.com**

FOCUS

🎏 **Bellringer**

Write the following message on the board for students to decode: *Gsv xlow dzi dzh z grnv lu hkrvh zmw xlwvh.*

Motivational Activity

Have students share their decoded message. *(If none have solved it, tell them this is an alphabet reversal code that says: "The cold war was a time of spies and codes.")* Tell students that in this chapter they will learn about the causes and effects of the cold war.

✓ **Reading Check Answer**
A **cold war** developed over the Soviet threat to spread communism beyond its borders.

GUIDE TO READING

Reading Strategy

Ask students to read "Why It's Important" and summarize the chapter's main theme. *(Tensions over the spread of communism led to a cold war and fears of all-out nuclear war.)*

Vocabulary Precheck

Ask students to define each of the "Terms to Learn." **L1** **ELL**

💾 Use the Vocabulary PuzzleMaker for Chapter 38 to create a crossword puzzle. **L1**

📁 Assign Chapter 38 Vocabulary and Guided Reading Activity.

📁 Assign Reading Essentials and Study Guide 38-1.

TEACH

Guided Practice

L2 **Critical Thinking** Ask students how a "cold" war might differ from a "hot" war. *(A cold war involves diplomatic relations rather than combat.)*

Reading Check Answer
Satellite nations that fell under Soviet control included Bulgaria, Czechoslovakia, Hungary, Poland, and Romania.

Reading Check Answer
The Soviets **blockaded** Berlin because they feared the Allies would unify Germany. The U.S. and Great Britain organized an **airlift** into Berlin.

ABC NEWS INTERACTIVE™

VIDEODISC
Communism and the Cold War

Side One
Chapter 3

Frames 2488-7305
Title: *End of Alliance*
Subject: Summary of events near end of World War II, which led to the cold war
Ask: Why did the United States view the Soviet Union as a threat?
(believed the Soviet Union was trying to spread communism)
Why did the Soviet Union view the United States as a threat? *(believed the U.S. was an imperialist power that wanted to destroy communism)*

Fun Facts . . . .

The Iron Curtain In a speech at Fulton, Missouri, in 1946, former British Prime Minister Winston Churchill declared: "From Stettin in the Baltic to Triest in the Adriatic an iron curtain has descended across the continent of Europe." Thereafter people used the term *iron curtain* to refer to the invisible barrier that split Europe into democratic Western Europe and Soviet-dominated Eastern Europe.

Reading Check
What **satellite nations** fell under Soviet control?

Reading Check
What was the reason that the Soviets **blockaded** Berlin? What nations organized an **airlift** to break the blockade?

AIRLIFT   The children in this photograph watch as an American plane brings food to Berlin during the Soviet blockade. **Why did the Soviet Union block off access to the city of Berlin?**

Workers from one nation could take jobs in any other member nation. Between 1957 and 1986, Denmark, Great Britain, Greece, Ireland, Portugal, and Spain also joined the European Common Market. Trade among the nations increased and living conditions improved.

The Start of the Cold War   Toward the end of World War II, the Soviet Union set up Communist governments in Bulgaria, Czechoslovakia, Hungary, Poland, and Romania. By 1948 these countries were Soviet **satellite nations,** or countries controlled by a stronger neighboring country. Yugoslavia, although Communist, refused to let itself be put under Soviet control.

The Soviet leader, Stalin, had originally promised the other Allies that he would allow free elections in these countries. When he broke his promise, the cold war began.

Berlin   The first cold war crisis took place over Berlin. In 1948 Great Britain, France, and the United States decided to unite their zones of Germany to encourage peace. The Soviet Union disagreed. It distrusted a united Germany because that nation had invaded the Soviet Union twice in 40 years. In June 1948, the Soviets **blockaded**, or closed off, all land and water traffic into Berlin. They hoped this would force the western powers to leave the city.

In response, the United States and Great Britain began an **airlift,** or a system of carrying supplies by airplane into Berlin.

626   UNIT 12 THE TWENTIETH CENTURY

EXTENDING THE CONTENT

After World War II, much of Europe was a wasteland. Help came in the form of the Marshall Plan which reconstructed cities of Europe. Many cities were a leveled landscape of gutted buildings, bombed-out bridges, and twisted rail track. As many as 45 million people were homeless. Damage to transportation networks made food distribution impossible. One-fourth of the farmland was out of production. Communication lines were destroyed. The war destroyed almost every major industrial region in the world except those in North America.

Each day planes flew in tons of food, fuel, and raw materials to the city. In May 1949, the Soviets finally lifted their blockade of Berlin. That same year, two separate governments were set up—a democratic one for West Germany, and a Communist one for East Germany. East Germany became a Soviet satellite nation.

The Berlin blockade convinced the western powers that the Soviets wanted to control Europe. In 1949 the United States, Great Britain, and France joined with nine other countries to form the North Atlantic Treaty Organization (NATO). All 12 countries agreed to help one another if attacked. Six years later, the Soviet Union and its satellites formed a similar organization called the Warsaw Pact.

Meanwhile, many people in East Germany were unhappy under Communist rule. About three million fled into West Berlin in search of political freedom and better living conditions. Because many of those who fled were well-educated professionals, the East German government wanted to stop these escapes. So in August 1961, it built a wall between East and West Berlin. The Berlin Wall, with Soviet soldiers guarding it, became a symbol of the split between Communist and non-Communist Europe. Many East Berliners continued to try escaping through the wall, risking their lives.

Korea   After World War II, Korea was also geographically divided. A Communist government was set up in North Korea and a non-Communist government was organized in South Korea. In 1950 North Korea invaded South Korea in an attempt to take over that country. Both the Soviets and Chinese sent the North Koreans military aid. The United Nations sent soldiers—mostly Americans— to help South Korea.

General Douglas MacArthur, the United Nations commander, suggested that dropping atomic bombs on Chinese bases and supply lines would gain a quick victory. However, President Harry S Truman refused. Truman did not want the Korean War to turn into World War III. In 1953 North Korea and South Korea signed a truce calling for the two countries and their governments to remain separate.

Cuba   In 1955 Fidel Castro (fē del′ kas trō) launched an unsuccessful revolution in Cuba against dictator Fulgencio Batista (fūl hen′ sē ō buh tēs′ tuh). In 1959 Castro tried again and finally succeeded—Batista was overthrown.

Castro at first promised free elections and social and economic reforms in Cuba. Many countries, including the United States, supported him. Most of the promises he made, however, were not kept. Cubans who had opposed Castro were jailed or executed. Thousands fled to the United States. Before long, Castro announced that his government would be Communist. He

Photograph of Fidel Castro

NATO Growth Although the Warsaw Pact ended in 1991, NATO continues to grow. In the late 1990s, NATO members voted to invite several former Soviet satellites—the Czech Republic, Hungary, and Poland—to join the organization. In addition, Russia and other members of the former Soviet Union, which dissolved in 1991, were accepted as partner nations.

Student Web Activity
Visit the *Human Heritage* Web site at **humanheritage.glencoe.com** and click on *Chapter 38— Student Web Activities* to find out more about the cold war.

VIDEODISC
Communism and the Cold War

‖‖‖‖‖‖‖ Side One
Chapter 15

Frames 26867-29413
Title: *Berlin Wall*
Ask: What reason did the Soviets give for blockading East and West Berlin? *(They were attempting to keep agents from the West from coming into the Soviet Union.)*

Glencoe Literature Library

The following novel from the **Glencoe Literature Library** may be used to enrich this unit:
• *So Far From the Bamboo Groove*, by Yoko Kawashima Watkins and Jean Fritz. (Exile of Japanese families from Korea during the Korean War.)

Student Web Activity objectives, goals, and answers can be found at the *Chapter 38 Web Activity Lesson Plan* at <u>humanheritage.glencoe.com</u>

L1 **Geography: Location** Tell students that Batista was backed by the U.S. government. Next, have students locate the U.S. and Cuba on a map of North America and measure the distance between the two countries. Then ask students why the U.S. would intervene in the affairs of Cuba? *(close location)*

EXTENDING THE CONTENT

The blockade of Berlin cut off all paths of communication. In order to get food, coal, and all other important supplies into Berlin, Western forces approached by air. Between June 1948 and May 1949 British and American air forces carried more than 1.5 million tons of goods into Berlin. One day a single load exceeded 12,000 tons. In this way civilians in both western and eastern sectors were aided. To the relief of British and U.S. pilots, the Soviets did not fire at incoming planes.

Photograph of Vietnam War Protesters

Satellite view of Venus

developed close ties with the Soviet Union which continued to send him economic aid.

In 1961 Cuban refugees who had been trained in the United States invaded Cuba. Their mission was to force Castro out of power. The invasion, in the area known as the Bay of Pigs, failed. Castro then asked the Soviet Union for more military aid. In 1962 Soviet nuclear missile bases were set up on the island. The United States blockaded Cuba and insisted the Soviets remove the missiles. The Soviets finally agreed and another world war was avoided.

Vietnam In 1941, Vietnam was a French colony and part of a larger region known as French Indochina. Japan invaded Vietnam in 1941 but pulled out of the country in 1945 at the end of World War II. At that time, the Vietnamese hoped to be independent but they were invaded again by the French. As a result, Communists and non-Communist Vietnamese nationalists joined together in a guerrilla war against the French. The guerrillas were led by a Communist named Ho Chi Minh (hō chē min'), a Vietnamese nationalist.

In 1954 the French were defeated and the country was temporarily divided into two parts—North and South Vietnam. North Vietnam became a Communist country headed by Ho Chi Minh. South Vietnam became a non-Communist country. A 1956 election meant to unite the two countries was never held. It was protested by the South Vietnamese government who feared it would show Ho's strength.

A war for the control of the country erupted between South Vietnam and North Vietnam. Guerrillas, known as the Vietcong, and the Soviet Union aided North Vietnam. The United States had already been sending military supplies to South Vietnam. It began sending combat troops there in 1965. Altogether, more than 3.3 million Americans fought in the Vietnam War. Eventually 58,000 of them lost their lives, and almost $200 billion was spent.

The Vietnam War deeply divided the American people. Many believed the United States should fight to help South Vietnam and prevent the spread of communism. Many others believed the fight was a civil war that the Vietnamese should settle themselves.

In 1973 an agreement between North Vietnam, South Vietnam, and the United States was reached. American troops pulled out of the country. Then, in 1975, troops from North Vietnam moved into South Vietnam and it came under Communist control.

The Space Race Part of the cold war between the Soviet Union and the United States involved the race to explore space. The Soviets took the first lead. In 1957 they launched *Sputnik I,* the first spacecraft to circle the earth. Four years later Soviet stronaut Yuri Gagarin (yū rē guh gahr′ uhn) became the first human being to circle the earth.

Then the United States took the lead. In 1969 American astronaut Neil Armstrong became the first person to walk on the moon. During the 1970s, the first landings on Venus and Mars were made by U.S. unmanned space vehicles. Later, these spacecraft explored Jupiter and Saturn.

Section 1 Assessment

- **Define:** cold war, satellite nations, blockaded, airlift.
- Why did Western European nations form the European Common Market?
- Why did East Germany build the Berlin Wall?
- Why did Castro have the support of the United States during his revolution? Why did he lose that support?

Critical Thinking

- **Demonstrating Reasoned Judgment** If you were living during the Vietnam War, would you have supported or opposed the war? Why?

Graphic Organizer Activity

6. Draw this diagram, and use it to summarize the issues in the following cold world crises: Soviet blockade of Berlin, construction of the Berlin Wall, Korean War, Cuban Revolution, Vietnamese civil war, launch of *Sputnik I*.

Crisis	Issue Involved

SECTION 2 Communist Powers

After World War II, China became a Communist nation. Later, however, both China and the Soviet Union made changes in the kind of communism they practiced.

Revolution in China   While the Soviet Union and the United States were competing in the cold war, communism was gaining support in China. The conditions that led to China's acceptance of communism developed over a long time.

Before the 1900s, there had been several revolts over control of the government. All had failed. In 1911, however, a revolt led by Sun Yat-sen (sun′ yaht sen′) overturned the government. He formed the Nationalist party which wanted China to be a free, democratic republic. He was ousted and Chinese warlords divided the country.

LINKING PAST TO PRESENT

When the Treaty of Versailles awarded the Shandong Peninsula to the Japanese, Chinese students in Beijing came together for a mass demonstration, urging the Chinese government not to sign the treaty. Similar demonstrations throughout the country culminated in a general strike in Shanghai. Under intense pressure from the students, the government at last yielded to their demands. China's students continue to protest and demonstrate—although not always successfully—as a means of gaining their government's attention.

DID YOU KNOW ??

In 1949 Taiwan was called Formosa.

Taiwan Taiwan was named Formosa, meaning "beautiful" by Portuguese explorers. In the 1600s, the island was controlled by the Dutch and then the Spanish. Still later it was acquired by China, then Japan, then China again. China, which regards Taiwan as a province, has strongly resisted Taiwanese moves toward independence.

INVASION   Japananese troops invaded the streets of Shanghai, China. Chinese soldiers united to fight the attack. **What major Chinese parties cooperated in this effort to fight the Japanese?**

After Sun died in 1925, Chiang Kai-shek (chyang kī shek') became the leader of the Nationalist party. He tried to unite China and wipe out the Communists. However, in 1927 the Chinese Communists who opposed the Nationalists began a movement to gain control of the country. Their leader was Mao Zedong (mow' dzuh dung').

The struggle between the two parties was interrupted by the Japanese invasion of China in 1937. The Nationalists joined the Communists to fight the Japanese. After the war, however, the struggle between them continued. In 1949 the Communists gained the support of the peasants with promises of land, and forced the Nationalists to leave the Chinese mainland to go to the island of Taiwan (tī wahn'). There Chiang set up a Nationalist government claiming it ruled China. The Communists set up their own government on mainland China headed by Mao Zedong. They called it the People's Republic of China.

China Under Mao   Mao's main goal was to make China a strong, modern country. In 1953 the Chinese began a series of plans to improve the country's economy. By the middle of the 1960s, the Chinese had more food and better health care. Many people had learned how to read and write. Also, under Mao the position of women in China changed. Women were now allowed to choose their own husbands, enter any occupation they chose, and receive equal pay. Men, however, continued to hold the highest positions in government and the best-paying jobs.

630   UNIT 12 THE TWENTIETH CENTURY

COOPERATIVE LEARNING

Divide the class into two groups to report on the influence of Chinese students on the politics of China. Each group should assign its members the tasks of researching, organizing, and reporting on the topic. Have one group examine the political role Chinese students played in the early part of this century. Have the other group research the role Chinese students have played in politics during the past decade. Have each group report its finding to the class. Then discuss how the Chinese student movement between 1900 and 1920 was similar to and different from the Chinese student movement of the 1980s.

Then Mao began to fear that the Chinese had lost their revolutionary spirit. As a result, in 1966 he carried out **purges** (per' juhs), or removals of undesirable members, of the Communist party. He also purged the country's *intellectuals* (in tuh lek' chū uhls), or scholars. This purge was called the Cultural Revolution. Students and young adults known as Red Guards attacked politicians, teachers, and others accused of not supporting communism. The purge soon got out of control, however, and there were battles between Red Guards and other citizens. The Red Guards were later broken up.

China After Mao   After Mao died in 1976, a group led by Deng Xiaoping (duhng' syow ping') came into power in China. Deng cared more about economic growth than about

☑ **Reading Check**
Who were some of the victims of Mao Zedong's **purges?**

CHINESE LEADERS   From 1928 to 1949, General Chiang Kai-shek (shown left) was a powerful leader in China. In 1949, the Communists, led by Mao Zedong (shown right), overthrew Chiang's government. Mao proclaimed the People's Republic of China on the Chinese mainland, while Chiang set up the Nationalist government on the island of Taiwan. **Why were the Nationalists unpopular with the Chinese peasants?**

CHAPTER 38 THE COLD WAR ERA   **631**

EXTENDING THE CONTENT

The Cultural Revolution was aimed against the bureaucracy and complacency that Mao Zedong feared had crept into the universities, the government, and the Communist Party. He thought special privileges for the educated elite worked against the ideal of a society in which everyone was equal. He wanted to purge "The Four Olds"—old thoughts, old culture, old customs, and old habits. The Cultural Revolution weakened Mao's leadership position. After Mao's death, Chinese historians began to regard the period as "the ten catastrophic years" and to view it as having been a serious setback.

☑ **Reading Check Answer**
Victims of **purges** by Mao Zedong included undesirable members of the Communist party, intellectuals, and scholars.

L2 **Culture** Discuss what it must have been like for the Chinese to go through the dramatic postwar changes in government policies. Ask students to imagine what would happen in the United States if the government started a Cultural Revolution. How do they think Americans would react? Which Americans would be most vulnerable in such a situation?

LINKING PAST TO PRESENT

During the Cultural Revolution, the Chinese educational system was nearly at a standstill, and the door was virtually closed to study at foreign institutions. Today, however, the Chinese constitute a majority of the foreign-student enrollment in U.S. universities.

CAPTION ANSWER

They did not make promises of bread and land, even though they wanted a democratic government.

THE HISTORY CHANNEL

The following videotape program is available from Glencoe to enrich Chapter 38:

• **Democracy Crushed: Tiananmen Square**

To find classroom resources to accompany this video, check the following home page:

A&E Television:
http://www.aetv.com

Glencoe Literature Library

The following novel from the **Glencoe Literature Library** may be used to enrich this chapter:

• *One Day in the Life of Ivan Denisovich*, by Alexander Solzhenitsyn. (Soviet labor camp in the 1950s.)

MAKING CONNECTIONS

➤➤ **History** China exploded its first atomic bomb in 1964. It became the fifth world atomic power, following the United States, the Soviet Union, Britain, and France.

✔ **Reading Check Answer**
Soviet **hard-liners** were people who stuck to communism regardless of the circumstances.

ABCNEWS INTERACTIVE™

VIDEODISC
Communism and the Cold War

Side Two
Chapter 19

Frames 46766-49626
Title: *Tiananmen Square*
Ask: What were the protests in Tiananmen Square about?
(democratic reform)

POLITICAL PROTEST   As crowds of Chinese demonstrators filled Tiananmen Square in 1989, government officials decided to attack them. **What were the demonstrators protesting against?**

Tibet Human rights are an issue in Tibet, seized by China in 1951. Eight years later, Tibetans waged an unsuccessful rebellion against Chinese control. Since then, the Dalai Lama, the religious leader of Tibet, has led a worldwide movement in support of Tibetan rights from his home in India. In 1989, the Dalai Lama received the Nobel Peace Prize.

✔ **Reading Check**
Who were the Soviet **hard-liners?**

revolutionary spirit. He encouraged foreign countries to invest money in China. He let many factory managers decide what goods to produce and what prices to charge. As a result of such changes, economic conditions in China improved greatly.

Political conditions, however, remained the same and many people were unhappy. They wanted the same control over politics that they had been given over the economy. Then beginning in April of 1989, a demonstration took place in Tiananmen (tyen′ ahn men) Square in Beijing. For seven weeks about one million Chinese people, mostly students, gathered in the square and demanded democracy.

The demonstration was peaceful but it frightened many Communist leaders. So Deng sent Red Army soldiers into Tiananmen Square to break up the gathering. Between 500 and 1,000 civilians were killed. Other students and labor leaders were imprisoned or executed. Since then, there have been changes in economic balance and trade in China, but not in human rights. Chinese leaders do not acknowledge that the people's human rights are being ignored.

Changes in the Soviet Union   Two groups of Communists existed in the Soviet Union after Stalin's rule. **Hard-liners** or people who stick to the rules regardless of the circumstances made up one group. They wanted to keep the Soviet Union as it

---

MULTICULTURAL PERSPECTIVES

Zhang Shuyan, a senior researcher in China's State Committee for Reforming the Chinese Written Language, has made a significant study of Chinese names. She found that during the Cultural Revolution, the single most common name was *Red.* Some people born during that time changed their revolutionary names as they entered adulthood. Since the Cultural Revolution, the most common name has been *Hua,* which means "magnificent and prosperous."

was. Reformers made up the other group of Communists. They were interested in economic growth, even if that meant introducing capitalism into the country. Under **capitalism,** most production is privately owned rather than owned by the government. After Stalin died in 1953, there was a Communist struggle for control.

In 1955 a reformer, Nikita Khrushchev (nuh kĕt' uh krŭsh chof'), became the leader of the Soviet Union. The following year, he began a program of **de-Stalinization** (dē stahl uh nuh zā' shuhn), or an attack on the policies established by Stalin. Many labor camps were shut down, and the secret police became less violent. More apartment houses were built, and consumer goods became more available.

In 1964 Leonid Brezhnev (lā uh nid brezh' nef) became the Soviet ruler. Under Brezhnev, life once again became less free for the Soviet people. In 1985, however, a reformer, Mikhail Gorbachev (mĕk' hī el gōr' buh chahf), came to power. Gorbachev adopted two policies to try to improve the growth of the economy in the Soviet Union.

Under Gorbachev's policy of *glasnost,* (glaz nōst) or openness, the Soviet people could say and write what they thought without fear of being punished. Free elections were held in which many non-Communist officials gained office. Under the policy of *perestroika,* (per uhs troi kuh) which means restructuring, Gorbachev changed the structure of the Soviet government and moved the country's economy toward capitalism.

As the Soviet Union continued toward democracy and capitalism, tensions within the country increased. Some people thought Gorbachev was moving too quickly with reform. Others thought he was not moving fast enough. At the same time, many ethnic groups within the country were demanding independence.

Reading Check
Who owns production under **capitalism?**

Reading Check
What changes took place under **de-Stalinization?**

Reading Check
What was the policy of *glasnost?*

Reading Check
What was the economic goal of *perestroika?*

Reading Check Answer
Under **capitalism,** most production is privately owned.

Reading Check Answer
Under **de-Stalinization,** labor camps were shut down, the secret police became less violent, new houses were built, and consumer goods became more available.

Reading Check Answer
The policy of *glasnost* was an openness to speak or write freely.

Reading Check Answer
The economic goal of *perestroika* was to move the Soviet economy toward capitalism.

💾 Use **Interactive Tutor Self-Assessment Software** to review Section 2.

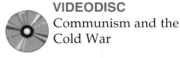

VIDEODISC
Communism and the Cold War

 Side One
Chapter 21

Frames 38662-44504
Title: *A New Soviet Union: Communist Rule Ends*
Subject: Chronicles the rise of Gorbachev and the end of the Soviet Union
Ask: What changes were made by Gorbachev's reforms? *(The people were allowed to vote, political prisoners were set free, and the ruling party was no longer required to support communism.)*

Section 2 Assessment

1. **Define:** purge, hard-liners, capitalism, de-Stalinization, *glasnost*, *perestroika*.
2. What was Mao Zedong's main goal for China?
3. Why did some people oppose the ideas of *glasnost* and *perestroika*?

Critical Thinking

4. **Predicting Consequences** Based on recent changes, do you think China will become a democracy or remain under strict Communist control? Explain.

Graphic Organizer Activity

5. Draw this diagram, and use it to compare the People's Republic of China under Mao Zedong and Deng Xiaoping.

China Under Mao — Both — China Under Deng

Section 2 Assessment Answers

1. purge, removal of undesirables (p. 631); hard-liners, inflexible people (p. 632); capitalism, privately owned economy (p. 633); de-Stalinization, erasing the influence of Stalin (p. 633), *glasnost,* Soviet openness (p. 633), *perestroika,* Soviet restructuring (p. 633)
2. to rebuild China, making it modern
3. they thought Gorbachev was moving too quickly
4. Answers will vary. Some students might cite the trend toward reform, especially those changes resulting from trade. Others might mention ongoing violation of human rights.
5. Diagrams will vary, but students should show the economic reforms initiated by Deng. Both Mao and Deng exercised strict control of government under the Communist Party and use of the Red Army to suppress protests.

Assign the Chapter 38 **Section 2 Quiz** in the TCR. Testmaker available.

Glencoe Literature Library

The following novel from the **Glencoe Literature Library** may be used to enrich this chapter:
• *Nectar in a Sieve,* by Kamala Markandaya. (Effect of industry on an Indian peasant village.)

VIDEODISC
Lessons of War

Side Two
Chapter 6

Frames 12636-20751
Title: *Philosophy of Nonviolence*
Subject: The philosophies of Mohandas Gandhi and Martin Luther King, Jr.
Ask: Identify two people in history who exemplified nonviolent protest.
(Mohandas Gandhi and Martin Luther King, Jr.)

Reading Check
What were most **developing nations** like right after independence?

Reading Check
How did Gandhi use **civil disobedience** to win independence from Great Britain?

SECTION 3 Developing Nations

Most of the countries in South Asia and Africa gained their independence after World War II. The majority of countries in Latin America gained independence in the early 1800s. All of these countries are considered to be **developing nations.** They generally have little industry and most of the people are poor, uneducated, and make their living from the land.

A great number of developing nations also have rapidly growing populations. They cannot produce enough food to feed their people and must buy it elsewhere. As a result, they do not have enough money to provide decent housing, health care, and education for their citizens.

India's Independence India, originally under British rule, was one of the first colonial countries of Asia in which nationalism grew. At first, several problems in India had to be dealt with. There were two major religions—Hinduism and Islam—many of whose followers did not like each other. The people also spoke hundreds of different languages. However, they had one thing in common—opposition to British rule.

In 1885 a political party called the Indian National Congress was formed. Its members called for more Indian self-government.

About that time, an Indian leader named Mohandas Gandhi (mah hahn' dahs gahn' dē) began a protest movement against British rule. Gandhi was a lawyer and a member of the upper class, but he identified himself with the common people. He went from village to village talking about self-government. The people called him Mahatma (muh haht' muh), which means Great Soul.

Gandhi did not believe in violence. He believed in **civil disobedience,** or refusing to obey laws considered unjust. He convinced millions of Indians to show their resistance to British rule through peaceful demonstrations and boycotts.

In 1947 Great Britain finally granted independence to its Indian colony. Instead of one country, however, two were formed. India, the larger country, had a majority of Hindus. A separate country, Pakistan, was created that had a majority of Muslims.

During the *partition,* or dividing, of India, fighting broke out between Hindus and Muslims. Many Hindus in Pakistan fled to India, while many Muslims in India fled to Pakistan. Of the more than 12 million people who changed homelands, nearly 1 million were killed in the fighting.

COOPERATIVE LEARNING

Divide the class into six groups. Assign three groups to design posters on three of the writers who influenced Gandhi: John Ruskin of England, Henry David Thoreau of the United States, and Leo Tolstoy of Russia. Have a fourth group prepare a poster on Gandhi, emphasizing his belief in nonviolence. Direct the remaining two groups to create posters on two leaders influenced by Gandhi: Nelson Mandela and Dr. Martin Luther King, Jr.

Arrange the posters in a display on the classroom wall. The poster on Gandhi should be in the center. Posters showing writers who influenced Gandhi should be on the left, while the posters of people influenced by Gandhi should be on the right. Have students connect the posters with arrows cut out of construction paper.

 Assign Chapter 38 *Cooperative Learning Activity* in the TCR.

INDUSTRIAL INDIA Industry has grown rapidly in India since the nation became independent in 1947. The government has encouraged the establishment of heavy industry in hopes of improving India's economy. Here, workers are employed at an automobile plant. **How do most of India's people make their living?**

In 1971 a civil war broke out between the eastern and western parts of Pakistan. Three years later, Pakistan recognized East Pakistan as the independent nation of Bangladesh.

India Since 1947 After independence, India's leaders worked to set up a stable government. In 1950 a democratic constitution was adopted. Under prime ministers Jawaharlal Nehru (juh wu' har lul nā' rū) and later Indira Gandhi (in dēr' ih gahn' dē) democracy advanced.

Since that time the Indian government has worked to improve people's living conditions. It has encouraged such industries as electric power, iron and steel manufacturing, and textiles. About 70 percent of the Indian people, however, still make their living by farming. Although some have small farms, most work on the estates of large landowners for low pay. Families in Indian villages are generally large although the government has encouraged people to have smaller families.

Many of India's large cities have two sections. One is modern with tall apartment and office buildings. The other section has narrow, twisting, crowded streets. These narrow avenues are lined with two- and three-story, old apartment buildings and hundreds of small businesses.

Mohandas Gandhi
1869–1948

Indian Leader

Trained as a lawyer, Gandhi practiced law in South Africa where he opposed prejudice against black South Africans. When he returned to India in 1915, he gave up his law practice for a more spiritual life. Using nonviolent resistance, Gandhi led the fight for the independence of India, opposed the caste system, and called for acceptance of all religions.

L1 **Economics** Have students research a major product from one of the developing countries such as coffee or cocoa, and create a flow chart of what happens to this product as it moves from producer to consumer. Have them share their charts with the class.

Biography

The following videotape program is available from Glencoe to enrich chapter 38:

- **Mahatma Gandhi: Pilgrim of Peace**

To find classroom resources to accompany this video, check the following home page:
A&E Television:
http://www.aetv.com

GEOGRAPHY AND HISTORY

Pakistan consisted of two regions, East Pakistan and West Pakistan, separated by India. Although the people in both regions were Muslims, they spoke different languages and belonged to different ethnic groups. In 1971, a civil war broke out between the two regions. As a result, East Pakistan became the new nation of Bangladesh.

CAPTION ANSWER

by farming

MAKING CONNECTIONS

➤➤ **History** Two years after Nehru's death his daughter, Indira Gandhi, was elected prime minister of India. She was instrumental in helping East Pakistan win its independence from West Pakistan.

MULTICULTURAL PERSPECTIVES

Indians dress according to their religion, the region in which they live, and how westernized they are. However, Indian men—except in large cities—usually wear a *dhoti*, or a white cotton garment wrapped between the legs. Most Indian women wear a sari. This is a long, straight piece of cotton or silk that is wrapped around the body and then draped over the head.

TECHNOLOGY SKILLS

TEACH

Using an Electronic Spreadsheet

To introduce this lesson, you might write the following information on the board:
Science 88, 90, 85, 98
Social Studies 100, 92, 80, 93
Math 84, 90, 81, 95

Tell students to imagine that these are their report card grades. Then challenge them to figure out their average grade in each subject. Have students use the classroom clock to record the length of time that it takes to complete the assignment.

When students are done, go over the method they used to figure out the averages. Use this discussion as a springboard to assign the skills lesson, which helps students use an electronic spreadsheet to compare birth rates in China, India, and the United States.

Performance Assessment

To encourage self-assessment of the multimedia presentation, have each student complete this individual task management plan.

Self-Management Plan

Name: _____

Task: _____

Steps to accomplish the task:

Problems to completing the task:

Solutions or attempted solutions:

Signed: _____

Using an Electronic Spreadsheet

People use electronic spreadsheets to manage numbers quickly and easily. You can use a spreadsheet any time a problem involves numbers that you can arrange in rows and columns.

Learning the Skill A spreadsheet is an electronic worksheet. All spreadsheets follow a basic design of rows and columns. Each column (vertical) is assigned a letter or a number. Each row (horizontal) is assigned a number. Each point where a column and row intersect is called a cell. The cell's position on the spreadsheet is labeled according to its corresponding column and row—Column A, Row 1 (A1); Column B, Row 2 (B2), etc.

Spreadsheets use standard formulas to calculate the numbers. You create a mathematical equation that uses these standard formulas, and the computer does the calculations for you.

Skill Practice

Suppose you want to compare the number of births in the three most highly populated nations—China, India, and the United States—over the past five years. Use these steps to create a spreadsheet that will provide this information:

1. In cells B1, C1, and D1 respectively, type the name of each of the three countries listed above. In cell E1, type the term *total*.
2. In cells A2–A6, type each year, starting with the most recent year for which statistics are available.
3. In row 2, enter the number of births that occurred in each nation for the year listed in A2. Repeat this process in rows 3 through 6.
4. Create a formula to calculate the number of children born for the first year on the spreadsheet. The formula for the equation tells what cells (2B + 2C + 2D) to add together.
5. Copy the formula down in the cells for the other four years.
6. Use the process in steps 4 and 5 to create and copy a formula to calculate the total births for each of the three countries over a five-year period.

636

TEAM TEACHING STRATEGY

Science Work with a science teacher to use the steps in this lesson to create spreadsheets on average yearly precipitation in several developing nations in the regions studied in Chapter 38. (At least one nation should be from a drought-stricken area of Africa, such as Sudan or Chad.) The spreadsheets can be the basis for a science lesson on climate and climate patterns. They can also be used for a social studies lesson linking climate to cash crops, special farming methods, ways of life, and so on. (Suggest that students check electronic encyclopedias and information on the Internet, including online almanacs, for precipitation figures.)

Malaysia   Malaysia is another developing Asian country that has gone through revolution and successfully built a cooperative government since World War II. Following riots in 1969 between the Malay and the Chinese, the country has become peaceful. With a prospering economy, it lies in a major shipping crossroads of the Pacific Ocean. Muslims, Christians, Buddhists, and Hindus live together, giving Malaysia its cultural richness. The three major ethnic groups of the country—Malays, Chinese, and Indians—cooperatively share power and resources.

Independence in Africa   World War II helped African nationalism grow. During the war, many Africans served in the armies of the European colonial powers. They were sent to fight in many different places around the world. The soldiers saw new sights and learned new skills. When they returned to Africa, they were not content with conditions there and wanted self-rule.

Nationalism grew quickly among educated Africans who worked for independence in different ways. They formed politi-

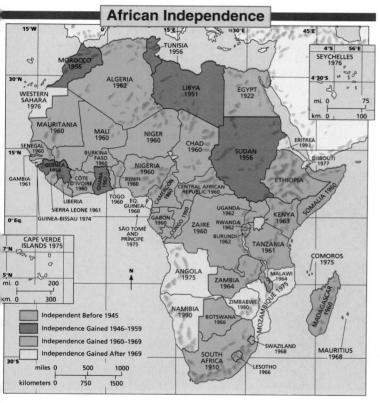

African Independence

Independent Before 1945
Independence Gained 1946–1959
Independence Gained 1960–1969
Independence Gained After 1969

miles 0 500 1000
kilometers 0 750 1500

MAP STUDY

REGIONS Between 1951 and 1991, more than 50 African colonies gained independence. **Which colonies gained independence after 1969?**

MULTICULTURAL PERSPECTIVES

There are many results of African influence in American culture. One of these is the celebration of Kwanzaa, the African American celebration of unity that takes place at the end of December. This week-long festival that calls attention to African American achievement and creativity is based on African harvest festivals that are centuries old.

Independent Practice

L1 **Geography: Region** Have students write five questions about the map "African Independence" on this page. Then have them gather in small groups and have students quiz each other with their questions. **ELL**

L2 **Government** Have students research more about the political history of the two countries showing no dates for independence: Ethiopia and Liberia. Have them write a report explaining what reasons there were for this situation.

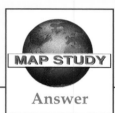

MAP STUDY

Answer

Western Sahara, Guinea-Bissau, Sao Tomé and Principe, Angola, Namibia, Zimbabwe, Mozambique, Djibouti, Comoros

Assign the Chapter 38 **Geography and Map Activity** in the TCR.

NATIONAL GEOGRAPHIC SOCIETY

CD-ROM
Picture Atlas of the World

You and your students can see and read about the physical features of Africa by clicking the "Photos" and "Essay" buttons of individual countries in the region.

Use the **Vocabulary Puzzle-Maker** to create crossword and word search puzzles.

L3 **Geography: Region** Point out to students that the newly independent nations of Africa had great difficulties in forming new governments partly as a result of the way European nations had drawn colonial boundaries in Africa without regard to ethnic differences. Have students compare the map "African Independence" with African maps that show ethnic groups. Have students write a brief paragraph that compares the boundaries of the African nations with the boundaries of these groups.

☑ Reading Check Answer
Subsistence farmers produce only enough food for their families. Africa's most important **cash crops** are cacao, coffee, peanuts, rubber, and tea.

DID YOU KNOW ???
Despite the cold war, both the United States and the Soviet Union supported independence for African nations.

CAPTION ANSWER
lack of education

NATIONAL GEOGRAPHIC SOCIETY

CD-ROM
Picture Atlas of the World
Click the "Video" button of Tanzania to view the Masai people and Serengeti National Park.

638

Then... **& Now**

Meaningful Names
Once they won freedom, many African nations took new names with deep historical meaning. Zimbabwe, for example, refers to the 1,000-year-old city of Great Zimbabwe. Massive, protective stone walls gave the city its name, which means "stone enclosure."

☑ Reading Check
What type of farming is done by **subsistence farmers?** What are some of Africa's most important **cash crops?**

cal parties and bargained with government leaders. They also boycotted goods from colonial countries. In some cases, violence broke out.

In 1960, 17 African countries became independent. The year became known as the "Year of Africa." Other African colonies freed themselves from European rule in following years.

At first most newly independent African countries set up democratic governments. Many did not last, however, and today most have one-party governments or are ruled by a military leader.

Many African countries—including Angola, Ethiopia, Mozambique (mō zam beek'), Nigeria, Rwanda (roo ahn' duh), Somalia, Sudan, Zaire (zīhr), and Zimbabwe (zim bahb' wā)—have suffered from civil war since they became independent. When Europeans originally drew colonial boundaries in Africa, they often put groups that had been fighting one another for hundreds of years in the same colony. Fighting often broke out among these groups.

Farming About 70 percent of all African workers make their living from farming. In the past, most farmers were **subsistence farmers.** They produced only enough food for their families. Today much of the land is used to grow **cash crops,** or crops that are sold in regional or world markets. In fact, more than half of Africa's income results from selling such crops as cacao (kuh kā' ō), coffee, cotton, peanuts, rubber, and tea.

Rural and Urban Africa Many Africans still live in small rural villages, such as the one in Zaire shown here (left), and hold onto their traditional ways. Africa also has many large, modern cities. **What differences face villagers who move to the city?**

638 UNIT 12 THE TWENTIETH CENTURY

MEETING SPECIAL NEEDS

Divide students with Limited English Proficiency into five groups, one group for each of the five regions of Africa. Have each group create a notebook, one page per country, for each region. Each page should consist of a map and legend, showing the major cities and geographic features. Refer students to an almanac and an atlas for other interesting statistics to include on their pages. Have them draw pictures of or

list several influential people (present or past) from each country, write a brief biography, and put them on a separate page. Have students share their notebooks.

📁 Refer to *Inclusion for the Middle School Social Studies Classroom: Strategies and Activities* for additional resources.

In recent years, because of poor farming methods, drought, disease, lack of fertilizer, and more cash crops being grown, there have been food shortages in Africa. Many African nations must buy food from other countries. Often this food is expensive and not plentiful. African governments have begun to teach farmers better farming methods but progress is slow. The United States has sent advisers also.

Large parts of Africa, however, are rich in energy resources. Coal, natural gas, oil, and hydroelectric power are plentiful. The continent also has large mineral deposits, such as copper, tin, iron, manganese, gold, and diamonds. To make full use of these resources, however, more money and skilled workers are needed. More roads and railroads are also needed to move the resources to market.

Ways of Life

Life has been changing in Africa since the 1960s. Most people still live in rural villages, where they belong to **extended families.** These are made up of parents, children, and other close relatives who live together in one house. Most houses in Africa consist of several buildings surrounded by a wall or fence. Rural village houses are often made of mud, clay, or tall grasses and might not have running water, electricity, or indoor plumbing. Large African cities, however, are modern active centers of growth and progress.

Children in rural areas may receive little or no formal schooling, but they have knowledge of and pride in their group's culture. Many leaders of emerging African nations have encouraged the pride each group within a nation shows in its heritage. Writers, musicians, artists, and scholars of African nations are recognized all over the world for their talent and achievements.

African heritage is also seen in the special body markings, and certain colors and kinds of clothing and jewelry African groups wear. For example, the Fulani (fū lah' nē) of West Africa wear royal blue, red, and yellow. The Masai (mah' sī) women of Kenya wear huge collars of brightly colored beads.

In recent years, many Africans have left their home villages and moved to the cities in search of jobs and better housing and education. Some high schools and colleges in the cities offer training in higher-level occupations and technology. They hope trained young people will return to the villages to improve their way of life. Lack of education, however, is a serious problem.

Foreign Influence in Latin America

Even after gaining independence, most Latin American countries remained under foreign control. Industrial nations such as Great Britain, France, Germany, and the United States organized businesses there. They produced such goods as bananas, sugar, coffee, metals, and oil which were sold in markets overseas.

CHAPTER 38 THE COLD WAR ERA **639**

Reading Check
What are **extended families?**

Photograph of Housing in Rio de Janeiro, Brazil

L2 **Language Arts** Have students research and create a simple outline map that shows the different languages that are spoken in Africa. Ask students to share their maps with the class and discuss the following: do language borders follow political borders? What language is most predominant? What language(s) seems to be most widely spread out? If possible, have students learn a word or two in an African language to teach to the class.

Reading Check Answer
Extended families are made up of parents, children, and other close relatives who live together in one house.

DID YOU KNOW

Many African nations changed their names once they gained independence. The new names had special meanings. For example, Rhodesia became Zimbabwe, which refers to the 1,000-year-old royal city of Great Zimbabwe. Massive, protective stone walls gave the city its name—*zimbabwe*—which means "stone enclosure." The city of 20,000 people contained palaces, religious buildings, markets, and the clay houses of Zimbabwe's citizens.

EXTENDING THE CONTENT

In addition to sculpture and painting, dance is an important traditional African art form. Although it varies from area to area, traditional African dance tends to have at least two characteristics in common. First, it expresses two vital concerns of African life—religion and community relationships. There are dances to celebrate the end of harvest, to mark the beginning of puberty, to honor the village gods, and to wish for a successful hunt. Another characteristic of African dance is that it responds to polyrhythms, or complex combinations of fairly simple but different rhythms played simultaneously.

L2 **Economics** Remind students that transportation is important to growing economies. Have students create a simple outline of South America and show on it where the major railway lines run. Ask them to explain, in a paragraph, any obstacles to railways that exist in undeveloped areas.

MAKING CONNECTIONS

➤➤ **History** The United States has tried to improve its relations with Latin America. In 1977, for example, the nation signed a treaty that pledged to return complete control over the Canal Zone to Panama in 1999—an agreement the United States kept.

✔ **Reading Check Answer**
Haciendas are large Latin American ranches. Most *campesinos* earn a living by working on the *haciendas*.

Biography ®

The following videotape program is available from Glencoe to enrich Chapter 38:

• **Evita: The Woman Behind the Myth**

To find classroom resources to accompany this video, check the following home page:

A&E Television:
http://www.aetv.com

LATIN AMERICAN FARMING   Although Latin America is primarily an agricultural region, wealthy landowners hold much of the land in large ranches. These haciendas are worked by peasants with few modern techniques or implements. Here, a Mexican farmer plows behind a team of oxen. **Why have most hacienda owners no desire to modernize their farms?**

Latin American nations benefited from foreign investments. Wages rose, and there were more jobs. Foreign business interests also built roads, railroads, and ports. They set up telephone systems and electric plants.

Still, there were problems. The economies of most of the countries depended on only one or two products. If the price of these products dropped, their incomes did too. Also, food, clothing, household goods, and other such items had to be brought in from other countries at high cost. In addition, Latin American nationalists who wanted their countries to be free of outside influence, resented foreigners.

Domestic Changes in Latin America   Since World War II, most Latin American countries have been trying to industrialize. They have greatly increased their production of such goods as steel, chemicals, oil, and automobiles. Argentina, Brazil, and Mexico are now fairly well-industrialized. Yet even they do not produce enough to meet the needs of their growing populations.

The Latin American economy depends on farming. Most land is held in *haciendas* (ah sē en' duhz), or large ranches. These are owned by a few very rich families. Most work on the *haciendas* is done by peasants known as *campesinos* (kam puh sē' nos).

✔ **Reading Check**
What are *haciendas?* How do the *campesinos* earn a living?

COOPERATIVE LEARNING

Have students form five teams, with each team making a poster of one area of challenge in Latin America studied in this section: population growth, urbanization, economic development, the growth of democracy, and Latin America's international and inter-American relationships. Ask students in each group to do research, plan the poster theme, create the art, and present the poster. Tell students to focus on these areas: the background or history of the challenge, a clear statement of the issue and its current status, any key individuals or countries involved with the issue, and possible solutions to the problems. Have students research current material and consolidate information in clearly organized posters.

Campesinos usually live in villages. Their small houses are made of wood, mud, sun-dried brick, or stone. Larger villages have a church and a few stores and hold open-air markets once a week. People meet there to exchange news as well as to buy and sell food and hand-made goods.

The *campesinos* farm the land in the same way their parents and grandparents did. They are not encouraged to learn new ways. Peasant labor is cheap, so most *hacienda* owners have no wish to modernize or reform the economic system. Often the result is that the land is poorly managed and crops are small.

The *hacienda* system holds back economic progress. Many Latin Americans would like to end it. They believe that farm production will rise if *campesinos* are allowed to own land and learn new ways of farming. In recent years, peasants in several Latin American countries have started revolutions for land reform. This reform has been opposed by the governments and wealthy landowners. Some of the worst violence has taken place in El Salvador, Nicaragua, and Peru. The demand for a voice in their governments by Latin American people, however, has increased.

Latin American cities have also grown larger in recent years. Poor farming methods, drought, warfare, or drops in farm prices have forced millions throughout Latin America off the land and into the cities. There are not enough jobs in the cities to go around, however.

Linking Across Time

Rain Forests   Rain forests once covered much of Central America. However, the clearing of land for ranches and farmland and the cutting of timber for export (right) reduced the rain forests of some nations by almost half. Starting in the late 1970s, Costa Rica set an example for other nations by creating parks and preserves to protect its remaining rain forests (left). **What other problems have resulted from Latin American dependence on cash crops?**

CHAPTER 38 THE COLD WAR ERA   **641**

Linking Across Time

EXTENDING THE CONTENT

The Organization of American States (OAS) includes every nation in the Western Hemisphere except Canada and Cuba, which was excluded in 1962. Its aims are to strengthen peace and security in the hemisphere and to encourage economic, social, and cultural cooperation. The OAS's 1948 charter states that an attack on any one member will be considered an attack on all. The three main organs of the OAS are the General Assembly, which meets annually; the Meeting of Consultation of Foreign Ministers, the emergency executive body; and the Permanent Council, consisting of an ambassador for each member state.

Evaluate

Assign the Chapter 38 **Performance Assessment Activity** in the TCR.

Administer the **Chapter 38 Test** in TCR. Testmaker available.

Reteach

Have students work in pairs to create crossword puzzles using key words or names of people from the chapter. Have pairs exchange and answer puzzles.

Assign the Chapter 38 **Reteaching Activity** in the TCR.

Enrich

Have students choose a country discussed in the chapter and read current magazine and newspaper articles about the country. Have students present an oral report about their findings.

Assign the Chapter 38 **Enrichment Activity** in the TCR.

CLOSE

Have students discuss the connection between improved health care and sanitation and overpopulation that has occurred in developing nations.

💾 Use **Interactive Tutor Self-Assessment Software** to review Section 3.

642

Section 3 Assessment

1. **Define:** developing nations, civil disobedience, subsistence farmers, cash crops, extended families, *haciendas*, *campesinos*.
2. How did Gandhi show his resistance to British rule?
3. Why is 1960 called the "Year of Africa"?
4. How does the *hacienda* system hold back economic progress in Latin America?

Critical Thinking

5. **Drawing Conclusions** How do you think civil wars have affected African nations in recent years?

Graphic Organizer Activity

6. Draw this diagram, and use it to show supporting details for this generalization: World War II helped spark the independence movement in Africa.

Generalization

Supporting Details
1. _____
2. _____
3. _____
4. _____

Chapter Summary & Study Guide

1. After World War II ended, a cold war developed between the United States and the Soviet Union, with the first crisis taking place during the 1948 blockade of Berlin.
2. The cold war turned hot when North Korean soldiers invaded South Korea, and U.N. troops led by the United States intervened in the conflict.
3. The 1959 Cuban Revolution led by Fidel Castro brought a communist government to Cuba.
4. Vietnam was the site of a war between the North Vietnamese and South Vietnamese that lasted until 1975.
5. Led by Mao Zedong, the Communists defeated Chinese Nationalists in 1949 and formed the People's Republic of China.
6. Although Deng Xiaoping relaxed some of China's economic policies, he limited political freedoms.

7. Under Mikhail Gorbachev, the policies of *glasnost* and *perestroika* moved the Soviet Union toward capitalism and greater freedom.
8. Most of the developing nations of South Asia, Africa, and Latin America have struggled with their lack of industry and their dependence on cash crops.
9. Since independence, Indian leaders have tried to set up a stable government and improve living conditions for the poor.
10. The nationalism triggered by World War II led African nations to seek independence. However, imperialism left these nations with numerous problems.

Section 3 Assessment Answers

1. developing nations, nations that have little industry (p. 634); civil disobedience, refusing to obey unjust laws (p. 634); subsistence farmers, produce only food for their families (p. 638); cash crops, raised to be sold (p. 638); extended families, parents, children, and other close relatives (p. 639); *haciendas,* large ranches (p. 640); *campesinos,* peasant-farmers (p. 640)
2. through civil disobedience
3. because many African nations became independent in that year

4. farm production might rise if *campesinos* owned their own land
5. Answers will vary, but civil wars empowered some African nations to develop their economies and governments.
6. Facts will vary but should reflect information on pages 637–638. To get students started, provide this example: Many Africans fought in the armies of colonial powers during World War II.

Assign the Chapter 38 **Section 3 Quiz** in the TCR. Testmaker available.

Using Key Terms

Imagine you are a newspaper reporter in the 1980s looking back on events in the world since World War II. Write a newspaper article describing the changes in the world since the war. Use the following words in your article.

cold war
blockaded
purges
glasnost
developing nations
haciendas

satellite nations
airlift
capitalism
perestroika
cash crops
campesinos

Understanding Main Ideas

1. How did the United States propose to rebuild Western Europe following World War II?
2. Why did the Soviet Union blockade Berlin in 1948?
3. What changes did Castro make once he came to power in Cuba?
4. Why did Mao Zedong order the Cultural Revolution?
5. What were the demonstrators at Tiananmen Square demanding?
6. What problems do most African nations face today?

Critical Thinking

1. Why do you think Chinese leaders restricted political freedom? Explain your reasoning.
2. What do you think might have happened if the Soviet Union had not introduced the policies of *glasnost* and *perestroika*?

3. If you were the leader of a developing Latin American country, what actions would you take to industrialize your country?

Graphic Organizer Activity

History Create a time line like the one shown, and use it to describe important events that occurred in each of the following years in the cold war: 1948, 1949, 1950, 1954, 1957, 1959, 1961. (Some years may have more than one event.)

```
1945 ──1948──1950──────1957──1961── 1965
        └1949─┘  └1954─┘  └1959─┘
```

Geography in History

Human/Environmental Interaction
Refer to the map tracing African independence on page 637. Note the locations of countries that gained their independence before 1945. Why might you expect revolutions for freedom to develop in coastal countries?

Using Your Journal

Review any details you may have noted about the challenges facing China, Latin America, and Africa. Choose one of these areas and write a paragraph describing what you think its biggest challenge is and what could be done to meet that challenge.

Bonus Test Question

For Chapter 38 Test
Choose one of the following countries and explain why it is considered a developing country: India, Brazil, Zimbabwe. *(Answers will vary but should offer details.)*

Using Your Journal

Paragraphs will vary. You might call on volunteers to read their paragraphs to the class and compile the suggested challenges on the board.

Geography in History

Answers will vary but could include that coastal areas are more accessible to outside influences and new ideas.

Using Key Terms

Newspaper articles will vary, but students should use all the key terms and present their article in newspaper style.

Understanding Main Ideas

1. through the Marshall Plan
2. to try and force Western powers to leave the city
3. Cubans who opposed him were jailed or executed. Castro announced his government would be communist.
4. because he began to worry that the Chinese people were losing their revolutionary spirit
5. democracy
6. *glasnost* and *perestroika*
7. how to produce enough food, utilize natural resources, educate people, stop warring clans

Critical Thinking

1. Answers will vary, but students could indicate that they might be afraid to give the people too much power.
2. Answers will vary but should include a slower economic growth and delayed independence.
3. Answers will vary but could include better use of resources and modernization.

Graphic Organizer Activity

Descriptions will vary, but events might include: 1948—Marshall Plan, establishment of Soviet satellites, blockade of Berlin, Berlin airlift; 1949—formation of NATO, flight of Chinese Nationalists from mainland; 1950—start of Korean War; 1954—formation of Warsaw Pact, defeat of French in Vietnam; 1957—formation of the European Common Market, launch of *Sputnik I*; 1959—Cuban Revolution; 1961—construction of Berlin Wall, Bay of Pigs invasion

Chapter 39 Planning Guide

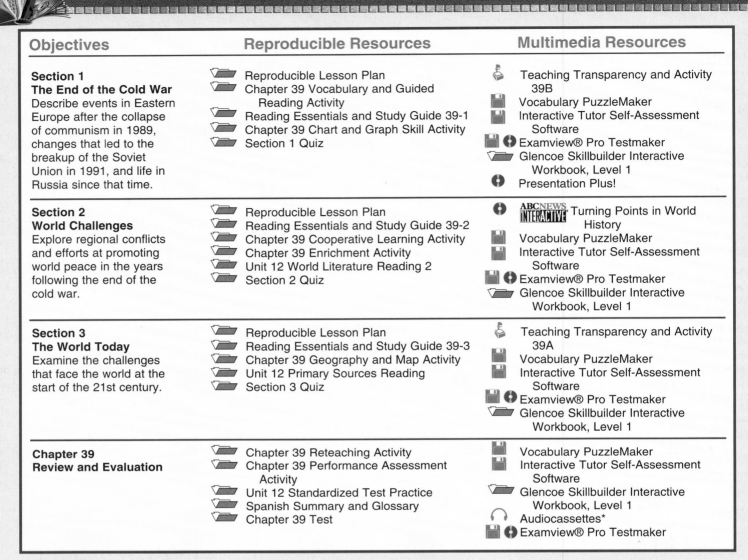

Objectives	Reproducible Resources	Multimedia Resources
Section 1 **The End of the Cold War** Describe events in Eastern Europe after the collapse of communism in 1989, changes that led to the breakup of the Soviet Union in 1991, and life in Russia since that time.	Reproducible Lesson Plan Chapter 39 Vocabulary and Guided Reading Activity Reading Essentials and Study Guide 39-1 Chapter 39 Chart and Graph Skill Activity Section 1 Quiz	Teaching Transparency and Activity 39B Vocabulary PuzzleMaker Interactive Tutor Self-Assessment Software Examview® Pro Testmaker Glencoe Skillbuilder Interactive Workbook, Level 1 Presentation Plus!
Section 2 **World Challenges** Explore regional conflicts and efforts at promoting world peace in the years following the end of the cold war.	Reproducible Lesson Plan Reading Essentials and Study Guide 39-2 Chapter 39 Cooperative Learning Activity Chapter 39 Enrichment Activity Unit 12 World Literature Reading 2 Section 2 Quiz	ABCNEWS INTERACTIVE Turning Points in World History Vocabulary PuzzleMaker Interactive Tutor Self-Assessment Software Examview® Pro Testmaker Glencoe Skillbuilder Interactive Workbook, Level 1
Section 3 **The World Today** Examine the challenges that face the world at the start of the 21st century.	Reproducible Lesson Plan Reading Essentials and Study Guide 39-3 Chapter 39 Geography and Map Activity Unit 12 Primary Sources Reading Section 3 Quiz	Teaching Transparency and Activity 39A Vocabulary PuzzleMaker Interactive Tutor Self-Assessment Software Examview® Pro Testmaker Glencoe Skillbuilder Interactive Workbook, Level 1
Chapter 39 **Review and Evaluation**	Chapter 39 Reteaching Activity Chapter 39 Performance Assessment Activity Unit 12 Standardized Test Practice Spanish Summary and Glossary Chapter 39 Test	Vocabulary PuzzleMaker Interactive Tutor Self-Assessment Software Glencoe Skillbuilder Interactive Workbook, Level 1 Audiocassettes* Examview® Pro Testmaker

*Also available in Spanish.

Presentation Plus!

Use Glencoe's **Presentation Plus!** multimedia teacher tool to easily present dynamic lessons that visually excite your students. Using Microsoft® PowerPoint, you can customize the presentations to create your own personalized lessons.

 Interactive Lesson Planner

Planning has never been easier! Using this CD-ROM, organize your week, month, semester, or year with all the help you need. The **Interactive Lesson Planner** gives you access to all of the blackline masters which accompany *Human Heritage*.

✓ PERFORMANCE ASSESSMENT ACTIVITIES

Videotape Assign students to select a global issue that concerns them—destruction of the rainforests, global warming, terrorism, human rights abuses, etc. Then direct them to research this problem, including information about groups seeking solutions. Have students present their findings in the form of a two-minute videotaped commercial urging people to volunteer their time and talents to resolving the issue.

CHAPTER RESOURCES

LITERATURE ABOUT THE PERIOD

The Learning Community. *A Journey to the Heart.* Rainbow Bridge/SSSS, 1991. Collection of experiences of American students who visited Kenya.

READINGS FOR THE STUDENT

Case, Dianne. *92 Queens Road.* Farrar Straus & Giroux, 1995. Story of a mixed-race child in Cape Town, South Africa.

READINGS FOR THE TEACHER

Gunn, Geoffrey C. *East Timor and the UN: The Case for Intervention.* Red Sea Press, 1997. An account of the crisis in East Timor and a collection of related primary sources.

Simes, Dimitri K. *After the Collapse: Russia Seeks its Place as a Great Power.* Simon & Schuster, 1999. Highly readable account of present-day Russia.

KEY TO ABILITY LEVELS

Teaching strategies have been coded for varying learning styles and abilities.

L1 Level 1 activities are **basic** activities and should be within the ability range of all students.

L2 Level 2 activities are **average** activities and should be within the ability range of the average to above-average student.

L3 Level 3 activities are **challenging** activities designed for the ability range of above-average students.

ELL ELL activities should be within the ability range of English Language Learning students.

NATIONAL GEOGRAPHIC SOCIETY — Teacher's Corner

INDEX TO NATIONAL GEOGRAPHIC MAGAZINE

The following articles relate to this chapter:

- "The Caspian Sea," by Robert Cullen, May 1999.
- "Beirut Rising," by Peter Theroux, September 1997.
- "Moscow: The New Revolution," by David Remmick, April 1997.
- "Kaliningrad," by Priit J. Vesilind, March 1997.
- "Sri Lanka," by Priit J. Vesilind, January 1997.
- "Reinventing Berlin," by Peter Ross Range, December 1996.
- "Gaza," by Alexandra Avakian, September 1996.

ADDITIONAL NATIONAL GEOGRAPHIC SOCIETY PRODUCTS

To order the following, call National Geographic at 1-800-368-2728:

- *Africa's Stolen River (Video)*
- *Amazon: Land of the Flooded Forest (Video)*
- *Great Lakes: Fragile Seas (Video)*
- *National Geographic's Atlas of World History (Book)*
- *National Geographic: Eyewitness to the 20th Century (Book)*
- *Technology's Price (Video)*

Access *National Geographic's* new dynamic MapMachine Web site and other geography resources at:
http://www.nationalgeographic.com/
http://www.nationalgeographic.com/maps/

The following videotape programs are available from Glencoe:

- **Israel: Birth of a Nation**
  0-7670-1107-4

- **Nelson Mandela: Journey to Freedom**
  0-7670-0113-3

- **Yitzhak Rabin**
  1-56501-714-5

To order, call Glencoe at 1-800-334-7344. To find classroom resources to accompany many of these check:

A&E Television: http://www.aetv.com
The History Channel:
http://www.historychannel.com

OVERVIEW

Chapter 39 discusses the end of the cold war and the challenges facing the global community at the start of the 2000s.

➤ **Section 1** describes the collapse of communism in Eastern Europe and the breakup of the Soviet Union.
➤ **Section 2** explores global crises following the cold war.
➤ **Section 3** summarizes global challenges and interaction among nations today.

CHAPTER OBJECTIVES

After reading Chapter 39, students will be able to:

1. discuss how independence came to Eastern Europe.
2. describe life in Russia after the breakup of the Soviet Union.
3. explain how nations responded to issues of war and peace after the cold war ended.
4. identify world challenges at the start of the 21st century.

EXAMINING ARTIFACTS

Ask students what these two artifacts tell them about the world since 1989. *(that communism is less of a force; that computers have increased contact among nations)* Call on students to brainstorm other events or inventions that they think may have shaped today's world. Record their ideas for review as you lead them through the chapter.

PERFORMANCE ASSESSMENT ✓

Use the Performance Assessment activity on page 644B to help you evaluate students as they complete the chapter.

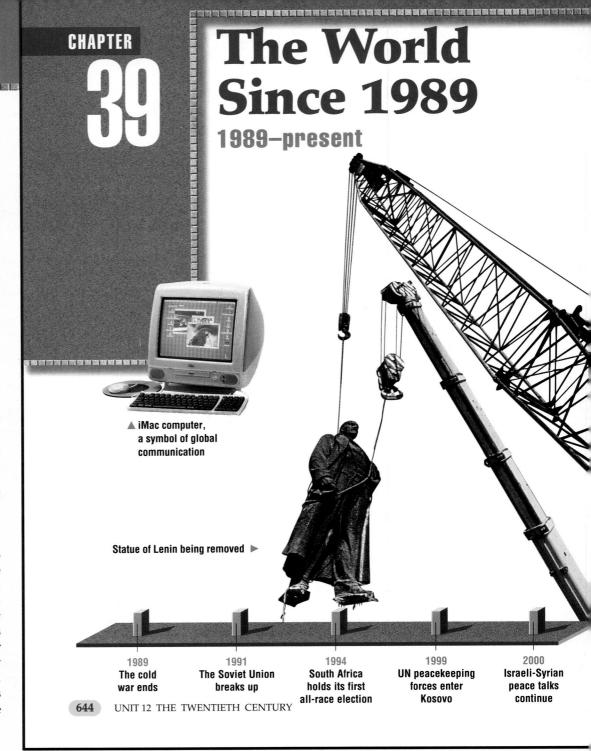

CHAPTER
39

The World Since 1989
1989–present

▲ **iMac computer, a symbol of global communication**

Statue of Lenin being removed ▶

1989	1991	1994	1999	2000
The cold war ends	**The Soviet Union breaks up**	**South Africa holds its first all-race election**	**UN peacekeeping forces enter Kosovo**	**Israeli-Syrian peace talks continue**

644 UNIT 12 THE TWENTIETH CENTURY

TEACHING RESOURCES

TEACHER PLANNING AND SUPPORT

📁 Reproducible Lesson Plan
📁 Block Scheduling Implementation Guide
📁 Videodisc Bar Code Correlation
💿 Presentation Plus!

REVIEW AND REINFORCEMENT

📁 Reading Essentials and Study Guide 39-1, 39-2, 39-3
📁 Chapter 39 Vocabulary and Guided Reading Activity
💾 Vocabulary PuzzleMaker Software
🖨 Teaching Transparencies 39A & 39B

📁 Chapter 39 Reteaching Activity
📁 Chapter 39 Cooperative Learning Activity
📁 Chapter 39 Activity Book Activity
📁 Chapter 39 Chart and Graph Skill Activity
💾 Interactive Tutor Self-Assessment Software
💿📼 Unit 12 MindJogger VideoQuiz

APPLICATION AND HANDS-ON ACTIVITIES

📁 Daily World History, Geography, and Culture Question
📁 Unit 12 Hands-On History Lab Activity

Chapter Focus

Read to Discover

- How independence came to the nations of Eastern Europe.
- What changes came to Russia after the breakup of the Soviet Union.
- How nations responded to issues of war and peace after the cold war ended.
- What challenges the world faces in the 2000s.

HISTORY Online
Chapter Overview

Visit the *Human Heritage* Web site at **humanheritage.glencoe.com** and click on *Chapter 39— Chapter Overviews* to preview this chapter.

Terms to Learn	People to Know	Places to Locate
aggression	Boris Yeltsin	Berlin
coup	Lech Walesa	Chechnya
sovereign	Saddam Hussein	Persian Gulf
secede	Slobodan	Sarajevo
autonomous	Milosevic	Kosovo
intifada	Yasir Arafat	Irish Republic
apartheid	Yitzhak Rabin	Hong Kong
euro	Nelson Mandela	Taiwan
		East Timor

Why It's Important

The 1980s and 1990s saw the end of the cold war and the collapse of the Soviet Union. People looked forward to a new era of peace. However, national and ethnic rivalries soon erupted around the world. Regional conflicts forced leaders to devise new rules for stopping **aggression,** or warlike acts, and intervening in the affairs of other nations.

As the 2000s opened, it had become clear that nations needed to work together to solve shared problems, such as a growing world population, a threatened environment, and a lack of opportunities for all of the earth's people.

> **Reading Check**
> What is **aggression**?

SECTION 1 · The End of the Cold War

The 1990s saw the collapse of communism in Eastern Europe and the breakup of the Soviet Union. Freed from Communist control, independent nations throughout the region struggled to develop new economic and political systems.

A Spirit of Democracy The Communist hold on government weakened under Soviet premier Mikhail Gorbachev. Earlier Soviet rulers had refused to publicly discuss problems facing the

CHAPTER 39 THE WORLD SINCE 1989 **645**

GEOGRAPHY ACTIVITIES
- Chapter 39 Geography and Map Activity
- Social Studies Outline Map Resource Book

INTERDISCIPLINARY CONNECTIONS
- Unit 12 World Literature Reading 2
- World Music: Cultural Traditions

ENRICHMENT AND EXTENSION
- Unit 12 Primary Sources Reading
- ABCNEWS INTERACTIVE Turning Points in World History
- World History Primary Source Document Library CD-ROM
- Foods Around the World

ASSESSMENT AND EVALUATION
- Chapter 39 Performance Assessment Activity
- Chapter 39 Section Quizzes 39-1, 39-2, 39-3
- Chapter 39 Test
- Unit 12 Standardized Test Practice
- Chapter 39 ExamView® Pro Testmaker Software
- Chapter 39 Digests Audiocassettes Activity and Tests

SPANISH RESOURCES
- Chapter 39 Spanish Chapter Summary and Glossary
- Chapter 39 Spanish Chapter Digests Audiocassettes Activities and Tests

---

HISTORY Online

Chapter Overview introduces students to chapter content and key terms. Have them access **Chapter 39 Overview** at **humanheritage.glencoe.com**

FOCUS

Bellringer
Have students list challenges facing the world today.

Motivational Activity
Compile students' lists on the board. Then help students to prioritize these challenges, encouraging them to reach a consensus on the top five issues. Tell students that issues such as the ones they have named form the subject of Chapter 39.

GUIDE TO READING

Reading Strategy
Ask students to read "Why It's Important" and summarize the chapter's main theme. *(Following the cold war, nations searched for ways to solve issues that threatened the earth's people.)*

Vocabulary Precheck
Ask students to define each of the "Terms to Learn." Have a volunteer consult the dictionary for any unfamiliar words. **L1** **ELL**

Use the Vocabulary PuzzleMaker for Chapter 39 to create a crossword puzzle. **L1**

Assign Chapter 39 Vocabulary and Guided Reading Activity.

Assign Reading Essentials and Study Guide 39-1.

>
> **Reading Check Answer**
> **Aggression** is warlike acts.

TEACH

Guided Practice

L1 **Chronology** Divide the class into small groups, and assign each group a subsection in Section 1. Instruct students to create an illustrated time line of the events discussed in their subsection. Display the time lines on a classroom wall.

Linking Across Time

Germany became reunited on October 3, 1990.

646

Soviet Union. Gorbachev, however, believed the only way t solve these problems was to talk about them freely.

As Gorbachev introduced his new policy of glasnost, o openness, to the Soviet Union, he urged leaders in the Sovie satellites to do the same. He indicated that the Soviet Unio would no longer use troops and tanks to support Communis governments, as had been done in Hungary in 1956 and i Czechoslovakia in 1968.

The first successful challenge to Communist rule came i Poland. In January 1989, the Polish government lifted its ban o Solidarity, a labor union that had been calling for reform sinc 1980. In June, Polish voters elected Solidarity members to two thirds of the seats in the Polish legislature. For the first time, Communist government in Eastern Europe had lost power as result of an election.

Fall of the Berlin Wall In East Germany, Communist leade Erich Honecker ignored the people's call for reform. In 1989, how ever, Hungary started reforms and opened its borders with Austri Thousands of East Germans—mostly young people—took thi chance to show their rejection of communism by fleeing throug Hungary into western Europe. Meanwhile, thousands of other Eas Germans held protest marches against the government.

Linking Across Time

Collapse of Communism The collapse of communism in Eastern Europe was symbolized by destruction of the Berlin wall in 1989 (below). Today pieces of the wall can be found on display in the United States (right) and in other places around the world. **When did Germany become reunited?**

SPOTLIGHT ON: POPE JOHN PAUL II

In 1978, the College of Cardinals elected the youngest man to become Pope since 1846 and the first non-Italian in 456 years. The new Pope—Karol Cardinal Wojtyla of Cracow—came from Poland. As a youth, Wojtyla had worked as a laborer, first in a quarry and later in a factory. During World War II, he studied for the priesthood at an illegal underground seminary and risked his life to shelter Jews from the Nazis.

The election of Wojtyla, known as Pope John Paul II, electrified Poland. In 1979, the staunch anti-communist Pope paid a personal visit to his homeland. He went on to become the most widely traveled Pope in history. In 1996, *Time Magazine* listed him in its biographical collection entitled *Great People of the 20th Century*.

In October 1989, Honecker resigned. On November 9, at the stroke of midnight, officials in East Berlin threw open the main gate in the Berlin Wall—a 28-mile-long, steel-and-concrete symbol of the cold war. A roar went up as people from both East and West Berlin climbed on top of the wall and danced with joy.

The next morning, a gigantic headline in a West Berlin newspaper declared "BERLIN IS BERLIN AGAIN!" That day, soldiers began to knock down the wall. Civilians joined them, whacking away with hammers, axes, and chisels. By December, the entire wall had disappeared.

The Last Satellites

East German demands for freedom sparked changes in other Eastern European nations. A week after officials opened the Berlin Wall, Bulgaria's hard-line Communist boss resigned. A little later, popular elections overturned Communist rule in Hungary and Czechoslovakia. When the Communist leader of Romania tried to crush the reform movement, rebels tried him and then executed him for crimes against the people.

As one Communist government after another collapsed in Eastern Europe, Gorbachev astounded the world by refusing to intervene. Throughout 1989, he worked with leaders in Europe and the United States to promote peace in the region.

In early 1990, East Germany held its first democratic election since the rise of Adolf Hitler in the 1930s. On October 3, it was reunited with West Germany. That December, Germans elected Helmut Kohl as the first chancellor of the reunited nation. The cold war, which had begun with the division of Germany after World War II, was over.

Conflict Within the Soviet Union

As former Soviet satellites celebrated their independence, trouble brewed within the Soviet Union. The new spirit of openness introduced by Gorbachev allowed **dissent**, or criticism, against the government for the first time since the 1917 Communist takeover.

Although widely popular in Europe and the United States, Gorbachev found himself attacked at home by both hard-liners and reformers. Hard-liners blasted Gorbachev for "giving up" Eastern Europe. They resisted reform, fearing both the loss of their jobs and the weakening of Soviet power. Because the hard-liners included many military leaders, Gorbachev moved carefully to avoid a takeover of government. The slow pace of change provoked criticism from reformers led by Boris Yeltsin.

Yeltsin's outspoken comments caused a break with Gorbachev, who dismissed him from important positions within the Communist party. Yeltsin responded by taking his case to the Soviet people. In May 1990, he won election as president of Russia, the largest of the 15 Soviet republics. For the first time, a Russian head of state

East Germany
On October 7, 1989, East Germany celebrated its 40th anniversary. When Gorbachev showed up to speak in East Berlin, thousands of protestors shouted, "Gorbi, help us!" They then started chanting a popular political slogan, "We are the people!"

 Reading Check
What is **dissent**?

Boris N. Yeltsin

L2 **Government** Guide students in naming the different countries in this section whose Communist regimes ended. *(Poland, East Germany, Romania, Hungary, Czechoslovakia)* Then have them create a chart on the board listing each country and the method that it used to achieve independence. Tell students to star those nations that had "peaceful rebellions."

L3 **Current Events** Assign students to research achievements and problems in former Soviet satellites in the 2000s. Have them present their findings in the form of a regional newspaper entitled *Eastern European News.* Headline stories should highlight the most important events or issues in the region. News articles and features should also cut across the region, with at least one article on each nation. Encourage students to include illustrations similar to those usually found in newspapers, especially political cartoons.

Reading Check Answer
Dissent is criticism, usually against the government.

MEETING SPECIAL NEEDS

Assign gifted students to read and report on literature written by Eastern European authors such as Vaclav Havel, Milovan Dijilas, Milan Kundera, Anna Swir, or other poets, playwrights, novelists, and essayists from this region. Ask these students to select a passage that interests them for reading to the class. Direct students to be prepared to answer questions or to explain difficult portions of the passage.

Refer to *Inclusion for the Middle School Social Studies Classroom: Strategies and Activities* for additional resources.

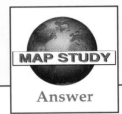

MAP STUDY

Answer

✓ **Reading Check Answer**
Hard-liners attempted a **coup** in 1991 because they wanted to rebuild the Communist state.

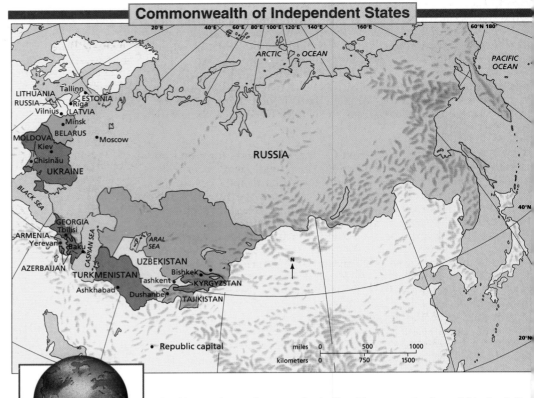

Commonwealth of Independent States

• Republic capital

MAP STUDY

LOCATION The Commonwealth of Independent States stretches from Europe through a large part of Asia. **What geographic factors made it easier for Russia to have power over the other former republics?**

✓ **Reading Check**
Why did Communist hard-liners attempt a **coup** in 1991?

had been chosen by popular ballot. Two months later, Yeltsin defied hard-liners by publicly quitting the Communist party.

Meanwhile, people in the other 14 Soviet republics talked openly of independence. In 1990, the Baltic states of Latvia and Estonia proclaimed their freedom. In March 1991, Lithuania—the third Baltic state occupied by Russia at the end of World War II—did the same. Instead of trying to suppress the revolt, Gorbachev responded by negotiating Lithuania's independence.

Hard-liners exploded at the breakup of what they called the "Soviet empire." In August 1991, the military and secret police arranged a **coup** (koo), or forced takeover of the government. They placed Gorbachev under house arrest and vowed to rebuild the Communist state.

In a tense, three-day struggle known as the "Second Russian Revolution," Yeltsin stepped in to restore order. He condemned the leaders of the revolt, who lost the support of the military. On August 24, Gorbachev returned to Moscow. The next day, he shut down the Communist party, thus ending 74 years of Communist rule.

COOPERATIVE LEARNING

Divide the class into three groups, assigning each group one of these time spans: 1989–1995, 1995–2000, 2000–present. Instruct each group to research important events in recent Russian history during the time span assigned, starting with the collapse of communism in Soviet satellites and ending with the most important issue or event in the news today. Have students present their findings in the form of a wall-sized time line. Students can use connected sheets of computer paper, newsprint, or posterboard to construct their time lines. Encourage them to illustrate selected events with copies of photographs or their own drawings.

Popular anger at the Communist party and secret police now boiled over. People tore down statues of Communist leaders such as Vladimir Lenin and Joseph Stalin. They rejected names given to cities to honor Communists. Leningrad, for example, returned to its pre-1924 name of St. Petersburg.

Independence and Ethnic Rivalries　By the end of 1991, all 15 Soviet republics had proclaimed their independence. In December, Gorbachev—a ruler without a country—resigned. Under the leadership of Yeltsin, 11 former Soviet republics formed the Commonwealth of Independent States (CIS)—a loose confederation of **sovereign**, or self-governing, nations.

The growth of independence went hand-in-hand with a revived spirit of nationalism among the many ethnic and religious groups in Eastern Europe and the former Soviet Union. Starting in 1991, Yugoslavia—a confederation of six individual republics—began to split apart as ethnic rivalries erupted in war. Two years later, Czechoslovakia peacefully split into the Czech Republic and the Republic of Slovakia. That same year, two republics quit the CIS, while Russia acted increasingly on its own.

Within Russia, rebels in the state of Chechnya tried to **secede**, or withdraw, to form their own government. Yeltsin responded by sending in troops and tanks. The drawn-out battle lasted throughout the Yeltsin presidency of the 1990s. The use of force and the failure to resolve the conflict left Yeltsin's reputation as a reformer badly battered.

Economic Hardships　Perhaps no single issue troubled the new governments more than the economy. In the effort to win the cold world, Communist leaders had neglected economic development. As a result, the new governments inherited outdated industries and a shortage of goods, such as household appliances.

Governments moved to **privatize**, or allow the private ownership of, state-owned stores, businesses, and factories. However, few people had acquired enough money or experience to run businesses based on free competition—the cornerstone of capitalism.

For many years, Communist governments had controlled prices, wages, and the production of goods. With the collapse of communism, however, the principle of supply and demand went into effect. In most places, consumer goods remained in short supply throughout the 1990s. This situation created a high demand, which in turn pushed up prices. Because governments no longer employed workers in state-owned businesses, unemployment soared and wages dropped.

By the mid-1990s, about 30 percent of the Russian population had fallen into poverty. Strikes shook Poland as workers demanded wage increases. Throughout the region, interest rates skyrocketed as investment money remained scarce.

Fast Food　In 1990, McDonald's opened its first restaurant in Moscow. By 1998 there were 15 McDonald's, serving more than a million orders of french fries each month.

✓ **Reading Check**
What are **sovereign** nations?

✓ **Reading Check**
How did Yeltsin respond when Chechnya tried to **secede?**

Chechnyan rebel

✓ **Reading Check**
What obstacles slowed Russian efforts to **privatize** businesses, shops, and factories?

✓ **Reading Check Answer**
Sovereign nations are self-governing nations.

✓ **Reading Check Answer**
When Chechnya tried to **secede,** Yeltsin sent in troops and tanks.

✓ **Reading Check Answer**
Russian efforts to **privatize** were slowed by a lack of money and experience to run businesses based on free competition.

ABCNEWS INTERACTIVE™

 Videodisc
Communism and the Cold War

 Side Two
Chapter 17

Frames 38033-42654
Title: *Challenge of Reform*
Subject: Challenges facing Eastern European countries
Ask: What happened as Poland tried to achieve a free market system?
(Prices and unemployment rose.)

SPOTLIGHT ON: CHECHNYA

The Chechens, a largely Muslim people, have a long history of resistance. They were the most active opponents of czarist Russian occupation of the Caucasus region during the years 1818 to 1917. When the Bolsheviks seized the region in 1918, the anti-communist Chechens immediately rebelled. Soviet troops occupied Chechnya, but they were forced to put down bloody rebellions in 1929 and 1940.

Fed up with resistance, Stalin exiled the entire Chechen nation to Siberia in 1944. In 1957, the remaining Chechens—those who had survived—were allowed to return home. The Soviets, however, treated the Chechen capital of Grozny as enemy territory. When the Soviet Union broke up in 1991, Chechens again declared their independence, triggering battles with Russia that lasted into the 2000s. Ask interested students to research the status of Chechnya today.

L2 **Current Events** Assign students to research political elections since the resignation of Boris Yeltsin on December 31, 1999. Have them examine the representation of Communists in the Duma, or Russian parliament, and the party affiliation of the current Russian president. Based on this information, would they say that Russia is more or less democratic today than it was on the day Yeltsin resigned?

CAPTION ANSWER

Economic challenges include: lack of money and experience to privatize businesses, shortages of consumer goods, high prices, soaring interest rates, and high unemployment. Political challenges include: rival political parties, Communist efforts to capitalize on economic hardships, and efforts to stabilize the office of the president.

Lech Welesa, the leader of Solidartiy

Lech Walesa Lech Walesa first worked as an electrician. He organized the trade union Solidarity, and later became Poland's first freely elected President. He won the Nobel Peace Prize in 1983.

Political Challenges At first, citizens expressed a willingness to endure the economic hardships. But as the excitement over independence cooled, the pains of poverty tested people's faith in democracy. Open elections allowed rival political parties to challenge the popular heroes of independence. In some nations, including Russia, the Communists reminded people of a time when the government put wages in their pockets and bread on their tables.

In 1994, Hungary elected a number of former Communists to the legislature. In 1995, a former Communist defeated Lech Walesa —the leader of Solidarity—in his bid for reelection as the president of Poland. In 1996, a half dozen candidates in Russia, including a Communist, tried to wrestle the presidency away from Boris Yeltsin.

By the end of the 1990s, however, none of those nations had returned to communism. In 1997, a coalition of groups led by Solidarity overwhelmingly defeated Communist candidates to the legislature. That year, the North Atlantic Treaty Organization (NATO) felt secure enough in the political future of Poland, Hungary, and the Czech Republic to admit all three former Soviet satellites as members.

Suddenly, on December 31, 1999, Russian president Boris Yeltsin resigned. Vladimir Putin was appointed acting president, and new elections were scheduled for March 2000. This peaceful transfer of power showed how much the political climate had changed since the days of Communist rule.

POLITICAL CHANGE Teenagers in Russia have more social and political freedom than their parents or grandparents. **What political and economic challenges does Russia face today?**

650 UNIT 12 THE TWENTIETH CENTURY

SPOTLIGHT ON: BORIS YELTSIN

The name Boris means "warrior," and Boris Yeltsin lived up the name at an early age. While still in primary school, he asked to speak to an assembled audience of teachers, parents, and students attending a graduation ceremony. Young Yeltsin took advantage of the opportunity to attack one of the teachers for "cruel, unusual punishment" of students. His outspoken speech earned Yeltsin an expulsion. However, he refused to accept the decision and demanded an appeal. In the end, Yeltsin, the child warrior, won the right to return to the school.

Reading A Demographic Map

In order to show information about where people live on the earth, mapmakers use **demographic maps.** Among other things, these maps can show population density, or the average number of people per square mile, or square kilometer, of land.

Some parts of the world have many people living in each square mile, or square kilometer. People generally live in areas with good physical environments. Other parts of the world have few people, and there are even some areas in which no people live. These are known as *uninhabited* areas.

For example, on the "World Population" map below, the color green indicates areas, such as Southeast Asia, with more than 250 people per square mile, or 97 people per square kilometer. This is the highest population density shown. The color light brown indicates areas, such as Antarctica, that are uninhabited.

Map Practice

1. **What color represents 60-125 people per square mile (25-50 per sq. km)?**
2. **What areas in South America have densities of 2-60 people per square mile (1-25 per sq. km)?**

World Population

Density

per sq. mile	per sq. km
More than 250	More than 100
125–250	50–100
60–125	25–50
2–60	1–25
Fewer than 2	Fewer than 1
Uninhabited	Uninhabited

NORTH AMERICA
SOUTH AMERICA
EUROPE
AFRICA
ASIA
AUSTRALIA
ANTARCTICA

180° 160°W 120°W 80°W 40°W 0° 40°E 80°E 120°E 160°E
80°N 40°N

miles 0 — 2000
kilometers 0 — 2000 — 4000

N

GO TO

Glencoe's **Skillbuilder Interactive Workbook, Level 1,** provides instruction and practice in key social studies skills.

651

TEACH

Reading a Demographic Map

Direct students to read the instructional part of the feature. Ask: Why do mapmakers use demographic maps? *(to show information about where people live on Earth)* Name one thing that a demographic map can show. *(population density)* What are uninhabited areas? *(places in which no people live)*

Next, tell students to study the map. Ask: What color indicates uninhabitable areas? *(gold)* What does the color green indicate on the map? *(more than 250 people per square kilometer)* What is the approximate population density of the area where you live? *(Answers will vary.)*

After asking these questions, have students work in pairs or in small groups to write questions and answers based on the map in the skill lesson. Call on a spokesperson from each pair or small group to pose their questions to the rest of the class.

Answers to Map Practice

1. salmon (pale orange)
2. much of the coastal area

SPOTLIGHT ON: WORLD POPULATION

The population of the world is computed only after a careful census has been taken. These counts must be made in a systematic way to record a *de jure* census, which tallies people according to their legal place of residence, or a *de facto* census, which counts them as residing where they spent the night of the day on which the census was taken. In either case, the census distribution is determined by where people sleep, rather than by where they work. Thus, it is a nighttime population count.

💾 Use **Interactive Tutor Self-Assessment Software** to review Section 1.

LINKING PAST TO PRESENT

UN peacekeeping troops, known as Blue Helmets, were originally formed to maintain peaceful conditions in areas where a cease-fire had been negotiated. Since the end of the cold war, however, Blue Helmets are being sent into situations where violence continues through a cease-fire, or where violence recurs after a cease-fire has been negotiated.

💾 Use the **Vocabulary Puzzle-Maker** to create crossword and word search puzzles.

Perhaps the most important change in Russia was the number of young people who grew up during the 1980s and 1990s. They lived at a time when Russians won the right to make their own decisions and to vote freely. As one Russian exchange student in the United States put it: "Let me tell you how Russia has changed. I'm not a Communist. My mother is not a Communist. My father is not a Communist. Do you think I could have said that in the old days?"

Section 1 Assessment

1. **Define:** aggression, dissent, coup, sovereign, secede, privatize.
2. What changes took place in Eastern Europe as a result of reforms introduced by Mikhail Gorbachev?
3. Why did hard-liners in the Soviet Union try to take control of the government?

Critical Thinking

4. **Making Predictions** Do you think the world has seen the last of communism in Russia? Why or why not?

Graphic Organizer Activity

5. Draw a diagram like this one, and use it to show some of the problems faced by former Soviet satellites.

SECTION 2 World Challenges

With the collapse of the Soviet Union, world peace was within reach—or so it seemed. However, the situation proved more complex. During the cold war, the United States and the Soviet Union had used their money, power, and influence to dominate events in other nations. Now, long-standing national and ethnic tensions erupted in violence and confusion.

As the world headed into the 2000s, nations struggled to find new ways of resolving regional threats to peace. Leaders in the United States tried to seek approval before acting, but crises in the Persian Gulf, the Balkans, Africa, and elsewhere showed that collective action was a hard course to follow. At times, global organizations such as the UN seemed unable to respond effectively to aggression. Even so, there were some bright spots. Progress in South Africa, Ireland, and the Middle East kept the dream of world peace alive.

The Gulf War One of the first major foreign-policy challenges of the post-cold war era took place in the area around the Persian Gulf. In August 1990, Iraqi dictator Saddam Hussein ordered the invasion of oil-rich Kuwait. He also moved Iraqi

Section 1 Assessment Answers

1. aggression, warlike acts (p. 645); dissent, criticism (p. 647); coup, takeover (p. 648); sovereign, independent (p. 649); secede, leave (p. 649); privatize, allow private ownership (p. 649)
2. collapse of communism, fall of the Berlin Wall, Eastern European independence
3. because they were angry that Gorbachev let Soviet satellite regimes collapse
4. Answers will vary. Some students might point to the continued presence of the Communist party, while others might point to the rise of a multi-party system and recent elections of non-Communists.
5. Sample problems: ethnic rivalries, soaring prices, high unemployment, low wages, worker strikes, skyrocketing interest rates, political challenges by the Communists.

Assign Chapter 39 **Section 1 Quiz** in the TCR. Testmaker available.

GULF WAR   As Allied forces put an end to Saddam Hussein's invasion of Kuwait, retreating Iraqi troops set fire to hundreds of oil wells. **What did Hussein hope to gain by the invasion?**

CAPTION ANSWER

Hussein hoped to pay off debts from the war with Iran, draw Iraqi attention off his own failed policies, and issue a strike against those Arab nations seeking better relations with the United States.

MAKING CONNECTIONS

➤➤ **History** When the Ayatollah Ruhollah Khomeini came to power in Iran in 1979, he condemned pro-Western and secular Arab leaders as enemies of Islam. Repeatedly, he urged Arab people in other nations to join in a struggle against their leaders. President Saddam Hussein of Iraq, fearful that revolution would sweep into Iraq, invaded Iran in September 1980. The eight-year war that followed is considered to be among the bloodiest in recent history. A UN cease-fire in 1988 ended the war, but by then the two countries had lost about 1 million people and suffered hundreds of billions of dollars in property damage.

troops close to the border of Saudi Arabia, site of the world's largest known oil reserves.

Hussein had several motives. He hoped to pay off debts from an eight-year war fought against Iran. He also wanted to get Iraqi attention off his own failed policies. Finally, he saw a chance to strike out at Arab nations seeking better relations with the United States.

The United States used the UN as a **forum**, or meeting place, to put together a coalition to free Kuwait. The UN set a deadline of January 15, 1991, for Iraq to withdraw its troops. When Iraq let the deadline pass, coalition forces backed heavily by the United States attacked Iraq. By late February, Kuwait was free from Hussein's grasp.

The Gulf War, named after Kuwait's location on the Persian Gulf, had mixed results. It stopped Iraqi aggression, but it still left Hussein in control of Iraq. He continued to violate the rights of opponents such as the Kurds, a people living in northern Iraq. He also refused to cooperate with UN inspectors assigned to make sure Iraq stopped producing deadly weapons, including poison gas and bombs that spread dangerous germs.

Because Hussein failed to comply with the terms for peace, the UN Security Council barred Iraq from selling oil, except in exchange for food and medicine. Hussein blamed the economic hardships suffered by the Iraqi people on the United States.

In August 1998, Hussein banned all UN inspections. The United States and Great Britain threatened to bomb Iraq unless it resumed inspections. Hussein let UN inspectors back into Iraq.

✔ **Reading Check**
What is a **forum?**

✔ **Reading Check Answer**
A **forum** is a meeting place.

DID YOU KNOW

Saddam Hussein claimed that his country invaded Kuwait because it was a historic part of Iraq and that Kuwait had unfairly drilled Iraqi oil. Although Iraq was fourth in the world in the production of oil, control of Kuwait would have given Iraq possession of one-fifth of the world's known oil reserves.

EXTENDING THE CONTENT

When the UN imposed a deadline for withdrawal, Hussein vowed not to leave Kuwait until Israel pulled out of its occupied territories and Syria left Lebanon. He also threatened to attack Israel if Iraq were attacked. The day after the UN deadline, the U.S. bombed the Iraqi capital of Baghdad. For the next month, the coalition forces conducted a massive air war aimed at destroying Iraq's war-making ability. Hussein responded by launching missiles at Israel, hoping to draw Israel into the war and split Arab support for the UN coalition. Israel resisted, however, and the U.S. provided Israel with an antimissile defense system.

To conduct the 1998 air attack against Iraq, the United States massed 24,100 troops, 201 aircraft, and 22 ships in the Persian Gulf. This was only a fraction of the arsenal used in the 1991 Gulf War. The Pentagon, however, believed its extensive knowledge of Iraq's war-making machinery and its smarter weapons would issue a more punishing strike by fewer troops and planes. As a result, they called the campaign "Operation Desert Fox."

L1 **Geography: Location** Ask students to locate each of the Balkan nations created by the breakup of Yugoslavia on a wall map of Europe. Then call on a volunteer to slowly read each paragraph aloud in "Fighting in Bosnia." Every time a place name is mentioned, request a volunteer to use a ruler or pointer to locate it on the wall map. Ask: Why do you think most European nations backed NATO involvement in the Bosnia conflict? *(because the region is near their borders; because of memories of other wars that started in the same area)* **ELL**

However, the U.S. member of the team reported that Hussein still blocked inspection of some weapon plants.

In late December 1998, the United States and Great Britain launched air strikes aimed at Iraqi missile factories and other military targets. Heavy bombing continued for four days. The action provoked strong criticism from many members of the UN. However, the United States and Great Britain continued to launch low-level air strikes throughout 1999.

As the 2000s opened, the crisis over arms inspections remained unresolved. The United States continued to support the ban on Iraqi oil sales. The suffering of the Iraqi people, however, caused deep division in the UN. Many experts felt that as long as Hussein stayed in power, the situation in Iraq would remain unstable.

Fighting in Bosnia As the UN argued over the fate of Iraq, another crisis took shape in the Balkan nation of Yugoslavia. The conflict reached back to 1980—the year Communist leader Josip Bronz Tito died. Ever since World War II, Tito had held Yugoslavia's six republics together with his iron-fisted rule. When Tito died, however, ethnic groups began to compete for power.

The republic of Serbia, led by president Slobodan Milosevic, tried to establish dominance over the confederation. His actions sparked bitter quarrels with non-Serbian groups. In 1991, Slovenia, Croatia, Bosnia-Herzegovina, and Macedonia declared their independence.

Serbs living in Croatia and Bosnia-Herzegovina opposed independence. They wanted to remain part of Yugoslavia, now made up of Serbia and Montenegro. With support from Serbia, they fought to take control of both Croatia and Bosnia-Herzegovina. In January 1992, a cease-fire ended fighting in Croatia. However, fighting in Bosnia-Herzegovina went on longer and with much greater violence.

Chilling reports out of Bosnia-Herzegovina raised world concern. Constant fighting in and around Sarajevo, the nation's capital, resulted in a huge loss of civilian life. Even more frightening was the Serbian policy of "ethnic cleansing," a planned effort to rid Bosnia-Herzegovina of its non-Serbian population. To achieve this goal, Serbian armies set up prison camps where they starved or executed non-Serbians, such as Bosnian Muslims and Croats.

With UN backing, NATO intervened in the conflict. NATO leaders used negotiation and air strikes to force the warring parties to take part in peace talks sponsored by the United States. In November 1995, leaders of Bosnia-Herzegovina, Yugoslavia, and Croatia met in Dayton, Ohio. Here they signed the Dayton peace accord, an agreement that divided Bosnia into two regions, a Croat-Muslim region and a Serb region.

NATO troops were scheduled to stay in the area until 1998. However, ongoing ethnic hatreds and an estimated 1 million

654 UNIT 12 THE TWENTIETH CENTURY

MEETING SPECIAL NEEDS

Many students will benefit from a strong visual and oral presentation that reinforces what they have read. Have small groups of students prepare a brief oral summary of each country in this section. Tell strong visual learners to collect or create images—photographs, illustrations, drawings, posters, collages—of the people, places, and politics they are studying. Have students use a large wall map to trace onto posterboard the outline of the region they have chosen. Direct them to paste the images on this outline map. Near the images, have them write a few key words—names, dates, or terms—to help them remember important facts about each country studied.

➥ Refer to *Inclusion for the Middle School Social Studies Classroom: Strategies and Activities* for additional resources.

KOSOVO CONFLICT Reports of destruction and violation of human rights in Kosovo led to intervention by NATO. **Why did many people believe that NATO troops would by required to enforce a long-term peace?**

refugees still without homes forced troops to remain past the deadline. As the 2000s opened, many people doubted that the peace would hold in Bosnia without outside intervention.

Kosovo Serbian nationalism still burned strong within Yugoslavia, where Slobodan Milosevic held on to power. The Serbs now tried to drive Muslim Albanians out of Kosovo, a self-governing province of Yugoslavia.

Kosovo held special meaning to the Serbs. It was the place where medieval Serbian kings had been crowned. Shrines of the Serbian Orthodox Church dotted the landscape. When Muslim Turks took control of the area in 1398, the Serbs resisted until they reconquered Kosovo in 1912.

Although part of Yugoslavia, Kosovo had been **autonomous**, of self-governing, since 1974. Its population consisted of about 90 percent Muslim Albanians. When ethnic conflicts broke up Yugoslavia, Serbia vowed to hold on to Kosovo. Led by Slobodan Milosevic, Serbia dissolved Kosovo's government and fired all Muslim Albanians from their jobs as teachers, civil servants, and police. Soon after, Albanian students were barred from university classes.

In 1997, the Kosovar Liberation Army (KLA)—a rebel group of Muslim Albanians calling for Kosovo's independence—attacked Serbs living in the province. By the summer of 1998, the KLA had seized control of about 40 percent of Kosovo. Milosevic now sent in the Yugoslav army and the Serbian police.

Because Kosovo was a legal province of Yugoslavia, NATO did not act right away. The situation changed, however, when

 Reading Check
What political right did Kosovo have to be an **autonomous** province of Yugoslavia?

CHAPTER 39 THE WORLD SINCE 1989 **655**

CAPTION ANSWER

As the 2000s opened, many people believed that ongoing ethnic hatreds and the refusal of Milosevic to give up the Yugoslav presidency would require the long-term presence of NATO peacekeeping forces in the area.

Reading Check Answer
Kosovo had been an **autonomous** province of Yugoslavia ever since 1974 and felt it had the right to continue self-government.

EXTENDING THE CONTENT

During the fighting that tore apart the former Yugoslavia, troops placed from 2 to 6 million antitank and antipersonnel mines throughout the area. Many of the mines were made of plastic, which hinders detection. As the war drew to a close, many land mines still lay hidden. The presence of land mines in this region and other former war-ring areas of the world led Jody Williams of Vermont to organize a grass-roots organization to prohibit land mines. By October 1997, her efforts had led 89 nations to sign an international treaty banning their use. That same month, the Nobel Prize committee awarded the U.S. activist its coveted award for peace.

During the 1999 conflict in Kosovo, Serbian armies pursued a "scorched-earth" policy, setting fire to towns and cities. At the start of the 2000s, a staggering 860,000 refugees struggled to rebuild their lives in the ruins of Kosovo or elsewhere in the Balkans.

At the end of the 1990s, Palestinians still accounted for the largest refugee group in the world. Their number totaled an estimatd 3,743,000 people.

Serbia unleashed a policy of ethnic cleansing against the Albanians. As hundreds of thousands of people fled Kosovo, NATO responded. For the first time ever, it intervened in the affairs of a sovereign nation.

Negotiators led by the United States tried to arrange a cease-fire. However, neither the KLA nor Serbia would compromise. Meanwhile, Serbia stepped up its policy of ethnic cleansing. Faced with a mass violation of human rights, NATO launched air strikes against Serbian military targets on March 24, 1999.

The UN became involved in the conflict and helped hammer out a peace agreement. On June 3, Serbia agreed to the terms and the 11-week war ended. A five-nation NATO peacekeeping force entered Kosovo to oversee the return of Albanian refugees.

The problem did not end there, however. Fearful for their lives, Kosovo's Serbs began to flee, creating yet another group of refugees. The UN charged Milosevic with war crimes against the Albanians, but he refused to resign the Yugoslav presidency. With ethnic hatreds running high, Kosovo faced an uncertain future. As the 2000s opened, the province remained under UN supervision—a status that most observers believed would continue for a long time.

Peace Efforts in the Middle East   Like the crisis in the Balkans, conflicts in the Middle East have deep roots. During World War I, many Arabs sided with Great Britain against the Turks of the Ottoman Empire. They hoped this would bring about the establishment of an independent Arab kingdom. However, only Saudi Arabia and Yemen became independent. The rest of the Turkish-ruled Arab world fell under European control. The disappointed Arabs then waged an undeclared war. They won independence for Iraq in 1932, for Lebanon in 1943, and for Syria in 1946.

The situation in Palestine was different. Jews as well as Arabs lived there. The Jews also fought with the British in World War I. When Jewish leaders asked for a Jewish homeland in Palestine, the British supported the idea.

In 1946, all of Palestine east of the Jordan River became the independent country of Transjordan, now known as Jordan. The following year, the UN gave part of Palestine west of the Jordan River to the Jews. In 1948, Jewish leaders established the nation of Israel.

Most Arabs did not accept Israel. As a result, a coalition of five Arab states invaded the new nation. The Israelis quickly defeated the Arab forces, causing about 450,000 Palestinian Arabs to flee Israel. Most settled in refugee camps on the West Bank of the Jordan River and in an area along the Mediterranean called the Gaza Strip.

Between 1948 and 1993, Arab nations and Israel fought four more wars. Boundaries shifted back and forth. The only Arab

PEACE ACCORD   Israeli leader Yitzhak Rabin (left) and PLO leader Yasir Arafat (right) shake hands as President Bill Clinton brings them together. **What was the result of the agreement signed by Israel and the PLO in 1993?**

nation that recognized Israel's right to exist was Egypt. The Palestinian Liberation Organization (PLO), led since 1969 by Yasir Arafat, carried out guerrilla attacks against Israel. In return, Israel bombed guerrilla bases and invaded PLO strongholds in Lebanon.

In 1987, a Palestinian uprising, known as the *intifada,* broke out in the West Bank. Workers went on strike, and street battles spread. The *intifada* focused world attention on the Palestinian issue.

The 1990 Gulf War proved an important turning point in Arab-Israeli relations. Israel and several Arab nations suddenly found themselves fighting on the same side. Afterwards, Arab and Israeli negotiators agreed to talk directly with one another.

In September 1993, Israel and the PLO signed an agreement that called for self-rule by Palestinian Arabs in the Gaza Strip and the West Bank city of Jericho. In 1994, Jordan's King Hussein and Israeli Prime Minister Yitzhak Rabin continued the peace process by ending the state of war that had existed between their two nations since 1948.

Although many Arabs and Israelis supported peace efforts, hatred and fears ran deep on both sides. In November 1995, an Israeli student who opposed the return of land to the Palestinians shot and killed Prime Minister Rabin—an event that shocked and saddened the world.

In elections held in June 1996, Israelis chose Benjamin Netanyahu as Prime Minister. At first, Netanyahu criticized the "land-for-peace" deals, pointing out that the PLO still opposed Israel. In January 1997, however, he agreed to further Israeli with-

> ✓ **Reading Check**
> What issue was highlighted by the *intifada*?

VIDEODISC
In the Holy Land

 Side One
Chapter 15

Title: *Arab Violence, 1919–1921*
Subject: Jewish and Palestinian perspectives of anti-Jewish rioting.
Ask: As a result of the Balfour Declaration, Jewish immigration to Israel increased. What was the effect of this movement on Arabs in the area? *(They felt threatened because others were claiming their homeland. This resulted in riots, strikes, and violence.)*

CAPTION ANSWER

self-rule by Palestinian Arabs in the Gaza Strip and the West Bank of Jericho; provided a framework for future peace talks

---

✓ **Reading Check Answer**
The *intifada* highlighted the demands of Palestinian refugees for a homeland.

Biography

The following videotape program is available from Glencoe to enrich Chapter 39:

- **Yitzhak Rabin**

To find classroom resources to accompany this video, check the following home page:

A&E Television:
http://www.aetv.com

COOPERATIVE LEARNING

Organize students into groups, and ask them to research—in the library or on the Internet—the number of people who follow these religions in the Middle East:

Sunni Muslim
Shi'ite Muslim
Christian
Jewish
Other

Direct groups of students to present the information they find in the form of a bar graph. When students have completed their graphs, ask: What is the largest religion in the Middle East? What is the smallest religion? Where, based on the text, do you think most Jews live?

📂 Assign Chapter 39 *Cooperative Learning Activity* in the TCR.

ABCNEWS INTERACTIVE™

 VIDEODISC
Turning Points in World History

 Side Two
Chapter 11

Title: *Middle East Peace Accords*
Ask: Why is it likely that the Middle East peace talks will be ongoing in the early 2000s? *(The disputes are decades old and many difficult issues are involved; thus, negotiations will likely take a long time.)*

CAPTION ANSWER

Under the peace accords signed in 1999, Catholics and Protestants in Northern Ireland formed a coalition government. Great Britain gave up demands that the IRA disarm, while the IRA dropped claims to lands in Northern Ireland.

drawals from the West Bank. Responding to criticism, he stopped the withdrawals in December 1998.

In May 1999, Israeli voters replaced Netanyahu with Ehud Barak. Barak called for a "peace of the brave" and vowed to pursue talks with the Palestinians and Syrians. In December 1999, Israel and Syria began the first round of peace talks in Washington, D.C. With great hope, Barak declared, "Making peace with Syria means a sea of change in the future of the Middle East."

Toward Peace in Ireland   In the late 1990s, the world also saw progress in the settling of a conflict dating back to the Protestant Reformation in the 1600s. For hundreds of years, Irish Catholics fought to be free from English rule. In 1922, the Catholic counties of southern Ireland became self-governing, while the Protestant majority in Ulster, or Northern Ireland, voted to remain under British rule.

Violent clashes between Catholics and Protestants in the 1960s and 1970s flared. The outlawed Irish Republican Army (IRA)—a group of radicals opposed to British rule—stepped up attacks on British military forces and civilians. In 1995, the British government made contact with the IRA in an effort to stop the violence, and negotiations began.

In April 1998, all sides in the dispute hammered out terms for peace, which were signed into law in December 1999. Catholics and Protestants in Northern Ireland agreed to joint rule, forming a coalition government. Great Britain gave up its demand that the IRA disarm. The Irish Republic dropped claims to lands in Northern Ireland.

NORTHERN IRELAND   After nearly 30 years of violence, Gerry Adams (center), a Protestant leader, joins with the people of Belfast in celebrating the peace accord. **What were the terms of peace?**

COOPERATIVE LEARNING

Assign a group of volunteers to update the following incomplete chronology of key events in the conflict between Protestants and Catholics in Ireland. Students should extend dates to the present year.

1534 Henry VIII declares himself "King of Ireland"; Irish Catholics resist Protestant rule.

1641 Oliver Cromwell puts down rebellion by Irish Catholics.

1688 Irish Catholics side with James II in the Glorious Revolution; Parliament awards Irish lands to its Protestant supporters.

1778 Irish nationalists rebel against English rule.

1800 Act of Union joins Ireland and England.

Distribute copies of the chronology to the rest of the class, and have two teams debate whether a lasting peace is possible.

Changes in China   In February 1997, Chinese leader Deng Xiaoping died at age 92. He was succeeded by Jiang Zemin. Jiang continued Deng's policies of economic reform, combined with tight political control by the Communist party.

On July 1, 1997, Jiang oversaw the return of Hong Kong to China. The return resulted from a 1984 agreement with Great Britain, which had seized Hong Kong from China in 1842. Under British rule, Hong Kong had become one of the world's largest financial centers and a leading exporter of manufactured goods. The Chinese government promised to allow Hong Kong to keep its capitalist system for 50 years. However, many citizens within Hong Kong worried about their political future.

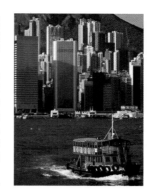

Port of Hong Kong

Fears over the fate of Hong Kong were enflamed by Communist actions toward Taiwan. The island has been ruled by Chinese Nationalists since 1949, when the Communists took over the mainland. Both Nationalists and Communists support the idea of "one China." However, people on Taiwan do not want to unite with the mainland while it is under Communist rule. Taiwan has a market economy, a free press, and democratic elections.

In July 1999, the president of Taiwan talked as if the island might declare itself an independent nation. China in turn responded with a threat to "smash" any attempts by Taiwan to break away. The United States, which has treaty obligations to Taiwan from the cold war era, urged both sides to show restraint.

Later in 1999, the United States entered into trade talks with China. Charges of the abuse of human rights within China triggered debate within the United States. However, supporters of trade between the two nations, including leaders in Hong Kong and Taiwan, felt that the only way to bring change to China was to speed up the development of a market economy.

Turmoil in Indonesia

For much of the past century, Indonesia has been the scene of turmoil. Comprised of more than 17,000 islands, Indonesia stretches along the equator from the Malaysian Peninsula toward Australia. Today it is the fourth most populous nation in the world. It is also the largest Muslim country and one of the world's leading oil producers.

Starting in the 1600s, the Dutch took increasing control of Indonesia, first for its spices and later for its oil. The Indonesians resisted, but they were not able to break the Dutch hold on the islands until the Japanese drove them out in World War II. When the Dutch tried to regain control in 1945, rebels led by Sukarno and Muhammad Hatta fought back. The fighting continued for four years until the UN pressured the two sides to reach an agreement. In November 1949, Indonesia received its independence, with Sukarno as president.

Sukarno tried to unite Indonesia's diverse islands under one government. However, he faced challenges from islands that

Macao On December 20, 1999, Portugal returned Macao—a peninsula and two islands on the south coast of China—to the People's Republic. Founded in 1557, the port was the oldest European outpost in China. As with Hong Kong, Chinese officials promised to respect Macao's way of life for 50 years after the start of Chinese rule.

SPOTLIGHT ON: TAIWAN

Taiwan, originally called Formosa, was "discovered" by Portugal, then controlled by the Dutch and later by Spain. Still later it was acquired by China, then Japan, and then China again. Despite its small size, it is considered a nuclear power, having six operational nuclear reactors and another under construction. In military strength, Taiwan ranks above Germany, Italy, Great Britain, and Japan in number of active troops in the military. The island also produces more motor vehicles than Australia, South Africa, or all of Malaysia.

Reading Check Answer
The **referendum** in East Timor set off a wave of violence because the East Timorese voted overwhelmingly to form their own nation.

CAPTION ANSWER

because Indonesians were mostly Muslim, while the East Timorese were largely Roman Catholics

Reading Check
Why did the **referendum** in East Timor set off a wave of violence?

wanted greater self-rule and from the Indonesian Communist party. The disorders led Sukarno to increase his own power at the expense of democracy. By the 1960s, he began to lean more toward the Communists. He quit the UN and opened talks with China.

In 1965, the Communists attempted a coup. However, it was quickly put down by army forces under General Suharto. In 1967, the legislature voted Sukarno out of office and named General Suharto acting president. Suharto was elected president in 1968 and reelected six more times.

Suharto also approved the takeover of East Timor, a Portuguese colony until 1975. He claimed that control of East Timor, which lay in the Indonesian archipelago, would block the spread of communism. The East Timorese, who are mostly Roman Catholic, immediately organized an independence movement. Over the next 25 years, an estimated 200,000 Timorese died from famine, disease, and fighting.

In 1996, two East Timorese activists, Bishop Carlos Filipe Ximenes Belo and Jose Ramos-Horta, received the Nobel Peace Prize for bringing the situation in East Timor to world attention. Meanwhile, in Indonesia, declining oil prices and corruption by Suharto's family had taken their toll. Amid massive student protests, the legislature forced Suharto to resign a short time after his 1998 reelection.

In February 1999, Suharto's successor, B.J. Habibie, unexpectedly announced that he would allow a **referendum**, or popular vote, on East Timorese independence. As expected, the East

INDONESIA A mosque rises above a modern street in Indonesia. **How did religious differences play a role in the conflict in East Timor?**

SPOTLIGHT ON: 1996 NOBEL PEACE PRIZE

Provide these details on the two winners of the 1996 Nobel Peace Prize:

José Ramos-Horta: Born December 26, 1949; one of eleven brothers and sisters, four of whom were killed by the Indonesian army; mandated in 1975 by pro-independence parties to represent East Timor abroad; spent more than 20 years speaking out at the UN and elsewhere against the Indonesian invasion; close friends with other human rights activists, such as Daw Aung San Suu Kyi (Burma), the Dalai Lama (Tibet), and Oscar Arias (Costa Rica).

Carlos Filipe Ximenese Belo: Born February 3, 1948 in East Timor; the fifth child of a rural school teacher; attended missionary schools in East Timor and studied for the priesthood in Portugal; became a bishop and head of East Timor's Roman Catholic Church at age 30; at great personal risk, pleaded with the world to save the East Timorese from "dying as a people and as a nation."

Timorese voted overwhelmingly to form their own nation. The announcement set off a wave of violence as pro-Indonesian militia killed or tried to force the East Timorese from the region. In September, Habibie agreed to involvement of a UN peacekeeping force.

In June 1999, Indonesia held its first free parliamentary elections in more than 40 years. On October 20, the freely elected legislators picked Abdurrahman Wahid as the new president of Indonesia. "I celebrate our independence and freedom," declared Wahid in his acceptance speech.

Struggles and Progress in Africa   As the 1990s drew to a close, most nations in Africa had been independent for less than 50 years. Lack of experience in self government had opened the door to **authoritarian rule**, or government in which one ruler or political party holds power. Like other parts of the world, ethnic differences also deeply split some African nations.

During the 1990s, Somalia, Rwanda, Sierra Leone, the Congo, and Liberia all experienced bloody conflicts with no easy solutions. Peacekeeping troops often arrived in these war-torn nations to find that there was no peace to keep. In some places, like Rwanda, warring parties refused to take part in peace talks. In others, peacekeepers had to disarm child soldiers.

Despite deep-rooted problems in many places, some experts feel that progress can still be seen. Today there are fewer civil wars in Africa than in the past. In 1996 nearly 20 nations held elections. Ten nations held them in 1997. In many African nations, newspapers enjoy greater freedom of the press than ever before. Perhaps the most remarkable strides toward freedom have taken place in South Africa.

Since its independence in 1926, South Africa had moved toward a system of **apartheid**, or forced separation of races. That system became law in 1948, ensuring that a white minority held power. To force an end to apartheid, the United States and other nations set up trade restrictions against South Africa in the 1980s.

The election of F. W. de Klerk as president of South Africa opened the door to change. In 1989, de Klerk bowed to world opinion and lifted the long-standing ban on the African National Congress (ANC), the political group that spoke for most black South Africans. In 1990, he released Nelson Mandela, the head of the ANC, from prison after 27 years. By 1992, most of the laws that defined apartheid had been thrown out. All South Africans, regardless of race, won the right to vote.

In 1994, the nation held its first all-race democratic election. The ANC won an overwhelming majority in the legislature. In turn, the legislature elected Nelson Mandela as president. In keeping with a campaign promise, he reached out to all black and white South Africans.

CHAPTER 39 THE WORLD SINCE 1989   661

Nelson Mandela
1918–PRESENT

South African Statesman

Born of royal parents, Nelson Mandela experienced apartheid while working in a South African gold mine. He went on to study law and to help found the ANC. Imprisoned in 1964 for his oppostion to apartheid, he emerged in 1990 to help F. W. de Klerk end the hated system. In 1993, the two men shared the Nobel Peace Prize. In 1994, Mandela became South Africa's first black president.

SPOTLIGHT ON: NELSON MANDELA

To extend People in History, provide these additional details on Nelson Mandela:

Nelson Mandela always expected to rule, but not the nation of South Africa. Mandela grew up the son of a Thembu chief and believed he would follow in his father's footsteps. Instead, the injustice of apartheid caused Mandela to join the fight that led to his imprisonment from 1964 to 1990.

When Mandela emerged from prison, his sense of tolerance and justice amazed the world. As South Africa's first black president, Mandela appointed not only his lifetime ANC colleagues to government, but also F.W. de Klerk and Mangosuthu Buthelezi, the Zulu leader who had loudly criticized Mandela for his support for all-race government. Through Mandela's leadership, South Africa experienced one of the most peaceful political revolutions in modern times.

Biography

The following videotape program is available from Glencoe to enrich Chapter 39:

- **Nelson Mandela: Journey to Freedom**

To find classroom resources to accompany this video, check the following home page:

A&E Television:
http://www.aetv.com

PRIMARY SOURCES
Library

You might assign "Freedom and Equality in South Africa," on pages 696–697 of the Primary Sources Library.

DID YOU KNOW

Thabo Mbeki joined the ANC's Youth League at age 14. Three years later, he was expelled from high school for participating in student strikes against apartheid. Later, under orders of the ANC, Mbeki left South Africa and coordinated resistance to apartheid from offices in London and in other African nations.

CAPTION ANSWER

Mandela respected the rights of South Africa's minorities, making sure they took part in the government.

💾 Use **Interactive Tutor Self-Assessment Software** to review Section 2.

662

Fun Facts...

Peace Prize In 1993 ANC leader Nelson Mandela and President F.W. de Klerk of South Africa shared the Nobel Peace Prize for their work to end apartheid.

SOUTH AFRICA Nelson Mandela congratulates Thabo Mbeki on his victory in South Africa's second all-race election. **How did Mandela help ensure a peaceful transition to black majority rule of South Africa?**

Throughout his term of office, Mandela worked for a peaceful transition to black majority rule. He also respected the rights of the nation's minorities, making sure that they took part in government as promised by the new South African constitution.

In 1999, South Africa held its second all-race democratic election. Mandela was succeeded by Thabo Mbeki. In his acceptance speech, Mbeki vowed to continue the hard work of undoing the economic and social injustices created by apartheid. He also held out a dream. Mbeki called on people all over the continent to contribute to what he called an "African Renaissance."

Section 2 Assessment

1. **Define:** forum, autonomous, *intifada*, referendum, authoritarian rule, apartheid.
2. How did religion play a part in the conflicts in Ireland and Indonesia?

Critical Thinking

3. **Making Predictions** What role do you think South Africa will play in world affairs during the next 100 years?

Graphic Organizer Activity

4. Draw this chart, and use it to summarize the responses of the world community to the global issues listed on the chart.

Global Issue	World Response
Invasion of Kuwait	
Fighting in Bosnia	
Fighting in Kosovo	
East Timor independence	
Apartheid in South Africa	

662 UNIT 12 THE TWENTIETH CENTURY

Section 2 Assessment Answers

1. forum, meeting place (p. 653); autonomous, self-governing (p. 655); *intifada*, name given to the 1987 Palestinian uprising on the West Bank (p. 657); referendum, popular vote (p. 660); authoritarian rule, control of government by one person or group (p. 661); apartheid, forced separation of the races (p. 661)
2. *Ireland*—Irish Catholics resisted rule by Protestants, both in England and in Ireland; *Indonesia*—East Timor, which is mostly Roman Catholic, resisted annexation and invasion by Indonesia, which is mostly Muslim.
3. Answers will vary, but many students may suggest that South Africa will take a leading role in helping to spread democracy in the region.
4. Charts will vary, but should reflect the trend toward collective action in responding to world crises.

Assign Chapter 39 **Section 2 Quiz** in the TCR. Testmaker available.

SECTION 3 The World Today

Today the world faces many challenges that call for cooperation among nations. The threat of war continues as new power relationships emerge. Tensions exist between industrial nations and developing nations over use of scarce resources, health care, and other issues. Continued global progress depends on the resolution of these and other problems.

Political Changes   As the 2000s began, the future of the world's remaining Communist nations was in doubt. Without Soviet aid, governments in Cuba and North Korea teetered on the edge of economic ruin. Meanwhile, China seemed to be moving toward capitalism. Young people, in particular, appeared more interested in consumer products than in politics.

The demise of communism, however, did not mean an end to the arms race. The presence of missile sites in the former Soviet Union remained a concern. So did the possession of nuclear bombs by China, India, and other nations.

A bigger threat was the growing number of **renegade nations**—countries that refused to reduce the weapons of war. Evidence pointed to the production of chemical weapons by Libya and Iraq. In 1999, North Korea, Pakistan, and Iran all tested their first missiles. Although North Korea denied the sale of missile technology, most experts believed North Koreans sold weapons to nations unfriendly to the United States.

> ✔ **Reading Check**
> How do **renegade nations** threaten world peace?

TERRORISM   The terrorist bombing of the U.S. embassy in Nairobi, Kenya, killed or injured hundreds of civilians and government workers. **How are nations combating terrorist activities in the world?**

MEETING SPECIAL NEEDS

DID YOU KNOW

In late 1999, the UN Environmental Program released a global health report known as GEO-2000. The report underscored the danger of global warming, targeting a new emergency for the 21st century—severe water shortages. The report placed some 50 nations at risk of running out of water. Causes included pollution, overuse, and climate changes.

Reading Check
What is **terrorism,** and how does it violate the rights of individual citizens?

Crowded street in India—a nation with over 1 billion people

Reading Check
What conditions help spread **communicable diseases**?

Reading Check
Why has the possibility of **pandemics** increased in recent years?

Reading Check
How does the **greenhouse effect** endanger our planet?

Global **terrorism**—violence to achieve a political objective—also remained a widespread concern. The 1998 bombings of the U.S. embassies in Kenya and Tanzania raised UN discussion of "freelance terrorists." These individuals or groups act on their own, usually without any formal government support. The bombings in East Africa, for example, were committed by individuals angry at U.S. policies in the Middle East.

Nations tried to combat the spread of weapons and terrorism in a number of ways. In some cases, the United States directly attacked suspected terrorist camps or weapons factories. In other cases, nations tried to curb the sale of weapons through trade agreements. In nearly all cases of terrorism, nations tried to locate the suspected terrorists and place them on trial for violating international law.

A Growing Population During the 1900s, a different kind of bomb exploded on Earth—a population bomb. In a single 100-year period, the earth's population quadrupled, or became four times as great. In October 1999, the earth's population topped 6 billion. Only 12 years had passed since it hit the 5-billion mark.

A number of reasons accounted for the growth: increased food production, improved medical care, and better living conditions. Around the world, fewer infants died and life spans increased.

Improving Health Care War, poverty, overcrowding, and poor sanitation promote the spread of disease. In many developing nations, millions of people still die from **communicable diseases**, or diseases passed along from an infected person or animal to another person or animal. In the mid-1990s, diseases such as tuberculosis, malaria, cholera, pneumonia, and measles claimed more than 11 million lives a year.

Increased contact among nations through improved travel has increased the possibility of **pandemics**, or epidemics spread over a wide region, such as the Black Death in the Middle Ages. Germs once confined to certain regions can now spread to all parts of the world.

No disease has made the world more aware of the importance of improving health care than Acquired Immunodeficiency Syndrome, or AIDS. In 1981, scientists identified the virus, known as HIV, that causes AIDS. However, as the 2000s opened, they had not yet discovered a cure for it.

Protecting the Environment In 1995, scientists at the UN-sponsored International Panel on Climate Change (IPCC) sounded an alarm. Scientists on the IPCC felt the buildup of carbon dioxide in the atmosphere was trapping heat released from the earth's surface, much like the glass in a greenhouse.

EXTENDING THE CONTENT

Some scientists believe that pollution has made a hole in the ozone layer—a thin layer of gas in the earth's atmosphere that protects the planet from harmful ultraviolet rays. In the 1970s, satellite pictures revealed that a hole in the ozone layer had formed over Antarctica. Some scientists blamed the hole on industrial chemicals called chlorofluorocarbons (CFCs). CFCs show up in a variety of products—air conditioners, aerosol sprays, and coolants in refrigerators—and in Styrofoam products such as polystyrene cups, packaging, and foam insulation. Groups such as Greenpeace have urged people worldwide not to buy products containing CFCs. Have students find out more about the current status of the ozone issue.

They believed this so-called **greenhouse effect** was pushing up the earth's temperatures to dangerous levels. They predicted that the polar ice caps might even melt. By the end of the century, most of the UN's member nations had signed a series of agreements to cut down on the production of greenhouse gases.

Global Links

Progress in the 21st century depends upon global cooperation. Issues that cut across national boundaries, such as water shortages, cannot be solved by one nation acting on its own. Nations also must rely upon each other to share resources. Few nations can fully meet all the needs of their people without global trade.

To promote trade, some nations have banned together to form trading blocs. In 1992, for example, 15 western European nations formed the European Union (EU). It was designed to help Europe become an economic superpower like the United States.

In 1999, 11 of the 15 EU nations adopted a common currency called the **euro** and set July 1, 2002, as the deadline for getting rid of their national currencies. The 11 nations also turned over control of their monetary policies to a new European Central Bank located in Frankfurt, Germany. Many economists believe the other four EU nations—Britain, Denmark, Greece, and Sweden—will eventually switch to the euro, too.

Other trade alliances have also formed. In 1993, the United States, Canada, and Mexico reduced trade barriers under the North American Free Trade Agreement (NAFTA). In 1995, blocs of nations in South America signed similar agreements. That same year, the Association of Southeast Asian Nations (ASEAN), organized in 1967, expanded its membership and cut regional tariffs.

Contact among nations has been further increased by a revolution in communications. Satellites have extended the reach of both telephones and the media. People almost anywhere on the earth can now contact each other, either by telephone, fax, or computer. The result has been the rise of what some experts call a *global culture.*

The speed at which goods, ideas, and people move is expected to increase in the years ahead. Cultures around the world will change as they influence each other. The most important force in bringing about the change, say some experts, is teenagers.

There are more than 800 million teens in the world today—the most there have ever been. They travel, watch television, buy things, and, most of all, talk. No other global generation has ever known each other better. They, more than other generation, have the chance to work together to solve some of the earth's most pressing problems.

Fun Facts....

Free Nations As 2000 started, a study revealed that 85 nations, or 44 percent of the world's total population, were "free." This was a higher percentage than at any time in history.

✓ **Reading Check**
How does the **euro** help create economic ties among the nations of Europe?

The global culture

✓ **Reading Check Answer**
The **greenhouse effect** endangers the planet by pushing up the earth's temperatures to dangerous levels.

✓ **Reading Check Answer**
The **euro** serves as a common currency for some European nations.

L2 Science Provide students with the background information in the "Did You Know??" feature on the previous page. Then divide them into groups and have them create a program in environmental education for their grade level. Tell students that the course will be taught as a morning lesson one day a week. It will cover approximately eight special topics. Challenge students to select these topics, along with suggestions for projects or field trips related to each topic. You might carry out some of the student suggestions as part of the activities surrounding Earth Day, held each April 22. **ELL**

ASSESS

Check for Understanding
Ask students to summarize the main points of the chapter, orally or in writing. Discuss the answers to the Section and Chapter Assessment questions.

COOPERATIVE LEARNING

Organize the class into five groups, and assign each group to design posters that show how each of the following inventions has helped link the world: communications satellites, telephones, fax machines, computers (the Internet), and jet airplanes. Display the completed posters on a classroom wall, and review them with students. Then hold a class vote ranking these inventions in terms of their importance to promoting a global culture.

Evaluate

Assign the Chapter 39 **Performance Assessment Activity** in the TCR.

Administer the **Chapter 39 Test.** Testmaker available.

Reteach

Assign the Chapter 39 **Reteaching Activity** in the TCR.

Enrich

Assign the Chapter 39 **Enrichment Activity** in the TCR.

CLOSE

Have students evaluate this statement: "The world has become a global village, and no country can be an island unto itself."

Use **Interactive Tutor Self-Assessment Software** to review Section 3.

Self-Check Quiz gives students an interactive chapter tutorial. Have them access **Chapter 39 Quiz** at humanheritage.glencoe.com

---

Section 3 Assessment

1. **Define:** renegade nations, terrorism, communicable diseases, pandemics, greenhouse effect, euro.
2. What health care challenges face the world during the 2000s?
3. What environmental challenges must be solved in the years ahead?

Critical Thinking

4. **Identifying Alternatives** What, if any, obligation do you think the United States has in reducing the gap between rich and poor nations in the world?

Graphic Organizer Activity

5. Draw this diagram, and use it to show the way your own life has been touched by increased contact and communication with other nations.

Influences on
My Life

Chapter Summary & Study Guide

1. Between 1989 and 1991, communism collapsed in Eastern Europe and the cold war came to an end.
2. By late 1991, the Soviet Union had dissolved into 15 separate republics.
3. Ethnic rivalries and economic hardships created many challenges for nations formerly under Soviet control.
4. In 1997, NATO offered membership to Poland, Hungary, and the Czech Republic.
5. The Iraqi invasion of Kuwait and use of chemical weapons tested the willingness of nations to stand up to an aggressor.
6. Ethnic conflicts in Bosnia and Kosovo led to NATO intervention and air strikes against Serbia.
7. In the Middle East, negotiations between Israel and the PLO, and between Israel and other Arab nations, helped bring peace to the region.
8. In 1999, Catholics and Protestants agreed to joint rule of Northern Ireland.
9. Hong Kong returned to China in 1997.
10. UN forces intervened in East Timor, while Indonesian leaders tried to undertake reforms to end political turmoil.
11. World opposition to apartheid paved the way for South Africa's first all-race election in 1994.
12. The world faces many challenges in the 2000s, including a growing population, environmental threats, the spread of disease, and other issues.

Self-Check Quiz

Visit the *Human Heritage* Web site at **humanheritage. glencoe.com** and click on *Chapter 39—Self-Check Quiz* to assess your understanding of this chapter.

Section 3 Assessment Answers

1. renegade nations, countries that refuse to reduce weapons of war (p. 663); terrorism, violence to achieve a political objective (p. 664); communicable diseases, diseases passed along from one infected person or animal to another (p. 664); pandemics, epidemics spread over a wide area (p. 664); greenhouse effect, buildup of heat-trapping carbon dioxide in the atmosphere (p. 664); euro, common currency for the European Union (p. 665)

2. Sample health care challenges: overpopulation, communicable disease, possibility of pandemics, AIDS
3. Sample environmental challenges: greenhouse effect, melting of polar ice caps, pollution, overpopulation
4. Students should think in terms of growing global interdependence.
5. Diagrams will vary.

Assign Chapter 39 **Section 3 Quiz** in the TCR. Testmaker available.

Using Key Terms

Imagine you are a historian in 2100. You have been asked to write an essay in which you describe the major challenges facing the world as the century opened 100 years ago. Use the following words in your essay.

aggression	dissent	coup
sovereign	secede	privatize
intifada	forum	autonomous
authoritarian	communicable	referendum
rule	diseases	renegade
terrorism	greenhouse	nations
apartheid	effect	pandemics
euro		

Understanding Main Ideas

1. What was the symbolic importance of destroying the Berlin Wall?
2. What problems did Russia face in reforming its government and economy?
3. What were the short-term and long-term outcomes of the Persian Gulf War?
4. What was the role of NATO in Bosnia and Kosovo?
5. What obstacles to peace exist in Africa?
6. What developments are linking nations in the 2000s?

Critical Thinking

1. Do you agree that trade is linked to the growth of democracy in the People's Republic of China? Why or why not?
2. Do you support the United States giving financial help to peacekeeping forces in places like Bosnia, Kosovo, and East Timor? Explain.
3. Do you think trading blocs help or hinder global trade? Explain.

Graphic Organizer Activity

Culture Create a diagram like this one, and use it to show some of the causes and effects of increased contact among the diverse cultures of the world.

Geography in History

Regions Look at the population map on page 651. Scientists are predicting great increases in the population by the year 2050. In what regions would you expect the most growth to take place? Explain.

Using Your Journal

Review any details you may have noted about the challenges facing the world. Then imagine you are a delegate attending a UN-sponsored conference on the most pressing issues of the early 2000s. Choose the issue that you consider the most important. Write a plan explaining the importance of this issue and outlining a proposed course of action.

 Bonus Test Question

For Chapter 39 Test
Think about the following challenges facing the world today, rank each, and explain your rankings: controlling renegade nations, producing enough food, protecting the environment, improving health care. *(Answers will vary.)*

Using Your Journal

Plans will vary, but students should indicate specific ways they would solve the problems. Have volunteers share their plans.

 Geography in History

Answers may vary but should indicate areas that are already heavily populated and likely to become more densely populated in the future.

Using Key Terms

Essays will vary, but students should use all the key terms in describing major challenges.

Understanding Main Ideas

1. symbolized the collapse of communism in Eastern Europe
2. shortages, high prices, high interest rates, wage disputes, unemployment
3. *short term*—stopped Iraqi aggression; *long term*—left Hussein in power, left Iraqi weapons production and related conflicts unresolved
4. forced negotiations, then remained to ensure the peace and protect returning refugees
5. lack of experience in self-government, ethnic differences
6. issues that cut across national boundaries, networks of communication and trade

Critical Thinking

1. Answers will vary, but some students may note that new ideas are spread through trade and that these ideas will influence the young people of China.
2. Answers will vary. Some students may argue that the money should be spent to solve problems at home, while others will cite the importance of peace in an interdependent world.
3. Answers will vary. Some students may say that trading blocs hinder free trade, while others may say they promote regional development and cooperation.

Graphic Organizer Activity

Sample responses: *causes*—increased global trade, increased speed of travel, a communications revolution; *effects*—rise of a global culture, chance for people to know each other better, increased cooperation to solve global problems

UNIT 12 Around

FOCUS

Objectives

After reading the Around the World for Unit 12, your students will be able to:

1. locate Nunavut and cite some of its unique geographic features.

2. explain why the creation of Nunavut was a milestone in history.

3. appreciate the importance of self-rule to preserving the Inuit identity and culture.

Bellringer

Have students write down a list of things they would pack for a trip to the Arctic Circle.

Motivational Activity

Go over student packing lists, exploring reasons for the various items. Then point out the location of Nunavut on the map on page 668. Based on the map and photographs on pages 668–669, what do students think it would be like to live in Nunavut?

TEACH

Geography: Region Assign students to find other lands that lie inside the Arctic Circle. Point out that the Inuit live in all these areas. Call on students to suggest reasons why Inuit groups in places as geographically scattered as Alaska, Canada, Greenland, and Russia might share similar cultures. *(shared Arctic location, environment that favors hunting rather than agriculture, importance of Arctic animals such as the caribou, and so on)*

NUNAVUT

On April 1, 1999, the Prime Minister of Canada greeted the birth of Nunavut—Canada's largest and newest self-governing territory. Nunavut was carved out of the existing Northwest Territories—a sprawling region of tundra, Arctic islands, and frozen waterways. It is the homeland of the Inuit, the native people who make up 85 percent of Nunavut's population. In the Inuit language, known as Inuktitut, Nunavut means "our land."

For the first time in Canada's history, a native people had won control of their own government and the right to send a territorial representative to the Canadian Parliament.

Nunavut

▲ Sprawling across three time zones, Nunavut covers nearly one-fifth of all Canadian land. More than half of the territory lies north of the Arctic Circle, one of the coldest inhabited regions in the world. It has such long winters that much of the land is permanently frozen.

The largest village in Nunavut is Iqaluit, the center of the new government. Montreal, the nearest Canadian city, lies over 1,250 miles away. Approximately 28 villages are scattered across Nunavut, with only a few hundred people living in each one. It is a region where the caribou, one of the animals traditionally hunted by the Inuit, outnumber humans by 25 to 1. ▼

668   UNIT 12

SPOTLIGHT ON: NUNAVUT

In setting up Nunavut, the Inuit have taken steps to preserve their traditional culture and the Inuktitut language. Some of these measures include:

• Flexible hours for civil workers to accommodate hunting schedules.

• Use of Inuktitut as the working language of government. (Other official languages are English and French.)

• Involvement of elders—those who possess *Inuit Qaujimajatuqangit*, or traditional knowledge—in setting government policies.

• Decision-making in the legislature by consensus of the majority, a practice used in traditional Inuit society.

• Continuation of traditional festivals, such as "Return of the Sun" celebrations in mid-January, and new holidays, such as Nunavut Day, held on July 9th.

DID YOU KNOW

In 1977, the Inuit formed the Inuit Circumpolar Conference (ICC) to represent the Inuit of Russia (Chukotka), the United States (Alaska), Canada, and Denmark (Greenland). The organization focuses its efforts on protection of the Arctic environment and preservation of the Inuit culture.

The Inuit of ▶ Nunavut trace their ancestry back more than 4,000 years. They share a culture with the Inuit who live in Arctic lands stretching from Greenland to eastern Siberia. The bone and ivory carvings made by Inuit artists today reflect this culture.

s their territorial symbol, eople of Nunavut chose *nukshuk*—the pile of stones by Inuit hunters to mark s. This symbol appears on erritory's new flag.

Just after midnight on April 1, 1999, ▶ a burst of fireworks lit up the sky in Iqaluit, the capital of Nunavut. The celebrants included some of the approximately 25,000 people who make up the territory's entire population. Of this number, about 56 percent are under the age of 25.

Glencoe Literature Library

The following novel from the **Glencoe Literature Library** may be used to enrich the Around the World feature:
• *Julie of the Wolves,* by Jean Craighead George. (Clash between Inuit and modern Western values.)

he creation of Nunavut gives the Inuit a chance to erve their culture in the century ahead. On a break school, a young Inuit boy camps out in an igloo he ed build during a winter hunt.

Taking Another Look

1. Where is Nunavut located?

2. Why was the creation of this territory a milestone in history?

Hands-On Activity

Creating a Magazine Cover Design the cover for a Canadian magazine announcing the creation of Nunavut—the nation's third and largest territory.

669

ASSESS

Check for Understanding

Have students answer the questions in Taking Another Look on page 669.

Enrich

Encourage interested students to take a virtual tour of Nunavut by visiting: http://www.arctic-travel.com/ Have them report their experiences in the form of a postcard to the rest of the class.

For other information on Nunavut, students can visit the territory's official Web site at: http://www.nunavut.com/

CLOSE

Explore with students why the creation of Nunavut represents a milestone in the spread of democracy. *(Sample response: It extends the right of self-government to a native people.)*

ANSWERS TO TAKING ANOTHER LOOK

1. Nunavut is located in the far northern regions of Canada, with more than half of its territory north of the Arctic Circle.

2. The creation of nunavut was the first time in Canadian history that a native people had won control over their own government and the right to send a territorial representative to the Canadian parliament.

Hand-On Activity

Magazine covers will vary, but designs should reflect Inuit pride in Nunavut and might include the use of traditional art forms or the new territorial flag.

Standardized Test Practice

Answers and Analyses

1C History

Page 604 states that World War I was different because civilians were attacked and new weapons were particularly destructive.

 TEST-TAKING TIP

This is a great example to illustrate the power of the process of elimination. It is very unlikely that choices A, B, and D were innovations of World War I. Remind students to read the question very carefully so they do not misunderstand what type of answer they should look for.

2J History

According to pages 610–611, the Russian people did support the revolution, and the poor did want equality, so choices F and H can be eliminated. Since the government was run by the Communist Party, and not democratically elected, the best choice is J.

3C History

According to page 614, Hitler *blamed many of Germany's troubles on the Jews and others.* This information best supports choice C.

4J History

According to page 620, President Truman *did not want to invade Japan* and he instead *approved the use of a new weapon—the atomic bomb.* This information best supports choice J.

Directions: Choose the *best* answer to each of the following multiple choice questions. If you have trouble answering a question, use the process of elimination to narrow your choices. Write your answers on a separate piece of paper.

1. Why was World War I different from earlier wars?

A It was the first war fought on European soil.

B It was the first time the United States fought in a war.

C New weapons made it the deadliest war ever.

D The war resulted in many political reforms.

> **Test-Taking Tip:** This question asks for a *comparison*. Although the war did result in political reforms (answer D), this fact does not make it *different* from other wars.

2. The Russian Revolution was different from the French and American revolutions in which of the following ways?

F The Russian Revolution was not fought because the poor wanted more equality.

G The Russian Revolution relied more on trench warfare.

H The people of Russia did not support the Russian Revolution.

J The goal of the Russian Revolution was not to put a democratically elected government in power.

> **Test-Taking Tip:** This question also asks you to find a *difference* by *comparison*. Ask yourself, how is *communism* different from *democracy*?

3. In which of the following ways did Hitler unite Germany?

A He gave voting rights to all males over the age of 18.

B He enacted a law requiring religion in Germany.

C He united the people of Germany against what he thought was a common enemy.

D He used various tactics from Soviet communism to improve the economy.

> **Test-Taking Tip:** Always read the question and all of the answer choices *carefully*. You may be tempted to choose answer D, since Hitler did promise to improve the economy. However, these tactics were not borrowed from Soviet communism—and they were not his most *significant* unifying action.

4. President Truman avoided sending American troops to invade Japan by

F signing a peace treaty with the emperor of Japan

G convincing other Allied nations to fight in Japan

H limiting the war to a fight for Midway Island

J releasing atomic bombs on Hiroshima and Nagasaki

> **Test-Taking Tip:** This question asks you to remember an important, pivotal event in World War II. President Truman did not limit the fighting just to Midway Island, though an important battle did take place there. Therefore, you can eliminate answer H.

670

5. The United Nations was formed at the end of World War II. The activities of the United Nations include all of the following EXCEPT

A providing medical care to people in poor countries

B preventing the spread of communism to western nations

C negotiating and keeping peace between nations

D lending money to poor countries

> **Test-Taking Tip:** Think about what you know about the United Nations. It is an organization made up of countries with many different types of governments. Which answer choice best fits this information? Remember, the question is asking for the EXCEPTION.

6. Why is Mohandas Gandhi considered a great leader?

F He convinced the Indian people to boycott British goods.

G He gained the respect of both the upper class and the common people.

H He believed in achieving peace without violence.

J He traveled through India convincing people to support democracy.

> **Test-Taking Tip:** Always read the question and *all* of the answer choices carefully. Even if you do not remember the answer to a fact-based question such as this one, it is usually a good idea to eliminate answers that you know are incorrect and then guess from the remaining choices.

Major Oil Producers in the Middle East

TURKEY
SYRIA
IRAQ
IRAN
MEDITERRANEAN SEA
EGYPT
KUWAIT
SAUDI ARABIA
UNITED ARAB EMIRATES
Persian Gulf
Red Sea
Arabian Sea
N

■ 10 million metric tons per year

miles 0   200   400
kilometers 0   200   400

7. According to this graph, how much oil does Kuwait produce annually?

F 6 metric tons

G 60 metric tons

H 6 million metric tons

J 60 million metric tons

> **Test-Taking Tip:** Use the map *legend*, or *key*, to understand the symbols used on the map. On this map, each barrel symbolizes a larger number to save space (and make them easier to count!). Make sure you double-check all the answer choices—this type of question can be tricky. However, all the information you need is on the graph: you just need to *interpret* it.

STOP

5B History

The UN is discussed on pages 621–622. There it states that the UN's responsibilities *were to prevent war, lend money to poor countries, and provide them with medical care and better education.*

> **THE PRINCETON REVIEW TEST-TAKING TIP**
>
> Students can often answer EXCEPT and NOT questions by association. Answers A, C, and D are all associated with the activities of the UN.

6H History

Gandhi is discussed on page 634. There it states that he *did not believe in violence. He believed in civil disobedience.* These are the principles for which Gandhi is best known, and therefore, answer H is the best choice.

7J Economics

The graph shows 6 barrels next to Kuwait. The legend indicates that each barrel represents 10 million metric tons of oil; therefore, the answer is 60 million metric tons (6 × 10 million).

> **THE PRINCETON REVIEW TEST-TAKING TIP**
>
> Students may notice that this graph is actually a map. Make sure that they read all labels carefully, so they understand which barrels correspond to each country.

Tested Objectives

Questions	Reading Objective
1, 2	Make comparisons
3	Evaluate information
4, 5	Identify central issues
6	Make inferences and generalizations
7	Analyze information

PRIMARY SOURCES
Library

Introduction

Have volunteers read and discuss the introduction to the Primary Sources Library. Have students complete the activities that follow to familiarize themselves with the types of primary sources.

Oral Histories

Work together with an English or language arts teacher to help students complete the following oral history activity. Provide the following guidelines: Interview a relative or friend who is much older than you. Your aim is to find out how much their lives differed from yours. Devise a list of interview questions, such as: What did you study in school? How did you and your friends spend your free time? What are some of the biggest changes you have seen in your lifetime? What was the most pressing world problem when you were my age?

Ask students to provide a transcript or written record of the interview. If a tape recorder is available, you may want students to record the interview. Have students discuss their findings in class.

WORKING WITH PRIMARY SOURCES

Suppose that you have been asked to write a report on changes in your community over the past 25 years. Where would you get the information you need to begin writing? You would draw upon two types of information—primary sources and secondary sources.

Definitions

Primary sources are often first-person accounts by someone who actually saw or lived through what is being described. In other words, if you see a fire or live through a great storm and then write about your experiences, you are creating a primary source. Diaries, journals, photographs, and eyewitness reports are examples of primary sources. **Secondary sources** are second-hand accounts. For instance, if your friend experiences the fire or storm and tells you about it, or if you read about the fire or storm in the newspaper, and then you write about it, you are creating a secondary source. Textbooks, biographies, and histories are secondary sources.

An ancient text

Checking Your Sources

When you read primary or secondary sources, you should analyze them to figure out if they are dependable or reliable. Historians usually prefer primary sources to secondary sources, but both can be reliable or unreliable, depending on the following factors.

Time Span

With primary sources, it is important to consider how long after the event occurred the primary source was written. Chances are the longer the time span between the event and the account, the less reliable the account is. As time passes, people often forget details and fill in gaps with events that never took place. Although we like to think we remember things exactly as they happened, the fact, is we often remember them, as we wanted them to occur.

Reliability

Another factor to consider when evaluating a primary source is the writer's background and reliability. First, try to determine how this person knows about what he or she is writing? How much does he or she know? Is the writer being truthful? Is the account convincing?

Opinions

When evaluating a primary source, you should also decide whether the account has been influenced by emotion, opinion, or exaggeration. Writers can have reasons to distort the truth to suit their personal purposes. Ask yourself: Why did the person write the account? Do any key

---

TEACHER NOTES

After studying the introduction to the Primary Sources Library, students should be able to meet the following objectives:
• explain the difference between primary sources and secondary sources.

• identify the different types of primary sources.
• understand that primary sources offer a unique view of people and events in a particular era.

Opera glasses,
late 1800s

words or expressions reveal the author's emotions or opinions? You may wish to compare the account with one written by another witness to the event. If the two accounts differ, ask yourself why they differ and which is more accurate.

Interpreting Primary Sources

To help you analyze a primary source, use the following steps:

- **Examine the origins of the document.**
  You need to determine if it is a primary source.

Classifying Primary Sources

Primary sources fall into different categories:

 Printed Publications

Printed Publications include books such as autobiographies. Printed publications also include newspapers and magazines.

 Personal Records

Personal Records are accounts of events kept by an individual who is a participant in or witness to these events. Personal records include diaries, journals, and letters.

 Oral Histories

Oral Histories are chronicles, memoirs, myths, and legends that are passed along from one generation to another by word of mouth. Interviews are another form of oral history.

- **Find the main ideas.**
  Read the document and summarize the main ideas in your own words. These ideas may be fairly easy to identify in newspapers and journals, for example, but are much more difficult to find in poetry.
- **Reread the document.**
  Difficult ideas are not always easily understood on the first reading.
- **Use a variety of resources.**
  Form the habit of using the dictionary, the encyclopedia, and maps. These resources are tools to help you discover new ideas and knowledge and check the validity of sources.

 Songs and Poems

Songs and Poems include works that express the personal thoughts and feelings or political or religious beliefs of the writer, usually using rhyming and rhythmic language.

 Artifacts

Artifacts are objects such as tools or ornaments. Artifacts present information about a particular culture or a stage of technological development.

For more primary sources to accompany this unit, use the **World History Primary Source Document Library CD-ROM.**

673

 Songs and Poems

Ask students to write a poem about an important event in their lives. Suggest that the poem be in a standard form such as limerick or other specific rhyming scheme.

 Personal Records

Tell students that a *journal* is a daily record of events kept by an individual who is a participant or witness to these events. Ask students to keep a journal of interesting events that they observed during a week's time. Encourage them to personalize the event by recording their own opinions or feelings of what they have witnessed.

Artifacts

To help students analyze artifacts, provide the following instructions: Find a primary source from your past—a photograph, a report card, an old newspaper clipping, your first baseball card, etc. Bring this source into class, and explain why you kept it and what it shows about the time from which the item comes.

 Printed Publications

To help students analyze printed publications, instruct them to read the first two paragraphs of the Preamble to the Declaration of Independence (found in the United States history text used in your school). Ask: What is the subject of these paragraphs? What do they tell you about the beliefs of the people who signed this document?

TEACHER NOTES

Through the study of the selections in the Primary Sources Library and their accompanying questions and activities, students should be able to:
- find the main idea in the selections.

- analyze information in a variety of written texts in order to make inferences and generalizations.
- provide an interpretation of the material in their own words.

Chapter Links

Use the primary sources selections on pages 674–675 to accompany the study of Unit 1. They provide students with the opportunity to extend their study of the following:

- Chapter 1, Section 4, "Archaeology," pp. 25–30.

- Chapter 2, Section 1, "The Paleolithic Age," pp. 33–40.

Reinforcing Vocabulary

Review the **Reader's Dictionary** with students to be sure they understand any unfamiliar terms. Call on a volunteer to explain what evidence of *bipedal* hominoids Mary Leakey is studying in the photograph on page 675.

Background Information

Artifacts Nearly every family has a collection of artifacts that links it with past generations or with their own history. Have students talk with the oldest friends or relatives that they know and have them find out what unique or special thing they have saved from the past. Tell students to record a description of the object, its approximate age, and reasons the person kept it. If possible, encourage students to photograph or sketch the object. Have students share their findings in a bulletin board display entitled "Pieces of the Past."

UNIT 1

AFRICAN ORIGINS

The work of one family—the Leakeys—helped uncover some of the earliest chapters in human history. Louis B. Leakey, born in Kenya in 1903, started the work. He believed that human history began in Africa. He also believed that this history was far older than anyone had ever imagined. His wife, Mary Nicol Leakey, joined him in his work. So did the couple's son, Richard. Together they made some of the most exciting archaeological and anthropological discoveries of the past 100 years.

■ Reader's Dictionary

petrified ash volcanic dust that has turned into stone

hominid member of a group that includes human beings and early human-like creatures

retained kept

bipedal walking on two feet

tuff pieces of volcanic rock

relief contrast with the surrounding area

haunt to reappear constantly

trek a long journey, usually by foot

perilous dangerous

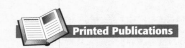
Printed Publications

Footprints in Time

The death of Louis Leakey in 1972 did not stop Mary and Richard Leakey from digging into the past. In 1978, Mary Leakey discovered a set of ancient footprints south of the Olduvai Gorge in present-day Tanzania. In a 1979 article for *National Geographic*, she describes a trail that carried her back in time.

This article . . . will cause yet another upheaval in the study of human origins. For in the gray, petrified ash . . . we have found hominid footprints that are remarkably similar to those of modern man. . . . Prints that were laid down an incredible 3,600,000 years ago! . . .

Two individuals, one larger, one smaller, had passed this way. . . . We have measured their footprints and the length of their stride. Was the larger one a male, the smaller one a female? Or was one mature, the other young? It is unlikely that we will ever know with certainty. . . .

The closeness of the two sets of prints indicates that their owners were not walking [side by side]. Other clues suggest that the hominids may have passed at different times. For example, the imprints of the smaller individual stand out clearly. The crispness of definition and sharp outlines convince me that they were left on a damp surface that retained the form of the foot.

On the other hand, the prints of the larger are blurred, as if he had shuffled or dragged his feet. In fact, I think that the surface when he passed was loose and dusty, hence the collapsed appearance of his prints. Nonetheless,

TEAM TEACHING STRATEGIES

Art Work together with an art teacher to help students illustrate the selection by Mary Leakey. Begin by telling students to imagine they are artists working for *National Geographic*. They have been asked to design a picture showing what the African landscape might have looked like on the day the footprints discovered by Leakey were made some 3,600,000 years ago. Encourage students to do additional research to determine what the region may have been like. To get students started, point out that it was a time of great volcanic activity and that the two walkers probably could see at least one volcano smoldering in the distance.

luck favored us again; the bigger hominid left one absolutely clear print, probably on a patch of once damp ash.

What did these footprints tell us? First, they demonstrate once and for all that at least 3,600,000 years ago, in Pliocene times, what I believe to be man's direct ancestor walked fully upright with a bipedal, freestriding gait. Second, that the form of his foot was exactly the same as ours.

Sometimes, . . . I go out and watch the dust settle over the gray tuff with its eerie record of time long past. The slanting light of evening throws the hominid prints into sharp relief, so sharp that they could have been left this morning.

I cannot help but think about the distant creatures who made them. Where did they come from? Where were they going? We simply do not know. It has been suggested that they were merely crossing this scorched plain toward the greener ridges to the north. Perhaps so.

In any case, those footprints out of the deep past, left by the oldest known hominids, haunt the imagination. Across the gulf of time I can only wish them well on that prehistoric trek. It was, I believe, part of a greater and more perilous journey, one that . . . culminated in the emergence of modern man.

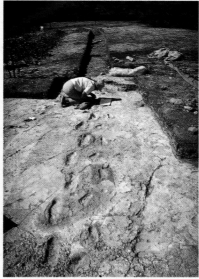

▲ Mary Leakey

Interpreting Primary Sources

1. What effect does Mary Leakey think her article will have?
2. Why does she feel this way?
3. How might a geographer describe the landscape at the time the footprints were made?
4. What does Mary Leakey mean when she says the footprints "haunt the imagination"?
5. What one important thing do you think the footprints revealed?

ACTIVITY

Writing a News Bulletin Write a 30-second news bulletin that a television or radio reporter might have given upon learning of Mary Leakey's discovery.

Block Schedule

Team Teaching These selections may be implemented in a team-teaching context, in conjunction with English/Language Arts.

Chapter Links

Use the primary source selections on pages 676–677 to accompany the study of Unit 2. They provide students with the opportunity to extend their study of the following:

• Chapter 3, Section 2, "Later Mesopotamian Empires," pp. 61–63.

Reinforcing Vocabulary

Review the **Reader's Dictionary** with students to be sure they understand any unfamiliar terms. Ask students what the word "justice" means to them.

Background Information

Symbols Point out that a *symbol* is a person, place, or object that has meaning in itself and also stands for something other than itself. Symbols communicate meaning even to those who cannot read. Refer students to the artifact from Hammurabi's Code on page 677. Ask: What symbols did the artist use to convey Hammurabi's importance? What did Hammurabi symbolize to the people of his empire?

UNIT 2

THE PURSUIT OF JUSTICE

Hammurabi's gift to civilization was his code of laws. Other rulers had enacted laws in the past, but Hammurabi was the first to collect them into a single written code. The code included nearly 300 legal decisions. Some were harsh—even brutal—by today's standards. However, the code made the state responsible for their enforcement. This was a great advance over a system in which people often took justice into their own hands. Under the Hammurabi Code, society began its long journey toward the ideal of "equal justice for all."

■ Reader's Dictionary

justified proven
commoner someone not of noble birth
thirtyfold thirty times (its value)
render pay
tenfold ten times (its value)
creditor person who has made a loan
interest fee charged on a loan
mina an ancient unit of weight
traffic trade
gored pierced with horns
plumbed tested or examined

676

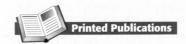

The Hammurabi Code

The Hammurabi Code touched on almost every aspect of life. The purpose of the code, said the prologue, was "to cause justice to prevail in the land, to destroy the wicked and the evil, that the strong may not oppress the weak." Here are some of the laws intended to achieve that goal.

1. If a man . . . bring a charge of murder against another man and has not justified himself, the accuser shall be put to death.

8. If a man has stolen ox or sheep . . . or pig or ship, whether from the temple or from the palace, he shall pay thirtyfold; if he stole from a commoner, he shall render tenfold. If the thief cannot pay, he shall be put to death.

15. If a man has helped a male or female palace slave, or a commoner's slave to escape out of the city gate, he shall be put to death.

21. If a man has broken into a house, he shall be killed . . . and walled in it.

48. If a man has a debt upon him and . . . the corn has not grown for lack of water, in that year he shall make no return of corn to his creditor . . . and he shall not pay interest for that year.

TEAM TEACHING STRATEGIES

Language Arts Work with a language arts teacher to introduce students to the meaning of *colloquial language,* or the everyday language we use in conversation. Then divide students into groups, and assign them to rewrite the laws in Hammurabi's Code so that they would be easy for a third grader to understand. Call on students to share their rewritten laws with the rest of the class.

104. If a merchant has lent a trader corn, wool, or oil or any sort of goods to traffic with, the trader shall write down the price and pay it back. . . .

195. If a man has struck his father, his hand shall be cut off.

200. If a man has made the tooth of a man that is his equal fall out, they shall take his tooth out.

201. If a man has made the tooth of a commoner fall out, he shall pay one third of a mina of silver.

229. If a builder has built a house and not made his work strong and the house he built has fallen and so has caused the death of the owner of the house, that builder shall be put to death.

250. If a wild bull in his charge has gored a man, and caused him to die, that case has no remedy.

▲ Hammurabi

 Artifacts   In December 1910, a team of French archaeologists working in Iran discovered three pieces of black stone covered with inscriptions. The stones fit together in a block nearly eight feet long. At the top, a king speaks with a seated god. The king introduces himself as a "god among kings," "a fighter without peer," and "the one who plumbed the depths of wisdom." The archaeologists had found the Hammurabi Code.

Interpreting Primary Sources

1. What do the pictures and inscriptions on the stone block reveal about Hammurabi's ideas about kingship?
2. How do you think discovery of the Hammurabi Code affected the way people viewed ancient Mesopotamia?
3. Which of the code's laws were intended to discourage theft?
4. Which were intended to promote fair business dealings?
5. Based on these laws, what social classes do you think made up Babylonian society?
6. Which, if any, of these laws would probably be upheld under our constitution?

ACTIVITY

Design a code of laws that you think should be implemented in your school. To be just, the code must take into account those rights guaranteed to defendants by the United States Constitution. (Study the Bill of Rights closely.) Present your code to the student government in your school.

677

Block Schedule

Team Teaching These selections may be implemented in a team-teaching context, in conjunction with English/Language Arts.

Chapter Links
Use the primary source selections on pages 678–679 to accompany the study of Unit 3. They provide students with the opportunity to extend their study of the following:

- Chapter 8, Section 2, "The Middle Kingdoms," pp. 132–134.

Reinforcing Vocabulary
Review the **Reader's Dictionary** with students to be sure they understand any unfamiliar terms. Refer students to the map on page 678. Ask: What evidence proves that the mapmaker saw Mansa Musa as the *sovereign* ruler of Mali?

Background Information
The Oral Tradition Ancient people handed down their culture, traditions, and histories through the oral tradition. Through storytelling, or word of mouth, they passed on their heritage from one generation to the next. Explain that family histories are often shared in the oral tradition. Ask volunteers to share family stories. Then explore how such stories might give insight into a certain period of time.

UNIT 3

THE EMPIRE OF MALI

Mali owed its success to two great conquerors—Sundiata Keita and Mansa Musa I. They helped build one of the largest empires in the world and by far the richest Africa has ever known. People from all over Africa and the Middle East traveled to see Mali. Generations of African storytellers have sung its praises.

■ Reader's Dictionary

eloquence beautiful speech
vanquished defeated
taboos forbidden acts
Keitas African people from which Sundiata came
ebony a type of dark wood
arms weapons
quiver case for holding arrows
score twenty
page a boy servant or attendant
sovereign all-powerful ruler
mitgals type of gold coin

The Father of Mali

A modern-day *griot*, or West African storyteller, celebrates the accomplishments of Sundiata Keita.

I am a griot, . . . master in the art of eloquence. . . . I teach kings the history of their ancestors so that the lives of the ancients might serve them as an example, for the word is old, but the future springs from the past.

My word is pure and free of all untruth; it is the word of my father; it is the word of my father's father. . . .

Listen, then, sons of Mali, . . . for I am going to tell you of Sundiata, . . . the master of a hundred vanquished kings. . . .

Sundiata was unique. In his own time no one equalled him, and after him no one had the ambition to surpass him. He left his mark on Mali, for all time, and his taboos still guide men in their conduct. . . .

Men of today, how small you are beside your ancestors. . . . Sundiata rests, . . . but his spirit lives on, and today the Keitas still come and bow before the stone under which lies the father of Mali.

The Sultan of Mali

An Arab scholar named Ibn Fadl Allah al Omari describes the court and army of Mansa Musa. He refers to Mansa Musa as *sultan*, the Arab word for "king."

TEAM TEACHING STRATEGIES

Art Have students locate present-day nations that once formed part of the empire of Mali. (Refer students to the map of early Africa on page 135 and to the map of present-day Africa on page 716.) Then, working with an art teacher, assign students to create commemorative stamps that one of these nations might print to celebrate its historic link with Mali.

The sultan of this kingdom presides in his palace on a great balcony, called *bembe*, where he has a seat of ebony that is like a throne fit for a large and tall person: on either side it is flanked by elephant tusks turned toward each other. His arms stand near him, being all of gold—saber, lance, quiver, bows, and arrows. He wears wide trousers made of about twenty pieces [of cloth], of a kind only he can wear.

Behind him stand a score of Turkish or other pages which are bought for him in Cairo. . . . His officers are seated in a circle about him, in two rows, one to the right and one to the left; behind them sit the chief commanders of his cavalry. . . .

Others dance before their sovereign, who enjoys this, and make him laugh. Two banners are spread behind him. Before him they keep two saddled and bridled horses in case he should wish to ride.

Arab horses are brought for sale to the kings of this country, who spend considerable sums in this way. Their army numbers 100,000 men of whom there are about 10,000 horse-mounted cavalry: the others are infantry having neither horses nor any other mounts. . . .

The officers of this king, his soldiers, and his guard receive gifts of land and presents. Some among the greatest of them receive as much as 50,000 *mitgals* of gold a year, besides which the king provides them with horses and clothing. He is much concerned with giving them garments and making his cities into capitals.

▲ An early map of North Africa showing Mansa Musa

Interpreting Primary Sources

1. Why does the griot say he is telling the story of Sundiata?
2. Why was Sundiata unique?
3. What conclusions can you draw about Mansa Musa's power?
4. Why do you think Mansa Musa treated his soldiers so well?
5. If you had the chance to meet one of these two leaders, whom would you choose—Sundiata Keita or Mansa Musa? Explain.

ACTIVITY

Storytelling   Write an account of Mansa Musa that a West African griot might tell to a group of children. (For more information on Mansa Musa, see pages 133–134.)

679

Portfolio Activity   Review the stories written by students in the Activity suggestion on page 679. Then assign them to turn these accounts into storyboards—a series of frames much like a comic strip. Explain that storyboards are often used to help decide on the main sequence of events for a video production. Have students present their storyboards, noting any changes that they made in their accounts when they switched from words to pictures. What details did they add? What details did they leave out?

Multiple Learning Styles

Auditory/Musical   Some students have problems processing what they hear. Students with this problem may look like they are not paying attention. Actually, they get "lost" in the confusion of language unless certain classroom modifications are made. To help students listen effectively, explain to them that you will cue them when you are coming to an important point with words such as "the definition of," "the main point," or "the most important." Then conduct a class discussion on Mali using these words.

ANSWERS TO INTERPRETING PRIMARY SOURCES

1. so that kings in the present might learn from the examples of the great leaders of the past
2. because no other person was his equal or could surpass him in ambition
3. Conclusions will vary in wording, but most students will say that Mansa Musa had absolute power.
4. Sample response: The soldiers helped Mansa Musa build and protect his empire. They were the source of his strength.

5. Students should offer reasons, based on the readings, why one leader interested them more than the other.
Activity Stories should accurately reflect details in the life of Mansa Musa while being told in a voice similar to that used by the *griot*. (For extra credit, you might assign interested students to find out more about the role of a *griot* in West African society.)

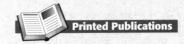

Block Schedule

Team Teaching These selections may be implemented in a team-teaching context, in conjunction with English/Language Arts.

Chapter Links

Use the primary source selections on pages 680–681 to accompany the study of Unit 4. They provide students with the opportunity to extend their study of the following:

- Chapter 10, Section 3, "Athens," pp. 168–175.

- Chapter 11, Section 2, "Science," pp. 185–190. (Socrates and Plato are covered here.)

Reinforcing Vocabulary

Review the **Reader's Dictionary** with students to be sure they understand any unfamiliar terms. Ask: What *regulations* do you think that women in Greek society probably had to follow?

Background Information

Persuasion   Point out to students that persuasive writing attempts to sway the reader to think or act in a particular way. Explain that Plato slanted the dialogues in *The Republic* to advance his own ideas on government and society. Ask students to decide how Plato viewed women.

UNIT 4

GREEK SOCIETY

Each of the Greek city-states had its own ideas on the rights of citizens. None of the city-states, however, gave women an equal voice in society or government. Even in Athens, which claimed to be a democracy, women had few legal rights. Parents arranged the marriages of their daughters, typically at ages 13 to 15, to men at least twice their age. Once married, women rarely appeared in public and took no part in politics. The philosopher Plato saw little justice in this situation and brought it to the attention of the ancient world.

■ Reader's Dictionary

regulations rules
flocks herds of animals, especially sheep and goats
nurture upbringing
gymnastic activities involving exercise or physical strength
inference a conclusion drawn through the use of reason
gymnasia buildings or rooms used for physical exercise or training
notions thoughts
jests jokes
attainments accomplishments

680

Printed Publications

The Rights of Women

In *The Republic*, Plato presents his ideas on a just society in the form of dialogues, or imaginary conversations, between Socrates and his students. In this dialogue, Socrates has just finished questioning his student about the type of men who might make the best "watchdogs" of Athenian government. He surprises his student by turning to the subject of women.

Let us suppose further the birth and education of our women to be subject to similar or nearly similar regulations [as men]. . . .

What do you mean?

What I mean may be put into the form of a question. . . . I said: Are dogs divided into hes and shes, or do they both share equally in hunting and in keeping watch and in the other duties of dogs? [O]r do we entrust to the males the entire and exclusive care of the flocks, while we leave the females at home, under the idea that the bearing and . . . [feeding of] their puppies is labour enough for them?

No, he said, they share alike; the only difference between them is that the males are stronger and the females weaker.

But can you use different animals for the same purpose, unless they are . . . [raised] in the same way?

You cannot.

Then, if women are to have the same duties as men, they must have the same nurture and education?

Yes.

TEAM TEACHING STRATEGIES

Science   Work with a science teacher to develop a lesson on the Socratic Method, which is covered on pages 185–186 of the text. Begin by reviewing the way Socrates uses a series of questions in the dialogue in the primary source reading to lead his student to a conclusion. Then, with the science teacher, have students form questions to plan an experiment on some topic they are currently studying in science.

The education which was assigned to the men was music and gymnastic.

Yes.

Then women must be taught music and gymnastic and also the art of war, which they must practise like the men?

That is the inference, I suppose.

I should rather expect, I said, that . . . our proposals, if they are carried out, being unusual, may appear ridiculous.

No doubt of it. . . .

Yes, and the most ridiculous thing of all would be the sight of women . . . exercising with the men . . . [who] frequent the gymnasia.

Yes, indeed, he said, according to present notions the proposal would be thought ridiculous.

But, then, I said, . . . we must not fear the jests . . . which will be directed against this sort of innovation; how they will talk of women's attainments both in music and gymnastic, and above all about their wearing armour and riding upon horseback!

Very true, he replied. . . .

Artifacts

Paintings on fifth-century vases give an inside look at Greek society. These vases took so much effort to make that an ancient Greek expression for working hard was "to make pottery." Careful studies of vase paintings show that at least some women managed to escape a world that said that they should "see as little, hear as little, and ask as few questions as possible."

Interpreting Primary Sources

1. What does Plato think will help to make men and women more equal?
2. How does he think most Athenians will react to this suggestion?
3. Based on this selection, what conclusions can you draw about the education of women in ancient Greece?
4. How do you think Plato might react to the scene shown in the vase painting? Explain.

ACTIVITY

Illustrating Ideas Design a vase painting illustrating Plato's ideas for reform of Athenian society.

681

Portfolio Activity

Assign students to review Plato's ideas on truth on page 187. Then have them present these views in a dialogue similar to that in the Primary Sources Library. Remind students that one speaker should be Socrates and the other should be a student.

Multiple Learning Styles

Verbal/Linguistic Students with language difficulties may have problems formulating questions. Assist these students by using the following strategy: Organize students into groups to develop questions that a pupil might have posed to Socrates about Athenian society or government. Help students vary their questions by offering the "clue" words *who, what, where, when, how,* and *why.*

ANSWERS TO INTERPRETING PRIMARY SOURCES

1. To become more equal, men and women should have an equal upbringing and education.
2. Athenians will joke about it.
3. Sample response: They received little or no training in the subjects studied by men.
4. Sample response: He may feel that the scene should also depict women wearing armor and fighting in battle.

Activity Vase paintings should accurately reflect Plato's beliefs rather than those of students. Drawings should also depict Greek culture—such as style of dress—as shown in artwork within the text or through independent research.

PRIMARY SOURCES
Library

Block Schedule

Team Teaching These selections may be implemented in a team-teaching context, in conjunction with English/Language Arts.

Chapter Links

Use the primary source selections on pages 682–683 to accompany the study of Unit 5. They provide students with the opportunity to extend their study of the following:

- Chapter 15, Section 2, *"Pax Romana,"* pp. 234–236.

- Chapter 15, Section 3, "Daily Life," pp. 236–240.

Note: This feature might also be used with the discussion on Pompeii in Chapter 1, Section 5, "Archaeology," pp. 25–30.

Reinforcing Vocabulary

Review the **Reader's Dictionary** with students to be sure they understand any unfamiliar terms. Have students speculate on what the woman on page 683 might be writing for *posterity.*

Background Information

Description   Point out that descriptive writing creates a picture of a person, place, or thing in a reader's mind. Have students individually or in small groups identify the descriptive language that Pliny the Younger uses to bring alive the eruption of Mount Vesuvius.

UNIT 5

ERUPTION OF MOUNT VESUVIUS

Early in August of 79 A.D., a series of small earthquakes shook the countryside around Mount Vesuvius, a volcano located along the Bay of Naples in southern Italy. On the morning of August 24, a cloud of ash formed over the volcano. Later that afternoon, Vesuvius exploded. Streams of molten rock shot upward as high as 17 miles. Then it rained back down on cities along the bay. The eruption lasted for about two days and formed one of the great natural disasters in Roman history.

■ Reader's Dictionary

posterity future generations
implored begged
inquiry search for knowledge
helmsman person who steers a ship
Fortune good luck
allay calm

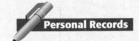
Personal Records

A Heroic Rescue Attempt

Pliny the Elder—a Roman admiral and well-known author and scientist—died attempting to rescue people trapped at the foot of Vesuvius. His nephew, Pliny the Younger, recorded his uncle's death in a letter written to a Roman historian named Tacitus. The letter forms an eyewitness account of the eruption and expresses Roman views of courage and duty.

Thank you for asking me to send you an account of my uncle's death so that you can leave an accurate account of it for posterity. . . .

On 24 August, in the early afternoon, my mother drew his attention to a cloud of unusual size and appearance. . . . It was not clear at the distance from which mountain the cloud was rising (it was afterwards known to be Vesuvius). . . . My uncle . . . saw at once that it was important enough for a closer inspection, and he ordered a boat to be made ready. . . .

As he was leaving the house he was handed a message from Rectina, . . . whose house was at the foot of the mountain, so that escape was impossible except by boat. She was terrified by the danger threatening her and implored him to rescue her. . . . He changed his plans, and what he had begun in a spirit of inquiry he completed as a hero. He gave orders for the warships to be launched and went on board himself with the intention of bringing help to many more people than Rectina. . . . He hurried to the place which everyone else was hastily leaving, steering his course straight for the danger zone. . . .

TEAM TEACHING STRATEGY

Science   Work with a science teacher to distinguish active, dormant, and extinct volcanoes. Then assign students to research active volcanoes in the world today. Have them locate these volcanoes on an outline map of the world. Ask: In which region are most of these volcanoes located? *(Students will discover that a large number of volcanoes lay along the Pacific Rim, giving it the nickname "ring of fire.")*

Ashes were already falling, hotter and thicker as the ships drew near. . . . For a moment my uncle wondered whether he should turn back, but when the helmsman advised this he refused, telling him that Fortune stood by the courageous. . . . The wind was . . . in my uncle's favor, and he was able to bring the ship in.

Meanwhile on Mount Vesuvius broad sheets of fire and leaping flames blazed at several points. . . . My uncle tried to allay the fears of his companions. . . . They debated whether to stay indoors or take their chances in the open, for buildings were now shaking with violent shocks, and seemed to be swaying. . . .

My uncle decided to go down to the shore and investigate on the spot the possibility of any escape by the sea, but he found the waves still wild and dangerous. A sheet was spread on the ground for him to lie down, and he repeatedly asked for cold water to drink. Then the flames and smell of sulfur which gave warning of the approaching fire drove the others to take flight. . . . He stood . . . and then suddenly collapsed, I imagine because the dense fumes choked his breathing. . . . When daylight appeared on the 26th—two days after the last day he had been seen—his body was found, . . . looking more like sleep than death. . . .

I will say no more, except to add that I have described in detail every incident which I either witnessed myself or heard about immediately after the event, when reports were most likely to be accurate.

 Artifacts The mud and lava that poured out of Vesuvius buried entire cities. When archaeologists uncovered the city of Pompeii, they got a firsthand look at life at the height of Roman power. The art and artifacts found at Pompeii reveal some of the comforts and pleasures enjoyed by the citizens of Pompeii.

Interpreting Primary Sources

1. Why did Pliny the Elder originally want to sail toward Vesuvius?
2. Why did he change his plans?
3. Why did Pliny the Younger consider his uncle a hero? Do you agree? Explain.
4. Why do you think historians consider Pompeii an important source of information about daily life in the Roman Empire?

ACTIVITY

Writing an Obituary Write an obituary for Pliny the Elder that might have appeared in a Roman newspaper. (Pliny the Elder was born around 23 A.D.)

683

ANSWERS TO INTERPRETING PRIMARY SOURCES

1. He wanted to inspect the source of the cloud—the smoking of Vesuvius—more closely.
2. He received a message from Rectina asking him to rescue her. Pliny the Elder then decided to help as many people as he could.
3. because he sacrificed his life to save those of others; students should support their opinions of Pliny with evidence from the selection
4. because Pompeii gives them a firsthand look at daily life during the Roman Empire
Activity Obituaries will vary, but students should try to model them after those found in their local newspaper.

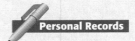
Block Schedule

Team Teaching These selections may be implemented in a team-teaching context, in conjunction with English/Language Arts.

Chapter Links

Use the primary source selections on pages 684–685 to accompany the study of Unit 6. They provide students with the opportunity to extend their study of the following:

- Chapter 20, Section 2, "Daily Life," pp. 301–303.

- Chapter 20, Section 3, "Raiders and Adventurers," pp. 304–308.

Note: This feature might also be used with the discussion of the Middle Ages in Chapter 24, Section 1, "Land and Government," pp. 367–369.

Reinforcing Vocabulary

Review the **Reader's Dictionary** with students to be sure they understand any unfamiliar terms. Refer students to the artifact on page 685. Ask: How did stolen *booty* allow the Vikings to make such jewelry?

Background Information

Annals Explain to students that annals are a record of events organized chronologically by year. (Tell students to keep in mind the word "annually.") Ask students how annals differ from diaries. *(Diaries are usually written each day or week.)* Explore with students reasons annals are useful for getting a sweeping picture of an era.

UNIT 6

THE AGE OF VIKING CONQUEST

The early Middle Ages was a time of disorder in Europe. Scattered communities throughout the region struggled to survive the hardships of daily life. In these unsettled times, the Vikings embarked on an age of conquest. They sailed out of Scandinavia and headed into lands that stretched from what is now Russia in the east to present-day Newfoundland in the west. They explored, traded, and set up colonies. They also attacked and robbed villages, earning a reputation as some of the most fearsome invaders of the early Middle Ages.

■ Reader's Dictionary

plundered robbed
booty stolen goods
heathen barbarian
famine time of great hunger
fodder food for livestock
entrenched well-established
razed leveled
hither and yon here and there
Flemings people from Flanders, a
    medieval country along the North Sea
kinsmen relatives

684

Plundering Europe

After the death of Charlemagne, central government again collapsed in western Europe. Records kept by a monastery near what is now Cologne, Germany, reveal the suffering caused by a new round of invasions by the Vikings, or the Northmen, as they were known at the time.

(846) According to their custom the Northmen plundered Eastern and Western Frisia and burned the town of Dordrecht, with two other villages. . . . The Northmen, with their boats filled with immense booty including men and goods, returned to their own country. . . .
(852) The steel of the heathen glistened; excessive heat; a famine followed. There was not fodder enough for the animals. . . .
(882) The Northmen in the month of October entrenched themselves at Condé and horribly devastated the kingdom of Carloman. . . .
    They destroyed houses, and razed monasteries and churches to the ground. . . . They killed the dwellers in the land and none could resist them.
    Abbot Hugo . . . gathered an army and came to aid the King. When the Northmen came back from a plundering expedition . . . he, in company with the King, gave them chase. They, however, . . . scattered hither and yon, and finally returned to their ships with little loss. . . .
(883) In the spring the Northmen left Condé and . . . forced the Flemings to flee from their lands and raged everywhere, laying waste to the country with fire and sword.

TEAM TEACHING STRATEGIES

Art Work with an art teacher to help students prepare a bulletin board display of Viking treasures—both things the Vikings made themselves and things they seized from other people. A good source of information on this topic is *What Life Was Like:* *When Longships Sailed*, by the editors of Time-Life, Time-Life Books (1998). Students should write captions to accompany each piece of art that they select for their display.

Artifacts The Vikings valued captured treasures. However, they also created their own beautiful works of art, including jewelry fashioned from precious metals seized in raids. This brooch shows the complicated designs for which the Vikings became famous.

Songs and Poems

Words of Praise

The Vikings celebrated their conquests in songs and verses written by *skalds*—professional poets hired by kings and nobles throughout Scandinavia.

Cattle die, kinsmen die,
one day you die yourself;
but the words of praise will not perish
when a man wins fair fame.

Interpreting Primary Sources

1. Why did the Vikings raid the villages and towns surrounding the monastery?
2. How did the Vikings avoid capture by the army raised by Abbot Hugo and the king?
3. In addition to Viking raids, what other problems did people living around the monastery face?
4. What do the lines written by a *skald* promise Vikings who win "fair fame"?
5. How did the Vikings use some of their plunder?

ACTIVITY

Writing a Song Imagine you are a *skald*. Write a song about a Viking expedition to explore the waters and lands to the west of Scandinavia.

685

Portfolio Activity After students have studied the monastery records, assign them to write entries that a Viking might have prepared for the same years and same events. Call on volunteers to read their entries aloud. Ask: How did the Viking view of this period in history differ from that of the abbot who kept the monastery records?

Multiple Learning Styles
Verbal/Linguistic Students with language difficulties may have difficulty distinguishing between essential and non-essential details. Explain that one way to identify essential details is to form questions to guide reading. Have students turn the title of this feature, "The Age of Viking Conquest," into a question. Then instruct them to find the essential details in the reading that answer this question.

ANSWERS TO INTERPRETING PRIMARY SOURCES

1. for booty and plunder
2. The Vikings split up and "scattered hither and yon." Then they made their way back to their ships and sailed away.
3. People around the monastery also suffered a famine and a lack of food for their animals.

4. that their great feats will be remembered forever
5. to create jewelry and other works of art
Activity Songs will vary, but details should reflect some of the actual expeditions, such as voyages to Greenland, mentioned on pages 304–308.

PRIMARY SOURCES
Library

Block Schedule

Team Teaching These selections may be implemented in a team-teaching context, in conjunction with English/Language Arts.

Chapter Links

Use the primary source selections on pages 686–687 to accompany the study of Unit 7. They provide students with the opportunity to extend their study of the following:

- Chapter 21, Section 1, "Constantinople," pp. 317–319.
- Chapter 21, Section 2, "Justinian I," pp. 320–324.

Reinforcing Vocabulary

Review the **Reader's Dictionary** with students to be sure they understand any unfamiliar terms. Refer students to the artifact on page 687, and ask: Who is the *sovereign* shown in this detail from a Byzantine altar?

Background Information

Bias Remind students of the importance of detecting bias, or viewpoints that may affect a writer's interpretation of events or people. (You might have students reread the skill lesson on page 170.) Then ask students what bias Anna Commena might have in retelling the story of her father's reign. Why do students think historians might want to check other sources of information about Alexius I?

UNIT 7

BYZANTINE WOMEN

The Byzantines valued intelligence, whether it be in a man or a woman. An emperor or noble might marry a woman as much for her education or political skills as for her royal birth. As a result, the women who belonged to the royal courts of the Byzantine Empire had a great deal of influence. Rarely did women elsewhere in the world exercise more power than the imperial women of Byzantium.

■ Reader's Dictionary

concealed kept hidden
confidant close friend
monastery religious community
endowed gifted
aptitude ability
sovereign ruler
reserved kept
ravaged damaged
undaunted fearless

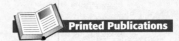
Printed Publications

A Woman on the Throne

In 1081, an able general named Alexius Commenus captured Constantinople. As Emperor Alexius I, he defended the Byzantine Empire against attacks from invaders in both the east and the west. His daughter, Anna Commena, retold the story of his reign in a book called the *Alexiad* (uh lek′ sē uhd). She begins her account by describing Alexius's decision to turn the government over to his mother Anna Dalassena. (The story refers to the Byzantine Empire as the Roman Empire.)

It was his desire that his mother should govern rather than himself, but . . . the plan had been concealed for fear that she, if she knew of it, might leave the palace. (Alexius was aware that she considered withdrawal to a monastery.) Nevertheless, in all matters however ordinary he did nothing without her advice: she became his confidant and co-partner in government. Gradually . . . he involved her more and more in state affairs; on occasions he even declared openly that without her brains and good judgement the Empire would not survive. . . .

The truth is that Anna Dalassena was in any case endowed with a fine intellect and possessed besides a really first-class aptitude for government. . . . For my grandmother had an exceptional grasp of public affairs, with a genius for organization and government; she was capable, in fact, of managing not only the

---

TEAM TEACHING STRATEGIES

Language Arts Invite a language arts teacher to explain the meaning of *memoirs*—a biography or historical account of events written from personal experience. Then assign students to imagine they are Empress Theodora. She has decided to compose her memoirs on the reign of her husband, Justinian I. Brainstorm with students a possible title for the book. Then assign students to compose a list of topics that Theodora might include. Have one group of students use this list to compose the memoirs, while another group of students designs the illustrations to accompany the writings.

Roman Empire, but every other empire under the sun as well. . . .

But, as I was saying, once he seized power my father reserved for himself the struggles and hard labour of war, while . . . he made her the sovereign. . . . I can sum up the whole situation thus: he was in theory the emperor, but she had the real power. She was the legislator, the complete organizer and governor. . . .

Such were the events that marked the beginning of the reign. . . . Alexius knew the Empire was almost at its last gasp. The east was being horribly ravaged by the Turks; the west was in bad condition. . . . The emperors before him, having little knowledge of war and military affairs, had reduced Roman prestige to a minimum. Indeed, I have heard it said by men who were soldiers themselves, and by some of the older men, that no other state in living memory had reached such depths of misery. Conditions were desperate then for the emperor. . . . However, being not only a courageous man and undaunted, but having excellent experiences in war, he wanted to restore his Empire. . . .

 Artifacts Some empresses were not handed power—they took it. This detail from an altar shows Empress Irene, the Byzantine Empire's first woman ruler. Supported by the generals, she seized the throne from her only son and ruled from 797 to 802. Although she held power for only five years, Irene put in place much-needed financial reforms.

Interpreting Primary Sources

1. Why did Alexius conceal his plans to turn government over to his mother?
2. How did Anna Dalassena help her son to strengthen the Byzantine Empire?
3. What do these two sources of information—the *Alexiad* and the coin—tell you about the role of women in the Byzantine Empire?

ACTIVITY

Writing a News Bulletin Write a short news bulletin announcing Alexius's decision to put his mother in charge of government while he fought invaders along the Byzantine borders.

687

Portfolio Activity Have students research women rulers in the past 50 years. Direct them to present their findings in short, illustrated biographies. Post these on the bulletin board. Then discuss whether students think they can expect to see a woman president of the United States in their lifetime.

Multiple Learning Styles

Verbal/Linguistic Students with problems decoding unfamiliar words often skip over them. Many times, however, they are successful in comprehending based on the context of the sentences. Ask students to scan "A Woman on the Throne" for words with which they are unfamiliar. Then ask them to write these words in their notebooks and to guess their meanings based on context. Have students check their answers in a dictionary, making any necessary corrections.

ANSWERS TO INTERPRETING PRIMARY SOURCES

1. because he feared that she might leave the palace and withdraw to a monastery
2. Answers will vary, but Anna Dalassena ruled the empire while her son fought to restore the empire to its former glory. She passed laws, governed, and did everything that any emperor would do.

3. Answers will vary, but most students will conclude that women played an important role in the government of the Byzantine Empire.
Activity News bulletins will vary but should state the qualifications of Anna Dalassena to rule in Alexius's absence.

Block Schedule

Team Teaching These selections may be implemented in a team-teaching context, in conjunction with English/Language Arts.

Chapter Links

Use the primary source selections on pages 688–689 to accompany the study of Unit 8. They provide students with the opportunity to extend their study of the following:

- Chapter 24, Section 2, "The Nobility," pp. 369–373.

- Chapter 24, Section 4, "The Manor," pp. 375–378.

Reinforcing Vocabulary

Review the **Reader's Dictionary** with students to be sure they understand any unfamiliar terms. Ask students how peasants helped nobles keep their *coffers* filled. (*by tilling the land and providing services that nobles might otherwise have had to buy with money from their treasuries*)

Background Information

Consonance Review with students what *vowels* and *consonants* are. Point out that *consonance* is the repetition of consonant sounds in a line of poetry or a song. Have students find the consonance in the poem on page 689. (For example: "I have no penny," said Piers, "to buy pullets, . . .")

UNIT 8

THE MEDIEVAL MANOR

During medieval times, nobody had an easy life. However, nobles and knights enjoyed more benefits than the peasants who worked the land. In exchange for protection, peasants kept a lord's castle well supplied with food, while they themselves lived on little or went hungry.

■ Reader's Dictionary

alms gifts for the poor
coffers treasury
whence from which
sup eat dinner
pullets young chickens
curds solid substance formed when milk sours; used to make cheese
hovels small, dirty, poorly built houses
charged made responsible for
spare save
meal powder made from grain
porridge hot cereal

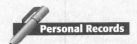
A Noble Household

Nobles often threw open their castles to travelers, who sought safety and a place to rest. In this passage, a French traveler describes his stay with a count, a high-ranking noble with close ties to the king.

I shall now tell you several particulars respecting the count and his household. . . . He had, every day, distributed, as alms at his gate, . . . small coin, to all comers. He was liberal and courteous in his gifts, and well knew how to take and how to give back. He loved dogs above all other animals; and during summer and winter amused himself much with hunting. . . . He chose twelve of his most able subjects to receive and administer his finances. . . . He had certain coffers in his apartment, whence he took money to give to different knights, squires, or gentlemen, . . . for none ever left him without a gift. . . . When he quitted his chamber at midnight for supper, twelve servants bore each a lighted torch before him. The hall was full of knights and squires, and there were plenty of tables laid out for any who chose to sup. No one spoke to him at table unless he first began the conversation. He ate heartily . . . [and] had great pleasure in hearing minstrels. . . . In short, . . . though I had before been in several courts, I never was at one which pleased me more. . . .

TEAM TEACHING STRATEGIES

Science Work with a science teacher to explain how each of these ideas or inventions helped increase agricultural production during the Middle Ages: the three-field system, heavy iron plows (mounted on wheels), and padded horse collars. Point out to students that each of these developments helped ensure a manor's self-sufficiency. Assign students to create before-and-after posters showing the changes that these inventions brought to agriculture. A possible source of information is *Cathedral, Forge, and Waterwheel: Technology and Invention in the Middle Ages*, by Frances and Joseph Gies, HarperCollins Publishers, 1994.

Songs and Poems

A Peasant's Life

The following selection comes from *The Vision of Piers Plowman*, written by English poet William Langland. The lines describe what it was like to be a medieval serf.

"I have no penny," said Piers, "to buy pullets,
No geese nor pigs, but two green cheeses,
A few curds of cream, a cake of oatmeal,
Two loaves of beans and bran, baked for my
     children;
And, by my soul, I swear I have no salt bacon,
But I have parsley and pot herbs and a plenty
     of cabbages,
And a cow and a calf, and a cart mare. . . .

The needy are our neighbors, if we note rightly;
As prisoners in cells, or poor folks in hovels,
Charged with children and overcharged by
     landlords.
What they spare in spinning they spend on
     rental,
On milk, or on meal to make porridge
To still the sobbing of the children at meal
     time."

▲ A peasant harvesting crops

Interpreting Primary Sources

1. What did the French traveler admire about the count?
2. Why do you think the count treated his knights and squires so well?
3. What hardships did serfs such as Piers Plowman face? Why do you think serfs were willing to bear such hardships?

ACTIVITY

Writing a Poem   Imagine you are a medieval poet. Write a poem about life on a medieval manor from the point of view of a noble, knight, or squire.

689

Portfolio Activity   Assign students to research pictures of the lettering used in illuminated manuscripts, especially capital letters. Then have them use this style to write their own names. Encourage students to include a picture inside at least one of the capital letters. (Refer them to the style in the artifact on this page.)

Multiple Learning Styles

Verbal/Linguistic   Auditory attention problems are often characterized by high levels of distractibility. Students may be surprised at the noise level in even quiet settings and how this noise can affect reading comprehension. Demonstrate this by having students read silently the selections on pages 688–689. While reading, direct students to jot down every noise they hear. Ask students to compare their lists. Which noises were most distracting? Ask: What does this show about trying to read with a television or radio on?

ANSWERS TO INTERPRETING PRIMARY SOURCES

1. He admired his generosity, his love of dogs and hunting, his selection of able subjects to collect and manage his finances, his pleasure in entertaining others, and so on.
2. Answers will vary, but under the system of feudal obligations, nobles provided economic support for those who helped defend their territory.
3. Hardships included poverty, hunger, rundown houses, high rents, and the sorrow of their children. They bore it to receive protection from nobles.

Activity Poems will vary, but should demonstrate the contrast in the life of these groups with the life of Piers Ploughman. They should also reflect some of the details from "A Noble Household" on page 688.

PRIMARY SOURCES
Library

THE FALL OF THE AZTEC EMPIRE

According to Aztec legend, a light-skinned god named Quetzalcoatl sailed across the sea in ancient times. He promised to return in the year One Reed on the Aztec calendar and reclaim his land. When Hernando Cortés and his army arrived in Mexico, the year was One Reed. Emperor Montezuma—spelled Motecuhzoma by some scholars—believed Cortés to be the returning god Quetzalcoatl, and so he invited the invaders into the Aztec capital of Tenochtitlán. The decision helped end his empire.

■ Reader's Dictionary

finery fancy clothes and jewelry worn on special occasions
installed placed
plunder stolen goods, usually taken in war
Mexicanos people of Mexico; term used by the translator to refer to the Aztec
shied avoided out of fear

690

Personal Records

Arrival of the Spaniards

Aztec accounts of the Spanish conquest of Mexico is recorded in *The Broken Spears*, edited and translated by Miguel Leon-Portilla. This selection describes the meeting of Motecuhzoma and Cortés. It also shows the role of La Malinche, a woman who came from a people conquered by the Aztec and who served as an interpreter for Cortés.

The Spaniards arrived . . . near the entrance to Tenochtitlán. That was the end of their march, for they had reached their goal.

Motecuhzoma now arrayed himself in his finery, preparing to go out to meet them. . . . Then he hung the gold necklaces around their necks and gave them presents of every sort as gifts of welcome.

When Motecuhzoma had given necklaces to each one, Cortés asked him: "Are you Motecuhzoma? Are you the king? . . ."

And the king said: "Yes, I am Motecuhzoma." Then he stood up to welcome Cortés; he came forward, bowed his head low and addressed him in these words: "Our lord, you are weary. The journey has tired you, but now you have arrived on the earth. You have come to your city, Mexico. You have come here to sit on your throne. . . ."

When the Spaniards were installed in the palace, they asked Motecuhzoma about the city's resources. . . . They questioned him closely and then demanded gold.

Motecuhzoma guided them to it. . . . When they entered the hall of treasures, it was as if they had arrived in Paradise. . . . All of

---

Chapter Links

Use the primary source selections on pages 690–691 to accompany the study of Unit 9. They provide students with the opportunity to extend their study of the following:

• Chapter 30, Section 2, "The Spanish," pp. 471–476.

Note: This selection might also be used to extend information on the Aztec in Chapter 8, Section 5, "Mesoamerica," pp. 138–140. It could also be used to supplement material on New Spain in Chapter 31, Section 2, "Spain," pp. 490–492.

Reinforcing Vocabulary

Review the **Reader's Dictionary** with students to be sure they understand any unfamiliar terms. Ask students which of Motecuhzoma's finery most interested Cortés? *(objects made of gold)*

Background Information

Translations Tell students that the selections on this page were written in Nahuatl, the language spoken by the Aztec. The translator, Miguel Leon-Portilla, is an expert in the Nahuatl language and culture. Instruct students to imagine that such translations were unavailable to historians. Ask: What would be our main source of information on the fall of the Aztec empire? *(Spanish accounts)* What information would be lost? *(Aztec eyewitness accounts and feelings about Spanish conquest)*

TEAM TEACHING STRATEGIES

Art Work with an art teacher to help students design a book cover that might be used for *The Broken Spears*. The cover should include copies of Aztec art or art drawn in the style of Aztec artists. You might use one of these covers for a booklet containing the poems suggested in the Portfolio Activity on page 691.

690

Motecuhzoma's possessions were brought out: fine bracelets, necklaces with large stones, ankle rings with little gold bells, the royal crowns and all the royal finery—everything that belonged to the king. . . . They seized these treasures as if they were their own, as if this plunder were merely a stroke of good luck. And when they had taken all the gold, they heaped up everything in the middle of the patio.

La Malinche called the nobles together. She climbed up to the palace roof and cried: "Mexicanos, come forward! The Spaniards need your help! Bring them food and pure water. They are tired and hungry; they are almost fainting from exhaustion! Why do you not come forward? Are you angry with them?"

The Mexicans . . . shied away . . . as if the hour were midnight on the blackest night of the year. Yet they did not abandon the Spaniards to hunger and thirst. . . . They delivered the supplies to the Spaniards with trembling hands, then turned and hurried away.

▲ An Aztec double-headed serpent charm

Songs and Poems

The Fall of Tenochtitlán

Aztec writers recorded the loss of their empire in a series of poems known as "songs of sorrow." This excerpt from a poem entitled "The Fall of Tenochtitlán" recalls their loss.

How can we save our homes, my people?
The Aztecs are deserting the city:
the city is in flames, and all
is darkness and destruction. . . .
Weep, my people:
know that with these disasters
we have lost the Mexican nation.
The water has turned bitter,
our food is bitter!
These are the acts of the Giver of Life. . . .

Interpreting Primary Sources

1. What gifts did Motecuhzoma give to Cortés?
2. Why do you think Motecuhzoma took Cortés to his personal treasury?
3. What does the poet tell you about the fate of the Aztec capital?
4. What do these two sources reveal about how the Aztec viewed the arrival of the *conquistadores* in what is now Mexico?

ACTIVITY

Writing Letters Write a letter that Cortés might have sent to the king of Spain describing his conquest. The letter should predict what this event means for the future of Spain.

691

Portfolio Activity Assign interested students to learn more about the final days of the Aztec empire, particularly an Aztec noble named Cuauhtemoc. Tell students that Cuauhtemoc, the last Aztec ruler, courageously resisted Cortés and is a hero of the Mexican people today. Have students present their findings in the form of a "song of sorrow," such as the one on this page.

Multiple Learning Styles
Intrapersonal Have students compile their own study guide. As students read the selections in this feature, direct them to write two multiple-choice questions for each reading. Compile the questions into a quiz—omitting repetitions—and distribute it to students as a study guide.

ANSWERS TO INTERPRETING PRIMARY SOURCES

1. Motecuhzoma gave them necklaces and "presents of every sort."
2. Answers will vary, but most students will note that Motecuhzoma thought that Cortés was the returning god Quetzalcoatl.
3. that the people deserted the city; that it was set on fire and destroyed
4. Answers will vary, but students should see that the Aztec came to see the Spanish arrival as a source of sorrow and destruction.

Answers Letters will vary, but Cortés would undoubtedly boast of the Aztec gold he had seized and of the power it would bring to Spain.

PRIMARY SOURCES
Library

UNIT 10

THE IRON HORSE

Invention of the railroad brought a revolution to transportation. The British led the way, with the first steam-powered railroads appearing in the early 1800s. However, like the Industrial Revolution itself, the idea soon spread. In the United States, inventors tried to replace the horse with one of the new steam-powered locomotives. Not surprisingly, the new locomotives won the nickname of "iron horse."

■ Reader's Dictionary

pistons metal cylinders that slide up and down, causing an internal combustion engine to work
laden heavily loaded
facility ease

Printed Publications

Riding the Railroad

In 1830, actress Frances Kemble took a ride on the Liverpool-Manchester Railway, the second passenger line in England. She had the pleasure of riding with George Stephenson, the railroad pioneer who invented the *Rocket* (see page 529). In *Record of a Girlhood*, Kemble describes the trip.

She [the engine] . . . consisted of a boiler, a stove, a small platform, a bench, and . . . a barrel containing enough water to prevent her being thirsty for fifteen miles. . . . She goes upon two wheels which are her feet and are moved by bright steel legs called pistons; these are propelled by steam. . . . This snorting little animal, which I felt rather inclined to pat, was then harnessed to our carriage, and Mr. Stephenson having taken me on the bench of the engine with him, we started at about ten miles an hour. . . . You can't imagine how strange it seemed to be journeying on thus, without any visible cause of progress other than the magical machine, with its flying white breath. . . . I felt as if no fairy tale was ever half so wonderful as what I saw. . . .

When I closed my eyes this sensation of flying was quite delightful and strange beyond description; yet strange as it was, I had a perfect sense of security and not the slightest fear. At one time, to exhibit the power of the engine, having met another steam carriage which was unsupplied with water, Mr. Stephenson caused it to be fastened in front of ours; moreover, a wagon laden with timber was also chained to us, and thus propelling the idle steam engine and dragging the loaded wagon . . . and our

692

Chapter Links

Use the primary source selections on pages 692–693 to accompany the study of Unit 10. They provide students with the opportunity to extend their study of the following:

• Chapter 33, Section 3, "Industrial Revolution," pp. 526–530.

• Chapter 33, Section 4, "Industrial Impact," pp. 530–533.

Reinforcing Vocabulary

Review the **Reader's Dictionary** with students to be sure they understand any unfamiliar terms. Ask students why *pistons* might make a good symbol for the Industrial Revolution. *(because they suggest the energy of the new machines, in this case an internal combustion engine)*

Background Information

The Diary Point out that Fanny Kemble's book was the product of a diary that she kept. Explain that some diaries are written self-consciously with an eye to readers. Some preserve ordinary thoughts in ordinary language. Ask students to discuss the differences between a diary account and a newspaper account of an event.

TEAM TEACHING STRATEGIES

Art Work with an art teacher to develop a multimedia presentation on the early days of railroads. Before beginning, have students review the guidelines in the Technology Skill on page 276. Then encourage them to find posters, songs, poems, eyewitness accounts, or any other memorabilia associated with railroads. When students have completed their assignment, you might arrange for them to show it to other social studies classes in your school.

own carriage full of people behind, this brave little she-dragon of ours flew on. Farther on she met three carts, which being fastened in front of her she pushed on before her without the slightest delay or difficulty; when I add that this pretty little creature can run with equal facility either backwards or forwards, I believe I have given you an account of all her capacities.

 Oral Histories

A Horse Race

In 1829, American inventor Peter Cooper tested his new steam-powered locomotive—the *Tom Thumb*—on some track laid down by the Baltimore and Ohio Railroad. The following year, a horse-drawn railcar challenged the *Tom Thumb* to a race. An observer later recalled the scene in a history of railroads compiled by the Baltimore and Ohio Railroad.

The horse was perhaps a quarter of a mile ahead before the engine started. The blower whistled, the steam blew off in vapory clouds, and the pace increased. Then the engine passed the horse, and a great hurrah hailed the victory. But it was not repeated. The engine began to wheeze and pant. Although the steam again did its best, the horse was too far ahead to be overtaken. But the real victory was with Mr. Cooper.

Interpreting Primary Sources

1. What impressed Frances Kemble about the new steam-powered locomotive?
2. What clues in the reading show that she viewed the engine as an "iron horse"?
3. What was the outcome of the race between the horse-drawn railcar and the *Tom Thumb*?
4. What do you think the observer meant by the remark that the "real victory was with Mr. Cooper"?

ACTIVITY

Writing a Diary Entry Imagine you are one of the passengers aboard the Liverpool-Manchester Railway shown in the picture on this page. Describe your trip in the form of a diary entry. Be sure to indicate whether you are a first-class or a second-class passenger and how you feel about your choice of railcar.

693

Portfolio **Activity** Assign students to brainstorm headlines that a newspaper might have run about the race between the *Tom Thumb* and a horse. Then have students use these headlines to write a short news article about the event. Point out that reporters try to get all the important facts to the reader as quickly as possible. The first paragraph of the story usually answers almost all of the six question words commonly used by reporters: *Who? What? Where? When? Why? How?*

Multiple Learning Styles

Verbal/Linguistic Some students who have difficulty retaining information or focusing their attention may benefit by audio versions of primary source selections. Request some of your more able readers to record the selections on a tape recorder. Then play the tape for the class as a whole. After every few sentences, turn off the tape recorder and say: "Tell me what you just heard." Repeat this process until the entire selection is read.

ANSWERS TO INTERPRETING PRIMARY SOURCES

1. Answers will vary, but most students will point out the railroad's great speed, which made Kemble feel like she was "flying."

2. Clues include Kemble's descriptions of locomotive parts. She compares wheels to "feet" and pistons to "legs." She also describes the locomotive as a "snorting little animal" that she felt like patting.

3. In the end, the horse won.

4. Answers will vary, but the race showed the potential of the locomotive, which had initially outrun the horse.

Activity Diary entries will vary but should reflect the different conditions of travel and perhaps some of the enthusiasm that most railroad riders felt at the time.

PRIMARY SOURCES
Library

Block Schedule

Team Teaching These selections may be implemented in a team-teaching context, in conjunction with English/Language Arts.

Chapter Links

Use the primary source selections on pages 694–695 to accompany the study of Unit 11. They provide students with the opportunity to extend their study of the following:

- Chapter 36, Section 3, "Asia," pp. 584–591.

Note: You might also use this feature as a bridge into the discussion of Indian independence in Chapter 38, "Developing Nations," pp. 634–641.

Reinforcing Vocabulary

Review the **Reader's Dictionary** with students to be sure they understand any unfamiliar terms. How might an opponent of British imperialism have used the postcard on page 695 as evidence of British *despotism*?

Background Information

Persuasion Point out that persuasive writing attempts to sway the reader to think or act in a particular way. Ask students to identify the course of action promoted in this selection. Then ask: Which argument used by the writer do you think is the most persuasive?

UNIT 11

BRITISH INDIA

The British brought many things to India, including a unified government and a railroad system that spanned a subcontinent. They made it possible for Indians to receive a British education and trained Indians as *civil servants*—the name given to people who work for the government. For the most part, however, the British looked down on Indian culture and denied Indians positions of importance. This attitude would be the undoing of British rule in India.

■ Reader's Dictionary

feeble weak
natives people born and raised in a place; in this case, the people of India
excluded left out
sent out graduated
aught all
material physical
convulsion upheaval
despotism cruel use of power

694

Stirrings of Nationalism

An early Indian nationalist named Dadabhai Naoroji admired British self-government. He feared, however, that colonial policies might prevent this system from ever coming to India. In 1880, he described these policies and their effect on India in a strongly worded memo to British officials.

Europeans occupy almost all the higher places in every department of government.... While in India they acquire India's money, experience, and wisdom, and when they go they carry both away with them, leaving India so much poorer.... Thus India is left without, and cannot have, those elders in wisdom and experience who in every country are the natural guides of the rising generations....

Every European is isolated from the people around him.... For any ... guidance or sympathy with the people, he might just as well be living in the moon. The people know not him, and he knows not nor cares for the people. Some honorable exceptions do now and then make an effort to do some good, ... but in the very nature of things, these efforts are always feeble ... and of little permanent effect....

The Europeans are not the natural leaders of the people. They do not belong to the people. They cannot ... sympathize with their joys or griefs.... There may be very few social institutions started by Europeans in which natives, however fit and desirous to join, are not deliberately and insultingly excluded. The Europeans ... make themselves strangers in every way....

TEAM TEACHING STRATEGIES

Art When students have analyzed the memo written by Naoroji, challenge them to convert his message into the form of a political cartoon. Work with the art teacher to present some of the tools commonly used by cartoonists—caricature, symbols, labels, and so on. When students are done, have them exchange cartoons for editorial review. Ask: What is the main issue addressed by this cartoon? What is the artist's opinion of this issue? What techniques has the artist used to get his or her opinion across?

. . . The thousands [of Indians] that are being sent out by the universities every year find themselves in a most [difficult] position. There is no place for them in their motherland. They may beg in the streets or break stones on the roads, for aught the rulers seem to care. . . .

. . . If the present material and moral destruction of India continues, a great convulsion must inevitably arise by which either India will be more and more crushed under the iron heel of despotism and destruction, or may succeed in shattering the destroying hand and power [that holds it down]. Far, far is it from my earnest prayer and hope that such should be the result of the British rule.

 Artifacts Like most visitors to a foreign land, the British sent postcards and bought souvenirs that reminded them of India. The postcard on the left from the 1890s shows a British traveler in India. The photo below shows the Victoria Memorial, built by the British in Calcutta.

Interpreting Primary Sources

1. What things does Naoroji say the British are taking from India?
2. Why does he feel the British are not the "natural leaders" of India?
3. What prediction does he make for the future if Great Britain does not change its policies?
4. What do the postcard and photograph show about the benefits and drawbacks of British rule?

ACTIVITY

Designing a Postcard Design a postcard that an Indian artist might create to capture some aspect of life in British India.

695

Assign students to draft a memo that a British official might have sent back to Naoroji. The memo should address or refute his arguments, pointing out the benefits of British rule. (Award extra credit to those students who do additional research on British colonial policy in India.)

Multiple Learning Styles

Visual/Spatial Some students may need concrete examples to understand abstract concepts such as *nationalism*. Ask students to look up a definition of this word in the dictionary. Then brainstorm some of the symbols that stir a sense of nationalism among people in the United States. *(the flag, the national anthem, etc.)* Assign interested students to research some of the national symbols adopted by India upon its independence. For example, what does the Indian flag look like?

ANSWERS TO INTERPRETING PRIMARY SOURCES

1. India's money, wisdom, and experience
2. because they isolate themselves from the people; because they cannot sympathize or understand the concerns of native-born Indians
3. that there will be a "great convulsion," or uprising, in which Indians will either throw off British rule or be subjected to even greater despotism

4. Sample response: Although the British used their wealth to initiate great building projects, they also kept Indians in a position of servitude.

Activity Postcards will vary but should accurately reflect the benefits and drawbacks of imperialism as it existed in India.

Block Schedule

Team Teaching These selections may be implemented in a team-teaching context, in conjunction with English/Language Arts.

Chapter Links

Use the primary source selections on pages 696–697 to accompany the study of Unit 12. They provide students with the opportunity to extend their study of the following:

• Chapter 39, Section 2, "World Challenges," pp. 652–662.

Note: You might also use this feature to extend information in Chapter 36, Section 2, "Africa," pp. 580–584.

Reinforcing Vocabulary

Review the **Reader's Dictionary** with students to be sure they understand any unfamiliar terms. Ask students what type of political *domination* Nelson Mandela spent his life resisting.

Background

Tone Point out that *tone* is the attitude a writer takes toward his or her subject and audience. Refer students to the song, "One Law for One Nation." What adjectives would students use to describe the tone of this song? *(hopeful, optimistic)*

UNIT 12

FREEDOM AND EQUALITY IN SOUTH AFRICA

On June 11, 1964, a South African judge sentenced Nelson Mandela and seven others to life in prison. The charge was *sabotage*—an active and often secret effort to undermine government. Their real "crime," as the government saw it, was opposition to apartheid, the system that denied black South Africans their rights. Nearly 25 years later—on February 11, 1990—South Africa bowed to world pressure and freed Mandela. Before the century ended, Mandela would realize his lifelong dream—a new South African government based on freedom and equality.

■ Reader's Dictionary

domination authority over others
preamble introductory statement
potential ability for future achievement
sovereign independent, self-governing

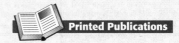
Printed Publications

"I Am Prepared to Die"

The following is a portion of a speech that Nelson Mandela delivered in his own defense before being sentenced to life in prison. It is considered one of the great democratic speeches in world history.

"During my lifetime I have dedicated myself to this struggle of the African people. I have fought against white domination, and I have fought against black domination. I have cherished the ideal of a democratic and free society in which all persons live together in harmony and with equal opportunities. It is an ideal which I hope to live for and to achieve. But if needs be, it is an ideal for which I am prepared to die."

Printed Publications

A New Constitution

In May 1994, South Africa held its first all-race election. The person chosen to build a new government was Nelson Mandela. As president of South Africa, he helped guide the nation in writing and approving a new constitution. Signed into law on December 10, 1996, the document began with a preamble stating the new government's political ideals.

TEAM TEACHING STRATEGIES

Language Arts Invite a language arts teacher to discuss the meaning of the term *democracy* with students—i.e., the free and equal right of every person to participate in government. Then have students come up with a list of reasons why the preamble to the South African constitution should be included in a book entitled, "Democratic Documents in World History." After students have gone over their list, brainstorm other documents that they would include in this book.

We, the people of South Africa,
Recognise the injustices of our past;
Honour those who suffered for justice and freedom in our land;
Respect those who have worked to build and develop our country; and
Believe that South Africa belongs to all who live in it; united in our diversity.
We therefore, through our freely elected representatives, adopt this Constitution as the supreme law of the Republic so as to
Heal the divisions of the past and establish a society based on democratic values, social justice and fundamental human rights;
Lay the foundation for a democratic and open society in which government is based on the will of the people and every citizen is equally protected by the law;
Improve the quality of life of all citizens and free the potential of each person; and
Build a united and democratic South Africa able to take its rightful place as a sovereign state in the family of nations.

Songs and Poems

The following lyrics come from a song entitled "One Law for One Nation." Composed in honor of the new South African constitution, it was originally sung by children.

We are positive about our future
Equality and dignity
Respect and help for one another
Our dreams will become reality

It's our new constitution
We're gonna make it work out right

One law for one nation
Giving us strength and harmony
Our hopes dreams and aspirations
Our people united as one
One law for one nation
One dream for all of us to share

▲ Nelson Mandela and Thabo Mvuyelwa Mbeki

Interpreting Primary Sources

1. What kind of government did Nelson Mandela say he wanted in 1964?
2. What are at least three goals expressed in the preamble to the South African constitution?
3. Why do you think the author of the new constitution song chose to call it "One Law for One Nation"?

ACTIVITY

Writing a Preamble Write a preamble—an introduction to a constitution—for your school or classroom.

697

REFERENCE ATLAS

NATIONAL
GEOGRAPHIC
SOCIETY

ATLAS KEY

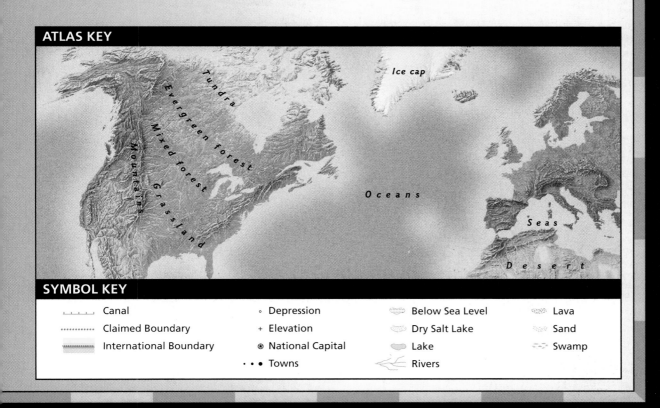

SYMBOL KEY

⌞⌟ Canal	∘ Depression	〰 Below Sea Level	〰 Lava
⋯ Claimed Boundary	+ Elevation	〰 Dry Salt Lake	〰 Sand
▦ International Boundary	⊛ National Capital	〰 Lake	⇢ Swamp
· · • Towns		〰 Rivers	

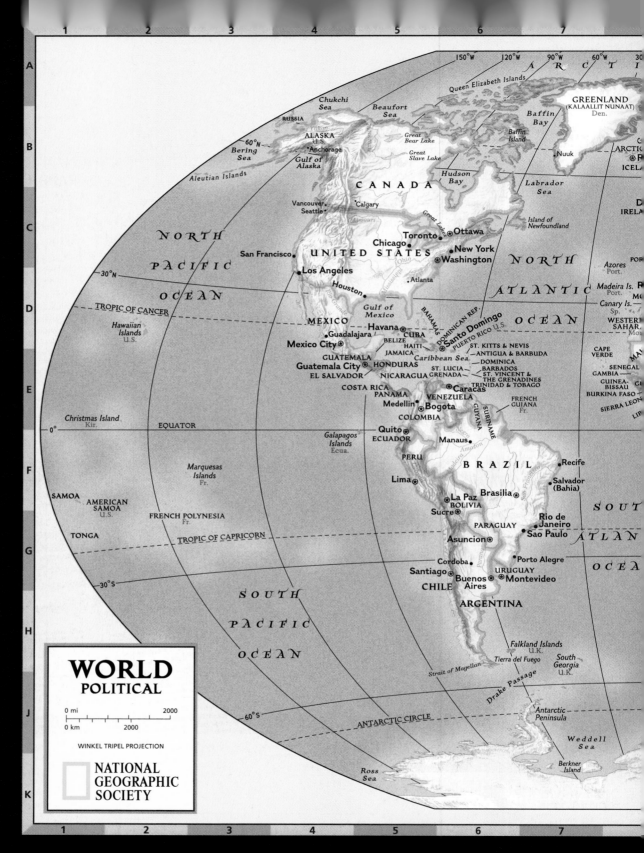

WORLD
POLITICAL

0 mi   2000
0 km   2000

WINKEL TRIPEL PROJECTION

NATIONAL
GEOGRAPHIC
SOCIETY

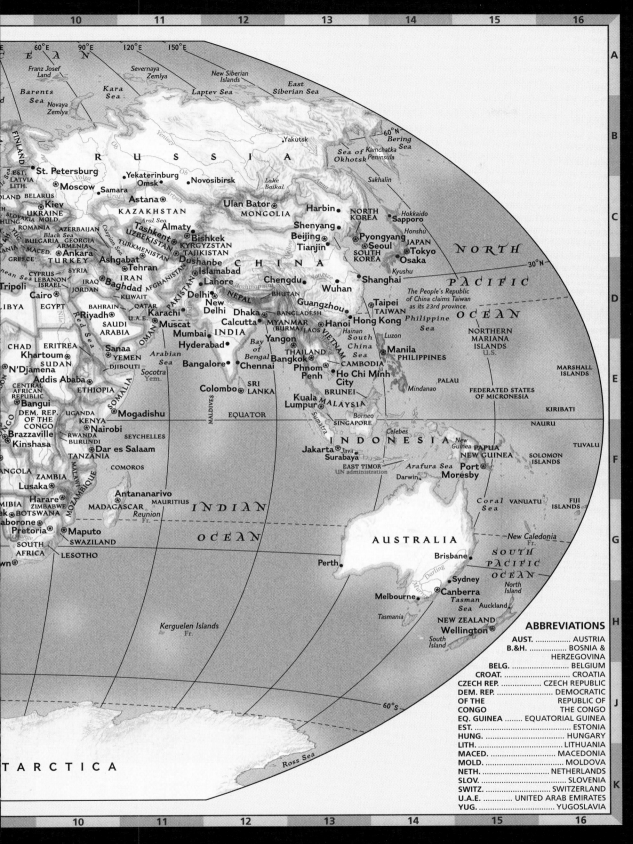

The People's Republic
of China claims Taiwan
as its 23rd province.

ABBREVIATIONS

AUST.	AUSTRIA
B.&H.	BOSNIA & HERZEGOVINA
BELG.	BELGIUM
CROAT.	CROATIA
CZECH REP.	CZECH REPUBLIC
DEM. REP. OF THE CONGO	DEMOCRATIC REPUBLIC OF THE CONGO
EQ. GUINEA	EQUATORIAL GUINEA
EST.	ESTONIA
HUNG.	HUNGARY
LITH.	LITHUANIA
MACED.	MACEDONIA
MOLD.	MOLDOVA
NETH.	NETHERLANDS
SLOV.	SLOVENIA
SWITZ.	SWITZERLAND
U.A.E.	UNITED ARAB EMIRATES
YUG.	YUGOSLAVIA

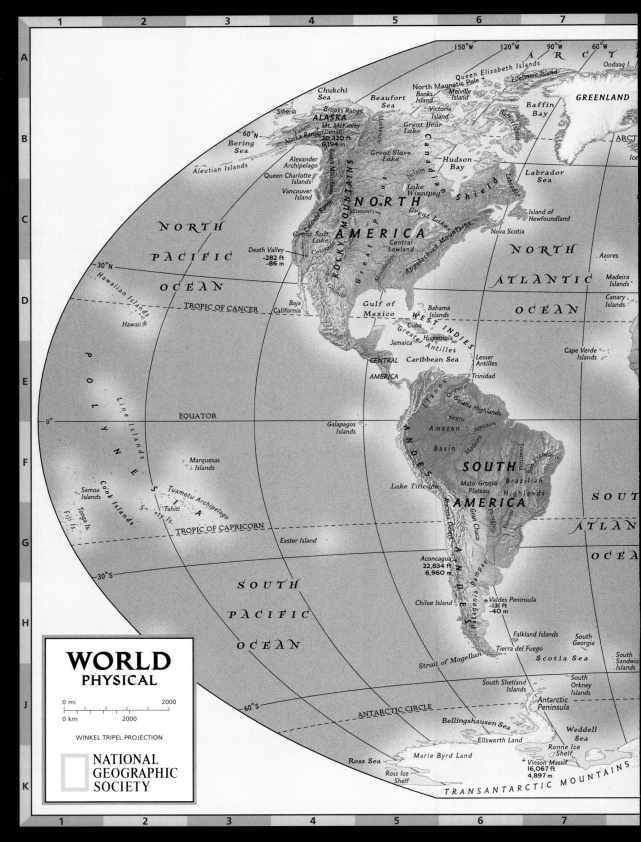

WORLD
PHYSICAL

0 mi   2000
0 km   2000

WINKEL TRIPEL PROJECTION

NATIONAL
GEOGRAPHIC
SOCIETY

A

B

C

D

E

F

G

H

J

K

60°E   90°E   120°E   150°E

Barents Sea

Novaya Zemlya

Kara Sea

Laptev Sea

East Siberian Sea

60°N

Bering Sea

Kamchatka Peninsula

Aleutian Is.

Yenisey

S I B E R I A

Central Siberian Plateau

Lena

Ural Mountains

West Siberian Plain

Irtysh

Ob

Angara

Lena

Amur

Sea of Okhotsk

Kuril Islands

Hokkaido

Sea of Japan

Japan

Honshu

NORTH

Eastern European Plain

E U R O P E

Volga

A S I A

The Steppes

Elbrus 18,510 ft 5,642 m

Aral Sea

Ob

Lake Baikal

Altay Mountains

G O B I

Tian Shan

Yellow

North China Plain

Korea

Yellow Sea

East China Sea

Nampo Shoto

Ryukyu Islands

30°N

PACIFIC

Danube

Black Sea

Caucasus Mts.

Caspian Sea

Zagros Mountains

Taklimakan Desert

Kunlun Shan

Plateau of Tibet

Yangtze

OCEAN

Sicily

Cyprus

nean Sea

Dead Sea -1,349 ft -411 m

ARABIAN PENINSULA

H I M A L A Y A

Brahmaputra

Mt. Everest 29,035 ft 8,850 m

Ganges

Salween

Taiwan

Philippine Sea

A R A

Red Sea

Libyan Desert

I C A

H E L

Gulf of Aden

Nile

Blue Nile

White Nile

Ethiopian Highlands

Somali Peninsula

INDIA

Arabian Sea

Deccan Plateau

Bay of Bengal

Andaman Islands

Andaman Sea

Hainan

Indochina Peninsula

Mekong

South China Sea

Luzon

Philippine Islands

Mariana Islands

M I C R O N E S I A

Sri Lanka

Nicobar Is.

Maldive Islands

EQUATOR

Malay Peninsula

Marshall Islands

Gilbert Islands

Congo

Lake Victoria

Kilimanjaro 19,340 ft 5,895 m

Seychelles

Sumatra

Borneo

Indonesia

Moluccas

Celebes

New Guinea

Bismarck Archipelago

M E L A N E S I A

Congo Basin

Lake Tanganyika

Greater Sunda Islands

Java

Arafura Sea

Solomon Islands

Madagascar

Zambezi

Mascarene Islands

INDIAN

Coral Sea

Vanuatu

Fiji Islands

Kalahari Desert

Drakensberg

OCEAN

Great Sandy Desert

AUSTRALIA

Lake Eyre -52 ft, -16 m

Great Victoria Desert

Great Dividing Range

New Caledonia

SOUTH

PACIFIC

Kerguelen Islands

Darling

Murray

Mt. Kosciuszko 7,310 ft 2,228 m

Tasman Sea

North Island

NEW ZEALAND

OCEAN

Tasmania

South Island

Auckland Islands

60°S

South Magnetic + Pole

aud Land

Transantarctic Mountains

Victoria Land

Ross Sea

A N T A R C T I C A

Ross Ice Shelf

ASIA

ARCTIC OCEAN

N

Chukchi Sea

Bering Sea

Bering Strait

Point Barrow

North Magnetic Pole

Queen Elizabeth Islands

Ellesmere Island

GREENLAND (KALAALLIT NUNAAT) Den.

Greenland Sea

EUROPE

ARCTIC CIRCLE

Beaufort Sea

Banks Island

Parry Islands

ALASKA U.S.

Gulf of Alaska

YUKON TERRITORY

Victoria Island

Boothia Peninsula

Baffin Bay

Qeqertarsuaq

Baffin Island

Davis Strait

Nuuk (Godthab)

NORTHWEST TERRITORIES

Great Bear Lake

Southampton Island

Labrador Sea

Great Slave Lake

CANADA

Hudson Bay

NEWFOUNDLAND

BRITISH COLUMBIA

Vancouver Island

PACIFIC OCEAN

ALBERTA

SASKATCHEWAN

MANITOBA

Lake Winnipeg

Churchill

ONTARIO

QUEBEC

LABRADOR

Gulf of St. Lawrence

P.E.I.

St.-Pierre & Miquelon Fr.

N.B.

NOVA SCOTIA

WASHINGTON

MONTANA

NORTH DAKOTA

MINN.

Lake Superior

Lake Huron

Ottawa

ME.

OREGON

IDAHO

WYOMING

SOUTH DAKOTA

WIS.

MICHIGAN

Lake Michigan

L. Ontario

L. Erie

N.H.

VT.

MASS.

NEW YORK

R.I.

CONN.

ATLANTIC OCEAN

Great Salt Lake

NEVADA

NEBRASKA

IOWA

ILL.

IND.

OHIO

PA.

N.J.

DEL.

MD.

W.VA.

Washington, D.C.

UTAH

COLORADO

KANSAS

MISSOURI

KENTUCKY

VA.

UNITED STATES

CALIFORNIA

ARIZONA

NEW MEXICO

OKLAHOMA

Arkansas

Mississippi

TENNESSEE

ARK.

MISS.

ALA.

GEORGIA

N.C.

S.C.

Bermuda Islands U.K.

Guadalupe I. Mex.

TROPIC OF CANCER

TEXAS

Rio Grande

LA.

FLORIDA

Gulf of Mexico

MEXICO

Havana

CUBA

BAHAMAS

Nassau

ANTIGUA AND BARBUDA

ST. KITTS AND NEVIS

BARBADOS

DOMINICAN REPUBLIC

Santo Domingo

PUERTO RICO U.S.

DOMINICA

Mexico City

Cayman Is. U.K.

HAITI

Port-au-Prince

ST. LUCIA

ST. VINCENT AND THE GRENADINES

GRENADA

BELIZE

Belmopan

JAMAICA

Kingston

Caribbean Sea

TRINIDAD AND TOBAGO

GUATEMALA

Guatemala City

HONDURAS

Tegucigalpa

San Salvador

NICARAGUA

Managua

EL SALVADOR

COSTA RICA

San Jose

PANAMA

Panama Canal

Panama City

SOUTH AMERICA

NORTH AMERICA POLITICAL

0 mi 1000

0 km 1000

AZIMUTHAL EQUIDISTANT PROJECTION

NATIONAL GEOGRAPHIC SOCIETY

Cocos I. C.R.

EQUATOR

10 11 12 13 14 15 16

120°W 110°W 100°W 90°W 80°W 70°W 60°W 50°W 40°W 30°W

70°N

GREENLAND
(KALAALLIT NUNAAT)
Den.

60°N

20°W

30°W

UNITED
STATES
POLITICAL

0 mi   600

0 km   600

OBLIQUE AZIMUTHAL EQUIDISTANT PROJECTION

NATIONAL
GEOGRAPHIC
SOCIETY

30°W

50°N

40°W

ARCTIC CIRCLE

C A N A D A

N

40°N

50°W

MAINE

Montpelier   Augusta

NEW   VT   Portland

NORTH
DAKOTA   MINNESOTA

Lake Superior

MICHIGAN

Lake Huron

Bismarck

Minneapolis   St. Paul

WISCONSIN

Pierre

SOUTH
DAKOTA

Milwaukee   Lansing

Madison

Detroit

L. Erie   Cleveland   PA.

Toledo

YORK   Concord, N.H.

Lake   Albany   Boston, MASS.
Ontario

Buffalo   Providence, R.I.

Hartford, CONN.

New York

Trenton, N.J.

Casper

Sioux City   IOWA   Chicago

Des Moines

NEBRASKA

Lincoln   Omaha

Denver

Kansas City

Topeka   MISSOURI

KANSAS   Jefferson City

ILLINOIS   IND.

Indianapolis

Springfield   Cincinnati

St. Louis   Louisville

KENTUCKY

Columbus   Pittsburgh   Harrisburg

OHIO   Baltimore

Dayton   W. VA.   Annapolis, MD.

Frankfort   Washington, D.C.

Charleston   Richmond

Philadelphia

Dover, DEL.

Virginia Beach

VIRGINIA

50°N

ATLANTIC OCEAN

40°N

ORADO

Oklahoma City

buquerque

OKLAHOMA

Tulsa

ARKANSAS   Memphis

Little Rock

Nashville

TENNESSEE

NORTH CAROLINA

Charlotte

SOUTH
CAROLINA   Columbia

Raleigh

Bermuda Is.
U.K.

30°N

Fort
Worth   Dallas

San Antonio

TEXAS

Austin

MISS.

Jackson

Atlanta

Birmingham

ALABAMA   GEORGIA

Montgomery

LOUISIANA

Baton Rouge

Houston

New Orleans

Tallahassee

Charleston

Savannah

Jacksonville

FLORIDA

Tampa

Rio Grande

Paso

San Antonio

Gulf of
Mexico

Straits of Florida

Miami

BAHAMAS

20°N

ANTIGUA
& BARBUDA

ST. KITTS
& NEVIS

CUBA

60°W

San Juan

DOMINICAN
REPUBLIC   PUERTO
RICO
U.S.

Caribbean

Sea   80°W   JAMAICA   70°W

HAITI

DOMINICA

O

100°W   90°W

10 11 12 13 14 15 16

CANADA
PHYSICAL/POLITICAL

0 mi   400
0 km   400

AZIMUTHAL EQUIDISTANT PROJECTION

NATIONAL
GEOGRAPHIC
SOCIETY

ICELAND

GREENLAND
(KALAALIT NUNAAT)
Den.

Baffin
Bay

Baffin Island

Davis Strait

Melville
Peninsula

Foxe
Basin

Southampton
Island

Iqaluit

Hudson Strait

Labrador
Sea

Ungava
Bay

udson

Bay

Belcher
Islands

Cartwright

Schefferville

Happy Valley-
Goose Bay

Smallwood
Reservoir

Churchill Falls

Island of
Newfoundland

St. John's
Avalon
Peninsula

James Bay

QUEBEC

SHIELD

Manicouagan
Reservoir
Sept-Iles

Anticosti I.

St.-Pierre & Miquelon
Fr.

TARIO

Lake
Nipigon

hunder
ay Lake
Superior

Gaspe
Pen.

Gulf of
St. Lawrence

PRINCE
EDWARD
ISLAND

Cape Breton I.

ATLANTIC

Chicoutimi

Rouyn-Noranda

Quebec

Fredericton

NEW
BRUNSWICK

Charlottetown

NOVA
SCOTIA

Sudbury

Lake
Huron

Montreal

Ottawa

St. Lawrence

Saint John

Bay of Fundy

Halifax

OCEAN

Lake Michigan

Toronto

L. Ontario

Niagara Falls

London

L. Erie

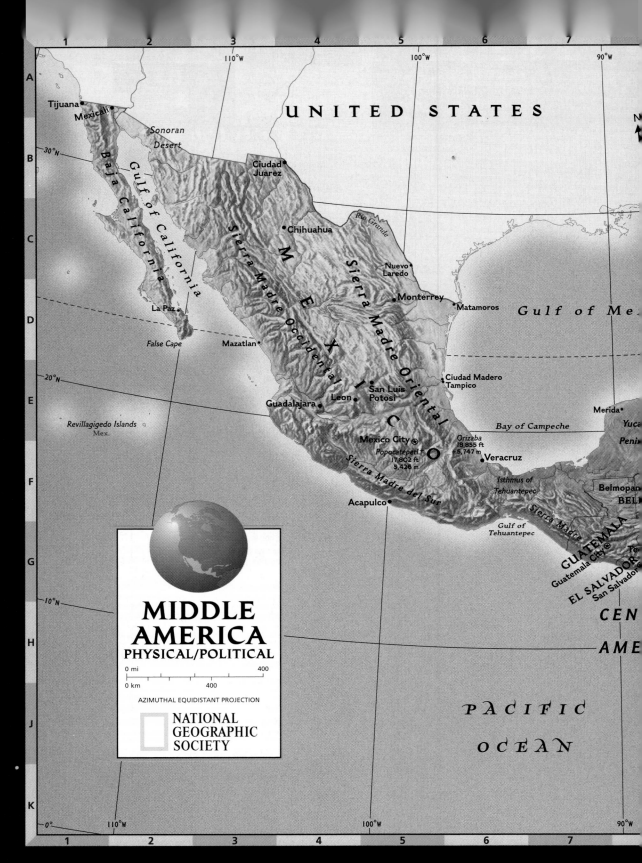

MIDDLE AMERICA

PHYSICAL/POLITICAL

0 mi   400

0 km   400

AZIMUTHAL EQUIDISTANT PROJECTION

NATIONAL GEOGRAPHIC SOCIETY

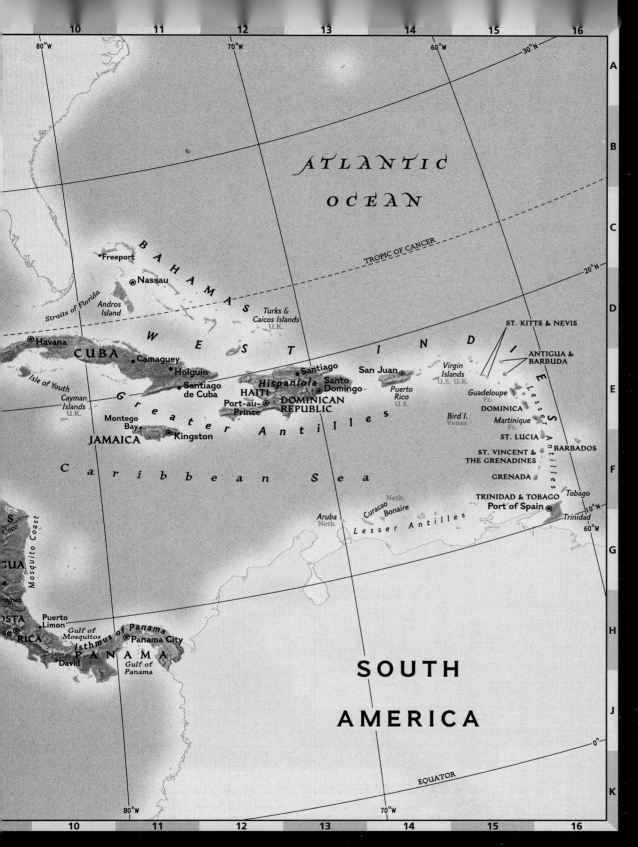

ATLANTIC
OCEAN

TROPIC OF CANCER

BAHAMAS

Freeport

Nassau

Andros
Island

Straits of Florida

Turks &
Caicos Islands
U.K.

ST. KITTS & NEVIS

WEST

INDIES

ANTIGUA &
BARBUDA

Havana

CUBA

Camaguey

Holguin

Santiago

San Juan

Virgin
Islands
U.S. U.K.

Santiago
de Cuba

Hispaniola

Santo
Domingo

Puerto
Rico
U.S.

Guadeloupe
Fr.

DOMINICA

HAITI

Port-au-
Prince

DOMINICAN
REPUBLIC

Isle of Youth

Cayman
Islands
U.K.

Greater

Bird I.
Venez.

Martinique
Fr.

ST. LUCIA

BARBADOS

Montego
Bay

Kingston

Antilles

ST. VINCENT &
THE GRENADINES

JAMAICA

Caribbean

Sea

GRENADA

Neth.

Curacao
Bonaire

TRINIDAD & TOBAGO
Port of Spain

Tobago

Aruba
Neth.

Lesser Antilles

Trinidad

Coco

Mosquito Coast

GUA
a
ogua

STA

RICA

Puerto
Limon

Gulf of
Mosquitos

Isthmus of Panama

Panama City

PANAMA

David

Gulf of
Panama

SOUTH

AMERICA

EQUATOR

EUROPE
POLITICAL

0 mi   400
0 km   400

AZIMUTHAL EQUIDISTANT PROJECTION

NATIONAL
GEOGRAPHIC
SOCIETY

ARCTIC CIRCLE

Norwegian Sea

MERIDIAN OF GREENWICH (LONDON)

N

• Akureyri
⊛ Reykjavik
ICELAND

Faroe Islands
Den.   • Torshavn

Shetland
Islands
Lerwick •

Rockall
U.K.

Isle of Lewis

Orkney Islands

Inverness •

UNITED   • Aberdeen
SCOTLAND
Glasgow •   ⊛ Edinburgh

NORTHERN
IRELAND   • Belfast

IRELAND   Irish
Dublin ⊛   Sea   • Liverpool
• Cork   • Manchester

KINGDOM   • Birmingham

Celtic   WALES   ENGLAND
Sea   Cardiff ⊛
• London
Land's End •   Southampton •
English Channel

Brest •

• Rennes

Nantes •

Bay of
Biscay   La Rochelle •
Bordeaux •

A Coruña •
• Vigo
Porto •   Donostia-
Bilbao •   San Sebastián

Coimbra •   Valladolid •   Pyrenees
ANDORRA
Madrid ⊛   • Zaragoza
Lisbon ⊛
SPAIN   • Barcelona
Cape
St. Vincent • Cordoba   Valencia •
Cadiz • • Seville   • Murcia   Palma •
GIBRALTAR • Malaga   • Cartagena   Balearic
U.K.   Strait of Gibraltar   Islands
Sp.

ATLANTIC
OCEAN

AFRICA

Mediterra

Trondheim •

Alesund •

Bergen •

Stavanger •

N
O
R
W

Oslo ⊛

Skagerrak

DENMARK   • Arhus
Copenhagen ⊛   • Malmo

• Kiel
• Hamburg

The   NETH.
Hague • ⊛ Amsterdam
Berlin ⊛

Brussels ⊛   GERMANY
BELGIUM   • Bonn   Wrocla
LUX.   • Frankfurt
Paris •   CZECH
Strasbourg •   Munich •   Vienna •
Zurich •   LIECH.
Bern ⊛   SWITZERLAND   AUSTRIA
Geneva •   A L P S
Lyon •   SLOVENI
• Milan   Ljubljana ⊛
• Turin   • Venice
Toulouse •   MONACO   • Genoa   SAN
Marseille • Nice   MARINO
Corsica   ITALY
Fr.
VATICAN ⊛ Rome
CITY
Sardinia
It.   • Naples

Cagliari •   Tyrrhenian
Sea
Palermo •
Sicily   • Mess
• Catani
Valletta •
MALTA

Goteb

Sto

N

Sto

Su

30°W
60°N
40°W
20°W
10°W   70°N
0°
10°E

30°W
50°N

20°W
40°N

10°W
0°
10°E
30°N

Prag
Bratis

CR
HE
Sa

Adriatic

A commonly accepted division between Asia and Europe—here marked by a gray line—is formed by the Ural Mountains, Ural River, Caspian Sea, Caucasus Mountains, and the Black Sea with its outlets, the Bosporus and the Dardanelles.

Europe–Asia boundary

A commonly accepted division between Asia and Europe—here marked by a gray line—is formed by the Ural Mountains, Ural River, Caspian Sea, Caucasus Mountains, and the Black Sea with its outlets, the Bosporus and the Dardanelles.

ASIA
POLITICAL

0 mi   1000
0 km   1000

TWO-POINT EQUIDISTANT PROJECTION

NATIONAL
GEOGRAPHIC
SOCIETY

NORTH AMERICA
Bering Strait

Chukchi
Sea

Wrangel I.

East
Siberian
Sea

New Siberian
Islands

Laptev
Sea

Cherskiy Range

Verkhoyansk Range

Magadan

Yakutsk

Lake
Baikal

Ulan Bator

MONGOLIA

GOBI

MTS.

Lanzhou

Xian

Chengdu

Guiyang

Kunming

CHINA

Boundary
claimed
by China

Gulf of
Anadyr

Anadyr

Bering

Sea

Commander Is.

Kamchatka
Peninsula

Sea of
Okhotsk

Sakhalin

Kolyma Range

MANCHURIA

Heilong

Changchun

Shenyang

Beijing

Shijiazhuang

Qingdao

Xuzhou

Nanjing

Nanchang

Fuzhou

Changsha

Guangzhou

Hong Kong

Macau

Hainan

Kuril Islands

Hokkaido

Sapporo

Sea of
Japan

Vladivostok

NORTH
KOREA

Pyongyang

Seoul

SOUTH
KOREA

Yellow

Sea

East
Shanghai
China

Sea

Taipei

TAIWAN

JAPAN

Honshu

Kyoto

Tokyo

Osaka

Hiroshima

Kyushu

Ryukyu Islands

Okinawa

PACIFIC OCEAN

Marcus I.
Jap.

TROPIC
OF CANCER

Bonin Is.
Jap.

Volcano Is.
Jap.

Parece Vela
Jap.

The People's Republic of China claims
Taiwan as its 23rd province.

Hanoi

Haiphong

South

China

Da Nang

THAILAND

Bangkok

CAMBODIA

Phnom Penh

Ho Chi Minh City

Bandar Seri
Begawan
BRUNEI

SABAH

SARAWAK

MALAYSIA

Borneo

MALAY

Luzon

Quezon City

Manila

Samar

PHILIPPINES

Leyte

Philippine

Sea

Mindoro

Panay

Negros

Palawan

Mindanao

Halmahera

Morotai

Biak

Jayapura

New Guinea

Kepi

Merauke

Dolak

EQUATOR

Buru

Ceram

Aru
Is.

Sea

Tanimbar
Is.

Following East Timor's vote for independence
from Indonesia, the United Nations,
in October 1999, established a UN transitional
administration to help East Timor's
870,000 people toward independence.

Dili

EAST TIMOR

Timor

UN admin.

AUSTRALIA

Kupang

Timor Sea

MYANMAR
(BURMA)

LAOS

Vientiane

VIETNAM

nan
nds

Gulf of Thailand

Kuala Lumpur

Medan

SINGAPORE

Sumatra

Jambi

Mentawai
Islands

INDONESIA

Celebes

GREATER
SUNDA ISLANDS

Java Sea

Jakarta

Java

Moluccas

AFRICA
POLITICAL

0 mi — 1000
0 km — 1000

AZIMUTHAL EQUIDISTANT PROJECTION

NATIONAL GEOGRAPHIC SOCIETY

ARCTIC OCEAN
PHYSICAL

0 mi — 800
0 km — 800

AZIMUTHAL EQUIDISTANT PROJECTION

NATIONAL
GEOGRAPHIC
SOCIETY

RUSSIA

GERMANY
LUX.
BELGIUM
FRANCE
NETH.
DENMARK
UNITED
KINGDOM
IRELAND

FINLAND
SWEDEN
NORWAY

Ob
Yenisey
Gulf
of Ob
White Sea
North
Sea
Barents
Sea
Kara Sea
Taymyr
Peninsula
Novaya Zemlya
Laptev Sea
Lena
North
Land
Franz
Josef
Land
Svalbard
Norwegian Sea
ARCTIC CIRCLE
50°N
60°N
70°E
60°E
30°E
0°
30°E
90°E
120°E
Greenland Sea
ICELAND
ATLANTIC OCEAN
New
Siberian
Islands
150°E
Oodaaq
Island
Lincoln
Sea
Denmark
Strait
30°W
ARCTIC
OCEAN
North Pole ★
GREENLAND
Sea of
Okhotsk
East Siberian Sea
180°
Queen
Ellesmere
Island
Hayes
Peninsula
60°W
Cape
Farewell
KAMCHATKA
PENINSULA
Wrangel Island
150°W
120°W
Elizabeth
90°W
Baffin
Bay
Davis Strait
Chukchi Sea
Devon I.
Chukchi
Peninsula
Melville
Island
Islands
Somerset I.
Baffin Island
Bering
Strait
Point Barrow
Prince of
Wales I.
Boothia
Peninsula
Melville
Peninsula
Foxe
Basin
Bering
Sea
St. Lawrence
Island
North Slope
Brooks Range
Beaufort
Sea
Banks
Island
Victoria
Island
Hudson Strait
Seward
Peninsula
Southampton
Island
Nunivak Island
Yukon
ALASKA
Mackenzie
CANADA
Hudson
Bay
Aleutian Islands
PACIFIC
OCEAN
Bristol
Bay
Great
Bear Lake

ANTARCTICA
PHYSICAL

0 mi — 600
0 km — 600

AZIMUTHAL EQUIDISTANT PROJECTION

NATIONAL
GEOGRAPHIC
SOCIETY

SOUTH
ATLANTIC
OCEAN
60°W
60°S
South Orkney Is.
45°W
30°W
15°W
0°
15°E
30°E
45°E
60°E
Fimbul
Ice Shelf
ANTARCTIC CIRCLE
Ruser–Larsen
Ice Shelf
QUEEN MAUD LAND
ENDERBY
LAND
75°E
South
Shetland
Islands
ANTARCTIC
PENINSULA
70°S
Weddell
Sea
COATS LAND
INDIAN
OCEAN
75°W
GRAHAM LAND
Larsen
Ice Shelf
Mt. Jackson
13,747 ft
4,190 m
Filchner
Ice Shelf
Valkyrie
Dome
PALMER LAND
Berkner
Island
Amery Ice Shelf
Alexander I.
Ronne
Ice
Shelf
AMERICAN
HIGHLAND
West
Ice Shelf
SOUTH
PACIFIC
OCEAN
90°W
Bellingshausen
Sea
ELLSWORTH LAND
Vinson Massif
16,067 ft
4,897 m
Ellsworth Mts.
TRANSANTARCTIC
ANTARCTICA
EAST
ANTARCTICA
90°E
WEST
Polar Plateau
South Pole ★
Bentley Subglacial Trench
−8,327 ft
−2,538 m
105°W
ANTARCTICA
MARIE BYRD LAND
MOUNTAINS
Dome
Circe
Shackleton
Ice
Shelf
WILKES LAND
Ross
Ice
Shelf
Roosevelt I.
120°W
INDIAN
OCEAN
105°E
VICTORIA LAND
Ross I.
Mt. Erebus
12,448 ft
3,794 m
135°W
Ross
Sea
Talos
Dome
120°E
150°W
165°W
180°
165°E
150°E
135°E

PACIFIC RIM
PHYSICAL

0 mi ——— 1500
0 km ——— 1500

MILLER CYLINDRICAL PROJECTION

NATIONAL
GEOGRAPHIC
SOCIETY

Glossary

Pronunciations are indicated in parentheses.

A

abbot (ab′ uht) Monastery head. (p. 255)

abdicate (ab′ duh-kāt) Give up the throne. (p. 565)

absolute location (ab sō lūt lō kā shun) Exact location of a place on the Earth's surface. (p. 5)

acropolis (uh krop′ uh lis) Fortified hill in ancient Greek cities. (p. 163)

act of homage (akt of om′ ij) Ceremony in which a vassal promises loyalty to a lord. (p. 368)

ages (ā′ juhs) Time periods. (p. 27)

aggression (uh greh′ shuhn) Warlike acts. (p. 645)

agora (ag′ uh ruh) Ancient Greek marketplace. (p. 163)

airlift (ār′ lift) System of carrying supplies into an isolated area by airplane. (p. 626)

alchemists (al′kuh mists) Scientists who try to turn metals into gold and silver. (p. 343)

alliances (uh lī′ uhn siz) Agreements between people or countries. (p. 195)

amendments (uh mend′ muhntz) Law changes. (p. 513)

ancestors (an′ ses terz) Family members from past generations. (p. 89)

annexation (an ek sā shuhn) Incorporating an area into an existing state. (p. 549)

anointed (uh noin′ tuhd) Blessed with holy oil. (p. 279)

anthropologists (an thruh pol′ uh jists) People who study human beings. (p. 24)

apartheid (uh pahr′ tāt) Separation of the races. (p. 661)

apostles (uh pos′ uhls) Men chosen by Jesus to teach his beliefs to others. (p. 253)

appeasement (uh pēz′ muhnt) Giving in to demands. (p. 615)

apprentice (uh pren′ tis) Person who is learning a craft or trade. (p. 406)

archaelogy (ar kē ol′ uh jē) Study of remains of past human cultures. (p. 25)

archaeologists (ar kē ol′ uh jists) People who study ruins and artifacts. (p. 24)

archbishops (arch′ bish uhps) Bishops at the head of churches in large cities. (p. 253)

aristocrats (uh rist′ ō kratz) Members of the upper class. (p. 164)

armada (ar mah′ duh) Fleet of warships. (p. 459)

armaments (ar′ muh muhnts) Military supplies. (p. 605)

armistice (ar′ muh stis) Agreement to stop fighting. (p. 605)

artifacts (ar′ tuh fakts) Products of human skill. (p. 25)

artillery (ar til′ uhr ē) Mounted guns. (p. 604)

artisans (art′ uh zuhnz) Skilled workers. (p. 57)

assembly line (uh sem′ blē līn) Work system in which each worker adds one part to a product until it is assembled. (p. 528)

astrolabe (as′ truh lāb) Navigational instrument used to determine latitude. (p. 467)

astronomers (uh stron′ uh muhrs) People who study the heavenly bodies. (p. 122)

authoritarian rule (aw thōr uh tār′ ē uhn rūl′) Government in which one ruler or political party holds power. (p. 661)

automation (aw tuh mā′ shuhn) Process in which machines replace workers. (p. 527)

autonomous (aw tah′ nuh muhs) Self-governing. (p. 655)

B

bailiff (bā′ lif) Medieval official who saw that peasants did their work. (p. 376)

balance of power (bal′ uhnts of pau′ uhr) Equal strength among countries. (p. 566)

balance of trade (bal′ uhns of trād) Difference between the amount of goods a country brings in and sends out. (p. 492)

bandeirantes (ban duh ran′ tās) Fortune hunters in colonial Brazil. (p. 488)

bands (bandz) Prehistoric groups that gathered food and lived together. (p. 34)

barbaroi (bar′ buh roi) People who did not follow Greek customs. (p. 197)

barter (bar′ ter) To exchange goods without using money. (p. 241)

berserkers (ber zerk′ erz) Viking warriors. (p. 301)

bishop (bish′ uhp) Diocese head. (p. 253)

blitzkrieg (blits′ krēg) Lightning war. (p. 616)

blockaded (blok′ ād uhd) Closed off. (p. 626)

blood feuds (bluhd fyūds) Longstanding quarrels between families. (p. 269)

bourgeoisie (bur zhwah zē) Middle class. (p. 514)

boyars (bō yahrs′) Members of the wealthy class in czarist Russia. (p. 350)

boycott (boi′ kot) Refuse to pay. (p. 509)

bull leaping (būl lēp′ ēng) Minoan bullfighting. (p. 152)

burgesses (ber′ jis ez) Elected representatives in colonial Virginia. (p. 495)

burghers (ber′ guhrz) Freemen or wealthy merchants who lived in medieval towns. (p. 404)

burgs (bergs) Medieval towns. (p. 403)

C

caliph (kā′ lif) Muslim ruler. (p. 336)

campesinos (kam puh sē′ nōz) Latin American farmers and peasants. (p. 640)

canon laws (kan′ uhn lahs) Church laws. (p. 382)

capitalism (ka pih tuhl izm) An economic system where most production is privately owned. (p. 633)

captaincies (kap′ tuhn sēs) Land in Brazil given to Portuguese nobles. (p. 488)

caravans (kar′ uh vans) Groups who traveled together for safety. (p. 121)

caravel (kar′ uh vel) Portuguese ship. (p. 468)

cash crops (kash krops) Crops sold in the market. (p. 638)

castles (kas′ uhlz) Large, fortified houses. (p. 370)

catacombs (kat′ uh kōmz) Underground cemeteries. (p. 214)

cathedrals (kuh thē′ druhlz) Churches headed by bishops. (p. 386)

caudillo (kau dē′ yō) Latin American military dictator. (p. 556)

census (sen′ suhs) Population count. (p. 234)

chancellor (chan′ suh luhr) English university head. (p. 387); Prime minister. (p. 614)

charters (char′ tuhrz) Documents that enabled towns to control their affairs. (p. 405)

chateaux (sha tōz′) French castles. (p. 440)

chieftain (chēf′ tuhn) Clan leader. (p. 267)

churches (cher′ chez) Groups of people who share the same religious beliefs. (p. 252)

circuit judges (ser′ kit juj′ iz) Judges who travel throughout a country. (p. 415)

citadel (sit′ uh duhl) Fortress. (p. 85)

city-states (sit′ ē stāts) Cities and the surrounding territories. (p. 57)

civil disobedience (siv′ uhl dis uh bē′ dē uhns) Refusal to obey government demands. (p. 634)

civilians (suh vil′ yuhnz) Non-soldiers. (p. 604)

civilization (siv′ uh luh zā shuhn) Society with a developed knowledge of farming, trade, government, art, and science. (p. 33)

civil wars (siv′ uhl wōrz) Wars between citizens of one nation. (p. 159)

clans (klans) Groups based on family ties. (p. 267)

classical writings (klas′ i′ kuhl rī tēngs) Ancient Greek and Roman writings. (p. 433)

clergy (kler′ jē) Religious leaders. (p. 367)

climate (klī′ mit) Average weather condition at a place over a period of years. (p. 14)

code of chivalry (kōd of shiv′ uhl rē) Rules knights had to live by. (p. 373)

cold war (kōld wōr) Non fighting hostility between nations. (p. 625)

collectivization (kuh lek ti vuh zā′ shuhn) Uniting small farms into large ones controlled by the government. (p. 611)

colonies (kol′ uh nēz) Permanent settlements. (p. 105)

colonize (kol′ uh nīz) Permanently settle in an area. (p. 487)

communes (kom′ yūnz) Political groups formed by townspeople in medieval Italy. (p. 405)

communicable diseases (kah mū ni kah bl dis ē zez) Diseases that are passed from an infected person or animal to another person or animal. (p. 664)

compass (kum′ puhs) Instrument used to tell direction. (p. 467)

concentration camps (kon suhn trā shuhn kamps) Prison camps for political enemies. (p. 620)

conquistadores (kon kē stuh dōr′ ēz) Spanish conquerors in the 1500s. (p. 473)

constitution (kon stuh tū′ shuhn) Written laws used to govern a state. (p. 169)

constitutional monarchy (kon stuh tū′ shuh nuhl mon′ uhr kē) Monarchy limited in its powers by a constitution. (p. 518)

consuls (kon' suhlz) Heads of the ancient Roman Republic. (p. 219)

continental drift (kon tuh nen' tl drift) Theory that the continents move. (p. 10)

convents (kon' vents) Communities of nuns. (p. 255)

converted (kuhn ver' tuhd) Changed. (p. 277)

coracles (kor' uh kuhls) Small Irish boats. (p. 290)

core (kōr) Central part of the Earth. (p. 10)

corregidores (kō rā hē dō' rās) Spanish royal officials. (p. 423)

cotton gin (kot' n jin) Cotton-cleaning machine. (p. 527)

counts (kounts) French law court officials. (p. 281)

coup (koo) Forced takeover of government. (p. 648)

cremation ovens (krē mā' shuhn uh' vuhns) Furnaces that burn bodies to ashes. (p. 621)

crusades (krū sāds') Wars fought to regain the Holy Land from Muslims. (p. 388)

crust (krust) Outer layer of the Earth. (p. 10)

culture (kuhl' chuhr) Way of life. (p. 61)

cuneiform (kyū nē' uh form) Sumerian writing made up of wedge-shaped signs. (p. 58)

czar (zahr) Russian ruler. (p. 355)

D

dauphin (do' fuhn) Eldest son of the king of France. (p. 417)

defensive league (di fen' siv lēg) Protective group formed by Greek city-states. (p. 173)

democratic (dem uh krat' ik) Favoring the equality of all people. (p. 169)

depression (di presh' uhn) Economic decline. (p. 608)

descendants (di sen' duhnts) Offspring. (p. 107)

de-Stalinization (dē stahl uh nuh zā' shuhn) Attack on Stalin's policies. (p. 633)

developing nations (duh vel' uh pēng nā shuns) Countries advancing in production, technology, and standard of living. (p. 634)

dictator (dik' tā tuhr) Absolute ruler of a state. (p. 228)

dictatorship (dik tā' tuhr ship) Government ruled by a dictator. (p. 613)

diet (dī' uht) Formal assembly. (p. 421)

diocese (dī' uh sis) Area under the control of a bishop. (p. 253)

direct tax (duh rekt' taks) Tax paid directly to a government. (p. 509)

dissent (dih sent') Criticism. (p. 647)

doge (dōj) Ruler of Renaissance Venice. (p. 439)

domesticated (duh mes' tuh kāt uhd) Tamed. (p. 42)

domestic system (duh mes' tik sis' tuhm) Manufacturing done in workers' cottages. (p. 526)

domus (dō' muhs) Roman house. (p. 236)

dowry (dow' rē) Wealth brought by a woman when she marries. (p. 322)

dubbing (dub' ēng) Ceremony in which a squire is made a knight. (p. 374)

dynasty (dī nuh stē) Series of rulers from the same family. (p. 88)

E

earthquake (erth' kwāk) Shaking or sliding of a portion of the Earth's crust. (p. 11)

Eddas (ed' uhz) Written poems based on stories of Viking gods. (p. 303)

elevation (el uh vā' shuhn) Altitude. (p. 9)

embalming (em bahm' ēng) Process used to keep dead bodies from decaying. (p. 73)

emigrated (em' uh grāt ed) Left one's country. (p. 200)

emigrés (em' uh grāz) French political exiles. (p. 518)

emirs (i miuhrs') Muslim army leaders. (p. 393)

emperor (em' phur uhr) Ruler of an empire. (p. 233)

empire (em' pīr) Territories governed by a single ruler or nation. (p. 117)

enclosure (en klō' zuhr) Fencing off common land for individual use. (p. 525)

erosion (i rō' zuhn) Wearing away by wind, water, and ice. (p. 12)

estates (e stāts') French social classes. (p. 513)

euro (yur' ō) Currency used by members of the European Union. (p. 665)

excavate (ek' skuh vāt) Uncover by digging. (p. 27)

excommunicated (ek skuh myū nuh kā ted) Barred as a member of the Roman Catholic Church. (p. 382)

extended families (ek sten' duhd fam' uh lēs) Parents, children, and other relatives living together in one house. (p. 639)

F

factories (fak' tuhr ēz) Buildings where goods are manufactured. (p. 200)

factory system (fak′ tuh rē sis′ tuhm) Workers and machines in one place to make goods. (p. 527)

fairs (fāuhrz) Medieval gatherings for trade. (p. 402)

fasces (fas′ ēz) Rods tied around an ax. (p. 215)

federal (fed′ uhr uhl) National government. (p. 546)

feudalism (fyū′ dl iz uhm) Medieval political system based on the relation of lords to vassals. (p. 367)

fiefs (fēfs) Pieces of land given to vassals by their lords. (p. 367)

flying shuttle (flī′ ēng shut′ l) Weaving device that carries thread quickly back and forth across the piece being woven. (p. 527)

foreign policy (fōr′ uhn pol′ uh sē) Relations with other countries. (p. 507)

forum (fōr′ uhm) Meeting place. (p. 653)

Forum (fōr′ uhm) Roman public square. (p. 215)

freemen (frē′ muhn) Peasants who paid the lord for the right to farm their own land. (p. 377)

freedmen (frēd′ muhn) Former slaves. (p. 234)

friars (frī uhrs) Preachers. (p. 385)

G

galleons (gal′ ē uhns) Spanish ships. (p. 459)

garrison (gar′ uh suhn) Military force stationed in an area. (p. 610)

genocide (jen′ uh sīd) Deliberate destruction of an entire people. (p. 620)

gentiles (jen′ tīls) Non-Jews. (p. 249)

geography (jē ahg ruh fē) Study of the Earth and the ways people live and work on it. (p. 5)

glaciers (glā′ shuhrz) Great Ice sheets. (p. 13)

gladiatorial games (glad′ ē uh tōr ē uhl gāmz) Roman games in which gladiators fought. (p. 215)

gladiators (glad′ ē ā tuhrz) Fighters in gladiatorial games. (p. 238)

glasnost (glaz nōst) Russian policy allowing openness. (p. 633)

grand jury (grand jūr′ ē) Jury that examines accusations and advises criminal charges. (p. 415)

Greek fire (grēk fīr) Chemical weapon used by the Byzantines. (p. 324)

greenhouse effect (grēn hows uh fekt) Carbon dioxide traps heat from the Earth's surface. (p. 664)

guerrilla warfare (guh ril′ uh wōr′ fār) Hit-and-run fighting. (p. 573)

guilds (gildz) Medieval craft organizations. (p. 406)

guillotine (gil′ uh tēn) Machine that cuts off a victim's head. (p. 518)

H

habitats (ha buh tats) Dwelling places. (p. 667)

haciendas (ah sē en′ duhz) Large ranches. (p. 640)

hajj (haj) Muslim journey to Makkah. (p. 336)

hard-liners (hahrd līnuhrz) People who stick to their ideas regardless of circumstances. (p. 632)

heavy industry (hev′ ē in′ duhs trē) Industry that manufactures machines. (p. 611)

helots (hel′ uhtz) Spartan slaves. (p. 164)

heresy (her′ uh sē) Religious belief at odds with church doctrine. (p. 253)

heretic (her′ uh tik) Church member who disagrees with official doctrine. (p. 451)

hieroglyphic (hī uhr uh glif′ ik) Egyptian writing system based on pictures. (p. 77)

Holocaust (hol′ uh kahst) Nazi program of genocide against the Jews. (p. 621)

holy of holies (hō′ lē of hō′ lēs) Innermost and most sacred chamber of a temple. (p. 104)

home territory (hōm ter′ uh tōr ē) Area where hunters and food gatherers lived. (p. 35)

hostage (hos′ tij) Person held by another until certain promises are carried out. (p. 193)

humanists (hyū′ muh nists) Philosophers who believe that people are important. (p. 433)

hypothesis (hī poth′ uh sis) Possible explanation for a problem. (p. 188)

I

icons (ī konz) Sacred pictures of Eastern Orthodoxy. (p. 325)

imam (i mam′) Muslim prayer leader. (p. 335)

immigrants (im′ uh gruhnts) People who settle permanently in a different country. (p. 534)

imperialism (im pir′ ē uh liz uhm) Establishing colonies and building empires. (p. 579)

indentured servants (in den′ chuhrd ser′ vuhntz) Settlers who pledged labor for their passage to the Americas. (p. 495)

indulgences (in dul′ juhnt sez) Church pardons that lessen punishment for sins. (p. 450)

industrialized (in dus′ trē uh līzd) Developed industry. (p. 533)

inflation (in flā shuhn) Period when prices go up and money value goes down. (p. 240)

interchangeable parts (in tuhr chān juh buhl parts) Machine parts made to a uniform size so they could be easily replaced. (p. 527)

internal combustion engine (in tuhr′ nuhl kuhm buhs′ chuhn en′ juhn) Engine that is fueled by gasoline. (p. 535)

intifada (in tuh fah′ duh) A 1987 Palestinian uprising. (p. 657)

isolationist (ī sō lā shun ist) A country that stays out of the affairs of other countries. (p. 607)

izbas (iz′ bahs) One-room wooden cabin built by Eastern Slavs. (p. 348)

J

jarls (yahrlz) Viking military leaders. (p. 301)

journeyman (jer′ nē muhn) Person who works under a master for a daily wage. (p. 406)

joust (jowst) Contest on horseback between two knights. (p. 374)

judge (juj) Hebrew tribe leader. (p. 112)

junker (jung′ kuhr) Rich Prussian landowner. (p. 574)

junta (hun′ tuh) Committee organized to take over a government. (p. 553)

juris prudentes (jū′ ruhs prū′ duhntz) Roman lawyers. (p. 236)

K

kaiser (kī′ zuhr) German emperor. (p. 574)

keep (kēp) Strongest part of a castle. (p. 371)

khan (kahn) Mongol leader. (p. 353)

king's peace (kings pēs) Protection extended to any area an Anglo-Saxon king visited. (p. 295)

knight (nīt) Warrior on horseback. (p. 369)

kremlin (krem′ luhn) Russian fortress. (p. 354)

L

labyrinth (lab′ uh rinth) Maze. (p. 153)

ladies (lā′ dēz) Noblewomen. (p. 372)

landforms (land′ forms) Physical features of the Earth's surface. (p. 9)

latifundias (lat uh fuhn′ dē uhs) Large Roman estates. (p. 225)

latitude (lat′ uh tūd) Imaginary lines that measure distance from the Equator. (p. 14)

legends (lej′ undz) Folktales or stories passed down from generation to generation. (p. 75)

legionaries (lē′ juh ner ēz) Roman soldiers. (p. 221)

legions (lē juhnz) Divisions of Roman soldiers. (p. 221)

liberals (lib′ uhr uhls) People who favor political reforms. (p. 566)

limited government (lim′ uh tid guv′ uhrn muhnt) Government has only powers given to it by the people. (p. 513)

lords (lordz) Medieval nobles. (p. 283)

M

macadam road (muh kad′ uhm rōd) Road made of layers of crushed rock. (p. 529)

manifest destiny (man′ uh fest des′ tuh nē) Belief that the United States should extend from coast to coast. (p. 548)

mandate (man′ dāt) Authority to govern. (p. 607)

manors (man′ uhrz) Medieval estates with a lord and tenants. (p. 375)

mantle (man′ tl) Part of the Earth beneath the crust and above the core. (p. 10)

martial law (mar′ shuhl lah) Rule by the army instead of by civil government. (p. 505)

mass (mas) Worship service. (p. 382)

masters (mas′ tuhrz) Experts. (p. 406)

megaron (meg′ uh ron) Square room in the center of a Mycenaean palace. (p. 155)

mercantilism (mer′ kuhn tēl iz uhm) System in which colonies provide wealth to their parent country. (p. 508)

mercenaries (mer′ suh nār ēz) Men hired to be soldiers for a foreign country. (p. 175)

messiah (muh′ sī′ uh) Savior. (p. 248)

mestizos (me stē′ zōz) People of mixed European and Native American Ancestry. (p. 490)

metropolitans (met ruh pol′ uh tuhns) Eastern Orthodox Church officials in charge of large cities. (p. 325)

migrate (mī′ grāt) To move from one place to another. (p. 34)

minerals (min′ uhr uhls) Nonliving substances found beneath the Earth's surface. (p. 19)

ministers (min′ uh stuhrz) Protestant religious leaders. (p. 451)

minstrels (min′ struhlz) Medieval traveling poets and singers. (p. 285)

missionary (mish′ uh ner ē) Person who tries to convert nonbelievers. (p. 250)

mobilize (mō′ buh līz) Prepare troops for action. (p. 604)

monarchies (mon′ uhr kēz) Countries ruled by a king or queen. (p. 411)

monasteries (mon′ uh ster ēz) Places where monks live. (p. 255)

monks (mungks) Men who live in a religious community. (p. 255)

monopoly (muh nop′ uh lē) Total control. (p. 508)

monsoons (mon sūnz) Seasonal winds that change direction. (p. 16)

mosaics (mō zā′ iks) Colorful pictures made of stone or glass. (p. 323)

mosque (mosk) Muslim house of worship. (p. 335)

multinational companies (mul tē na shun ul kum pun ēz) Companies that operate across national boundaries. (p. 661)

mummy (mum ē) Wrapped body of preserved dead person. (p. 73)

mundus (muhn′ duhs) Meeting point of the worlds of the living and the dead for the Romans. (p. 216)

municipal (myū nis′ uh puhl) Relating to a city. (p. 215)

mutiny (myūt′ n ē) Revolt against officers. (p. 472)

N

nationalists (nash′ uh nuhl ists) People in favor of national independence. (p. 566)

national workshops (nash′ uh nuhl wuhrk′ shops) Factories run by workers but paid for by the government. (p. 570)

natural resources (nach′ uhr uhl rē′ sōr sez) Materials found in nature. (p. 19)

necropolis (nek rop′ uh luhs) Etruscan cemetery. (p. 214)

nobles (nō′ buhlz) People having high rank in a kingdom. (p. 90)

nomadic (nō mad′ ik) Wandering. (p. 106)

nonrenewable resources (non ri nū′ uh buhl rē sōr sez) Irreplaceable natural resources. (p. 20)

nuns (nunz) Women belonging to a religious order. (p. 255)

O

oath-helpers (ōth help′ erz) Germans who swore an accused person was telling the truth. (p. 269)

ocean current (ō′ shun kur′ uhnt) Water that flows in the ocean in a steady stream. (p. 16)

oligarchy (ol′ uh gahr kē) Government in which a few people rule. (p. 169)

omens (ō′ muhnz) Signs believed to indicate the future. (p. 214)

open-hearth process (ō′ puhn hahrth prah′ ses) Process that uses a special kind of furnace to make steel inexpensively. (p. 529)

oracles (ōr′ uh kuhlz) Greeks through whom the gods spoke. (p. 179)

oracle bones (ōr′ uh kuhl bōnz) Bones used by the Shang to receive messages from ancestors. (p. 90)

orator (ōr′ uh ter) Public speaker. (p. 195)

ordeal (ōr dēl) Painful test used by the Germans to decide innocence or guilt. (p. 269)

orders (ōr′ duhrs) Groups of friars. (p. 386)

P

page (pāj) Person who helped knights care for their horses and armor. (p. 373)

pancratium (pan krā′ shē uhm) Olympic event that combined boxing and wrestling. (p. 183)

pandemics (pan dem′ icks) Epidemics spread over a wide region. (p. 664)

papal line of demarcation (pā′ puhl līn ov dē mahr kā′ shuhn) Line drawn in 1493 dividing Spanish and Portuguese land claims. (p. 473)

papyrus (puh pī′ ruhs) Egyptian paper. (p. 78)

parchment (parch′ muhnt) Material made from thin animal skin used for windows and as paper. (p. 153)

parish (par′ ish) Area assigned to a local church. (p. 253)

patriarchs (pā′ trē arks) Most important bishops in the early Christian church. (p. 253)

patricians (puh trish′ uhnz) Powerful upper-class citizens of ancient Rome. (p. 219)

peninsulares (puh nin sū la′ rās) Colonials born in Spain who later came to the Americas. (p. 490)

pentathlon (pen tath′ luhn) Olympic game made up of five events. (p. 183)

perestroika (pār uhs troi kuh) Russian system of restructuring. (p. 633)

perioeci (pār ē ē′ sī) Merchants and artisans in Spartan villages. (p. 166)

phalanx (fā′ langks) Greek infantry formation. (p. 194)

pharaoh (fār′ ō) Egyptian ruler. (p. 70)

philosophes (fē luh zofs′) French philosophers of the 1700s. (p. 514)

philosophia (fi la sō fē′ ya) The love of wisdom, according to the Greeks. (p. 185)

piazza (pē aht′ suh) Italian city square. (p. 436)

pilgrimage (pil′ gruh mij) Religious journey to a shrine or holy place. (p. 133)

pilgrims (pil′ gruhms) People who travel to a holy place to worship. (p. 332)

pillars of faith (pil′ uhrs of fāth) Five Muslim duties as described in the Quran. (p. 335)

planned communities (pland kuh myū′ nuh tēz) Cities built to a definite plan. (p. 85)

plebeians (pli bē uhnz) Poor and lower-class citizens of ancient Rome. (p. 219)

plebiscite (pleb′ uh sīt) Popular vote. (p. 563)

polar zone (pō′ luhr zōn) Climate zone more than 60° north or south of the Equator. (p. 15)

polis (pah′ lis) Greek city-state. (p. 163)

political parties (puh lit′ uh kuhl par′ tēz) Groups with set ideas about government. (p. 546)

political science (puh lit′ uh kuhl sī′ uhns) Study of government. (p. 187)

popular sovereignty (pop′ yuh luhr sov′ ruhn tē) Idea that government derives its powers from the people. (p. 513)

population (pop ū lā shuhn) Number of living things in a particular area. (p. 42)

population explosion (pop ū lā′ shuhn ek splō′ zhuhn) Sudden growth in the number of people. (p. 136)

precipitation (prē sip uh tā shuhn) Falling moisture such as snow or rain. (p. 16)

prehistory (prē′ his tuh rē) Time before people began to keep written records. (p. 33)

prevailing winds (pri vā′ lēng winds) Winds that blow mostly from one direction. (p. 16)

priest (prēst) Religious leader, usually Roman Catholic or Eastern Orthodox. (p. 253)

priest-king (prēst king) Sumerian governmental and religious leader. (p. 59)

printing press (prin′ tēng pres) Machine for printing books, using movable type. (p. 441)

privatize (prī vuh tīz) Allow private citizen ownership. (p. 649)

proletariat (pro luh tār′ ē uht) Industrial working class. (p. 568)

prophecy (prof′ uh sē) Statement of what might happen in the future. (p. 179)

prophets (prof′ its) People claiming to have messages from God. (p. 112)

protectorate (pruh tek′ tuhr it) Country that gives up foreign policy to an imperial authority. (p. 582)

provinces (prah′ vins uhs) Political districts. (p. 119)

psalms (sahms) Sacred songs. (p. 112)

publicans (pub′ luh′ kuhnz) Ancient Roman tax collectors. (p. 225)

purges (per′ juhs) Removals of undesirable members. (p. 631)

pyramids (pir′ uh midz) Large Egyptian tombs. (p. 71)

Q

quipus (k′ pūz) Inca counting devices. (p. 142)

R

referendum (ref ah ren′ duhm) Popular vote. (p. 660)

reformation (ref uhr mā′ shuhn) Change. (p. 449)

reform (rē form) Change that leads to improvement. (p. 61)

reign (rān) Period of power. (p. 63)

relative location (rel uhtiv lō kā shun) Location of place in relation to other places. (p. 6)

relics (rel′ iks) Sacred objects from the past. (p. 319)

relief (ri lēf′) Differences in height between a region's summits and lowlands. (p. 9)

renegade nations (ren′ ah gāde na′ shunz) Countries that refuse to reduce the weapons of war. (p. 663)

renewable resources (ri nū′ uh buhl rē sōr sez) Replaceable natural resources. (p. 20)

repealed (ri pēld′) Abolished or called back. (p. 507)

representative government (rep ri ent′ uht iv guv′ uhrn muhnt) System of ruling in which officials are elected. (p. 546)

republic (ri pub′ lik) Government in which citizens choose their leaders. (p. 219)

revolution (rev uh lū′ shuhn) Activity designed to overthrow a government. (p. 503)

right of extraterritoriality (rīt ov ek struh ter i tōr ē al′ uh tē) Right of an accused person in a different country to be tried in a court of his or her own nation. (p. 587)

river system (riv′ uhr sis tuhm) River and all streams that flow into it. (p. 14)

rule by divine right (rūl bī duh vīn′ rīt) Rule based on the theory that a monarch's right to rule comes from God. (p. 243)

runes (rūnz) Letters of the Viking alphabet. (p. 303)

S

sabbath (sab′ uhth) Day of the week used for rest and worship. (p. 113)

sans-culottes (san skū' lahts) French city workers and peasants in the 1700s. (p. 518)

satellite nations (sat' l īt nā shuhns) Countries controlled by another, stronger country. (p. 626)

scientific method (sī uhn tif' ik meth' uhd) Process used by scientists for study. (p. 188)

scorched-earth policy (skōrchd uhrth pahl' uh sē) Tactic of destruction used by a retreating army. (p. 564)

scribe (skrīb) Sumerian writer. (p. 58)

scriptures (skrip' churz) Sacred writings. (p. 247)

sea dog (sē dahg) Veteran sea captain in Tudor England. (p. 477)

seceding (si sēd' ēng) Withdrawing. (p. 551)

seminary (sem' uh ner ē) School for training priests. (p. 454)

seneschal (sēn' uh shuhl) Medieval official who looked after the noble's fiefs. (p. 375)

sepoys (sē' pois) Indian soldiers in the British army. (p. 585)

serfs (serfz) Medieval poor people bound to the land. (p. 285)

shadoof (shuh dūf') Egyptian machine used to raise water. (p. 68)

sheriff (sher' if) English government official in charge of a shire. (p. 295)

shires (shīrz) Districts in England. (p. 295)

shrines (shrīns) Sacred places to worship. (p. 154)

silent barter (sī luhnt bahr' ter) Method of exchanging goods without talking; used in the middle kingdoms of Africa. (p. 132)

slums (slumz) Run-down city areas. p. 551)

smelting (smel' tēng) Heating iron or metals to remove impurities. (p. 118)

social justice (sō' shuhl jus' tis) Fair treatment of all people in a society. (p. 110)

social order (sō' shuhl ōr' der) Social divisions according to wealth and other factors. (p. 213)

social security laws (sō shuhl si kyūr' uh tē lahz) United States laws that provided for people's welfare. (p. 613)

Socratic method (sō krat' ik me' thuhd) Form of questioning developed by Socrates. (p. 186)

soothsayers (sūth' sā uhrz) People who are believed to be able to fortell the future. (p. 214)

sovereign (sah' vuh ruhn) Independent and self-governing. (p. 649)

soviets (sō' vē ets) Communist committees that represent workers and soldiers. (p. 610)

specialization (spesh uh luh zā' shuhn) Development of occupations. (p. 45)

spheres of influence (sfērs of in' flū uhns) Areas in one country in which another country has special rights. (p. 585)

spinning jenny (spin' ēng jen' ē) Machine for spinning that uses many spindles.(p. 527)

spirits (spēr' itz) Supernatural beings. (p. 89)

squire (skwīr) Young noble under the care and training of a knight. (p. 373)

stable government (stā' buhl guv' uhrn muhnt) Firmly established government. (p. 545)

strike (strīk) Stop work. (p. 569)

subsistence farmers (suhb sis stuhns far muhrs) People who produce only enough food for their own use. (p. 638)

swastika (swos' tuh kuh) Hooked black cross used as a Nazi symbol. (p. 614)

syllogism (sil' uh jiz uhm) Form of reasoning developed by Aristotle. (p. 188)

T

tariffs (tar' ifz) Taxes placed on goods entering one country from another. (p. 235)

tectonic plates (tek ton' ik plāts) Slow-moving sections of the Earth. (p. 10)

temperate zone (tem' puhr it zōn) Climate zone between 30° and 60° north or south of the Equator. (p. 15)

tenants (ten' uhnts) People who live and work on someone else's land. (p. 155)

tenements (ten' uh muhnts) Apartments that meet minimum standards. (p. 551)

terrorism (tār' ōr izm) Violence to achieve a political goal. (p. 665)

textile (tek' stuhl) Woven cloth. (p. 526)

theology (thē ol' uh jē) Study of religion. (p. 320)

theses (thē' sēz) Statements written by Luther criticizing Church practices. (p. 450)

tithes (tīthz) Payments to the church. (p. 384)

tournaments (tur' nuh muhnts) Contests to test the skill of knights. (p. 374)

trade unions (trād yū' nyuhns) Associations of workers. (p. 533)

treaties (trē' tēz) Formal agreements between nations. (p. 103)

trench warfare (trench wōr' fāuhr) Warfare in which opposing forces attack from a system of trenches. (p. 604)

trial jury (trī uhl jūr' ē) Group of people that decide whether a person accused of a crime is innocent or guilty. (p. 415)

tribunes (trib' yūnz) Roman officials elected to protect the lower class. (p. 220)

triremes (trī' rēmz) Greek warships. (p. 172)

triumph (trī' uhmf) Parade to welcome home a Roman hero. (p. 215)

triumvirate (trī um' vuhr it) Group of three people who rule with equal power. (p. 228)

tropical zone (trop' uh kuhl zōn) Climate zone between 30° north and 30° south of the Equator. (p. 15)

tyranny (tir' uh nē) Unjust use of power. (p. 517)

U

unions (yūn' yuhns) Groups of people joined together for a common cause, especially medieval students and teachers. (p. 387)

universal male suffrage (yū nuh ver' suhl māl suhf' rij) Right of all men to vote. (p. 569)

universities (yū ni ver' suh tēs) Institutions of higher learning. (p. 387)

urbanization (uhr buh nuh zā' shuhn) Growth of cities. (p. 551)

utopian socialists (yū tō' pē uhn sō' shuh lists) People who want to set up ideal communities based on economic cooperation. (p. 568)

V

vassal (vas' uhl) Medieval noble who served a lord of higher rank. (p. 368)

veche (ve' chuh) Russian town assembly. (p. 350)

veto (vē' tō) Refuse consent. (p. 219)

viceroy (vīs roi) Ruler of a viceroyalty. (p. 490)

viceroyalties (vīs' roi uhl tēz) Districts in Spain's colonies in the Americas. (p. 490)

vizier (vi zir') Chief adviser to the caliph of the Abbasids. (p. 338)

volcano (vol kā' nō) Opening in the Earth's crust through which, when active, steam, ashes, and lava are forced. (p. 11)

W

wergeld (wuhr' geld) Fine paid by the family of a German who committed a crime. (p. 269)

witan (wi' tuhn) Member of the witenagemot. (p. 295)

witenagemot (wit uhn uh' guh mōt) Anglo-Saxon council that advised the king. (p. 295)

Z

zaibatsu (zī bah tsū) Industrialist families in Japan. (p. 589)

zakah (zuh kah') Muslim charitable giving. (p. 335)

ziggurat (zig' uh rat) Mesopotamian temple. (p. 57)

Index

Church, Middle Ages, 253, 281, 324–26, 381–95, 423
  Inquisition, 382–83
  learning, 254–56, 386–88
  see also Roman Catholic Church
Churchill, Winston, 616
Church of England, 455–58, 504
Circumnavigation of world, 476
City–states, 103, 136, 327, 419–20
  Greece, 13, 162–76, 193, 195, 199–200, 222, 224
  Renaissance, 433–39
  Sumer, 55–57, 61, 63–64
Clovis, 275, 277, 284
Cluny, 385–86
Coins, 126, 167, 174, 338, 402, 412
Cold war, 624–29, 632–33, 645–46
College of Cardinals, 385
Columbus, Christopher, 471–73, 476
Commonwealth of Independent States, 648–49
Communists, 568, 601, 611, 624–33, 645–52, 659–60, 663
Communist Manifesto, 568
Compass, 467
Concentration camps, 620
Confucianism, 145, 586
Confucius, 145, 586
Conquistadores, 473–74
Conquerors, eastern, 341
Constantine I, 241, 243, 252, 317, 318
Constantinople, 243, 314, 317–19, 395, 439
Constitution, French, 518–19
Constitution, U.S., 512–13
Continental Congresses, 510, 512
Copernicus, Nicolaus, 523, 525
Coronado, Francisco, 473–74
Cortés, Hernando, 466, 473
Cranmer, Thomas, 456
Crécy, Battle of, 417
Crete, 151–52, 157
Critical Thinking Skills
  bias, 170
  cause and effect, 29
  comparing, 111
  conclusions, 461
  fact and opinion, 60
  predicting, 571
  generalizations, 321
  main idea, 242
Croatia, 654–55
Cro-Magnons, 33, 37, 39–40
Cromwell, Oliver, 505–6
Crossbow, 393, 417
Crusades, 364–65, 388–95, 412, 420
  Children's, 395
  Kings', 393, 420
  Nobles', 391
  Peasants', 389, 393
Cuba, 472, 627–28, 663
Cultural Revolution, 631
Czechoslovakia, 601, 607, 615, 626, 646–47, 649
Czech Republic, 649–50

D

Danelaw, 294, 307
Danes, 293–94, 307–8
Dante, 407
Darius, 98, 123–24, 171
Da Gama, Vasco, *see* Gama
David (Israel), 112
Da Vinci, Leonardo, *see* Vinci
Dayton peace accord, p. 654
Declaration of Independence, U.S., 485, 512
Declaration of Rights, 507
Declaration of the Rights of Man and the Citizen, 517–518, 553
Declaratory Act, 509–10
Delian League, 173–74
Democracy, 169, 415, 610, 635, 645
Demosthenes, 194–95
Deng Xiaoping, 631–32
Denmark, 299, 463
de Klerk, Frederick W., 661
de Soto, Hernando, 473
Developing nations, 634–42
  Africa, 637–39, 661–62
  India, 634–35
  Indonesia, 659–61
  Latin America, 639–42
  Malaysia, 637
Dias, Bartolomeu, 467, 469–70, 475
Diet, German, 421, 451
Diocletian, 241, 243
Discovery, Age of, 466–78
Domesday Book, 414
Domestic system, 526
Dorians, 159
Draco, 169
Drake, Sir Francis, 460

E

Eastern Orthodox Church, 253, 255, 324–26, 350–55, 388
  conflict with Pope, 253, 326
  icons, 325–26, 351
Eastern Slavs, 347–49
East Frankish Kingdom, 285
East Goths, 270–72
East India Company, 510, 585
East Timor, 660–61
Education, 351, 407, 434, 552, 557, 562
  see also Learning, Schools
Edward I (England), 416
Edward III, 417
Edward VI, 456
Edward the Confessor, 413
Egypt, 25, 66–81, 83, 582
  hieroglyphics, 26–27, 77–78, 105, 130
  invasions, 53, 73–74, 78, 130
  Middle Kingdom, 73–74
  New Kingdom, 53, 74, 76–78, 129
  Old Kingdom, 52, 69–73
  pyramids, 71–72
Eleanor of Aquitaine, 392, 414

Elizabeth I, 444, 457–58, 503
  Armada, 459–60
El Salvador, 554
England, 288–97, 443–46
  Anglo-Saxons, 289–96, 413
  Danish invasion, 293–94, 307
  expansion, 489, 508–9, 582–83
  monarchy, 295, 413–16, 418, 518–20
  Revolution, 503–7, 518
  see also Great Britain
English language, 295, 407
Enlightenment, Age of, 503
Enslavement, 134, 139, 213, 580
  Americas, 484, 509
  Athens, 168
  Latin America, 553
  Nazi Germany, 614–15
  Roman Empire, 236, 238
  Rome, 219–20, 224–25, 236, 238, 251, 270
  Sparta, 164, 166–67
  trade, 470, 580
  triangular, 509
  United States, 548, 551
Environment, 7, 664–65
Erasmus, 441
Eratosthenes, 197–98
Eriksson, Leif, 302, 305
Estates-General, 412, 514–15
Ethiopia, 131, 638
Etruscans, 206, 210–16
Euclid, 197
Euphrates River, 27, 53, 55, 106
Euripides, 183–84
European Common Market, 625–26
European Union (EU), 665

F

Factory system, 527
Farming, 20, 41–42, 56, 84, 98, 225, 283, 285, 339, 525–26, 611, 638–42
Fascists, 610
Ferdinand (Aragon), 365, 423, 471
Ferdinand II (Germany), 462–63
Feudalism, 285, 364–79, 395, 403, 405, 407–8, 414
Fire, discovery, 33, 36
Flanders, 401, 441
Florence, 433, 436–37, 438
Fourteen Points, 605
France, 9, 307–8, 411–13, 440, 509, 513–15, 517–20, 534, 561–69, 604–6, 625
  expansion, 563–65
  government, 562–63
  July Revolution (1830), 568–69
  monarchy, 411–12, 518–19
  revolution, 508, 513–15, 517–20, 552–53, 561
  three estates, 513–14
Francis I, 440, 460
Francis of Assisi, 386
Franks, 274–87
Franz Ferdinand, 604
Frederic I (Barbarossa), 365, 393, 419–20

INDEX   **731**

Jews, 113, 248–49, 340, 391, 656
    Nazi Germany, 614
    Spain, 340, 423
    see also Hebrews
Joan of Arc, 417–18
Jordan, 656
Juárez, Benito, 557
Judah, 112
Judaism, 106
Julius Caesar, *see* Caesar, Gaius
Justinian I, Emperor, 314, 320, 322–24
    law code, 322

K

Ka'bah, 332–33
Kampuchea, 591
Kenya, 5–6, 8, 470, 639
Khrushchev, Nikita S., 633
Kiev, 349
Kievan Rus, 349–352
King James Bible, 504
Knights, 373–74
Knossos, 152–55
Koran, *see* Quran
Korean War, 627
Kosovo, 665–66
Kublai Khan, 362–63
Kurds, 653
Kush, 129–31
Kuwait, 652–53

L

Land bridge, Asia to America, 34, 137
Laos, 591
La Salle, Sieur de, 499
Latin America, 552–57, 591–93, 639–42
Latins, 206, 209–10, 213, 215
Latitude, 14–15, 135
Law, 235–36, 405, 412, 562–63
    canon, 382
    common law's origins, 268–69
    England, 294–95, 414–15, 505
    feudal, 377
    German, 268–69
    Roman, 220, 235–36, 268–69
League of Nations, 607, 615, 621
Leakey, Mary Nicol, 28
Lebanon, 101, 000
Legends, 22–24, 57–59, 88, 103–5, 155,
    158–59, 209–10, 292, 332
Lenin, Vladimir Ilyich, 610–11
Leningrad, 611
Leo III, Byzantine Emperor, 326
Leo X, Pope, 449–51
León, Ponce de, 473–74
Leopold II (Belgium), 581–82
Liliuokalani, 591
Lithuania, 606, 648
Livingstone, David, 580–81
Locke, John, 507
Lombards, 279
London, 294, 507, 532
Longbow, 417

Longitude, 156
Lothair, 285
Louis VI (the Fat), 411
Louis VII, 390
Louis IX, 412
Louis XVI, 514–15, 518–19
Louis XVIII, 566, 568
Louisiana Purchase, 547–48
Louis-Philippe, 569–70
Louis the Pious, 285
Loyola, Ignatius of, 453
Lucy, 35
Luther, Martin, 448–51
Lutheran Church, 451
Luxembourg, 625
Lydia, 126, 210

M

Macedonia, 176, 193–94, 654
Madina, 333–34, 336–37
Magellan, Ferdinand, 474–76
Magna Carta, 365, 415–16
Makkah, 332–36
Malaria, 664
Mali, 99, 132–34
Mamelukes, 341
Mandela, Nelson, 661–62
Manor, 375–78
Mansa Musa I, 133–34
Mao Zedong, 630–31
Map Skills, 467–68
    demographic, 651
    direction, 44
    grids, 394
    historical, 306, 356, 567
    inset, 284
    latitude, 135
    legends, 75, 475
    location, 41, 394
    longitude, 156
    mercator, 13
    military, 511
    physical, 62, 165
    political, 211
    projections, 17
    scale, 108
Marathon, Battle of, 171–72
Marcus Aurelius, *see* Aurelius
Marie Antoinette, 514, 518–19
Marius, Gaius, 227–28
Marshall Plan, 625
Martel, Charles, 277–79, 367
Marx, Karl, 568
Mary I, 456–57
Maximilian I, Holy Roman Emperor,
    421–22
Maximilian, Emperor (Mexico), 557, 592
Mayas, 99, 138–39
Mayflower Compact, 495
Mayors of the Palace, 278
Mbeki, Thabo, 662
Mecca, *see* Makkah
Medici, Catherine de, 460

Medici, Lorenzo de, 436–37
Medicine, 79–80, 111, 190, 343, 373, 392
Medina, *see* Madina
Mercantilism, 401–3, 508–9
Mesoamerica, 138–40
Mesopotamia, 53–65, 83, 94, 101, 117
Mexico, 12, 42, 139–40, 548–49, 554, 557
Michelangelo Buonarroti, *see* Buonarroti
Middle East, 55, 656–58
Milan, Edict of, 252
Milosevic, Slobodan, 654–55
Minoans, 148, 151–55, 157
Missionaries, Roman, 250, 292
Moche, 260–61
Mogul Empire, 461, 585–86
    see also Mongols
Mohenjo-daro, 85–86
Monarchy, rise of, 410–25
Mongols, 315, 341, 353–54, 461
Monks, 255–56, 282, 290–92, 325–26, 351,
    353, 381, 384–86
Monroe Doctrine, 592
Montezuma II, 140, 466, 473
Moors, 340, 423, 471
Moscow, rise, 315, 354–55
Moses, 109–10
Mozambique, 638
Muhammad, 331–37, 342
Muscovy, 354, 608
Muslims, 262, 278–79, 327, 332, 391–93,
    400, 461, 470, 634
    Shi'ah, 338
    Sunni, 338
    see also Islam
Mussolini, Benito, 613
Mycenaeans, 148, 151, 155, 157–60

N

NAFTA, *see* North American Free Trade
    Agreement
Nagasaki, atomic bomb, 620
Nantes, Edict of, 462
Napoleon Bonaparte, *see* Bonaparte
Napoleon III, 570, 572, 574
Napoleonic Code, 562–63
Narmer, king of Egypt, 69
National Assembly, France, 517–18, 520
National Socialist party (Nazis), 614–15
Nationalism, 566, 568, 572–76, 580, 634
Native Americans, 305, 472–73, 493–94
NATO, *see* North Atlantic Treaty
    Organization
Natural resources, 19–21, 639, 664–65
Neanderthals, 33, 37–38
Nicaragua, 554
Nebuchadnezzar, 120–21
Nehru, Jawaharlal, 635
Neolithic Age, 33, 41–43, 45–46
Netherlands, 462
Newton, Sir Isaac, 525
New Zealand, 538–541
Nicaragua, 554
Nicholas II (Russia), 609–610

Spanish Glossary

A

abbot / abad jefe de monasterio. (pág. 255)

abdicate / abdicar dejar al trono. (pág. 565)

absolute location / localización absoluta posición exacta de un lugar en la superficie de la tierra. (pág. 5)

acropolis / acrópolis colina fortificada en las ciudades de la antigua Grecia. (pág. 163)

act of homage / acto de homenaje ceremonia en la cual un vasallo promete lealtad a su señor. (pág. 368)

ages / épocas períodos de tiempo. (pág. 27)

aggression /agresión actos violentos (pág. 645)

agora / ágora plaza pública en las ciudades de la antigua Grecia. (pág. 163)

airlift / puente aéreo sistema de transportar provisiones por avión a un área aislada. (pág. 626)

alchemists / alquimistas científicos que trataron de cambiar los metales a oro y plata. (pág. 343)

alliances / alianzas acuerdos entre pueblos o países. (pág. 195)

amendments / enmiendas cambios de ley. (pág. 513)

ancestors / antepasados miembros de la familia de generaciones pasadas. (pág. 89)

annexation / anexión incorporación de áreas dentro de un estado existente. (pág. 549)

anointed / ungido untado con aceite bendito. (pág. 279)

anthropologists / antropólogos personas que se dedican al estudio de los seres humanos. (pág. 24)

apartheid / *apartheid* separación de las razas. (pág. 661)

apostles / apóstoles hombres escogidos por Jesús para enseñar sus creencias a otros. (pág. 253)

appeasement / apaciguamiento cederse a demandas (pág. 615)

apprentice / aprendiz persona que está aprendiendo una artesanía u oficio. (pág. 406)

archaeology / arqueología estudio de los restos de culturas humanas antiguas. (pág. 25)

archaeologists / arqueólogos personas que se dedican al estudio de ruinas y artefactos. (pág. 24)

archbishops / arzobispos obispos titulares en las iglesias de las grandes ciudades. (pág. 253)

aristocrats / aristócratas miembros de la clase alta. (pág. 164)

armada / armada flota de buques de guerra. (pág. 459)

armaments / armamentos equipo militar. (pág. 605)

armistice / armisticio acuerdo para suspender peleas. (pág. 605)

artifacts / artefactos productos de habilidades humanas. (pág. 25)

artillary / artillería armas montadas. (pág. 604)

artisans / artesanos trabajadores expertos. (pág. 57)

assembly line / línea de montaje sistema de trabajo en el cual cada trabajador agrega una parte a un producto hasta que está ensamblado. (pág. 528)

astrolabe / astrolabio instrumento de navegación usado para determinar la latitud. (pág. 467)

astronomers / astrónomos personas que estudian los cuerpos celestes. (pág. 122)

authoritarian rule / régimen autoritario gobierno en que una persona o partido político tiene todo el poder. (pág. 661)

automation / automatización proceso en el cual las máquinas reemplazan a los trabajadores. (pág. 527)

autonomous / autónomo que se gobierna por sí solo. (pág. 655)

B

bailiff / mayordomo oficial medieval que vigilaba que los campesinos hicieran su trabajo. (pág. 376)

balance of power / equilibrio de poder fuerza igual entre países. (pág. 566)

balance of trade / equilibrio de comercio diferencia entre la cantidad de mercancía que un país exporta a la que importa. (pág. 492)

***bandeirantes* / bandeirantes** aventureros de fortuna del Brasil colonial. (pág. 488)

bands / bandas grupos prehistóricos que colectaban comida y vivían juntos. (pág. 34)

barbaroi* / *barbaroi personas que no seguían las costumbres griegas. (pág. 197)

barter / trocar cambiar artículos sin el uso de dinero. (pág. 241)

berserkers* / *berserkers guerreros vikingos. (301)

bishop / obispo jefe de diócesis. (pág. 253)

blitzkrieg / *blitzkrieg* guerra relámpago. (pág. 616)

blockaded / bloqueado cerrado. (pág. 626)

blood feuds / enemistad hereditaria pleitos antiguos entre familias o clanes. (pág. 269)

bourgeosie / burguesía clase media. (pág. 514)

boyars / boyardos miembros de la clase rica en la Rusia zarista. (pág. 350)

boycott / boicotear rehusar a pagar. (pág. 509)

bull leaping / salto de toros tauromaquia minoica. (pág. 152)

burgesses / diputados representantes elegidos de Virginia en la época colonial. (pág. 495)

burghers / burgueses hombres libres o adinerados que vivían en pueblos medievales. (pág. 404)

burgs / burgos pueblos pequeños medievales. (pág. 403)

C

caliph / califa gobernante musulmán. (pág. 336)

campesinos / **campesinos** paisanos y granjeros latinoamericanos. (pág. 640)

canon laws / leyes canónicas leyes de la iglesia. (pág. 382)

capitalism / capitalismo sistema económico donde la mayoría de la producción es de propiedad privada. (pág. 633)

captaincies / capitanías territorios de Brasil dados a los nobles portugueses. (pág. 488)

caravans / caravanas grupos que viajaban juntos para la seguridad. (pág. 121)

caravel / carabela embarcación portuguesa. (pág. 468)

cash crops / cultivo comercial cosecha vendida en el mercado. (pág. 638)

castles / castillos grandes casas fortificadas. (pág. 370)

catacombs / catacumbas cementerios subterráneos. (pág. 214)

cathedrals / catedrales iglesias dirigidas por obispos. (pág. 386)

caudillo / caudillo dictador militar latinoamericano. (pág. 556)

census / censo escrutinio de la población. (pág. 234)

chancellor / rector director de universidad inglesa. (pág. 387); primer ministro. (pág. 614)

charters / cartas documentos que permitían a las ciudades el control de sus asuntos. (pág. 405)

chateaux / *chateaux* castillos franceses. (pág. 440)

chieftain / cacique jefe de clan. (pág. 267)

churches / iglesias grupos de personas que comparten sus mismas creencias religiosas. (pág. 252)

circuit judges / jueces de distrito jueces que viajan a través de un país. (pág. 415)

citadel / ciudadela fuerte. (pág. 85)

city-states / ciudades estados ciudades y los territorios de sus alrededores. (pág. 57)

civil disobedience / desobediencia civil el negar a obedecer las demandas del gobierno. (pág. 634)

civilians / civiles que no son soldados. (pág. 604)

civilization / civilización sociedad con conocimiento desarrollado de agricultura, comercio, gobierno, arte, y ciencia. (pág. 33)

civil wars / guerras civiles guerras entre los ciudadanos de una nación. (pág. 159)

clans / clanes grupos fundamentados en sus lazos familiares. (pág. 267)

classical writings / obras clásicas escrituras de la antigua Grecia y Roma. (pág. 433)

clergy / clero líderes religiosos. (pág. 367)

climate / clima promedio de las condiciones del tiempo en un lugar a través de un período de años. (pág. 14)

code of chivalry / código de caballerosidad reglamentos que tenían que seguir los caballeros. (pág. 373)

cold war / guerra fría hostilidad entre naciones sin pelear. (pág. 625)

collectivization / colectivización la unión de granjas pequeñas en granjas grandes controladas por el gobierno. (pág. 611)

colonies / colonias poblaciones permanentes. (pág. 105)

colonize / colonizar establecerse permanentemente en un lugar. (pág. 487)

communes / comunes grupos políticos formados por ciudadanos en la Italia medieval. (pág. 405)

communicable diseases / enfermedades contagiosas enfermedades que son transmitidas de una persona o animal infectado a otra persona o animal. (pág. 664)

compass / brújula instrumento usado para determinar direcciones. (pág. 467)

concentration camps / campos de concentración prisiones para enemigos políticos. (pág. 620)

conquistadores / **conquistadores** vencedores españoles en los años 1500. (pág. 473)

constitution / constitución leyes escritas usadas para gobernar un estado. (pág. 169)

constitutional monarchy / monarquía constitucional monarquía limitada en sus poderes por una constitución. (pág. 518)

consuls / cónsules jefes de la antigua República Romana. (pág. 219)

continental drift / deriva continental teoría de que se mueven los continentes. (pág. 10)

convents / conventos comunidades de monjas. (pág. 255)

converted / convertido cambiado. (pág. 277)

coracles / barcos de cuero pequeños barcos irlandeses. (pág. 290)

core / núcleo parte central de la tierra. (pág. 10)

corregidores / corregidores oficiales de la realeza española. (pág. 423)

cotton gin / desmotadora de algodón máquina para limpiar el algodón. (pág. 527)

counts / condes oficiales del tribunal de justicia francés. (pág. 281)

coup / golpe de estado toma del gobierno por la fuerza. (pág. 648)

cremation ovens / hornos de cremación hornos para quemar los cuerpos y quedarlos reducidos en cenizas. (pág. 621)

crusades / cruzadas guerras hechas para recuperar de los musulmanes la Tierra Sagrada. (pág. 388)

crust / corteza terrestre capa exterior de la tierra. (pág. 10)

culture / cultura modo de vida. (pág. 61)

cuneiform / cuneiforme escritura sumeria hecha con signos en forma de cuña. (pág. 58)

czar / zar soberano ruso. (pág. 355)

D

dauphin / dauphin hijo mayor del rey de Francia. (pág. 417)

defensive league / liga defensiva grupo protector formado por las ciudades estados griegas. (pág. 173)

democratic / democrático que favorece la igualdad de toda la gente. (pág. 169)

depression / depresión decadencia económica. (pág. 608)

descendants / descendientes progenitura. (pág. 107)

de-Stalinization / de-Stalinización ataque a las políticas de Stalin. (pág. 633)

developing countries / países en desarrollo países progresando en la producción, la tecnología, o la norma de vida. (pág. 634)

dictator / dictador gobernante absoluto de un país. (pág. 228)

dictatorship / dictadura gobierno manejado por un dictador. (pág. 613)

diet / dieta asamblea formal. (pág. 421)

diocese / diócesis área bajo el control de un obispo. (pág. 253)

direct tax / impuesto directo impuesto pagado directamente a un gobierno. (pág. 509)

dissent / disensión crítica. (pág. 647)

doge / doge gobernante de la Venecia del Renacimiento. (pág. 439)

domesticated / domesticado sumiso. (pág. 42)

domestic system / sistema doméstico fabricación hecha en las casas de los trabajadores. (pág. 526)

domus / domus casa romana. (pág. 236)

dowry / dote riqueza que lleva la mujer cuando se casa. (pág. 322)

dubbing / armar ceremonia en la cual un escudero se hace caballero. (pág. 374)

dynasty / dinastía sucesión de soberanos de la misma familia. (pág. 88)

E

earthquake / terremoto temblor o deriva de una porción de la corteza terrestre. (pág. 11)

Eddas / Eddas poemas escritos basados en las historias de los dioses vikingos. (pág. 303)

elevation / elevación altitud. (pág. Pág. 9)

embalming / embalsamar proceso usado para mantener los cuerpos muertos sin que se descompusieran. (pág. 73)

emigrated / emigrado haber dejado el país de uno. (pág. 200)

emigrés / emigrés exiliados políticos franceses. (pág. 518)

emirs / emirs jefes del ejército musulmán. (pág. 200)

emperor / emperador gobernante de un imperio. (pág. 233)

empire / imperio territorios gobernados por un solo gobernante o nación. (pág. 61)

enclosure / cercado encierro de terrenos comunes para uso individual. (pág. 525)

erosion / erosión desgaste de la tierra por el viento, el agua, y el hielo. (pág. 12)

estates / estados clases sociales francesas. (pág. 513)

euro / euro moneda usada por los países miembros de la Unión Europea. (pág. 665)

excavate / excavar dejar al aire libre por medio de remover tierra. (pág. 27)

excommunicated / excomulgado excluido como miembro de la Iglesia Católica. (pág. 389)

extended families / familia extendida padres, hijos, y otros parientes viviendo juntos en un mismo hogar. (pág. 639)

F

factories / fábricas edificios donde artículos son manufacturados. (pág. 200)

factory system / sistema de fábricas trabajadores y maquinarias en un lugar para elaborar la mercancía. (pág. 527)

fairs / ferias recaudaciones medievales para el comercio. (pág. 402)

fasces / fasces varas atadas alrededor de un hacha. (pág. 215)

federal / federal gobierno nacional. (pág. 546)

feudalism / feudalismo sistema político medieval basado en la relación de los señores y sus vasallos. (pág. 367)

fiefs / feudos terrenos dados a los vasallos por sus señores. (pág. 367)

flying shuttle / lanzadera aparato tejedora que lleva el hilo rápidamente hacia adelante y de regreso a través de la pieza que se está tejiendo. (pág. 527)

foreign policy / política exterior relaciones con otros países. (pág. 507)

forum / foro lugar para reuniones. (pág. 653)

Forum / Foro plaza pública romana. (pág. 215)

freemen / hombres libres campesinos que pagaron a su señor por el derecho de sembrar su propia tierra. (pág. 377)

freedmen / libertos ex-esclavos. (pág. 234)

friars / frailes predicadores. (pág. 385)

G

galleons / galeones barcos españoles. (pág. 459)

garrison / guarnición fuerza militar estacionada en un área. (pág. 610)

genocide / genocidio destrucción deliberada de toda una población. (pág. 620)

gentiles / gentiles que no son judíos. (pág. 249)

geography / geografía estudio de la tierra y las maneras en que viven y trabajan en ella la gente. (pág. 5)

glaciers / glaciares grandes mantos de hielo. (pág. 13)

gladiatorial games / juegos de gladiadores juegos romanos en los cuales luchaban los gladiadores. (pág. 215)

gladiators / gladiadores luchadores en los juegos de gladiadores. (pág. 238)

glasnost / *glasnost* política rusa para permitir franqueza. (pág. 633)

grand jury / gran jurado jurado que examina las acusaciones y aconseja los cargos criminales. (pág. 415)

Greek fire / fuego griego arma química usada por los bizantinos. (pág. 324)

greenhouse effect / efecto invernadero el bióxido de carbono retiene el calor de la superficie de la tierra. (pág. 664)

guerrilla warfare / guerra de guerrillas peleas de asaltar y esconderse. (pág. 573)

guilds / gremios organizaciones medievales de artesanos. (pág. 406)

guillotine / guillotina aparato que quita la cabeza de una víctima. (pág. 518)

H

habitats / hábitats lugares de vivir. (pág. 660)

haciendas / **haciendas** grandes ranchos. (pág. 640)

hajj / *hajj* jornada musulmana hacia la Meca. (pág. 336)

hard-liners / extremistas personas que se apegan a sus ideas sin preocuparse de las circunstancias. (pág. 632)

heavy industry / industria pesada industria que fabrica la maquinaria. (pág. 611)

helots / ilotas esclavos espartanos. (pág. 164)

heresy / herejía creencias religiosas en contra de la doctrina de la iglesia. (pág. 253)

heretic / hereje miembro de la iglesia que no está de acuerdo con la doctrina oficial. (pág. 451)

heiroglyphic / jeroglífico sistema de escritura egipcia basada en figuras. (pág. 77)

Holocaust / Holocausto programa nazi de genocidio en contra de los judíos. (pág. 621)

holy of holies / santo de santo la cámara más profunda y más sagrada de un templo. (pág. 104)

home territory / territorio de hogar lugar donde vivían los cazadores y recolectores de comidas. (pág. 35)

hostage / rehén persona detenida por otra hasta que se cumplan ciertas promesas. (pág. 193)

humanists / humanistas filósofos que creen que la gente es importante. (pág. 433)

hypothesis / hipótesis explicación posible para un problema. (pág. 188)

I

icons / iconos dibujos sagrados del ortodoxo oriental. (pág. 325)

imam / *imam* guía musulmán de oración. (pág. 335)

immigrants / inmigrantes personas que se quedan a vivir permanentemente en un país diferente al suyo. (pág. 534)

imperialism / imperialismo establecer colonias y construir imperios. (pág. 579)

indentured servants / sirvientes escriturados colonos que prometían trabajar a cambio de su viaje a las Américas. (pág. 495)

indulgances / indulgencias perdones de la iglesia que disminuyen el castigo por pecados. (pág. 450)

industrialized / industrializado industria desarrollada. (pág. 533)

inflation / inflación período cuando se suben los precios y se baja el valor de dinero. (pág. 240)

interchangeable parts / partes intercambiables partes maquinarias hechas de un tamaño uniforme para que puedan ser reemplazadas fácilmente. (pág. 527)

internal combustion engine / motor de combustión interna motor que trabaja con gasolina. (pág. 535)

intifada / intifada insurrección palestina de 1987. (pág. 657)

isolationist / aislacionista país que se mantiene afuera de los asuntos de otros países. (pág. 607)

izbas / izbas cabañas de un cuarto construidas por los eslavos orientales. (pág. 348)

J

Jarls / jarls jefes militares vikingos. (pág. 301)

journeyman / oficial persona que trabaja bajo un maestro por un salario diario. (pág. 406)

joust / justa combate en caballo entre dos caballeros. (pág. 374)

judge / juez líder de tribu hebrea. (pág. 112)

junker / *junker* terrateniente rico prusiano. (pág. 574)

junta / junta comité organizado para tomar posesión de un gobierno. (pág. 553)

juris prudentes / juris prudentes abogados romanos. (pág. 236)

K

kaiser / káiser emperador alemán. (pág. 574)

keep / torre de homenaje la parte más fuerte de un castillo. (pág. 371)

khan / khan líder mongol. (pág. 353)

king's peace / paz del rey protección extendida en cualquier área que visitara un rey anglosajón. (pág. 295)

knight / caballero guerrero a caballo. (pág. 369)

kremlin / kremlin fuerte ruso. (pág. 354)

L

labyrinth / laberinto caminos que entrecruzan, de manera que es difícil orientarse. (pág. 153)

ladies / damas mujeres de la nobleza. (pág. 372)

landforms / formas de tierra características físicas de la superficie de la tierra. (pág. 9)

latifundias / latifundios grandes estados romanos. (pág. 225)

latitude / latitud líneas imaginarias que miden la distancia desde el ecuador. (pág. 14)

legends / leyendas cuentos o historias populares que se han pasado de generación en generación. (pág. 22)

legionaries / legionarios soldados romanos. (pág. 221)

legions / legiones divisiones de los soldados romanos. (pág. 221)

liberals / liberales personas que están a favor de las reformas políticas. (pág. 565)

limited government / gobierno limitado gobierno que tiene solamente los poderes otorgados por la gente. (pág. 513)

lords / señores nobles medievales. (pág. 283)

M

macadam road / calle de macadán camino hecho de capas de roca triturada. (pág. 529)

manifest destiny / destino manifiesto creencia que los Estados Unidos deberían extenderse de costa a costa. (pág. 548)

mandate / mandato autoridad para gobernar. (pág. 607)

manors / feudos estados medievales con un señor y habitantes. (pág. 375)

mantle / capa terrestre parte de la tierra debajo de la corteza y arriba del núcleo. (pág. 10)

martial law / ley marcial dominio del ejército en lugar de mando del gobierno civil. (pág. 505)

mass / misa servicio de alabanza. (pág. 382)

masters / maestros artesanos expertos. (pág. 406)

megaron / megaron sala cuadrada al centro de un palacio micénico. (pág. 155)

mercantilism / mercantilismo sistema en el cual las colonias proveían de riquezas a su país patrón. (pág. 508)

mercenaries / mercenarios hombres pagados para servir de soldados de parte de un país extranjero. (pág. 175)

messiah / mesías salvador. (pág. 248)

mestizos / mestizos personas de ascendencia mixta europea e indígena americana. (pág. 490)

metropolitans / metropolitanos oficiales de la Iglesia Ortodoxo Oriental a cargo de ciudades grandes. (pág. 325)

migrate / migrar trasladarse de un lugar a otro. (pág. 34)

minerals / minerales substancias no vivas encontradas bajo la superficie de la tierra. (pág. 19)

ministers / ministros líderes religiosos protestantes. (pág. 451)

minstrels / trovadores poetas y cantores ambulantes medievales. (pág. 285)

missionary / misionero persona que trata de convertir a los que no creen. (pág. 250)

mobilize / movilizar preparar a las tropas para acción. (pág. 604)

monarchies / monarquías países gobernados por un rey o una reina. (pág. 411)

monasteries / monasterios lugares donde viven monjes. (pág. 255)

monks / monjes hombres que viven en una comunidad religiosa. (pág. 255)

monopoly / monopolio control total. (pág. 508)

monsoons / monzones vientos estacionales que cambian de dirección. (pág. 16)

mosaics / mosaicos dibujos llenos de color hechos de piedra o vidrio. (pág. 323)

mosque / **mezquita** casa de alabanza musulmana. (pág. 335)

multinational companies / compañías multinacionales compañías que operan a través de fronteras nacionales. (pág. 661)

mummy / momia cuerpo envuelto y preservado de una persona muerta. (pág. 73)

mundus / *mundus* para los romanos, el lugar donde se reúnen el mundo de los vivos y el mundo de los muertos. (pág. 216)

municipal / municipal tocante a una ciudad. (pág. 215)

mutiny / motín rebelión en contra de los oficiales. (pág. 472)

N

nationalists / nacionalistas personas a favor de la independencia nacional. (pág. 566)

national workshops / talleres nacionales fábricas dirigidas por los obreros pero pagadas por el gobierno. (pág. 570)

natural resources / recursos naturales materiales encontrados en la naturaleza. (pág. 19)

necropolis / necrópolis cementerio etrusco. (pág. 214)

nobles / nobles personas de clase alta en un reino. (pág. 90)

nomadic / nómada ambulante. (pág. 106)

nonrenewable resources / recursos no renovables recursos naturales irreemplazables. (pág. 20)

nuns / monjas mujeres que pertenecen a una orden religiosa. (pág. 255)

O

oath-helpers / colaboradores de juramento alemanes que prestaron juramento de que una persona acusada estaba diciendo la verdad. (pág. 269)

ocean current / corriente oceánica agua que fluye en el océano en un chorro constante. (pág. 16)

oligarchy / oligarquía gobierno en el cual varias personas gobiernan. (pág. 169)

omens / presagios signos que se creen indicar el futuro. (pág. 214)

open-hearth process / proceso de hogar abierto proceso que usa una clase especial de horno para producir económicamente el acero. (pág. 529)

oracles / oráculos griegos por los cuales hablaron los dioses. (pág. 179)

oracle bones / huesos del oráculo huesos usados por el Shang para recibir mensajes de los antepasados. (pág. 90)

orator / orador uno que habla públicamente. (pág. 195)

ordeal / prueba muy dura prueba dolorosa usada por los alemanes para determinar la inocencia o la culpa. (pág. 269)

orders / órdenes grupos de frailes. (pág. 386)

P

page / paje persona que ayudaba a los caballeros en cuidar sus caballos y sus armaduras. (pág. 373)

pancratium / pancracio evento olímpico que combinaba el boxeo y la lucha. (pág. 183)

pandemics / pandemias epidemias que se propagan por una región extensa. (pág. 664)

papal line of demarcation / línea papal de demarcación línea trazada en 1493 dividiendo las tierras demandadas por España y Portugal. (pág. 473)

papyrus / papiro papel egipcio. (pág. 78)

parchment / pergamino material hecho de pieles delgadas de animales usado para ventanas y papel. (pág. 153)

parish / parroquia área designada para una iglesia local. (pág. 253)

patriarchs / patriarcas los obispos más importantes de la iglesia cristiana antigua. (pág. 253)

patriarchs / patricios ciudadanos poderosos de la clase alta de la Roma antigua. (pág. 219)

peninsulares **/ peninsulares** colonos nacidos en España que vinieron luego a las Américas. (pág. 490)

pentathlon / pentatlón juego olímpico con cinco eventos. (pág. 183)

peristroika **/ perestroika** sistema ruso de reestructuración. (pág. 633)

perioeci */ perioeci* mercaderes y artesanos de pueblos espartanos. (pág. 166)

phalanx / falange formación de infantería griega. (pág. 194)

pharaoh / faraón gobernante egipcio. (pág. 70)

philosophes */ philosophes* filósofos franceses de los años 1700. (pág. 514)

philosophia */ philosophia* el amor a la sabiduría, según los griegos. (pág. 185)

piazza */ piazza* zócalo italiano. (pág. 436)

pilgrimage / peregrinaje jornada religiosa a un santuario o lugar santo. (pág. 133)

pilgrims / peregrinos personas que viajan a un lugar santo para alabar. (pág. 332)

pillars of faith / pilares de fe cinco deberes musulmanes descritos en el Corán. (pág. 335)

planned communities / comunidades planeadas ciudades construidas según un plan definido. (pág. 85)

plebeians / plebeyos ciudadanos pobres y de baja clase de la Roma antigua. (pág. 219)

plebiscite / plebiscito voto popular. (pág. 563)

polar zone / zona polar zona atmosférica a más de 60° al norte o al sur del ecuador. (pág. 150)

polis */ polis* ciudad estado greco. (pág. 163)

political parties / partidos políticos grupos con ideas establecidas sobre el gobierno. (pág. 546)

political science / ciencia política estudio del gobierno. (pág. 167)

popular sovereignty / soberanía popular la idea de que el gobierno saca sus poderes de la gente. (pág. 513)

population / población número de habitantes que viven en una zona en particular. (pág. 42)

population explosion / explosión demográfica crecimiento inesperado del número de personas. (pág. 136)

precipitation / precipitación humedad cayendo tal como la lluvia o la nieve. (pág. 16)

prehistory / prehistoria la época antes de que las personas empezaron a mantener historias escritas. (pág. 33)

prevailing winds / vientos predominantes vientos que soplan principalmente de una dirección. (pág. 16)

priest / sacerdote líder religioso, generalmente católico romano u ortodoxo oriental. (pág. 253)

priest-king / rey sacerdote líder religioso y gubernamental sumerio. (pág. 59)

printing press / prensa máquina para imprimir libros usando tipos movibles. (pág. 441)

privatize / privatizar permitir propiedades privadas a los ciudadanos. (pág. 649)

proletariat / proletariado clase industrial trabajadora. (pág. 568)

prophecy / profecía declaración de lo que podría suceder en el futuro. (pág. 179)

prophets / profetas personas que pretenden tener mensajes de Dios. (pág. 112)

protectorate / protectorado país que deja su política exterior a cargo de una autoridad imperial. (pág. 582)

provinces / provincias distritos políticos. (pág. 119)

psalms / salmos cantos sagrados. (pág. 112)

publicans / publicanos colectores de impuestos de la Roma antigua. (pág. 225)

purges / purgas despidos de miembros indeseables. (pág. 631)

pyramids / pirámides grandes tumbas egipcias. (pág. 71)

Q

quipus / quipos artefactos con que contaban los inca. (pág. 142)

R

referendum / referéndum plebiscito o voto popular. (pág. 660)

reformation / reforma cambio. (pág. 449)

reform / reforma cambio que se hace para mejorar. (pág. 61)

reign / reinado período de poder. (pág. 63)

relative location / localización relativa localización de un lugar en relación a otros lugares. (pág. 6)

relics / reliquias objetos sagrados del pasado. (pág. 319)

relief / relieve diferencias de altura entre las cimas y las tierras bajas de una región. (pág. 9)

renegade nations / naciones renegadas países que se niegan a reducir las armas de guerra. (pág. 663)

renewable resources / recursos renovables recursos naturales reemplazables. (pág. 20)

repealed / anulado revocado. (pág. 507)

representative government / gobierno representativo sistema de gobierno en el cual los oficiales son elegidos. (pág. 546)

republic / república gobierno en el cual los ciudadanos escogen a sus dirigentes. (pág. 219)

revolution / revolución actividad planeada para derrocar un gobierno. (pág. 503)

right of extraterritoriality / derecho extraterritorial derecho de una persona acusada en diferente país de ser procesado en un tribunal de su propia nación. (pág. 587)

river system / sistema de río un río y todas las corrientes que desembocan en él. (pág. 14)

rule by divine right / dominio por derecho divino mando basado en la teoría de que el derecho de gobernar de un monarca viene de Dios. (pág. 243)

runes / runas letras del alfabeto vikingo. (pág. 303)

S

sabbath / sábado día de la semana usado para descansar y venerar. (pág. 113)

sans-culottes / sans-culottes trabajadores municipales y campesinos franceses en los años 1700. (pág. 518)

satellite nations / naciones satélites países controlados por otro país más poderoso. (pág. 626)

scientific method / método científico proceso usado por los científicos para estudiar. (pág. 188)

scorched-earth policy / política de tierra quemada (táctica de avance) táctica de destrucción usada por un ejército al retroceder. (pág. 564)

scribe / escribiente escritor sumerio. (pág. 58)

scriptures / libros sagrados escrituras sagradas. (pág. 347)

sea dog / lobo de mar veterano del mar en Tudor, Inglaterra. (pág. 477)

seceding / separándose retirándose. (pág. 551)

seminary / seminario escuela para el entrenamiento de sacerdotes. (pág. 454)

seneschal / senescal oficial medieval que vigilaba los feudos de un noble. (pág. 375)

sepoys / cipayos soldados indios al servicio del ejército inglés. (pág. 585)

serfs / siervos gente pobre medieval vinculada a la tierra. (pág. 285)

shadoof / cigoñal maquinaria egipcia usada para levantar el agua. (pág. 68)

sheriff / gobernador civil oficial del gobierno inglés a cargo de un condado. (pág. 295)

shires / condados distritos de Inglaterra. (pág. 295)

shrines / capillas lugares sagrados para la veneración. (pág. 154)

silent barter / cambio silencioso método de cambiar artículos sin hablar; usado en los reinos medios de África. (pág. 132)

slums / barrios bajos áreas arruinadas de la ciudad. (pág. 551)

smelting / fundición calentamiento del hierro o de metales para remover impurezas. (pág. 118)

social justice / justicia social tratamiento justo a toda la gente de una sociedad. (pág. 110)

social order / orden social divisiones sociales de acuerdo a la riqueza y otros factores. (pág. 213)

social security laws / leyes de seguridad social leyes de los Estados Unidos proporcionadas para el bienestar de la gente. (pág. 613).

Socratic method / método socrático forma de cuestionamiento desarrollado por Sócrates. (pág. 186)

soothsayers / adivinos gente que se creen habilitados para predecir el futuro. (pág. 214)

sovereign/ soberano país independiente que se gobierna a sí mismo. (pág. 649)

soviets / soviéticos comités comunistas que representan a trabajadores y soldados. (pág. 610)

specialization / especialización desarrollo de profesiones. (pág. 45)

spheres of influence / esferas de influencia áreas en un país en los cuales otro país tiene derechos especiales. (pág. 585)

spinning jenny / máquina de hilar máquina para hilar algodón que utiliza muchos ejes. (pág. 527)

spirits / espíritus seres sobrenaturales. (pág. 89)

squire / escudero noble joven bajo el cuidado y entrenamiento de un caballero. (pág. 373)

stable government / gobierno estable gobierno establecido firmemente. (pág. 545)

strike / huelga paro laboral. (pág. 569)

subsistance farmers / agricultores de subsistencia personas que solamente producen comida suficiente para su propio consumo. (pág. 638)

swastika / esvástica cruz negra ganchuda usada como símbolo nazi. (pág. 614)

syllogism / silogismo forma de razonamiento desarrollado por Aristóteles. (pág. 188)

T

tariffs / tarifas impuestos exigidos para mercancía al entrar de un país a otro. (pág. 235)

tectonic plates / tectónica de placas secciones de la tierra que se mueven lentamente. (pág. 10)

temperate zone / zona templada zona climatológica entre 30° y 60° al norte y al sur del ecuador. (pág. 15)

tenants / arrendatarios personas que viven y trabajan en la tierra de otra persona. (pág. 155)

tenements / casas de vecindad apartamentos que cumplen con los mínimos requisitos para vivir. (pág. 551)

terrorism / terrorismo uso de violencia para llevar a cabo metas políticas. (pág. 664)

textile / textil tela de tejido. (pág. 526)

theology / teología estudio de la religión. (pág. 320)

theses / tesis declaraciones escritas por Lutero criticando las prácticas de la Iglesia. (pág. 450)

tithes / diezmo pagos a la iglesia. (pág. 384)

tournaments / torneos concursos para examinar las destrezas de los caballeros. (pág. 374)

trade unions / gremios asociaciones de trabajadores. (pág. 533)

treaties / tratados acuerdos formales entre naciones. (pág. 103)

trench warfare / guerra de trincheras guerra en la cual fuerzas enemigas atacan desde un sistema de trincheras. (pág. 604)

trial jury / jurado grupo de personas que deciden entre la inocencia o la culpabilidad de una persona acusada de un crimen. (pág. 415)

tribunes / tribunos oficiales romanos elegidos para proteger a las clases bajas.

triremes / trirremes buques de guerra griegos. (pág. 172)

triumph / triunfo desfile de bienvenida a casa para un héroe romano. (pág. 215)

triumvirate / triunvirato grupo de tres personas que gobiernan con igualdad de poderes. (pág. 228)

tropical zone / zona tropical zona climatológica entre 30° al norte y 30° al sur del ecuador. (pág. 15)

tyranny / tiranía uso injusto de poder. (pág. 517)

U

unions / sindicatos grupos de personas unidas por una causa común, especialmente estudiantes y maestros en la época medieval. (pág. 387)

universal male suffrage / sufragio universal masculino derechos de todo hombre para votar. (pág. 569)

universities / universidades instituciones de la educación superior. (pág. 387)

urbanization / urbanización crecimiento de las ciudades. (pág. 551)

utopian socialists / socialistas utópicos personas que quieren establecer comunidades ideales basadas en la cooperación económica. (pág. 568)

V

vassal / vasallo noble medieval que servía a un señor de rango más alto. (pág. 368)

veche / veche asamblea en un pueblo ruso. (pág. 330)

veto / vetar rehusar permiso. (pág. 219)

viceroy / virrey gobernante de un virreinato. (pág. 490)

viceroyalties / virreinatos distritos de las colonias de España en las Américas. (pág. 490)

vizier / visir primer consejero al califa de los abasidas. (pág. 338)

volcano / volcán una abertura en la corteza terrestre por la cual están forzados vapor, cenizas, y lava, cuando está activa. (pág. 11)

W

wergeld / wergeld multa pagada por la familia de un alemán que cometió un crimen. (pág. 269)

witan / *witan* miembro de la *witenagemot*. (pág. 295)

witenagemot / *witenagemot* concilio anglosajón que aconsejaba al rey. (pág. 295)

Z

zaibatsu / zaibatsu familias industriales en el Japón. (pág. 589)

zakah / zakah dádivas caritativas musulmanas. (pág. 335)

ziggurat / *ziggurat* templo mesopotámico. (pág. 57)

Photo Credits

744